Turkey

a travel survival kit

Tom Brosnahan

Turkey - a travel survival kit
3rd edition

Published by
Lonely Planet Publications
Head Office: PO Box 617, Hawthorn, Victoria 3122, Australia
US Office: PO Box 2001A, Berkeley, CA 94702, USA

Printed by
Colorcraft, Hong Kong

Photographs by
Tom Brosnahan
Front cover: Heads at Nemrut Daği, by Robert Cheves

First Published
July 1985

This Edition
January 1990

Back cover quote reprinted courtesy of The Boston Globe

National Library of Australia Cataloguing in Publication Data

Brosnahan, Tom.
  Turkey, a travel survival kit.

  3rd ed.
  Includes index.
  ISBN 0 86442 083 8.

  1. Turkey - Description and travel - 1981 - - Guidebooks. I. Title.

915.61'0438

text © Tom Brosnahan 1989
maps © Lonely Planet 1989
photos © photographers as indicated

Tom Brosnahan

Tom Brosnahan was born and raised in Pennsylvania, went to college in Boston, then set out on the road. His first two years in Turkey, during which he learned to speak fluent Turkish, were spent as a US Peace Corps Volunteer. He studied Middle Eastern history and the Ottoman Turkish language for eight years, but abandoned the writing of his PhD dissertation in favour of travelling and writing guidebooks. So far his twenty books for various publishers have sold over two million copies in twelve languages. *Turkey – a travel survival kit* is the result of over nine years' experience and travel in the country. Tom Brosnahan is also the author of Lonely Planet's *Turkish Phrasebook*.

Dedication

For my Mother and Father, this one too.

From the Author

Several people and organisations have provided very useful assistance in the tremendous task of revising the tens of thousands of facts in this guide, and expanding it for its 3rd edition. Warm thanks are due to my longtime friend Cem Tarhan of the Turkish Information Office in Washington; also to Pamela Hanlon, Corporate Communications, Pan American World Airways, and Elizabeth Manners of that same office. They helped without attempting to exert any editorial influence whatsoever; the opinions expressed in this guide are my own.

Lonely Planet Credits

Editors	Diana Saad
	Tom Smallman
Maps	Graham Imeson
	Chris Lee Ack
	Ralph Roob
Cover Design	Chris Lee Ack
Design	Trudi Canavan
Typesetting	Ann Jeffree

Thanks also to: Gillian Cumming, Mark Ellis, Hugh Finlay and Frith Pike for copy editing; James Lyon and Lyn McGuarr for proofreading and corrections; Gaylene Miller for additional typesetting; Sharon Wertheim for indexing; Richard Nebesky and Sue Tan for coping with the readers' letters; and Trudi Canavan, Graham Imeson, Ann Jeffree and Valerie Tellini for illustrations.

A Warning & a Request

Things change – prices go up, schedules change, good places go bad and bad places go bankrupt – nothing stays the same. So if you find things better or worse, recently opened or long since closed, please write and tell us and help make the next edition better!

Your letters will be used to help update future editions and, where possible, important changes will also be included as a Stop Press section in reprints.

All information is greatly appreciated and the best letters will receive a free copy of the next edition, or any other Lonely Planet book of your choice.

From the publisher

Thanks must go to all the travellers who

used the last edition of this book and wrote to us with information, comments and suggestions. Their names are listed in the back of the book.

Preface to the Third Edition

Turkey is undergoing a tourism boom as travellers from many countries discover its natural and historical attractions. This, the 3rd edition of *Turkey – a travel survival kit*, has been brought fully up to date and greatly expanded. But Turkey is changing rapidly. If you find new things of interest to travellers, please let me know so I can include them in the next edition. I'm very grateful for letters, I read each one, and I reply as soon as I can.

A note on money: as I write this, prices in Turkey's tourism sector are in turmoil. Besides 100% annual inflation, prices are being driven up by shortages of services in some areas. Though daily small devaluations of the Turkish lira keep your costs down, it is impossible to predict whether the prices given in this book will remain the same, change slightly, or change significantly.

Many people have mentioned that the unfamiliar Turkish language can be the biggest stumbling block to full enjoyment of a journey through Turkey. This is the only guidebook to Turkey which has extensive translations of unfamiliar Turkish words and phrases right in the text, along with pronunciation guidance. In addition, there is a large Turkish Language Guide chapter. I hope this method will minimise any difficulty for you. For more complete and systematic help in getting along in Turkish, pick up a copy of Lonely Planet's new *Turkish Phrasebook* (available mid 1990). To help you learn correct pronunciation, I've made up a cassette keyed to both this guidebook and the Lonely Planet Turkish Phrasebook. For a copy of the cassette, please send your name and address, and a cheque (payable to Tom Brosnahan) for US$10, A$12.50, UK£6, C$12 or SFr 16, to Turkish Cassette, c/o Tom Brosnahan, PO Box 563, Concord, MA 01742, USA.

Tom Brosnahan

Contents

Introduction

In the minds of most western visitors, the mention of Turkey conjures up vague stereotype visions of oriental splendour and decadence, of mystery and intrigue, of sultans and harems, of luxury and wickedness. Once in the country, these outdated stereotypes quickly give way before the truth. Though still a third world country, Turkey is a rapidly modernising, secular and western-oriented country with a vigorous economy. Its people are disarmingly friendly to foreign visitors, the cuisine is outstanding, the cities dotted with majestic old buildings, the countryside often as beautiful as a national park. For almost 70 years the Turkish Republic has been working to put its imperial past behind it while preserving the best parts for posterity, and has done remarkably well.

The old stereotype of oriental, imperial decadence originated at least partly from reality. In the last years of the Ottoman Empire, the entire Middle East ruled by the Turkish sultan was up for grabs, and the western powers did whatever they could to gain advantage. This included putting pressure on the sultan by portraying him in the western press as little better than a monster. This negative image built easily on the notion of the 'terrible Turk' left from the days, in the 1600s, when Ottoman armies threatened the gates of Vienna, and thus all of central Europe.

By contrast with this outdated European stereotype, tourists coming to Turkey today from the Arab countries formerly ruled by the sultan have a view of İstanbul as the glittering imperial capital, fount of culture and seat of the last Caliph of Islam. İstanbul is to an eastern Muslim what Rome is to a western Christian.

The Turks themselves are proud of their imperial past, not the last centuries, but the times of Mehmet the Conqueror and Süleyman the Magnificent, when the Turkish Empire was the richest, most powerful, most civilised state in the world. And they are fascinated by the depth of history in their homeland, the progression of kingdoms and empires which fostered a dozen great cultures: Hittite, Hellenic, Hellenistic, Roman, Christian, Byzantine, Seljuk, Ottoman and more. But Turks harbour no romantic visions of reclaiming past glories or territories. Kemal Atatürk, founder of the modern republic, set forth the plan in no uncertain terms: preserve the high culture of the past, but get on with the work of the future in a democratic nation-state.

The history of Anatolia, the Turkish homeland, is simply incredible. In fact, the world's oldest 'city' was discovered here, at Çatal Höyük (7500 BC). The Hittite Empire, little known in the west, rivalled that of ancient Egypt, and left behind breathtaking works of art. The heartland of classical Hellenic culture is actually in Turkey, including cities such as Troy, Pergamum, Ephesus, Miletus and Halicarnassus. Most modern Turkish cities have a Roman past, and all have a Byzantine one. The Seljuk Turkish Empire could boast of men like Omar Khayyam and Celaleddin Rumi ('Mevlana'), the poet, mystic and founder of the order of Whirling Dervishes.

On a typical day in Turkey, after you've had your day's dose of history and culture, you can head out to the beach. At many resorts on the Aegean and Mediterranean coasts, the ruins are right *on* the beach. Or have dinner at a small fish restaurant on the shores of the Bosphorus in İstanbul. Or sit in a shady tea garden for what the Turks call *keyf*. Order a tiny, tulip-shaped glass of hearty Turkish tea, enjoy the pleasant surroundings, think over the day's good times, and let it all come together: that's keyf. There's no adequate translation; pleasure, contentment, positive outlook, relaxation? It's all part of a normal day in Turkey.

PLANNING WHERE TO GO

Any itinerary is an expression of interest, energy, time and money. You can see an awful lot of the country if you spend six to eight weeks, but if your time is limited, here are some suggestions to help you plan your travels in Turkey. These are *minimal* times, moving fast.

Less Than a Week (3-5 days)

İstanbul, with an overnight trip to İznik and Bursa, or Troy and the Dardanelles.

Basic One-Week (7-9 day) Itinerary

İstanbul (two nights), Bursa (one), Dardanelles and Troy (one), Bergama, İzmir and Kuşadası (two) with excursions to Ephesus, Priene, Miletus, Didyma; return to İstanbul (one). Spend any extra time in İstanbul.

Two Weeks

Add an excursion from Kuşadası via Aphrodisias to Pamukkale and Hierapolis (one to two nights); also take a loop excursion to Ankara, Konya and Cappadocia. Visit the Hittite cities. If you have time left over, spend a day or two on the Turquoise Coast (Kaş, Antalya, Side, Alanya).

Three Weeks

Add a yacht cruise or coastal highway excursion from Kuşadası south to Bodrum (Halicarnassus), Marmaris, Fethiye, Kaş, Finike, Kemer and Antalya; or second-best, an excursion along the Black Sea coast. Another option is a tour to the south-east, Şanlıurfa, Mardin and Diyarbakır, best done outside of the blazing-hot months of July and August.

Eastern Tour

A 14 to 21-day tour for mid-May to early October only: a circuit beginning in Ankara or Cappadocia going to Adıyaman and Nemrut Dağı (Mt Nimrod), Diyarbakır, Van, Doğubeyazıt and Mt Ararat, Erzurum, Kars, Artvin, Hopa, Rize, Trabzon, Samsun, Amasya, and returning to Ankara via Boğazkale (Hattuşaş).

Facts about the Country

HISTORY

Turkey's history is astoundingly long – almost 10,000 years. Before giving a summary, here is a table so you can keep the various periods in the right places:

Historical Table

7500 BC Earliest known inhabitants; earliest human community at Çatal Höyük.

5000 BC Stone-and-Copper Age; settlement at Hacılar.

2600 to 1900 BC Old Bronze Age; Proto-Hittite Empire in central and southeastern Anatolia.

1900 to 1300 BC Hittite Empire, wars with Egypt; the Patriarch Abraham departs Harran, near Şanlıurfa, for Canaan.

1250 BC Trojan War.

1200 to 600 BC Phrygian and Mysian invasions, followed by the great period of Hellenic civilisation; Yassı Höyük settlement flourishes; King Midas and King Croesus reign; coinage is invented; kingdoms of Ionia, Lycia, Lydia, Caria, Pamphylia; Empire of Urartu.

550 BC Cyrus of Persia invades Anatolia.

334 BC Conquest of simply everything and everybody by Alexander the Great from Macedon.

279 BC Celts (or Gauls) invade and set up Galatia near Ankara.

250 BC Rise of the Kingdom of Pergamum (Bergama).

129 BC Rome establishes the Province of Asia, with its capital at Ephesus (near İzmir).

47 to 57 AD St Paul's trips in Anatolia.

330 AD Constantine dedicates the 'New Rome' of Constantinople, and the centre of the Roman Empire moves from Rome to the Bosphorus.

527 to 565 Reign of Justinian, greatest Byzantine emperor; construction of Sancta Sophia, greatest church in the world.

570 to 622 Muhammed's birth; revelation of the Koran; flight ('Hijra') to Medina.

1037 to 1109 Empire of the Great Seljuk Turks, based in Iran.

1071 to 1243 Seljuk Sultanate of Rum, based in Konya; life and work of Celaleddin Rumi ('Mevlana'), founder of the Whirling Dervishes.

1000s to 1200s Age of the Crusades.

1288 Birth of the Ottoman Empire, near Bursa.

1453 Conquest of Constantinople by Mehmet II.

1520 to 1566 Reign of Sultan Süleyman the Magnificent, the great age of the Ottoman Empire; most of North Africa, most of Eastern Europe and all of the Middle East controlled from İstanbul; Ottoman navies patrol the Mediterranean and Red seas and the Indian Ocean.

1876 to 1909 Reign of Sultan Abdül Hamid, last of the powerful sultans; the 'Eastern Question' arises: which European nations will be able to grab Ottoman territory when the empire topples?

1923 Proclamation of the Turkish Republic.

1938 Death of Atatürk.

Earliest Times

The Mediterranean region was inhabited as early as 7500 BC, during Palaeolithic, or Old Stone Age, times. By 7000 BC a Neolithic (New Stone Age) city had grown up at what's now called Çatal Höyük, 60 km south-east of Konya. These early Anatolians developed fine wall paintings, statuettes, domestic architecture and pottery. Artefacts from the site, including the wall paintings, are in Ankara's Museum of Anatolian Civilisations.

The Chalcolithic (Stone-and-Copper Age) period saw the building of a city at Hacılar (HA-juh-LAHR), near Burdur, in about 5000 BC. The pottery here was of finer quality, and copper implements rather than stone or clay were used.

Hittites: The Bronze Age

The Old Bronze Age (2600-1900 BC) was the time when Anatolians first developed cities of substantial size. An indigenous people now named the Proto-Hittites, or Hatti, built cities at Nesa, or Kanesh (today's Kültepe), and Alaca Höyük. The first known ruler of Kanesh was King Zipani (circa 2300 BC), according to Akkadian texts. You can visit the archaeological site near Kültepe, 21 km north-east of Kayseri. As for Alaca Höyük, 36 km from Boğazkale (bo-AHZ-kahl-eh), it was perhaps the most important pre-Hittite city and may have been the first Hittite capital.

The Hittites, a people of Indo-European language, overran this area and established themselves as a ruling class over the local people during the Middle Bronze Age (1900-1600 BC). They took over existing cities and built a magnificent capital at Hattuşaş (Boğazkale), 212 km east of Ankara near Sungurlu. The early Hittite Kingdom (1600-1500 BC) was replaced by the greater Hittite Empire (1450-1200 BC). They captured Syria from the Egyptians (1380-1316), clashed with the great Rameses II (1298), and meanwhile developed a wonderful culture.

Their graceful pottery, ironwork ornaments and implements, gold jewellery and figurines now fill a large section of the Museum of Anatolian Civilisations in Ankara. The striking site of Boğazkale, set in dramatic countryside, is worth a visit, as is the religious centre of Yazılıkaya nearby. The Hittite religion was based upon worship of a Sun Goddess and a Storm God.

The Hittite Empire was weakened in its final period by the cities of Assuwa ('Asia'), subject principalities along the Aegean coast, which included the city of Troy. The Trojans were attacked by Achaean Greeks in 1250 – the Trojan War –

which gave the Hittites a break. But the *coup de grâce* came with a massive invasion of 'sea peoples' from various Greek islands and city-states. Driven from their homelands by the invading Dorians, the sea peoples flocked into Anatolia by way of the Aegean coast. The Hittite state survived for a few centuries longer in the south-eastern Taurus mountains, but the great empire was dead.

Phrygians, Urartians, Lydians & Others

With the Hittite decline, smaller states filled the power vacuum. About 1200 BC the Phrygians and Mysians, of Indo-European stock, invaded Anatolia from Thrace and settled at Gordium (Yassı Höyük), 106 km south-west of Ankara. This Hittite city became the Phrygian capital (circa 800 BC). A huge Hittite cemetery and a royal Phrygian tomb still exist at the site. King Midas (circa 715 BC), he of the golden touch, is Phrygia's most famous son.

At the same time (after 1200 BC), the Aegean coast was populated with a mixture of native peoples and Greek invaders. The region around İzmir became Ionia, with numerous cities. To the south was Caria, between modern Milâs and Fethiye, a mountainous region whose people were great traders. The Carians sided with the Trojans during the Trojan War. When the Dorians arrived they brought some Greek culture to Caria, which the great Carian king, Mausolus, developed even further. His tomb, the Mausoleum, was among the Seven Wonders of the Ancient World. Of his capital city, Halicarnassus (modern Bodrum), little remains.

Further east from Caria was Lycia, a kingdom stretching from Fethiye to Antalya; and Pamphylia, the land east of Antalya.

As the centuries passed, a great city grew up at Sardis, 60 km east of İzmir. Called Lydia, it dominated most of Ionia and clashed with Phrygia. Lydia is famous not only for Sardis, but for a great invention: coinage. It's also famous for King Croesus, the world's first great coin collector. Lydia's primacy lasted only from 680 to 547 BC, at which date Persian invaders overran everybody.

Meanwhile, out east on the shores of salty Lake Van, yet another kingdom and culture arose. Not much is known about the Urartians who founded the Kingdom of Van (860-612 BC), except that they left interesting ruins and vast, bewildering cuneiform inscriptions in the massive Rock of Van just outside the modern town.

The Cimmerians invaded Anatolia from the west, conquered Phrygia and challenged Lydia, then settled down to take their place as yet one more ingredient in the great mulligan stew of Anatolian people. The stew was simmering nicely, but in 547 BC the Persians brought it to a boil. Though the Ionian cities survived the invasion and lived on under Persian rule, the great period of Hellenic culture was winding down. Ionia, with its important cities of Phocaea (Foça, north of İzmir), Teos, Ephesus, Priene and Miletus, and Aeolia centred on Smyrna (İzmir), had contributed a great deal to ancient culture, from the graceful scrolled capitals of Ionic columns to Thales of Miletus, the first recorded philosopher in the west.

While the great city of Athens was relatively unimportant, the Ionian cities were laying the foundations of Hellenic civilisation. It is ironic that the Persian invasion which curtailed Ionia's culture caused that of Athens to flourish. On reaching Athens, the Persians were overextended. By meeting the Persian challenge, Athens grew powerful and influential, taking the lead in the further progress of Hellenic culture.

Cyrus & Alexander

Cyrus, emperor of Persia (550-530 BC), swept into Anatolia from the east, conquering everybody and everything.

Alexander the Great

Though he subjected the cities of the Aegean coast to his rule, this was not easy. The independent-minded citizens gave him and his successors trouble for the next two centuries.

The Persian conquerors were conquered by Alexander the Great, who stormed out of Macedon, crossed the Hellespont (Dardanelles) in 334 BC, and within a few years had conquered the entire Middle East from Greece to India. Alexander, so it is said, was frustrated in untying the Gordian knot at Gordium, so he cut it with his sword. It seems he did the right thing, as the domination of Asia – which he was supposed to gain by untying the knot – came to be his in record time. His sword-blow proved that he was an impetuous young man.

Alexander's effects on Anatolia were profound. He was the first of many rulers who would attempt to meld western and eastern cultures (the Byzantines and the Ottomans followed suit). Upon his death in 323 BC, in Babylon, his empire was divided among his generals in a flurry of civil wars. Lysimachus claimed western and central Anatolia after winning the battle of Ipsus (301 BC), and he set his mark on the Ionian cities. Many Hellenistic buildings went up on his orders. Ancient Smyrna was abandoned and a brand-new city was built several km away, where the modern city stands.

But the civil wars continued, and Lysimachus was slain by Seleucus (King of Seleucid lands, 305-280 BC), another of Alexander's generals, at the Battle of Corupedium (281 BC). Though Seleucus was in turn slain by Ptolemy Ceraunus, the kingdom of the Seleucids, based in Antioch (Antakya), was to rule a great part of the Middle East for the next century.

Meanwhile, the next invaders, the Celts (or Gauls) this time, were storming through Macedonia on their way to Anatolia (279 BC) where they established the Kingdom of Galatia. The Galatians made Ancyra (Ankara) their capital, and subjected the Aegean cities to their rule. The foundations of parts of the citadel in Ankara date from Galatian times.

While the Galatians ruled western Anatolia, Mithridates I had become king of Pontus, a state based in Trebizond (Trabzon) on the eastern Black Sea coast. At its height, the Pontic kingdom extended all the way to Cappadocia in central Anatolia.

Still other small kingdoms flourished at this time, between 300 and 200 BC. A leader named Prusias founded the Kingdom of Bithynia, and gave his name to the chief city: Prusa (Bursa). Nicaea (İznik, near Bursa) was also of great importance. And in south-eastern Anatolia an Armenian kingdom grew up, centred on the town of Van. The Armenians, a Phrygian tribe, settled around Lake Van after the decline of Urartian power.

A fellow named Ardvates (ruled 317-284 BC), a Persian satrap (provincial governor) under the Seleucids, broke away from the Seleucid kingdom to found the short-lived Kingdom of Armenia. The Seleucids later regained control, but lost it again as Armenia was split into two kingdoms, Greater and Lesser Armenia.

Reunited in 94 BC under Tigranes I, the Kingdom of Armenia became very powerful for a short period (83-69 BC). Armenia finally fell to the Roman legions not long afterwards.

But the most impressive and powerful of Anatolia's many kingdoms at this time was Pergamum. Gaining tremendous power around 250 BC, the Pergamene king picked the right side to be on, siding with Rome early in the game. With Roman help, Pergamum threw off Seleucid rule and went on to challenge both King Prusias of Bithynia (186 BC) and King Pharnaces I of Pontus (183 BC).

The kings of Pergamum were great warriors, governors and also mad patrons of the arts, assembling an enormous library which rivalled that of Alexandria. The Asclepion, or medical centre, at Pergamum was flourishing at this time, and continued to flourish for centuries under Rome. Greatest of Pergamene kings was Eumenes II (197-159 BC), who ruled an enormous empire stretching from the Dardanelles to the Taurus mountains near Syria. He was responsible for building much of what's left on Pergamum's acropolis, including the grand library.

Roman Times

The Romans took Anatolia almost by default. The various Anatolian kings couldn't refrain from picking away at Roman holdings and causing other sorts of irritation, so finally the legions marched in and took over. Defeating King Antiochus III of Seleucia at Magnesia (Manisa, near İzmir) in 190 BC, the Romans were content for the time being to leave 'Asia' (Anatolia) in the hands of the kings of Pergamum. But the last king, dying without an heir, bequeathed his kingdom to Rome (133 BC). In 129 BC, the Romans established the Province of Asia, with its capital at Ephesus.

An interesting postscript to this period is the story of Commagene. This small and rather unimportant little kingdom in central Anatolia, near Adıyaman, left few marks on history. But the one notable reminder of Commagene is very notable indeed: atop Nemrut Dağı (NEHM-root dah-uh, Mt Nimrod), Antiochus I (62-32 BC) built an astounding memorial. His mammoth, cone-shaped funerary mound is framed by twin temples filled with huge stone statues portraying himself and the gods and goddesses who were his 'peers'. A visit to Nemrut Dağı, from the nearby town of Kâhta, is one of the high points of a visit to Turkey.

Roman rule brought relative peace and prosperity to Anatolia for almost three centuries, and provided the perfect conditions for the spread of a brand-new, world-class religion.

Early Christianity

Christianity began in Roman Palestine (Judaea), but its foremost proponent, St Paul, came from Tarsus in Cilicia, in what is now southern Turkey. Paul took advantage of the excellent Roman road system to spread the teachings of Jesus. When the Romans drove the Jews out of Judaea in 70 AD, Christian members of this Diaspora may have made their way to the numerous small Christian congregations in the Roman province of Asia (Anatolia).

On his first journey in about 47-49 AD, Paul went to Antioch, Seleucia (Silifke), and along the southern coast through Pamphylia (Side, Antalya) and up into the mountains. First stop was Antioch-in-Pisidia, today called Yalvaç, near Akşehir. Next he went to Iconium (Konya), the chief city in Galatia; Paul wrote an important 'Letter to the Galatians' which is now the ninth book of the New Testament.

From Iconium, Paul tramped to Lystra, 40 km south, and to Derbe nearby. Then it was back to Attaleia (Antalya) to catch a boat for Antioch. His second journey took him to some of these same cities, and later north-west to the district of Mysia where Troy (Truva) is located; then into Macedonia.

Paul's third trip (53-57) took in many of these same places, including Ancyra, Smyrna and Adramyttium (Edremit). On the way back he stopped in Ephesus, capital of Roman Asia and one of the greatest cities of the time. Here he ran into trouble because his teachings were ruining the market for silver effigies of the local favourite goddess, Cybele/Diana. The silversmiths led a riot, and Paul's companions were hustled into the great theatre for a sort of kangaroo court. Luckily, the authorities kept order: there was free speech in Ephesus; Paul and his companions had broken no laws; they were permitted to go freely. Later on this third journey Paul stopped in Miletus.

Paul got his last glimpses of Anatolia as he was being taken to Rome as a prisoner, for trial on charges of inciting a riot in Jerusalem (59-60). He changed ships at Myra (Demre); further west, he was supposed to land at Cnidos, at the tip of the peninsula west of Marmaris, but stormy seas prevented this.

Other saints played a role in the life of Roman Asia as well. Tradition has it that St John retired to Ephesus to write the fourth gospel near the end of his life, and that he brought Jesus' mother Mary with him. John was buried atop a hill in what is now the town of Selçuk, near Ephesus. The great, now ruined basilica of St John marks the site. As for Mary, she is said to have retired to a mountaintop cottage near Ephesus. The small chapel at Meryemana ('Mother Mary') is the site of a mass to celebrate her Assumption into heaven on 15 August.

The Seven Churches of the Revelation were the Seven Churches of Asia: Ephesus (Efes), Smyrna (İzmir), Pergamum (Bergama), Sardis (Sart, east of İzmir), Philadelphia (Alaşehir), Laodicea (Goncalı, between Denizli and Pamukkale) and Thyatira (Akşehir). 'Church' of course meant 'congregation', so don't go to these sites looking for the ruins of seven buildings.

The New Rome

Christianity was a struggling faith during the centuries of Roman rule. By 250 AD, the faith had grown strong enough and Roman rule so unsteady that the Roman emperor Decius decreed a general persecution of Christians. Not only this, but the empire was falling to pieces. Goths attacked the Aegean cities with fleets, and later invaded Anatolia. The Persian Empire again threatened from the east. Diocletian (284-305) restored the empire somewhat, but continued the persecutions.

When Diocletian abdicated, Constantine battled for succession, which he won in 324. He united the empire, declared equal rights for all religions, and called the first Ecumenical Council to meet at Nicaea in 325.

Meanwhile, Constantine was building a great city on the site of Hellenic Byzantium. In 330 he dedicated it as New Rome, his capital city; it came to be called Constantinople. The emperor died seven years later in Nicomedia (İzmit), east of his capital. On his deathbed he adopted Christianity.

Justinian

While the barbarians of Europe were sweeping down on weakened Rome, the eastern capital grew in wealth and strength. Emperor Justinian (527-565) brought the Eastern Roman, or Byzantine, Empire to its greatest strength. He reconquered Italy, the Balkans, Anatolia, Egypt and North Africa, and further embellished Constantinople with great buildings. His personal triumph was the Church of the Holy Wisdom, or Sancta Sophia, which remained the most splendid church in Christendom for almost 1000 years, at which time it became the most splendid mosque.

Justinian's successors were generally good, but not good enough, and the empire's conquests couldn't be maintained. Besides, something quite momentous was happening in Arabia.

Birth of Islam

Five years after the death of Justinian, Muhammed was born in Mecca. In 612 or so, while meditating, he heard the voice of God command him to 'recite'. Muhammed was to become the Messenger of God, communicating His holy word to people. The written record of these recitations, collected after Muhammed's death into a book by his family and followers, is the Koran.

The people of Mecca didn't take to Muhammed's preaching all at once. In fact, they forced him to leave Mecca, which he did, according to tradition, in the year 622. This 'flight' (*hijra* or hegira) is the starting-point for the Muslim lunar calendar.

Setting up house in Medina, Muhammed organised a religious commonwealth which over 10 years became so powerful that it could challenge and conquer Mecca (624-630). Before Muhammed died two years later, the Muslims (adherents of Islam, 'submission to God's will') had begun the conquest of other Arab tribes.

The story of militant Islam is one of history's most astounding tales. Fifty years after the Prophet's ignominious flight from Mecca, the armies of Islam were threatening the walls of Constantinople (669-678), having conquered everything and everybody from there to Mecca, plus Persia and Egypt. The Arabic Muslim empires that followed these conquests were among the world's greatest political, social and cultural achievements.

Muhammed was succeeded by caliphs or deputies, whose job was to oversee the welfare of the Muslim commonwealth. His close companions got the job first, then his son-in-law Ali. After that, two great dynasties emerged. The Umayyads (661-750) based their empire in Damascus, the Abbasids (750-1100) in Baghdad. Both continually challenged the power and status of Byzantium.

Coming of the Turks

The history of the Turks as excellent soldiers goes back at least to the reign of the Abbasid Caliph Al-Mutasim (833-842). This ruler formed an army of Turkish captives and mercenaries that became the empire's strength, and also its undoing. Later caliphs found that their protectors had become their masters, and the Turkish 'praetorian guard' raised or toppled caliphs as it chose.

The Seljuk Empire

The first great Turkish state to rule Anatolia was the Great Seljuk Turkish Empire (1037-1109), based in Persia (Iran). Coming from Central Asia, the Turks captured Baghdad (1055). In 1071, Seljuk armies decisively defeated the Byzantines at Manzikert (Malazgırt), taking the Byzantine emperor as a prisoner. The Seljuks then took over most of Anatolia and established a provincial capital at Nicaea. Their domains now included today's Turkey, Iran and Iraq. Their empire developed a distinctive culture, with especially beautiful architecture and design; the Great Seljuks also produced Omar Khayyam (died 1123). Politically, however, the Great Seljuk Turkish Empire declined quickly, in the style of Alexander the Great's empire, with various pieces being taken by generals.

A remnant of the Seljuk empire lived on in Anatolia, based in Iconium. Called the Seljuk Sultanate of Rum ('Rome', meaning Roman Asia), it continued to flourish, producing great art and great thinkers until overrun by the Mongol hordes in 1243. Celaleddin Rumi, or 'Mevlana', founder of the Mevlevi (Whirling) Dervish order, is perhaps the Sultanate of Rum's outstanding thinker.

The Crusades

These 'holy wars', created to provide work for the lesser nobles and riffraff of Europe, proved disastrous for the Byzantine emperors. Although a combined Byzantine and Crusader army captured Nicaea from the Seljuks in 1097, the Crusaders were mostly an unhelpful, unruly bunch. The Fourth Crusade (1202-1204) saw European ragtag armies invade and plunder Christian Constantinople. This was the first and most horrible defeat for the great city, and it was carried out by 'friendly' armies.

Having barely recovered from the ravages of the Crusades, the Byzantines were greeted with a new and greater threat: the Ottomans.

Founding of the Ottoman Empire

Byzantine weakness left a power vacuum which was filled by bands of Turks fleeing from the Mongols. Warrior bands, each led by a warlord, took over parts of the Aegean and Marmara coasts. The Turks who moved into Bithynia, around Bursa, were followers of a man named Ertuğrul. His son, Osman, founded (in about 1288) a principality which was to grow into the Osmanlı (Ottoman) Empire.

The Ottomans took Bursa in 1326. It served them well as their first capital city. But they were vigorous and ambitious, and by 1402 they moved the capital to Adrianople (Edirne) because it was easier to rule their Balkan conquests from there. Constantinople was still in Byzantine hands.

The Turkish advance spread rapidly to both east and west, despite some setbacks. By 1452, under Mehmet the Conqueror, they were strong enough to think of taking Constantinople, capital of eastern Christendom, which they did in 1453. Mehmet's reign (1451-1481) began the great era of Ottoman power.

Süleyman the Magnificent

The height of Ottoman glory was under Sultan Süleyman the Magnificent (1520-1566). Called 'The Lawgiver' by the Turks, he beautified İstanbul, rebuilt Jerusalem and expanded Ottoman power to the gates of Vienna (1529). The Ottoman fleet under Barbaros Hayrettin

Paşa seemed invincible, but by 1585 the empire had begun its long and celebrated decline. Most of the sultans after Süleyman were incapable of great rule. Luckily for the empire, there were very competent and talented men to serve as grand viziers, ruling the empire in the sultans' stead.

The Later Empire

By 1699, Europeans no longer feared an invasion by the 'terrible Turk'. The empire was still vast and powerful, but it had lost its momentum, and was rapidly dropping behind the west in terms of social, military, scientific and material progress. In the 19th century, several sultans undertook important reforms. Selim III, for instance, revised taxation, commerce and the military. But the Janissaries (members of the sultan's personal guard) and other conservative elements resisted the new measures strongly, and sometimes violently. It was tough to teach an old culture new tricks.

Affected by the new currents of ethnic nationalism, the subject peoples of the empire revolted. They had lived side-by-side with Turks for centuries, ruled over by their heads of communities (chief rabbi, patriarch, etc) who were responsible to the sultan. But decline and misrule made nationalism very appealing. The Greeks gained independence in 1830; the Serbs, Bulgarians, Rumanians, Albanians and Arabs would all seek their independence soon after.

As the empire broke up, the European powers (Britain, France, Italy, Germany, Russia) hovered in readiness to colonise or annex the pieces. They used religion as a reason for pressure or control, saying that it was their duty to protect the Catholic, Protestant or Orthodox subjects from misrule and anarchy. The Holy Places in Palestine were a favourite target, and each power tried to obtain a foothold here for colonisation later.

The Russian emperors put pressure on the Turks to grant them powers over all

Süleyman the Magnificent

Ottoman Orthodox subjects, whom the Russian emperor would thus 'protect'. The result of this pressure was the Crimean War (1853-56), with Britain and France fighting on the side of the Ottomans against the Russians.

More reforms were proposed and carried out in the Ottoman Empire in an attempt to 'catch up' several centuries in a few years. The last powerful ruler, Abdül Hamid II (1876-1909), was put on the throne by Mithat Paşa, who also proclaimed a constitution in 1876. But the new sultan did away both with Mithat Paşa and the constitution, and established his own absolute rule.

Despite Abdül Hamid's harsh methods, the empire continued to disintegrate, with nationalist insurrections in Crete, Armenia, Bulgaria, Macedonia and other parts of the empire. The situation only got worse. The Young Turk movement for western-style reforms gained enough power by 1908 to force the restoration of the constitution. In 1909, the Young Turk-led Ottoman Parliament deposed Abdül Hamid and put his weak brother on the throne.

In its last years, though a sultan still sat on the throne, the Ottoman Empire was ruled by three members of the Young Turks' Committee of Union & Progress named Talat, Enver and Jemal. Their rule was vigorous, but harsh and misguided, and only worsened an already hopeless situation. When WW I broke out, they sided with Germany and the Central Powers. The Central Powers were defeated, and the Ottoman Empire along with them.

The victorious Allies had been planning, since the beginning of the war, how they would carve up the Ottoman Empire. They even promised certain lands to several different peoples or factions in order to get their support for the war effort. With the end of the war, the promises came due. Having promised more than they could pay, the Allies decided on the dismemberment of Anatolia itself in order to get more land with which to pay 'claims'. The Turks were about to be wiped off the map. As for the last sultans, they were under the control and occupation of the Allies in İstanbul, and thought only of their own welfare.

The Turkish Republic
The situation looked very bleak for the Turks as their armies were being disbanded and their country taken under the control of the Allies. But a catastrophe turned things around.

Ever since gaining independence in 1831, the Greeks had entertained the *Megali Idea* ('Great Plan') of a new Greek empire encompassing all the lands which had once had Greek influence – in effect, the refounding of the Byzantine Empire. During WW I, the Allies had offered Greece the Ottoman city of Smyrna. King Constantine declined for various reasons, even though his prime minister, Eleutherios Venizelos, wanted to accept. After the war, however, Alexander became king, Venizelos became prime minister again, and Britain encouraged the Greeks to go

ahead and take Smyrna. On 15 May 1919, they did.

The Turks, depressed and hopeless over the occupation of their country and the powerlessness of the sultan, couldn't take this: a former subject people capturing an Ottoman city, and pushing inland with great speed and ferocity. Even before the Greek invasion, an Ottoman general named Mustafa Kemal had decided that a new government must take over the destiny of the Turks from the powerless sultan. He began organising resistance on 19 May 1919. The Greek invasion was just the shock needed to galvanise the people and lead them to his way of thinking.

The Turkish War of Independence lasted from 1920 to 1922. In September 1921 the Greeks very nearly reached Ankara, the nationalist headquarters, but in desperate fighting the Turks held them off. A year later, the Turks began their counter-offensive and drove the Greek armies back to İzmir by 9 September 1922.

Victory in the bitterly fought war made Mustafa Kemal even more a national hero. He was now fully in command of the fate of the Turks. The sultanate was abolished and after it, the Ottoman Empire. A Turkish republic was born, based in Anatolia and eastern Thrace. The treaties of WW I, which had left the Turks with almost no country, were renegotiated. Venizelos even came to terms with Kemal, signing a treaty in 1930.

Atatürk's Reforms
Mustafa Kemal undertook the job of completely remaking a society. After the republic was declared in 1923, a constitution was adopted (1924); polygamy was abolished and the fez, mark of Ottoman backwardness, was prohibited (1925); new, western-style law codes were instituted, and civil (not religious) marriage was required (1926); Islam was removed as the state religion, and the Arabic alphabet was replaced by a

modified Latin one (1928). In 1930, Constantinople officially became İstanbul, and other city names were officially Turkified (Angora to Ankara, Smyrna to İzmir, Adrianople to Edirne, etc). Women obtained the right to vote and serve in parliament in 1934.

In 1935, Mustafa Kemal sponsored one of the most curious laws of modern times. Up to this time, Muslims had only one, given name. Family names were purely optional. So he decided that all Turks should choose a family name, and they did. He himself was proclaimed Atatürk, or 'Father Turk', by the Turkish parliament, and officially became Kemal Atatürk.

Atatürk lived and directed the country's destiny until 10 November 1938. He saw WW II coming, and was anxious that Turkey stay out of it. His friend and successor as president of the republic, İsmet İnönü, succeeded in preserving a precarious neutrality. Ankara became a hotbed of Allied-Axis spying, but the Turks stayed out of the conflict.

Recent Years

In the beginning years, Atatürk's Republican Peoples' Party was the only political party allowed. However, between 1946 and 1950 true democracy was instituted, and the opposition Democratic Party won the election in 1950.

By 1960 the Democratic Party had acquired so much power that the democratic system was threatened. The army, charged by Atatürk to protect democracy and the constitution, stepped in and brought various Democratic Party leaders to trial on charges of violating the constitution. The popular Peron-like party leader, Adnan Menderes, was executed, though all other death sentences were commuted. Elections were held in 1961.

In 1970 there was a gentlemanly coup d'état again because the successor to the Democratic Party had overreached its bounds. High-ranking military officers entered the national broadcasting head-

quarters and read a short message, and the government fell.

Under the careful watch of those same officers, democracy returned and things went well for years, until political infighting and civil unrest brought the country to a virtual halt in 1980. On the left side of the political spectrum, Soviet-bloc countries pumped in arms and money for destabilisation and, it is claimed, supported Armenian terrorist elements who murdered Turkish diplomats and their families abroad. On the right side of the spectrum, fanatic Muslim religious groups and a neo-Nazi party caused havoc.

In the centre, the two major political parties were deadlocked so badly in parliament that for months they couldn't even elect a parliamentary president. The economy was in bad shape, inflation was 130% per year, the lawmakers were not making laws, crime in the streets by the fringe elements of left and right was epidemic. The military stepped in again on 12 September 1980, much to the relief of the general population, and restored civil, fiscal and legal order.

The constitution was rewritten so as to avoid parliamentary impasses. In a plebiscite, it was approved overwhelmingly by the voters. The head of the military government, General Kenan Evren, resigned his military commission (as Atatürk had done) and was elected to be the country's new president. Under the interim Consultative Assembly and National Security Council, laws stalemated for years were passed. The old political leaders, seen by the new government to have been responsible for the breakdown of society, were tried (if they had committed crimes) or excluded from political life for 10 years. The indictment against the head of the now-outlawed neo-Nazi party ran to nearly 1000 pages; he was subsequently convicted.

In 1983, elections under the new constitution were held, and the centre-right Anavatan Partisi (Motherland

Party), the one less favoured by the military caretakers, won easily. The new prime minister was Turgut Özal, a former World Bank economist. Under the new government, Turkey continues on the course it has pursued since Atatürk: a persistent drive towards an industrialised western economy. How successful this will be is, as with many small countries who pursue such a course, more in the hands of world banks and world markets than in the efforts of the countries themselves.

ATATÜRK - THE NATIONAL HERO

It won't take you long to discover the national hero, Kemal Atatürk. Though he died on 10 November 1938, his picture is everywhere, a bust or statue (preferably equestrian) is in every park, and quotations from his speeches and writings are on

Kemal Atatürk

every public building. He is almost synonymous with the Turkish Republic.

The best popular account of his life and times is *Atatürk: The Rebirth of a Nation* by Lord Kinross (Weidenfeld & Nicolson, London, 1964). As portrayed by Kinross, Atatürk is a man of great intelligence and even greater energy and daring, possessed by the idea of giving his fellow Turks a new lease on life. Like all too few leaders, he had the capability of realising his obsession almost single-handedly. His achievement in turning a backward empire into a forward-looking nation-state was taken as a model by Egypt's Gamal Abdel Nasser, the shahs of Iran and other Islamic leaders. None had the same degree of success, however.

Early Years

In 1881, a boy named Mustafa was born into the family of a minor Turkish bureaucrat living in Salonika, now the Greek city of Thessaloniki, but at that time a city in Ottoman Macedonia. Mustafa was smart, and a hard worker in school. His mathematics teacher was so impressed that he gave him the nickname Kemal (excellence). The name Mustafa Kemal stuck with him as he went through a military academy and the War College, and even as he pursued his duties as an officer.

Military Career

He served with distinction and acquired a reputation as something of a hothead, perhaps because his commanders were not as bold as he was. By the time of the Gallipoli battle in WW I, he was a promising lieutenant colonel of infantry.

The defence of Gallipoli, which saved Constantinople from British conquest (until the end of the war, at least), was a personal triumph for Mustafa Kemal. His strategic and tactical genius came into full play; his commanders had little to do but approve his suggestions; he led with utter disregard for his own safety. A vastly superior British force (mostly Anzacs) was driven away, and Mustafa Kemal became an Ottoman folk hero.

Though he was promoted to the rank of *paşa* ('pasha', general), the powers-that-be wanted to keep him under control. They saw him as a 'dangerous element', and they were right. When the war was lost and the empire was on the verge of being disarmed and dismembered, Mustafa Kemal Paşa began his revolution.

The Revolution

He held meetings and congresses to rally the people, began to establish democratic institutions, and held off several invading armies (French, Italian and Greek), all at the same time and with severely limited resources. Several times the whole effort almost collapsed. Many of his friends and advisers were ready to ride out of Ankara for their lives, but Kemal never flinched and was always ready to dare the worst. He was skilful – and fortunate – enough to carry through.

Many great revolutionary leaders falter or fade when the revolution is won. Atatürk was fortunate enough to live 15 years into the republican era, and he had no doubts as to what the new country's course should be. He introduced reforms and directed the country's progress with surprising foresight.

Most importantly, he gave Turks a new, positive image of themselves with which to replace the negative western image of the Ottoman Turk as decadent, sombre, ignorant and incompetent. This western image, which replaced that of the 'Terrible Turk' once there was no longer a threat that Turkey would conquer Europe, was based on a little truth and a lot of politics, but also on religious grounds: Turks were not Christian, and therefore unworthy. Atatürk replaced the Ottoman Turk with a new person who was European and modern in outlook.

Atatürk was the right man at the right time, and many Turks believe that without him there is no way Turkey could be what it is today. Rather, it might have

ceased to exist; at the least, it would be like one of its Islamic neighbours, with less material and social progress, and no real grounding in democratic traditions. The Turks look around them at their Islamic neighbours and thank their lucky stars they had a leader of such ability and foresight.

What This Means to You

This all means something to the visitor. There is a law against defaming the national hero, who is still held in the highest regard by the Turks. You won't see cartoons or caricatures of him, and no-one mentions him in jest. The battle for nationhood was just too close ever to be anything but a serious matter. A slight directed toward Atatürk is virtually the same as insulting the Turks and their country.

GEOGRAPHY & CLIMATE

Most first-time visitors come to Turkey expecting to find deserts, palm trees and camel caravans. In fact, the country is geographically diverse, with snow-capped mountains, rolling steppe, broad rivers, verdant coasts and rich agricultural valleys.

It's interesting to note that Ankara, the country's capital, is at a latitude similar to those of Naples, Lisbon, Beijing and Philadelphia. The southernmost shore of Turkey is similar in latitude to Tokyo, Seoul, Gibraltar, Norfolk (USA) and San Francisco.

Distances

Turkey is big: the distance by road from Edirne on the Bulgarian border to Kars on the Russian one is over 1700 km. From the Black Sea shore to the Mediterranean is almost 1000 km. Now, 1000 km on flat ground might take only one very long day to drive, but Turkey has many mountain ranges which can lengthen travel times considerably.

Geographic Statistics

Turkey is located between 35° and 42° north latitude, and 25° and 44° east longitude. It covers an area of 779,452 square km, and has borders with Bulgaria, Greece, Iran, Iraq, Syria and the Soviet Union. Its coastline totals almost 8400 km; the Aegean coastline alone is 2800 km long. As for mountains, the highest is Ağrı Dağı (Mt Ararat) at 5165 metres (17,275 feet). Uludağ (Mt Olympus) near Bursa is 2543 metres (8343 feet). Under the empire, snow and ice could be taken from Uludağ, sailed across the Sea of Marmara, and presented to the sultan in İstanbul to cool his drinks.

Climatic Regions

Going from west to east, here's the lay of the land:

Marmara This region includes eastern Thrace from Edirne to İstanbul, rolling steppe and low hills good for grazing, some farming and industry. The peninsula of Gelibolu (Gallipoli) forms the north shore of the Çanakkale Boğazı (Dardanelles, Hellespont). On the southern shore of the Sea of Marmara are low hills and higher mountains (including Uludağ). The land is very rich, excellent for raising fruits such as grapes, peaches and apricots. The average rainfall is about 670 mm; this is Turkey's second most humid region, with an annual average of 73% humidity.

Aegean This is a region of fertile plains and river valleys, low hills and not-so-low mountains. The ancient river Meander, now called the Menderes, is a good example of the Aegean's rivers. When you see it from the heights of ruined Priene, you'll know where the word 'meander' comes from. For travelling, the Aegean region presents constantly changing views of olive, fig and fruit orchards on hillsides; and broad tobacco and sunflower fields in the valleys.

Mediterranean The Mediterranean coast is mountainous without much beach between Fethiye and Antalya, but then opens up into a fertile plain between Antalya and Alanya before going to mountains again. All along the south coast, mountains loom to the north. The great Taurus (Toros) range stretches all the way from Alanya east to Adana. Temperatures at Antalya are a few degrees warmer than at İzmir.

Central Anatolia The Turkish heartland is a vast high plateau broken by mountain ranges, some being volcanoes with snow-capped peaks. The land is mostly rolling steppe good for growing wheat and grazing sheep. Ankara's elevation is 900 metres above sea level. In summer, Ankara is hot and dry; in winter, chilly and often damp. Late spring and early autumn are perfect.

Black Sea The coast, 1700 km long, has a climate you might not expect in this part of the world. Rainfall is two to three times the national average, and temperatures are moderate. You will see hazelnut groves (on which the economy depends heavily), cherry orchards and tobacco fields. The root word of 'cherry' is the Latin *cerasus* (Turkish *kiraz*), and this is where they came from, getting their name in Roman times. The cattle on the outskirts of every town provide milk, cream and butter famous throughout Turkey. At the eastern end of the Black Sea coast, the mountains come right down to the sea, and the slopes are covered with tea plantations. Rainfall and humidity are highest here. All in all, the Black Sea coast is like central Europe, but pleasantly warmer.

South-East Anatolia This region is dry (382 mm rainfall per year) and very hot in summer, as hot as 47°C. The land is rolling steppe with rock outcrops. The major rivers are the Tigris (Dicle) and the Euphrates (Fırat), both of which spring in

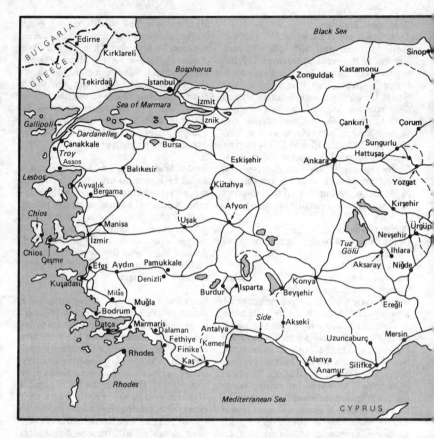

Turkey. In the next few years, the mammoth South-East Anatolia Project (*GAP*) will come on line, providing irrigation to thousands of hectares of farmland and millions of kilowatt-hours of electricity for industry. Huge new lakes will be formed and new recreational facilities built. All of this activity should change the face of this historically poor and heavily Kurdish region, making it among the most prosperous in the country.

Eastern Anatolia A mountainous and somewhat forbidding zone, this is wildly beautiful like no other region in Turkey. The average temperature is a cool 9°C, but varies between a hot 38°C and a daunting –43°C. Rainfall is average for Turkey, about 560 mm. It's cold out here except from June to September. The people are not as rich as in other regions, but they do well enough grazing sheep, raising wheat and producing a few other crops.

When to Visit
Spring and autumn are best, roughly from April to June and September to October. The climate is perfect on the Aegean and

Mediterranean coasts then, and in İstanbul. It's cooler in Central Anatolia, but not unpleasantly so. Normally, there is little rain between May and October except along the Black Sea coast.

The best months for water sports are, of course, the warmest: July and August. But the water is just right in May, June, September and October too.

In the hottest months on the coasts you may have to take a siesta during the heat of the day between 12 noon and 3 pm. Get up early in the morning, clamber around the local ruins, then after lunch and a siesta come out again for *piyasa vakti*,

'promenade time', when everyone strolls by the sea, sits in a café, and watches the sunset.

If you plan a trip to eastern Turkey, do it in late June, July or August. As a general rule, you should not venture into the east before June or after September unless you're prepared, as there will still be lots of snow around, perhaps even closing roads and mountain passes. Unfortunately, the trip to eastern Turkey in high summer usually includes a pass through the south-east, which is beastly hot at that time.

The following chart shows the average daily minimum and maximum temperatures (in C°) for the main centres in Turkey.

city	Jan	March	May	July	Sept	Nov
Ankara	-4 – 4	0 – 11	9 – 22	15 – 30	11 – 26	2 – 13
Antalya	6 – 15	8 – 18	15 – 25	23 – 34	19 – 31	11 – 21
Bursa	2 – 9	4 – 13	11 – 23	17 – 31	14 – 27	7 – 16
Edirne	-1 – 6	2 – 12	12 – 24	17 – 31	13 – 27	5 – 13
İstanbul	3 – 8	3 – 10	12 – 21	18 – 29	16 – 25	9 – 15
İzmir	5 – 12	6 – 16	14 – 26	21 – 33	17 – 29	10 – 29
Silifke	7 – 14	9 – 18	15 – 26	22 – 32	20 – 31	12 – 22
Trabzon	5 – 11	5 – 11	13 – 17	20 – 26	18 – 23	10 – 16

POPULATION

Turkey has a population estimated at 56 million in 1990. Though the great majority of its people are Turks, ethnically and linguistically, there is a significant Kurdish population in the south-eastern region. The Kurds, though Muslims, have their own language and close tribal and family affiliations. Turkey also has small groups of Greeks, Armenians, Laz (a Black Sea people), Assyrians and Jews. The Turkish Jewish community is the remnant of a great influx which took place in the 1500s when the Jews of Spain were forced by the Inquisition to flee their homes. They were welcomed into the Ottoman Empire, and brought with them knowledge of many recent European scientific and economic discoveries and advancements. Commemoration of the Jewish emigration to Turkish lands will be celebrated in 1992.

RELIGION

The Turkish population is 99% Muslim, mostly of the Sunni creed; and there are groups of Shiites in the east and south-east. A small community of Sephardic Jews, descendants of those who were driven out of Spain by the Inquisition and welcomed into the Ottoman Empire, exists in İstanbul. There are groups of Greek Orthodox, Armenian Orthodox, Byzantine Catholic, Armenian Roman Catholic, Armenian Protestant and a few even smaller sects. But all of these non-Muslim groups make up less than 1% of the population, so to talk about Turkish religion is to talk about Islam.

The story of Islam's founding is covered in the History section.

Principles of Islam

The basic beliefs of Islam are these: God (Allah) created the world and everything in it pretty much according to the biblical account. In fact, the Bible is a sacred book to Muslims. Adam, Noah, Abraham, Moses and Jesus were prophets. Their teachings and revelations are accepted by Muslims, except for Jesus' divinity and his status as saviour. Jews and Christians are called 'People of the Book', meaning those with a revealed religion that preceded Islam. The Koran prohibits enslavement of any People of the Book. Jewish prophets and wise men, Christian saints and martyrs, are all accepted as holy men in Islam.

However, Islam is the 'perfection' of this earlier tradition. Though Moses and Jesus were great prophets, Muhammed was the greatest and last, the Prophet. To him, God communicated his final revelation, and entrusted him to communicate it to the world. Muhammed is not a saviour, nor is he divine. He is God's messenger, deliverer of the final, definitive message.

Muslims do not worship Muhammed, only God. In fact, muslim in Arabic means, 'one who has submitted (to God's will)'; *islam* is 'submission (to God's will)'. It's all summed up in the *ezan*, the phrase called out from the minaret five times a day and said at the beginning of Muslim prayers: 'God is great! There is no god but God, and Muhammed is his Prophet.'

The Koran

God's revelations to Muhammed are contained in the *Kur'an-i Kerim*, the Holy Koran. Muhammed recited the *suras* (verses or chapters) of the Koran in an inspired state. They were written down by followers, and are still regarded as the most beautiful, melodic and poetic work in Arabic literature, sacred or profane. The Koran, being sacred, cannot be translated. It exists truly only in Arabic.

The Islamic Commonwealth

Ideally, Islam is a commonwealth, a theocracy, in which the religious law of the Koran is the only law – there is no secular law. Courts are religious courts. In Turkey and several other Muslim countries, this belief has been replaced by secular law codes. By contrast, Ayatollah Khomeini attempted to do away with secular law and return to the exclusive use of Islamic

Two calligraphic versions of the **Basmallah** – phrase 'Bismillah al-rahman al-rahim': In the name of God the Compassionate the Merciful

law in the Islamic Republic of Iran. In Saudi Arabia, religious law rules as well.

Religious Duties & Practices

To be a Muslim, one need only submit in one's heart to God's will, and perform a few basic and simple religious duties:
– One must say, understand and believe, 'There is no god but God, and Muhammed is His Prophet'.
– One must pray five times daily: at dawn, at noon, at mid-afternoon, at dusk and after dark.
– One must give alms to the poor.
– One must keep the fast of Ramazan, if capable of doing so.
– One must make a pilgrimage to Mecca once during one's life, if possible.

Muslim prayers are set rituals. Before praying, a Muslim must wash hands and arms, feet and ankles, head and neck in running water; if no water is available, in clean sand; if there's no sand, the motions will suffice. Then he must cover his head, face Mecca and perform a precise series of gestures and genuflexions. If he deviates from the pattern, he must begin again.

In daily life, a Muslim must not touch or eat pork, or drink wine (interpreted as any alcoholic beverage), and must refrain from fraud, usury, slander and gambling. No sort of image can be revered or worshipped in any way.

Islam has been split into many factions and sects since the time of Muhammed. Islamic theology has become very elaborate and complex. These tenets, however, are still the basic ones shared by all Muslims.

CUSTOMS & PRACTICES

Under the Ottoman Empire (1300s to 1923), Turkish etiquette was highly organised and very formal. Every encounter among people turned into a mini-ceremony full of the flowery 'romance of the East'. Though the Turks have adapted to the informality of 20th-century life, you'll still notice vestiges of this courtly state of mind. Were you to learn Turkish, you'd find dozens of polite phrases – actually rigid formulas – to be repeated on cue in many daily situations. Some are listed in the language section at the back of this book. Use one of these at the proper moment, and the Turks will love it.

Turks are very understanding of foreigners' different customs, but if you want to behave in accordance with local feelings, use all the polite words you can muster, at all times. This can get laborious, and even Turks complain about how one can't even get out the door without five minutes of politenesses. But even the complainers still say them.

Also note these things: don't point your finger directly towards any person. Don't show the sole of your foot or shoe towards anyone (ie, so they can see it). Don't blow your nose openly in public, especially in a restaurant; instead, turn or leave the room and blow quietly. Don't pick your teeth openly, but cover your mouth with your hand. Don't do a lot of kissing or hugging with a person of the opposite sex in public. All of these actions are considered rude and offensive.

Mosque Etiquette

Always remove your shoes before stepping on a mosque's carpets, or on the clean area just in front of the mosque door. This is not a religious law, just a practical one. Worshippers kneel and touch their foreheads to the carpets, and they like to keep them clean. If there are no carpets, as in a saint's tomb, you can walk right in with your shoes on.

Wear modest clothes when visiting mosques, as you would when visiting a church. Don't wear tatty blue jeans, shorts (men or women) or weird gear. Women should have head, arms and shoulders covered, and modest dresses or skirts, preferably to the knees. At some of the most visited mosques, attendants will lend you long robes if your clothing doesn't meet a minimum standard. The loan of the robe is free, though the attendant will probably indicate where you can give a donation to the mosque. If you donate, chances are that the money actually will go to the mosque.

Visiting Turkish mosques is generally very easy, though there are no hard and fast rules. Most times no-one will give you any trouble, but now and then there may be a stickler for propriety guarding the door, and he will keep you out if your dress or demeanour is not acceptable.

Avoid entering mosques at prayer time, (ie, at the call to prayer – dawn, noon, mid-afternoon, dusk and evening, or 20 minutes thereafter). Avoid visiting mosques at all on Fridays, especially morning and noon. Friday is the Muslim holy day.

When you're inside a mosque, even if it is not prayer time, there will usually be several people praying. Don't disturb them in any way; don't take flash photos; don't walk directly in front of them.

Everybody will love you if you drop some money into the donations box.

Body Language

Turks say 'yes' (*evet*, eh-VEHT) by nodding the head forward and down.

To say 'no' (*hayır*, HAH-yuhr), nod your head up and back, lifting your eyebrows at the same time. Or just raise your eyebrows: that's 'no'.

Another way of saying 'no' is *yok* (YOHK), literally 'It doesn't exist (here)', or 'We don't have any (of it)'. Same head upward, raised eyebrows.

Remember, when a Turk seems to be giving you an arch look, he's only saying 'no'. He may also make the sound 'tsk', which also means 'no'. There are lots of ways to say 'no' in Turkish.

By contrast, wagging your head from side to side doesn't mean 'no' in Turkish; it means 'I don't understand'. So if a Turk asks you, 'Are you looking for the bus to Ankara?' and you shake your head, he'll assume you don't understand English, and will probably ask you the same question again, this time in German.

There are other signs that can cause

confusion, especially when you're out shopping. For instance, if you want to indicate length ('I want a fish this big'), don't hold your hands apart at the desired length, but hold out your arm and place a flat hand on it, measuring from your fingertips to the hand. Thus, if you want a pretty big fish, you must 'chop' your arm with your other hand at about the elbow.

Height is indicated by holding a flat hand the desired distance above the floor or some other flat surface such as a counter or table top.

If someone – a shopkeeper or restaurant waiter, for instance – wants to show you the stockroom or the kitchen, he'll signal 'Come on, follow me' by waving his hand downward and toward himself in a scooping motion. Waggling an upright finger would never occur to him, except perhaps as a vaguely obscene gesture.

HOLIDAYS & FESTIVALS

The official Turkish calendar is the western, Gregorian one as in Europe, but religious festivals, some of which are public holidays, are celebrated according to the Muslim lunar Hijri (HIJ-ree) calendar. As the lunar calendar is about 11 days shorter than the Gregorian, the Muslim festivals arrive that many days earlier each year.

Actual dates for Muslim religious festivals are not completely systematic. Rather, they are proclaimed by Muslim authorities after the appropriate astronomical observations and calculations have been made, and then the civil authorities decide how many days should be civil holidays. To help you know what's going on, the approximate dates of all major festivals for the near future are listed at the end of this section. No matter what month or year you visit Turkey, you can see at once when a lunar-calendar festival will be held.

Muslim days, like Jewish ones, begin at sundown. Thus a Friday holiday will begin Thursday at sunset and last until Friday sunset. For major religious and civic holidays there is also a half-day vacation for 'preparation', called *arife* (ah-ree-FEH), preceding the start of a festival; shops and offices close about noon, and the festival begins at sunset.

Friday is the Muslim Sabbath, but it is not a holiday. Mosques and baths will be crowded, especially Friday morning. The day of rest, a secular one, is Sunday.

Only two religious holidays are public holidays: Şeker Bayramı and Kurban Bayramı.

Festivals

Regaip Kandili According to the lunar calendar, Regaip Kandili is the first Friday in the month of Recep, the traditional date for the conception of the Prophet Muhammed. Mosques are illuminated and special foods prepared. You'll see packets of small, sweetish *simit* bread rings, wrapped in coloured paper, for sale on the streets.

Miraç Kandili The 26th of the month of Recep, Miraç Kandili celebrates Muhammed's miraculous nocturnal journey from Mecca to Jerusalem and to heaven astride a winged horse named Burak. Mosques are illuminated and special foods eaten.

Berat Kandili The 'sacred night' between the 14th and 15th of the month of Şaban, this has various meanings in different Islamic countries, like Hallowe'en (All Saints, Day of the Dead). There are mosque illuminations and special foods.

Ramazan The Holy Month, called Ramadan in other Muslim countries, is similar in some ways to Lent. For the 30 days of Ramazan, a good Muslim lets *nothing* pass the lips during daylight hours: no eating, drinking, smoking, or even licking a postage stamp. A cannon shot, and these days a radio announcer, signal the end of the fast at sunset. The fast is broken traditionally with flat pide bread if possible. Lavish dinners are given and may last far into the night. Before dawn, drummers circulate through town to awaken the faithful so they can eat before sunrise.

Ramazan can be an ordeal when it falls in hot weather; *Ramazan kafası* ('Ramazan head', meaning irritability) can cause arguments to break out. Restaurants may be closed till nightfall, and in conservative towns it's bad form for anyone – non-Muslims included – to smoke, munch snacks or sip drinks in plain view. Business hours may change and be shorter. As non-Muslims, it's understood that you get to eat and drink when you like, and in the big cities you'll find lots of non-fasting Muslims right beside you, but it's best to be discreet and to maintain a polite low visibility.

The fasting of Ramazan is a worthy, sacred act and a blessing to Muslims. Pregnant or nursing women, the infirm and aged, and travellers are excused, according to the Koran, if they feel they cannot keep the fast.

Kadir Gecesi The 27th day of the Holy Month of Ramazan is the 'Night of Power', when the Koran was revealed and Muhammed was appointed to be the Messenger of God. His duty was to communicate the Word of God to the world. Mosque illuminations, special prayers and foods celebrate the day.

Şeker Bayramı Also called Ramazan Bayramı or İd es-Seğir, this is a three-day festival at the end of Ramazan. *Şeker* (shek-EHR) is sugar or candy; during this festival children traditionally go door to door asking for sweet treats. Muslims exchange greeting cards and pay social calls. Everybody enjoys drinking lots of tea in broad daylight, after fasting for Ramazan. The festival is a three-day national holiday when banks and offices are closed. Hotels, buses, trains and airplanes are heavily booked.

Kurban Bayramı The most important religious and secular holiday of the year, Kurban Bayramı (koor-BAHN, sacrifice) is equivalent in importance to Christmas in Christian countries. The traditional date for its beginning is the 10th day of the month of Zilhicce.

The festival commemorates Abraham's near-sacrifice of Isaac on Mt Moriah (Genesis 22; Koran, Sura 37). In the story, God orders Abraham to take Isaac, the son of his old age, up to Mt Moriah and sacrifice him. Abraham takes Isaac up the mountain and lays him on the altar, but at the last moment God stops Abraham, congratulates him on his faithfulness, and orders him to sacrifice instead a ram tangled in a nearby bush. Abraham does so.

Following the tradition today, 2½ million rams are sacrificed on Kurban Bayramı in Turkey each year. For days beforehand you'll see herds of sheep parading through streets or gathered in markets. Every head of household who can afford a sheep buys one and takes it home. Right after the early morning prayers on the actual day of Bayram, the head of the household slits the sheep's throat. It's then flayed and butchered, and family and friends immediately cook up a feast. A sizeable portion of the meat is distributed to the needy, and the skin is often donated to a charity; the charity sells it to a leather products company. Lots of people take to the road, going home to parents or friends. Everybody exchanges greeting cards. At some point you'll probably be invited to share in the festivities.

Kurban Bayramı is a four-day national holiday which you must plan for. Banks may be closed for a full week, though one or two branches will stay open in the big cities to serve foreigners. Transportation will be packed, and hotel rooms, particularly in resort areas, will be scarce and expensive.

Mevlid-i Nebi The 12th of Rebi ul-evvel is the anniversary of the Prophet's birth (in

570 AD). There are special prayers and foods, and mosque illuminations.

THE CALENDAR
January
All Month Rainy and cold throughout the country, and not usually a pleasant time to visit. Eastern Turkey is in the icy grip of winter; Ankara and the rest of the Anatolian plateau may be covered in snow. Camel wrestling at various locations in the province of Aydın, south of İzmir.
Religious Holidays The movement of the Muslim lunar calendar makes January and February a time of *kandil* festivities, brightening an otherwise dour season. In 1992, Regaip Kandili is on 10 January; in 1991, it is on 18 January. Miraç Kandili is celebrated on 31 January 1992, and 21 January 1993.
1 January New Year's Day is a public holiday. Decorations in shops, exchanges of gifts and greeting cards, make it a kind of surrogate Christmas, good for business.
15-16 January Camel-wrestling festival in the village of Selçuk, next to Ephesus, south of İzmir.

February
In February it rains almost everywhere and is chilly and cheerless. The only fun to be had is indoors or at the ski slopes on Uludağ near Bursa. Another ski resort is in the Beydağları mountains near Antalya.
Religious Holidays Regaip Kandili falls on 2 February 1990. Miraç Kandili is on 23 February 1990, and 12 February 1991. Berat Kandili is on 18-19 February 1992 and 7-8 February 1993. The holy month of Ramazan begins on 23 February 1993, and lasts until 24 March 1993.

March
Still rainy in most of the country, though there may be some good periods on the south Aegean and Mediterranean coasts. It's still bitterly cold in the east.
Religious Holidays Berat Kandili occurs on 12-13 March 1990, and 1-2 March 1991.

March signals the beginning of the holy month of Ramazan these days. Ramazan is from 28 March to 26 April 1990, 17 March to 15 April 1991, 5 March to 3 April 1992, and 23 February to 24 March 1993. Kadir Gecesi, the 'Night of Power', is 31 March 1992, and 21 March 1993. Şeker Bayramı, the important three-day holiday following Ramazan, falls on 25-28 March 1993, so adjust your travel plans accordingly.

April
April can be delightful throughout the country, except in the east, where it's still cold. There may be some rain, but there may also be virtually none, and in any case the wild flowers will be out on the Anatolian plateau. The waters of the Aegean and Mediterranean are approaching a comfortably swimmable temperature. The south-east (Gaziantep, Urfa, Mardin, Diyarbakır), so torrid and parched in high summer, is very pleasant now, but there may still be snow atop Nemrut Dağı. April is when the bus tours begin in earnest.
Religious Holidays The movement of the lunar calendar brings Ramazan in coincidence with at least part of April. Ramazan is from 28 March to 26 April 1990, 17 March to 15 April 1991, and 5 March to 3 April 1992. Kadir Gecesi, the Night of Power, is 24 April 1990, and 12 April 1991. The Şeker Bayramı holiday will screw up your travel plans 27-30 April 1990; 16-18 April 1991 (but expect disruptions of your plans anytime in the period 13-21 April 1991); and 4-6 April 1992 (but expect disruptions 3-7 April).
20-30 April Manisa Power Gum Festival, when a traditional remedy called *mesir macunu* or *kuvvet macunu* ('power gum'), said to restore health, youth and potency, is concocted and distributed in Manisa, near İzmir.
23 April The big national holiday is National Sovereignty Day, when the first Grand National Assembly, or republican parliament, met in Ankara in 1920; it's also Children's Day. An international

children's festival, with kids from all over the world, is held in Ankara.

Late April to early May Tulip Festival in Emirgân, the Bosphorus suburb of İstanbul.

May

May usually brings perfectly beautiful weather throughout the country, with little chance of rain, though it's still chilly out east. May is a good month to visit the hot, dry south-east. This month begins the tourist season in earnest, and also includes important civil holidays. Bus tours are everywhere. Sound and light shows begin at the Blue Mosque in İstanbul and last until October.

In Konya, the javelin-throwing game of *cirit* (jirid), played on horseback, takes place every Saturday and Sunday until October.

First Week Selçuk Ephesus Festival of Culture & Art at Selçuk, south of İzmir; folk dances, concerts, exhibits, some in the Great Theatre at Ephesus.

19 May Youth & Sports Day, held to commemorate Atatürk's birthday (1881).

29 May In İstanbul, celebrations remember the conquest of the city from the Byzantines in 1453.

Last Week Festival of Pergamum at Bergama, north of İzmir – drama in the ancient theatre, folk dancing and handicrafts exhibits. In 1993, the important holiday of Kurban Bayramı begins on 29 May.

June

The weather is perfect throughout the country, but getting hot. There is little chance of rain except along the Black Sea coast. Bus tours drop off as the height of the tourist season approaches. Sound and light shows take place at the Blue Mosque in İstanbul all month.

Religious Holidays Kurban Bayramı, the most important holiday all year, will disrupt your travel schedule as millions of Turks head for the beaches, the mountains, and Grandma's house. The holiday tends to shut down the country for most of a week. Dates are 24-28 June 1991 (but expect disruptions from 23 to 30 June); 12-15 June 1992 (expect disruptions from 12 to 16 June); and 1-4 June 1993 (expect full buses and hotels from 29 May to 6 June 1993).

First Week The International Mediterranean Festival takes place in İzmir usually at this time.

4-5 June Traditional Rose-growing Competition at Konya, when roses grown in the region are judged.

7-13 June Music & Art Festival at Marmaris – musical performances, folk dances, exhibitions.

Second Week Traditional Kırkpınar Oiled Wrestling Competition at Edirne; Festival of Troy at Çanakkale, on the Dardanelles near Troy.

Late June to Mid-July The world-class İstanbul International Festival, with top performers in the arts and special exhibitions.

July

The weather is hot, the sky is always blue, the sea water is warm, and everything is crowded with holiday-makers, both Turkish and foreign. In İstanbul, sound and light at the Blue Mosque continues, as does the İstanbul Festival. These are the two highlights of the month, but watch out for Kurban Bayramı, which runs from 4 to 8 July 1990.

1 July The first day of the month is Denizcilik Günü (Navy Day), when mariners, ships and various maritime pursuits are celebrated. It commemorates the day when Turkey regained the right to operate its own ships along its own shores. (Under what are called the Capitulations, Ottoman sultans had granted this right of cabotage exclusively to foreign shipping companies.) You'll see decorations, hear speeches, and share in a moment of silence (except for ships' sirens and car horns) at 10 am. No public holiday, though.

5-10 July Nasreddin Hoca Celebrations,

in honour of the semilegendary humorous master of Turkish folklore legends and tales; held in Akşehir, his traditional birthplace. (Dates may be changed in 1990 due to the conflict with Kurban Bayramı).

7-12 July At Bursa, the Folklore & Music Festival is one of Turkey's best folk-dancing events of the year; the Bursa Fair (trade and tourism) starts about the same time.

29-31 July Music, Folklore & Water Sports Festival in Foça, north of İzmir.

August

It's hot and sunny all month, and crowded too. This is the best time to be in eastern Turkey, when the weather is fine and crowds are smaller than along the western beaches. In İstanbul, sound and light continue at the Blue Mosque. Similar shows begin at the Anıtkabir, Atatürk's mausoleum, in Ankara.

Religious Holidays Mevlid-i Nebi celebrations occur on 30 August 1993.

15 August A special mass celebrates the Assumption of the Virgin Mary, at the House of the Virgin Mary (Meryemana) near Ephesus. The Catholic Archbishop of İzmir says mass.

15-18 August Çanakkale Troy Festival at Çanakkale, near Troy – folk dances, music, tours of Mt Ida and Troy.

20 August to 9 September The biggest festival is the İzmir International Fair; for a month the city's hotels are packed and transportation is crowded. The fair has amusements, cultural and commercial-industrial displays.

26 August Armed Forces Day with speeches and parades.

30 August Zafer Bayramı (zah-FEHR, Victory), commemorating the decisive victory at Dumlupınar of the republican armies over the invading Greek army during Turkey's War of Independence in 1922. Several foreign countries, including Greece, invaded Anatolia after WW I. Towns and cities celebrate their own Kurtuluş Günü (koor-too-LOOSH gew-new, Day of Liberation) on the appropriate date when Atatürk's armies drove out the foreign troops during July and August 1922.

September

Weather is still hot and fine, moderating a bit toward the end of the month. Swimming is still wonderful, crowds are still fairly heavy, and the bus tours begin to make a comeback. Sound and light shows continue at the Blue Mosque in İstanbul and at the Anıtkabir in Ankara. The İzmir Fair goes on until 9 September.

Religious Holidays The Prophet's birthday, Mevlid-i Nebi, is celebrated on 21 September 1991, and 10 September 1992.

1-9 September Bodrum Culture & Art Week, Turkish classical music concerts in Bodrum Castle, art exhibits and water sports shows.

2-4 September Kırşehir Ahi Evran Crafts & Folklore Festival at Kırşehir, when Turkish handicrafts are displayed and modelled in shows.

9 September In İzmir it's Kurtuluş Günü, or Liberation Day. In 1922, Atatürk's armies pushed the Greek invaders into the sea. Lots of parades, speeches and flags.

11-12 September Çorum Hittite Festival, crafts shows, musical performances, tours of Hittite archaeological sites at Çorum near Ankara.

15-18 September Cappadocia Tourism Festival, a grape harvest and folklore festival highlighting the 'fairy chimneys' and underground cities of Cappadocia.

15 September to 5 October Textile & Fashion Fair at Mersin with fashion shows, handicrafts exhibitions, musical and folk-dancing performances.

22-30 September Konya hosts a culinary contest.

26-29 September At Diyarbakır, the Watermelon Festival. One year when I attended, everybody was disappointed because the prize-winning watermelon weighed in at a mere 32 kg. A bad year, they said – no rain.

October

The weather is perfect again, and crowds are diminishing, though bus tours begin again in earnest. The rains begin sometime in mid or late October, and it can rain for a week or two nonstop. There may also be freak snowstorms on the Anatolian plateau. There will be a **census** carried out on one Sunday in October, 1990, and there will be an **all-day curfew** on that day. Foreigners are supposedly excluded from the curfew, but most of the country will be closed up tight so there will be little to see or do. Plan to be in a hotel with dining facilities, or buy some food. The curfew usually ends in late afternoon or early evening. If you do go out, carry your passport. Sound and light shows are supposed to continue in İstanbul at the Blue Mosque, but check in advance.

Religious holidays The Prophet Muhammed's birthday, Mevlid-i Nebi, falls on 2 October 1991; kandil-like celebrations and illuminations.

1-9 October The 'Golden Orange' Film & Art Festival in Antalya, with a competition for best Turkish film of the year; other exhibits.

21-29 October Turkish Troubadours' Week at Konya – bards who continue the traditional poetic forms hold contests in repartee, free-form composition and riddles.

29 October Cumhuriyet Bayramı (joom-hoor-ee-YEHT, Republic Day), commemorating the proclamation of the republic by Atatürk in 1923; biggest civil holiday, lots of parades and speeches.

November

Weather is very pleasant, with cool to warm days and chill nights, but one must play cat and mouse with the rain, which may or may not become a bore. If your luck holds, you can have a marvellous late-year beach holiday.

10 November The most important day of the month, it is the day Atatürk died in 1938. At precisely 9.05 am, the moment of his death, the entire country comes to a screeching halt for a moment of silence. Literally everything stops in its tracks (you should too), just for a moment. Car horns and sirens blare. In schools, in the newspapers (the names of which are normally printed in red, but are all in black on this day), on radio and television, the national hero's life and accomplishments are reviewed.

December

Weather is chilly throughout the country, though milder along the Mediterranean coast. You must expect some rain, perhaps heavy rain. There are few visitors. In rare years, the warmth and pleasantness of a good November will stretch into early December.

All Month Camel wrestling at various locations in the province of Aydın, south of İzmir.

6-8 December St Nicholas Festival, when commemorative ceremonies are held in the 4th-century church of St Nicholas, the original Santa Claus, in Demre near Antalya.

14-17 December (approx) The Mevlana Festival, honouring Celaleddin Rumi, the great poet and mystic who founded the Mevlevi order of Whirling Dervishes, is held in Konya. Hotel space is tight, so try to pin down a room in advance, or be prepared to take a room below your normal standard.

LANGUAGE

Turkish is the dominant language in the Turkic language group which also includes such less-than-famous tongues as Kirghiz, Kazakh and Azerbaijani. Once thought to be related to Finnish and Hungarian, the Turkic languages are now seen as comprising their own unique language group. You can find people who speak Turkish, in one form or another, from Belgrade, Yugoslavia all the way to Sinkiang, China.

In 1928, Atatürk did away with the Arabic alphabet and adopted a Latin-based alphabet much better suited to easy learning and correct pronunciation. He also instituted a language reform to purge Turkish of abstruse Arabic and Persian borrowings, in order to rationalise and simplify it. The result is a logical, systematic and expressive language which has only one irregular noun (*su*, water), one irregular verb (*etmek*, to be) and no genders. It is so logical, in fact, that Turkish grammar formed the basis for the development of Esperanto.

Word order and verb formation are very different from those belonging to the Indo-European languages, which makes Turkish somewhat difficult to learn at first despite its elegant simplicity. Verbs, for example, consist of a root plus any number of modifying suffixes. Verbs can be so complex that they constitute whole sentences in themselves, though this is rare. The standard blow-your-mind example is, *Afyonkarahisarlılaştıramadıklarımızdanmısınız?* 'Aren't you one of those people whom we tried – unsuccessfully – to make to resemble the citizens of Afyonkarahisar?' It's not the sort of word you see every day.

Turks don't expect any foreigner to know Turkish, but if you can manage a few words you'll delight them. For their part, they'll try whatever foreign words they know, usually English or German, but some French, Dutch or Swedish as well. In this guide I've written the necessary Turkish words into the text wherever possible, so that you won't be at a loss for words. For a full collection of words, see the Turkish Language Guide section at the back of this book.

To help you in your travels, you might want to buy a copy of Lonely Planet's forthcoming Turkish phrasebook. To help you learn correct pronunciation, I'm offering an audio cassette keyed to both this guidebook and the Lonely Planet Turkish phrasebook. For a copy of the cassette, please send your name and address, and a cheque payable to Tom Brosnahan for US$10, A$12.50, UK£6, CN$12, or SFr 16, to Turkish Cassette, c/o Tom Brosnahan, PO Box 563, Concord, MA 01742, USA.

Facts for the Visitor

VISAS

If you have a valid passport, chances are good that you can enter Turkey and stay for three months, no questions asked. Citizens of Australia, Canada, Eire, Japan, New Zealand, the UK, the USA and virtually all the countries of western and central Europe have that privilege. Citizens of some other places – Hong Kong, Jamaica, etc – have it as well. If in doubt, check with the Turkish Embassy in your country (for addresses of Turkish embassies abroad, see Overseas Reps in the Tourist Information section).

Don't overstay your visit. If you're going to stay a year, you might want to apply for a residence permit (*İkamet tezkeresi*), in which case you will have to show means of support. This means savings, a steady income from outside the country, or legal work within the country. The last is very difficult to find. Most people staying for a shorter period, or working without a valid permit (as private tutors of English, for example), cross the border into Greece for a day or two every three months rather than bother with the residence permit.

For visas to East European countries, which you may need if you are travelling overland into or out of Turkey, refer to the relevant information in the Tourist Information section.

CUSTOMS

Upon entering the country, customs inspection is often very cursory for foreign tourists. They may spot-check, but you probably won't even have to open your bags.

Arrival

A verbal declaration is usually all you need. You can bring in up to one kg of coffee, five litres of liquor and two cartons (400) of cigarettes. Things of exceptional value (jewellery, unusually expensive electronic or photographic gear, etc) are supposed to be declared, and may be entered in your passport to guarantee that you will take the goods out of the country when you leave.

Vehicles Automobiles, minibuses, trailers, towed watercraft, motor cycles and bicycles can be brought in for up to three months without a carnet or triptyque. Drivers must have a valid driving licence; an International Driving Licence is useful, but not normally required. Your own national driving licence should pass all right. Third-party insurance such as a 'green card' valid for the entire country (not just for Thrace or European Turkey) or a Turkish policy purchased at the border is obligatory.

Departure

It is illegal to buy, sell, possess or export antiquities! Read on.

You may export valuables (except antiquities) that have been registered in your passport on entry, or that have been purchased with legally converted money. For souvenirs, the maximum export limit is US$1000 of all items combined; if two or more similar items are exported, a licence may be required. Also, you may need to show proof of exchange transactions for at least these amounts. Save your currency exchange slips, and have them ready for the customs officer in the departure area.

Your bags may well be checked when you leave the country (both for customs and security reasons), and searching questions will be asked about whether or not you are taking any antiquities with you. Only true antiquities are off limits, not the many artful fakes. If you buy a real Roman coin from a shepherd boy at an archaeological site, can you take it home with you? Legally not. What happens if you get caught trying to smuggle out a significant piece of ancient statuary? Big trouble.

Turkey is one of those countries with treasure-troves of antiquities, some of which are smuggled out of the country and fed into the international contraband art market. The Turkish government takes vigorous measures to defend its patrimony against theft. Antiquity smuggling, like drug smuggling, is a dirty business. Keep away from it.

Arrival Home My own advice, given after decades of travel, is to realise that customs officials in your home country may encounter hundreds of travellers returning from Turkey every week; they see what travellers have bought; they know pretty well what was paid. You are not the expert on souvenirs and prices, *they are!* Keep this in mind to avoid expensive unpleasantness.

British readers have written to warn that you should get official-looking receipts from Turkish shopkeepers for any expensive item you purchase to take home to Britain. British customs officers may expect you to underdeclare, asking 'What did you *really* pay?' If you budge from your original price (as on the receipt), they'll read you the riot act, and you'll have to cough up some duty. If you try to smuggle dutiable goods through the 'green' channel and are caught, they may offer you a choice: pay a fine equal to the price you paid for the goods abroad, or face criminal prosecution.

MONEY

The unit of currency is the Turkish *lira*, or TL, which was called the Turkish pound (LT) in the Ottoman Empire. The lira is supposedly divided into 100 *kuruş* (koo-ROOSH), but inflation has rendered the kuruş obsolete.

Coins are rare, but you may come across coins of 50 and 100 liras, and even higher denominations as time goes by. Banknotes

come as 100, 500, 1000, 5000, 10,000 and 20,000 liras, and soon even higher, no doubt.

The exchange rates at the time of writing were:

US$ 1 =	2200TL
UK£1 =	3417TL
A$ 1 =	1667TL
NZ$ 1 =	1284TL
C$ 1 =	1867TL
DM 1 =	1104TL

Changing Money

Wait until you arrive in Turkey to change your home currency (cash or travellers' cheques) into Turkish liras. Exchange bureaus in other countries (eg UK, USA) usually offer terrible rates of exchange. When in doubt, check the foreign exchange listings in the business section of any important daily newspaper, or call a commercial bank. A proper tourist exchange rate will be only a few percentage points less than this published rate.

Always have your passport with you when you change money in Turkey.

Many tourist shops, travel agencies, expensive restaurants and some hotels have licences to accept foreign currency. The rate may not be quite as good as you get at the bank, though all rates will be pretty close. Most post office (PTT) branches will give you liras for foreign cash, but not for travellers' cheques. Eurocheques are readily accepted by banks and also by many shops. With the value of the Turkish lira constantly dropping, it's wise to change money every few days rather than all at once at the beginning of your visit.

Travellers' Cheques There is no problem in exchanging travellers' cheques for Turkish liras in a bank, as long as you have your passport with you. The more expensive hotels, restaurants and shops will accept the cheques, as will car rental agencies and travel agencies. Generally it's better to change cheques to Turkish liras in a bank, although some may charge a fee (see Commissions in the Banks section).

Although a wide range of cheques is accepted, the more familiar your cheques are, the better. American Express, Thomas Cook, Eurocheques and the like go quickly. I once changed some Swiss Bankers' travellers' cheques with little trouble; the clerk just had to look up the example in a book and compare them.

Exchange Receipts Save your currency exchange receipts (*bordro*). You will need them to change back Turkish liras at the end of your stay. Turkish liras may be worth a lot less outside the country, so you won't want to take them with you.

Credit Cards

Turks are beginning to learn about living on plastic. The big hotels and expensive shops will accept your credit card. Car rental agencies certainly will. Make sure in advance because not all establishments accept all cards. If you have American Express, Visa, Diners Club, MasterCard, Access and Eurocard, you're probably equipped for any establishment that takes cards. If you only have one or two, ask. Turkish Airlines, for instance, may accept only Visa, MasterCard, Access and Eurocard. The Turkish State Railways doesn't accept credit cards at present, but it may soon do so. A souvenir shop may accept all major cards.

A shopkeeper may require you to pay the credit card fee of 5% to 7%, or the charges (up to US$3 or US$4) for making credit card arrangements (*provizyon*, pro-veez-YOHN) with a bank: he may not see it as a normal cost of business. Any price, whether marked or haggled for, is assumed to be for cash. As he must pay the credit card company a percentage, and the bank a fee, he may reason that these charges should be passed on to you.

Banks

Banks are open from 8.30 am till 12 noon,

and from 1.30 to 5 pm, Monday to Friday. Outside those times it's difficult to change money, so plan ahead. There are currency exchange desks at the major entry points to Turkey by road, air and sea. The rate at the entry point will be pretty close to the one in town, so it's a good idea to change some money when you enter – US$25 or US$50 at least.

Almost any bank will change money for you. Look for a sign on or near the front door reading 'Kambiyo – Exchange – Change – Wechsel', which says it all. In the large cities, big banks have branches everywhere, even within 100 metres of one another, and exchange facilities may be limited to the more convenient branches. If a bank tells you it can't change your money, don't worry. You won't have to walk very far to reach the next one.

Many banks will post the daily exchange rates for all the major European currencies, plus the Japanese yen and the US dollar. You'll have no trouble exchanging US dollars, pounds sterling, marks, francs, guilders, kroner, etc. Dollars, marks and sterling seem to go fastest. Eurocheques are readily accepted.

Procedures Changing money, either banknotes or travellers' cheques, can take anywhere from two to 15 minutes. It depends upon the bank and how cumbersome its procedures are. Sometimes a clerk must type up a form with your name and passport number, you must sign it once or twice, it must be countersigned by one or two bank officers, and then a cashier in a glass booth (*vezne*) will give you your money. Always take your passport when changing money, and be prepared to wait a while.

Commissions Some banks charge a fee for changing travellers' cheques (though not for changing cash notes). The Türkiye İş Bankası, for instance, charges up to 3%, plus the cost of official stamps. Most other banks charge nothing and have the same rate of exchange, so try elsewhere. To find

out before you begin, ask *Komisyon alınır mı?* (koh-meess-YOHN ah-luh-NUHR muh, 'Is a commission taken?')

Transferring Money
The speed with which you need to transfer money determines the cost of the transfer. If you have months, send a letter home, ask for a cheque, deposit the cheque in a Turkish bank for clearance, then wait. Of course, banks can telex or wire money in a matter of a day or two (usually), but this may cost as much as US$30 per transfer. Sometimes the transfer fee is a percentage of the amount transferred. Still, if you're in a hurry, you may have to do it.

Though the PTT in Turkey handles postal money orders, I would not recommend this route for anything more than token amounts. The PTT is often difficult to deal with. You'll do better with a bank.

Before transferring money, consider these alternatives: some shopkeepers and other businesses will accept a personal cheque in exchange for a purchase. If you have a Turkish friend to countersign a cheque, you may well be able to get cash from a bank. With some credit cards, you may be able to get a cash advance on the card from a bank, or use the card as security to cash a cheque at the card's company office. Even if the amount is limited (US$100 to US$150 per day), it doesn't take many days to build up a substantial sum. A bank may require you to pay a telex charge of a few dollars for a credit card cash advance.

If it comes to transferring money by bank wire, walk into a large bank, preferably in a large town, find someone who speaks English and explain the problem. The bank may be able to telex your bank and request the funds, or you may have to call your bank (or a friend) and do it yourself. When the funds arrive at the Turkish bank, take your passport and pick up your money.

The Black Market

There is no currency black market to speak of as the Turkish government is heading toward full convertibility of the Turkish lira.

COSTS

All costs in this book are given only in US dollars as prices in Turkish liras are ever changing.

Inflation is about 75% to 100% per annum, though the government swears it is trying hard to bring it down. The exchange rates for hard currency reflect a slow, 'creeping' devaluation which offsets this inflation and keeps the actual cost for a foreign tourist reasonable. An adventurous traveller can live on as little as US$8 or US$10 a day, easily on US$15 a day. For US$25 to US$50 a day, you can live in comfort and even style. If you go luxury class, the sky's the limit. Spending US$500 is not impossible, though it would be bizarre.

Special Discounts

Holders of International Student Identity Cards (ISICs) used to be admitted to museums at reduced fees, but recent revisions in the regulations now allow that privilege only to students with Turkish student cards.

Students with ISICs get discounts of 10% on the Turkish State Railways and on Turkish Maritime Lines ships. Turkish Airlines, which used to give very good student discounts, does not do so any more. However, the airline does offer a 10% 'family discount' to any husband-and-wife couple, with or without children.

Turkey is part of the Wasteels and Inter-Rail Youth discount schemes for rail.

TIPPING

Restaurants

Most of the tipping you'll do will be in restaurants. In the cheapest places tipping is not necessary, though some people do leave a few coins in the change plate. In more expensive restaurants, tipping is more usual.

Some places will automatically add a service charge (*servis ücreti*) of 10% or 15% to your bill, but this does not absolve you from the tip, oddly enough. The service charge goes either into the pocket of the *patron* (owner), or to the maître d'hôtel. Leave 5% on the table for the waiter, or hand it directly to him.

If service is included, the bill may say *servis dahil* (service included). Still, a small tip is expected. In any situation, 5% to 10% is fine. Only in the fancy foreign-operated hotels will waiters expect those enormous 15% to 20% American-style tips. In the very plain, basic restaurants you needn't tip at all, though the price of a soft drink or a cup of coffee is always appreciated.

Hotels

In the cheapest hotels there are few services and tips are not expected. In most hotels, a porter will carry your luggage and show you to your room. For doing this he'll expect about 3% or 4% of the room price. So if your room costs US$25, give about US$0.75 to US$1. For any other chore done by a porter, a slightly smaller tip is in order.

Taxis

Don't tip taxi drivers unless they've done some special service. Turks don't tip taxi drivers, though they often round off the metered fare. Thus, if the meter reads 7860TL, it's common to give the driver 8000TL. Taxi drivers may look for a tip from you, but that's only because you're a foreigner and foreigners tip taxi drivers. A driver of a *dolmuş* – a cab or minibus that departs only when all seats are filled – never expects a tip or a fare to be rounded upwards.

Hairdressers

In barbershops and hairdressers, pay the fee for the services rendered (which goes to the shop), then about 15% to the person who cut your hair, and smaller tips to the others who provided service, down to the one who brushes stray locks from your clothing as you prepare to leave (5% for that).

Turkish Baths

In a Turkish bath or *hamam* there will be fees for the several services, and in baths frequented mostly by Turks these will be sufficient. However, in baths with a clientele that includes tourists, everyone will expect and await tips. You needn't go overboard in this. Share out about 30% or 35% of your total bath bill to the assembled staff (and they will indeed be assembled for tips as you depart). In a few of the more tourist-frequented baths in İstanbul, the attendants are insistent. Don't let them browbeat you. Look firm and say, *Yeter!* (yeh-TEHR, 'It's sufficient!').

Sleeping Cars

If you take a sleeping compartment on a train, the porter will come around near the end of the trip, request an official 10% service charge, give you a receipt for it and expect an additional tip for himself. If you give him 5% extra, he'll be pleased.

Other Situations

There are other situations in which a tip is indicated, but these must be handled delicately. For instance, at a remote archaeological site, a local person may unlock the gate and show you around the ruins. He will probably have official admission tickets, which he must sell you. If that's all he does, that's all you pay. But if he goes out of his way to help you, you may want to offer a tip. He may be reluctant to accept it, and may refuse once or even twice. Try at least three times. He may well need the money, but the rules of politeness require several refusals. If he refuses three times, though, you can assume that he truly wants to help you only for friendship's sake. Don't press further, for this will insult his good intentions.

In many of these situations, a token gift will be just as happily received as a cash tip. If you have some small item, particularly something distinctive from your home country, you can offer it in lieu of money.

TOURIST INFORMATION
Local Tourist Offices

Every Turkish town of any size has a Tourism Information Office run by the Ministry of Tourism. The ministry's symbol is the fan-like Hittite sun figure. There may also be an office operated by a local tourism association called 'turizm derneği'.

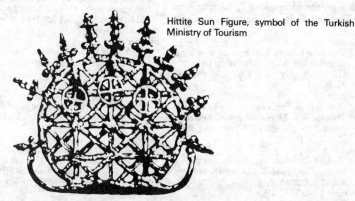

Hittite Sun Figure, symbol of the Turkish Ministry of Tourism

In addition, a town may also have a municipal or provincial government tourism office. If you need help and you can't find an office, ask for the Belediye Sarayı (behl-eh-DEE-yeh sah-rah-yuh, Town Hall). They'll rummage around for someone who speaks some English, and will do their best to solve your problem.

In İstanbul, there is a Tourism Information Office at Atatürk Airport in the international arrivals area (tel 573-7399, 573-4136); in Sultanahmet Square at the northern end of the Hippodrome (tel 522-4903); in the Hilton Hotel arcade two long blocks from Taksim Square (tel 140-6300, 140-6864); and in the İstanbul Bölge Müdürlüğü building on Meşrutiyet Caddesi, near Galatasaray Square and the British Consulate General.

In İzmir, the Tourism Information Office (tel 14 21 47) is on Gazi Osman Paşa Bulvarı at Cumhuriyet Meydanı (Cumhuriyet Square), right next to the Turkish Airlines office in the shops built beneath the Büyü Efes Oteli. Cumhuriyet Meydanı is the square with the equestrian statue of Atatürk.

In Ankara you can go to the ministry itself. It's on Gazi Mustafa Kemal Bulvarı several blocks west of Kızılay, on the south (left) side of the street. Ask for the Turizm Bakanlığı (tel 129-0965).

Overseas Reps

Here are the addresses of Turkish tourism offices and diplomatic missions abroad:

Austria
    Turkische Botschaft Informationsabteilung, Singerstrasse 2/VIII, 1010 Wien (tel (222) 512-2128/9; fax 513-8326; telex 111281 TUINF)
Belgium
    Conseiller de l'Information, Ambassade de Turquie, Rue Montoyer 4, 1040 Bruxelles (tel (2) 513-8230/9; fax 511-7951; telex 25973 TURKTA B)
Denmark
    Turkish Embassy Information Counsellor Bureau, Vesterbrogade 11A, 1620 Kobenhavn V (tel (1) 223-100, 228-374; fax 229-068; telex 19562 THY DK)

France
    Turquie, Service d'Information, Champs Elysées 102, 75008 Paris (tel (1) 45 62 78 68, 45 62 79 84, 45 62 26 10; fax 45 63 81 05; telex 29 06 39 TURTANT)
Italy
    Ambasciata di Turchia, Ufficio Informazione, Piazza della Republica 56, 00185 Roma (tel (6) 462-957; fax 474-1697; telex 612131 TURTANIT)
Japan
    Turkish Tourism & Information Office, 33-6, 2-Chome Jingumae, Shibuya-Ku, Tokyo (tel (3) 470-6380, 470-5131; telex J-22856 EMBTURK)
Kuwait
    Turkish Embassy, Office of the Information Counsellor, PO Box 15518, 35456 Deaya, Kuwait, 35456 (tel 242-4248; fax 242-4298; telex 46228 TURKISM, KT)
Netherlands
    Turkish Embassy, Information Counsellor's Office, Herengracht 451, 1017 BS Amsterdam (tel (20) 266-810, 244-006; fax 222-283; telex 15521 TANIT NL)
Saudi Arabia
    Turkish Embassy, Information Office, Medina Rd, Km 6, Arafat St, PO Box 6966, Jeddah (tel (2) 665-4578; fax 665-2606; telex 602631 CIBMEM-SJ)
Spain
    Oficina de Información y Turismo de Turquía, Plaza de España, Torre de Madrid, Planta 3, Oficina 3, 28008 Madrid (tel (1) 248-7014, 248-7114; telex 47288 OTTR E)
Sweden
    Turkiska Statens Informationsbyra, Kungsgatan 3, 11143 Stockholm (tel (8) 218-620, 218-630; fax 723-1828; telex 11083 A TELEKC S)
Switzerland
    Türkisches Generalkonsulat, Talstrasse 74, 8001 Zurich (tel (1) 221-0810/12; telex 813752 COTU CH)
UK
    Turkish Tourism & Information, 170-173 Piccadilly, 1st floor, London W1V 9DD (tel (1) 734-8681/2; fax 491-0773; telex 895-4905 TTIOFC G)
USA
    Tourism Information Office, Turkish Consulate-General, 821 United Nations Plaza, New York, New York 10017 (tel (212) 687-2194; fax 599-7568; telex 426428 TTINY)

Turkish Information Office, 1714 Massachusetts Ave NW, Washington, DC 20036 (tel (202) 429-9409, 429-9844, 833-8411; fax 429-5649; telex 251544 VKTM UR)

West Germany

Informationsabteilung des Türkischen Generalkonsulats, Baselerstrasse 37, 6 Frankfurt M1 (tel (69) 233-081/2; fax 232-751; telex 4170-081 IDTG D)

Informationsabteilung des Türkischen Generalkonsulats, Karlsplatz 3/1, 8000 München 2 (tel (89) 594-902, 594-317; telex 528190 INTU D)

Foreign Embassies

İstanbul has many palatial consulates left from the days of Ottoman glory, when foreign powers built splendid embassy compounds to impress the sultan. The embassies are all now in Ankara, the modern capital, but there are helpful consulates or consular agents in İstanbul, İzmir, Adana and a few other port cities.

Call before you visit any of these embassies or consulates. Diplomats keep very odd business hours sometimes, and they close up on both Turkish and their own national holidays. Also, you may learn that you need passport photos or some other documentation before coming to the embassy or consulate.

For instance, before approaching the Syrian Embassy or consulate for a visa, obtain a letter of introduction from your own embassy or consulate. Visa applications are accepted by the Syrians from 9 to 11 am; you'll need two photos of yourself and a fee of US$6 to US$16, depending on your nationality. Arrive early to beat the line. You can pick up your passport, complete with visa, the following day from 1.30 to 3.30 pm.

If you plan to travel from Turkey to Europe by way of Bulgaria, you'll save time and money by picking up a Bulgarian transit visa in İstanbul or Ankara. Do not depend upon getting one at the border; you are required to have your Bulgarian visa in advance (see East

European Visas in this section for details).

In many cases, the Turkish travel agency which sells you the bus or train ticket through Bulgaria will also be able to get a Bulgarian transit visa for you. To obtain a visa yourself, take bus No 56 from Eminönü to the last stop at Esentepe, and ask for Yıldız Posta Sokak. The visa fee depends upon reciprocal agreements between Bulgaria and your home country, but should be in the range of US$5 to US$10.

Iranian transit visas are, in principle, available to citizens of many countries. Availability may depend upon current politics.

Note If your passport bears any evidence (ie stamps) that you have been in the Turkish Republic of Northern Cyprus, you will be denied entry to Greece. Have the TRNC official stamp on a piece of paper instead.

Here is a list of diplomatic missions. To find one, use these phrases:

'Where is the .... embassy?'
.... *Büyükelçiliği nerede?*
(........ bew-YEWK-ehl-chee-lee neh-reh-DEH)

'Where is the .... consulate?'
.... *Konsolosluğu nerede?*
(KOHN-sohl-lohs-loo-oo)

Australia (*Avustralya*)
Embassy: Nene Hatun Caddesi 83, Gazi Osman Paşa, Ankara (tel 136-1240/3)

Austria (*Avusturya*)
Embassy: Atatürk Bulvarı 189, Kavaklıdere, Ankara (tel 134-2172/4)
Consulate: Silâhhane Caddesi 59/4, Teşvikiye, Şişli, İstanbul (tel 146-3769)

Bulgaria (*Bulgaristan*)
Embassy: Atatürk Bulvarı 124, Kavaklıdere, Ankara (tel 126-7456)
Consulate: Yıldız Posta Sokak 15, Esentepe, İstanbul (tel 166-2605)

Canada (*Kanada*)
Embassy: Nene Hatun Caddesi 75, Gazi Osman Paşa, Ankara (tel 136-1275/9)

Denmark (*Danimarka*)
Embassy: Kırlangıç Sokak 42, Gazi Osman
Paşa, Ankara (tel 127-5258)
Consulate: Silâhhane Caddesi, İzmir Palas
Apt 31/1, Teşvikiye, Şişli, İstanbul
(tel 140-4217)
France (*Fransa*)
Embassy: Paris Caddesi 70, Kavaklıdere,
Ankara (tel 126-1480)
Consulate: İstiklal Caddesi 8, Taksim,
İstanbul (tel 143-1852/3)
Greece (*Yunanistan*)
Embassy: Ziya-ul-Rahman Sokak, Gazi
Osman Paşa, Ankara (tel 136-8861)
Consulate: Ağahamam Sokak, Kuloğlu,
Beyoğlu, İstanbul (tel 145-0596)
India (*Hindistan*)
Embassy: Cinnah Caddesi 77/A, Çankaya,
Ankara (tel 138-2195)
Iran (*İran*)
Embassy: Tahran Caddesi 10, Kavaklıdere,
Ankara (tel 127-4320)
Consulate: Ankara Caddesi, Cağaloğlu,
İstanbul (tel 512-0090/2)
Israel (*İsrail*)
Embassy: Farabi Sokak 43, Çankaya,
Ankara (tel 126-3904)
Consulate: Valikonağı Caddesi 73/4,
Nişantaşı, İstanbul (tel 146-4125/6/7)
Netherlands (*Holanda*)
Embassy: Köroğlu Sokak 16, Gazi Osman
Paşa, Ankara (tel 136-1074)
Consulate: İstiklal Caddesi 393, Tünel,
Beyoğlu, İstanbul (tel 149-5310/1)
Pakistan (*Pakistan*)
Embassy: İran Caddesi 37, Çankaya,
Ankara (tel 127-1410)
Consulate: Ihlamur Sergi Sarayı, Blok A,
Kat 3, Otim Binası, Barbaros Hayrettin
Paşa, İstanbul (tel 172-1636/7)
Sweden (*İsveç*)
Embassy: Kâtip Çelebi Sokak 7, Kavaklıdere,
Ankara (tel 128-6735)
Consulate: İstiklal Caddesi 497, Tünel,
Beyoğlu, İstanbul (tel 143-5770/1/2)
Switzerland (*İsviçre*)
Embassy: Atatürk Bulvarı 247, Çankaya,
Ankara (tel 127-4316)
Consulate: Hüsrev Gerede Caddesi 75/3,
Teşvikiye, Şişli, İstanbul (tel 159-1115/8)
Syria (*Suriye*)
Embassy: Abdullah Cevdet Sokak 7,
Çankaya, Ankara (tel 138-8704)
Consulate: Silâhhane Caddesi 59/5, Ralli
Apt, Teşvikiye, Şişli, İstanbul
(tel 148-3284)

UK (*İngiltere, Birleşik Krallığı*)
Embassy: Şehit Ersan Caddesi 46/A,
Çankaya, Ankara (tel 127-4310)
Consulate: Meşrutiyet Caddesi 26, Tepebaşı,
Beyoğlu, İstanbul (tel 149-8874, 144-7540)
USA (*Amerika Birleşik Devletleri, Amerika*)
Embassy: Atatürk Bulvarı 110, Kavaklıdere,
Ankara (tel 126-5470)
Consulate: Meşrutiyet Caddesi 106,
Tepebaşı, Beyoğlu, İstanbul (tel 151-3602)
USSR (*Sovyetler Birliği, Rusya*)
Embassy: Karyağdı Sokak 5, Çankaya,
Ankara (tel 139-2122/3)
Consulate: İstiklal Caddesi 443, Tünel,
Beyoğlu, İstanbul (tel 144-2610, 144-1693)
West Germany (*Federal Almanya*)
Embassy: Atatürk Bulvarı 114, Kavaklıdere,
Ankara (tel 26 54 65)
Consulate: İnönü (Gümüşsuyu) Caddesi,
Selim Hatun Camii Sokak 46, Ayazpaşa,
Taksim, İstanbul (tel 151-5404)

East European Visas

If you travel to Turkey by rail or road (bus,
car, motor cycle, bicycle), you will
have to deal with the problem of visas for
transit of East European countries. Costs
of visas, and the level of hassle you must
endure to get them, are usually governed
by reciprocity. For example, if the Dutch
government charges a Yugoslav 21
guilders (about US$10) for a visa, the
Yugoslav government will charge a Dutch
traveller 89,000 dinars (about US$10) for a
visa. If the US government charges
Yugoslavs nothing for an American visa,
the Yugoslavs will charge Americans
nothing for a Yugoslav visa. Thus, visa
cost (and sometimes availability) depends
entirely on which passport you carry.

Bulgaria You will need a transit visa (good
for 48 hours), both on the trip from Europe
to Turkey and on the trip back, because
the train and the highway pass through
Bulgaria (unless you take the roundabout
route via Thessaloniki, Greece). It is
about US$8 one way, US$15 two ways
(more or less, depending upon your
passport) for the privilege of passing
through.

Get your visa in advance so as to avoid

hassle, delay and possible refusal. Visas can be obtained from your nearest friendly Bulgarian diplomatic representative at home or in Europe. If you arrive at the border without a visa, you will be taken from your train or bus (which will go on without you), and told to wait 12 to 24 hours while a visa is obtained for you.

In Australia contact the Bulgarian Consulate General (tel (2) 327-7581), 4 Karlotta Rd, Double Bay, NSW 2028. In the UK, go to the Bulgarian Legation, 24 Queen's Gate Gardens, London SW7. In the USA, contact the Consular Section, Bulgarian Embassy, 1621 22nd St NW, Washington, DC 20008 (tel (202) 387-7969).

Passport holders from Scandinavian and East European countries do not need visas for Bulgaria. If you carry a South African passport you can't get a visa: you must go around Bulgaria through Greece.

Yugoslavia Holders of UK, Irish and most European passports need no visa; those from the US, Canada, Australia and New Zealand need a transit visa, good for seven days, obtainable at the border. Israeli passport holders may run into problems, and may not be granted a visa. South African, Taiwanese and South Korean passport holders will not be granted visas.

GENERAL INFORMATION
Post & Telecommunications
Postal and telecommunication services in Turkey are handled by the PTT (peh-teh-TEH), which stands for *posta, telefon, telgraf*. Look for the yellow signs with black 'PTT' letters.

Letter boxes and postal vehicles are yellow as well. Every town has a PTT, usually close to the main square. Go there to buy stamps and telephone tokens, to send letters and telegrams, or to make telephone calls if no other phone is available.

Convenient PTT branches are located in Taksim, Galatasaray, Aksaray and the

Kapalı Çarsı ('Covered Market' also called Grand Bazaar).

Many railway stations and bus stations in Turkey have their own branch PTTs.

Turkish postal and telephone personnel have a reputation for surliness, bad temper and incompetence which is, in many cases, richly deserved.

Postal Rates The constant creeping devaluation of the Turkish lira results in frequent rises in postal rates. Ask at the post office to learn current rates.

Express Mail The PTT now operates an express mail, courier-type service called *acele posta servisi* (AH-jeh-leh POHSS-tah sehr-vee-see). If you must have something reach its destination in the fastest, most secure possible manner, ask for this. Don't confuse this courier service with the traditional *ekspres* (special delivery) service, which is slower.

Parcels To mail packages out of the country from İstanbul, or to receive dutiable merchandise, you must go to the special Paket Postahane (parcel post office) near Karaköy. You must have your package open for customs inspection, and you may have to endure a bit of frustrating red tape.

Postal clerks in Turkey are, as a rule, cold and curt, often rude and sometimes even nasty, though foreigners get better treatment than Turks do. You can't be rude back because there's a law against 'insulting a public official'.

If you want to make certain that a parcel will get to its destination intact, send it *kayıtlı* (by registered mail).

Poste Restante For poste restante mail, go to İstanbul's Merkez Postahane (Mehr-KEHZ POHS-tah-neh, Central Post Office) in the section called Eminönü, several blocks west of Sirkeci Station. If you are having mail sent, have it addressed this way:

```
Name
Poste Restante
Merkez Postahane
Eminönü
İstanbul
TURKEY
```

Addresses Turkish postal addresses are usually written with the name of the main street first, then the minor street and then the number of the building. For example:

```
Bay Mustafa Adıyok
Geçilmez Sokak, Bulunmaz Çıkmazı
Lüks Apartımanı No 23/14
80200 Tophane
İSTANBUL
```

In this example, *Bay* means 'Mr' (for 'Mrs' or 'Miss', it's *Bayan*, pronounced like the English phrase 'buy an ....'). The next line has the name of a largish street, 'Geçilmez Sokak', followed by the name of a smaller street, alley, mews or

dead end, 'Bulunmaz Çıkmazı', which runs off it. The third line has the name of an apartment building, 'Lüks Apartımanı'. As for the numbers, the first one, '23', is the street number of the building; the second, '14', is the apartment or office number within the building. The district, 'Tophane', comes next, then the city. *Kat* in an address means floor, as in Kat 3, '3rd floor' (4th floor up if you count street level as the 1st floor).

The address can be written more simply when the desired building is on a large, well-known street. For example:

```
Bay Mustafa Adıyok
Büyük Caddesi No 44/10
80090 Taksim
İSTANBUL
```

In some cases, the district of the city is put at the beginning of the second line, eg 'Taksim, Büyük Caddesi No 44/10'. In any case, you've got to be familiar with the district names to find a certain address.

Turkey has a system of five-digit postal codes (*posta kodu*), but they have yet to come into general use. Use the postal code if you have it.

Telephones
You will find the telephone useful in Turkey. The PTT operates two different telephone systems, the traditional operator-assisted type and an automatic direct-dial type. You will find yourself using the automatic system more often, as it is more widespread, faster, cheaper and easier. Automatic phones are yellow and have push buttons rather than dials. You pay for a call with a *jeton* (zheh-TOHN, token), or perhaps several, or a *telekart* debit card. Calls are measured in usage units, each of which costs about US$0.10; a local call of several minutes' duration costs one usage unit.

If you want to place a reverse-charge call, you will have to use the slower operator-assisted phone network.

Tokens Tokens come in three sizes. The small one usage units (*küçük jeton*, kew-CHEWK zheh-TOHN) are equivalent to US$0.10 and are used for local calls. The middle-sized five usage units (*normal jeton*, nohr-MAHL), about US$0.40, are useful mostly for long-distance calls within Turkey. The large 10 usage units (*büyük jeton*, bew-YEWK), about US$0.85, are necessary for international calls. Buy your jetons at the post office, or from a disabled person outside a PTT or near a rank of public telephones. Most PTTs have a sign saying *Satılmış jeton geri alınmaz*, which means 'Jetons, once sold, cannot be returned'. If they insist on this, try exchanging the jetons for stamps, or sell the jetons to another traveller.

Telekarts A telekart is a plastic-and-metal telephone debit card sold at post offices. You pay for the card in advance of calling, and then as you call, your telephone usage is electronically deducted from the value of the card. Telekarts come in values of 20, 60, 120, or 180 telephone usage units. Special telekart phones take only these cards, inserted in a slot in the centre of the front panel. These phones are not yet found everywhere in Turkey; you'll see them mostly in the heavily frequented tourist areas. Try to find them, because they are by far the easiest phones to use.

After you've found a phone and bought a card, insert it in the slot and a liquid crystal display in the upper left-hand corner will show you the number of usage units for which the card is valid. A normal local call usually costs one usage unit; a long-distance call, four or five usage units; an international call takes lots of units. Buy only the most expensive 180-unit telekarts (US$15.30) for international calls. After you've finished your call, your telekart will be ejected from the slot and a mark on the white band on its face will show how many units remain on the card (the liquid crystal phone display gives you this same information). When that mark

is at zero, the card is worthless and you can throw it away.

Types of Telephones Yellow automatic push-button phones are the most common units. They take either jetons or telekarts, but not both. The yellow phones have pictographs on them demonstrating their use, and sometimes also instructions in English. For a local call, punch the buttons for the local number, and you're on your way.

You may also come across any of several older types of phones. The desk phones with a small box attached take normal jetons for local calls. These are the ones you find in grocery shops and offices. They are more expensive because they take normal rather than small jetons. Long-distance calls can be made from these phones only through the slower, more expensive operator-assisted system, and usually must be reverse-charge calls.

The following sorts of phones are being phased out and replaced by the yellow push-button phones. With the old black wall-telephones, don't put the jeton in the slot on top until your party answers. With the red or gun-metal grey phones, put the jeton in before you dial; if you don't get through, it will be returned to you. These older phones are good mostly for local or reverse-charge calls.

Long-Distance Calls For long-distance calls, use a yellow automatic phone. It may have a sign above it saying *Şehirlerarası* (Inter-city); or *Uluslararası* or *Milletlerarası* (International). You'll need to know the city and country codes for the place you're calling. These are on display in most PTTs and in some phone booths.

Look for the little square red light below the push buttons. If it's lit, tough luck – the phone is broken. Let's assume the phone works instead. Lift the receiver and deposit a jeton. The yellow phones have slots for all three sizes of jetons. Sometimes the jeton may fall straight through and out the return hole, so reinsert it very gently and let it fall as slowly as possible. If all else fails, try another phone or another size of jeton. The fault is with the phone, not with the jeton.

For a long-distance call, look for the little round light in the last box, to the right of the pictorial instructions above the push buttons. When this light goes out, push '9'. Then, when you hear the inter-city long-distance tone, push the buttons for the city code and the local number. For international calls, push '9' twice, then the country code, followed by the city code and local number. For instance, for London, after pushing '9' twice, push '44', then the area code ('1'), then the number. For Melbourne, dial thus: 9-9-61-3 plus local number. For the USA and Canada, dial 9-9-1 plus area code plus local number.

Here are some frequently-used country codes:

Australia	61
Austria	43
Belgium	32
Canada	1
Denmark	45
Eire	353
Finland	358
France	33
Greece	30
India	91
Israel	972
Italy	39
Japan	81
Netherlands	31
New Zealand	64
Norway	47
Portugal	351
South Africa	27
Spain	34
Sweden	46
Switzerland	41
Turkey	90
UK	44
USA	1
Yugoslavia	38

As you talk, watch that little round red light up top, and listen for chimes on the line. Both are indications that it's time to deposit another jeton or telekart.

With all other phones, place the call with the operator, then wait for the operator to ring you back. The call will go through according to the speed which you designate: *normal* (nohr-MAHL) means 'slowest' in this instance; *acele* (ah-jeh-LEH) means twice as fast; *yıldırım* (yuhl-duhr-RUHM) means 'lightning', five times as fast as normal (and costs five times as much). After you place the call, you wait a minute or two, or an hour or two – the operator can estimate the wait.

Telegraph

You can send a telegram from any post office in Turkey. Ask for a *telgraf kâğıdı* (tehl-GHRAHF kyah-uh-duh, telegram form), fill it out, and hand it over. For most foreign countries, there is only one rate of service: fast and expensive. A simple telegram to North America may cost US$15 to $20, for instance.

If you're sending your wire within Turkey, the clerk will ask you at what speed you want it sent. As with the phone service, normal is quite slow; acele is fast and twice as expensive; and yıldırım costs five times as much as normal. Remember that the address of the recipient is included in the word count.

Fax & Telex

The larger cities have some post offices with telex (*teleks*, TEHL-eks) and facsimile (*faks* or *elektronik mektup*) machines. If your recipient has a telex or fax machine, this can be cheaper than sending a telegram. Write out your message, including the telex number if you have it, find a post office with a machine, and the attendant will send the message and give you a receipt and confirmation copy. There are telex and fax machines in İstanbul's major PTTs and in the branch post office in Ankara's Kızılay Square.

The price for a fax or telex, as for a telephone call, depends upon the actual time spent using the line. The PTT telex operator may make mistakes and have to retype the entire message, and you will have to pay for his incompetence and all of this time on the line. Fax is easier in this regard. Many businesses in Turkey, including many hotels, have fax machines these days.

Electricity

Electricity in Turkey is 220 volts, 50 cycles, as in Europe. Plugs are of the European variety with two round prongs, but there are two sizes in use. Most common is the small-diameter prong, so if you have these you're in fine shape. The large-diameter, grounded plug used in Germany and Austria is also in use, and you'll find some outlets of this type. Plugs for these won't fit the small-diameter outlets.

Adapters are not easily available. You've got to rig something up yourself unless you've brought an adapter from Europe and it happens to be the right one. (Adapters for the flat-prong North American-type plugs are sold in many electrical shops. If you have these plugs, and 220-volt appliances, you're unusual and in luck.)

For those who have the good sense to plan ahead, here are the 'vital statistics of the Turkish plug': prongs 4 mm in diameter, 19 mm long; distance from the centre of one prong to the centre of the other, 19 mm; distance between the prongs 15 mm. The European grounded plug, by contrast, has prongs 4.5 mm in diameter, 19 mm apart from centre to centre, but only 14 mm long.

Time

Turkish time is East European Time, two hours ahead of GMT, except in the warm months, when clocks are turned ahead one hour. Daylight saving time usually begins at 1 am on the last Sunday in March, and ends at 2 am on the last Sunday in September. When it's 12 noon in İstanbul, Ankara or Erzurum, the time elsewhere is:

city	winter	summer
Paris, Rome	11 am	11 am
London	10 am	10 am
New York	5 am	5 am
Los Angeles	2 am	2 am
Perth, Hong Kong	7 pm	5 pm
Sydney	9 pm	7 pm
Auckland	11 pm	9 pm

Weights & Measures

Turkey uses the metric system. For those used to the British-American systems of measurement, conversion information can be found at the back of this book.

Laundry

There are no coin-operated automatic laundries in Turkey yet, but getting laundry (çamaşır, chahm-mah-SHUR) cleaned is a simple matter. At any hotel or boarding house, ask at the reception desk, or just short-circuit it and ask a staff member. They'll quickly find someone to do laundry. Agree on a price in advance. The classier the hotel, the more exorbitant their laundry rates. Even so, the rates are no higher than at home.

Figure at least a day to get laundry done. It may be washed in a machine or by hand, but it will be dried on a line, not in a drying machine. In summer, drying takes no time at all. If you wash a T-shirt at 10.30 am in İzmir and hang it in the sun, it'll be dry by 11 am.

By the way, the word çamaşır also means 'underwear' in Turkish. This can be confusing at times.

Dry-cleaning shops (kuru temizleme, koo-ROO tehm-eez-lem-MEH) are found here and there in the big cities, usually in the better residential sections or near the luxury hotels. Service is similar to that in Europe and America: fast service takes an hour or two if you're willing to pay 50% more; otherwise, overnight or two-day service is normal. Prices are very reasonable, and you'll save money by taking the garments yourself rather than having the hotel staff do it.

MEDIA

Newspapers & Magazines

The Turks are great readers of newspapers. The local dailies are produced by up-to-date computerised methods, in full colour. A few decades ago, İstanbul could boast more than a dozen Turkish-language dailies, two in Greek, one in Armenian, one in French and two in Ladino Spanish (spoken by Jews who came from Spain to the Ottoman Empire in the Middle Ages). As everywhere, the number of dailies is dwindling as the more successful papers grow. Several of the Turkish-language dailies now have editions printed in Germany for Turkish workers there, as well as numerous local editions.

Of prime interest to visitors is the *Turkish Daily News*, an English-language daily newspaper published in Ankara and sold for US$0.30 in most Turkish cities where tourists go. It is the cheapest source

of English-language news in print. Another local effort is *Dateline*, a weekly news digest priced at US$0.75. A similar weekly news digest in French is *La Revue d'Orient*. The big international papers such as the *International Herald Tribune, Le Monde, Corriere della Sera, Die Welt*, etc are on sale in tourist spots as well, but are much more expensive (US$1.75 for the *Herald Tribune*). Check the date on any international paper before you buy it. If it's more than a day old, look elsewhere.

Large-circulation magazines including *Newsweek, Time, Der Spiegel* and the like, are also sold in tourist spots.

If you can't find the foreign publication you want, go to a big hotel's newsstand or check at a foreign-language bookstore (see the Bookshops section at the end of this chapter for addresses).

Radio & Television

TRT, for Türkiye Radyo ve Televizyon, controls all broadcasting. It's a quasi-independent establishment modelled on the BBC. Western classical and popular music, along with Turkish classic, folk, religious and pop music, are played regularly on both AM (medium-wave) and FM channels. Short news broadcasts in English, French and German are given each morning and evening.

The BBC World Service is often receivable on AM as well as on short-wave. The Voice of America broadcasts in English on AM, relayed from Rhodes, each morning. The rest of the medium-wave band is a wonderful babel of Albanian, Arabic, Bulgarian, Greek, Hebrew, Italian, Persian, Romanian and Russian.

There are two TV channels broadcasting mostly in Turkish from breakfast time to about midnight. The familiar Los Angeles-made series and many of the films are dubbed in Turkish. Occasionally you'll catch a film in the original language. There is a short news broadcast in English at 10 pm. In addition to the Turkish channels, many of the larger and more expensive hotels have satellite hook-ups to receive European channels, mostly in German, but often including the European service of the American Cable News Network (CNN).

HEALTH

Medical services are fairly well distributed in Turkey, though often fairly basic. Some doctors in the larger cities speak English, French or German, and have studied in Europe or America. Your consulate can recommend a good doctor or dentist.

For minor problems, it's customary to ask at a pharmacy (*eczane*, edj-zahn-NEH) for advice. Sign language usually suffices to communicate symptoms, and the pharmacist will prescribe on the spot. Even 'prescription' drugs are sometimes sold without a prescription.

Though Turkey manufactures most modern prescription medicines, it's not good to risk running out. If you take a drug regularly, bring a supply. If your medicine is available in Turkey, it may be less expensive here than at home. The drug's name may not be exactly the same, though the substance may be.

Pre-Departure Preparations

Health Insurance A travel insurance policy to cover theft, loss and medical problems is a wise idea. There are a wide variety of policies and your travel agent will have recommendations. The international student travel policies handled by STA or other student travel organisations are usually good value. Some policies offer lower and higher medical expenses options, but the higher one is chiefly for countries like the US with extremely high medical costs. Check the small print:

1. Some policies specifically exclude 'dangerous activities' which can include scuba diving, motor cycling, even trekking. If these activities are on your agenda you don't want that sort of policy.
2. You may prefer a policy which pays doctors or hospitals direct rather than you

having to pay now and claim later. If you have to claim later make sure you keep all documentation. Some policies ask you to call back (reverse charges) to a centre in your home country where an immediate assessment of your problem is made.
3. Check if the policy covers ambulances or an emergency flight home. If you have to stretch out you will need two seats and somebody has to pay for it!

Medical Kit A small, straightforward medical kit is a wise thing to carry. In many countries if a medicine is available at all it will generally be available over the counter and the price will be much cheaper than in the west. A possible kit list includes:

1. Aspirin or panadol – for pain or fever.
2. Antihistamine (such as Benadryl) – useful as a decongestant for colds, allergies, to ease the itch from insect bites or stings or to help prevent motion sickness.
3. Antibiotics – useful if you're travelling well off the beaten track, but it must be prescribed and you should carry the prescription with you.
4. Kaolin preparation (Pepto-Bismol), Imodium or Lomotil – for stomach upsets.
5. Rehydration mixture – for treatment of severe diarrhoea, this is particularly important if travelling with children.
6. Antiseptic, mercurochrome and antibiotic powder or similar 'dry' spray – for cuts and grazes.
7. Calamine lotion – to ease irritation from bites or stings.
8. Bandages and band-aids – for minor injuries.
9. Scissors, tweezers and a thermometer – mercury thermometers are prohibited by airlines.
10. Insect repellent, sunblock cream, suntan lotion, chapstick and water purification tablets.

Vaccinations

You need no special inoculations before entering Turkey, unless you're coming from an endemic or epidemic area. If you want to get preventive shots (tetanus, typhoid, etc) get cholera too. The chances are small that you'll run into cholera, but it may come in handy when crossing borders. Health officers far removed from the scene may not keep track of which countries have it.

Also, if you plan to live very cheaply and travel extensively in the eastern regions, you might consider getting a gamma globulin injection as some protection against hepatitis.

Officially, malaria is present in southeast Anatolia from Mersin on the Mediterranean coast eastward to the Iraqi border, but the highest danger is in the muggy agricultural areas from Mersin to Gaziantep. If you just pass through, or spend most of your time in cities, the danger is low; but if you plan to spend lots of time in rural areas and camp out, consider taking chloroquine tablets weekly (consult a doctor first). At present there are no known chloroquine-resistant strains of mosquitoes in this area. I have visited south-east Anotolia repeatedly and never had a problem, but you must make your own decision.

Food & Water

Turkey is generally a safe country as far as food and water are concerned, but there are always bouts of travellers' diarrhoea to contend with. You should take precautions for several reasons.

The first is obvious: sanitary practices are not universally observed, no matter where you are in the world.

The second reason has to do not with the cleanliness of the food but with its familiarity. Most people suffer some consequences from drastic change of diet and water, for each area and each cuisine has its own 'normal' bacteria and its own composition. Some people find it difficult to digest olive oil, or even to stomach pure water that has a high limestone content. Any experienced traveller knows that getting sick from food is mostly by chance, but there are still a few things you can do to improve your chances.

Dining Precautions Take the normal travel precautions. Choose dishes that look freshly prepared and sufficiently hot. You can go into almost any Turkish kitchen (except in the very posh places) for a look at what's cooking. In fact, in most places that's what the staff will suggest, the language barrier being what it is. Except for grilled meats, Turkish dishes tend to be cooked slowly for a long time, just the thing to kill any errant bacteria. If the dishes don't sell on the day they're cooked, they might be saved, and the oil may congeal and become harder to digest. Most of the time meals are reasonably fresh.

As for grilled meats, these may be offered to you medium rare. They'll probably be all right, but if they really look pink, send them back for more cooking (no problem in this). The words you'll need are *biraz daha pişmiş* (beer-ahz da-HAH peesh-meesh) for 'cooked a bit more', and *iyi pişmiş* (ee-EE peesh-meesh) or *pişkin,* (peesh-KEEN) for 'well done'.

Beware of milk products and dishes containing milk that have not been properly refrigerated. Electricity is expensive in Turkey, and many places will scrimp on refrigeration temperature. If you want a rice pudding (*sütlaç*) or some such dish with milk in it, choose a shop that has lots of them in the window, meaning that a batch has been made recently and thus guaranteeing freshness. In general, choose things from bins, trays, cases, pots, etc that are fairly full rather than almost empty. If you make a point of eating some yoghurt every day, you'll keep your digestive system in excellent condition.

Drinking Precautions As for water, you'll find it preferable to stick to bottled spring water as much as possible. It's sold everywhere in clear plastic bottles in sizes of one-third of a litre, 1-½ litres and three litres. Check the date on the bottle, and don't buy water that's been around for a while as it may taste of the plastic.

Tap water in Turkey is chlorinated and not particularly poisonous (as in some countries), but neither does it taste good.

At a roadside *çeşme* (CHESH-meh, fountain or spring), look out for the word *içilmez* (eech-eel-MEHZ, 'not to be drunk') near the water. If what you see is *içilir* (eech-eel-LEER, 'drinkable'), or *içme suyu* (EECH-meh soo-yoo, 'drinking water'), or *içilebilir* (EECH-eel-eh-bee-LEER, 'can be drunk') then it may be all right, but I'd avoid these if possible unless you think you really know what's upstream from them.

Alternatives to spring water include *maden suyu*, naturally fizzy mineral water, and *maden sodası* (or just *soda*), artificially carbonated mineral water. The latter just has bigger bubbles, and more of them, than the former. Both come from mineral springs, and both are truly full of minerals. The taste is not neutral. Some people like it, some don't. It's supposed to be good for you, clean out your kidneys, etc.

Packaged fruit juice (*meyva suyu*), soft drinks, beer and wine are reliably pure, except in rare cases. As for wines, you'll have no trouble with the big names: Doluca, Kavaklıdere, Tekel and Efes Güneşi.

Toilets

Virtually every hotel above the lowest class, most apartments, many restaurants, train stations and airports have the familiar raised-bowl commode toilet. You may also meet with the traditional flat 'elephant's feet' variety, a porcelain or concrete rectangle with two oblong foot-places and a sunken hole. This may be daunting at first, but it is actually the best kind of toilet from a physical standpoint.

It is also sanitary, in that only your shod feet contact the vessel – you squat, you don't sit on anything.

Using it takes some getting used to, but is not as difficult as you may think. As for the apparent lack of dignity involved in this process, remember that the urbane Ottoman sultans and the gracious Harem ladies did it this way for centuries and never thought twice about it. Just make sure all the stuff doesn't fall out of your pockets when you squat.

Also, bring your own toilet paper. In the government-rated hotels there should be paper. In public conveniences, if there's no attendant, there will be no paper; there will be a spigot and a can for washing (with the left hand). It's a good idea to carry enough paper or tissues with you at all times.

Sometimes the plumbing is not built to take wads of paper, and the management will place a wastepaper basket or can next to the toilet for used paper. Signs in Turkish will plead with you not to throw the paper down the toilet. What you do depends upon your feelings on the matter. If the toilet doesn't flush, use a bucket or plastic container of water to do the job.

Serviceably clean public toilets can be found near the very big tourist attractions such as Topkapı Palace and the Covered Market. In other places, it depends. Look first. Every mosque has a toilet, often very basic, but it may be better than nothing, depending upon the urgency of Nature's call.

Health Precautions

There are occasional cases of salmonella (food poisoning) and hepatitis. The way to combat them is to remain generally strong, well rested and well fed, and to avoid eating in places which seem to ignore basic rules of sanitation.

Food Poisoning The symptoms of food poisoning are headaches, nausea and/or stomach ache, diarrhoea, fever and chills. If you get it, go to bed and put as many covers on as possible (stay warm no matter what). Drink lots of fluids, preferably hot tea without sugar or milk. Camomile tea, *papatya çay*, is a specific against a queasy stomach. Some teahouses serve it, herbal markets sell the dried camomile, and in many parts of Turkey you can even pick the fragrant little daisy-like camomile flowers along the roadside and make the tea yourself.

Until the bout of food poisoning has run its course (24 to 30 hours), drink nothing but plain tea (no milk or sugar), and eat nothing but dry toast or rusks and maybe a little yoghurt. The day after, you'll feel weak, but the symptoms will have passed except perhaps for the diarrhoea. If you take it easy and eat only bland, easily digested foods for a few days, you'll be fine.

In almost every case, the few people who get food poisoning while abroad compound the problem by ignoring it, or by continuing to travel or see the sights, or by eating whatever is easiest. Medicines, available with or without a prescription from any *eczane*, can help a serious bout of the illness. But nothing can rebuild your intestinal flora, necessary to good digestion, except time and tender loving care. Most medicines for food poisoning are strong antibiotics. They kill the poisonous bacteria (which your body would have killed on its own, in time), but they also kill all the normal, healthful digestive bacteria. Thus antibiotics can actually *prolong* the diarrhoea by making it difficult for your digestive system to do its work.

Travellers' Diarrhoea The standard treatments for travellers' diarrhoea, as recommended by the US Public Health Service, include antibiotics, bismuth subsalicylate (Pepto-Bismol), and difenoxine (Lomotil). Each of these medicines has side effects; you should consult a physician before taking any of them, and you should not take any medicine as a preventative, but only if you actually become ill.

Bismuth subsalicylate coats your stomach lining and helps get rid of the harmful bacteria, but it must not be taken by people allergic to salicylates, or by those with kidney problems. The standard dosage is 30 ml of the liquid, or a similar quantity in tablet form, every half-hour for four hours.

Difenoxine usually comes as diphenoxylate (Lomotil) or loperamide (Imodium), synthetic opiate anti-motility agents. They drug your gut into passivity and also dull your senses. Don't take these pills for longer than two days, and don't take them if you have a high fever or blood in the stool.

Antibiotics can help in a bad case of travellers' diarrhoea. How do you know it's 'bad'? The Public Health Service says that if you have three or more loose stools in an eight-hour period, especially if you also suffer from nausea, vomiting, abdominal cramps, and/or fever, you probably should have a doctor prescribe an antibiotic. The normal prescription is for doxycycline, 100 mg twice daily; or Bactrim F (Roche), tablets of TMP and SMX (trimethoprim 160 mg and sulfamethoxazole 800 mg) twice daily. These drugs are powerful and should not be taken carelessly. Be sure not to take them if hepatitis is suspected.

Hepatitis Hepatitis (*sarılık*, SAH-ruh-LUHK) is a serious viral infection which must be treated carefully. The chief symptoms are fatigue, loss of energy, a yellow cast to the eyes and skin, and odd-coloured brownish urine. If you rest when your body tells you to, you will have no trouble curing yourself. If you push on, the disease can cause serious liver damage or even death. Being a virus, there is no known drug to combat it. Antibiotics can actually make it worse, even fatal, as they put great stress on the already over-burdened liver which must detoxify them.

If you think you have hepatitis, go to a doctor and get an examination and a blood test. If the diagnosis is positive, go to bed and stay there. Eat only easily digestible non-fatty foods such as toast, yoghurt, cooked fruits and vegetables. Don't drink any alcohol for six months after diagnosis. You will have to figure on at least a week or two of bed rest, then an easy life for several months. The doctor may prescribe vitamins, especially B-complex. If he prescribes any other medicine, go to another doctor. This is no joke.

Sexually Transmitted Diseases Sexual contact with an infected sexual partner spreads these diseases and while abstinence is the only 100% preventative, use of a condom is also effective. Gonorrhoea and syphilis are the most common of these diseases and sores, blisters or rashes around the genitals, discharges or pain when urinating are common symptoms. Symptoms may be less marked or not observed at all in women. The symptoms of syphilis eventually disappear completely but the disease continues and can cause severe problems in later years. Treatment of gonorrhoea and syphilis is by antibiotics.

There are numerous other sexually transmitted diseases for most of which effective treatment is available. There is no cure for herpes and there is also currently no cure for AIDS, which is most commonly spread through male homosexual activity. Using condoms and avoiding certain sexual practices such as anal intercourse are the most effective preventatives.

AIDS can also be spread through infected blood transfusions or by dirty needles – vaccinations, acupuncture and tattooing can potentially be as dangerous as intravenous drug use if the equipment is not clean. If you do need an injection it may be a good idea to buy a new syringe from a pharmacy and ask the doctor to use it.

Doctors, Dentists & Hospitals
You can find good doctors and dentists in Turkey's big cities. Ankara has a medical centre called Hacettepe (hah-JEHT-tehp-peh) plus other hospitals (*hastane*, hahs-tahn-NEH) and clinics (*klinik*, klee-NEEK). Government-supported hospitals are called *devlet hastanesi* (dehv-LEHT hass-tah-neh-see), and you can find them by following the standard international road sign with a large 'H' on it.

Clinics run by the Red Crescent (Kızılay, the Turkish equivalent of the Red Cross) are marked by a red crescent. *İlk yardım* on one of these signs means 'first-aid', which may or may not be competent; a *sağlık ocağı* is a simple dispensary. All hospital and clinic costs are controlled by the government, and are quite low, even at private hospitals.

In every city and town of any size you will see signs marking the medical offices of doctors and giving their specialities. *Operatör* means surgeon. A doctor (*tıbbî doktor*, medical doctor) might treat *göz hastalıkları*, eye diseases; *dahili*, internal medicine; *kadın hastalıkları*, gynaecological ailments; *çocuk hastalıkları*, children's ailments.

By the way, half of all the physicians in Turkey are women, and women might prefer to be seen by a female doctor. If a woman visits a male doctor, it's customary to have a companion present during any physical examination or treatment. There is not always a nurse available to serve in this role.

İstanbul has several foreign-run hospitals:

American
    Amiral Bristol Amerikan Hastanesi, Güzelbahçe Sokak, Nişantaş (tel 148-6030)
French
    La Paix Hastanesi, Büyükdere Caddesi, Şişli, (tel 148-1832)
German
    Alman Hastanesi, Sıraselviler Caddesi, Taksim (tel 143-5500)

Care in Turkish hospitals is sometimes not of the highest standard in terms of comfort or convenience. But medical care, as always, depends upon the particular staff members (doctors and nurses) involved. These can be quite good or not so good. The lower staff echelons may be low paid and trained on the job. As a foreigner, you will probably be given the best possible treatment and the greatest consideration.

DANGERS & ANNOYANCES

Turkey is a safe country relative to most of the world. Crime is not a big problem – yet. You may feel safer here than at home.

Police

You'll see a lot of soldiers in Turkey. This is partly because soldiers make up the *jandarma* (gendarmerie) force, and partly because Turkey has universal male military service – every man serves, even if he is partly disabled. With all these men in arms, jobs have got to be found for them. Other reasons include NATO commitments, borders with sometimes hostile neighbours, and a long, proud military tradition which began when Turks formed the elite units under the later Arab caliphs in the 10th and 11th centuries. The military presence is large in Turkey, but not really sinister.

Here's the rundown on the police forces:

Polis The green-clad officers with white caps, both men and women, are part of a national force called Polis (poh-LEES), which controls traffic, patrols highways and attends to other police duties in cities and towns. Under normal circumstances you will have little to do with these people. If you do have reason to deal with them, you should know that they will judge you partly by your clothes and personal appearance. If you look tidy and 'proper', they'll be on your side. If you're dressed carelessly, they may turn a jaundiced eye.

Belediye Zabıtası The blue-clad officers are called Belediye Zabıtası (municipal inspectors), or market police. These officers are the modern expression of an age-old Islamic custom of special commercial police who make sure a loaf of bread weighs what it should, that 24-carat gold is indeed 24 carats, that scales and balances don't cheat the customer. You'll see them patrolling the markets and bazaars, and if you have a commercial problem they'll be glad to help. They may not speak much of a foreign language, though.

Jandarma Soldiers in the standard Turkish army uniforms may be of three types. Without special insignia, they're regular army. With a red armband bearing the word 'Jandarma', they're gendarmes, whose job is to keep the peace, catch criminals on the run, stop smuggling, etc. If the soldiers have white helmets emblazoned with the letters 'As İz', plus pistols in white holsters connected to lanyards around their necks, they're Askeri İnzibat, or military police who keep off-duty soldiers in line. (A lot of these fellows are from the Kurdish areas, and have a reputation for toughness and discipline.)

Most of these soldiers are draftees inducted into the enormous Turkish army, put through basic training, and sent out to guard jobs that are usually pretty unexciting. They look ferocious – life in the Turkish army is no joke – but basically they are hometown boys waiting to get out. Every single one of them can tell you the precise number of days he has left to serve. Any request from a foreign tourist for help or directions is received as though it were a marvellous privilege.

Theft

In general there is not much problem with theft if you take the normal precautions. These include keeping track of your wallet or other valuables on crowded buses and trains and in markets; not leaving valuables in your hotel room, or at least not in view; and not walking into unknown parts of town when nobody else is around. I've received one report that a reader had his flight bag quietly slashed in İstanbul's Covered Market. Don't let Turkey's relative safety lull you into complete trustfulness.

Actually, the biggest danger of theft is probably in dormitory rooms and other open accommodation where other foreigners can see what sort of camera you have (and can guess its value pretty accurately), or where you stash your money.

Women Alone

Women must be more careful, as in any Mediterranean country. Turkish social customs dictate that a young woman (eg a high school student) not go to a major shopping street without friends or mother; college-aged women usually stroll with friends; women in their prime look purposeful, ignore catcalls and don't walk on lonely streets after dark. If you're approached by an eastern Romeo, ignore, ignore, ignore. It's best not to say or do anything.

The key is respectability: if you look and act respectable according to Turkish standards, you'll have the best chance to fend off unwanted advances. A wedding ring may help. It definitely helps to dress more formally. If you must say something at a would-be romeo, say *Ayıp!* (ah-YUHP), which means 'shameful'. Use it all you want to on young kids. But men may take exception if you call them shameful when they're certain that you'll find their masculine charms irresistible.

When you buy a bus ticket, the ticket agent will automatically seat you next to another woman or will leave the seat next to you empty. Should you want to confirm that this is the case, you can request it by saying *Yanımda erkek oturtmayın* (YAH-nuhm-DAH ehr-KEK oh-TOORT-mah-yuhn, 'Please don't seat a man next to me'). On some buses there are single seats set aside specifically for women.

When searching for a hotel, look for one catering to families. The word 'family' in Turkish can mean either wife, or husband and wife, or husband, wife and children. When you go out, look for the section of the tea garden or restaurant reserved for families or women alone; sometimes this is a separate upstairs room. The magic word for a respectable spot is always *aile* (family), as in *aile salonu* (family dining room) or *aile çay bahçesi* (family tea garden) or *aileye mahsustur* (reserved for families).

Over the years I have received numerous letters from women relating their experiences at the hands (literally) of Turkish men. Some say they had no problems whatsoever, others say they thought themselves in real danger at times. I think it's fair to predict that many unescorted women will have some annoying and unpleasant moments during their travels, but that they will also be treated in a civil, even courtly, manner by many Turkish men. There's a real clash of cultures: a traditionally patriarchal eastern society meets the modern, liberated western woman. Less than a century ago, a proper Turkish woman was veiled from head to toe; today, most female tourists in Turkey go topless at the beach. The cultural adjustment may take some time.

Disputes

In general, Turks view foreigners as cultured, educated and wealthy – even if many foreign visitors don't deserve such a view. This means that you will sometimes be given special consideration, jumped to the heads of queues, given the best seat on the bus, etc. In a dispute, if you keep your cool and act dignified, you will generally be given the benefit of the doubt. If it is thought you have powerful friends, you will definitely be given that benefit.

It's difficult to imagine a dispute involving a foreigner coming to the point of blows, as Turks are slow to anger. Don't let it happen. A Turk rarely finds it necessary to fight, but if he does, he wants to win, *whatever* the cost. Knowing that horrible things could happen, bystanders will pull two quarrelling men apart, even if they've never seen them before.

In the case of women travellers in disputes with Turks, you should know that Turkish men feel acutely any insults to their manhood, and will retaliate. Insults to them can include being shouted at or browbeaten by a woman who is not (in their eyes) unquestionably of a higher social status. In general, keep it all formal.

Lese-Majesty

The battle to form the Turkish Republic out of the ruins of the Ottoman Empire was a very tough one, and Turks have great respect for the accomplishments of Atatürk and the republic. There are laws against insulting, defaming or making light of Atatürk, the Turkish flag, the Turkish people, the Turkish republic, etc. These are normal for many countries. Any difficulty will probably arise from misunderstanding. At the first sign that you've inadvertently been guilty of lese-majesty, be sure to make your apologies. It may seem a trivial thing to you, but if it's important to someone else, you should apologise. An apology will be readily accepted.

Natural Hazards

Earthquakes Turkey sometimes has very bad ones. The big quakes only seem to hit every eight or 10 years, though, and the same thing happens in many parts of the world, so it's up to Allah.

Undertow & Riptide At some of the swimming areas, particularly in the Black Sea near İstanbul, this is a real danger. Undertow can kill you by powerfully pulling you beneath the surface, and a riptide does the same by sweeping you out to sea so that you exhaust yourself trying to regain the shore. There may be no signs warning of the danger. Lifeguards may not be present, or may be untrained or not equipped with a boat. Don't trust to luck.

You can't necessarily see these hazards or predict where they will be. In either situation, remain calm, as panic can be fatal. Don't exhaust yourself by trying to swim straight back to the beach from a riptide, because you'll never make it. Rather, swim to the left or right to escape the riptide area, and make for land in that direction. These dangers are usually a problem only on long stretches of open-sea beach with surf. In coves and bays, where waves are broken or diverted by headlands, you probably won't be in danger.

Insects, Snakes & Other Animals Turkey has mosquitoes, scorpions and snakes. You will not see many of them, but be aware, as you tramp around the ruins of Ephesus or Priene, that such beasts do live here and may be nearby, at least in summer. There are also wild boar and wolves around, though you won't encounter these unless you hike deep into the bush.

The Imperial Auto

Give way to cars and trucks in all situations, even if you have to jump out of the way. The sovereignty of the pedestrian is unrecognised in Turkey. If a car hits you, the driver (if not the courts) will blame you for not getting out of the way. This does not apply on a recognised crosswalk controlled by a traffic officer or a traffic signal. If you've got a 'Walk' light, you've got the right of way. Watch out, all the same. The insistence of every Turkish driver that you, as a pedestrian, are merely an annoyance composed of so much vile protoplasm, will get to you after a while. Grit your teeth and bear it, murmuring 'When in Rome', etc. A dispute with a driver will get you nowhere and may escalate into an even bigger problem.

The Pungent Weed

If you're allergic to cigarette smoke, you will have some unpleasant moments in Turkey. Though the local cancer prevention society fields a brave effort to stop smoking, this is the land of aromatic

Turkish tobacco. Smoking is the national passion. No-smoking areas are virtually unheard of, and would not really be observed if they were, even on planes and trains. (Recently a progressive minister of transport decreed a ban on smoking aboard all domestic airline flights; after a few months he was turfed out and the ban lifted.) OK, some people don't smoke next to the fuel pumps in petrol stations. But in general, position yourself near a fresh-air source if possible. And help in my campaigns to have separate smoking and no-smoking areas: ask for no-smoking whenever you board a plane or a bus.

Noise

Noise is a source of annoyance in cities. As in many third world countries, the noise level in Turkey is frequently high. Turks seem either immune to the annoyance of a high noise level, or even to enjoy it. Choose hotel rooms with noise in mind.

Among the most persistent and omnipresent noises is that of the call to prayer, amplified to ear-splitting levels. In the good old days before microphones and amplifiers, it must have been beautiful to hear the clear, natural voices of the muezzins calling from a hundred minarets, even before dawn, when the first call is given. Now you hear a cacophony of blaring noise five or more times a day. If there's a minaret right outside your hotel window, you'll know it.

Also, Turks are addicted to nightlife and think nothing of staying up until 1 or 2 am in the middle of the week, so watch out for highly amplified bands and singers. Nightclub noise is particularly insulting when you have spent good money to upgrade your accommodation only to find that the better the hotel, the louder its nightclub. In some resorts, atomic-powered discos rock the entire town until dawn, making sleep virtually impossible. When in doubt, ask *Sakin mi?* (sah-KEEN mee, 'Is it quiet here?').

Air Pollution

In winter, air pollution is a problem in the big cities. In Ankara it is a very serious problem, rivalling that of Tokyo and Mexico City. The traditional heating fuel is lignite (soft brown coal), which produces enormous clouds of heavy, choking particles. The situation is now improving because of a new natural gas pipeline from the Soviet Union which brings clean heating fuel to buildings in Ankara and İstanbul. But air quality in winter may still be substandard for a while. If you find your nose running, your eyes watering and itching, and your head aching, that's the pollution. The heating season lasts from 15 October to 1 April. In summer there is some pollution from autos, but it's no worse than in other big cities.

ACCOMMODATION
Hotels

The cheapest hotels in Turkey are rated by each local municipality. These are the basic places that provide bed, heat, light and water. They are used mostly by working-class Turkish men travelling on business. Virtually all hotels above this basic standard are rated by the Ministry of Tourism according to a star system. One-star hotels are just a step above the cheap places rated by the municipalities. At the top, rating five stars, are the international-class places, such as the Hiltons, Sheratons, Pullman Etaps and Ramadas.

In this guide hotels are listed according to price, except in places with only a few hotels which must be used by all visitors regardless of preference.

Bottom End Lodgings in this group are priced from US$2 per bed up to US$20 or US$25 for a double room. For Turks, these are the rooms used by farmers in town for the market, workers in town looking for a job, or working-class families on holiday at the seaside. Not surprisingly, the most difficult place to find a truly cheap and good low-budget room is İstanbul. In most other cities, good, cheap beds can be found fairly easily. In out-of-the-way villages the price for a bed is surprisingly low.

Rooms priced below about US$7 do not usually have a private shower or toilet in the room, but may have a *lavabo* (washbasin). Above that price, in small towns you may get private plumbing. Cold-water showers are usually free, as they should be. Hot-water showers may cost about US$1 in lodgings where a fire must be built in the hot-water heater. If there is solar water-heating, hot showers are often free, but the water may only be warm, as the solar tanks are generally uninsulated off season. On cloudy days, or if everyone else has preceded you to the showers, expect tepid water. With solar water-heating, plan to shower in the evening when the water is hottest, rather than in the morning.

At the lowest prices, the rooms will be quite bare and spartan, but functional. Prices may be quoted per bed rather than per room. For privacy, you may have to pay for all of the beds in the room. If you find used sheets on the bed, request clean ones; the owner has got to change them sometime, and it may as well be for you. Say *Temiz çarşaf lâzım* (teh-MEEZ chahr-SHAHF lyaa-zuhm, 'Clean sheets are necessary'). Bedbugs are not unheard of; let me know of any bug banquets you host so I can warn other readers.

Using your own equipment and bedding, it is sometimes possible to sleep on the roof of a pension or hotel, or camp in the garden, for a minimal fee of US$1 to US$3 per person, which includes use of bathing and other hotel facilities. Another way to save lodging money is to take night buses or trains on long hauls.

Middle Turkey has lots of modern and comfortable hotels rated at one to three stars by the Ministry of Tourism. Facilities in this range include lifts, staff capable of a smattering of German, French and English, rooms with a private

shower or bath and toilet, perhaps balconies to enjoy the view, and maybe guarded car parks. Prices in this range are from US$25 to US$75.

A one-star hotel will have these facilities and little else, and will price its double rooms with a bath at around US$25. A two-star hotel will probably have a restaurant and bar, a TV lounge, obsequious staff, and some pretensions to decor and architecture. Double rooms with a private bath would be priced from US$25 to US$45.

A three-star hotel may provide colour TVs and mini-bar refrigerators in all guest rooms, and may have haughty but multilingual staff, a swimming pool, nightclub, pastry shop, or other special facilities as well. Double rooms with a bath would be priced at US$45 to US$75. Fairly prosperous Turks look upon a hotel room in this range as quite luxurious accommodation.

Top End Turkey's tourism boom has produced a frenzy of hotel-building in all price ranges, including the luxury market. Hotels in this 'Top End' classification are priced at US$75 to US$250 and up for a double room.

Hotels of an international standard, such as the Hiltons, Sheratons, Ramadas, Pullman Etaps, Swissôtels, etc, are rated at five stars and are mostly to be found in the three largest cities (İstanbul, Ankara, İzmir) and in the most famous tourist destinations (Antalya, Cappadocia). Just below the international chains in luxury are the Turkish chain hotels such as Turban, Emek, Dedeman and others, rated at four or five stars. These hotels often provide almost the same degree of luxury as some of the top places, but at prices about 20% to 40% lower.

Besides these very expensive places, Turkey has a number of smaller, very comfortable hotels where you'll enjoy more personal and attentive service at much lower prices. These four-star luxury hotels may not have swimming pools, health clubs, ballrooms and convention centres, but they have most of the comforts an individual traveller would normally require. Prices for a double room range from $100 to $175.

Hostels

The term *yurt* (hostel or lodge) or *öğrenci yurdu* (student hostel) usually defines an extremely basic and often dingy dormitory lodging intended for low-budget Turkish students from the provinces who are attending university classes. With hotels and *pensions* (boarding houses) so cheap, few tourists stay at these student hostels. However, as the boom in travel to Turkey continues, better hostels are being opened and drab ones spruced up. Basic hostels may have hot water only at certain times of the day.

The Ministry of Youth Affairs & Sports operates a number of hostels and camps in İstanbul, Ankara, İzmir, Bolu, Çanakkale and Bursa. Hostel arrangements change from season to season and year to year. Ask at a Tourism Information Office, or at Gençtur Tourism & Travel Agency Ltd (tel 528-0734), Yerebatan Caddesi 15/3, Sultanahmet, İstanbul. Gençtur works closely with the Ministry of Youth Affairs & Sports.

Other Accommodation

Perhaps the most interesting development in the Turkish hotel business is the flourishing of 'boutique' hotels. These are usually old Ottoman mansions, caravanserais, or other historic buildings which have been refurbished or even completely rebuilt, and equipped with modern conveniences. Charm, atmosphere and history are the attractions here, and they provide it in abundance, at prices from US$75 to US$175 for a double room, breakfast included. Because of their unique character, these hotels may not be rated according to the star system. Most would rate three or four stars if they were.

Choosing a Hotel

Here are some points to watch:

Inspect the Rooms Don't judge a hotel by its facade. Look at the rooms. I've never had a desk clerk refuse to show me a room. Among the middle range of Turkish hotels there is a tendency to put money into the lobby rather than into the rooms, and so looking at the lobby does not give you an accurate idea of the quality of the guest quarters.

Know the Price Next, prices should be posted prominently at the reception desk. Sometimes, particularly in low-budget hotels, the posted prices will be above what the proprietor actually expects to get for a room. Haggling is often in order, particularly if the hotel doesn't seem to be particularly busy. Another way to lower the price is to haggle for a price that does not include breakfast. In some places the hotel requires you to take breakfast, and then charges exorbitantly for it. Raise a stink and they'll back down, and you can have breakfast in a teahouse nearby for next to nothing.

Whether you haggle or not, make sure you understand the price. Is it per bed (*beher yatak*, beh-HEHR yah-TAHK) or per room (*oda fiyatı*, OH-dah fee-yah-tuh)? Is breakfast (*kahvaltı*) included (*dahil*) or excluded (*hariç*)? Is there an extra fee for a hot shower (*duş ücreti*, DOOSH urj-reh-tee)? Is the tax included (*vergi dahil*, vehr-GEE dah-HEEL)? It usually is (and should be).

Beware of Noise Turkish cities and towns are noisy places, and you will soon learn to choose a hotel and a room with quiet in mind. In this guide I have done some of the work for you by recommending mostly the quieter places, but you will have to be aware when you select your room. The front rooms in a hotel, those facing the busy street, are usually looked upon as the most desirable by the hotel management, and are sometimes priced higher than rooms at the rear. Take advantage of this. Ask for *sakin bir oda* (sah-KEEN beer oh-dah, 'a quiet room') and pay less.

Water Pressure In some cities, and particularly in summer, there may be temporary water problems. Water may be cut off for several hours at a time, though many hotels have roof tanks which do away with this problem. The other problem with water pressure is when the pressure remains high, but the fixtures are not in good repair, and the toilet tinkles all night.

Hot Water Except in the fanciest hotels, do not trust hot water to come out of the left-hand tap and cold water out of the right-hand one. Every time you settle into a hotel room, or use a shower, experiment with the taps. It means nothing that the left-hand one is marked in red, it may yield cold water, while the right-hand one, marked in blue, gives hot water. In the same bathroom, the washbasin may be marked correctly and the shower incorrectly. It's a daily struggle. Open both taps and let them run full force for a minute or so, close them, then open one and next the other to see what you get. If both are cold, let them run a few minutes more and check again. Still cold? OK, now it's time to complain to the management.

As for hot water, it's often difficult to find in summer in the cheaper hotels, unless they have solar water-heaters. Many small hotels have only a single furnace for both hot water and central heating, and they really don't want to run that furnace in summer. Since the summers are warm, even hot, this doesn't present much of a problem. Early spring and late autumn are another matter, though. Every desk clerk will say, 'Yes, we have hot water', but when you try to take a shower the new fact will be, 'Ah, the furnace just this minute broke down!'

Believe it or not, the most dependable hot water is in the cheapest pensions, because in these places the owner builds a little fire in the bottom of the hot-water tank 30 minutes before your shower appointment, and you bathe in as much steaming water as you want. The extra charge for this luxury is about US$0.75 to US$1.

An alternative, fairly dependable hot-water method is the *şofben* (SHOHF-behn), or flash heater. This type runs on gas, and flashes into action as soon as you turn on the hot-water tap. It's activated by water flowing through the hot-water pipe. Obviously this sort of heater is not dependent on a central furnace, but it does have other problems. Gas pressure must be sufficient to heat the water, which it sometimes is not; and the flow of water must be strong enough to activate the *şofben*, which it sometimes is not. Often it's a balancing act, keeping the flow of water fast enough to activate the heater, yet slow enough to make sure the water is hot.

Lifts If you push the wrong button, you'll never get to ride. 'Ç' stands for *çağır* (call) which is what you want to do to the lift – call it to where you are. 'G' is for *gönder* (send), and if you push this one, you'll send the lift to the end of its run (usually to the ground floor). A little illuminated 'M' means the lift is *meşgül* (engaged); wait until the light goes out before pushing 'Ç'. If there's a little illuminated 'K', it means the car is *katta* (positioned at your floor). 'Z' or *zemin* in lift parlance means ground floor; this is the button to push to get there. If you push '1', you'll end up on the 1st floor above ground level. If the ground floor button is not 'Z' it's probably 'L' for *lobi*.

If you stay in hotels with lifts, at least once you will have the idiotic feeling that comes when you press the 'Ç' button only to have the lift respond 'K', meaning, 'The car's already here, stupid. Just pull the door open and get in.'

Electricity Electricity may go off for short periods in some locations. This is not much of a problem, however. What is a problem is the lack of reading lights in all but the more expensive hotels. Your bedside lamp will never have more than a 25-watt bulb in it. Apparently Turks don't read in bed. However, you will almost always find a *gece lambası* in your room, a low-wattage bulb, perhaps even one in a lurid colour, perhaps high on the wall. The function of this 'night light' (as the term translates) is to give an eerie glow to the room so that you do not sleep in total darkness.

Unmarried Couples Unmarried couples sharing rooms usually run into no problems, even though the desk clerk sees the obvious when he takes down the pertinent information from your passports onto the registration form. The cheaper the hotel, the more traditional and conservative its management tends to be. Very simple hotels which are clean and 'proper' want to maintain their reputations. If you look clean and proper, and act that way, there should be no trouble. Lots of allowances are made for odd foreign ways.

Single Women Single women travelling alone or in pairs should look for family hotels. Men travel much more than do women in Turkey, and many hotels, from moderate to rock bottom, cater mostly to men on business. No sharp dividing line, no key word in the hotel's name lets you know that one hotel is good and another not so good. In principle, every hotel accepts all potential guests. In practice, you may feel uncomfortable in a place which customarily is filled with men; and they may wonder why you're staying there when there are better aile hotels nearby. To locate a suitable hotel, look to see if there are matronly types waiting in the lobby, or just ask, *Bu otel aile için mi?* (BOO oh-tehl ah-yee-LEH ee-cheen mee, 'Is this hotel for families/ladies?') If it's not, the clerk should direct you to a more suitable place nearby.

TURKISH BATHS
The history of steam baths goes back millennia. Many of the natural spas in Turkey were enjoyed by the ancient Greeks and Romans. Seljuk and Ottoman Turks built beautiful, elaborate baths to serve their communities, partly because Islam demands good personal hygiene, and partly because bathing is such a pleasure.

Public baths were required in ancient times because private residences did not have bathing facilities. Everybody, rich and poor alike, went to the baths. For a workman, it was simply to get clean. For a high-born lady, it was a ritual of attendants, accessories and polite courtesies. Some baths are very fancy, others simpler, but there are still public baths to be found in virtually every neighbourhood of every town in Turkey.

The custom of going to the baths continues because the public facilities are so much grander than what is available at home, and because to the Turks it is still a social occasion. To steam clean, have a massage, relax and read, sip tea and chat with friends, is looked upon as a wonderful, affordable luxury. Baths are male or female, but not male and female together. Sex, whether heterosexual or homosexual, has no place in the baths.

The Turkish bath procedure is this: you will be shown to a cubicle where you can undress, store your clothes and wrap around you the cloth that's provided. An attendant will lead you through the cool room and the warm room to the hot room, where you sit and sweat for a while, relaxing and loosening up. You can have a massage here. Haggle with a masseur or masseuse on a price before beginning.

When you are half-asleep and soft as putty from the steamy heat, you have a choice. The cheapest bath is the one you do yourself, having brought your own soap, shampoo and towel. But the true experience is to have an attendant wash you, providing all the necessaries. You'll be led to the warm room, doused with warm water, then lathered with a sudsy swab. Next, the attendant will scrub your skin with a coarse cloth mitten loosening dirt you never suspected you had. Next comes a shampoo, another dousing with warm water, then one with cool water. water.

When the scrubbing is over, head for the cool room, there to be swathed in Turkish towels, then led back to your cubicle for a rest or a nap. You can order tea, coffee, a soft drink or a bottle of beer. For a nap, tell the attendant when to wake you.

Bath etiquette requires that men remain clothed with the bath-wrap at all times. During the bathing, they wash their private parts themselves, without removing the modesty wrap. In the women's section modesty is less in evidence.

FOOD

It is worth travelling to Turkey just to eat. Turkish cuisine is the very heart of eastern Mediterranean cooking, which demands excellent, fresh ingredients and careful, even laborious preparation. The ingredients are often very simple, but are of the highest quality, and in recipes they are harmonised with great care. Turkish farmers, herders and fishers bring forth a wealth of truly superb produce from this agriculturally rich land and its surrounding seas. Being one of only seven countries on earth which produces a surplus of food, the Turks have enough good produce to feed everyone here, with some left over for export.

Good as it is, Turkish cooking can get to be a bit monotonous after a while, as the variety of dishes found in restaurants is not as great as that found in home kitchens. And when you'd like a change from charcoal-grilled lamb, you won't find an Indonesian or Mexican or Indian or Japanese restaurant just around the corner. Despite the extent of the Ottoman Empire the Turks did not trade extensively with other nations during the 18th and 19th centuries, and never received an influx of foreign populations and cuisines. This is changing, though. Some Chinese restaurants have opened, Japanese ones are sure to follow, and you can now – for better or worse – get authentic Yankee hamburgers in the largest cities.

Saving Money

Several tips can save you lots of money on food. First, order as you eat. Turks order appetisers, eat them, then decide what to have next, and order it. There is no need to order your entire meal at the beginning, except perhaps in the international hotels.

Second, don't 'overeat with your eyes'. Often you will be directed to a steam table or stove to select your meal, and there's a tendency to order too many courses. Order them one at a time, and remember that it takes at least 20 minutes for food to 'make you feel full' after you've eaten it.

Third, eat bread. Turkish bread is delicious, fresh, plentiful and cheap. Many Turkish dishes come in savoury

sauces; dip and sop your bread and enjoy. For instance, a meal of *kuru fasulye* (beans in a rich tomato sauce with meat stock) with bread and water is delicious, nutritious and ridiculously cheap at about US$0.75 or US$1.

Fourth, don't accept any plate of food which you have not specifically ordered. For example, in İstanbul's Çiçek Pasajı, near Galatasaray Square, itinerant vendors may put a dish of fresh almonds on your table. They're not a gift. They'll show up on your bill at a premium rate. The same goes for unwanted appetisers, butter, cheese, etc. If you haven't ordered it, ask *Hediye mi?* (heh-dee-YEH mee, 'Is it a gift?') or *Bedava mı?* (beh-dah-VAH muh, 'Is it free?'). If the answer is no, say *Istemiyorum* (eess-TEH-mee-oh-room, 'I don't want it').

Finally, always check your restaurant bill for errors. As tourism comes to Turkey, so do the common sins of ripping off the tourist. The more touristy a place is, the more carefully you must check your bill.

Restaurants

Restaurants (*restoran, lokanta*) are everywhere, open early in the morning until late at night. Most are very inexpensive, and although price is always some determinant of quality, often the difference between a US$4 meal and a US$15 meal is not great, at least as far as flavour is concerned. Service and ambience are fancier at the higher price. In any restaurant in Turkey, whether fancy or simple, there is a convenient washbasin (*lavabo*) so that you can wash your hands before eating. Just say the word and the waiter will point it out. Also, if you're a woman or are travelling with a woman, ask for the *aile salonu* (often upstairs) which will be free of the sometimes oppressive all-male atmosphere to be found in some cheap Turkish eateries.

Many Turkish waiters have the annoying habit of snatching your plate away before you're finished with it. This may be due to a rule of eastern etiquette which holds that it is impolite to leave a finished plate sitting in front of a guest. If a waiter engages in plate-snatching, say *Kalsın* (kahl-SUHN, 'Let it stay').

Full Service First there is the familiar sort of restaurant with white tablecloths and waiter service. It may be open for three meals a day, and will probably be among the more expensive dining places. Most full-service restaurants have some 'ready food' and also prepare grilled meats, particularly in the evening. They also usually serve liquor, wine and beer, and are sometimes called *içkili* (EECH-kee-LEE, serving drinks) because of this.

Hazır Yemek Next there is the *hazır yemek* (hah-ZUHR yeh-mehk, 'ready food') restaurant. Although all restaurants offer some dishes prepared in advance, these places specialise in an assortment of dishes, prepared in advance of meal time and served on demand. They are basically working-class cafeterias, but with waiter service. You pass by a steam table, which is often in the front window of the restaurant to entice passers-by, you make your choices, and a waiter brings them to you. Usually there are no alcoholic beverages served in these places, but occasionally, if you order a beer, the waiter will run to a shop nearby and get one for you.

There will always be *çorba* (CHOR-bah, soup), often *mercimek çorbası* (mehr-jee-MEHK, lentil soup). *Ezo gelin çorbası* (EH-zoh GEH-leen) is a variation of lentil soup, with rice and lemon juice. *Domates çorbası* (doh-MAH-tess) is creamy tomato soup. *Şehriye* (SHEH-ree-yeh) is vermicelli soup, made with a chicken stock.

Pilav (pee-LAHV) of some sort will always be available. Plain pilav is rice cooked in stock. There may also (or instead) be *bulgur pilav*, cracked bulghur wheat cooked in a tomato stock.

Many of the dishes will be vegetables

and meat. Most popular are *salçalı köfte* (sahl-chah-LUH kurf-teh), meatballs of lamb stewed in a sauce with vegetables; *patlıcan kebap* (paht-luh-JAHN keh-bahp), eggplant and chunks of lamb; or *orman kebap* (ohr-MAHN keh-bahp), lamb chunks, vegetables and potatoes in broth. *Kuzu haşlama* (koo-ZOO hahsh-lah-mah) is lamb hocks in a stew.

Sometimes grilled meats are available in *hazır yemek* restaurants. *Döner kebap* (durn-NEHR keh-bahp), <u>lamb roasted on a vertical spit and sliced off in thin strips as it cooks, is the closest thing you'll find to a national dish</u>. *Şiş kebap* (SHEESH keh-bahp) is meat only, small pieces of lamb grilled on real charcoal.

Sometimes beer is served in these restaurants; more often, it's not. Decor may be nonexistent and the letters on the front window may only say 'Lokanta', but the welcome will be warm, the food delicious and very cheap.

With your meal you will receive as much fresh bread as you can eat, for a nominal charge. <u>It's easy to 'overeat with your eyes' in these places, especially when the bread is so good. Soup, pilav, a main course and bread make for a big meal.</u>

Hazır yemek restaurants prepare most of their daily dishes for the midday meal and then just keep them heated (one hopes) until supper time. <u>The best reason to eat a big meal at midday is that the food is freshest and best then.</u> If you want grilled fish or meat, have it in the evening.

Kebapçı, & Köfteci Two other sorts of restaurant are the *kebapçı* (keh-BAHP-chuh) and *köfteci* (KURF-teh-jee). A kebapçı is a person who cooks *kebap* (roast meat). A köfteci roasts *köfte*, which are rissoles or meatballs of ground lamb made with savoury spices. Though they may have one or two ready-food dishes, kebapçı and köfteci restaurants specialise in grilled meat, plus soups, salad, yoghurt and perhaps dessert. Döner kebap and şiş kebap are the two most common kinds of

kebap. *Kuşbaşı* (KOOSH-bah-shuh, 'bird's head') is a smaller and finer lamb şiş kebap. *Çöp kebap* (CHURP keh-bahp) is tiny morsels of lamb on split bamboo skewers.

If you want any sort of kebap or köfte well done, say *iyi pişmiş* or *pişkin*.

Kebapçıs can be great fun, especially the ones that are *ocakbaşı* (oh-JAHK bah-shuh, fireside). Patrons sit around the sides of a long rectangular firepit and the kebapçı sits enthroned in the middle, grilling hundreds of small skewers of şiş kebap and şiş köfte, which is köfte wrapped around a flat skewer; *adana köfte* (ah-DAHN-nah) is the same thing, but spicy hot. The chef hands them to you as they're done, and you eat them with flat bread, a salad and perhaps *ayran* (ah-yee-RAHN), a drink of yoghurt mixed with spring water. Alcoholic beverages are not usually served.

Pideci For those on an adventurer's budget, the Turkish *pideci* (pizza place) is a godsend. At a pideci, the dough for flat bread is patted out and shaped something like a boat, then dabbed with butter and other toppings, immediately baked in a wood-fired oven, and served at once. It's fresh, delicious, inexpensive, sanitary and nutritious. As toppings, if you want cheese say *peynirli* (pehy-neer-LEE); if you want eggs, say *yumurtalı* (yoo-moor-tah-LUH); *kıymalı* or *etli* means with ground lamb. In some parts of Turkey a *pide* (pizza) with meat is called *etli ekmek*, but it's still the same freshly baked flat bread.

I've recommended numerous pidecis in the various places covered by this book. To find your own, ask *Buralarda bir pideci var mı?* ('Is there a pideci around here?'). Alcoholic beverages are usually not served in pidecis.

Büfe & Kuru Yemiş Besides restaurants, Turkey has millions of little snack stands and quick-lunch places known as *büfe* (bew-FEH, buffet). These serve sandwiches, often grilled, puddings, portions of *börek* (bur-REHK, flaky pastry), and perhaps *lahmacun* (LAHH-mah-joon), an Arabic soft pizza made with chopped onion, lamb and tomato sauce. In the bigger büfes in İstanbul, you may have to pay the cashier in advance and get a *fiş* (FEESH, receipt), hand it to the cook and order your snack. Just tell the cashier *İki lahmacun*, pay, give the fiş to the cook, and repeat the order. You'll end up with two of the soft pizzas.

A *kuru yemiş* (koo-ROO yeh-MEESH) place serves dried fruits and nuts. These places are wonderful! Along İstiklal Caddesi in İstanbul you'll find little kuru yemiş shops selling pistachios (shelled or unshelled), walnuts, hazelnuts, peanuts (salted or unsalted), dried figs and apricots, chocolate, sunflower seeds and a dozen other good things. Prices are displayed, usually by the kg. Order 100 grams (*yüz gram*, YEWZ grahm), which is a good portion, and pay exactly one-tenth of the kg price displayed.

Another good place for kuru yemiş is the Mısır Çarşısı, the Egyptian Market or Spice Bazaar, in İstanbul's Eminönü district. Kuru yemiş shops here will also have *pestil* (pehs-TEEL), fruit which has been dried and pressed into flat, flexible sheets. Odd at first, but delicious, it's also relatively cheap and comes made from *kayısı* (apricots), *dut* (mulberries) and other fruits.

Hotel Restaurants

These, in general, do not offer good value in Turkey. You may want to have breakfast here for convenience (or because breakfast has been included in the room price), but most other meals should be taken in independent, local places. There are exceptions, of course, as in those remote towns where the one nice hotel in town also has the one nice restaurant.

Meals

Breakfast

In a hotel or pastry shop, breakfast (*komple kahvaltı*, kohm-PLEH kah-vahl-TUH) consists of fresh, delicious *ekmek* (ek-MEHK, Turkish bread) with jam or honey, butter, black olives, white sheep's milk cheese and *çay* (CHAH-yee, tea). Sometimes a wedge of processed cheese, like the French 'La Vache Qui Rit', is added or substituted for the sheep's milk cheese.

You can always order an egg (*yumurta*, yoo-moor-TAH), soft-boiled (*üç dakikalık*, EWCH dahk-kah-luhk) or hard-boiled (*sert*, SEHRT). Fried eggs are *sahanda yumurta* (sah-hahn-DAH yoo-moor-tah). Sometimes your bread will come toasted (*kızarmış*, (kuh-zahr-MUSH). This is the standard breakfast for tourists. If you order an egg or another glass of tea, you may be charged a bit extra. You can order fried eggs in most places.

Breakfast is not always included in the hotel room rate, though some hotels do include it. When breakfast is included, the desk clerk will mention it as he quotes the price of the room. *Kahvaltı dahil* (kah-vahl-TUH dah-HEEL) means 'Breakfast is included'.

Turkish bread and tea are usually fresh and good, but because any breakfast can get dull after a while there are alternatives. Turks may have a bowl of hot soup which, with lots of fresh bread, makes quite a delicious breakfast for a very low price. If that's not for you, find a place serving *su böreği* (SOO bur-reh-yee), a many-layered noodle-like pastry with white cheese and parsley among the layers, served warm.

Hot, sweetened milk (*sıcak süt*, suh-JAHK sewt) is also a traditional breakfast drink, replaced in winter by *sahlep* (sah-LEHP), which is hot, sweetened milk flavoured with tasty orchid-root (Orchis mascula) powder and a sprinkle of cinnamon.

Bacon is difficult to find as any pork product is forbidden to Muslims. You may find it in the big hotels in the biggest cities.

Turkish coffee (*Türk kahvesi*, TEWRK kah-veh-see) is better as an after-dinner drink than a breakfast drink. You may find some places willing to serve you *Amerikan kahvesi* (ah-mehr-ee-KAHN kahh-veh-see), a less concentrated brew than Turkish coffee. *Fransız kahvesi* (frahn-SUHZ kahh-veh-see, 'French coffee') can be either strong Amerikan kahvesi served black or it can be coffee with milk, which may also be called *sütlü kahve* (sewt-LEW kahh-veh).

Instant coffee, called *neskafe* (NEHS-kah-feh) or *hazır kahve* (hah-ZUHR kahh-veh), is also served nearly everywhere now, but can be surprisingly expensive.

Lunch The midday meal (*öğle yemeği*) can be big or small. In summer, many Turks prefer to eat a big meal at midday and a light supper in the evening. You might want to do this, too.

Dinner The evening meal can be a repeat of lunch, a light supper, or a sumptuous repast. In fine weather the setting might be outdoors.

Turkish Specialities

Meze A big meal starts with *meze* (MEH-zeh), all sorts of appetisers and hors d'oeuvres. You'll find börek pastry rolls, cylinders, or 'pillows' filled with white cheese and parsley, then deep-fried. There will be *zeytin* (olives), white cheese, *turşu* (toor-SHOO, pickled vegetables), *patates tava* (pah-TAH-tess tah-vah, fried potatoes) or light potato fritters called *patates köfte*. The famous stuffed vine leaves (*dolma*) come either hot or cold. The hot ones have ground lamb in them. The cold ones are made without meat, but 'with olive oil' (*zeytinyağlı*).

Salads The real stars of the meze tray, however, are the salads and purées. These are mystifying at first because they all look about the same: some goo on a plate decorated with bits of carrot, peas, parsley, olives or lemon slices. Here's where you'll need words to understand:

Amerikan salatası – a Russian salad with mayonnaise, peas, carrots, etc.

Beyin salatası – sheep's brain salad, usually the whole brain served on lettuce. Food for thought.

Cacık – that's 'jah-JUHK', yoghurt thinned with grated cucumber, then beaten and flavoured with a little garlic and a dash of olive oil.

Çoban salatası – a 'shepherd's salad', this is a mixed, chopped salad of tomatoes, cucumbers, parsley, olives and peppers (sometimes fiery). If you don't want the peppers, order the salad *bibersiz* (bee-behr-SEEZ, without pepper). But as the salad was probably chopped up all together at once, this order means some kitchen lackey will attempt to pick out the peppers. He may miss some. Be on guard.

Karışık salata – same as a çoban salatası.

Patlıcan salatası – this is puréed eggplant, perhaps mixed with yoghurt. The best of it has a faintly smoky, almost burnt flavour from the charcoal grilling of the eggplant.

Pilâki – broad white beans and sliced onions in a light vinegar pickle, served cold.

Rus salatası – a Russian salad. See Amerikan salatası.

Söğüş – pronounced 'sew-EWSH', this indicates raw salad vegetables such as tomatoes or cucumbers peeled and sliced, but without any sauce or dressing.

Taramasalata – red caviar, yoghurt, garlic and olive oil mixed into a smooth paste, salty and delicious.

Yeşil salata – a green salad of lettuce, oil and lemon juice or vinegar.

Main Courses After the meze comes the main course. The fish is marvellous all along the coast, especially in the Aegean. Ankara has some excellent fresh fish restaurants, too.

The most popular fish are the *palamut* (tunny or bonito), a darkish, full-flavoured baby tuna. *Lüfer* (bluefish), *levrek* (sea bass), *kalkan* (turbot), *pisi* (megrim or brill) and *sardalya* (fresh sardines) are other familiar fish.

Many fish will be grilled (*ızgara*) or fried (*tava*), especially turbot and tunny. Lüfer and levrek are particularly good poached with vegetables (*buğlama*). Fresh sardines are best if deep-fried in a light batter.

If you prefer meat, you can order a *karışık ızgara* (kahr-uh-SHUK uhz-gahr-ah), mixed grill of lamb. For beef, order *bonfile* (bohn-fee-LEH), a small fillet steak with a pat of butter on top. *Kuzu pirzolası* (koo-ZOO peer-zohl-ah-suh) is tiny lamb chops, charcoal-grilled.

Besides grilled meats there are numerous fancy kebaps, often named for the places where they originated. Best of the kebaps is *Bursa kebap* (BOOR-sah), also called *İskender kebap*, since it was invented in the city of Bursa by a chef named İskender (Turkish for Alexander). The kebap is standard döner spread on a bed of fresh, chopped, flat pide bread, with a side order of yoghurt. After the plate has been brought to your table, a man comes with savoury tomato sauce and pours a good helping on top. Then another man comes with browned butter, which goes on top of the sauce. This stuff is addictive.

Of the other fancy kebaps, *Urfa kebap* comes with lots of onions and black pepper; Adana kebap is spicy hot, with red pepper the way the Arabs like it (Adana is down near the Syrian border).

Cheese Cheeses are not a strong point in the Turkish kitchen. Although there are some interesting peasant cheeses such as *tulum peynir*, a salty, dry, crumbly goat's milk cheese cured in a goatskin bag, or another dried cheese which looks just like twine, these interesting cheeses rarely make it to the cities, and almost never to restaurant tables. What you'll find is the ubiquitous *beyaz peynir* (bey-AHZ pey-neer), white sheep's milk cheese. To be good, this must be full-cream (*tam yağlı*)

cheese, not dry and crumbly and not too salty or sour. You may also find *kaşar peynir* (kah-SHAHR pey-neer), a firm, mild yellow cheese which comes *taze* (tah-ZEH, fresh) or *eski* (ess-KEE, aged). The eski is a bit sharper, but not very sharp for all that.

Desserts Turkish desserts tend to be very sweet, soaked in sugar syrup. Many are baked, such as crumpets, biscuits or shredded wheat, all in syrup.

Baklava comes in several varieties: *cevizli* is with chopped walnut stuffing; *fıstıklı* is with pistachio nuts; *kaymaklı* is with clotted cream. Sometimes you can order *kuru baklava*, 'dry' baklava which has less syrup. True baklava is made with honey, not syrup, and though the home-made stuff may contain honey, the store-bought stuff rarely does.

As an alternative to sweet desserts, Turkish fruits can't be beaten, especially in mid-summer when the melon season starts, and early in winter when the first citrus crop comes in. *Kavun* is a deliciously sweet, fruity melon. *Karpuz* is watermelon.

The standard unsweetened dessert, available in most restaurants, is *krem karamel* (crème caramel or flan).

Vegetarian Food
Vegetarianism is not prevalent in Turkey. If you merely want to minimise consumption of meat, you will have no problem, as Turkish cuisine has many, many dishes in which meat is used merely as a flavouring rather than as a principal element. However, if you wish to avoid meat utterly, you will have to choose carefully. A good dish to try is *menemen* (MEH-neh-MEHN), tomatoes topped with eggs and baked; it is fairly spicy. Salads, cheeses, pilavs and yoghurt can fill out the menu. Note that many of the bean dishes such as *nohut* (chickpeas) and kuru fasulye are prepared with lamb as a flavouring.

Here are some phrases so that you can

explain to the waiter or the chef what you want: *Hiç et yiyemem* (HEECH eht yee-YEH-mehm, 'I can't eat any meat'); *Et suyu bile yiyemem* (EHt soo-YOO bee-leh yee-YEH-mehm, 'I can't even eat meat juices'); *Etsiz yemek var mı?* (eht-seez yeh-mehk VAHR muh, 'Do you have any dishes without meat?')

Chicken is an ingredient in two dessert puddings, and you wouldn't know it from looking at them or even eating them: *tavuk göğsü* and *kazandibi*. *Yiyemem* means 'I can't eat'. Depending upon your requirements, use it with *et* (meat), *tavuk* or *piliç* (chicken), yumurta or *balık* (fish) to make yourself understood.

DRINKS
Tea & Coffee
The national drink is not really Turkish coffee as you might expect, but çay (tea). The Turks drank a lot of coffee as long as they owned Arabia, because the world's first (and best) coffee is said to have come from Yemen. With the collapse of the Ottoman Empire coffee became an imported commodity. You can get Turkish coffee anywhere in Turkey, but you'll find yourself drinking a lot more çay.

The tea plantations are along the eastern Black Sea coast, centred on the town of Rize. Turkish tea is hearty and full-flavoured, served in little tulip-shaped glasses which you hold by the rim to avoid burning your fingers. Sugar is added, but never milk. If you want your tea weaker, ask for it *acık* (ah-CHUK, clear); for stronger, darker tea, order *koyu* (koh-YOO, dark). You can get it easily either way because Turkish tea is made by pouring some very strong tea into a glass, then cutting it with water to the desired strength.

The tiny glasses may seem impractical at first, but in fact they assure you of drinking only fresh, hot tea. Few Turks sit down and drink only one glass. For a real tea-drinking and talking session, they'll go to an outdoor tea garden and order a

semaver (samovar) of tea so they can refill the glasses themselves, without having to call the *çaycı* (CHAH-yee-juh, tea-man).

A few years ago a brand-new beverage, *elma çay* (apple tea) was introduced, and it caught on quickly. Tourists love it as much as Turks do, and you may even see street vendors selling packets of it for tourists to take home with them. It's delicious, caffeine-free, slightly tart, with a mild apple flavour. Surprisingly, the list of ingredients yields no mention of apple, only sugar, citric acid, citrate, food essence and vitamin C.

As for Turkish coffee, it is always brewed up individually, the sugar being added during the brewing. You order it one of four ways: *sade* (sah-DEH, plain, without sugar), *az* (AHZ, with a little sugar), *orta* (ohr-TAH, with moderate sugar), *çok şekerli* (CHOHK sheh-kehr-LEE, with lots of sugar).

Order *bir kahve, orta* (BEER kah-VEH, ohr-TAH) for the first time, and adjust from there. The pulverised coffee grounds lurk at the bottom of the cup – stop drinking before you get to them.

Water
Turks are connoisseurs of good water, and stories circulate of old men able to tell which spring it came from just by tasting it. *Menba suyu*, spring water, is served everywhere, even on inter-city buses. The standard price for a 1½-litre bottle of any brand, sold in a grocery, probably chilled, is US$0.65. If you order it in a restaurant there will be a mark-up of 100% to 300%.

Tap water is supposedly safe to drink because it is treated, but it's not as tasty or as trustworthy as spring water. (For more information on water, see Food & Water in the Health section.)

Non-Alcoholic Drinks
Soft drinks include the usual range of Coca-Cola, Pepsi, clear lemon-flavoured soft drinks like Seven-Up, orange soda, and others. Most Turks make little distinction between Coke and Pepsi, and

if you ask for one will serve you the other without thinking. Few places carry both brands, so you might as well just ask for *kola*, which will yield whatever the shop or restaurant carries.

If you want unflavoured fizzy water, ask for soda. Fizzy mineral water is maden suyu.

Fruit juice is a favourite refresher, and can be excellent. These used to be only thick juices full of pulp and flavour, but with the advent of modern marketing you will also find watery, sugared drinks of almost no food value. These are usually the ones in the paper containers. The good fruit juices tend to come in glass bottles and are so thick that you may decide to dilute them with spring water.

Traditional drinks include ayran, which is tart, refreshing and healthful. *Şıra* (shur-RAH), unfermented white grape juice, is delicious but is served in only a few places, and only during the summer. *Boza* is a thick, slightly tangy, very mild-flavoured drink made from fermented millet and served only in winter. *Sahlep* or *salep* is a hot drink made with milk, flavoured with orchid root and served with a dusting of cinnamon on top. It's sweet and fortifying; it, too, is served mostly in winter.

Alcohol

Beer Strictly observant Muslims don't touch alcoholic beverages at all, but in Turkey the strictures of religion are moderated by the 20th-century lifestyle. *Bira* (BEE-rah, beer) is served almost everywhere. Tuborg makes light (*beyaz*, bey-AHZ) and dark (*siyah*, see-YAH) beer in Turkey under licence. A local company with a European brewmaster is Efes Pilsen, which also makes light and dark beer. The light is a good, slightly bitter pilsener. Tekel, the Turkish State Monopolies company, makes Tekel Birası (teh-KEHL bee-rah-suh), a small-bubbled (sort of flat), mildly flavoured brew that may be an acquired taste. As of this writing, beer is available in returnable

bottles, and also in disposable cans at a premium price. You'll save money, get better flavour, and not contribute to the litter problem if you buy bottled beer.

Wine Turkish wines are surprisingly good and delightfully cheap. Tekel makes all kinds in all price ranges. Güzel Marmara is the cheap white table wine. Buzbağ (BOOZ-baah) is a hearty Burgundy-type wine with lots of tannin. Restaurants seem to carry mostly the wines of the two big private firms, Doluca (DOHL-oo-jah) and Kavaklıdere (kah-vakh-LUH-deh-reh). You'll find the premium Villa Doluca wines, white (*beyaz*) and red (*kırmızı*, KUHR-muh-ZUH) in most places. Kavaklıdere wines include the premium white named Çankaya and the medium-range wines named Kavak (white), Dikmen (red) and Lâl (rose). Some Turkish wines have won prizes in international competitions in recent years.

Among the more popular regional table wines are those under the Doruk and Dimitrakopulo labels.

Strong Liquor Hard liquor has traditionally been a government monopoly in Turkey, and what's not made by Tekel is imported by them. This may change as the government carries out its privatisation programme. Duties on imported spirits used to be very high but have now dropped significantly, so that your favourite brand will probably cost about the same in Turkey as it does at home, or may even be cheaper. Even so, the locally made drinks will be much cheaper than the imported brands.

The favourite ardent spirit in Turkey is *rakı* (rah-KUH), an aniseed-flavoured grape brandy similar to the Greek ouzo, French pastis and Arab arak. Rakı comes under several labels, all made by Tekel, the standard one being Yeni Rakı. It's customary (but not essential) to mix rakı with cool water, half-and-half, perhaps add ice, and to drink it with a meal.

Tekel also makes decent *cin* (JEEN, gin), *votka* and *kanyak* (kahn-YAHK, brandy). When ordering kanyak, always specify the *beş yıldız* or *kaliteli* ('five-star' or 'quality') stuff, officially named Truva Kanyak. The regular kanyak is thick and heavy, the five-star much lighter.

There is a Tekel *viski* (VEES-kee, whisky) named Ankara. You might try it once.

For after-dinner drinks, better restaurants will stock the local sweet fruit-brandies, which are OK but nothing special.

BOOKS & BOOKSHOPS
Books
Everyone from St Paul to Mark Twain and Agatha Christie has written about Turkey. It's one of those Middle Eastern countries with an incredibly deep history and culture. You will get far more out of your visit if you read up on the history, the culture and the people before you go. In a few cases, you might want to carry a specialised guide or history with you on your visit.

Biography *Atatürk, The Rebirth of a Nation* (Weidenfeld & Nicolson, London, 1964) by Lord Kinross (J P D Balfour) is essential reading for anyone who wants to understand the formation of the Turkish Republic and the reverence in which modern Turks hold the father of modern Turkey. It's well written and more exciting than many novels. The American edition is *Atatürk: A Biography of Mustafa Kemal* (Morrow, New York, 1965).

For a fascinating look into the last years of the Ottoman Empire and the early years of the Turkish Republic, read İrfan Orga's *Portrait of a Turkish Family* (Eland Books, London; Hippocrene Books (new edition), New York, 1988). First published in 1950 and recently republished with an afterword by the author's son, it's an absorbing portrait of a family trying to survive the collapse of an old society and the birth of a new one.

Anthropology For a good overview of life during the great days of the empire, look for *Everyday Life in Ottoman Turkey* (B T Batsford, London; G P Putnam's Sons, New York, 1971) by Raphaela Lewis. The book has many photographs, but is not easily found in bookshops these days; go to a library.

Archaeology *Ancient Civilisations & Ruins of Turkey* (Haşet Kitabevi, İstanbul, 1973 and later editions) by Ekrem Akurgal is a very detailed and fairly scholarly guide to most of Turkey's ruins 'from Prehistoric Times until the End of the Roman Empire'. The book, which costs about US$10, has 112 pages of photographs and is a good, readable English translation of the original. This is the best handbook for those with a deep interest in detailed classical archaeology.

George Bean (1903-1977) was the dean of western travel writers on Turkish antiquities. His four books with maps, diagrams and photos, cover the country's greatest wealth of Greek and Roman sites in depth, but in a very readable style. These four works were written as guidebooks to the ruins. They contain plenty of detail, but not so much that the fascination of exploring an ancient city or temple is taken away.

If you'd like to go deeply into a few sites, but not make the investments of time, energy and money necessary to cover the entire coast from Pergamum to Silifke, just buy Bean's *Aegean Turkey* (Ernest Benn, London; W W Norton, New York, 1979). It covers İzmir and its vicinity, Pergamum, Aeolis, sites west of İzmir to Sardis, Ephesus, Priene, Miletus, Didyma, Magnesia on the Menderes River (formerly Meander), and Heracleia. It costs about US$16.

Other books by George Bean (and from the same publishers) include:

Lycian Turkey (1978), which covers the Turkish coast roughly from Fethiye to Antalya, and its hinterland, and costs about US$16.

Turkey Beyond the Meander (1980), which covers the region south of the Menderes River, excluding Miletus, Didyma and Heracleia (covered in *Aegean Turkey*) but including sites near Bodrum, Pamukkale, Aphrodisias and Marmaris, and to the western outskirts of Fethiye. The book costs about US$22.

Turkey's Southern Shore (1979), which overlaps with *Lycian Turkey* a bit, and covers eastern Lycia, Pisidia and Pamphylia, or roughly the coast from Finike east to Silifke.

Besides these archaeological guides, you'll find shorter, locally produced guides on sale at each site. Most of these include colour photographs but of varying quality. The text, however, is often badly translated, or else doesn't go into much depth. Look closely at one before you buy.

History *The Ottoman Centuries* (Morrow Quill, New York, 1977) by Lord Kinross covers the greatness of the empire without weighing too heavily on your consciousness. At US$15, the paperback reads easily and has many illustrations and maps.

Professor Stanford Shaw's excellent and authoritative *History of the Ottoman Empire & Modern Turkey* (Cambridge University Press, New York, 1977 & 1984) comes in two volumes. Volume One is *Empire of the Gazis: The Rise & Decline of the Ottoman Empire 1280-1808*; Volume Two is *Reform, Revolution & Republic: The Rise of Modern Turkey 1808-1975* both by Stanford Shaw & Ezel Kural Shaw.

The Emergence of Modern Turkey (Oxford University Press, London & New York, 1968) by Bernard Lewis is a scholarly work covering Turkey's history roughly from 1850 to 1950, with a few chapters on the earlier history of the Turks. It tells you nearly everything you want to know about modern Turkey's origins.

Turkey (Frederick A Praiger, New York, 1966) by Geoffrey Lewis is a good general introduction to the country, the people and the culture through their history, but it's not easily found these days.

Gallipoli (Ballantine, New York, 1982) by Alan Moorhead is the fascinating story of the battles for the Dardanelles, which figured so significantly in the careers of Atatürk and Winston Churchill, and in the histories of Australia and New Zealand.

The Harvest of Hellenism (Simon & Schuster, New York, 1971; Allen & Unwin, London, 1972) by F E Peters details Turkey's Hellenic heritage. *Byzantine Style & Civilisation* (Penguin, New York & London, 1975) by Sir Steven Runciman is the standard work on the later Roman Empire.

The thorny subject of the Armenian tragedy is rarely dealt with in a purely scholarly fashion. Turkish and Armenian writers and scholars regularly issue 'proofs' that the other side is ignoring facts, or falsifying records, or refusing to admit the 'truth' as they see it. When a dispassionate account of the Turkish-Armenian conflict is presented, its author may find himself to be *persona non grata* with one side or the other. (When the Shaws' *History of the Ottoman Empire & Modern Turkey* was published, their house in California was fire-bombed and they were forced into hiding for a time.)

It is certainly true that the more one learns on this subject, the more confusing it all becomes as rumour, fiction, press release, memory, questionable statistic, hyperbole and propaganda are all put forth as absolute truth. One work which has been favourably received by the unbiased scholarly community as a dispassionate summary of Turkish-Armenian disputes is Professor Michael M Gunter's *Pursuing the Just Cause of Their People: A Study of Contemporary Armenian Terrorism* (Greenwood Press, London & New York, 1986). Though most of the book deals with the modern problem of terrorism, the first chapter is an admirably brief and straightforward summary of both the Turkish and Armenian positions on this historical quandary.

Fiction Everybody knows about Agatha Christie's *Murder on the Orient Express*, and so they should. It has some scenes in Turkey itself, though most of the train's journey was through Europe and the Balkans. In any case, it helps to make vivid the 19th-century importance of the Turkish Empire.

Among Turkish authors, the one with the world-class reputation is Yaşar Kemal, whom some compare to Kazantzakis. Kemal's novels often take Turkish farming or working-class life as their subject matter, and are full of colourful characters and drama. There are translations in English (done by Kemal's wife) of *Memed, My Hawk, The Wind from the Plains* and several others.

Many modern 'harem' novels trade on the romance (real or wildly imagined) of the sultan's private household. Most are facile. The exception is *The Bride of Suleiman* (St Martin's Press, New York, 1981) by Aileen Crawley. The author, who lives in Northern Ireland, has written a historically faithful and very absorbing fictionalised account of the relationship between Hürrem Sultan ('Roxelana') and her husband Süleyman the Magnificent, greatest of the Ottoman sultans. She brings alive the life of the Ottoman Empire during its golden age.

You might also want to look at *An Anthology of Modern Turkish Short Stories* (Bibliotheca Islamica, Minneapolis & Chicago, 1978) edited by Fahir İz.

Dictionaries & Phrasebooks Several companies publish Turkish-English pocket dictionaries, including Langenscheidt and McGraw-Hill. The most useful thing to have is not a dictionary, but a good phrasebook. Lonely Planet's forthcoming *Turkish Phrase Book* is truly a 'language survival kit', as it contains words and phrases useful to real-life situations. Besides including all the common words and phrases needed during travel, it covers the 'unmentionable' situations in which you need to know the word for tampon or condom.

For a more detailed dictionary, look to *The Concise Oxford Turkish Dictionary*. Similar in scope and easier to find in Turkey is the *Portable Redhouse/Redhouse Elsözlüğü*; this 500-page work on thin paper was actually intended for Turkish students learning English, but it does the job well when you graduate from the pocket dictionary.

For grammar books, there's *Teach Yourself Turkish* in the popular English series, an excellent brief guide to learning the language. Also excellent is Yusuf Mardin's *Colloquial Turkish*. Longer, more expensive, and even more interesting is *Turkish Grammar* (Oxford University Press, London, 1967) by Geoffrey L Lewis. You've got to be pretty interested in Turkish (and in grammar) to get this far into it, but if a grammar book can be said to read like a novel, this one does.

Travel Guides This book was written to tell you just about everything you'd need to know on a first or even subsequent trip to Turkey. Other excellent guides exist, however, each with its own special interest.

An essential tool for hikers going to Turkey is Lonely Planet's *Trekking in Turkey* by Marc Dubin & Enver Lucas (South Yarra, 1989). It does not duplicate any of the information given in this book, but rather supplements it with detailed information on the best places to hike, the finest mountains to climb, and the perfect places to camp. If you want trail maps, details on hiring guides for the trek up Mt Ararat, facts on traditional village life, and lists of essential trekking gear, this is the book in which to find them.

For the literary-minded, *Istanbul – a traveller's companion* (Atheneum/Macmillan, New York, 1987) by Laurence

Kelly is a delight. The editor has combed through the writings of two millennia and collected the choicest bits, by the most interesting writers, relating to Byzantium, Constantinople and Istanbul. History, biography, diary and travellers' observations are all included.

The excellent French series of Blue Guides published by Hachette (English edition by Prentice Hall Press, New York) has a commendable volume on Turkey, good for dense background information on historical sights. The practical information is out of date, however.

Otherwise, the most interesting travel guides on Turkey are those published by the Redhouse Press of İstanbul. Founded under the Ottoman Empire as part of an American missionary effort, the Redhouse Press now does an admirable job of publishing dictionaries, guidebooks and general works designed to bridge the gap between the Turkish and English-speaking realms. Some of the Redhouse guides have been translated into German, French and Italian. Though only a few Redhouse books turn up in bookshops outside of Turkey, you'll find them readily within the country itself, in decent editions at moderate prices. A good example of a Redhouse work is *Biblical Sites in Turkey* (1982) by Everett C Blake & Anna G Edmonds. It has colour photos, maps and costs about US$6. Other guides cover İstanbul and day trips from it.

Travellers' Accounts The published diaries and accounts of travellers in Turkey provide fascinating glimpses of Ottoman life. One of the more familiar of these is Mark Twain's *Innocents Abroad* (New American Library/Signet Classics, New York 1982, and other editions). Twain accompanied a group of wealthy tourists on a chartered boat which sailed the Black Sea and eastern Mediterranean over a century ago. Many of the things he saw in İstanbul haven't changed much.

A more modern account of a foreigner's life in Turkey is *Scotch & Holy Water*

(St Giles Press, Lafayette, Calif, 1981) by John D Tumpane. The author lived in Turkey for eight years as an employee of an American company, and has written a humorous and sympathetic account of his Turkish friends and adventures.

Bookshops
As far as Turks are concerned, their country is part of Europe. Western culture is their culture, and if they learn a foreign language it will be English, French or German. Thus it is easy to find bookshops (*kitabevi*) selling works in these languages. The major cities, and most of the resort towns, have bookshops which sell some foreign-language books, newspapers and magazines.

İstanbul In general, the place to find foreign-language books is in and around Tünel Square, at the southern end of İstiklal Caddesi, and from there northward to Galatasaray.

Sander Kitabevi has a small branch a few doors north-east of the PTT in Galatasaray, on the same side of İstiklal Caddesi. The main store is at Hâlâskargazi Caddesi 275-277, Osman Bey, north of Taksim Square. Books are in English, French and German.

Haşet Kitabevi (Hachette), İstiklal Caddesi 469, Tünel, Beyoğlu, has perhaps the best selection of French and English books and periodicals. Haşet has branches in several of the larger hotels, including the Hilton (in the arcade at the entrance) and the Divan.

Redhouse Kitabevi at Rıza Paşa Yokuşu, Uzun Çarşı, in the Old City down the hill from the Covered Market, publishes books in English and Turkish, including excellent guides and dictionaries. It has an English-language bookstore as well. You will find Redhouse books for sale in many English-language bookshops in Turkey.

Sahaflar Çarşısı, the used-book bazaar, is great fun for browsing. It's just west of the Covered Market across Çadırcılar

Caddesi, sandwiched between that street and the Beyazıt Camii. One shop here specialises in used foreign-language paperbacks; much of the stock is worthless, however.

The big hotels – Hilton, Sheraton, Etap, Divan – all have little bookshops or newsstands.

Ankara Tarhan Kitabevi on Sakarya Caddesi at Atatürk Bulvarı, a few steps north (down the hill) out of Kızılay, is perhaps Turkey's best foreign-language bookstore. It has a predominance of books in English, but some in French and German as well. To find it, walk out of Kızılay toward Ulus and the old part of Ankara along Atatürk Bulvarı, and take the first turn to the right (a pedestrian street).

İzmir There are several foreign-language bookstores on Cumhuriyet Caddesi, or İkinci Kordon, the second street in from the waterfront. Look near the NATO headquarters. The Büyük Efes (Grand Ephesus) hotel also has a small shop.

Other Towns If tourists go there in any numbers, you'll find a newsstand selling international papers and at least some paperback novels, perhaps second hand.

MAPS

Turkish-produced maps are not of very good quality, generally speaking, and you'd be well advised to bring a good map from home. The British *AA/ESR Tourist Map Turkey* is a good one. It covers the whole of the country at a scale of 1:2,000,000; the south-west coast at 1:750,000; and includes street plans of İstanbul, İzmir and several tourist resorts. The French *Turquie* (Série Internationale No 331) by Recta Foldex covers the entire country at 1:1,600,000.

SHOPPING

Most shops and shopping areas close on Sunday. This includes the Covered Market and the Egyptian Market (or Spice Bazaar) in İstanbul, and the bazaars in other cities and towns. Grocers' shops may be open on Sunday, though, and there will always be one pharmacy open in town, known as the *nöbetçi eczane* (nur-BEHT-chee edj-zah-neh, 'duty pharmacy').

Haggling

For the best buy in terms of price and quality, know the market. Spend some time shopping for similar items in various shops, asking prices. Shopkeepers will give you pointers on what makes a good *kilim* (flat-woven mat), carpet, meerschaum pipe or alabaster carving. In effect, you're getting a free course in product lore. This is not at all unpleasant, as you will often be invited to have coffee, tea or a soft drink as you talk over the goods and prices.

You can, and should, ask prices if they're not marked, but you should not make a counter-offer unless you are seriously interested in buying. No matter how often the shopkeeper asks you, 'OK, how much will you pay for it?', no matter how many glasses of tea you've drunk at his expense, don't make a counter-offer if you do not intend to buy. If the shopkeeper meets your price, you should buy. It's considered very bad form to haggle over a price, agree, and then not buy.

Some shopkeepers, even in the 'haggle capital of the world' (İstanbul's Covered Market), will offer a decent price and say, 'That's my best offer'. Many times they mean it, and they're trying to do you a favour by saving time. How will you know when they are, and when it's just another haggling technique? Only by knowing the market, by having shopped around. Remember, even if they say, 'This is my best offer', you are under no obligation to buy unless you have made a counter-offer, or have said, 'I'll buy it'. It's perfectly acceptable to say a pleasant good-bye and walk out of the shop, even after all that free tea, if you cannot agree on a price. In fact, walking out is one of the best ways to test the authenticity of the shopkeeper's price. If they know you can surely find the item somewhere else for less, they'll stop you and say, 'OK, you win, it's yours for what you offered'. And if he doesn't stop you, there's nothing to prevent you from returning in a half-hour and buying the item for what he quoted.

If any shopkeeper puts extraordinary pressure on you to buy, even though you can't agree on price, walk out of the shop, and consider reporting the shop to the Market Police (see Belediye Zabıtası in the Dangers & Annoyances section).

Commissions

Read and believe: *if a Turk accompanies you into a shop, he will expect a commission from the shopkeeper on any purchase you make*. Your guide may be a wonderful person, the owner of your pension, a cheery and engaging soul, but after you buy and depart, the guide will take his cut. This is money that comes out of your pocket. It's better to go alone and strike a bargain on your own, because then you have a better chance of getting a lower price from the shopkeeper, who will have no commission to pay.

Value Added Tax

Turkey has a Value Added Tax (VAT), called Katma Değer Vergisi or KDV, added to and hidden in the price of most items and services, from souvenirs through hotel rooms to restaurant meals. Most establishments display a sign saying *Fiatlarımızda KDV Dahildir*, 'VAT is included in our prices'. Thus, it is rare that the VAT is added to your bill separately, and you should be suspicious if it is.

There is a scheme whereby tourists can reclaim the amount paid in VAT on larger purchases such as leather garments, carpets, etc. Not all shops participate in the scheme, so you must ask if it is possible to get a *KDV Iade Özel Fatura*

(keh-deh-VEH ee-ah-DEH err-ZEHL fah-too-rah, Special VAT Refund Receipt). Ask for this during the haggling rather than after you've bought. The receipt can be converted to cash at a bank in the international departures lounge at the airport (if there is a bank open!), or at your other point of exit from Turkey; or, if you submit the form to a customs officer as you leave the country, the shop will (one hopes) mail a refund cheque to your home after the government has completed its procedures (don't hold your breath).

Shipping Parcels Home

If practicable, carrying your parcels with you is the best idea, as you may escape extra duty payments when you return to your home country; parcels arriving separately may be dutiable. If you decide to ship something home from Turkey, don't close up your parcel before it has been inspected by a customs or postal official, who will check to see if you are shipping antiquities out of the country. Wrap it very securely and insure it. Sending it by registered mail is not a bad idea, either. Unless you buy from a very posh shop (eg in one of the luxury hotels,) it's best to ship your own parcels. At least one reader has had the sad experience of buying a beautiful kilim and agreeing to have the shopkeeper ship it, only to discover that the kilim shipped was not the one bought, but a much cheaper item.

THINGS TO BUY
Alabaster

A translucent, fine-grained variety of either gypsum or calcite, alabaster is pretty because of its grain and colour, and because light passes through it. You'll see ashtrays, vases, chess sets, bowls, egg cups, even the eggs themselves carved from the stone. Cappadocia is a major producing and carving area, and towns like Ürgüp and Avanos specialise in it. But in fact you will find it wherever good souvenirs are sold.

Antiques

Turkey harbours a lot of fascinating stuff left over from the empire: vigorous peasant jewellery, water-pipe mouthpieces carved from amber, old Korans and illuminated manuscripts, Greek and Roman figurines and coins, tacky furniture in the Ottoman Baroque style. However, *it is illegal to buy, sell, possess or export any antiquity*, and you can go to prison for breaking the law. All antiquities must be turned over to a museum immediately upon discovery. You may be offered Greek and Roman coins and figurines for sale. Refuse at once. Items only a century or two old are not usually classed as antiquities, though, and only true antiquities are off limits, not the many artful fakes.

Carpets & Kilims

Turkey has lots of marvellous carpets and kilims, sometimes at good prices. However, with the flood of tourists, dealers sometimes lose sight of reality and charge prices higher than you'd pay to a reputable dealer at home. They may also offer you inferior goods. Unless you're willing to research prices, patterns, dyes, knots-per-square-cm and so forth, you'll buy what you like for a price that seems reasonable. But please learn at least the basics of carpet-buying before you put your money down.

The very basic examination of a carpet, so that you can look like you know what you're doing, involves the following procedures. Turn a corner over and look at the closeness of the weave. Ask, 'How many knots per square cm?' The tighter the weave, the smaller the knots, the higher the quality and durability. Compare the colours on the back with the colours on the front. Spread the nap with your fingers and look to the bottom of the carpet's pile. Are the colours more vivid there than on the surface? If so, the surface has faded in the sun considerably. Take a white handkerchief, wet it a bit, and rub it on the top surface of the carpet.

Is there colour on the handkerchief? There shouldn't be; if there is, the carpet's dyes are runny.

Check the ends of the warp (lengthwise) cords: are they of wool (*yün*) as they should be, or cotton (*pamuk*), which is weaker and inferior? The pile should definitely be of wool; in fact, a good-quality, long-lasting carpet is 100% wool (*yüz de yüz yün*). If the pile is of cotton or 'flosh' (mercerised cotton), sometimes misleadingly called 'floss silk', then the carpet will wear badly and be of little value in a few years. (A real silk carpet, by the way, even a small one, will cost thousands of dollars.) Look at the carpet from one end, then from the other; the colours will be different because the pile always leans one way or the other. Take the carpet out into the sunlight and look at it there.

That's about all you can do without becoming a rug expert. If you don't trust the dealer's sworn oath that the rug is all wool, and you're serious about buying, ask him to clip a bit of the tassel and burn it for you – that is if you can differentiate between the odours of burning silk, wool, cotton or nylon.

Carpet prices are determined by demand, age, material, quality, condition, enthusiasm of the buyer and debt load of the seller. New carpets can be skilfully 'antiquated'; damaged or worn carpets can be rewoven (good work, but expensive), patched or even painted. Worn carpets look fairly good until the magic paint washes out. Give the carpet a good going-over, decide if you think it's a good price, and go from there.

The method of payment can be a bargaining point, or a point of contention. Some dealers will take personal cheques, but all prefer cash or travellers' cheques. If you pay with a credit card (and not all shops will have facilities for this), the dealer may require you to pay the fee which the credit card company will charge him, and even the cost of the phone call or telex to check on your credit. If he doesn't require you to pay these charges, it means that you've paid a hefty enough price so that another 6% to 8% doesn't bother him.

If all this seems too much trouble, be advised: it isn't. A good wool Turkish carpet will easily outlast the human body of its owner, and become an heirloom.

Ceramics

The best Turkish ceramics were made in İznik in the 17th and 18th centuries. İznik tiles from the great days are now museum-pieces, found in museums throughout the world.

Today most of the tile-making is done in Kütahya, a pleasant town with few other redeeming qualities for the tourist. For the

Ceramic Mosque Lamp

very best ceramics, you must go there. Souvenir shops will also have attractive, hand-made tiles, plates, cups and bowls. They're not really high-fired so they're vulnerable to breaks and cracks, but they are still attractive.

The real, old İznik tiles from the 16th and 17th centuries qualify as antiquities and cannot be exported. If you go to İznik, you will find a reviving tile industry on a small scale. Some of the items are quite pretty and reasonably priced.

Copper

Gleaming copper vessels will greet you in every souvenir shop you peep into. Some are old, sometimes several centuries. Most are handsome, and some are still eminently useful. The new copperware tends to be of lighter gauge; that's one of the ways you tell new from old. But even the new stuff will have been made by hand.

'See that old copper water pipe over there?' my friend Alaettin asked me once. We were sitting in his impossibly cluttered, closet-sized shop on İstanbul's Çadırcılar Caddesi, just outside the Covered Market. 'It dates from the time of Sultan Ahmet III (1703-1730), and was used by the *Padişah* (sultan) himself. I just finished making it yesterday.'

Alaettin was a master coppersmith, and had made pieces for many luminaries, including the late Nelson Rockefeller. His pieces might well have graced the sultan's private apartments – except that the sultanate was abolished in 1922. He charged a hefty price for his fine craftwork but not for the story, which was the gift-wrapping, so to speak.

Copper vessels should not be used for cooking or eating unless they are tinned inside: that is, washed with molten tin which covers the toxic copper. If you intend to use a copper vessel, make sure the interior layer of tin is intact, or negotiate to have it tinned (*kalaylamak*). If there is a *kalaycı* shop nearby, ask about the price of the tinning in advance.

Inlaid Wood

Cigarette boxes, chess and *tavla* (back-gammon) boards and other items will be inlaid with different coloured woods, silver or mother-of-pearl. It's not the finest work, but it's pretty good. Make sure there is indeed inlay. These days, alarmingly accurate decals exist. Also, check the silver: is it silver, or aluminium or pewter? Is the mother-of-pearl actually 'daughter-of-polystyrene'?

Jewellery

Turkey is a wonderful place to buy jewellery, especially the antique stuff. None of the items sold here may meet your definition of 'chic', but window-shopping is great fun. Jewellers' Row in any market is a dazzling strip of glittering shop windows filled with gold. Light bulbs, artfully rigged, show it off. In the Covered Market, a blackboard sign hung above Kuyumcular Caddesi ('Street of the Jewellers') bears the daily price for unworked gold of so-many karats. Serious gold-buyers should check out this price, watch carefully as the jeweller weighs the piece in question, and then calculate what part of the price is for gold and what part for labour.

Silver is another matter. There is sterling silver jewellery (look for the hallmark), but nickel silver and pewter-like alloys are much more common. Serious dealers don't try to pass off alloy as silver.

Leather & Suede

On any given Kurban Bayramı (Sacrifice Holiday), over 2,500,000 sheep get the axe in Turkey. Add to that the normal day-to-day needs of a cuisine based on mutton and lamb and you have a huge amount of raw material to be made into leather items. Shoes, bags, cushions, jackets, skirts, vests, hats, gloves and trousers are all made from soft leather. This is a big industry in Turkey, particularly in and around the Grand Bazaar. So much leather clothing is turned out that a good deal of it will be badly cut or carelessly made, but there are lots of fine pieces as well.

The only way to assure yourself of a good piece is to examine it carefully, taking time. Try it on just as carefully; see if the sleeves are full enough, if the buttonholes are positioned well, if the collar rubs. If something is wrong, keep trying others until you find what you want. Made-to-order garments can be excellent or disappointing, as the same tailor who made the ready-made stuff will make the ordered stuff; and will be making it fast because the shopkeeper has already impressed you by saying 'No problem. I can have it for you tomorrow'. It's better to find something off the rack that fits than to order it, unless you can order without putting down a deposit or committing yourself to buy (this is often possible).

Leather items and clothing are standard tourist stuff, found in all major tourist destinations.

Meerschaum

If you smoke a pipe, you know about meerschaum. For those who don't, meerschaum ('sea foam' in German; *lületaşı*, LEW-leh-tahsh-uh in Turkish) is a hydrous magnesium silicate, a soft, white, clay-like material which is very porous but heat-resistant. When carved into a pipe, it smokes cool and sweet. Over time, it absorbs residues from the tobacco and turns a nut-brown colour. Devoted meerschaum pipe smokers even have special gloves with which to hold the pipe as they smoke, so that oil from their fingers won't sully the fine, even patina of the pipe.

The world's largest and finest beds of meerschaum are found in Turkey, near the city of Eskişehir. Artful carving of the soft stone has always been done, and blocks of meerschaum were exported to be carved abroad as well. These days, however, the export of block meerschaum is prohibited because the government realised that exporting uncarved blocks was the same as exporting the jobs to carve them. So any carved pipe will have been carved in Turkey.

Carving is of a very high quality, and you'll marvel at the artistry of the Eskişehir carvers. Pipes portraying turbaned paşas, wizened old men, fair maidens and mythological beasts, as well as many pipes in geometrical designs, will be on view in any souvenir shop. Pipes are not the only things carved from meerschaum these days. Bracelets, necklaces, pendants, earrings and cigarette holders all appear in souvenir shops.

When buying, look for purity and uniformity in the stone. Carving is often used to cover up flaws in a piece of meerschaum; do look over it carefully. For pipes, check that the bowl walls are uniform in thickness all around, and that the hole at the bottom of the bowl is centred. Purists buy uncarved, just plain pipe-shaped meerschaums that are simply but perfectly made.

Prices for pipes vary, but should be fairly low. Abroad, meerschaum is an expensive commodity, and pipes are luxury items. Here in Turkey meerschaum is cheap, the services of the carver are low-priced, and nobody smokes pipes. If you can't get the pipe you want for US$10 to US$20, or at least only half of what you'd pay at home, then you're not working at it hard enough.

Postcards

Turkey produces hundreds of thousands of colour postcards each year, and many of the images are candidates for the pantheon of kitsch. The heart of the hilarious postcard trade is Ankara Caddesi, up the hill from Sirkeci Station, in İstanbul. Walk up the street, and as you round the curve look in the shop windows for the postcards, then go into the printery and look at more. They're amazing. Besides kitsch, the printers turn out very handsome art and note cards with traditional Turkish designs and images of Turkish carpets and tiles.

WHAT TO WEAR

For tips on the weather, month by month, refer to The Calendar section in the Facts About the Country chapter.

In high summer, that is mid-June to mid-September, you'll need light cotton summer clothes, and a light sweater or jacket for the evenings or to wear up on the Central Anatolian plateau. You won't need rain gear at all, except perhaps on the Black Sea coast. You would do better to duck between the showers rather than haul rain gear during your entire trip just for a possible day or two of rain on the Black Sea coast.

In spring and autumn, summer clothing will still be OK, but the evenings will be cooler. If you plan to travel extensively in Central Anatolia (Ankara, Konya, Cappadocia, Nemrut Dağı), pack a heavier sweater and perhaps a light raincoat.

Winter wear – December to March – is woollens and rain gear. Though it doesn't get really cold along the Mediterranean, it does get damp, rainy and chilly in most of the country, including the south coast. İstanbul and İzmir get dustings of snow; Ankara gets more. Nemrut Dağı and the eastern region are frigid and covered in snow.

Formal or Informal?

How does one dress in a Muslim country? In this one, you dress pretty much as you would for Europe. In high summer, no-one will really expect men to have a coat and tie, even when visiting a government official. For the rest of the year, Turks tend to dress formally in formal situations such as at the office or in a good restaurant or nightclub, but informally at other times. Neat and tidy dress is still admired here. Tatty or careless clothes, a sign of nonchalance or independence in other societies, are looked upon as tatty or careless in Turkey.

Anyone can visit a Turkish mosque so long as they look presentable. Clothes must be neat. No shorts or sleeveless shirts on either men or women; women require skirts of a modest length (knees) and a headscarf. Before you enter a mosque where people are praying, remove your shoes to protect the carpets from soil. Muslims pray on the carpets, so they must be kept clean.

SPORTS

Turks are sports enthusiasts. Football (soccer), basketball and wrestling are the favoured sports. Every city of any size has a large football stadium which fills up on match days.

The famous oiled wrestling matches, where brawny strongmen in leather breeches rub themselves down with olive oil and grapple with equally slippery opponents, take place each June in Edirne. Another purely Turkish sight is the camel-wrestling matches held in the province of Aydın, south of İzmir, in the winter months. Konya is the setting for cirit, the javelin-throwing game played on horseback.

Water sports are big in Turkey because of the beautiful coasts and beaches. Yachting, rowing, water-skiing, snorkelling, diving (with or without scuba gear) and swimming are well represented. Because of the many antiquities in the depths off the Turkish coasts, scuba diving is regulated. Diving shops in Marmaris, Bodrum and other coastal towns can provide details. A diver friend of mine tells me that Turkish divers are very safety-conscious, so bring your diving credentials to prove that you are certified to the depth you want to explore. An experienced diver in Marmaris is Mr Feyyaz Subay (tel (6121) 2524, 3200) c/o German-Tur, Kordon Caddesi 10/2, Marmaris.

Mountain-climbing (dağcılık, DAAH-juh-LUHK) is practised by a small but enthusiastic number of Turks, and Turkey has plenty of good, high mountains for it. For complete information, with addresses of outfitters, guides, and Turkish climbing clubs, buy a copy of *Trekking in Turkey* (see Travel Guides in the Books & Bookshops section).

Turkey is a good country for hunting animals, from small game to wild boar (there's a boar-hunting festival at Ephesus each spring). However, the Turks are touchy about people bringing guns into the country. Check with a Turkish consulate about regulations and permits for importing a sporting gun.

Skiing is decent on Uludağ, near Bursa, and at a few resorts in the Beydağları mountain range near Antalya. Equipment can be rented at the slopes. There are plans for a new ski resort near Erzurum in eastern Turkey, where the snow is good during nine months of the year.

Bicycling through Turkey is possible, and mostly delightful. For details, see the Getting Around chapter.

Getting There

You can get to Turkey by air, rail, road or sea. Note that if you travel by land you will have to deal with the problem of transit visas for East European countries. (See the Foreign Embassies and East European Visas sections in the Facts for the Visitor chapter.)

AIR

Most international flights arrive at İstanbul's Atatürk Airport, the country's busiest with a big new terminal. Other international airports are at Ankara, İzmir, Adana (down near the Syrian border), Antalya and Dalaman (on the southern coast). Most foreign visitors arrive in İstanbul because it has the most flights and is also the first place tourists want to see. İzmir has its shiny new Menderes Airport south of the city on the road to Ephesus. Antalya and Dalaman receive mostly charter flights filled with vacationers headed for the south coast.

Turkish Airlines (Türk Hava Yolları, flight symbol TK) has flights to New York, Singapore, most major cities in Europe, the Middle East and North Africa. The airlines of these destination countries also fly into and out of Turkey. Other Turkish airlines flying from Europe (mostly Germany) to Turkey include İstanbul Airlines and Toros Air.

All the fares mentioned here are subject to change, but they will give you an idea of what to expect.

From Greece

Olympic Airlines and Turkish Airlines share the Athens/İstanbul route, offering at least four flights per day in summer. Fares for the 70-minute flight are US$121 one way, US$167 for an excursion (round-trip) ticket.

From Europe

Most of the European international airlines have flights to Turkey. The busiest airports, with lots of airlines offering lots of fares, are London and Frankfurt.

The normal one-way fare from London to İstanbul is UK£467 (US$794), but there are excursion fares as low as UK£232 (US$400) in spring and autumn. Peak-season (summer) excursion fares are higher, but there are still bargains to be had. Among the scheduled carriers, JAT, the Yugoslavian airline, seems to have the lowest fares via Belgrade to İstanbul. Lots of people know this, however, and the flights are often full. Reserve your seat well in advance for this one. Also, look at the schedules and fares of other East European airlines such as Tarom of Rumania, and also Pakistan International Airlines (PIA).

Don't neglect the European and Turkish charter lines such as Condor (German) and Toros Air (Turkish). Toros Air, for instance, flies to Turkey from several European points including Maastricht Airport in southern Holland, often for round-trip fares as low as US$250 or US$300.

British Airways (BA) and Turkish Airlines fly from London to İstanbul, and Turkish Airlines seem to have many discount fares from the British capital. Pan American World Airways (Pan Am), Air France and Turkish Airlines fly from Paris.

From the Eastern Mediterranean

Here is the data on fares to İstanbul from various Middle East cities:

Amman Turkish Airlines and Royal Jordanian share the traffic, with about two flights per day; the nonstop 2½-hour flight costs US$160 one way, US$184 to US$319 for a round-trip excursion ticket.

Cairo EgyptAir and Turkish Airlines have flights about four days per week, charging US$185 one way, US$368 for a round-trip excursion ticket on the nonstop, two-hour flight.

Damascus Syrian Arab Airlines and Turkish Airlines make the 2½-hour flight four days per week and charge US$168 one way, US$194 to US$227 for a round-trip excursion.

Nicosia (Turkish Side) Turkish Airlines and Cyprus-Turkish Airlines operate nonstop flights connecting Ercan Airport in Nicosia (Lefkoşa in Turkish) with Adana (four flights weekly), Ankara (five flights weekly), Antalya (one flight weekly), İstanbul (daily, twice daily in summer) and İzmir (four flights weekly). Fares are subsidised and very reasonable. In Nicosia, contact Turkish Airlines at Osman Paşa Caddesi 32 (tel (20) 71 382, 71 061, 77 124, 77 344); the Cyprus-Turkish Airlines (*Kıbrıs-Türk Hava Yolları*) office is in Bedrettin Demirel Caddesi (tel (20) 71 901).

İstanbul Airlines (tel (20) 77 140/1) at Osman Paşa Caddesi, Mirata Apt 4 and at Ercan Airport (tel (23) 14 714/5) flies between Nicosia, Antalya (two flights weekly) and İstanbul (eight flights weekly), at fares lower than Turkish Airlines.

Tel Aviv El Al has flights three times weekly, charging US$283 one way, US$368 to US$380 for round-trip excursions.

From India

There is not much traffic at this writing. Turkish Airlines has one flight per week stopping in Delhi, but it is one of Turkish Airlines' two flights per week to Singapore. These flights are very popular, and are booked up weeks in advance. BA sometimes runs an İstanbul/Delhi flight as well. A full-fare ticket costs US$569 one way. You might also contact Aeroflot, the Soviet airline, to see what they offer via Moscow.

From the USA

New York has the most direct flights, the most airlines, and the most elaborate spread of fares, so you should be able to find a fare to suit your budget. Pan Am has been flying the New York/İstanbul route for almost 60 years, and still provides efficient and convenient daily service via Europe. The regular cabin-class fare is US$1355 one way; excursion fares range from US$889 to US$1725 depending upon season, stopovers, etc. Occasionally, even lower promotional fares are offered. On the Europe to İstanbul portion of the flight, the Pan Am crews are mostly Turkish.

Trans World Airlines (TWA) also operates between New York and İstanbul via Europe. Call for schedules and fares.

Turkish Airlines operates four flights per week in summer on the New York/Brussels/İstanbul route. Turkish Airlines' North American operations are still relatively new, and they may add or subtract flights as the traffic demands.

Most of the European national airlines fly from New York to their home countries, then on to İstanbul, at fares similar to the Pan Am ones. KLM's connections are particularly good, with a layover in Amsterdam of little more than one hour.

PIA has a one-stop service from New York to İstanbul, with an even lower excursion fare, but some passengers find the service less than luxurious.

From New York and Chicago, particularly during the summer months, group fares to İstanbul are sold by various tour operators. You do not have to be part of a group, nor do you have to take a tour or buy nights in a hotel. You pay only for the flight (which is on a regular, scheduled airline, not a charter), but you get your ticket at a special low group rate. There may be some restrictions, such as perhaps having to stay more than seven nights and less than 180 nights. From New York, fares are about US$300 to US$400 one way, US$500 to US$800 round trip; from Chicago they are US$350 one way, US$630 round trip. For more information contact a travel agent or get a copy of the monthly *JAXFAX Travel Marketing Magazine*, 397 Post Rd, PO Box 4013, Darien, CT 06820-1413, USA (tel (203) 655-8746); a subscription costs $12 per year. Or contact one of these tour operators:

ABC Travel & Tours
    60 East 42nd St, Suite 631, New York, NY 10165 (tel (800) 222-4605, (212) 986-2220; fax (800) 635-0612)
HTI Tours
    1015 Chestnut St, Suite 820, Philadelphia, PA 19107 (tel (800) 441-4411, (215) 629-9997)
Hürtürk Travel & Tours
    509 Madison Ave, Suite 2301, New York, NY 10022 (tel (800) 247-8875, (212) 750-1170)
Sunbeam Travel
    265 Madison Ave, New York, NY 10016 (tel (800) 247-6659, (212) 573-8980; fax (212) 573-8878)
Tursem Tours International 420 Madison Ave, Suite 804, New York, NY 10017 (tel (800) 223-9169, (212) 935-9210.
Union Tours
    3175 North Lincoln Ave, Chicago, IL 60657 (tel (800) 331-6221, (312) 472-4620)

It is also worth investigating the East European airlines, as well as alternative fares such as the 'open-jaw' ones that let you fly to one city (eg Vienna) and return from another (eg İstanbul). You have to make separate arrangements for transport between the two cities, but the overall savings can be considerable. For example, Tarom always advertises a stand-by fare of US$205 from New York to Vienna nonstop. JAT often has the lowest direct fare from New York to İstanbul, though you may have to stay overnight in Belgrade.

From Australia

There is no direct route by air from Australia to İstanbul, though there are connecting flights via Athens, London and Singapore on Qantas, Olympic and British Airways. Round-trip fares via Athens, the closest and most convenient connection to İstanbul, range from A$1569 in the off season, to A$1757 in the shoulder season and A$1851 in the peak season. If you can get a cheap fare to London, you might do well to look for a cheap London/Turkey round-trip fare once you arrive there.

The cheapest way to get to Turkey directly from Australia is to fly to Athens (not on a charter flight! see next paragraph) and take a boat to one of the islands (Lesbos, Chios, Samos, Kos or Rhodes) and then a ferry to the Turkish mainland. This route proves the dictum that the smaller the price the greater the inconvenience.

Charter Flights

You cannot take a charter flight to Greece and then go to Turkey without paying a huge penalty! Several countries (such as Greece) which benefit greatly from charter-flight traffic have enacted a regulation which prohibits charter passengers from leaving the charter destination country for the duration of their stay. Thus, if you fly to Athens on a charter and then legally enter Turkey (ie have your passport stamped), the officials at the airport in Athens will not allow you to board your return charter flight. You will have to pay for another whole ticket to get home. (If you just take a day excursion to Turkey, and the Turkish immigration officials do not stamp your passport, you will have no problem boarding your return charter flight.) The regulation is enforced so that the charter destination country reaps all of the benefits of the low charter fare. This regulation does not apply to regular or excursion-fare flights, only to charters.

Thus, if you want to go by charter flight, you must go directly to Turkey. By the way, I have had no news that the Turkish officials enforce the charter regulation, which means that if you take a charter to Turkey, you probably *can* visit Greece, return to Turkey and have no trouble boarding your return charter flight. But ask in advance so as to avoid disappointment and expense.

OVERLAND
Car

Car ferries (see the Boat section) from Italy, Cyprus and Syria can shorten driving time considerably. No special car documents are required for visits of up to three months. The car will be entered in the driver's passport as imported goods, and must be driven out of the country by the same visitor within the time period allowed. *Do not drive someone else's car into Turkey.* Normally, you cannot rent a car in Europe and include Turkey (or many other East European countries) in your driving plans. If you want to leave your car in Turkey and return for it later, the car must be put under customs seal.

For stays longer than three months, contact the Turkish Touring & Automobile Association (*Türk Turing ve Otomobil Kurumu*) (tel (1) 140-7127), Halâskârgazi Caddesi 364, Şişli, İstanbul.

The E5 highway makes its way through the Balkans to Edirne and İstanbul, then onward to Ankara, Adana and the Syrian frontier. Though the road is good in most of the countries it passes through, you will encounter heavy traffic and lots of heavy vehicles along the route, as this is a very important freight route between Europe and the Middle East.

Insurance Your Green Card third-party insurance must be endorsed for *all* of Turkey, both European and Asian, not just the European portion (Thrace). If it is not, you will have to buy a Turkish insurance policy at the border.

Bus
The construction of good highways between Europe and Turkey has opened the Middle East to all sorts of vehicles.

Turkish bus companies operate frequent passenger services.

To/From Europe The past decade has seen the rise of frequent, fairly comfortable and moderately priced bus travel along this route. Several of the best Turkish companies (Bosfor Turizm, Ulusoy, Varan) operate big Mercedes buses which are at least as comfortable as the now-neglected trains (usually more so), comparable in price, often faster and perhaps safer. The major discomfort on the trip may be cigarette smoke.

Bosfor Turizm operates from Paris and Lyon (US$80), Geneva, Milan and Venice (US$63), departing from Paris on this route Monday evening and arriving in İstanbul around midday on Thursday. From Munich they have an express service which departs each Friday and Sunday at 12 noon and arrives in İstanbul about 48 hours later. The cost is US$80, plus US$25 to US$30 for a hotel the second night. From Vienna, an express service departs Tuesday and Friday evenings, arriving in İstanbul Thursday and Sunday evenings (US$63). Bosfor Turizm, Ulusoy and Varan have sales desks or representatives in the international bus terminals of several European cities; or you can contact them at these addresses:

İstanbul
  Bosfor Turizm, Mete Caddesi, Taksim (tel (11) 143-2525; telex 24324 IBOS TR)
Munich
  Bosfor Turizm, Seidlstrasse 2, 8 München 2 (tel (89) 59 40 02, 59 24 96; telex 529388 MBOS)
Paris
  Bosfor Turizm, Gare Routière Internationale, 8 Place de Stalingrad, 75019 Paris (tel (1) 12 01 70 80, 12 05 12 10; telex 210192)
Vienna
  Bosfor Turizm, Argentinierstrasse 67, Südbahnhof, 1040 Wien (tel (222) 65 65 93, 65 96 02; telex 136878 WBOS)

Other Turkish companies ply similar routes, and more are getting into the act all the time.

The Ulusoy bus company teams up with the Harris Coaches (UK), Touring (Germany) and L'Epervier (Belgium) companies to operate connecting service on routes joining London, Antwerp, Brussels, Paris, Namur, Luxembourg, Völkingen, Saarbrücken, Kaiserslautern, Ludwigshafen, Karlsruhe and İstanbul. Reservations must be made at least three days in advance. One-way fares range from US$175 (London to İstanbul) to US$115 (Karlsruhe to İstanbul). Children two years and under pay 30% of the full fare, children 12 years and under pay 50% of the full fare. Students 25 and under get a reduction of 10% off the full fare. For details, contact these offices:

İstanbul
  Ulusoy Turizm, Topkapı Otogar No 13, Topkapı (tel (1) 143-1903, 144-8457)
  Ulusoy Turizm, İnönü Caddesi 59, Taksim (tel (1) 144-1271, 144-2823)
Brussels
  Ulusoy Turizm, Place de la Reine 19 (tel (1) 217-6382)
Karlsruhe
  Ulusoy Turizm, Sophienstrasse 126 (tel (721) 85 62 31)
London
  Harris Coaches, Manor Rd, West Thurrock, Grays, Essex (tel (708) 86 49 11), or any National Travel Bureau
Paris
  Ulusoy Turizm, Gare Routière Internationale, 8 Place de Stalingrad, 75019 Paris (tel (1) 12 05 12 10)

Varan Turizm operates from Metz, Nancy, Strasbourg, Colmar and Mulhouse in France, with buses departing these cities for İstanbul on Wednesday; from St Gallen, Winterthur and Zurich in Switzerland, with departures for İstanbul on Wednesday; from Bregenz, Dornbirn, St Pölten, Linz, Salzburg, Wiener Neustadt, Vienna, Graz and Innsbruck in Austria, with departures on Wednesday, Friday or Saturday. The trip between

Europe and Turkey takes anything from 32 hours (Graz to İstanbul) to 48 hours (Metz to İstanbul). Here are some addresses:

İstanbul
  Varan Turizm, İnönü Caddesi 29/B, Taksim (tel (1) 143-1903, 144-8457)
Innsbruck
  Varan Turizm, Hofgasse 2 (tel (5222) 35 378)
Salzburg
  Varan Turizm, Bahnhof Vorplatz Kaiserschützenstrasse 12 (tel (662) 75 068)
Strasbourg
  Varan Turizm, 37 Faubourg de Pierre 67000 (tel (88) 22 03 87)
Vienna
  Varan Turizm, Südbahnhof Südtirolerplatz 7 (tel (222) 65 65 93)
Zurich
  Varan Turizm, Josefstrasse 45, 8005 Zurich (tel (1) 44 04 77)

To/From Greece For a bus to İstanbul, go to the railway station (OSE Hellenic Railways Organisation, Plateia Peloponisu), from which the buses depart. Among other companies running to Turkey you will find Varan Turizm (tel (1) 513-5768) which operates buses to and from İstanbul via Thessaloniki twice daily, departing Athens at 8 am, departing Thessaloniki at 6.30 pm, and arriving İstanbul at 6.30 am the next day; and departing Athens at 8 pm, departing Thessaloniki the next morning at 4.30 am, and arriving İstanbul later that day at 6.30 pm. Return trips depart İstanbul for Athens daily at 10 am and 8 pm, arriving 22½ hours later. In summer, when traffic is heavy, they may put on extra buses. Reserve your seat in advance if you can. A one-way ticket costs US$40 from Athens, US$25 from Thessaloniki.

Bosfor Turizm also runs buses from Athens to Turkey. Other companies operating buses between İstanbul and Athens can be contacted through these offices:

Athens
    Rika Tours, Marni 44, Platia Vathis (tel (1) 523-2458, 523-3686, 523-5905; telex 21-9473)
İstanbul
    Ast Turizm, Beşir Fuat Caddesi 8, Tepebaşı (tel (1) 144-2006)
Thessaloniki
    Simeonidis Tours, 26 October St No 14 (tel (31) 54 09 71, 52 14 45)

Train

Fares Fares are competitive with the buses. If you're young, you can take advantage of the Wasteels BIGE Youth Train, with special low fares. In İstanbul, buy your tickets at window (*Gişe*) No 5 in Sirkeci Railway Station. Also, people under 26 years of age using the Inter-Rail Youth pass should know that the pass is valid only on Turkey's European lines (which means just between the border at Edirne or Kapıkule and İstanbul); it is *not* valid for any Turkish train east or south of İstanbul. Nor is it valid in Bulgaria. Thus if you travel on the Inter-Rail pass, you must go around Bulgaria by taking the Belgrade to Edirne route via Thessaloniki, which can take a long 55 hours from Munich. The alternative is to pay full fare through Bulgaria, plus the cost of a transit visa, for the 39-hour İstanbul Express trip.

Orient Express Route The Orient Express lives on in special excursion trains with various names, but the fares for these deluxe tours are between US$2500 and US$5500 one way. These packages include transportation from European points to İstanbul aboard restored railway coaches, with lectures and optional side-trips. By the way, the train which now bears the name 'Orient Express' goes nowhere near İstanbul on its run between London and Venice.

Otherwise, there is a daily train service from Europe. In 2nd class it is fairly cheap, which is why the carriages are usually packed with Turkish 'guest workers' and their families. They want to stash away as much as possible from a stint of hard factory work in Europe, so they don't mind discomfort.

There is no romance left on this famed Orient Express route. You may be able to resurrect a bit of romance if you have the money to travel 1st class, preferably in a sleeping car as far as Belgrade, then in a couchette to İstanbul. Another tip is to get off the train in Edirne, the first stop in Turkey. It's an interesting city, well worth a stop. From Edirne to İstanbul the train takes at least six hours, but the bus takes less than four.

For several years I received reports of thieves who sprayed sleeping gas under compartment doors at night, and when the occupants were knocked out, stripped them of their valuables; it happened to close friends of mine. But I haven't had any reports of the chemical warriors recently.

To/From Greece I'm not sure why they still run the train between Athens and İstanbul. Neither country cares much about it. The schedule says that the 1400-km journey takes a day and a half, departing Athens or İstanbul in the evening, arriving mid-morning about 35 hours later. This schedule (if indeed the train is on time) is about an hour faster than the scheduled run in 1908 under the Ottoman Empire. My guess is that the Ottoman train ran on time much more frequently than today's does. The train hauls 2nd-class carriages only.

Don't think you'll cut this excruciating time much by going from Thessaloniki to İstanbul. That trip is still about 25 hours – if it's on time. You'd be well advised to take a bus.

To/From Italy You can take a late afternoon train from Venice which reaches Belgrade the next morning; but then you must wait until mid-afternoon to catch an onward train to İstanbul. From Belgrade to İstanbul alone is 26 hours, and thus the entire Venice to İstanbul trip takes a full two days.

To/From Germany & Austria The İstanbul Express from Munich is a bit better, taking 39 hours from Munich to İstanbul, 30 hours from Vienna to İstanbul; it hauls couchettes and, between Munich and Belgrade, sleeping carriages. All these travel times apply only if the trains are on time, which they rarely are.

To/From France There is a daily train from Paris which takes 57 hours to reach İstanbul.

BOAT

Without question, the most romantic way to arrive in İstanbul is by sea. The panorama of the Old City's skyline, with rows of minarets and bulbous mosque domes rising above the surrounding houses, is an incomparable sight. If you can't arrive by sea, don't despair. A trip on a Bosphorus ferry will reveal a similar panorama.

Though steamers still ply the Mediterranean from port to port, eventually turning up at İzmir or İstanbul, schedules are erratic. Sometimes fares are not particularly low, as passenger accommodation tends to be deluxe. The Black Sea Steamship Company, a Soviet outfit, runs very comfortable, modern cruise ships during the summer months. You can sometimes book a place on one, and prices will be moderate, but everything will be in Russian, including the chitchat of your fellow passengers. The occasional Turkish Maritime Lines freighter may take passengers at low fares, but this is not dependable either. Going to Turkey by sea, then, you have three choices.

To/From Italy

Turkish Maritime Lines Turkish Maritime Lines (T C Denizyolları, or TML) operates modern, comfortable car-and-passenger ferries from Venice to İzmir, departing Venice every Saturday evening

from April to October, arriving in İzmir on Tuesday morning. The return trip from İzmir departs Wednesday afternoon, arriving in Venice Saturday morning. The one-way fare in cabins ranges from US$220 to US$460 per passenger, breakfast and port taxes included. In 'Pullman' class you get not a cabin, but a reclining seat in a large room for US$205, breakfast and port tax included. Students can claim a 10% reduction on the fare only (not on meals). For lunch and dinner, add another US$35 to the fare. Fare for a normal car, port tax included, is about US$190; for a motor cycle about US$90.

For more information, contact TML at these addresses:

İstanbul
    Turkiye Denizcilik Isletmeleri, Rihtim Caddesi, Karaköy (tel (1) 144-0207, 149-7178)
İzmir
    Turkiye Denizcilik Isletmeleri Acenteligi, Yeniliman, Alsancak (tel (51) 21 00 94, 21 00 77)
London
    Sunquest Holidays Ltd, Aldine House, 9/15 Aldine St, London W12 8AW (tel (1) 749-9911)
Venice
    Bassani SPA, via 22 Marzo 2414 (tel (41) 522-9544)

British Ferries The MV *Orient Express* is a luxury car ferry that follows a similar cruise route on its weekly cruises from Venice, departing Saturday at dinner time, through the Corinth Canal to Piraeus (Monday), İstanbul (Tuesday), Kuşadası and Patmos (Wednesday), then to Katakolon in the Peloponnesus (Thursday), and back to Venice, arriving Saturday at breakfast time. The cruises begin in the first week of May and continue until the first week in November. You can travel from Venice to Piraeus, Venice to İstanbul, Piraeus to İstanbul, or take the entire week-long cruise.

There is time to leave the vessel and explore the port and nearby areas on each day. All meals and port taxes are included in the per-person fares which, between Venice and İstanbul or Kuşadası are UK£175 to UK£425 (US$260 to US$627) one way, UK£315 to UK£765 (US$465 to US$1129) round trip. The top fares are for double-bed staterooms; the rest are for cabins in which two, three or four persons share. The charge for a car is UK£130 to UK£145 (US$192 to US$214) one way, UK£234 to UK£261 (US$345 to US$385) return.

Passenger prices in two-berth cabins, including all meals and port taxes, but not including the cost of transporting your car, range from US$210 to US$360 per person from Piraeus to İstanbul, or US$460 to US$810 per person from Venice to İstanbul. Price differentials depend upon when you travel and how luxurious and well-placed your cabin is. Highest fares are in effect from mid-July to mid-September. For more information, contact a travel agent or Venice Simplon-Orient Express, One World Trade Center, Suite 2565, New York, NY 10048 (tel (800) 524-2420, (212) 938-6830; in Canada, tel (800) 451-2253).

To/From the Greek Islands

In the past, Greeks have at times been unwilling to provide information on transport to Turkey, but recent reports are better and it is now fairly easy to find and to buy tickets on the ferries from the Greek islands to Turkey. I have heard that Greek regulations require that passengers originating trips in Greece must travel on Greek-flag vessels, which means that you may not be allowed to hop aboard a convenient Turkish vessel for your trip from the Greek islands to the Turkish mainland. (If you've come over from Turkey for the day, you may return on the Turkish boat.) With the boom in Turkish tourism, the traffic from the Greek islands to the Turkish mainland is intense in the warm months.

There are five regular ferry services: Lesbos to Ayvalık, Chios to Çeşme, Samos to Kuşadası, Kos to Bodrum, and Rhodes to Marmaris.

The procedure is this: once you've found the ticket office, buy your ticket a day in advance. You may be asked to turn in your passport the night before the trip. The next day, before you board the boat, you'll get it back.

Here are the routes, fares and ticket agencies:

Lesbos to Ayvalık Aeolic Cruises Travel Agency (tel 23 960), at the port in Mytileni, is one of the ticket agencies. Both Greek and Turkish boats make this run daily in summer (late May or early June to September), charging US dollars for the fares. In spring, autumn and winter, boats operate about once or twice a week, weather permitting. The one-way fare is US$15; a return ticket costs US$25.

Chios to Çeşme Boats run daily except Monday from mid-July to mid-September. In spring and autumn, service is thrice weekly on Tuesday, Thursday, and Sunday (mid-May to mid-July and mid-September to the end of October). Winter service is once a week, on Thursday, if the weather allows and if there are sufficient passengers to make the trip worthwhile. Sometimes the companies put on extra boats when demand warrants. The voyage lasts about 45 minutes. The local boats (Greek boats from Chios, Turkish boats from Çeşme) depart at 9.30 or 10 am, making the return trip at 4 pm.

The one-way fare is US$18, same-day return fare is US$20; a return ticket valid for one year costs US$30. Children four to 12 years old are entitled to a 50% reduction on the fare. Motor cycles, cars, small caravans or minibuses can be transported on some boats. Fares for vehicles vary from US$40 to US$60, depending on size. For details, contact Chios Tours at the port in Chios, or Ertürk Travel Agency (tel (5492) 6768, 6876), Cumhuriyet Meydanı 11/A, in Çeşme's main square next to the fortress, facing the docks.

Samos to Kuşadası Boats operate between the settlements of Samos (daily, 8.30 am and 5 pm, a 30-minute trip) and Pythagorion (thrice weekly in summer, 8.30 am, a 45-minute trip) on the island of Samos, and Kuşadası, near Ephesus, in Turkey. In spring and autumn there are four trips weekly from the town of Samos.

There is no scheduled service in winter, though this may change; check with a travel agency in Samos or Kuşadası for the latest information. The voyage costs US$25 one way, US$30 return.

Kos to Bodrum Greek ferries leave the outer harbour of Kos for Bodrum on Monday, Wednesday and Friday mornings in summer, and on other days if there are sufficient passengers. Tickets cost US$21 one way. The Greek authorities usually require you to take a Greek-flag vessel rather than the Turkish excursion boat which has come over for the day, but sometimes you can talk them into letting you take the afternoon Turkish boat. If so, buy your ticket right on the boat.

Rhodes to Marmaris This is the busiest ferry service of all, with numerous boats flying Greek or Turkish flags competing for business. The Rhodes ticket office is the ANKA Travel Centre (tel (241) 25 095), 13 Odos Galias, near the New Market. It is open from 8.30 am to 2 pm and 5.30 to 9.30 pm in summer, closed on Sunday. In Turkey, buy your tickets at any travel agency. There are several daily boats (except Sunday) in each direction during the summer, and if lots of passengers are waiting, they may even put on Sunday boats. The fare is US$15 one way, US$20 same-day return, US$27 open-date return. The ferry service operates all year, though service does dwindle to only one or two trips weekly in winter. Some of the ferries are large enough to carry cars; reserve space in advance.

To/From Cyprus

You should be aware that relations between the Greek Cypriot-administered Republic of Cyprus and the Turkish Republic of Northern Cyprus (TRNC) are not good, and that the border between the two regions will probably be closed. Also, if you enter the TRNC and have your passport stamped you will later be denied entry to Greece. The Greeks will reject only a stamp from the Turkish Republic of Northern Cyprus, *not* a stamp from Turkey proper.

Famagusta to Mersin The large, comfortable MF *Yeşilada* car ferry operated by TML departs Famagusta (Magosa or Gazimagosa, Turkish Cyprus) on Tuesday, Thursday and Sunday at 10 pm, all year round. Departures from Mersin (Turkey) are at 10 pm on Monday, Wednesday and Friday. The overnight trip takes 10 hours, arriving at 8 am. Fares between Famagusta and Mersin range from US$35 per person in luxury cabins to US$18 for a reclining Pullman seat; port taxes are included, but meals cost a few dollars extra. To transport a car one way costs about US$17.

Saturday departures from Famagusta (11 pm) go to Lattakia (Lâzkiye), Syria, arriving the next day at 7 am, departing Lattakia for Famagusta at 12 noon on Sunday. The TML agent in Syria is the Lattakia Shipping Agencies Company (tel 33 163, 34 263, 34 213), Port Said St, PO Box 28, Lattakia.

Kyrenia to Taşucu Kyrenia (Girne in Turkish) and Taşucu, near Silifke, are connected by daily hydrofoil and car ferry service.

The 250-passenger MV *Barbaros* is a *deniz otobüsü* (sea bus) operated by the Kıbrıs Express company (tel (7593) 1434, 1334), Atatürk Bulvarı 82, Taşucu. It departs Kyrenia daily at 2.30 pm on the two-hour run to Taşucu. Departures from Taşucu for Kyrenia are daily at 11.30 am. The MV *Barbaros* has comfortable airplane-style seats, air-con, a bar and a snack counter. Tickets cost US$18 one way, US$32 return. Children younger than five travel free; from five to 12 years old, the one-way fare is US$13. You must pay a US$7 port tax as well.

The Kyrenia office for the Kıbrıs Express hydrofoil (tel (81) 53 544, 52 900) is at İskenderun Caddesi 4, Kyrenia; in Nicosia (Lefkoşa in Turkish) there's another office across from the İş Bankası. There's also an office in Turkey, at İnönü Bulvarı, Güvenç İş Merkezi 10, Mersin (tel (741) 16 731, 11 550).

The *Ertürk* car ferry runs from Kyrenia at 12 noon on Monday, Tuesday, Wednesday, Thursday and Friday, arriving in Taşucu at 4 pm. Trips from Taşucu to Kyrenia depart at midnight on Sunday, Monday, Tuesday, Wednesday and Thursday, arriving in Kyrenia the next morning at 7.30 am. One-way tickets cost US$22; a return is US$33. Contact Fatih Feribot (tel (81) 54 880, 54 977, 52 840) in Kyrenia; in Nicosia call the Şen-Tur agency (tel (20) 78 824). The ticket agent in Taşucu is Fatih Feribot (tel (7593) 1249, 1386) on the main square just off the dock. There is also an agent for the line in London called Gir-Taş Shipping (tel (1) 946-2828).

A similar car-ferry service is provided by the MV *Girne Sultanı*, operated by the Fergün Denizcilik company (tel (81) 53 866, 52 344, 53 377) in Kyrenia and in Taşucu (tel (7593) 1717, 1204). The MV *Girne Sultanı* departs Kyrenia for Taşucu at 1 pm on Monday, Wednesday and Friday, arriving at 5 pm. Departures from Taşucu are at midnight on Tuesday and Thursday, arriving the next morning at 7.30 am; and at 12 noon on Saturday, arriving in Kyrenia at 4 pm. Cabin berths are priced at US$14 to US$19 for a one-way ticket, plus US$7 port tax. Discounts are offered on return tickets and for students.

LEAVING TURKEY
Departure Tax

As of this writing, Turkey does not levy a departure tax on departing travellers.

Getting Around

Turkey has an elaborate public transport system, as private cars are still quite expensive and Turks love to travel all the time. Even the sleepiest village seems to have minibuses darting in and out throughout the day, and buses running between İstanbul and Ankara depart every few minutes.

AIR
Local Air Services
Turkish Airlines Turkish Airlines operates flights throughout the country. Most routes begin and end in İstanbul, travelling via Ankara. Thus there are 10 or more flights per day between these two cities, and continuing flights to many other points. One-way fares (in US dollars) and frequencies from İstanbul are:

city	flights/week	fare
Adana	14	$82
Ankara	80	$62
Antalya	20	$67
Dalaman	10	$60
Diyarbakır	9	$77
Erzurum	8	$77
Gaziantep	6	$80
İzmir	47	$62
Kayseri	2	$74
Konya	2	$70
Malatya	4	$80
Sivas	2	$80
Trabzon	10	$82
Van	4	$82

At present, there are few Turkish Airlines flights which connect Turkish cities directly without going through İstanbul or Ankara, and the few flights that exist are very vulnerable to change. The only such flight currently is from Sivas to Malatya (Tuesday and Sunday); there is no Malatya to Sivas service.

İstanbul Airlines İstanbul Airlines (İstanbul Hava Yolları) operates between its namesake city and Antalya, Dalaman, İzmir and Trabzon. There are also flights connecting Antalya with Dalaman and İzmir. You can buy tickets at the airport, or from these İstanbul Airlines offices:

Ankara
    İstanbul Airlines, Atatürk Bulvarı 83, Kızılay (tel (4) 132-2234)
    Ankara's Esenboğa Airport (tel (4) 312-2820, ext 285)

Antalya
    İstanbul Airlines, Anafartalar Caddesi 2, Selekler Çarşısı 82 (tel (31) 12 48 88)
    Antalya Airport (tel (31) 12 24 44)

Dalaman
    İstanbul Airlines, Yat Limanı 27, Marmaris (tel (612) 14 714)
    Dalaman Airport (tel (6119) 1780)

İstanbul
    İstanbul Airlines, İncirli Caddesi 50, Bakırköy (tel (1) 561-3466/7)
    İstanbul's Atatürk Airport tel (1) 573-4093, 574-2443)

İzmir
    İstanbul Airlines, Gazi Osman Paşa Caddesi 2/E (across from the Büyük Efes Oteli), Alsancak (tel (51) 19 05 41/2)
    İzmir's Menderes Airport (tel (51) 51 30 65, 51 26 26, ext 1202 or 1352)

Trabzon
    İstanbul Airlines, Kazazoğlu Sokak 9, Sanat İş Hanı (facing Atatürk Alanı) (tel (031) 23 806, 23 346)
    Trabzon Airport (tel (031) 23 327)

As you can see from the following table, İstanbul Airlines' flight frequency is less than Turkish Airlines, but the one-way fares are considerably cheaper:

city	flights/week	fare
İstanbul/Antalya	7	$50
İstanbul/Dalaman	6	$45
İstanbul/İzmir	6	$44
İstanbul/Trabzon	3	$58
Antalya/Dalaman	1	$44
Antalya/İzmir	1	$45

Sönmez Holding Airlines Called Sönmez Holding Hava Yolları in Turkish, this is a small airline set up by a large holding company for the convenience of its employees and visitors, but they are perfectly happy to fly you between Bursa and İstanbul. The airline has one small C-212 aircraft which wings from Bursa to İstanbul and back each morning, and again each evening; there's an extra flight on Saturday, but no flights at all on Sunday. Buy tickets at the airport or at these offices:

Bursa
     Ottomantur, Kızılay Pasajı, Çakırhamam (tel (24) 21 00 99, 22 20 97)
İstanbul
     Moris Seyahat Acentalığı, Tünel Pasajı 11, Beyoğlu (tel (1) 149-8510/1)

A bus departs the Ottomantur office in Bursa 45 minutes prior to flight time. To get to İstanbul's Atatürk Airport, take the airport bus from the Turkish Airlines terminal in Şişhane, or use a taxi.

Other Airlines Deregulation of Turkey's air transport system has resulted in the birth of many small commuter, charter and air-taxi firms. These companies come and go, and rarely operate scheduled flights, but you might find them of use in special circumstances.

EmAir (tel (4) 229-0440, 229-0757), Necatibey Caddesi 88/6, Ankara, provides air-taxi services in twin-engine Cessna 421C 'Golden Eagles'. They fly frequently between İstanbul and Bodrum. Contact them in İstanbul at the Atatürk Airport domestic terminal desk No 16 (tel (1) 574-4318, 573-7220, ext 2728). In Bodrum, the office is at Neyzen Tevfik Caddesi 138/A (tel (6141) 2100).

SancakAir (tel (1) 580-1517, 580-1074; fax 579-0727), Londra Asfaltı, Şefaköy, İstanbul, offers corporate jets and helicopters for hire.

Check-in Procedures
It's a good idea to get to the airport *at least* 45 minutes before flight time. Things can get a bit chaotic. Signs and announcements are not always provided, or understandable, so you need to keep asking to make sure you end up at the proper destination. Also, you need to make sure that your checked baggage is tagged and sent off to the plane. Sometimes when you hand it over to the agents, they just assume you want them to keep it for you until you return.

As of this writing, there is open seating on all domestic flights; you are not assigned a specific seat number, but may sit wherever you choose. This also means that there is smoking throughout the plane. For a short time in 1988, a non-smoking minister of transport abolished smoking on all domestic flights, but smoking was brought back by popular demand and he lost his job. When you check in, ask for the no-smoking section anyway, if that's what you prefer. Sooner or later the Turkish airline companies will get the hint and divide the seating sections accordingly.

Security
As you approach the airport perimeter, your bus or taxi will be stopped and spot-checked by police looking for terrorists. On a bus, your passport and ticket will be inspected.

As you enter the terminal, you will have to put your luggage through an x-ray machine. Before you leave the terminal you will be frisked for weapons and your hand baggage will be searched. Don't try to carry even a pocketknife aboard, as they will probably find it, and they certainly won't allow you to carry it aboard. Rather, pack it in your checked luggage.

As you approach the aircraft, all passengers' luggage will be lined up, and you will be asked to point out your bag. It will then be put on board. This is to prevent someone from checking a bag in with a bomb inside it, then not boarding the plane. So if you forget to point out your bag to the baggage handler, it may not be loaded on board and may be regarded with distrust.

Turkish Airlines has an enviable record of terror-free flights.

BUS

The bus and the dolmuş (minibus) are the most widespread and popular means of transport in Turkey. Buses go literally everywhere, all the time. Virtually every first-time traveller in Turkey comments on the convenience of the bus and minibus system. The bus service runs the gamut from plain and very inexpensive to very comfortable and moderately priced. It is so cheap and convenient that many erstwhile long-distance hitchhikers opt for the bus. The eight-hour, 450-km trip between İstanbul and Ankara, for example, costs only US$5 to US$8, depending on the bus company. Though bus fares are open to competition among companies, and even to haggling for a reduction, the cost of bus travel in Turkey works out to around US$1.25 per 100 km – a surprising bargain.

The Otogar

Most Turkish cities and towns have a central bus terminal called variously otogar, otobüs garajı, otobüs terminalı, santral garaj or sehir garajı (city garage). In this book I'll stick to otogar. Besides inter-city buses, the otogar often handles minibuses to outlying districts or villages. Otogars are often equipped with their own PTT branches, telephones with an international service, restaurants, snack stands, pastry shops, tourism information booths and left-luggage offices called *emanet* (eh-mah-NEHT).

İstanbul has several mammoth garages; Ankara and İzmir each have a mammoth one. Bus companies aiming at the high-class trade may have their own small, private terminals in other parts of town, to save their privileged patrons the hassle of dealing with large crowds at the main terminal. These are mentioned in the text where appropriate.

A few small towns have only a collection of bus line offices rather than a proper garage.

Buying Tickets

Though you can often just walk into an otogar and buy a ticket for the next bus out, it's wise to plan ahead. At the least, locate the companies and note the times for your destination a day in advance. Buses on some routes may fill up, so buying tickets a day in advance is good if you can do it. This is especially important along the south coast, where long-distance bus traffic is less frequent than in some other parts of the country.

Some bus companies will grant you a reduction on the fare if you show your ISIC student card. This may not be official policy, but just an excuse for a reduction – in any case you win.

The word for 'tomorrow', very handy to know when buying bus tickets a day in advance, is *yarın* (YAHR-uhn). Bus departure times will be given using the 24-hour clock system, eg 1830 instead of 6.30 pm.

When you enter an otogar you'll see lots of people and baggage, buses and minibuses, plus rows of little ticket offices. Competition on some routes is stiff. In most cases, more than one company will run to your desired destination; the cities and towns served by the company will be written prominently at the company's ticket office. It's a good idea to check several ticket offices, asking when the company's next bus leaves. Hawkers near the entrance to the otogar will approach you as soon as you enter, asking your destination. Tell them, and they'll lead you to a particular company's ticket office. This company may or may not have the next departure. A few times I have been sold a ticket for the company's next bus (in two hours) when another company had a bus departing – with seats available – in 40 minutes. Let the hawkers lead you, but then ask around at other companies before you buy.

All seats are reserved, and your ticket will bear specific seat numbers. It's very important that you plan your seat strategy rather than leave it up to the ticket seller. He'll have a chart of the seats in front of him. The ones already taken will be indicated. Let the ticket seller know that you want to see the chart, and indicate on it your seating preference.

The preferable seats, according to Turkish conventional wisdom, are in the middle of the bus (that is, not right over the wheels, which can be bumpy), and also on the side which will not get the full sun. However, unless you absolutely adore inhaling cigarette smoke, you may prefer to seize one of the front seats (Nos 1 to 4) near the driver's open window, perhaps the only fresh-air source on the bus. On the Mercedes 0302 bus, avoid if possible the front rows over the wheels and the last three rows (Nos 33 to 43); seats Nos 9 to 28 are the best, but on the shady side. On the single-deck Neoplan bus, wheel seats are Nos 5 to 8 and Nos 33 to 36; Nos 31 to 32 are right by the rear door, and Nos 45 to 48 are right atop the motor. Avoid these. On the double-decker Neoplan bus, lower deck seats are Nos 53 to 72; you should avoid wheel seats Nos 57 to 60, and rear seats Nos 69 to 72; all of the upper deck seats are good, though Nos 31 to 36 and Nos 39 to 40 are next to the door. The problem with the front seats, however, is that they are most vulnerable in case of a traffic accident.

Turks, it seems, are constitutionally opposed to air draughts of any strength, even on a sweltering hot day. Even if the ventilation or air-con system of the bus is excellent, it may not be turned on. 'Better to swelter than take any chance of sitting in a draught' is the Turkish rule. Thus you must choose your seat with care, keeping the glare of the hot midday sun in mind. On a four-hour summer afternoon trip from Ankara to Konya, for instance, you'll be too warm if you're on the right-hand (western) side of the bus, while the seats on the left (eastern) side will remain comfortable.

You can also join in my fresh-air campaign. Summon the *yardımcı* (assistant) and say *çok sıcak!* ('choke' suh-jahk, 'It's very hot'). Indicate the ventilation system and say *Havalandırma açın!* (hah-vah-lahn-duhr-MAH ah-chun, 'Open the ventilation system'). If you can't manage that, just point to it here, in the book, and let the yardımcı read it. Sometimes this works.

Once you've bought a ticket, getting a refund can be difficult, though it's possible. Exchanges for other tickets within the same company are easier.

About Bus Travel

A bus trip in Turkey is usually a fairly pleasant experience if it's not too long. Buses are big, modern and comfortable. As Turks are great cigarette smokers, you may encounter a significant amount of smoke on the trip. Passengers in the seats near you will offer you cigarettes as an ice-breaker, hoping to strike up a conversation. There's no stigma in refusing. Say *Hayır, teşekkür ederim, içmem* ('No, thank you, I don't smoke') or, if this is a mouthful, just *İçmem* (eech-MEHM) with a smile. Turks, like most people, think it laudable that someone doesn't smoke (or has given up smoking). Besides, the offer was intended as a politeness, a welcome and a conversation opener. It serves this purpose whether you smoke or not.

On the subject of cigarette smoke, please join my crusade (holy war?) against smoke-filled buses. Whenever you buy an inter-city bus ticket in Turkey, ask for a *sigara içilmez otobüsü* (see-GAH-rah ee-cheel-MEHZ oh-toh-bur-sur, a 'no smoking' bus). The larger companies have begun to institute smoke-free buses on some major routes, a trend that must be encouraged as buses do not lend themselves to the 'smoking' and 'no smoking' divisions common on trains and airplanes.

Most of your inquiries will elicit a sad smile and a *maalesef* ('unfortunately'), indicating that there aren't any no-smoking buses on that route yet. But Turks are quick to recognise demand for a service, and future travellers may not have to suffer so much.

Once en route, your fellow passengers will be curious about where you come from, what language you speak, and how you're enjoying the country. Openers may be in German. It's polite to exchange at least a few sentences.

Shortly after you head out, the yardımcı will come through the bus with a bottle of lemon cologne with which to refresh his *sayın yolcular* (honoured passengers). He'll dribble some into your cupped hands, which you then rub together, and then rub on your face and hair, ending with a sniff to clear your nasal passages. You may not be used to the custom, but if you ride buses in Turkey much you will get used to it quickly, and probably love it.

If you want a bottle of cool spring water at any time during the trip, just signal to the yardımcı and ask *Su, lütfen* ('Water, please'). There's no charge.

Stops will be made every 1½ hours or so for the toilet, snacks or meals and the inevitable çay. At some stops boys rush onto the bus selling sweets, nuts, sandwiches and the like, or a waiter from the teahouse (buses always stop at a teahouse) may come through to take orders. Most people, however, welcome the chance to stretch their legs.

Keep your bus ticket until you reach your absolutely final destination. In some cases, companies have *servis arabası* (sehr-VEES ah-rah-bah-suh, service cars) – a minibus service that will shuttle you from the bus station into the city at no extra charge, provided you can show a ticket on the company's line.

You can save money by taking night buses on long hauls (eight or 10 hours or more). Cigarette smoke will be less, the bus will be cooler, and you will save money

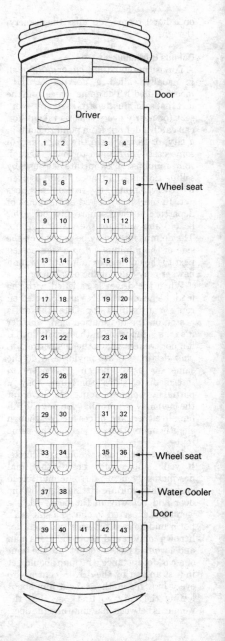

on a hotel room. You miss the scenery, though.

Dolmuş & Minibus

A Turkish minibus (*minibüs* or *münübüs*), is usually called a *dolmuş* (DOHL-moosh, 'filled'). The name comes from the fact that a dolmuş departs as soon as every seat (or nearly every seat) is taken. You can catch a dolmuş from point to point in a city, or from village to village, and in some cases from town to town. Though some minibus routes operate like buses by selling tickets in advance (perhaps even for reserved seats), the true dolmuş does not. Rather, it is parked at the point of departure (a town square, city otogar or beach) and waits for the seats to fill up. The dolmuş route may be painted on the side of the minibus, or on a sign posted next to the dolmuş, or in its window; or a hawker may call out the destination.

When the driver is satisfied with the load, he heads off. Fares are collected en route or at the final stop. Often the fare is posted on the destination sign, whether it's on a signpost or in the car window. If it's not, watch what other passengers to your destination are paying and do the same, or ask. Though passengers to intermediate stops sometimes pay a partial fare, on other routes the driver (or the law) may require that you pay the full fare. In either case, prices are low, though slightly more than a bus on the same route.

Here are some rules of dolmuş etiquette. If your stop comes before the final destination, you may do some shuffling to ensure that you are sitting right by the door and not way in the back. Also, a woman is expected to choose a side seat, not a middle seat between two men, for her own comfort and 'protection'. If a man and a woman passenger get into the front of a car, for instance, the man should get in first and sit by the driver (contrary to everything his mother taught him about letting the lady go first), so that the woman is between 'her' man and the door.

This is not a gesture against women, but rather the opposite, to show respect for her honour.

Collection of fares will begin after the car starts off, and the driver will juggle and change money as he drives. This thrilling practice costs no extra. If you're still not sure about your fare, hand over a bill large enough to cover the fare but small enough not to anger the driver, who will never have enough change and will not want a large bill. Should there be any doubt about fares or problem in payment (rare), you can always settle up at the last stop.

To signal the driver that you want to get out, say *İnecek var*. Other useful words are *durun* (DOOR-oon, 'stop') and *burada* (BOO-rah-dah, 'here').

TRAIN

The Turkish State Railways (T C Devlet Demiryolları, or TCDD) run to many parts of the country, on lines laid out by German companies which were supposedly paid by the km. But some newer, more direct lines have been laid during the republican era, shortening travel times for the best express trains.

It's not a good idea to plan a train trip all the way across Turkey in one stretch. Turkey is a big country, and the cross-country trains are a lot slower than the buses. The Vangölü Ekspresi from İstanbul to Lake Van (Tatvan), a 1900-km trip, takes almost two full days, for example – and that's an express! The bus would take less than 24 hours. Train travel between Ankara, İzmir and İstanbul is another matter, however. The top trains on these lines are a pleasure to ride, whether by night or day.

Whenever you take an inter-city train in Turkey, you'd do well to take only *mavi tren* (blue train), *ekspres* or *mototren* trains. These are fairly fast, comfortable, and about the same price as the bus. The *yolcu* (passenger) trains are much slower and the *posta* (mail) trains move at the

Top: Village family in Karatay
Left: Istanbul craftsman at work on a coffee pot
Right: Entry-way niche in Avanos

Top: Cotton pickers near Side
Left: Back streets of Antalya
Right: A Çayci (tea waiter) in his filigree vest

Logo of the TCDD – the Turkish State Railways

speed of cold treacle; neither is very comfortable.

Note that Turkish train schedules indicate *stations*, not cities; the station name is usually, but not always, the city name. Thus you may not see İstanbul on a schedule, but you will see Haydarpaşa and Sirkeci, the Asian and European stations in İstanbul. For İzmir, the stations are Basmane and Alsancak. I'll mention the station names in this guide where appropriate.

Top Trains
Full information on trains is given at the end of each city section, but here is a summary of the top trains:

İstanbul to Ankara Mavi Tren Daily 1st-class express between Ankara and İstanbul, about 7½ hours, departing each city at 1.30 pm, arriving 9 pm, and departing 11 pm, arriving the next morning at 7.30 am; a bit faster than the bus, more expensive, more comfortable.

Boğaziçi Ekspresi Daily all-Pullman 1st-class express between Ankara and İstanbul, about nine hours, departing each city at 8 am, arriving at 5.05 pm; a bit slower than the bus, but more comfortable.

İzmir (Basmane) to Ankara Mavi Tren Daily overnight express, about 14 hours, departing each city at 8.05 pm, arriving the next morning at 10.06 am.

İzmir Ekspresi Nightly coach and sleeping-car train between Ankara and İzmir (Basmane), about 15½ hours, departing each city at 6.05 pm, arriving the next morning at 9.40 am.

Anadolu Ekspresi Nightly sleeping-car, couchette and coach train between Ankara and İstanbul, about 11 hours, departing each city at 9.05 pm, arriving the next morning at 8.10 am.

Ankara Ekspresi Nightly 1st-class all-sleeping-car train between Ankara and İstanbul, about 11 hours, departing each city at 9.40 pm, arriving the next morning at 8.30 am.

Buying Tickets
Most seats on the best trains, and all sleeping compartments, must be reserved. This is done when you buy your ticket. Turkish State Railways have installed a computerised reservations system for use in selling tickets for reserved seats, sleeping berths and couchettes on the top trains. Look for the *bilgisayar gişeleri* (computer ticket windows).

Turkish words useful in the railway station are given in the Turkish Language Guide at the back of this book.

As the best trains are very popular, particularly the sleeping-car trains, and as rail travel is often cheaper than bus travel, you should make your reservation and buy your ticket as far in advance as possible. A few days will usually suffice. If you can't do this, check at the station anyway. There may be cancellations, even at the last minute. I once boarded a night train expecting to sleep in a seat, but I mentioned to the sleeping-car conductors that I preferred a bed. They came and found me after the train departed, and sold me a vacant compartment left by someone who didn't show up.

Weekend trains, from Friday evening to Monday morning, seem to be busiest.

Youth & Student Discounts Student discounts of 10% are available on most trains and most routes. In listings of fares, look for the *öğrenci* or *talebe* (student) fare.

If you are under 26 years of age, you can buy an Inter-Rail card which allows you unlimited 2nd-class rail travel in Turkey and 19 other European countries plus Morocco, and also a 50% reduction on private trains. Ask at Sirkeci Station in İstanbul, or at the station in Ankara.

Cancellation Penalties If you decide not to travel and you seek a refund for your rail ticket up to 24 hours before train departure, you must pay a cancellation fee of 10% of the ticket price. Within 24 hours of departure the fee rises to 25%. After the train has departed the fee is 50%.

Fares

In general, train fares are about the same as bus fares for the same journey. But as train fares are set in liras, which devalue daily, and are not revised frequently, chances are that you will find trains cheaper than buses. The exceptions are the fast mavi tren and the couchette and

sleeping-car trains when you avail yourself of those facilities.

Here is a sampling of fares (in US dollars) for seats on express trains from İstanbul's Haydarpaşa Station to:

city	full fare	student fare	return fare
Adana	$10	$ 9	$17
Ankara	$ 6	$ 5.50	$10
Denizli	$ 8	$ 7.20	$13
Diyarbakır	$10	$ 9	$17
Edirne	$ 3.50	$ 3	$ 5.75
Erzurum	$12	$10.50	$20
İzmir	$ 6	$ 5.50	$10

Tickets for a trip on one of the many mavi tren super-expresses cost about 50% more than for the same trip on a normal express train.

You must also pay considerably more for a berth in a sleeping car, but the price compares well to that for a night in a moderately good hotel. The prices in the following list are given *per person* in US dollars for sleeping compartments with one, two, three or four berths, from İstanbul (Haydarpaşa) to:

city	single	double	triple/quad
Ankara	$38	$32	$24
Diyarbakır	$42	$36	$28
Erzurum	$42	$36	$28
Kayseri	$32	$26	$22
Tatvan	$50	$40	$32

Thus, the total cost for a comfortable private 1st-class sleeping compartment for the 12-hour trip aboard the nightly all-sleeper Ankara Ekspresi between Ankara and İstanbul (Haydarpaşa) for two people is about US$80; this price includes the train tickets, the sleeping-car fees and the porter's service charge and tip. When you realise that this includes both the night's lodging and the night's travel, the price seems very reasonable. If there's a dining car, table d'hôte meals are fairly good and not overly expensive. Breakfast in the dining car is about US$3.

TAXI

Inter-city taxis are expensive, but if you must catch a plane, train or bus in town and you're in a village, you may have to use one. Municipalities set inter-city (and for that matter, intra-city) taxi rates. Before you engage a taxi, if it does not have a meter ask to see the official rate card or *tarife* (tah-ree-FEH). If your destination is not on the tarife, you've got to strike a bargain. You needn't tip unless the driver has provided some extra service for you.

BOAT

Turkish Maritime Lines (TML) cruise ships sail along the Black Sea, Aegean and Mediterranean coasts. With the advent of good highways and a very frequent, inexpensive, speedy bus service, the coastal boat trips have become cruises rather than mere passenger transport. Cabins are few and in great demand, so you may have to make reservations well in advance.

Ferries

İstanbul to İzmir The overnight car ferries running between İstanbul and İzmir (19 hours) demand advance reservations for both car space and cabins. Schedules are like this: Friday departure from İstanbul at 3 pm, arriving in İzmir on Saturday at 9 am; departing İzmir on Sunday at 2 pm, arriving İstanbul on Monday at 9 am, year round. In high summer, extra trips are added on Monday and Wednesday from İstanbul departing at 2 pm, Tuesday and Thursday from İzmir departing at 2 pm; arrivals are at 9 am the next morning. Fares range from US$12 for a Pullman reclining seat to US$50 per person in the most luxurious cabin. You can turn the trip into a mini-cruise by staying aboard and using the ship as your hotel in İzmir for a night, then returning to İstanbul. The extra charge for this night in port is 80% of the regular fare. Meals cost extra, about US$3 for breakfast, and US$8 for

lunch or dinner. Fare for an car is US$26, for a motor cycle US$6.

İstanbul to Trabzon Car and passenger ferries operate each week all year round, departing İstanbul Monday at 5.30 pm, arriving Samsun on Tuesday at 7.30 pm and departing at 9 pm, arriving in Trabzon on Wednesday at 8 am, departing on the return voyage to İstanbul at 10 pm. The returning ferry arrives in Samsun Thursday at 8 am, departs at 9.30 am, and arrives in İstanbul on Friday at 11 am. Per-person fares between İstanbul and Trabzon are US$12 for a Pullman seat, US$18 to US$50 for cabin berths. Cars cost US$26, motor cycles US$6.

Another Black Sea ferry departs İstanbul on Thursday evening for Zonguldak, Sinop, Ordu and Giresun (arrival Saturday morning), and returns from Giresun on Saturday afternoon with the same ports of call, reaching İstanbul by Monday morning. This route operates from mid-May to late September.

İstanbul to Bursa If you're headed from İstanbul to Bursa, you'll doubtless want to take the enjoyable and very cheap ferry across the Sea of Marmara and the Bay of İzmit to Yalova, where you catch the bus for İznik or Bursa. Details on this route are given in the Near İstanbul chapter. There is also a fast, more expensive hydrofoil service between İstanbul and Mudanya, whence buses trundle you on the half-hour trip inland to Bursa.

Cruises

İstanbul to Alanya There are 10 cruises lasting 10 days each, run by TML from mid-May to mid-September, on the route İstanbul, Dikili (Bergama), İzmir, Marmaris, Alanya, Antalya, Fethiye, Datça, Bodrum, Kuşadası, İzmir and İstanbul. It's a wonderful way to see the Turkish Aegean and Mediterranean coasts, but tickets sell out well in advance. The cruise price for most cabins includes all meals and tours to the various sites along the way, and the entire trip from İstanbul to İstanbul. Tickets costing US$250 to US$600 per person are for the better and best cabins, and include meals and sightseeing. Cabins priced at US$90 to US$175 include meals, but not sightseeing. 'Deck-class' tickets entitle you to a bed in a dormitory cabin, and cost only US$75, but include no meals nor sightseeing.

Rumour has it that a private company has leased the TML's vessel MV *Ankara*, and will be offering similar, more expensive cruises on this same run. Ask a travel agent about these cruises.

By Boat & Train

Turkish State Railways and TML team up to provide an inexpensive and enjoyable ride between İstanbul and İzmir. Trains run between İzmir and the railhead-port of Bandırma, on the Sea of Marmara; ships connect Bandırma and İstanbul. There are two boat-train trips daily in each direction. Departures from İstanbul on the 11-hour trip are at 9.30 am and 9 pm, reaching the port of Bandırma about four hours later. Transfer from ship to train takes about 90 minutes, and the train trip takes another 5½ hours, arriving in İzmir at 8.30 pm and 8.50 am respectively. Departures from İzmir are at 8.15 am and 8 pm, arriving at Bandırma about 1.45 pm and 1.30 am, then arriving in İstanbul at 6.45 pm and 7 am respectively. As you can see, one of these schedules requires you to make the train to boat switch in the middle of the night. A single ticket costs US$8. Should you want to sleep in a cabin aboard the ship, you'll have to pay somewhat more.

DRIVING

You don't really need an International Driving Permit (IDP) while you drive in Turkey, despite what some travel books say. Your home driving licence, unless it's something weird, will be accepted by traffic police officers and by car rental firms. If you'd feel more secure against

bureaucratic hassle by carrying an IDP, you can get one through your automobile club at home.

Road Safety

Turkish highways are of passable quality. The Türkiye Cumhuriyeti Karayolları (Turkish Republic Highways Department, or TCK) undertakes ambitious improvements constantly, but despite their efforts most roads are still of two lanes, perhaps with overtaking lanes on long uphill grades. Motorways are to be found mostly near the four largest cities; a new motorway will soon connect İstanbul and Ankara. In eastern Turkey, with its severe winter weather, roads are easily destroyed by frost, and potholes can be quite a nuisance.

The major commerce routes (E5, E24) are often busy but not impossible, but city streets are positively thronged and parking can be a real problem. Turkish drivers are not particularly discourteous out on the highway, but they are inexperienced, they drive at high speed, they simply must overtake you whatever the cost, and, most regrettably, they all believe absolutely in *kısmet* (fate). If a Turkish driver, careening along a slippery highway in a car with smooth tyres, the accelerator pedal to the floor, his mind engaged in heated conversation, swerves to avoid an errant sheep and crashes into a tree, that's kısmet, and it can't be helped. Moderating speed, getting better tyres or paying attention to the road are not really possible options, as kısmet will get you if it's going to, no matter what you do. So why bother?

In the cities, illogic, discourtesy and madness among drivers are universal. In addition to the customary and very appropriate *Allah Korusun* (May God Protect Me) emblazoned somewhere on every Turkish car, bus and truck, you should imagine the additional motto *Önce Ben* (Me First).

Spares & Repairs

Spare parts for most cars may be available, if not readily so, outside the big cities. European models, especially Renaults, Fiats and Mercedes, are preferred, though ingenious Turkish mechanics contrive to keep all manner of huge American models – some half a century old – in daily service.

If you have a model with which Turkish mechanics are familiar, such as a Mercedes, simple Renault or Fiat, repairs can be swift and very cheap. Don't be afraid of little roadside repair shops, which can often provide excellent, virtually immediate service, though they (or you) may have to go somewhere else to get the parts. It's always good to get an estimate of the repair cost in advance. Ask *Tamirat kaç para?* (How much will repairs cost?). For tyre repairs find a *lâstikçi* (tyre-repairer). Repair shops are closed on Sunday, but even so, if you go to the repair shop district of town (every town has one) and look around, you may still find someone willing and able to help you out.

Traffic Police

Police in black-and-white cars (usually Renaults) and green uniforms with white peaked caps set up checkpoints on major highways in order to make sure that vehicle documents are in order and that vehicle safety features are in working condition. They busy themselves mostly with trucks and buses, and will usually wave you on, but you should slow down and prepare to stop until you get the wave.

If you are stopped, the officer may ask for your car registration, insurance certificate and driving licence. He may ask you to turn on your headlamps (high and low beam), hoot your horn, switch on your turning signals and windscreen wipers, etc, to see that all are working properly. He'll certainly ask your nationality, and try to chat, because one of the reasons he stopped you was to break up the monotony of checking trucks by throwing in a curious foreigner.

Car Rental

Cars may be rented in Adana, Alanya, Ankara, Antalya, Bodrum, Bursa, Çeşme, Dalaman, Gaziantep, İstanbul, İzmir, Kuşadası, Marmaris, Mersin, Samsun, Side and Trabzon from the larger international rental firms (Hertz, Avis, National Europcar, Budget and Dollar InterRent) or from smaller local ones. Avis has the most extensive and experienced network of agencies and staff. The most popular rental cars are the Fiat Murat 131 (Şahin), 131SW (Kartal), Mirafiori (Doğan), the Ford Taunus 1.6 and the Renault 12. The cheapest cars are the Fiat 131 and Renault 12, built in Turkey. They can carry four passengers in a modicum of comfort, with adequate storage space for luggage. The Kartal and Doğan are more comfortable, more powerful and a bit larger. Most rental cars are equipped with radio-cassette tape players, but only the most expensive ones have air-con.

Costs Total costs for a week with unlimited km, including full insurance and tax, might be US$300 to US$400; in addition, you'll pay about US$0.35 per litre for fuel. The fuel cost to operate a small car is about US$0.04 per km.

When you look at a rental company's current price list, keep in mind that the daily or weekly rental charge is only a small portion of what you will actually end up paying, unless it includes unlimited km. The charge for km normally ends up being higher, per day, than the daily rental charge. By the way, VAT (KDV) should be included in the rental, insurance and km prices quoted to you. It should not be added to the bottom of your bill.

You should not be afraid to try (with caution) one of the small local agencies, which offer much lower prices than the big firms. I've had good experience with Seytur Ltd (tel (711) 44157, 44216),

Ziyapaşa Bulvarı, Libya Dostluk Derneği Yanı, 290 Sokak 40, Adana. Though there is little fluency in English and no far-flung network for repairs, they are friendly, helpful and 10% to 20% cheaper than the large firms. Other small agencies, in more convenient cities, may do as well.

MOTOR CYCLE

Motor cycles and mopeds are becoming more popular in Turkey because they are cheaper than cars to buy and to run. These days, Austrian and German mopeds are the popular items. Motor cycles tend to be large old Czechoslovak Jawa models that make a distinctive hollow putt-putt.

You can bring your motor cycle to Turkey and have a fine time seeing the country. Spare parts will probably be hard to come by, so bring what you may need, or rely on the boundless ingenuity of Turkish mechanics to find, adapt or make you a part. Or else be prepared to call home, have the part flown in, and endure considerable hassles from customs.

BICYCLE

Though Turks use bicycles primarily as utilitarian vehicles to go short distances, long-distance bicycling for sport is being introduced by European tourists, mostly Germans with mountain bikes. You can bike pleasurably through Turkey if you plan ahead, pick your routes carefully and avoid certain perils.

The pleasures are in the spectacular scenery, the friendly people, the easy access to archaeological sites and the ready availability of natural camping sites both official and unofficial. The best routes are those along the coasts, particularly the western Mediterranean coast between Marmaris and Antalya. You may be wheeling merrily along, overtaken by a truck loaded with fruit, and handed some on the run by the laughing children who have just picked it.

The perils are more specific. Road conditions are not ideal. The road surface, particularly on the newer roads, is of rough limestone and marble chips. Turkish car and bus drivers tend to believe more in kısmet than in good driving to protect them; truck drivers are usually more reasonable, if only because their heavily overladen vehicles can't go very fast. *Every* driver will hoot at you (this is safe but annoying). Maps available in Turkey are sometimes incorrect on such things as grades and altitudes, so search out a suitable map before leaving home.

As a cyclist, you may find your relations with Turks somewhat extreme. Along the road, some children not used to cyclists may toss stones. This is often more of an annoyance than a danger, and as cyclists become more familiar sights it should subside. In hotels and pensions, and on those occasional bus and train rides, you may find people so accommodating and helpful in storing your valuable cycle 'safely' that lights, carriers and reflectors may get damaged unintentionally, so supervise and say *yavaş yavaş*, (yah-VAHSH yah-VAHSH, 'slowly') frequently. Whenever you stop for a rest or to camp, the rural staring squads of the curious will appear, instantly, as if by magic. You may find, like the royal family, that constant scrutiny, even if friendly, can be wearisome.

Here are some tips on equipment and repairs. High-pressure pumps are not yet available in Turkey; petrol-station pumps may or may not go to 90 psi (high pressure). Inner tubes of 69 cm by 3 cm are available, but not everywhere; most of the tubes sold are larger, and they won't fit 69 cm by 2½ cm rims because of the large valve seat. Be prepared for frequent chain maintenance due to dust and mud. Moped and motor cycle repair shops are often helpful, and if they can't do the repairs they will seek out someone who can.

HITCHING

When you hitchhike (*otostop*), Turkish custom requires that you offer to pay for your ride. If a car or truck stops to pick you up, the driver will expect you to share expenses, the amount being more or less equivalent to the bus fare on the same route. (Say *Borcum kaç?*, bohr-JOOM kahtch, 'How much do I owe you?' as you prepare to get out). Truck drivers depend on their passenger trade for spending money, and will not like it if you occupy one of their paying seats and then refuse to pay. Thus it's not surprising that long-distance hitchhiking, though possible in Turkey, is not all that common. The bus and minibus network is so elaborate and cheap that most people opt for that, figuring that if bus fare must be paid, bus comforts might as well be enjoyed. Private cars are not as plentiful as in Europe, and owners here are not as inclined to pick up hitchers.

Short-distance hitching is somewhat different. As the country is large and vehicles not so plentiful outside the towns, short-distance country hops are the norm. If you need to get from the highway (where the bus dropped you) into an archaeological site (Ephesus, Troy or wherever), you hitch a ride with whatever comes along. Again, private cars are the least amenable, but delivery vans, heavy machinery, oil tankers, farm tractors, etc are all fair game. *You must offer to pay for the ride*; in most cases your offer will be declined (though appreciated) because you are a 'guest' in Turkey.

The signal used in hitchhiking is not an upturned thumb. In Turkey, you face the traffic, hold your arm out toward the road, and wave your hand and arm up and down as though bouncing a basketball.

Women Hitchhikers

When it comes to women hitchhiking, Turkey is like the rest of the world, perhaps a bit more so: it is done, but you really should not do it, especially alone. A Turkish woman would rather die than hitchhike; she'd feel like she was offering herself to every man in every car that picked her up. With buses so cheap, why set yourself up for hassle?

Hitching as a couple is usually OK, but

I'd avoid vehicles with more than one or two men in them. Two women hitching together is preferable to one alone. If you're determined to hitch, take the normal precautions: don't accept a ride in a car or truck which is already occupied by men only (especially if it's only one man, the driver). Look for vehicles carrying women and/or children as well as men. Act appreciative and polite, but cool, dignified and formal, to the driver who picks you up. Avoid hitching across long, empty spaces, and never hitch at night. As for regional variances, you'll have the easiest time where foreigners and their strange customs are most familiar, naturally. The Aegean coast is the least dangerous. The further east you go, the more misunderstood you'll be.

LOCAL TRANSPORT
Airport Transport
Transport to and from each airport in Turkey is covered within the section on each city.

Bus
Turkish cities have lots of buses, but they are usually crowded to capacity. Buses run by the city government often have *belediyesi* (municipality) marked on them. Most municipal bus systems now work on a ticket system, and you must buy a ticket (*otobüs bileti*, or simply *bilet*, 'bee-LEHT'), at a special ticket kiosk. These kiosks are at major bus termini or transfer points.

What usually happens is that the unsuspecting foreign tourist tries to climb onto a bus, discovers that money is not accepted for the fare, and a nearby passenger saves the day by handing the tourist a ticket from his own booklet. The tourist offers payment, the Turk sometimes declines it. You can avoid embarrassment by tracking down a kiosk and buying a few tickets whenever you arrive in a new city. The cost is minimal: US$0.12 to US$0.25, depending on which city.

Dolmuş

Besides the inter-city dolmuş system, a similar system exists within every town of any size. You'll find yourself using it frequently as it is usually faster, more comfortable and only slightly more expensive than the bus (and still very cheap). Intra-city dolmuş stops are near major squares, termini or intersections, and you'll have to ask: (name of destination) *dolmuş var mı?* (...DOHL-moosh VAHR muh?) If you are at Sirkeci Station in İstanbul, for instance, and you want to get to Taksim Square, you ask, *Taksim dolmuş var mi?* Someone will point you to the dolmuş stand, just out the station door and to the right.

Often there is not a direct dolmuş route from where you are to where you're going. Maps of the system don't exist. If the person you ask seems to hem and haw, they're probably trying to tell you that you must take one dolmuş to a certain point, and then another.

Once you know a few convenient routes, you'll feel confident about picking up a dolmuş at the curb. In the larger cities, stopping-places are regulated and marked by signs saying 'Dolmuş İndirme Bindirme Yeri' (Dolmuş Boarding and Alighting Place). You'll see minibuses, old American cars and new little Turkish-made cars stopping. A true city dolmuş has a solid-colour band, usually yellow or black, painted horizontally around the car just below the windows. Sometimes taxis with a black and yellow chequered band operate like the dolmuş. You've got to be careful. If you climb into an empty car, the driver might assume (honestly, or for his own benefit) that you want a taxi, and he will charge you the taxi fare. Always ask, *Dolmuş mu?* (dohl-MOOSH moo? 'Is this a dolmuş?') when you climb into an empty car.

You'll get the hang of the dolmuş way of life after only a few days in Turkey, and will find it very useful.

Taxi

Most taxis in most cities have digital meters, and they use them. If yours doesn't, mention it right away by saying, *Saatiniz* (saa-AHT-EE-NEEZ, 'Your meter'). The starting rate is about US$0.50, slightly more at night. The average taxi ride costs US$1 to US$2 in the daytime, more at night.

With the flood of tourists arriving in Turkey, some taxi drivers – especially İstanbul's many crooks-on-wheels – have begun to demand flat payment from foreigners. In some cases the driver will actually offer you a decent fare, and will then pocket all the money instead of giving the owner of the cab his share. But most of the time the driver will offer an exorbitant fare, give you trouble, and refuse to run the meter. City regulations against this sort of behaviour are strict, and the fines are huge, so drivers don't want to be caught at it. All the same, do you want to get into a guy's cab just after having chewed him out for illegal gouging? If you call the police, they'll probably smooth it over, and the driver will agree to take you to your destination, and you'll feel obliged to accept the offer, and then the driver will take you where you're going by way of the Paris suburbs, running up an astronomical fare. Perhaps the best course of action if you are asked to pay a flat fare is to find another cab.

Ferries

In İstanbul and İzmir, public transport is delightfully augmented by ferries. White with orange trim (the TML's colours), these sturdy craft steam up, down and across the Bosphorus and the Bay of İzmir, providing city dwellers with cheap, convenient transport, views of open water and (in summer) fresh cool breezes. They are not nostalgic transport toys but a real, even vital, part of each city's transport system. You should take the ferry in each city at least once, enjoying the cityscapes that are revealed from the decks, sipping a glass of fresh tea or a soft drink. The ferries can be crowded during rush hour but there's still lots of air and scenery; and while buses sit trapped in traffic the ferries glide through the water effortlessly, at speed.

In İstanbul, special ferry sailings on a touristic route are operated daily, and the price for a 1¾-hour cruise all the way from İstanbul to the Black Sea is only about US$3.

TOURS
As Turkey's tourist boom continues, the number of companies offering guided tours of cities or regions expands apace. Along with legitimate operators, the sleazy ones are moving in, so you should be careful when choosing a tour company. The actual tour you get depends greatly on the competence, character and personality of your particular guide; but it's difficult to pick a tour by guide rather

than company, so you must go by the tour company's reputation.

The best course of action is to ask about at your hotel for recommendations. Other foreign visitors may be able to give you tips on which companies to use and which to avoid.

Watch out for these rip-offs: a tour bus that spends the first hour or two of your 'tour' circulating through the city to various hotels, picking up tour participants; a tour that includes an extended stop at some particular shop (from which the tour company or guide gets a kickback); a tour that includes a lunch which turns out to be mediocre. Most of the time, it is a lot cheaper and quicker to see things on your own by bus, dolmuş, or even taxi. Tours can cost US$20 to US$40 per person; you can probably hire a taxi and driver for the entire day for less than that, after a bit of haggling.

İstanbul

For many centuries this city was the capital of the civilised world. Even though Ankara became the capital of the newly proclaimed Turkish republic in 1922, İstanbul continues to be the Turkish metropolis. It is the largest city (about six million people), the business and cultural centre, the largest port and the first destination for tourists, Turkish or foreign.

In recent years İstanbul has yielded some of its pre-eminence to up-and-coming towns such as Ankara, İzmir and Adana. However, it is still, without doubt, the heartbeat of the Turkish spirit. For Ankara, the up-tempo, 20th-century capital city, Turks feel pride; but it is İstanbul, the well-worn but still glorious metropolis, which they love. Its place in the country's history, folklore, commerce and culture is unchallenged.

The First Glimpse

No matter how you arrive, you'll be impressed. The train skirts the southern coast of the Thracian peninsula, following the city walls until it comes around Seraglio Point and terminates right below Topkapı Palace. The bus comes in along an expressway built on the path of the Roman road. From the bus station, you'll approach the city walls and pass through the Topkapı (Cannon Gate, not to be confused with the palace of the same name). Flying in on a clear day may reveal the great mosques and palaces, the wide Bosphorus (Boğaziçi, boh-AHZ-ee-chee, 'Inside the throat') and the narrower Golden Horn (Haliç), in a wonderful panorama.

But nothing beats 'sailing to Byzantium' – gliding across the Sea of Marmara, watching the slender minarets and bulbous mosque domes rise on the horizon. Even Mark Twain, who certainly had control of his emotions, waxed rhapsodic in his *Innocents Abroad* on the beauties of arriving by sea. Today, though a cloud of fumes from fossil fuels may obscure the view a bit, it's still impressive. (If you take the boat-train from İzmir via Bandırma, or the ferry from Bursa and Yalova, you'll approach the city by sea.)

İstanbul has grown ferociously in the past decade, and now sprawls westward as far as the airport, 23 km from the centre, northward halfway to the Black Sea, and eastward deep into Anatolia. It is crowded. The Bosphorus, the strait which connects the Black Sea and the Sea of Marmara, is more than 1½ km wide, and the narrower Golden Horn, a freshwater estuary, also helps to preserve a sense of openness and space. More than that, the Bosphorus provides an uncrowded maritime highway for transport to various sections of the city. For several thousand years before the construction of the Bosphorus Bridge (1973), the only way to go between the European and Asian parts of the city was by boat. The second Bosphorus bridge, named Fatih Köprüsü, north of the first one, was finished in 1988. A third bridge, farther north, is in the works.

As an introduction to Turkey and the Turks, İstanbul is something of a rich diet – too rich for some people. You might enjoy the city more if you come here after having first seen some smaller, more comprehensible and easily manageable Turkish town, such as Edirne or a port on the Aegean Sea.

History

İstanbul today is interesting as the

Turkish metropolis, but nobody visits just for that reason when the city is 3000 years old. The greatest part of the city's fascination comes from its place in history and from the buildings that remain from ancient times. Without knowing something of its history, a tour of İstanbul's ancient monuments will leave you impressed but bewildered.

Here's a quick summary of its past, so that you'll be able to distinguish a hippodrome from a harem.

1000 to 657 BC Ancient fishing villages on this site.
657 BC to 330 AD Byzantium, a Greek city-state, later subject to Rome.
330 to 1453 AD Constantinople, the 'New Rome', capital of the Later Roman ('Byzantine') Empire. Reached its height in the 1100s.
1453 to 1922 İstanbul, capital of the Ottoman Turkish Empire, which reached the height of its glory in the 1500s.
1922 to 1984 Ankara becomes the capital of the Turkish Republic. İstanbul continues to be the country's largest city and port, and its commercial and cultural centre.
1984 to Present İstanbul begins to enjoy a renaissance as 'capital of the East'. A new municipal government undertakes vast schemes to modernise and beautify the city, and to attract international business operations. New parks, museums and cultural centres are opened, old ones are restored and refurbished.

Early Times The earliest settlement, Semistra, was probably around 1000 BC, a few hundred years after the Trojan War and in the same period that kings David and Solomon ruled in Jerusalem.

This was followed by a fishing village named Lygos, which occupied Seraglio Point where Topkapı Palace stands today. Later, about 700 BC, colonists from Megara (near Corinth) in Greece settled at Chalcedon (now Kadıköy), on the Asian shore of the Bosphorus.

Byzantium The first settlement to have historic significance was founded by another Megarian colonist, a fellow named Byzas. Before leaving Greece, he asked the oracle at Delphi where he should establish his new colony. The enigmatic answer was 'Opposite the blind'. When Byzas and his fellow colonists sailed up the Bosphorus, they noticed the colony on the Asian shore at Chalcedon. Looking to their left, they saw the superb natural harbour of the Golden Horn, on the European shore. Thinking, as legend has it, 'Those people in Chalcedon must be blind', they settled on the opposite shore, on the site of Lygos, and named their new city Byzantium. This was in 657 BC.

The legend might as well be true. İstanbul's location on the waterway linking the Sea of Marmara and Black Sea, and on the 'land bridge' linking Europe and Asia, is still of tremendous importance today, 2600 years after the oracle spoke. The Megarian colonists at Chalcedon must certainly have been blind to have missed such a site.

Byzantium submitted willingly to Rome and fought Rome's battles for centuries, but finally got caught supporting the wrong side in a civil war. The winner, Septimius Severus, razed the city walls and took away its privileges (196 AD). When he relented and rebuilt the city, he named it Augusta Antonina.

Constantinople Another struggle for control of the Roman Empire determined the city's fate for the next 1000 years. Constantine pursued his rival Licinius to Augusta Antonina, then across the Bosphorus to Chrysopolis (Üsküdar). Defeating his rival (324 AD), Constantine solidified his control and declared this city to be 'New Rome'. He laid out a vast new city to serve as capital of his empire, and inaugurated it with much pomp in 330 AD. The place which had been first settled as a fishing village over 1000 years earlier was now the capital of the world, and would remain so for almost another 1000 years.

The Later Roman, or Byzantine, Empire lasted from the re-founding of the city in 330 AD to the Ottoman Turkish conquest in 1453, an impressive 1123 years. A lot remains of ancient Constantinople, and you'll be able to visit churches, palaces, cisterns and the Hippodrome during your stay. In fact, there's more of Constantinople left than anyone knows about. Any sort of excavation reveals streets, mosaics, tunnels, water and sewer systems, houses and public buildings. Construction of a modern building may be held up for months while archaeologists investigate. Rediscovering Byzantium, to a modern real-estate developer, is an unmitigated disaster.

The Conquest Westerners usually refer to 'The Fall of Constantinople', whereas to Muslims it was 'The Conquest of İstanbul'. Though the Byzantine Empire had been moribund for several centuries, the Ottomans were quite content to accept tribute from the weak Byzantine emperor as they progressively captured all the lands which surrounded his well-fortified city. By the time of the conquest, the emperor had control over little more than the city itself and a few territories in Greece.

When Mehmet II, 'the Conqueror' (*Fatih*), came to power in 1451 as a young man, he needed an impressive military victory to solidify his dominance of the powerful noble class. As the Ottomans controlled all of Anatolia and most of the Balkans by this time, it was obvious that the great city should be theirs. Mehmet decided it should be sooner rather than later.

The story of the conquest is thrilling, full of bold strokes and daring exploits, heroism, treachery and intrigue. Mehmet started by readying the two great fortresses on the Bosphorus. Rumeli Hisar, the larger one, on the European side, was built in an incredibly short three

months. Anadolu Hisar, the smaller one on the Asian side, had been built half a century earlier by Yıldırım Beyazıt, so Mehmet had it repaired and brought to readiness. Together they controlled the strait's narrowest point.

The Byzantines had closed the mouth of the Golden Horn with a heavy chain to prevent Ottoman boats from sailing in and attacking the city walls on the north side. In another bold stroke, Mehmet marshalled his boats at a cove (now covered by Dolmabahçe Palace) and had them transported overland on rollers and slides, by night, up the valley (where the Hilton now stands) and down the other side into the Golden Horn at Kasım Paşa. He caught the Byzantine defenders completely by surprise and soon had the Golden Horn under control.

The last great obstacle was the mighty bastion of the land walls on the western side. No matter how Mehmet's cannons battered them by day, the Byzantines would rebuild them by night, and the impetuous young sultan would find himself back where he started come daybreak. Then he received a proposal. A Hungarian cannon founder named Urban had come to offer his services to the Byzantine emperor, for the defence of Christendom, to repel the infidel. Finding that the emperor had no money, he went to Mehmet and offered to make the most enormous cannon ever. Mehmet, who had lots of money, accepted the offer, and the cannon was cast and tested in Edirne.

The first shot, which terrified hundreds of peasants, sent a huge ball 1½ km, where it buried itself two metres in the ground. The jubilant sultan had his new toy transported to the front lines and set to firing. A special crew worked hours to ready it for each shot, for every firing wrecked the mount, and the gun had to be cooled with buckets of water.

Despite the inevitability of the conquest, the emperor refused surrender terms offered by Mehmet on 23 May 1453, preferring to wait in hope that Christendom would come and save him. On 28 May the final attack began, and by the evening of the 29th Mehmet's troops were in control of every quarter. The emperor, Constantine XI Dragases, died in battle fighting on the walls.

Mehmet's triumphant entry into 'the world's greatest city' on the evening of 29 May is commemorated every year in İstanbul. Those parts of the city which did not resist his troops were spared, and their churches guaranteed to them. Those that resisted were sacked for the customary three days, and the churches turned into mosques. As for Sancta Sophia, the greatest church in Christendom (St Peter's in Rome was not begun until 1506), it was converted immediately into a mosque.

The Ottoman Centuries Mehmet the Conqueror began at once to rebuild and repopulate the city. He saw himself as the successor to the glories and powers of Constantine, Justinian and the other great emperors who had reigned here. He built a mosque (Fatih Camii) on one of the city's seven hills, repaired the walls and made İstanbul the administrative, commercial and cultural centre of his growing empire.

Süleyman the Magnificent (1520-1566) was perhaps İstanbul's greatest builder. His mosque, the Süleymaniye (1550), is Turkey's largest. Other sultans added more grand mosques, and in the 19th century numerous palaces were built along the Bosphorus: Çirağan, Dolmabahçe, Yıldız, Beylerbeyi, Küçük Su.

As the Ottoman Empire grew to include all of the Middle East and North Africa as well as half of eastern Europe, İstanbul became a fabulous melting pot. On its streets and in its bazaars, people spoke Turkish, Greek, Armenian, Ladino, Russian, Arabic, Bulgarian, Rumanian, Albanian, Italian, French, German, English and Maltese. The parade of national costumes was no less varied.

However, from being the most civilised city on earth in the time of Süleyman, the city and the empire declined. By the 19th century it had lost some of its former glory, though it was still the 'Paris of the East'. Its importance was reaffirmed by the first great international luxury express train ever run, which connected İstanbul with Paris – the famous Orient Express.

Republican İstanbul Atatürk's campaign for national salvation and independence was directed from Ankara. The founder of the Turkish Republic decided to get away from the imperial memories of İstanbul, and also to set up the new government in a city which could not easily be threatened by gunboats. Robbed of its importance as the capital of a vast empire, İstanbul lost a lot of its wealth and glitter. From being the East's most cosmopolitan place, it relaxed into a new role as an important national, rather than international, city. But during the 1980s it began to return to its former role. More liveable than Cairo or Beirut, more attractive than Tel Aviv, more in touch with the Islamic world than Athens, it is fast becoming the 'capital' of the eastern Mediterranean again.

Orientation

It's a daunting prospect to arrive in a strange city of more than six million people whose language is a complete mystery to you. In general, Turks are friendly and helpful, even amidst the frustrations of a language barrier. It shouldn't take you long to get set up in a suitable hotel.

The first thing you'll see in İstanbul will be the impressive skyline of the Old City. It will take you at least three days to get around and see the major sights. You can easily spend a week at it, for İstanbul offers a great deal to see.

The sightseeing plan here is organised to show you the most important and accessible sights first, so you can see as much as possible in even a short time. If you have a week, you should be able to see just about everything described.

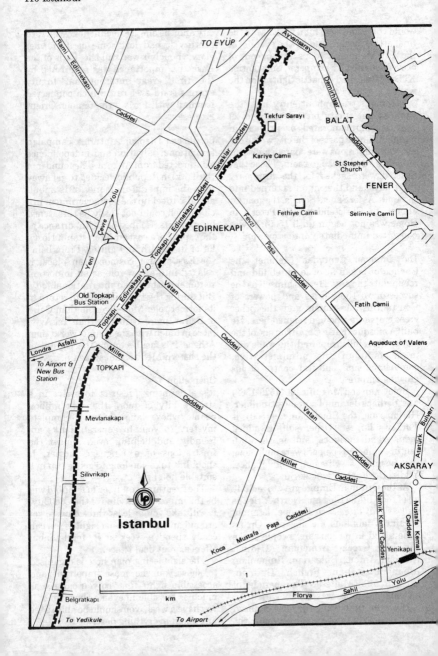

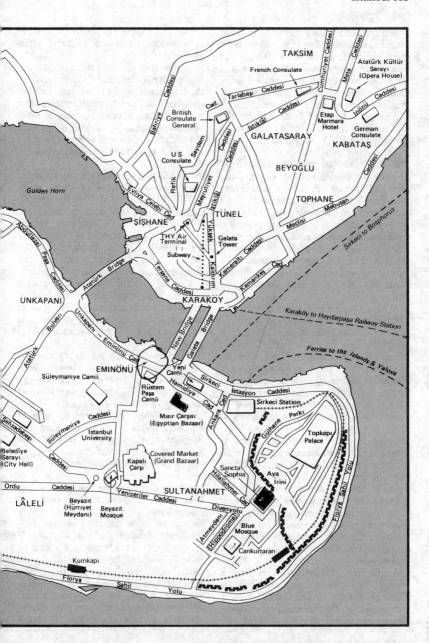

TAKSİM

French Consulate

Atatürk Kültür Sarayı (Opera House)

Tarlabaşı Caddesi

Cumhuriyet Caddesi

Mete Caddesi

İnönü Caddesi

British Consulate General

Bahriye Caddesi

Cad.

İstiklâl

Caddesi

Etap Marmara Hotel

German Consulate

U S Consulate

Saydam

Refik

Meşrutiyet Caddesi

İstiklâl Caddesi

GALATASARAY

BEYOĞLU

KABATAŞ

Caddesi

Golden Horn

Evliya Çelebi Cad

TÜNEL

TOPHANE

Meclisi

Mebusan

ŞİŞHANE

THY Air Terminal

Subway

Galata Tower

Yüksek

Kaldırım

Kemeraltı Caddesi

Kemankeş Cad

Sirkeci to Bosphorus

Abdülezel Paşa Caddesi

Atatürk Bridge

Tersane Caddesi

KARAKÖY

Karaköy to Haydarpaşa Railway Station

UNKAPANI

Unkapanı - Eminönü Cad.

Bulvarı

New Bridge

Galata Bridge

Ferries to the Islands & Yalova

Atatürk

Süleymaniye Camii

EMINÖNÜ

Yeni Camii

Hamidiye

Sirkeci

İstasyon Caddesi

Rüstem Paşa Camii

Antara Cad

Sirkeci Station

Parkı

Şehzadebaşı

Süleymaniye Caddesi

İstanbul University

Mısır Çarşısı (Egyptian Bazaar)

Gülhane

Topkapı Palace

Belediye Sarayı (City Hall)

Caddesi

Covered Market (Grand Bazaar)

Kapalı Çarşı

Sancta Sophia

Aya İrini

Ordu Caddesi

Yeniceriler Caddesi

Hilaliahmer Cad

SULTANAHMET

Florya Sahil Yolu

LÂLELİ

Beyazıt (Hürriyet Meydanı)

Beyazıt Mosque

Divanyolu

Atmeydanı (Hippodrome)

Blue Mosque

Cankurtaran

Kumkapı

Florya

Sahil

Yolu

A glance at the map will show you that İstanbul is divided down the middle, from north to south, by the wide strait of the Bosphorus. The areas of prime attraction for hotels, restaurants and sightseeing are in the European portion of the city, on the western shore of the Bosphorus.

European İstanbul is divided by the Golden Horn into the Old City to the south and Beyoğlu (BEY-oh-loo) to the north.

Old City This is ancient Byzantium/ Constantinople/İstanbul. It's here, from Seraglio Point (*Saray Burnu*) jutting into the Bosphorus to the mammoth land walls some seven km eastward, that you'll find the great palaces and mosques, hippodromes and monumental columns, ancient churches and the Covered Market. The Old City also harbours the best areas for inexpensive and moderate hotel choices: Laleli near Aksaray, and Sultanahmet.

When referring to the Old City, Turks usually mention the name of a particular district such as Sultanahmet, Aksaray or Beyazıt. They do not say Stamboul, as Europeans sometimes do. Nor do they use the term Old City – in Turkish this is Eskişehir which is also the name of a completely different municipality hundreds of km away in Anatolia. Get used to asking for a district, not for a Stamboul.

Beyoğlu North of the Golden Horn is Beyoğlu, the Turkish name for the two old cities of Pera and Galata, or roughly all the land from the Golden Horn to Taksim Square. Here is where you'll find the Hilton, the Sheraton and other luxury hotels; airline offices and banks; the European consulates and hospitals; Taksim Square, the very hub of European İstanbul; and the 19th-century palace of Dolmabahçe.

Under the Byzantines, this was a separate city built and inhabited by Genoese traders. Called Galata then, it extended from the shore up to the Galata Tower, which still stands and which now

serves as a convenient landmark. Galata is now usually called Karaköy (KAHR-ah-keuy).

Under the sultans, the non-Muslim European population of Galata spread up the hill and along the ridge, founding the sister city of Pera. In modern times this part of the city has been the fastest growing and has stretched far beyond the limits of old Galata and Pera. The name Beyoğlu still refers to just those two old cities.

Galata Bridge One landmark you will get to know at once is the Galata Köprüsü (gahl-AH-TAH KEUP-reu-seu, Galata Bridge). Connecting Karaköy with Eminönü (eh-MEEN-eu-neu), it is İstanbul's jugular vein, always packed with traffic and lively with activity. Views of the Old City, Beyoğlu, the Golden Horn and the Bosphorus are fantastic from the bridge.

The old, floating pontoon bridge here since the beginning of the century, is being augmented by a new bridge. The plan at present is for vehicles to use the new bridge, while the old one is reserved for pedestrians.

Karaköy and Eminönü, by the way, are the areas from which Bosphorus ferries depart. The ferries from Karaköy go exclusively to Haydarpaşa Station and Kadıköy (a lighted signboard tells you which one is the destination); ferries from the Eminönü side go to Üsküdar, the Bosphorus, the Princes' Islands and Yalova. See Getting Around at the end of this chapter for more information.

The Asian Side The Asian part of the city, on the eastern shore of the Bosphorus, is of less interest to tourists, being mostly bedroom suburbs such as Üsküdar (EU-skeu-dahr, Scutari) and Kadıköy (KAH-duh-keuy). One landmark you'll want to know about is Haydarpaşa İstasyonu (HIGH-dahr-pah-shah ee-stahs-yohn-oo), right between Üsküdar and Kadıköy. This is the terminus for Anatolian trains, which means any Turkish train except the one from Europe via Edirne. If you're headed for Ankara, Cappadocia or any point east of İstanbul, you'll board at Haydarpaşa.

Information

Most museums are closed on Monday, but some – including the most important one of all, Topkapı Palace – are closed on Tuesday instead; Dolmabahçe Palace is closed on both Monday and Thursday at present, but I expect that this may change. Holders of International Student Identity Cards are no longer admitted free to sites controlled by the Ministry of Tourism. Only a few scattered sites in Turkey now grant reductions to foreign students. Usually, you may pay the 'student' entry fee only if you have Turkish student identification.

Tourist Offices The Ministry of Tourism maintains several Tourism Information Offices in the city. Besides the ones at Atatürk Airport (tel 573-7399, 573-4136) and the Karaköy Yolcu Salonu (International Maritime Passenger Terminal, tel 149-5776), there is a third office at the western end of the Hippodrome in Sultanahmet Square (tel 522-4903), near the Blue Mosque, Sancta Sophia and Topkapı Palace (open from 9 am to 5 pm daily).

In Beyoğlu, the office is in the Hilton Hotel arcade (tel 133-0592), just off Cumhuriyet Caddesi (open from 9 am to 5 pm, closed Sunday). Get to Taksim Square, ask for 'joom-hoor-ee-YEHT jad-dess-see' or simply 'HEEL-tohn oh-tehl-ee', walk two rather long blocks in the direction indicated, and you'll see the Hilton arcade, with the hotel behind it, on the right-hand side of the street.

Post İstanbul's Central Post Office is in the section called Eminönü, several blocks west of Sirkeci Railway Station. Other convenient PTT branches are located in Taksim, Galatasaray, Aksaray and the Covered Market.

Banks For information on banks, see the Money section in the Facts for the Visitor chapter.

OLD İSTANBUL

In the Old City, Topkapı Palace is right next to Sancta Sophia, which is right next to the Blue Mosque, which is right on the Hippodrome, which is right next to the Cistern Basilica, which is only a few steps from the museum complex, which is right next to Topkapı Palace. You can spend at least two days just completing this loop. Start with the palace, which is among the world's greatest museums.

You can get there from Aksaray and Laleli by dolmuş, by bus or on foot along Ordu Caddesi, which changes its name to Yeniçeriler Caddesi, and finally to Divan Yolu. Ask the driver if he's going to Sultanahmet. From Taksim it's a bit more difficult. Get a dolmuş to Sirkeci and walk up the hill for 10 minutes (take a short cut to the palace through Gülhane Park); or take a T1 or T4 circle route bus, which stops right in Sultanahmet. The dolmuş is faster.

Topkapı Palace

Topkapı Sarayı (TOHP-kahp-uh sah-rah-yuh) or Topkapı Palace was the residence of the sultans for almost three centuries. Mehmet the Conqueror built the first palace shortly after the Conquest in 1453, and lived here until his death in 1481. Sultan after sultan played out the drama of the Ottoman sovereign here until the 19th century. Mahmut II (1808-1839) was the last emperor to occupy the palace. After him, the sultans preferred to live in new European-style palaces – Dolmabahçe, Çirağan, Yıldız – which they built on the Bosphorus. Under the republic, the palace became Turkey's finest museum.

The palace is called the Seraglio by foreigners, an Italian word for the Turkish *saray* (palace). Mozart's famous opera 'Abduction from the Seraglio' is performed

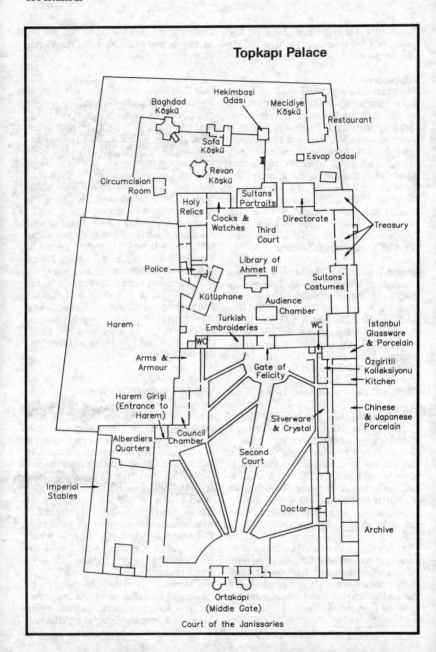

Topkapı Palace

Baghdad Köşkü

Hekimbaşi Odası

Mecidiye Köşkü

Restaurant

Sofa Köşkü

Revan Köşkü

Esvap Odasi

Circumcision Room

Holy Relics

Sultans' Portraits

Clocks & Watches

Directorate

Treasury

Third Court

Police

Library of Ahmet III

Sultans' Costumes

Kütüphane

Audience Chamber

Harem

Turkish Embroideries

İstanbul Glassware & Porcelain

WC

WC

Arms & Armour

Gate of Felicity

Özgiritli Kolleksiyonu

Kitchen

Harem Girişi (Entrance to Harem)

Council Chamber

Silverware & Crystal

Chinese & Japanese Porcelain

Alberdiers Quarters

Second Court

Imperial Stables

Doctor

Archive

Ortakapı (Middle Gate)

Court of the Janissaries

in the palace every summer during the İstanbul International Festival.

It will take you the better part of a day to explore Topkapı Palace (tel 512-0480). You should be at the door when it opens if you plan to visit in the busy summer months. Though it's tempting to nip into Sancta Sophia for a look as you go by on your way to Topkapı, I strongly recommend that you resist the urge. Sancta Sophia has been there for 1500 years, and it will be there when you come out of Topkapı.

Topkapı Palace is open from 9.30 am to 7 pm during July and August, till 5 pm the rest of the year; closed Tuesday. Admission to the palace costs US$7; you will buy a separate ticket for the Harem tour (US$2) at the Harem entrance as you begin the tour. I suggest that you head straight for the Harem when you enter the palace, note the tour times posted on the board by the entry, buy your ticket, and return in time to catch the next tour.

In summer this may not work; the crowds are so thick and the tour groups so numerous that individual travellers sometimes are out of luck as the groups book all of the Harem tours in advance. I expect that in seasons to come the palace (and the Harem) will have to remain open on Tuesday in order to accommodate the crowds. Also, it may be possible to schedule a Harem tour with a private guide. The cost is about US$8 for a group of six or so. Ask at the Harem ticket kiosk.

Court of the Janissaries Topkapı grew and changed with the centuries, but its basic four-courtyard plan remained the same. As you pass through the great gate behind Sancta Sophia, you enter the first court, the Court of the Janissaries. On your left is the former **Aya İrini Kilisesi** or Church of Divine Peace (tel 520-6952), Sarayiçi 35, now a concert hall where recitals are given during the İstanbul International Festival, and soon perhaps to be a museum dedicated to Atatürk's life and career.

There was a Christian church here from earliest times, and before that a pagan temple. The early church was replaced by the present one during the reign of the Byzantine emperor Justinian in the 540s, so the church you see is as old as Sancta Sophia. When Mehmet the Conqueror began building his palace, the church was within the grounds and thus couldn't be used for worship. Ironically, it was used as an arsenal for centuries, then as an artillery museum.

The large Court of the Janissaries, stretching from the church to the Middle Gate, is now a shady park and tour bus parking area, but in the old days this was where the sultan's elite corps of guards gathered to eat the hearty pilav provided by him. When they were dissatisfied with the sultan's rule (which meant his treatment of them), they would overturn the great cauldrons of pilav as a symbol of revolt. After that the sultan usually didn't last too long. Food was the most important symbol – so important, in fact, that the Janissary corps was organised on commissary lines. Some of the officers had kitchen titles, and the corps was called the *ocak*, 'hearth' or 'cookfire'.

'Janissary' comes from *yeni çeri* (YEHN-ee chehr-ee), 'new levies'. These soldiers were personal servants of the sultan, 'owned' by him, paid regularly and fed by him, and subject to his will. They were full-time soldiers in an age when most soldiers were farmers in spring and autumn, homebodies in winter, and warriors only in summer.

The Janissaries were mostly recruited as boys of 10 years old from Christian families in the Balkans. Though Islam forbids the enslavement or forcible conversion of Christians and Jews, the Balkans were looked upon as an exception. Saints Cyril and Methodius, 'Apostles to the Slavs', converted the pagan Slavic peoples to Christianity in the 800s, after the revelation of the Koran to Muhammed. So it was very convenient for the Ottoman religious authorities to rule that Slavic Christians 'had made the wrong choice' in converting to Christianity. Since they had been pagans when the Koran was revealed, they could be enslaved now.

The boys were taught Turkish and were instructed in Islam. The brightest went into the palace service, and many eventually rose to the highest offices, including grand vizier. This ensured that the top government posts were always held by 'slaves' of the sultan. Those not quite so bright made up the Janissary corps. More than once, in the later years of the empire, they proved that the sultan was their 'slave', and not the other way around.

The reforming sultan, Mahmut II, decided to do away with this dangerous and corrupted palace guard in 1826. Risking his throne, his life and his dynasty, he readied a new, loyal European-style army, then provoked a revolt of the Janissaries and wiped them out, ending their 3½ centuries in this courtyard headquarters.

Janissaries, merchants and tradespeople could circulate as they wished in the Court of the Janissaries, but the second court was different. The same is in a way true today, because you must buy your tickets before entering the second court. The ticket booths are on your right as you approach the entrance. Just past them is a little fountain where the imperial executioner used to wash the tools of his trade after decapitating a noble or rebel who had displeased the sultan. The head of the unfortunate was put on a pike and exhibited above the gate you're about to enter.

Ortakapı & Second Court The Ortakapı ('Middle Gate', also called the Gate of Greeting) led to the palace's second court, used for the business of running the empire. Only the sultan was allowed through the Ortakapı on horseback. Everyone else, including the grand vizier, had to dismount. The gate you see was constructed by Süleyman the Magnificent in 1524, utilising architects and workers he had brought back from his conquest of Hungary.

Within the second court is a beautiful, park-like setting. You'll see at once that Topkapı is not a palace on the European plan, one large building with outlying gardens. Rather, it is a series of pavilions, kitchens, barracks, audience chambers, kiosks and sleeping quarters built around a central enclosure, much like a fortified camp. It is a delightful castle and palace all in one.

As you walk into the second court, the great **palace kitchens** will be on your right. They now contain a small portion of Topkapı's incredibly large and varied collection of Chinese celadon porcelain. The greater part of the collection, which is quite vast, is in storage. Another room holds a fine collection of European and especially interesting Ottoman porcelain and glassware. The last of the kitchens, the Helvahane in which all the palace sweets were made, is now set up as a kitchen, and you can easily imagine what went on in these rooms as the staff prepared food for the 5000 inhabitants of the palace.

On the left side of the second court is the ornate **Kubbealtı** or Imperial Council Chamber where the grand vizier met with the Imperial Divan (council) on matters of state. The sultan did not participate in these discussions, but kept track sometimes by sitting behind a screen and listening. Kubbealtı means 'beneath the cupola'. The squarish tower which is one of Topkapı's most noticeable features is just above the Council Chamber.

Harem The entrance to the Harem is just behind the Kubbealtı. You will have to buy a ticket and take the guided tour. Tour times are listed on a board at the Harem ticket office. A little snacks and drinks stand here serves refreshments to those waiting for the tour. It's a good idea to see the Harem as soon as possible, because it is open only from 10 am to 4 pm. Reserve your place for the Harem tour before visiting the other parts of the

palace. Make sure the guide will be speaking a language that you understand.

Fraught with legend and wild romance, the Harem is everything that you've imagined, even though the legends and stories are not really quite true.

The usual stereotype has an army of gorgeous women petting and caressing, amusing and entertaining, and doing their best to exhaust, a very pampered man. Well, there's no denying that the sultan had it good, but every detail of Harem life was governed by tradition, obligation and ceremony. The sultan could not, unfortunately, just leap into a roomful of beauties and go to it.

Every traditional Muslim household had two distinct parts: the *selamlık* ('greeting room') where the master greeted friends, business associates and tradespeople; and the *harem* ('private apartments'), reserved for himself and his family. The Harem, then, was something akin to the private apartments in Buckingham Palace or the White House. The selamlık was what outsiders saw when they visited.

The women of the Harem had to be foreigners, as Islam forbade enslaving Muslims, Christians or Jews (Christians and Jews could be enslaved if taken as war prisoners, or if bought as slaves in a legitimate slave market). Besides war prisoners, girls were bought as slaves (often sold by their parents at a good price), or received as gifts from nobles and potentates. A favourite source of girls was Circassia, north of the Caucasus Mountains in Russia, as Circassian women were noted for their beauty, and parents were often glad to sell their 10-year-old girls.

Upon entering the Harem, the girls would be schooled in Islam and Turkish culture and language, plus such arts as make-up and dress, music, reading and writing, embroidery and dancing. They then entered a meritocracy, first as ladies-in-waiting to the sultan's concubines and children, then to the sultan's mother and finally, if they were good enough, to the sultan himself.

Ruler of the Harem was the 'valide sultan' or queen mother, the mother of the reigning sultan. She often owned large landed estates in her own name and controlled them through black eunuch servants. She was allowed to give orders directly to the grand vizier. Her influence on the sultan, on the selection of his wives and concubines, and on matters of state, was very great.

The sultan was allowed by Islamic law to have four legitimate wives, who received the title of *kadın* (wife). If one bore him a child, she was called 'haseki sultan' if it was a son, 'haseki kadın' if it was a daughter. Each lady of the Harem would do almost anything to get her son proclaimed heir to the throne, thus assuring her own role as the new valide sultan. (The Ottoman dynasty did not observe primogeniture, succession by the first-born son. The throne was basically up for grabs to any imperial son.)

As for concubines, Islam permits as many as a man can support in proper style. The Ottoman sultan could support a lot. Some of the early sultans had as many as 300 concubines, though not all in the Harem at the same time. The domestic thrills of the sultans were usually less spectacular. Mehmet the Conqueror, builder of Topkapı, was the last sultan to have the four official wives. After him, sultans did not officially marry, but instead kept four chosen concubines without the legal encumbrances, thereby saving themselves the embarrassments and inconveniences suffered by another famous Renaissance monarch, Henry VIII.

The Harem was much like a small village with all the necessary services. About 400 or 500 people lived in this distinct section of the palace at any one time. Not many of the ladies stayed in the Harem forever: sometimes the sultan granted them their freedom, and they were snapped up as wives by powerful men who wanted the company of these supremely graceful and intelligent women, not to mention their connections with the palace.

The 'kızlarağası ' (kuhz-LAHR-ah-ah-suh, chief black eunuch), was the sultan's personal representative in the running of the Harem and other important affairs of state. In fact, he was the third most powerful official in the empire, after the grand vizier and the supreme Islamic judge.

The imperial princes were brought up in the Harem, taught and cared for by the women. The tradition of the *kafes* (kah-FESS, cage) was one of many things which led to the decline of the great empire. In the early centuries imperial princes were schooled in combat and statecraft by direct experience: they practised soldiering, fought in battles and were given provinces to administer.

In the later centuries they spent their lives more or less imprisoned in the Harem, where the sultan could keep an eye on them and prevent any move to dethrone him. This meant that the princes were prey to the intrigues of the women and eunuchs; and when one of them did succeed to the throne he was corrupted by the pleasures of the Harem, and completely ignorant of war and statecraft. Luckily for the empire in this latter period, there were very able generals and grand viziers to carry on.

When you walk into the Harem, think of it as the family quarters; as a place of art, culture and refinement; and as a political entity subject to intense manoeuvring and intrigue. Much of it was constructed during the reign of Süleyman the Magnificent (1520-1566), but a lot was added over the years.

The door through which you enter was for tradespeople, who brought their wares here to the black eunuch guards. The tilework in the second room is some of Turkey's finest: the green and yellow colours are unusual in İznik faïence (tin-glazed earthenware). A corridor leads past the rooms of the black eunuchs who guarded the sultan's ladies. In the early days white eunuchs were used, but black eunuchs sent as presents by the Ottoman governor of Egypt later took control. As many as 200 lived here, guarding the doors and waiting on the women.

The sultan, when he walked these corridors, wore slippers with silver soles. They were noisy, and that was the point: no woman was allowed to show herself to the 'imperial regard' without specific orders. When they heard the clatter of silver on stone, they all ran to hide. This rule no doubt solidified the valide sultan's control: *she* would choose the girls to be presented to the sultan. There was to be no flirting in the hallways.

You enter a small courtyard, around which were the private apartments of the four kadıns. A larger courtyard beyond was the domain of the valide sultan. Besides being the centre of power in the Harem, this was where each new sultan came after accession to the throne, to receive the allegiance and congratulations of the people of the Harem.

The sultan's private Turkish bath is next. His mother and his four wives each had their own private bath. Other private baths went to the lady responsible for discipline in the Harem and to her assistant, the treasurer. After that, all the women shared common baths.

Next you enter a few of the sultan's private chambers. There is a 17th-century room with a beautifully decorated fireplace, and a reception room with a fountain. Here the sultan received the ladies of the Harem, or his married female relatives – sisters, cousins and aunts. The fountain obscured the sounds of their conversation so that no one, in this hotbed of intrigue, could eavesdrop.

The sultan's private chamber was first built by Sinan, Süleyman the Magnificent's great architect, but the present decor dates from the 18th century.

Sultan Ahmet I (1603-1617), builder of the Blue Mosque, added a nice little library. In 1705 his successor Ahmet III added the pretty dining room with all the appetising bowls of fruit painted on the walls.

The Veliaht Dairesi is the 'cage', or

apartment of the crown prince, where in later centuries he was kept secluded from the world. Note the ingenious little fountains in the windows and the leather-covered domed ceiling. Next to the crown prince's suite are the sumptuous rooms of his mother, the haseki sultan.

These are the last rooms you see on the tour. You exit into the third, innermost courtyard.

Third Court If you enter the Third Court through the Harem, and thus by the back door, you should head for the main gate into the court. Get the full effect of entering this holy of holies by going out through the gate, and back in again.

This gate, the **Bab-i Saadet** or Gate of Felicity, also sometimes called the Akağalar Kapısı, or Gate of the White Eunuchs, was the entrance into the sultan's private domain. A new sultan, after girding on the sword which symbolised imperial power, would sit enthroned before this gate and receive the congratulations and allegiance of the empire's high and mighty. Before the annual military campaigns in summertime, the sultan would appear before this gate bearing the standard of the Prophet Muhammed to inspire his generals to go out and win for Islam. Today the Bab-i Saadet is the backdrop for the annual performance of Mozart's 'Abduction from the Seraglio' during the İstanbul International Festival in late June and early July.

The Third Court was staffed and guarded by white eunuchs, who allowed only very few, very important people to enter. Just inside the Bab-i Saadet is the **Arz Odası** or Audience Chamber. The sultan preserved the imperial mystique by appearing in public very seldom. To conduct official business, important officials and foreign ambassadors came to this little room. An ambassador, frisked for weapons and held on each arm by a white eunuch, would approach the sultan. At the proper moment, he knelt and

kowtowed; if he didn't, the white eunuchs would urge him ever so strongly to do so. After that, he could speak to the sultan through an interpreter.

The sultan, seated on the divans whose cushions are embroidered with over 15,000 seed pearls, inspected the ambassador's gifts and offerings as they were passed by the small doorway on the left. Even if the sultan and the ambassador could converse in the same language (sultans in the later years knew French, and ambassadors often learned Turkish), all conversation went through an interpreter. One couldn't have just anybody putting words into the imperial ear.

During the great days of the empire, foreign ambassadors were received on days when the Janissaries were to get their pay. Huge sacks of silver coins were brought to the Kubbealtı. High court officers would dispense them to long lines of the tough, impeccably costumed and faultlessly disciplined troops as the ambassadors looked on in admiration. It all worked for a while.

As you stroll into the Third Court, imagine it alive with the movements of imperial pages and white eunuchs scurrying here and there in their palace costumes. Every now and then the chief white eunuch or the chief black eunuch would appear, and all would bow deferentially. If the sultan walked across the courtyard, all activity stopped until the event was over.

Right behind the Arz Odası is the pretty little **Library of Ahmet III** (1718). Walk to the right as you leave the Arz Odası, and enter the rooms which were once the **Turkish baths** of the Third Court staff. They now contain a fascinating collection of imperial robes, kaftans and uniforms worked in thread of silver and gold. You'll be surprised at the oriental, almost Chinese design of these garments. The Turks came originally from the borders of China, and their cultural history was tied closely with that of the Persian Empire and Central Asia. In fact, tribes in China's westernmost province of Shinjiang still speak a dialect of Turkish.

Next to the baths are the chambers of the **Imperial Treasury**. This you won't believe. After a while the display cases filled with rubies, emeralds, jade, pearls and more diamonds than you ever imagined will cause you to think, 'These are not all real, they must be plastic'. They're real.

One of my favourite items in the Imperial Treasury is the solid gold throne of Shah Ismail, encrusted with thousands of precious stones. It was captured by Sultan Selim I (1512-1520) in a war with the Persians. Other thrones are almost as breathtaking. Look also for the tiny figurine of a sultan sitting under a baldachin (canopy). His body is one enormous pearl. The Kaşıkçının Elması or Spoonmaker's Diamond is an 86-carat mammoth surrounded by several dozen smaller stones. But the prize for biggest precious stone goes to the uncut emerald which weighs 3.26 kg.

In the midst of all this heavy-duty show of wealth, don't lose sight of the fact that the craftwork, design and artistry exhibited in many of these items is extraordinary in itself.

Next door to the Treasury is the **Hayat Balkonu** or Balcony of Life. Here the breeze is cool, and it offers a marvellous view of the Bosphorus and the Sea of Marmara.

Fourth Court To reach the palace **restaurant and café**, walk along the rear side of the Third Court and look for the narrow alley which goes north between the buildings. Down the slope and on the right is the **Mecidiye Köşkü** or Kiosk of Sultan Abdül Mecit. Have a look at the view, enter the kiosk and go down the stairs to reach the restaurant. Tour groups fill it up around lunch time, so plan your visit after noon, or at least half an hour before.

Four imperial pleasure domes occupy the north-easternmost part of the palace, sometimes called the gardens, or Fourth

Court. The Mecidiye built by Abdül Mecit (1839-1861), you've already seen as entrance to the restaurant. In the other direction (north-east) is the **Mustafa Paşa Köşkü** or Kiosk of Mustafa Pasha, sometimes called the Sofa Köşkü. Also here is the room of the **hekimbaşı** or chief physician to the sultan, who was always one of the sultan's Jewish subjects.

The gardens around it were once filled with tulips. In fact, the reign of Sultan Ahmet III (1703-1730) is named the Tulip Period because of the rage which spread through the upper classes. Gardens such as this held hundreds of varieties of tulips. Little lamps would be set out among the flowers at night. A new variety of the flower earned its creator fame, money and social recognition. Tulips had been grown in Turkey from very early times, having come originally from Persia. Some bulbs were brought to Holland during the Renaissance. The Dutch, fascinated by the possibilities in the flower, developed and created many varieties, some of which made their way back to Turkey and began the tulip craze there.

Up the stairs at the end of the tulip garden are two of the most enchanting kiosks. Sultan Murat IV (1623-1640) built the **Revan Köşkü** or Erivan Kiosk in 1635 after reclaiming the city of Erivan (now in the Soviet Union) from Persia. He also constructed the **Bağdat Köşkü** or Baghdad Kiosk in 1638 to commemorate his victory over that city. Notice the İznik tiles, the inlay and woodwork, and the views from all around.

Just off the open terrace with the wishing well is the **Sünnet Odası** or Circumcision Room, used for the ritual which admits Muslim boys to manhood. Circumcision is usually performed at the age of nine or 10. Be sure to see the beautiful tile panels.

Back in the Third Court Re-enter the Third Court for a look at yet another set of wonders, the holy relics in the **Hırka-i Saadet** or Suite of the Felicitous Cloak.

These rooms, sumptuously decorated with İznik faïence, in a way constituted a holy of holies. Only the chosen could enter the Third Court, but entry into the Hırka-i Saadet rooms was for the chosen of the chosen on special ceremonial occasions. For in these rooms reside the cloak of the Prophet Muhammed himself, his battle standard, two of his swords, a hair from his beard, a tooth, his footprint and a letter in his own handwriting.

The 'felicitous cloak' itself resides in a golden casket in a special alcove along with the battle standard. This suite of rooms was opened only once a year so that the imperial family could pay homage to the memory of the Prophet on the 15th day of the holy month of Ramazan. Even though anyone, prince or commoner, faithful or infidel, can enter the rooms now, you're supposed to acknowledge the sacred atmosphere by reverent behaviour.

Other exhibits in the Third Court include **Ağalar Camii** or Mosque of the Eunuchs, another little **library**, miniature paintings, imperial seals and arms, clocks, watches and costumes. These exhibits are sometimes moved around or closed to make room for special exhibits. In the room with the seals, notice the graceful, elaborate *tuğra* (TOO-rah, monogram) of the sultans. The tuğra was at the top of any imperial proclamation. It actually contains elaborate calligraphic rendering of the names of the sultan and his father. The formula reads like this: 'Abdül Hamid Khan, son of Abdül Mecit Khan, Ever Victorious'.

Imperial Stables Enter the Imperial Stables (Has Ahırları) from the Second Court, just to the north-east of the main entrance (Ortakapı). Go down the cobbled slope.

The stables are now a museum for the carriages, saddles and other horse-related gear used by the sultans. The usual collection of gold-encrusted coaches, diamond-studded bridles, etc fill the rooms. One gets the impression that the imperial lifestyle was at least soft, even though it had its complications.

As you leave the palace proper through the Ortakapı, you can walk to your right and down the slope to the museums, or straight to Sancta Sophia. I'll assume, for the moment, that you're heading to Sancta Sophia, only a few steps away. Thus you can ignore the taxi drivers who will confront you with ever more original ways of increasing the cost of a simple ride from point A to point B.

Just after you leave the tall gate of the Court of the Janissaries, take a look at the ornate little structure on your left. It's the **Fountain of Ahmet III**, the one who liked tulips so much. Built in 1728, it replaced a Byzantine one at the same spring. There's no water these days, though.

The fancy gate across the road from the fountain was where the Sultan entered Sancta Sophia for his prayers. It led to a special elevated imperial pavilion inside, which you will see when you explore the inside.

Down the narrow street along the palace walls are the **Ayasofya Pansiyonları** or Sancta Sophia Pensions. These are old İstanbul houses which have been rebuilt under the auspices of the Turkish Touring & Automobile Association and now serve as lodgings. The street, Soğukçeşme Sokağı (Street of the Cold Fountain), was named after a little public fountain dedicated in 1800. One of the houses was once the home of Fahri Korutürk, sixth president of the Turkish republic. At the far (western) end of the street is the entrance to the **Restaurant Sarnıç** or Cistern Restaurant, in a restored Byzantine cistern.

Sancta Sophia

The Church of the Divine Wisdom (Hagia Sofia in Greek, Aya Sofya in Turkish) was not named for a saint; *sofia* means wisdom. Emperor Justinian (527-565) had it built as yet another effort to restore the greatness of the Roman Empire. It was completed in 548 and reigned as the

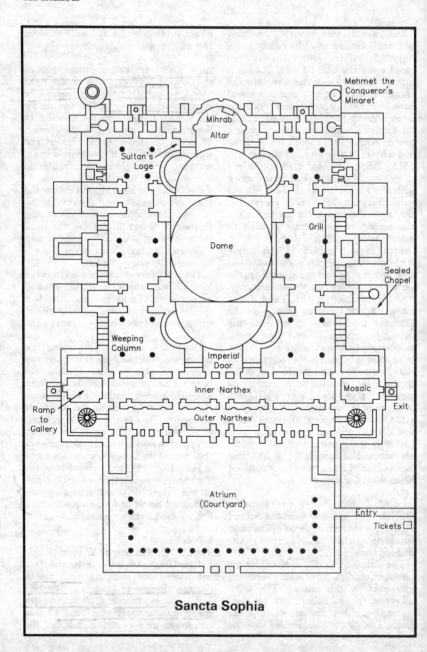

Mehmet the
Conqueror's
Minaret

Mihrab
Altar

Sultan's
Loge

Dome

Grill

Sealed
Chapel

Weeping
Column

Imperial
Door

Inner Narthex

Mosaic

Exit

Ramp
to
Gallery

Outer Narthex

Atrium
(Courtyard)

Entry

Tickets □

Sancta Sophia

greatest church in Christendom until the conquest of Constantinople in 1453. St Peter's in Rome is larger than Sancta Sophia, but it was built more than 1000 years later.

A lot can happen to a building in 1400 years, especially in an earthquake zone, and a lot has certainly happened to Sancta Sophia. But it is still a wonder and a joy to behold. Ignore the clutter of buttresses and supports, kiosks, tombs and outbuildings which hug its massive walls. Try to see the church as it was meant to be seen by its creators.

You can no longer approach the church exactly as a Byzantine would have, walking along a street which led up a hill and straight to the great main door, but you can still marvel at the genius of the architecture. Enter on the side by Sultanahmet, through the open square which was once the Forum of Augustus.

The church was originally a pale rose colour, and this is to be restored during the renovations now under way.

Sancta Sophia (tel 522-0989) is open daily except Mondays, from 9.30 am to 4.30 pm (to 7 pm in July and August); the galleries are open from 9.30 to 11.30 am and from 1 to 4 pm; there's a multivision show at 3 pm daily except Saturday. Entrance costs US$5.

Now, to recapture the feeling that Justinian had when he first entered his great creation, walk down to the main entrance and stop. Here are the sunken ruins of a Theodosian church (404-415), and the low original steps.

If you enter the church slowly, one step at a time, you will at first see only darkness broken by the brilliant colours of stained-glass windows. As your eyes adjust to the dark, two more massive doorways appear, and far beyond them in the dim light, a semi-dome blazing with gold mosaics portraying the Madonna and Child, she as Queen of Heaven. Just inside the threshold of the first door the mosaic is clear and beautiful, and the apse beneath it makes a harmonious whole.

From where you are standing now, the mosaic of Christ as Pantocrator (Ruler of All) above the third and largest door, is visible except for the august expression on the face.

As you approach, the face of the Pantocrator becomes visible, and in the distance you can also see the apse and lofty semi-dome above it which, big as they are, are dwarfed by a gigantic dome above them. At the same time you are facing the Pantocrator in all his majesty.

When you walk through the second door and toward the immense Imperial Door, the 'gigantic dome' turns out to be only another semi-dome. Halfway to the Imperial Door, a row of windows peeks out above the larger semi-dome and betrays the secret. As you approach the Imperial Threshold the magnificent dome soars above you and seems to be held up by nothing. Justinian, when he entered his great creation for the first time, came this far and exclaimed, 'Glory to God that I have been judged worthy of such a work. Oh Solomon! I have outdone you!'

During its years as a church (almost 1000), only imperial processions were permitted to enter through the central, Imperial Door. You can still notice the depressions in the stone by each door just inside the threshold where imperial guards stood. It was through the Imperial Door that Mehmet the Conqueror came in 1453 to take possession for Islam of the greatest religious edifice in the world. Before he entered, so historians tell us, he sprinkled earth on his head in a gesture of humility. Aya Sofya remained a mosque for almost 500 years. In 1935 Atatürk proclaimed it a museum; the wisdom in this decision is apparent when you consider that both devout Muslims and Christians would like to have it as a place of worship for their religions.

There are bigger buildings, and bigger domes, but not without modern construction materials such as reinforced concrete and steel girders. The achievement of the architects, Anthemius of Tralles and Isidorus of Miletus, is unequalled. The dome, constructed of special hollow bricks made in Rhodes of a unique light, porous clay, was a daring attempt at the impossible. The sense of air and space in the nave and the apparent lack of support for the dome made the Byzantines gasp in amazement. Indeed, it almost was impossible, because the dome lasted only 11 years before an earthquake brought it down in 559.

Over the centuries it was necessary for succeeding Byzantine emperors and Ottoman sultans to rebuild the dome several times, to add buttresses and other supports and to steady the foundations. The dome is supported by massive pillars incorporated into the interior walls. In order to appreciate how this works, compare it with the Blue Mosque. And for an acoustic thrill, stand right beneath the centre of the dome and clap your hands.

The Ottoman chandeliers, hanging low above the floor, combined their light with the rows and rows of little oil lamps which lined the balustrades of the gallery and even the walkway at the base of the dome. When all were lit, it must have been an impressive sight.

Justinian ordered the most precious materials for his church. Note the matched marble panels in the walls, and the breccia columns. The Byzantine emperor was crowned while seated in a throne placed within the square of inlaid marble in the main floor. The nearby choir gallery is an Ottoman addition, as is the *mihrab*, or prayer niche, which shows the faithful the direction in which Mecca lies. The large alabaster urns were added by Sultan Murat III (1574-1595) as a place where worshippers could perform their ritual ablutions before prayer.

The large medallions inscribed with gilt Arabic letters were added in the mid-1800s. Calligraphy is a highly prized art in Islam, and these were done by Mustafa İzzet Efendi, a master calligrapher of the time. You'll see these words over and over in Turkish mosques. They are the names of God (Allah), Muhammed and the early caliphs Ali and Abu Bakr.

The curious elevated kiosk, screened from public view, is the Hünkâr Mahfili or Sultan's Loge. Ahmet III (1703-1730) had it built so he could come, pray, and go unseen, preserving the imperial mystique.

If you wander around enough you'll come to the 'weeping column'. A copper facing with a hole in it has been put on a column (to the left after you enter through the Imperial Door). Stick your finger in the hole and make a wish. Legend has it that if the tip of your finger emerges damp, you're supposed to get your wish. If your wish is that a feeling of silliness sweep over you as soon as you poke your finger in the hole, your wish is certain to be fulfilled, damp or dry.

Mosaics Justinian filled his church with gorgeous mosaics. The Byzantine church and state later went through a fierce civil war (726-787) over the question of whether images were to be allowed or not. (The debated biblical passage was Exodus 20:4, 'Thou shalt not make unto thee any graven image, or any likeness of anything that is in heaven above, or that is in the earth beneath, or that is in the water under the earth: Thou shalt not bow down thyself to them, nor serve them.') Though the Bible seems clear, the people liked images a lot, and the iconoclasts ('image-breakers') were defeated. It's interesting to speculate whether iconoclastic Islam, militant and triumphant at this time, had any influence on Byzantine theology.

When the Turks took Constantinople there was no controversy. The Koran repeatedly rails against idolatry, as in Sura 16: 'We sent a Messenger into every nation saying, Serve God and give up idols'. Consequently Islamic art is supposed to have no saints' portraits, no pictures of animals, fish or fowl, nor anything else with an immortal soul, and the mosaics had to go. Luckily they were covered with plaster rather than destroyed. Restoration work is still going on.

From the floor of Sancta Sophia you can see several saints' portraits high up in the semicircles of the side walls. The best are in the galleries, reserved for female worshippers in Byzantine times. Climb to the galleries by a switchback ramp which starts at the northern end of the narthex.

Some of the work, though partially lost, is superb. The best mosaics are in the southern gallery. Most famous of all is the beautiful Deesis, dating from the early 1300s. Christ is at the centre, with the Virgin Mary on one side, John the Baptist on the other.

Be sure to go all the way to the far ends of the galleries. At the apse end of the south (right-hand) gallery are portraits of emperors, with a difference. The Empress Zoe (1028-1050), for instance, had three

husbands. When her portrait was put here in mosaic her husband was Romanus III Argyrus, but he died in 1034. So when she married Michael IV in that year, she had Romanus's portrait taken out and Michael's put in, but Michael didn't last that long either. In 1042 his portrait was removed to make way for that of Constantine IX Monomachus. Constantine outlived Zoe, so it is his portrait that you see today. The inscription reads, 'Constantine, by the Divine Christ, Faithful King of the Romans'.

As you leave Sancta Sophia, pass all the way through the corridor-like narthex and through the door at the end of it. Then turn and look up. Above the door is one of the church's finest mosaics, a Madonna and Child dating from the late 900s; on the left, Constantine the Great offers her

Sancta Sophia

the city of Constantinople; on the right, Justinian offers her Sancta Sophia.

A few more steps and you're out of the museum. The fountain to the right was for Muslim ablutions. Immediately to your left is the church's baptistry, converted after the Conquest to a tomb for sultans Mustafa and İbrahim. Other tombs are clustered behind it: those of Murat III, Selim II, Mehmet III and various princes. By the way, the minarets were added by Mehmet the Conqueror (1451-1481), Beyazıt II (1481-1512) and Selim II (1566-1574).

Haseki Hürrem Hamamı Across the road to the left (east) of the park with the fountain is the Haseki Hürrem Hamamı or Turkish bath of Lady Hürrem, now fixed up as a government-run carpet gallery and shop. Every mosque has a steam bath nearby; this was Sancta Sophia's, built in 1556 by the great Sinan. There were both men's and women's baths here, separated by a centre wall. The beautiful building is worth visiting for its architecture, and also to learn about traditional Turkish carpets and how to get the real thing when you buy. Carpets are sold here at a fixed price.

Set into Sancta Sophia's enclosing fence, directly across the road from the Haseki Hürrem Hamamı, is a *sebil*. A sebil was a place where sweet spring water and other refreshing drinks were sold; this one has just been adapted for modern ways. You'll recognise it as a little café, with an ornate kiosk, sidewalk tables and chairs. You'll see many others scattered throughout the Old City, mostly closed up, though.

The Blue Mosque

There used to be palaces where the Blue Mosque now stands. The Byzantine emperors built several of them, stretching from near Sancta Sophia all the way to the site of the mosque. You can see a mosaic from one of these palaces, still in place, in the Mosaic Museum (described later).

Sultan Ahmet I (1603-1617) set out to build a mosque that would rival and even surpass the achievement of Justinian. He succeeded, but only in part. The Sultan Ahmet Camii or Mosque of Sultan Ahmet, the Blue Mosque, is a triumph of harmony, proportion and elegance, but it comes nowhere near the technical achievements of Sancta Sophia.

The mosque is best appreciated if entered as at Sancta Sophia – by the main gate, slowly. In this case don't just walk across the park between the two structures, and in the side door. Rather, go out to the Hippodrome, and approach the mosque from the front.

The Blue Mosque is the only one in Turkey with six minarets. When it was built, between 1609 and 1616, the sacred Haram esh-Sharif in Mecca had six, and another had to be added so that it would not be outdone. Walk toward the mosque, through the outer gate (the hanging chains prevented men from riding in on horseback). As you walk up the steps to the courtyard door, you will see the domes of the Blue Mosque rise heavenward, one after the other. The effect is marvellous. Its architect, Mehmet Ağa, achieved on the exterior what Sancta Sophia's architects had achieved on the interior: an ascension of eyes and spirit toward the heavens.

The layout of the Blue Mosque is the classic Ottoman design as it evolved over the centuries. The forecourt contains an ablutions fountain in its centre. The portico around three sides could be used for prayer, meditation or study during warm weather.

The Blue Mosque is such a popular tourist sight that worshippers were in danger of being lost in the tourist crowds. So you'll be asked to turn left and enter through the north side door, not through the main door. At the side door an attendant will take your shoes; if your clothing is unpresentable, he'll lend you a robe to wear while you see the mosque. There's no charge for this, but you may be asked for a donation for the mosque, to which the money will actually go.

Though the stained-glass windows are replacements, they still create the marvellous coloured effects of the originals. The semi-domes and the dome are painted in graceful arabesques. The 'blue' of the mosque's name comes from the İznik tiles which line the walls, particularly in the gallery (which is not open to the public). You'll be able to get up close to equally beautiful tiles in the Rüstem Paşa Camii.

You can see immediately why the Blue Mosque, constructed in 1609-1616, over 1000 years after Sancta Sophia, is not as great an architectural triumph as Sancta Sophia. Although the four massive pillars which hold up the dome don't detract from the mosque's breathtaking beauty, they show what an impressive achievement Sancta Sophia is, by showing what's usually needed to hold up a massive dome.

Other things to notice are: the imperial loge, covered with marble latticework, to the left; the piece of the sacred Black Stone from the Kaaba in Mecca, embedded in the mihrab; the grandfather clock, to be sure the faithful know the exact times of the five-times-daily prayers; the high, elaborate chair (*mahfil*) from which the *imam* or teacher gives the sermon on Friday; and the *mimber*, or pulpit. The mimber is the structure with a curtained doorway at floor level, a flight of steps and a small kiosk topped by a spire. This one is particularly notable because of its fine carving (it's all marble), and because it was from here that the destruction of the Janissary corps was proclaimed in 1826 (see the Topkapı Palace section).

Mosques built by the great and powerful usually included numerous public-service institutions. Clustered around the Sultan Ahmet Camii were a *medrese* or theological school; an *imaret* or soup kitchen serving the poor; a hamam so that the faithful could wash on Friday,

the holy day; and shops, the rent from which supported the upkeep of the mosque. The tomb of the mosque's great patron, Sultan Ahmet I, is here as well. Buried with Ahmet are his brothers, Sultan Osman II and Sultan Murat IV.

Textile Museum Parts of the Blue Mosque cellars have been turned into a textile museum officially called the **Kilim ve Düz Dokuma Yaygılar Müzesi** or Museum of Kilims & Flat-Woven Rugs. The cellars, entered from the north side (toward Sancta Sophia), are where you buy your ticket (9 am to 4 pm, closed Sunday and Monday; less than US$1).

Inside the building are impressive stone-vaulted chambers. Huge kilims are stretched on boards, with descriptive tags written in Turkish and English.

The napped carpets are housed upstairs in the Halı Müzesi or Carpet Museum, at the end of the stone ramp which you can see from the side door where you entered the mosque. The ramp was so that the sultans could ride their nobly caparisoned steeds right up into the shelter of the mosque, dismount, and walk to their loge in safety and imperial privacy.

Turkish oriental carpets are among the finest works of art. The collection here provides a look at some of the best examples.

Mosaic Museum Before the Blue Mosque was built, its site was occupied by the palaces of the Byzantine emperors. The Roman art of mosaic moved, with most other Roman traditions, to Byzantium, and so the palace floors were covered in this beautiful artwork. Though the palaces have long since disappeared, some of the mosaics have survived.

When archaeologists from the University of Ankara and the University of St Andrew (in Scotland) dug at the back (east) of the Blue Mosque in the mid-1950s, they uncovered a mosaic pavement dating from early Byzantine times, about 500 AD. The pavement, filled with wonderful hunting and mythology scenes and emperors' portraits, was a triumphal way which led from the palace down to the harbour of Boucoleon. The dust and rubble of 1500 years have sunk the pavement considerably below ground level.

Other 5th-century mosaics were saved providentially when Sultan Ahmet had shops built on top of them. The row of shops, called the **Arasta**, was intended to provide rent revenues for the upkeep of the mosque. Now they house numerous souvenir vendors, a little teahouse, and the entrance to the Mosaic Museum. The museum is open daily except Tuesday from 9 am to 5 pm, for less than US$2.

After you've paid your admission, descend to the walkways around the sunken mosaics. The intricate work is impressive, with lots of hunters and beasts and maidens and swains. Note the ribbon border with heart-shaped leaves which surrounds the mosaic. In the western-most room (farthest from the entrance) is the most colourful and dramatic picture, that of two men in leggings carrying spears and holding off a raging tiger. If you can convince the custodian to wipe the mosaics with a wet cloth, the colours will become much more vivid.

The museum is designed so that you can walk beneath the Arasta, up the steps on the other side and past the postcard stand to the exit. But at my last visit the exit was locked, and I had to walk back through and leave by the entrance. In any case, there are diagrams near the postcard stand of the great palace of the Byzantine emperors, but labelled in Turkish and German only.

The Hippodrome

This was the centre of Byzantium's life for 1000 years and of Ottoman life for another 400. The Hippodrome (At Meydanı, in Turkish, 'Horse Grounds') was the scene of countless political and military dramas during the long life of this city.

History In Byzantine times, the rival chariot teams of 'Greens' and 'Blues' were politically connected. Support for a team was the same as membership in a political party, and a team victory had important effects on policy. A Byzantine emperor might lose his throne as the result of a post-match riot.

Ottoman sultans kept an eye on activities in the Hippodrome. If things were going badly in the empire, a surly crowd gathering here could signal the start of a disturbance, then a riot, then a revolution. In 1826, the slaughter of the debased and unruly Janissary corps was carried out by the reformer-sultan, Mahmut II. Almost a century later, in 1909, there were riots here which caused the downfall of Abdül Hamid II and the repromulgation of the Ottoman constitution.

Though the Hippodrome might be the scene of their downfall, Byzantine emperors and Ottoman sultans outdid one another in beautifying it. Many of the priceless statues carved by ancient masters have disappeared. The soldiers of the Fourth Crusade sacked Constantinople (a Christian ally city!) in 1204, tearing all the bronze plates from the magnificent stone obelisk at the Hippodrome's southern end, in the mistaken belief that they were gold. The crusaders also stole the famous 'quadriga', or team of four horses cast in bronze, which now sits atop the main door to Saint Mark's Church in Venice.

Monuments Near the northern end, the little gazebo done in beautiful stonework, is actually **Kaiser Wilhelm's fountain**. The German emperor paid a state visit to Abdül Hamid II in 1901, and presented this fountain to the sultan and his people as a little token of friendship. According to the Ottoman inscription, the fountain was built in the Hijri (Muslim lunar calendar) year of 1316 (1898-1899 to us). The monograms in the stonework are those of Abdül Hamid II and Wilhelm II.

Top: The Mosque of Sultan Ahmet III (Blue Mosque), İstanbul
Left: The Grand Bazaar (Kürkçüler Çarşısı), İstanbul
Right: A hazy view of the Golden Horn

Top: Sancta Sophia, İstanbul
Bottom: A spice merchant in the Egyptian Bazaar

The impressive granite obelisk with hieroglyphs is called the **Obelisk of Theodosius**, carved in Egypt around 1500 BC. According to the hieroglyphs, it was erected in Heliopolis (now a suburb of Cairo) to commemorate the victories of Thutmose III (1504-1450 BC). The Byzantine emperor, Theodosius, had it brought from Egypt to Constantinople in 390 AD. He then had it erected on a marble pedestal engraved with scenes of himself in the midst of various imperial pastimes. Theodosius' marble billboards have weathered badly over the centuries. The magnificent obelisk, spaced above the pedestal by four bronze blocks, is as crisply cut and as shiny bright as when it was carved from the living rock in Upper Egypt 3500 years ago.

Many obelisks were transported over the centuries to Paris (Place de la Concorde), London (Cleopatra's Needle), New York, Rome and Florence. A few still remain in Egypt as well.

South of the obelisk is a strange **spiral column** coming up out of a hole in the ground. It was once much taller and was topped by three serpents' heads. Originally cast to commemorate a victory of the Hellenic confederation over the Persians, it stood in front of the temple of Apollo at Delphi from 478 BC, until Constantine the Great had it brought to his new capital city about 330 AD. Though badly bashed up in the Byzantine struggle over the place of images in the church (called the Iconoclastic Controversy), the serpents' heads survived until the early 1700s. Now all that remains of them is one upper jaw in the Archaeological Museum.

The level of the Hippodrome rose over the centuries, as civilisation piled up its dust and refuse here. The obelisk and serpentine column were cleaned out and tidied up by the English troops who occupied the city after the Ottoman defeat in WW I.

No-one is quite sure who built the large **rough-stone obelisk** at the southern end of the Hippodrome. All we know is that it was repaired by Constantine VII Porphyrogenetus (913-959), and that the bronze plates were ripped off by the boys in the Fourth Crusade.

Turkish & Islamic Arts Museum

The Palace of İbrahim Paşa (1524) is on the western side of the Hippodrome. Now housing the Türk ve İslam Eserleri Müzesi or Turkish & Islamic Arts Museum, it gives you a glimpse into the opulent life of the Ottoman upper class in the time of Süleyman the Magnificent. İbrahim Paşa was Süleyman's close friend, son-in-law and grand vizier. He was enormously wealthy and so powerful that the sultan was finally convinced by İbrahim's enemies to have him murdered. Roxelana, Süleyman's wife, had convinced the sultan that İbrahim was a rival and a threat.

The museum is open from 10 am to 5 pm daily; closed Monday. Admission costs US$2. Labels are in Turkish and English. A video show on the first floor of the museum gives you a quick summary of Turkish history, and explains the sultan's tuğra and *ferman* (imperial edict). The coffee shop in the museum is a welcome refuge from the press of crowds and touts in the Hippodrome.

Highlights among the exhibits, which date from the 8th and 9th centuries up to the 19th century, are the decorated wooden Koran cases from the high Ottoman period; the calligraphy exhibits, including fermans with tuğras, Turkish miniatures, and illuminated manuscripts. You'll also want to have a look at the *rahles* or Koran stands, and the many carpets from all periods.

The lower floor of the museum houses ethnographic exhibits. At the entry is a black tent (*kara çadır*) like those used by nomads in eastern Turkey. Inside the tent is an explanation of nomadic customs, in English. Inside the museum building are village looms on which carpets and kilims are woven, and an exhibit of the plants and materials used to make natural textile dyes for the carpets. Perhaps most fascinating are the domestic interiors, including a yurt or Central Asian felt hut, a village house from Yuntdağ, and a late-19th-century house from Bursa. One display shows women shopping for cloth, and another a scene of daily life in an İstanbul home of the early 20th century.

The buildings behind and beside İbrahim Paşa's palace are İstanbul's law courts and legal administration buildings.

'Little' Sancta Sophia

The southern end of the Hippodrome is artificially supported by a system of brick arches called the **Sphendoneh**. Take a detour into İstanbul's lively little back streets for a look at this Byzantine feat of engineering. While you're down there, you can visit the Little Sancta Sophia Mosque or Küçük Aya Sofya Camii (formerly the Byzantine Church of St Sergius & St Bacchus), and also the Sokollu Mehmet Paşa Camii.

Facing south, with the Blue Mosque on your left, go to the end of the Hippodrome and turn left, then right, onto Aksakal Sokak. Soon you'll be able to recognise the filled-in arches of the Byzantine Sphendoneh on your right. Follow the curve around to the right and onto Kaleci Sokak. The next intersecting street is Mehmet Paşa Sokak; turn left and the Küçük Aya Sofya Camii is right there. If the mosque is not open, just hang around or signal to a boy on the street, and someone will come with the key.

Justinian and Theodora built this little church sometime between 527 and 536. Inside, the layout and decor are typical of an early Byzantine church, though the building was repaired and expanded several times during its life as a mosque, after the conquest of Constantinople in 1453. Repairs and enlargements to convert the church to a mosque were added by the Chief White Eunuch Hüseyin Ağa around 1500. His tomb is to the left as you enter.

Go north on Mehmet Paşa Sokak, back up the hill to the neighbouring **Sokollu Mehmet Paşa Camii**. This one was built during the height of Ottoman architectural development (1571) by the empire's greatest architect, Sinan. Though named for the grand vizier of the time, it was really sponsored by his wife Esmahan, daughter of Sultan Selim II. Besides its architectural harmony, typical of Sinan's great works, the mosque is unique because the medrese is not a separate building but actually part of the mosque structure, built around the forecourt.

If the mosque is not open, wait for the German-speaking guard to appear. When you enter, notice the harmonious architecture, the coloured marble, and the beautiful İznik tiles, some of the best ever made. Also, check out the four fragments from the sacred Black Stone in the Kaaba at Mecca: one above the mosque entrance (framed in gold), two in the mimber, and one in the mihrab. The marble pillars by the mimber revolve if the foundations have been disturbed by earthquake, an ingenious signalling device.

Walk back up the hill on Suterazisi Sokak to return to the Hippodrome.

Yerebatan Saray

Cross the main road, Divan Yolu, from the Hippodrome. On the north side of the street is a little park with a curious stone tower rising from it. The tower is part of an ancient aqueduct, a segment of this timeless city's elaborate water system. Beneath the park, entered by a little doorway on its north side (on the corner of Hilaliahmer and Yerebatan Caddesis) is the Yerebatan Saray ('Sunken Palace') formerly called the Cistern Basilica.

The Yerebatan Saray is actually a grand Byzantine cistern, 70 metres wide and 140 metres long. It has been completely restored, and now has atmospheric low lighting, classical music playing from hidden speakers, and a maze of walkways spreading throughout the 'palace'. The Byzantines never had it so good.

Admission costs US$2.50; at this writing, they still accept the ISIC student card for a discount. Yerebatan Saray (tel 522-1259) is open daily from 9 am to 5 pm, till 8 pm in summer. You can stay down in the cool darkness as long as you want. If you have a hand torch (flashlight), take it along, as the lights tend to go out for short periods every now and again.

The cistern was built by Justinian the Great (527-565), who was incapable of thinking in small terms. The roof is held up by 336 columns. At the back of the cistern is a column with an upside-down capital as its plinth, an anomaly that's rated as one of the big attractions here. But the mood of the place is what you'll remember; water still drips and tinkles in the dank shadows as it has for centuries.

Gülhane Park & Sublime Porte

Walk down the hill from Yerebatan Saray, along the main street called Alemdar Caddesi. Sancta Sophia will be on your right. Just past a big tree in the middle of the road, the street turns left, but just in front of you is the arched gateway to Gülhane Park.

Before entering the park, look to the left. That bulbous little kiosk built into the park walls at the next street corner is the **Alay Köşkü** or Parade Kiosk, from which the sultan would watch the periodic parades of troops and trade guilds which commemorated great holidays and military victories.

Across the street from the Alay Köşkü (not quite visible right from the Gülhane gate) is a gate to the Sublime Porte. The gate leads into the precincts of what was once the grand vizierate, or prime ministry, of the Ottoman Empire. Westerners called the Ottoman prime ministry the 'sublime porte' because of a phrase in Ottoman official documents: 'The Ambassador of (wherever) having come to my Sublime Porte. . .'

In Islamic societies, and in other societies with strong clan roots, it was customary for the chief or ruler to adjudicate disputes and grant favours. To petition the leader, you went to his tent, or house, or palace, stood at the door (hence 'porte'), and waited for a chance to lay it on him. When a western ambassador arrived at the sultan's 'sublime porte', he was looked on as just another petitioner asking favours. In later centuries, ambassadors reported not to the palace but to the grand vizierate, which was thus thought to be the Sublime Porte. Today the buildings beyond the gate house the Ottoman archives and various offices of the İstanbul provincial government.

Back up the street and inside the gates of Gülhane Parkı, you'll find a shady refuge. Gülhane was once the palace park of Topkapı; admission is free. There's a small zoo here, a somewhat kinky place with dogs, cats, pigs and cows as well as monkeys and exotic birds. Conditions at the zoo have improved in recent years, but still have a long way to go. At the far (north) end of the park, up the hill, is a flight of steps used as seats, and a small tea garden. Few tourists (except Lonely Planet readers) know about this quiet refuge, where you can sip a bracing glass of tea or a cool drink, gaze at the Bosphorus, and shake off the stresses of travel.

Museums

İstanbul's major collection of 'serious' museums is right behind Gülhane and Topkapı. As you pass beneath the arched gateway from Alemdar Caddesi into Gülhane, bear right and walk up the slope along a cobbled road, Osman Hamdi Yokuşu, which then turns to the right. After the turn you'll see a gate on the left. Within the gate are the İstanbul Archaeological Museum, Tiled Kiosk and Museum of the Ancient Orient.

You can also reach the museum complex from Topkapı. As you come out the Ortakapı from the palace, walk into the Court of the Janissaries, then turn right and walk down the hill before you get to Aya İrini, the Church of Divine Peace.

These museums were the palace collections, formed during the 19th century and added to greatly during the republic. While not immediately as dazzling as Topkapı, they contain an incredible wealth of artefacts from the 50 centuries of Anatolia's history.

The **Arkeoloji Müzesi** or Archaeological Museum houses a vast collection of statues and sarcophagi. One of the most beautiful sarcophagi was once thought to be that of Alexander the Great; today that theory is not held by all. Signs in the museum are in Turkish and French. The Ottoman Turkish inscription over the door of this imposing structure reads 'Eser-i Atika Müzesi', or Museum of Ancient Works. At present, extensive renovations are under way.

Across the court from the Archaeological Museum is the **Çinili Köşkü**, or Tiled Kiosk of Sultan Mehmet the Conqueror. Though once completely covered in fine tilework, you'll see tiles only on the facade these days. Mehmet II had this built (1472) not long after the conquest, which makes it the oldest surviving non-religious Turkish building in İstanbul. It now houses an excellent collection of Turkish faïence, including many good examples of fine İznik tiles from the period in the 1600s and 1700s when that city produced the finest coloured tiles in the world.

Last of the museums in the complex is the **Eski Şark Eserler Müzesi** or Museum of the Ancient Orient. Go here for a glimpse at the gates of ancient Babylon in the time of Nebuchadnezzar II (604-562 BC), for clay tablets bearing Hammurabi's famous law code (in cuneiform, of course), ancient Egyptian scarabs, and artefacts from the Assyrian and Hittite empires.

The museum complex (tel 520-7740/1) is open daily from 9.30 am to 5 pm, closed Monday. At present, the Tiled Kiosk is open only from 9.30 am to 12 noon, and the Museum of the Ancient Orient is open

Relief of Alexander (Sarcophagus, Archaeological Museum)

only in the afternoon from 1 to 5 pm.
Admission to the complex, and thus to all
three museums, costs US$3.

Divan Yolu

The main thoroughfare of the Old City
stretches between the gate named
Topkapı and the palace named Topkapı.
Starting from the Hippodrome and
Yerebatan Saray, it heads due west, up
one of İstanbul's seven hills, past the
Covered Market, through Beyazıt Square
and past İstanbul University to Aksaray
Square. Turning north a bit, it continues
to the Topkapı (Cannon Gate) in the
ancient city walls. In its progress through
the city, its name changes from Divan
Yolu to Yeniçeriler Caddesi, Ordu Caddesi
and Millet Caddesi. At the eastern end,
near the Hippodrome, it's Divan Yolu, the
Road to the Imperial Council.

The street dates from the early times of
Constantinople. Roman engineers laid it
out to connect with the great Roman roads
heading west. The great milestone from
which all distances were measured was
near the tall shaft of stones which rises
above Yerebatan Saray. The street held
its importance in Ottoman times, as
Mehmet the Conqueror's first palace was
in Beyazıt Square, and his new one,
Topkapı, was under construction.

If you start from Sancta Sophia and the
Hippodrome and walk up the slope on
Divan Yolu, you will see the little **Firuz Ağa
Camii** on the left. Firuz Ağa was chief
treasurer to Beyazıt II (1481-1512). The
mosque was built in 1491, in the simple
style of the early Ottomans: a dome on a
square base, with a simple porch out front.
The Ottomans brought this style with
them from the east or borrowed it from the
Seljuk Turks. It changed greatly after
they conquered İstanbul, inspected
Sancta Sophia and put the great architect
Sinan to work.

Just behind Firuz Ağa Camii are the
ruins of the **Palace of Antiochus** (5th
century), not much to look at these days.

The first major intersection on the right

is with Babiali Caddesi. Turn right here
and after walking a block you'll be in
Cağaloğlu Square, once the centre of
İstanbul's newspaper publishing. Most of
the publishers have moved to large,
modern buildings outside the walls. The
Cağaloğlu Hamamı, is just off the square,
on the right (see the Entertainment
section for details).

If instead you turn left (south) from
Divan Yolu, you'll be on Klodfarer
Caddesi (not a German word, but the
name of the Turcophile French novelist,
Claude Farrère). It leads to a large open
area beneath which lies the Byzantine
cistern now called **Binbirdirek**,
'A Thousand-and-One Columns'. You'll
see the little doorway to the stairs. If the
door is locked, call to a child, who will find
the guard. Not as large as Yerebatan
Saray, Binbirdirek is still very impressive,
but woefully neglected these days.

Back on Divan Yolu, the impressive
enclosure right at the corner of Babiali
Caddesi is filled with **tombs** of the
Ottoman high and mighty. First to be
built here was the mausoleum of Sultan
Mahmut II (1808-1839), the reforming
emperor who got rid of the Janissaries and
revamped the Ottoman army. After
Mahmut, other notables chose to be
buried here, including sultans Abdül Aziz
(1861-1876) and Abdül Hamid II
(1876-1909).

Right across Divan Yolu from the tombs
is a small stone **library** built by the Köprülü
family in 1659. The Köprülüs rose to
prominence in the mid-1600s and furnished
the empire with an outstanding succession
of grand viziers, generals and grand
admirals for centuries. They basically ran
the empire during a time when the scions
of the Ottoman dynasty did not live up to
the standards of Mehmet the Conqueror
and Süleyman the Magnificent.

Stroll a bit further along Divan Yolu.
On the left, the curious tomb with
wrought-iron grillework on top is that of
Köprülü Mehmet Paşa (1575-1661).
Across the street, that strange building

with a row of streetfront shops is actually an ancient Turkish bath, the **Çemberlitaş Hamamı** (1580).

The derelict, time-worn column rising from a little plaza is one of İstanbul's most ancient and revered monuments. Called **Çemberlitaş** ('The Banded Stone') or the Burnt Column, it was erected by Constantine the Great (324-337) to celebrate the dedication of Constantinople as capital of the Roman Empire in 330. This area was the grand Forum of Constantine, and the column was topped by a statue of the great emperor himself. In an earthquake zone erecting columns can be a risky business. This one has survived, though it needed iron bands for support within a century after it was built. The statue crashed to the ground almost 1000 years ago.

The little **mosque** nearby is that of Atik Ali Paşa, a eunuch and grand vizier of Beyazıt II.

The Covered Market

İstanbul's Kapalı Çarşı ('Covered Market' or Grand Bazaar) is 4000 shops and several km of streets, mosques, banks, police stations, restaurants and workshops. Today it is very touristy, with touts badgering bus tour groups everywhere. For real shopping in a more relaxed atmosphere, the Egyptian Market in Eminönü is better. But you must take a spin through the Covered Market in any case, or you haven't seen İstanbul.

Starting from a small *bedesten* or warehouse built in the time of Mehmet the Conqueror, the bazaar grew to cover a vast area as neighbouring shopkeepers decided to put up roofs and porches so that commerce could be conducted comfortably in all weather. Great men built *hans*, or caravanserais, at the edges of the bazaar so that caravans could bring wealth from all parts of the empire, unload and trade right in the bazaar's precincts. Finally, a system of locked gates and doors was provided so that the

entire mini-city could be closed up tight at the end of the business day.

Though tourist shops now crowd the bazaar, it is also still a place where an *İstanbullu* (citizen of İstanbul) may come to buy a few metres of printed cloth, a gold bangle for a daughter's birthday gift, an antique carpet or a fluffy sheepskin. Whether you want to buy or not, you should see the bazaar (remember that it's closed on Sunday). Also, I've had a report from a reader that his flight bag was slashed while strolling in the bazaar, and again while walking down the busy market streets to the Egyptian Market. Guard your belongings.

Turn right off Divan Yolu at the Çemberlitaş and walk down Vezir Hanı Caddesi. The big mosque before you is **Nuruosmaniye** or Light of Osman Mosque, built between 1748 and 1755 by Mahmut I and his successor Osman III, in the style known as Ottoman Baroque. It's one of the earliest examples of the style.

Turn left through the mosque gate. The courtyard of the mosque is peaceful and green, but with a constant flow of pedestrian traffic heading through it, to and from the bazaar.

Out the other side of the courtyard, you're standing in Çarşıkapı Sokak, Bazaar Gate St, and before you is one of several doorways into the bazaar. The glorious gold emblem above the doorway is the Ottoman armorial emblem with the sultan's monogram.

While here, you might want to see an interesting little street behind Nuruosmaniye Camii. If you turn right after leaving the mosque courtyard, then right again, you'll be on **Kılıççılar Sokak**, Swordmakers' St. The dingy workshops on both sides of the street have fiery forges in the rear. They no longer make swords here, except the miniature ones to be used as letter openers. Most of the metalwork is brass souvenirs. Once you've taken a look, head back to the doorway with the Ottoman arms above it.

Inside the bazaar, the street you're on is

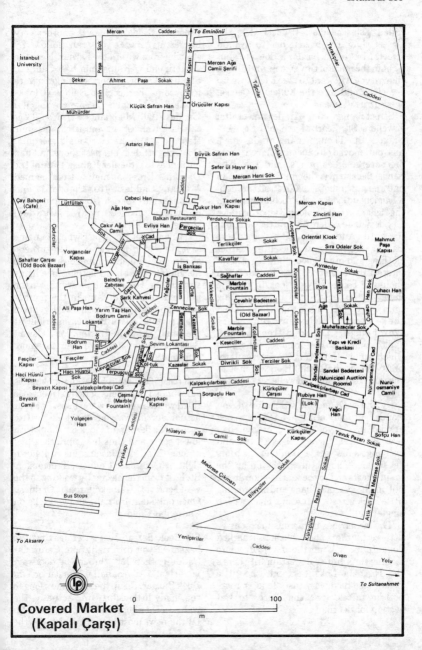

Covered Market
(Kapalı Çarşı)

0   100
m

called **Kalpakçılarbaşı Caddesi**. It's the closest thing the bazaar has to a main street. Most of the bazaar is down to your right in the maze of tiny streets and alleys, though you will want to take a left turn up the steps and into the **Kürkçüler Çarşısı**, the Furriers Bazaar.

Street names refer to trades and crafts: Jewellers St, Pearl-Merchants St, Fez-Makers St. Though many trades have died out, moved on or been replaced, there are several areas you should see. The **Sandal Bedesteni** is the municipal auction hall and pawn shop – take a stroll through. **Kuyumcular Caddesi**, the second street on the right as you walk along Kalpakçılarbaşı Caddesi, is Jewellers St, aglitter with tons of gold and gems. The Furriers Bazaar now houses shops selling leather clothing and other goods, but it's still an interesting corner of the bazaar. You should of course have a look in the **Old Bazaar** at the centre of the bazaar, dating from the 1400s. This is sometimes called the Cevahir Bedesteni (Jewellery Warehouse). I'd also recommend explorations into one or more of the hans which adjoin the bazaar. A particularly pretty one is the **Zincirli Han**, which is at the far (north) end of Jewellers St, on the right.

By the way, no one will mind if you wander into any of these hans for a look around. In fact, you may well be invited to rest your feet, have a glass of tea and exchange a few words. Don't let the touts get to you. They'll approach you on the main streets and in the tourist-shop areas, but in the bazaar's hans and interesting little back streets you won't meet with a single one.

The bazaar has numerous inexpensive little restaurants and cookshops (marked 'lokanta' or 'lok' on the map). If you're looking for a full-scale restaurant there's the Havuzlu Lokantası, but the little places also have very tasty food at rock-bottom prices. (See the Places to Eat section for details.)

Uzunçarşı Caddesi There is another very interesting route you can follow by starting from within the bazaar. Near the western end of Kalpakçılarbaşı Caddesi, Sipahi Sokak heads north, changes names to become Feraceciler Sokak (Cloak-makers St), then becomes Yağcılar Caddesi (Oil Merchants St). You'll see the Şark Kahvesi on your left, then some steps up to a *mescit* (small mosque). Continue straight on, past shops and han entrances to Örücüler Kapısı, Gate of the Darners. Cross a main street named Mercan Caddesi (to the left) and Çakmakçılar Yokuşu (to the right), and continue on Uzunçarşı Caddesi (Longmarket St).

'Longmarket St' is just what its name says: one long market of wood-turners' shops, clog-makers' cubbyholes, bakeries for simits, second-hand clothing merchants and the like. Follow it all the way down the hill and you will end up in the market district in Eminönü, near the Egyptian Market and Galata Bridge, and right at the small, exquisite Rüstem Paşa Camii. See the section on Eminönü for more information.

Çadırcılar Caddesi The Kapalı Çarşı is surrounded by dozens of little streets also filled with stores and workshops. For your actual purchases, you might do well to escape the bazaar and look for shops with lower rents and thus lower prices. Chief among these, and fascinating in its own right, is Çadırcılar Caddesi, Tentmakers St. Exit from the bazaar by walking to the west end of Kalpakçılarbaşı Caddesi. Once outside, turn right and you'll be on Çadırcılar Caddesi.

Old Book Bazaar Just after leaving the bazaar, if you turn right onto Çadırcılar Caddesi, then left through a doorway, you'll enter the Sahaflar Çarşısı or Old Book Bazaar. Go up the steps and along to the shady little courtyard. Actually, the wares in the shops are both new and old. Of the new, most are in Turkish. Of the old, many are in other languages. It's unlikely that you'll uncover any treasures here, but you can certainly find a curiosity or two.

The book bazaar dates from the Byzantine Empire. Many of the booksellers are members of a dervish order called the Halveti after its founder, Hazreti Mehmet Nureddin-i Cerrahi-i Halveti. Their *sema* or religious ceremony includes chanting from the Koran, praying, and rhythmic dancing and breathing to the accompaniment of classical Turkish liturgical music. As with all dervish orders, the sema is an attempt at close knowledge of and communion with God. The Mevlevi dervishes attempt it by their whirling dance, the Halveti through their circular dance and hyperventilation. Don't, however, expect to wander into a den of mystics. What you'll see are normal Turkish booksellers who just happen to be members of this dervish order.

Out the north gate of the Sahaflar Çarşısı is (in summer) a pretty tea garden filled with café tables under colourful umbrellas; university students studying, talking or flirting; and waiters in traditional costume scurrying around carrying trays packed with tiny glasses of fresh tea. It's a good place for a rest. If you want tea, just signal the waiter when you see him with a full tray. For a soft drink, order anytime. In the cooler months, this area hosts a daily flea market; on Sunday the flea market expands and spills out into Beyazıt Square.

Beyazıt & İstanbul University

The aforementioned tea garden is right next to **Beyazıt Camii**, or Mosque of Sultan Beyazıt II (1481-1512). Beyazıt used an exceptional amount of fine stone in his mosque, which he built in 1501-1506 on a plan similar to that for Sancta Sophia, but smaller. It's well worth a look.

The main street here, which started out as Divan Yolu, is now called Yeniçeriler Caddesi. It runs past Beyazıt Square, officially called Hürriyet Meydanı (Freedom Square), though everyone knows it simply as Beyazıt. The plaza is backed by the impressive portal of İstanbul University.

Under the Byzantines, this was the largest of the city's many forums, the **Forum of Theodosius**, built by that emperor in 393. Mehmet the Conqueror built his first palace here, a wooden structure which burnt down centuries ago. After Mehmet built Topkapı he used his wooden palace as a home for aging harem women.

The grand gates, main building and tall tower of the university were originally built as the Ottoman War Ministry, which explains why they are so grandiose and somewhat martial. You used to be allowed up into the tower, which is no doubt still used as a fire lookout post.

The small building at the west side of the square is now **Beyazıt Hat Sanatları Müzesi** or Beyazıt Calligraphy Museum, open from 9.30 am to 4 pm every day, for US$0.25 admission. Though you may not be fascinated by Ottoman calligraphy, the building, once a theological college, is certainly worth a look.

Laleli & Aksaray

As you continue west along the main street, now named Ordu Caddesi (Army or 'Horde' Ave), notice the huge broken marble columns decorated with peacocktail designs on the left-hand side of the roadway. These were part of the decoration in the Forum of Theodosius. There was a monumental arch hereabouts.

A bit further along, on the right, are more university buildings, and beyond them the hotel district of Laleli. Stay on Ordu Caddesi and you'll soon come to the **Laleli Camii**, an Ottoman baroque mosque built (1759-1763) by Sultan Mustafa III. The ornate baroque architecture houses a sumptuous interior. Underneath it are shops and a plaza with a fountain. These were partly to produce rent for the upkeep of the mosque, partly to show off the architect's skill and cunning.

Continue down the hill on Ordu Caddesi and you will enter the confused clamour of Aksaray Square, where there's nothing particularly interesting to see or do. The **Valide Camii** on the square's northwest side is, well, highly ornamented to say the least. It does not date from any great period of Ottoman architecture, having been built in 1871 by Valide Sultan Pertevniyal, mother of Sultan Abdül Aziz. It used to be attractive, in a way, because it looked like a white wedding cake among the dull, normal structures of Aksaray, but now – with all the exhaust fumes – it's not even white anymore, and traffic flyovers block a good, full view.

Süleymaniye Camii

The Süleymaniye Camii or Mosque of Sultan Süleyman the Magnificent, is İstanbul's largest. To the west is the quaint old Municipal Museum. To get to the Süleymaniye from Beyazıt Square, walk around the university. The mosque is directly north of (behind) the university enclosure. Facing the university portal in Beyazıt, go to the left along Takvimhane Caddesi.

The Süleymaniye crowns one of İstanbul's hills, dominating the Golden Horn and providing a magnificent landmark for all of the city. This, the grandest of all Turkish mosques, was built between 1550 and 1557 by the greatest, richest, and most powerful of Ottoman sultans, Süleyman I (1520-1566), 'The Magnificent'. The Turks call this sultan Kanuni, 'The Lawgiver', and remember him more for his codification of the empire's laws than for his magnificent style.

Süleyman was a great builder who restored the mighty walls of Jerusalem (an Ottoman city from 1516) and built countless other monuments throughout his empire. He was the patron of Mimar Sinan, Turkey's greatest architect. Though the smaller Selimiye Camii in Edirne is generally counted as Sinan's masterpiece, the Süleymaniye is without doubt his grandest work.

Ottoman imperial mosques were instrumental in repopulating the capital after its conquest. In 1453, much of the city had been abandoned, the Byzantine population had shrunk, and huge areas were vacant or derelict. When a sultan built an imperial mosque, it quickly became the centre of a new quarter. Residences and workshops were soon built nearby.

Each imperial mosque had a *külliye*, or collection of charitable institutions, clustered around it. These might include a hospital, insane asylum, orphanage, soup kitchen, hospice for travellers, religious school, library, baths and a cemetery in which the mosque's imperial patron, his family and other notables could be buried. The külliye of the Süleymaniye is particularly elaborate, and includes all of these institutions. Those are the impressive buildings you see surrounding the mosque.

Unfortunately, most visitors enter the mosque precincts by a side door. Though this is the most convenient entrance, coming from Beyazıt, the effect of entering from the north-west side and seeing the four towering minarets and the enormous, billowing domes is better.

Inside, the mosque is breathtaking in its size and pleasing in its simplicity. There is little in the way of decoration, except for some very fine İznik tiles in the mihrab, gorgeous stained-glass windows done by one İbrahim the Drunkard, and four massive columns, one from Baalbek, one from Alexandria and two from Byzantine palaces in İstanbul. The painted arabesques on the dome are 19th-century additions, recently renewed.

At the south-east wall of the mosque is the cemetery. Ask for the *bekçi* (BEHK-chee, caretaker) so you can see the *türbeler* (tewr-beh-LEHR, tombs) of Süleyman and his wife Haseki Hürrem Sultan (known in the west as Roxelana), and of his architect, the great Mimar Sinan (MEE-mahr see-NAHN). The tombs are high points of rich, high Ottoman decoration. The İznik tiles in Hürrem's tomb are particularly fine. Tombs are usually closed and inaccessible on Monday and Tuesday, when the caretaker takes his 'weekend'.

Şehzadebaşı Caddesi

Aqueduct of Valens Walk along Süleymaniye Caddesi, which goes south-west from the mosque, and turn right onto Şehzadebaşı Caddesi. You can see remnants of the high Bozdoğan Kemeri or Aqueduct of Valens on the left side of the street. It's not really certain that the aqueduct was constructed by the emperor Valens (364-378), though we do know it was repaired in 1019, and by several sultans in later times. After the reign of Süleyman the Magnificent, parts of it collapsed, but restoration work was begun in the late 1980s.

Şehzade Camii On the south side of the aqueduct is the Şehzade Camii, the Mosque of the Prince. Süleyman had it built in 1544-1548 as a memorial to his son Mehmet, who died in 1543. It was the first important mosque to be designed by Mimar Sinan, who spent the first part of his long career as a military architect. Among the many important people buried in tile-encrusted tombs here are Prince Mehmet, his brothers and sisters, and Süleyman's grand viziers, Rüstem Paşa and İbrahim Paşa.

Municipal Museum If you have a few minutes to spare, walk west on Şehzadebaşı Caddesi. The dusty modern building on the left is Belediye Sarayı, İstanbul's Town Hall. Turn right and pass under the aqueduct, then take your life in your hands and cross Atatürk Bulvarı. Just on the other side of the street is the former medrese of Gazanfer Ağa (1599), now the Belediye Müzesi or Municipal Museum. It has an odd and eclectic assortment of city memorabilia which you might find interesting.

EMİNÖNÜ

No doubt you've already seen Eminönü. The view of the Galata Bridge, crowded with ferries and dominated by the Yeni Cami (YEHN-nee jahm-mee, New Mosque), also called the Pigeon Mosque because of the ever present flocks of birds, is a favourite for advertisements and magazine articles about İstanbul. The Yeni Cami sits comfortably and serenely in the midst of bustling Eminönü as the traffic, both vehicular and pedestrian, swirls around it. Visitors to İstanbul find themselves passing through Eminönü time after time.

In a way, Eminönü is the inner city's transportation hub. Not only do the Bosphorus ferries dock here, not only does all Galata Bridge traffic pass through, but Sirkeci Station is just around the corner.

Galata Bridge

The dusty bridge which has rested here for many decades may not be very impressive at first glance, but it was once a true microcosm of İstanbul, full of little unexpected surprises. By the time you arrive, the old bridge should be relegated to traffic by pedestrians only, and a new bridge just west of it should be bearing the heavy streams of vehicles.

Though the new bridge will be stationary, the old bridge floated on pontoons. This is so that the central section could be removed to allow larger ships to enter the Golden Horn and reach its shipyards. The central section, unlatched and driven by small motors, was floated out and to the side each morning at 4.30 am. For a half-hour ships steamed out, then for another half-hour ships steamed in. At 5.30 am the central section was floated back into place.

Underneath the bridge are small fish restaurants which get their provisions directly from the fishmongers who approach the bridge in boats. Itinerant pedlars sell fishing tackle so you can try your luck in the murky waters. There's even a teahouse where you can get tea,

Turkish coffee, soft drinks or a bubbling *nargile* (NAHR-gee-leh, water pipe).

In Byzantine times the Golden Horn provided a perfect natural harbour for the city's commerce. Suppliers of fresh vegetables and fruits, grain and staple goods set up shop in the harbour. Until only a few years ago, their successors in İstanbul's wholesale vegetable, fruit and fish markets performed the same services, in the same area to the west of the Galata Bridge in Eminönü. With the drive to clean up and beautify the Golden Horn, the wholesale markets have been moved to the outskirts.

Still picturesque and interesting is the retail market district which surrounds the Egyptian Market. But before wandering into this maze of market streets, take a look inside the Yeni Cami.

Yeni Cami

This imperial mosque was begun in 1597, commissioned by Valide Sultan Safiye, mother of Sultan Mehmet III (1595-1603). The site was earlier occupied by a community of Karaite Jews, radical dissenters from orthodox Judaism. When the valide sultan decided to build her grand mosque here, the community was moved to Hasköy, a district further up the Golden Horn which still bears traces of the Karaite presence.

The valide sultan lost her august position when her son the sultan died, and the mosque had to be completed (1663) six sultans later by Valide Sultan Turhan Hatice, mother of Sultan Mehmet IV (1648-1687).

In plan, the Yeni Cami is much like the Blue Mosque and the Süleymaniye Camii, with a large forecourt and a square sanctuary surmounted by a series of half-domes crowned by a grand dome. The interior is richly decorated with gold, coloured tiles and carved marble. The mosque and its tiles are 'late', past the period when Ottoman architecture was at its peak. The tilemakers of İznik were turning out slightly inferior products by the late 1600s. Compare these tiles to the ones in the Rüstem Paşa Camii, which are from the high period of İznik tilework. Only in İstanbul would a 400-year-old mosque be called 'New'.

Mısır Çarşısı

The Mısır Çarşısı (MUH-suhr chahr-shuh-shuh, Egyptian Market) is also called the Spice Bazaar because of the many spice shops within. A century or two ago, it was twice as fascinating as it is now. Its merchants sold such things as cinnamon, gunpowder, rabbit fat, pine gum, peach pit powder, sesame seeds, sarsaparilla root, aloe, saffron, liquorice root, donkey's milk and parsley seeds, all to be used as folk remedies.

Gunpowder, for instance, was prescribed as a remedy for haemorrhoids: you'd boil a little gunpowder with the juice of a whole lemon, strain off the liquid, dry the powder and swallow it the next morning with a little water, on an empty stomach. It was also supposed to be a good cure for pimples when mixed with a little crushed garlic. Whatever its values as a pharmaceutical, it was finally banned from the market because the shops in which it was sold kept blowing up.

The market was constructed in the 1660s as part of the Yeni Cami complex, the rents from the shops going to support upkeep of the mosque and its charitable activities. These included a school, baths, hospital and public fountains.

Enter the market (open Monday to Saturday from 8.30 am to 6.30 pm, closed Sunday) through the big armoured doors which open onto Eminönü Square. Just inside the doors, to the left, is the little stairway which leads up to the Pandeli restaurant (see the Places to Eat section). Readers of this book have found that the little büfe on the left-hand side of the entrance serves the best lahmacun in the city (stand-up dining only).

Strolling through the market, you can still see numerous shops which sell *baharat* (bah-hah-RAHT, spices), and even a few which specialise in the old-time remedies. Some of the hottest items are bee pollen and royal jelly, used to restore virility. You'll see also shops selling nuts, candied fruits, chocolate and other snacks. Try some _incir_ (een-JEER, figs) or _lokum_ (low-KOOM, Turkish delight). Fruit pressed into sheets and dried (looks like leather) is called pestil; often made from apricots or mulberries, it's delicious and relatively cheap. Buy 50 grams or 100 grams to start.

When you come to the crossroads within the market, you have a choice. I'd suggest you turn left, see the rest of the market, then return to the crossroads and take the street to the right.

Turning left will reveal shops selling toys, clothing and various household goods. You may see a shop which specialises in the white outfits little boys wear on the day of their circumcision (_sünnet_). The white suit is supplemented with a pillbox hat and a red sash which bears the word _Maşallah_ (MAH-shah-lah, 'What wonders God has willed!'). When you see a little kid in such an outfit, you'll know that today he's going to get his. He will probably be riding around in the midst of musicians and merrymakers, for a boy's circumcision (at age eight to 10 or so) is his coming of age and an excellent excuse for a tremendous party.

Turn left again at the first opportunity, and you'll leave the bazaar and enter its busy courtyard, backed by the Yeni Cami. This is the city's major market for flowers, plants, seeds and songbirds. There's a WC to your left, down the stairs, subject to a small fee. To the right, across the courtyard, is the **tomb** of Valide Sultan Turhan Hatice, founder of the Yeni Cami. Buried with her are no less than six other sultans, including her son Mehmet IV, plus dozens of imperial princes and princesses.

Now, back at that crossroads within the bazaar, take the right turning and exit through another set of armoured doors. Just outside the doors is another crossroads of bustling market streets. You can always smell coffee here, because right across the intersection is the shop of Kurukahveci Mehmet Efendi. Clerks wrap customer's parcels with lightning speed (they take great pride in this), and there always seems to be a line waiting to make a purchase. To the right, down toward the Golden Horn, is a small fish market with a few butchers' shops thrown in for good measure. Up to the left, the shops and street pedlars sell mostly household and kitchen items.

Head out the bazaar doors and straight across the intersection. This is **Hasırcılar Caddesi**, Mat Makers St. Shops along it sell fresh fruits, spices, nuts, condiments, knives and other cutlery, coffee, tea, cocoa, hardware and similar retail necessities. The colours, smells, sights and sounds make this one of the liveliest and most interesting streets in the city.

A few short blocks along Hasırcılar Caddesi, on the right-hand side, you'll come to the **Rüstem Paşa Camii**. Keep your eyes peeled – it's easy to miss as it is not at street level. All you'll see is a tidy stone doorway and a flight of steps leading up; there is also a small marble fountain and plaque. This mosque is used heavily by the merchants and artisans of the bazaar. As with most mosques, you should not visit during prayer-time, so if the müezzin has just given the call to prayer, come back in half an hour.

At the top of the steps is a terrace and the mosque's colonnaded porch. You'll notice at once the panels of dazzling İznik faïence set into the mosque's facade. The interior is covered in similarly gorgeous tiles, so take off your shoes (women should also cover heads and shoulders), and venture inside. Particularly beautiful, the mosque was built by Sinan, the greatest Ottoman architect, for Rüstem Paşa, son-in-law and grand vizier of Süleyman the Magnificent. Ottoman power, glory, architecture and tilework were all at their zenith when the mosque was built (1561). You won't forget this one.

After your visit to the mosque, you might want to spend some more time wandering the streets of this fascinating market quarter. If you need a goal, head up the hill (south) on Uzunçarşı Caddesi, which begins right near the Rüstem Paşa Camii and ends at the Covered Market (see that section earlier for more details).

The Outer City

From early times the heart of this ancient city has been near the tip of Seraglio Point. As the city grew over the centuries, its boundaries moved westward. That process continues.

There are several points of interest farther out, and if you have at least four days to tour the city you should be able to see all the centre's essential sights and still have time for these. They include the Fatih Camii, the Church of the Holy Saviour in Chora (Kariye Müzesi) famous for its Byzantine mosaics, the Palace of Constantine Porphyrogenetus (Tekfur Saray), several other mosques, the mammoth City Walls, and the village of Eyüp up the Golden Horn. On your way back downtown you can stop at the Ecumenical Orthodox Patriarchate and also at a curious Bulgarian church made of cast iron.

A detour to Yedikule is described at the end of this section.

Fatih Camii The Mosque of the Conqueror or Fatih Camii is just west of the Aqueduct of Valens, on Fevzi Paşa Caddesi. You can get a dolmuş from Aksaray or Taksim to the City Hall (ask for the Belediye Sarayı, behl-eh-DEE-yeh sar-rah-yuh) near the Aqueduct and walk five blocks; or you can catch any bus that has 'Fatih' or 'Edirnekapı' listed on its itinerary board. Buses and trolley buses going to Edirnekapı pass frequently through Sultanahmet Square.

When Mehmet the Conqueror entered Constantinople in 1453, he found a once-great city depopulated and shrunken in size within the walls. Large tracts of urban land had reverted to grass and shrubs, and many buildings were in ruins. He sought to repopulate the city with groups from the various nations of his empire, sometimes commanding that they move to İstanbul.

A prime method of repopulating a district was to commission the construction of an imperial mosque there. The mosque would become the nucleus of a city quarter, first providing work for construction crews and the merchants and pedlars who served them, then providing a focus of religious and social life. The mosque's külliye would also encourage people to move to the quarter.

The Fatih Camii was the first great imperial mosque to be built in İstanbul following the conquest. For its location, Fatih Sultan Mehmet (Mehmet the Conqueror) chose the hilltop site of the ruined Church of the Apostles. The mosque complex, finished in 1470, was enormous, and included in its külliye 15 charitable establishments – religious schools, a hospice for travellers, a caravanserai, etc. The mosque you see, however, is not the one he built. The original mosque stood for 300 years before toppling in an earthquake (1766). It was rebuilt, but to a completely different plan. The exterior of the mosque still bears some of the original decoration; the interior is not all that impressive.

While you're here, be sure to visit the tomb of Mehmet the Conqueror behind the mosque. His wife Gülbahar, whose tomb is next to the sultan's, is rumoured to have been a French princess.

When you're finished at the mosque, go back to Fevzi Paşa Caddesi and catch a bus or dolmuş headed north-west toward Edirnekapı. Get off the bus just before the massive city walls. You'll see the **Mihrimah Camii**, a mosque built by Süleyman the Magnificent's favourite daughter, Mihrimah, in the 1560s. The architect was Sinan, and the mosque marks a departure from his usual style. The inevitable earthquakes worked their destruction, and the building has been restored several times, the latest being around 1900. Mihrimah married Rüstem Paşa, Süleyman's brilliant and powerful grand vizier (his little tile-covered mosque is down by the Egyptian Market). You can visit her tomb on the south-east side of the mosque.

Take a look at the **city walls** (you can hardly help it!). You'll get a closer look, and even a climb up top, in a little while.

Cross the road from the Mihrimah Camii and, still inside the walls, head north toward the Golden Horn. You'll see signs, and children pointing the way, to the Chora Church.

Chora Church Mosaics If we translate the original name (*Chora*) for this building, it comes out 'Church of the Holy Saviour Outside the Walls' or 'in the Country', because the original church on this site was indeed outside the walls built by Constantine the Great. But just as London's Church of St Martin-in-the-Fields is hardly surrounded by bucolic scenery these days, the Church of the Holy Saviour was soon engulfed by Byzantine urban sprawl. It was enclosed within the walls built by the Emperor Theodosius II in 413, less than 100 years after Constantine. So the Holy Saviour in the Country was 'in the country' for about

80 years, and has been 'in the city' for 1550 years. It was not only the environs of the church which changed: for four centuries it served as a mosque (Kariye Camii), and is now a museum, the Kariye Müzesi.

The Kariye Müzesi (tel 523-3009) is open daily from 9.30 am to 4.30 pm, closed Tuesday; admission costs US$4.

The building you see is not the original church-outside-the-walls. Rather, this one was built in the late 11th century, with lots of repairs and restructuring in the following centuries. Virtually all of the interior decoration – the famous mosaics and the less renowned but equally striking mural paintings – dates from about 1320. Between 1948 and 1959 the decoration was carefully restored under the auspices of the Byzantine Society of America.

The mosaics are breath-taking. There is a definite order to the arrangement of the pictures. The first ones are those of the dedication, to Christ and to the Virgin Mary. Then come the offertory ones: Theodore Meto-chites, builder of the church, offering it to Christ. The two small domes of the inner

ora Church

narthex have portraits of all Christ's ancestors back to Adam. A series outlines the Virgin Mary's life, and another, Christ's early years. Yet another series concentrates on Christ's ministry. There are lots of saints and martyrs everywhere.

In the nave are three mosaics: of Christ, of the Virgin as Teacher, and of the Dormition of the Blessed Virgin (turn around to see this one – it's over the main door you just entered). By the way, the baby in the painting is actually Mary's soul, being held by Jesus, while her body lies 'asleep' on its bier.

South of the nave is the Parecclesion, a side chapel built to hold the tombs of the church's founder and his relatives, close friends and associates. The frescos, appropriately, deal with the theme of death and resurrection. The striking painting in the apse shows Christ breaking down the gates of Hell and raising Adam and Eve, with saints and kings in attendance.

Kariye Pudding Shop Just across from the Kariye Müzesi is the Kariye Muhallebicisi or Pudding Shop, an old İstanbul structure restored by the Turkish Touring & Automobile Club. *Muhallebi* (Arabic) means pudding, and there were lots of such 'pudding shops' in Ottoman İstanbul. Today the word generally refers to a bland rose-water jelly served alone as a sweet. You can have some or another sweet or beverage on the patio on the ground floor, or on the neighbouring shady terrace with its dovecote. The upper floor of the building has been arranged as a traditional Ottoman salon. One room of the structure serves as a souvenir shop.

Constantine's Palace From Kariye, head west to the city walls, then north again, and you'll soon come to the Palace of Constantine Porphyrogenetus, the Tekfur Saray (tehk-FOOR sar-rah-yuh). It's nominally open on Wednesday, Thursday and Sunday from 9 am to 5 pm, but you can usually just wander in on any day.

The caretaker may appear and sell you a ticket (US$0.25).

Though the building is only a shell these days, it is remarkably preserved for a Byzantine palace built in the 1300s. Sacred buildings often survive the ravages of time because they continue to be used even though they may be converted for use in another religion. Secular buildings, however, are often torn down and used as quarries for building materials once their owners die. The Byzantine palaces which once crowded Sultanahmet Square are all gone; so is the great Palace of Blachernae, which adjoined the Tekfur Saray. Only this one remains.

The caretaker may have put a ladder against the wall for you, and you can climb up onto the walls for a view of the palace, the city walls, the Golden Horn, and much of the city.

The City Walls Since being built in the 400s, the city walls have been breached by hostile forces only twice. The first time was in the 1200s, when Byzantium's 'allies', the armies of the Fourth Crusade, broke through and pillaged the town, deposing the emperor and setting up a king of their own. The second time was in 1453 under Mehmet the Conqueror. Even though Mehmet was ultimately successful, he was continually frustrated during the siege as the walls withstood admirably even the heaviest bombardments by the largest cannon in existence at the time. The walls were kept defensible and in good repair until about a century ago, when the development of mighty naval guns made such expense pointless: if İstanbul was going to fall, it would fall to ships firing from the Bosphorus, not to soldiers advancing on the land walls.

During the late 1980s, the city undertook to rebuild the major gates for the delight of tourists. Debates raged in the Turkish newspapers over the style of the reconstruction. Some said the restorations were too theatrical, while others said that if the walls never actually did look like that, perhaps they *should* have. Anyway, the work allows you to imagine what it must have looked like in the Middle Ages. The gates which have been completed include the Topkapı, Mevlanakapı, and Belgrat Kapısı.

For a look at the most spectacular of the defences in the walls see Yedikule later.

By now you've seen the high points in this part of the city. If you've still got time and stamina, take your bearings for these places while you're up on the walls: outside the walls, on the Golden Horn, is the suburb of Eyüp, with a famous mosque and coffee house. Inside the walls, near the Golden Horn but back toward the centre, is the Rum Patrikhanesi, the seat of the Ecumenical Patriarch of the Orthodox Church. You can't see it, but you'll notice the prominent cupola of a Greek school near it.

Heading North or East Heading north, you can make your way to the Golden Horn at Balat or Ayvansaray and then take a bus, dolmuş or ferry to Eyüp. Otherwise, return to the Kariye Müzesi and make your way through the maze of streets to the Fethiye Camii, where there are more magnificent Byzantine mosaics. From the Fethiye Camii it's only a few minutes' walk to the seat of the Ecumenical Orthodox Patriarchate.

Fethiye Camii This, the Mosque of the Conquest, was built in the 1100s as the Church of the Theotokos Pammakaristos, or Church of the Joyous Mother of God. To reach it, ask someone to point you toward Draman Caddesi; follow this street until it changes names to become Fethiye Caddesi, then look left (north) to see the mosque, set in the midst of an open space.

The original monastery church was added to several times over the centuries, then converted to a mosque in 1591 to commemorate Sultan Murat III's victories in Georgia and Azerbaijan. Before its conversion it served as the headquarters of the Ecumenical Orthodox Patriarch (1456-1568); Mehmet the Conqueror visited to discuss theological questions here with Patriarch Gennadios not long after the conquest of the city. They talked things over in the side chapel known as the parecclesion, which has been restored to its former Byzantine splendour; the rest of the building remains a mosque. Visit the parecclesion to see the wonderful mosaics showing Jesus, the Apostles, the Virgin Mary, St John the Baptist, angels and saints. Entry to the parecclesion costs US$1; it is open daily from 9.30 am to 4.30 pm, closed Tuesday.

From the Fethiye Camii, ask directions for the walk of three short blocks to the Ecumenical Orthodox Patriarchate. If your goal is Eyüp, catch a bus or ferry from Fener, near the patriarchate.

Eyüp This suburb, once a village outside the walls, is named for the standard-bearer of the Prophet Muhammed. Eyüp Ensari (Ayoub in Arabic, Job in English) fell in battle here while carrying the banner of Islam during the Arab assault and siege of the city in 674-678. Eyüp had been a friend of the Prophet and a revered member of Islam's early leadership. His tomb and the **Eyüp Sultan Camii** are very sacred places for most Muslims, almost on a rank with Mecca, Medina and Jerusalem.

The most pleasant way to reach Eyüp is aboard a Golden Horn ferry, boarded at Galata Bridge (Eminönü side) or at one of the little landing stages along the route westward. Otherwise, take bus No 55 (Taksim to Eyüp Üçşehitler) or bus No 99 (Eminönü to Alibeyköyü), and get off at the 'Eyüp' stop. There are also dolmuşes: Edirnekapı to Eyüp, Topkapı to Eyüp, Aksaray to Eyüp, or Aksaray to Alibeyköyü. The mosque is open long hours every day, for free; avoid visits on Friday and on Muslim holy days, when the mosque and tomb will be very busy with worshippers, and infidels may be looked upon as interlopers. For a snack or a lunch, there are little pastry shops and snack stands on Kalenderhane Caddesi across from the mosque.

Ironically, Eyüp's tomb was first venerated by the Byzantines after the Arab armies withdrew, long before the coming of the Turks.

When Mehmet the Conqueror besieged the city in 1453, the tomb was no doubt known to him, and he undertook to build a grander and more fitting structure to commemorate it. A legend persists though, that the tomb had been lost and was miraculously rediscovered by Mehmet's Şeyh-ül-İslam (Supreme Islamic Judge). Perhaps both are true. If the tomb was known to Mehmet Fatih and his leadership, but not generally known by the common soldiers, it could be used for inspiration: have it miraculously 'rediscovered', and the army would take it as a good omen for the holy war in which they were engaged.

Whatever the truth, the tomb has been a very holy place ever since the Conquest. Mehmet had a mosque built here within five years of his victory, and succeeding sultans came to it to be girded with the Sword of Osman, a coronation-like ceremony signifying their supremacy. Mehmet's mosque was levelled by an earthquake in 1766, and a new mosque was built on the site by Sultan Selim III in 1800.

From the open space next to the complex, enter the great doorway to a large courtyard, then to a smaller court shaded by a huge, ancient plane tree. Note the wealth of brilliant İznik tilework on the walls here. To the left, behind the tilework and the gilded grillwork, is Eyüp's tomb; to the right is the mosque. Be careful to observe the Islamic proprieties when visiting: decent clothing (no shorts), and modest dresses for women, who should also have head, shoulders and arms covered. Take your shoes off before entering the small tomb enclosure, rich with silver, gold, crystal chandeliers, and coloured tiles. Try not to stand in front of those at prayer; act respectful; don't use a camera.

During your visit you may see boys dressed up in white satin suits with spangled caps and red sashes emblazoned with the word Maşallah. These lads are on the way to their circumcision and have made a stop beforehand at this holy place. After the actual operation, they'll be treated to huge celebration parties.

Across the court from the tomb is the **Eyüp Sultan Camii**, or Mosque of the Great Eyüp, where for centuries the Ottoman princes came for the Turkish equivalent of coronation: to gird on the Sword of Osman, signifying their power and title as *padişah* ('king of kings'), or sultan. The baroque style of the mosque, gilding, marble, windows, calligraphy and other decoration lavished on it, is elegant and even simple - if baroque can ever be described as simple.

As the Eyüp Sultan Camii is such a sacred place, many important people wanted to be buried in its precincts, including lots of grand viziers. Between the mosque-tomb complex and the Golden Horn you will see a virtual 'village' of octagonal tombs. Even those who were not to be buried here left their marks. The Valide Sultan Mihrişah, Queen Mother of Selim III, built important charitable institutions such as schools, baths and soup kitchens. Sokullu Mehmet Paşa, among the greatest of Ottoman grand viziers, donated a hospital which still functions as a medical clinic to this day.

Pierre Loti Café Up the hill to the north of the mosque is a café where 'Pierre Loti' (Louis Marie Julien Viaud, 1850-1923) used to sit and admire the city. Loti pursued a distinguished career in the French navy, and at the same time became his country's most celebrated novelist. Though a hard-headed mariner, he was also an inspired and incurable romantic who fell in love with the graceful and mysterious way of life he discovered in Ottoman İstanbul.

Loti set up house in Eyüp for several years and had a love affair, fraught with peril, with a married Turkish woman whom he called Aziyadé, the title of his most romantic and successful novel. He was transferred back to France and forced to leave his mistress and his beloved İstanbul, but he decorated his French home in Ottoman style and begged Aziyadé to flee and join him. Instead, her infidelity was discovered and she 'disappeared'.

Pierre Loti's romantic novels about the daily life of İstanbul under the last sultans introduced millions of European readers to Turkish customs and habits, and helped to counteract the politically inspired Turkophobia then spreading through Europe.

Loti loved the city, the decadent grandeur of the empire, and the fascinating late-mediaeval customs of a society in decline. When he sat in this café, under a shady grapevine, sipping some çay, he saw a Golden Horn busy with caiques, schooners and a few steam vessels. The water in the Golden Horn was still clean enough for boys to swim in, and the vicinity of the café was all pastureland.

The café which today bears his name may not have any actual connection to Loti, but it occupies a spot and enjoys a view which he must have enjoyed. It's in a warren of little streets on a promontory surrounded by the Eyüp Sultan Mezarlığı (Cemetery of the Great Eyüp), just north of the Eyüp mosque. The surest way to find it is to ask the way to the café via Karyağdı Sokak. Walk out of the mosque enclosure, turn right, and walk around the mosque complex keeping it on your right until you see the street going uphill into the cemetery. There's a little sign, 'Pierre Loti'. Hike up the steep hill on Karyağdı Sokak for 15 minutes to reach the café. If you take a taxi, it will follow a completely different route because of one-way streets. At my last visit, tea was US$0.35, soft drinks about twice as much. They serve a few snacks and sandwiches as well.

Back to the Centre

The ferry service on the Golden Horn will take you from the dock at Eyüp, not far from the mosque, down to the Galata Bridge at Eminönü. Ferries are not frequent, however, and you may instead find yourself going by bus or taxi. You can get a bus or dolmuş from Eyüp along the shore of the Golden Horn or up along the walls and into the city that way.

From the ferry, you'll view the old city walls, shipyards, warehouses, residential and industrial quarters, a government dry dock, naval buildings and the cast-iron Bulgarian church. Until a few years ago the Golden Horn was quite a sewer, but now a cleanup of the waters has begun, and green parks line much of its banks. Taking the shore road allows you to stop at the Ecumenical Orthodox Patriarchate, the Sultan Selim Camii and the Bulgarian church, all very interesting sights.

Balat

The quarter on the Golden Horn called Balat used to hold a large portion of the city's Jewish population. Spanish Jews driven from their country by the judges of the Spanish Inquisition found refuge in the Ottoman Empire in the late 1400s and early 1500s; the quincentenary (500th anniversary) of their migration to Ottoman lands is to be celebrated in 1992. As the sultan recognised, they were a boon to his empire: they brought news of the latest western advances in medicine, clock-making, ballistics and other means of warfare. The refugees from the inquisition set up the first printing presses in Turkey. Like all other religious 'nations' within the empire, they were governed by a supreme religious leader, the Chief Rabbi, who oversaw their adherence to biblical law and who was responsible to the sultan for their good conduct.

Though you can still find a few traces of Jewish life in this quarter, such as inscriptions in Hebrew over doorways, most of the city's Jewish residents have long since moved to more attractive quarters or emigrated to Europe or Israel. There is one İstanbul newspaper published in Ladino Spanish, the language brought by the immigrants in Renaissance times and still spoken in this city today.

Church of St Stephen

The Church of St Stephen of the Bulgars, between Balat and Fener on the Golden Horn, is made completely of cast iron. Most of the interior decoration is of cast iron as well. The building is unusual, and its history even more so.

During the 19th century the spirit of ethnic nationalism swept through the Ottoman Empire. Each of the many ethnic groups in the empire wanted to rule its own affairs. Groups identified themselves on the bases of language, religion and racial heritage. This sometimes led to problems, as with the Bulgarians.

The Bulgars, originally a Turkic-speaking people, came from the Volga in about 680 AD and overwhelmed the Slavic peoples living in what is today Bulgaria. They adopted the Slavic language and customs, and founded an empire which threatened the power of Byzantium. In the 800s they were converted to Christianity.

The head of the Orthodox church in the Ottoman Empire was an ethnic Greek; in order to retain as much power as possible, the patriarch was opposed to any ethnic divisions within the Orthodox church. He put pressure on the sultan not to allow the Bulgarians, Macedonians and Rumanians to establish their own groups.

The pressures of nationalism became too great, and the sultan was finally forced to recognise some sort of autonomy for the Bulgars. What he did was establish not a Bulgarian patriarchate, but an 'exarchate'. The Bulgarian Exarch would be 'less important' than, but independent of, the Greek Orthodox Patriarch. In this way the Bulgarians would get their desired ethnic recognition, and would get out from under the dominance of the Greeks.

St Stephen's is the Bulgarian Exarch's church; the former exarchate headquarters is directly across the street, and is still the office of St Stephen's clergy. The Gothic church was cast in Vienna, shipped down the Danube on 100 barges, and assembled here in 1871. A duplicate church, erected in Vienna, was destroyed by aerial bombing during WW II. The Viennese cast-iron church factory produced no other products, so far as we know.

A number of years ago St Stephen's was repaired and repainted. The first coat, of course, was metal primer. The whole procedure seemed to fit in well, what with a shipyard on the opposite shore of the Golden Horn.

The church is open for services on most mornings, but come on Sunday to be certain. If it's not open, the priest or sacristan may be present to let you in so you can enjoy the pretty garden, tap a coin on the church wall to verify that it's metal, and admire the interior.

Fener

Next quarter along the Golden Horn from Balat is Fener (fehn-EHR, Phanari in Greek: lantern or lighthouse), where the Ecumenical Orthodox Patriarch has his seat. To find the patriarchate (patrikhane, pah-TREEK-hah-neh), you'll have to head inland from the Fener ferry dock on the Golden Horn, and ask. People will point the way.

Ecumenical Orthodox Patriarchate The Ecumenical Patriarch is a ceremonial head of the Orthodox churches, though most of the churches – in Greece, Cyprus, the Soviet Union and other countries – have their own patriarchs or archbishops who are independent of İstanbul. Nevertheless, the 'sentimental' importance of the patriarchate, here in the city which saw the great era of Byzantine and Orthodox influence, is considerable.

These days the patriarch is a Turkish citizen. He is nominated by the church and appointed by the Turkish government to be an official in the Directorate of Religious Affairs. In this capacity he is the religious leader of the country's Orthodox citizens.

Assuming you don't have any business with the patriarchate, your reason for visiting is to look at the **Church of St George**, within the patriarchate compound. Like the rest of the buildings here, it is a modest place, built in 1720. The ornate patriarchal throne may date from the last years of Byzantium. The patriarchate itself has been in this spot since about 1600. In 1941 a disastrous fire destroyed many of the buildings, but spared the church.

Selimiye Camii

Only a few blocks south-east of the patriarchate (ask someone to point the way) is the mosque of Yavuz Selim (Selim I, 1512-1520) on a hilltop overlooking the Golden Horn. Sultan Selim 'the Grim' laid the foundations of Ottoman greatness for his son and successor, Süleyman the Magnificent. Though he ruled for a very short time, Selim virtually doubled the empire's territory, solidified its institutions and filled its treasury. He came to power by deposing his father, Beyazıt II (1481-1512), who died 'mysteriously' soon thereafter. To avoid any threat to his power, and thus the sort of disastrous civil war which had torn the empire apart in the days before Mehmet the Conqueror, Selim had all his brothers put to death, and in the eight years of his reign he had eight grand viziers beheaded. So 'Grim' is indeed the word.

But all of this violence was in the interests of empire-building, at which he was a master. He doubled the empire's extent during his short reign, conquering part of Persia, and all of Syria and Egypt. He took from Egypt's decadent, defeated rulers the title Caliph of Islam, which was borne by his successors until 1924. In his spare time he liked to write poetry in Persian, the literary language of the time. When he died, the empire was well on the

way to becoming the most powerful and brilliant in the world.

The mosque was built mostly during the reign of Selim's son Süleyman. It is especially pretty, with lots of fine, very early İznik tiles (the yellow colour is a clue to their 'earliness') and a shallow dome similar to that of Sancta Sophia. Selim's tomb behind the mosque is also very fine. Among the others buried nearby are Sultan Abdül Mecit (1839-1861) and several children of Süleyman the Magnificent.

To the Galata Bridge

You can walk back down the hill to the Fener ferry dock and catch a ferry down to the bridge. They aren't all that frequent, so check the schedule first. Otherwise, catch a bus or dolmuş along the waterfront street, Abdül Ezel Paşa Caddesi, headed for Eminönü.

Yedikule

Yedikule or The Fortress of the Seven Towers is a long way from most other sights of interest in İstanbul, and involves a special trip. Situated where the great city walls meet the Sea of Marmara, it's accessible by cheap train from Sirkeci; take any *banliyö* (that's the French *banlieue* in Turkish guise) train and hop off at Yedikule, then walk around to the entrance at the north-east. You can take bus No 80 ('Yedikule') from Eminönü, Sultanahmet and Divan Yolu, but the ride may take the better part of an hour if there's any sort of traffic. The castle is open every day from 9.30 am to 5 pm; admission costs US$1.

If you arrived in İstanbul by train from Europe, or if you rode in from the airport along the seashore, you've already had a glance of Yedikule towering over the southern approaches to the city.

Theodosius I built a triumphal arch here in the late 300s. When the next Theodosius (408-450) built his great land walls, he incorporated the arch. Four of the fortress' seven towers were built as part of the Emperor Theodosius' walls; the other three, inside the walls, were added by Mehmet the Conqueror. Under the Byzantines, the triumphal arch became known as the **Golden Gate**, and was used for triumphal state processions into and out of the city. For a time, its gates were indeed plated with gold. The doorway was sealed in the late Byzantine period.

In Ottoman times the fortress was used for defence, as a repository for the imperial treasury, as a prison and as a place of execution. Diplomatic practice in Renaissance times included chucking into loathsome prisons the ambassadors of countries with which yours didn't get along. For foreign ambassadors to the Sublime Porte, Yedikule was that prison. Latin and German inscriptions still visible in the Ambassadors' Tower bring the place's history to light. It was also here that Sultan Osman II, a 17-year-old youth, was executed in 1622 during a revolt of the Janissary corps. The kaftan he was wearing when he was murdered is now on display in Topkapı Palace's costumes collection.

The best view of the city walls and of the fortress is from the **Tower of Sultan Ahmet III**, near the gate in the city wall.

Beyond the fortress are the city's leather-tanning industries. Even in mediaeval times, the tanners were required to work outside the city walls because their work generated such terrible odours. Plans now call for them to be moved to the Asian suburbs (downwind) soon.

Right down at the shoreline, where the land walls meet the Sea of Marmara, is the **Marble Tower**, once part of a small Byzantine imperial seaside villa.

BEYOĞLU

Beyoğlu (BEY-oh-loo) is fascinating because it holds the architectural evidence of the Ottoman Empire's frantic attempts to modernise and reform itself, and the evidence of the European powers' attempts

to undermine and subvert it. The Ottomans were struggling for their very existence as a state; the Europeans were struggling for domination of the entire Middle East, and especially its oil (already important at that time), holy places and sea lanes through the Suez Canal to India.

New ideas walked into Ottoman daily life down the streets of Pera (which with Galata comprises Beyoğlu). The Europeans, who lived in Pera, brought new fashions, machines, arts and manners, and rules for the diplomatic game. The Old City across the Golden Horn was content to sit tight and continue living in the Middle Ages with its oriental bazaars, great mosques and palaces, narrow streets and traditional values. But Pera was to have telephones, underground trains, tramways, electric light and modern municipal government. Even the sultans got into the act. From the reign of Abdül Mecit (1839-1861) onward, no sultan lived in Mehmet the Conqueror's palace at Topkapı. Rather, they built opulent European-style palaces in Pera and along the shores of the Bosphorus to the north.

The easiest way to tour Beyoğlu is to start from its busy nerve-centre: Taksim Square. You can get a dolmuş directly to Taksim from Aksaray or Sirkeci; buses to Taksim are even more plentiful.

History

Often called the New City, Beyoğlu is 'new' just in a relative sense. There was a settlement on the northern shore of the Golden Horn, near Karaköy Square, before the birth of Jesus. By the time of Theodosius II (408-450), it was large enough to become an official suburb of Constantinople. Theodosius built a fortress here, no doubt to complete the defence system of his great land walls, and called it Galata (gah-LAH-tah), as the suburb was then the home of many Galatians. During the height of the Byzantine Empire, Galata became a favourite place for foreign trading

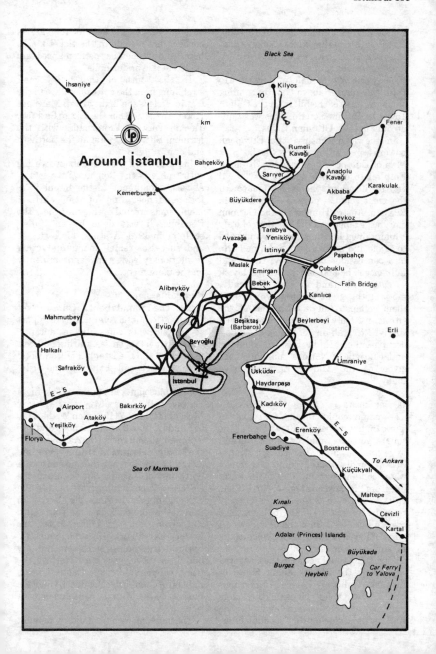

Around İstanbul

companies to set up business. To this day, it still harbours the offices of many non-Muslim businesses and foreign representatives.

The word 'new' actually applies more to Pera, the quarter above Galata, running along the crest of the hill from the Galata Tower to Taksim Square. This was built up only in later Ottoman times.

In the 19th century, the European powers were waiting eagerly for the 'Sick Man of Europe' (the decadent Ottoman Empire) to collapse so that they could grab territory and spheres of influence. All the great colonial powers – the British, Russian, Austro-Hungarian and German empires, France and the kingdom of Italy – maintained lavish embassies and tried to cajole and pressure the Sublime Porte into concessions of territory, trade and influence. The embassy buildings, lavish as ever, still stand in Pera. Ironically, most of the great empires which built them collapsed along with that of the Ottomans. Only the British and French survived to grab any of the spoils. Their occupation of Middle Eastern countries under League of Nations 'mandates' has given us the Middle East we have today.

Taksim Square

The name could mean 'my taxi' in Turkish, but it doesn't; after a look at the square, you may wonder why not. Rather, it is named after the *taksim* (tahk-SEEM), or distribution point, in the city's water-conduit system. The main water line from the Belgrade Forest, north of the city, was laid to this point in 1732 by Sultan Mahmut I (1730-1754), and the branch lines lead from the taksim to all parts of the city. You'll get a glance at the taksim in a moment.

First thing you'll notice in the elongated 'square' is the **Atatürk Kültür Sarayı** or Atatürk Cultural Palace (sometimes called the Opera House), the large building at the eastern end. In the summertime, during the İstanbul Inter-

national Festival, tickets for the various concerts are on sale in the ticket kiosks here, and numerous performances are staged in its various halls.

To the south of the grassy mall stretching from the cultural palace to the traffic circle is the luxury Etap Marmara Hotel. To the north is the **Taksim Gezi Yeri**, Taksim Park or Promenade, with the İstanbul Sheraton Hotel at the northern end of it.

In the midst of the roundabout swirling with traffic is the **Cumhuriyet ve İstiklal Abidesi**, Monument to the Republic & Independence, one of the earliest monuments erected during the time of the Republic. It was done by an Italian sculptor in 1928. Atatürk, his assistant and successor İsmet İnönü and other revolutionary leaders appear prominently on the monument.

North of Taksim

From the roundabout, Cumhuriyet Caddesi (Republic Ave) leads north past several sidewalk cafés and restaurants, banks, travel agencies, airline offices, nightclubs and the İstanbul Hilton Hotel to the districts called Harbiye and Şişli.

Military Museum A km north of Taksim in Harbiye is the Askeri Müzesi or Military Museum (tel 148-7115), open Wednesday to Sunday, from 9 am to 12 noon and 1 to 5 pm; admission costs US$2. Concerts by the *Mehter* or Ottoman Military Band are at 3 and 4 pm. To reach the museum, walk north out of Taksim Square along the eastern side of Cumhuriyet Caddesi (by Taksim Park). During the 10 or 15 minutes' walk you'll pass, on your right, the Divan Oteli, the Hilton Hotel, the Radyo Evi (Turkish radio and TV broadcasting studios), and several military buildings. When you come to Harbiye, the point where Valikonağı Caddesi bears right off of Cumhuriyet Caddesi, you'll see the gate to the Military Museum on your right.

The museum, within a military complex,

is of two parts. Entering from Cumhuriyet Caddesi, you'll come first to the new section. On the ground floor are displays of weapons, a 'heroes' gallery' (*şehit galerisi*) with artefacts from fallen Turkish soldiers of many wars, displays of Turkish military uniforms through the ages, and many glass cases holding battle standards, both Turkish and captured. The captured ones include Byzantine, Greek, British, Italian, Austro-Hungarian, and Imperial Russian. Perhaps the most interesting of the exhibits are the *sâyebânlar,* or imperial pavilions. These luxurious cloth shelters, heavily worked with thread of silver and gold, jewels, precious silks and elegant tracery, were the battle headquarters for sultans during the summer campaign season.

The upper floor of the new section has fascinating displays of Ottoman tents, and more imperial pavilions, as well as a room devoted to Atatürk who was, of course, a famous Ottoman general before he became founder and commander-in-chief of the Turkish republican army, and first president of the Turkish republic.

To reach the old section of the Military Museum, walk out of the new section, turn right, and walk down the hill past displays of old cannon, then turn right again, and climb the steps into the museum. Signs along the way read 'To the Other Departments'. The cannons, by the way, include Gatling guns bearing the sultan's monogram, cast in Vienna.

The old section is where you really feel the spirit of the Ottoman Empire. It has exhibits of armour (including cavalry), uniforms, field furniture made out of weapons (chairs with rifles for legs, etc), and a *Türk-Alman Dostluk Köşesi* (Turco-German Friendship Corner) with mementoes of Turkish and German military collaboration before and during World War I. Some of the exhibits here are truly amazing. My favourites are the great chain that the Byzantines spread across the mouth of the Golden Horn to keep Mehmet the Conqueror's ships out

during the battle for Constantinople in 1453; and a tapestry woven by Ottoman sailors (who must have had lots of time on their hands) showing the flags of all of the world's important maritime nations.

Perhaps the best reason to visit the Military Museum is for a little concert by the Mehter. The Mehter, according to historians, was the first true military band in the world. Its purpose was not to make pretty music for dancing, but to precede the conquering Ottoman paşas into vanquished towns, impressing upon the defeated populace that everything was going to be different now. They would march in with a steady, measured pace, turning all together to face the left side of the line of march, then the right side. With tall Janissary headdresses, fierce moustaches, brilliant instruments and even kettledrums, they did their job admirably.

South of Taksim

To the south, two streets meet just before the roundabout. Sıraselviler Caddesi goes south and İstiklal Caddesi goes southwest. The famous **taksim** is to the southwest of the roundabout, just to the right of İstiklal Caddesi. It is a little octagonal building of stone. You'll also notice a wall with fountains and a pool, a little public celebration of the city's water system.

Nestled in the small triangle formed by the two mentioned streets, rising above the shops and restaurants which hide its foundations, is the **Aya Triada Kilisesi** or Greek Orthodox Church of the Holy Trinity. If it's open, as it is often during the day, you can visit: take either street out of Taksim Square, and look for the first possibility to turn toward the church.

Now head down İstiklal Caddesi for a look at the vestiges of 19th-century Ottoman life.

İstiklal Caddesi

Stretching between Taksim Square and Tünel Square, İstiklal Caddesi (ees-teek-

LAHL, Independence Ave) was once known as the Grande Rue de Pera. It was the street with all the smart shops, several large embassies and churches, many impressive office buildings and a scattering of tea shops and restaurants. Some vignettes of this glory still survive. For decades İstiklal Caddesi was heavy with traffic, its buildings cracked and dusty, but renovation and restoration efforts are under way, and it will soon be a street for pedestrians only.

As you stroll along İstiklal, try to imagine it during its heyday a century ago, peopled by frock-coated merchants and Ottoman officials, European officers in colourful uniforms, women with parasols, and even some lightly veiled Turkish women.

Just out of Taksim Square, the first building you'll come to on your right is the former French plague hospital (1719), for years used as the **French Consulate General** in İstanbul. There's a **French library** here as well.

İstiklal Caddesi is packed with little restaurants and snack shops, bank branches, clothing stores, itinerant pedlars, shoppers and strollers. If you have the time, take a few detours down the narrow side streets. Any one will reveal glimpses of Beyoğlu life. The street names alone are intriguing: Büyükparmakkapı Sokak, 'Gate of the Thumb St'; Sakızağacı Sokak, 'Pine-Gum Tree St'; Kuloğlu Sokak, 'Slave's Son St'.

This used to be the cinema centre of İstanbul. With the advent of television, the cinemas found it necessary to appeal to baser appetites, which is what many of them do now. Baser appetites are also satisfied by going up some of the stairways which lead from the back streets. Though I wouldn't recommend doing a lot of wandering along narrow, dark streets here late at night, the area is perfectly safe during the day and early evening.

A few streets before coming to Galatasaray Square, look on the left for Suterazisi Sokak. Turn into this street,

and at its end you'll find the **Tarihi Galatasaray Hamamı** or Historical Galatasaray Turkish Bath. The bath is one of the city's best, with lots of marble decoration, comfy little cubicles for resting and sipping tea after the bath, pretty fountains and even a shoeshine service. However, the staff is very hungry for tips. If you go, you'll enjoy it more if you don't go alone; best of all, go with a Turkish friend. The women's part of the bath, by the way, is not nearly so elegant as the men's.

Galatasaray Square Halfway along the length of İstiklal Caddesi is Galatasaray (gah-LAH-tah-sah-rah-yee), named for the imperial lycée you can see behind the huge gates on your left. This building once housed the country's most prestigious school, established in its present form by Sultan Abdül Aziz in 1868, who wanted a place where Ottoman youth could hear lectures in both Turkish and French. Across İstiklal from the school is a branch of the PTT.

Çiçek Pasajı Before coming into the square (really just an intersection) of Galatasaray, you'll notice on your right a small street with some flower-sellers' stalls. This is İstanbul's renowned Çiçek Pasajı (chee-CHEHK pah-sah-zhuh), or 'Flower Passage'. Besides the flowers, there is a charming market called the Balık Pazar, literally the 'fish market', although meats, fruits, vegetables, condiments and kitchen items are sold as well. You can do a lot of interesting exploring here.

Turn right from İstiklal into Sahne Sokak, the flower-lined street, and then right again into a courtyard. On the lintel of the doorway into the courtyard you can see the legend 'Cité de Pera', for this was at one time the municipal headquarters of a 'modern' building which symbolised Pera's growth as the 'modern' European-style city. For years the courtyard held a dozen cheap little restaurant-taverns. In good weather beer barrels were rolled out onto the pavement, marble slabs were balanced on top, little stools were put around, and enthusiastic revellers filled the stools as soon as they hit the ground.

Now, the restoration of İstiklal has reached the venerable Çiçek Pasajı. The makeshift tables and little stools have been replaced by comfortable, solid wooden tables and benches, the broken pavement has been replaced with smooth tiles, and the courtyard has been covered with a glass canopy to keep out foul weather. The clientele is better behaved now, and its smattering of adventurous tourists has become a significant proportion. It's a favourite destination for local guys who have picked up foreign women and want to show them some tame İstanbul nightlife. But for all that, the Çiçek Pasajı is still OK for an evening of beer drinking, food and conversation.

Pick a good place, pull up a stool and order a mug of (beyaz or siyah) beer. For something stronger, ask for *Bir kadeh rakı* (BEER kah-deh rah-KUH), 'A shot of rakı'. As for food, printed menus, even if you can find them, mean little here. If you already know a few Turkish dishes you like, order them, but ask prices first. Otherwise, the waiter will lead you to the kitchen so you can see what's cooking. As you eat and drink, at least three nearby revellers will want to know where you are from; when you tell them, the response is always *Çok iyi*, 'Very good!'

Many regulars have now abandoned the Çiçek Pasajı to the tourists and their attendant carpet and leather-apparel touts, opting instead to dine at little *meyhanes* (tavernas) deeper in the market.

Balık Pazar Walk out of the courtyard to the flower stalls on Sahne Sokak, turn right, then look for a little passage off to the left. This is the Avrupa Pasajı, the 'European Passage', a small gallery with marble paving and little shops selling this and that. In Pera's heyday it was undoubtedly very elegant.

Further up the market street, another little street (Duduodalari Sokak) leads off to the left, down to the British Consulate General (more of that in a moment). Continuing along Sahne Sokak, though, near this junction on your right is the entrance to the **Üç Horan Ermeni Kilisesi**, the Armenian Church of Three Altars. You can visit if the doors are open.

Past the Armenian church, Sahne Sokak changes names to become Balık Sokak. Leading off to the right from Balık Sokak are narrow streets harbouring numerous meyhanes where the old-time life of the Çiçek Pasajı continues, untrammelled by the glossy overlays of tourist İstanbul. Feel free to wander in and have a meal and a drink. You will probably not encounter much English, either on menus or on waiters' lips.

Unless you want to continue down the slope among the fishmongers on Balık Sokak, turn back and then right into Duduodalari Sokak, and stroll down this little street past fancy food shops, butchers', bakers', and greengrocers' shops to the British Consulate General. Along the way you may notice small stands where *midye* (MEED-yeh, skewered mussels) are frying in hot oil, and others where *kokoreç* (koh-koh-RETCH, lamb intestines packed with more lamb intestines) is being grilled over charcoal. I recommend the mussels, but get a skewer that's been freshly cooked.

At the end of the market street you emerge into the light. Right in front of you is Meşrutiyet Caddesi, which makes its way down to the Pera Palas Oteli and the American Consulate General. On the corner here are the huge gates to the **British Consulate General**, an Italian palazzo designed by Sir Charles Barry and built in 1845. Sir Charles is the one who did the Houses of Parliament in London.

Walk past the British Consulate General along Meşrutiyet Caddesi. Watch for an iron gate and a small passage on the left, leading into a little courtyard with a derelict lamppost in the centre. Enter the courtyard, turn right up the stairs, and you'll discover the Greek Orthodox **Church of Panaya Isodyon**. It's quiet and very tidy, hidden away in the midst of other buildings. The doors are open to visitors most of the day.

When you've seen the church, go down the stairs *behind* it (not the stairs you came up). Several little streets here are lined with tiny shops, many bearing their Greek proprietors' names. Turn right, and just past the church property on the right-hand side you will see the entrance to the **Yeni Rejans Lokantası** or New Regency Restaurant. Founded, as legend would have it, by three White Russian dancing girls who fled the Russian Revolution, the restaurant is still operated by their Russian-speaking descendants. This area of Beyoğlu was a favourite with Russian émigrés after the revolution. The Yeni Rejans, by the look of it, was a cabaret complete with orchestra loft and grand piano. Lunch and dinner are still served except on Sunday. The food is good, though you pay a certain amount for the seedy nostalgia.

When you go out the restaurant door, down the steps, turn right, then left along the narrow alley called Olivo Çikmazı, which brings you back to İstiklal Caddesi.

Back on İstiklal Across İstiklal, notice the large Italian Gothic church behind a fence. The Franciscan **Church of San Antonio di Padua** was founded here in 1725; the brick building dates from 1913.

Cross over to the church, turn right, and head down İstiklal once more. After the church you will pass Eskiçiçekçi Sokak on the left, then Nuriziya Sokak. The third street, a little cul-de-sac, ends at the gates of the **Palais de France**, once the French embassy to the Ottoman sultan. The grounds of the palace are extensive. The buildings include the chapel of St Louis of the French, founded here in 1581, though the present chapel building dates from the 1830s. You can get a better look at the palace and grounds another way: read on.

A few steps along İstiklal brings you to the pretty **Netherlands Consulate General** (1855), built by the former architect to the Russian tsar. The first embassy building here dated from 1612. Past the consulate, turn left down the hill on Postacılar Sokak. You'll see the **Dutch Chapel** on the left side of the street. If it's open, take a look inside. The chapel is now the home of the Union Church of İstanbul, a multinational Protestant congregation that holds services in English.

The narrow street turns right, bringing you face to face with the former **Spanish Embassy**. The little chapel, founded in 1670, is still in use though the embassy is not.

The street then bends left and changes names to become Tomtom Kaptan Sokak. At the foot of the slope, on the right, is the **Palazzo di Venezia**, once the embassy for Venice, now the Italian Consulate. Venice was one of the great Mediterranean maritime powers during Renaissance times, and when Venetian and Ottoman fleets were not madly trading with one another, they were locked in ferocious combat.

To the left across the open space is a side gate to the Palais de France. Peek through the gates for another, better view of the old French embassy grounds. Then you've got to slog back up that hill to İstiklal Caddesi.

Continuing along İstiklal, the **Church of St Mary Draperis** (1678, 1789) is behind an iron fence and down a flight of steps. It's rarely open to visitors. Past the church, still on the left-hand side, is the grand **Soviet Consulate General**, once the embassy of imperial Russia. It is still a busy place as the Soviet Union has a common border with Turkey, and dozens of Soviet ships pass through the Bosphorus and the Dardanelles each day.

Now take a detour: turn right (north-west) off İstiklal Caddesi along Asmalı Mescit Sokak, a narrow, typical Beyoğlu street which holds some fusty antique shops, food shops, suspect hotels and little eateries. After 50 metres the street intersects Meşrutiyet Caddesi. To the left of the intersection is the American Library & Cultural Center, and just beyond it the pretty marble mansion which was first the American embassy, now the **American Consulate General**. Built as a pleasure palace for a rich man's mistress, it is now heavily fortified. To the right of the intersection is the grand old Pera Palas Oteli.

Pera Palas Oteli The Pera Palas (peh-RAH pah-LAHS, Pera Palace) was built in the 1890s by Georges Nagelmackers, the Belgian entrepreneur who founded the Compagnie International des Wagons-Lits et Grands Express Européens (1868). Nagelmackers, who had succeeded in linking Paris and Constantinople by luxury train, found that once he got his esteemed passengers to the Ottoman imperial capital there was no suitable place for them to stay. So he built the hotel here in the section today called Tepebaşı. It opened in the 1890s, advertised as having 'a thoroughly healthy situation, being high up and isolated on all four sides', and 'overlooking the Golden Horn and the whole panorama of Stamboul'.

It's a grand place, with huge public rooms, a sympathetic bar, a good dining room and a birdcage lift. Atatürk often stayed here; his luxurious suite on the 2nd floor (room No 101) is now a museum, preserved as it was when he used it (open from 2 to 5 pm, or ask at the reception desk). The hotel was a favourite of Agatha Christie. The author usually stayed in room No 411, which at the time enjoyed a view of a little park and wooden theatre building. The view is now of the city's new meeting and exhibition centre. Once you've taken a turn through the hotel, and perhaps had a drink in the bar or tea in the salon (not for the budget-minded), head back to İstiklal Caddesi.

Near Tünel Square When you reach İstiklal, go straight across it and down the hill on Kumbaracı Yokuşu to reach the **Crimean Memorial Church**. The Anglican church was built as a memorial to English troops of the Crimean War, and designed by C E Street. Lord Stratford de Redcliffe, the very influential British ambassador of the time, was instrumental in the church's foundation. The building is not often open to visitors.

Back on İstiklal, you will notice two good **bookstores** on the left-hand side. The ABC Kitabevi has Turkish and foreign-language books, and Haşet (Hachette) has books, magazines and newspapers in French, English and Turkish.

Next along the avenue, on your left, is the **Royal Swedish Consulate**, once the Swedish embassy. After that the Four Seasons Restaurant. The road curves to the right; the open space here is Tünel Square.

Tünel

You now have a chance to take a peek at İstanbul's underground railway. Built by French engineers in 1875, the Tünel (teu-NEHL, Tunnel) allowed the European merchants to get from their offices in Galata to their homes in Pera without hiking up the steep hillside. Up to a few decades ago, the cars were of dark wood with numerous coats of bright lacquer. A modernisation programme replaced them with modern rubber-tyred Paris metro-type trains. Modernisation also swept away the quaint Swiss-chalet lower station and replaced it with a concrete bunker; and signs which once said, 'It is requested that cigarettes not be smoked' were exchanged for new ones that say 'No Smoking'.

The fare is US$0.18. Trains run as frequently as necessary during rush hours, about every five or 10 minutes other times. Though you may want to use the Tünel later to ascend the hill, right now you should stay on foot. There's a lot to see as you descend slowly toward Karaköy: a

Whirling Dervish monastery, the Galata Tower and fascinating glimpses of Beyoğlu daily life.

Whirling Dervish Monastery Though the main road (İstiklal Caddesi) bears right as you come into Tünel Square, you should continue walking straight on. The surface turns to paving stones, the street narrows and takes the name of Galip Dede Caddesi, and on your left you'll notice the doorway into the Galata Mevlevi Tekkesi. The Dervishes no longer whirl here, the Dervish orders having been banned in the early days of the republic because of their ultraconservative religious politics. Though a few orders still survive unofficially, this hall is now officially the Museum of Divan Literature and holds exhibits of *hattat* (Arabic calligraphy). It's open from 9.30 am to 4.30 pm, closed Monday; admission costs US$0.75.

The Whirling Dervishes, or Mevlevi, took their name from the great Sufi mystic and poet, Jelaleddin Rumi (1207-1273). Rumi was called Mevlana ('Our Leader') by his disciples. Sufis (Muslim mystics) seek mystical communion with God through various means. For Mevlana, it was through a sema, involving chants, prayers, music and a whirling dance. The whirling induced a trance-like state which made it easier for the mystic to 'get close to God'. The Dervish order, founded in Konya during the 1200s, flourished throughout the Ottoman Empire and survives in Konya even today. The Galata Mevlevihane (Whirling Dervish Hall) was open to foreign, non-Muslim visitors, who could witness the sema. The Dervishes stressed the unity of mankind before God regardless of creed.

The Turks are passionate gardeners, as you'll see when you enter the grounds. In the midst of the city is this oasis of flowers and shady nooks, where you can sit and have a glass of tea. As you sip, notice the tomb of the sheik by the entrance passage, and also the *şadırvan* (ablutions fountain).

The modest frame *tekke* (a place where

Dervishes hold religious meetings and ceremonies) was restored in 1967-1972, but the first building here was erected by a high officer in the court of Sultan Beyazıt II in 1491. Its first *şeyh* (sheik, or leader) was Şeyh Muhammed Şemai Sultan Divani, a grandson of the great Mevlana. The building burned in 1766, but was repaired that same year by Sultan Mustafa III.

As you approach the building, notice the little graveyard on the left. The stones are very beautiful with their graceful Arabic lettering. The shapes on top of them are of hats of the deceased; each hat denotes a different religious rank.

Inside the tekke, the central area was where the Dervishes whirled. In the galleries above, visitors could sit and watch. Separate areas were set aside for the orchestra and for female visitors (behind the lattices). Don't neglect the exhibits of calligraphy, writing instruments and other paraphernalia associated with this highly developed Ottoman art.

Leaving the Whirling Dervish monastery, turn left down Galip Dede Caddesi, lined with shops selling books, Turkish and European musical instruments, plumbing supplies and cabinetmakers' necessities such as wood veneers. The hillside here is covered with winding streets, little passageways, alleys of stairs and European-style houses built mostly in the 19th century. There are some older houses, a glimpse of what life was like for the European émigrés who came to live here and make their fortunes centuries ago. A few minutes' walk along Galip Dede Caddesi will bring you to Beyoğlu's oldest landmark, the Galata Tower.

Galata Tower
The Galata Kulesi or Galata Tower was the highpoint in the Genoese fortifications of Galata. The tower, rebuilt many times, is ancient. Today it holds an observatory and a restaurant/nightclub. The circular tower's lofty **panorama balcony** is open to

visitors from 10 am to 6 pm every day, for a fee of US$1. In the evening the restaurant, bar and nightclub swing into action.

Daily life in the vicinity of the tower is a fascinating sight. There are woodworking shops, turners' lathes, workshops making veneer and other materials for interior decoration, a few dusty antique stores. This neighbourhood is also one of the last inhabited by the city's Spanish-speaking Jewish population. There's a synagogue named **Neve Shalom** only a block north-east of the Galata Tower, toward Şişhane Square. This was the site of a horrible massacre by Palestinian gunmen during the summer of 1986.

From the Galata Tower, continue downhill on the street called Yüksek Kaldırım to reach Karaköy.

Karaköy

In order to avoid 'contamination' of their way of life, both the later Byzantine emperors and the Ottoman sultans relegated European traders to Galata. Under the late Byzantines, Genoese traders got such a hold on the town that it was virtually a little Genoa. Though Galata, now usually called Karaköy, still harbours many shipping and commercial offices, and some large banks, it is also busy with small traders.

As you approach the Galata Bridge from Karaköy, the busy ferry docks and also the docks for Mediterranean cruise ships are to your left. To your right are a few fishmongers' stands and a warren of little streets filled with hardware stores and plumbing-supply houses. Scattered throughout this neighbourhood are Greek and Armenian churches and schools and a large synagogue, reminders of the time when virtually all of the empire's businesspeople were non-Muslims.

At the far end of the square from the Galata Bridge, right at the lower end of Yüksek Kaldırım, Voyvoda Caddesi (also called Bankalar Caddesi) leads up a slope to the right toward Şişhane Square. This street was the banking centre during the days of the empire, and many merchant banks still have headquarters or branches here. The biggest building was that of the Ottoman Bank, now a branch of the Turkish Republic's Central Bank.

Karaköy has busy bus stops, dolmuş queues and the lower station of the Tünel. As of this writing the place is pure chaos, as work goes forward to reorganise the square around the traffic patterns required by the new Galata Bridge. To find the Tünel station descend into the hubbub of the square from Yüksek Kaldırım, and turn into the next major street on the right, Sabahattin Evren Caddesi. The Tünel is a few steps along this street, on the right, in what looks like a concrete bunker.

THE BOSPHORUS

The strait which connects the Black Sea and Sea of Marmara, 32 km long, 500 metres to 3 km wide, 50 to 120 metres (average 60 metres) deep, has determined the history not only of İstanbul, but even of the empires governed from this city. In earlier centuries it was one of the city's strongest defences. Until the age of armoured gunboats, the city was never seriously threatened from the sea.

In Turkish, the strait is the Boğaziçi, from *boğaz*, throat or strait, and *iç*, inside or interior: within the strait.

The Bosphorus provides a convenient boundary for geographers. As it was a military bottleneck, armies marching from the east tended to stop on the eastern side, and those from the west on the western. So the western side was always more like Europe, the eastern more like Asia. Though the modern Turks think of themselves as Europeans, it is still common to say that Europe ends and Asia begins at the Bosphorus.

Except for the few occasions when the Bosphorus froze solid, crossing it always meant going by boat – until 1973. Late in that year, the Bosphorus Bridge, fourth longest in the world, was opened to travellers. For the first time in history there was a firm physical link across the straits from Europe to Asia. (Interestingly, there had been a plan for a bridge during the late years of the Ottoman Empire, but nothing came of it.) Traffic was so heavy over the new bridge that it paid for itself in less than a decade. Now there is a second bridge, the Fatih Köprüsü, (named after Mehmet the Conqueror, *Mehmet Fatih*) just north of Rumeli Hisar. A third bridge, even farther north, is already in the works.

History

Greek legend recounts that Zeus, unfaithful to his wife Hera in an affair with Io, tried to make up for it by turning his erstwhile lover into a cow. Hera, for good measure, provided a horsefly to sting Io on the rump and drive her across the strait. In ancient Greek, *bous* is cow, and *poros* is crossing place, giving us Bosphorus: the place where the cow crossed.

From earliest times it has been a maritime road to adventure. It is thought that Ulysses' travels brought him through the Bosphorus. Byzas, founder of Byzantium, explored these waters before the time of Jesus. Mehmet the Conqueror built two mighty fortresses at the strait's narrowest point so he could close it off to allies of the Byzantines. Each spring, enormous Ottoman armies would take several days to cross the Bosphorus on their way to campaigns in Asia. At the end of WW I, the defeated Ottoman capital cowered under the guns of Allied frigates anchored in the strait. And when the republic was proclaimed, the last sultan of the Ottoman Empire sneaked quietly down to the Bosphorus shore, boarded a launch, and sailed away to exile in a British man-of-war.

Touring the Bosphorus

You could spend several days exploring the sights of the Bosphorus. It holds five Ottoman palaces, four castles, the mammoth suburb of Üsküdar, and dozens of interesting little towns. But if you're pressed for time, you can see the main points in a day.

The essential feature of any Bosphorus tour is a cruise along the strait. You just can't appreciate its grandeur and beauty completely if you're in a bus or car. On the other hand, it's time-consuming to take a ferry to a certain dock, debark, visit a palace or castle, and return to the dock to wait for the next boat, so a trip combining travel by both land and sea is best. I recommend that you begin your explorations with a ferry cruise up the strait. This will give you a glimpse of everything, and allow you to decide which sites you'd like to visit and see in more detail. Following is a description of the cruise, after which detailed information is given on the more important sites.

A Bosphorus Cruise

Though tour agencies and luxury hotels have private boats for cruises on the Bosphorus, it's considerably cheaper and much more fun to go the authentic way, on one of the orange-and-white ferries of the Denizyolları (Turkish Maritime Lines). Special Bosphorus cruise trips are operated twice daily on summer weekdays and Saturdays, and five times a day on summer Sundays and holidays. If you can't afford the time for the whole trip, you can get off at one of the four stops en route.

Reading the Ferry Schedule The special cruise ferries are called Boğaziçi Özel Gezi Seferleri. Look for this heading on the schedules, which are posted in the waiting area of each ferry dock. By tradition, European ports of call are printed on the schedules in black, Asian ports in red.

Times will be close to the following, but check to be sure: Eminönü departures are on summer weekdays at 10.30 am, 12.30 and 2.10 pm; in winter daily at 10.30 am and 1.30 pm; Anadolu Kavağı departures are on summer weekdays at 1.30, 3 and 5.10 pm; in winter daily departures at 3 and 5.10 pm. On Sunday and holidays in summer, departure times from Eminönü are 10 and 11 am, 12 noon, 1.30 and 3 pm. From Anadolu Kavağı, Sunday departures are at 12.30, 1.30, 2.30, 4 and 5.30 pm.

The fare for the 1¾-hour cruise from Eminönü to Anadolu Kavağı, or vice versa, is US$3. Prices are printed on all tickets. Save your ticket to show the ticket-collector when you leave the ferry at your destination. The special cruise ferries call at only five docks: Barbaros Hayrettin Paşa on the European shore, Kanlıca on the Asian shore, Yeniköy and Sarıyer on the European shore, and Anadolu Kavağı on the Asian shore (turn-around point).

If you visit in the cooler months and the special ferries aren't running, look at the schedule for the heading 'Boğaz'a Gidiş' ('To the Bosphorus'), and also 'Boğaz'dan Geliş' ('From the Bosphorus'), for long-distance boats that make good substitutes. Heaviest travel will naturally be southward down the Bosphorus in the morning rush hour, and northward up the Bosphorus in the evening.

These special cruise ferries are popular, and they fill up early and quickly. It's a good idea to get to the dock well ahead of departure (say, 30 minutes or even more), locate the boat, board and seize a seat. Keep the sun in mind when you choose your place; you may want some shade as you head north.

Heading Out As you steam out from the mouth of the Golden Horn, **Galata** will be on your left and **Seraglio Point** on your right with **Topkapı Palace** rising above it. Down at the water's edge is an **Ottoman shipyard** (*tersane*). For sights on the Asian shore, refer to the Üsküdar and Beylerbeyi Palace sections.

Soon you'll be gliding past the incredible facade and sea-fence of **Dolmabahçe Palace** on the European side. After that, the main square of **Barbaros Hayrettin Paşa** comes into view. Barbaros Bulvarı, a wide highway, cuts a swath up the hill westward. To its right (north) is

the green expanse of **Yıldız Park**. At the water line is **Çirağan Palace**, only a few years ago a burnt-out hulk, now restored and converted into a luxury hotel. (See the later European Shore section for more details.)

The handsome Neo-Renaissance mosque nestled at the foot of the Bosphorus Bridge's European pylons is the **Ortaköy Camii**. Though it has hardly anything to do with Turkish architecture, it's very attractive and well sited. Within the mosque hang several masterful examples of Arabic calligraphy executed by Sultan Abdül Mecit, an accomplished calligrapher who had the mosque built in 1854.

Above the town you'll notice the New England 19th-century architecture of the **Boğaziçi Üniversitesi**, Bosphorus University, on a hilltop above the town of Bebek. Founded as Robert College in the mid-19th century by the American Board of Foreign Missions, the college had an important influence on the modernisation of political, social, economic and scientific thought in Turkey. Though donated by the board to the Turkish Republic in the early 1970s, instruction is still in English and Turkish.

Robert College survives as a special school to prepare bright students for university, having joined forces with the American College for Girls in nearby Arnavutköy.

Just north of Bebek on the European shore is **Rumeli Hisar** (roo-mehl-LEE hee-sahr), the Fortress of Europe. Here at the narrowest part of the Bosphorus, Mehmet the Conqueror had this fortress built in a mere four months (1452), in preparation for his planned siege of Byzantine Constantinople. In concert with Anadolu Hisar on the Asian shore just opposite, the cannon of Rumeli Hisar controlled all traffic on the Bosphorus, and cut the city off from resupply by sea from the north. Built just for use in the conquest of the city, the mighty citadel served as a glorified toll booth for a while, and was then more or less abandoned. It was restored and is now used for folk dancing, drama and other performances in the summertime, particularly during the İstanbul International Festival.

Across the strait from Rumeli Hisar is the **Anadolu Hisar** (ahn-nah-doh-LOO hee-sahr, Fortress of Asia). This small castle had been built by Sultan Beyazıt I in 1391. It was repaired and strengthened by Mehmet the Conqueror in preparation for the great siege. These days a picturesque village crowds its foundations, and the second Bosphorus bridge, the Fatih Köprüsü, soars overhead.

Each spring a Tulip Festival takes place in **Emirgan**, a well-to-do suburb of İstanbul on the European side. North of Emirgan, at İstinye, is a cove with a dry dock. A ring ferry service runs from İstinye to Beykoz and Paşabahçe on the Asian shore, soon to be replaced by a third Bosphorus bridge. Across on the Asian shore lies **Kanlıca**, a town famous for its yoghurt. The mosque in the town square dates from 1560.

On a point jutting out from the European shore is **Yeniköy**, first settled in classical times. This place later became a favourite summer resort, indicated by the lavish 19th-century Ottoman *yalı* or seaside villa, of the one-time grand vizier, Sait Halim Paşa. Not too many of these luxurious timber villas survive. Fire destroyed many. Economics and desire for modern conveniences caused many others to be torn down before preservation laws were promulgated. Today it is against the law to remove a yalı from the Bosphorus. It must either be repaired or rebuilt.

Across from Yeniköy are the Asian towns of **Paşabahçe** and **Beykoz**. Much of Turkey's best glassware is produced at the famous Paşabahçe factory – you'll see the name as a brand in shops selling glassware. In Beykoz, legend says that one of Jason's Argonauts, Pollux by name, had a boxing match with the local king, Amicus. Pollux was the son of Leda (she of the swan); Amicus was a son of Poseidon. Pollux won.

Originally called Therapeia for its healthful climate, the little cove of **Tarabya** has been a favourite summer watering place for İstanbul's well-to-do for centuries. Now there is a big hotel here, the Grand Tarabya (Büyük Tarabya Oteli). Little restaurants, specialising in fish, ring the cove (for details, see the Places to Eat section). North of the village are some of the old summer embassies of foreign powers. When the heat and fear of disease increased in the warm months, foreign ambassadors and their staffs would retire to palatial residences, complete with lush gardens, on this shore. The region for such embassy residences extended north to the next village, Büyükdere.

The quaint, pretty town of **Sarıyer** is a logical place to end your cruise up the Bosphorus, or to begin your cruise down. Sarıyer has several good fish restaurants, an interesting little marketplace, and good transportation down the Bosphorus or north to the Black Sea coast at Kilyos.

North of **Rumeli Kavağı**, the village farthest north on the European shore, is a military zone. The sleepy little town gets most of its excitement from the arrival and departure of ferries. There is a little public beach named Altınkum (ahl-TUHN-koom) near the village.

Perched above the village of **Anadolu Kavağı** on the Asian side are the ruins of a Genoese castle. As the straits are narrow here, it was a good choice for a defensive site to control traffic. Two more fortresses, put up by Sultan Murat IV, are north of here. But Anadolu Kavağı is the final stop on the special cruise ferry route, and the land to the north is in a military zone. If you have a picnic lunch, climb up to the fortress, which provides a comfortable picnic location with spectacular views.

From Sarıyer you can get a bus (No 151, US$0.25) or dolmuş ('Sarıyer-Kilyos', US$0.30) to **Kilyos**, on the Black Sea coast. The 15 or 20-minute ride takes you up into the hills past posh villas built by Arab oil potentates and traders, and little impromptu open-air roadside restaurants featuring *kuzu çevirme* (spit-roasted lamb). I can recommend the lamb highly. These places are usually open every day in high summer, but weekends only in the off season. Prices are low to moderate.

There are some little pensions, hotels and guest houses in Kilyos, open during the summer for beach fanciers (see the Places to Stay section for details). This entire area is under the control and protection of the Ministry of Tourism to prevent overdevelopment. The best beach is the fenced one in front of the Turban Kilyos Moteli, which you can use without staying at the motel if you pay a fee; it's open daily in warm weather from 8 am to 6 pm. The beach is very crowded on summer weekends, but during the week it's not bad. Entrance to the beach costs US$3.50 per person, a private changing cabin for two costs US$7.50. Parking costs US$2, so if you drive, park elsewhere in the village and walk over to the beach.

If you go to Kilyos for swimming, keep in mind that the waters of the Black Sea are fairly chilly. More important, there is a deadly undertow on many beaches. Swim only in protected areas or where there is an attentive lifeguard, and don't swim alone.

Sights on the European Shore

If you've cruised up the Bosphorus on a ferry, catch any bus or dolmuş headed south. To be safe, mention the name of your destination, Rumeli Hisar for example, when you board, and this way you won't miss your stop.

Coming from Aksaray, Sultanahmet, or Eminönü to visit the sights along the Bosphorus, your best bet is to take a bus or dolmuş to reach Dolmabahçe, one km down the hill from Taksim Square. From Taksim, the downhill walk is short (about 10 minutes) and pleasant with views of the Bosphorus and the palace. Starting in Taksim Square, walk toward the Atatürk Cultural Palace (Opera House). As you stand facing it, the tree-lined, divided

street on your right is İnönü Caddesi, formerly called Gümüşsuyu Caddesi. It leads directly to Dolmabahçe. On the right-hand side of İnönü Caddesi, just out of Taksim, you'll see ranks of dolmuşes. Routes are mostly long ones up the European Bosphorus shore, but you may find one going to Barbaros Hayrettin Paşa. Take this one to Dolmabahçe if you need to ride.

Coming from other parts of the city, catch a bus that goes via Eminönü and Karaköy to Barbaros Hayrettin Paşa. Any bus heading out of Karaköy along the Bosphorus shore road will take you to Dolmabahçe. Get off at the Kabataş stop. Just north of the stop you will see the Dolmabahçe Camii, and beyond it the palace.

Dolmabahçe Palace For centuries the padişah, the Ottoman sultan, had been the envy of all other monarchs in the world. Cultured, urbane, sensitive, courageous; controller of vast territories, great wealth and invincible armies and navies, he was the Grand Turk. The principalities, city-states and small kingdoms of Europe, Africa and the Near East cowered before him, and all stood in fear of a Turkish conquest. Indeed, the Turks conquered all of North Africa, parts of southern Italy, and eastern Europe to the gates of Vienna. The opulent palace of Dolmabahçe might be seen as an apt expression of this Ottoman glory – but it's not.

Dolmabahçe was built between 1843 and 1856, when the homeland of the once-mighty padişah had become 'the Sick Man of Europe'. His many peoples, aroused by a wave of European nationalism, were in revolt; his wealth was mostly mortgaged to, or under the control of, European interests; his armies, while still considerable, were obsolescent and dis-organised. The European, western, Christian way of life had triumphed over the Asian, eastern, Muslim one. Attempting to turn the tide, 19th-century sultans 'went European', modernising the army and civil service, granting autonomy to subject peoples, and adopting – sometimes wholesale – European ways of doing things.

The name Dolmabahçe, 'filled-in garden', dates from the reign of Sultan Ahmet I (1607-1617), when a little cove here was filled in and an imperial pleasure kiosk built on it. Other wooden buildings followed, but all burned to the ground in 1814. Sultan Abdül Mecit, whose favourite architects were an Armenian family named Balyan, wanted a 'European-style' marble palace. What he got is partly European, partly oriental, and certainly sumptuous and heavily overdecorated.

When you arrive, look for the ornate **clock tower** between Dolmabahçe Camii and the palace. The gate near the clock tower is the one you enter. The palace is open from 9 am to 12 noon and from 1.30 to 4.30 pm, closed Monday and Thursday; I predict that the press of crowds will soon force them to open it on Monday and/or Thursday as well, at least in the summertime. Entry costs US$5. There is a camera fee, but you should check your camera rather than pay the fee as the palace interior is too dark to photograph (even with fast film) and flash and tripod are not allowed. Rather, take your photos

Dolmabahçe Palace

from the small garden near the clock tower. You must take a guided tour here; it lasts between 60 and 90 minutes. Get here and get in line early: even so, you may wait in line an hour in high summer because of the crowd. Make sure the palace tour leader will be speaking a language you understand.

The palace gardens are very pretty. High-stepping guards by the main gate add a martial note. The fence along the Bosphorus and the palace facade go on for almost half a km. Inside, you'll see opulent public and private rooms, a harem with steel doors, lots of stuff like Sèvres vases and Bohemian chandeliers, and also a staircase with a crystal balustrade.

One room was used by Sultan Abdül Aziz (1861-1876), an enormously fat fellow who needed an enormously large bed. You will see just how large. The magnificent throne room, used in 1877 for the first meeting of the Ottoman Chamber of Deputies, has a chandelier that weighs over 4000 kg. The place is awesome.

Don't set your watch by any of the palace clocks, however. They are all stopped at the same time: 9.05 am. On the morning of 10 November 1938, Kemal Atatürk died in Dolmabahçe. You will be shown the small bedroom which he used during his last days. Each year on 10 November, at 9.05 am, Turkey – the entire country – comes to a dead halt in commemoration of the Republic's founder.

After you've boggled your mind at Dolmabahçe, go back to the vicinity of the clock tower and turn right, heading north along the palace wall, down an avenue lined with poplars. Soon on your right you'll come to the **Kuşluk ve Sanat Galerisi** or Aviary & Art Gallery, open daily from 9.30 am to 4 pm, closed Monday and Thursday. Only mad palace-lovers need spend the money, however, because there is not a lot to see. This section of the palace was the aviary, with its birdhouse and cages now restored, and a pretty garden restaurant added. The art gallery, lined with paintings by 19th and 20th-century Ottoman artists (many of them from the nobility), is actually an old passageway leading from one part of the palace to another. That accounts for its extraordinary shape, a single corridor over 100 metres long.

Barbaros Hayrettin Paşa When you've finished at the aviary and gallery, turn right (north) again and walk for five minutes to the suburb of Barbaros Hayrettin Paşa. It's not a long walk if you're willing, but the heavy traffic in this corridor between two walls is noisy and smelly. When you emerge from the walls, you'll be in the suburb now officially named Barbaros Hayrettin Paşa, which used to be named Beşiktaş. Most people still call it by its former name.

Naval Museum The Deniz Müzesi or Naval Museum, is on the Bosphorus shore just south of the flyover in Barbaros Hayrettin Paşa. Among its exhibits are an outdoor display of cannon (including Selim the Grim's 21-tonne monster) and a statue of Barbaros Hayrettin Paşa (1483-1546), the famous Turkish admiral known also as Barbarossa who conquered North Africa for Süleyman the Magnificent. The admiral's tomb, designed by Sinan, is close by.

There are two parts to the museum, one entered from the main road, the other from the Bosphorus shore. You must pay an admission fee for each part. The Naval Museum (tel 161-0225) is open from 9.30 am to 5 pm, closed Monday and Tuesday. Admission costs US$0.75 in each part.

Though the Ottoman Empire is most remembered for its conquests on land, its maritime power was equally impressive. During the reign of Süleyman the Magnificent (1520-1566), the eastern Mediterranean was virtually an Ottoman lake. The sultan's navies cut a swath in the Indian Ocean as well. Sea power was instrumental in the conquests of the Aegean coasts and islands, Egypt and

North Africa. Discipline, well-organised supply and good ship design contributed to Ottoman victories.

However, the navy, like the army and the government, lagged behind the west in modernisation during the later centuries. The great battle which broke the spell of Ottoman naval invincibility was fought in 1571 at Lepanto, in the Gulf of Patras off the Greek coast. (Cervantes fought on the Christian side, and was badly wounded.) Though the Turkish fleet was destroyed, the sultan quickly produced another, partly with the help of rich Greek shipowners who were his subjects.

In the Bosphorus section of the museum, be sure to see the sleek, swift imperial barges, in which the sultan would speed up and down the Bosphorus from palace to palace (in those days the roads were not very smooth or fast). Over 30 metres in length but only two metres wide, with 13 banks of oars, the barges were obviously the rocket boats of their day. The ones with latticework screens were for the imperial ladies. There's also a war galley with 24 pairs of oars.

You may also be curious to see a replica of the Map of Piri Reis, an early Ottoman map (1513) which purports to show the coasts and continents of the New World. It's assumed that Piri Reis ('Captain Piri') got hold of the work of Columbus for his map. The original map is in Topkapı; this one is on the wall above the door as you enter the Bosphorus section. Colourful copies are on sale here in the museum.

Ihlamur Kasrı Inland to the north of Dolmabahçe Palace and the Naval Museum, sheltered in a narrow valley surrounded by a maze of twisting little streets, is the Ihlamur Kasrı (UHH-lah-moor kahss-ruh, Ihlamur Kiosk), or Kiosk of the Linden Tree (tel 161-2991). The pretty park actually has two small, ornate imperial pavilions rather than one.

The park and two kiosks are open from 9.30 am to 4 pm every day except Monday and Thursday. Admission to the park and kiosks costs US$0.50, or US$0.15 if you just want to stroll through the park. Fee for use of a camera is US$6. The easiest way to find this place in its maze of streets is to take a taxi which, from Dolmabahçe or Barbaros Hayrettin Paşa, should cost only US$1 or so. Bus No 26 (Dikilitaş to Eminönü) departs Eminönü, stops at Karaköy, Dolmabahçe and Barbaros Hayrettin Paşa , before heading inland to the Ihlamur stop and continuing to Dikilitaş (DEE-kee-LEE-tahsh), which is not far past Ihlamur. Other buses are Nos 26A, 26B or 26C.

Once a quiet, sheltered valley neighbouring the imperial palaces of Yıldız and Dolmabahçe, the Ihlamur valley now hums with the noise of traffic and is surrounded by modern apartment blocks. It's not difficult to imagine, however, what it must have been like when these two miniature palaces stood here alone, in the midst of a forest, waiting for the sultan to drop by for a few hours away from his duties. Near the entry gate the park is open and formal, with grassy lawns, ornamental trees, and a quiet pool. To the right behind the Maiyet Köşkü the gardens are more rustic, shady and cool, with naturalistic spring-like fountains.

As you enter, look across the pool to find the **Merasim Köşkü**, or Sultan's Kiosk, built on the orders of Sultan Abdül Mecit between 1849 and 1855 by Nikogos Balyan, of the family of imperial architects. As you enter, a guide will approach to offer you a free guided tour. Up the marble stairway and through the ornate door is the Hall of Mirrors, with crystal from Bohemia and vases from France. The Baroque decor includes patterns of shells, flowers, vines, fruits and lots of gold leaf.

The music room to the right of the entrance has precious Hereke fabrics on the chairs and a beautiful enamelled coalgrate fireplace painted with flowers. You'll see similarly beautiful fireplaces in the other rooms as well. The 'marble' walls of the music room are fake.

Next comes the Imperial Water Closet, with an interesting flat Turkish toilet, demonstrating that even the sultan had to hunker down.

The room to the left of the entrance was a reception salon with a sofa-throne and 'marble' decoration of plaster with gold flecks. The tour ends downstairs, where displays of photographs show details of the restoration work carried out in the 1980s.

The **Maiyet Köşkü** or Retinue Kiosk, was for the sultan's suite of attendants, guests or harem. It's now a teahouse serving tea (US$0.40), coffee (US$0.50), Nescafé (US$0.85) and snacks. Downstairs are WCs and a shop selling books and other publications.

Çirağan Palace From the Naval Museum and the flyover in Barbaros Hayrettin Paşa, you can walk north for 10 minutes, or catch a bus or dolmuş heading north along the shore, to reach the entrance to Yıldız Park (bus stop Galatasaray Lisesi). Before you reach the entrance, you'll be passing Çirağan Palace on your right; the palace, now restored as a posh hotel, is hidden from the road by a high wall, though you can get a glimpse of it through the huge gates.

Unsatisfied with the architectural exertions of his predecessor at Dolmabahçe, Sultan Abdül Aziz (1861-1876) had to build his own palace. He built Çirağan on the Bosphorus shore only a km north of Dolmabahçe, replacing an earlier wooden palace. The architect was the self-same Balyan as for Dolmabahçe. The sultan didn't get to live here much, however. Instead, it served as a detention place for his successor, the mentally unbalanced Sultan Murat V, who was deposed before he had even reigned a year. Later the palace housed the Ottoman Chamber of Deputies & Senate (1909), but in 1910 it was destroyed by fire under suspicious circumstances.

Yıldız Palace & Park Sultan Abdül Hamid II (1876-1909), who succeeded Murat V, also had to build his own palace. He added considerably to the structures built by earlier sultans in Yıldız Park, on the hillside above Çirağan. The kiosks and summer palaces, as well as the park itself, have been restored by the Turkish Touring & Automobile Association, and several now serve as delightful restaurants and teahouses.

The park is open from 9 am to 6 pm every day; admission costs US$0.20 for pedestrians, US$0.65 for cars (including taxis). The park began life as the imperial reserve for Çirağan Palace, but when Abdül Hamid built the Şale Köşkü, the park served that palace. Under Abdül Hamid, the park was planted with exotic and valuable trees, shrubs and flowers, and was provided with manicured paths and a superior electric lighting and drainage system. The sultan could reach Çirağan Palace by a private bridge over the roadway from the park. If you come to the park by taxi, you might as well have it take you up the steep slope to the Şale Köşkü. You can visit the other kiosks on the walk down. A taxi from Taksim Square to the top of the hill might cost about US$4 or $5.

As you toil up the hill along the road, near the top of the slope to the left you'll see the **Çadır Köşkü**. This pretty, ornate little kiosk was built between 1865 and 1870 as a place for the sultan to enjoy the view, rest from a walk, and have a cup of tea or coffee. It serves the same purpose today for visitors. Only drinks are served (no food), but you can enjoy them on the marble terrace overlooking the Bosphorus, and afterwards walk around the artificial lake, complete with island.

To the right (north) as you are hiking up the road from the gate, you will notice two greenhouses and another kiosk. These are the **Kış Bahçesi** (Winter Garden), the **Yeşil Sera** (Green Nursery), and the **Malta Köşkü** (Malta Kiosk) (tel 160-2752). The Malta Kiosk, restored in 1979, is now a café serving refreshments, alcoholic drinks and light meals. The view here is

the best in the park, much better than that at the Çadır Köşkü. If you sit down to a plate of grilled lamb and then finish up with something sweet, your bill will add up to US$3.75 to $5.

Also to the right are the **Yıldız Porselen Fabrikası** or Yıldız Porcelain Factories, constructed to manufacture dinner services for the palace. They still operate and are open to visits.

At the very top of the hill, enclosed by a separate, lofty wall, is the **Şale Köşkü** or Chalet Kiosk, a 'guest house' put up in 1882 and expanded in 1898 by Abdül Hamid for use by Kaiser Wilhelm II of Germany during a state visit. You must pay a separate admission fee of US$3 to see the Chalet Kiosk (tel 158-3080), which is open from 9.30 am to 4 pm daily; closed Monday.

I expect the Kaiser had enough space to move in, as the 'chalet' has 64 rooms. After his imperial guest departed, the sultan became quite attached to his 'rustic' creation, and decided to live here himself, forsaking the more lavish but less well-protected palaces on the Bosphorus shore. Abdül Hamid was paranoid, and for good reason. Fate determined that his fears would come true. He was deposed, departed this wooden palace in April 1909 and boarded a special train which took him to house arrest in Ottoman Salonika (today Thessaloniki, in Greece). He was later allowed by the Young Turks government to return to İstanbul and live out his years in Beylerbeyi Palace, on the Asian shore of the Bosphorus.

As though this were not enough dolorous history for the place, the last sultan of the Ottoman Empire, Mehmet V (Vahideddin), lived here until, at 6 am on 11 November 1922, he and his first chamberlain, bandmaster, doctor, two secretaries, valet, barber and two eunuchs, accompanied by trunks full of jewels, gold and antiques, boarded two British Red Cross ambulances for the secret journey to the naval dockyard at Tophane. There they boarded the British battleship HMS

Malaya for a trip into exile, ending the Ottoman Empire forever. On the way to the quay one of the tyres on the sultan's ambulance went flat; while it was being changed, the Shadow of God on Earth quaked, fearing that he might be discovered.

In the Republican era, the Chalet Kiosk has served as a guest house for visiting heads of state, including Charles de Gaulle, Pope Paul VI, Nikolai Ceausescu and the Empress Soraya. The gravel walkways along which you approach the palace are said to have been ordered by Abdül Hamid as a security measure. It's impossible for anyone to walk on them without making a lot of noise. As you enter the palace, a guide will approach you to give you the tour, which is required. The guide will tell you that all of the carpets in the palace are from the imperial factory at Hereke, east of İstanbul.

The first section you visit was the original chalet, built in 1882. The first room on the tour was used by Abdül Hamid's mother for her religious devotions, the second was her guest reception room, with a very fine mosaic tabletop. Then comes a women's resting room, and afterwards a tearoom furnished with furniture having a gold star on a blue background, which reminds one that this was the 'star' (*yıldız*) palace.

In 1898 the chalet was expanded, and the older section became the harem (with steel doors), while the new section was the selamlık. In the selamlık are a bathroom with tiles from the Yıldız Porcelain Factories, and several reception rooms, one of which has furniture made by Abdül Hamid himself, an accomplished wood-worker. The grand hall of the selamlık is vast, its floor covered by a 7½-tonne Hereke carpet woven just for this room. So huge is the rug that it had to be brought in through the far (north) wall before the building was finished and the wall was closed.

Other buildings at Yıldız include the **Merasim Köşkü** or Ceremonial Kiosk and

barracks. Part of the Ceremonial Kiosk was restored (1988) and opened as the **İstanbul Şehir Müzesi** or Istanbul City Museum, open daily except Monday from 9 am to 5 pm; admission costs US$1. It's reached from Barbaros Bulvarı, the road along the south side of the park, not from within the park itself.

After seeing Yıldız, you can take a bus or dolmuş north to Bebek and Rumeli Hisar, or return to Barbaros Hayrettin Paşa to catch a shuttle ferry over to Üsküdar, on the Asian side, in order to continue your sightseeing. The ferries operate every 15 or 20 minutes in each direction, from 6 am to midnight. There are also boats between Üsküdar and Eminönü. Ferries to Eminönü may bear the sign 'Köprü' or 'Bridge', meaning the Galata Bridge.

Rumeli Hisar This impressive fortress, completed in the summer of 1452, was built in only four months. To speed its completion in line with his impatience to conquer Constantinople, Mehmet the Conqueror ordered each of his three viziers to take responsibility for one of the three main towers. If the tower's construction was not completed on schedule, the vizier would pay with his life, or so legend has it. Not surprisingly, the work was completed on time, with Mehmet's three generals competing fiercely with one another to finish. Once completed, the mighty fortress' useful military life was less than one year. After the conquest of Constantinople, it was used as a barracks, a prison, and an open-air theatre, but never again as a fortress.

Rumeli Hisar is open from 9.30 am to 5 pm daily; closed Monday. Admission costs US$2.50, half-price on Sundays and holidays.

Sarıyer The villagers of Sarıyer occupied themselves for most of their history by fishing in the currents of the Bosphorus. Fishing is still a pastime and a livelihood here, and Sarıyer is justly noted for its several good fish restaurants. Turn right as you leave the ferry dock, stay as close to the shore as possible, and you will soon come to the village's active fish market and several fish restaurants both cheap and expensive (see the Places to Eat section for details). Dolmuşes for the beach at Kilyos leave from a point just to the north of the ferry dock.

Also of interest in Sarıyer is the **Sadberk Hanım Müzesi** (tel 142-3813), Piyasa Caddesi 27-29, Büyükdere, a private museum of Anatolian antiquities and Ottoman heirlooms from one of Turkey's richest families. If you come to Sarıyer by ferry, look to the left as you leave the dock, and you will see a yellow wooden house on the shore road about 300 metres to the south – that's the museum. It's open in summer from 10.30 am to 6 pm, in winter from 10 am to 5 pm; it's closed on Wednesday all year. Admission costs US$1. Plaques in the museum are in English as well as Turkish.

Sadberk Hanım, who gathered the collections now housed in the museum, was the wife of Mr Vehbi Koç, one of the country's foremost businessmen, who made much of his fortune as Turkish agent for many international firms such as Coca-Cola, Avis and IBM. After her death in the 1970s, the family established the museum in this graceful old Bosphorus yalı, once the summer residence of Manuk Azaryan Efendi, an Armenian who was at one time Speaker of the upper house of the Ottoman Parliament.

At the time of my last visit, the collections were being rearranged and the museum expanded to include the house immediately to the rear. The original part of the museum now houses only artefacts and exhibits from Turkey's Islamic past. The non-Islamic collections are displayed in the new building.

In my opinion, the most fascinating of the museum's collections are those in the original yalı, dating from Ottoman times: worry beads of solid gold; golden,

bejewelled tobacco boxes and watches (one bears the sultan's monogram in diamonds); beautiful Kütahya pottery; even a table that once belonged to Napoleon (he's pictured on it, surrounded by his generals). A number of rooms in the great old house have been arranged and decorated in Ottoman style – the style of the ruling class, obviously. There's a sumptuous maternity room with embroidered cloth and lots of lace, a salon with all the paraphernalia of the Ottoman coffee ceremony, and a third set up as a circumcision room. A display case holds a fine collection of Ottoman spoons (the prime dining utensil) made from tortoise-shell, ebony, ivory, and similarly precious materials.

The collections in the new building include very choice artefacts dating from as early as the 500s BC, and continuing through Roman and Byzantine times. There is also a well-chosen collection of Chinese celadon ware from the 1300s to 1500s, later Chinese blue-and-white porcelain, and some 18th-century Chinese porcelain made specifically for the Ottoman market.

Sights on the Asian Shore

The best and most pleasant means of transport is a ferry from Eminönü (Dock No 2). They run every 20 minutes between 6 am and midnight, even more frequently during rush hours. A similar, frequent ferry service operates between Üsküdar and Barbaros Hayrettin Paşa. There are also city buses and dolmuşes departing Taksim Square for Üsküdar. The ferries are much faster and much more enjoyable, though.

If you take the ferry to Üsküdar, you'll notice **Leander's Tower**, called the Kız Kulesi (Maiden's Tower) in Turkish. The tower was a toll booth and defence point in ancient times; the Bosphorus could be closed off by means of a chain stretching from here to Seraglio Point. The tower has really nothing to do with Leander, who was no maiden, and who swam not the

Bosphorus but the Hellespont (Dardanelles), 340 km from here. The tower is subject to the usual legends: oracle says maiden will die by snakebite, concerned father puts maiden in snake-proof tower, fruit vendor comes by in boat, sells basket of fruit (complete with snake) to maiden, maiden gets hers, etc. The legend seems to crop up wherever there are offshore towers, and maidens. Anyway, it's a pretty tower, and an İstanbul landmark.

Another landmark for travellers is the German-style **Haydarpaşa Station**, İstanbul's terminus for Asian trains. During the late 19th century, when Kaiser Wilhelm was trying to charm the sultan into economic and military cooperation, he gave him the station as a little gift.

You will also notice the large **Selimiye Kışlası**, Selimiye Barracks, a square building with towers at the corners. It dates from the early 19th century, when Selim III and Mahmut II reorganised the Ottoman armed forces along European lines. Not far away is the **Selimiye Camii** (1805). During the Crimean War (1853-56), when Britain and France fought on the Ottoman side against the Russian Empire, the Selimiye Barracks served as a military hospital as well. It was here that the English nurse Florence Nightingale, horrified at the conditions suffered by the wounded, established with 38 companion nurses the first model military hospital with modern standards of discipline, order, sanitation and care. In effect, her work at the Selimiye laid down the norms of modern nursing, and turned nursing into a skilled, respected profession. A small museum in the barracks, open daily except Sunday, is dedicated to her work.

That other highly ornamented building, very storybook Ottoman, was formerly a rest home for aging palace ladies. It's now a school.

Üsküdar Üsküdar (ER-sker-dahr) is the Turkish form of the name Scutari. Legend has it that the first ancient colonists established themselves at Chalcedon, the modern Kadıköy, south of Üsküdar. Byzas, bearing the oracle's message to found a colony 'Opposite the blind', thought the Chalcedonites blind to the advantages of Seraglio Point as a townsite, and founded his town on the European shore. Still, people have lived on this, the Asian shore, longer than they've lived on the other.

Today Üsküdar is a busy dormitory suburb for İstanbul, and you will enjoy an hour's browse through its streets, markets and mosques. You should definitely see the Çinili Cami, with its brilliant tiles, and the attractive little palace of Beylerbeyi.

Hop off the ferry in Üsküdar. The **main square** is right before you. North of the square, near the ferry landing, is the **Mihrimah Camii** (1547), built by Sinan for a daughter of Süleyman the Magnificent. To the south of the square is the **Yeni Valide Camii**, or New Queen Mother's Mosque (1710), built by Sultan Ahmet III for his mother. It resembles the Rüstem Paşa Camii near the Egyptian Market in Eminönü. Built late in the period of classical Ottoman architecture, it is not as fine as earlier works.

West of the square, overlooking the harbour, is the **Şemsi Paşa Camii** (1580), designed by Sinan.

Walk out of the busy square along the main road, called Hakimiyeti Milliye Caddesi, or Popular Sovereignty Ave. (After six centuries of monarchy, the idea of democracy, of the people ruling, is enough to inspire street names.) Watch on the left for Tavukçu Bakkal Sokak, and turn into it. When you reach Çavuşdere Caddesi, turn right and walk less than a km to the little **Çinili Cami** (chee-nee-LEE jahm-mee, Tiled Mosque).

The mosque doesn't look like too much from the outside: just a shady little neighbourhood mosque with the usual collection of bearded old men sitting around. Inside, it is brilliant with İznik faïence. It is the work of Mahpeyker Kösem (1640), wife of Sultan Ahmet I (1603-1617) and mother of sultans Murat IV (1623-1640) and Ibrahim (1640-1648).

From the European shore of the Bosphorus, you may have noticed a hill or two behind Üsküdar, and a television transmission tower. The hills are **Büyük Çamlıca** (bew-YEWK chahm-luh-jah, Big Pine Hill) and **Küçük Çamlıca** (kew-CHEWK, Little Pine Hill). Büyük Çamlıca, especially, has for years been a favourite picnic place for İstanbullus, restored in recent times through the efforts of the Turkish Touring & Automobile Association. You can get there from the main square in Üsküdar on an Ümraniye bus or dolmuş. Get off at Kısıklı. You can walk to the top on Büyük Çamlıca Caddesi or take a taxi; if it's a busy time (weekend or holiday), there will be dolmuşes running.

Beylerbeyi Palace Catch a bus or dolmuş north along the shore road from Üsküdar's main square to reach Beylerbeyi, just north of the Asian pylons of the Bosphorus Bridge. Get off at the Çayırbası stop. Beylerbeyi Palace (tel 333-6940) is open from 9 am to 5 pm, closed Monday and Thursday; admission costs US$2.50.

Every emperor needs some little place to get away to, and Beylerbeyi was the place for Abdül Aziz (1861-1876). Mahmut II had built a wooden palace here, but Abdül Aziz wanted stone and marble, so he ordered Serkis Balyan to get to work on Beylerbeyi. The architect came up with an Ottoman gem, complete with fountain in the entrance hall, and two little tent-like kiosks in the sea wall.

One room is panelled in wonderful marquetry (woodwork), all done by the sultan himself. Woodwork was not just a hobby. Under the laws of Islam, every man should have an honest skill with which to make a living. Being a soldier was a duty and an honour, not a living. So was being king. Thus every sultan had to develop a skill by which, theoretically, he could earn his living. Frequently the sultans chose calligraphy; Abdül Aziz chose woodwork.

Abdül Aziz spent a lot of time here. But so did other monarchs and royal guests, for this was, in effect, the sultan's guest quarters. Empress Eugénie of France stayed here for a long visit in 1869. Other royal guests included Nasruddin, Shah of Persia; Nicholas, Grand Duke of Russia; and Nicholas, King of Montenegro. Its last imperial 'guest' was none other than the former sultan, Abdül Hamid II, who was brought here to spend the remainder of his life (1913 to 1918), having spent the four years since his deposition (1909) in Ottoman Salonika. He had the dubious pleasure of gazing across the Bosphorus at Yıldız, and watching crumble before his eyes the great empire which he had ruled for over 30 years.

Küçüksu Kasrı If Beylerbeyi was a sultan's favourite getaway spot, Küçüksu was preferred for picnics and 'rustic' parties. Sultan Abdül Mecit was responsible for building this tiny palace, actually an ornate lodge, in 1856. Earlier sultans had wooden kiosks here. The Büyük Göksu (Great Heavenly Stream) and Küçük Göksu (Small Heavenly Stream) were two brooks which descended from the Asian hills into the Bosphorus. Between them was a flat, fertile delta, grassy and shady, just perfect for picnics. The Ottoman upper classes would get away from the hot city for rowing and picnics here. Foreign residents, referring to the place as 'The Sweet Waters of Asia', would often join them.

Take a bus or dolmuş along the shore road north from Beylerbeyi to reach Küçüksu. The kiosk was restored and opened to the public in 1983, having been closed for decades. Küçüksu Kasrı (tel 332-0237) is open from 9.30 am to 5 pm, closed Monday and Thursday; admission costs US$2.

The next village north of Beylerbeyi is Çengelköy. To the north, ferries run on a ring route from İstinye on the European side to the Beykoz and Paşabahçe village docks on the Asian side. Another ring operates from Sarıyer and Rumeli Kavağı in Europe to Anadolu Kavağı in Asia. These ferries run about every hour. Check the schedules. If you can't catch one of them, you can always hire a boatman to take you across the Bosphorus for a few dollars.

If the timing's right, you might want to take a bus or dolmuş north all the way to Anadolu Kavağı and catch the Bosphorus cruise ferry as it heads back down toward the city.

PLACES TO STAY

İstanbul is well provided with hotels in all categories, particularly in the middle price range. Hotel clusters in various areas of the city make it easy to find the room you want at an affordable price. If the first hotel you look at is full, there will be another one around the corner, or even right next door.

Turkey's tourism boom is affecting the hotel situation in a number of ways, however. At present there is a shortage of rooms during the height of the summer season. This not only makes rooms difficult to find, it also allows hotel owners to raise prices considerably, thus making İstanbul's hotel rooms the most expensive in the country. Hotel construction is booming, however, and in a short while there should be enough rooms to take pressure off prices. Unfortunately for low-budget travellers, the trend in hotels is to modernise and upgrade cheap hotels to higher price brackets. But there will always be cheap beds to be found in İstanbul.

The prices given here were carefully researched, but they may rise or fall according to İstanbul's volatile hotel situation.

As everywhere in Turkey, you should inspect the hotel room before you register.

It may be better or worse than the lobby or facade. Also, one room may be better than another. If you don't like what you see, you can look at something else; just ask, *Başka var mı* (BAHSH-kah VAHR-muh, 'Are there others?').

Generally speaking, the lowest-priced hotels and hostels are near Sultanahmet or Sirkeci Station. The best selection of moderate rooms is in the quarter named Laleli. The moderate to luxury places are around Taksim Square and Tepebaşı in Beyoğlu. Camping areas are in the beach sections named Ataköy and Florya. The Bosphorus' shores hold some moderate and luxury hotels. Kilyos, on the Black Sea coast, has moderate pensions and small hotels.

Places to Stay – bottom end

Among the hotels in this section are those which will provide you with a place to roll out your sleeping bag on the roof for as little as US$3 to US$6, and those offering double rooms with private hot-water shower for as much as US$35. Mostly though, these places have simple, but adequate double rooms with a washbasin or private shower for US$16 to US$22.

Sultanahmet The Blue Mosque is officially the Sultan Ahmet Camii. It gave the square and the quarter its name, contracted to Sultanahmet. The Blue Mosque faces the ancient Hippodrome, now a public park.

Around the Hippodrome are grouped the premier sights of İstanbul: Topkapı Palace, Sancta Sophia, the Blue Mosque and the Yerebatan Saray, so when you stay here the sights are mere steps from your hotel door. Knowing this, hotel and pension operators in this area charge more, for less, than in other parts of the city.

The thickest concentration of low-budget hotels is on and off Yerebatan Caddesi, the street which begins at Sancta Sophia and runs north-westward in front of the entrance to Yerebatan

Saray. To locate the street, walk to the northern end of the Hippodrome, cross Divan Yolu, and walk to the northern side of the little park.

Now find the entrance to Yerebatan Saray, on the north side of the little park, and start walking away from Sancta Sophia. You'll soon come to the *Sultan Tourist Hostel 1* (tel 520-7676), Yerebatan Caddesi 35, 34400 Sultanahmet. Rooms here are somewhat beat up, but fairly clean and usable, priced at US$18 a double, hot showers included. Breakfast costs another US$1 or US$2. As with the other hotels facing Yerebatan Caddesi, this one can be noisy.

Next door is the *Hotel Ayasofya* (tel 522-7126). Rooms here are somewhat better and more modern, but also pricier at US$24 a double, with private bath.

Also right here is the *Hotel Stop* (tel 527-6795), with lower prices because none of its rooms has a private bath. Doubles go for US$18, and hot showers are free. Breakfast can be had in the hotel's basement Restaurant Elif.

Across the street from these places is a little street named Salkım Söğüt Sokak which has several cheap hotels which tend to be a bit quieter than those facing Yerebatan Caddesi.

The *Elit Hotel* (tel 511-5179, 519-0466; fax 511-4437), Yerebatan Caddesi, Salkım Söğüt Sokak 14, 34400 Sultanahmet, has 12 clean, simple, fairly quiet rooms with private facilities, above a carpet shop. The price is US$22 a double.

Down Salkım Söğüt Sokak a few more steps and the street narrows. At this point, on the right, is the *Hotel Anadolu* (tel 512-1035), Salkım Söğüt Sokak 3, 34000 Cağaloğlu, perhaps the oldest hotel in the quarter, but also the quietest. By the front door are a few little tables overlooking a car park, a good place to sip a tea or write a letter. The rooms are tiny and just have washbasins, but beds are priced at only US$8 per person, and hot showers are free.

Very near the Anadolu is the *Hotel Mola* (tel 526-7604, 527-3073), Alayköşkü

Caddesi 15, 34000 Cağaloğlu; it's virtually across the street from the Anadolu, but the street changes names here. It's certainly quieter than most, and the hotel has rooms both with washbasin (US$17 double) or with private shower (US$20 to US$23 double), but use the Mola only if all the others are full.

Right beside Sancta Sophia, running along its western side, is Caferiye Sokak, which has two bottom-end lodging choices. The location is superb.

The *Yücelt Interyouth Hostel* (tel 513-6150/1), Caferiye Sokak 6/1, 34400 Sultanahmet, is literally across the street from the front door of Sancta Sophia. The Yücelt is where many backpackers head when they first arrive in İstanbul, because it is affiliated with the International Youth Hostel Federation, and also the Federation of International Youth Travel Organisations. But it would better be described as a student hotel than a hostel. It has a cafeteria, laundry room, bulletin board, public showers, TV and video room, library, games room, garden terrace, and a Turkish bath. Prices are not as low as in hostels: double rooms with bath cost US$22, rooms with three or four beds go for US$10 per person, and dormitory beds cost US$8 each.

Virtually next door to the Yücelt is the *Hotel Büyükayasofya* (tel 522-2981), Caferiye Sokak 5, 34400 Sultanahmet, a budget travellers' hostelry of long standing. It's quiet as the street gets little traffic, and the hotel is set back a bit from the roadway in any case. Rooms are nothing fancy, let me tell you, and the crowd here seems to be mostly men, but prices are good: US$7 for a bed in a room without private shower, or US$9 in a room with shower. Sometimes they'll allow you to sleep on the roof for $2; the roof is noisier, but will do for a night if you're stretched for cash.

You'll notice several hotels right on Divan Yolu facing the Hippodrome – *Hotel Güngör, Hotel Pırlanta, Hotel Holiday*, etc. While these do have fairly

174 İstanbul

low prices, they are extremely noisy. Keep this in mind if you look at a room here. I recommend that you find a place off the main street.

One such place is the tiny *Optimist Guesthouse* (tel 519-2091), Atmeydanı 68, 34400 Sultanahmet. Hippodrome in Turkish is *Atmeydanı* ('Horse Square'), which explains the mailing address of this private home turned pension. Look for it down near the southern end of the Hippodrome on the western side, across the Hippodrome from the Blue Mosque. The six rooms (two with private shower) are priced at US$30 to US$38 a double, breakfast included.

West of the Hippodrome are the İstanbul law courts, and beyond the courts a warren of little streets, some of which hold cheap hotels. It is here that you will find the *Hotel Klodfarer* (tel 528-4850/1), Klodfarer Caddesi 22, 34000 Binbirdirek, off Divan Yolu facing the Binbirdirek Underground Cistern (*sarnıç*). Old-fashioned and dark, it is fairly quiet, has a lift and a cheap restaurant, and offers rooms with a shower for US$13/19/25 a single/double/triple.

Another area of low-budget hotels near Sultanahmet is down toward the Bosphorus, east of Sancta Sophia and the Blue Mosque. This neighbourhood is called Cankurtaran (Life Saver) because of the naval life-saving station which was once here. To reach this area, follow Mimar Mehmet Ağa Caddesi, the street which runs between Sancta Sophia and the Blue Mosque, to the right of the park with the fountain. The street curves to the right, then to the left, and goes downhill.

The *Sultan Tourist Hostel 2* (tel 520-7676), Akbıyık Caddesi, Terbıyık Sokak 3, 34400 Cankurtaran, is operated by the same people who run the Sultan Tourist Hostel 1 on Yerebatan Caddesi. The rooms in this former private home are small, clean and simple, with private baths or showers. Price for a room is US$18 a double, hot showers included. Breakfast costs another US$1 or US$2. As

you walk down Mimar Mehmet Ağa Caddesi from the Hippodrome, look for Akbıyık Caddesi and turn left. The hostel is on Terbıyık Sokak, the second street on the right.

Other cheap lodgings are in this same area, but most easily reached by walking around Sancta Sophia and heading for Topkapı Palace. Before entering the first portal, turn right and walk down the hill, with the palace walls on your left. Soon you'll come to the *Topkapı Hostel* (tel 527-2433), İshak Paşa Caddesi, 34400 Cankurtaran, above a carpet shop. The carpets make it attractive, but more attractive is the range of prices. A room for one or two people costs US$20 with a private shower, but you can also get a bed in a dormitory for only US$8, or sleep on the roof with your own bedding for US$6. Breakfast is available if you want it.

One last place to try, somewhat more expensive, is the *Berk Guest House* (tel 511-0737), Kutlugün Sokak 27, 34400 Cankurtaran, more or less behind the famous (and expensive) Yeşil Ev Hotel. To find it, walk down either of the two little streets by the Yeşil Ev – Dalbastı Sokak or Seyithasan Sokak. Or, you can get to it by following the directions given for the Topkapı Hostel, turning into the first street on the right as you walk down the hill with the palace walls on your left. The Berk is family-run and has only half a dozen rooms, but each room has its own bath. Doubles are priced at US$30.

Also down in this area is the *Hotel Park* at Utangaç Sokak 26, brand new in 1989, clean, with friendly staff and rooms going for US$12 a double.

In the summer (July and August), several university dormitories open their doors to foreign students. These tend to be extremely basic and cheap. They're not for all tastes, but if you want to look into one, ask for the latest information from the Tourism Information Office in Sultanahmet, right at the northern end of the Hippodrome next to the bus stop on Divan Yolu.

Sirkeci Railway Station Most of the hotels near Sirkeci tend to be noisy, run down or off colour, but there is a street full of good hotels only five minutes' walk from the station. Walk out of the station's main (west) door, turn left, then left again onto Muradiye-Hüdavendigar Caddesi. A block up on the right you'll see Orhaniye Caddesi going up a gentle slope. Follow it up to the top, two very short blocks. At the top is the İpek Palas Hotel and İbni Kemal Caddesi. Turn left onto İbni Kemal, where there are eight hotels, all fairly quiet, all pretty cheap.

Hotel Fahri (tel 522-4785, 520-5686), İbni Kemal Caddesi 14-16, 34000 Sirkeci, is modernish, clean, not fancy but suitable, and charges US$12/18 a single/ double for rooms with shower. It's quiet because the street in front of it is used as an unofficial car park.

Nearby is the *Hotel Meram* (tel 527-6295), İbni Kemal Caddesi 19, 34000 Sirkeci, which is simpler, but even cheaper, with singles/doubles for only US$8/15, with washbasins, but without private bath.

Should you have a mind to spend some money on comfort, the *Hotel Karacabey* (tel 526-0902), İbni Kemal Caddesi 38, 34000 Sirkeci, is the 'high-priced' lodging on the block. Though posted prices are considerably higher, I haggled them down to US$29 for a double room with private shower, breakfast included. A similar single would have cost US$19. The advantages here are many: a restaurant and bar, a roof terrace with views of Sancta Sophia, and some rooms even have TVs. With these facilities, price will depend upon the trade. If the hotel is busy, you may not be able to haggle them down.

The *İpek Palas Oteli* (tel 520-9724/5), Orhaniye Caddesi 9, 34000 Sirkeci, at the corner with İbni Kemal, is a period piece straight out of the 1950s. Some new furniture has been added, but it blends into the style. Rooms have either washbasins or private bathrooms; the cheaper rooms, without bath, cost US$24 for one or two people in one bed, US$30 for a room with two beds. Rooms with private bath cost about US$4 more.

Laleli The district of Laleli (LAA-leh-LEE) is just east of Aksaray, just west of İstanbul University and north of Ordu Caddesi, about 1½ km west of Sancta Sophia. The landmark here is the Ramada Hotel İstanbul, fitted into a large old apartment building beautifully restored. Laleli is a pleasant residential and hotel district with relatively quiet, shady, narrow streets and with a life and character all its own. Itinerant pedlars patrol the streets looking for tourists to sell their wares to, and tailors' shops advertise their services in Polish (for some reason Laleli is full of Polish and Yugoslav tourists who've come to take advantage of cheap Turkish tailoring).

Several dozen little hotels sit here cheek by jowl, and new places open every year. To the north lies the district named Şehzadebaşı (sheh-ZAH-deh-bosh-uh). It's really all one area, but some hotels will have Laleli in their addresses, others Şehzadebaşı. Refer to the map of this area to find your way.

The trend in recent years is for Laleli hotels to upgrade facilities and raise prices, but it is still possible to find a clean, quiet double room that's within our low-budget price range. Off season, or if you intend to stay for more than just a few days, you can haggle for a reduction. Most will grant it willingly.

Start your explorations by walking up Harikzadeler Sokak from Ordu Caddesi. This will take you past several inexpensive hotels and into the heart of Laleli.

The *Hotel Neşet* (tel 526-7412, 522-4474), Harikzadeler Sokak 23, 34470 Laleli, across the street from the Hotel Oran, is now among the area's older hotels, having been built several decades ago. But the rooms are maintained OK, staff are exceptionally friendly and accommodating,

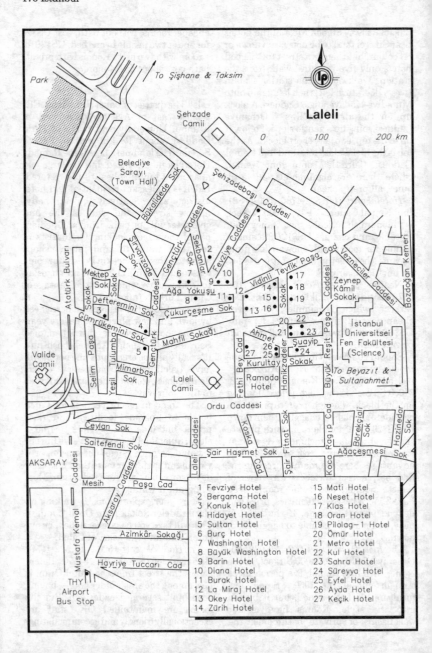

Park

To Şişhane & Taksim

Şehzade Camii

Laleli

0   100   200 km

Belediye Sarayı (Town Hall)

Şehzadebaşı Caddesi

Büyükalidede Sok

Gençtürk Caddesi

Sekbanlar Sok

Fevziye Caddesi

Sırvanzade Sok

Vezneciler Caddesi

Bozdoğan Kemeri

1

2

Mektep Sok

6 7

9 10

Ağa Yokuşu

Vidinli Sok

Tevfik Paşa Cad

• 17

• 18

• 19

Zeynep Kâmil Sokak

Defteremini Sok

8

11 12

14

• 15

Çukurçeşme Sok

13 16

3

Gümrükemini Sok

4

Mahfil Sokağı

20 22

21 • 23

Ahmet

İstanbul Üniversitsei Fen Fakültesi (Science)

Selim Paşa

Gençtürk

5

Ayda

26

27 25

Suayip

• 24

Büyük Reşit Paşa

To Beyazıt & Sultanahmet

Valide Camii

Yeşil Tulumba Sok

Mimarbaşı Sok

Laleli Camii

Kurultay Sokak

Hanikzadeler

Fethi Bey Cad

Ramada Hotel

Ordu Caddesi

Ceylan Sok

Saitefendi Sok

Laleli Caddesi

Koska Cad

Şair Haşmet Sok

Şair Fitnat Sok

Koca Ragıp Cad

Börekçiağı Sok

Ağaçeşmesi Sok

Hazinedar Sok

AKSARAY

Mesih Paşa Cad

Aksaray Caddesi

Azimkâr Sokağı

Mustafa Kemal Caddesi

Hayriye Tuccarı Cad

THY Airport Bus Stop

1 Fevziye Hotel	15 Mati Hotel
2 Bergama Hotel	16 Neşet Hotel
3 Konuk Hotel	17 Klas Hotel
4 Hidayet Hotel	18 Oran Hotel
5 Sultan Hotel	19 Pilolag-1 Hotel
6 Burç Hotel	20 Ömür Hotel
7 Washington Hotel	21 Metro Hotel
8 Büyük Washington Hotel	22 Kul Hotel
9 Barin Hotel	23 Sahra Hotel
10 Diana Hotel	24 Süreyya Hotel
11 Burak Hotel	25 Eyfel Hotel
12 La Miraj Hotel	26 Ayda Hotel
13 Okey Hotel	27 Keçik Hotel
14 Zürih Hotel	

and until renovation raises prices, you can get a room here for only US$14 to US$18 a single, US$22 a double.

Just across the street from the Neşet is the *Hotel Pilolag-1* (tel 511-8914/5), Harikzadeler Sokak 30, 34470 Laleli, which may have rooms if the others are full. If it doesn't have rooms, it's because there's a Polish or Yugoslav tour group in town. The price is a moderate US$28 for a double room with private bath. Breakfast costs extra.

The side street named Ahmet Şuayip Sokak, to the right (east) as you walk up Harikzadeler, holds the last grouping of Laleli hotels to survive (so far) the 'upgrade and raise prices' rage. It's here that you'll see the very cheap *Hotel Süreyya* (tel 520-7715), Ahmet Şuayip Sokak 8/2, 34470 Laleli, a very basic place with no pretensions to decor or style, just rooms, beds and running water. The price is right, though: a mere US$15 for a double room with shower. The *Hotel Paksoy* (tel 528-5848), Ahmet Şuayip Sokak 6, 34470 Laleli, right nearby, is quite similar in accommodation and price.

The *Hotel Sahra* (tel 526-0222), Ahmet Şuayip Sokak 8/1, 34470 Laleli, is marginally nicer than the Süreyya and the Paksoy, charging slightly more for that extra comfort: US$14 for a single room with shower, US$17 to US$20 for double rooms with private shower, or US$9 per person in rooms with three or four beds.

Hotel Ayda (tel 526-7867), Harikzadeler Sokak 11, 34470 Laleli, is simple but quite liveable and not expensive: double rooms with shower are priced at US$18. The Ayda and the more expensive Mati Pension nearby are under the same management.

The *Ömür Hotel* (tel 526-3030, 520-9728), at the intersection of Zeynep Kâmil Sokak and Harikzadeler Sokak, 34470 Laleli, has quite suitable rooms priced at US$12/20 a single/double, with private shower. I've had complaints about staff harassing single women, however, which

makes it a better choice for men and for couples.

Turn right onto Zeynep Kamil Sokak to find the *Hotel Kul* (tel 526-0127, 528-2892), Büyük Reşit Paşa Caddesi, Zeynep Kamil Sokak 27, 34470 Laleli, a very basic, old-fashioned place renting rooms for US$15/22 a single/double, with shower. The *Hotel Kaya* nearby is cheaper, and looks it, but it's usually full, as is the similar *Hotel Berlin* across the street.

Fethi Bey Caddesi is the street parallel to Harikzadeler Sokak, but one block to the west. Turn left onto Zeynep Kamil Sokak and walk west to Fethi Bey Caddesi, then turn right and you'll see the *Hotel La Miraj* (tel 511-2445/6), Fethi Bey Caddesi 28, 34470 Laleli, which has two parts, an older section on Fethi Bey Caddesi and a newer one right at the corner with Tevfik Paşa Sokak. The hotel is nothing fancy, with a bit of fray and fade, but it's clean and cheap, charging only US$14 for a single, US$19 for a double with one bed, US$23 for a double with two beds, and US$26 for a triple in a room with one double and one single bed. All of these prices are for rooms that have private showers.

Hotel Burak (tel 522-7904, 511-8679), Ağa Yokuşu Sokak 1-3, 34470 Laleli, is older than many of the other hotels in this area, with prices that reflect this difference. Furnishings are well used, and the decor is perhaps a bit drabber than others, but the tiny private bathrooms are bright and shiny. There's a lift and the staff are friendly. The best rooms in the hotel are the corner rooms, whose numbers end in '3' (203, 303, 403, etc); try to get one of these. In any case, you'll pay US$24/30 a single/double for any room, with breakfast included.

Finally, for those who'd like to spend a bit more for modernity and comforts, there's the *Hotel Diana* (tel 526-9621), Fethi Bey Caddesi, Ağa Yokuşu 2, 34470 Laleli, which is patronised largely by an Arab clientele. It has fairly modern rooms with private baths, a lobby, TV lounge and bar, and reasonable prices (usually quoted to guests in dollars) of US$25/32 a single/double.

Aksaray Across Ordu Caddesi from Laleli, to the south, are dozens of other small hotels. In recent years this area has become popular with tourists, students and job seekers from Iran and the Arab countries south and east of Turkey. Some of the hotels are accustomed to westerners, but most cater to Middle Eastern tourists.

Near the Covered Market Just across the main boulevard (Yeniçeriler Caddesi) from Beyazıt Camii, Tiyatro Caddesi runs downhill toward the Kumkapı quarter. Find the mosque, which is just west of the Covered Market and just east of İstanbul University and Beyazıt Square, then cross the street and walk one long block down Tiyatro Caddesi to find the *Hotel Radar* (tel 526-5150), Tiyatro Caddesi 18, 34000 Beyazıt, on the right-hand side of the street on the corner with Pehlivan Sokak. The Radar has been here for years, serving mostly a Yugoslavian clientele who come for shopping and who like being very close to the 4000 shops in the Covered Market. Though nothing fancy, it's clean and comfortable enough, considering the price: US$19 for a double room with shower. Breakfast is available as well.

Taksim Believe it or not, there are a few inexpensive hostelries near up-market Taksim Square, amid the banks, airline offices, nightclubs and towering luxury hotels.

The *Otel Avrupa* (tel 150-9420), Topçu Caddesi 32, Talimhane, 80090 Taksim, at the corner of Şehit Muhtar Caddesi, is in a warren of little streets not far from the Divan Hotel. It's a converted apartment house with an entrance at street level, a cheerful breakfast room one flight up, and guest rooms of varying sizes on the upper floors. Hallways are dingy, but the guest rooms are fine. Prices are the best in the Taksim area: US$22/28 a single/double without private shower, or US$32 a double with private shower. To find the Avrupa, locate the Air France office, and walk north on either Şehit Muhtar Caddesi or Lamartin Caddesi which are nearby. When you come to Topçu Caddesi, look for the hotel's sign.

More pleasant but also more expensive is the *İstanbul Plaza Hotel* (tel 145-3273/4), Sıraselviler, Aslan Yatağı Sokak 19/21, 80090 Taksim. From Taksim, walk down Sıraselviler Caddesi and turn left at a sign reading 'Plaza Hotel' just before the Alman Hastanesi (German Hospital). The hotel, hidden away on quiet Aslan Yatağı Sokak ('Lion's Bed St'!), has a nice marble facade, some marvellous views of the Bosphorus, and older, unrenovated but clean 1950s-style rooms and facilities. Rooms are priced at US$28/44 a single/double for a room with bath, or a few dollars less for a room without private bath. Rooms Nos 21, 31, 41, etc, all large corner rooms with little sun-porches and big baths with nice white tiles, offer excellent value for money. The staff speak French, Greek and Turkish. The hotel has a lift, a restaurant and even a few parking spaces. Go there if you want that Bosphorus view and are willing to pay just a bit more to get it.

Tepebaşı There is one hotel in Tepebaşı, near the American Consulate General and the grand old Pera Palas Oteli, that can still qualify for the low-budget range, though it too is in danger of renovation and price rises. It's the *Otel Alibaba* (tel 144-0781), Meşrutiyet Caddesi 119, 80050 Tepebaşı, next door to the Büyük Londra Oteli (Grand London Hotel). The Alibaba's reception desk is one flight up, its rooms several flights up, and fancy is certainly not the word to describe them, but the price is a mere US$18 for a double with shower.

Topkapı Bus Station İstanbul's chaotic Topkapı Bus Station is due to be replaced by a modern facility farther out of the city. Just in case you arrive before the new bus station is finished, here are the names of two cheap hotels near Topkapı Bus Station and Topkapı Gate in the City Walls. (Remember: Topkapı Gate is five km west of Topkapı Palace). To find these hotels, go through the Topkapı Gate on Millet Caddesi, the main road. Pass a military police post (Askeri İnzibat or As İz) on the right, then turn right just before the fancy Hotel Olcay. The cheap hotels are directly behind the Olcay.

Best of the two is the *Hotel Ulubat* (tel 585-4694/5), Kalburcu Çeşme Sokak 10, 34000 Topkapı. Simple but suitable rooms with bath and breakfast cost US$25/36 a single/double. The hotel has a restaurant and car park.

The very basic *Hotel Emir Sultan* (tel 585-6482), Kalburcu Çeşme Sokak 14, 34000 Topkapı, next door to the Ulubat, is dingy and male-dominated, but if you're desperate a double room with washbasin costs only US$10.

Kilyos On the Black Sea coast, an hour's drive (35 km) north of the Galata Bridge, lies Kilyos, a seaside resort village protected from development by the Ministry of Tourism. The village itself is not particularly charming, but the sand beach is a nice one, and the waters of the Black Sea are wonderfully cooling on a hot summer's day. Several hotels, motels, and pensions provide lodging; most are priced in our middle range, but there are a few in the bottom end. On summer weekends all Kilyos lodgings are likely to be filled from advance reservations. You will have a better chance of finding a room at Kilyos if you plan your visit for the middle of the week, reserve ahead, or visit outside of the high season (mid-July to the end of August).

To get to Kilyos from Taksim Square, you can take bus No 40 ('Sarıyer-Taksim') and then bus No 151 ('Sarıyer-Kilyos') for a total cost of US$0.55; or a dolmuş from Taksim to Sarıyer, and another dolmuş

from Sarıyer to Kilyos, for only a little more; or a taxi all the way (US$10).

The *Yuva Motel* (tel 882-1043), Kilyos, İstanbul, near the beach, has a few rooms with views of the sea. All rooms have little porches, but the rooms on the sea side of the motel are preferable. The price for a small double room with private shower, breakfast included, is US$25.

The *Yalı Pansiyon* (tel 882-1018), Kilyos, İstanbul, is a tidy little place at the eastern end of the beach. The rooms are simple, neat and clean, but have no running water; washing facilities are down the hall. Rooms on the lower level, with no sea view, cost US$22 a double; upstairs, with sea views, the price is US$28 a double. The upstairs rooms have one double and one single bed each, perfect for a couple with one child. The pension's kitchen facilities are available for your use. Ahmet, the manager, doesn't speak much English, but guests seem to overcome this obstacle.

Camping İstanbul's camping areas are ranged along the shore in Florya, Yeşilköy and Ataköy near the airport, about 20 km from Sancta Sophia. They have good sea view locations and average prices of US$8 for two persons in a tent. All are served by the frequent commuter trains (*banliyö trenleri*) which run between Sirkeci Station and the suburb of Halkalı. Thus, once you've set up camp you can hop on the train and ride to within 400 metres of Sancta Sophia and Topkapı Palace for a fraction of a dollar. (From Ataköy, hitch or take a bus east along the shore road about four km to Kazlıçeşme, where there's a train station; otherwise, rely on bus No 81 to trundle you between Eminönü and Ataköy, or bus Nos 71 or 72 to and from Taksim Square.)

Yeşilyurt Kamping (yeh-SHEEL-yoort) (tel 572-4961) is on the shore road, Sahil Yolu, near the village of Yeşilköy.

In Ataköy is the camping place closest to the city, the *Ataköy Mokamp* (AH-tah-kury) (tel 572-4961), part of a hotel, restaurant and beach complex with all sorts of facilities. The cost is US$10 for two in a tent.

Londra Mokamp, on the Londra Asfaltı highway between the airport and Topkapı Gate, is in a bad location which is near to city-bound traffic, noisy and fairly unpleasant.

There are also several camping places south of the E-5 highway in the suburb of Küçükçekmece, on the Sea of Marmara shore.

Places to Stay – middle

Middle-range hotels vary in size from 40 or 50 to 150 rooms, and charge from US$35 to US$85 for a double room with bath; but most rooms fall in the range of US$45 to US$65. Except for the few hotels in Sultanahmet, virtually all of these middle-range places can be depended upon to have lifts, restaurants, cocktail lounges, car parks and staff who speak foreign languages. Many provide TVs in their guest rooms. They're usually newer buildings constructed during the past decade or so.

Sultanahmet This prime sightseeing area does not have many middle-range lodging places; the hotels hereabouts tend to be low-budget ones. There are, however, a few places you should consider.

The *Otel Pamphylia* (tel 526-8935, 522-9069), Yerebatan Caddesi 47, 34400 Sultanahmet, at Çatalçeşme Sokak, just a short walk from the entrance to Yerebatan Saray, is near the Hotel Stop and Sultan Tourist Hostel 1. Its location is convenient, only steps from the major sights of Sultanahmet. The hotel is actually an apartment building which was renovated and converted during the late 1980s. A lift was added, and accommodations now have white tile bathrooms with a short bathtub and shower going for US$25/35/40 a single/double/triple; a few quieter rooms on the top floor have partial views, and thus cost US$40 a double.

Barut's Guesthouse (tel 520-1227), İshak Paşa Caddesi 8, 34400 Cankurtaran, is a favourite hostelry for young people who like the carpet-filled lobby-lounge, the family atmosphere, the quiet location near Topkapı and Sancta Sophia, and the clean, simple rooms. There are less than two dozen rooms in all, priced at US$32/36/50/60 a single/double/triple/quadruple, with a private shower. Each room is different in terms of size, shape and shower facilities, so look at several and choose the best if possible. Breakfast is served on a rooftop terrace with views of Sancta Sophia and the Bosphorus. To find Barut's, walk behind Sancta Sophia and turn right just before coming to the first gate into Topkapı Palace. Go down the hill on İshak Paşa Caddesi and you'll see Barut's on the right-hand side, at the corner with Kutlugün Sokak.

Laleli This area has far more middle-range hotels than low-budget ones. In fact, it has so many little hotels that local residents have complained in the newspapers about its becoming virtually one huge hotel, filled with foreigners. Though it sometimes appears to be a 'foreign ghetto', Laleli is still the best place to stay.

Many of the hotels in the Laleli quarter are of the perfect size for tour groups, and you may find many hotels filled during the summer months. Still, there are usually rooms available if you look. For your search, I suggest you follow a route similar to that outlined in the section on 'bottom end' places to stay. Start by walking up Harikzadeler Sokak from Ordu Caddesi.

One block up from Ordu Caddesi, just off Harikzadeler Sokak on the corner of Kurultay Sokak, is the two-star *Hotel Eyfel* (tel 520-9788/9), Kurultay Sokak 19, 34470 Laleli. It's an old favourite and has a lift, restaurant, cocktail lounge and 90 guest rooms with tiled showers for US$32/42 a single/double, US$12 for an extra bed in a room. Breakfast costs another US$3. The Eyfel has been here some time and has a few musty corners, but it has mostly gotten more comfortable over the years; staff are experienced and cordial.

The *Metro Oteli* (tel 511-3019, 520-6448), Ahmet Şuayip Sokak 17, 34470 Laleli, just off the right-hand side of Harikzadeler Sokak on the corner with Ahmet Şuayip, is a new three-star hotel, thoroughly modern in architecture and decor. The comfortable rooms have their own small tiled private bath, TV and fan. Prices are US$40/52 a single/double, US$12 for an extra bed, breakfast included.

The *Mati Pansiyon* (tel 526-4299, 526-8654), Harikzadeler Sokak 29, 34470 Laleli, right next door to the Hotel Zürih, is a new place operated by the management of the Hotel Ayda. Though small, it is attractive and well built. Honey-coloured natural wood is used extensively in the decoration, the private bathrooms are all tiled, and a small, pleasant breakfast room provides the first meal of the day. Though it calls itself a pension, this is actually a small, simple hotel of very good quality. The bed arrangements make the Mati a good choice for families: every room has a double bed and a single bed, or three single beds. Rooms are priced at US$40/50 a single/double, breakfast included.

Oran Hotel (tel 513-8200; fax 513-8205), Harikzadeler Sokak 36-42, 34470 Laleli, is directly across the street from the Hotel Neşet. Once a fairly simple hostelry, the Oran has been upgraded, and now all of the rooms have modern decors seemingly inspired by the Art Deco movement, private 'tub and shower' combination baths, TVs, mini-bar drinks refrigerators and direct-dial telephones; room service is available 24 hours a day (so they say). The hotel has a lift, nice lobby, restaurant and bar and a separate breakfast salon. With all of these improvements, the prices represent good value for money: US$36/45 a single/double, breakfast included.

The *Klas Hotel* (tel 511-7874),

Harikzadeler Sokak 48, 34470 Laleli, is at the northern end of Harikzadeler Sokak where it meets Vidinli Tevfik Paşa Caddesi, right across the street from the Hotel Zürih. The advantages here are a new building, good location, 60 tidy rooms with little balconies, two lifts, restaurant and bar and even a sauna, all for good prices of US$35/50/60 a single/double/triple.

Finally, the fancy three-star, 105-room *Hotel Zürih* (tel 512-2350), Harikzadeler Sokak 37, 34470 Laleli, on the corner with Vidinli Tevfik Paşa Caddesi, is the luxury place on the block. It's very shiny and clean, with several services usually only available in four and five-star hotels. Every room has a TV connected to the hotel's satellite antenna which can pick up European (mostly German) stations. The private baths have tubs of good size, not the short mini-tubs so often found in Laleli hotels. In the very comfortable restaurant, there's live entertainment most nights of the week (watch out for noise from this). The handsome rooms with bath are US$65/85 a single/double, breakfast included.

Turn left around the Hotel Zürih and onto Vidinli Tevfik Paşa Caddesi. Walk one short block, and the street changes names to become Ağa Yokuşu Sokak, running between Fethi Bey Caddesi and Gençtürk Caddesi. Ağa Yokuşu is packed solid with middle-range hotels.

One of the nicer places is the *Hotel Barın* (tel 522-8426, 526-4440), Fevziye Caddesi 25, 34470 Şehzadebaşı, a 65-room hostelry built a decade or so ago. When it opened, it was the most luxurious place in the quarter, but now it ranks solidly in the middle of the comfort range, with lifts, a nice lobby and decent restaurant. All of the guest rooms have showers, some have tubs as well. Families travelling with children should consider staying in one of the moderately priced suites. Prices are US$35/42 a single/double, or US$55 for a suite sleeping three; breakfast is US$3.50 per person extra.

Hotel Washington (tel 520-5990/1/2), Ağa Yokuşu Sokak 12, 34470 Laleli, has been here for a long time, which you may note from the 1960s decor. The hotel has been decently maintained though. The '60s rooms are larger than many built in the '80s and all have little balconies, TVs and mini-tubs as well as showers in the private bathrooms. There's a restaurant and bar, a spacious lobby and a lounge. The Washington is still very popular with tour operators, who tend to fill the better hotels hereabouts. Because of its reputation and comforts, the Washington gets away with charging US$36/52 a single/double.

Hotel Büyük Washington (tel 511-6371/2/3/4/5), Ağa Yokuşu 7, 34470 Laleli, is directly across the street from the similarly named Washington, and indeed is operated by the same people. Büyük means 'great' or 'grand', so this is the Grand Hotel Washington. Prices are higher here, but then you get more for your money, including a restaurant, nightclub, tearoom and café, hairdresser's shop and car park. The 148 attractive rooms have pretensions to style and even some luxury, with mini-tubs and showers in the baths, colour cable TVs and direct-dial telephones. Prices are a reasonable US$48/65 a single/double, breakfast included.

Hotel Burç (tel 513-8186/7/8), Ağa Yokuşu Sokak 18, 34470 Laleli, is virtually next door to the Hotel Washington, but charges much less: US$25/36 a single/double, US$10 for an extra bed, breakfast included. It's not as fancy, but then neither is the price, and the quiet, convenient location is just as good.

There are a few other hotels in the area, several just a few steps off Ağa Yokuşu Sokak. Two streets intersecting Ağa Yokuşu are Fethi Bey Caddesi to the south and Fevziye Caddesi to the north. Both have several hotels worth your consideration. Fethi Bey Caddesi is the street which runs from Ordu Caddesi (the main boulevard) between the Ramada Hotel and the Laleli mosque. Let's start there and head north.

Hotel Keçik (tel 511-2310, 528-1400), Fethi Bey Caddesi 18, 34470 Laleli, is almost next door to the fancy Ramada Hotel, on the right-hand (east) side of Fethi Bey Caddesi. Perhaps because of its propinquity to the class act in this area, the three-star Keçik looks and feels a bit more elegant than the rest. You enter to find a modern lobby with nice antique touches, like the little marble fountain. The 75 guest rooms are attractively modern, with solid-colour drapes and spreads, and all have halo-light vanity mirrors, colour TV and bathrooms with mini-tub and shower combinations. Guests can avail themselves of services including men's and women's hairdressers, a restaurant, bar, lounge, small outdoor terrace, TV room and even a fitness room equipped with sauna and Turkish bath. Prices for all this, just steps from the Ramada, are US$46/68 a single/double, US$17 for an extra bed, breakfast included.

Hotel Okey (tel 511-2162/3), Fethi Bey Caddesi 65, 34470 Laleli, just a short walk farther up Fethi Bey Caddesi, is more modest, friendlier and cheaper. It has 36 rooms going for US$16 to US$22 a single, US$30 to US$40 a double, breakfast included. The bathrooms here have both mini-tubs and showers.

Otel Bergama (tel 520-8411, 513-1443), Fevziye Caddesi 34, 34470 Şehzadebaşı, is around to the side of the aforementioned Hotel Washington, and more or less across the street from the Hotel Barın. This place is a perfect example of how Turkish architects and hotel owners tend to spend more on the lobby than on the guest rooms. The lobby is quite OK and rich-looking, but the guest rooms are small and pretty plain. Still, they'll do, and the prices are more in tune with the comforts of the rooms than the beauties of the lobby. Rates are US$16/32 a single/double, breakfast included.

The large, 220-room, three-star *Hotel Hamidiye* (tel 519-4150), Fevziye Caddesi 1, 34470 Şehzadebaşı, on the corner with

Şehzadebaşı Caddesi, is unique in this area in that its plan is completely different from that of a normal Turkish hotel. The lobby is vast, long, airy and fairly formal. A bank of three lifts takes guests up to the wide, spacious hallways and the rooms. All of the rooms have balconies, and some have views of the Şehzade Camii across the street. The Hamidiye's rates reflect its three-star status: US$46/60 a single/double, US$22 for an extra bed, breakfast included. Unfortunately, the Hamidiye caters largely to tour groups, and the reception desk staff tend to be curt with individual travellers.

Gençtürk Caddesi, the next street to the west of (and parallel to) Fethi Bey Caddesi, is broad and busy. There are several good hotel choices here as well.

The three-star, 130-room *Sultan Oteli* (tel 513-5890; fax 513-0305), Gençtürk Caddesi 29, 34470 Laleli, is at the top of our middle-range budget, but offers comforts – even luxuries – worthy of its prices. Marble, copper, wood and chromium steel are used lavishly throughout the decor, the staff are multilingual and hotel services abound. You'll find a good restaurant, a bar, a hairdresser's, a tearoom and a gift shop. The guest rooms have two double beds or one queen-size bed, colour TV with European channels via satellite, and bathrooms richly furnished with marble. For all this, the rates are US$60/84 a single/double, US$25 for an extra bed, breakfast included.

Hotel Hidayet (tel 513-4940), Gençtürk Caddesi 23, 34470 Laleli, on the corner of Gümrükemini Sokak, could be considered a smaller and less deluxe version of the aforementioned place. It's modern, but the rooms are smaller and there are not quite so many services. This means, though, that you pay only US$38/47/54 a single/double/triple for room and breakfast.

Go along Gümrükemini Sokak west one block to Yeşil Tulumba Sokak and you'll come to the *Otel Konuk* (tel 520-6135/6), Yeşil Tulumba Sokak 39, 34470 Laleli. It's a small, 25-room two-star place that stands out for the quality and taste of its decor. Rooms are small but comfortable enough and there's a restaurant. You'll pay US$30/42 a single/double, breakfast included.

Aksaray Across the traffic circle in Aksaray Square are other hotel areas. Because Laleli is becoming so popular, it might be a good idea for you to search for suitable accommodation here when Laleli seems full. In general, I cannot recommend the hotels on the south side of Ordu Caddesi, but several readers of this book have enjoyed their stays at the *Hotel İkbal* (tel 526-1667/8, 526-0794), Koska Caddesi 45, 34470 Laleli; Koska Caddesi is the southward continuation of Fethi Bey Caddesi. A good, clean room with bath and shower combination costs about US$35 a double, breakfast included. The hotel is sometimes used by British tour groups.

Look also on the west side of Mustafa Kemal Caddesi. To reach this area, walk south on Aksaray Caddesi to Azimkâr Sokak and turn right. Cross Mustafa Kemal Caddesi and continue straight on along Tiryaki Hasan Paşa Sokak to Namık Kemal Caddesi.

The *Hotel Fuar* (tel 525-9732, 525-9859), Namık Kemal Caddesi, Aksaray, boasts four stars though it has only 60 rooms. The comforts provided are aimed partly at business travellers: rooms have three closed-circuit colour TV channels, many have mini-bars, and all have comfortable furnishings and modern bathrooms. Prices for these comforts are US$78/115 a single/double; breakfast costs another US$5.50. If the hotel is not full, you can and should haggle to get a reduction, by which you can bring these four-star comforts down to a three-star price.

Much less expensive is the nearby three-star *Hotel Tamsa* (tel 523-8616), Manastırlı Rıfat Sokak 33, Aksaray. It's a modern, 120-room establishment with restaurant, terrace café, restaurant and bar, and comfortable rooms with bath on a quiet street renting for US$50/68 a single/double, US$30 for an extra bed; breakfast is included in these rates. Manastırlı Rıfat Sokak, by the way, is the westward continuation of Tiryaki Hasan Paşa Sokak. As this area develops, no doubt many more hotels will be built, and it will become a 'second Laleli' as far as hotels are concerned.

Taksim Though the city has changed greatly in a century, Beyoğlu is still, generally speaking, the centre of European-style living. The airline offices, foreign banks and luxury hotels are all here. The Pullman Etap Marmara (formerly the Inter-Continental) hotel is right in Taksim; the Sheraton is a block away, as is the Hyatt, and the Hilton is two long blocks north. All these places charge 'international rates' of US$175 to US$250 for a double room.

There are several smaller hotels near Taksim which charge more reasonable rates, but even these suffer from price inflation due to location. They all charge a bit more because they're in the shadow of the 'big boys'. A hotel room that costs US$75 at a nice little place in Laleli will cost US$115 near Taksim.

Hotel Keban (keh-BAHN) (tel 143-3310/1/2/3), Sıraselviler Caddesi 51, 80090 Taksim, is just out of Taksim Square near İstiklal Caddesi. Look for the Maksim theatre – that's at the beginning of Sıraselviler Caddesi, and the hotel is just a few doors down from it. The three-star Keban has English-speaking staff, 87 rooms with air-con, combination tub and shower, colour TVs and mini-bar drinks refrigerators. For all this posh stuff you pay US$50/68 a single/double.

The three-star *Dilson Hotel* (DEEL-sohn) (tel 143-2032), Sıraselviler Caddesi 49, 80090 Taksim, a few steps down from the Keban, is very similar. Its 90 rooms are priced at US$48/62 a single/double;

family rooms with several beds are also available.

The *Hotel Star* (tel 145-0050), Sağlık Sokak 11, 80090 Taksim, is very close to Taksim, though on a back street and therefore fairly quiet. Although the building has eight floors, it holds only 24 rooms, all of which are quite small, as are the hallways, lifts, lobby and every other part of the hotel. But for all that the accommodations are pleasant, with private showers, and most are sunny and cheery. Rates are a moderate US$35/50 a single/double, with breakfast included. An extra person in a room pays US$25. Rooms with numbers ending in '4' are the corner ones, larger and lighter, so ask for one of them and try to get one on an upper floor. To find the hotel, stand in front of the big Pullman Etap Marmara Hotel, walk toward the Atatürk Cultural Palace at the northern end of the square, and bear right down İnönü Caddesi, walking on the right-hand side of the road. Pass the Toros Air airline office, then look on the right for the hotel's sign.

A unique lodging near the Hotel Star is the *Family House* (tel 149-7351, 149-9667), Kutlu Sokak 53, Gümüşsuyu, 80090 Taksim, with five three-room apartments for rent in a pleasant and very well-kept building. The atmosphere here is one of a well-bred family's home, as the manager, Mr Atıl Erman, is available to answer any question or solve any problem quietly and decorously; he'll even meet you at the airport and bring you to Family House.

Apartments come with two twin beds and one double bed, telephone, colour TV with video hook-up, kitchen with refrigerator, two-burner gas hotplate, utensils, and even an apron. The price per apartment in summer is US$95 per day for up to four people, in winter US$80 per day; reductions of 10% are offered on stays of a month or longer. Breakfast (at an extra charge) is available in Family House's pleasant breakfast room, or you can prepare your own meals in your apartment's kitchen. To find Family House, follow the directions to the Hotel Star, then go downhill one more flight of steps, following the signs.

The *Hotel Cihangir* (tel 151-8215, 151-5317), Aslan Yatağı Sokak 33, Cihangir, is less than a 10-minute walk from Taksim. Walk out of the square along Sıraselviler Caddesi past the afore-mentioned Keban and Dilson hotels, turn left at the sign for the Plaza Hotel and go straight down the hill turning to right and left as the road does. Soon the narrow cobbled street will intersect a wide street opening to your right, and you'll see the hotel on the left-hand side. The Cihangir is only a few years old, and all of its rooms are attractive and modern, with tile baths or showers. However, some have a view of the Bosphorus and others don't, and this determines the room price. Without the view, the price is a moderate US$50 for a double; with the view, it rises to US$85 a double, but for this price you also get a nice little balcony from which to admire the view. Hotel services include a restaurant and bar, a TV lounge and a car park.

Near the Hilton, just off Cumhuriyet Caddesi, is the *Hotel Konak* (tel 148-4744/5), Nisbet Sokak 9, 80230 Elmadağ, a three-star hotel several decades old which benefits from an experienced staff and an up-market location. The Konak is popular with young business executives and some small European tour groups, who like being near the airline offices, nightclubs and posh hotels. The hotel has its own restaurant and bar. Rooms have been upgraded over the years, and now boast colour TVs, mini-bars, and direct-dial phones. Singles/doubles/triples with bath are priced at US$58/74/95, breakfast included.

To find the hotel, walk up the left-hand (west) side of Cumhuriyet Caddesi from Taksim Square. After you pass the Divan Oteli, look for these landmarks: Titibank, Planet Travel and İlhan Şerif's men's store. The narrow side street going left

(west) off Cumhuriyet Caddesi is at this place, just opposite a pedestrian crossing – the only possible place to cross busy Cumhuriyet Caddesi.

Tepebaşı Between Galatasaray Square and Tünel Square, west of İstiklal Caddesi, is the district called Tepebaşı (TEH-peh-bah-shuh), which was the first luxury hotel district in the city. The main road through Tepebaşı is Meşrutiyet Caddesi, where one finds the British and American Consulates General, the Pera Palas Oteli and the Pullman Etap İstanbul Hotel. So if you stay here, you're in good company. The best way to get here is by taxi, or failing that, by dolmuş from Taksim; you may have to use a dolmuş that goes past Tepebaşı (say, to Aksaray) and pay the full fare. You can catch a bus along Tarlabaşı Caddesi (TAHR-la-bash-uh), just out of Taksim near the Air France office. Coming from Karaköy, take the Tünel to the top station and walk the several blocks to the hotels.

Just behind the towering Etap İstanbul Hotel is the older *Yenişehir Palas* (tel

Ceramic Dish

152-7160), Meşrutiyet Caddesi, Oteller Sokak 1/3, 80050 Tepebaşı, renovated in recent times and now in the three-star class. It is a hotel of eight floors, with little in the way of views but in a good location, with 90 comfortable and attractive rooms with baths. Its moderate prices have made it popular with Greek tourists, whom you may hear talking in the lobby. Rooms are priced at US$30 to US$40 a single, US$40 to US$50 a double with shower or bath.

The *Büyük Londra Oteli* (tel 149-1025, 145-0670) is on Meşrutiyet Caddesi 117, 80050 Tepebaşı. It dates from the same era as the Pera Palas Oteli, has much smaller rooms and bathrooms, and is a bit the worse for wear, but it does preserve some of the Victorian-era glory (in the public rooms at least) at a price considerably below that of its larger and more famous neighbour. A room with shower costs US$50 with one double bed, US$60 with two beds.

Down the hill a few steps from the Pera Palas Oteli and behind the American Consulate General is the *Otel Bale* (tel 150-4912), Refik Saydam Caddesi, 80050 Tepebaşı, another good choice if you're careful to avoid the noisier rooms. Luckily, the quieter rooms are also the ones which have views of the Golden Horn; ask for one of these. Rooms with bath are priced at US$35 a single, US$45 to US$50 a double.

Kariye Here is a hotel that is pretty much in the middle of nowhere – unless you want to be right next door to the marvellous mediaeval mosaics in the Kariye Müzesi. The Turkish Touring & Automobile Association, which earlier restored the Ottoman Pudding Shop facing the museum, has now restored a mansion just to the right of the museum as a nice little Ottoman-style hotel.

The *Kariye Oteli* (tel 524-8864/8881/9806, 521-6631) Kariye Camii Sokak 18, 34240 Edirnekapısı, has smallish but perfectly comfortable guest rooms with

showers furnished in pleasant (though not opulent) 19th-century Ottoman style. The staff speak some English and provide careful, friendly service in the restaurant and bar. There is no traffic noise in this working-class İstanbul neighbourhood out by the city walls. Prices are moderate and the lowest of all the Turkish Touring & Automobile Association hotels: US$50/66/80 for a single/double/triple, US$90 for a suite, breakfast included. (Note that you must pay in cash: credit cards are not accepted.)

So what could be wrong with this place? Well, you must take a 15 to 25-minute bus or taxi ride to reach any other sightseeing area such as Sultanahmet or Taksim Square. Even the airport is a long way off, but actually it is closer to the Kariye than it is to any hotels in Laleli, Sultanahmet or Taksim. To get to the Kariye Oteli, take a taxi (US$5 or so from the airport, US$2 or US$3 from other points in the city) or hop aboard bus No 80 (to Edirnekapı) travelling up Fevzi Paşa Caddesi from the quarters of Fatih, Şehzadebaşı (Laleli) or Beyazıt. Take the same bus to get back to the centre of the city.

Topkapı Bus Station Though the bus station at Topkapı will probably have moved by the time you arrive, you still may have use for a moderately priced hotel just inside Topkapı Gate. The following hotel is often used by people whose planes are delayed and who must stay another night in the city, then head out to Atatürk Airport early in the morning.

Right next to the Hotel Ulubat is the *Hotel Olcay* (OHL-jahyee) (tel 585-3220/1/2/3/4; fax 585-6405), Millet Caddesi 187, Topkapı. It's a bright, modern four-star place with smooth service, a large restaurant and 182 very comfortable air-con rooms with baths priced at US$60/84 a single/double; breakfast costs another US$6. To make your waiting time more pleasant, the hotel has a heated indoor swimming pool, sauna, fitness room, jacuzzi whirlpool bath, TV lounge, restaurant and bar.

Bebek The *Hotel Bebek* (tel 163-3000), Cevdetpaşa Caddesi 113-115, Bebek, İstanbul, is in a charming suburb of the city midway up the European shore of the Bosphorus, 10 km from the Galata Bridge. The town and the hotel are right on the shore overlooking the water. Steep hillsides rise to the west just inland from the shore road; atop the slopes is the Bosphorus University, and just to the north of it is the fortress of Rumeli Hisar. Bebek has many cosmopolitan, wealthy residents who moor their yachts, large and small, just offshore. Should you have a reason to get out of the city for a few days, Bebek may be the place to get away to.

The two-star hotel has wonderful Bosphorus views from many of its rooms, as well as from the restaurant and bar. Prices are quite reasonable at US$45 for a double room with bath, breakfast included. Bus No 23 runs up the Bosphorus from Taksim Square. Make sure you get one signed as 'Bebek-Taksim'; some other buses on route No 23 only go as far as Barbaros Hayrettin Paşa or Ortaköy. There are also cheap dolmuşes from Taksim Square, departing from İnönü Caddesi in front of the Toros Air office. A taxi from Taksim to Bebek costs around US$4.

Kilyos For a description of Kilyos and how to get there from the Galata Bridge, refer to the Kilyos section in Places to Stay – bottom end.

The prime hostelry in Kilyos is the *Turban Kilyos Moteli* (tel 142-0288, 142-2464/5; fax 882-1259), right on the beach. The several two-storey motel buildings hold 144 rooms of three types. There are twin-bedded rooms with bath, rooms with twin beds and a double bed, and two-room four-bedded suites. All of the rooms, designed in a simple, modern Mediterranean style with white stucco walls, dark wood and plaid blankets, have

bathrooms and porches with some sea views.

Prices depend upon the number of beds, the position of the building (whether it's nearer or farther from the beach), and the season of the year; you are required to take breakfast and dinner with your room. Services at the motel include a tennis court, sea-view restaurant and bar, tea terrace and beer garden, and of course the fine beach just steps away. In the high summer season from mid-July to the end of August, prices range from US$40 to US$45 a single, US$62 to US$68 a double, breakfast and dinner included. In rooms with four beds, three people pay US$100, four pay US$120, breakfast and dinner included. Prices in 'mid-season' (mid-May to early July and all of September) are 20% lower; off-season (early to mid-May) prices are 33% lower. The motel is closed from October to April.

The next-best lodging at Kilyos is the *Kilyos Kale Hotel* (tel 882-1054, 882-1295), Kale Caddesi 78, Kilyos, İstanbul, up the hill from the centre of the village. This modern, comfortable but simple hotel has 27 rooms with bath, many of which have beach and sea views; there's a fine view from the restaurant as well. Rooms cost US$25/35 a single/double; add US$4.50 more per person for breakfast, US$8.50 per person for breakfast and dinner, or US$12.50 per person for all three meals.

The *Gurup Hotel* (tel 882-1194, 882-1251), Kilyos, İstanbul, has a nice hillside location with fine views of the sea and the beach, a sunny patio and a vine-covered restaurant. It's a small place of 30 tidy little rooms, each with twin beds, a private shower and vine-covered porch with sea view (in late summer you can pick the grapes right on your own porch!). The aptly named Gurup ('abundant') is a favourite with British holiday groups. You must take breakfast and dinner with your room; the price for room and half board is US$36 a double.

The *Kilyos Erzurumlu Motel* (tel

882-1003), Kilyos, İstanbul, is next door to the Kilyos Kale Hotel. It's somewhat older but very tidy and quiet. Rooms have splendid views and cost US$36 a double with breakfast.

Places to Stay – top end

The centre of the posh hotel district is certainly Taksim Square, but there are numerous luxury hotels in other parts of the city as well. Prices range from US$100 to US$250 and higher a double, but most rooms fall into the range of US$100 to US$175. Sultanahmet has several extremely attractive hotels set up in restored Ottoman mansions, such as the Yeşil Ev. In Tepebaşı is the famous Pera Palas Oteli, built for the passengers on the original Orient Express. And up the Bosphorus at Çubuklu is the Hidiv Kasrı, the former mansion of the khedives of Egypt, now converted into a fabulous villa hotel. Here you can sleep in the bed of King Faruk if you like.

Sultanahmet The Turkish Touring & Automobile Association has been restoring historic buildings throughout the city, including an Ottoman mansion very near Sancta Sophia and the Blue Mosque. This is the Yeşil Ev (tel 528-6764, 511-1150/1), Kabasakal Caddesi 5, 34400 Sultanahmet. The house is simply lovely, a graceful old Ottoman place perfectly restored (virtually rebuilt) and furnished with period pieces and antiques in exquisite taste. To its right is the Istanbul Handicrafts Centre, a restored Ottoman medrese in which the rooms that were once student cells are now shops selling authentic handicrafts. Behind the hotel is a lovely shaded garden terrace with restaurant and beverage service.

Alas, the Yeşil Ev has only 22 rooms, and so it is usually very difficult to get a reservation here, but if you do, you'll pay US$110/140/175 a single/double/triple or US$200 for the Pasha's Room, with its own private Turkish bath. Breakfast, service and tax are included in the rates;

they may not accept credit cards, so be prepared to pay with cash or travellers' cheques.

Not far from the Yeşil Ev, behind Sancta Sophia against the walls of Topkapı Palace, is a row of Ottoman houses which have also been rebuilt and refitted by the Turkish Touring & Automobile Association people as lodgings for travellers. These are the Ayasofya Pansiyonları (tel 513-3660), Soğukçeşme Sokak, 34400 Sultanahmet. The location is unbeatable, which is why all the rooms are often filled and reservations difficult to obtain.

The 58 accommodations with private baths here are somewhat simpler, but still in 19th-century Ottoman style with brass or antique wooden beds, frilly glass lamps, Turkish carpets and period wall hangings. Prices are US$65 to US$85 a single, US$100 to US$120 a double, US$120 to US$140 a triple, breakfast included; they may not accept credit cards. The cheaper rooms are the ones at the back, with little in the way of views or light. The complex's dining rooms provide good food and moderate prices, and the Sarnıç Restaurant, set up in a Roman cistern, is right next door (see Places to Eat for details). The reception desk, by the way, is at the north-western end of the street, on the way to Gülhane Park.

Similar in feeling but lower in price is the Hotel Sokullu Paşa (tel 512-3753/6/7/8), İshak Paşa Mahallesi, Mehmet Paşa Sokak 10, 34400 Sultanahmet, an old frame townhouse on a back street, off the southern end of the Hippodrome. The house has been completely rebuilt and is now beautiful with stained and etched glass, antique prints, turn of the century-style furniture, Turkish carpets and beaten copper utensils as accent pieces. The hotel's private walled garden terrace has a beautiful marble fountain pool; the terrace is good for tea or a meal or writing postcards.

The hotel has obliging English-speaking staff, a nice restaurant and wine cellar with rough stone walls, a lobby bar and Turkish bath (right off the lobby, unfortunately). Though it is very nice, the rooms are small and quite crowded together, with some loss of privacy. Prices for all of this atmosphere are US$75/95/115 a single/double/triple, breakfast included. The Sokullu Paşa is owned and managed by Konuk Otelcilik Co.

Another of Konuk Otelcilik's hotels is the beautiful *Hotel Sümengen* (tel 512-6162, 512-9088; fax 512-9584), Mimar Mehmet Ağa Caddesi, Amiral Tafdil Sokak 21, 34400 Sultanahmet, down behind the Blue Mosque. Here, another Ottoman townhouse with its own pretty little marble fountain in front has been beautifully restored and features a marble-covered Turkish bath, an airy and light restaurant with excellent views of the Sea of Marmara, an ornate lobby with parquet floors and Turkish carpets everywhere, and Turkish-style sofas to relax upon. On the top floor is an open-air terrace with the same fine views of the Sea of Marmara. The location, at the end of a quiet street, is very good. The 30 guest rooms are small with tiny but very tidy showers and twin or double beds. A few of the rooms have views of the sea but many rooms open only onto corridors, giving their inhabitants little privacy. Rates are US$75/95/115 a single/double/triple, breakfast included.

Laleli The Tayyare Blok was a large apartment complex built across a side street from the Laleli mosque almost a century ago. In the late 1980s the building was renovated and is now the *Ramada Hotel İstanbul* (tel 519-4050; fax 512-6390; for reservations, 512-8120), Ordu Caddesi 226, 34470 Laleli. The narrow courtyards and walks of the Tayyare Blok have been enclosed and covered with lofty glass canopies, and the small apartment rooms furnished with luxurious modern fabrics and furniture.

This hotel is one of the most architecturally fascinating luxury hostelries in

the city. There's a complete roster of services, of course, including shops, a courtyard pastry-shop café and bar, enclosed heated swimming pool and fitness centre, a Turkish restaurant and a formal Chinese restaurant. The 275 guest rooms tend to be small by luxury standards, with small bathrooms, but they are certainly comfortable. Some overlook the enclosed courtyards, others the busy street or side streets. Prices are up there: US$135/155 a single/double for 'standard' rooms which are the smaller ones; larger, deluxe rooms cost US$285 single or double, tax and service included, but breakfast costs extra.

Taksim The *Hotel Pullman Etap Marmara* (tel 151-4696; fax 144-0509), Taksim Square, 80090 Taksim, is right in the busy square. A tall rectangular tower, its height and position provide splendid views of the Old City, Beyoğlu and the Bosphorus from its middle and upper floors. You enter the lobby past the pastry-shop café, the shopping arcade and the casino entrance, then up a long escalator.

Several restaurants, an enclosed swimming pool, a sun deck, a nightclub and a rooftop restaurant and bar are among the luxury services here. The 424 guest rooms have colour TVs with European satellite channels (including one in English), mini-bar refrigerators and nice tiled bathrooms. Prices are US$175 to US$200 a single, US$200 to US$250 a double, with tax, service and buffet breakfast included.

The 437-room *İstanbul Sheraton Hotel and Towers* (tel 131-2121; fax 131-2180), Taksim Park, 80174 Taksim, is a 23-storey asymmetrical tower rising right over Taksim Park. It provides wonderful Bosphorus and Golden Horn views and is only a few minutes' stroll from Taksim Square. All conceivable luxury hotel services are here, including an enclosed heated swimming pool, health club, rooftop restaurant and bar and an indoor car park. Rooms are large, airy and furnished with every luxury including marbled bathrooms. Prices depend partly upon the view from the room: singles cost US$135 to US$185, doubles are US$175 to US$225, tax and service included.

A bit farther from Taksim along Cumhuriyet Caddesi on the right is the *Hilton International İstanbul* (tel 131-4650; fax 140-4165), Cumhuriyet Caddesi, 80200 Harbiye, set in its own spacious park with tennis courts, swimming pool, helicopter pad and even its own large convention centre. It gives one the feeling of staying at a private luxury club, albeit a very large club.

Though the oldest luxury hotel in the city, the Hilton has been renovated frequently and remains, in my mind, the city's prime luxury hotel. The public rooms and guest rooms are done lavishly with creamy marble, gleaming brass and rich textiles. Guest rooms are in several locations, with various decors and special services, and so the price range is broad: US$190 to US$215 a single, US$225 to US$260 a double, tax and service included. Pricier rooms have more services (hair dryers, TVs with remote controls, etc), are larger, and have Bosphorus views. Weekend prices can be as low as US$170 a double per night, tax, service and continental breakfast included.

There is a middle ground for those who want some of the comforts of a luxury hotel but don't want to pay 'international' prices. A few steps out of Taksim Square along the western side of Cumhuriyet Caddesi is the office of Air France, and to the left of the office is the beginning of Şehit Muhtar Caddesi. Walk along this street for two short blocks and you'll come to the *Otel Eresin* (tel 156-0803), Topçu Caddesi 34, 80090 Taksim. It's a very comfortable seven-floor, 60-room hotel done in natural wood and muted colours, with bathtubs, TVs and little refrigerators in all the guest rooms. The street is quiet and the price is US$80/100 a single/double, breakfast included.

Similar but more stylish is the *Riva*

Hotel (tel 156-4420), Aydede Caddesi 8, 80090 Taksim, on the corner of Lamartin Caddesi. The Riva is modern and highly polished, nine storeys of shiny glory, with all the comforts. The clientele are mostly travelling on business. Prices for rooms, including a full buffet breakfast, are US$98/130 a single/double. If you think the price is too high, and if the hotel doesn't seem busy, you can negotiate a reduction.

The *Divan Oteli* (dee-VAHN) (tel 131-4100, 131-4070), Cumhuriyet Caddesi 2, Elmadağ, 80090 Taksim, was founded by Vehbi Koç, Turkey's millionaire industrialist whose family also founded the Sadberk Hanım Museum in the Bosphorus town of Sarıyer. Though it is one of the city's older luxury hotels, and with only 96 rooms one of the smaller ones, it has built an enduring reputation as a small European-style hotel with personal service by well-trained English-speaking staff and excellent cuisine. Besides the acclaimed dining room, there is the less formal Divan Pub (actually a full-service restaurant) and the Divan pastry-shop café. Rooms have all the comforts, including colour TV with satellite channels (mostly German), mini-bar refrigerators and simple modern furniture. The location, right across the street from the Sheraton and only a short stroll from Taksim Square or the Hilton, is very convenient. Prices here are US$140 a single, US$195 a double.

Tepebaşı In the heart of Beyoğlu, midway between Galata and Taksim, is Tepebaşı.

The prime, modern, high-rise hostelry here is undoubtedly the *Hotel Pullman Etap İstanbul* (tel 151-4646; fax 149-8033), Meşrutiyet Caddesi, 80050 Tepebaşı. It's run by the same French hotel group as the Pullman Etap Marmara in Taksim Square, which is the more luxurious of the two. But the Etap İstanbul has its own advantages: 200 simple, attractive modern rooms with satellite TVs and mini-bars in a 22-storey air-con tower. Many rooms have splendid views of the Golden Horn, the bulbous mosques and slender minarets of the Old City, and of the Bosphorus. The view from the rooftop's tiny swimming pool is the best of all.

The Etap İstanbul has a pastry-shop café, disco, restaurant, coffee shop, bar and lounge. Another distinct advantage here is that room prices are substantially lower than at the other, larger Etap hotel. For the price, which is US$100/135 a single/double, this is the best hotel in the city, and it's often booked solid. Reserve well in advance if you can.

Though it is no longer 'isolated on all four sides', the *Pera Palas Oteli* (PEH-ra pa-LAHS) (tel 151-4560), Meşrutiyet Caddesi 98-100, 80050 Tepebaşı, is still open and thriving. It fills up regularly with individual tourists and groups looking to relive the great age of Constantinople. It is a worthy place.

It used to be fairly cheap, too, but the management have discovered what foreigners will pay for nostalgia (a lot) and have upped the prices. The Pera Palas Oteli has 120 rooms with high ceilings, period furnishings and some bathrooms to match; the bathrooms, made with British fixtures a century ago, are still in excellent condition. Some rooms have views of the Golden Horn. Nostalgia and atmosphere are what you're paying for here, as there are no luxury services such as air-con, TV sets or sound-proofing; but the atmosphere in the public salons and the wonderful bar is certainly bewitching. Rooms with bath and breakfast are priced at US$95 to US$115 a single, US$135 to US$160 a double. Rooms on the lower floors can be very noisy, and west-facing rooms can get quite hot from the setting sun in summer.

While we're on the subject of the Pera Palas Oteli, I should let you know that Agatha Christie's favourite room was No 411, while the great Atatürk preferred No 101, a vast suite which, kept just as he used it, is now a museum (ask at the reception desk for admission).

Near Atatürk Airport The *Çınar Hotel* (chuh-NAHR, tel 573-2910), PO Box 12, 34800 Yeşilköy, İstanbul, is on the Sea of Marmara shore, and at this writing is the nearest luxury hotel to the airport, though other hotels are being built. If you have flight delays or cancellations, you can get to this four-star, 200-room hotel in 15 minutes by taxi (US$2.50). You'll find an older building, decently maintained, with several restaurants and bars, swimming pool, sauna, disco and shops. Many of the comfortable guest rooms have fine views of the sea, and most have balconies so you can enjoy the view. The rooms in the newer wing at the poolside have more up-to-date furnishings, including mini-bars. Rates are US$115/125 a single/double.

Bosphorus The shores of the Bosphorus have several hotels which may be of use to you.

Drawing the most interest these days is the restoration of *Çirağan Palace*, to be opened in 1991 as the Çirağan Palace Kempinski İstanbul Hotel. The rebuilt palace will hold VIP suites, a ballroom, casino, restaurants and boutiques. Connected to the palace will be a modern 312-room luxury hotel annex. Work is still in progress at this writing, but the hotel may well be open and receiving guests by the time you arrive in İstanbul.

Halfway up the Bosphorus on the European side, 20 km north of the Galata Bridge, is the pleasant little village of Tarabya on a salt-water cove. Dominating the northern reaches of the village is the *Büyük Tarabya Oteli* (Grand Hotel Tarabya, tel 162-1000; fax 162-2260), Kefeliköy Caddesi, Tarabya, İstanbul. It's a curving mammoth of a building put up several decades ago and now operated by one of Turkey's larger hotel chains, Emek. The Tarabya has 216 rooms, a good seafood restaurant, another restaurant on the terrace, a nightclub, café, bars, its own post office branch and several other services. Many of the guest rooms face the Bosphorus; those that do are priced at

US$145/175 a single/double. Rooms facing inland cost about 20% less. You may be able to haggle.

But certainly the most enchanting lodgings on the Bosphorus (besides those in palaces) are the ones in the villa built by the king of Egypt. Herewith a little history:

Having ruled Egypt for centuries, the Ottomans lost control to an adventurer named Muhammed Ali, who took over the government of Egypt and defied the sultan in İstanbul to dislodge him. The sultan, unable to do so, gave him quasi-independence and had to be satisfied with reigning over Egypt rather than ruling. The ruling was left to Muhammed Ali and his line, and the ruler of Egypt was styled *hidiv*, 'khedive' (not 'king', as that would be unbearably independent). The khedives of Egypt kept up the pretence of Ottoman suzerainty by paying tribute to İstanbul.

The Egyptian royal family, who looked upon themselves as Turkish and spoke Turkish rather than Arabic as the court language, often spent their summers in a traditional yalı on the Bosphorus shore. In 1906, Khedive Abbas Hilmi built himself a palatial villa on the most dramatic promontory on the Bosphorus, a place commanding a magnificent view.

The *Hidiv Kasrı* (hee-DEEV kahss-ruh, 'Khedive's Villa', tel 331-2651), Çubuklu, İstanbul, set in its own large park, is in pure, delicious Art Nouveau style, with a circular entry hall complete with fountain. A semicircular facade looks toward the sunset across the Bosphorus. The ground floor is now the restaurant; the upper floor is still the master bedroom.

There is room for only 50 guests in the hotel, but every single one has an unforgettable stay. Rooms with bath are priced from US$75 to US$100 for a double on the top (servants') floor, through US$130 for a large bedroom as used by the royal family, to US$250 for the Khedive's Suite. You'll need a taxi to reach the hotel. Çubuklu is about a 30 to 45-minute drive north of the city centre, which costs US$8 or so in a taxi.

PLACES TO EAT

In İstanbul you will eat some very tasty food, no matter if you eat in a simple workers' cafeteria or in a luxury restaurant. Good food has been a Turkish passion for centuries. In fact, the fearsome Janissary corps, the sultan's shock troops, were organised along the lines of a kitchen staff. They had a habit of signalling revolt by overturning the cauldrons which held their dinner of pilav. The message from these elite troops to their sovereign might be phrased, 'If you call this food, we have confidence in neither your taste buds nor your leadership'.

İstanbul's restaurants are everywhere. Price, by the way, has little to do with flavour in Turkish restaurants. In the posh places you will get somewhat finer food, elegant presentation and European-style service. But in the moderate, inexpensive and even very cheap places, the food will still be savoury and delicious.

Little neighbourhood places, mostly hazır yemek (ready-food) restaurants, kebapçıs and pidecis, will charge between US$1.50 or US$2 for a simple main-course lunch to perhaps US$4 or US$5 for a several-course budget tuck-in. These are the places listed in the 'bottom end' section.

In slightly nicer places with white tablecloths and attentive waiters, if you order something more expensive such as a good portion of meat or fish, wine or beer, dessert, etc, expect to pay US$6 to a top of US$12 per person. These are the restaurants listed in the 'middle' section.

In the 'top end' section are those restaurants in which a meal will normally cost between US$12 and US$20 per person, all included. A meal costing more than US$25 per person is a rarity in Turkey except in the big international-class hotels.

Places to Eat – bottom end
Sultanahmet Several little restaurants are open along Divan Yolu, the main street

which goes from Sultanahmet Square up the hill toward the university and the Covered Market.

Perhaps the most popular place on Divan Yolu is the *Vitamin Restaurant* (VEE-tah-meen) (tel 526-5086) at Divan Yolu 16, opposite the Hippodrome. It's a ready-food eatery with all sorts of savoury dishes (some pretty oily) displayed in the street-side windows. Choose a meal such as *taze fasulye* (green string beans), *kabak dolması* (stuffed marrow), flat pide bread and fruit juice, and the meal will cost US$3 or so. Check your bill carefully.

Just down Divan Yolu from the Vitamin is the *Meshur Halk Köftecisi*, Divan Yolu 12/A, a classic Turkish workers' eatery which has somehow survived in the midst of this touristy area. The reason may be that it serves delicious grilled lamb köfte, şiş kebap, salad, lentil soup, bread and soft drinks at very low prices. That's pretty much the entire menu. For a beverage, have the traditional ayran.

You order your köfte or şiş kebap by the *porsyon*: if you're not all that hungry, order *bir porsyon* (BEER porss-yohn, one portion), if you'd like a bit more, ask for *bir buçuk porsyon* (BEER boo-CHOOK, one and a half); if you're hungry, order a *duble porsyon* (DOOB-leh, double). A meal of lentil soup, an order of köfte, a plate of salad, bread and a glass of ayran should cost around US$3.

On the other (south) side of the street, up the hill on Divan Yolu, is the *Çamlık Restaurant* (tel 528-1739), Divan Yolu 15/A, with large windows looking out onto the street. It's a modest and old-fashioned place, but the selection of food arrayed on the steam tables and grills near the front windows is particularly large and interesting, and prices are moderate. Have a look at what's cooking, indicate the dishes you want, ask the prices, and your bill need not exceed US$4 or US$5 for a full, delicious meal.

If this seems too pricey, walk a few steps

farther up the hill on Divan Yolu to the *Dedem Börekçisi*, Divan Yolu 21, a sidewalk booth selling savoury börek filled with cheese made from white sheep's milk, eaten either hot or cold. You order by weight, so you can have as much as you like; a normal serving is 200 grams, 250 if you're quite hungry. With a soft drink, lunch would cost US$1.

Across Divan Yolu from the Hippodrome is the famous *Pudding Shop*, where the drop-out generation of the 1960s kept alive and happy on various nutritious, tasty, inexpensive puddings such as sütlaç or its even tastier baked version, *fırın sütlaç* (FUH-ruhn SEWT-latch), served cold. Today the Pudding Shop has changed its approach, and it's now a self-service cafeteria serving all sorts of meals. Prices are higher and food quality not the same as in the hippy heyday, but if you want to be in the centre of things, you can have a meal here for US$4 or US$5. Tea costs US$0.60, Nescafé twice as much, soft drinks somewhere in between. A sandwich and soft drink should cost less than US$2. The traffic on busy Divan Yolu out front is objectionable.

So much for the tourist-frequented restaurants along Divan Yolu. For some very cheap and good places patronised largely by local people, walk toward the far (south-west) end of the Hippodrome. Before coming to the end of the Hippodrome, turn right onto Terzihane Sokak, and walk up the slope to find two small full-service restaurants patronised mostly by lawyers pleading cases before the law courts facing the Hippodrome.

The first is the *Lezzet Lokantası* ('Flavour Restaurant'), Terzihane Sokak 13; the second is the *Bitirim Lokantası* ('Summation Restaurant'), on the corner with Klodfarer Caddesi. Both establishments are simple but have very tasty food, waiter service and quite low prices. My lunch of kuru fasulye, pilav, bread, and melon for dessert, along with a soft drink, cost US$3. The Bitirim, by the way, is only steps from the Hotel Klodfarer.

Even less expensive? Walk back to the Hippodrome, turn right, and at the very end of the Hippodrome turn right again onto Haci Tahsin Bey Sokak, a narrow street which soon changes names to become Üçler Sokak. In the first block of this little street are two good, cheap places. The *Akdeniz Lokantası* is a little ready-food restaurant with savoury collations in steam tables awaiting your appetite at breakfast, lunch and dinner. For breakfast, have the traditional hot soup and bread, or börek. At lunch or dinner, the menu is more varied. A full meal can be had here for US$2 or so. Nearby is the *Karadeniz Aile Pide Salonu*, where hot, made-to-order Turkish pizza is served up for US$1 or less. The price depends upon the toppings you request, which may include cheese, minced lamb or eggs. There are other inexpensive places farther along Üçler Sokak.

Sultanahmet Cafés For refreshments and snacks, the most obvious place to go to is the *Sultan Sofrası*, a café-restaurant facing the Hippodrome on its north-west side, with good people-watching possibilities. Though it is a restaurant with indoor and outdoor seating areas, most customers are here for drinks: coffee, tea, beer or fizzy refreshers. Most of the food served is snacks and sandwiches: hamburgers, fried cheese toast and plates of chips. A drink and a sandwich should not cost much over US$1. Directly across the Hippodrome from the Sultan Sofrası, hugging the wall of the Blue Mosque, is another small teahouse operated by the same management.

If you prefer shade to sun, seek out the *Derviş Aile Çay Bahçesi* (Dervish Family Tea Garden), Kabasakal Caddesi 2/1 near the Yeşil Ev Hotel. In the cool, dark shadows cast by big old trees, this pleasant café offers tea for US$0.25, coffee for US$0.50, small sandwiches (*sandviç*) or grilled sandwiches called *tost* for US$0.55. Try a *peynirli tost*, a cheese sandwich mashed in a vice-like sandwich cooker. Prices are listed on the menu placed at each table.

Behind the Blue Mosque, near the Mosaic Museum in the row of shops known as the Arasta, is the *Kent Café*, with five tiny sidewalk tables, one of them an upside-down marble column capital. This is a standard Turkish teahouse, providing the national beverage to nearby shopkeepers and their guests. A row of shops or an office building without a teahouse is unthinkable in Turkey. This one is nice because of the old-time street, the huge, shady tree and the quiet atmosphere. Tea, coffee, soft drinks and perhaps a few biscuits are the only items served.

For more substantial café fare, try the *Arasta Café* at the northern end of the Arasta street (you'll recognise it by its sidewalk café tables with umbrellas). Here, cheeseburgers, chicken burgers, Nescafé and ice cream cost about US$1 each.

Sirkeci & Eminönü There are lots of good small restaurants in the Sirkeci area. Leave the railway station by the main (west) door. The busy street before you is Ankara Caddesi. Turn left (south), cross busy Muradiye Caddesi and walk up the slope on Ankara Caddesi, turning into the second or third little street on the left (the second street leads into the third street). This will bring you to İbni Kemal Caddesi, one of those areas of workshops and offices with half a dozen eateries, all delightfully low in price.

Walk up İbni Kemal Caddesi to Hoca Paşa Camii (that's HO-jah pah-shah), and you'll reach a little open place (just before the mosque) where several streets meet. Within a few steps of the mosque are one dozen small restaurants.

The *Bozkurt Döner Kebap Salonu* serves that succulent lamb roasted on a vertical spit; the *Yıldız Et Lokantası* (Star Meat Restaurant) serves a variety of grilled meats; the *Hocapaşa Köftecisi* specialises in savoury grilled lamb meatballs; the *Hocapaşa Pidecisi* specialises in freshly made Turkish pizza. There are others: *Fahri Kebap*, another grilled-meat restaurant, the *Kardeşler Anadolu Lokantası* and the ready-food *Karadeniz Gençlik Lokantası*. At the Kardeşler Anadolu I was served a meal of lentil soup, *biber dolma* (green pimiento pepper stuffed with rice and lamb), bread and spring water for less than US$2. The köfteci and the pideci will have meals for about the same, or even less.

If you want something to finish off your meal at the lowest possible price, buy fresh fruit from a vendor and wash it at the tap by the mosque.

Facing the plaza in Eminönü, to the right of the Denizcilik Bankası and to the left of the Yeni Cami, is a tiny stand which bears the name *Vefa Bozacısı*. Glasses of boza is all they serve here, except in summer when they may switch to grape juice. A fortifying glass of boza, favourite drink of the Ottoman Janissary corps, costs US$0.40; prices are posted prominently. By the way, Vefa is also noted for its flavourful vinegar (*sirke*). Don't mistake this for grape juice or boza!

For another traditional Ottoman treat, walk through the archway to the left of the Yeni Cami in Eminönü, and turn left onto Hamidiye Caddesi. One short block along, on the right-hand (south) side of the street near the corner with Şeyhülislam Hayri Efendi Caddesi, is the original shop of Ali Muhiddin Haci Bekir, inventor of Turkish delight.

History notes that Ali Muhiddin came to İstanbul from the Black Sea mountain town of Kastamonu and established himself as a confectioner in the Ottoman capital in the late 1700s. Dissatisfaction with hard candies and traditional sweets led the impetuous Ali Muhiddin to invent a new confection that would be easy to chew and swallow. He called his soft, gummy creation *rahat lokum*, the 'comfortable morsel'. 'Lokum', as it soon came to be called, was an immediate hit with the denizens of the imperial palace, and anything that goes well with the palace goes well with the populace. Lokum was a hit.

Ali Muhiddin elaborated on his original confection, as did his offspring (the shop is still owned by his family), and now you can buy lokum made with various fillings: *cevizli* (JEH-veez-LEE, with walnuts), *şam fıstıklı* (SHAHM fuhss-tuhk-LUH, with pistachios), *portakkallı* (POHR-tah-kahl-LUH, orange-flavoured), or *bademli* (BAH-dehm-LEE, with almonds). You can also get a *çeşitli* (CHEH-sheet-LEE, assortment). Price is by weight; a kg costs US$3, more or less, depending upon which flavour you choose. If you'd like to taste before you buy, ask for a free sample by indicating your choice and saying *Denelim!* (DEH-neh-LEEM, 'Let's try it').

During the winter, a cool-weather specialty is added to the list of treats for sale. *Helvah*, a crumbly sweet block of sesame mash, is flavoured with chocolate or pistachio nuts or sold plain. Ali Muhiddin Haci Bekir has another, more modern shop on İstiklal Caddesi between Taksim Square and Galatasaray.

About the cheapest way to enjoy fresh fish from the waters round İstanbul is to buy a fish sandwich from a boatman. Go to the Eminönü end of the old Galata Bridge, and on the right-hand (Bosphorus) side, tied to the quay railing just east of the bridge, you'll see a boat bobbing in the water. In the boat, two men tend a tinplate cooker and fry fish fillets in oil. The quick-cooked fish is slid into the cleft made in a quarter loaf of fresh Turkish bread, the whole is wrapped in newspaper, and handed up to a hungry, waiting customer, who forks over about US$1 for the meal. Once you get over the shock of seeing a fire in a boat, order one. I've never been disappointed, nor made sick, by one of these.

Karaköy & Galata Bridge On shore at Karaköy, facing the ferry docks, are numerous snack shops, including several *börekçis.* A börekçi (bur-REK-CHEE) makes various sorts of flaky pastries filled with cheese and chopped parsley. Each type of börek has its own name. *Su böreği* (SOO bur-reh-yee, water pastry) is a thick, noodle-like affair with sprinklings of cheese made from white sheep's milk and chopped parsley. Ask for 200 grams (ee-KEE yewz gram), and the clerk will cut out a square, chop it into manageable bites, and hand it to you on a plastic plate with a fork. It will cost perhaps US$0.75.

Other sorts of börek are the more familiar flaky pastries with filling, like *sosisli* (soh-sees-LEE, sausage) or cheese. In Karaköy's many börekçi shops they're cheap, fresh and good.

For more substantial fare, you might try one of the little fish restaurants beneath the old Galata Bridge. If you walk from Eminönü or Karaköy along the waterside walkways on the Bosphorus (east) side of the bridge, you'll pass one after another of these modest eateries. Waiters and touts will dart out to cajole you in several languages, boasting of the freshness of the fish and the lowness of the price, both of which facts you should ascertain for yourself: price, especially, should be understood and agreed to. Don't let the waiter put anything on your table that you did not order, or you will be expected to pay for it.

Of the fish restaurants beneath the Galata Bridge, I favour the ones on the Karaköy side because they seem to importune you less and offer a bit more quiet, good service as well as lower prices. Bearing the aforementioned caveats in mind, try the fish at the *Duba* or the *Yıldızlar*.

For even cheaper fish, buy a fish sandwich from a boatman, as described in the section on Eminönü restaurants.

Karaköy is also noted for its baklava. The baklava comes with all sorts of stuffings. Prices are marked per kg and per portion (usually 150 grams, though you can order as little or as much as you like for a portion). Stuffings include pistachios, walnuts and even clotted cream. İstanbul's most famous pastry shop, called a *baklavacı* (BAHK-lah-vah-juh, 'baklava-maker'), is *Güllüoğlu* (GEW-loo-oh-loo), in a shop on the street level of the big parking garage across from the Yolcu Salonu (International Maritime Passenger Terminal), 100 metres east of the Galata Bridge.

Covered Market You will come across several little restaurants in this area. With one exception, these are tiny, basic places where bazaar workers eat or from which prepared meals are taken to their workshops on trays.

Some of these little places rarely see a foreign tourist, but some are accustomed to serving foreigners. All will welcome you and make extra efforts to please. The ones that are used to foreigners, where the menus may be in English and where the waiter will know at least a few words of a foreign language, are grouped on Koltuk Kazazlar Sokak and Kahvehane Sokak. The most prominent one is the *Sevim Lokantası*, founded (a sign proudly states) in 1945. Take a seat in the little dining room, or sit at a table set out in one of the little streets and order two or three plates of food. The bill won't exceed US$4 and will probably be less.

Another place is the *Balkan Restaurant* at Perdahçılar Sokak 60, on the corner of Takkeciler. Don't let its tiny entrance fool you, as the dining room is larger and there is another dining room upstairs. Choose one of the ready-food items or order döner kebap. I had a *çerkez kebabı* (chehr-KEHZ, circassian) of peas, aubergine, lamb, potatoes, tomatoes and peppers in a rich sauce, plus bulgur pilav with beans, ayran and bread for US$3.50.

Should you be longing for a taste of the US, there's a regulation *McDonald's* hamburger shop facing Beyazıt Camii across Yeniçeriler Caddesi from the Covered Market. A Big Mac, chips and soft drink will cost about US$3 or so.

Covered Market Cafés You will no doubt pass the *Şark Kahvesi* (SHARK kahh-veh-see, Oriental Café), at the end of Fesçiler Caddesi. Always filled with locals and tourists, it can be difficult to find a seat in. But this is the real bazaar, noisy with traders' conversations, backgammon games and the shouted orders of the waiters. The arched ceilings betray its former existence as part of a bazaar street; some enterprising *kahveci* (coffee-house owner) walled up several sides and turned it into a café. On the grimy walls hang paintings of Ottoman scenes and framed portraits of sultans and champion Turkish freestyle wrestlers. A cup of Turkish coffee, a soft drink or a glass of tea costs US$0.23 to US$0.50; Nescafé is overpriced at US$1.

In fine weather, head out of the bazaar and next door to the Beyazıt Camii (between the bazaar and the university gates). You can go through the Sahaflar Çarşısı, the Old Book Bazaar. In the summertime, on the east side of the mosque is a lovely tea garden, which is a plaza filled with mostly shaded tables. Waiters in traditional coffee-house costumes circulate through the sea of tables carrying trays filled with the pretty little glasses of tea. Signal to the waiter when you see him with a tray and you'll get your tea right away; or order and have your drink brought to you. As this garden is patronised by university students, the drinks are not overly expensive.

Laleli Laleli is a good place to look for low-priced eats because İstanbul University is close by. You'll see several places stuffed with students, serving good food at low prices. Down the slope in Aksaray are dozens of little restaurants, neighbourhood places catering not to tourists, but to a local clientele.

Perhaps the best and most popular ready-food restaurant in this area at this writing is the *Murat Lokanta ve Kebap Salonu* (tel 528-1928), Ordu Caddesi 212/A, half a flight down from street level near the Ramada hotel. Bright, clean and attractive, the Murat is open for all three meals and is busy with tourists and locals all day. Meal bills usually come to US$3 to US$5, depending upon what and how much you eat. Everything is available.

For kebaps, a favourite in this district has the daunting name of *Hacıbozanoğulları Kebap Salonu* (tel 528-4492), Ordu Caddesi 214. Ordu Caddesi is the main thoroughfare, and the restaurant is up the hill from the big Ramada hotel, on Ordu Caddesi between Harikzadeler Sokak and Büyük Reşit Paşa Caddesi. Though this quarter is somewhat fancied up, prices are still very moderate. The restaurant is one flight up from the street; menus at street level by the doorway show pictures of various kebap is 100 grams and costs only about US$1.50; you may want to order a about US$1.50; you may want to order a double portion. With your kebap you may get *yufka*, the paper-thin unleavened peasant flat bread; or *pide*, the thicker, leavened flat bread. For a drink, try ayran. Hacıbozanoğulları (that's ha-JUH-bo-ZAHN-oh-ool-lah-ruh) also has a separate baklavacı across the street and down the hill one block, on the corner of Ordu Caddesi and Laleli Caddesi. Besides baklava the shop features other Turkish sweets.

Kebap restaurants abound in the little side streets off Ordu Caddesi. The *Hacı Dayı Kebap Salonu* (tel 528-2043), Harikzadeler Sokak, is deep in the midst of the Laleli hotel district, next door to the Hotel Oran. Fairly dressy as kebap restaurants go, it is still quite small (narrow actually), modest and low in price, with a meal of soup, kebap, bread and beverage costing US$4.

The *Gaziantep Emek Saray Kebapçısı* (tel 522-4556), Gençtürk Caddesi 6, just a few steps north from Ordu Caddesi, will serve you a portion of urfa kebap plus a glass of ayran for US$3. When you order your kebaps here, specify whether you want them *acısız* (ah-juh-SUHZ, without hot pepper) or *acılı* (ah-juh-LUH, with hot pepper). The restaurant's specialty is *çiğ köfte* (CHEE kerf-teh), uncooked ground lamb with spices.

There are cheaper places. Facing the Chemistry Faculty on Büyük Reşit Paşa Caddesi is the *Şar Lokantası* at No 62, a tidy little ready-food cafeteria where soups cost US$0.75 and kebaps are priced from US$2.25 to US$2.75. The *Pehlivan Büfe 2*, Büyük Reşit Paşa Caddesi 50, near the corner with Kurultay Sokak, offers simple meals such as sandwiches, grilled sausages and chips, and putting together a satisfying lunch for US$2 to US$3 is a possibility. Almost next door to the Pehlivan is the *Hasan Paşa Fırını*, Büyük Reşit Paşa Caddesi 52, with a display window full of delicious-looking breads, rolls, buns, pastries and cakes.

Not far from these eateries is the *Paradise Café*, on the corner of Büyük Reşit Paşa Caddesi and Ahmet Şuayip Sokak. As the name suggests, this is a students' hangout where İstanbul University's youth come to see and be seen. Essentially, it's an American-style burger spot with a Turkish twist. Decor is plastic laminate, with illuminated signs instead of menus. A typical lunch here would be a döner kebap sandwich, a plate of chips and a soft drink, costing US$3.50.

Aksaray As Aksaray is only a five-minute walk from Laleli, the restaurants of Aksaray are quite accessible to anyone staying in a Laleli hotel. At present, the advantages of Aksaray dining involve roast chicken and Turkish kebabs.

From the traffic flyover in Aksaray, a major street, Mustafa Kemal Caddesi, runs south to the Sea of Marmara. Two blocks south, on the corner of Mustafa Kemal Caddesi and Mesih Paşa Caddesi, are several eateries specialising in spit-roasted chicken. To find them walk from Laleli along Ordu Caddesi to Aksaray Caddesi. Walk down Aksaray Caddesi to Mesih Paşa Caddesi (the second street),

turn right, and walk to Mustafa Kemal Caddesi.

The best of these places is *Arjantin Piliç* (tel 512-1475), Mustafa Kemal Caddesi 76, with marble floors and a quieter, more sedate dining room upstairs for women, couples and families. You can order a quarter chicken (US$1.75), half chicken (US$3) or whole chicken (US$5), other dishes such as salads, pilav, etc (less than US$1), and a glass of draught lager (US$1). Directly across the street is the similar *Şölen Piliç* (tel 528-6166), Mustafa Kemal Caddesi 78. A few steps up Mesih Paşa Caddesi is *Mudurnu Fried Chicken*, part of a chicken-selling chain. Prices and food are similar. A piliç, by the way, is a pullet (young chicken); a tavuk is a stewing chicken, tough as a football.

Across Mustafa Kemal Caddesi from the chicken restaurants are the kebap places. Taking your life in your hands, cross the street, and walk west along İnkilap Caddesi, the continuation of Mesih Paşa Caddesi.

İskender Kebapçısı (tel 586-6073), İnkilap Caddesi 4, serves Bursa-style döner kebap, with the meat spread on a bed of fresh flat pide bread, and the whole topped with savoury tomato sauce and browned butter. The restaurant is nothing fancy, just a little neighbourhood eatery, but there are still tablecloths and placemats, fresh flowers on the tables, and waiters in black trousers, white shirts and burgundy waistcoats (vests). The kebap is delicious and, with a bowl of soup and a drink, makes a fine meal for US$3 or US$4.

A few doors to the west is *Konyalı Kebabcı Osman* (tel 586-6083), İnkilap Caddesi 10, specialising in Konya's *fırın kebap* (rich chunks of oven-roasted mutton), and etli ekmek, the type of Turkish pizza made in Konya, topped with ground lamb. At the *Güneş Kebap & Baklava Salonu* right next door, the specialty is *tandır kebap*, a savoury lamb and vegetable stew traditionally cooked in an earthenware crock. The crock should be buried in a fire pit, but here in the city they settle for an oven. Etli ekmek is served here as well and is the cheapest choice for a good, simple meal.

For cheap seafood, or at least for seafood as cheap as it's going to come in this city, head for the *Dergâh Restaurant* (tel 588-0895), İnkilap Caddesi 39. Portions are huge, the fish is good, and service is courteous – at least until it is discovered by more tourists. A meal with wine might cost only US$6.

Taksim Taksim Square has dozens of restaurants, some of them quite cheap. As Turkish dishes are so varied and their names so incomprehensible, you might want to start off at the *Antep Restaurant*, İstiklal Caddesi 3, just off the traffic roundabout. This bright, plain place has the standard cafeteria line, steam tables and low prices. They're not as low as they might be, however: this is Taksim. Be careful not to order too much: three selections (two will usually suffice), plus that good Turkish bread, is plenty for anyone. You can always go back. Fill up at lunch or dinner for US$3 to US$5.

The *McDonald's* hamburger restaurant next to the PTT by Taksim Park is the real thing, usually filled with students talking, munching and smoking. The sidewalk terrace makes it part café, part burger joint. A Big Mac, chips and drink costs around US$3.

Continuing along İstiklal takes you past several little side streets. Perhaps the best and most plentiful food for the lowest price in the Taksim area is to be found at the *Ada Lokantası* (tel 145-1633), at No 25 on a narrow side street called Büyükparmakkapı Sokak (Thumb Gate St) going south from İstiklal opposite the posh Beymen clothing store; it's the third little street on the left as you come from Taksim. A bright, fairly large restaurant, it is open seven days a week from early morning to late evening, with lots of ready-food choices on which you can fill up easily for very little. Soups cost

US$0.50 the bowl, kebaps are US$1.40 the plate, and meals for US$2 to US$4 an easy matter.

Büyükparmakkapı Sokak, by the way, is a colourful introduction to the neighbourhood street life of Beyoğlu, with a shoe repair shop, barber shop, bridge salon, record shop, sporting goods shop and cheap nightclubs. The population of the street seems to be 99% male, but all are good natured, and though the scene looks like something out of an oriental movie, it's safe enough.

For sweets, try the *Saray Muhallebi ve Tatlı Salonu* (tel 144-5724), İstiklal Caddesi 102, on the right-hand side of İstiklal as you come the few short blocks from Taksim. A tall glass facade shields a high-ceilinged, airy salon with a mezzanine floor. The baklava, puddings and other sweets are in refrigerator cases at the front. Look them over, point out your choice to a waiter, order a beverage (tea, coffee, a soft drink or just water), take a table, and enjoy. My usual here is *burma kadayıf* (BOOR-mah kah-dah-yuf), a shredded wheat roll stuffed with pistachios and doused in honey and syrup, plus a *büyük çay*, (ber-YERK chah-yee), a large glass of tea, costing US$2.

Tepebaşı From Galatasaray, Meşrutiyet Caddesi leads north, then west, then south, roughly parallel to İstiklal Caddesi. Several restaurants are of interest on these two streets, most of them in the middle range; there's not a lot of good, cheap eating to be had. For a light lunch or snack, go to the pideci behind and to the left of the Etap İstanbul Hotel, where you can get a fresh pide with butter and cheese for US$1.

Bosphorus Fish is expensive, but in the Bosphorus fishing village of Sarıyer, several restaurants serve it up at affordable prices.

The *Sahil Aile Lokantası*, next to the sea just north of the town's fish market, is extremely simple. You'll recognise it by the several rickety little tables set out under a shady grapevine, or by its combination 'sign and menu' chalk slate. Prices are marked (if something's not priced, be sure to ask), and depending upon the fish in season, you should be able to have a tasty fish dinner here for less than US$6. The cheapest thing to have is simply a grilled or fried fish fillet of whatever's in season, with salad – the Turkish equivalent of fish & chips.

Even closer to the Sarıyer fish market is the *Çağanoz Aile Balık Restaurant* (that's CHAH-nose), a few steps south of the Sahil. Dining areas are a bit fancier here, but prices and fare are similar and the clientele is mostly Turkish. The upstairs dining area is quite pleasant.

Places to Eat – middle
Sultanahmet With few exceptions, eateries around Sultanahmet fall into our 'bottom end' price category, and happily so.

For a bit more atmosphere (but not much), try the *Sultan Pub* (tel 526-6347), Divan Yolu 2, between the Pudding Shop and the small park atop Yerebatan Saray. The café is on the ground floor, the nicer restaurant is one flight up. A sandwich and soft drink in the café, patronised mostly by tourists, costs about US$3 or US$4. A full meal upstairs costs between US$6 and US$8. Alcoholic and other drinks are served in both places.

Topkapı Palace Everyone who visits Topkapı Palace has a problem: since it can take almost a whole day to see the palace properly (including the Harem), where does one eat lunch? There is a restaurant in the palace, the *Konyalı Restaurant* (tel 526-2727), all the way at the northern end; find the *Mecidiye Köşkü*, the Kiosk of Sultan Abdül Mecit, and enter the restaurant through it. Tables are both inside and outside under an awning, with very fine views of Üsküdar, the Bosphorus and the Sea of Marmara from the outside tables.

Because the restaurant has a captive market of tourists (not locals, who might complain), food and service are not quite what they might be, though the restaurant is always crowded at lunch time. The trick is to arrive by 11.30 am to beat the lunch rush, or to come later in the afternoon. For a meal of soup, şiş kebap, salad and drink with tax and tip included, figure on paying about US$10 or US$12.

If it's just a good seat, a sandwich and a cool drink you're looking for, go to the café terrace just below the restaurant, where there are even better views, and a snack won't set back your budget so much.

The only other food in the palace is at the little snacks-and-drinks stand by the entrance to the Harem.

Sirkeci & Eminönü Go out the station door, turn left, then left again onto Muradiye Caddesi. The first street to the right is Orhaniye Caddesi. Across the street from the Küçük Karadeniz Oteli is the *Şehir Lokantası* (sheh-HEER), with white tablecloths, waiter service, decent surroundings, lots of ready-food choices as well as grilled-to-order kebaps, at prices of US$4 to US$6 for a full meal.

In Sirkeci Station there is a restaurant offering good meals at similar prices.

Karaköy & Galata Bridge The Yolcu Salonu (YOHL-joo sah-loh-noo, International Maritime Passenger Terminal), on Kemankeş Caddesi 100 metres north-east of Galata Bridge, contains two of İstanbul's best restaurants. As headquarters for Turkish Maritime Lines, the Yolcu Salonu must have a showplace seafood restaurant. In fact, it has two. Enter on the building's right (south-west) end and go to either the *Liman Lokantası* or the *Liman Kafeteryası* (tel 144-1033). Both are open from 12 noon to 4 pm (lunch only) every day except Sunday.

The Kafeteryası is a less elegant, less expensive version of the restaurant. You pay a set price (about US$8) and help yourself to the various courses at the steam tables.

Upstairs in the Liman Lokantası, a spacious, simple, somewhat old-fashioned dining room overlooks the mouth of the Golden Horn and the Old City. (If there's a cruise ship moored at the Yolcu Salonu dock, the ship will block the view.) Service is polite and refined, fish is the specialty, and a full, elegant, delicious lunch from soup to baklava and coffee, with wine, will cost between US$12 and US$16 per person.

Covered Market Though most Covered Market eateries are low budget, at the *Havuzlu Lokantası* (tel 527-3346), Gani Çelebi Sokak 3, prices are in the moderate range. The food is about the same as at the bottom-end places in this area, but you get a lofty dining room made of several bazaar streets (walled off for the purpose long ago) and a few tables set out in front of the entrance by a little stone pool (*havuzlu* means 'with pool'), which I suspect was a deep well centuries ago. Waiter service here is much more polite and unhurried. If you want to escape the activity of the bazaar into a haven of quiet and calm, spend a little more (US$5 to US$8) and go to the Havuzlu. It's next to the PTT. Follow the yellow-and-black signs and ask for the PTT or the restaurant.

Taksim & Galatasaray Taksim Square and the surrounding area have numerous restaurants and sweets shops. I'll start by describing some full-service restaurants, and then give you a few hints on where to have a light meal or refreshments.

The *Hacı Baba Restaurant* (ha-JUH bah-bah) (tel 144-1886) at İstiklal Caddesi 49, deserves special mention. The nondescript doorway opens onto a flight of stairs leading to the restaurant, which is much nicer than the appearance of the entrance suggests. For a better first impression, continue down İstiklal, turn left at the next corner, and enter the Hacı Baba from the side street (Meşelik Sokak).

It's here, on Meşelik Sokak, that you'll see the restaurant's strong point: a pleasant little outdoor porch set with tables overlooking the courtyard of the Greek Orthodox Church of the Holy Trinity next door – a bit of open space, peace and quiet in the midst of the city. Hacı Baba is a full-menu, full-service restaurant with fish and grilled meats, ready-food dishes and specialties. The food is good, the service usually competent; some English is spoken. Expect to pay US$9 to US$13 per person for a full lunch or dinner with wine or beer.

Two other good full-service restaurants are a short walk from the square, down the hill on İnönü Caddesi by the Atatürk Cultural Palace. Walk down the hill on the right-hand side of the tree-lined street and around the curve until you see the huge rectangular bulk of the German Consulate General on the opposite side of the road. These restaurants are more or less opposite the consulate.

The *C Fischer Restaurant* (tel 145-2576, 145-3375), İnönü Caddesi 51/A, is the latest expression of a famous old İstanbul dining-place which was previously located near the British Consulate General in Galatasaray. Now the pleasant dining room, a half-flight down from street level, caters to the German diplomats with Turkish and continental dishes including lamb şiş kebap and delicious tiny lamb chops, beef tournedos and wienerschnitzel. The traditional starter course at Fischer's is savoury borshch, and for a sweet, apple strudel or *palaçinka* (crêpes filled with fruit jam). Lunch or dinner at the Fischer costs US$6 to US$9 per person, with a wine or beer, tax and tip included.

In the same block is the *Reyşin Restaurant* (tel 143-4892), İnönü Caddesi 77/1. Walk down the hill to the end of the block and turn left onto Miralay Şefik Bey Sokak, from which you enter the restaurant's small low-ceilinged dining room with white-clothed tables. The feeling here is of a neighbourhood bistro. Many years ago, when I first came to İstanbul and lived in this quarter, one could buy a big bowl of borshch here for TL1. Well, the lira has fallen, but the borshch has improved considerably. The restaurant has retained its Russian menu and still features chicken Kiev (boned chicken stuffed with spiced butter, rewrapped around a bone, dusted with batter and deep fried), beef stroganoff or beefsteak with mushrooms. Your bill at the Reyşin might be US$6 to US$9 per person, all included, for a very full meal. It opens from 11 am to 10 pm daily, 2 to 10 pm on Sunday.

İstanbul has few 'ethnic' restaurants. But in every major city in the world there has got to be at least one Chinese restaurant. In this city it is the *Çin Lokantası* ('China Restaurant') (tel 150-6263), Lamartin Caddesi 17/1, near the Eresin and Riva hotels, more or less behind the Air France office off Cumhuriyet Caddesi. Standard Chinese restaurant decorations bring some gaiety to this little place, and white tablecloths add a touch of elegance. The standard fare is offered, nothing too adventurous: wonton soup and egg rolls, then beef, shrimp, chicken and fish prepared with various vegetables. The food is good, if slightly less than authentic, but prices are a bit high for this city; alcoholic beverages are served. A full meal, including tea, tax and tip, might cost US$10 per person. Avoid the coffee which, at US$1 per cup, is overpriced. The Çin Lokantası is unusual among Turkish restaurants in that it has set mealtimes. It is open from 12 noon to 3 pm and 7 to 11 pm, closed Sunday.

Is there anywhere one can sit and watch the passing pedestrian traffic while dining? The row of restaurants along the right-hand (east) side of Cumhuriyet Caddesi just off the traffic roundabout offers several possibilities, including an authentic *McDonald's* (see Places to Eat – bottom end). Most of the other restaurants are heavy on decor and pretension, catering to İstanbul's gilded youth eager to see and be seen.

Among these places, the *Taksim Gezi Cafeteria & Pizza Restaurant* (tel 144-6890), Taksim Square, has edible if undistinguished fare in slightly gaudy surroundings at reasonable prices. Sidewalk tables provide the proper venue for people-watching; if the day is very warm, sit inside as it has air-con. The printed menu here is supplemented by illuminated photographs of dishes mounted on the walls. The offerings are heavy with meat, including hamburgers, şiş kebap, chops and cutlets. The 'special meze plate' gives you a sampling of numerous Turkish hors d'oeuvres. Pizzas come in several variations on the classic cheese-and-tomato theme. Beer comes in mugs, very cold. A two or three-course meal, drinks included, costs from US$6 to US$9.

Facing the roundabout on its south side is *Taksim Sütiş* (tel 143-7204, 143-7268), Taksim Square, which is primarily a sweets shop but also serves some more substantial meat dishes such as döner kebap, fried chicken and sausages. Most of the customers are young İstanbullus, male and female, who come to chat and to enjoy a plate of baklava or *kadayıf* (crumpet in syrup) or some other Turkish sweet with a glass of tea. If you have kadayıf, have it with clotted cream; another wonderful Turkish sweet is kazandibi (kah-ZAHN-dee-bee, bottom of the pot), a delicious caramelised pudding rolled into little cylinders. One would never guess from its creamy texture and sweet flavour that it contains a certain amount of pounded chicken meat. A sweet and tea costs US$2 or so. Taksim Sütiş is open from 7 am to 1 am every day.

Now head west along İstiklal Caddesi to reach the renowned Çiçek Pasajı. Halfway along the length of this street is Galatasaray, an intersection so named because of the big Galatasaray Lisesi (Galatasaray Lycée) on the south side of the street. On the north side is an entrance to the Çicek Pasajı, the 'Flower Passage' described in the Things to See section. I strongly recommend that you come for an evening here, and that you come early so as to find a table. The ones in the courtyard are most in demand, but most of the little restaurants also have family dining rooms where you can usually find a table, and they will be quieter as well. If you order seafood, expect to pay US$10 to US$13 per person for the meal, drinks included. Meat will be about half that amount.

Tepebaşı & Tünel The special place in this district is the *Yeni Rejans* (yeh-NEE rehzhahnss, New Regency) restaurant (tel 144-1610), Olivo Geçidi 15, reached from İstiklal Caddesi. Walk south on İstiklal from Galatasaray toward Tünel, and turn right at No 244 down the dingy little passageway. The restaurant is up a set of stairs at the far end of the passage.

Founded in 1930 by Russian émigrés (there were many living in this district at the time), the Yeni Rejans has been serving the same French-inspired Russianmodified food, in the same location, ever since. It is not at all fancy, though there are white tablecloths and white-jacketed waiters; rather, it is a bit of living İstanbul history.

To relive the old days authentically, as soon as you are seated you should order a half-bottle of *limonlu votka*, Turkish vodka with lemon rind soaked in it. As for food, one of the favourite choices here is the chicken Kiev, but you can have any number of meat or fish dishes as well. If you start with a bowl of borshch with sour cream, and perhaps a side order of *piroçki* (croquettes), go on to a main course and something to follow, order a half-bottle of wine, add the tip, then your bill will be about US$10 to US$14 per person. The Yeni Rejans is open for lunch and dinner; closed Sunday.

Popular with the diplomatic set at lunch time is the *Dört Mevsim* (DEWRT mehv-seem, Four Seasons) restaurant (tel 145-8941). It's at İstiklal 509, very near Tünel. Founded and operated by an international couple (he's Turkish, she's English), it is well located to draw diners from the Swedish, Soviet, Dutch, British

and American consulates. Lunch is served from 12 noon to 3 pm, dinner from 6 pm to midnight; closed Sunday. If you order the fixed menu at lunch, you might pay US$8, drink and tip included. Ordering from the regular menu at dinner can drive your bill up to US$12, but it will be money well spent.

On Meşrutiyet Caddesi between the Büyük Londra Hotel and the Etap İstanbul Hotel are three serviceable restaurants. The *Restaurant Tuncel* (toon-JEHL) (tel 145-5566) at Meşrutiyet 129, is a small place with an attractive, modern decor and black-coated waiters. Have a meal of soup, grilled meat, a side dish of vegetables and something to drink, and you'll pay about US$5 to US$8 per person.

The *İrfan Restaurant* (eer-FAHN) (tel 144-2597), somewhat closer to the Etap İstanbul, is a similar place, at similar prices. The *Kardeşler Restaurant* (tel 143-6130), in the same area, is bright and airy, with a high-ceilinged dining room. Prices tend to be quite high for what you get: my last three-course meal here cost US$14.

Bosphorus The Bosphorus is lined with villages, each with its several little seafood restaurants catering to a more or less distinguished clientele. Some of these places charge prices at the top end of the price scale, a very few charge at the bottom end (see those sections for details).

Places to Eat – top end

Sultanahmet When the Turkish Touring & Automobile Association restored the row of houses behind Sancta Sophia along the Topkapı Palace walls and turned them into a hotel, they also restored an adjoining Byzantine cistern. It's now the *Sarnıç Taverna-Restaurant* (tel 512-4291), Soğukçeşme Sokak, open for lunch and dinner Wednesday to Sunday. The echoing stone cistern makes an interesting dining room, and the recently added fireplace confuses the senses – a fireplace in a cistern? Anyway, it's cool in here on a hot summer's afternoon. The food is OK but not exciting, the service competent and the prices fairly high. The menu is international, with goulash, bouillabaisse, borshch, şiş kebap and canard à l'orange all listed. The entertainment in the evenings seems loud, unless you like that sort of thing. A complete meal with wine may cost US$15 to US$20 per person.

If the weather is fine, don't descend into a darkish cistern, walk to the *Yeşil Ev Hotel* on Kabasakal Caddesi, and go to their lovely terrace restaurant at the back. You can have anything from tea or coffee to a light meal or a full repast for about US$12 per person. Many readers have found the food undistinguished, but the setting is certainly first rate. Similar value is assured at the dining rooms of the *Ayasofya Pansiyonları* (tel 513-3660), on Soğukçeşme Sokak. Several small salons in house No 4 provide pleasant places to have a set-menu lunch or dinner at a moderate price.

Kumkapı For a meal of seafood in an unforgettable İstanbul atmosphere, the place to go is Kumkapı (KOOM-kah-puh, Sand Gate).

In Byzantine times, the fishers' harbour called Kontoscalion was located due south of Laleli. The gate into the city from that port came to be called Kumkapı by the Turks. The harbour has been filled in and the gate is long gone, but the district is still filled with fishers who moor their boats in a more modern version of the old harbour, then pass beneath the railway to reach their homes in one of İstanbul's most colourful neighbourhoods.

Where there are fishers, there are fish restaurants, and Kumkapı is famous for them. Before the mid-1970s fish was the poor person's protein throughout the world. Since that time demand has exceeded supply, and a fish dinner, even in a modest restaurant, has become

something of a luxury. You should, however, stroll around Kumkapı one evening, choose a likely place for dinner, and expect to part with US$12 to US$20 per person for the meal, appetisers, salads, wine, sweet, tax and tip all included.

Here are a few tips on seasons. From March to the end of June is a good time to order *kalkan* (turbot), *uskumru* (mackerel), and *hamsi* (fresh anchovies), but July to mid-August is spawning season for many species, and fishing them is prohibited. In high summer, these are the easiest to find in the markets and on the restaurant tables: *çinakop* (a small bluefish), *lüfer* (medium-size bluefish), *palamut* (bonito), *tekir* (red mullet: *Mullus surmuletus*), *barbunya* (red mullet: *Mullus barbatus*), and *istavrit* (scad, horse mackerel).

Kumkapı has at least two dozen seafood restaurants, many operated by Turkish citizens of Greek or Armenian ancestry. Among the favourite things to order is swordfish şiş kebap, chunks of fresh fish skewered and grilled over charcoal, but there are fish soups and stews, fish poached with vegetables, pan-fried fish and pickled fish.

Typical of Kumkapı's seafood eateries is the *Minas Restaurant* (MEE-nahss) (tel 522-9646) at Samsa Sokak 7, Kumkapı, facing the square. It has white tablecloths, airy windows with lacy curtains, and on one wall a cartoon of a vengeful giant fish about to dine on an embarrassed and frightened fellow lying, fishlike, on a plate. Minas is not one of the cheaper places; you can dine for less money elsewhere. If you're not in the mood for seafood but would like to explore Kumkapı in any case, come for a kebap, and you'll spend a mere US$4 or so.

Also facing the square is *Köşem Cemal Restaurant* (tel 520-1229), Samsa Sokak 1, Kumkapı, with similar prices, cuisine and advantages. Here there are white tablecloths, good careful service and a mixed clientele of Turks and tourists. Upstairs is another pleasant dining room.

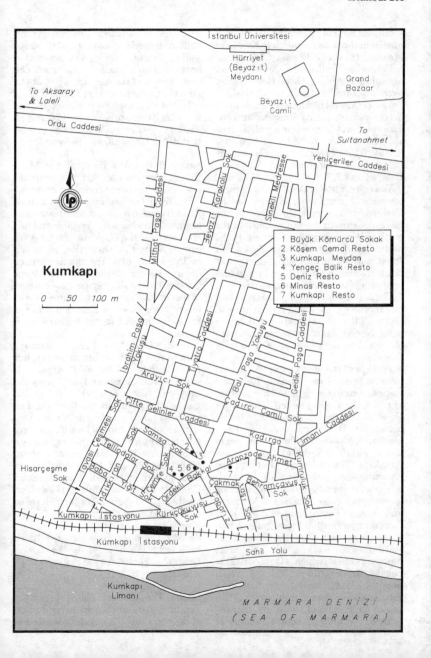

To Aksaray & Laleli

Ordu Caddesi

İstanbul Üniversitesi

Hürriyet (Beyazıt) Meydanı

Beyazıt Camii

Grand Bazaar

To Sultanahmet

Yeniçeriler Caddesi

Kumkapı

0   50   100 m

1 Büyük Kömürcü Sokak
2 Köşem Cemal Resto
3 Kumkapı Meydan
4 Yengeç Balik Resto
5 Deniz Resto
6 Minas Resto
7 Kumkapı Resto

Beyazıt Pasa Caddesi

Sinekli Medresse

Karakolu Sok

Mithat Paşa Caddesi

İbrahim Paşa Yokuşu

Tiyatro Caddesi

Bali Paşa Yokuşu

Gedik Paşa Caddesi

Arayıcı Sok

Çadırcı Camii Sok

Çifte Gelinler Caddesi

Samsa Sok

Kadırga Limanı Caddesi

Hisarçeşme Sok

Havyar Çeşmesi Sok

Telliodalar Sok

Baba Sok

Fındıkkıran Sok

Yiğit Sok

Gençre Sok

Ördekli Bakkal

Çakmak Sok

Arapzade Ahmet

Kadırga Limanı Caddesi

Kumkapı Sok

Behramçavuş Sok

Kürkçükuyusu Sok

Çapariz Sok

Kumkapı İstasyonu

Kumkapı İstasyonu

Sahil Yolu

Kumkapı Limanı

MARMARA DENİZİ
(SEA OF MARMARA)

Ördekli Bakkal Sokak, the street which runs from the railway station to Kumkapı Meydanı (as the little square is named), has another half-dozen good seafood restaurants. Among them is the *Deniz Restaurant* (tel 528-0858), Ördekli Bakkal Sokak 12/A, which can be recommended. Yet other side streets hold more restaurants. Two that have been recommended to me are the *Yengeç Balık Lokantası* (tel 527-5414), Telli Odalar Sokak 6, and the *Kumkapı Restaurant* (tel 522-6590), Üstad Sokak 7.

You can get to Kumkapı by one of three methods. From Laleli, Beyazıt or the Covered Market, walk. Just opposite the Beyazıt Camii in Beyazıt Square, on the south side of Yeniçeriler Caddesi, is the beginning of Tiyatro Caddesi. Follow this street south for 10 short blocks (for the last block, it veers to the left), and you'll find yourself in Kumkapı's main square.

You can also take a taxi, but it may be a bit expensive as the driver might choose to cruise all the way around the old city in order to enter this congested district from the sea side; figure on US$3 or so from Sultanahmet.

Perhaps the most enjoyable way to go is by train from Sirkeci Station. Enter the station, bear to the right and buy a ticket at one of the kiosks marked 'Banliyö' for US$0.20, and board any of the electric commuter trains on the right-hand platforms. Most will be for Halkalı, but in fact any train will do, as they all pass Kumkapı. The trains are run-down and uncomfortable, but the ride is short.

You will round Seraglio Point, offering marvellous views of the Sea of Marmara and Topkapı Palace, and stop briefly at Cankurtaran Station before pulling into Kumkapı Station. Leave the train and the station, and walk down the most prominent street, which is Ördekli Bakkal Sokak, (Grocer with a Duck St). You'll pass the *Gönül Pastanesi* on the left, a good place for a sweet after dinner. Then you're in Kumkapı, with its market, Orthodox church, itinerant vendors of

delicious fresh almonds (*taze badem*) and stuffed mussels (*midye tavası*), shops selling fishing tackle and wellington boots, and many, many restaurants. The main square of the quarter, is just at the far end of Ördekli Bakkal Sokak.

By the way, the next station on the rail line after Kumkapı is Aksaray (Yenikapı). You can use the train to come and go from that district, as well, for the same fare.

Sirkeci & Eminönü Here, at the Mısır Çarşışı, Egyptian Market, a famous old restaurant has been serving for decades.

Nearly a century ago, a man named Pandeli opened a modest little restaurant down by the wholesale vegetable and fish markets on the Golden Horn. After gaining a citywide reputation, he moved to the rooms over the main entrance (facing Galata Bridge) of the Mısır Çarşışı. The small chambers are covered in beautiful faïence, and some of the tables have views of Eminönü and the bridge, or inward to the bazaar's main street.

Pandeli Usta ('Chef Pandeli') long ago went to that great kitchen in the sky, but his restaurant (tel 522-5534) remains. It still serves only lunch and you'll enjoy the fresh fish (the specialty) or the grilled meats, all of which are excellent. I had an absolutely delicious *beğendi kebap* here (şiş kebap on top of warm, buttery aubergine purée). Other choices include a white aubergine salad, taramasalata, grilled prawns, and *levrek kâğıtta* (sea bass cooked in paper). Plan to spend US$10 to US$12 for a full meal based on meat, at least 50% more for fish, even more if you order the prawns.

Karaköy The place for a good fish lunch here (and lunch only) is the *Liman Lokantası*. For details see Places to Eat – middle.

Taksim The fanciest places to eat in Taksim Square are the various restaurants of the big hotels. These offer good food at prices that are extremely high for Turkey. But to sample the pleasures of the international hotels without throwing budgetary caution to the wind, have a seat in the *Opera Pastanesi* (tel 151-4696), Taksim Square, on the ground floor of the Hotel Pullman Etap Marmara. A tiny outdoor marble patio and indoor tables behind a glass facade provide a choice of seating. Refrigerator cases are laden with sweet delights and chocolate treats. With a cup of coffee, tea or chocolate, a portion of pastry might cost US$4 or US$5.

Sea of Marmara İstanbul's longtime favourite for kebaps and other grilled meats is *Beyti* (tel 573-9373, 573-9212), Orman Sokak 33, in the suburb of Florya, just west of Atatürk Airport (Yeşilköy). A dramatic, modern, even opulent place with a domed stained-glass canopy and a dozen different dining rooms, Beyti has been famous for decades. It was founded in the village of Büyükçekmece, farther to the west, when that was the butchery for İstanbul, so all the best meats were readily available.

Vegetarians and seafood-lovers should stay away, but if you love to eat meat, you must not miss it. Lots of kebaps are offered, the speciality being the *Beyti kebap*, a feast of successive plates of various meats prepared in various ways – you finish one and another appears, hot and savoury, and then another, until you can't eat one more thing. Beyti is open for lunch and dinner (closed Monday); expect to pay about US$20 to US$25 per person for a full dinner, wine, tax and tip included.

To get to Beyti, take a taxi (US$8 to US$10 each way), or take any banliyö train from Sirkeci Station to the Yeşilköy or Florya stop. Fare on the rattling train costs only a few pennies. Then take a taxi for the short ride to the restaurant; taxis are more easily found at the Yeşilköy Station.

Bosphorus The shores of the Bosphorus bear many excellent restaurants. Here are my favourites at the top of the price spectrum. These 'high' Turkish prices would be considered low in any other major European city.

In the interesting Bosphorus village of Bebek is the *Yeni Bebek Restaurant* (yeh-NEE beh-BEHK) (tel 163-3447), Cevdet Paşa Caddesi 123, next to the Hotel Bebek on the shore road. Heavy velvet drapes, white high-backed chairs and tables spread with snowy cloths make for a formal atmosphere, and the quiet, careful service reinforces the formality. But it is not a stiff formality, and the wonderful Bosphorus views lighten everything.

The array of dishes offered is vast. Start with a selection of appetisers, then continue with a main course – it really should be fish in such a setting, but the meat dishes are equally tasty and much cheaper. With a bottle of wine or a few glasses of beer, your meal might cost US$15 to US$20 per person. To reach the restaurant, take bus No 23 from Taksim Square. Make sure you get one signed as 'Bebek-Taksim'; some other buses on route No 23 only go as far as Barbaros Hayrettin Paşa, or Ortaköy. There are also cheap dolmuşes from Taksim Square, departing from İnönü Caddesi in front of the Toros Air airline office. A taxi from Taksim to Bebek costs about US$4.

İstanbul's old standard is the *Abdullah Lokantası* (tel 163-6406), Koru Caddesi 11, in the Bosphorus hills above the town of Emirgân. Founded a century ago, it was located for most of that time on İstiklal Caddesi, but moved to the outskirts several decades ago in order to achieve a more bucolic setting. The cuisine at Abdullah is Turkish with continental influences. Thus, you can expect the menu to include grilled lamb, but also sturgeon; börek, but also caviar. It's a good place to try some of the more unusual Turkish dishes such as *mantı*, a lamb ravioli in a light yoghurt sauce. I've gotten mixed reports from readers on Abdullah lately, except for one subject upon which all agree: it is expensive. You can expect to pay US$25 to US$35 per person for a fine dinner here, all included.

The dining room is a modern semicircle of glass designed to provide good Bosphorus views. You must reach the restaurant by taxi. The ride from the city centre might take 20 to 40 minutes and might cost US$5 to US$7. The restaurant is open for lunch (12 noon to 3 pm) and dinner (from 8 pm to midnight) every day. Call for reservations.

Farther north along the European shore of the Bosphorus is the village of Tarabya, which takes its name from the Greek word 'Therapia', or treatment for an illness. Under the Byzantines and Ottomans, this little village surrounding a cove was a favourite resort from the ills of the big city. Today the cove is surrounded with seafood restaurants, and in summer a carnival atmosphere prevails.

On the south side of the cove is the famous *Garaj Restaurant* (tel 162-0032, 162-0474), Yeniköy Caddesi 30, which was once located above a petrol station in Bebek, but later moved to this much more suitable location. Several old-fashioned dining rooms have partial views of the cove; however, it is not the surroundings or view that bring customers, but the fish. Fresh and in vast array, you will see it displayed as you enter. Take a few moments to look it over, ask some questions, and determine price before you order. Note that the waiters here have a tendency to load your table with items you did not order. Keep them if you want them, but send them back immediately if you do not, or they will be added to your bill. A very full and very delicious seafood lunch or dinner here costs US$14 to US$20 per person, wine, tax and tip included.

On the north side of the cove, the inland side of the road is lined solidly with little seafood restaurants. All have sidewalk tables, but the traffic makes these unpleasant at times, unfortunately.

My favourite here is the *Palet 1* (tel 162-0118), Kefeliköy Caddesi 110, a small and overdecorated place that dares to be different (a thing rare among Turkish restaurants) by offering such continental dishes as seafood soufflé, shrimp in a Mexican barbecue sauce, octopus in a cheese sauce, and even paella. In trying these exotic items, I would not expect authenticity, though they will be tasty enough. If you're not in the mood for fish, you can have meat and cut the cost of your meal in half. A fish dinner is about US$15 or US$20 per person, all included. The Palet's sister establishments, *Palet 2* and *Palet 3*, provide additional seating when Palet 1 is heavily booked. The restaurants, like most Turkish restaurants, are open every day, all day.

Even farther up the Bosphorus, in Sarıyer, are several cheap seafood restaurants described in Places to Eat – bottom end.

Just north of these places is the fancier, more expensive, but very satisfying *Urcan Balık Lokantası* (tel 142-0367, 142-1677). As you enter, the display of live fish in aquaria, fresh fish laid out on beds of crushed ice, baskets of live crabs and lobsters, buckets of shellfish and shrimp may dazzle your taste buds. There is great profusion here. Choose a table in the large dining room (try to get a table right next to the windows overlooking the Bosphorus), return to the seafood display, consult with the waiter, choose a fish, have it weighed, determine the price, then sit down to order wine, soup or mezes and salads. An unforgettable meal at the Urcan costs US$16 to US$24 per person, all included. Lobster, by the way, is fairly expensive. Be sure you know what you're paying before you say 'yes' to any suggestion.

If the Urcan Balık is filled, you might try the very similar *Mücahit Körfez Balık Lokantası* right next door.

On the eastern, Asian shore of the Bosphorus, on a promontory above the village of Çubuklu, is the *Hidiv Kasrı*, described in Places to Stay. The dining room of the villa is a wonderful place to enjoy a lunch or dinner, with the blue of the Bosphorus glistening below you. In the evening, a string trio plays songs from between the two world wars as you dine. The cuisine here is pure Turkish. Soup, or a selection of appetisers, followed by a lamb dish, then a sweet, will cost US$12 to US$16 per person, drinks included. Allow enough time (and daylight) to stroll around the grounds and inspect the marvellous villa as well. The only practical way to the Hidiv Kasrı is by taxi. From the city, this should cost about US$10 each way. Lunch and dinner are served every day.

ENTERTAINMENT

The name 'İstanbul' often conjures up thoughts of mysterious intrigues in dusky streets, dens in which sultry belly dancers do what they do, and who knows what else? As with most aged stereotypes, the reality is somewhat different.

İstanbul International Festival

This, the most prominent entertainment event in İstanbul, begins in late June and continues to mid-July. World-class performers – soloists, orchestras, dance companies, etc – give recitals and performances in numerous concert halls, historic buildings and palaces. The highlight is Mozart's 'Abduction from the Seraglio' performed in Topkapı Palace, with the Sultan's private Gate of Felicity as a backdrop. Don't miss it. Check at the box offices in the Atatürk Cultural Palace for schedules, ticket prices and availability.

Another good bet during the festival, and on other warm summer evenings as well, is a performance of drama or folk dance given in Rumeli Hisar, up the Bosphorus. Several years ago, I saw a fine English company do Shakespeare's 'A Midsummer Night's Dream' here. The performance was excellent, the setting simply spectacular.

Another open-air theatre, the Açık Hava Tiyatrosu, is just north of the İstanbul Hilton Hotel, off Cumhuriyet Caddesi.

Folklore

Turks are enthusiastic folklore fans, and many are still close enough in tradition to their regional dances to jump in and dance along at a performance. It's usually pretty easy to find a dance performance. University groups, good amateur companies and professionals all schedule performances throughout the year. The Turkish Folklore Association usually has something going on. For current offerings, ask at a Tourist Information Office or at one of the larger hotels.

High Culture

There are symphony, opera and ballet seasons, and occasional tour performances by the likes of Jean-Pierre Rampal or Paul Badura-Skoda. Many but not all of these performances are given in the Atatürk Cultural Centre in Taksim Square. The box offices there will have schedules.

Theatre

The Turks are enthusiastic theatre-goers, and as a people they seem to have a special genius for dramatic art. The problem, of course, is language. If you're a true theatre-buff you might well enjoy a performance of a familiar classic, provided you know the play well enough to follow the action without benefit of dialogue.

Cinema

İstiklal Caddesi used to be the centre of İstanbul's cinema (sinema, SEE-neh-mah) district, with many foreign films being shown. The advent of television changed all that, and now some of İstiklal's cinemas screen the racier movies, plus the much-beloved Turkish melodramas. Many first-run feature films do make it to İstanbul, however, and you will be able to enjoy them at bargain prices in certain cinemas. Some are along Cumhuriyet Caddesi between Taksim and Harbiye. Others are in the section called Nişantaşı (nee-SHAHN-tah-shuh): head north on Cumhuriyet Caddesi past the Hilton to Harbiye, and bear right on Valikonağı Caddesi. The cinemas are along this street in the first few blocks.

You may need some words on your cinema outing. Look on the cinema posters for the words 'Renkli' and 'Türkçe' or 'Orijinal' (ohr-zhee-NAHL). If you see 'Renkli Orijinal', that means the film is in colour and in the original language with Turkish subtitles. If you see 'Renkli Türkçe', the film is in colour, but has been dubbed in Turkish, in which case you may understand nothing.

There are three general seating areas, and you pay according to which you choose: *koltuk* (kohl-TOOK), on the floor in the mid-section to the rear; *birinci* (beer-EEN-jee), on the floor near the screen; and *balkon* (bahl-KOHN), in the balcony where the young lovers congregate. If you're going to the cinema to watch the film, ask for koltuk.

When possible, buy your tickets a few hours in advance. Tickets cost US$1 to US$2.50. Also, the usher will expect a small tip for showing you to your seat.

Nightclubs

Belly dancers do still perform in Turkey, of course. Many of the nightclubs along Cumhuriyet Caddesi between Taksim and the Hilton feature belly dancers, folk dance troupes, singers and bands. The usual arrangement is that you pay one price and get dinner and the show; drinks are extra. With Turkish prices being what they are, the price is not all that unreasonable at the independent clubs, perhaps US$20 to US$25 per person. At the large hotels, which also have belly dancers in their nightclubs, the cost may be twice as high.

The trick is to find a good, legitimate club. The *Kervansaray*, on the north side of the Hilton, has been catering to both Turks and tourists for years. This is not the cheapest, but it's reasonable and the show is good. Actually, it may be among the cheaper ones when you remember that at the sleazy ones you may tussle over the bill.

İstiklal Caddesi and the side streets running from it have many clubs where you can watch a show (more or less). Choose only clubs where you see couples entering. In some clubs males should be careful because they might meet ladies of the night and get suckered into paying big money for their drinks. The procedure is this: a male wanders in, perhaps at the behest of a tout who has accosted him along İstiklal Caddesi, and sits down. Immediately there are girls seated on either side of him, and they order champagne which is added to his bill despite his protests. When he refuses to pay the exorbitant charge, several hefty fellows urge him ever so forcefully to do so. It's a situation to avoid.

Gazinos

Turkish gazinos have nothing to do with gambling. Rather, they are open-air nightclubs popular in the summertime. (Some have been built up and operate in winter to the point that they are actually nightclubs with a gazino heritage.) The best of these are along the European shore of the Bosphorus. You won't find much belly dancing here. The shows are mostly Turkish popular singers. Dinner and drinks are served. If the name of the place has the word 'aile' in it, as in Bebek Aile Gazinosu, it means the proprietor wants to appeal to a respectable, mixed crowd and avoid all-male or heavy-drinking audiences.

Dinner on the Bosphorus

For my money, the most enjoyable thing you can do in İstanbul at night is have a long, leisurely seafood dinner at a little restaurant overlooking the Bosphorus. As Turks very often have the same idea, there are lots of little restaurants to choose from. Most, it must be stated, are in the moderate price range, not extremely cheap. Among the Bosphorus villages with a good selection of restaurants are Arnavutköy, Bebek, Tarabya and Sarıyer, all on the European side. The Asian coast has its share of little places as well. See Places to Eat for some specific suggestions.

Night Cruise

About the cheapest yet most enjoyable night-time activity is to take a Bosphorus ferry somewhere. It doesn't really matter where, as long as you don't end up on the southern coast of the Sea of Marmara or out in the Princes' Islands. Catch one over to Üsküdar or any town up the Bosphorus, and enjoy the view, the twinkling lights, the fishing boats bobbing in the waves, the powerful searchlights of the ferries sweeping the sea lanes. Have a nice glass of tea (a waiter will bring it round regularly). Get off anywhere, and take a bus or dolmuş home if you can't catch a ferry back directly.

Perhaps the easiest ferry to catch for this purpose is the one from Eminönü to Üsküdar. Just go to Eminönü's Dock No 2, buy a ticket to Üsküdar, and walk aboard. (If you want a ticket there and back, say *Üsküdar, gidiş dönüş* (EW-skew-dahr, gee-DEESH dur-NEWSH). From Üsküdar, just come back; or wait for one of the frequent ferries to Barbaros Hayrettin Paşa. From Barbaros you can catch a bus or dolmuş back to your part of town. There are dolmuş ranks right outside the ferry dock.

A fail-safe evening ferry ride is the one to Haydarpaşa or Kadıköy, from Karaköy's Dock No 7 or No 8. These two Asian suburbs are the only destinations for ferries from these docks, so you can't end up way off somewhere. Return boats bring you back to Karaköy. Each way, the voyage takes 20 minutes and costs US$0.25.

Turkish Bath

For a description of taking a Turkish bath, see the Facts For the Visitor chapter. Actually, you're not confined to bathing only in the evenings, but it does feel wonderful after a tiring day. Some readers have written to say that service is much better and fees much lower at less famous baths in other cities. This may be true, but the baths in İstanbul are quite fancy and worth a look and a bathe.

Two baths attract foreigners. First is the *Cağaloğlu Hamamı* (jaa-AHL-oh- loo) (tel 522-2424), on Yerebatan Caddesi at Babiâli Caddesi, just 200 metres from Sancta Sophia near Cağaloğlu Square. Built over three centuries ago, it boasts that King Edward VIII, Kaiser Wilhelm II, Franz Liszt and Florence Nightingale have all enjoyed its pleasures. Any day between 7 am and 10 pm (men) or 8 am to 9 pm (women), descend the stairs and enter the bath. Some readers have commented that service in the women's section was somewhat grudging, with much bickering over price on extra little services which should have been included in the 'complete bath' price.

The other bath is the *Tarihi Galatasaray Hamamı* (tel 144-1412) at the end of Suterazi Sokak, a little street going southeast from İstiklal Caddesi, just north of Galatasaray. Look for the sign on İstiklal Caddesi, which points the way. This is a beautiful old bath filled with gleaming marble.

The price for the entire experience can range from about US$3 or US$4 if you bring your own soap, shampoo and towel, and bathe yourself; through US$8 to US$10 for an assisted bath; to US$16 to US$20 for the deluxe service, including a massage. Tips will be expected all around, and I've included them in these estimates. Don't let yourself be pressured into tipping heavily; tip on a Turkish scale, not a foreign one.

After you're all done, you'll be utterly refreshed, squeaky clean, and almost unable to walk due to the wonderful relaxation of muscles, mind and spirit.

GETTING THERE & AWAY

All roads lead to İstanbul. As the country's foremost transportation hub, the question is not how to get there (see the Getting There chapter at the front of this book), but how to negotiate this sprawling urban mass when you arrive. Here is the information you may need on arrival.

Air

Atatürk Airport, formerly known as Yeşilköy Airport, has a decent, modern terminal for international flights, and an upgraded domestic terminal. A new, larger airport is already under construction at a site nearby.

The Ministry of Tourism maintains an information office in the international arrivals terminal and will be happy to help with questions or problems. There is also a hotel reservation desk in the arrivals terminal, but some readers of this guide have written to say that they always recommend the same expensive, inconvenient hotel to everyone, regardless

of their preference. This may change, so check anyway.

Also in the arrivals terminal are various currency exchange offices operated by Turkish banks. If you change money here, count your money carefully and make sure it agrees with the total on the exchange slip. These guys will often short-change you by several thousand liras, relying upon your confusion as a new arrival to get away with it. Also, don't accept an excuse that they 'have no change'. It's their business to have the proper change.

Before you pass through customs, avail yourself of the opportunity to buy duty-free goods at decent prices, with no transcontinental carrying problems. They're on sale at the Tekel shop; sales are for foreign currency only.

For examples of airfares from İstanbul to other Turkish cities, and for airport transport details, see the Getting Around chapter.

Road

The E5 from Europe brings you by Atatürk Airport and a bypass heading north and east to cross the Bosphorus bridges. If you're headed for Aksaray, don't take the bypass, but rather head straight on and you'll end up at Topkapı Gate. Continue straight on through the gate along Millet Caddesi, and you will end up in Aksaray Square. For Laleli, continue straight through the square and turn left just before the big university buildings on the left. For Taksim, stay on the bypass and follow the signs.

If you're a bit more daring, leave the expressway at the airport, following signs for Yeşilköy or Ataköy. You can make your way to the shore of the Sea of Marmara and drive into the city along the water's edge. You'll pass the city walls near Yedikule, the Fortress of the Seven Towers and the Marble Tower, which has one foot in the water. The city's southern wall will be on your left as you drive. Across the Bosphorus, the view of Üsküdar,

Haydarpaşa and Kadıköy is impressive. You can turn left onto Mustafa Kemal Caddesi for Aksaray and Laleli; or continue around Seraglio Point to Sirkeci, Eminönü and the Galata Bridge.

Bus

Coming from Europe or Edirne, your bus will drop you at İstanbul's main bus station. At this writing, this is still the Topkapı Otogar, right outside the city walls next to the Topkapı or Cannon Gate. This is nowhere near Topkapı Palace, which lies five km to the east, on the Bosphorus. It seems that two gates, at very different places in the city walls, had cannons associated with them. The Topkapı Otogar at this writing is nothing but a bewildering chaos of little bus offices, snack stands, taxi shills, mud, dust, noise and air pollution.

The better bus lines such as Bosfor Turizm and Varan will provide a servis arabası, or minibus, to take you from the bus station into the city. Both Bosfor Turizm and Varan have their main ticket offices near Taksim Square, so that's where the minibus will end up. But if you ask to be dropped in Aksaray or Laleli, the driver will doubtless oblige.

A new, modern bus terminal is being built at Ferhat Paşa Çiftliği in Esenler, on the new Edirne to İstanbul motorway (expressway). It's almost completed, and will probably have opened by the time you arrive. It is a good, modern facility quite a distance west of the city.

If you do arrive at the old bus station in Topkapı and, if your bus company doesn't have a servis arabası, you'll have to make your own way into the city. Taxi drivers will be waiting to buttonhole you as you alight. You might want one if your bags are heavy. Otherwise, make your way out of the bus station and across to the Topkapı Gate itself. Just inside the gate (on the other side of the walls from the bus station) is a city bus stop, from which you can catch a bus or a dolmuş to Aksaray. If Aksaray or Laleli is not your final

destination, you must change in Aksaray for a bus or dolmuş to Sultanahmet, Eminönü or Taksim.

There is also a bus station on the eastern shore of the Bosphorus at Harem, between Üsküdar and Haydarpaşa. Many buses entering and leaving the city make a stop at Harem to serve residents of the Asian suburbs.

Bus Ticket Offices Bus company ticket offices are found clustered in Laleli on Ordu Caddesi, and near Sirkeci Station on Muradiye Caddesi.

In Taksim, try the offices of the Pamukkale company (tel 145-2946) at Mete Caddesi 16, to the left (north) of the Atatürk Cultural Palace. Pamukkale has a reputation as one of Turkey's best bus companies. It operates routes to many points in Turkey, as well as to Europe.

Three more offices near Taksim are to the right (south) of the Cultural Centre, down the hill a block along İnönü Caddesi, on the left-hand side of the road. Varan (tel 149-1903, 144-8457), at İnönü Caddesi 29/B is also one of Turkey's best companies; its routes include those to Ankara, Athens, Çanakkale, Dornbirn, Edirne, Innsbruck, İzmir, Salzburg, Strasburg and Zurich, and to the more popular holiday destinations in Turkey.

Kamil Koç, another good line, is represented by Arama Turizm (tel 145-2795), İnönü Caddesi 31, where you can also buy tickets for the TCDD (Turkish State Railways). Ulusoy (tel 149-4373, 148-8449), also among the best, has an office down the hill another block along İnönü Caddesi, facing the German Consulate General. Also here are As Turizm and Hakiki Koç lines (tel 145-4244).

Here are some examples of bus fares and travel times from İstanbul to:

Ankara – 450 km, eight hours, US$6.50 to US$8.50
Antalya – 725 km, 12 hours, US$11 to US$13
Antakya – 1115 km, 20 hours, US$14 to US$16

Bodrum – 830 km, 14 hours, US$12 to US$14

Bursa – 230 km, four hours, US$4

Denizli (for Pamukkale) – 665 km, 10 hours, US$10 to US$12

Edirne – 235 km, four hours, US$3.50

Fethiye – 980 km, 15 hours, US$15 to US$18

Gaziantep – 1150 km, 20 hours, US$14 to US$16

İzmir – 605 km, nine hours, US$8

Kuşadası – 700 km, 11 hours, US$9 to US$11

Marmaris – 900 km, 15 hours, US$13 to US$15

Side – 790 km, 14 hours, US$12 to US$14

Trabzon – 1110 km, 19 hours, US$14 to US$16

Train

All trains from Europe terminate at Sirkeci (SEER-keh-jee) Station, right next to Eminönü in the shadow of Topkapı Palace. The station has its own small Tourism Information Office, post office and currency exchange booth, as well as a restaurant and café.

The main (west) station door of Sirkeci now is a modern structure. But take a look on the north side of the station, facing the Bosphorus: this more ornate facade was the original front of the station, more in keeping with the romantic ideas of what the terminus for the Orient Express should look like.

Right outside the station door and across the street (use the overhead walkway) you can catch a bus or dolmuş going to Sultanahmet, Beyazıt, Laleli and Aksaray.

If you're headed for Taksim, go out the station door and turn right. Walk toward the sea and you'll see the Eminönü bus ranks to your left. Catch a bus to Taksim from here.

Departures: the İstanbul Express, the train for Athens and for cities in Europe, departs Sirkeci Station, on the European side of the Bosphorus, at 8.50 pm each evening in summer, at 6.15 pm in winter, arriving at the Turkish frontier the following morning about 9½ hours later (check these times, as they may change). The Orient Express no longer runs between İstanbul and Paris, but this evening train carries with it a whiff of the old romance, with cars destined for points in Romania, Hungary, Germany, Austria, Turkey, Greece, Yugoslavia and Bulgaria. It carries 1st and 2nd-class seats to Belgrade and Munich, couchettes to Munich and Vienna; sleeping cars once a week to Bucharest and Moscow; extra couchettes to Munich on Tuesday and Wednesday, and extra couchettes to Sofia on Sunday and Monday.

To continue a train journey deeper into Turkey (meaning Anatolia), you must get to Haydarpaşa Station on the Asian side. The best way is by ferry from Karaköy. Cross the Galata Bridge from Eminönü to Karaköy (by bus, dolmuş or taxi if your luggage is heavy), go to the prominent ferry dock, buy a token, go through the turnstile and look for the illuminated sign saying Haydarpaşa. Some ferries stop both at Haydarpaşa and Kadıköy; but you should be careful not to get a ferry that goes *only* to Kadıköy. If in doubt, just say *Haydarpaşa ya mü?* ('To Haydarpaşa?') to anyone while pointing at the boat. By the way, don't let anyone suggest that you take a taxi to Haydarpaşa. Ferries are scheduled to depart Kadıköy and arrive at Haydarpaşa in time for the departure of all major trains. The ferry is cheap, convenient, pleasant and speedy. A taxi would be expensive and slow.

Ferries depart Kadıköy for Haydarpaşa every 15 to 30 minutes; the special ferries, timed to connect with the departures of the major expresses, leave Karaköy about a half-hour before express train departures. The fare is US$0.25.

The major trains departing Haydarpaşa for Ankara are these:

Boğaziçi Ekspresi Departs daily at 8 am, arriving in Ankara at 6.10 pm

Mavi Tren I Departs daily at 1.30 pm, arriving in Ankara at 9 pm

Doğ Ekspresi Departs daily at 11.40 pm, arriving in Ankara at 9.57 am the following day, then continuing to Erzurum and Kars

Anadolu Ekspresi Departs daily at 9 pm, arriving Ankara at 8.10 am

Ankara Ekspresi An all-sleeping-car train, departs daily at 9.40 pm, arriving Ankara at 8.30 am the following morning

Mavi Tren II Departs daily at 11 pm, arriving Ankara at 7.30 am

Vangölü Ekspresi (Monday, Wednesday, Saturday) Departs 7.10 pm, arriving Ankara at 5.40 am, then continuing onward to Sivas, Malatya, Elâzığ and Tatvan, with a lake steamer to Van

Güney Ekspresi (Tuesday, Thursday, Friday, Sunday) Departs 7.10 pm, arriving Ankara at 5.40 am, then continuing onward to Sivas, Malatya, Elâzığ and Tatvan, with a lake steamer to Diyarbakır and Kurtalan

The fare from İstanbul to Ankara is US$6, US$10 return (US$5.50 one-way for a student) on an express train, US$9 one-way on a Mavi Tren.

In addition, there are trains departing Haydarpaşa for Gaziantep, Denizli and Konya:

Toros Ekspresi Departs Tuesday, Thursday and Sunday at 9 am, arriving Gaziantep at 2.52 pm the following day

Pamukkale Ekspresi Departs daily at 6 pm, arriving Denizli at 8.25 am

Anadolu Mavi Tren Departs daily at 11.30pm, arriving Konya at 12.16 pm

Meram Ekspresi Departs daily at 8.25 pm, arriving Konya at 10.15 am

From İstanbul to İzmir take the boat-train. You depart İstanbul aboard a comfortable passenger ship bound for Bandırma, four hours away on the south shore of the Sea of Marmara, midway between Bursa and Çanakkale. At Bandırma you board a motor-train for the 5½-hour trip to İzmir. Though you can do this trip at night, the daytime run is preferable because you get to see the countryside (which is lovely), and you don't have to change from boat to train in the middle of the night. Cabins are available both day and night so you can have some privacy, and even get some sleep, if you like. Reserve your cabin when you buy your ticket.

There are two trips daily in each direction. Boats depart the dock at Sarayburnu northeast of Sirkeci Station at 9.30 am and 9 pm, with the train arriving in İzmir at 8.30 pm and 8.50 am respectively. Departures from İzmir are at 8.15 am and 8 pm, arriving 6.45 pm and 7 am respectively. The 11-hour journey costs US$7. For tickets and schedules in İstanbul, go to Sirkeci Station or to the Turkish Maritime Lines offices in the Yolcu Salonu in Karaköy. In İzmir, go to Basmane Station. By the way, when you head for Sarayburnu dock to board your boat, be advised that you can't get there by walking through the staging area of the car-ferry dock just north of Sirkeci; you must stay on the street until you reach Sarayburnu dock.

Boat

Passenger ships dock at Karaköy, near the Yolcu Salonu (YOHL-joo sahl-oh-noo, International Maritime Passenger Terminal) on Rıhtım Caddesi. The Ministry of Tourism has an information office in the Yolcu Salonu, near the front (street) doors.

The international dock is next to the Karaköy ferry dock and only 100 metres east of Galata Bridge. Bus and dolmuş routes to Taksim pass right in front of the Yolcu Salonu; for those to destinations in the Old City such as Sultanahmet, Laleli and Aksaray, go to the western side of Karaköy Square itself, right at the end of the Galata Bridge. You'll have to find the pedestrian underpass to get to the dolmuş and bus stops.

Some domestic-line ships dock at

Kabataş (KAH-bah-tahsh), about two km north of Karaköy on the Bosphorus shore, very near Dolmabahçe Palace and Mosque. As you leave the dock at Kabataş, buses and dolmuşes heading left will be going to Karaköy and the Old City; those travelling right will be going to Taksim or north along the Bosphorus shore.

Boats arriving from Bandırma on the İzmir to İstanbul train-boat route dock at Sarayburnu (Seraglio Point), one km east of the Galata Bridge north and east of Sirkeci Station.

GETTING AROUND

Transport within İstanbul moves slowly. The mediaeval street patterns do not receive automobiles well, let alone buses. Several conflagrations in the 19th century cleared large areas of the city and allowed new avenues to be opened. Were it not for these providential disasters, traffic would be even slower.

A subway system has been in the planning for years, but the costs, astronomical in any case, increase dramatically when İstanbul's hilly terrain and water bodies are taken into account. Then there are the ruins: every time a Roman or Byzantine structure is discovered, construction must be halted and the archaeologists brought in for weeks, perhaps months of study. Still, the work progresses, and at some point the city will have a more modern public transport system.

Airport Transport

The fastest way to get into town from the airport is by taxi, but this may cost as much as US$7 or US$10, depending upon what part of the city you're headed for. A far cheaper alternative is the airport bus (operated by Havaş) for US$1, which departs the domestic terminal and goes into the city, stopping at Bakırköy (Cevizlik) in Aksaray (near Laleli), before ending its run at the Turkish Airlines terminal in Şişhane Square, near the

Galata Tower and Tepebaşı in Beyoğlu. Buses leave every half-hour from 6.30 to 10 am, every hour from 10 am to 2 pm, and every half-hour from 2 pm to 10 pm. The journey, depending upon the traffic, may take between 25 and 45 minutes. Free shuttle buses leave the airport's international terminal for the domestic terminal every 10 minutes or so throughout the day. Just walk out of the international arrivals terminal and look for the Havaş shuttle bus.

You can cut the cost by a few pennies if you take the red-and-beige city bus into town, but they leave infrequently and take a long time to deliver you to the town centre. Catch the bus by the taxi parking area across from the domestic terminal.

For the return trip to the airport, catch the Havaş bus at the Şişhane terminal. You must be at the airport for check-in *at least* 30 minutes before departure time for domestic flights, and it's not a bad idea to be there earlier, say 45 to 60 minutes before. For international flights, be at the airport at least an hour before take-off or, better yet, 1½ or two hours before. Remember, there are three security checks, customs, check-in and immigration procedures to pass through before you board, and if the aircraft is a wide-body, the officials will have to process about 400 passengers before boarding is completed.

Bus

İstanbul's red-and-beige city buses run almost everywhere. Fares are US$0.25 per ride, or about half price for students with Turkish ID cards. Fares are paid on a ticket system (see the Getting Around chapter). The route name and number appear on the front of the bus; also on the front, or on the curb side, is a list of stops along the route.

Some buses fill to capacity right at the departure point, leaving no room for passengers waiting along the route. It's frustrating to wait five or 10 minutes for a bus, only to have it pass right by due to wall-to-wall flesh inside. Even if the driver does stop, is it worth it to jam in? If you're jammed in the middle of the bus when your stop comes, you may not be able to get off. (What you do in this situation is let the driver and other passengers know you must get out by saying, *İnecek var!* (een-eh-JEK vahr, 'Someone will alight!').

Dolmuş

The dolmuş and minibus system is preferable to the city buses for several reasons. As cars or minibuses have a set number of seats, they are rarely overcrowded like buses. It's against the law carry more than the designated number of passengers. Also, they tend to be faster. Finally, they tend to run on short routes between the major squares, so the tourist unfamiliar with İstanbul's maze of streets can be sure of ending up at the chosen destination. Pluck up your courage and try a dolmuş early on in your stay. Soon you'll find them a great help.

Fares are only slightly more expensive than the buses on short routes, somewhat more expensive on the longer routes; but it is on the longer routes that one appreciates the comfort more.

Major dolmuş termini of use to tourists are: Taksim, Karaköy, Eminönü and Beyazıt. Sultanahmet, near the majority of İstanbul's most important sights, is not well-served by dolmuşes except from Aksaray and Beyazıt. Coming from Galata Bridge, Eminönü and Sirkeci, they tend to pass a few blocks west of Sultanahmet. But a few blocks out is better than walking all the way, so ask for Cağaloğlu (jah-AHL-oh-loo) and you'll be close.

At these major dolmuş termini, look for the rows of cars and lines of people being matched up. If there's no sign indicating your destination, look in the cars' front windows, or ask just by saying the name of your destination. A hawker or driver will point you to the appropriate car.

Tünel

İstanbul's little underground train, the Tünel, runs between Karaköy and the southern end of İstiklal Caddesi called Tünel Meydanı (Tünel Square). The fare is US$0.20.

There are only two stations on the line, the upper and lower, so there's no getting lost. Buy a token, enter through the turnstile and board the train. They run every five or 10 minutes from early morning until about 10 pm.

Taxi

Taxis are plentiful, and it is usually not difficult to find one, though finding an honest driver can be a lot more difficult. All taxis have digital meters, and it is an offence (punishable by a very high fine) to take a passenger and refuse to run the meter. Some drivers, however, particularly those who loiter in areas frequently visited by tourists, may demand that you pay a flat rate (see the warning under Taxi in the Getting Around chapter). The base (drop) rate is US$0.50 during the daytime (*gündüz*); the night-time (*gece*) rate is higher, and you should be careful that the driver is not running the night-time rate on his meter during the day. A trip between Aksaray and Sultanahmet costs about US$1; between Taksim and Karaköy about US$2; between Taksim and Sultanahmet about US$3.

Ferry

Without doubt the nicest way to go any considerable distance in İstanbul is by ferry. You will (and should) use the boats whenever possible. The alternatives are bus and dolmuş along the coastal roads or across the Bosphorus Bridge. These can be faster, but they will also be less comfortable and sometimes more expensive. Most ferry rides cost about the same as a bus ticket.

The mouth of the Golden Horn by the Galata Bridge is a seething maelstrom of the white ferries at rush hour. The Eminönü docks are being reorganised at this writing, so some of the dock information which follows may have changed by the time you arrive.

First of all, each dock serves a certain route, though a few routes may overlap. At each dock is a framed copy of the *tarife* (tah-ree-FEH, timetable) outlining service. It's only in Turkish, so I'll give you the necessary translations. Each route (*hat* or *hattı*) is designated by the names of the principal stops. Please note that the tarife has two completely different parts, one for weekdays (*normal günleri*) and Saturday (*Cumartesi*), and another for Sunday (*Pazar*) and holidays (*bayram günleri*). Make sure you're looking at the proper part.

The ferry you're most likely to use is the Eminönü-Kavaklar Boğaziçi Özel Gezi Seferleri (Eminönü Special Touristic Excursion) up the Bosphorus. These depart Eminönü daily at 10.30 am, 12.30 and 2.10 pm each weekday (10 and 11 am, 12 noon, 1.30 and 3 pm on Sunday and holidays), with more trips in summer, and go all the way to Rumeli Kavağı and Anadolu Kavağı at the Black Sea mouth of the Bosphorus. The entire trip takes about 1¾ hours one way and costs US$3. You may want to go only as far as Sarıyer, about two hours' ride, then take a dolmuş back down, stopping at various sights along the way. These boats fill up early, so buy your ticket and walk aboard at least 30 or 45 minutes prior to departure in order to get a seat.

Otherwise, if you just want to take a little ride around Seraglio Point (good for photos of Topkapı Palace, Sancta Sophia and the Blue Mosque) and across the

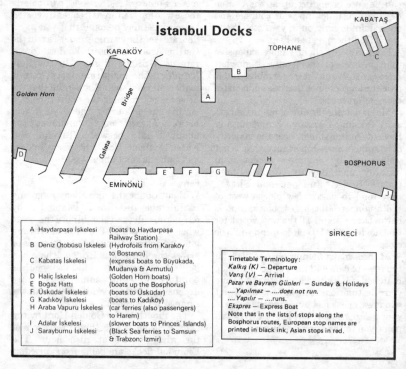

İstanbul Docks

KABATAŞ

KARAKÖY   TOPHANE

Golden Horn

Bridge

Galata

BOSPHORUS

EMİNÖNÜ

SİRKECİ

A Haydarpaşa İskelesi   (boats to Haydarpaşa Railway Station)
B Deniz Otobüsü İskelesi   (Hydrofoils from Karaköy to Bostancı)
C Kabataş İskelesi   (express boats to Büyükada, Mudanya & Armutlu)
D Haliç İskelesi   (Golden Horn boats)
E Boğaz Hattı   (boats up the Bosphorus)
F Üsküdar İskelesi   (boats to Üsküdar)
G Kadıköy İskelesi   (boats to Kadıköy)
H Araba Vapuru İskelesi   (car ferries (also passengers) to Harem)
I Adalar İskelesi   (slower boats to Princes' Islands)
J Sarayburnu İskelesi   (Black Sea ferries to Samsun & Trabzon; İzmir)

Timetable Terminology:
Kalkış (K) — Departure
Varış (V) — Arrival
Pazar ve Bayram Günleri — Sunday & Holidays
....Yapılmaz — ....does not run.
....Yapılır — ....runs.
Ekspres — Express Boat
Note that in the lists of stops along the Bosphorus routes, European stop names are printed in black ink, Asian stops in red.

Bosphorus, catch any boat from Dock No 7 or No 8 in Karaköy. The trip over to Haydarpaşa or Kadıköy and back will take about an hour.

Hydrofoil
Called *deniz otobüsü* (sea-bus) in Turkish, hydrofoils are running on an increasing number of routes in and around the city. Hydrofoil trips cost several times more than ferries, but are much faster. There are presently hydrofoil docks at Kabataş (the main one), Karaköy and Yenikapı (east of Kumkapı on the Sea of Marmara shore). Yenikapı is slated to become the main hydrofoil port in coming years.

On Foot
With an overburdened public transport system, walking can often be faster and more rewarding. The street scenes are never dull, and the views from one hill to the next are often extraordinary. While walking, watch out for broken pavement, bits of pipe sticking a few centimetres out of the pavement, and all manner of other obstacles. Don't expect any car driver to stop for you in any situation. In Turkey, the automobile seems to have the right of way virtually everywhere, and drivers get very annoyed at pedestrians who assert ridiculous and specious rights. It is obvious, isn't it? The automobile, being such a marvellous and expensive machine, should go wherever its driver is capable of taking it, without hindrance from mere pedestrians. This, at least, seems to be the common belief.

The Princes' Islands

The Turks call these islands, which lie about 20 km south-east of the city in the Sea of Marmara, the Kızıl Adalar, 'Red Islands'. Most İstanbullus get along with 'Adalar' (AH-dah-LAHR, 'The Islands'), however, as there are no other islands nearby.

It's convenient to have islands near a big city, as they serve all sorts of useful purposes. In Byzantine times, so the story goes, refractory princes, deposed monarchs and others who were a threat to the powers that be, were interned here. A Greek Orthodox monastery and seminary on Heybeliada turned out Orthodox priests until only a decade or two ago.

Under the Ottomans, stray dogs were rounded up from the city's streets and shipped out to Köpek Adası (Dog Island), where they were released. After that, their fate was up to God. (Muslim belief holds that animals, too, have immortal souls, and that it is not the business of humans to take animal lives needlessly; that is, to kill dogs just to get them off city streets.) From one of the islands, copper was mined. Another was used as a self-contained rabbit farm: bunnies were released on the deserted island to breed, and the 'crop' gathered at leisure.

In the 19th century the empire's business community of Greeks, Jews and Armenians favoured the islands as summer resorts. The population was heavily Greek up to the end of the empire. Many of the pretty Victorian holiday villas and hotels built by these wealthy Ottoman subjects survive, and make the larger islands, Büyükada and Heybeliada, charming places.

BÜYÜKADA
The first thing you will notice about this delightful place is that cars are not allowed. Except for the necessary police, fire and sanitation vehicles, transportation is by bicycle, horse-drawn carriage and foot. It's wonderful!

Something you may not notice, but that you should be aware of, is that there is no fresh water in the islands; it must be brought in tanks from the mainland.

Walk from the ferry to the clock tower and the main street. The business district, with some fairly expensive restaurants, is to the left. For a stroll up the hill and through the lovely old houses, bear right.

If you need a goal for your wanderings, head for the Greek Monastery of St George, in the 'saddle' between Büyükada's two main hills.

Horse-drawn carriage tours of the island are available. You can take either the 'long tour' (*büyük tur*) for about US$10, or the 'short tour' (*küçük tur*) which gives you a look mostly at the town, not the shores or hills, for US$7.

Between the islands of Büyükada and Heybeliada there are fairly frequent ferries on the 15-minute trip.

HEYBELİADA

Called Heybeli for short, this small island holds the Turkish Naval Academy. The presidential yacht is often anchored off the academy landing. Within the academy grounds is the grave of Sir Edward Barton (died 1598), ambassador of Queen Elizabeth I to the Sublime Porte.

Getting There & Away

If you have the time and want a leisurely, relaxing outing with no heavy sightseeing or scheduling, by all means cruise out to the islands. The summer schedules are heavily in favour of commuters, with frequent morning boats from the islands and frequent evening boats from the city. But you'll have no trouble getting a convenient boat if you check the schedules ahead of time. The few morning boats from the city to the islands fill up quickly, and though you'll almost certainly get aboard, you may have to stand the whole way unless you board the boat and seize a seat at least half an hour before departure time.

The fastest way to reach the islands is by hydrofoil, operating between Kabataş and Büyükada. The voyage takes 22 minutes, and costs US$3 one way.

Cheaper and more leisurely are the express ferries to the islands, which depart from Kabataş (Dock B, near Dolmabahçe Camii) at 9.30 am, 2.30 and 6.20 pm; on Saturday there's an extra morning boat to Heybeliada (but not Büyükada) at 9.45 am. Returning express ferries depart Büyükada for Kabataş at 7.10 and 9.10 am, 2.40 and 6.10 pm, and, on Saturday only, at 10 pm. The trip from Kabataş to Heybeliada, the first express ferry stop, takes 50 minutes. Büyükada, the main island, is 15 minutes' cruise past Heybeliada. The express round-trip fare between Kabataş and Büyükada is US$1.50. The best plan is to go outbound as far as Büyükada, see the island, take a local boat over to Heybeliada, see that one, then take a returning express ferry to Kabataş.

Cheaper still are the slower local ferries to the islands from Galata Bridge (Sirkeci), departing at 6.50, 8.30, 10.05, and 11.10 am, and 12.50, 3, 4.30, 5.30, 6.10 pm and even later. The trip from Galata Bridge to Büyükada can take as long as 1½ hours, as the local boats stop at each island in the archipelago.

The ferry steams out of the Golden Horn, with good views all around. To the right is a magnificent panorama of Topkapı Palace, Sancta Sophia and the Blue Mosque; to the left, Üsküdar, Haydarpaşa and Kadıköy. Along the southern coast of Asia are more suburbs of İstanbul, some of them industrial. Before coming to the bigger islands, you'll pass the small ones named **Kınalı** and **Burgaz**. Heybeliada is next. Finally, you debark at Büyükada.

If you don't have the time for this excursion, you still have a chance for a look: if you're heading off to İznik and Bursa, you'll probably take a ferry from Kabataş to Yalova. It will pass, and may call at, both Heybeliada and Büyükada.

Edirne

The land to the north of the Aegean Sea was called Thrace by the Romans. Today this ancient Roman province is divided among Turkey, Bulgaria and Greece, with Turkey holding the easternmost part.

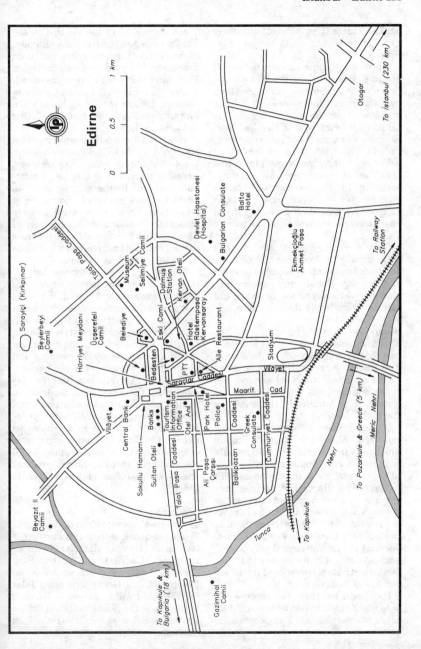

Edirne

Sarayiçi (Kırkpınar)

Beyerbeyi Camii

Beyazıt II Camii

Gazimihal Camii

To Kapıkule & Bulgaria (18 km)

Tâclâr Paşa Caddesi

Museum
Selimiye Camii
Dolmuş Station
Kervan Oteli

Devlet Haastanesi (Hospital)
Bulgarian Consulate
Balta Hotel

Ekmekçioğlu Ahmet Paşa

To İstanbul (230 km)
Otogar

Hürriyet Meydanı
Üçşerefeli Camii
Belediye
Eski Cami
Hotel Rüstempaşa (Kervansaray)
Aile Restaurant

Bedesten
PTT
Saraçlar Caddesi
Stadyum
Vilâyet

To Railway Station

Vilâyet
Central Bank
Banks
Sultan Oteli
Sokullu Hamam

Talat Paşa Caddesi
Otel Anıl
Tourism Information Office
Ali Paşa Çarşısı
Balıkpazarı
Park Hotel
Police
Maarif Caddesi
Greek Consulate
Cumhuriyet Caddesi
Cad

Tunca
To Kapıkule

Nehri
Meriç Nehri
To Pazarkule & Greece (5 km)

0   0.5   1 km

Turkish Thrace (Trakya) is not particularly exciting except for its major city, Edirne.

A glance at the map seems to tell you all about Edirne (eh-DEER-neh): it's the first town you come to if you're travelling overland from Europe to Turkey, it's a way-station on the road to İstanbul. It wouldn't be surprising if this had been Edirne's role throughout history, even in the old days when the town was called Adrianople. But there's more to Edirne than this. Because of its role in history, several of the finest examples from the greatest periods of Turkish mosque architecture were built here, and if you have the chance you should take time to visit.

If you're coming from İstanbul, you can make the 250-km, four-hour trip to Edirne and back (another four hours) to İstanbul in a long day. Get an early morning bus, plan to have lunch and see the sights, and catch a return bus in the late afternoon.

History

This town was indeed built as a defence post for the larger city on the Bosphorus. The Roman emperor Hadrian founded Edirne in the 2nd century as Hadrianopolis, a name which was later shortened by Europeans to Adrianople, then again by the Turks to Edirne.

It played a very important role in the early centuries of the Ottoman Empire which grew from a small Turkish emirate in north-western Anatolia. By the mid-1300s, the emirate of the Ottomans with its capital at Bursa had become very powerful, but not enough to threaten the mighty walls of Constantinople. Bent on more conquest, the Ottoman armies crossed the Dardanelles into Thrace, skirting the great capital. Capturing Adrianople in 1363, they made it their new capital and base of operations for military campaigns in Europe.

For almost 100 years, this was the city from which the Ottoman sultan would set out on his campaigns to Europe and Asia.

When, at last, the time was ripe for the final conquest of the Byzantine Empire, Mehmet the Conqueror set out from Edirne on the road to Constantinople. Even after this great city was captured, Edirne played an important role in Ottoman life and society, for it was still a forward post on the route to other conquests in Europe.

When the Ottoman Empire disintegrated after WW I, the Allies had decided to grant all of Thrace to the Greek kingdom. Constantinople was to become an international city. In the summer of 1920, Greek armies occupied Edirne. But Atatürk's republican armies were ultimately victorious and the Treaty of Lausanne left Edirne and Eastern Thrace to the Turks. Edirne returned to its role as 'the town on the way to İstanbul'.

Edirne is largely disregarded by tourists, which has helped preserve its Turkish character and appeal. While the towns along the Aegean and Mediterranean coasts are clogged with foreigners and with vast new European-style building projects, Edirne attracts the discerning few who come to enjoy the harmony and history of its mosques, covered bazaars, bridges and caravanserais, and the easy pace of life. These days it has also taken on a little importance as an international shopping town. As many Turkish prices are lower than those in neighbouring Greece, Greeks from border towns cross over to Edirne to do their shopping. You'll see numerous shops in Edirne's market streets with window notices written in Greek.

Orientation

The centre of town is Hürriyet Meydanı or Freedom Square, at the intersection of the two main streets, Saraçlar Caddesi/ Hükümet Caddesi and Talat Paşa Caddesi. Just west of the square is the Üçşerefeli Cami. Going north along Talat Paşa Caddesi will bring you to Edirne's masterpiece, the Selimiye Camii. On the way to the Selimiye, you'll pass the Eski

Cami and south of Hürriyet Square is the Ali Paşa Çarşısı, Edirne's covered bazaar.

The main dolmuş station downtown is right next to the Eski Cami and the Hotel Rüstempaşa Kervansaray. There is a major city bus stop across the street from the Eski Cami which is only a few minutes' walk from most important points in town.

Information
There is a Tourism Information Office (tel (181) 11518) a half-block south-west of Hürriyet Meydanı on Talat Paşa Caddesi; there's another at the Kapıkule border post. The office in town can help you with finding places to stay (many of these are within finger-pointing distance) and transport questions. The staff speak some English and have maps and brochures in English.

Üçşerefeli Cami
The principal reason to stop in Edirne is to see mosques, so start out from Hürriyet Meydanı and go the few steps to the Üçşerefeli Cami.

The name means 'mosque with three galleries (balconies)'. Actually it's one of the mosque's four minarets which has the three balconies. The minarets, built at different times, are all wonderfully varied.

Enter at the far end of the courtyard rather than through a side gate. That way you can enjoy the full effect of the architect's genius. The courtyard at the Üçşerefeli (EWCH-sheh-reh-feh-LEE) with its şadırvan was a prototype for the courtyards of the Ottoman mosques built in later centuries.

Construction of this mosque was begun in 1440 and finished by 1447. It exemplifies a transition from the Seljuk Turkish type of architecture of Konya and Bursa to a truly Ottoman style, which would be perfected later in İstanbul. The Seljuks were greatly influenced by the Persian and Indian styles prevalent in their empire to the east. The Ottomans learned

much from the Seljuk Turks, but also from the Byzantines, for whom Sancta Sophia (with its wide, expensive dome covering a great open space) was the purest expression of their ideal. After the Ottomans took Constantinople in 1453, they assimilated the architecture of Sancta Sophia into their tradition and the transition from Seljuk to pure Ottoman accelerated.

In the Seljuk style, smaller domes are mounted on square rooms. But at the Üçşerefeli, the wide (24 metres) dome is mounted on a hexagonal drum and supported by two walls and two pillars. Keep this transitional style in mind as you visit Edirne's other mosques which reflect earlier or later styles.

Across the street from the mosque is the **Sokollu Mehmet Paşa Hamamı**, or Turkish bath, built in the late 1500s and still in use. Designed by the great Mimar Sinan for Grand Vizier Sokullu Mehmet Paşa, it is actually two hamams in one: one for men (*erkekler kısmı*), one for women (*kadınlar kısmı*). (At most Turkish baths there is only one system of bathing rooms, used by men and women on different days.)

Eski Cami
Now head back to Hürriyet Meydanı, and walk north-east on Talat Paşa Caddesi to the Eski Cami (ehs-KEE jah-mee), or Old Mosque. On your way you'll pass the bedesten, another covered market, this one dating from the early 1400s. Behind it to the east is the Rüstem Paşa Hanı, a grand caravanserai built 100 years after the bedesten.

The Eski Cami (1414) exemplifies one of two principal mosque styles used by the Ottomans in their earlier capital, Bursa. Like Bursa's great Ulu Cami, the Eski Cami has rows of arches and pillars supporting a series of small domes. Inside, there's a marvellous mihrab and huge calligraphic inscriptions on the walls. The columns at the front of the mosque were lifted from some Roman building, a common practice over the centuries.

Selimiye Camii

Up the hill past the Eski Cami stands the great Selimiye (seh-LEE-mee-yeh), the finest work of the great Ottoman architect Sinan – or so the architect himself considered. Though smaller than Sinan's tremendous Süleymaniye in İstanbul, the Selimiye is wonderfully harmonious and elegant. Crowning its small hill, it can be seen from a good distance across the rolling Thracian steppeland and makes an impressive sight.

The Selimiye was constructed for Sultan Selim II (1566-1574) and was finished just after his death. Sinan's genius guided him in designing a broad and lofty dome, supported by pillars, arches and external buttresses. He did it so well that the interior is very spacious and the walls can be filled with windows because they don't have to bear all of the weight. The result is a wide, airy, light space for prayer, similar to that of the Süleymaniye.

Part of the Selimiye's excellent effect comes from its four slender, very tall (71 metres) minarets. The fluted drums of the minarets add to the sense of height. You'll notice that each is *üçşerefeli*, or built with three balconies – Sinan's respectful acknowledgement, perhaps, to his predecessor who designed Edirne's Üçşerefeli Cami.

As you might expect, the interior furnishings of the Selimiye are exquisite, from the delicately carved marble mimber to the outstanding İznik faïence in and around the mihrab.

The Selimiye had its share of supporting buildings – religious schools, libraries, etc. However, all that survive are a medrese (theological seminary) and a gallery of shops, called the arasta, beneath the mosque. The shops have been restored and are still in use; rents are dedicated to the upkeep of the mosque, as they have been for over 400 years. The medrese is now a museum of Turkish and Islamic arts, called the Türk-İslâm Eserleri Müzesi, open daily except Monday from 8 am to 12 noon and from 1.30 to 6 pm, for a small admission charge.

Beyazıt II Camii

Edirne's last great imperial mosque is that of Sultan Beyazıt II (1481-1512), on the far side (north-west) of the Tunca River (TOON – jah). From Hürriyet Meydanı, the pleasant walk to the mosque will take you about 15 or 20 minutes. Walk along Hükümet Caddesi beside the Üçşerefeli Cami (on your right), and turn left immediately after its Turkish bath. Walk one block and bear right at the ornate little fountain. This street is Horozlu Bayır Caddesi; it changes names later to İmaret Caddesi, but it will take you right to the bridge (1488) across the Tunca to Sultan Beyazıt's mosque.

The Beyazıt complex (1484-88) was fully restored in the late 1970s, so it now looks as good as new. The architect, a fellow named Hayrettin, didn't have the genius of Mimar Sinan, but did a very creditable job nonetheless.

The mosque's style is between that of the Üçşerefeli and the Selimiye, moving back a bit rather than advancing: its large prayer hall has one large dome, more like in Bursa's mosques, but it has a courtyard and sadırvan like the Üçşerefeli Cami's. Though it's certainly of a high standard, it can't compare with the Selimiye, built less than a century later.

The mosque's külliye is extensive and includes a *tabhane* (hostel for travellers), medrese, imaret (soup kitchen) and *darüşşifa* (hospital).

Eski Saray & Sarayiçi

Saray means 'palace' in Turkish. Upriver (east) from the Sultan Beyazıt II mosque complex are the ruins of the Eski Saray or Old Palace. Begun by Sultan Beyazıt II in 1450, this palace once rivalled İstanbul's Topkapı in luxury and size. Today, little is left of it: only a few bits of the kitchen buildings. But it's a pleasant walk along the river (less than a half-hour) to reach

Top: İstanbul as seen from the Süleymaniye minaret
Bottom: Dolmabahçe Palace

Top: The rooftops of the Covered Bazaar
Bottom: Fishing skiffs on the Bosphorus at sunset

Eski Saray from the Beyazıt mosque, and if the day is nice you might want to go there. From the Eski Saray, Saraçhane Köprüsü (bridge) will take you back across the Tunca; Saraçhane Caddesi then leads directly back to Hürriyet Meydanı.

East of Eski Saray, across a branch of the Tunca (there's a bridge called Fatih Sultan Köprüsü), is Sarayiçi ('within the palace'). This scrub-covered island, once the sultans' hunting preserve, is now the site of the famous annual Kırkpınar Oiled Wrestling Matches or *Tarihi Kırkpınar Yağlı Güreş Festivali* ('yah-LUH gew-RESH', oiled wrestling). In late May and early June, huge wrestlers slathered with olive oil and clad only in leather knickers take part in freestyle matches. An early sultan is said to have invented the sport to keep his troops in shape. Whatever the origin, a *pehlivan* (wrestler) at the Kırkpınar matches is something to behold. Folk-dancing exhibitions are organised as part of the festivities.

If you've made it all the way to Sarayiçi, look for the Kanuni Köprüsü to get you back to the south bank of the Tunca. Bear right coming off the bridge, and the road will lead you to Hükümet Caddesi, and eventually to Hürriyet Meydanı.

The Old Town

While you're here, don't forget to take a stroll through the old town of Edirne to discover some scenes of Turkish daily life. The Old Town, called Kale İçi ('within the fortress') by the locals, was the original mediaeval town with streets laid out on a grid plan. Some fragments of Byzantine city walls are still visible at the edges of the grid, down by the Tunca River. The Old Town, bounded by Saraçlar Caddesi and Talat Paşa Caddesi, is basically the area behind and to the west of the Ali Paşa Çarşısı.

Places to Stay

It's relatively easy to find inexpensive pensions and rooming houses in Edirne,

as this is the first stop within Turkey on the route from Europe. Travellers who know the route will often push on through northern Greece or Bulgaria in order to get into Turkey so they can enjoy the lower prices and incomparably better food. Edirne is where they spend their first night.

However, this route is heavily travelled by Turkish workers on their way to and from Europe, and by international lorry-drivers heading to or from Iran and the Arabic countries. So your companions in the inexpensive hostelries may be mostly bachelors. Also, many places will be filled by crowds at holiday time.

Places to Stay – bottom end

The first area to look for low-cost lodging is behind the Tourism Information Office along Maarif Caddesi. Several grand old town houses here have been converted into budget hotels.

First along the street is the *Otel Anıl* (tel (181) 21482), Hürriyet Meydanı, Maarif Caddesi 8, 22100 Edirne, a clean and proper hostelry with simple but acceptable waterless rooms costing US$12 a double. Bathrooms are down the hall; showers here have electric shower heads for heating the water.

Next door to the Anıl is the *Konak Hotel* (tel (181) 11348), Hürriyet Meydanı, Maarif Caddesi 6, 22100 Edirne. Rooms here are also waterless but clean; some have five or six beds, renting for US$3.50 per person.

Only slightly more expensive is the *Otel Açıkgöz* (tel (181) 11944), Tüfekçiler Çarşısı, Sümerbank Arkası 74, 22100 Edirne, a block off Saraçlar Caddesi behind the Sümerbank building. Modest but cheerful, the price for a clean room with private shower is US$14.

Camping The *Fifi Mocamp* (tel (181) 11554), E-5 Karayolu, Demirkapı Mevkii, 22100 Edirne, is eight km east of town on the İstanbul road, and is open from April to mid-October. It has a full range of hook-ups and services for tents and caravans, and even a few motel rooms available for rent the year round.

Places to Stay – middle

Were you to ask any Edirneli the name of the best hotel in town, they would no doubt answer with the name of the two-star, 80-room *Balta Hotel* (tel (181) 15210), Talat Paşa Caddesi, 22100 Edirne, half way from the bus terminal to Hürriyet Meydanı. This is where the important business executives and government officials stay. It does offer the town's newest and most comfortable rooms, a bar, restaurant and similar two-star services, but it has the disadvantage of being several km from Hürriyet Meydanı, facing a noisy street. Rooms are priced at US$26 a single, US$36 a double with breakfast included.

A more convenient choice is the 83-room *Sultan Oteli* (tel (181) 11372; fax 15763), Talat Paşa Caddesi 170, 22100 Edirne. It's several decades old but very nicely renovated. The advantages here are two-star comforts just off Hürriyet Meydanı across the street from the Tourism Information Office. The Sultan has a restaurant and bar and a clientele that's a mix of Turkish and foreign, tourist and business travellers. Rooms are priced at US$25 a single, US$32 a double.

Less posh, but still quite comfortable, very quiet and less expensive is the *Park Hotel* (tel (181) 14610), Maarif Caddesi 7, 22100 Edirne, down the end of this street of bottom-end lodgings which starts behind the Tourism Information Office. Though this hotel does not face a park, it's still quiet, clean, comfortable and convenient. Rooms cost US$22 a single, US$28 a double for a room with bath, breakfast included; rooms with only a washbasin go for US$16 a single, US$22 a double.

The *Kervan Oteli* (tel (181) 11382) on Talat Paşa Caddesi, Kadirhane Sokak 134, 22100 Edirne, was the city's prime place to stay several decades ago. Even though it is now a bit faded and old-fashioned, it still provides comfortable and convenient rooms with bath for US$30 a double in summer, and less in the off season. They have a car park, a good restaurant and a front terrace with beverage service.

The most intriguing place to stay is undoubtedly the *Hotel Rüstempaşa Kervansaray* (tel (181) 12195), Eski Cami Yanı, 22100 Edirne, to the right of the Eski Cami beyond the dolmuş lot. The hotel's name means 'Caravanserai of Rüstem Paşa'. The eponymous Rüstem Paşa was a grand vizier of Süleyman the Magnificent who ordered the caravanserai be built in the mid-1500s. The camel caravans on the road between Europe, İstanbul and points further east rested here for the night, their valuable freight safe within the building's massive stone walls and great armoured doors.

Several decades ago the caravanserai was renovated and turned into a hotel for a tourist boom that has yet to arrive; tourists come to Edirne in twos and threes, not by the busload. Though the rooms are comfortable enough and certainly atmospheric, it is the hotel's nightclub which brings in the profit. The club can be noisy, which can make the rooms less than suitable; so if you stay here, get a quiet room. The price is US$44 a double, breakfast included.

Places to Eat

The hotels have the best dining rooms in town, and it may be possible to spend from US$8 to US$10 per person for a meal in one. In the rest of Edirne, it's very difficult to spend that much on dinner.

My longtime favourite is the *Aile Restaurant*, Saraçlar Caddesi, Belediye İş Hanı. To find it, walk south from Hürriyet Meydanı along Saraçlar Caddesi, looking for the building named Belediye İş Hanı on the left-hand side; it's just past the PTT. The entrance is on the side street by the post office. Climb the stairs to the upper level where you'll find a pleasant, if simple, dining room with windows overlooking Saraçlar Caddesi. This is perhaps the longest established restaurant in town: it has been serving food for decades; the waiters are efficient and experienced, the food good and the prices low. Kebaps, stews and other traditional Turkish dishes are served, and a meal need cost no more than US$4 or US$5 per person. If you need help deciding what to have, just go to the kitchen and point.

On the opposite side of the PTT from the Aile is the *Café M Restaurant* (tel 23448), Saraçlar Caddesi, Vakıf İş Hanı, on the upper floor of a building named the Vakıf İş Hanı. Actually, there are two establishments here: the Café Muharipler (Veterans' Café), and the Café M Restaurant. The first is a typical no-nonsense Turkish teahouse, always filled with men and smoke. The second is the genteel gathering-place of Edirne's young, well-dressed and upwardly-mobile types. The decor is white: little café tables, bentwood chairs and wall benches. The menu features snacks and confections, coffee, tea and soft drinks. You can have an omelette, a sausage plate, chips or some other light fare for about US$3, with a drink included.

For simple, tasty fare at simple, low prices, stop in at a kebap or köfte place on Saraçlar Caddesi or anywhere else in town for that matter. Side by side on Saraçlar Caddesi, a few steps from Hürriyet Meydanı just past the park, are the *Rümeli Köftecisi* and the *Serhad Köftecisi*, two plain little places selling those good grilled Turkish meatballs with yoghurt, salad, bread and drink for US$2 or so. Down the street a bit farther, just past the PTT but on the opposite (right-hand) side of the street, is the *Şark Kebap ve Lahmacun*, a tiny, very basic place with a few tables downstairs and a few more upstairs in the aile salonu. I had a filling meal of soup, pide with cheese (Turkish pizza), salad, a soft drink and a glass of tea for US$3.25. The pide was freshly made and delicious.

Getting There & Away

Border Posts Edirne has both Bulgarian and Greek consulates – ask at the tourist office and they'll give you details. You can get a Bulgarian transit visa here fairly easily. It's good for 30 hours (enough time to travel through) and costs about US$8.

There are two frontier crossing-points on the outskirts of Edirne. On the E5 highway from Svilengrad, Bulgaria, you come to the busy border post of Kapıkule. After the formalities, you enter the town by crossing the Tunca at the Gazi Mihal bridge and passing some fragments of Byzantine city walls. The red-and-cream city bus No 1 runs along the route from Kapıkule to the Eski Cami; there are dolmuşes on this route as well, but both are infrequent in early morning and late at night. By the way, you may not be allowed to walk to the border on the Bulgarian side; you may be required to hitch a ride or rent a taxi.

From Greece, the major road goes to Kastaneai (Greece) and Pazarkule (Turkey), south-west of Edirne on the Maritsa (Meriç, mehr-EECH) River, to a border post originally meant to serve the railway line. The frontier, as determined at the Treaty of Lausanne (1923), left the Turkish line passing through Greece on its way to Edirne! A bypass line was built in the 1970s, though. The problem here is that the Greeks have declared the border area a military zone and do not permit anyone to walk in it without a military escort, so you will probably have to take a taxi to the actual border. On the Turkish side, you can walk to Pazarkule.

From Pazarkule, or from the nearby railway station, you will probably have to take a taxi into town as there is not much traffic and hitching is not too easy, though you may be lucky.

Road The E5 highway between Europe and İstanbul follows very closely the ancient road which connected Rome and Constantinople. It follows the river valleys past Niš and Sofia, on between the mountain ranges of the Stara and Rhodopi to Plovdiv, and cruises along the Maritsa riverbank into Edirne which stands alone on the gently undulating plain, snuggled into a bend of the Tunca River. After Edirne, the road heads out into the rolling, steppe-like terrain of eastern Thrace toward İstanbul.

Bus Inter-city buses operate very frequently throughout the day (about every 20 minutes or so) and take four hours to make the 235-km journey to İstanbul; tickets cost between US$3 and US$3.50. In Edirne, buses operate out of the city's Otobüs Garajı on the outskirts of town. Take a city bus or dolmuş from the Eski Cami to get to the Otobüs Garajı.

Along the way, the bus will stop in Lüleburgaz and Çorlu before joining the new motorway into İstanbul.

The terminus in İstanbul is the Topkapı Otogar, the big bus station just outside the city walls at Topkapı gate, on the E5 highway (also called the Londra Asfaltı). When the new bus station at Esenler is completed, this will no doubt be the terminus.

Train You may be coming to Turkey by train, in which case you will probably be ready for a break. Except for the luxurious tour group re-creation of the Orient Express (Paris to İstanbul costs US$5000 one-way), rail service is slow and tedious. The international train can take another six to 10 hours to reach İstanbul. Get off. Don't miss Edirne. (The train may only stop at the Kapıkule border station, not the Edirne city station – ask the conductor to be sure).

The service between Edirne and İstanbul is slow and inconvenient. The train leaves İstanbul at 3.50 pm, arriving in Edirne at 10 pm. From Edirne, the train departs for İstanbul at 8 am, arriving at 2.45 pm. The railway station is out of town, reachable by dolmuş, bus or taxi. Tickets on the Edirne to İstanbul run cost US$2 one-way, with a 10% discount for students. You'd be better off taking the bus.

It's interesting to note that the original Midnight Express ran between İstanbul and Edirne through Greece. When the Ottoman Empire collapsed, the new Turkish-Greek border was drawn so that the old rail line was partly in Greece. Greek border police would board when the train entered Greek territory and get off when it re-entered Turkish territory. There used to be a slow, late-night train on this run. Foreigners convicted of drug-related offences in Turkey would be released by the Turkish government while their convictions were being appealed. They'd be given all of their possessions except their passports, and told in a whisper about the 'Midnight Express.'

They'd climb aboard and jump off the train in Greece, where Greek border police would pick them up and jail them. They'd call their consulate, arrange for a new passport, be let out of jail and sent on their way. This system allowed the Turkish government to meet foreign governments' demands that it be strict with drug smugglers, but it avoided the expense and bother of actually incarcerating the convicted smugglers. In the late 1970s, the Turkish State Railways built a bypass line and the Greek corridor route was abandoned. The truth of the Midnight Express is quite different from that portrayed in the blatantly anti-Turkish movie of the same name.

If you've come from İstanbul, it might make sense to head due south after looking around Edirne and go directly to the Dardanelles and Troy. Buses do not run frequently on this route, and by doing this you miss the ferry cruise across the Sea of Marmara as well as the delightful cities of İznik, ancient Nicaea and Bursa, the first Ottoman capital. So if you've got the time, head back to İstanbul and catch a ferry to Yalova, first stop on your explorations of the south Marmara shore.

South of the Sea of Marmara

The southern shore of the Sea of Marmara is a land of small villages surrounded by olive groves, orchards, sunflower fields, rolling hills and rich valleys. During the time of the Ottoman Empire the choice olives for the sultan's table came from here, as did snow to cool his drinks. The latter came from the slopes of Bursa's Uludağ (the Bithynian Mt Olympus). The region's few cities are of moderate size, but of significant interest to visitors.

You can enjoy this region and its sights in only two days: catch an early ferry from İstanbul to Yalova, make a quick tour of İznik (the ancient city of Nicaea) and spend the night in Bursa. After seeing the sights of Bursa, the next morning catch a bus westward to Çanakkale. You'll reach that town on the Dardanelles in time for a late supper. But three days is a more realistic time in which to see all there is to see.

If you have another day, you can truly enjoy the Marmara's southern shore. Plan to spend most of your extra time in Bursa, where the mosques and museums are particularly fine (this was the Ottomans' first capital city, before Edirne and İstanbul). You can even bask in hot mineral baths at Çekirge, a spa suburb, and take the cablecar to the top of Uludağ, which is snow-capped for most of the year, and offers skiing in winter.

If you must, you can rocket down to Bursa from İstanbul just for the day. But this means a lot of travel time for only a few hours' sightseeing, when the city really deserves an overnight stay.

On your way to Bursa, you will probably pass through the Sea of Marmara port of Yalova.

YALOVA

This small town (pronounced YAH-loh-vah) with a population of 60,000, is a

farming and transportation centre. The highway between the industrial cities of Bursa and İzmit (not to be confused with İznik) passes near here, as does the ferry/bus link between Bursa and İstanbul. It's a pleasant enough town, with a few modest hotels and restaurants, most within two blocks of the ferry dock. Everything else you'd need is here as well, including banks, chemists/drugstores, etc. The market area is a short stroll straight from the wharf.

Other than these few amusements, there's nothing to detain you in Yalova. You can plan to head for the spa at Termal, the ancient city of İznik or booming Bursa without delay.

Getting There & Away

Bus On arrival in Yalova, disembark from the ferry, and as you walk from the wharf you will see a traffic circle centred on an enormous statue of Atatürk. Just off the dock, look to the left. You'll see rows of buses and minibuses. Approach them, and a man will approach you to find out where you're going. Say 'İznik' (EEZ-neek) or 'Bursa' (BOOR-sah) as the case may be, and he'll lead you to a waiting minibus. Be certain that your bus is going to İznik, not İzmit, which is a different city entirely. Climb in and find a seat. In a few minutes the bus will be full and will set off. The fare is US$1.50 to İznik, US$2 to Bursa, and it will be collected en route.

Yalova city bus No 4 (Taşköprü-Termal) will take you to Termal for US$0.25; a dolmuş charges US$0.35. Both leave from a parking area only a block from the ferry dock. Coming off the ferry, walk to the traffic circle with the statue and turn right, walk a block and the parking area is on the left.

Boat To reach Yalova, Termal, İznik and Bursa from İstanbul, most people choose the express ferries across the Sea of Marmara. An alternative method, involving less expense but more time and bother, is to take the car ferry from Kartal. If you miss the express ferry, consider taking the car ferry which, though a bit slower, leaves more often. Least often (only once a day) a hydrofoil departs İstanbul for the port of Mudanya on the south shore of the Sea of Marmara. From Mudanya, buses take you to Bursa.

The best and most enjoyable way to get to Bursa is by express ferry across the Sea of Marmara. The ferries depart Eminönü Dock 5 (near Sirkeci) daily. Check the schedules for times and frequency, as this changes often.

The voyage takes about two hours if there are no stops, and costs US$1.50 for a one-way ticket. Board the boat *at least* a half-hour before departure time (45 minutes or an hour is not too early in summer) if you want to be assured of a seat.

Whether you have a car or not, you can take a car ferry as part of your travel to Yalova. Take the passenger ferry from Karaköy to Haydarpaşa Station, then take any banliyö train (US$0.20) as far as Kartal. The trains begin at 6 am and run every 20 minutes (until around midnight); the journey from Haydarpaşa to Kartal takes about 40 minutes. Leave the train at Kartal Station and walk downhill to the shore and left to the car-ferry dock. Purchase a ticket (US$0.75 single), then board one of the ferries which depart every hour on the hour (except 2 and 4 am). The voyage takes 1¼ hours and lands you right in Yalova. (If you don't want to bother with the train, you can take a taxi from İstanbul to Kartal for about US$6.)

Return car-ferry voyages from Yalova are at the same times and prices as those from Kartal.

TERMAL

Twelve km west of Yalova, off the road to Çınarcık, is Termal (tehr-MAHL), a spa. The baths here take advantage of hot, mineral-rich waters that gush from the earth and were first exploited in Roman times. The Ottomans used the baths from the 1500s and Abdül Hamid II repaired and refurbished them in 1900 to celebrate the 25th anniversary of his accession to the throne.

He had the work done in the wonderfully gaudy Ottoman Baroque style. Atatürk added a simple but comfortable spa hotel, where time seems to stand still: at luncheon you may still hear a violin-and-piano duo play a lilting rendition of 'Santa Lucia', as though the great Turkish leader were resting and taking the waters here, as he did in the 1930s. You can come just to stroll through the shady gardens and have a look at the facilities, or you can come to bathe or stay the night.

Things to See

The gardens and greenery at Termal are worth the trip. But then there are the baths. At the Valide Banyo you get a locker for your clothes, then take a shower and enter a pool. An admission charge of US$1 or so gets you 1½ hours of bathing. Soap and shampoo cost extra, so bring your own. The Sultan Banyo is even grander and much pricier at US$3 a single, US$4 a double; you can rent a swimsuit here. The Kurşunlu Banyo features an open-air pool for US$2, an enclosed pool and sauna for US$2.50, and small private cubicles for US$2/2.50 a single/double.

Atatürk had a small house here, which is now a museum you can visit.

Places to Stay – bottom end

The villages several km from the centre of Termal have numerous modest little pensions charging from US$3 to US$5 per person for rooms with and without running water. The only problem with these places is that they are a long walk from the baths. You may find yourself hitchhiking in, or waiting for the infrequent buses and dolmuşes.

Places to Stay – top end

Though fairly simple, befitting a health resort, the two hotels here are extremely pleasant, but both are in the upper price range. The *Turban Yalova Termal Hotel* (tel 4905) and the *Çınar Oteli* (same telephone) charge from US$40 to US$55 a single, US$45 to US$60 a double, the price depends on whether the room is at the front or the back of the hotel; breakfast is included in these high-season summer prices. Off-season rates are 25% to 30% lower, but do not include breakfast.

Places to Eat

Termal has several restaurants and cafés, but all are fairly pricey. A cup of Nescafé, for example, costs around US$1.

İZNİK

The road from Yalova to İznik, home to 16,000 people, runs along fertile green hills punctuated by tall, spiky cypress trees, passing peach orchards, cornfields and vineyards. The journey of 60 km takes about 1½ hours.

As you approach İznik you may notice fruit-packing plants among the orchards. You will certainly have admired the vast *İznik Gölü*, or İznik Lake. Watch for the great Byzantine city walls: the road passes through the old İstanbul Kapısı (İstanbul Gate) and then becomes Atatürk Caddesi, and leads to the ruined Sancta Sophia Church (now a museum) in the very centre of town. The otogar is a few blocks south-east of the church.

History

This ancient city may well have been founded around 1000 BC. We know for sure that it was revitalised by one of Alexander the Great's generals in 316 BC.

Another of the generals, Lysimachus, soon got hold of it and named it for his wife Nikaea. It became the capital city of the province of Bithynia.

Nicaea lost some of its prominence with the founding of Nicomedia (today's İzmit) in 264 BC, and by 74 BC the entire area had been incorporated into the Roman Empire.

Nicaea flourished under Rome; the emperors built a new system of walls, plus temples, theatres and baths. But invasions by the Goths and the Persians brought ruin by 300 AD.

Ecumenical Councils With the rise of Constantinople, Nicaea took on a new importance. In 325, the First Ecumenical Council was held here to condemn the heresy of Arianism. During the great Justinian's reign, Nicaea was grandly refurbished and embellished with new buildings and defences, which served the city well a few centuries later when the Arabs invaded. Like Constantinople, Nicaea never fell to its Arab besiegers.

In 787 yet another Ecumenical Council, the 7th, was held in Nicaea's Sancta

Sophia Church. The deliberations solved the problem of iconoclasm: henceforth it would be church policy not to destroy icons. Theologians who saw icons as 'images', prohibited by the Bible, were dismayed. But Byzantine artists were delighted, and went to work on their art with even more vigour.

Nicaea and Constantinople did, however, fall to the Crusaders. During the period from 1204 to 1261 when a Latin king sat on the throne of Byzantium, the true Byzantine emperor Theodore Lascaris reigned over the 'Empire of Nicaea'. When the Crusaders cleared out, the emperor moved his court back to the traditional capital.

The Turks The Seljuk Turks had a flourishing empire in Central Anatolia before 1250, and various tribes of nomadic warriors had circulated near the walls of Nicaea during those times. In fact, Turkish soldiers had served as mercenaries in the interminable battles which raged among rival claimants to the Byzantine throne. At one point, a Byzantine battle over Nicaea ended with a Turkish emir as its ruler!

It was Orhan, son of Osman and first true sultan (1326-1361) of the Ottoman Empire, who conquered İznik on 2 March 1331. The city soon had the honour of harbouring the first Ottoman college. Proussa (Bursa) had fallen to the Ottomans on 6 April 1326, and became their first capital city. In 1337 they took Nicomedia and effectively blocked the Byzantines from entering Anatolia.

Sultan Selim I (1512-1520), a mighty conqueror nicknamed 'The Grim', rolled his armies over Azerbaijan in 1514 and took the Persian city of Tabriz. Packing up all of the region's artisans, he sent them westward to İznik. They brought with them a high level of expertise in the making of coloured tiles. Soon İznik's kilns were turning out faïence which is unequalled even today. The great period of İznik faïence continued almost to 1700.

At one point, artisans were sent to Tunisia, then an Ottoman possession, to begin a high-quality faïence industry there.

The art of coloured tile-making is being revived in İznik today; you can buy some good examples at moderate prices in the shops. Be aware that true İznik tiles from the great period are considered antiquities, and cannot legally be exported from Turkey.

Orientation

In İznik the famous Sancta Sophia Church is at the very centre, a good vantage-point from which to consider the town's classical Roman layout: two dead-straight boulevards, north-south (Atatürk Caddesi) and east-west (Kılıçaslan Caddesi), leading to the four principal gates in the city walls. To the north is the İstanbul Kapısı, to the south is the Yenişehir Kapısı, to the east is Lefke Kapısı and to the west, the Göl Kapısı. More details about the walls and gates follow.

Information

İznik's Tourism Information Office (tel (2527) 1933) is on the main east-west street, Kılıçaslan Caddesi 168, east of Sancta Sophia – follow the signs. Hours are from 8.30 am to 12 noon and from 2 to 5.30 pm every day in the warm months, with shorter hours during the off-season.

Sancta Sophia

Start your sightseeing in the centre of town, at the Sancta Sophia Church or Church of the Divine Wisdom.

Sancta Sophia is open from 9 am to 12 noon and from 2 to 5 pm daily, closed Monday. If there's no one about when you visit, continue with your tour. The key is probably at the museum. After visiting there, ask to be let into the church.

This former church is hardly striking in its grandeur, but it has a fascinating past. What you see is the ruin of three different buildings. Inside you can inspect a mosaic

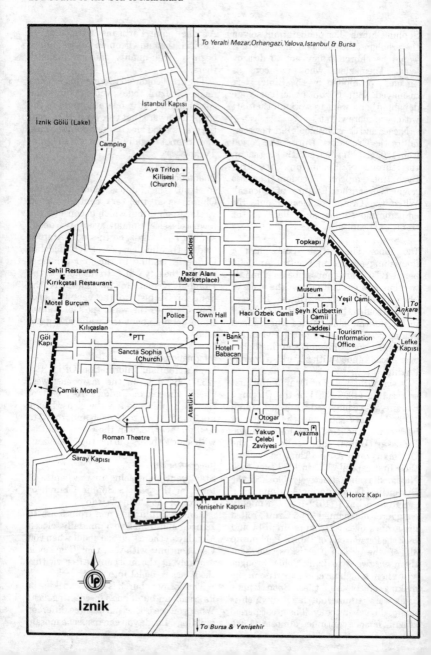

To Yeralti Mezar,Orhangazi,Yalova,Istanbul & Bursa

İznik Gölü (Lake)

İstanbul Kapısı

Camping

Aya Trifon
Kilisesi
(Church)

Caddesi

Topkapı

Pazar Alanı
(Marketplace)

Museum

Yeşil Cami

Sahil Restaurant

Kırıkçatal Restaurant

Motel Burçum

Şeyh Kutbettin
Camii

To
Ankara

Kılıçaslan

Police

Town Hall

Hacı Özbek Camii

Caddesi

Tourism
Information
Office

Göl
Kapı

PTT

Bank

Lefke
Kapısı

Sancta Sophia
(Church)

Hotel
Babacan

Çamlik Motel

Atatürk

Otogar

Roman Theatre

Yakup
Çelebi
Zaviyesi

Ayazma

Saray Kapısı

Horoz Kapı

Yenişehir Kapısı

İznik

To Bursa & Yenişehir

floor and a mural of Jesus with Mary and John the Baptist which date from the time of Justinian (500s). That original church was destroyed by earthquake in 1065 but later rebuilt. Mosaics were set into the walls at that time. With the Ottoman conquest (1331), the church became a mosque. A fire in the 1500s ruined everything, but reconstruction was carried out under the expert eye of Mimar Sinan, who added İznik tiles to the decoration.

Behind Sancta Sophia is the II Murat Hamamı, also called the Hacı Hamza Hamamı, a Turkish bath constructed during the reign of Sultan Murat II, in the first half of the 15th century. It's still in operation.

The Main Street
Now walk east toward Lefke Kapısı (Lefke Gate), along İznik's main street, Kılıçaslan Caddesi. On the left is the Belediye Sarayı or Town Hall, with a sign out the front that reads (in Turkish) 'Our motto is, Clean City, Green City'. It really is a very pleasant, quiet, peaceful and agreeable place with its big poplars shading the commercial district from the summer sun.

A bit farther along on the left is the Hacı Özbek Camii, one of the town's oldest mosques, dating from 1332.

A short detour along the street opposite the Hacı Özbek Camii, to the south, will bring you to the Süleyman Paşa Medresesi. Founded by Sultan Orhan shortly after he captured Nicaea, it has the distinction of being the very first college (actually a theological seminary) founded by a member of the Ottoman dynasty.

Back on the main street, you will come to the Tourism Information Office on the right-hand side. Soon, to the left, you can see the tile-covered minaret of the Yeşil Cami.

Yeşil Cami
Built in the year that Columbus discovered America (1492), the Yeşil Cami or Green Mosque has Seljuk Turkish proportions influenced more by Persia (the Seljuk homeland) than by İstanbul. The green-glazed bricks of the minaret foreshadowed the tile industry that arose a few decades after the mosque was built. Sultan Selim, impatient to have a tile industry of his own, simply moved a large number of artisans from Tabriz.

Museum
Across the road from the Yeşil Cami is the Nilüfer Hatun İmareti or Soup Kitchen of Lady Nilüfer (1388), now set up as the town's museum. Hours are from 9 am to 12 noon and from 1.30 to 5 pm, closed Monday. Admission is US$0.50. I'll wager that Lady Nilüfer would be pleased to see her pious gift in its present state. Though intended as a place where the poor could come for free food, it now dispenses culture to the masses. The front court is filled with marble statuary, bits of cornice and column, and similar archaeological flotsam and jetsam. In the lofty, cool halls are exhibits of İznik faïence, Ottoman weaponry, embroidery and calligraphy. Many of the little signs are in French and English, but you'll need to know the word *yüzyıl* – 'century', as in 'XVI Yüzyıl', '16th century'.

While at the museum, inquire about a visit to the Byzantine tomb Yeraltı Mezar or Katakom on the outskirts of town. You must have a museum official accompany you with the key; there is a small charge for admission, and the official should receive a small tip. Also, you will have to haggle with a taxi-driver for a return-trip price. But once these arrangements have been made, you're in for a treat. The little tomb, discovered by accident in the 1960s, has delightful Byzantine murals covering walls and ceiling. There is another tomb nearby, but it's not really worth the bother or expense to see.

Across the road to the south of the museum is the Şeyh Kutbettin Camii (1492), now undergoing restoration.

City Walls

Go back to Kılıçaslan Caddesi and continue east to the **Lefke Kapısı**. This charming old monument is actually three gates in a row, all dating from Byzantine times. The middle one has an inscription which tells us it was built by Proconsul Plancius Varus in 123 AD. It's possible to clamber up to the top of the gate and the walls here, a good vantage-point for inspecting the ancient walls.

Outside the gate is an aqueduct, and the tomb of Çandarlı Halil Hayrettin Paşa (late 1300s), with the graves of many lesser mortals nearby.

Lefke, by the way, is now called Osmaneli. In Byzantine times it was a city of considerable size, though now it's just a small town.

Re-enter the city through the Lefke Kapısı, and turn left. Follow the walls south and west to the **Yenişehir Kapısı**. On the way you will pass near the ruined **Church of the Koimesis**, which dates from about 800. Only some bits of the foundation remain, but it is famous as the burial-place of the Byzantine emperor, Theodore I Lascaris. When the Crusaders took Constantinople in 1204, Lascaris fled to Nicaea and established his court here. He never made it back to his beloved capital. When the court did move back to Constantinople in 1261, it was under the guidance of Michael VIII Palaeologus. By the way, it was Lascaris who built the outer ring of walls, supported by over 100 towers and protected by a wide moat. No doubt he didn't trust the Crusaders, having lost one city to them.

Near the church is an ayazma (*aghiasma*) or **sacred fountain**, also called a *yeralt çeşme* (underground spring).

After admiring the Yenişehir Kapısı, start toward the centre along Atatürk Caddesi. Halfway to Sancta Sophia, a road on the left leads to the ruins of a Roman theatre. Nearby is the **Saray Kapısı** or Palace Gate in the city walls. Sultan Orhan had a palace near here in the 1300s.

The Lake

Make your way to the lakeshore where there's a bathing beach (the water tends to be chilly except in high summer), teahouses and little restaurants. This is the place to rest your feet, and have an ice cream, soft drink or glass of tea, and ponder the history of battles which raged around this city. It is obviously much better off as a sleepy fruit-growing centre.

Places to Stay – bottom end

İznik has a few modest hostelries good for a one-night stay. In the centre, just across the street from the Town Hall, is the plain *Hotel Babacan* (tel 1211) at Kılıçaslan Caddesi 104. Thirty of the rooms come with washbasins and are priced at US$7/9 a single/double. With private shower, the prices are US$9 and US$12, respectively.

Camping Both of the following places have very basic camping areas.

Places to Stay – middle

Motel Burcum (tel 1011) has tidy rooms, some with views of the lake, for US$15 a double, breakfast included. Get a room on the 2nd or 3rd floor if you want that view.

The tidy *Çamlık Motel* (CHAHM-luhk) (tel 1631) at the southern end of the lakefront road, has nice rooms and a pretty restaurant, with prices similar to those at the Burcum.

Places to Eat

The lakeside restaurants are the most pleasant for a light meal, if the weather is fine. A snack of white cheese (beyaz peynir), bread and a bottle of beer will cost less than US$2, full meals will cost more because of the beautiful location. Of the restaurants along the lakeshore, the *Dostlar* (tel 1585) is perhaps the busiest; it's near the Motel Burcum. Readers have liked the *Dallas Restaurant*, across from the Çamlık Motel, as well. Yes, it is named after the TV series.

You'll find a greater selection of hot

dishes along the main street in the centre, though. Near the Town Hall, look for the *Köşk* and *Çiçek* restaurants, facing one another across the main street. The Çiçek serves no alcohol; the Köşk (tel 1843) perhaps has the edge in terms of attractiveness. At either place, a very filling meal can be had for US$4 or less.

Another choice near the Town Hall is the *İnegöl*. It specialises in İnegöl köftesi, rich grilled rissoles of ground lamb in the style used in the nearby town of İnegöl.

There are also several pastahanes hereabouts, including the *Saray Pastanesi*, good for breakfast or a snack.

Things to Buy
Coloured tiles, of course, are the natural souvenir from İznik. Several small shops along the main street sell these. There is also embroidery, a local cottage industry.

Getting There & Away
Bursa has a much better selection of hotels and restaurants than does İznik. Unless you are unusually interested in İznik, take one of the hourly buses from İznik's otogar to Bursa. Don't wait until too late in the day, however, as the last bus heads out at 6 or 7 pm on the 1½-hour trip. A ticket costs US$1.75.

BURSA
Bursa, with a population of one million, has a special place in the hearts of the Turks. It was the first capital city of the enormous Ottoman Empire and, in a real sense, the birthplace of modern Turkish culture. The city, at an altitude of 155 metres, has its pretty parts despite its industrial base.

History
Called Prusa by the Byzantines, Bursa is a very old and important city. It was founded – according to legend, by Prusias, king of Bithynia – before 200 BC; there may have been an even older settlement on the site. It soon came under the sway of

Eumenes II of Pergamum, and thereafter under direct Roman control.

Bursa grew to importance in the early centuries of Christianity, when the thermal baths at Çekirge were first developed on a large scale and when a silk trade was founded here. The importation of silkworms and the establishment of looms began an industry which survives to this day. It was Justinian (527-565) who really put Bursa on the map. Besides favouring the silk trade, he built a palace for himself and bathhouses in Çekirge.

With the decline of Byzantium, Bursa's location near İstanbul drew the interest of would-be conquerors, including the Arab armies (circa 700 AD) and the Seljuk Turks. The Seljuks, having conquered much of Anatolia by 1075, took Bursa with ease that same year, and planted the seeds of the great Ottoman Empire to come.

With the arrival of the First Crusade in 1097, Bursa reverted to Christian hands, though it was to be conquered and reconquered by both sides for the next 100 years. When the rapacious armies of the Fourth Crusade sacked Constantinople in 1204, the Byzantine emperor fled to İznik and set up his capital there. He succeeded in controlling the hinterland of İznik, including Bursa, until he moved back to Constantinople in 1261.

Ever since the Turkish migration into Anatolia during the 11th and 12th centuries, small principalities had risen here and there around Turkish military leaders. A *gazi* (warrior chieftain or 'Hero of the Faith') would rally a group of followers, gain control of a territory, govern it and seek to expand its borders. One such prince was Ertuğrul Gazi (died 1281), who formed a small state near Bursa. Under the rule of his son Osman Gazi (1281-1326) the small state grew to a nascent empire and took Osman's name (*Osmanlı*, 'Ottoman'). Bursa was besieged by Osman's forces in 1317 and was finally starved into submission on 6 April 1326 when it immediately became the Ottoman capital.

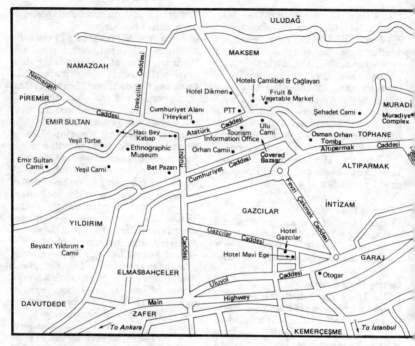

After Osman had expanded and enriched his principality, he was succeeded by Orhan Gazi (1326-1361) who, from his base at Bursa, expanded the empire to include everything from Ankara in Central Anatolia to Thrace in Europe. The Byzantine capital at Constantinople was thus surrounded, and the Byzantine Empire had only about a century to survive. Orhan took the title of *sultan* (lord), struck the first Ottoman coinage and near the end of his reign was able to dictate to the Byzantine emperors. One of them John VI Cantacuzene was Orhan's close ally and later even his father-in-law (Orhan married the Princess Theodora).

Even though the Ottoman capital moved to Adrianople (Edirne) in 1402, Bursa remained an important, even revered, Ottoman city throughout the long history of the empire. Both Osman and Orhan were buried there; their tombs

are still proud, important monuments in Turkish history.

With the founding of the Turkish Republic, Bursa's industrial development began in earnest. What really brought the boom was the automobile assembly plants, set up in the 1960s and 1970s. Large factories here assemble Renaults, Fiats (called Murat) and a Turkish car called the Anadol. Also, Bursa has always been noted for its fruits; it was logical that a large fruit juice and soft drink industry should be centred here. Tourism is also important.

Orientation

Bursa clings to the slopes of Uludağ and spills down into the fertile valley. The major boulevards are Uluyol and Atatürk Caddesi, which run across the slope, not up and down it.

Bursa's main square is Cumhuriyet

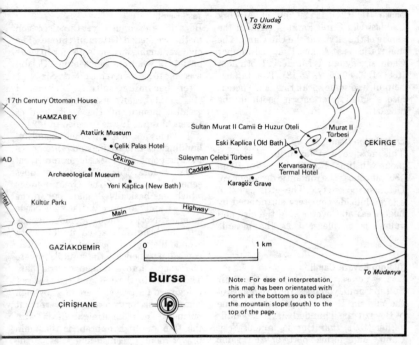

To Uludağ 33 km

17th Century Ottoman House

HAMZABEY

Atatürk Museum
• Çelik Palas Hotel
Çekirge

AD

Archaeological Museum
Yeni Kaplica (New Bath)

Kültür Parkı

Main   Highway

GAZİAKDEMİR

Bursa

ÇİRİŞHANE

Sultan Murat II Camii & Huzur Oteli
Eski Kaplica (Old Bath)
Süleyman Çelebi Türbesi
Caddesi
Karagöz Grave

Murat II
Türbesi

ÇEKİRGE

Kervansaray
Termal Hotel

0   1 km

To Mudanya

Note: For ease of interpretation, this map has been orientated with north at the bottom so as to place the mountain slope (south) to the top of the page.

Alanı (joom-hoor-ee-YEHT ah-lahn-uh, Republic Square), where you will see an equestrian statue of Atatürk. Most people refer to the square as Heykel (hey-KEHL, statue), and that's what you will see written on a little plastic sign in the windscreens of dolmuşes waiting just outside the otogar. Hop in a dolmuş to get up the hill to Heykel.

Bursa's main street, Atatürk Caddesi, runs west from Heykel to the Ulu Cami (oo-LOO jah-mee, Great Mosque), a distance of perhaps half a km. This is the business section, the centre of Bursa. The westward continuation of Atatürk Caddesi becomes Cemal Nadir Caddesi, then Altıparmak Caddesi, then Çekirge Caddesi. It leads to the spa suburb of Çekirge, about a 10-minute ride.

You can see most of Bursa's sights in one full day, though a leisurely tour will take a little more time. Start with the city's most famous architectural monuments, located east of the city centre.

Bursa's most famous mosque is the Yeşil Cami. Past it, up a hill on the same road, is the Emir Sultan Camii. The way to see these sights is to hop on a bus or dolmuş departing Heykel (look for them on a side street 100 metres west of the square) or Atatürk Caddesi and bound for Emir Sultan. Get off at the end of the line. You'll pass by the Yeşil Cami and Yeşil Türbe before coming to the Emir Sultan Camii, but this way you can walk *down* the hill, not up.

From Heykel and Atatürk Caddesi you can get dolmuşes and buses to all other parts of the city, including hotel and sightseeing areas.

Information

The Tourism Information Office has a

booth (tel (24) 11 29 59) at Atatürk Caddesi Ulu Cami Parkı 7, right in the centre of the city near the Ulu Cami. The main office is at Ahmet Hamdi Tanpınar Caddesi, Saydam İş Merkezi 21, 5th floor (tel (24) 22 80 05, 22 75 13). The staff are helpful, and some speak English. There is also a small information booth in the otogar.

Emir Sultan Camii

This mosque is a favourite of Bursa's pious Muslims. Rebuilt by Selim III in 1805, it echoes the romantic decadence of Ottoman rococo style. The setting, next to a large hillside cemetery surrounded by huge trees and overlooking the city and valley, is as pleasant as the mosque itself.

Yıldırım Beyazıt Camii

Gazing across the valley from the Emir Sultan Camii, you'll see the two domes of the Yıldırım Beyazıt Camii, the Mosque of Beyazıt the Thunderbolt. It was built earlier (1391) than Bursa's famous Yeşil Cami, and forms part of the same architectural evolution. You can walk through the city to this mosque if you like, but go and see the Yeşil Cami first.

Next to the Yıldırım Beyazıt Camii is its medrese, once a theological seminary, now a public health centre. Here also are the tombs of the mosque's founder, Sultan Beyazıt I, and his son İsa. This peaceful spot gives one no sense of the turbulent times which brought Beyazıt to his death.

Yıldırım Beyazıt (Sultan Beyazıt I, 1389-1402) led his Ottoman armies into Yugoslavia and Hungary, and captured even more of Anatolia for the Ottomans. But he was brought down by Tamerlane, who defeated him and took him prisoner at the Battle of Ankara in 1402. Beyazıt died a year later in captivity, and Tamerlane marched all the way to İzmir and Bursa. The empire was just about finished.

Yeşil Cami

Beyazıt's sons argued over the succession to the weakened Ottoman throne. The civil war amongst them lasted for 10 years until 1413, when one son, Mehmet Çelebi, was able to gain supreme power. Six years after becoming sultan, Mehmet I (1413-1421) began construction of Bursa's greatest monument, the Yeşil Cami or Green Mosque. It was finished in 1424.

The mosque is a supremely beautiful building in a fine setting and represents a turning-point in Turkish architectural style. Before this, Turkish mosques echoed the style of the Great Seljuks which was basically Persian, but in the Yeşil Cami a purely Turkish style emerges. Notice the harmonious facade and the beautiful carved marble work around the central doorway. As you enter, you will pass beneath the sultan's private apartments into a domed central hall. The rooms to the left and right, if not being used for prayer, were used by high court officials for transacting government business. The room straight ahead, with the 15-metre-high mihrab, is the main prayer room. Greenish-blue tiles on the interior walls gave the mosque its name.

Much of Bursa, including the Yeşil Cami, was destroyed in an earthquake in 1855 but the mosque was restored, authentically, by 1864.

Just inside the mosque's main entrance, a narrow stairway leads up to the **hünkâr mahfili** or sultan's loge, above the main door. The loge is sumptuously tiled and decorated. This is where the sultan actually lived (or at least it was one of his residences), with his harem and household staff in less plush quarters on either side. The caretaker used to choose single travellers or couples, give them a conspiratorial wink, and lead them up for a peek, after which he would receive a tip. Somebody higher up must have caught on, as he no longer seems to be doing it.

Yeşil Türbe

Walk around the Yeşil Cami, noticing the

slender minarets rising from bulbous bases, across the road and up the steps to the Yeşil Türbe or Green Tomb. It's not green, of course. The blue exterior tiles were put on during restoration work in the 1800s; the lavish use of tiles inside is original work, however. No need to remove your shoes to enter here. The tomb is open from 8.30 am to 12 noon and from 1 to 5.30 pm, for free.

The most prominent tomb is that of the Yeşil Cami's founder, Mehmet I. Others include those of his children. The huge tiled mihrab here is very impressive. Take a walk around the outside of the tomb to look at the tiled calligraphy above several windows.

After seeing the mosque and the tomb, you might want to take a rest and have something to drink at one of the cafés on the east side of the mosque. They have wonderful views of the valley.

Ethnographic Museum

Down the road a few steps from the Yeşil Cami is its medrese, now used as the Bursa Etnoğrafya Müzesi or Bursa Ethnographic Museum. The building is in the Seljuk style of religious schools, and the museum collection contains many local craft items. The museum is open from 8.30 am to 12 noon and 1 to 5.30 pm, closed Monday; admission costs US$1.50.

Bat Pazarı

From the square at Heykel, walk down the hill on İnönü Caddesi until you come to a small mosque set partly in the roadway. The section to your right – a warren of little streets – is the Bat Pazarı or Goose Market. The one thing you won't find here today are geese, but you will find ironmongers' shops and pedlars of old clothes, carpets, rope, utensils, potions and just about everything else. This market section is lively and colourful, perfect for photographing. When you snap a shot of the blacksmith at his forge, chances are he will ask you to send him a

copy. It's only fair; you should try to do so.

Bedesten

After an hour's stroll through the Bat Pazarı, head back to İnönü Caddesi and ask someone to point out the Bedesten or Covered Bazaar. Cross İnönü Caddesi and head into the side streets, following their directions.

The Bedesten was originally built in the late 1300s by Yıldırım Beyazıt, but the earthquake of 1855 brought it down. The reconstructed Bedesten retains the look and feel of the original, though it is obviously much tidier. This is not a tourist trap; most of the shoppers are local people. As you wander around, look for the **Eski Aynalı Çarşı**, which was once a Turkish bath; the domed ceiling with many small lights shows this.

In the Eski Aynalı Çarşı is a shop called Karagöz (tel 21 87 27), run by a man named Şinasi Çelikkol. Şinasi specialises in quality goods (copper and brass, carpets and kilims, knitted gloves and embroidery, old jewellery, etc) at fair prices, as did his father before him. This is the place to find the delightful Karagöz shadow-play puppets. Cut from flat, dried camel leather, painted in bright colours and oiled to make them translucent, the puppets are an authentic Turkish craft item. The Karagöz shadow play originated in Bursa. Şinasi Bey periodically organises performances of the shadow plays in English for groups, charging several dollars for admission. If you're interested, ask at the shop about the next shows.

The raising of silkworms is a cottage industry in Bursa. Each April, villagers buy the worms from their cooperatives, take them home and raise them on mulberry leaves. After a month the worms spin their cocoons and are soon ready for the trip to the **Koza Han** or Silk Cocoon Caravanserai, just outside the Bedesten's eastern entrance, which is lively with cocoon dealers in June and also in

September when there is a second harvest.

When you visit, you may well see huge sacks of the precious little white cocoons being haggled over by some of the 14,000 villagers who engage in the trade. In the centre of the Koza Han's courtyard is a small mosque constructed by Yıldırım Beyazıt in 1493, restored by the guild of silk traders in 1948 and again in 1985 by the Aga Khan. The product of all this industry, silk cloth (ipek, ee-PEHK), is for sale in the Bedesten.

Another place you ought to visit in the Bedesten is the **Emir Han**, a caravanserai used by many of Bursa's silk brokers, as it has been for centuries. Ask directions by saying Emir Han nerede? (eh-MEER hahn neh-reh-deh, 'Where's the Emir Han?'). There's a lovely fountain in the centre of the courtyard, and a tea garden for refreshments. Camels from the silk caravans used to be corralled in the courtyard, while goods were stored in the ground-floor rooms and drovers and merchants slept and did business in the rooms above.

Ulu Cami

Next to the Bedesten is Bursa's Ulu Cami or Great Mosque. This one is completely Seljuk in style, a big rectangular building with immense portals and a forest of supporting columns inside. The roof is a mass of 20 small domes. A şadırvan (ablutions fountain) is right within the mosque. It was Yıldırım Beyazıt who put up the money for the building in 1396. Notice the fine work of the mimber and the preacher's chair, also the calligraphy on the walls.

Legend has it that one of the men working on construction of the mosque was a hunch-back called Karagöz (Black-eye). He and his straight-man Hacivat indulged in such humorous antics that the other workmen abandoned their tasks to watch. This infuriated the sultan, who had the two miscreants put to death. Their comic routines (many of them

bawdy) live on in the Karagöz shadow-puppet theatre, a Bursa tradition that later spread throughout the Ottoman lands. The puppets are manipulated behind a white cloth onto which their coloured shadows are cast by a light behind them.

Hisar

From the Ulu Cami, walk west and up a ramp-like street to the section known as Hisar ('Fortress'). Coming by bus or dolmuş from Heykel, get a vehicle labelled 'Muradiye'.

The main street here is Pınarbaşı Caddesi. This section is among the oldest in Bursa, once enclosed by stone ramparts and walls. Some picturesque old frame houses and neighbourhood quarters survive here.

In a little park near the edge of the cliff, overlooking the boulevard (Cemal Nadir Caddesi) and the valley, are the **tombs of sultans Osman and Orhan**, founders of the Ottoman Empire. The originals were destroyed in the earthquake of 1855 and rebuilt in Ottoman Baroque style by Sultan Abdül Aziz in 1868. The tomb of Orhan Gazi was built on the foundations of a small Byzantine church, and you can see some remnants of the church's floor. The park here is attractive, as is the view of the city.

Muradiye

The Sultan Murat II Camii, also called the Hüdavendigar Camii, is further west and up the slope from the tombs. With a shady park in front and a quiet cemetery behind, the place is pretty and peaceful. The mosque proper dates from 1426 and follows the style of the Yeşil Cami.

Beside the mosque are a dozen tombs dating from the 1400s and 1500s, including that of Sultan Murat himself. Tomb-visiting may not be high on your list of priorities but you should see the beautiful decoration, especially the porch of the **Murat II Türbesi**, the tilework in the **Cem Türbesi** and the beautiful coloured tiles in the **Şehzade Mahmut Türbesi**. Also here is the **Tarihi Murat II Hamamı**, or Historic Turkish Bath of Sultan Murat II, still in use.

Across the park from the mosque is an old Ottoman house (the sign says '17 Y Y Ev', or '17th-century House'. Now a museum, it gives you a fascinating glimpse into the daily life of the Ottoman nobility in the 1600s. Carpets and furnishings are all authentic. Don't miss this one. It's open from 8.30 am to 12 noon, and from 1 to 5 pm, closed on Monday; there's a small admission charge of US$0.40.

Kültür Parkı

Bursa's Kültür Parkı (kewl-TEWR pahr-kuh) or Cultural Park, is laid out to the north of the Muradiye complex, down the hill some distance. You can reach it from Heykel by any bus or dolmuş going to Çekirge. Besides offering a pleasant stroll, the Kültür Parkı is good for lunch in one of its shady outdoor restaurants (see Places to Eat).

The park also houses the Bursa Archaeological Museum. Bursa's history goes back to the time of Hannibal (200 BC), and Roman artefacts are preserved here. The collection is nice, but not at all exceptional. If you've seen another good Turkish collection, this is more of the same. Find the bus stop named 'Arkeoloji Müzesi', and enter the park by the gate nearby. The museum is open from 8.30 am to 12 noon and from 1 to 5.30 pm, closed Monday; admission costs US$2.

Çekirge & The Baths

The warm, mineral-rich waters which spring from the slopes of Uludağ have been famous for their curative powers since ancient times. Today the ailing and the infirm come here for several weeks at a time, taking a daily soak or two in the tub, spending the rest of the time chatting, reading or dining. Most stay in hotels which have their own bathing facilities.

There are independent baths (*kaplıca*) as well, some of historical importance.

The Yeni Kaplıca is a bath built in 1522 by Sultan Süleyman the Magnificent's grand vizier, Rüstem Paşa, on the site of a much older one built by Justinian. The Kükürtlü bath is noted for its high sulphur content. At the Kaynarca ('Boiling') bath, it's the extreme heat of the water that is outstanding.

Bathing arrangements vary. Some baths have private steam rooms, some have rows of tubs, some have a common steam room and pool, some have several of these all under one roof. Bathing fees are low, though tips to the staff can run up the final tab somewhat. Baths will be crowded on Friday, the Muslim sabbath, as local people clean up for the holy day.

For details on bathing procedure, see the Turkish Baths section of the Facts for the Visitor chapter. Perhaps the most attractive place is the **Eski Kaplıcaları** or Old Baths, right next door to the new Kervansaray Termal Hotel on the eastern outskirts of Çekirge. Beautifully restored, the baths now cater to an up-market clientele of business travellers, tourists and local notables who stay at or socialise in the new hotel.

The bathing rooms are covered in creamy marble; in the hot room on the men's side there's a plunging pool (I haven't seen the women's side). The cool room has lounge chairs for relaxing, and a bar with waiter service. Prices are higher here than at unrestored neighbour-hood baths, but the style is deluxe. Hours are daily from 7 am to 11 pm for men, from 7.30 am to 11 pm for women. There's an entry fee of US$4, and a similar fee to have an attendant wash you; the cost of soap is additional, so figure US$20 for the works, including massage and tips. You can bring your own soap and wash yourself for little more than the basic entry fee.

Places to Stay

Though there are a few hotels in the centre of town, many of Bursa's best lodgings in terms of both quality and price are in the western suburb of Çekirge. Hotels atop Uludağ are mentioned in the section (following) describing the mountain.

Places to Stay – bottom end

In Bursa You can find a very cheap room in Bursa near the otogar, in the centre, or in Çekirge, but you must choose carefully. Hotels near the otogar tend to be outrageously noisy and not well kept; noise is a problem in the section as well.

I strongly recommend that you look for lodgings away from the otogar. If you must stay here, at least find a quiet place. Walk out the front door of the otogar and cross Uluyol. There are several hotels here, but they are noisy and expensive. Turn left, then right, and walk along this small street to the *Mavi Ege Oteli* (mah-VEE eh-GEH) (tel 14 84 20), Fırın Sokak 17. The 'Blue Aegean' is very plain and simple, but quieter than most, and charges from US$4 to US$6 a single, US$7 to US$8 a double, US$9 to US$10 a triple. Some rooms have sinks. Check the sheets and have the management change them if they've been used. A better bet is the *Hotel Belkis* (tel 14 83 22) Gazcılar Caddesi 168. Just a few steps up the street from the Mavi Ege is Gazcılar Caddesi. Turn right and you'll see the Belkis, which charges the same as the Mavi Ege, but has nicer rooms; there's no running water in the rooms, though.

For much better accommodation, continue walking along the small street to Gazcılar Caddesi, turn left and you'll see the *Gazcılar Oteli* (GAHZ-juh-LAHR) (tel 14 94 77), Gazcılar Caddesi 156. Neat and clean, the Gazcılar has central heating and a *lüks* (deluxe) rating from the municipal government. Prices are US$12/15 a single/double; with private shower, rates are US$15/21 a single/ double.

In the centre, the traditional choice is the *Otel Çamlıbel* (CHAHM-luh-behl) (tel 11 25 65, 12 55 65), İnebey Caddesi 71, an old and well-worn place with these advantages: a quiet location, rooms with constant hot water and good cross-ventilation, a lift and a few parking places in front of the hotel. Rates are not bad, at US$12/15/18 a single/double/triple; or US$15/21/26 a single/double/triple with private shower. You can have breakfast served in the hotel. To find the Çamlıbel, walk one block west from the PTT on Atatürk Caddesi (it's across from the Ulu Cami), pass the Türkiye Emlak Kredi Bankası and turn left. This is İnebey Caddesi. Walk two blocks up the hill on İnebey, and the hotel is on the right-hand side.

Just before the Çamlıbel on İnebey Caddesi is the *Hotel Çağlayan* (tel 21 14 58), İnebey Caddesi 73, which at the moment is a bit cleaner and newer-looking than the well-used Çamlıbel. Prices are identical, so the Çağlayan is preferable; note that it does not have a lift.

Bursa has a 206-bed student hostel, the *Özyurt Öğrenci Yurdu* (tel 23 05 44, 23 11 00), Fevzi Çakmak Caddesi 46, with cafeteria, kitchen, laundry, games and luggage storage facilities. Prices are US$3 per bed in a dormitory, US$4 for a bed in a triple or quad room, US$5 per person in a double room. To find it, go up the hill on Fevzi Çakmak Caddesi, also called Maksem Caddesi, past the Hotel Dikmen.

In Çekirge Most Çekirge hotels have their own facilities for 'taking the waters', since that's the reason people come here. You may find that the bathtub or shower in your hotel room runs only mineral water, or there may be separate private or public bathing-rooms in the basement of the hotel. One day's dip in the mineral waters is no great thrill. The therapeutic benefits are acquired over a term of weeks. All the same, you may find that a soak in a private tub is included in the price of the room, even in the very cheapest hotels, so take advantage of it.

For all of the Çekirge hotels, get a bus or dolmuş from Heykel or along Atatürk

Caddesi, and get out at the bus stop mentioned.

In Çekirge, my choices are the *Huzur Oteli* (hoo-ZOOR) (tel 36 80 21), Birinci Murat Camii Aralığı 2, Çekirge, on the east side of the Sultan Murat II Camii, more or less behind the Ada Palas Hotel near the entrance to Çekirge. The Huzur has it all: tidiness, quietness, friendly staff and mineral baths included in the rates of US$5/9/12 a single/double/triple in rooms without running water.

More or less next door to the Huzur is the *Konak Palas Oteli* (tel 36 51 13, 35 52 74), Birinci Murat Arkası 11, Çekirge, which is similar and charges US$6 per person for bed and breakfast in a room with washbasin. The acceptable, if unexciting, *Hotel Eren* (tel 36 80 99, 36 71 05), Birinci Murat Camii Aralığı 2, is up the hill a few steps from the Konak Palas, behind the Ada Palas. It has rooms with showers, and charges substantially more for them: US$12/16 a single/double.

The *Yeşil Yayla Oteli* (tel 36 80 26), Çekirge Caddesi, behind the Yıldız Hotel at the upper end of the village just off the main road, has similar simple rooms at identical prices. Daily use of the hotel's mineral bath facilities is included, as always.

Places to Stay - middle

In Bursa In central Bursa noise is a big problem, but it won't bother you much at the *Hotel Dikmen* (deek-MEHN) (tel 21 49 95/6/7), Fevzi Çakmak Caddesi 78 (it leads ultimately to Uludağ). The hotel's airy lobby is pleasant, with a small enclosed garden terrace, complete with fountain, at the back. Rooms have many little luxuries, including tubs in many of the bathrooms, TVs and mini-bar refrigerators. The Dikmen is popular with tour groups, but if there's a room, you can rent it for US$24/30 a single/double with shower, US$34 a double with bath. The hotel is about 50 metres up the hill on the street that begins beside the main PTT (across from the Ulu Cami).

In Çekirge The *Büyük Yıldız 2 Oteli* (yuhl-DUHZ) (tel 36 66 05/6/7), Selvinaz Sokak 1, Çekirge, at the upper end of the village, used to be a small and exceedingly modest place but is now more posh, proud and expensive. Lavish refurbishing has produced a comfortable 34-room hotel with some antique touches. Prices are US$36/48 a single/double, breakfast included; also included is use of the hotel's mineral baths, of course. A half km farther along the road, on the outskirts of Çekirge, is its sister establishment, the modern three-star, 124-room *Büyük Yıldız Oteli* (tel 36 66 00), Uludağ Caddesi 6, Çekirge. It offers the finest views of the valley, a wonderfully quiet location and a price of US$48/62 a single/double, including breakfast and baths.

The 60-room *Termal Hotel Gönlü Ferah* (GEWN-lew feh-RAH) (tel 36 27 00/1), I Murat Caddesi 24, Çekirge, in the very centre of the village, is one of the old reliables, and is among the more deluxe three-star hotels in the village. Some rooms have wonderful views over the valley, all have very comfortable furnishings and TVs. The ambience here is 'European spa', the service attentive and experienced. Rates are US$56 a double on the street side, US$62 a double on the panoramic side, with breakfast included.

Next door, the *Hotel Dilmen* (DEEL-mehn) (tel 36 61 14), I Murat Caddesi, Çekirge, rates four stars, boasts a lobby replete with stained glass, a pleasant garden terrace with restaurant and bar service, an exercise room with sauna and mineral-water baths, and 100 modern, posh rooms complete with satellite TV hook-ups. Prices are US$75 a double for a room facing the village, US$85 a double for a room with a valley view. Take a room with the valley view, for sure.

Places to Stay - top end

Bursa's most famous spa hotel is the five-star, 173-room *Hotel Çelik Palas* (tel 35 35 00; fax 36 19 10), Çekirge Caddesi 79, Bursa. Given its name in 1935 by Atatürk himself, the hotel had been a favourite resort for the Turkish leader and his peers; King Idris of Libya was taking the waters here when he was ousted by Colonel Muammar Gaddafi. Set in pretty grounds, the hotel consists of a historic older building dating from between the wars, and a newer section. Decor is an odd combination of the modern and the traditional elements.

All rooms have colour television sets, mini-bars, direct-dial phones, air-con and bathrooms with separate mineral-water taps. The Çelik Palas's mineral-water bath facilities are the most sumptuous in town, with lots of marble and tile, stained glass and a huge circular pool. Restaurants, bars, nightclub and disco, shopping and exercise room are all available. Though not on a par with the great spa hotels of Europe, it is quite comfortable. Rates range from US$70 to US$98 a single, from US$90 to US$125 a double. Breakfast costs US$7, other meals from around US$10 to US$16. The Çelik Palas is part of the Emek chain.

Çekirge's other five-star hotel is the *Hotel Kervansaray Termal* (tel 35 30 00), Çekirge Meydanı, Çekirge, opened in late 1988. The architecture and decoration here is updated, subdued Art Deco, and your first impression will be one of comfort and old richness. Marble, brass and mirrors make the public rooms gleam. Outside, tawny travertine with brick and wood trim links the building with the countryside and its past; a nice little swimming pool is open for use in summer. Bathrooms have bidets, full bathtubs, big mirrors and rich marble vanities.

The Eski Kaplıcaları mineral baths are right next door to the hotel, which is on the eastern outskirts of Çekirge set well back from a major crossroads. Rates are US$75/105 a single/double. It's part of the Kervansaray hotel chain, which also has a hotel in Bursa, and another atop Uludağ.

Places to Eat

Bursa's culinary specialities include fresh fruit (especially peaches in season), candied chestnuts (*kestane şekeri*) and two types of roast meat. *Bursa kebap* or *İskender kebap* is the most famous, made from döner kebap laid on a bed of fresh pide bread and topped with savoury tomato sauce and browned butter. When I'm in Bursa, I have this every single day. The other speciality is *İnegöl köftesi*, a type of very rich grilled rissole (ground meat patty) which is actually the speciality of the nearby town called İnegöl. You will see several restaurants which specialise in these dishes exclusively, called *Bursa kebapçısı* or *İnegöl köftecisi*.

Most of Bursa's eateries are quite inexpensive and would suit a bottom-end budget, while the food is good enough for the top end. The exceptions are in Çekirge, where you really pay for the marvellous views.

Bursa Kebapçıs An old favourite Bursa kebapçı is *Hacı Bey* (hah-JUH bey) (tel 21 64 40) on Ünlü Cadde, a small street just east of Heykel (ask in the square for 'hah-JUH bey BOOR-sah keh-bahp-chuh-suh'). It's just a few steps down the street, on the right – you'll recognise it by the döner turning in the window. Simple, but neat and tidy, the restaurant serves Bursa kebap in one, 1½ and two-portion sizes. A single portion with yoghurt (yoğurtlu), a dab of smoky aubergine purée on the side, a bottle of mineral water or a glass of grape juice, and Turkish coffee, tip included, will cost about US$5. Remember – after your kebap is served, don't begin eating until the waiter brings the tomato sauce and browned butter.

Hacı Bey has two other restaurant locations as well, one in the Kültür Parkı and another on the road to the Yeşil Cami, a half-block from the Ethnography Museum; but I think the original location is the best.

Bursa kebap was invented in a small restaurant now called *Kebabcı İskenderoğlu*

(İskender's Son) at Atatürk Caddesi 60, in the centre of town. The famous kebap sells for about US$2 per portion here. Another restaurant under the same management, with a wood facade making it look like a paşa's palace, is just a few steps past the Hacı Bey on Ünlü Cadde, marked by a sign, 'İskender İskenderoğlu.'

İnegöl Köfteçi For İnegöl köftesi, try the *İnegöl Köftecisi* on a little side street by Atatürk Caddesi 48. On your second visit you might try the köfte made with onions or cheese as a variation on the basic stuff. A full lunch need cost only US$3.

Another good köfteci is the *Özömür*, on the western side of the Ulu Cami, in the arasta, the complex of shops attached to the mosque. Here you can dine in an old stone building, for about US$3.50.

Hazır Yemek Those cheap and tasty meals you sampled in İstanbul are readily available in Bursa's many hazır yemek restaurants. Look for these down side streets near Heykel. Also, the *Şehir Lokantası* (sheh-HEER) (tel 22 62 03) at İnebey Caddesi 85, a half-block up from Atatürk Caddesi, is near the Çamlıbel and Yeni Ankara hotels. Simple, clean and attractive, it serves filling hazır yemek meals for less than US$3.

Kültür Parkı Strolling around the Cultural Park is pleasant, and having a meal here is more so. The *Selçuk Restaurant* is good, quiet, shady and inexpensive. I paid US$5 for a full lunch here, beverage and tip included. There are lots of other pleasant little restaurants in the park as well.

Çekirge The more expensive hotels in Çekirge have their own dining rooms. Besides these, there's the *Sezen Restaurant* (tel 36 91 56), on Çekirge Caddesi to the right of the Ada Palas Hotel. Plain white walls, white tablecloths, white plates – in short, very simple surroundings. But the food is fine and the prices fairly low, at US$5 or US$6 for a full meal.

Markets There's a nice little fruit and vegetable market district west of the Çamlıbel and Çağlayan hotels, south of the Ulu Cami. Look in this area for pidecis also.

Things to Buy

I've already mentioned those Bursa exclusives, silk cloth (especially scarves), hand-knitted woollen mittens, gloves and socks, Karagöz shadow puppets and candied chestnuts. If you're in the market for English-language books, try the ABC Kitabevi (that's ah-beh-JEH KEE-tah-beh-vee) (tel 21 08 93), at Altıparmak Caddesi 69/A, several hundred metres west of the Ulu Cami on the road to Çekirge.

Getting There & Away

The best way to reach Bursa is by ferry and bus. Though there is limited air service, there is no rail service.

Air Bursa has an air service from İstanbul on Sönmez Holding Hava Yolları (tel (24) 21 00 99, 22 20 97); at Bursa's airport (tel (24) 36 46 23, 36 44 77 ext 29); in İstanbul, (tel (1) 573-9323, 573-7240 ext 712). There are flights at 8.30 am and 5 pm from Monday to Friday, and 9 am Saturday; no flights Sunday. Buy your tickets in İstanbul at the Moris Seyahat Agentalığı (tel (1) 149-8510, 149-8511), Tünel Pasajı 11, Beyoğlu, opposite the upper station of the little Tünel subway at the southern end of İstiklal Caddesi.

To get to İstanbul's Atatürk Airport, take the airport bus from the Turkish Airlines terminal in Şişhane, just down the hill a block from the Moris Seyahat Agentalığı, or use a taxi. In Bursa, tickets can be bought at Ottomantur (tel (24) 21 00 99, 22 20 97), Kızılay Pasajı, Çakırhamam. A bus departs from the Ottomantur office 45 minutes prior to flight time.

Bus You will probably arrive in Bursa by bus or minibus from the ferry dock at

Yalova, or from İznik. These services come into Bursa's otogar, sometimes called the Şehir Garajı. For local transport, see the following Getting Around section.

When the time comes to leave Bursa, go to the otogar. Buses, minibuses and dolmuşes leave frequently for İznik (US$1.50) and for the İstanbul ferries at Yalova (US$2). If you plan to catch a boat at Yalova, get a bus that departs at least 90 minutes before the scheduled ferry departure. If you miss the express ferry you can always take the car ferry. See the Yalova section for details.

For other destinations, buy your ticket in advance to ensure a good seat and departure time. Here are some details about bus trips from Bursa:

Ankara – 400 km, 6½ hours, US$5; hourly buses

Çanakkale (for Troy and Gallipoli) – 310 km, six hours, US$4.50; a dozen buses daily

Kütahya – 200 km, three hours, US$3; several buses daily

İstanbul – 230 km, four hours, US$3.50; hourly buses

İzmir – 375 km, six hours, US$5; hourly buses

Getting Around

Outside the front of the otogar is a big street named Uluyol (oo-LOO-yohl, 'Great Road') or Ulu Caddesi. Here you will find dolmuşes, taxis and city buses. For the city buses, you will need to buy a ticket US$0.20 *before* you board the bus. Look for the ticket kiosk.

You will be looking for transport to the centre of town and its hotels, or the hotels at Çekirge. To reach Heykel, walk out the front door of the otogar, cross Uluyol, and look for the rank of cars filling up with people; most of these dolmuşes go to Heykel US$0.25. To get to the Ulu Cami from the otogar, go out the door, turn right, walk to the big intersection, cross the avenue and catch a bus or dolmuş

heading up the slope. Most will pass the Ulu Cami (ask for OO-loo JAH-mee).

The fastest way to travel between Heykel and Çekirge is by dolmuş; they run frequently and charge according to how far you travel. Also, city bus No 1 travels the entire 'tourist route', from the Emir Sultan Camii at the eastern end of town, through Heykel and along Atatürk Caddesi, past the Kültür Parkı and the Turkish baths to Çekirge.

ULUDAĞ

Bursa's Mt Olympus dominates the city. There were numerous mountains named Olympus in the ancient world. This was the one in the Kingdom of Bithynia, later the Roman province of Mysia.

The gods no longer live atop Uludağ, but there is a cable car (*teleferik*), a selection of hotels, a national park, cool forests and often snow. Even if you don't plan to hike to the summit (three hours each way from the hotel zone) or to go skiing (winter only), you might want to take the cable car up for the view and the cool, fresh air.

Cable Car

For a summer visit to Uludağ, getting there is most of the fun. Take a Bursa city bus, a dolmuş (from about 100 metres west of the statue in Heykel) or a taxi to the lower terminus, called Teleferuç (tel 21 36 35), a 15-minute ride away at the eastern edge of town. In summer when crowds abound, the cars depart when full or at least every 30 to 45 minutes, weather and winds permitting. The trip to the top takes about 30 minutes each way and costs US$2.50 one way, twice that for the round trip.

The cable car stops at an intermediate point named Kadıyayla, from whence you continue upward to the terminus at Sarıalan (sah-RUH-ah-lahn) at an altitude of 1635 metres. From Sarıalan, there is a smaller ski lift (*telekabin*) which runs to Çobankaya, but it's not worth the time or money.

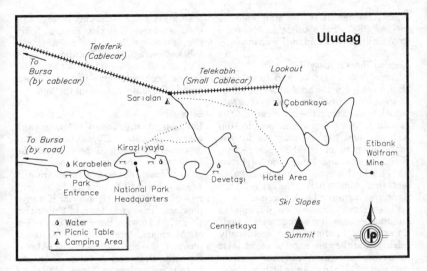

At Sarıalan there are a few snack and refreshment stands, a national park camping area (full at all times, it seems), some walking trails and the occasional dolmuş to the hotel zone (called the *Oteller Mevkii*), six km farther up the mountain slope. That's all there is to do, except enjoy the scenery.

Skiing Uludağ

Though a fairly sleepy place in summer, the hotel and ski area on Uludağ comes to life during the ski season from late December to March. Hotels have equipment to rent; boots and skis cost about US$6 per day. Each hotel also has its own ski lift, so when you buy a day pass, you are buying it for that lift alone. If you want to try other slopes, buy only a few rides on any particular lift.

Places to Stay

More than a dozen inns are scattered about the mountaintop. All are meant for skiers, so they close for much of the year. A few stay open all the time, though they have little business in summer unless they can schedule a commercial meeting.

Among the better places to stay is the *Otel Beceren* (BEH-jeh-REHN) (tel 1111). The hotel consists of two buildings, one of which closes in summer, the other staying open. For US$35 a double you get a room with bath, plus breakfast; the room has a TV and six channels of video programming. For US$50 two people can have a room and all three meals in summer. Prices rise substantially in winter, to about US$100 per couple, all three meals included.

One reader of this book found the *Hotel Aylin Yalçın*, farthest up the road on the right, to be good value. Rooms and meals are simple but acceptable, and the price during ski season is US$65 a double, meals included.

Of the other hotels, the *Büyük Otel* (bew-YEWK) (tel 1216/7/8) is a traditional favourite. It's an older place with small rooms, with showers or baths, renting for US$35/50 a single/double in winter, breakfast and dinner included; prices are lower in summer, of course.

The status address on the mountain is the *Grand Hotel Yazıcı* (YAH-zuh-juh) (tel 1050), where a lot of the status is in the lobby, the minds of the staff and the prices: US$75/100 a single/double, for a room with shower and no TV or meals.

Getting There & Away

Dolmuş You can take a dolmuş from Bursa's otogar to the hotel zone on Uludağ; it costs about US$5 per person to the top, which is more than the cable car. On the winding, 22-km trip you'll have to stop (11 km) and pay an entry fee for the national park of US$0.35 per person, US$1 for a car and driver. The hotel zone is 11 km farther up from the national park entrance. Almost half of the entire 22 km is on rough granite-block pavement.

The return ride can be difficult in summer as there are few dolmuşes or taxis in evidence. In winter there are usually plenty, and they are eager to get at least some fare before they head back down, so you may be able to go for as little as US$4.

HEADING WEST

Bandırma

This port town of 75,000 people is a 20th-century creation with little to offer the tourist except the junction between the İzmir to Bandırma rail line and the Bandırma to İstanbul ferry line. Few tourist services are available.

Kuşcenneti Milli Parkı Though Bandırma will not hold your interest for very long, bird fanciers will want to make a detour to Kuşcenneti Milli Parkı, the Bird Paradise National Park, centred on the Kuş Gölü (Bird Lake), 15 km due south of Bandırma. The towns of Manyas and Aksakal provide the best approaches to the park, which boasts from two to three million feathered visitors, of 239 different varieties, each year.

Places to Stay I've found no recommendable cheap hotels or restaurants. The best hotel in town, the *Hotel Eken* (tel (198) 10840/1/2), Soğuksu Caddesi 11, has a decent restaurant and a nightclub which is guaranteed to keep you awake until at least midnight. It's the only hotel of this class in the region, and has 78 clean, fairly simple rooms with tiny bathrooms (mini-tubs), as well as a sauna, hairdresser's and TV lounge. Rooms cost US$33/42 a single/double. Look for the hotel just a half-block west of the main square, up the hill.

Balıkesir

Balıkesir, at an altitude of 147 metres and with a population of 175,000, is the capital of the triangle-shaped province of the same name. The province's odd shape gives it coastlines on the Marmara and Aegean seas, and a mountainous eastern region bordering on neighbouring Kütahya province. The resort town of Erdek and the railhead town of Bandırma, on the Sea of Marmara, are both in Balıkesir province, as are the resorts at Akçay, Edremit, Ören and Ayvalık. There are historic hot springs at Gönen, used since Roman times. At Sındırgı, 63 km south of Balıkesir town, the famous *Yağcıbeydir* Turkish carpets are woven by descendants of early Turkish nomads who came to this area from Central Asia.

Balıkesir is at least 5000 years old, and was known as Palaeokastron to the Romans and Byzantines. Though there are a few old buildings in Balıkesir, including the **Zağanos Paşa Camii** (1461), the **Yıldırım Camii** (1388), the **Umur Bey Camii** (1412) and the **Karesi Bey Türbesi** (1336), this is not really a touristic town. No doubt you will just be passing through on the bus or train.

For answers to questions, contact the Tourism Directorate (tel (661) 11820, 17611, 10505), Gazi Bulvarı, Kamil Bey Apt 27.

There are numerous cheap hotels near the bus station. The best hotel rated by the Ministry of Tourism is the two-star *İmanoğlu Hotel* (tel 17144), Örücüler Caddesi, a 36-room place charging US$20/26 a single/double for its rooms.

HEADING SOUTH

From Bursa, a highway skirts the

northern edge of Uludağ, heading inland to İnegöl (46 km), Eskişehir (150 km) and Ankara (400 km). İnegöl is famous for its savoury köfte, and Eskişehir is where they mine meerschaum. The soft white stone is artistically carved into bracelets, earrings, necklaces and cigarette holders, but the most popular form meerschaum takes is that of a pipe. A short detour of 90 km south-east of Eskişehir brings you to Kütahya, centre of Turkey's faïence industry.

Kütahya

Set in the midst of hill country, at an altitude of 949 metres, Kütahya, with a population of 125,000, is a small city spread beneath the walls of an imposing hilltop fortress.

History No one knows for sure when Kütahya was founded; its earliest known inhabitants were Phrygians. In 546 BC it was captured by the Persians, and then saw the usual succession of rulers, from Alexander the Great to the kings of Bithynia, to the emperors of Rome and Byzantium, who called the town Cotyaeum. The first Turks to arrive were the Seljuks, in 1182. They were later pushed out by the Crusaders, but they returned to found the Emirate of Germiyan (1302-1428), with Kütahya as its capital. The Emirs cooperated with the Ottomans in nearby Bursa, and upon the death of the last emir, his lands were incorporated in the growing Ottoman Empire. When Tamerlane swept in at the beginning of the 15th century, he upset everyone's applecart, made Kütahya his headquarters for a while and then went back to where he came from.

As an Ottoman province, Kütahya settled down to tile-making. After Selim I took Tabriz in 1514, he brought all of its ceramic artisans to Kütahya and İznik, and set them to work. The two towns rivalled one another in the excellence of their faïence.

After the collapse of the 1848 Hungarian revolution, the great leader Lajos Kossuth fled to the Ottoman Empire, where he was given refuge and settled in Kütahya for a short time.

During the Turkish War of Independence, Greek armies pushed inland from İzmir, occupied Kütahya and threatened the fledgling Republican government at Ankara. Twice the Greek advance was checked by the Turks at the village of İnönü, north-east of Kütahya, but the invading forces finally broke through and took Eskişehir and Afyon. On 26 August 1922, the Turkish forces began a bold and risky counterattack, breaking through the Greek defences along the valley of Dumlupınar, due south of Kütahya, near the highway from İzmir to Afyon. In the battle for the valley, half of the Greek expeditionary force was annihilated or imprisoned, while the other half was soon beating a hasty retreat toward İzmir. The Dumlupınar victory (30 August 1922) was the turning point in the war.

Orientation After the confusing layout of İstanbul and Bursa, Kütahya's uncomplicated street plan is a joy. The roundabout with the vase in the fountain is the city's main square, called Belediye Meydanı (Town Hall Square), with the *Vilayet* (the provincial government headquarters) here as well. The bus station, called the Kütahya Çinigar (Tile-Garage) is less than one km from Belediye Meydanı; go out the otogar's front gateway (which is tiled, naturally), turn right and walk straight on to reach Belediye Meydanı. At the time of writing, Kütahya did not have a bona fide Tourist Information Office.

Information When you arrive in the main square, you can see what this town does for a living. There before you, in the middle of a traffic roundabout, is a huge coloured-pottery vase in a circular fountain. You'll see faïence (coloured tiles) used everywhere in this city, on facades of buildings, in floors and walls, and in some unexpected places. Every year scholars come here from many countries to attend the International Faïence & Ceramics Congress. The Dumlupınar Fuarı, held each year in the fairgrounds of the same name not far from the otogar, is Turkey's largest handicrafts fair. Besides decorative tiles, Kütahya's factories turn out industrial ceramics such as water pipes and conduits.

Things to See You can find Kütahya pottery in any souvenir shop in Turkey, but the shops in the city's bazaar have the widest selection and the lowest prices. Surprisingly, tile shops are not the city's proudest feature. Rather, Kütahyans pride themselves on the old houses, picturesque places of wood and stucco found in several old neighbourhoods near Belediye Meydanı. The city hosts a Historic Turkish Houses week each year. Many of these buildings have been beautifully restored, among them the **Kossuth Evi**, where Lajos Kossuth lived while in Kütahya.

The best way to see what there is to see in town is to follow signs to the **Archaeology Museum**. This will also lead you to the **Ulu Cami** (1411), 750 metres from Belediye Meydanı, right at the edge of a neighbourhood of historic houses. The museum (open from 9.30 am to 12 noon and from 1.30 to 5 pm, closed Monday) is in the former medrese of the mosque, the **Vecdiye Medresesi**. Exhibits are mostly ethnographic, with some Roman, Byzantine and Ottoman artefacts.

In the bazaar area, you might come across the **Kavaflar Pazarı**, a 16th-century market building; the **İşak Fatih Camii** (1434) and the **İmaret Mescidi** (1440), a former medrese.

Follow signs to the **kale** to find your way to the top of the hill and Kütahya's fortress.

If you're in the mood for an off-beat archaeological exploration, take a dolmuş from the Çinigar to the village of Çavdarhisar, 57 km up in the mountains

west of Kütahya, for a visit to **Aezani** (Aizanoi), which has one of the best-preserved Roman temples in all of Anatolia. The **Temple of Jupiter** dates from the time of Hadrian (117-138 AD), and was dedicated to the worship of Zeus and also the Anatolian fertility goddess Cybele. Be sure to have a look at the underground chamber beneath the temple. In the area around the temple are ruins of a stadium, baths (with some mosaics) and a theatre.

Places to Stay As tourism has yet to hit Kütahya, the range of lodgings is limited, but usually adequate.

Among the cheapest places is the *Hotel İstanbul*, on the main street, on the right-hand side just before Belediye Meydanı as you walk from the otogar. Rooms here go for US$6/8 a single/double. The town's old standards are the old-fashioned *Gül Palas 1* (tel (231) 11759, 11233), Belediye Meydanı, and newer *Gül Palas 2* (tel 12325) Lise Caddesi, just around the corner. Both hotels have lifts and simple but serviceable rooms with showers going for US$8/12 a single/double. In some rooms, the shower is a 'phone' attached to the washbasin faucet. Gül Palas 1 has seen better days, but offers views of the square. Gül Palas 2 is newer and also quieter. Staff at both are as yet unjaded by tourists, and thus are quite eager to please.

In between the two Gül Palases is the *Otel Cumhuriyet* (tel 13502), Belediye Meydanı, charging slightly less for similar rooms.

The top place to stay is the new *Hotel Erbaylar* (tel 36960; fax 11046), Afyon Caddesi 14, a modern, three-star, 42-room place which is simple but quite comfortable. All rooms have solid-colour carpeting, bedspreads and drapes, private baths (without any Kütahya tiles!), and some rooms have TVs with satellite hook-ups receiving German and American programmes. There's a restaurant and the Çini Bar (Faïence Bar); tiles are used as decorative accents throughout, naturally.

Rates are US$32/35 a single/double in one bed, US$40 a double in twin beds. Breakfast costs extra.

Places to Eat The *Hotel Erbaylar* has the poshest dining in town. For cheaper meals, try the very decent restaurant in the otogar, or *Çınar Köfte* (tel 11130), Lise Caddesi 7, near the Hotel Gül Palas 2 and the Otel Cumhuriyet. Köfte, soup, salad, bread and beverage are yours for US$2 or so. The Otel Cumhuriyet has a cheap restaurant, right on the corner.

Getting There & Away Because it is a provincial capital, Kütahya's otogar supports fairly busy traffic. Here are details on trips from Kütahya to:

Afyon - 100 km, under two hours, US$2.25; many buses daily

Ankara - 315 km, five hours, US$4.25; a dozen buses daily

Antalya - 375 km, eight hours, US$6.50; a few buses daily in summer, fewer in winter

Bursa - 190 km, three hours, US$3.75; a dozen buses daily

İstanbul - 355 km, six hours, US$5.50; a dozen buses daily

İzmir - 385 km, six hours, US$5.50; a dozen buses daily

Konya (via Afyon) - 335 km, five hours, US$6; several direct buses, or change at Afyon

Afyon

Formerly called Afyonkarahisar (The Black Fortress of Opium), this workaday agricultural and carpet-weaving town (at an altitude of 1015 metres, with a population of 100,000) and capital of the province of the same name, hardly lives up to its sinister moniker. There is indeed a steep hill, crowned with a fortress, in the historic centre of town. This is still an important region for producing legal opium for legitimate pharmaceutical use. But Afyon's claim to fame among Turks is its kaymak or clotted cream.

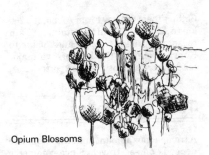
Opium Blossoms

The story is this: Afyon's opium farmers never used the stuff themselves, but they used every other part of the plant. The juice was made into opium, the tender leaves were good in salads and the left-over plants were fed to the cattle. The cattle became very, very contented and produced rich cream in abundance. The clotted cream became famous perched atop a serving of *kadayıf* (crumpet in syrup), or used in baklava, or even stuffed in lokum (Turkish delight).

Today the opium is grown legally by the 'poppy straw' method, which is easier to police and control. The young plants are cut down before the narcotic sap begins to flow, and the 'straw' is processed in special government-operated factories. But the local cattle still seem to be contented.

Places to Stay Should you be passing through and need a place to stay, about the best you can find is the *Ece Hotel* (tel 16070), formerly called the Emek Oteli, on the main square at Ordu Bulvarı 2. It's a 38-room, nominally two-star place charging US$20/25 a single/double, but open to haggling if business is slow. It's the best place in town at this writing, but it's still pretty simple. The *Oruçoğlu Oteli* (tel 20120/1/2; fax (491) 19765), Bankalar Caddesi on the main square (actually a traffic roundabout), is older and quite simple, but serviceable. Prices here are US$18 a single, US$23 a double. Meals are available in either hotel, or at little kebapçıs facing the square.

Getting There & Away From Afyon, it's 260 km to Ankara, 300 km to Antalya, 165 km to Isparta, 340 km to İzmir and 235 km to Konya. Being at the hub of five major roads, there's plenty of transportation.

The Dardanelles

A tremendous amount of world commerce depends on sea travel. Since commerce means wealth and wealth means power, the people who control the sea have enormous commercial – not to mention military – power. The best place for a small group of people to control an awful lot of sea is at a strait.

The story of the Çanakkale Boğazı (cha-NAH-kah-leh boh-ah-zuh), or the Dardanelles, is one of people battling each another for control of this narrow passage which unites the Mediterranean and Aegean seas with the Marmara and Black seas. In ancient times it was the Achaeans attacking the Trojans; in modern times the Anzacs facing Atatürk at Gallipoli. The name 'Dardanelles' comes from Dardanus, ruler of a very early city-state at Çanakkale, who controlled the straits.

The story of the Dardanelles is not all war and commerce; romance, too, has been central to its mythical associations: legend says that the goddess Helle fell from a golden-winged ram into the water here, giving the straits the name of Hellespont. The lovesick Leander, separated from his beloved Hero, swam to her through the fierce currents each night, until one night he didn't make it. 'Swimming the Hellespont' is a challenge for amateur and professional swimmers to this day.

The height of romance is the story of two ancient peoples battling over the love and honour of Helen, the most beautiful woman in the world. Historians now tell us that Helen was just a pawn in the fierce commercial and military rivalries between Achaea and Troy. Still, no one says she

wasn't beautiful, or that the Trojan horse didn't actually fool the Trojans and lead to their defeat by the Achaeans.

The area of the straits holds these attractions: the town of Çanakkale with a population of 45,000, a fast-growing agricultural centre on the south-east shore; the fortifications, ancient and modern, which guarded the straits; the battlefields of Gallipoli on the north-west side of the straits; and the excavated ruins of ancient Troy 32 km to the south. For a week in mid-August, the Çanakkale Festival fills the hotels in town. If you plan to be here around mid-August, arrive early in the day and start your search for a hotel room at once.

ÇANAKKALE
Orientation
You can easily walk to Çanakkale's interesting sights. Everything you need is within two blocks of the ferry docks and the clock tower, except for the otogar and the Archaeological Museum.

To get from the otogar to the centre of town near the clock tower and car-ferry docks, leave the otogar by the front doors, turn left, walk to the first turning to the right and follow signs straight to the 'Feribot' (ferryboat!). Just before you come to the docks you'll see the vaguely Teutonic clock tower, Saat Kulesi (sah-AHT koo-leh-see), on your left. To reach the market area, walk behind the clock tower and turn into one of the streets on the left-hand side.

Information
The town's Tourism Information Office (tel (196) 11187) is in a little booth near the quay, between the clock tower and the ferry docks.

Cannon Monument
In the broad main street at the centre of the town is a monument constructed of old WW I cannons. The words on the plaque translate as 'Turkish soldiers used these cannons on 18 March 1915 to ensure

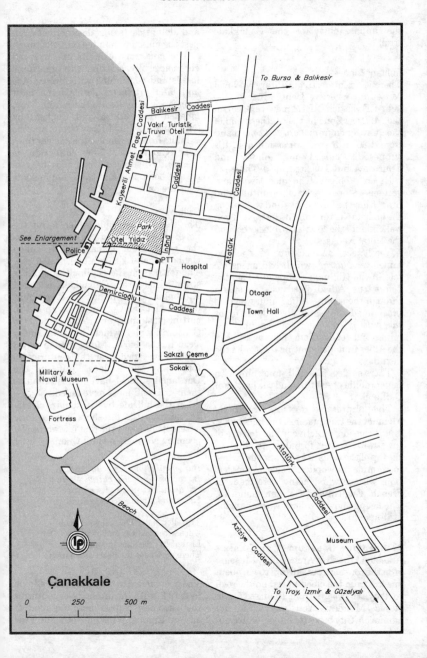

To Bursa & Balıkesir

Balıkesir Caddesi

Vakıf Turistik
Truva Oteli

Kayserili Ahmet Paşa Caddesi

İnönü Caddesi

Atatürk Caddesi

Park
Otel Yıldız

See Enlargement
Police

PTT

Hospital

Demircioğlu

Caddesi

Otogar

Town Hall

Sakızlı Çeşme
Sokak

Military &
Naval Museum

Fortress

Atatürk

Caddesi

Beach

Azizye Caddesi

Museum

Çanakkale

0   250   500 m

To Troy, İzmir & Güzelyalı

the impassability of the Çanakkale strait'.

Military Zone

There is an interesting Military & Naval Museum (Askerî ve Deniz Müzesi, ahs-kehr-EE veh deh-NEEZ mew-zeh-see), in the Military Zone at the southern end of the quay, open from 9 am to 12 noon and from 1.30 to 5 pm, admission free. It's supposedly closed on Monday and Thursday, but I visited on a Thursday with no problem. The nice lawns and gardens are open for strolling until 10 pm. Start from the ferry docks and walk along the quay to the zone and its fortress. If you walk inland, the zone is two blocks beyond the Hotel Konak.

You'll see a mock-up of the old minelayer *Nusrat*, which had an heroic role in the Gallipoli campaign. The day before the Allied fleet was to steam through the straits, Allied minesweepers proclaimed the water cleared. At night the *Nusrat* went out, picked up loose mines and relaid them, helping to keep the Allies from penetrating the straits the next day.

There's also a small museum with memorabilia of Atatürk and the battles of Gallipoli.

The impressive fortress, built by Mehmet the Conqueror in the mid-1400s, is still considered active in the defence of the straits. So it is forbidden to climb to the top of the walls or keep, but you're free to examine the wonderful old cannons left from various wars; many were made in French, English and German foundries. The keep is now a gallery with changing exhibits.

Archaeology Museum

Çanakkale's Arkeoloji Müzesi or Archaeology Museum is on the southern outskirts of town, about one km from the clock tower, on the road to Troy. Hours are from 10 am to 5 pm, closed Monday. You pay US$1 for admission. City buses (to İntepe, Güzelyalı)

and dolmuşes (same destinations) run past the museum from the centre of town.

The museum's exhibits are arranged chronologically, starting with prehistoric fossils and continuing with Bronze Age and later artefacts. Perhaps the most interesting exhibits are those from Troy, labelled (in Turkish and English) by 'city', that is, Troy I, Troy II, etc; and the exhibits from Dardanos, the ancient town near Çanakkale. The collection is pleasantly displayed. Don't miss the glass case of bone pins and small implements near the exit.

Gallipoli

The slender peninsula which forms the north-western side of the straits, across the water from Çanakkale, is called Gelibolu (geh-LEE-boh-loo) in Turkish. The fortress on the Gallipoli side of the strait, visible from Çanakkale, is called Kilitbahir, 'Lock on the Sea'. It was built by Mehmet the Conqueror as an aid to cutting off supplies and reinforcements to Constantinople, which he held under siege in the 1450s. Many foreign naval forces have tried over the centuries to force any such 'lock' put on the Dardanelles. Most have had İstanbul as their goal, and most have failed.

On the hillside by Kilitbahir, clearly visible from the far shore, are gigantic letters spelling out the first few words of a poem by Necmettin Halil Onan.

Dur yolcu! Bilmeden gelip bastığın
Bu toprak bir devrin battığı yerdir.
eğil de kulak ver, bu sessiz yığın
bir vatan kalbinin attığı yerdir.

Traveller, halt! The soil you tread
Once witnessed the end of an era.
Listen! In this quiet mound
There once beat the heart of a nation.

The poem refers to the battles of Gallipoli in WW I. With the intention of capturing the Ottoman capital and the road to eastern Europe, Winston Churchill, First

Top: The walls of Ancient Troy
Left: A latter-day Trojan Horse in Troy
Right: The minaret of the Green Mosque in İznik

Top: A burst cannon and a commemorative mural in Çanakkale (Dardenelles)
Bottom: A caravanserai courtyard in Bursa

Lord of the Admiralty, organised a naval assault on the straits. A strong Franco-British fleet tried first to force them in March 1915 but failed. Then, in April, British, Australian and New Zealand troops were landed on Gallipoli, and French troops near Çanakkale. After nine months of disastrous defeats the Allied forces were withdrawn.

The Turkish success at Gallipoli was partly due to disorganisation on the Allied side, and partly due to reinforcements under the command of General Liman von Sanders. But a crucial element in the defeat was that the Allied troops happened to land in a sector where they faced Lieutenant-Colonel Mustafa Kemal (Atatürk). Though a relatively minor officer, he had General von Sanders' confidence. He guessed the Allied battle plan correctly when his commanders did not, and stalled the invasion by bitter fighting which wiped out his division. Though suffering from malaria, he commanded in full view of his troops and of the enemy, and miraculously escaped death several times. At one point a piece of shrapnel tore through the breast pocket of his uniform, but was stopped by his pocket watch (now in the Çanakkale Military & Naval Museum). His brilliant performance made him a folk hero and paved the way for his promotion to general.

Both the Turkish and the Allied troops fought desperately and fearlessly and devastated one another. The action was decided not by bravery, but by luck and chance.

The Gallipoli campaign lasted for nine months, until January 1916, and resulted in huge numbers of casualties on both sides. The British Commonwealth nations suffered over 200,000 casualties, with the loss of some 36,000 lives. French casualties of 47,000 were over half of the entire French contingent. Of the half-million Turkish troops who participated in the battle, one out of every two was a casualty, with more than 55,000 dead. There are now 31 war cemeteries on the peninsula, as well as several important monuments. You can visit Turkish, British and French monuments to the war dead at Seddülbahir, as well as Australian and New Zealand cemeteries at Arıburnu. Other points you'll want to see include Anzac Cove, and the memorials at Cape Helles, Lone Pine, Twelve Tree Copse, Hill 60 and Chunuk Bair.

Troy

The approach to Troy or Truva (TROO-vah) is across low, rolling countryside of grainfields, with a small village here and there. This is the Troad of ancient times, all but lost to legend until a German-born Californian entrepreneur and amateur archaeologist named Heinrich Schliemann (1822-1890) rediscovered it in 1871. The poetry of Homer was at that time assumed to be based on legend, not history, but Schliemann got permission from the Ottoman government to excavate here at his own expense. He uncovered four superimposed ancient towns and went on to make notable excavations at other Homeric sites.

History The first people lived here during the Early Bronze Age. The cities called Troy I to Troy V (3000-1800 BC) had a similar culture, but Troy VI (1800-1275 BC) took on a new character, with a new population of Indo-European stock related to the Mycenaeans. The town doubled in size and carried on a prosperous trade with Mycenae. It also held the key, as defender of the straits, to the prosperous trade with Greek colonies on the Black Sea. Troy VI is the city of Priam which engaged in the Trojan War. A bad earthquake brought down the walls in 1275 and hastened the Achaean victory.

This heroic Troy was followed by Troy VII (1275-1100 BC). The Achaeans may have burned the city in 1240; an invading Balkan people moved in around 1190 BC and Troy sank into a torpor for four centuries. It was revived as a Greek city

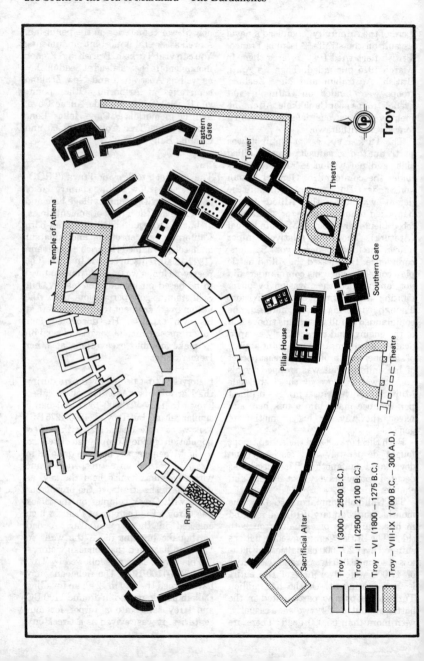

Troy

Eastern Gate

Tower

Temple of Athena

Theatre

Southern Gate

Pillar House

Theatre

Ramp

Sacrificial Altar

Troy – I (3000 – 2500 B.C.)
Troy – II (2500 – 2100 B.C.)
Troy – VI (1800 – 1275 B.C.)
Troy – VIII-IX (700 B.C. – 300 A.D.)

(Troy VIII, 700-300 BC) and then as a Roman one (Troy IX, 300 BC-300 AD). At one point Constantine the Great thought of building his new eastern Roman capital here, but he chose Byzantium instead. As a Byzantine town, Troy didn't amount to much.

Now for Homer's history of Troy. In the *Iliad*, this is the town of Ilium. The battle took place in the 13th century BC, with Agamemnon, Achilles, Odysseus (Ulysses), Patroclus and Nestor on the Achaean (Greek) side, and Priam with his sons Hector and Paris on the Trojan side. Homer alludes to no commercial rivalries as cause for the war. Rather, he says that Paris kidnapped the beautiful Helen from her husband Menelaus, King of Sparta, and the king asked the Achaeans to help him get her back.

The war went on for a decade, during which Hector killed Patroclus and Achilles killed Hector. When the time came for Paris to kill Achilles, he was up to the task. Paris knew that Achilles' mother had dipped her son in the River Styx, holding him by his heel, and had thus protected Achilles from wounds anywhere that the water had touched. So Paris shot Achilles in the heel.

Even this carnage didn't end the war, so Odysseus came up with the idea of the wooden horse filled with soldiers. That's the way Homer reported it.

One theory has it that the earthquake of 1275 BC gave the Achaeans the break they needed, bringing down Troy's formidable walls and allowing them to battle their way into the city. In gratitude to Poseidon, the Earth-Shaker, they built a monumental wooden statue of his horse. Thus there may well have been a real Trojan horse, even though Homer's account is less than fully historical.

The last people to live here were Turkish soldiers and their families, subjects of the Emir of Karası, in the 1300s. After them, the town disappeared until Schliemann arrived.

Touring the Ruins Today at Troy you'll find a parking area, a huge replica of the wooden Trojan horse (put here so you'll have something distinctive to photograph) and Troy itself. The excavations by Schliemann and others have revealed nine ancient cities, one on top of another, going back to 3000 BC. Though there are few thrilling sights here (and some visitors say it's not worth the trip), Troy is interesting because of the Troad's beauty, great antiquity and semilegendary character. Just half a km before the archaeological site is the village of **Tevfikiye**, with a Tourism Information Office, drink stands, simple restaurants, souvenir shops, replicas of the Trojan treasure, etc. There are a few little pensions and camping areas as well.

Troy is open to visitors from 8 am to 5 pm daily; admission costs US$3.50.

The identifiable structures at Troy are well marked. Notice especially the walls from various periods, the **bouleterion** or council chamber built about Homer's time (c 800 BC) and the **Temple of Athena** from Troy VIII, rebuilt by the Romans. Also, don't miss the beautiful views of the Troad, particularly over toward the straits. On a clear day you can see the Gallipoli war memorials on the far shore and ships passing through the Dardanelles. You can almost imagine the Achaean fleet beached on the Troad's shores, ready to begin a battle that would be remembered over 3000 years later.

Places to Stay

Çanakkale has a good, if small, selection of hotels in all price ranges. There are also comfortable hotels in a seaside setting on the road to Troy.

Places to Stay - bottom end

The hotels in the centre of town are clustered near the clock tower. Perhaps the most friendly is the funky old brick *Hotel Kervansaray* (no phone), Kemal Paşa Mahallesi, Fetvahane Sokak 13, 17100 Çanakkale, just behind the clock tower. The Kervansaray, run by an energetic woman who welcomes backpackers, is in the 200-year-old home of a Turkish paşa. It has a delightful garden with a fountain, cooking facilities you can use, and rooms for US$4/6 a single/double without running water, or US$12 a triple with shower.

The Küçük Truva Oteli (kew-CHEWK TROO-vah) (tel 11552), very near the Kervansaray, has similar rates for rooms without shower. The hotel has flyscreens (sineklik) on its windows, but these do not keep the bedbugs out. Some readers have enjoyed staying here. The nearby Hotel Efes (eh-FEHS) (tel 13256) is a similar place; it's good and cheap, clean and airy and has also been praised by readers.

The Hotel Konak (koh-NAHK) (tel 11150), Fetvahane Sokak, 17100 Çanakkale, just behind the clock tower and facing the Hotel Kervansaray, boasts central heating, constant hot water and prices of US$6 a double, or US$8.50 a double with private shower, but it is no longer up to its old standard. Take a good look around before you settle in.

For a clean, friendly family pension, the place to go is the Avrupa Pansiyon (ahv-ROO-pah) (tel 14084), Matbaa Sokak 8, 17100 Çanakkale, past the Hotel Kervansaray a bit further on from the clock tower. It's quiet here, as the pension is on a block-long side street. It is run by Mehmet Özcan's family; it's clean and safe, and you can use the kitchen for your own cooking. The basic charge for a double is US$10, or US$15 a double with private bath. Breakfast costs extra. If the Avrupa is full, try the Otel Turing, directly across the street, which shares the advantage of the quiet location.

Camping There are several small camping places 16 km from Çanakkale along the Troy road at Güzelyalı, and also a few across the straits near the fortress of Kilitbahir. Much of the area around Kilitbahir is a nature reserve and there's a good beach as well. The village of

Tevfikiye, just before Troy, also has simple camping areas.

Places to Stay – middle

The best two hotels in town are fairly simple, but comfortable enough. You can't miss the two-star, 70-room Otel Anafartalar (ah-nah-fahr-tah-LAHR) (tel 14454/5/6), İskele Meydanı, 17100 Çanakkale, on the north side of the ferry docks. The front rooms in this seven-floor structure have good views of the water and cost US$20/28 a single/double with bath. The hotel has a pleasant restaurant on its roof, and a supremely convenient location.

The Vakıf Turistik Truva Oteli (tel 11024, 11886), Kayserili Ahmet Paşa Caddesi, Yalıboyu, 17100 Çanakkale, sometimes called simply the Truva Hotel, is a special two-star place as it is owned and operated by a hotel training school. Most of the staff are students for whom serving you well means good grades in class, so the service is careful, if perhaps a bit earnest. The 66 rooms are comfortable without being fancy; some in the older front section have sea views, while the ones at the back are newer. Rates are from US$18 to US$22 a single, US$25 to US$30 a double, breakfast included. Higher-priced rooms have bathrooms, with tub and shower, while lower-priced rooms have shower alone. The hotel is a short 200-metre walk north-east of the main square, along the waterfront.

The one-star, 35-room Hotel Bakır (bah-KUHR) (tel 12908, 14088/9), Rıhtım Caddesi 12 (also called Yalı Caddesi), 17100 Çanakkale, is very near the clock tower. A clean double room with bath and view of the straits, breakfast included, costs US$25/32/38 a single/double/triple.

Just a block from the ferry docks is the one-star, 33-room Otel Yıldız (yuhl-DUHZ) (tel 11793, 11069), Kızılay Sokak 20, 17100 Çanakkale, on a quiet side street. It is a comfortable enough place renting rooms with private shower for US$15 with a double bed, US$17 with twin beds. A restaurant, bar, a lift and

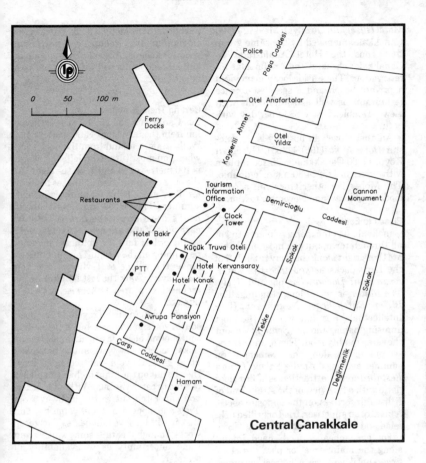

Central Çanakkale

several English-speaking staff make your stay pleasant here. To find the hotel, get to the front door of the Hotel Anafartalar, walk out that door and head straight down the side street and you'll see it.

Only someone with a car would be interested in the motels on the outskirts in the seaside district called Güzelyalı. The old faithful here is the *Tusan Truva Motel* (TOO-sahn TROO-vah) (tel 14987), Güzelyalı Mevkii, 17100 Çanakkale, located in a pine forest at the end of a road. The motel is 2 km further on. Most rooms have views of the straits and the establishment has more the ambience of a small, quiet retreat than of a highway motel. Rooms are priced at US$26 a double with shower and US$30 a double with bath. To find the motel, leave Çanakkale by the road to Truva, drive about 14 km and take the turning for Güzelyalı, then follow the motel's signs for about 2½ km from the turning.

Other hotels and motels are being built here as Turkey's tourism boom continues. Among the newer ones is the two-star

Motel Güzelyalı, Güzelyalı Mevkii, 17100 Çanakkale, managed by the same group that runs the Hotel Anafartalar in Çanakkale; check at the Anafartalar for reservations. The seaside location provides a private beach and a sea-view terrace restaurant, as well as some rooms with views. Doubles cost US$30 per day with bath.

Another Güzelyalı hostelry is the one-star *Hotel Mola* (196) 11495), Güzelyalı Köyü, 17100 Çanakkale, a 35-room place with prices of US$24/30 a single/double. The Mola, like other Güzelyalı accommodation, closes from November to March.

Places to Eat

Çanakkale has inexpensive places to eat all through town, but the most enjoyable are those right along the quay to the left of the ferry docks as you face the water. *Restaurant Dardanel* is big and lively. The *Rıhtım* is one of long-standing. The *Bizim Entellektüel Restaurant* (Our Intellectuals' Restaurant!) has the most amusing name, and the *Şehir* has about the same quality food. These, and others, set out tables along the promenade on summer evenings. At the *Yalova Liman Restaurant* the attraction is a 3rd-floor patio with a fine view of the straits and of Kilitbahir fortress on the opposite shore. A meal of an appetiser, fried or grilled fish, salad and a bottle of beer might cost US$5.

For even cheaper food, head inland along the main street or past the clock tower until you see a köfteci or pideci shop. At a pideci, fresh flat pide bread is topped with such things as whole eggs, cheese or ground lamb, dabbed with butter, then baked. It's filling, delicious and very cheap. Price depends on the toppings. Ask for pide yumurtalı, peynirli or kıymalı.

The Hotel Bakır, beside the clock tower, has both seafront and clock-tower entrances. Across from the clock-tower entrance is the *Öz Yalova Restaurant*, a cheap hazır yemek place where a three-course meal costs only US$3 or so. Right next door to the Hotel Küçük Truva is the *Gaziantep Aile Kebap ve Pide Salon*, good for kebaps. A meal of soup, pide or köfte, bread and a soft drink should cost about US$2.

Getting There & Away

Bus Çanakkale has an otogar less than a km from the ferry docks and clock tower. Walk straight inland from the docks and when you must turn, turn left; the otogar is 100 metres or so along, on the right. At the otogar you will find dolmuşes heading for Troy every 30 to 60 minutes in high summer. Troy is 30 km, less than an hour's drive away; the fare is US$1.50 each way. If you are here in winter, early spring or late fall, the dolmuşes may not be running all the way to Troy, but only as far as the village of Tevfikiye, and you may have to walk the last half km to the archaeological area. Otherwise, it's a tour by taxi.

If you plan to visit Troy and then head south, you should try to buy a ticket on a southbound bus a day in advance, let the ticket seller know you want to be picked up at Troy, do your sightseeing at Troy, then be out on the main highway in plenty of time to catch the bus. Without a ticket, you can hitch out to the highway from Troy and hope a bus will come by, and that it will have vacant seats. This often works, though it entails some waiting and some uncertainty as to availability of seats.

By the way, you can buy bus tickets at the otogar, or at the bus company offices on the main street in the centre of Çanakkale near the ferry docks.

Here are some times and distances from Çanakkale:

Ankara – 700 km, 12 hours, US$8; several buses daily
Behramkale (change to dolmuş at Ayvacık) – 100 km, two hours (or more, depending upon dolmuşes), US$2.25; many buses

Ayvalık – 200 km, 3½ hours, US$3.50; many buses

Bursa – 310 km, six hours, US$4.50; a dozen buses daily

Edirne (change at Uzunköprü or Keşan) – 230 km, 3½ hours, US$3.50; five buses daily

İstanbul – 340 km, six hours, US$5; a dozen buses daily

İzmir – 340 km, six hours, US$5; many buses daily

Boat Two ferry services run across the straits. The northern one is between the towns of Gelibolu and Lâpseki. Ferries leave Gelibolu at 1, 6, 7, 8, 9 and 10 am; 12 noon and 2, 4, 5, 6, 7, 8, 9, 10 and 11 pm. From Lâpseki, ferries are at 2, 6, 7, 8, 9, 10 and 11 am; 1, 3, 5, 6, 7, 8, 9 and 10 pm and midnight.

The southern car-ferry service runs between Çanakkale and the town of Eceabat (eh-jeh-AH-baht) near the battlefields of Gallipoli. Between 6 am and 11 pm, boats run in each direction every hour on the hour; there are also boats at midnight and 2 am from Eceabat, and at 1 and 3 am from Çanakkale.

Passengers as well as cars are carried on the boats for fares of US$0.25 per person, US$4.50 and up for a car and driver. The crossing from Çanakkale to Eceabat takes about 25 minutes in good weather.

Because of the schedules, a return trip takes 1½ hours. Buses running along the highway between Çanakkale, Bandırma and Bursa often stop at the Lâpseki ferry landing to pick up passengers.

You can shorten the time it takes to cross the straits by climbing aboard a *motor* (moh-TOHR, motorboat). These small craft ply between Çanakkale's docks and the village of Kilitbahir, at the foot of the fortress on the opposite shore. The voyage over takes from 15 to 20 minutes; the motorboat will leave as soon as it has enough passengers.

Getting Around
Tours Many readers of this book have written commending Troy-Anzac Tours (tel (196) 15047, 15049), Saat Kulesi Yanı 2, Çanakkale, near the clock tower, for their excellent tours. I've also received letters saying that other Gallipoli tour operators do not offer good value for money. I'd stick with Troy-Anzac, which has been in business for more than 20 years, and avoid the others. Troy-Anzac's three-hour tours of the battlefields include car, driver and guide for from US$8 to US$16 per person, depending upon the number of people signed up to go. It's best to have a car and guide, as the battlefields are spread out and a guide can fill in the exciting details of the battles.

Aegean Turkey

The Aegean coast is a beautiful procession of golden wheat fields, fig and olive orchards, fishing villages and holiday resort towns. Assos (Behramkale) is an out-of-the-way village built on an ancient city. Ayvalık is a pleasant fishing and resort town with good beaches, good seafood restaurants and beautiful panoramas of pine forest and Aegean islands. At Bergama, the ancient Pergamum, you should see the impressive ruins of the Acropolis and the Asclepion, an early medical centre. Many visitors make their base in İzmir and go north to Bergama or east to Sardis for the day.

South of İzmir the main attractions are the many Ionian cities, including Ephesus, the best-preserved classical city in the world, and also Priene, Miletus, Didyma, Labranda, Aphrodisias, Hierapolis and several others. The resort town of Kuşadası can serve as a base for visits to many of these sites. A bonus is the spa at Pamukkale.

At the southern end of the Aegean coast is the beautiful little resort and yachting port of Bodrum, with its Crusader castle, just across the water from the Greek island of Kos.

Here's what you'll find on the coastal highway (E24), heading south from Troy.

The North Aegean

ASSOS (Behramkale)

It's 73 km from Çanakkale to Ayvacık (AHY-vah-juhk, not to be confused with nearby Ayvalık), a ride of less than two hours. From Ayvacık, dolmuşes run the 19 km to Behramkale. Called Assos in ancient times, the village and the ruins share a gorgeous setting overlooking the Aegean and the nearby island of Lesbos (Midilli, MEE-dee-lee in Turkish). The main part of the village and the acropolis ruins are perched atop a hill, but down the far (sea) side of the hill a tiny cluster of little stone buildings clings to the cliff in an incredibly romantic, not to mention unlikely, setting. It's a picture-postcard sight, but crowded with tourists in summer. The swimming is difficult here, but there's a good beach at Kadırga, four km to the east.

History

Assos was founded in the 8th century BC by colonists from Lesbos. Aristotle stayed here for three years, and St Paul visited briefly. In its long history, Assos has flourished as a port, agricultural town and centre for Platonic learning. Today the main part of the village atop the hill is just a Turkish farming village. The tiny port settlement on the seaside is crammed if a few dozen foreigners show up.

Things to See

There's a fine Ottoman **hump-back bridge**, built in the 1300s, to the left of the road as you approach the village. When you get to a fork in the road, go left up to the village proper, or right to see the massive city walls, necropolis and port hamlet.

Taking the village road, you wind up to a small square with a few shops and a small restaurant or two. Continue upward on the road, and you'll come to a small square with a teahouse and a bust of Atatürk; at the very top of the hill you will get a spectacular view, and perhaps meet some village girls crocheting lace and importuning you to buy some.

Aegean Turkey

You also get a look at the **Murad Hüdavendigâr Camii** (1359-1389). This early mosque is very simple, a dome on squinches set atop a square box of a room. The mihrab is nothing special. The Ottomans had not yet conquered Constantinople and begun to elaborate on the theme of Sancta Sophia at the time this mosque was built. Curious, though, is the lintel above the entrance, which bears Greek crosses and inscriptions. It probably was left over from a Byzantine church.

The principal sight atop the hill is the **Temple of Athena**, presently under restoration. There wasn't much left for tourists to see, so the government is obliging by making it photogenic again.

By taking the right fork of the entry road, you'll reach the impressive **city walls** and the **necropolis** or cemetery. Just 2½ km past the fork, on a block-paved road which winds down the cliff side, is the **port hamlet**, the most picturesque spot in Assos. There are a few little pensions and restaurants here, and crowds of bodies in summer. Try to plan your Assos visit for spring or fall.

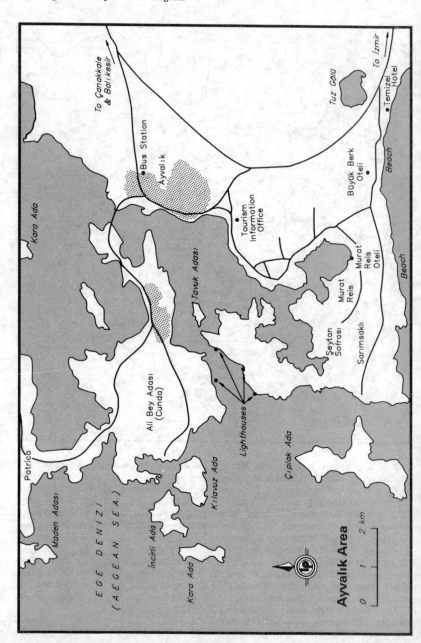

Ayvalık Area

0   1   2 km

To Çanakkale & Balıkesir

To İzmir

Temizel Hotel

Beach

Tuz Gölü

Bus Station

Ayvalık

Büyük Berk Oteli

Kara Ada

Tourism Information Office

Murat Reis Oteli

Tavuk Adası

Murat Reis

Şeytan Sofrası

Sarımsaklı

Ali Bey Adası (Cunda)

Lighthouses

Patrica

Çıplak Ada

Maden Adası

İncirli Ada

Kılavuz Ada

Kara Ada

EGE DENİZİ (AEGEAN SEA)

Places to Stay

The building boom has hit Assos with hotels, motels and pensions opening up all over.

Places to Stay - bottom end

The cheapest way to stay in Assos is to camp in the olive groves where there are five small camp grounds in a row charging about US$1 per person; there are small restaurants here as well. The upper town, near the Temple of Athena, has some pensions, including the cheap *Gök Köşe Pansiyon*. In the port hamlet are the *Hotel Yıldız* (yuhl-DUHZ) (tel 18) and the *Motel Assos*, where double rooms with shower go for about US$18. The *Aristo Motel* charges about the same for a double with shower and breakfast.

Places to Stay - middle

Hotel Behram (BEHH-rahm) (tel 12753) is the most comfortable place in town, and will rent you quite a pleasant room for US$24/36 a single/double, breakfast included.

Places to Eat

Each of the hotels has its own restaurant perched at quay-side beneath a shade of reeds. The Hotel Behram's is the most expensive, with meals for US$4 to US$8; there's also the very basic *Sahil Lokantası* to the right by the Jandarma post. The Sahil is one of the cheapest places in town, but in fact everything is at city prices, as it all must be transported from Ayvacık or beyond.

Getting There & Away

Dolmuşes depart Ayvacık hourly in high summer for Assos. Off season, they are less frequent, perhaps only a few times per day. If you visit off season (which I recommend), leave Ayvalık or Çanakkale early in the day, get to Ayvacık as soon as possible, then hang out on the road to Assos to catch a dolmuş or hitch a ride.

After you've seen Assos and are back on the highway, heading south, you will come round the Bay of Edremit. At the eastern end of the bay are the holiday resorts of **Küçükkuyu, Altınoluk, Akçay** and **Ören**, with moderately priced hotels and motels. At Akçay is a fine five-km-long beach with sulphur springs issuing from parts of it; the beach at Ören is nine km long. Ayvalık, your most likely destination, is 130 km (over two hours) from Assos, 110 km (two hours) from Ayvacık.

AYVALIK

Across a narrow strait from the Greek island of Lesbos, Ayvalık ('EYE'-vah-luhk) is a beach resort, fishing town, olive oil and soap-making centre, and terminus for boats to and from Lesbos. The coast here is cloaked in pine forests and olive orchards, the offshore waters sprinkled with 23 islands.

Orientation

The town of Ayvalık is small and manageable, but with some inconveniences: the otogar is 1½ km north of the centre, the Tourism Information Office one km to the south. Three km farther to the south are the areas called Çamlık and Orta Çamlık, with a scattering of pensions popular with Turkish vacationers. Eight km south of the centre is Sarımsaklı Plaj (SAHR-uhm-SAHK-luh plahzh, Garlic Beach), a nice if not spectacular beach lined with hotels, motels and a few pensions.

Information

The Tourism Information Office (tel (663) 12121) is a km south of the main square around the curve of the bay, opposite the yacht harbour.

Things to See & Do

Ayvalık is about 350 years old. It was inhabited by Ottoman Greeks until after WW I. When the nations formerly incorporated in the Ottoman Empire decided to exchange minority populations, Ayvalık's Turkish-speaking Greeks went to Greece, and Greek-speaking Turks

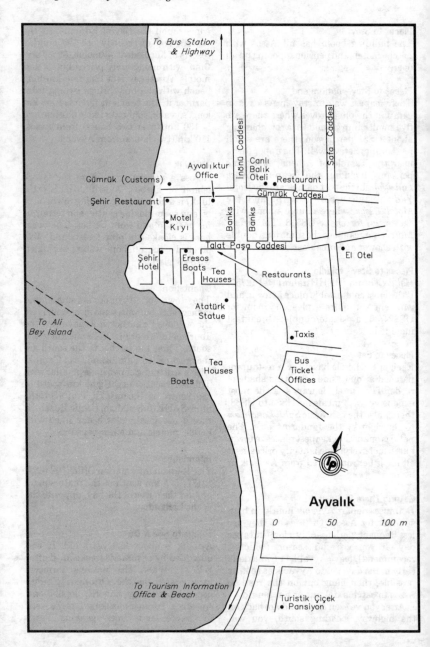

To Bus Station & Highway

İnönü Caddesi

Safa Caddesi

Gümrük (Customs)

Ayvalıktur Office

Canlı Balık Oteli

Restaurant

Şehir Restaurant

Gümrük Caddesi

Motel Kıyı

Banks

Banks

Talat Paşa Caddesi

El Otel

Şehir Hotel

Eresos Boats

Tea Houses

Restaurants

To Ali Bey Island

Atatürk Statue

Taxis

Tea Houses

Bus Ticket Offices

Boats

Ayvalık

0   50   100 m

To Tourism Information Office & Beach

Turistik Çiçek Pansiyon

came here from Lesbos, the Balkans and Crete. A few locals still speak some Greek, and most of the town's mosques are converted Orthodox churches. You can take a look in one of these curiosities as you stroll around town. The **Saatli Camii**, or Mosque With a Clock, was once the church of Agios Yannis (St John); the **Çınarlı Camii** used to be the Agios Yorgos (St George) church.

In summer, boats depart the harbour at the centre of town for **Ali Bey Adası**, an island just across the bay where there are pleasant little seaside restaurants. A causeway links the island to the mainland, so you can go by city bus or taxi any time of the year, but this isn't nearly so much fun as the boat.

Among the standard tourist activities are daytime and evening boat tours around the dozens of islands that fill the bay. The average tour is priced at US$3.50, or US$12 with a meal.

Another goal for excursions is **Şeytan Sofrası** (shey-TAHN soh-frah-suh, Devil's Dinnertable), a hilltop south of the town from which the view is magnificent. There's a snack stand. As no bus or dolmuş runs here regularly, you'll have to take a taxi.

City buses run through the centre of town and south to Sarımsaklı Plaj.

Travelling 41 km south from Ayvalık along the coast road, there is a turning on the right for **Dikili**, four km west of the E24 highway, on the seacoast. A new wharf capable of serving ocean liners is bringing cruise ships to Dikili; the passengers then bus to Bergama to see the ruins. There are a few small, inexpensive hotels and pensions, and some nice waterfront restaurants here. Dikili has been largely undiscovered by the tourist hordes (as yet), and is a nice place to hang out for a few days away from the crowds. The beach is good.

Places to Stay

There are numerous beach resort hotels, motels and camping areas on Sarımsaklı

Plaj, several km south of the centre. You'll also see many pensions, camping areas and little hotels along the road to Sarımsaklı Plaj. Other, quieter camping areas are located along the road to Ali Bey Adası; take the city bus of that name. The hotels in the town centre are convenient, simple and cheap.

Places to Stay – bottom end

There's the *Motel Kıyı* (tel 11438) at 18 Gümrük Meydanı (Customs House Square), where rooms without private bath cost US$10/14/16 a single/double/triple. The motel (actually a tiny hotel) is just off the main square by the harbour, out along the quay in the warren of little streets. The front rooms have nice water views. Right on this same square is the old *Şehir Oteli*, with very cheap, basic rooms for US$3.50 per person. The plumbing (with hot water) is down the hall. This place may be noisy because of the restaurant below.

El Otel (tel 12217) is a block off the main street near the main square, at Safa Caddesi 3, overlooking the intersection with Talat Paşa Caddesi which leads to a church-like mosque. It is very clean and correct, run by God-fearing types who will rent you a room with washbasin for US$7/10/14 a single/double/triple. Some rooms with showers go for the same prices.

Not far from the El Otel is the *Canlı Balık Oteli* (tel 12292), next door to the Canlı Balık Restaurant at 20 Gümrük Caddesi. Prices are slightly less than at the El Otel, but rooms may be quieter here, although they have no running water. On the ground floor of the hotel is a cheap, good restaurant.

The *Turistik Çiçek Pansiyon* (tel 11201) is about 200 metres south of the main square, a half-block off the main road, hidden somewhat by a larger building. There is lots of fluorescent lighting here, and bare but bright corridors leading to simple, clean rooms with a washbasin, renting for US$14/18 a single/double, breakfast included. This place is popular with working-class Turkish families on holiday.

The *Yalı Pension*, behind the PTT, is a fine old Greek house now operated as a pension by a retired Turkish army officer. It has a pretty garden and faces the sea. Pleasant rooms in a clean and caring atmosphere cost US$16 a double, showers and breakfast included.

Places to Stay – middle

The resort hotels in Ayvalık are pleasant and not expensive. One is near Çamlık on the way to Şeytan Sofrası, the others are on Sarımsaklı Plaj.

The *Murat Reis Oteli* (moo-RAHT reh-yeess) (tel 11680, 12788), Sarımsaklı Mevkii, is set apart in its own pine grove with its own beach at the foot of Şeytan Sofrası. This gives it an air of splendid isolation and tranquillity except for the French tour groups which daily come and go. Double rooms including a bath cost US$40 with breakfast, US$52 with breakfast and dinner, or US$60 for two with all meals included. The food here is good. In the busy summer season, if the hotel is nearly full, you will probably have to pay the full-board price. Note also that the groups may monopolise the attentions of the staff, and you may have to fend for yourself sometimes. It's a 15-minute walk to the top of Şeytan Sofrası.

Down on Sarımsaklı Plaj, a mere 50 metres from the water, are numerous good hotels. The 100-room *Otel Ankara* (tel 11195, 41048) has rooms with balcony and bath priced at US$30 a single, US$35 to US$40 a double, breakfast included. A room with full board will cost a total of US$50 or US$55. The hotel has a card-and-game room, bar, café and terrace restaurant.

The *Büyük Berk Oteli* (tel 12311, 41045; fax 41194) is a modern building with lots of facilities, including a swimming pool and water sports paraphernalia, discotheque, playground for children, billiard and table-tennis room. It's right next door to the Ankara.

The 112 guest rooms have private baths, balconies (some with sea views) and prices of US$32 to US$40 a double, breakfast included; or US$42 to US$56 a double, breakfast and dinner included.

The Büyük Berk now has a sister establishment, the fancier *Hotel Club Berk* (tel 41046, or call the Büyük Berk), with even more comfortable and up-to-date guest rooms, a posh lobby done in black marble, golden travertine and soft grey textiles. All of the Büyük Berk's facilities are shared with the new hotel, though the Club Berk does have its own small swimming pool. Room prices here are presently the same as at the Büyük Berk, although I predict the Club Berk will cost more than its sister establishment in future years.

The new *Hotel Zeytinci* should be completed by the time you arrive. Prices and facilities should be similar to the aforementioned three places.

Places to Stay – top end

There's lots of construction in Ayvalık these days, particularly on Sarımsaklı Plaj. At the western end of the beach, not far from the north-south highway, the four-star, 170-room *Temizel Hotel* should be finished by the time you arrive. Prices should be about US$50 to US$70 a single, US$60 to US$80 a double.

Places to Eat

Right on the main square are numerous teahouses, with views of the harbour.

The tiny streets just north of the harbour, around the agencies selling tickets to Lesbos, have several small, simple restaurants with good food and low prices. Try looking on the street which starts between the Tariş Bankası and the Yapı ve Kredi Bankası. You'll find the *Ayvalık Restaurant, Anadolu Pide ve Kebap Salonu* (tel 16759), where I had a lunch of lentil soup, *türlü* (mixed baked vegetables), pilav, a soft drink, lots of fresh bread and tea for US$2.75. The nearby *Sultan Pastanesi* is good for biscuits or pastries and tea.

The full-service restaurant in the area is the *Sahil Restaurant* (tel 11418), on Gümrük Meydanı near the Motel Kıyı. With both indoor and outdoor dining areas, the Sahil serves in all weather. Seafood is the specialty, but you'll pay a lot less if you order meat. A full dinner based on meat, beverage and tip included, costs about US$3; for seafood, figure at least twice as much.

Getting There & Away

Bus Ayvalık is served by the frequent bus service running up and down the Aegean coast between Çanakkale and İzmir, but you may have to hitchhike in from the highway. See the following Getting Around section.

When it comes time to leave Ayvalık, you should know that you can buy bus tickets at offices in the main square. Check departure times and availability early in the day. Bus activity may die down quickly in late afternoon.

Here are some routes, from Ayvalık to:

Assos (Behramkale, via Ayvacık) – 130 km, over two hours, US$2.50; many buses to Ayvacık
Bergama – 50 km, 45 minutes, US$1; many buses to highway junction, few into town
Bursa – 300 km, 4½ hours, US$4; a dozen buses daily, continuing to İstanbul or Ankara
Çanakkale – 200 km, 3½ hours, US$3.50; many buses
İzmir – 240 km, 3½ hours, US$3; many buses

Boats to Lesbos Greek and Turkish boats share the trade and make the two-hour voyage daily in summer (roughly from late May/early June to the end of September). Thus you can leave from Ayvalık on any day at 9 am with the Turkish boat, or 5 pm with the Greek boat. From Lesbos the weekday times are 8.30 am

for the Greek boat and 1.30 pm for the Turkish boat (I've heard that Greek law states you must leave Greece on a Greek-flag vessel, unless you arrived on a Turkish-flag vessel with a round-trip ticket; thus, you may not be able to take the Turkish boat). On weekends the times are different: Saturday at 5.30 am, Sunday at 6 pm from Ayvalık; Saturday at 9 am, Sunday at 8 or 9 pm from Lesbos for the Turkish boat. Off-season (October to April) boats operate about three times a week, but may halt completely in bad winter weather.

The cost of a one-way ticket is US$20 to US$24, a round-trip ticket costs US$28 to US$35. Usually you must buy your ticket and hand over your passport for paperwork a day in advance of the voyage, whether you are departing from Turkey or from Greece. For information and tickets, contact one of the several shipping agencies in the warren of little streets north and west of the main square, near the Motel Kıyı and the Sahil Restaurant. Eresos Tur has an agent, Ali Barış Erener (tel 11756), Talat Paşa Caddesi 67, who can fill you in on schedules and fares, as can Ayvalık Tur (tel 12740). When I last checked, Eresos quoted a lower fare.

Amphitheatre at Pergamum

In summer there are often afternoon boats departing Lesbos at 4 pm for Piraeus, which means that you may be able to leave Ayvalık by the morning boat, spend a pleasant day in Lesbos, depart for Piraeus in the late afternoon, and arrive in Athens about 24 hours after leaving Ayvalık.

Getting Around

Buses along the highway will drop you at the northern turning for Ayvalık, exactly five km from the centre, unless the bus company specifically designates Ayvalık Otogar as a stop. From the highway you must hitchhike into town; most vehicles will understand your situation and stop to give you a lift. If you are dropped in town, it will be at the Şehirlerarası Otobüs Garajı (Intercity Bus Garage), which is 1½ km (15 or 20 minutes' walk) north of the main square. City buses marked 'Ayvalık Belediyesi' run all the way through the town from north to south and will carry you from the bus station to the main square, south to the Tourism Information Office, and farther south to Çamlık, Orta Çamlık and Sarımsaklı, for a minimal fare.

BERGAMA (Pergamum)

Modern Bergama (BEHR-gah-mah) has a population of 60,000 and is part of the province of İzmir. It's an agricultural market town in the midst of a well-watered plain. There has been a town here since Trojan times, but Pergamum's heyday was during the period after Alexander the Great and before Roman domination of all Asia Minor. At that time, Pergamum was one of the richest and most powerful small kingdoms in the Middle East. Its ruins are very impressive.

History

Pergamum owes its prosperity to Lysimachus and to his downfall. Lysimachus, one of Alexander the Great's generals, controlled much of the Aegean region when Alexander's far-flung empire fell apart after his death in 323 BC. In the battles over the spoils Lysimachus captured a great treasure, which he secured in Pergamum before going off to fight Seleucus for control of all Asia Minor. But Lysimachus lost and was slain (281 BC), so Philetarus, the commander he had posted at Pergamum to protect the treasure, set himself up as governor.

Philetarus was a eunuch, but he was succeeded by his nephew Eumenes I (263-241 BC), and Eumenes was followed by his adopted son Attalus I (241-197 BC). Attalus took the title of king, expanded his power and made an alliance with Rome. He was succeeded by his son Eumenes II, and that's when the fun began.

Eumenes II (197-159 BC) was the man who really built Pergamum. Rich and powerful, he added the library and the Altar of Zeus to the hilltop city, and built the 'middle city' on terraces halfway down the hill. The already-famous medical centre of the Asclepion was expanded and beautified as well.

The Pergamum of Eumenes II is remembered most of all for its library. Said to have held more than 200,000 volumes, it was a symbol of Pergamum's social and cultural climb. Eumenes was a mad book collector. His library came to challenge the world's greatest in Alexandria (700,000 books). The Egyptians were afraid Pergamum and its library would attract famous scholars away from Alexandria, so they cut off the supply of papyrus from the Nile. Eumenes set his scientists to work, and they came up with *pergamen* (Latin for 'parchment'), a writing surface made from animal hides rather than pressed papyrus reeds.

The Egyptians were to have their revenge, however. When Eumenes died, he was succeeded by his brother Attalus II (159-138 BC). Things went pretty well under him, but under Attalus II's son Attalus III (138-133 BC) the kingdom was falling to pieces. Attalus III had no heir so he willed his kingdom to Rome. The

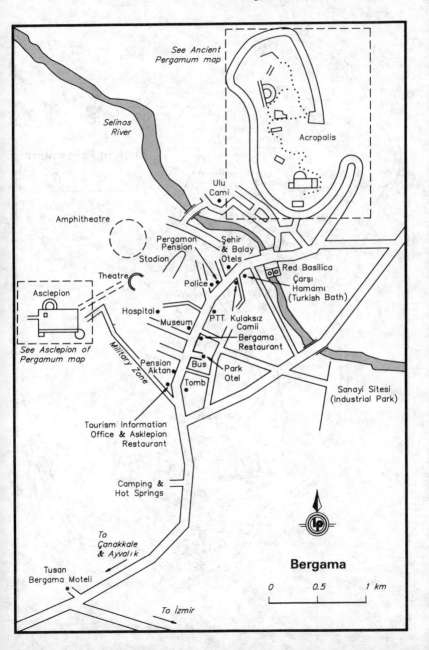

Selinos River

See Ancient
Pergamum map

Acropolis

Ulu
Cami

Amphitheatre

Pergamon
Pension

Şehir
& Balay
Otels

Red Basilica
Çarşı
Hamamı
(Turkish Bath)

Stadion

Theatre

Police

Asclepion

Hospital

Museum

PTT

Kulaksız
Camii

Bergama
Restaurant

See Asclepion of
Pergamum map

Military Zone

Pension
Aktan

Bus

Park
Otel

Tomb

Sanayi Sitesi
(Industrial Park)

Tourism Information
Office & Asklepion
Restaurant

Camping &
Hot Springs

To Çanakkale
& Ayvalık

Tusan
Bergama Moteli

Bergama

0   0.5   1 km

To İzmir

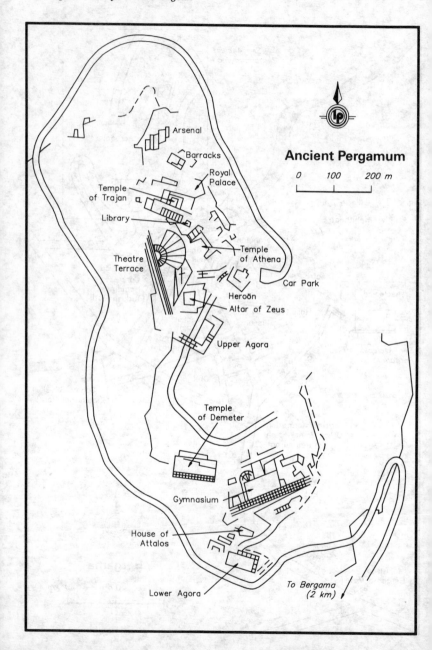

Ancient Pergamum

0   100   200 m

Arsenal

Barracks

Royal Palace

Temple of Trajan

Library

Temple of Athena

Theatre Terrace

Car Park

Heroön

Altar of Zeus

Upper Agora

Temple of Demeter

Gymnasium

House of Attalos

Lower Agora

To Bergama (2 km)

Kingdom of Pergamum became the Roman province of Asia in 129 BC.

In the early years of the Christian era the great library at Alexandria was damaged by fire. Marc Antony, out of devotion to Cleopatra, pillaged the library at Pergamum for books to replace those of the Egyptian queen.

Orientation

Bergama's layout is pretty easy to figure out. Everything you'll need is between the bus station to the west and the market to the east, including hotels, restaurants and the Archaeology Museum. The two principal archaeological sites are out of town, several km in each case. The 'centre of town', for our purposes, is the Archaeology Museum on the main street. The main street, by the way, is called İzmir Caddesi, İzmir Yolu, Cumhuriyet Caddesi, Hükümet Caddesi, Bankalar Caddesi, or Uzun Çarşı Caddesi, depending upon whom you ask.

Information

Bergama's Tourism Information Office (tel (541) 11862), Zafer Mahallesi, İzmir Yolu Üzeri 54, is two km west of the centre of town, on the main road out to the highway, at the turning for the Asclepion.

Bergama has four sites to visit. Only one is in the centre of town; the others require some healthy hiking or the hire of a taxi.

Acropolis

Much of what was built by the ambitious kings of Pergamum did not survive, but what did survive is certainly impressive.

The bitumen road up to the Acropolis winds five km from the centre of town (ie, the museum), around the north side of the hill, to a car park at the top. Next to the car park are some souvenir and soft-drink stands, and a ticket seller (US$3). You can visit the Acropolis any day from 9 am to 5 pm (till 7 pm in summer); the road is open from 8.30 am to 5.30 pm (till 7.30 pm in summer).

While you're up here on the Acropolis, don't forget to look for the Asclepion, across the valley to the west, on the north edge of town near an army base. You'll also see the ruins of a small theatre, a larger theatre and a stadium down in the valley.

The outstanding structures on the Acropolis include (of course) the **library**, being rebuilt with West German aid to its former glory. The great **theatre** is impressive (10,000 seats) and unusual. Pergamum borrowed from Hellenistic architecture, but in the case of the theatre it made major modifications. To take advantage of the spectacular view and to conserve precious building space atop the hill, it was decided to build the theatre into the hillside. Hellenistic theatres are usually more rounded, but because of its location, rounding was impossible, so it was heightened instead. Below the stage of the theatre is the ruined **Temple of Dionysus**.

The **Altar of Zeus**, south of the theatre, shaded by evergreen trees, is in an idyllic setting. Most of the building is now in Berlin, taken there (with the sultan's permission) by the 19th-century German excavators of Pergamum. Only the base remains.

Otherwise, several piles of rubble atop the Acropolis are marked as the **palaces** of Attalus I and Eumenes II, and there is an **agora** as well as fragments of the defensive **walls**.

Walk down the hill from the Altar of Zeus, through the **Middle City**, and you will pass the **Altar and Temple of Demeter**, **gymnasium or school**, **Lower Agora** and **Roman bath**. The path down is not well marked.

Asclepion

The road to the Asclepion is at the western edge of town on the way to the highway. The ruins are 3½ km from the Archaeology Museum, about 1½ km from the Tourism Information Office. To reach the Asclepion you must pass through a military zone.

Don't take photographs or leave the road in the zone. The Asclepion is open during the same hours and for the same admission fee as the Acropolis.

The Asclepion of Pergamum was not the first nor the only ancient medical centre. In fact, this one was founded by Archias, a citizen of Pergamum who had been treated and cured at the Asclepion of Epidaurus in Greece. But Pergamum's centre came to the fore under Galen (131-210 AD), who was born here, studied in Alexandria and Greece as well as in Asia Minor, and set up shop as physician to Pergamum's gladiators. Recognised as perhaps the greatest early physician, Galen added considerably to knowledge of the circulatory and nervous systems, and also systematised medical theory. Under his influence, the medical school at Pergamum became renowned. His work was the basis for all western medicine well into the 1500s. About 162 AD, he moved to Rome and became personal physician to Emperor Marcus Aurelius.

As you walk around the ruins, you'll see bas-reliefs or carvings of a snake, the symbol of Aesculapius, god of medicine. Just as the snake shed its skin and gained a 'new life', so the patients at the Asclepion were supposed to 'shed' their illnesses. Diagnosis was often by dream analysis. Treatment included massage and mud baths, drinking sacred waters, and the use of herbs and ointments.

A **Sacred Way** leads from the car park to the centre. Signs mark a **Temple to Aesculapius, library** and **Roman Theatre**. Take a drink of cool water from the **Sacred Well**, then pass along the vaulted underground corridor to the **Temple of Telesphorus**. It is said that patients slept in the temple hoping that Telesphorus, another god of medicine, would send a cure, or at least a diagnosis, in a dream. Telesphorus, by the way, had two daughters named Hygeia and Panacea.

Other Sights

The **Arkeoloji Müzesi** or Archaeology Museum is in the town centre next to the hillside tea gardens, not far from the Park Otel. It has a substantial collection of artefacts for so small a town, and an excellent ethnology section as well. It's open from 9 am to 12 noon and 1 to 7 pm in summer (to 5.30 pm in winter), every day; admission costs US$3.

The **Kızıl Avlu** (KUH-zuhl ahv-loo), Red Basilica or Red Courtyard, was originally a temple built in the 2nd century AD to Serapis, an Egyptian god. It was converted to a Christian basilica by the Byzantines and now holds a small mosque, proving the theory that sacred ground tends to remain sacred even though the religion may change. You'll notice the curious red flat-brick walls of the large, roofless structure if you take the main road to the Acropolis; or you can see it from atop the Acropolis. You can walk to the Kızıl Avlu, or stop your taxi there on your way to or from the Acropolis.

Places to Stay

Bergama has one mid-range motel on the outskirts of town, a cheap hotel and several pensions in the town centre. This is a surprisingly small number of lodging places for a town of this importance. Try to arrive early in the day to claim one of the scarce rooms.

Places to Stay – bottom end

The central hotels are very basic, plain and cheap. The *Park Otel* (tel 11246), Park Otel Sokak 6, is closest to the bus station and the first place where most people look for a room. Walking east into town from the bus station, turn right after several blocks; there's a sign, and it's easy to find. Rooms are quite bare and plain but tidy, and in fierce demand at US$6/8 a single/double without any private facilities. Hot showers cost another US$0.75, and breakfast goes for US$1.75. There's a shady sitting area in front, and the location is fairly quiet.

The *Pension Aktan* (tel 14000), İzmir Caddesi 18, is conveniently located on the

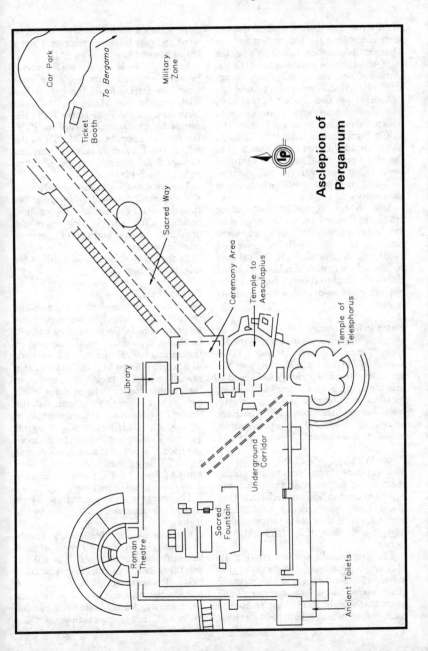

Asclepion of Pergamum

main street 120 metres west of the bus station, between the bus station and the Tourism Information Office; it's on the right-hand side as you come from the bus station. Clean and friendly, they charge US$10 for a double room with twin beds.

Another pension is a bit farther east, past the museum, and it also caters to backpackers. The *Pergamon Pension* (tel 12395), Bankalar Caddesi 3, Polis Karakolu Yanı, is in an old stone house right next to the city's police station in the centre of town. Doubles without running water go for US$8; meals are available at tables in the courtyard.

Also in the centre of town along Hükümet Caddesi, on the left-hand side, are the *Şehir Oteli* (tel 11031), Uzun Çarşı Caddesi 45 and the *Balay Oteli* (tel 11334), Uzun Çarşı Caddesi 47, next door to one another, with similar rooms and prices identical to those at the Park Otel but not quite as desirable and certainly noisier.

Places to Stay – middle

Bergama's fanciest place to stay is the 42-room *Tusan Bergama Moteli* (TOO-sahn) (tel 11173), Çatü Mevkii, near the junction of the E24 highway and the road into town. It has a restaurant and a quiet location with pretty gardens, in the middle of nowhere. Rooms with a bath are priced at US$25/30 a single/double; breakfast costs another US$4.

Places to Eat

You will pass several restaurants on the main street as you walk through town. Most are used to tourists and are at that stage when you should ask prices, remonstrate if they seem unreasonable, and check your bill thoroughly for 'errors'.

The *Bergama Restaurant* (tel 11274), Hükümet Caddesi, has a fancyish sidewalk terrace dining area with plentiful street noise, and a large interior dining room that's fairly plain. They're used to tourists here, which is both good and bad,

as they may assume they know what you want and may be somewhat curt. I had a three-course dinner here for US$7.

Simpler places, with lower prices, perhaps better food and certainly more quiet, are farther along the main street past the museum. Look for the *Zeus Lokantası*, to the right of the PTT, the *Lezzet Lokantası* to the left of the PTT, the *Osman Lokantası* (tel 12395) to the left of the Pergamon Pension, and the *Doyum 2 Restaurant*, two doors to the right of the Şehir Oteli.

The main street also has several pastry shops, including the *Café Manolya* across from the Tekel (Turkish State Monopolies) building. You might come here for breakfast, or for tea and a pudding or cake later in the day.

At the ruins there are soft drinks for sale, but no food.

Getting There & Away

Whether you approach Bergama from the north or south, check to see if your bus actually stops *in* Bergama. Any bus will be glad to drop you along the highway at the turning to Bergama, but you will have to hitchhike seven km into town in this case. The hitch is pretty easy, except in the evening. Better to be on a bus which goes right to Bergama's otogar. Ask the driver, *Bergama Santral Garajına gidiyor musunuz?* (BEHR-gah-mah sahn-tral gah-rah-zhuh-nah gee-dee-YOHR moo-soo-nooz, 'Do you go to Bergama's central garage?') Be advised that many drivers will nod *Evet!* (Yes!), and then blithely drop you out at the highway.

The otogar is on the main street, which is also the road from town out to the highway.

Bergama municipal buses run frequently every day (6 am to 7.30 pm) between Bergama and İzmir's otogar. The 100-km trip takes less than two hours and costs US$1. It's not too difficult to travel between Bergama and Ayvalık or Bergama and İzmir, but buses to other destinations are not all that frequent. In winter, you may find yourself travelling via İzmir or Balıkesir to change buses.

There is a frequent dolmuş service between Bergama and Dikili, 30 km to the east.

Getting Around

Taxi Because many tourists come to Bergama from İzmir on day-trips, Bergama doesn't have many hotels. You can easily see the sights of Bergama in a day and get to İzmir in the evening, especially if you use a taxi to travel among the far-flung ruins. If you plan to walk everywhere (there are no buses to the various ruins), it will be a long day. To walk it all, plan to stay overnight.

If you're in good shape and don't mind walking, but you want to see everything in a day, find others to share a taxi to the top of the Acropolis, then walk down the hill to the Kızıl Avlu. Walking down through the various levels of the ruined city is the best way to see the site, in any case. From the Kızıl Avlu, walk through the market district into town, have lunch and take a taxi, or hitch, or walk to the Asclepion, depending upon your budget, your fatigue and your schedule.

The standard taxi-tour rates and times are: up to the Acropolis and return, plus one hour's waiting time at the top, US$7 per *carload*, not per person. To the Asclepion, a half-hour's wait and back to tour is both of these for US$10. Just to drive to the top of the Acropolis should drive to the top of the Acropolis should cost only about US$4, but you may have to haggle for this.

SOUTH TOWARD İZMİR

The coast between Bergama and İzmir was once the Ionian and Aeolian shore, thick with Hellenic cities and busy with trade. Of these ancient cities very few traces remain. Instead, what you'll see are farming towns and villages, plus the occasional beach resort.

The farming village of Çandarlı is 20 km south of Dikili, and about 15 km westward

along a side road. It has a little restored Genoese fortress of the 1300s and numerous pensions. It's a popular weekend and holiday resort for middle-class İzmirlis, so the pensions tend to be priced about US$5 to US$8 per person.

North of Menemen, a road leads west to **Foça**, sometimes called Eski Foça, the ancient Phocaea, a town founded before 600 BC. Nothing remains of the ancient city. In recent centuries this was an Ottoman Greek fishing and trading town, but it's now a middle-class Turkish resort with yachts bobbing in the harbour. Near Yenifoça, to the north of Foça, there's a Club Méditerranée holiday village (*tatil köyü*).

Menemen

Menemen (MEHN-eh-mehn), 33 km north of İzmir, is famous for a reactionary riot which took place in 1930. Atatürk's cultural reforms such as abolishing religious law, separating religion from the state and recognising the equality of women were not received well by religious conservatives. A band of fanatical dervishes staged a riot in Menemen's town square. When a young army officer named Mustafa Fehmi Kubilay attempted to quell the disturbance, he was shot and beheaded by the dervishes. The government took immediate action to quash the fanatics' revolt, and proclaimed Kubilay a republican hero. The statue here honours the young officer.

Manisa

A road goes east 30 km to the town of Manisa (mah-NEES-ah), the ancient town of Magnesia ad Sipylus. It lies at an altitude of 74 metres and has a population of 130,000. It is a modern little city with an ancient past. An early king here was Tantalus, from whom we get the word 'tantalise'. The early, great Ottoman sultans favoured it as a residence, and for a while the province of Manisa was the training ground for crown princes.

During the War of Independence,

retreating Greek soldiers wreaked terrible destruction on Manisa. After they passed through, Manisa's 18,000 historic buildings had been reduced to only 500.

Near the end of April each year, Manisa has a special festival celebrating kuvvet macunu (kew-VEHT mah-joo-noo, 'power gum'). Manisa power gum, a local concoction made from who-knows-what, is distributed. It is supposed to restore health, youth and potency.

Things to See As you might expect, there are several old mosques, among them the **Muradiye** (1586) with nice tilework, a small museum and near it the tomb of Saruhan Bey; the **Sultan Camii** (1572) with some gaudy painting, but an agreeable hamam next door; and, perched on the steep hillside above the town, the **Ulu Cami** (1366), ravished by the ages, and not as impressive as the view from the teahouse next to it. Other mosques in town are the **Hatuniye** (1490) and the **İlyas Bey** (1363).

Places to Stay Manisa has one nice hotel, the 34-room two-star *Hotel Arma* (tel 11980), Doğu Caddesi 14, with a willing and helpful staff, restaurant and bar, clean and presentable rooms, a lift and prices of US$20/28 a single/double. Other than the Arma, there are few places to stay (everyone stays in İzmir and drives here for the day, whatever their business). The *Hotel Yılmaz* near the bus station charges about US$5/8 a single/double, and is OK, but noisy.

Into İzmir

If you approach İzmir from Menemen along the E24, you will pass a road at Çiğli to İzmir's old airport. İzmir's new Adnan Menderes Airport – the one you'll use – is at Cumaovası, south of the city half-way to Ephesus. Past Çiğli, the highway passes the suburb of Karşıyaka (KAHR-shuh-YAH-kah), then curves around the end of the bay to the otogar.

Coming from Manisa, the road passes through the suburb of Bornova, once the residence of wealthy Levantine traders. Some of their mansions still stand, most now converted to public use such as municipal offices and schools. There's a university here. İzmir city buses run from Bornova to the centre of İzmir.

İZMİR (Smyrna)

İzmir (EEZ-meer), with a population of 2,000,000, is Turkey's third-largest city and its major port on the Aegean. It has a different feeling about it, something Mediterranean, something more than just being a large and prosperous Turkish city. The setting is certainly dramatic, for İzmir rings a great bay and is backed to the east and south by mountains. Most of the city is quite modern and well laid out, with broad boulevards radiating from a series of hubs. The streets are lined with waffle-front, stucco-and-glass apartment and office blocks, and dotted with shady sidewalk cafés, though here and there the red-tile roof and bull's-eye window of a 19th-century warehouse hide in the shadow of an office tower. When you see an old mosque in İzmir it comes as a surprise, as though it doesn't really fit in.

You may enjoy a short stay in İzmir, with its palm-lined waterfront promenade. The city can be explored and enjoyed in a fairly short time because there's not a whole lot to see: most of the remains from its long and eventful history have been swept away by war, fire and earthquake. Compared to most Turkish towns, İzmir does not have a large number of antiquities. You can also use İzmir as a base for excursions to a few nearby points: Sardis, for instance. But in most cases you will be ready to move on in a day, as you may find İzmir to be just a big, busy, noisy and impersonal Turkish city.

History

İzmir owes its special atmosphere, indeed its entire appearance, to an eventful and turbulent history. What you see today is new because it has risen on the ashes of

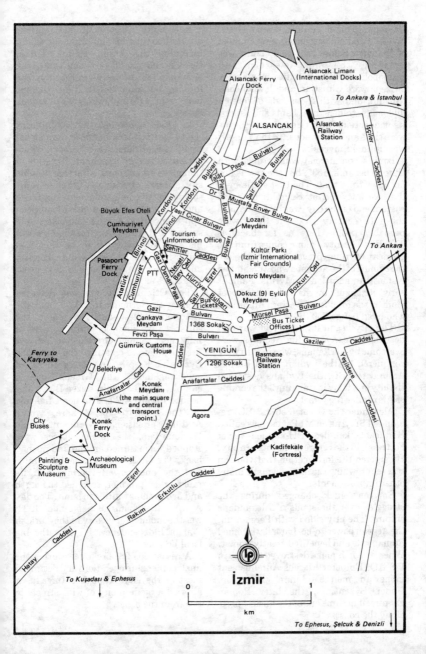

To Ankara & İstanbul

Alsancak Limanı
(International Docks)

Alsancak Ferry
Dock

ALSANCAK

Alsancak
Railway
Station

Caddesi

Talât Paşa Bulvarı

Dr Pleyne

Sair Eşref Bulvarı

Mustafa Enver Bulvarı

İşçiler

Caddesi

Büyük Efes Oteli

Cumhuriyet
Meydanı

Yasif Çınar Bulvarı

(İkinci) Kordon

(Birinci) Kordon

Tourism
Information Office

Lozan
Meydanı

Kültür Parkı
(İzmir International
Fair Grounds)

To Ankara

Pasaport
Ferry
Dock

Atatürk Cumhuriyet

PTT

Gazi Osman Paşa Blvd

Şehitler

1296 Sokak

(Necati) Bey Cad

Caddesi

Sair Eşref

Hürriyet Bulvarı

Montrö Meydanı

Bozkurt Cad

Gazi

Bulvarı

Çankaya
Meydanı

1368 Sokak

Dokuz (9) Eylül
Meydanı

Mürsel Paşa

Bulvarı

Bus
Tickets

Bus Ticket
Offices

Gaziler

Caddesi

Fevzi Paşa
Bulvarı

Gümrük Customs
House

YENİGÜN

1296 Sokak

Basmane
Railway
Station

Yeşildere

Caddesi

Ferry to
Karşıyaka

Anafartalar Cad

Belediye

Anafartalar Caddesi

City
Buses

KONAK

Konak
Meydanı
(the main square
and central transport
point.)

Agora

Kadifekale
(Fortress)

Paşa

Painting &
Sculpture
Museum

Konak Ferry
Dock

Archaeological
Museum

Eşref

Rakım

Erkutlu

Caddesi

Hatay

Caddesi

To Kuşadası & Ephesus

0   1

km

İzmir

To Ephesus, Şelcuk & Denizli

Ottoman İzmir since 1923, when a Greek invasion and a disastrous fire razed most of the city. Before that year, İzmir was Smyrna, the most western and cosmopolitan of Turkish cities, where more citizens were Christian and Jewish than Muslim, and with thousands of foreign diplomats, traders, merchants and sailors. Its connections with Greece and Europe were close and continuous. To the Turks it was 'Infidel Smyrna'.

İzmir's commercial connections with Europe began in 1535, but the city is far, far older than that. The first settlement that we know of, at Bayraklı near the eastern end of the bay, was by Aeolians in the 10th century BC, but there were probably people here as far back as 3000 BC. The city's name comes from the goddess Myrina, prevalent deity before the coming of the Aeolians who worshipped Nemesis in addition to Myrina. Famous early citizens of Smyrna included the poet Homer, the founder of western literature, who lived before 700 BC.

The city began its history of war and destruction early, for the Aeolians were overcome by the Ionians, who in turn were conquered by the Lydians from Sardis. Around 600 BC, the Lydians destroyed the city and it lay in ruins until the coming of Alexander the Great.

Alexander the Great (356-323 BC) re-founded Smyrna on Mt Pagus, now called Kadifekale (kah-dee-FEH-kah-leh, Velvet Fortress), in the centre of the modern city. He erected the fortification that you can still see crowning the hill, and made many other improvements.

Smyrna's luck changed during the struggles over the spoils of Alexander's empire. The city sided with Pergamum, the Aegean power-to-be. Later it welcomed Roman rule and benefited greatly from it. When an earthquake destroyed the city in 178 AD, Emperor Marcus Aurelius sent money and men to aid in reconstruction. Under Byzantium, the later Roman Empire, it became one of the busiest ports along the coast.

As Byzantium's power declined, various armies marched in, and often out again, including the Arabs, Seljuk Turks, Genoese and Crusaders. When Tamerlane arrived in 1402 he destroyed the city, true to form, but after he left, the Ottomans took over (1415) and things began to look better.

In 1535, Süleyman the Magnificent signed the Ottomans' first-ever commercial treaty (with François I of France), which permitted foreign merchants to reside in the sultan's dominions. After that humble start, İzmir became Turkey's most sophisticated commercial city. Its streets and buildings took on a quasi-European appearance, and a dozen languages were spoken in its cafés. Any merchant worth his salt was expected to be fluent in Turkish, Greek, Italian, German, English and Arabic, and perhaps a few other languages as well.

The Ottoman Empire was defeated along with Germany in WW I, and the victorious Allies sought to carve the sultan's vast dominions into spheres of influence. Some Greeks had always dreamed of re-creating the long-lost Byzantine Empire. In 1920, with Allied encouragement, the Greeks took a gamble, invaded İzmir, seized Bursa and headed toward Ankara. In fierce fighting on the outskirts of Ankara, where Atatürk's provisional government had its headquarters, the foreign forces were stopped, then turned around and pushed back. The Greek defeat turned to a rout, and the once-powerful army, half its ranks taken prisoner, scorched the earth and fled to ships waiting in İzmir. The day Atatürk took İzmir, 9 September 1922, was the moment of victory in the Turkish War of Independence. It's now the big local holiday.

A disastrous fire broke out during the final mopping-up operations and destroyed most of the city. Though a tragedy, it allowed a modern city of wide streets to rise from the ashes.

Orientation

İzmir has wide boulevards and an apparent sense of orderliness, but it is in fact somewhat difficult to negotiate. This is because the numerous roundabouts (traffic circles), with their streets radiating like spokes from a hub, don't give you the sense of direction a street grid does. Here are some tips on getting your bearings.

First of all, the city's two main avenues run parallel to the waterfront, downtown. The waterfront street is officially Atatürk Caddesi, which is what you will see in written addresses, but everyone in town calls it the Birinci Kordon (beer-EEN-jee kohr-DOHN, First Cordon). Just inland from it is Cumhuriyet Bulvarı (joom-hoor-ee-YEHT bool-vahr-uh, Republic Blvd), which is called by everyone the İkinci Kordon (ee-KEEN-jee, Second Cordon).

The city's two main squares are located along these two parallel avenues. The very centre of town is Konak Meydanı (koh-NAHK mey-dah-nuh, Government House Square), or simply Konak. Here you will find the municipality buildings, the Ottoman clock tower (İzmir's symbol), a little old tiled mosque, pedestrian bridges over the busy roadway and a dock for ferries to Karşıyaka (kahr-shuh-YAH-kah), the suburb across the bay.

Konak is the city's bus and dolmuş hub, so you can pick up a vehicle to any part from here. You can also board buses for Selçuk, Ephesus and Kuşadası here as well as at the otogar. Konak also has an entrance to the bazaar. Anafartalar Caddesi, the bazaar's main street, winds through İzmir's most picturesque quarters all the way to the Basmane (bahs-mah-NEH) Railway Station.

The other main square holds the equestrian statue of Atatürk and is called Cumhuriyet Meydanı. It is about a km north of Konak along the two kordons. The PTT, Tourism Information Office, Turkish Airlines office and Büyük Efes Oteli are here. The 19th-century building right on the quay is called Pasaport, and used to be the entry point for foreign ships. It is now a ferry dock used during rush hours only. From Pasaport to Konak along the Birinci Kordon is an active shipping centre for local commerce, with colourful kayık (kah-YUK) boats moored along its length. The offices of the Turkish Maritime Lines are here as well.

The section called Çankaya (CHAN-kah-yah) is two long blocks inland, south-east of Cumhuriyet Meydanı.

Another İzmir landmark is the Kültür Parkı (kewl-TEWR pahr-kuh), site of the annual İzmir International Fair, an amusement and industry show which takes place from about 20 August to 9 September each year. Hotel space is very difficult to find during the fair. When it's not fair time the grounds provide a pleasant, shady place to walk, sit and rest, with some amusements.

Finally, the hill directly behind the main part of town is crowned by Kadifekale.

Information

The Tourism Information Office (tel (51) 19 92 78) is next to the Büyük Efes Oteli, in the row of offices which includes the Turkish Airlines office. The bus station has a small office as well. The main office (tel (51) 21 68 41, 22 02 07, 22 02 08) is at Atatürk Caddesi 418, Alsancak.

Agora

The marketplace built on the orders of Alexander was ruined in an earthquake (178 AD), but there is much remaining from the Agora as it was rebuilt by Marcus Aurelius just after the quake. Corinthian colonnades, vaulted chambers and a reconstructed arch fill this conspicuously open spot in the midst of the crowded city, and give you a good idea of what a Roman 'bazaar' looked like.

To reach it, walk up Eşref Paşa Caddesi from Fevzi Paşa Bulvarı one short and one long block, to 816 Sokak, on the left. This street of bakeries and radio repair shops leads to the Agora, one short block away, which is open from 8.30 am to 5.30 pm daily; admission costs US$0.50. You can also reach the Agora via 943 Sokak, off Anafartalar Caddesi near the Hatuniye Camii in the bazaar. Follow the signs.

Bazaar

İzmir's bazaar is large and fascinating. An hour or two of exploration along Anafartalar Caddesi is a must. You can pick up this street easily from Eşref Paşa Caddesi, after your visit to the Agora, or enter the street from Basmane or Konak. Just get lost in the bazaar, enjoy its sights and sounds, and when you're ready to get out, ask for directions to Basmane, Çankaya, or Konak. Note that virtually all bazaar shops close on Sunday, and there's little to see on that day.

Kadifekale

The time to ride up the mountain is an hour before sunset. Catch a dolmuş in Konak (it may say only 'K Kale' on the sign) and allow 15 or 20 minutes for the ride. The view on all sides is spectacular. Look inside the walls, and even climb up on them if you like. Just at sunset, the muezzins will give the call to prayer from İzmir's minarets. A wave of sound rolls across the city as the lights twinkle on.

Near the gate in the walls are a few little terrace teahouses where you can have a seat and a tea, soft drink or beer.

Archaeology & Ethnology Museums

These two museums are just a short walk up the hill from Konaklong, along the road up to Kadifekale called the Varyant. The entrance is positioned on the one-way road which brings traffic down the hillside, so to reach the museums, walk up that way. If you walk up the road carrying uphill traffic, you'll walk all the way around the museums but you won't be able to enter.

The two museums are open from 9 am to 5.30 pm every day; admission costs US$1 per museum.

The Arkeoloji Müzesi or Archaeology Museum is in a modern building. You enter on a floor with quite fine exhibits of Egyptian, Greek and Roman statuary, then move to an upper level dedicated to terracotta objects, tools and vessels, glassware, metalwork and jewellery of silver and gold. The lower level has tomb statuary and sarcophagi, and also the head of a gigantic statue of Domitian which once stood at Ephesus. Be sure to see the beautiful frieze from the mausoleum at Belevi (250 BC), south of İzmir, and also the high relief of Poseidon and Demeter dating from 200 AD. All plaques in the museum are in English and Turkish.

Perhaps of even more interest is the Etnoğrafya Müzesi or Ethnography Museum, in the old stone building next door. Once İzmir's Department of Public Health, this interesting old building now houses colourful displays demonstrating the folk arts, crafts and customs of the city and its surrounding province. You'll learn about camel wrestling, the potter's craft as practised here, the important craft of tin-plating whereby toxic copper vessels were made safe for kitchen use, felt-making, wood block printing for scarves and cloths, and embroidery. You can even see how those curious little blue-and-white 'evil eye' beads are made; this craft goes back hundreds, perhaps even thousands of years.

Other exhibits include an Ottoman chemist's shop, a fully decorated salon from a 19th-century Ottoman residence, an Ottoman bridal chamber, a circumcision celebration room from the same period and a kitchen. Carpet-making is explained, and there are displays of armour, weapons and local costumes. The museum is well worth a visit.

Other Sights

As you make your way around town, you will certainly see the equestrian statue of Atatürk in Cumhuriyet Meydanı. It symbolises Atatürk's leadership as he began the counter-offensive from Ankara.

His battle order to the troops on the first day of the offensive (26 August 1922) read 'Soldiers, your goal is the Aegean'.

A few blocks north of Cumhuriyet Meydanı is the South-Eastern Head-quarters of NATO, in a building with a long row of flags in front. Here and there along the Birinci Kordon you can see the few old stone houses which survived the Great Fire of 1922.

The Kültür Parkı or Culture Park is pleasant, and you can dodge in here any time of day for a quiet walk or picnic away from the city bustle. In late August and early September, the fairgrounds hold centre stage in this city, as the İzmir International Fair is in session.

Had it with the crowded, noisy city? Head down to the ferry dock on the waterfront in Konak, and board a ferry for the ride over to Karşıyaka, on the far side of the bay. The view is beautiful, the air fresh and cool. The voyage over and back takes an hour, perhaps 75 minutes, and costs less than US$0.50 return.

Places to Stay

İzmir has lots and lots of good, very cheap places to stay, and several nice expensive places. The middle-range establishments, unfortunately, often suffer from street noise so you must choose your room carefully. The magic word for low prices is Basmane; there are several middle-range places near that railway station as well. The top-end places tend to be on the waterfront near Cumhuriyet Meydanı.

Places to Stay – bottom end

The quarter named Yenigün – bounded by Fevzi Paşa Bulvarı, Basmane Meydanı, Anafartalar Caddesi and Eşref Paşa Caddesi, and right next to Basmane, İzmir's main railway station – is a low-budget traveller's dream come true. Several entire streets are lined with clean, cheap, safe places to stay.

Walk out the front door of Basmane Station, turn left, fight your way across the flood of traffic and walk up the shady Anafartalar Caddesi. After you cross the road, turn right then left almost immediately, keeping the little Basmane Camii on your left. Take the first street on your right, which is 1296 Sokak. (All these directions sound complicated, but in fact you're just across the road from the railway station.)

Now, 1296 Sokak is nothing but small hotels, some in new buildings, others in grand old İzmir houses with coloured glass, fancy woodwork and mosaic floors. Though there is some spread in prices, most tend to charge between US$3 and US$6 per bed in a room with a washbasin only, or about US$5 to US$8 per bed in a room with a private shower.

A few steps along 1296 Sokak, on the left-hand side, is the Yıldız Palas Oteli (yuhl-DUHZ pah-lahss) (tel 25 15 18), 1296 Sokak No 50, reputedly a family hotel favouring couples and women travellers, though one reader says the 'aile' designation just makes it easier for the local Romeos to know where the girls are. Bright and airy, it is quite simple, but so are its prices: US$7 for a double bed without running water, US$10 for twin beds with a washbasin and telephone.

Slightly farther along 1296 Sokak, look left down a side street and you'll see the Otel Gümüş Palas (gerr-MERSH pah-lahss) (tel 13 41 53), 1299 Sokak No 12, a more modern place (but hardly ultramodern) where a double room without running water costs only US$3 per bed.

Right next door to the Gümüş Palas is the Hotel Enka (tel 12 24 57), 1299 Sokak, also advertising itself as an aile hotel, and charging about the same for beds, as does the Otel Yeşil Palas nearby on 1296 Sokak.

These suggestions are only the tip of the iceberg. In the unlikely event that you don't find what you want on 1296 Sokak, look on the parallel 1294 Sokak, between 1296 and Fevzi Paşa Bulvarı.

Should you want a slightly better class of hotels, head for a different area equally near Basmane Station, packed with

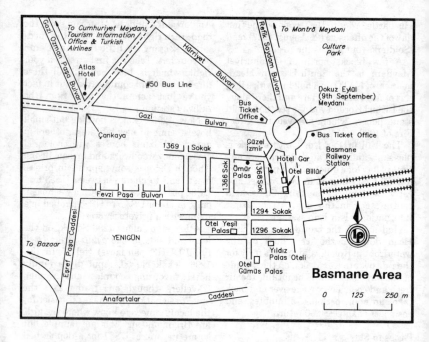

To Cumhuriyet Meydanı,
Tourism Information
Office & Turkish
Airlines

Gazi Osman Paşa Bulvarı

Atlas
Hotel

#50 Bus Line

Çankaya

Hürriyet Bulvarı

Refik Saydam Bulvarı

To Montrö Meydanı

Culture
Park

Gazi   Bulvarı

Bus Ticket
Office

Dokuz Eylül
(9th September)
Meydanı

Bus Ticket Office

1369 | Sokak

1366 Sok

Güzel
İzmir

Ömür
Palas

1368 Sok

Hotel Gar

Otel Billûr

Basmane
Railway
Station

Fevzi Paşa Bulvarı

1294 Sokak

Esref Paşa Caddesi

To Bazaar

YENİGÜN

Otel Yeşil
Palas

1296 Sokak

Yıldız
Palas Oteli

Otel
Gümüş Palas

Basmane Area

Anafartalar   Caddesi

0   125   250 m

---

hotels and with good restaurants as well. Go out the station door and straight down the right-hand side of Fevzi Paşa Bulvarı to the three-star Hotel Hisar. Turn right and you will be on 1368 Sokak, which is lined with little hotels charging about US$12 to US$20 for a double room with a private shower.

The *Otel Özcan* (ERZ-jahn) (tel 13 50 52), 1368 Sokak No 3, is typical, being an older building with clean, quiet rooms renting for US$10 a double without a private shower, or US$12 with one. The *Güzel İzmir* (tel 13 50 69, 14 66 93), 1368 Sokak 8, is fancier by the look of its lobby, but the rooms are about the same and go for US$6 to US$9 per person in a room with washbasin or with shower. Try also the *Yeni Park Oteli* (tel 13 52 31) and the *Bilen Palas* (tel 13 92 46), 1369 Sokak 68; the latter is on the corner, and charges US$13 for a double with washbasin.

Walk along 1368 Sokak and at the end,

on 1369 Sokak, are several more: the *Otel Akgün* (tel 13 55 63) and the clean and friendly *Otel Oba* (tel 13 54 74), 1369 Sokak 59, just to name two. Most of these hotels give you a choice between rooms with a shower and rooms without, and most are very quiet, even in this noisy city.

Places to Stay – middle

Basmane Of the moderately priced hotels in the Basmane area, the most readily found is the two-star, 60-room *Otel Billûr* (bee-LYOOR) (tel 13 62 50, 13 97 32), Basmane Meydanı 783, facing the railway station. The rooms are fine and the prices not bad – US$24 to US$32 a single, or US$28 to US$40 a double, US$45 to US$50 for a suite with a shower or bath, and breakfast. However, many of the rooms facing the street will be noisy, so be sure to look at and listen in the room before you rent it. Just to the right of the Billûr is the similar *Hotel Gar*.

Hotel Nil (NEEL) (tel 13 52 28, 13 56 20), Fevzi Paşa Bulvarı 155, Basmane, is just a block or so along the boulevard from the railway station, on the right-hand side. Though the facade and entrance have been modernised, most of the hotel is actually older, which accounts for its moderate prices: US$20/26 a single/double with shower. There's a lift.

Right next door, the three-star, 63-room *Hotel Hisar* (tel 14 54 00), Fevzi Paşa Bulvarı, 1368 Sokak 2, charges a surprisingly high US$64/78 a single/double, and up to US$135 for other rooms. These prices include bath, TV, mini-bar and air-con. The small Turkish carpet in the shape of a US$100 note, hanging behind the reception desk, may be a hint as to the philosophy of hospitality here.

Just around the corner on 1368 Sokak, which is much quieter, is the new two-star, 36-room *Hotel Zeybek* (tel 19 66 94, 19 74 71), 1368 Sokak 5, Basmane. It's a handsome new place with light wood, gleaming brass and coloured marble used unstintingly in the decor. The hotel has its own restaurant and bar, which puts it in a class apart from the other small, modest hotels on this street. Guest rooms at the Zeybek come with little luxuries such as TVs, fans and bathrooms with small tubs, and cost US$36/42 a single/double.

Cumhuriyet Meydanı *Hotel Anba* (AHN-bah) (tel 14 43 80/4), Cumhuriyet Bulvarı 124, is on the İkinci Kordon just a block south of Cumhuriyet Meydanı and the Büyük Efes. Air-con and bath-equipped rooms with breakfast in this status location cost US$40/62 a single/double.

The *Kilim Oteli* (kee-LEEM) (tel 14 53 40), right in front of the Anba on Birinci Kordon is similar, but charges a bit less for sea-view rooms. Those on the 1st floor are noisy but cheap at US$32/42 a single/double; on less noisy upper floors the price is US$40/55 a single/double. The hotel has a nice little restaurant and a clientele mostly of people travelling on business.

Behind the Büyük Efes Oteli, in a fairly

quiet residential section, is the three-star, 73-room *Otel Karaca* (tel 14 44 45, 14 44 26), Necati Bey Bulvarı 1379 Sokak 55, just a short walk from the corner of Gazi Osman Paşa Bulvarı and Necati Bey Bulvarı. The attractions here are the quiet yet convenient location, the comfortable, modern rooms with TVs and mini-bars, and the English-speaking staff. The neighbourhood has lots of NATO military and diplomatic families whose friends and families patronise the Karaca, so they're used to foreigners. Rooms cost US$48/68 a single/double, breakfast included.

Menderes Airport Should you find yourself caught at the airport overnight, check out the *Dal-Pet Motel* (tel (5461) 1449), İzmir-Aydın Karayolu Km 22, Kısıkköy, İzmir, in the BP fuel station and restaurant complex on the main highway about a five-minute drive from the air terminal. This new hotel has a swimming pool, restaurant and good rooms going for about US$35 a double with bath. There is room for campers as well.

Places to Stay – top end
For a long time no new luxury hotels were built in İzmir, but that is now changing as Turkey's tourism boom intensifies. Expect several new hotels of an international standard to open within the next few years.

İzmir's best so far is the five-star, 400-room *Büyük Efes Oteli* (bew-YEWK eh-FEHS, Grand Ephesus Hotel) (tel 14 43 00/29; fax 25 86 95), Gazi Osman Paşa Bulvarı 1, 35210 İzmir, on Cumhuriyet Meydanı. Though not as luxurious as a Hilton or Sheraton, it is comfortable and has these advantages: pretty, private gardens with a swimming pool, good dining room and patio restaurant, nightclub and some rooms with a bath, TV, mini-bars, air-con and perhaps a view of the bay. Rates vary with the seasons and with the location of the room within the hotel (rooms with sea views and pool views are most expensive, those with street views are the cheapest). April to October is the summer season, with rooms renting for US$65 to US$145 a single, US$85 to US$155 a double. Winter prices are a few dollars cheaper.

The four-star, 127-room *Pullman Etap İzmir Hotel* (eh-TAHP) (tel 14 40 90/9; fax 19 40 89) is just around the corner, across from the PTT, at Cumhuriyet Bulvarı 138, 35210 İzmir. Pastryshop-cafés are the latest thing among luxury hotels in Turkey, and the Etap has a good one in its lobby; there's also a nice, garden-style ground-floor restaurant serving buffet luncheon and dinner daily. Part of the worldwide French chain, its air-con, mini-bar and TV-equipped rooms cost US$78/98/118 a single/double/triple in high summer; lower rates are offered off season.

Places to Eat – bottom end

The lowest priced meals are to be found in the same areas as the lowest priced hotels. Some of the most delightful are along Anafartalar Caddesi in the bazaar. Start from the Basmane end, and hazır yemek restaurants, kebapçıs and köftecis will appear all along the way as you wander. A few will have one or two small tables outside.

Check out *Osman'in Birahanesi*, Anafartalar 806, which serves alcoholic beverages and therefore may have a bit heavier atmosphere, but at least you can get a beer with lunch. A few steps farther on is the *Ömür Lokantası*, bright, clean and cheap, with a good selection of hazır yemek dishes.

Just before you come to a little open square with a mosque, look for the *Ege Lezzet Lokantası* on Anafartalar Caddesi. The front window is filled by steam tables holding hearty pilav, stews and vegetable dishes. Lunch for US$2.50 or US$3 is a simple matter. The *Konya Lezzet Lokantası*, 50 metres past the little Hatuniye Camii and park, is a bit fancier, but priced about the same. No alcohol is served at these two.

For slightly more pleasant restaurants, go to that section with slightly better hotels on 1368 Sokak near Basmane Station, described in Places to Stay. The *Zeybek Mangal Restaurant* (tel 13 52 31), 1368 Sokak 6/A, specialises in döner kebap and has pleasant sidewalk tables. A portion of döner or one of their many other kebaps, with a salad and something to drink, costs US$4 or US$5.

The *Güzel İzmir Restaurant* (tel 14 05 01), 1368 Sokak 8/B, across the street from the Zeybek Mangal, has more hazır yemek dishes, sidewalk tables and similar prices.

Places to Eat – middle

Birinci Kordon For medium-priced meals, the city's most interesting section is the waterfront north of Cumhuriyet Meydanı. Many of the restaurants here, along the Birinci Kordon, have sidewalk tables, views of the harbour activity, lots of good meze dishes and fresh fish prepared various ways.

South of Cumhuriyet Meydanı there used to be several little restaurants overlooking the water, but development and construction have wiped out a number of them, and the others are being

threatened. Still, as long as it exists, the *Mangal Restaurant* (tel 25 28 60), Atatürk Caddesi 110, will serve a good seafood dinner with white tablecloths and experienced service for US$10 to US$12 per person, all included; if you order lamb as your main course, the cost will only be half that much. The small number of sidewalk tables fill up early in the evening, so come early or late if you want one of them. The *Ahtapot* and *Kazan* restaurants right next door are similar in all regards.

Up past the NATO building are numerous sidewalk cafés where young people come to sip drinks, talk, flirt and have something to eat. Prices are similar here, with a serving of the ubiquitous şiş kebap going for only US$2.50; seafood, of course, costs much more. The *Sirena* at Atatürk Caddesi 194 is one such place, the *Orfoz Balık Restaurant* another.

New at my last visit was the *Chinese Restaurant* (tel 25 73 57/8), 1379 Sokak, Efes İş Hanı, a branch of the Turkish chain located more or less behind the Büyük Efes Oteli. The narrow dining room has rows of tables with red cloths, bits of Chinese decoration and a menu listing the more popular Chinese dishes. Expect to pay US$10 to US$14 per person for a full dinner. The restaurant is open every day.

Konak A special place for sweets is the *Ali Galip Pastanesi* (ah-LEE gah-LEEP), just a few steps along Anafartalar Caddesi from Konak, on the right-hand side. This is one of the city's oldest and best confectioneries, justly famed for its baklava, helvah and other treats.

Getting There & Away

Air The Turkish Airlines office (tel 14 12 26; for reservations 25 82 80) is located in the arcade of shops in the Büyük Efes Oteli on Gazi Osman Paşa Bulvarı. To İzmir's Adnan Menderes Airport there are four to six daily non-stop flights from İstanbul (US$62), and one daily non-stop flight

from Ankara (US$68). Other Ankara/İzmir flights go via İstanbul.

Non-stop flights connect İzmir and Amsterdam, Athens, Cologne, Frankfurt, Hamburg, Lefkoşe (Nicosia, Turkish Cyprus), London, Lyon, Milan, Munich, Paris, Rome and Zurich, with at least one flight per week.

İstanbul Airlines flies between İstanbul and İzmir daily except Sunday, charging only US$44 for the flight. They also have a weekly flight between İzmir and Antalya (US$35). Contact them at İstanbul Airlines (tel 19 05 41/42), Gazi Osman Paşa Caddesi 2/E (across from the Büyük Efes Oteli), Alsancak. They can also be contacted at Menderes Airport (tel 51 30 65, 51 26 26, ext 1202, 1352).

For airport transport, see Getting Around.

Bus Buses arrive at İzmir's otogar, a mammoth and seemingly chaotic establishment north-east of the city's centre. Buses roar around outside while throngs of passengers move through the interior past rows of shops selling snacks, trinkets and refreshing lemon cologne (an absolute necessity for a Turk on the road). There's a small Tourism Information Office and complaints office near the terminal's main gate; ask to be directed to it. If you're at the otogar to buy a ticket to another city, ask for directions to the *bilet gişeleri* (bee-LEHT gee-sheh-leh-ree, ticket windows).

If you've come on a premium line such as Varan, there may be a servis arabası to take you into town at no extra charge. Otherwise, a taxi, dolmuş or city bus (No 50, 'Konak-Yeni Garaj'; ask for the *şehir otobüsü*, city bus) can be found just outside the terminal grounds. Easiest is the dolmuş marked 'Mersin', which will take you to the bus ticket offices on Gazi Bulvarı at Dokuz (9) Eylül Meydanı (doh-KOOZ ey-LEWL), just a few steps from Basmane Station. For inexpensive hotels get something to Basmane Station. For the moderate and more expensive hotels, get something to Konak, but get out at Cumhuriyet Meydanı.

To buy bus tickets in the town centre without having to drag yourself all the way out to the otogar, go to Dokuz (9) Eylül Meydanı. Here, at the beginning of Gazi Bulvarı, are numerous bus ticket offices, including those for Aydın, Dadaş, Hakiki Koç, İzmir Seyahat, Kâmil Koç, Karadeveci, Kent, Kontaş, Vantur and others. You should be able to buy a ticket to any point in the country from here.

For buses to Bergama, go to the otogar and catch the next bus out: they run frequently. If you're headed for Sardis, catch the next bus from the otogar to Salihli (sah-LEEHH-lee), the large town just beyond Sardis.

Here are details on travel from İzmir to:

Ankara – 600 km, 8½ hours, US$8.50; buses at least every hour

Antalya – 550 km, nine hours, US$8.50; buses at least every two hours

Athens – Varan has direct service for US$50; the trip takes nearly two days

Bergama – 100 km, two hours, US$1; frequent Bergama municipal buses from 6 am to 7.30 pm

Bodrum – 250 km, four hours, US$4; buses every hour in summer

Bursa – 375 km, six hours, US$5; hourly buses

Çanakkale – 340 km, six hours, US$5; buses at least every two hours

Çeşme (for Chios) – 85 km, 1½ hours, US$1; frequent buses (at least hourly) depart a separate terminal in Güzelyalı, west of Konak

Denizli – 250 km, four hours, US$4; buses every hour

Erzurum – 1520 km, 21 hours, US$16; several buses daily

İstanbul – 610 km, nine hours, US$8.50; buses at least every hour

Konya – 575 km, eight hours, US$8; buses at least every two hours

Kuşadası – 95 km, 1½ hours, US$1.50; buses at least every hour

Marmaris – 320 km, six hours, US$5; buses at least every two hours

Sardis – 90 km, 1¼ hours, US$1; buses at least every 30 minutes

Selçuk (for Ephesus) – 80 km, 1¼ hours, US$1.25; buses at least every hour

Trabzon – 1375 km, 22 hours, US$17; several buses daily

Van – 1600 km, 28 hours, US$23; several buses daily

Train Arrival by rail is easy. Most intercity trains come into Basmane Station, whence there are buses and dolmuşes to other sections, and numerous hotels close by. İzmir's other railway depot, at Alsancak (AHL-sahn-jahk), at the northern end of the city near the international passenger ship docks, is mostly for commuter and suburban lines.

Trains departing Basmane include the three daily mototrens to Denizli at 8.10 am, 3.30 and 6 pm; these are the best trains to take to Selçuk (for Ephesus and Kuşadası). A single ticket as far as Selçuk costs US$0.75, slightly less if you have a student card. For more information on trains along the İzmir, Menderes, Selçuk, Denizli route, see the train schedule in the section on Ephesus.

For Ankara and points east, the İzmir (Basmane) to Ankara Mavi Tren departs each city at 8.05 pm, arriving the next morning at 10.06 am. It hauls only comfortable Pullman-type coaches, no sleeping cars. The İzmir Ekspresi is the nightly coach and sleeping-car train between Ankara and İzmir (Basmane) taking about 15½ hours, departing each city at 6.05 pm, arriving the next morning at 9.40 am. A one-way ticket on the İzmir Ekspresi costs US$5.50, on the Mavi Tren US$8. Sleeping-car berths on the İzmir Ekspresi are priced between US$20 and US$30.

The train-boat route between İzmir and İstanbul is served by the Marmara Ekspresi to Bandırma on the Sea of Marmara coast, then by ship to İstanbul. Departures from İzmir are at 8.15 am and

8 pm, arriving at Bandırma about 1.45 pm and 1.30 am, then arriving in İstanbul at 6.45 pm and 7 am respectively. As you can see, one of these schedules requires you to make the train-boat switch in the middle of the night. A one-way ticket for the entire journey costs US$8. Should you want to sleep in a cabin aboard the ship, you'll have to pay somewhat more.

Boat If you are lucky enough to arrive in İzmir by sea, the city will present itself to you wonderfully as you glide by, and your ship will come into Alsancak Limanı (AHL-sahn-jahk lee-mah-nuh, Alsancak Harbour), also called Yeni Liman (yeh-NEE lee-mahn, New Harbour), at the northern tip of the city's central section. The harbour is about equidistant from the otogar and the centre of the city, Konak. For transport, turn left as you leave the dock area and walk the block to Alsancak Railway Station, from which buses, dolmuşes and taxis will take you to the centre.

Getting Around

Airport Transport You can travel between the centre of İzmir and Menderes Airport, 25 km south of the city near Cumaovası on the road to Ephesus and Kuşadası, by airport bus, city bus, intercity bus or commuter train. Airport buses leave from the Turkish Airlines office periodically throughout the day on the half-hour trip. Plan to catch a bus that leaves at least 90 minutes before domestic flight departures, or two hours before international departures; the bus fare is US$0.75. City buses trundle – fairly slowly – between Menderes Airport and Montrö Meydanı, next to İzmir's Kültür Parkı, every half-hour throughout the day for even less, but the trip takes twice as long. A taxi between İzmir and Menderes Airport can cost between US$10 and US$25, depending upon your haggling abilities.

There are frequent diesel railcar and suburban trains which connect the station at Menderes Airport with Alsancak Station, so you'll probably wait between 30 and 60 minutes to catch one. There are also a few intercity express trains which arrive at Basmane Station (for a schedule of these expresses, see the section on Ephesus). Train fare is a low US$0.40. From Alsancak or Basmane there are city buses and dolmuşes to other parts of town. The aforementioned schedule in the Ephesus section includes trains heading south and east to Selçuk (for Ephesus), and Denizli (for Pamukkale).

Most intercity buses running between İzmir and points south such as Selçuk, Kuşadası, or Denizli, will shuttle you between the airport and İzmir's bus station. You may have to walk the 600 metres from the highway to the air terminal. Also, if you're heading south from the airport, just walk out to the highway, cross to the other side, and catch the appropriate bus to Selçuk, Kuşadası, Denizli, Pamukkale, Bodrum, or Marmaris.

To return to the airport at the end of your stay, take the same bus, 90 minutes prior to any domestic flight departure, 120 minutes prior to an international departure.

City Transport Within the city, blue-and-silver city buses lumber along the major thoroughfares, but dolmuşes are much faster. Dolmuşes in İzmir tend to be Fiat taxis. One of these running between Alsancak station and Konak via Cumhuriyet Meydanı charges US$0.22.

SARDIS (Sart)

The phrase 'rich as Croesus' made its way into language early, in the 6th century BC to be precise. Croesus was the king of Lydia, and Sardis was its capital city. It was here that one of humankind's most popular and valuable inventions appeared: coinage. No doubt the Greeks thought Croesus (560-546 BC) rich because he could store so much wealth in such a small place. Rather than having vast estates and far-ranging herds of livestock,

Croesus kept his wealth in his pockets, and they were deep pockets at that.

History

For all his wealth, Croesus was defeated and captured by Cyrus and his Persians, after which he leapt onto a funeral pyre. Even Croesus couldn't take it with him.

The Lydian kingdom had dominated much of the Aegean area before the Persians came. Besides being the kingdom's wealthy capital, Sardis was a great trading centre as well, obviously because coinage facilitated trade.

After the Persians, Alexander the Great took the city in 334 BC and embellished it even more. The inevitable earthquake brought its fine buildings down in 17 AD, but it was rebuilt by Tiberius and it became a thriving provincial Roman town. It became part of the Ottoman Empire at the end of the 14th century.

Orientation

There are actually two small villages at Sardis, nestled in a valley rich in vineyards (for sultanas, not wine grapes), olive groves, melon fields and tobacco fields. Sartmustafa (SART-MOOS-tah-fah) is the village on the highway, with a few teahouses and grocery shops. Sartmahmut (SART-mah-MOOT) is north of the highway, clustered around the railway station. The station is precisely one km north of the highway.

During the day the farmers come into town, park their tractors in front of the teahouses, sit down for a few glasses and discuss the crops. In early August the harvest is in progress, and little stalls by the roadside, attended by children, sell huge bunches of luscious, crisp, sweet sultanas to passers-by.

The teahouses in town are where you wait to catch a bus back to İzmir.

Things to See

The ruins of Sardis are scattered throughout the valley which lies beneath the striking ragged mountain range to the south. Two concentrations of ruins are of interest.

Just east of the village (away from İzmir), on the north side of the highway, lies the most extensive part of the ruins, open virtually all the time during daylight hours, every day, for US$3.

Buy your ticket at the little booth, then enter the ruins along the Marble Way past rows of Byzantine-era shops – note the elaborate drainage system, with pipes buried in the stone walls. Some of the shops have been identified from inscriptions. There's a restaurant, Jacob's Paint Shop, an office, a hardware shop, the shop of Sabbatios and the shop of Jacob, an elder of the synagogue. At the end of the Marble Way is an inscription on the marble paving-stones done in either 17 or 43 AD, honouring Prince Germanicus.

Turn left from the Marble Way and enter the synagogue, impressive because of its size and beautiful decoration. It has lots of fine mosaic paving, and coloured stone on its walls. A modern plaque lists donors to the Sardis American Excavation Fund, who supported the excavations carried out during the period from 1965 to 1973.

The striking facade to the right of the synagogue is that of the gymnasium. Note especially the finely chiselled inscriptions in Greek, and the serpentine fluting on the columns. Behind the facade is a swimming pool and rest area.

Just over one km south of the village (take the road beside the teahouse) is the Temple of Artemis, a once-magnificent building which was actually never completed. Today only a few columns stand untoppled, but the temple's plan is clearly visible and quite impressive. Next to the temple is an altar used since ancient times, refurbished by Alexander the Great and later by the Romans. Clinging to the south-eastern corner of the temple is a small brick Byzantine church. From archaic times through the Hellenistic, Roman and Byzantine periods, this was a sacred spot, no matter what the religion.

Getting There & Away

Sardis is 90 km east of İzmir along the Ankara road. In high summer, start out early so you're not tramping the ruins in the heat of the day, which can be oppressive.

Bus Buses depart frequently – at least every 30 minutes – for the 1¼-hour trip from İzmir's otogar. You needn't buy a ticket in advance, just go out to the bus station and buy a ticket for the next bus to Salihli (US$1). Tell them you want to get out at Sardis.

Dolmuş minibuses run between Sartmustafa and Manisa for US$0.80 per ride.

Train There are several daily trains from İzmir (Basmane) which stop here; they are slower than the buses. Take the bus out to Sardis, but then ask in town about trains returning to İzmir, as you may find one at a convenient time.

Tours Alternatively, local travel agencies in İzmir operate full-day tours to Sardis and Manisa for about US$30, lunch included.

Heading East If your itinerary takes you eastward into Anatolia, refer to the South of the Marmara Sea chapter for information on the cities of Afyon and Kütahya.

ÇEŞME

The name of this town and resort area, 85 km due west of İzmir, means 'fountain' or 'spring' (çeşme, CHESH-meh). It has a population of 12,000. From the town, it's only about 10 km across the water to the Greek island of Chios. The ferries to the Greek islands are the main reason people go to Çeşme, though the fast-growing resort area encircling the town is popular with weekend-trippers from İzmir.

Çeşme itself is a pleasant enough little Aegean seaside village, but the land to the east of it is rolling steppe, a foretaste of Anatolia and Central Asia, though this barrenness subsides as one approaches İzmir, giving way to wheat fields, lush orchards, olive groves and tobacco fields. About 23 km east of Çeşme is the pretty Uzunkuyu Piknik Yeri, a roadside picnic area in a pine forest. One passes the official city limits of İzmir a full 30 km west of Konak Meydanı (50 km east of Çeşme).

Orientation

Çeşme is right on the coast. Ilıca, a seaside resort town six km to the east of Çeşme, has lots of hotels in all price ranges, from family pensions to the big Turban Çeşme Oteli. Dolmuşes run between Ilıca and Çeşme frequently (US$0.25), but unless you want to spend time at the beach you're better off staying in Çeşme proper.

Çeşme's otogar is less than one km south of the main square and the fortress. In Çeşme everything you need is very near the main square, with its inevitable statue of Atatürk on the waterfront. The Tourism Information Office, Customs House (Gümrük), ferry ticket offices, bus ticket offices, restaurants and hotels are all here, or within two blocks.

Information

The Tourism Information Office (tel (549) 26653) is down by the dock at İskele Meydanı No 6.

Things to See

The old fortress in the centre of town was built by the Genoese but repaired by Beyazıt, son of Sultan Mehmet the Conqueror, to defend the coast from attack by the Knights of St John based on Rhodes, and from pirates. It now holds the museum and is called the **Çeşme Kalesi ve Müzesi** or Çeşme Fortress & Museum, open every day from 8.30 to 11.45 am and from 1 to 5.15 pm, for US$1. The entrance is up the hill on the right-hand side as you face the fort from the main square.

Facing the main square, with its back to the fortress, is a **statue** of Cezayirli Gazi Hasan Paşa (1714-1790), together with a lion which symbolises his temperament.

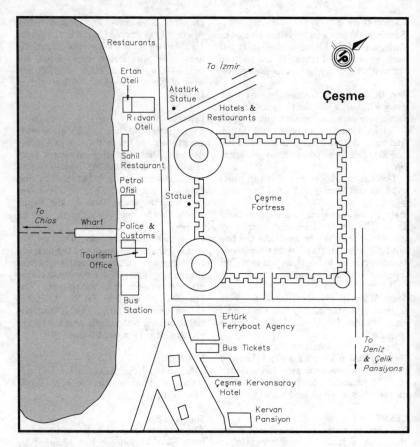

As a boy he was captured in a battle on the Iranian border, sold into slavery by the Ottoman army and bought by a Turkish tradesman who raised him with his own sons. Having joined the Janissary corps at 25, he began a brilliant military, naval and political career which included fierce battles with the Russian fleet off Çeşme. He retired an extremely wealthy man, having served as the sultan's grand vizier and having built public monuments, fountains and mosques on Lesbos, Limnos, Chios, Kos and Rhodes (all were Ottoman islands at the time).

In the evening the people of Çeşme still observe the custom of dressing up and coming down to the main square for a stroll, a glass of tea, a bit of conversation and some people-watching. That's nightlife in Çeşme, and it's pleasant enough. The men, some with their wives, will linger in the seaside restaurants and teahouses.

The area around Çeşme is developing rapidly. Some say Çeşme is spoiled already, and the place to spend your time is in **Alaçatı** instead (dolmuşes run the two km to Alaçatı from Ilica). There's a nice beach about three or four km out of the village.

Places to Stay

Çeşme has several inexpensive pensions and hotels, several moderately priced hotels, a restored caravanserai and a luxury resort. All charge more than normal, and many lodgings are often booked solid in the summer season. The lodging situation in Çeşme is thus not particularly good in any respect.

Places to Stay – bottom end

The best, cheap lodgings are at the several little pensions in private homes.

Walk up the hill along the walls of the fortress and follow the signs to reach the *Anıt Pansiyon,* in a nicely restored old Çeşme house across from the fortress museum entrance. If it's full, follow the signs from the Anıt to the *Çelik Pansiyon* (cheh-LEEK) (tel 26153), and the *Kısaoglu Pansiyon,* which charge US$7.50/12 a single/double for a room without private shower. The *Kervan Pansiyon* (tel 26061), just south of the main square and the docks past the Kervansaray Hotel, charges the same, but will allow you to roll out your sleeping bag on the roof for US$3. Just past the Kervan pension is the town's hamam, and beyond it are even more cheap pensions.

There are several small, fairly noisy and severely plain hotels along the main shopping street, which heads inland toward İzmir. These are last-ditch lodgings, unless some renovation is done to them.

The *Dilek Pension* in Alaçatı has been recommended by one reader.

Places to Stay – middle

Right on the shore, facing the main square, is the two-star *Ertan Oteli* (ehr-TAHN) (tel 26795/6), Cumhuriyet Meydanı 12, with a lift, an open-air terrace bar, an air-con restaurant, and 60 guest rooms with bath, some of them facing the sea, priced at US$35/45 a single/double. This is a bit expensive for what you get, but demand is high in Çeşme, rooms are scarce and the Ertan is often filled with tour groups.

Next door to the Ertan, the newer 35-room *Rıdvan Oteli* (tel 26336/7) also rates two stars and has similar facilities, but here most rooms have balconies. Prices are identical at US$35/45 a single/double.

The *Çeşme Kervansaray* (kehr-VAHN-sah-rah-yee) (tel 26490/1/2; in İzmir call (51) 14 17 20), just south of the main square, dates from the reign of Süleyman the Magnificent (1528). Recently restored by the same company that operates the Golden Dolphin resort, it is now a beautiful hotel decorated with a mixture of modern and traditional Turkish styles. Rates for room with a bath, breakfast included, in the summer season (mid-June to mid-September) are US$42/58/76 a single/double/suite; off season, rates are about 20% lower. Note that the hotel is closed from October to the end of March. A table d'hôte meal in the hotel is priced at US$8 to US$10.

At Ilica, four km from Çeşme proper, is the *Turban Ilica Motel* (tel 32183; fax 32128), Çeşme, Ilica, İzmir. It's a newer two-storey motel at the seaside with 65 rooms going for US$45/65 a single/double in the high summer season (early July to the end of August), tax and service, breakfast and dinner included. Off-season prices are substantially lower; the hotel is closed November to April. The motel is moderately well kept up, with a swimming pool, beach, sun deck, restaurant, bar and games room.

Places to Stay – top end

About four km outside of Çeşme proper is the luxury *Golden Dolphin Holiday Village* (Altın Yunus Tatilköyü) (tel 31250), Boyalık Mevkii, Ilica, İzmir, a complete resort with facilities for all water sports, a yacht harbour and luxury accommodation. Facilities at this lavish spread include 540 guest rooms in three buildings, five restaurants, cafés and bars, a disco, seven tennis courts (two of them floodlit), two swimming pools and another for children, a health and fitness centre and facilities for water sports, hunting, horseback riding and bicycling. Rates change with the seasons but are about US$75 to US$100 a double per night with tax, service charge, breakfast and dinner included.

Places to Eat

Except for meals in the more expensive hotels, Çeşme's restaurants are all fairly cheap, but some are cheaper than others. The *Imren Lokantası* on the main street inland from the main square has white tablecloths, fluorescent lights and grilled meats for US$2 to US$3. The *Lezzet Aş Evi* ('Flavour Cook-House') a bit farther along the same street is much cheaper, with vegetable plates for US$0.50, and salçalı köfte for US$0.75.

The *Hasan Abi Lokantası*, on the right (east) side, is similar. Tiny, ugly, crowded and always busy, 'Big Brother Hasan' (that's the name) serves kebaps and hazır yemek dishes throughout the day. I had *salçalı kebap* (a stew in a rich sauce), pilav, a glass of ayran, bread and water for US$2.25.

Also on the main street, the *Nil Patisserie* serves breakfast for less than US$1; it's across the street from the Tekbank in the second block in from the main square.

Down on the waterfront at the main square is the *Sahil Restaurant*, perhaps the most popular eatery, with lots of outdoor tables, some facing the square, others the sea. The bill of fare includes a lot of seafood, and full meals are US$4 to US$6, more if you order fish. They serve an early breakfast but it's a bit expensive at US$3 for the same bread, honey, tea, cheese and olives that you get inland for US$2.

For a local taste treat, try the *sakızlı dondurma* (sah-kuhz-LUH dohn-doormah), ice cream flavoured with pine resin, the same stuff they put in Greek retsina wine. It tastes like you think it's going to taste, there's no mystery or discovery involved. If you like retsina, you may like this weird incarnation of the flavour.

Getting There & Away

Bus It's simple. Çeşme Turizm buses and minibuses make the 85-km 1½-hour run into the big city every 15 minutes or so from 6 am to 6 pm, for US$1. Çeşme buses operate out of a separate terminal in Güzelyalı, a neighbourhood west of Konak, and not out of İzmir's big otogar. From Güzelyalı, you take city buses and dolmuşes into the centre of town.

Chios Ferry The reason you've come to Çeşme is probably to catch the ferry between this town and the Greek island of Chios. Boats run on Thursday at 10 am during the winter months, weather and customers permitting; Sunday and Thursday in early May; Tuesday, Thursday, Friday and Sunday from mid-May till mid-July. In high summer there are daily boats (except Monday) from mid-July to mid-September; from mid-September to the end of October the boats run on Tuesday, Thursday, and Sunday. At other times, extra boats may run if there is enough traffic. Most of these boats depart in the morning at 9.30 or 10 am, but a few depart at 4 pm.

A one-way fare between Çeşme and Chios is US$25, a same-day return trip costs US$30 and a return ticket valid for one year costs US$45. Children four to 12 years old get a 50% reduction. Motor cycles, cars, even caravans, minibuses and buses can be carried on some of the ferries. The fare for a car is between US$45 and US$80.

Some boats can also serve as a day trip to Chios; you leave Çeşme in the morning, spend the better part of the day on Chios and return to Çeşme in the evening.

For details, reservations and tickets, contact the Ertürk Travel Agency (EHR-tewrk) (tel 26768, 26876) in Çeşme's main square at Cumhuriyet Meydanı 11/A, near the fortress and across from the docks; the head office is at İnkilap Caddesi 42/1 (tel 26147, 26223). It's a good idea to buy your ticket at least a day in advance, if possible. By the way, the Ertürk people usually have information about onward connections from Chios to Piraeus (daily except Saturday at 8 pm), to Athens by air, and to Samos, Lesbos and Thessaloniki by boat, as well as multiple connections to other Greek islands.

In the past, you had to go through İzmir to get anywhere else, but the route from Çeşme via Seferihisar and Gümüldür to Pamucak beach, Ephesus, Selçuk and Kuşadası (about 150 km) is now passable, and it cuts out the worst of İzmir's city traffic. At this writing there are no direct Çeşme to Selçuk buses, but they will no doubt begin one day. For now, take a bus to Urla and the Seferihisar turning, and wait there to get something else. On the beach near Seferihisar are the ruins of ancient Teos, and along the route south you'll pass near the ruins of Colophon, Claros and Notion before coming to the Pamucak, Selçuk, Kuşadası intersection.

Ephesus

It's often said that Turkey has more ancient cities and classical ruins than does Greece. Well, it's true, and the Aegean coast holds a great number of sites, including Ephesus, the grandest and best preserved of them all.

Even if you are not fascinated by archaeology, there's great pleasure in riding through a countryside rich in fields of tobacco, passing orchards of fig trees, tramping among verdant fields bright with sunflowers, resting in little village teahouses, and strolling along marble streets which once witnessed the passing of the men who practically invented architecture, philosophy, mathematics and science. And when it gets hot, there's always the beach.

History

This was Ionia. About 1000 BC, colonists from Greece arrived on these shores,

fleeing an invasion by the Dorians. The Ionian culture flourished, and its cities exported these cultural refinements back to Greece.

The history of Ionia is much the same as that of İzmir, with the original Ionian league of cities being conquered by the Lydians of Sardis, then the Persians, then Alexander. They prospered until their harbours silted up, or until the predominance of İzmir siphoned off their local trade.

Ephesus (Efes, EFF-ess) was a great trading and religious city, centre for the cult of Cybele, the Anatolian fertility goddess. Under the influence of the Ionians, Cybele became Artemis, the virgin goddess of the hunt and the moon, and a fabulous temple was built in her honour. When the Romans took over and made this the province of Asia, Artemis became Diana and Ephesus became the Roman provincial capital. Its Temple of Diana was counted among the Seven Wonders of the World.

As a large and busy Roman town with ships and caravans coming from all over, it had an important Christian congregation very early. St Paul visited Ephesus and later wrote the most profound of his epistles to the Ephesians.

Ephesus was renowned for its wealth and beauty even before it was pillaged by Gothic invaders in 262 AD, and it was still an important enough place in 431 AD that a church council was held here. There is a lot of the city's glory left for you to see. As for the other Ionian ports, sometimes a sleepy Turkish village rose among the ruins, sometimes not. Today several of those once-sleepy villages are bustling seaside resort towns.

Orientation

The region around Ephesus is rich in attractions. The city itself is an archaeological zone, but only four km away is Selçuk, a Turkish town of 20,000 people, where you catch buses and dolmuşes, have meals and find pensions to sleep for the night. On a hilltop 10 km south of Selçuk is Meryemana, the House of the Virgin Mary. About seven km from Selçuk, past Ephesus, is the Aegean coast and Pamucak beach, a long, wide swath of dark sand backed by some beach-shack eateries and hotels.

Farther south along the coast, 20 km from Selçuk, is Kuşadası, a resort town of 40,000 people and a port for Aegean cruise ships doing the Greek islands route. Kuşadası is also where you can catch a ferry to Samos. Inland 15 km from Kuşadası and about 35 km due south of Selçuk is the farming town of Söke with a population of 50,000. It's a Turkish town, of interest as a transportation point on the way to three nearby archaeological sites of great importance: Priene, Miletus and Didyma.

It is easy to spend at least three days seeing the sights in this region. Plan a day for Selçuk and Ephesus, another for Priene, Miletus and Didyma, and a third for Pamucak, Kuşadası and the beach.

Accommodation

You can make your base in Selçuk, the small town four km from the ruins, or you can stay in the nearby seaside resort of Kuşadası, 20 km away. Selçuk is closer to Ephesus proper and has a large number of inexpensive pensions, but Kuşadası is closer to Priene, Miletus and Didyma, and has a greater number and variety of lodgings, especially in the higher price ranges. Details appear in the Places to Stay sections of each town.

Getting There & Away

İzmir is the transportation hub for the region. It has the only air service, and the only rail service from İstanbul and Ankara except for one İstanbul-Denizli train.

Bus Buses, of course, go everywhere. Direct services run from İzmir otogar to:

Selçuk - 80 km, 1¼ hours, US$1.25
Kuşadası - 100 km, 1⅔ hours, US$1.50
Söke - 125 km, two hours, US$1.75

Selçuk, being on the main highway, is a stopping-place for most through buses between İzmir and Denizli, Pamukkale, Marmaris, Bodrum, Fethiye, Antalya and other south-western points. Kuşadası has lots of direct bus services to İzmir, some direct bus services to Denizli and Pamukkale, and minibus dolmuş services to many other parts of the region.

Train Here's the schedule for long-distance ekspres and mototren trains on the İzmir to Denizli run, and return. Check these times locally before you ride, as they are subject to change.

Fares are low, about US$0.50 between İzmir and Menderes Airport, US$0.75 between İzmir and Selçuk, US$1.75 between İzmir and Denizli, and US$1.45 between Selçuk and Denizli.

İzmir (Basmane)	Menderes Airport	Selçuk (Ephesus)	Denizli
8.10 am	8.39 am	10.01 am	1.30 pm
3.30 pm	3.59 pm	5.12 pm	9.14 pm
6 pm	6.30 pm	7.52 pm	11.55 pm
6.45 pm	7.15 pm	8.58 pm	–
Denizli	Selçuk (Ephesus)	Menderes Airport	İzmir (Basmane)
5.27 am	8.45 am	10.10 am	10.40 am
7.55 am	12.29 pm	1.50 pm	2.20 pm
3.35 pm	7.53 pm	9.22 pm	9.54 pm

Car Rental It's simple but expensive to rent a car in İzmir or Kuşadası. You will probably have to return the car to the same city. If you give it up in Antalya or Ankara, you may have to pay a hefty charge to get the car back to its home base. Figure US\$50 per day, all in, to rent a small Renault or Fiat ('Murat').

SELÇUK

Before going to Ephesus, take an hour or two to visit the ancient buildings in Selçuk. The best place to start is the St John Basilica atop the hill; look for signs pointing the way to St Jean.

Information

Selçuk has a nice little Tourism Information Office (tel (5451) 1328) in a group of modern shops near the museum and across the highway from the bus station. It's open every day from 8.30 am to 6.30 or 7 pm (outside the busy summer months, Sunday hours are from 9 am to 2 pm). They'll be glad to help you with accommodation here, particularly if you want a bed in a small, inexpensive pension.

Ayasoluk Hill

It is said that St John came to Ephesus at the end of his life and wrote his Gospel here. A tomb built in the 300s was thought to be his, so Justinian erected this magnificent church above it in the 500s. Earthquakes and scavengers for building materials had left the church a heap of rubble until a century ago when restoration began. Virtually all of what you see is restored. The church site is open every day; admission costs US\$1.

This hill, including the higher peak with the fortress, is called Ayasoluk. The view is attractive. Look west: at the foot of the hill is the İsa Bey Camii, built in 1307 by the Emir of Aydın in a transitional style which was post-Seljuk and pre-Ottoman. Keep a picture of it in your mind if you plan to venture deep into Anatolia for a look at more Seljuk buildings. There are many in Konya.

Beyond the mosque you can see how the Aegean Sea once invaded this plain, allowing Ephesus to prosper by maritime commerce. When the harbour silted up, Ephesus began to lose its famous wealth.

Early in the town's existence it had earned money from pilgrims coming to pay homage to Cybele or Artemis. The many-breasted Anatolian fertility goddess had a fabulous temple, the **Artemision**, to the south-west of the St John Basilica. A sign marks the spot today, and you can see a re-erected column and the outline of the foundation. When you visit the huge temple at Didyma you can get an idea of what the great temple looked like, as the one at Didyma is thought to be very similar. But the cult of the fertility goddess has now moved from Ephesus to men's magazines.

By the way, the **citadel** atop the hill to the north of the St John Basilica was originally constructed by the Byzantines in the 500s, rebuilt by the Seljuks and restored in modern times. A small Seljuk mosque and a ruined church are inside.

Ephesus Museum

Don't miss the beautiful museum in the centre of Selçuk just a few steps from the Tourism Information Office. The collection is a significant one, and its statuary, mosaics and artefacts are attractively displayed. Among the prime attractions in this rich collection are several marble statues of Cybele/Artemis, with a row of eggs representing fertility, elaborate headdresses and several effigies of Priapus, the phallic god. There are also good mosaics and frescoes. The museum is open every day from 9.30 am to 6.30 pm; admission costs US\$3.50.

Other Sites

Selçuk has some **tombs** and a little **mosque** dating from the Seljuk period; these are near the bus station. Also, on the streets between the highway and the railway station you can see the remains of a

Byzantine **aqueduct**, now a favourite nesting-place for a large population of storks (late April to September).

Places to Stay - bottom end

Selçuk has numerous small pensions, a complete list of which is painted on a signboard in front of the Tourism Information Office. Rooms in these modest, friendly, cheap places cost US$3.50 to US$5 a single, US$7 to US$10 a double without bath; or US$4 to US$6 a single, US$10 to US$12 a double with private shower. In some cases it's possible to sleep on the roof or camp in the garden for US$2 to US$3 per person.

The *Australian Pension* (tel 2972), on the second street behind the museum, advertises 'Vegemite breakfasts available', and deserves special mention as it is run by a Turk who spent 12 years Down Under, and who enjoys visits by his former compatriots. He hosts barbecues sometimes.

Pensions that readers have liked in the past include the *Anatolia Pension 1* and *Anatolia Pension 2*, the *Pamukkale Pension*, the *Semiramis* and the *Manolya* (tel 1690), Atatürk Mahallesi, Professor Mitler Sokak 6, where you can have meals on the terrace, the showers are hot and there's a roof for cheap sleeping.

The *Pension Akançay* is another favourite; Veli Akançay speaks English and treats guests like family. The *Pension Tomurcuk*, near the railway station, is good, as is the *Gamaze Pension*. The *Pension Çubikoğlu* is airy and cool, surrounded by shady fruit trees; the *Lale Pension* has bright rooms, hot showers and both Turkish and European-style toilets.

Yet another good one is the *Filiz Pansiyon* (tel 1585), Zafer Mahallesi, İkinci Bademlik Sokak 10, operated by Mehmet Noyan. For a quiet place, find the *İsabey Pension*, across from the Hotel Akay near the İsa Bey Camii, well off the highway. The *Amazon Pension* is another quiet one on this same street. The *Pension*

Akbulut (tel 1139) continues to treat readers of this book well, also.

Camping The *Tusan Efes Moteli*, the closest lodging to the ruins of Ephesus, has the prime site for camping. Here you're only a few minutes' walk from the ruins, and also within walking distance of Selçuk. Dolmuşes to Kuşadası pass right by the motel. There's also camping at Pamucak.

Places to Stay - middle

The lodgings most convenient to the Ephesus ruins are at the *Tusan Efes Moteli* (tel 1060), Efes Yolu 38, Selçuk, İzmir 35920, at the turning from the Selçuk to Kuşadası road into the ruins of Ephesus. The location is excellent, a 10-minute walk from the archaeological zone entrance. According to what the traffic will bear, the 12 rooms cost US$35 to US$45 a double with shower, breakfast included. Although the motel is an older one, it has been decently maintained and has its own gardens. Prices are lower off season.

In Selçuk proper, the two-star *Victoria Hotel* (tel 3203/4), Cengiz Topel Caddesi 4, Selçuk, İzmir 35920, is about the best. It's a new place decorated in light natural wood and creamy marble, with a decent dining room on the ground floor and a lift to take you up to your room. The small rooms are simple but comfy enough; all have private showers and toilets with red seats. Rates are US$35 a double with shower, breakfast included, in the high summer season. By the way, some rooms here have views of the storks' nests in the old aqueduct, but the storks are in residence only during the warm months (mid-April to September).

Not far from the railway station, behind the Victoria Hotel, is the simple *Ürkmez Otel* (ewrk-MEHZ) (tel 1312), Namık Kemal Caddesi 18, with willing staff, some rooms with balconies, all rooms with shower, and a price of US$25 a double.

Near the museum in Selçuk is the *Ak Otel* (tel 2161), Kuşadası Caddesi 14,

Selçuk, İzmir 35920. It also boasts two stars and has 25 rooms with showers. It's priced slightly lower than the aforementioned places.

The 16-room *Hotel Akay* (tel 3009, 3172), İsa Bey Camii Karşısı, Serin Sokak 3, Selçuk, İzmir 35920, is near the İsa Bey Camii and thus well away from the noise of the town. A TV thrums in the lounge, and a waiter takes orders at the rooftop (3rd floor) terrace restaurant. The simple guest rooms are built around an interior court and reached by walkways, motel-style. All is white stucco except for the honey-coloured pine doors, windows, and other trim. All rooms have tiled baths with telephone booth-style showers, and go for US$16/25 a single/double.

Places to Eat

The place to look for an inexpensive meal is Cengiz Topel Caddesi (jehn-GEEZ toh-PEHL), between the highway and the railway station. It has numerous restaurants, including several with pleasant outdoor tables by the street. A full meal of two courses plus bread and beverage need cost only US$3 or so, though you can spend as much as US$4 or US$5 if you're not careful.

The *Seçkin Restaurant* (tel 1698), Cengiz Topel Caddesi 22, was the town favourite on my last visit because of its good food, attractive dining room and decent service. The menu covers a wide range, there are some sidewalk tables. A normal meal here costs about US$4 or US$5. The *Bizim Restaurant* just along the street has lower prices, however. Cheaper still is the *Bayraklı Pide Salonu*, up at the end of the street.

By the railway station there are some shaded tea gardens where you can sit, sip tea and watch the storks atop the aqueduct. A popular place opposite the Hotel Aksoy is the *Turan Köfteci*.

For better surroundings, head for the *Villa Restaurant* (tel 1299, 1331), at the beginning of the road to Ephesus. Vines and lattices shade the tables here. In summer there is a wooden rig out front which holds a large barrel-like churn for ayran, as the best of this drink is churned (*yayık ayran*), not simply mixed. Prices for meals are not high, as meat dishes range from US$1.75 to US$3. Try *çöp şiş* (churp sheesh), delicate small morsels of lamb grilled on little wooden skewers. The Villa Restaurant is only open in the summer.

In the town proper, the street-level dining room of the *Victoria Hotel* is the place to try, at similar prices.

Getting Around

There's a small bus and dolmuş station right in the centre, on the highway opposite the turning for Kuşadası and the Tourism Information Office, from which you can get minibuses to Ephesus, Pamucak, Kuşadası and Söke.

It's a good idea to do your travelling early in the day. The dolmuş service from Selçuk to Kuşadası (US$0.50), for instance, may stop at around 6 or 7 pm. After that time you hitch, or pay for a taxi unless you can find enough fellow travellers to hire a whole minibus or car and share the cost. Should you find yourself in this predicament, look for taxis lurking near the museum in Selçuk. Sometimes there's a driver who lives in Kuşadası on his way home, looking for some fares so he doesn't travel empty. He'll be amenable to bargaining.

Taxi drivers charge about US$1.50 to take you the four km to the Ephesus ruins, about US$6 to Meryemana and back. For US$12, they'll take you to the main ruins, wait, take you to Meryemana, and return you to Selçuk. All of these rates are per carload, not per person. Dolmuş drivers at the Selçuk bus station will organise a tour to Priene, Miletus and Didyma, lasting from 10 am to 7.30 pm, including lunch and a few hours' swimming time at Altınkum Beach for US$12 to US$15 per person.

EPHESUS

Half a day will do you for sightseeing at

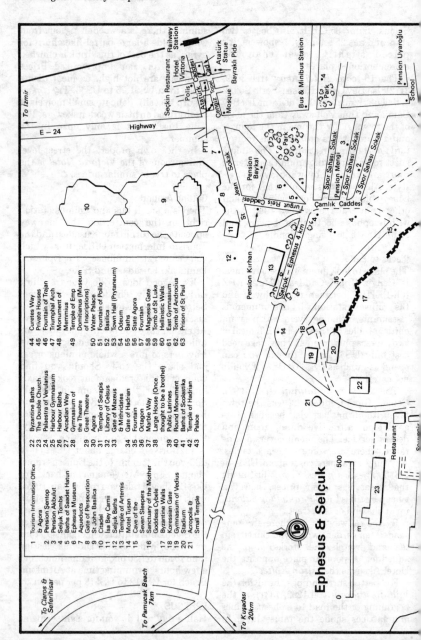

1 Tourism Information Office & Agora
2 Pension Sentop
3 Pension Akbulut
4 Seljuk Tombs
5 Baths of Saadet Hatun
6 Ephesus Museum
7 Aqueducts
8 Gate of Persecution
9 St John Basilica
10 Citadel
11 Isa Bey Camii
12 Seljuk Baths
13 Temple of Artemis
14 Motel Tusan
15 Cave of the Seven Sleepers
16 Sanctuary of the Mother Goddess Cybele
17 Byzantine Walls
18 Koressian Gate
19 Gymnasium of Vedius
20 Stadium
21 Acropolis & Small Temple

22 Byzantine Baths
23 The Double Church
24 Palaestra of Verulanus
25 Harbour Gymnasium
26 Harbour Baths
27 Arcadian Way
28 Gymnasium of the Theatre
29 Great Theatre
30 Agora
31 Temple of Serapis
32 Library of Celsus
33 Gate of Mazeus & Mithridates
34 Gate of Hadrian
35 Fountain
36 Octagon
37 Marble Way
38 Large House (Once thought to be a brothel)
39 Public Latrines
40 Round Monument
41 Baths of Scolastika
42 Temple of Hadrian
43 Palace

44 Curetes Way
45 Private Houses
46 Fountain of Trajan
47 Triumphal Arch
48 Monument of Memmius
49 Temple of Emp Domitianus (Museum of Inscriptions)
50 Water Palace
51 Fountain of Pollio
52 Basilica
53 Town Hall (Prytaneum)
54 Odeum
55 Baths
56 State Agora
57 Fountain
58 Magnesia Gate
59 Tomb of St Luke
60 Hellinistic Walls
61 East Gymnasium
62 Tomb of Androclus
63 Prison of St Paul

Ephesus & Selçuk

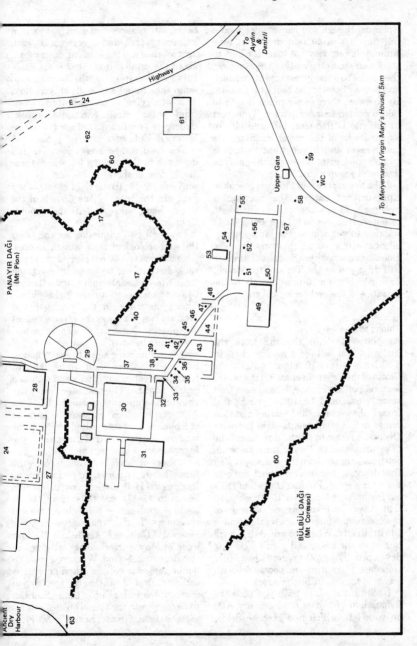

Ephesus, though you can easily spend a full day if you go into detail. In high summer it gets very hot here. It's best to start your tramping early in the morning, then retire to a shady restaurant for lunch and to your hotel or the beach for a siesta. By the way, there is not much reason to take a guided tour of Ephesus. Transport to the site is frequent, fast and cheap; explanations of the major buildings are given here; and if you want to hear a guide's spiel, just tag along with one of the dozens of group tours.

I like to walk the four km from Selçuk to Ephesus, but only in the morning or evening. The walk takes about 45 minutes. But as you'll be doing a lot of walking to get around the large archaeological site, you might want to ride. Dolmuşes headed from Selçuk to Pamucak will drop you at the Tusan Efes Moteli, from which it's a 10-minute walk to the entrance of the archaeological zone.

Things to See

As you walk into the site from the highway, you will see a road to the left. This leads (after a 10-minute walk) to the Grotto of the Seven Sleepers, on the northeast side of Mt Pion. A legend says that seven persecuted Christian youths fled from Ephesus in the 3rd century and took refuge in this cave. Agents of the Emperor Decius, a terror to Christians, found the cave and sealed it. Two centuries later an earthquake broke down the wall, awakening the sleepers, and they ambled back to town for a meal. Finding that all of their old friends were long dead, they concluded that they had undergone a sort of resurrection. Ephesus was by this time a Christian city. When they died they were buried in the cave, and a cult following developed. The grotto is actually a fairly elaborate Byzantine-era necropolis with scores of tombs cut into the rock.

Back on the entry road you pass the Gymnasium of Vedius (2nd century AD) on your left, which had exercise fields, baths, latrines, covered exercise rooms, a swimming pool and a ceremonial hall. Just south of it is the Stadium, dating from about the same period. Most of its finely cut stones were taken by the Byzantines to build the citadel and walls of Ayasoluk. This 'quarrying' of precut building stone from older, often earthquake-ruined structures continued through the entire history of Ephesus.

The road comes over a low rise and descends to the parking lot, where there are a few teahouses, restaurants and souvenir shops. To the right (west) of the road are the ruins of the Church of the Virgin Mary, also called the Double Church.

Pay the US$6 admission fee and enter the archaeological zone, which is open from 8.30 am to 5.30 pm every day. As you walk down a lane bordered by evergreen trees, a few colossal remains of the Harbour Gymnasium are off to the right (west). Then you come to the marble-paved Arcadian Way. This was the grandest street in Ephesus. Constructed with water and sewer lines beneath the paving, installed with street lighting along the colonnades, lined with shops and finished with triumphal columns, it was and still is a grand sight. The builder was the Byzantine emperor Arcadius (395-408). At the far (western) end was the harbour of Ephesus, long since silted up. Near the western (harbour) end of the street is the Nymphaeum, a fountain and pool.

At the east end of the Arcadian Way is the Great Theatre, still used for performances. Its design is Hellenistic; construction was begun in 41 AD and finished in 117. It could – and can – hold almost 25,000 spectators. During the Selçuk Ephesus Festival of Culture & Art, held in the first week of May, performances are given in this dramatic setting. When you visit, no doubt someone will be standing on the orchestra floor of the theatre, speaking to someone seated high up in the auditorium to demonstrate the fine acoustics.

Behind the Great Theatre is Mt Pion,

Statue of Diana the Huntress from the Roman period at Ephesus

which bears a few traces of the ruined city walls.

From the theatre, continue along the marble-paved **Sacred Way**, also called the Marble Way. Note the remains of the city's elaborate water and sewer systems. The large open space to the right, once surrounded by a colonnade and shops, was the **Agora** (3 BC) or marketplace, heart of Ephesus' business life.

At the end of the Sacred Way, Curetes Way heads east up a slope. This corner was 'central Ephesus'. The beautiful **Library of Celsus** is here, carefully restored with the aid of the Austrian Archaeological Institute.

Across the street is an elaborate building with rich mosaics and several fountains. It was once thought to be the brothel, but some say it was just a grand private residence. In the maze of ruined walls you'll come upon a **spring** served by a hand pump from which, with a little effort, you can coax the most deliciously refreshing cool water.

As you head up Curetes Way, a passage on the left leads to the **public latrines**, their design demonstrating their function unmistakably. These posh premises were for men only. The women's were elsewhere.

On the right side of Curetes Way, the hillside is covered in **private houses**. Most of these were small, as houses in classical times were mostly for sleeping and dressing. Bathing, amusements, socialising and business were all conducted in public places. The houses are still being excavated and restored. A few of the ones along the street belonged to wealthy families and have elaborate decoration.

You can't miss the impressive **Temple of Hadrian**, on the left. It's in Corinthian style, with beautiful reliefs in the porch and a head of Medusa to keep out evil spirits. The temple was finished in 138 AD. Across the street is an elaborate house from the same period.

Further along Curetes Way, on the left, is the **Fountain of Trajan**, who was Roman emperor from 98 to 117 AD.

To the right is a side street leading to a colossal temple dedicated to the Emperor Domitian (81-96 AD), which now serves as the **Museum of Inscriptions**.

Up the hill on the left (north) are the very ruined remains of the **Prytaneum**, a municipal hall; and the **Temple of Hestia Boulaea**, in which the perpetual flame was guarded. Finally you come to the pretty little marble **Odeum**, a small theatre used for lectures, musical performances and meetings of the town council.

There is another entrance to the archaeological zone here, near the Odeum at the Upper Gate, on the road which leads to Meryemana (mehr-YEHM-ah-nah), the House of the Virgin Mary, also called Panaya Kapulu. You will need a taxi for the five km to Meryemana.

MERYEMANA

Legend has it that the Virgin Mary, accompanied by St Paul, came to Ephesus at the end of her life, around 37 to 45 AD. Renaissance church historians mentioned the trip, and it is said that local Christians venerated a small house near Ephesus as Mary's. Then a German woman named Catherine Emmerich (1774-1824) had visions of Mary and of her surroundings at Ephesus. When Lazarist clergy from İzmir followed Emmerich's detailed descriptions, they discovered the foundations of an old house in the hills near Ephesus; a tomb, also described by Emmerich, was not found. In 1967 Pope Paul VI visited the site, where a chapel now stands, and confirmed the authenticity of the legend. A small traditional service, celebrated by Orthodox and Muslim clergy on 15 August each year in honour of Mary's Assumption into heaven, is now the major event here. To Muslims, Mary is Meryemana, Mother Mary, who bore İsa Peygamber, the Prophet Jesus.

The site is now a Selçuk municipal park; there is no regular dolmuş service, so you'll have to hitch, rent a taxi or take a tour. The park is seven km from Ephesus' Lower Gate (or 5½ km from the Upper Gate, nine km from Selçuk), up steep grades. The views of Ephesus, Selçuk, Ayasoluk Hill, and the surrounding countryside are wonderful along the way. At the top of the hill you must pay a small park entrance fee of US$0.15, and a fee for the site of US$0.40, then ride or walk down the other side a short way to the site.

Along the approach to the house are signboards explaining its significance in various languages. The house is usually busy with pilgrims, the devout and the curious. A small restaurant and snack stand provide meals at fairly moderate prices. If you're travelling on a budget, bring picnic supplies and enjoy lunch on your own in the shady park.

PAMUCAK

About nine km west of Selçuk lies Pamucak (PAH-moo-jahk) beach, a long wide crescent of dark sand. Pamucak is undergoing the standard tourism boom, with big hotels rising here and there, and a growing litter problem. In summer, it can get pretty busy with sun and surf seekers, both Turkish and foreign. As of this writing, you can still camp on the beach (along with the mosquitoes), but that may change soon.

Places to Stay

The first and oldest hotel on the beach is the *Dereli Motel* (tel 1749), Pamucak, Selçuk, İzmir. It has little double or twin-bedded motel-style rooms with bath, facing the beach (US$25) or the land (US$20); slightly more comfortable rooms in bungalows inland a bit cost US$30 a double. The whole place could do with a bit more maintenance, but it does offer a restaurant, food shop and camping area. The Dereli is to the left as you come to the beach.

To the right of the access road, inland from the beach about 250 metres, is the four-star, 150-room *Otel Tamsa Pamucak* (tel 1190, 2282), Çorak Mevkii, Pamucak, Selçuk, İzmir, the first of several new and modern places to open on the beach. It's a big, white box designed for the pleasure of tour groups, and offers quite comfortable rooms with TV, bath and refrigerator, and the many services of an upper-bracket hotel, including tennis court, water sports equipment, restaurant and bar. Rates are US$60/80 a single/double during the high summer season.

Getting There & Away

Transport to Pamucak is fairly easy in summer, as there are regular dolmuşes (US$0.25); hitching is easy, as well. Out of season, it's hitching and hiking, or taxi.

ŞİRİNCE

This little village up in the hills, seven km east of Selçuk, is in the midst of peach and apple orchards. The old-fashioned stone-and-stucco houses have red-tile roofs, and the villagers, who were moved here from Salonica and its vicinity during the exchange of populations (1924) after WW I, are ardent fruit farmers; they make an interesting apple wine. People here will regale you proudly with the story that this village used to be named Çirkince ('ugliness'), but that it was changed to Şirince ('pleasantness') shortly after they arrived.

There's not much to do in Şirince

except look at a few old Byzantine churches and monasteries, walk in the hills, and hang out, but that's exactly why people come here, away from the touristy bustle of Selçuk. If you need a place to stay, there's one cheap pension, the *Village of Maria's Pension* (tel 1430), Şirince Köyü, Selçuk, İzmir, run by Metin Ozan. Beds go for US$2 and meals are similarly cheap. Dolmuşes run to Şirince daily from Selçuk's bus station.

KUŞADASI

On the Aegean coast, 20 km from Selçuk, is Kuşadası (koo-SHAH-dah-suh, Bird Island). A seaside resort town with a population of 40,000, it is a base for excursions to the ancient cities of Ephesus, Priene, Miletus and Didyma, and even inland to Aphrodisias.

Many Aegean cruise ships on tours of the Greek islands stop at Kuşadası so that their passengers can take a tour to Ephesus and haggle for trinkets in Kuşadası's shops. The town's appearance, not to mention its economy, has been affected by this cruise business, to the point where Kuşadası has lost a lot of the pleasant, easy atmosphere which made it popular.

Today in high summer the town is crowded, bustling and noisy. Its centre is all shops, and in front of the shops, beside the shops, in the streets, on the waterfront and climbing the walls are *işportacılar*, itinerant pedlars ready to sell you anything and everything. But Kuşadası is still a mixture of hotels and pensions for Turks and foreigners on holiday, and of businesses serving the farmers, beekeepers and fishers who still make up a portion of the town's population.

Kuşadası gets its name from a small island, now connected to the mainland by a causeway, called Güvercin Adası (gew-vehr-JEEN ah-dah-suh, Pigeon Island). You can recognise it by the small stone fort, now a supper club, which is the tiny island's most prominent feature. As for central landmarks, the biggest is the Öküz

Mehmet Paşa Kervansarayı, an Ottoman caravanserai which is now a hotel called the Club Caravansérail, operated by Club Méditerranée. It's at the intersection of the two main streets.

Orientation

The waterfront road is named Atatürk Bulvarı. During high summer, a horse-drawn buggy rolls along this street carrying people from the centre to the northern beach. The main street heading from the wharf into town is officially named Barbaros Hayrettin Caddesi, but many locals still call it by its former name of Tayyare Caddesi. The street changes names to become Kahramanlar Caddesi as it progresses inland past the police station, which is in a little stone tower that was once part of the town's defensive walls. The bus and dolmuş station is north on Kahramanlar Caddesi, near the prominent mosque named the Hacı Hatice Hanım Camii, about one km from the sea.

Information

The Tourism Information Office (tel (636) 11103), İskele Meydanı, is down by the wharf where the cruise ships dock, about 100 metres in front of the Club Caravansérail.

Things to Do

Besides a stroll through the Kervansaray and out to Güvercin Adası, and a short ride to the beaches, the thing to do is take dolmuşes to the nearby ruined cities. While you're in Kuşadası, however, you might want to shop for onyx, meerschaum, leather clothing and accessories, copper, brass, carpets and jewellery. Don't shop while the cruise ships are in port, however, as prices are higher and dealers ruder.

Should you feel in need of a scrubbing, the town's **Belediye Hamamı** is up the hill behind the Hotel Akdeniz; take the street which goes along the left side of the hotel. (For a description of traditional Turkish

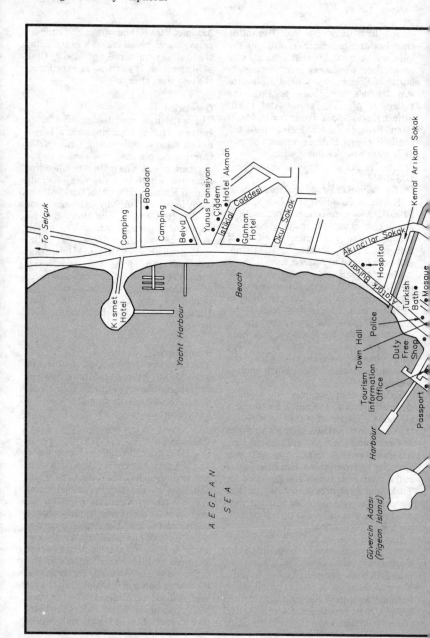

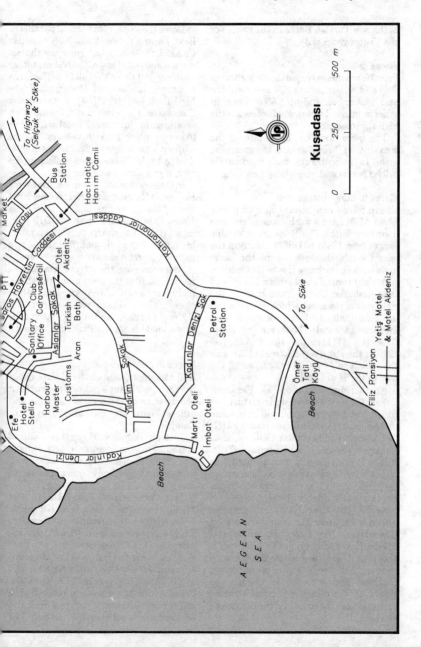

Kuşadası

500 m

250

0

To Highway
(Selçuk & Söke)

Market

Karasu

Bus
Station

Hacı Hatice
Hanım Camii

Kahramanlar Caddesi

PTT

Club Caravaserail

Baros Hayrettin Caddesi

Sanitary
Office

Otel
Akdeniz

Aslanlar Sokak

Turkish
Bath

Aran

Customs

Harbour
Master

Hotel
Stella

Efe

Yıldırım Sokak

Kadınlar Denizi Sok

Petrol
Station

To Söke

Martı Oteli

İmbat Oteli

Ömer
Tatil
Köyü

Beach

Filiz Pansiyon

Yetiş Motel
& Motel Akdeniz

To Söke

Beach

Kadınlar Denizi

Beach

A E G E A N
S E A

baths, see Turkish Baths in the Facts For the Visitor chapter.)

Places to Stay

Prices for rooms in Kuşadası are highest in July and August, about 20% lower in June and September, and up to 50% lower in other months. Rates quoted below are the high summer rates.

The more luxurious hotels are on the outskirts of town, as are the camping areas. In the centre are small, moderately priced hotels and very cheap pensions.

Places to Stay – bottom end

Cheap rooms can be very nice or pretty basic. Most have a washbasin, a few have a private bath. The price for a double ranges from US$7 to US$11. Many of the cheap establishments are in the same area: walk up Barbaros Hayrettin Caddesi, turn right toward the Akdeniz Hotel, and take Arslanlar Caddesi, the road on the right side of the hotel, which will take you up past half a dozen pensions and inexpensive hotels. Look for the *Hotel Rose* (tel 11111); the *Hotel Ada* (tel 12491); the *Pansiyon Su* (tel 11453); and the *Pansiyon Dinç* (tel 14249), along the way to the Hotel Stella.

Another such area is on Eski Pazaryeri Sokak: facing the Akdeniz Hotel, turn left (don't just bear left). You will soon come to the popular *Öven Pansiyon* (ewr-VEHN) (tel 13963), Kahramanlar Caddesi, Eski Pazaryeri Sokak 15, Kuşadası 09402 Aydın. It has a friendly management, lots of hot water and bathless rooms renting for US$5.50/9/12 a single/double/triple. Breakfast is available at cheap rates.

Across the street is the moderately priced *Hotel Güler Tur*. You'll also see, on this street, the *Hotel Kuşadası* (tel 11315), Eski Pazaryeri Sokak 15, which is cheap at US$6/10 a single/double with shower, but needs some management coaching and someone to change the sheets. If you consider staying here, be sure to look at the room and the bed before you rent.

Down the slope, north of and parallel to Eski Pazaryeri Sokak, is Kahramanlar Caddesi, the street which runs past the bus station and out of town. On Kahramanlar Caddesi, just down the hill from the Öven Pansiyon, is the *Otel Demiroğlu* (deh-MEER-oh-loo) (tel 11035), Kahramanlar Caddesi 58, Kuşadası, 09402 Aydın. It's a small, plain, functional hotel such as is found in many Turkish villages. Rooms without a bath cost US$8/11/14 a single/double/triple. There's room to sleep on the roof, if you have a sleeping bag.

In the centre of town on Barbaros Hayrettin Caddesi is an inexpensive hotel which, though cheap, is also noisy. The *Hotel Pamuk Palas* (pah-MOOK pah-lahss) (tel 11080) charges US$16 a double, breakfast included, but for this extra money you get a shower in your room.

As for camping, there are several areas a few km north of the town along the shore, including a *BP Mocamp* and other, cheaper places. There is also one opposite the yacht harbour and others south of the centre, near Kadınlar Plajı and beyond.

Places to Stay – middle

Mid-range hotels are scattered throughout the town, with some out on the northern beach, some on the southern hillside and others right off Barbaros Hayrettin Caddesi.

Just off Barbaros Hayrettin Caddesi opposite the caravanserai is Cephane Sokak (JEHP-hah-neh), with three good, convenient, relatively quiet places to stay.

The *Alkış Oteli* (ahl-KUSH) (tel 11245), Cephane Sokak 4/A, Kuşadası, 09402 Aydın, is the first one you'll come to. The 19 tidy rooms with shower here are priced at US$30 in season.

A few steps farther on is the two-star, 45-room *Minik Otel* (mee-NEEK) (tel 12359, 12043), Cephane Sokak 8, Kuşadası, 09402 Aydın. It's a modern place with a self-service restaurant, bar, roof deck and 45 guest rooms with private showers. The price for a double, breakfast included, is US$32.

Next door is the *Bahar Pansiyon* (bah-HAHR) (tel 11191), Cephane Sokak 12, Kuşadası, 09402 Aydın, a newer establishment with a facade full of balconies and flower boxes, and a rooftop restaurant. The 13 rooms offer a step up in comfort, and also in price, at US$20/25 a single/double, breakfast included. Note that the Bahar is closed from November to February.

Up at the end of Barbaros Hayrettin Caddesi is the *Otel Akdeniz* (AHK-deh-neez) (tel 11120) with a pleasant vine-shaded patio in front, a spacious lobby and 42 rooms of varying sizes, shapes, and number of beds, with or without a bath. Tour groups sometimes fill the hotel. If you find a room vacant, look at it and listen to the noise level, as some face heavily trafficked streets. A double without a bath costs US$26, with a bath US$32 to US$38; breakfast is included in room prices.

Face the Otel Akdeniz, turn left, and walk down Eski Pazaryeri Sokak to find the *Otel Güler Tur Center* (gew-LEHR toor) (tel 12996), Eski Pazaryeri Sokak 26, Kuşadası, 09402 Aydın, a newish hotel with friendly management who always seem to be reading newspapers. The rooms are plain but tidy and fairly quiet, with relatively low prices of US$18/26 a single/double, with bath. Facing the Güler Tur Center across the narrow street is the *Otel Güler Tur City*, with the same prices and similar rooms.

Walk up Arslanlar Caddesi, which mounts the slope next to the Otel Akdeniz, and turn right (west) toward the sea to find the two-star, 22-room *Hotel Stella* (tel 11632, 13787), Bezirgan Sokak 44, Kuşadası, 09402 Aydın. It's a tidy, airy place with fabulous views of the town and the harbour, friendly and personable management, and bright, modern rooms priced at US$54 a double with shower, breakfast included.

Less charming but also less expensive is the *Hotel Pamuk Palas* (pah-MOOk pah-lahss) (tel 13191), near the bus station (not to be confused with its plainer sister hotel downtown on Barbaros Hayrettin Caddesi). New and shiny, with its own swimming pool and another for children, it charges US$38 for a double room with shower, breakfast included.

About one km north of the centre is another group of moderately priced lodgings, either on the waterfront street or west of it a block or two. Most can be found by following their signs.

The *Günhan Hotel* (GEWN-hahn) (tel 11050) faces the sea at Atatürk Bulvarı 52, Kuşadası, 09402 Aydın, and charges US$22/26 a double/triple with bath, breakfast included.

Nearby is a group of other good places, including the 20-room *Çidem Pansiyon* (chee-DEHM) (tel 11895), İstiklal Caddesi 9, Kuşadası, 09402 Aydın, next to the Yunus Pansiyon. It's a clean and cheerful place with single rooms for US$22 with washbasin or US$26 with shower, and doubles for US$28 with washbasin, US$34 with shower.

The 18-room *Posacı Turistik Pansiyon* (POHSS-ah-juh) (tel 11151), Leylak Sokak 5, Kuşadası, 09402 Aydın, back inland from the shore road a few blocks, has tidy rooms for US$14 a single, US$26 a double, without bath, but with breakfast.

The nearby *Hotel Akman* (AHK-mahn) (tel 11501) is at İstiklal Caddesi 13, Kuşadası, 09401 Aydın. It's a neat and modern little two-star, 46-room place open from mid-March to the end of October, used by tour groups. Some rooms have bathtubs, and all are priced at US$28/36 a single/double, breakfast included.

Places to Stay – top end

Kuşadası's poshest place to stay is the refurbished Ottoman caravanserai, now a hotel operated by the Club Méditerranée called the *Club Caravansérail* (tel 14115), Öküz Mehmet Paşa Kervansaray, Kuşadası, 09402 Aydın. It's in the centre of town at the seaside end of Barbaros

Hayrettin Caddesi. Rooms are attractive, if small and simple, the courtyard is lush, the ambience superb. A double costs US$75, with room, breakfast, tax and service included, but you're usually required to book half-board (breakfast and dinner), which brings the daily tab up to US$95. If you don't stay here, at least come for a meal (expensive), a drink or a free look around.

On Kadınlar Plajı south of town are other comfortable hotels priced at US$60 to US$90 a double. These include the four-star, 250-room İmbat Oteli (EEM-baht) (tel 12000/1/2), Kadınlar Denizi Mevkii, Kuşadası, 09402 Aydın, at the high end of that price range; and the Martı Oteli (mahr-TUH) (tel 13650), Kadınlar Denizi 69, Kuşadası, 09402 Aydın, a three-star, 60-room place that's somewhat lower in price.

Places to Eat

Restaurant prices stretch across the full range in this resort and farming town. As you get away from the sea, prices drop dramatically and quality stays high.

Places to Eat – bottom end

Go up Barbaros Hayrettin Caddesi past the little police station in the stone tower, continue on Kahramanlar Caddesi, and prices drop even more. The Konya Restoran and Nazilli Pideci are places where you can fill up for US$2 to US$4.

As usual, the very cheapest eateries are next to the market, which is one block north off Kahramanlar Caddesi, next to the bus station. Little restaurants here such as the Kısmet equal or undercut those on Kahramanlar as far as price is concerned. In between Kahramanlar and the bus station, in the narrow street beside the Hacı Hatice Hanım Camii, are little cookshops serving delicious köfte, flat pide bread, salad and soft drinks, all for less than US$2.

For a cheap kebapçı, find the Hotel Alkış; facing it across the street is the Öz Urfa Kebapçısı (tel 13244).

Places to Eat – middle

The Çatı on Barbaros Hayrettin Caddesi is on the roof of a building, has a fine view of town life and costs US$10 to US$12 for a full fish dinner with wine. However, it's actually more pleasant to sit at one of the fish restaurants next to the wharf. This is the town's prime dining location, so a full fish dinner with wine at the Toros Canlı Balık (tel 11144), Kâzım Usta'nın Yeri (tel 11226) or Diba (tel 11063) may cost US$12 to US$18 per person. Perhaps the best prices, with equally good food, are at the Çam Restaurant (tel 11051).

Places to Eat – top end

Most expensive is definitely the Club Caravansérail, where a meal can easily set you back US$20 to US$30 per person.

Getting Around

Bus & Dolmuş Buses of the Elbirlik company run between İzmir and Kuşadası every hour or so in each direction from about 7 am to 6 or 7 pm, charging US$1.50 for the 1½-hour trip. Dolmuşes buzz off from Kuşadası to Ephesus and Selçuk every 30 minutes, on the hour and half-hour, charging US$0.50 for the ride. There are dolmuşes to Söke (US$0.50) as well; this is what you take if your ultimate destination is Priene, Miletus or Didyma. Catch an onward dolmuş in Söke. Or you can take a tour minibus from the Kuşadası bus station for US$3 per person, much the easiest way.

Minibus drivers at the Kuşadası bus station run tours to Ephesus and Meryemana for about US$10 per person.

Dolmuşes for Kadınlar Plajı, south of town, and for Pamucak, to the north, depart from the bus station as well.

Boats to Samos Any travel agency in Kuşadası will sell you a ticket for a boat to Samos. You can go over for the day and return in the evening, or go there to stay. Boats depart each port, Samos and Kuşadası, at 8.30 am and 5 pm daily in high summer; about four times weekly in spring and autumn. Service is usually suspended in winter except for special excursions. The trip costs a high US$35 one way, US$50 return. In most cases, you must surrender your passport for immigration processing the evening before you travel; the same thing happens if you're coming from Samos to Kuşadası.

PRIENE, MILETUS & DIDYMA

South of Kuşadası lie the ruins of three very ancient and important settlements well worth a day trip. Priene occupies a dramatic position overlooking the plain of the River Menderes. Miletus preserves a great theatre, and Didyma's Temple of Apollo is among the world's most impressive religious structures.

Priene

As you approach the archaeological zone, you'll come to a shady rest-spot in a romantic setting: water cascades from an old aqueduct next to the Priene Şelale Restaurant, where you can get a cool drink or hot tea, make a telephone call or have a meal. This is where you recover from your tramp through the ruins. A motto painted on one of their garbage receptacles reads, 'Tourists want a smiling face and pleasant speech'.

The site at Priene is open from 9 am to 6 pm daily for US$2.

Priene was important around 300 BC because it was where the League of Ionian Cities held its congresses and festivals. Otherwise, the city was smaller and less important than nearby Miletus, which means that its Hellenistic buildings were not buried by Roman buildings. What you see in Priene is mostly what one saw in the city over 2000 years ago.

The setting is dramatic, with steep Mt Mykale rising behind the town, and the broad flood plain of the River Menderes spread out at its feet.

Priene was a planned town, with its streets laid out in a grid (the grid system originated in Miletus). Of the buildings which remain, you should see the

bouleterion (city council meeting place); Temple of Athena, designed by Pythius of Halicarnassus and looked upon as the epitome of an Ionian temple; Temple of Demeter; theatre; ruins of a Byzantine church; and the gymnasium and stadium. As you gaze across the river's flood plain, you will see why the name of this river came to signify a river which twists and turns (meanders) back and forth across its flood plain.

Miletus

Miletus' Great Theatre rises to greet you as you approach the flood plain's southern boundary and turn left, riding through swampy cotton fields to reach the archaeological zone. It is the most significant building remaining of this once-grand city, which was an important commercial and governmental centre from about 700 BC till 700 AD. After that time the harbour filled with silt, and Miletus' commerce dwindled. The 15,000-seat theatre was originally a Hellenistic building, but the Romans reconstructed it extensively during the 1st century AD. It's still in very good condition and very impressive to explore.

The ticket booth in front of the theatre sells tickets from 9 am to 6 pm, any day, for US$2. The site is open, at least unofficially, until dusk. There is also a little museum about a km south of the theatre. Across the road from the ticket booth is a small restaurant where you can get snacks and beverages and drink them in a shady grove.

A Seljuk caravanserai, a hundred metres south of the ticket booth, is currently under restoration and is to be opened as a souvenir bazaar.

Climb to the top of the theatre for a view of the entire site, with several groups of ruins scattered about, among them a stadium; two agoras, northern and southern; the Baths of Faustine, constructed upon the order of Emperor Marcus Aurelius' wife; and a bouleterion. To the south of the main group of ruins, nearer to the

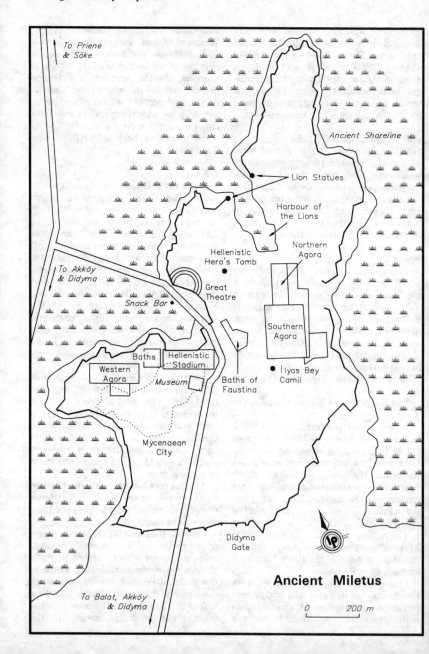

To Priene
& Söke

Ancient Shoreline

Lion Statues

Harbour of
the Lions

Northern
Agora

Hellenistic Hero's Tomb

To Akköy
& Didyma

Great
Theatre

Snack Bar

Southern
Agora

İlyas Bey
Camii

Baths

Hellenistic
Stadium

Western
Agora

Museum

Baths of
Faustina

Mycenaean
City

Didyma
Gate

To Balat, Akköy
& Didyma

Ancient Miletus

0   200 m

museum, is the **İlyas Bey Camii** (1404), a mosque dating from the Emirate period. After the Seljuks but before the Ottomans, this region was the Emirate of Menteşe. The mosque's doorway and the mihrab inside are pleasant, but perhaps nicest of all is the ambience of the place. A small gem of a building when new, it is now partly in ruins, its roof a favourite nesting-place for storks. Grass and weeds grow in the courtyard, and a romantic, ageless melancholy surrounds the place.

From Miletus, head south again to Akköy (seven km) and Didyma (14 km farther). Transportation may be infrequent in these parts, and it may take some time to reach Akköy by hitchhiking. South of Akköy there is more traffic, however, and most of it goes past Didyma to Altınkum Beach.

Didyma

Called Didim in Turkish, this was the site of a stupendous temple to Apollo, where lived an oracle as important as the one at Delphi. The temple and the oracle were important since very early times, but the great temple you see is the one started in the late 300s AD. It replaced the original temple which was destroyed in 494 BC by the Persians, and the later construction which was done by Alexander the Great.

The Temple of Apollo was never finished, though its oracle and its priests were hard at work until Christianity became the state religion of the Byzantines and they put an end to all such pagan practices. Fourteen hundred years of operation is a pretty good record, however.

When you approach Didyma today, you come into the village of Yenihisar (yeh-NEE-hee-SAHR). A few teahouses and restaurants across the road from the temple provide drinks and meals. Admission hours and fee are the same as at Priene and Miletus.

Ancient Didyma was not a town, but the home of a god. People did not live here, only priests. I assume that the priests, sitting on the temple treasure (which was considerable) had a pretty good life. The priestly family here, which specialised in oracular temple management, originally came from Delphi.

The temple porch held 120 huge columns, the bases of which are richly carved. Behind the porch is a great doorway at which the oracular poems were written and presented to petitioners. Beyond the doorway is the *cella* or court, where the oracle sat and prophesied after drinking from the sacred spring. We can only speculate on what that water contained to make someone capable of prophesies. The cella is reached today by a covered ramp on the right side of the porch.

In the temple grounds are fragments of its rich decoration, including a striking head of Medusa (she of the snakes for hair). There used to be a road lined with statuary which led to a small harbour. The statues stood there for 23 centuries but were then (1858) taken to the British Museum.

Altınkum Beach

Five km south of Didyma is, Altınkum Beach (AHL-tuhn-koom, Golden Sand), with little restaurants, pensions and hotels. It's nice, but not as convenient for transport as Kuşadası.

Getting Around

If you start early in the morning from Kuşadası or Selçuk, you can get to all three of these sites by dolmuş, returning to your base at night. If you have a car, you can see all three on your own and be back by mid-afternoon.

Guided tours of these sites can save you time and uncertainty; one that covers these three sites, including lunch and a swim at Altınkum Beach, will cost US$12 per person; a minibus 'tour' which merely trundles you around to the sites costs US$3 per person.

If you want to do it yourself, begin by catching a dolmuş from Kuşadası (15 km) or Selçuk (35 km) to Söke, then another onward to Priene.

When you've finished at Priene, wait for a passing dolmuş or hitchhike across the flat flood plain to Miletus (22 km). The dolmuş may bear a sign saying 'Balat' (the village next to Miletus) or 'Akköy', a larger village beyond Balat.

From Miletus, catch something to Akköy or, if you can, something going all the way to Didyma or Altınkum. For the return trip from Didyma or Altınkum get a dolmuş to Söke, and change for another to your base. If you do it all by dolmuş the fares will total about US$3.

SÖKE

The modern bus and dolmuş station in this transport town is divided into separate bus and dolmuş sections. From the bus side of the station, Söke municipal buses depart for İzmir every hour on the half-hour until 4 pm for US$1.50. Others head east to Denizli and Pamukkale, south to Bodrum and to Muğla (for Marmaris).

The dolmuş side of the station serves vehicles going to Güllübahçe (the village next to Priene, 14 km, US$0.40); Balat (the village near Miletus, 35 km, US$0.85); Davutlar (US$0.60); Milâs, on the way to Bodrum (82 km, US$1); Didyma (56 km, US$0.80); Aydın, on the way to Aphrodisias, Denizli and Pamukkale (55 km, US$0.85); Altınkum Beach (61 km, US$1); and Güzelçamlı, where there is a national park (Milli Park).

Aphrodisias & Pamukkale

At the spa named Pamukkale (pah-MOO-kah-leh, Cotton Fortress), 220 km due east of Kuşadası, hot mineral waters burst from the earth to run through a ruined Hellenistic city before cascading over a cliff. The cascades of solidified calcium from the waters form snowy white travertines, waterfalls of white stone, which give the spa its name. Nearby are the ruins of Laodicea, one of the Seven Churches of Asia.

On the way to Pamukkale you can make several detours to significant archaeological sites, including the hilltop city of Nyssa about 100 km east of Kuşadası. About 150 km east of Kuşadası is Aphrodisias, one of Turkey's most complete and elaborate archaeological sites, with several buildings exceptionally well preserved.

From Denizli, the city near Pamukkale, you can catch a bus onward to Ankara, Konya or Antalya, but you'll miss the lovely Aegean Coast if you do. Only those pressed for time and anxious to see Central Anatolia should consider such a short cut. Everyone else should plan to visit Pamukkale as a one or two-night side trip from Selçuk or Kuşadası before continuing down the coast to Bodrum, Marmaris, Fethiye and Antalya.

As you begin your trip you may pass through the ruins of Magnesia ad Meander, which lie on the road between Söke and Ortaklar. This ancient city is not really worth a stop, but the fragments of wall easily visible from the road are certainly impressive.

From Ortaklar to the provincial capital of Aydın (ahy-DUHN) is 33 km. Aydın has a population of 100,000 and is a farming town with little to detain you. Should you have to stay, the one-star, 28-room *Hotel Orhan* (tel (631) 11781), Gazi Bulvarı 63, will put you up in some modicum of comfort for US$18/22 a single/double.

East of Aydın, you are deep in the fertile farming country of the Büyük Menderes river valley. Cotton fields sweep away from the road in every direction. During the cotton harvest in late October, the highways are jammed (dangerously so) with tractors hauling wagons overladen with the white puffy stuff. Other crops prevalent in the valley, all the way to Denizli, are pomegranates, pears, citrus fruits, apples, melons, olives and tobacco.

Getting There & Away

Bus and train services are good on the route from İzmir through Selçuk, Aydın and Nazilli to Denizli. There is no air service.

From Kuşadası, get a direct bus to Denizli or a dolmuş to Selçuk, Söke or Ortaklar, and transfer to a bus or train; at Ortaklar you wait on the road for a bus. If you plan to take the side trip to Aphrodisias, hop on a bus or train and go as far as Nazilli; otherwise, go all the way to Denizli.

See also the Getting There & Away sections of each town.

NYSSA

Heading 31 km east from Aydın brings you to the town of Sultanhisar and, three km to the north, the site of ancient Nyssa, set on a hilltop amid olive groves. You'll have to walk or hitch to the site, as there is no public transport. When you reach the ruins you'll find a water fountain, public toilets, a guard and no admission fee. The guard will show you around the site if you wish; a tip is expected.

The major ruins here are of the **theatre**, next to the parking area, which has olive trees growing from its tiers of seats, and a long **tunnel** beneath the road. A five-minute walk up the hill along the road and through a field brings you to the **bouleterion**, which has some nice fragments of sculpture.

What you will remember about Nyssa, however, is the peacefulness and bucolic beauty of its site, very different from tourist metropolises such as Ephesus.

NAZİLLİ

Nazilli (NAH-zee-lee), 14 km east of Nyssa and Sultanhisar, has a population 95,000 and is the transfer point for a trip to Aphrodisias. The bus station is just north of the main highway.

Places to Stay

This farming town boasts a comfortable three-star hotel, the 54-room *Nazilli Ticaret*

Odası Oteli (Chamber of Commerce Hotel) (tel (637) 19678/9, 19680/1), Hürriyet Caddesi, Nazilli, Aydın, 500 metres up the main street from the bus station. Quite decent rooms with a bath and balcony rent for US$26 a double, breakfast included. There's a restaurant and bar of course, and also a decent pastry-shop adjoining the hotel. If you want a quick, cheap snack before heading out to Aphrodisias, this is the place. Otherwise, there are several little eateries in the bus station area.

Getting There & Away

Bus There are a few direct buses a day between Karacasu and İzmir (210 km, 3½ hours, US$2) and Selçuk (130 km, two hours, US$1.75). If you don't get one of these, take a bus from İzmir, Selçuk, Ortaklar, Aydın or Denizli to Nazilli, and from there a dolmuş to Geyre (GEHY-reh), a village 55 km from Nazilli and right next to the ruins. If you can't find a dolmuş to Geyre or Aphrodisias, take one to Karacasu, 42 km from Nazilli, and take a dolmuş, hitch a ride or hire a taxi in Karacasu for the final 13 km to Geyre and the ruins. You should be able to hitch easily in summer.

Nazilli is the local transportation hub, with buses to and from İzmir and Selçuk about every 45 minutes or less in the morning and afternoon, but infrequent in the evening. Here are some other destinations from Nazilli:

Ankara – 545 km, eight hours, US$6; several buses daily
Antalya – 360 km, six hours, US$4; several buses daily
Bodrum – 225 km, four hours, US$3; several buses daily
Denizli – 65 km, one hour, US$0.75; very frequent buses and dolmuşes
İstanbul – 600 km, 12 hours, US$9; several buses daily
İzmir – 170 km, 2½ to three hours, US$2; very frequent buses

Konya – 505 km, eight hours, US$6; several buses daily

Kuşadası – 150 km, 2½ hours, US$2; several buses daily

Pamukkale – 85 km, 1½ hours, US$1; several buses daily

Selçuk – 130 km, 1½ hours, US$1.75; buses at least every hour

Car For those driving, Aphrodisias is 55 km from Nazilli, 101 km from Denizli and 38 km off the E24 highway. By the way, after you've visited Aphrodisias, it's advisable to return to the main highway rather than follow the narrow, rough, winding mountain road to Denizli via Tavas.

APHRODISIAS

You come to Aphrodisias from Nazilli by way of the town of Karacasu (KAH-rah-jah-soo), surrounded by tobacco fields, fig trees and fruit orchards. The site and museum at Aphrodisias, 13 km past Karacasu, are open from 8 am to 6.30 or 7 pm in summer, 8.30 am to 5.30 pm in winter, for US$3. One ticket gets you into both the site and the museum. No photography is permitted in the museum, and you are also prohibited from photographing excavations in progress here. Signs in the car park advise that no camping is allowed; they're afraid of antiquity thieves hereabouts.

The city's name quickly brings to mind 'aphrodisiac'. Both words come from the Greek name for the goddess of love, Aphrodite, called Venus by the Romans. Aphrodite was many things to many people. As Aphrodite Urania she was the goddess of pure, spiritual love; as Aphrodite Pandemos she was the goddess of sensual love, married to Hephaestus but lover also of Ares, Hermes, Dionysus and Adonis. She got around. Her children included Harmonia, Eros, Hermaphroditus, Aeneas and Priapus, the phallic god. All in all, she was the complete goddess of fertility, fornication and fun.

History

The temple at Aphrodisias was famous and a favourite goal of pilgrims for over 1000 years, from the 8th century BC. The city prospered. (How could it not, with such a popular goddess? Just think what worship entailed!) But under the Byzantines the city changed substantially: the steamy Temple of Aphrodite was transformed into a chaste Christian church, and ancient buildings were pulled down to provide building stones for defensive walls (circa 350 AD). The town, diminished from its former glory, was attacked by Tamerlane on his Anatolian rampage (1402) and never recovered.

Ruins lay abandoned and mostly buried until French, Italian, American and Turkish archaeologists began to resurrect them. What they found was a city that held a surprisingly well-preserved stadium, odeum and theatre. The National Geographic Society (USA) supported some of the excavation and restoration. Articles on Aphrodisias are in the August '67, June '72 and October '81 issues of their magazine.

Museum

On the way to the ruins is a tidy modern museum with a good collection of pieces from the ruins. Check your camera at the door. During Roman times there was a school for sculptors here, which accounts in part for the rich collection. Beds of high-grade marble are nearby. Note especially the 'cult statue of Aphrodite, second century' and the 'cuirassed statue of an emperor or high official, second century'.

Ruins

Unfortunately the site is not yet well marked, so it can be confusing to get around, even with our handy map.

The dazzling white marble **theatre** is beautiful, and virtually complete. Behind it, the **odeum** is more or less the same, in miniature. During your walk around you'll discover the elaborate but well-ruined **Baths of Hadrian** (circa 200 AD) and

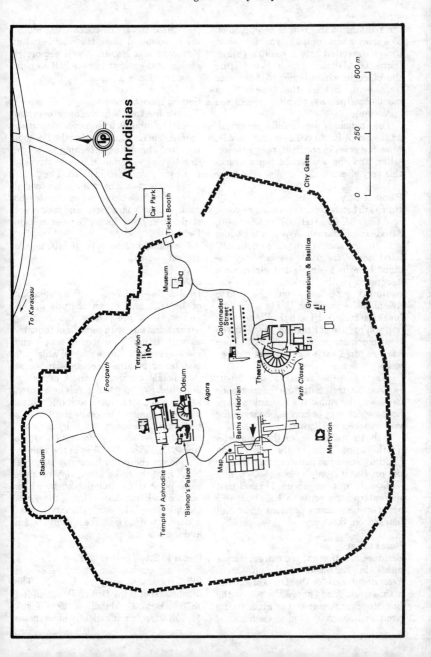

320 Aegean Turkey – Aphrodisias & Pamukkale

the remains of the **Temple of Aphrodite**. The temple was completely rebuilt when it was converted into a basilica church (circa 500 AD), so it's difficult to picture the place in which orgies to Aphrodite were held. Behind the temple is a **monumental gateway** which led to a sacred enclosure.

The **stadium** is wonderfully preserved, and most of its 20,000 seats are usable. Mow the grass in the field, post a ticket-seller, and one could hold chariot races this very afternoon.

Places to Stay

Half a km before coming to the ruins you'll spot *Chez Mestan* (tel (6379) 1430, 1446), Afrodisias, Karacasu, Aydın, a big house with an airy, shady front porch on the left-hand side of the road. You can stay the night here in a simple but clean room decorated with Turkish crafts and equipped with a private hand-held 'telephone' shower for US$14 a double, breakfast included, less if they're not busy or if you're good at haggling. Meals on the front porch are priced about US$3. They have an area set aside for camping as well.

Also near the ruins is the *Bayar Pension*, 200 metres up from the crossroads closest to the ruins. It's a simple village house which may or may not be receiving visitors when you arrive.

In the town of Karacasu, there is an *otel* on the upper floor of the bus station building where you can sleep for US$3 per person. But it is only a place to sleep, and really only for emergencies. I expect that the enterprising souls in Karacasu will begin opening comfy pensions and small hotels soon, though.

Places to Eat

Besides *Chez Mestan*, you can get simple meals in Karacasu at the *Köseoğlu Restaurant* and at the *Öztekin* on the main street. A cut above the rest is the *Bonjour Restaurant* at the main traffic circle in Karacasu. Similar restaurants,

patronised mostly by coach tour groups, are to be found along the road between Karacasu and Nazilli. You'll get better service at these if you arrive half an hour before or after a group.

Getting There & Away

The Pamukkale bus company operates special minibuses in summer, departing Pamukkale Köyü at 10 am on the 1½-hour trip to Aphrodisias, returning at 3 pm, thus leaving you ample time to explore the ruins and have a picnic lunch. The cost is US$4 per person. The minibus is a special service for those based in Pamukkale who want to visit Aphrodisias, and it does not stop to take on or discharge passengers in Denizli.

For transport from other points, see the section on Nazilli.

DENİZLİ

Denizli (deh-NEEZ-lee), with a population of 185,000, and at an altitude of 354 metres, is a prosperous and bustling agricultural city with some light industry as well. It has a number of hotels and restaurants in all price ranges, which are of interest because accommodations at Pamukkale are usually more expensive and often full up. Denizli can be a noisy, smoky place sometimes, so it offers little to hold your interest except as a transportation centre and lodging spot.

Denizli's Tourism Information Office (tel (621) 13532, 20046) is in the railway station on the main highway, only one block from the bus station, very near the three-point traffic roundabout by which one goes to Pamukkale 19 km to the north. Delikli Çınar Meydanı, the city's main square, is two km from the railway station and the bus station.

Places to Stay – bottom end

If all accommodation at Pamukkale is full, you must stay in Denizli. The favourite spot is the *Denizli Pansiyon* (tel 18738), Deliktaş Mahallesi, 1993 Sokak 14, 20100 Denizli. It's slightly more than a

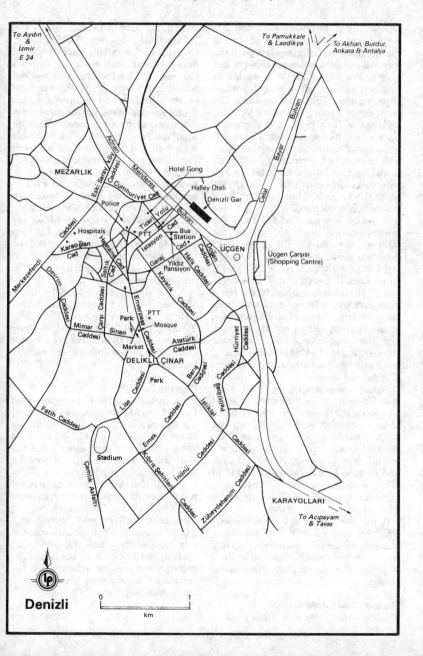

To Aydın
&
İzmir
E 24

To Pamukkale
& Laodikya

To Akhan, Burdur,
Ankara & Antalya

MEZARLIK

Hotel Gong

Halley Oteli

Denizli Gar

Police

Cumhuriyet Cad

Menderes

Adnan

Eski Saray Köy Caddesi

Bulvarı

Celal Bayar Bulvarı

Caddesi

Hospitals

Karaoğlan Cad

Hastane Cad

Saltık Cad

Devrim

Merkezefendi

Caddesi

Ticaret Yolu

Bulvarı

Cad

PTT

Istasyon

Bus
Station

Cad

Doğan Caddesi

Halk Caddesi

ÜÇGEN

Üçgen Çarşısı
(Shopping Centre)

Garaj

Yıldız
Pansiyon

Kevalik Caddesi

Enverpaşa Caddesi

Çarşı Caddesi

Mimar
Sinan
Caddesi

Park

PTT

Mosque

Market

Atatürk
Caddesi

DELİKLİ ÇINAR

Park

Lise Caddesi

Barış Caddesi

İstiklal Caddesi

Pelitlibağ Caddesi

Hürriyet Caddesi

Fatih Caddesi

Emek Caddesi

Kıbrıs Şehitleri Caddesi

İnönü Caddesi

Caddesi

Zübeydehanım Caddesi

Stadium

Çamlık Asfaltı

KARAYOLLARI

To Acıpayam
& Tavas

Denizli

0   1
km

km (a 15-minute walk) from the bus station, away from the centre of town in the section called Deliktaş; signs point the way. All rooms have private showers and toilets, and go for US$18 a double in summer, cheaper off season; breakfast costs another US$2 per person. The pension has a courtyard with a fountain and lots of fruit trees, and it's quiet; there's space for camping, too. The owner, Süleyman Can (pronounced 'john'), also sells carpets; he'll sometimes shuttle you to and from the bus station in his car. His wife cooks delicious Turkish meals for about US$3 each. Many readers have stayed here quite happily.

Walk up İstasyon Caddesi from the railway station and turn left at the intersection marked by the Halley Oteli. Soon you should see the *Yıldız Pansiyon* (tel 18216), Halk Caddesi, 452 Sokak 13, 20100 Denizli. Located on a side street just off the main drag, this place is fairly quiet and only a five-minute walk from the bus station. The old building has been spruced up a bit with paint and carpeting, and the guest rooms have tidy tiled showers. Rates are US$18 a double in a room with a shower; breakfast is included. The pension has no lift.

Other choices are nearby. Turn right onto Cumhuriyet Caddesi from İstasyon Caddesi at the Halley Oteli, and one block along on the left is the *Otel Gong* (tel 111178, 38803), Cumhuriyet Caddesi 13, 20100 Denizli, an older hotel that's recently had a face-lift. It now has a lift and suitable rooms renting for US$12 to US$16 a single, US$16 to US$22 a double, breakfast included; the higher prices are for rooms with private shower.

Across the street is the *Hotel Gökdağ*, which is also suitable and somewhat cheaper; rooms with twin beds, balcony and washbasin cost US$14 a double. Both of these hotels suffer from street noise, though.

Places to Stay – middle
The two-star, 60-room *Halley Oteli* (HAHL-ley, named for the comet) (tel 19544, 21843), İstasyon Caddesi, 20100 Denizli, is a five-minute walk up the hill from the railway station. Popular with bus tour groups, its advantage to individual travellers is that it is the two-star hotel nearest the bus and railway stations. Rooms are comfortable but not particularly fancy, and prices are somewhat high for what you get: US$30/48 a single/double with bath and TV. The hotel is one of Denizli's status addresses and boasts two lifts, a rooftop restaurant and bar, a mezzanine breakfast room and French-speaking staff at the reception desk. Even so, most of the rooms are fairly noisy.

Up the hill on İstasyon Caddesi are several similar hotels, such as the two-star, 30-room *Keskinkaya Oteli* (tel 11325), İstasyon Caddesi 83, 20100 Denizli, at slightly lower prices, with the same noise problem.

Just a step or two off Delikli Çınar Meydanı, two km from the bus and train stations, is the *Kuyumcu Oteli* (koo-YOOM-joo) (tel 13749/50), Delikli Çınar Meydanı, 20100 Denizli. It has a two-star rating, 75 rooms with bath, and slightly lower prices.

Places to Eat
If you're staying in the Kuyumcu Oteli in Delikli Çınar Meydanı, there's a restaurant a few steps away. The *Sevimli Kardeşler Döner Kebap Salonu* (tel 14700) will serve you a portion of döner kebap, soft drink and slice of watermelon (in season) for about US$2.50.

Denizli's bus station has an inexpensive restaurant called the *Doyuran Kafeterya* (DOY-yoo-RAHN, 'filling-up'), serving kıymalı pide (flat bread topped with ground lamb) for US$0.75. I recommend this because they bake the bread and make up the pide fresh to your order. The *Self-Servis Hamburg* restaurant in the bus station is quite drab, with so-so food but is open long hours.

Getting There & Away

Bus There are frequent buses between İzmir and Denizli Belediyesi Oto Santral Garajı, the Denizli Municipal Central Bus Station; these buses take a route via Selçuk, Ortaklar, Aydın and Nazilli. City buses and dolmuş minibuses depart frequently from the otogar for Pamukkale, though service drops off in late afternoon and ceases in the evening.

For your onward journey, you can catch a bus in Denizli for virtually any major city in Turkey, including these:

Ankara – 480 km, seven hours, US$6; frequent buses daily

Antalya – 300 km, five hours, US$4; several buses daily

Bodrum – 290 km, five hours, US$4; several buses daily

İstanbul – 665 km, 13 hours, US$10; several buses daily

İzmir – 250 km, four hours, US$2.75; frequent buses daily

Konya – 440 km, seven hours, US$5.50; several buses daily

Kuşadası – 215 km, 3½ hours, US$3; frequent buses daily

Selçuk – 195 km, three hours, US$2.50; hourly buses

Train Three trains a day ply between Denizli and İzmir; for the schedule, refer to the beginning of the Ephesus section. Tickets go on sale in Denizli station an hour before departure. The Pamukkale Ekspresi is a nightly couchette train between Denizli and İstanbul, departing İstanbul (Haydarpaşa) at 6 pm, arriving Denizli the next morning at 8.25 am. Departure from Denizli is at 6.05 pm, arriving İstanbul (Haydarpaşa) at 9.40 am the next morning. A 1st-class ticket costs US$3.50, a 2nd-class ticket US$2.75. There is also a daily mototren between Denizli and Afyon, departing Denizli at 6.25 am on the five-hour journey, returning in the late afternoon.

When you arrive at the railway station, walk out the front door, go out to the highway, cross over, turn left and walk one block to the otogar, where you can catch a a dolmuş or bus to Pamukkale. İstasyon Caddesi, an important thoroughfare for hotels, begins just on the other (south) side of the main highway from the railway station.

PAMUKKALE

As you approach Pamukkale from Denizli (19 km), the gleaming travertines form a white scar on the side of the ridge. As you come closer, the road winds through the midst of them up to the plateau. It's an unlikely landscape, beautiful and yet somehow unsettling. The travertines form shallow pools supported by stalactites of white and black, and filled with the warm, calcium-rich mineral waters.

Beneath the travertines in the valley is the village of Pamukkale Köyü, filled with little pensions charging low rates. On the plateau above are several motels lining the ridge, a municipal bathing establishment with various swimming pools and bath houses, and the ruined city of Hierapolis. An overnight stay here is recommended for several reasons. The site is beautiful, the waters deliciously warm and inviting, the accommodation good and the ruins – especially the restored theatre – worth visiting.

Today at Pamukkale you'll find a Tourism Information Office, a PTT, souvenir shops, a museum and a first aid station.

Pamukkale Travertines

Swimming

Virtually all the lodgings have a place where you can swim, even most of the cheap pensions in Pamukkale Köyü. If you want to try the motel pools atop the ridge, you can usually do so by paying a day-use fee. The pool at the Pamukkale Motel, with its submerged fragments of fluted marble columns, is the most charming. A pass for a two-hour swim costs US$1, but they rarely check your pass so you may be able to stretch it out for a longer time.

Similar rates are charged at the Belediye Turistik Tesisleri, the municipal baths, but these, though bigger, are hardly as picturesque. Don't have a bathing suit? You can rent one for the day at the Belediye. By the way, *umumi havuzlar* (US$1 for two hours' swimming) are the large public pools; *özel aile havuzu* is a private family pool (US$2.50 per hour).

Signs at the edges of the travertines forbid anyone to enter or wade in these natural pools, but everyone seems to ignore the signs, and the travertines are in danger of being abused. They will no doubt enforce the prohibition at some point in the future.

Hierapolis

After you've sampled the warm mineral waters, tour the ruins of Hierapolis, which are extensive. To inspect the ancient city can take a full day. It was a cure centre founded about 190 BC by Eumenes II, king of Pergamum, which prospered under the Romans and even more under the Byzantines. It had a large Jewish community and therefore an early Christian church. Earthquakes did their worst a few times, and after the one in 1334 the people decided it was actually an unhealthy spot to live, and moved on.

The ancient city's **Roman baths**, parts of which are now the **Pamukkale Museum**, are next to the modern motels, closest to the Pamukkale Motel. The museum is open from 9 am to 5 pm for US$2.

Near the museum is a ruined **Byzantine church** and a **Temple of Apollo**. As at Didyma and Delphi, the temple had an oracle attended by eunuch priests. But the source of inspiration was a **spring** which gave off toxic vapours, potentially lethal, so the priests took it easy on the heavy breathing.

The **theatre** dates from Roman times and, appropriately, has been restored exquisitely by Italian stonecutters. The plan is to hold performances here, and you may find some scheduled.

For a health spa, it has a surprisingly large **necropolis** or cemetery, extending several km to the north, with many striking, even stupendous tombs.

Karahayıt

Five km to the north of Pamukkale is the village of Karahayıt (KAH-rah-hah-yuht), which has no spectacular travertines but boasts healthful mineral waters nonetheless. The waters of Karahayıt leave clay-red deposits. You can get cured (and stained red) at any of several small family pensions, camping places or motels here, patronised mostly by ageing locals in search of the fountain of youth. Or you can flee to Karahayıt just to get away from the crush of tourist traffic in Pamukkale. The dolmuş from Denizli to Pamukkale usually continues as far as Karahayıt.

Places to Stay

On weekends you may find the pensions and motels at Pamukkale full, and may have to seek lodgings in Denizli. But the point of a trip to Pamukkale is to sleep there, so plan to come during the week, or very early in the day on Friday or Saturday, and preferably in spring or autumn, not high summer.

Of the best motels, several may be filled by tour groups during the summer, so if you plan to live well, reserve in advance.

Places to Stay – bottom end

Pamukkale Köyü, the village at the base of the ridge, is filled with little family

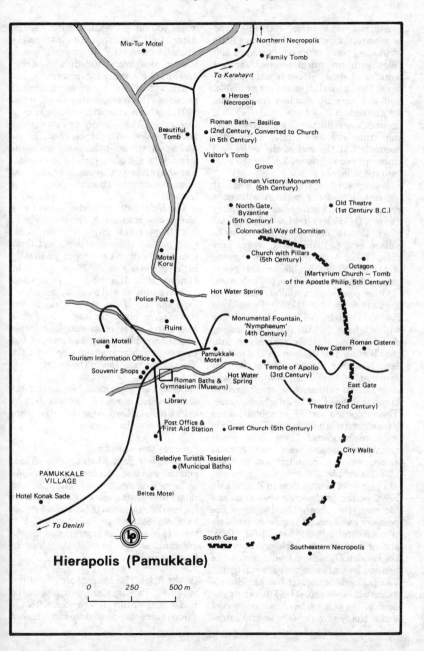

Mis-Tur Motel

Northern Necropolis

Family Tomb

To Karahayıt

Heroes' Necropolis

Roman Bath – Basilica (2nd Century, Converted to Church in 5th Century)

Beautiful Tomb

Visitor's Tomb

Grove

Roman Victory Monument (5th Century)

North Gate, Byzantine (5th Century)

Old Theatre (1st Century B.C.)

Colonnaded Way of Domitian

Motel Koru

Church with Pillars (5th Century)

Octagon (Martyrium Church – Tomb of the Apostle Philip, 5th Century)

Police Post

Hot Water Spring

Ruins

Monumental Fountain, 'Nymphaeum' (4th Century)

Tusan Moteli

Roman Cistern

New Cistern

Tourism Information Office

Souvenir Shops

Pamukkale Motel

Roman Baths & Gymnasium (Museum)

Hot Water Spring

Temple of Apollo (3rd Century)

East Gate

Library

Theatre (2nd Century)

Post Office & First Aid Station

Great Church (5th Century)

City Walls

Belediye Turistik Tesisleri (Municipal Baths)

PAMUKKALE VILLAGE

Hotel Konak Sade

Beltes Motel

To Denizli

South Gate

Southeastern Necropolis

Hierapolis (Pamukkale)

0   250   500 m

pensions, some more elaborate and expensive than others. Many have little swimming pools, often oddly shaped and filled with the warm calcium mineral water, and shady places to sit, read, sip tea or have a meal. If rooms are available, you will have no problem finding one, as pension owners will crowd around your bus as it arrives and importune you with offers. Those with rooms left at the end of the mêlée will intercept you as you walk along the road into the village.

If you want to spend the very smallest amount, look for a pension without a swimming pool. Such a place is the *Halley Pension* (HAH-ley) (tel 1204), Pamukkale Köyü, Denizli, next to the mosque in the village centre. Plain, clean rooms here cost US$12 a double without running water, or US$18 a double for their newer 'motel-style' rooms with nice tile showers.

Other pensions are similar, such as the *Ziya Pension* (tel 1195), Pamukkale Köyü, Denizli, which offers rooms without bath for US$5/10/15 a single/double/triple; if their rooms are full, they'll allow you to sleep on the roof for less. Near the highway is the *Pension Mustafa* (tel 1240, 1096) in which anyone over 140 cm tall must be careful not to bump their head on the interior staircase. The rooms are sort of jerry-built; some have showers, others do not. The owner is open to haggling. There is a small swimming pool and restaurant. A room alone, without running water, costs US$12 a double.

The rule of thumb here in Pamukkale Köyü is: the farther you walk from the highway, the cheaper and quieter the pensions are. Among the quietest pensions is the *Anatolia Pension* (tel 1052, 1085), almost a km from the highway down past the Pension Ziya. Signs leading you to the pension let you know that it's run by the village English-language teacher. Simple rooms with shower cost US$10/14 a single/double. The pension has a swimming pool and a shady terrace with several tables

where you can get meals and drinks. The *Aster Motel*, down the road a bit from the Anatolia, charges US$16 for a double with shower, breakfast included; it has a pool and lots of hot water for showers.

The village has many more, similar pensions. The *Kervansaray Pension* (tel 1209) has been a favourite with readers of this guide. The friendly owners have a house-pension with simple, cheap rooms and a fancier modern building across the street with a rooftop terrace restaurant. They have received favourable comments from readers; the *Paradise Pension* has not.

The *Hotel Göreme* is cheap and has a nice rooftop restaurant. The *Hotel Turku* (tel 1181) is fancier, with very tidy rooms with private shower, a pool, and tasty meals in the dining room, but for slightly higher prices (about US$25 a double). The *Pension Rose* (tel 1205), has a small camping area as well as cheap rooms.

At the top of the ridge, there is one inexpensive place to stay. The *Beltes Motel* (tel 1014) rents simple A-frame structures which sleep two people but have no plumbing at all, for US$15 double. You use the facilities in the motel.

Camping This is permitted for a small fee at sites along the road to Pamukkale, and in Pamukkale Köyü. Atop the ridge, there are camp sites in Karahayıt.

Places to Stay – middle

The motels at Pamukkale are often filled, and this can lead to a drop in quality. As no more lodgings may be built atop the ridge, the existing motels have a lock on the market. Demand is heavy and prices have skyrocketed in recent years. But there is competition emerging as motels are built at the base of the ridge in Pamukkale Köyü.

On the Ridge The *Pamukkale Motel* (tel 1024/5/6), Pamukkale, Denizli, is in the midst of the ruins; it's the one with the garden swimming pool littered with broken marble columns that you see in photographs so often. The entire establishment was renovated and made luxurious several years ago, and a large new restaurant added to accommodate the omnipresent tour groups. With its column-studded pool, the Pamukkale Motel is about the most expensive place to stay; rooms with bath rent for US$65/85 a single/double. I've had several complaints that the service was lackadaisical, though. For that price, it certainly shouldn't be.

The three-star, 47-room *Tusan Moteli* (tel 1010/1), Pamukkale, Denizli, was the first very comfortable motel here, and still commands premium prices of US$65/80 a single/double. The Tusan is off by itself a bit, surrounded by gardens and away from the crowds, yet still very close to the ruins of Hierapolis. Service here also leaves something to be desired.

The *Mis-tur Motel* (MEES-toor) (tel 1013), Pamukkale, Denizli, is another middle-range choice. It is at the northern end of 'motel row', slightly away from things. Its odd beehive rooms produce unnerving echoes (you will scare yourself silly if you snore), but it's a nice place for all that. Rates are US$40/58 a single/double, breakfast included; these lower rates reflect the motel's slightly inconvenient location, a bit of a walk from the centre of things.

At the *Beltes Motel* (BEHL-tess) (tel 1014/5/6/7), Pamukkale, Denizli, you can choose from several styles of accommodation. The older rooms (Nos 101 to 129) are arranged so that you have your own individual section of swimming pool right near your room, with a magnificent view of the valley. Newer rooms (Nos 130 and up) do not share this fabulous valley view, but rather surround a big swimming pool. All are simple Turkish-style motel rooms, comfortable but fairly basic. In the busy summer season the Beltes Motel, with one of the best situations on the ridge, can get away with charging US$50 a double for a room around the main pool, or US$75 for a room with an individual pool.

Breakfast and dinner are included in these prices.

To one side of the main swimming pool, an 'antique bar' has caryatid (draped female-statue) barstools so tacky they're good; the bar is a fine pergola-observatory for gazing at the valley or watching the sunset.

The conveniently located, 130-room *Motel Koru* (kohr-OO) (tel 1020/1/2), Pamukkale, Denizli, is the largest lodging-place here, with a big, beautiful swimming pool and pleasant gardens. It's a mecca for bus tours, and always seems to be thronged with groups settling in, chowing down or hauling out. Service to individual travellers may suffer as a result; the food seems mass produced.

Pamukkale Köyü At the base of the ridge, motels are squeezing out some cheap pensions as the demand for accommodation at the spa grows. The best place here at this writing is the 30-room *Yörük Motel* (tel 1073), Pamukkale Köyü, Denizli, just a few steps off the highway and down the hill, in the village centre. Guest rooms are on two levels, surrounding a courtyard with swimming pool. Balconies allow you to sit outside and enjoy the sun while watching the swimmers. The restaurant is often busy with group tours. Double rooms with shower, breakfast included, cost US$45 a double in summer.

Right at the entrance to Pamukkale Köyü, just off the highway, is a different sort of place. The *Hotel Konak Sade* (tel 1002), Pamukkale Köyü, Denizli, was the first lodging-place in the village, having opened more than 20 years ago. It's an old village house decorated with Turkish carpets, kilims and copperware. The shady rear garden holds a small swimming pool surrounded by tables and chairs for drinks, snacks or meals; the view of the travertines from here is the best around. The rooms are simple, in character with the old village house, but many have private showers. You pay US$35 a double with breakfast, or US$45 a double with breakfast and dinner. As there are few decent restaurants in the village, taking meals with your room is a good idea.

Places to Eat – bottom end

As with lodgings, so with meals. The inexpensive places (and they're not all that cheap for what you get) are at the bottom of the ridge in Pamukkale Köyü. Most of the pensions serve meals, and I recommend that you take a room with half-board (breakfast and dinner) included. Chances are very good that your pension will serve you better food, with larger portions at lower prices, than any of the crude, overpriced eateries in the village.

The famous *Pizzeria* was built to resemble a Pizza Hut in Australia, in which its builder worked for several years. Don't expect a shiny plastic fast-food place; this one's far more 'Turkish villagey', with prices to match, and excellent fresh pizza. The upper deck gives you a view with your meal. I should mention that the pizza place is becoming something of a pick-up joint, though.

In the village square by the mosque and the Halley Pension is the *Teras Restaurant*, the favourite hangout on my last visit. Kebap, salad, bread and beverage cost US$3.

Readers have found the *Blue Moon Pastanesi* to be a good place for coffee or tea and baklava.

Atop the ridge there is a pideci restaurant and a café selling soft drinks, with tables overlooking the travertines, but at resort prices somewhat higher than those in the valley.

Places to Eat – middle

All of the motels atop the ridge have dining rooms, most geared to the bus tour trade. The *Tusan Moteli*, being too small for most tours, may have the most pleasant dining room. The *Mis-Tur* is another possibility, though it is a walk from the other motels. You might also look at the *Beltes Motel*. You can expect to pay US$6 to US$10 for a full meal at any of these places.

Getting There & Away

Bus Because it is a resort, Pamukkale has a surprising number of direct buses from other cities. The Pamukkale ticket kiosk in Pamukkale Köyü near the Hotel Nebioğlu sells tickets to Antalya, Fethiye, Göreme, İzmir, Kuşadası and Selçuk. Pamukkale also operates special minibuses to Aphrodisias, departing the Pamukkale Köyü ticket kiosk at 10 am on the 1½-hour trip to Aphrodisias, returning at 3 pm. This leaves you ample time to explore the ruins and have a picnic lunch. The cost is US$4 per person. The minibus is a special service for those based in Pamukkale who want to visit Aphrodisias; it does not stop in Denizli.

For many itineraries, however, Denizli is the transportation hub. Municipal buses make the half-hour trip between Denizli and Pamukkale every 45 minutes or so, more frequently on Saturday and Sunday, for US$0.40; dolmuşes go more frequently, and faster, and charge US$0.50. If you arrive in the evening the dolmuşes and buses may have ceased to run, and you may have to take a taxi, which will cost about US$8.

Car If you're driving from Aphrodisias and Nazilli, you might want to know that there's a short cut to Pamukkale. About 600 metres after you pass the exit sign from Sarayköy ('Sarayköy' with a red diagonal stripe through it), there is a narrow road on the left going to Pamukkale via the villages of Sığma (SUH-mah), Akköy, and Karahayıt. The road is not well marked, so you should ask directions for Pamukkale in each village. If enough people ask, they might erect signs.

LAODİKYA

Laodicea was a prosperous commercial city at the junction of two major trade routes running north to south and east to west. Famed for its black wool, banking and medicines, it had a large Jewish community and a prominent Christian congregation. Cicero lived here a few years before he was put to death at the request of Marc Antony.

To reach the ruins of Laodikya, you will need a car, a taxi, a hired minibus, or good strong legs. Head north toward Pamukkale from the Üçgen, the large traffic roundabout near Denizli's bus station. Take the left turn marked for Pamukkale, and then almost immediately another left marked (badly) for Laodikya. From this point it is just over three km to the edge of the archaeological site, or just over four km from Laodikya's most prominent theatre. There are actually several routes to the ruins, but this one takes you through a little farming village; the road is unmarked, so ask, or when in doubt, go to the right. You should soon come to a level railway crossing; on the other side of the tracks, the ruins are visible. (Another route leaves the main road closer to Pamukkale, and brings you to the theatre first.)

At present there is no guard at the site, no fee and no appointed visiting hours, so you can come anytime during daylight.

Though the city was a big one, as you see by the ruins spread over a large area, there is not much of interest left for the casual tourist. The **stadium** is visible, but most of the cut stones were purloined for construction of the railway. One of the **two theatres** is in better shape, with many of its upper tiers of seats remaining, though the bottom ones have collapsed. Unless you have a car or are interested in church history, you can bypass Laodikya.

AK HAN

While you're digging about out here, consider taking a look at the Ak Han, or White Caravanserai, a marble Seljuk Turkish caravan 'motel' just one km past the Pamukkale turn-off from the main road. (Heading north from the Üçgen in Denizli, don't take the Pamukkale road, but continue in the direction marked for Dinar for one more km.) The caravanserai

is set just off the highway on the left as you come down the slope of a hill. Somewhat neglected these days, the caravanserai awaits preservation, but it is still in quite marvellous shape considering that it dates from the early 1250s.

The South Aegean

The south-western corner of Anatolia is mountainous and somewhat isolated. In ancient times this was the Kingdom of Caria, with its own people and customs, who later took on a veneer of Hellenic civilisation. Later, Christian anchorites (hermits) sought out the mountains and lake islands of Caria to be alone, and to escape the invading Arab armies. Ottoman sultans used the mountainous region to exile political troublemakers in Bodrum, secure in the belief that they could raise no turmoil from such a remote spot.

Today the region is not at all forbidding, though still remote enough so that development has not ruined the beautiful scenery or polluted the air.

Your goal is Bodrum, the seacoast town in which sleek yachts are anchored in twin bays beneath the walls of a mediaeval Crusaders' castle. Along the way are a number of ancient cities and temples worth stopping to see.

SÖKE TO BODRUM

The 130-km ride from Söke, near Selçuk and Kuşadası, to Bodrum need take only three hours if you go nonstop. But there are so many interesting detours and stops to make that it may take you several days.

About 35 km south of Söke there is a turning, on the right, for Akköy, Miletus and Didyma, described in the section on Kuşadası. Soon afterwards, the highway skirts the southern shore of Lake Bafa (Bafa Gölü). The lake was once a gulf of the Aegean Sea, but became a lake as the sea retreated. Along the shore are a few isolated little restaurants and teahouses. At the second such cluster (heading south-east) is *Ceri'nin Yeri*, a good restaurant for sea bass, eel, carp and grey mullet which find their way into the lake to spawn. Ceri'nin's has a camp site as well. No doubt a motel will follow soon.

Latmos

At the south-eastern end of the lake is a settlement named Çamiçi, from which an unsealed road on the left is marked for **Kapıkırı**, 10 km to the north, though it's actually only eight km. You will have to hike or hitch unless you can catch one of the infrequent dolmuşes. The road is rough and dusty but easily drivable (30 kph), unless it's very wet. At the end of the road, in and around the village of Kapıkırı, are the ruins of **Herakleia ad Latmos**. Behind the village is **Beşparmak Dağı**, the 'Five-fingered Mountain (1500 metres), named for its five peaks. This was the ancient Mount Latmos.

As you enter the village, a yellow sign in German announces that the road only continues for another 30 metres, so you should park in the car park by the sign and explore on foot.

A path behind the car park leads westward up to the **Temple of Athena**, on a promontory overlooking the lake. Also from the car park, paths lead eastward to the **agora**, and then several hundred metres through stone-walled pastures and across a valley to the unrestored **theatre**. The theatre is oddly sited, with no spectacular view; it's badly ruined. Its most interesting feature is the several rows of seats and flights of steps cut into the rock. You will also see many remnants of the **city walls** dating from 300 BC.

Much of the fun of a visit to Latmos is to observe real Turkish farming village life, as you will when you walk about this untouristed spot.

When you're done in the village, follow the road down to the lake, past the **Endymion Temple** built partly into the rock, the ruins of a **Byzantine castle** and the city's **necropolis**.

Down at the lakeside, near the ruins of a Byzantine church, are several small restaurants for fish (if they've caught any that day). You can camp here, using the primitive facilities. There's a small beach of coarse white sand. Just offshore is an 'island' which is often connected to the shore as the level of the lake has fallen in recent years. Around its base are foundations of ancient buildings.

Latmos is famous because of Endymion, the legendary shepherd-boy. As the story goes, the incredibly handsome Endymion was asleep on Mt Latmos when Selene, the moon goddess, fell in love with him. The myth-sayers tend to disagree on what happened next, though you can easily imagine. It seems that Endymion slept forever, and Selene (also called Diana) got to come down and sleep with him every night. What Endymion did in the hot daytime sun, when Selene was hidden, is not reported. Selene somehow saw to the care of his flocks, and on he slept. No more to report. When the male lead is catatonically inactive, it makes for a short play.

This area, ringed by mountains, was one of refuge for Christian hermits during the Arab invasions of the 700s AD, which accounts for the ruined churches and monasteries. The monks reputedly thought Endymion a Christian saint because they admired his powers of self-denial. It seems to me that it doesn't take much willpower to deny yourself something when you're completely out of it.

Euromos

About 15 km past the lake and one km south of the village of Selimiye, keep your eyes open for the extremely picturesque great **Temple of Zeus**, and two men's religious gathering places, the **First Andron** of Euromos. The Corinthian colonnades set in green olive groves seem too good to be true, like a Hollywood idea for a classical setting. Once there was a town here, but now only the temple remains. But it's enough, and well worth a stop.

If you're interested in ruins, you can explore the slopes around to find other bits of the town. Look north-east (more or less toward İzmir) and find the big, stone fortification walls up on the hillside. Climb up to them through the olive groves, go over the wall, and continue at the same altitude (the path dips a bit, which is OK, but don't climb higher). After 100 metres you'll cross another stone wall and find yourself on flat ground which was the stage of the ancient **theatre**. It's badly ruined now, with olive trees growing among the few remaining rows of seats. Besides the theatre, the town's **agora** is down by the highway to the north of the temple, with only a few toppled column drums to mark it.

There are no facilities whatsoever at Euromos. The temple is open to visit for free. About 12 km past the temple is Milâs, but before you come to this city, there are other ruins.

Iasos

Several km south of Euromos is a road on the right marked for **Kıyıkışlacık** (Iasos) about 18 km to the south-west over an unpaved road. The Turkish name means 'Little Barracks on the Coast', but Iasos was in fact a fine city set on its dramatic perch several centuries before Christ. Earliest settlement may date from the Old Bronze Age, and may have included a civilisation much like the Minoan one on Crete. Recent excavations have revealed the city's theatre and agora, a gymnasium, a basilica, a Roman Temple of Artemis Astias (190 AD) and numerous other buildings besides the prominent Byzantine fortress.

Some little restaurants here provide sustenance. No doubt there will soon be places to stay and to camp as well, since this wonderful bit of coastline will not remain undiscovered for long. Already, boats come over to Iasos from nearby Güllük.

Labranda

Just before coming into Milâs, 12 km south of Euromos, you will pass a turning for Labranda, 14 km along a very rough and slow but scenic road which winds tortuously up into the mountains, to an area from which the ancient city of Mylasa and the modern town of Milâs took their water supplies. The road can be rough going in wet weather. Perhaps this road will be paved soon, which will make Labranda easily accessible. For now, you can try hitching a ride to the village of Kargıcak about eight km along, then walk, or hope for another ride, for the remaining six km; or you can hire a taxi in Milâs for about US$10 for the whole car, round trip.

Labranda was a sanctuary to Zeus Stratius, controlled for a long time by Milâs. There may have been an oracle here. It's known that festivals and Olympic games were held at the site. Set into a steep hillside, Labranda today is surrounded by fragrant pine forests peopled by beekeepers. Late in the season (October) you can see their tents pitched in cool groves as they go about their business of harvesting the honey and rendering the honeycombs.

This was a holy place, not a settlement, and today there is no settlement here either, just a caretaker who will welcome you, have you sign his guest book and show you around the site. There is the great **Temple of Zeus**, and two men's religious gathering places, the **First Andron** and the **Second Andron**, as well as a large **tomb** of fine construction, and other buildings. The ruins, excavated by a Swedish team in the early part of this century, are interesting, but it is the site of the sanctuary which is most impressive. The view out over the valley is spectacular.

Milâs

Milâs (MEE-lahs) is a town of very great age. As Mylasa, it was capital of the Kingdom of Caria (except when Mausolus ruled from Halicarnassus, now Bodrum).

Today it is an agricultural town with a population of 35,000 and has many homes in which carpets are woven by hand.

Things to See

Approaching Milâs from the north, you come to an intersection from which the Labranda road goes off to the left, and another marked 'Şehir Merkezi' ('City Centre') goes off to the right. Your dolmuş or bus will head for the centre; follow the same route if you're driving. This route passes the city's new **museum** on the left, after which you'll see a little yellow-arrow sign on the left pointing the way to the **Baltalı Kapı**, or Gate With Axe. Follow the sign, cross a little bridge, and you come to a 'T' intersection. Look to the right to see a ruined gate in ancient Milâs' defensive walls, but turn left to reach the more impressive and well-preserved Baltalı Kapı, which has marble posts and lintel and Corinthian capitals.

Continuing into the centre of town, you'll come to a traffic roundabout next to a verdant park. Follow the little yellow-arrow signs from the roundabout to the **Gümüşkesen**, about one km from the roundabout on a hill west of the centre. The Gümüşkesen, set in a little park, is a Roman tomb dating from the first century AD, modelled after the great Tomb of Mausolus at Halicarnassus. A guardian will let you into the enclosure, set in a little park, and allow you to climb a ladder up to the platform; the view of the city from this perch is very good. The Corinthian columns support a pyramidal roof, just as at the Tomb of Mausolus. Beneath the platform is the tomb chamber, which you can enter. A hole in the platform floor allowed devotees to pour libations into the tomb chamber to quench the dead soul's thirst.

You might also want to see some of Milâs' fine mosques, the **Ulu Cami** (1378) and **Orhan Bey Camii** (1330), built during the time when Milâs was the capital of the Turkish principality of Menteşe. The larger, more impressive **Firuz Bey Camii**

(1394) was built shortly after Menteşe became part of the new and growing Ottoman Empire.

Places to Stay & Eat

Milâs is hardly a tourist mecca, so accommodation is scarce and primitive, but you might try the *Turan* and the *Akdeniz* hotels. In the bazaar at the centre of town there are several good, cheap hazır yemek restaurants.

Güllük

Three km south of Milâs is an intersection: right to Bodrum, left to Muğla and Marmaris. Turn right and after another 15 km you come to the turning for Güllük, a beach resort with several little pensions.

Eight km west of the highway through olive groves lies Güllük, a little fishing village with a harbour occupied predominantly by fishing boats, not yachts or excursion ships. Fishers still repair their nets on the quays, and town life still centres on the teahouse, not the noisy disco. There are actually three little bays here, with the central bay at the centre of town. To the left, the Türk Petrol company has a company resort which monopolises the southern bay; to the right, the northern bay is lined mostly with posh summer villas. The north bay is the best for swimming, but in fact there is no beach here.

One comes to Güllük for a few days' easy relaxation after the trials of life on the road. It's quieter and more laid back than Bodrum or Marmaris, and relatively undeveloped. Most of the activity has to do with fishing, with the quiet Türk Petrol resort, and with the nearby Etibank bauxite mines. A few simple pensions and restaurants provide the necessities. Dolmuşes run to Güllük from the village of Koru, on the highway a few km north of the Güllük turnoff. Take a bus or dolmuş from Milâs to Koru, then another one to Güllük.

For an excursion, haggle with a boatowner to take you north across the bay to

Iasos for the day, a voyage of less than an hour each way.

Approaching Bodrum

On the way to Bodrum, you cruise through pine forests and along beautiful, completely unspoilt coastline. Those curious little dome-topped structures which appear here and there, low to the ground, are cisterns. Rain falls on the dome, collects in a groove, and runs inside; the dome helps keep evaporation to a minimum.

Finally, the road climbs a hill and starts down the other side, and the panorama of Bodrum with its striking castle spreads before you.

BODRUM

It is strange that a town should owe its fame to a man long dead and a building long since disappeared, but that's the way it is with Bodrum (boh-DROOM). With a population of 20,000, it's the South Aegean's prettiest resort town with a yacht harbour and a port for ferries to the Greek island of Kos.

History

Following the Persian invasion, Caria was ruled by a satrap named Mausolus (circa 376-353 BC), who moved the capital from Mylasa to here and called this town Halicarnassus. After the satrap's death, his wife undertook construction of a monumental tomb which Mausolus had planned for himself. The Mausoleum, an enormous white marble tomb topped by a stepped pyramid, came to be considered one of the Seven Wonders of the World. It stood relatively intact for almost 19 centuries, until it was broken up by the Crusaders and the pieces used as building material in 1522.

Bodrum's other claim to fame comes from Herodotus (485?-425? BC), the 'Father of History', who was born here. Herodotus was the first person to write a comprehensive 'world history', and all other histories in western civilisation owe him a debt.

Orientation

The bus station is several hundred metres inland from the water, on the main street into the centre. Walk down from the bus station toward the castle, and you will come to a small white mosque called the Adliye Camii (AHD-lee-yeh jah-mee, Courthouse Mosque), or Yeni Cami. Turn right, and you'll be heading west on Neyzen Tevfik Caddesi toward the Yat Limanı (Yacht Marina); turn left and you will go through the bazaar, then pass dozens of hotels and pensions in all price ranges. The array of lodgings continues all the way around the bay, then along the shore of another bay farther on.

Go straight on toward the castle and you'll be walking along Cevat Şakir Caddesi, the tourist axis of Bodrum, lined with boutiques selling clothing, carpets, souvenirs and such. At the end of Cevat Şakir Caddesi beneath the castle walls, is Oniki Eylül Meydanı (12 September Square), also called İskele Meydanı (Dock Square), the main plaza. It has the Tourism Information Office, customs office, teahouses and lots of activity.

Information

The Tourism Information Office (tel (6141) 1091) is in Oniki Eylül Meydanı, with yachts moored alongside. Summer hours are Monday to Friday from 8 am to 8 pm, Saturday from 9 am to 12 noon and 3.30 to 7.30 pm, closed Sunday. They're helpful and well informed, with bus and ferry schedules and accommodation lists. Several bus and ferry companies have ticket offices nearby; the Karadeveci bus line ticket office is right next door.

The Bodrum Festival is held annually during the first week in September. Lodgings may be especially crowded then.

Herodotus and the Mausoleum are long gone, but Bodrum has many other attractions. Most striking is the fairytale Crusaders' castle in the middle of town, guarding twin bays now crowded with yachts. Palm-lined streets ring the bays,

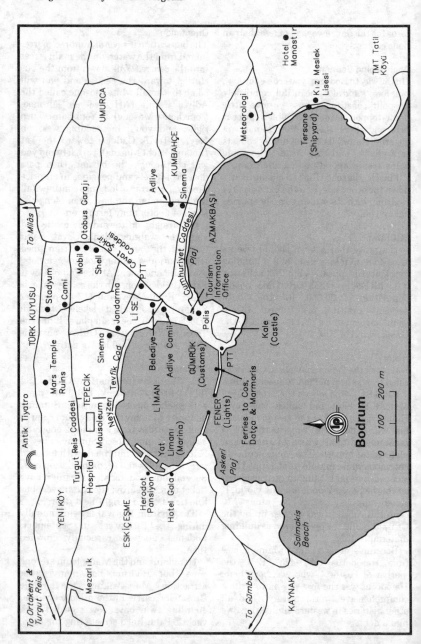

Bodrum

0   100   200 m

To Miläs

To Ortakent &
Turgut Reis

To Gümbet

UMURCA

Hotel
Manastır

Kız Meslek
Lisesi

TMT Tatil
Köyü

Meteorolagi

Tersane
(Shipyard)

KUMBAHÇE

Adliye

Sinema

Otobus Garajı

AZMAKBAŞI

Cevat Şakir Caddesi

Cumhuriyet Caddesi

Plaj

Mobil

Shell

PTT

Tourism
Information
Office

Stadyum

Cami

TÜRK KUYUSU

Jandarma

LİSE

Polis

Kale
(Castle)

Mars Temple
Ruins

Sinema

Adliye Camii

PTT

TEPECİK

Belediye

GÜMRÜK
(Customs)

Antik Tiyatro

Neyzen Tevfik Cad

LİMAN

Turgut Reis Caddesi

Mausoleum

FENER
(Lights)

Ferries to Cos,
Datça & Marmaris

YENİKÖY

Hospital

Yat
Limani (Marina)

Askeri
Plaj

Herodot
Pansiyon

Hotel Gala

ESKİÇEŞME

Mezarlık

Salmakis
Beach

KAYNAK

and white sugar-cube houses are scattered on the hillside. Yachting, boating, swimming, snorkelling and scuba diving are prime Bodrum activities. So is just hanging out and enjoying life. Bodrum's economy is now dedicated to tourism, though in winter there is a bounteous citrus crop (especially tangerines), and you will still see a few sponge fishers' boats. For diversion, you can take boat or jeep trips to nearby secluded beaches and villages (see The Bodrum Peninsula section), or over to the Greek island of Kos.

Castle of St Peter

The castle, of course, is first on anyone's list. When Tamerlane invaded Anatolia in 1402, throwing the nascent Ottoman Empire off balance for a time, the Knights Hospitaller of St John of Rhodes took the opportunity to capture Bodrum. They built the Castle of St Peter, and it defended Bodrum (not always successfully) all the way to the end of WW I. It now holds Bodrum's famous **Museum of Underwater Archaeology** and an open-air theatre. Hours are from 8.30 am to 12 noon and 3 to 7 pm every day from June to mid-September; 8 am to 12 noon and 1 to 5 pm in winter. Admission costs US$4.

Perhaps the best plan is to head straight for the French Tower, the castle's highest point. After enjoying the view, descend through the museum exhibit rooms.

As you find your way up into the castle, you'll pass several coats of arms carved in marble and mounted in the walls. Many of the stones in these walls came from the ruined Mausoleum. As always, the question which the knights put to themselves was this: with all this lovely cut stone from some old fellow's tomb, why bother to cut our own?

Many of the museum's exhibits are the result of underwater archaeology conducted by Professor George Bass of Texas A & M University and his international team of marine archaeologists. Numerous ancient coastal cargo ships have been found sunk off Bodrum, and divers have recovered

many artefacts. One of these was the oldest shipwreck ever discovered. Construction is underway on an exhibit which will include an ancient ship raised from the bottom of the Aegean off Bodrum.

Within the French Tower is the Sub-Mycenaean Archaic Age Hall, with the very oldest finds. The Italian Tower holds the Hellenistic Hall and the Classical Hall. Then, in descending order, you come to the Mediaeval Hall, the Hall of Coins and Jewellery, a collection of tombstones (outdoors), and the Snake Tower with a collection of ancient amphorae. Finally, there is the Bronze Age Hall.

Mausoleum

Though the Mausoleum is long gone, you might like to pay the site a visit. In a handsome gallery here, archaeologists have arranged models, drawings and documents to give you an idea of why this tomb was among the seven wonders of the ancient world. It's located a few blocks inland from Neyzen Tevfik Caddesi. Turn near the little white Tepecik Camii on the shore of the western bay, then left onto the road to Turgut Reis and Gümüşlük, following the signs.

The site is open every day from 8 am to 5 or 6 pm; though officially closed on Monday, you can usually get in by asking at the little grocery shop across the street. Admission costs US$0.50. Most labels and documents are in English as well as Turkish; a few are in French.

The site has pleasant gardens, with the excavations to the right and the exhibition galleries to the left. Exhibits include bits of sculpted marble found at the site, a model of Halicarnassus at the time of King Mausolus, a model of the Mausoleum and its precincts, and various diagrams and plans.

Written descriptions taken from ancient documents (1581) tell the alarming story: The Knights of St John of Rhodes discovered the Mausoleum, largely buried and preserved by the dust of ages. They

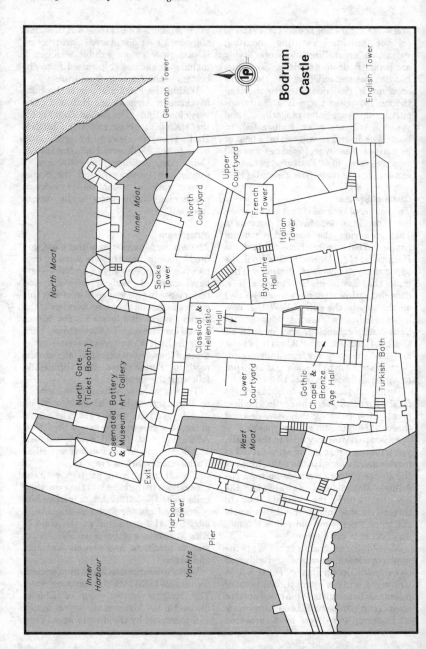

Bodrum Castle

German Tower

English Tower

Upper Courtyard

North Courtyard

French Tower

Italian Tower

Byzantine Hall

Inner Moat

North Moat

Snake Tower

Classical & Hellenistic Hall

Lower Courtyard

Gothic Chapel & Bronze Age Hall

Turkish Bath

North Gate (Ticket Booth)

Casemated Battery & Museum Art Gallery

Exit

West Moat

Harbour Tower

Pier

Yachts

Inner Harbour

uncovered it, admired it for a while, then went back to the castle for the night. During the night, pirates broke in and stole the tomb treasures, which had been safe as long as the Mausoleum was buried. The next day the knights returned and broke the tomb to pieces for use as building stone. Some of the bits were pulverised to make lime for mortar. They used these materials to repair their castle in anticipation of an attack by Süleyman the Magnificent. They knew he would attack, and they knew they would lose and have to abandon the castle, but they saw the effort as a holding action. So the Mausoleum was sacrificed to the honour of a Crusader military order.

In the large exhibition room is a copy of the famous frieze found in the castle walls; the original is now in the British Museum. Four fragments of the frieze here are original, having been discovered more recently.

In the archaeologists' hole itself there is little to see: a few pre-Mausolean stairways and tomb chambers, the Mausolean drainage system, the entry to Mausolus' tomb chamber, a few bits of precinct wall and some large, fluted, marble column drums.

Theatre

The theatre, behind the town up on the hillside by the bypass road, is cut into the rock of the hillside. The show these days is entitled 'Bodrum at Sunset'. There are no ticket-sellers, no ushers, no actors and no sets except the pretty town itself. Hike up here in the evening and take it in.

Hamam

Bodrum's Turkish bath is near the mosque beneath the castle walls just off of İskele Meydanı. Hours are from 8 am to 5 pm; the hamam is open to women on Wednesday and Saturday, to men on the other days. Admission and a wash cost US$2.

Boat Excursion

Dozens of yachts are moored along Neyzen Tevfik Caddesi on the western bay, and most have sales agents who will try and cajole you into taking a day-trip. Most boat excursions departs at 10 or 11 am, return at 4.30 or 5 pm and cost US$6.

Here's a typical itinerary. First you sail to Karaada (Black Island) due south of Bodrum, where there are hot springs issuing in a strong current from a cave. Swimmers here rub the orange mud from the springs on their bodies, hoping for some aesthetic improvement. After a half-hour stop at Karaada, the boat makes for the coarse sand and pebble beach at Ortakent Yalısı, due west of Bodrum. There's a lovely little cove here with a few beach-front restaurants, small pensions and camping areas. Big construction projects inland will change the character, though. You can have lunch at the Ökalyptos Restaurant for about US$5 or US$6. After Ortakent, the boat sails to the 'Aquarium', a small cove deserted except for other excursion boats. The water is beautifully clear, and the idea is that you'll see lots of fish, but much of the time the boating and swimming activity scares the fish away. After the Aquarium, it's back to Bodrum.

Places to Stay

As mentioned, most of Bodrum's lodgings are on the bay east of the castle, along the street called Cumhuriyet Caddesi. Most people find a room by simply walking along, asking prices and inspecting rooms. In high summer, especially on weekends, Bodrum can fill up with holiday-makers. Try to arrive early in the day to find a room. The Tourism Information Office may be able to help you find a room if space is tight.

Places to Stay – bottom end

The 17-bed Kemer Pansiyon (keh-MEHR) (tel 1473), at 30 Uslu Çıkmazı, a small street off Cumhuriyet Caddesi, is typical of Bodrum's little pensions. Rooms here have just beds and no plumbing, and cost US$16 a double, but

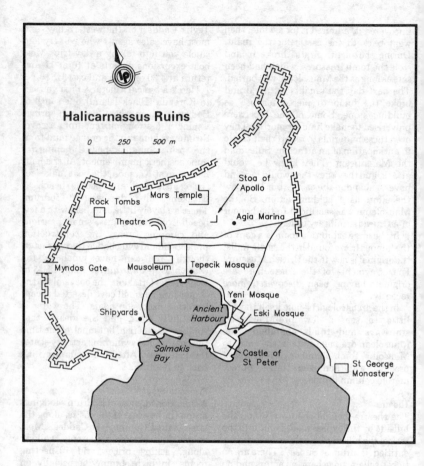

Halicarnassus Ruins

0   250   500 m

Rock Tombs

Mars Temple

Stoa of Apollo

Theatre

Agia Marina

Myndos Gate

Mausoleum

Tepecik Mosque

Yeni Mosque

Shipyards

Ancient Harbour

Eski Mosque

Salmakis Bay

Castle of St Peter

St George Monastery

the location on a back street is quiet. If the Kemer is full, the *Aşkın Pansiyon* (tel 1499) and the *Billûr Pansiyon* on the same street may have rooms. The Billûr has some rooms with a private shower. The nearby *Martı Pansiyon* (tel 2605), Cumhuriyet Caddesi 92, is a similar, simple, place right on the main street by the seaside, charging the same price.

Other pensions along Cumhuriyet Caddesi include the *Mercan* (mehr-JAHN) (tel 1111), and the *Uslu Pansiyon* (ooss-LOO) (tel 1486).

For a step up in price, consider the *Neptün Oteli* (tel 1544), Cumhuriyet Caddesi, which also calls itself the Neptune Hotel. Right on the water, many of its bare but clean rooms enjoy views of the castle and the bay. Room No 3 has a nice balcony with fabulous views. Rates are US$35 to US$45 a double in season, breakfast included, but you can haggle for a considerable reduction in spring and autumn. You're paying for the location, the lobby and the water views.

For other small pensions, look for

'pansiyon' signs along Neyzen Tevfik Caddesi, on the west side of the castle.

Camping Though Bodrum should offer all sorts of camping possibilities, this is not yet the case. There are two camp sites at Gümbet, west of the centre, but neither is particularly recommendable. More camp sites should be opening in the future, so perhaps the situation will improve. If you don't feel tied to the town, take off to one of the smaller villages on the peninsula. Bitez Yalısı and Ortakent Yalısı, for instance, are beach villages west of Bodrum with many small pensions and camp sites. There are more on the peninsula's north shore.

Places to Stay – middle

Western Bay Facing the western bay, along Neyzen Tevfik Caddesi, you'll find the *Herodot Pansiyon* (HEHR-oh-doht) (tel 1093), Neyzen Tevfik Caddesi 116, 48400 Bodrum, Muğla, with 15 rooms near the marina priced at US$15/20 a single/double. It's quiet and tidy, and therefore usually full up. Also on Neyzen Tevfik Caddesi, at No 164/1, is *Seçkin Konaklar* (setch-KEEN koh-nahk-lahr) (tel 1351) with multi-bed apartments sleeping up to six persons priced at US$18 to US$20 per person; this is a good choice for families or small groups.

Next door is the *Hotel Gala* (tel 2216, 1673), Yat Limanı, 48400 Bodrum, Muğla, nothing fancy, but cheap at US$35 a double with shower, breakfast included. The lobby, bar and garden-terrace breakfast area are more attractive than the guest rooms, which are pretty simple and small.

The three-star *Otel Bodrum* (tel 2269, 2270, 2347), Yat Limanı Karşısı, Neyzen Tevfik Caddesi 212, 48400 Bodrum, Muğla, is fancier than these other places, and advertises that 'there is no disco close by, and the windows are double insulated'! Besides the 84 comfortable guest rooms with wall-to-wall carpeting and private baths with showers, the hotel has two fresh-water swimming pools, two restaurants and three bars. Decor is in the standard Bodrum idiom of white stucco and natural wood with Turkish carpets, textiles and crafts for colour. A double room with breakfast and dinner costs US$75 in the high season, and is well worth it.

Eastern Bay Along Cumhuriyet Caddesi on the eastern bay you'll see the two-star *Otel Baraz* (bah-RAHZ) (tel 1857, 1714; fax 4430), Cumhuriyet Caddesi 62, 48400 Bodrum, Muğla, right on the water. It has 24 clean and comfortable rooms with private bath priced at US$35/48 a single/double, breakfast included. Get one with a sea view. The Baraz is open all year. The neighbouring *Hotel Mercan* takes the overflow from the Baraz.

Farther east along Cumhuriyet Caddesi is the *Artemis Pansiyon* (AHR-teh-mees) (tel 2530), Cumhuriyet Caddesi 117, 48400 Bodrum, Muğla, a 22-room place facing the bay and charging US$38 a double, breakfast included. The 16-room *Dinç Pansiyon* (DEENCH) (tel 1141, 2051), Cumhuriyet Caddesi 123, 48400 Bodrum, near the Artemis, is similar. There's a narrow strip of beach shaded by palm trees just across the street from these places. The Artemis and Dinç are comfy, but in this area the dreaded disco at the nearby Hotel Halikarnas blares its music at hundreds of decibels all night long.

This area is called Kumbahçe (KOOM-bahh-cheh); turn off Cumhuriyet Caddesi following the signs to find the *Feslegen Pansiyon* (fehs-leh-EHN) (tel 2910) at Papatya Sokak 18/1; any one of the 13 double rooms costs US$32.

A bit farther east, up on the hillside, is the three-star *Hotel Manastır* (tel 2854, 2775/6; fax 2772), Barış Sitesi Mevkii, Kumbahçe Mahallesi, 48400 Bodrum, Muğla. It's a modern holiday hotel with 51 pleasant guest rooms, all with baths and water views. There's a sun deck, a nice swimming pool and tennis court as well.

Prices are higher than at the aforementioned places, but you get more for your money here. In high summer, a room with breakfast and dinner costs US$65/85 a single/double. Off-season prices are 15% to 20% lower.

The traditional top of the line accommodation in Bodrum is a 'holiday village' on the eastern outskirts past Kumbahçe, in the section named Akçabük, two km to the east of the centre. It's the *TMT Tatil Köyü* (TEH-meh-TEH tah-TEEL keryur) (tel 1207), a large place (171 rooms) set in nice gardens by the beach, with its own swimming pools and tennis courts, large dining room and several bars. Airy guest rooms with sea views cost US$68 a double, breakfast and dinner included.

Gümbet Other hotel possibilities are to be found at Gümbet, the bay to the west of Bodrum over the hills. Dolmuşes run regularly between Bodrum and Gümbet, or you can take a short taxi ride or hitchhike. Atop the hill above Gümbet and commanding fantastic views is the *Kıvanç Motel* (kuh-VAHNCH) (tel 2043/4), Esentepe Mevkii, Gümbet, 48400 Bodrum, Muğla, the better maintained and more pleasant of the two hotels here. All rooms have private baths and balconies with that fabulous view, and cost US$40 a double in summer, breakfast included, but they usually require that you take dinner as well. This raises the price a bit, but as restaurants are scarce in Gümbet, it's not a bad plan in any case.

Down the hill a few steps, the *Hotel Mafar* (tel 1837), the *Hotel Gümbet* (tel 5935, 5936) and several similar places provide clean, if spartan, double rooms with shower for about US$35. They're popular with young British and German holiday-makers on package trips.

Right down by the beach at Gümbet is the new little *Hotel Seray* (tel 1969, 4891, 6544), Gümbet, 48400 Bodrum, Muğla. It's a welcoming family-run hostelry with pleasant little two-storey stucco units grouped around a small swimming pool.

Jasmine, bougainvillea and other flowers surround the shaded terrace dining area and bar. Guest rooms have brown tile floors, honey-coloured wood furniture, balconies with clotheslines for drying things, insect screens, and – surprise of surprises – decent reading lamps by the beds. The little marble-floored bathrooms have showers. Rooms go for US$35 to US$45 in season, breakfast included. It's an easy walk to the beach. The adjoining *Hotel Serhan* (tel 3044) is quite similar. Both hotels close at the end of October, re-opening in April.

Places to Eat

You will have no trouble finding places to eat, but you may encounter a good deal of mediocre food. Many of the restaurants are seasonal, with part-time staff. I'll give you some recommendations, and hope that these places uphold the quality I found when I visited.

Places to Eat – bottom end

For cheap food, look for the little eateries in the bazaar, the grid of market streets just to the east of Adliye Camii. About the best here is the *Portakal Restaurant,* which you can recognise by its orange-coloured umbrellas and outdoor wooden benches. They offer various meze plates, fish, fried octopus and octopus salad, meat-and-vegetable stews, grilled lamb and several other choices. Food and prices are written on a signboard, so you'll know what you're spending. For soup or a meze plate, main course, salad and beverage, the bill will be about US$5.

Next door to the Portakal is the *Bodrum Restaurant* (tel 2740), which takes the overflow from the Portakal, at similar prices. The *Durak Lokantası* (tel 1880), just a few steps east of Adliye Camii, has even cheaper prices, and a full meal for US$2.50 or US$3 is a possibility. Just around the corner from the Portakal is the *Sakallı Köfteci,* near the Garanti Bankası, serving full meals of grilled lamb meatballs, salad, bread and a drink for

US$2.50 or so. The few outdoor tables here permit you to enjoy the market atmosphere as you eat.

The *Kardeşler* (kahr-desh-LEHR) and the *Yıldız* (yuhl-DUHZ), near the Türkiye İş Bankası have hazır yemek food, outdoor tables, usually a TV and similarly low prices.

Just east of the bazaar is Hilmi Uran Meydanı, called Kilise Meydanı ('Church Square') by the locals. The square used to be dominated by an old church, but years ago the disused church was razed and replaced by a bank (significance?). Today Kilise Meydanı is chock-a-block with cheap cafés, snack shops, pidecis, restaurants and tavernas. The *Nazilli,* the *Şahin,* and the *Karadeniz* all serve cheap pide, kebaps, or hazır yemek and all have sidewalk seating areas good for people-watching. Fresh pides and Italian-style pizzas are priced between US$1.50 and US$2.50. For very cheap eats, buy a *dönerli sandviç* (dur-nehr-LEE sahn-DVEECH, sandwich with roast lamb). You may also want to try the ice cream. The filling of the cone is a great show, done with a long-handled paddle.

On Cumhuriyet Caddesi, the *Kumbahçe Köftecisi,* just a few doors east of the Hotel Baraz, has köfte, *piyaz* (a salad of white beans and onions in a light vinegar pickle), *cacık* (a cold yoghurt and cucumber soup) and similar simple fare at low prices. You should be able to eat well for US$2.

For breakfasts, snacks or picnics, walk along Cumhuriyet Caddesi to the *Yunuslar Karadeniz Fırını* (Dolphins Black Sea Bakery). It has a selection of breads and rolls in the window.

For sitting and sipping, the teahouses in İskele Meydanı, near the castle, are the best places, though prices tend to be high. You're paying for the location. There are also numerous little teahouses along the promenade on Neyzen Tevfik Caddesi.

Places to Eat – middle

Remember always to ask the price of fish, and choose those in season, as out-of-season fish are much more expensive than the already-expensive seasonal ones. When in doubt, ask *Mevsimli mi?* (mehv-seem-LEE mee, Is it in season?).

The *Amphora Restaurant* (tel 2368) is at Neyzen Tevfik Caddesi 164, across from the yacht marina and near the Herodot Pansiyon on the western bay. It's a pleasant place with streetside tables under a broad awning and several inside dining rooms in an old, stone, commercial building. Turkish carpets here and there add colour, and bits of seafaring equipment add visual interest to the decor. The clientele is drawn largely from the yachting crowd, who seem to want meat when they come ashore after days of cruising and eating fish, so the Amphora serves very little fish, though they do have fish soup. Grilled meats are the thing here, but start with a selection of mezes. You can expect to spend US$7 to US$10 per person for a full dinner with wine or beer. If you can't find a table at the Amphora, try the nearby *Gemibaşı Restaurant.*

Not far from the Amphora is the prominent *Chinese Restaurant* (tel 3136/7), Neyzen Tevfik Caddesi 220, on the ground floor and mezzanine of a large white building. If you dined in the Chinese Restaurant in İzmir, you know what this one is like, as it's run by the same people. Tablecloths are red or white, Chinese lamps and prints make the mood, and the menu lists such traditional favourites as wonton soup, fried rice with fish, meat, chicken or vegetables, and several Chinese fish dishes. If you're used to excellent and authentic Chinese cuisine, this may seem a bit pale, but it does make for variety. Prices are higher than at Turkish restaurants. A full meal here costs about US$10 to US$14 per person, with drinks.

Half-way between Adliye Camii and the Amphora Restaurant on Neyzen Tevfik Caddesi is the *Mauzolos Restaurant,* a modest place with a simple indoor dining room (used in winter), and an awning-shaded seaside open-air dining area across the street. The seaside tables are much more pleasant. Though they do serve meat here, the fish is usually delicious and reasonably priced, about US$8 to US$10 per person for a full three or four-course fish dinner with wine.

On the other side of town, along Cumhuriyet Caddesi, are more good restaurants, these specialising in seafood as well. Some get so many British customers that they write their menus in English with the prices in pounds sterling. About the best in this area is the *Kortan Restaurant* (tel 1300), right across Cumhuriyet Caddesi from the Uslu Pansiyon. Fresh fish is the forté, and the cold cases near the entrance are usually full of it. You can order your fish whole, steamed, as a fillet, or as şiş kebap, grilled on a skewer. Have a few meze plates to start, order a bottle of white wine to wash it down, and the bill should be between US$8 and US$12 per person.

Readers of this book have also found the *Restaurant Italiano* on Cumhuriyet Caddesi to have good food and service, and fair prices.

Bodrum's best pastry-shop is the *Han Pastanesi*, on Cevat Şakir Caddesi, the tourist-shop street which runs between Adliye Camii and İskele Meydanı, on the left-hand side as you walk toward the castle. The display cases show you the rolls, cakes, tarts and biscuits available, and a signboard tells you prices: *kuru pasta* ('dry' pastries) are about US$0.50 per portion, *yaş pasta* ('wet' pastries) are about US$1.25 per portion. Prices are posted by the kg as well; divide by four to get the price for 250 grammes, a good take-away amount. You might have to do some tricky translating here to order. One pastry was advertised as *kiwili-frabuazlı*, meaning that it was made with kiwi fruit and *framboises* (French for raspberries).

The pastry-shop building, by the way, is Bodrum's old han. Its interior courtyard is now a carpet shop, but it was once filled with artisans and traders who conducted their businesses out of the ground-floor rooms. Itinerant merchants slept in the rooms above. It was still a real han in 1968 when I first arrived in Bodrum, and you could get a room upstairs, as I did, with a straw-filled mattress, one light bulb and no plumbing, for US$0.25.

Getting There & Away

There are a few boat routes serving Bodrum, and a small commuter airline operates planes from İstanbul, but most transport is by bus. There is no rail service south of Söke.

Air The nearest large airports to Bodrum are at İzmir, 220 km away, and Dalaman (near Fethiye), 220 km away, though Muğla, the provincial capital, only 110 km from Bodrum, may get an airport soon. Turkish Airlines flies to Dalaman from İstanbul daily.

An air taxi company called EmAir operates single-engine Cessna 172 and 206, and twin-engine Cessna 412C aircraft carrying four to seven passengers between İstanbul's Atatürk Airport and Bodrum's small airstrip on weekends in summer. Prices are high, because this is basically an aircraft charter. Contact them at Atatürk Airport, Desk 16 in the Domestic Terminal (tel (1) 574-4318, 573-7220 ext 2728); in Bodrum the office is at Neyzen Tevfik Caddesi 138/A (tel 2100); headquarters is in Ankara at Necati Bey Caddesi 88/6 (tel (4) 229-0440, 229-0757).

Bus As usual, Bodrum's bus service is frequent and far flung. Companies serving the Bodrum bus station include Aydın Turizm, Hakiki Koç, Kamil Koç, Karadeveci, Kontaş, Pamukkale and Varan. Here are some destinations; there are lots of others as well:

Ankara – 785 km, 13 hours, US$12; a dozen buses daily
Antalya – 640 km, 11 hours, US$10; one bus daily

Dalaman – 220 km, four hours, US$5; six buses daily

Fethiye – 265 km, 4½ hours, US$6; six buses daily

Gökova – 135 km, 2½ hours, US$4; Marmaris bus, then a dolmuş or hitch

İzmir – 250 km, four hours, US$4; buses almost every half hour in summer

İstanbul – 855 km, 15 hours, US$12; hourly buses in summer

Kaş – 400 km, six hours, US$6.50; Fethiye bus, then change

Konya – 750 km, 12 hours, US$12; one bus daily

Kuşadası – 150 km, three hours, US$3; buses every half hour in summer

Marmaris – 165 km, three hours, US$3.50; hourly buses in summer

Ören – 95 km, two hours, US$2.50; bus to Milâs and change

Pamukkale – 310 km, five hours, US$6; two direct buses daily

Trabzon – 1565 km, 28 hours, US$16; one bus daily

Boat You can take boats to the Greek island of Kos, and to the Datça Peninsula west of Marmaris.

Ferries carry passengers and cars on the short voyage (less than an hour) to Kos at 9 am on Monday, Wednesday and Friday in summer, and on other days if demand warrants; return trips from Kos are at 5 pm. Make reservations and buy tickets at least a day in advance at the boat offices in İskele Meydanı, the square just beneath the castle walls, or farther along out by the harbour entrance. Fares are US$20 one way, US$24 same-day round trip, or US$40 open-date round trip. These prices include the Greek taxes of US$8 per person per trip.

Ferries between Bodrum and Datça, west of Marmaris, operate daily in summer, taking 1½ to two hours, depending upon the boat. Passenger fares are US$12 one way, US$16 round trip; cars are carried as well.

THE BODRUM PENINSULA

If tourist-crowded Bodrum is not your cup of tea, escape to one of the little seaside villages on the Bodrum Peninsula. Some have fragments of ancient ruins, others have small beaches. There are no really splendid beaches easily accessible on the peninsula, but there are at least several serviceable ones, and the slow, easy pace of life in the villages is in marked contrast to the crowded streets and noisy discos of cosmopolitan Bodrum. Dolmuşes depart Bodrum's bus station several times daily to all of these points.

Southern Shore

The southern shore of the peninsula has many small bays and inlets, but a number of them are being developed as tourist resorts, and the land behind the beaches is covered in construction. The beach at **Gümbet**, backed by lots of hotels and

Castle of St Peter, Bodrum

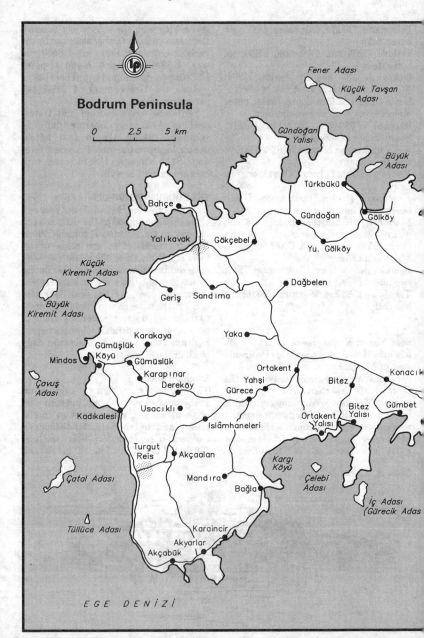

Bodrum Peninsula

0   2.5   5 km

Fener Adası

Küçük Tavşan Adası

Gündoğan Yalısı

Büyük Adası

Türkbükü

Gündoğan

Gölköy

Bahçe

Yalıkavak

Gökçebel

Yu. Gölköy

Küçük Kiremit Adası

Dağbelen

Büyük Kiremit Adası

Geriş

Sandıma

Karakaya

Yaka

Gümüşlük Köyü

Mindos

Gümüşlük

Ortakent

Bitez

Konacık

Karapınar

Yahşi

Çavuş Adası

Dereköy

Gürece

Bitez Yalısı

Gümbet

Kadıkalesi

Usacıklı

İslâmhaneleri

Ortakent Yalısı

Turgut Reis

Akçaalan

Kargı Köyü

Çelebi Adası

Çatal Adası

Mandıra

Bağla

İç Adası (Gürecik Adas

Tüllüce Adası

Karaincir

Akyarlar

Akçabük

EGE DENİZİ

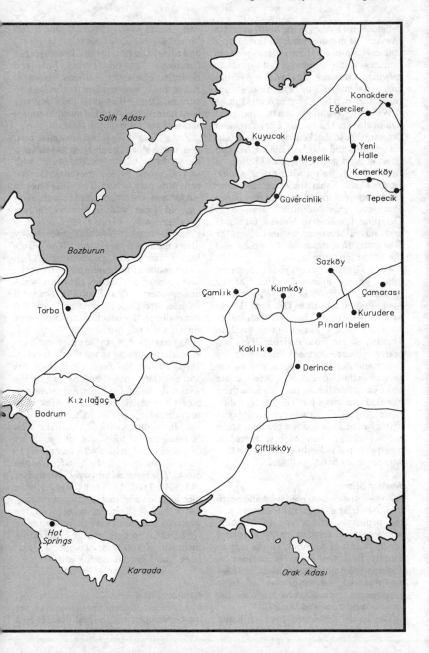

pensions, with more being built, is only a five-km, 10-minute ride from Bodrum; or you can walk to Gümbet in about 45 minutes. It has numerous restaurants to provide sustenance. The beach is good but crowded sometimes by British tour groups travelling with Sun-Med and Intasun.

West of Gümbet, past the next peninsula, are the bays of **Bitez Yalısı** and **Ortakent Yalısı**, backed by white hotels, resort villas and holiday villages, but still offering good swimming possibilities. At Bitez Yalısı there's a windsurfing school. At Ortakent Yalısı there are numerous small pensions, including the *Erkal Bahçe Pansiyon*, the *Nautilus Pansiyon & Camping*, the *Zeferya Motel & Camping* and several restaurants including the *Ökaliptus Restaurant & Camping* and the *Yalım Restaurant*.

From Ortakent Yalısı you must travel inland to continue your circuit of the peninsula, as there is not yet a coastal road. Take a dolmuş to Ortakent, 13 km west of Bodrum, then via Gürece to Akçaalan, where you can hitch south to **Akyarlar**, 30 km from Bodrum. This is a pretty village, formerly inhabited by Ottoman Greeks, with a narrow beach, several little pensions and hotels and a small yacht and fishing port. It's something like Bodrum was a half century ago. Just east of Akyarlar is **Karaincir**, a similar cove with a beach, hotels, a few pensions and a holiday village. East of here there are rough dirt roads leading to construction sites for more holiday villages.

Western Shore

Following the coastal road west and north from Akyarlar at the southernmost tip of the peninsula brings you to **Akçabük**, where there is another pretty cove and beach. North of Akçabük all the way to Turgut Reis the coast is covered in Turkish holiday villages. Most of these are reserved for employees of large government organisations such as the various ministries and the PTT.

The newly developed town of **Turgut**

Reis, 20 km west of Bodrum, has a nice beach, several little hotels and pensions, and a few little restaurants. Dolmuşes run frequently between Turgut Reis and Bodrum. The town, formerly known as Karatoprak, was renamed for the Turkish admiral Turgut Reis (died 1560) who was born here. A statue of the admiral stands south of the town on the shore.

From Turgut Reis, an unsealed road goes north along the shore to **Kadıkalesi**, a sleepy little village on the water with several small pension-restaurants. You can camp here as well. The village has an old fortress, cistern, disused church, a few big old trees and new condominium developments.

Farther north is **Gümüşlük**, reachable by direct dolmuş from Bodrum. The village has a few little pensions and fish restaurants, a fine beach and, on the rocky islet south of the hamlet, the ruins (some underwater) of ancient **Mindos**. All vehicles are stopped at a car park 100 metres from the beach so as to preserve the village's tranquillity.

As you walk down to the beach you'll see several restaurants to your right (north): *Tertib'in Yeri*, the *Yacht Club*, the *Teras* and the *Batı*, with tables set out by the water. To the left (south) are several small hotels and pensions, and also a few more restaurants. The *Gümüşlük Motel* has simple rooms with balconies. The restaurants include the *Batık Şehri* (Sunken City), which also has rooms to rent, *Nazim'in Yeri*, the *Mindos* and the *Siesta*. The *Fenerci Pansiyon & Restaurant* (tel (6141) 1420/51), out on the point, has a nice location and rooms without running water but with insect screens on the windows and nice views of the water, for US$8/12 a single/double, breakfast included. If you want the simple, laid-back, quiet life, Gümüşlük is it.

Northern Shore

The northern shore of the peninsula is the least developed and the best place to go if you want simple, authentic life 'alla Turca' at low prices.

On the north-western corner of the peninsula, 18 km from Bodrum, is **Yalıkavak**. It has several old windmills, a village square with taxis, teahouses, tractors, farmers and other evidence of normal Turkish life. Though there are several moderately priced hotels on the outskirts, look for the cheap pensions in town.

Arrayed along a perfect little bay, 17 km north of Bodrum, is the small Turkish village of **Gölköy**. It's like Gümüşlük without the ruins. Family pensions accom-modate most arrivals, though there is also the little *Sahil Motel* with pretty gardens, and fancier hotels under construction on the outskirts. Wooden boat docks serve the fishing boats; the boat-owners will also take you out for short excursions if you wish.

About 1½ km around the point from Gölköy is **Türkbükü**, another beautiful, simple little village with a few modest pensions and motels, a PTT and a few simple restaurants and shops for the yachters who stop here. There are signs of more construction of course, but for now it's wonderful.

Mediterranean Turkey

The southern coast of Turkey is delightful: a succession of scenic roads, interesting villages and picturesque ancient ruins. Only a few decades ago one had to explore parts of this coast with a rugged vehicle, pack animal or boat. New highway construction has changed all that and now you can ride easily from Marmaris, where the Aegean meets the Mediterranean, to Antakya on the Syrian border, enjoying the countryside rather than battling it.

For all its natural beauty, the coast is still relatively undeveloped. This is no Riviera with miles of waffle-front hotels, but a succession of small settlements separated by miles of rocky coastline, with the occasional sweep of beach.

The most idyllic way to explore the coast is by private yacht – not as outrageous as it sounds. While yachts chartered in the Greek islands may charge over US$100 per person per day, you can charter a beautiful wooden yacht in Turkey in spring or autumn for as little as US$35 to US$60 per person per day, meals included. The meals, made by the crew, will include fish and octopus pulled fresh from the blue waters, and herbs gathered along the shore. There's more information on yacht chartering in the Marmaris section.

You can spend as much or as little time as you like on the coast. Those without a lot of time can see the coast from Marmaris as far as Alanya pretty well in a week. The Greek island of Rhodes is close enough for a day trip from Marmaris. In this chapter I'll describe the towns and sights along the coast, from west to east.

Getting There & Away

Air The airport at Dalaman, 120 km east of Marmaris and 50 km west of Fethiye, is used mostly for charter flights from abroad, though Turkish Airlines does operate daily flights in summer linking

Dalaman with İstanbul. For detailed information on land transport from Dalaman to other points on the Mediterranean coast refer to the Dalaman section.

The other south coast airports are at Antalya and Adana.

Bus Your coastal explorations will be by bus, car or hired yacht. With the yacht and car you can make progress as you like. With the bus you must be aware that traffic is sparse along the coast. There may be only a few buses a day between points. As with most parts of Turkey, service dwindles and disappears in late afternoon or early evening, so do your travelling early in the day, and relax in the evening. With fewer buses it's all the more important to buy your reserved-seat tickets a day or so in advance.

Train There is no rail service south of Söke, Denizli and Isparta; trains do run from Ankara to Adana and Mersin, however. See the sections on Ankara and Adana for details.

BODRUM TO MARMARİS

The trip from Bodrum takes you back to Milâs, then up into the mountains through the towns of Yatağan and Muğla. The land is rich and heavily cultivated, with vast fields of sunflowers and frequent colonies of beehives. Thirty km north of Marmaris the road descends by switchbacks into a fertile valley. It then turns right and crosses the valley floor, beside a magnificent double lane, over two km in length, of

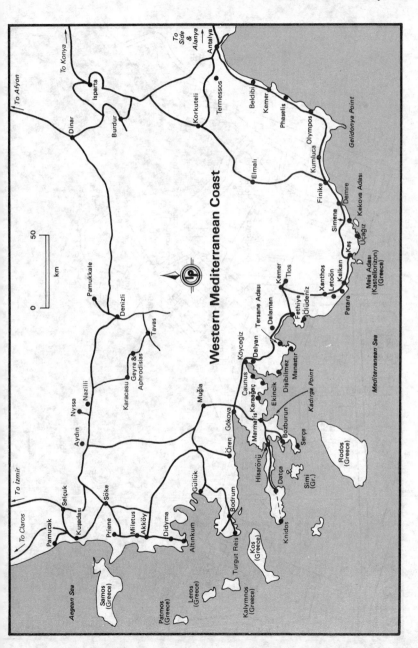

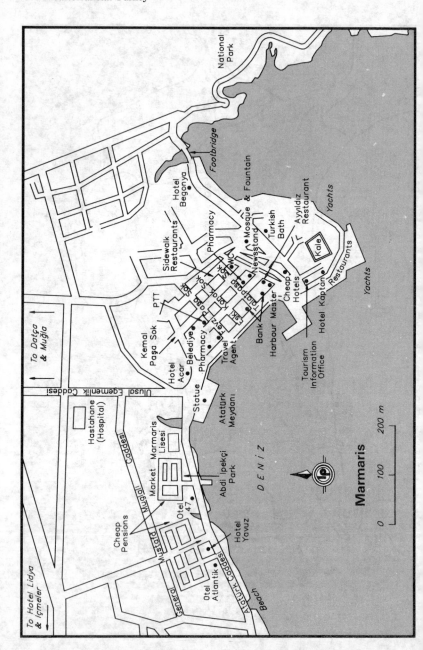

Marmaris

great eucalyptus trees. The old highway went right between the trees; the new one bypasses them on the west side. At the far end of the trees the road ascends into the hills again before coming down into Marmaris.

MARMARİS

The once-quaint fishing village of Marmaris (MAHR-mahr-ees, population 10,000) has in recent years become a busy holiday resort. This is due partly to the boat connection with Rhodes and partly to local enthusiasm. It's now the 'in' place for Turkey's rich and famous, who are followed in their choice of holiday places by the hoi polloi.

Why Turkey's movie stars and magnates chose Marmaris is something of a mystery. It is not as cosmopolitan as Kuşadası, it does not have a fine castle as at Bodrum, nor does it have impressive ruins as at Side. The choice may have something to do with the yachting trade, as Marmaris has a fine little marina in its centre and is one of Turkey's busiest yacht chartering ports.

Besides the throngs of middle-class locals and the occasional newsworthy Turk, the streets and shores of Marmaris play host to an interesting variety of international tourists and yachties, from Saudi princes to university students. There are also day-trippers from Rhodes who – ignoring the dire warnings of Greeks that Turkey is expensive, unfriendly and dangerous – come over to find just the opposite. But Marmaris is also local village people – some are farmers and fishers, others waiters and shopkeepers. It is not a flashy resort. If it's idyllic little fishing towns you're looking for, take only a brief look at Marmaris then rush on to Datça.

Orientation

Except for its shoreline development, Marmaris is a small village and a short stroll will show you the layout of the downtown section. The very heart of town

is the little plaza next to the ferry dock. Here you'll find the customs house, tourism office, currency exchange booths, many small hotels and the market district.

The waterfront road is officially named Atatürk Caddesi, though most locals refer to it as Kordon Caddesi. A landmark here is the equestrian statue of Atatürk on Kordon Caddesi. Plaques on the plinth bear the sayings 'Türk Ögün Çalış Güven' (Turk! Be Proud, Work, Trust) and 'Ne Mutlu Türküm Diyene' (What joy to him who says, 'I am a Turk'). Both sayings were meant to dispel the Ottoman inferiority complex. Another plaque bears the words 'Egemenlik Ulusundur' (Sovereignty belongs to the Nation), Atatürk's statement signifying that the Turkish people, and not the imperial House of Osman, were in charge of the country's destiny. The final plaque in this statuary history lesson reads 'İzindeyiz' (We Follow in Your Footsteps); the 'footsteps' are Atatürk's, of course.

Information

Tourist Office The Tourism Information Office (tel (612) 11035) is at İskele Meydanı 39 by the yacht harbour, the wharf for boats to Greece and the market – in short, right at the centre. Though it nominally closes at 6.30 pm, it often stays open later during the summer months. Some of the staff members here are not very helpful.

Post The PTT is open until about 8 pm and will change foreign cash (but not travellers' cheques).

Banks The Türkiye Halk Bankası exchange booth at the wharf, next to the tourism office, is usually open on summer evenings and weekends when other banking facilities are closed.

Beaches

There are beaches along the Kordon in Marmaris, and even better, cleaner ones outside of town, although they are all small. The better beaches are near the fancy hotels, and still others can be reached by boat from near the tourism office.

Menzilhane

Take a look at the *menzilhane*, behind and to the left of the tourism office. It's an Ottoman 'pony express' way-station which now serves as a shopping centre for souvenirs. The nice old historic stone building has been somewhat ruined by the commercialism. Look for the Ottoman Turkish inscription in Arabic letters, on a plaque on the doorway, which records that the menzilhane was built by Sultan Süleyman the Magnificent in 1545.

İçmeler

Catch a dolmuş just inland from the Atatürk statue to İçmeler, a beautiful little seaside holiday spot eight km west and south around the bay from Marmaris. You may decide you like İçmeler better than Marmaris, and can then move to one of the hotels or camp grounds there.

Fortress

Marmaris has a little ruined fortress on the hill just above the yacht harbour. It has recently been under restoration; perhaps it will be open by the time you arrive. To reach it walk up the narrow street to the left of the menzilhane opposite the Hotel İmbat, then go around the back of the menzilhane and through a village-scape very reminiscent of the Greek islands.

Boat Excursions

Besides the daily boats to Rhodes there are numerous boats ranged along the waterfront offering day tours of the harbour, its beaches and islands. Departures are usually at 9 am. About half an hour before then, walk along Kordon Caddesi, check out the boats and talk to the captains about the *gezi* (excursion): where it goes, what it costs,

whether lunch is included and, if so, what's on the menu. An average price for a day's pleasure outing is about US$5 to US$8, more if lunch is included.

There are longer, more serious excursions by boat, including trips to Datça and Knidos, well out along the hilly peninsula west of Marmaris. Ask at a travel agency or haggle with a boatman for a day's excursion to the secluded coves, beaches and ruins scattered along the peninsula. For full information on the peninsula see the Datça and Knidos sections.

Yacht Charters

You can charter a comfortable yacht in Turkey and, out of season, the cost can be as low as US$35 to US$60 per person daily. The larger the yacht (up to 12 berths) and the earlier (in spring) or later (in autumn) the cruise, the cheaper it is. For instance, an 11-berth yacht rented for a week in late April can cost a mere US$35 per person per day. The same yacht rented in July or August would cost several times as much. You can have the crew make the meals (at an extra charge) or you can plan to buy supplies and cook them on board yourself, planning also to eat in little village restaurants much of the time. It is much cheaper to do your own meals, especially if you have booked your charter through a yacht charter-broker abroad. The broker will mark up the price of meals to well above the actual cost.

Smaller boats tend to be more expensive per person but even if you hire a larger yacht and cruise with some of the berths empty the charges are still quite reasonable. A yacht designed to sleep eight people (10 in a pinch) will be all the more comfortable for five or six people. In May or October, with crew and meals included, the charge for such a boat will still be only US$55 to US$70 daily per person, compared to US$45 if there were eight people. Considering that this includes lodging, meals, transport and a luxurious, unforgettable experience, the cost is quite moderate.

Top: A driveway to a former mansion in İzmir
Bottom: An antique and carpet shop in Side, Antalya

Top: Ancient columns litter a swimming pool, Pamukkale
Left: Rock tombs at Demre
Right: Distinctive Ottoman gravestone

Occasionally, charter yachts sell berths individually, allowing you to enjoy a cruise even if you can't find half a dozen people to share the cost. Prices depend upon the season, the yacht, the number of people signed up and the length of the cruise. For current information ask at any travel agency in town.

As for yachting itineraries, virtually everything described in this book from Bodrum to Antalya is open to you, as well as many secluded coves and islands. Any trip in this area becomes what is called a Blue Cruise, which means a cruise along the ancient Carian and Lycian coasts.

Places to Stay

Marmaris has more than 200 lodging places. The cheapest are very convenient, right in the centre. There are a few moderately priced hotels a short walk from town. Most of the expensive hotels are well around the bay from the town, some as far as the beach suburb of İçmeler, eight km from the Marmaris main square. Transport around the bay is easy though: in summer the municipality operates an open-air 'trailer-train' between the distant hotels and the centre, and dolmuşes run frequently to İçmeler. There is sometimes also a launch running across the bay.

Places to Stay – bottom end

The very cheapest lodgings are called ev pansiyon (home pensions), where you rent a room in a private home. The Tourism Information Office can help you locate one of these, or you can find your own by merely proceeding inland from the waterfront for 50 or 100 metres anywhere in town. This simple, homey accommodation is where thrifty Turkish families and couples stay, paying only US$8 to US$12 for a double room without running water. Some rooms have three and four beds.

To find one 'hidden' area of pensions, walk from the Tourism Information Office to the right, along the water past the yachts. Eventually you'll see a wooden footbridge heading off to the right. Don't cross the footbridge, but follow the street opposite, at the end of the footbridge, which heads back into town. Along this street are several cheap, quiet pensions which tend to fill up last, including the Ufuk, Dilek and Işıksal. You're really only a short walk from the centre, but I guided you around the waterfront because it's virtually impossible to guide you through the maze of tiny streets in the town.

Another good area in which to search for pensions is out along the shore road behind Abdi İpekçi Park. Walk along the shore road until you see the little park on the right-hand side; the Çubuk Hotel is here as well. Walk through the park and explore the little back streets. You should easily find the Aksoy, the Akın, the Olca and others.

Next cheapest are the small, plain hotels by the main square at İskele Meydanı (Wharf Square), such as the Sema (seh-MAH) (tel 11595), İmbat (EEM-baht) and the Karaaslan (kah-RAH-ahss-lahn) (tel 11867). These face the menzilhane. The Kalyon (kahl-YOHN) (tel 11085) faces the main square next to the Tourism Information Office. All these hotels are ranked as 2nd class by the Municipality and charge US$8 to US$10 for a double room without private bath, or US$13 to US$16 for a double with shower.

Despite its expensive reputation, the area called Uzunyalı, near the Hotel Lidya, has some inexpensive pensions. The Motel Küçükevler (kew-CHEWK-ehv-lehr) (tel 11856) offers pleasant little whitewashed, tile-roofed bungalows surrounded by flowers and equipped with toilet and shower, for US$22 a double, breakfast included.

Camping Camping areas are scattered all along the shore, mixed in with the hotels, but as the local building boom progresses, last year's camp ground becomes this year's construction site – see what's available when you arrive. If you don't mind being eight km from town, and you'd like to be near the beach, find a camp ground at İçmeler, around the bay.

Places to Stay – middle

The Municipality's 1st-class hotels offer significant improvements over the 2nd-class ones. These are the cheapest and simplest of middle-range hotels. At the very centre of all the action is the *Hotel Kaptan* (kahp-TAHN) (tel 11251) facing the wharf for boats to Rhodes. A double with shower and breakfast costs US$34. Right next door to the Tourism Information Office, facing İskele Meydanı, is the *Hotel Anatolia* (tel 12665, 12851), with small but decent rooms and tiled showers for the same price.

Just a short walk out along the shore road from the main square is the *Hotel Acar* (ah-JAHR) (tel 11117), on Kordon Caddesi behind the equestrian statue of Atatürk. This place charges US$26 for doubles at the back, US$32 for doubles with little balconies at the front, all with private showers (hot water) and breakfast included. Rates are lower off season.

The *Hotel Begonya* (tel 14095), Kısayalı Hacı Mustafa Sokak 71, is a different and delightful place. Here an old village house on a quiet back street has been renovated, its rooms equipped with tiled showers and decorated simply. Outside the house is a delightful private garden terrace with fountain and lots of greenery. Prices are US$32 a double; breakfast (taken at tables on the terrace) costs an extra US$2.50 per person. Unfortunately, the Begonya is open only from April to October, and it's often full in high summer, but check anyway. From the mosque and fountain in the market (see map) head north along the narrow street for 200 metres; the hotel is on the left.

Among the newer hotels out along Atatürk Caddesi is the *Otel Karaca* (KAH-rah-jah) (tel 11663, 11992) at No 48. Many rooms have sea views and all have bathrooms served by solar water-heaters. With breakfast, singles cost

US$38, doubles US$45 and triples are US$55 to US$60. A similarly new and modern place is the two-star, 46-room *Karadeniz Hotel* (kah-RAH-deh-neez) (tel 11064, 12837), popular with German and Finnish tour groups, which charges US$45 a double with shower and breakfast. It's got a sidewalk restaurant as well.

The *Otel Yavuz* (tel 12937), Atatürk Caddesi 10, in this same area despite its lower street number, has three-star comforts, 54 rooms and a small swimming pool atop the building. Chances are good that your room (with bath) will have a balcony with a view of the bay. The price for such a double, breakfast included, is US$50. For reservations in İstanbul contact the hotel's office at Halaskargazi Caddesi 94/4, Gül Han, Şişli (tel (1) 147-4460, 131-6137).

An older mid-range favourite is the one-star, 63-room *Otel Marmaris* (tel 11308), Atatürk Caddesi 32, on the waterfront street. It's 15 minutes' walk from İskele Meydanı. Double rooms with bath cost US$50, a bit less if you take a room facing the rear. The front-facing rooms have that lovely sea view, but they also get a tremendous amount of street noise. Next door is the two-star, 44-room *Otel Atlantik* (aht-lahn-TEEK) (tel 11218, 11236), Atatürk Caddesi 34, catering mostly to Turkish families. Singles with shower go for US$34, doubles with shower are priced at US$44, breakfast included.

A block inland from these hotels near Abdi İpekçi Park is the *Çubuk Otel* (tel 16774/5/6/7), Atatürk Caddesi. To find it follow signs to the 'Pension Honeymoon'. A newer hotel done in the standard Turkish-Mediterranean idiom of white stucco and varnished pine trim, the hotel's six floors of rooms are tidy, simple and less noisy than the more expensive hotels right on the Kordon. Prices for singles/doubles are US$32/42, breakfast and shower included.

On Atatürk Caddesi is the shiny three-star *Otel 47* (kirk-yeh-DEE) (tel 11700,

12730), Atatürk Caddesi 10, a polished and comfortable place with streetside restaurant, shops and comfortable rooms with balconies overlooking the bay for US$40/50 for singles/doubles including breakfast.

Other hotels are out along the western shores of the bay. The grande dame here is the three-star *Hotel Lidya* (LEED-yah) (tel 12940/1/2), a comfortable if not posh place of 220 rooms surrounded by lovely gardens. It's around the bay from the town in the section called Uzunyalı. Lodgings include suites, motel-style rooms, apartments, and rooms looking onto the sea or the gardens. Prices range from US$50 to US$75 for double rooms (twice as much for an apartment) from mid-June to mid-September. Off-season reductions are about 35%.

Places to Stay - top end

The poshest place to stay so far is the *Marmaris Altın Yunus Hotel* (tel 13617, 11102), Pamucak Mevkii, almost five km around the bay to the west and south from İskele Meydanı. This five-star, 350-room place has many resort services, including several restaurants and bars from the formal to the very casual, a pastry-shop/ café, its own beach and swimming pools, extensive hillside gardens, a fitness centre, sauna, Turkish bath and a nightclub. The long, narrow rooms are comfortable enough, with mini-bar, twin beds and balconies, but the building's long rectangular design is oddly uncomfortable: to get to your room, you must walk what seems like a full km down a dark hallway, and rooms are not positioned so as to take full advantage of the marvellous views. Still, it's the most comfortable place in Marmaris. Prices reflect the facilities: US$90/135/180 for a single/double/triple, breakfast and dinner included.

Places to Eat - bottom end

As always, for less expensive fare head into the market area and look for a pideci.

One of the best streets for pidecis is the narrow one leading into the market from the Atatürk statue; look for the *İstanbul Pideci*. Besides these Turkish pizza places there are small and cheap restaurants. The *Ayyıldız Lokantası* (AHY-yuhl-duhz) (tel 12158) has tables set outside beneath the market awnings. A meal of döner kebap, bulgur pilav, salad and drink costs US$3 to US$4. The *Şadırvan* (SHAH-duhr-vahn) on İsmet Paşa Sokak is even cheaper and very popular. The *Tat Restaurant* (tel 15903), on Mustafa Kemal Paşa Sokak in the market, is a bright, clean cafeteria with ready food. A full meal costs US$3 to US$5. In fact, Kemal Paşa Sokak has lots of other cheap restaurants, on both sides of Fevzi Paşa Sokak.

The back streets of the market area have many kebapçıs, small cookshops with larger outdoor sidewalk seating areas shaded by awnings. Some of these places translate kebapçı as 'meat house', a particularly unappealing term. One such place is the *Özyalçın Meat House* (tel 12934), where a portion of döner kebap with yoghurt, bread and a glass of ayran costs US$5. The food is good though the waiters seem to look after passing girls better than the restaurant customers.

If you must eat out on the waterfront look for a pideci or restaurant which is full of Turks, as it will have the lower prices. The cheapest places tend to be those between the Tourism Information Office and the Acar Pide restaurant.

Even cheaper? Walk through Abdi İpekçi Park, turn right, then left onto Fikri Öztan Sokak. The street soon turns to the left and you'll see a string of cheap eateries patronised exclusively by Turks and by readers of this book. There's *Aslan'in Yeri* and *Metin Usta'nin Yeri* where you can dine on kebaps, salads and mezes, and the *Mutlu Şarküteri* where you can buy picnic supplies. The local fruit and vegetable market is just a few steps farther along the street. Another way to reach this area is by walking inland from the Çubuk Hotel; you'll see the fruit and vegetable market. Turn right to find the restaurants.

Places to Eat – middle

Downtown restaurants near the yacht harbour have pleasant outdoor dining areas and moderate prices. The *Birtat* (BEER-taht, 'one taste') (tel 11076) is well established, with a good reputation, and the food was good when I last had dinner there. The best strategy, however, is to stroll along the waterfront and look for a restaurant which is busy and popular. You can expect to spend about US$12 per person for a full fish dinner with wine.

Things to Buy

Marmaris is a honey-producing region. Those who know honey will want to sample several of the local varieties, most famous of which is *çam balı* (CHAHM bah-luh, also called *wald*, from the German). It's a pine-scented honey from young forest growth; rich, dark and full-flavoured. There's also *siyah çam balı*, black-pine honey, with a deep, rich flavour and a colour almost as dark as molasses. Others are *portakkal*, orange-blossom, very light-coloured, thin in texture, with a light, sweet flavour; *akasya balı*, locust-tree blossom; slightly darker and more flavourful *çiçek* (flower honey); and *oğul balı*, virgin honey (the first honey from a new swarm). You can buy the honey in jars priced from US$2 to US$4, or in larger tins for US$5 to US$10. One shop which has many varieties is Balcı Gözpınar (tel 11533), a block inland from the PTT and the Belediye building on Fevzi Paşa Sokak, on the left-hand (north-west) side. The owner can explain the different types of honey to you in English because he spent some time in the USA during his military training.

Speaking of shopping, Marmaris has lots of possibilities. Because the boats from Rhodes bring lots of shoppers on day-trips, Marmaris merchants stock everything: onyx, leather clothing and accessories, carpets, jewellery, crafts, Turkish delight, meerschaum pipes and baubles, sandals, apple tea powder, copper and beach-wear.

Getting There & Away

Marmaris is somewhat remote but that's part of its charm. In any case, transport by bus is not inconvenient and there is even a regional airport.

Air The airport at Dalaman is 120 km from Marmaris. Turkish Airlines has daily flights between Dalaman and İstanbul in summer. From the village bus station in Dalaman buses run fairly frequently to other places along the coast, from Marmaris and Bodrum to Fethiye and Kaş. Hitch or take a taxi from the airport to the bus station, a distance of less than six km.

Bus As yet Marmaris has no otogar. Bus company ticket offices are concentrated on the waterfront street near the equestrian statue of Atatürk; look for the names Pamukkale, Kamil Koç, Kontaş and Köseoğlu. The Varan office is farther west along the Kordon, near the Yavuz and Karadeniz hotels.

In the summer months bus traffic is furiously active, with dozens of the huge growling machines rolling in and out of town all day long, but in winter service drops off to that required by a small farming town. Some destinations include:

Adana – 1025 km, 20 hours, US$16; change buses at Antalya
Ankara – 780 km, 13 hours, US$12; a dozen buses daily in summer
Antalya – 590 km, nine hours, US$8; a few buses daily
Bodrum – 165 km, three hours, US$3; hourly buses in summer
Dalaman – 120 km, 2½ to three hours, US$2.50 to US$3; hourly buses in summer

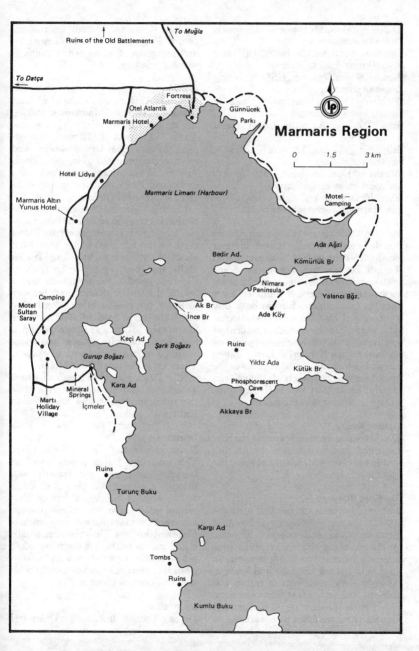

Datça - 75 km, 1¾ hours, US$2; hourly buses in summer
İstanbul - 900 km, 16 hours, US$14; a dozen buses daily in summer
İzmir - 300 km, 5½ hours, US$4.50; hourly buses in summer
Fethiye - 170 km, three hours, US$2.50; hourly buses in summer
Kaş - 305 km, five hours, US$4; several buses daily
Köyceğiz - 75 km, 1½ hours, US$1.25; several buses daily
Muğla - 60 km, one hour, US$0.75; very frequent buses and dolmuşes
Pamukkale - 325 km, eight hours, US$6; via Marmaris, several buses daily

Boats to Rhodes Boats to and from Rhodes run daily except Sunday in high summer on the 2½-hour voyage, with Greek and Turkish boats sharing the service. Some of these ferries are capable of carrying cars as well as passengers. If traffic is heavy they may also put on a Sunday boat. Buy your ticket (US$25 one-way, US$30 same-day return, US$40 open-date return) at any travel agency in Marmaris (you'll see them along the Kordon) at least a day in advance if you can. At other times of the year there may be fewer boats but you can depend on at least two boats per week except in times of stormy weather.

Getting Around
Dolmuşes run frequently around the bay, beginning just inland from the Atatürk statue near İskele Meydanı and going the eight km to İçmeler.

The Road Eastward
Leaving Marmaris and heading north the road climbs into mountains with beautiful panoramas and fertile valleys in between. At the end of the long rows of eucalyptus trees is a highway junction where you can turn right toward Köyceğiz and Fethiye. Along the way are fields of cotton and tobacco, and orchards of fruits and nuts, as well as cool pine forests. At Kadırga and Günlük there are forest picnic areas.

Near Köyceğiz, a local agricultural centre, is the town of Dalyan, with an archaeological site named Caunus - worth a side-trip.

DATÇA
A narrow, mountainous finger of land points westward from Marmaris, stretching 100 km to touch the edge of the Aegean. About 75 km west of Marmaris through pine forests lies the pleasant and relatively untouristed village of Datça. Another 35 km brings you to the hamlet and ruins of Knidos, the ancient city of the great sculptor Praxiteles.

Leaving Marmaris for the trip along the peninsula takes you up into the mountains. Not too long after leaving town you'll see a road on the left marked for Bozburun, about 40 very bumpy km along. It's an idyllic spot, best reached by boat, where there's a small hotel, restaurant and a 'yacht club' with showers and laundry facilities for the yachters. Continuing along the main road to Datça, at the 22-km mark is Çubucak Dinlenme Yeri, a rest area, camping place and park operated by the Directorate of Forests. There's also the small Fırat Motel.

After 70 km you reach Reşadiye, where a road goes off to the left for Datça while the main road continues westward to Knidos.

Orientation
Datça is essentially a one-street town. The road into Datça passes near the hospital, past the gendarmerie and through a commercial district of shops selling scented honey and spices. Past several small teahouses and restaurants, you reach the main plaza with its market-place and bus area. The street then climbs a hill, curves to the left down the other side, scoots across an isthmus and ends on a hill at the end of a short peninsula. This whole distance is about one km.

Information
Datça's Tourism Information Office (tel

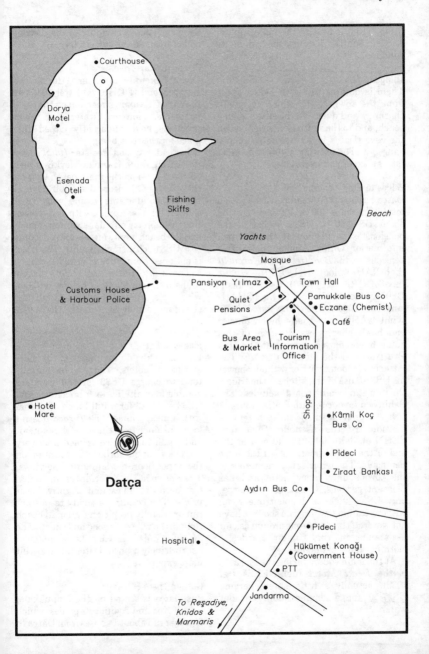

(6145) 1163) is next to the main square. Accommodation lists are posted in its windows.

Things to See

There is nothing to see in Datça apart from the town itself, which is small, charming and quiet. To the east is a long beach, and to the south is another one on the cove. Datça is a place to relax and hang out. For exciting sights you must take an excursion to Knidos.

Places to Stay – bottom end

Datça has about 50 small pensions with a total of perhaps 400 or 500 beds costing about US$2.50 to US$4. A list of the pensions is on display at the Tourism Information Office. Among the quieter pensions are the *Bora* (tel 1327), *Karaoğlu* (kah-RAH-oh-loo) (tel 1079), *Huzur* (hoo-ZOOR) (tel 1052), *Sadık* (sah-DUHK) (tel 1196) and *Çağla* (CHAH-lah) (tel 1084). The *Pansiyon Yılmaz* (yuhl-MAHZ) is actually much fancier and has higher prices. Readers of this guide have enjoyed staying at the *Oya Pansiyon* and the *Pansiyon Şahin*. The latter offers rooms with or without shower for US$10, use of the kitchen, the fridge, the iron and ironing board included. The Şahin is a favourite with British tours.

If you prefer a small, cheap hotel to a pension try the *Esenada Oteli* (eh-SEHN-ah-dah) (tel 1014), almost at the end of the main street, out on the little peninsula. Though it's right next door to the town's only fancy hotel and has pleasant gardens, the Esenada charges only US$8/12 for a double/triple room without running water. The showers have hot water. If there's no-one around ask for assistance in the Çimen Kardeşler clothing shop next door.

At the main square facing the bus area is the *Deniz Motel* (deh-NEEZ) (tel 1038), actually a little hotel charging US$7.50 for a double room without water.

Camping There's camping in the district called Ilıca, on the eastern bay.

Places to Stay – middle

Datça's premier place used to be the *Dorya Motel* (DOHR-yah) (tel 1036) at the end of the main street, out on the little peninsula. However, water and sewer problems have apparently closed this place for the time being.

Instead, try the three-star *Hotel Mare* (tel 1211), Yanık Harman Mevkii, a new 50-room hotel on the main beach (not on the peninsula) near the Club Datça. Besides comfortable rooms with tiled showers and balconies with sea views, there is a pretty circular swimming pool, and the beach is only metres away. Rooms cost US$45/60 a single/double. The hotel is not open from November to March.

The *Club Datça* (tel 1170), İskele Mahallesi, is a 95-room holiday village, with lots of water-sports facilities, charging somewhat more than the Mare.

Places to Eat

Except for the dining rooms at the more expensive hotels, Datça's restaurants tend to charge US$2 for the standard komple kahvaltı Turkish breakfast, and US$3 to US$6 for a full lunch or dinner with a meat course. The *Taraça* doesn't look like much from the street, but enter it and you'll find a nice terrace with very good views of the harbour. The *Liman*, on the upper floor, has similarly fine views. The *Köşem* has bits of sculpture in front, a few outdoor tables and slightly lower prices. The *Dutdibi*, a shady restaurant run by friendly people on the small beach right in the village, is good and cheap. The *Marina Café* by the yacht harbour is good – surprisingly posh for Datça but also a bit more expensive.

Getting There & Away

Bus Datça is served by the Pamukkale, Kâmil Koç and Aydın companies, which together run about 14 buses from Datça to

Marmaris (75 km, 1¾ hours, US$2), eight buses to Muğla (3½ hours, US$3), seven buses to İzmir (eight hours, US$7) and one or two direct buses daily to İstanbul and Ankara. Virtually all of this traffic stops in Marmaris.

Boat There are often boat excursions to Datça from Marmaris and sometimes you can buy a one-way ticket.

There are scheduled ferry services between Bodrum and Datça during the summer months, organised by Karya Tour Yachting & Travel Agency (tel (6141) 1759, 1914), Karantina Caddesi 13, Bodrum. Daily departures are at 8.30 am from Bodrum, 5 pm from Datça, with these exceptions: on Friday there is a second boat which leaves Bodrum at 5.30 pm; on Saturday the boat departs Bodrum at 6 pm and Datça at 8 am; on Sunday boats depart Datça at 7.30 am and 5 pm. The one-way fare is US$12, return is US$15.

KNİDOS

At Knidos, 35 km west of Datça at the very tip of the peninsula, are ruins of a prosperous port town dating from about 400 BC. The Dorians who founded it were smart: the winds change as one rounds the peninsula and ships in ancient times often had to wait at Knidos for good winds. This happened to the ship carrying St Paul to Rome for trial.

Being rich, Knidos commissioned the great Praxiteles to make a large statue of Aphrodite. It was housed in a circular temple in view of the sea. The statue, said to be the sculptor's masterpiece, has been lost.

Other than the ruins, Knidos consists of a tiny jandarma post with a telephone for emergencies, four little makeshift restaurants (the *Bora* and the *Knidos* were most popular on my last visit), a repository for artefacts found on the site (no entry), and the *Bora Pansiyon*, which will put you up for US$4 per person in a room without running water if space is

available; or you can camp nearby and use the Bora's facilities for a small fee. You can swim in the bays from wooden piers, but the beaches are several km out of town. The nearest PTT is in Çeşme Köyü, the last village you pass through on the road to Knidos.

The Ruins

The ruins are scattered along the three km at the end of the peninsula. The setting is also dramatic - steep hillsides terraced and planted with groves of olive, almond and fruit trees - and the peninsula here is occupied by goatherds and the occasional wild boar. All this surrounds two picture-perfect bays in which a handful of yachts rest at anchor. Few of the buildings are in recognisable shape, but you can appreciate easily the importance of the town by exploring the site. The guardian will show you around for a small tip.

Getting There & Away

The trip to Knidos must be made by private car, taxi (about US$30 for a day-trip from Datça) or boat. There is not really any dependable minibus service. A ferry departs Datça each morning in summer at 9 am for a day-trip to Knidos, returning at 5 pm and charging US$8 per person.

KÖYCEĞİZ

Less than 50 km east of the turn-off from the Muğla to Marmaris road lies Köyceğiz (population 7000), a small lakeside town only now being discovered by foreign tourists. Turks in on the secret of Köyceğiz's beauty have been coming here quietly for years.

Köyceğiz sits at the northern end of the large Köyceğiz Gölü (lake), which connects to the Mediterranean via the Dalyan Çayı stream. The attraction here is the lake - broad, beautiful and serene.

Except for its small (but growing) tourist trade, Köyceğiz is a farming and fishing town. Among the goods produced here are citrus fruits, olives, honey and cotton. This region is also famous for its liquidambar trees, the sort which produced that precious petrified gum ages ago. The government is now sponsoring large-scale reafforestation projects in this region using liquidambar evergreens.

Orientation

The village centre, at the lake's edge, is two km south of the highway. The local hospital is near the highway turn-off. Proceed along the tree-lined boulevard until you reach a small mosque right by the waterfront park. Just west of the mosque is the Belediye, or town hall.

Information

The town's Tourism Information Office (tel (6114) 1703) is opposite the mosque, at the eastern edge of the square. They have a simple map and several historical hand-outs.

Walks

Walk along the lakeshore on the promenade, officially called the Atatürk Kordonu, past the pleasant town park, a children's playground, tea gardens and several lakeside restaurants. If there's not a lot of activity on the lake, you can see the fish jump. Enjoy the quiet pace of the town.

Boat excursions

When you get restless take a boat excursion on the lake; boats can be hired along the promenade. Take a boat to the **Sultaniye Kaplıcaları** or thermal springs, 30 km by road or eight nautical miles across the lake on the southern shore. The hot mineral waters are rich in calcium, sulphur, iron, nitrates, potassium and other mineral salts; temperatures sometimes reach 40°C. Other than the hot springs, you can take boat trips to Dalyan and its ruins, and to points along the Mediterranean coast. For details see the Dalyan section which follows.

Places to Stay – bottom end

As you come into town there are many signs advertising pensions along the main

boulevard. There are also lots around the main square and the mosque. Rooms in small house pensions cost about as much as in Datça or Marmaris. The *Star Pension*, run by a man named Rami, offers excellent value, with double rooms for US$6 and use of the kitchen to boot. Other places offer more, at somewhat higher prices. The *Malibu Pension* (tel (6114) 1280) behind the Hotel Kaunos is similar.

Most prominent of the pensions is the *Pension & Café Deniz Feneri* (tel 1777), an old-fashioned building recently fixed up with white stucco, Ottoman-style lattice screens on the windows and decorations of handicrafts and carved wood. The ground-floor café has been fixed up as a frontier saloon of sorts; Turkish and Greek flags fly happily together behind the bar. Wooden tables outside allow you to enjoy the fresh air. The high-ceilinged rooms are similarly decorated with handicrafts and, though simple, are fairly authentic period pieces, but with the useful addition of insect screens. Bath and shower are down the hall, and are primitive but serviceable. The owner, Hüseyin Hava, is a retired teacher who just loves his guest house. Rates are US$16 for a double off season, US$20 in season, breakfast included.

Behind the Hotel Kaunos is the *Pansiyon Beyaz Konak* (tel 1893), which was in the process of changing ownership when I visited, so all may change. Right now it's a simple, modern building with double rooms renting for US$15 with shower. It's popular with German visitors.

The owners of the *Hotel-Pension Villa* (tel 1117, 1802), and the *Turist Pension* (tel 1894) have written to me saying that they have 100 rooms, all with shower, priced from US$10 to US$15 a double. They're next to the Hotel Kaunos's parking lot.

Camping One km to the west of the mosque is a forest camp ground among liquidambar trees, with a small beach nearby.

Places to Stay - middle

Walk past the mosque and the Belediye to the two-star, 20-room *Hotel Özay* (tel 1300, 1361), Kordon Boyu 11, a nice little modern place with a small pool in front surrounded by shady vine-covered arbours. Rooms have private showers, tiny balconies with partial lake views, and prices of US$35 for a double in season, breakfast included.

Farther along in the same direction (west) is the *Hotel Kaunos* (tel 1288, 1835, 3637), Cengiz Topel Caddesi 37, also rated at two stars. The 40 rooms have private showers and balconies overlooking the placid lake. In front of the hotel is a pretty terrace for relaxing and enjoying the view. There's a restaurant and bar as well. Rates are US$38 for a double, breakfast included.

Places to Eat

As always, the market has the cheapest eats. For special occasions, the *Gölbaşı*, next to the Tourism Office, is good for fish. The *Şamdan*, near the Hotel-Pension Villa, is as good but doesn't have the lakeshore location.

Getting There & Away

Buses run from Marmaris to Köyceğiz several times daily. Unless you don't mind walking that last two km into town, make sure they drop you at the centre of town. Dolmuşes also run frequently to Dalyan.

DALYAN/CAUNUS

About 70 km east of Marmaris, at a place called Yuvarlak Çay, signs point south (right) to 'The Graves of Likya' and 'The Ruins of Caunus', nine km down a side road. Coming by bus, get out at Ortaca and catch a dolmuş to Dalyan. The road brings you to the settlement - a small farming and fishing town with a sideline in tourism - through lush cotton and vegetable fields, along the winding course of a stream, the Dalyan Çayı.

Boat Excursions

On the town's tidy quay you can choose an excursion boat for a cruise to the ruins of Caunus, the pretty cove at Ekincik, the beach at İztuzu on the Mediterranean coast or up the Dalyan Çayı stream to Köyceğiz Lake. A two-hour tour just to the Caunus ruins costs US$12 to US$18 for the entire boat; if you want to visit the Sultaniye hot springs as well, figure on three hours and US$25 for the boat. If you would also like to go to İztuzu beach for a swim, it'll take four to five hours and cost US$36 for the boat. Do some haggling to get the best price, particularly if there are many boats without work. The river excursion boats can carry about 12 people.

Boats belonging to the Dalyan Kooperatifi operate a 'river dolmuş' service between the town and İztuzu beach, charging US$1 for the round trip. In high summer there may be five or more boats per day, heading out from 9 to 11 am, returning between 4 and 6 pm. Take some food as you might not like the few little kebap stands on the beach, which has a few other facilities. The beach, by the way, is renowned as a

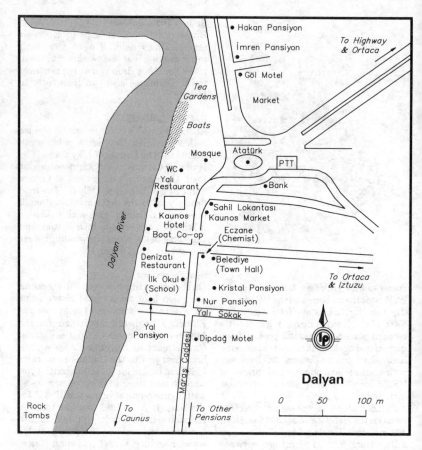

Dalyan

nesting-place for sea turtles – an endangered species.

Caunus

This was an important Carian city by 400 BC. Right on the border with the kingdom of Lycia, its culture shared aspects of both kingdoms. The **tombs**, for instance, are in Lycian style (you'll see many more of them at Fethiye, Kaş and other points east). If you don't hire a boat for a cruise on the river, walk south from town along Maraş Caddesi and you can get a fairly good view of the tombs.

Though of good size, Caunus suffered from endemic malaria.

Besides the tombs, the **theatre** is very well preserved; parts of an **acropolis** and other structures (baths, a basilica, defensive walls) are nearby. Those curious wooden structures in the river are **fishing weirs** (*dalyan*). No doubt the ancient Caunians benefited from such an industry as well. Caunus was once a Mediterranean port city but over the centuries the silt from the Dalyan Çayı choked the harbour, and today the city lies several km from the sea.

Places to Stay

Dalyan's accommodation is very simple, though a new and fancier hotel is being built on the outskirts of town. Besides numerous homey pensions, the town has several hotels.

There are several pensions right near the centre of town, including the *Hakan, Kyane* and *Ekrem*. The *Miletos* is one of the nicer pensions. To find the cheapest pensions head south along Maraş Caddesi. The road continues for just over one km before ending at the river bank and the *Gel Gör Pension* ('Come See Pension'), right on the river bank. The Gel Gör has a little restaurant as well, offering good food at good prices in very pleasant surroundings. It's worth the walk. Along the way are many small home pensions such as the *Çiğdem, Sahil, Gözde, Aktaş, Ada* and *Huzur*, all marked by signs. Beds cost US$2.50 to US$4.

The *Kaunos Otel & Restaurant* (tel (6116) 1057), between the mosque and the river bank, is the town's poshest place at present. With tea gardens and a terrace restaurant it's pleasant if simple. Double rooms with shower go for US$18, breakfast included.

The *Dipdag Motel* (tel 1070) is 250 metres south of the mosque, several blocks along pension-lined Maraş Caddesi. It is presently the town's most comfortable lodging-place, charging US$14 for a double room with shower and breakfast. It's a newer building; rooms have balconies, lace curtains and wood trim to add colour to the featureless stucco. Some of the upper-storey rooms have views of the river. Breakfast is taken in a sunny courtyard on the landward side.

The *Göl Motel* (say 'girl') (tel 1062, 1096), across from the quay and next to the market, is right in the centre of town and charges US$12 for a double with shower. It has triples as well. Your room may even have a view of the river. If not, the hotel has a rooftop terrace with a good view. One reader had a tussle over the price here.

You can also stay in the nearby town of Ortaca, by the highway, at the *Altınkum Hotel* (tel 1369), a modern place just north of the main traffic roundabout in that town. They charge US$20 for a double with shower, breakfast included.

Places to Eat

The *Sahil Lokantası* (sah-HEEL, shore) is not on the shore but near the mosque, beneath a shady tree. It is very plain and simple and the hard-working cook serves up good food at rock-bottom prices. I had salçalı köfte (ground lamb meatballs in a rich sauce), pilav, bread, mineral soda and the yoghurt drink ayran for a total of US$2.25.

A big step up in class is the *Denizatı Restaurant* (deh-NEEZ-ah-tuh, seahorse) on the riverbank, which prides itself on serving the best fish in town at prices that are low when measured against those of Marmaris.

Try also the *Gel Gör Restaurant* at the pension of the same name.

DALAMAN

This agricultural town (population 15,000) was quite sleepy until the regional airport was built on the neighbouring river delta. Now the town stirs whenever a jet arrives, but otherwise slumbers as in the past. Most visitors pass right through, as they should.

Orientation

It is 5½ km from the airport to the town, and another five km from the town to the east-west highway. The road connecting the highway with the airport is called Kenan Evren Bulvarı. The town itself has one main street named (surprise!) Atatürk Caddesi, about 500 metres long, running east from Evren Bulvarı, with banks, shops and simple restaurants. The bus station, served by the Pamukkale, Aydın and Köseoğlu companies, is near the junction of Evren Bulvarı and Atatürk Caddesi. The PTT is a block north of Atatürk Caddesi.

Places to Stay

As its air traffic grows Dalaman grows along with it. There are now several decent hotels, including the *Belediye Hotel*, under construction on the west side of Evren Bulvarı near the traffic roundabout with Atatürk Caddesi.

The more modest *Deniz Apart-Motel* (tel (6119) 1073), Kenan Evren Bulvarı, is not far away, just a few hundred metres south toward the airport. Tidy rooms with private shower cost US$28 a double, breakfast included.

Dalaman also has several little pensions. Look for the *Dalaman Pansiyon* (tel 1543, 1550), 200 metres south of the traffic roundabout near the bus station, out toward the airport. They charge about US$3.50.

Getting There & Away

Unless you can hitch a ride into town from the airport, take a taxi to the bus station (US$2). Most of what you need in town is within walking distance of the bus station. Every hour or two buses stop here to pick up passengers going east and west along the coast.

THE ROAD EAST

The highway east of Dalaman winds through mountains cloaked in fragrant evergreen forests, with many liquidambar trees, before reaching Fethiye 50 km to the south-east. About 20 km east of Dalaman a road on the right (south) is marked for **Göçek**, a delightful little hamlet on a bay at the foot of the mountains. Yachts stop in the harbour and fishing boats ply their trade. Near the village is a wharf from which chromium ore is shipped by the Etibank company. Several cheap little pensions (US$8 a double) and the *Zakkum Motel* can put you up, and small waterfront restaurants provide sustenance.

At a place called Küçük Kargı, 33 km east of Dalaman, is a forest picnic area with a camping place and beach. Two km farther east is Katrancı, another picnic and camping spot with a small restaurant, on a beautiful little cove with a beach. If you can plan it, stop here. It's a further 15 km to Fethiye.

FETHİYE

Fethiye (FEH-tee-yeh, population 25,000) is a very, very old town with few old buildings. An earthquake in 1958 levelled the town, leaving very little standing. Most of what was left were tombs from the time when Fethiye was called Telmessos (400 BC), but that's good since one of the things Fethiye is famous for is its tombs.

The bay of Fethiye is an excellent harbour, well protected from storms. Beaches are good here, and even better at Ölüdeniz, one of Turkey's seaside hot spots. You may want to stop in Fethiye, spend an afternoon or two at Ölüdeniz, climb up to the rock tombs and then head east.

Orientation

The centre of town is about 3½ km from the highway; the bus station is just over one km west of the highway, and one km east of the centre. Mid-range and top-end hotels are near the centre, but most inexpensive pensions are either east of the centre near the bus station, or west of the centre overlooking the yacht harbour. Dolmuşes run to and fro along Fethiye's main street, Atatürk Caddesi.

The all-important beach at Ölüdeniz is 15 km south of Fethiye. For full information see the Ölüdeniz section.

Information

Fethiye's Tourism Information Office (tel (6151) 1051) is at İskele Meydanı next to the Dedeoğlu Hotel, near the yacht harbour at the downtown end of Atatürk Caddesi. They will help you with lodgings and inexpensive yacht charters. Right next door is the office of the Fethiye Turizm Derneği (Fethiye Tourism Association), a local group which can also provide helpful information. On Atatürk Caddesi across from the Kordon Oteli is the Fethiye Belediyesi Turizm Ofisi, the city's contribution to the tourism info game.

Excursions

Hotels and travel agencies in town will want you to sign up for the 12-island tour, a boat trip around Fethiye Bay which takes most of a day and costs between US$4 and US$6 per person.

North-east of the centre is Çalış, a long swath of beach with some little hotels and pensions, now somewhat ignored by the crowds racing to Ölüdeniz.

You can arrange to take a boat or minibus tour to some of the archaeological sites and beaches along the nearby coasts. Standard tours are those which go west to Günlük, Pınarbaşı, Dalyan and Caunus, and east to Letoön, Kalkan, Kaş, Patara and Xanthos.

The old city of Karmylassos near the village of Kaya is reached by a road which climbs the hillside behind Fethiye to the south, passing the Crusader castle ruins and offering wonderful views. The shore at Karmylassos is protected by Gemile Island, so the swimming is good, warm and safe, though there's not a lot of sandy beach. On Gemile are unexcavated ruins of an ancient city with a large necropolis. This is a favourite anchorage for yachts embarked on a Blue Voyage.

Other Sights

On the hillside behind the town, notice the ruins of a **Crusader fortress** constructed by the Knights of St John on earlier (400 BC?) foundations.

In the town you will notice curious Lycian stone **sarcophagi** dating from about 450 BC. There is one near the PTT, others in the middle of streets or in private gardens; the town was built around them.

Carved into the rock face behind the town is the **Tomb of Amyntas** (350 BC), in the Doric style. Other smaller tombs are near it. Walk up or take a taxi for a look at the tomb and the fine view of the town and bay.

Fethiye's **museum** (*müze*) is open from 8 am to 5 pm daily and charges US$0.35 for admission.

Places to Stay

Fethiye has a good selection of lodgings but you must choose one of three areas. For a night or two, stay right in the town. For a beach holiday of three days or more, stay at Ölüdeniz.

Places to Stay – bottom end

Fethiye has 15 small downtown hotels and almost 100 small pensions so you're sure to find suitable cheap lodgings.

For real savings find a pension. There are lots of them in Fethiye, left from the time before Ölüdeniz was discovered and developed. In those halcyon days Turks on beach holiday would stay in Fethiye's homes, bringing welcome income to the town's matrons. Since Ölüdeniz the trade has dropped off but the pensions remain and they're better bargains than ever. The Tourism Information Office will help you find one, or you can simply explore the area of the bus station, or walk up the hill behind the Likya Hotel along Karagözler Caddesi and look for the little 'pansiyon' signs. The houses are all about the same, as are the rates: about US$3 to US$5 per bed in rooms without running water; the price of a cold shower is included in the charge. Soap and towels are not normally provided. The *Aygen Pansiyon* up here (take the right fork as you go up the hill) is a good one; breakfast is also available.

For a pension in the midst of the market try the *Halley Pansiyon* (tel 1158), Eski Cami Sokak 6, on a pedestrians-only street off Çarşı Caddesi, the main street through the market area. Rooms are simple, without plumbing, but quiet except for the nearby minaret. The energetic manager, Mr Arif Acar, charges US$10 for a double.

If you want a downtown hotel try the tidy, modern little *Hotel Kaya* (KAH-yah) (tel 1161, 2469), Cumhuriyet Caddesi 6, a block inland from the main

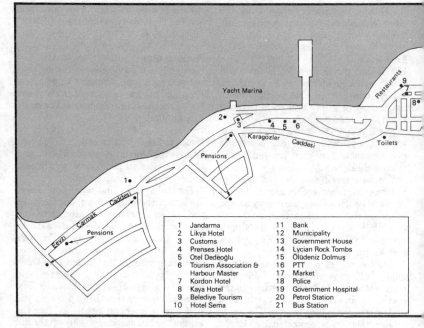

1	Jandarma	11	Bank
2	Likya Hotel	12	Municipality
3	Customs	13	Government House
4	Prenses Hotel	14	Lycian Rock Tombs
5	Otel Dedeoğlu	15	Ölüdeniz Dolmuş
6	Tourism Association &	16	PTT
	Harbour Master	17	Market
7	Kordon Hotel	18	Police
8	Kaya Hotel	19	Government Hospital
9	Belediye Tourism	20	Petrol Station
10	Hotel Sema	21	Bus Station

road on a narrow market street. Graced with a wonderful jasmine vine on its facade, the Kaya charges US$12 for a double, US$15 for rooms with private shower. Some rooms open right onto the jasmine vine, which gives the air a wonderful scent. The *Hotel Kent* facing the Kaya is similar in price and comforts.

Off Çarşı Caddesi not far from Atatürk Caddesi is the *Hotel Özgün* (tel 4469), Çarşı Caddesi 9/4, charging US$18 for double rooms with shower, breakfast included. If the Özgün is full, the *Hotel Ankara* (tel 1742) right across the street is similar.

The fancy-looking *Otel Ulvi* (OOL-vee) (tel 1650) on Atatürk Caddesi, half a block east of the statue of Atatürk, is not actually all that fancy and charges US$14 for a double with shower and breakfast, but watch out for street noise. Similar is the *Kordon Oteli* (tel 1834, 1217), Atatürk

Caddesi 8, with rooms overlooking the bay. From the street it looks fancier than it is. Double rooms with shower go for US$18, breakfast included.

Places to Stay – middle

Perhaps the best place in town is the *Hotel Se-Sa Eine Rose* (tel 4326), Akdeniz Caddesi 17, a new hotel at the Fethiye end of Çalış beach just off Atatürk Caddesi. Many rooms face the bay and you should ask for one of these as the street-side rooms may be noisy. All rooms have private bath, most have balconies and there's a good terrace restaurant on the beach side. Prices are the highest in Fethiye: US$42 for a double with breakfast.

High marks for service and friendliness go to the experienced staff at the two-star *Otel Dedeoğlu* (deh-DEH-oh-loo) (tel 4010), İskele Meydanı, next to the Tourism Information Office. The 41

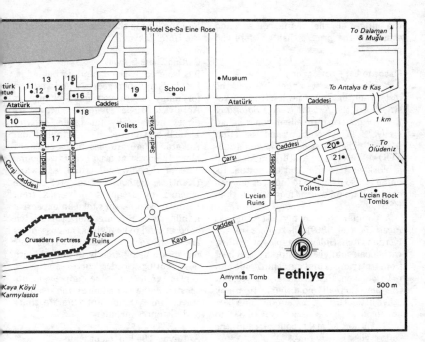

rooms with sea view and private bathrooms are priced at US$26/34 for singles/doubles, breakfast included. It's far from elegant, with a leather shop crowding the lobby, but it's among Fethiye's best.

A few steps westward is the newer *Prenses Hotel* (PRENN-sess) (tel 1013, 1305), Yat Limanı Yanı, which charges about the same for its rooms, but which has a long way to go in order to equal the comfort and congeniality of its older neighbour. Service here is very inept.

In town at the intersection of Çarşı Caddesi and Atatürk Caddesi stands the *Hotel Sema* (tel 1015). Though it was among the first hotels built in the city, it has been kept up-to-date and its modest comforts are yours for US$30 a double.

Finally, just opposite the yacht harbour is Fethiye's old standard, the one-star, 40-room *Likya Hotel* (LEEK-yah) (tel 1169, 1690), Karagözler Mahallesi. Its older rooms open onto the sea and Fethiye's

most pleasant gardens, and cost US$38/48/66 for singles/doubles/triples, breakfast included. The high price results from the Likya's gardens, its status address by the yacht harbour, and its swimming pool – the only one in town. Surprisingly, the hotel has a Chinese restaurant and the chef is in fact Chinese. The Likya, by the way, may be filled by bus tours when you visit.

Places to Eat

In recent years Fethiye has seen numerous quayside restaurants set up for business along its waterfront, and these are perhaps the most pleasant places to have breakfast or an evening meal. The quayside restaurants, however, tend to be more expensive than the ones which crowd the narrow market streets. If you're trying to save money, use the quayside restaurants only for breakfast. At any restaurant be sure to ask prices – at least the price of the main course, and especially the price of fish – before you order.

Places to Eat – bottom end

Among the least expensive of the restaurants on Çarşı Caddesi (the market street) are the *Kristal Kebap Salonu & Restaurant* (with excellent döner kebab for US$1.75 per portion) and the *Tuna Merkez*. There's also the *Doyum* (doh-YOOM, 'fill-up') on Atatürk Caddesi half a block east of the Atatürk statue. Its name is also its claim to fame, as one can easily fill up on decent food for less than US$4.

A popular spot on my last visit was *Pizza 74* (tel 1869), next door to the Kordon Oteli. Sidewalk tables were filled with locals and visitors sipping cold beer from frosty mugs and munching pide and roast chicken. Pizzas are served, yes, but this place is really no different from any other little Turkish restaurant. The beer and food are good and cheap (US$1 to US$1.75 for a meat course), and the sunset view is very fine.

Places to Eat – middle

For local colour, the most pleasant place to dine is the *Yacht Restaurant*, facing the yacht harbour just by the Hotel Likya. It's not fancy, with fluorescent lights and a noisy TV, but the outdoor tables are very pleasant, the service polite and the food quite good. A fish dinner might cost about US$4.50, drinks included.

Typical of the restaurants in the market area between Çarşı Caddesi and the harbour is the *Restaurant Güneş* (tel 2776), Likya Caddesi 4, with outdoor tables, English-speaking waiters and a wide selection of cold meze and salads. Main courses include everything from spicy-hot adana kebap through chicken and lamb chops to octopus and *trança şiş* (skewer-grilled chunks of bonito). Ask prices so they don't mistake you for Rockefeller.

For fancier meals dine in the *Hotel Se-Sa Eine Rose* or the Chinese restaurant at the *Hotel Likya*.

Getting There & Away

Bus Isolated by the mountains behind it, Fethiye's transport goes east and west and for many routes you must change at Antalya or Muğla. There are, however, six direct buses daily for İzmir, one for Denizli and one each for İstanbul and Ankara. There are also buses eastward along the coast at least every two hours. The archaeological sites eastward (Xanthos, Letoon, Patara, etc) can be reached by frequent dolmuşes from Fethiye – you needn't take an expensive minibus tour. Bus fares along this stretch of coast tend to be high as the passengers are mostly tourists. The highways in this region are being greatly improved, with new routings, wider curves and more gentle grades. These improvements shorten highway distances and decrease travel times. Some approximate times and distances include:

Antalya – 295 km, eight hours
Dalaman – 50 km, 45 minutes
Demre – 155 km, 3½ hours
Kalkan – 81 km, two hours
Kaş – 110 km, 2½ hours
Kemer – 250 km, six hours
Letoon – 60 km, 1½ hours
Marmaris – 170 km, three hours
Muğla – 150 km, three hours
Patara – 75 km, two hours
Xanthos – 65 km, 1½ hours

Dolmuş For Ölüdeniz catch a dolmuş from beside the PTT, just off Atatürk Caddesi, for the 15-km, 25-minute ride (US$0.65).

ÖLÜDENİZ

Ölüdeniz (eur-LUR-deh-neez, Dead or 'Calm' Sea) is not dead like its biblical namesake. Rather, it is a very sheltered lagoon not at all visible from the open sea. The scene as you come down from the pine-forested hills is absolutely beautiful: in the distance is open sea, in the

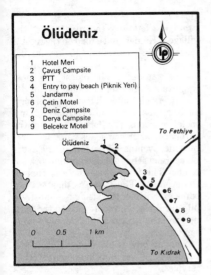

Ölüdeniz

1 Hotel Meri
2 Çavuş Campsite
3 PTT
4 Entry to pay beach (Piknik Yeri)
5 Jandarma
6 Çetin Motel
7 Deniz Campsite
8 Derya Campsite
9 Belcekız Motel

Ölüdeniz

To Fethiye

To Kıdrak

0   0.5   1 km

foreground a peaceful lagoon bordered by forest, in the middle a long sand spit of perfect beach. Yachts stand at anchor in the blue water, or glide gracefully along the hidden channel out to sea. The discordant note is the rampant and unplanned development taking place all along the road to the beach.

The development of Ölüdeniz has been somewhat haphazard, with a jumble of makeshift camping areas and rentable shacks beginning several km inland from the shore. The bright spots in the development are the parks operated by the Directorate of Forests, which include the excellent section of beach on the sand spit called the Ölüdeniz Piknik Yeri, and Kıdrak Orman Parkı, the forest park at the south-eastern end of the bay.

Orientation

The great and beautiful swath of beach speaks for itself. Even in high season it's too big to be really crowded. When you wind down the mountainside and reach the beach you are at the centre of things. To your right (north-west) is a jandarma post, a PTT and the entrance to the Ölüdeniz Piknik Yeri (US$0.50 admission fee per person) with free showers and toilets. One km past this point is the only fancy hotel at Ölüdeniz, the Motel Meri, overlooking the lagoon.

To your left (south-east) are most of the camping areas, restaurants and cheap 'motels'. At the far end of the beach the road climbs up a slope and clings to the mountainside for two km before descending to Kıdrak Orman Parkı.

You can rent canoes on the main beach for about US$2 per half-hour. Excursion boats leave the main beach to explore the coast, charging US$4 to US$6 per person.

Places to Stay – bottom end

Camping is the thing to do here and the cheapest and best place to do it is at the *Ölüdeniz Kamp Yeri*, a five-minute walk beyond Kıdrak Parkı. The cost is only US$1.50 per person in a tent. Kıdrak Parkı is the place to hang out, however; it has a spring water source and sanitary facilities. It is idyllic and usually fairly crowded.

Otherwise there are various commercial camping areas, along and inland from the beach, charging about US$3 per person. Some of the better, shadier ones are out past the PTT on the road to the Motel Meri and are undiscovered by most foreign tourists, who tend to stay on the main beach rather than on the lagoon.

Places to Stay – middle

Several of the camping areas have makeshift little 'bungalows' which they rent for premium prices in high season. Much of the time, despite the high prices, they are occupied. Try the *Belcekız Motel* (BELL-jeh-kuhz) (tel 1430/9) which is nothing great but which nonetheless charges US$35 to US$45 for a room with shower, breakfast and dinner included.

The *Çetin Motel* (cheh-TEEN) (tel 1430/2/3) is even simpler, charging US$16 for a double room without private shower, US$22 with shower, breakfast included.

In high season chances are good that all of
the rooms with shower will be reserved
long before you arrive.

The two-star *Hotel Meri* (meh-REE)
(tel 4388/9) has 75 rooms scattered down a
steep hillside amidst pretty gardens. The
views from many of the rooms are very
fine. Some of the rooms are a bit musty,
but this place has a lock on the market
here so the price for a double with bath,
breakfast and dinner included is US$72;
similar singles cost US$50, triples are
US$92. The motel has its own beach and
seaside restaurant. For reservations in
Fethiye contact the hotel office at Atatürk
Caddesi 34 (tel 1482, 2575, 4444).

Places to Eat

All of the restaurants at Ölüdeniz charge
resort prices so a portion of döner kebap
which might cost US$1.50 in Fethiye costs
US$2.75 here. The quality of restaurant
food and service changes constantly. On
my last visit the *Han Restaurant* at Han
Camping was the cheapest and most
popular beachfront spot. You can save a
bit of money by walking inland along the
access road to the *Pirate's Inn Restaurant
& Bar* which, because it is 100 metres from
the beach, has much lower prices.

FETHİYE TO KAŞ

This portion of the Lycian coast,
sometimes called the Lycian Peninsula
because it extends well south into the
Mediterranean, is littered with the
remains of ancient cities. If you have your
own car you can visit as many as you like
by making a few short detours. Without a
car you can still make your way to many of
them by dolmuş or bus, with perhaps a bit
of a hike here and there.

Leave Fethiye on Atatürk Caddesi.
About 23 km along, near the town of
Kemer, the road forks. The right fork goes
to 'Kaş-Antalya'; take the left fork to
'Korkuteli-Antalya' if you want to have a
look at the ancient city of Tlos.

Tlos

From the left fork the road enters the
village of Kemer, and a road on the right is
marked for Tlos, about 15 km farther
along.

Tlos was one of the oldest and most
important cities in ancient Lycia. Its
prominence is matched by its promontory,
as the city has a dramatic setting high on a
rocky outcrop. The **fortress** crowns the
acropolis; what you see is Turkish work,
but the Lycians had a fort in the same
place. Beneath it are the familiar **rock-cut
tombs**. The fanciest of these is that of
Bellerphon. The town's **theatre** and
baths are visible; the **stadium** is mostly a
pile of rubble. The **necropolis** on the path
up to the fortress has many stone
sarcophagi.

You can buy drinks and snacks in the
small village here but there are few other
services.

Back on the highway heading south
toward Kaş, the road takes you up into
fragrant evergreen forests and down to
fertile valleys. Herds of sheep and goats
(and a few cattle) skitter along the road
near the villages. The road is curvy and
the journey somewhat slow. Farm tractors
pulling trailers can slow you down as well.

Pınara

Some 37 km east of Fethiye, near the
village of Esen, is the turning (right) for
Pınara, which lies up in the mountains.
The road winds through tobacco and
maize fields and alongside irrigation
channels for over three km, then takes a
sharp turn to climb the slope. The last two
km are extremely steep and rough, and
not all cars can make it. If yours has
trouble, try doing it in reverse as that is
often a car's lowest gear; or get out
and walk.

At the top of the slope is an open
parking area, and near it a cool, shady
spring with refreshing water. The guardian,
Mr Fethi Parça, may appear and offer to
show you around the ruins, and it is wise to

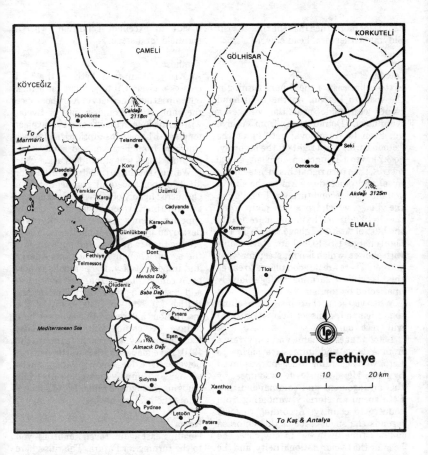

Around Fethiye

```
0        10        20 km
```

take him up on his offer as the path around the site is not easy to follow. The site is always open; there is no admission fee, though you may want to tip the guardian if he gives you a tour.

Pınara was among the most important cities in ancient Lycia and, though the site is vast, there are only a few features which make a lasting impression. The sheer column of rock behind the site, and the rock walls to its left, are pock-marked with many rock-cut tombs. To reach any one of them would take several hours. Other tombs are within the ruined city

itself. The one called the Royal (or King's) Tomb has particularly fine reliefs, including several showing walled cities.

Pınara's theatre is in good condition; its odeum badly ruined. The temples of Apollo, Aphrodite and Athena (with heart-shaped columns) are also badly ruined, but in a fine location.

The village at Esen has a few basic pensions and restaurants.

A few km south of Esen is a turning for **Sidyma**, 12 km over a rough dirt road. The ruins are not spectacular. If you've seen all the other Lycian cities and are simply aching for more, then take the time to visit Sidyma. Otherwise, head onward.

Letoön

Sixteen km east of the Pınara turning is the road to Letoön, on the right-hand (south-west) side near the village of Kumluova. (Dolmuşes run from Fethiye via Esen to Kumluova; get out at the Letoön turn.) Turn right off the highway, go 3.2 km to a T-junction, turn left, go 100 metres, then turn right (this turn is easy to miss) and proceed one km to the site. If you miss the second turn you'll end up in the village, which has a very plain hotel, the *Otel Yıldız*, on the main square next to the bust of Atatürk, above the PTT. The hotel charges US$10 for bare, stark rooms with shower, which is a bit steep for what you get. There are no good places to eat as this is still a farming village largely unaffected by tourism.

When you get to the ruins, a man selling soft drinks and admission tickets (US$0.75) will greet you.

Letoön takes its name and importance from a large and impressive shrine to Leto, who according to legend was loved by Zeus. Hera, Zeus' wife, was upset by this arrangement and commanded that Leto spend an eternity wandering from country to country. According to local legends she spent a lot of this enforced holiday time in Lycia. In any case, she became the Lycian national deity, and the federation of Lycian cities built this impressive religious sanctuary for worship of her.

The site consists of three **temples** side by side, to Apollo (on the left), Artemis (in the middle) and Leto (on the right). The Temple of Apollo has a nice mosaic showing a lyre and a bow and arrow; a boy will uncover it for you, then wait breathlessly for your tip. There's also a **nymphaeum** which is permanently flooded and inhabited by frogs, which is appropriate as worship of Leto was somehow associated with water. Nearby is a large Hellenistic

theatre in excellent condition, with a cornfield for a stage.

Xanthos

At Kınık, 63 km from Fethiye, the road crosses a river. Up to the left on a rock outcrop is the ruined city of Xanthos, once the capital and grandest city of Lycia, with a fine **Roman theatre** and **Lycian pillar tombs** with Lycian inscriptions. Dolmuşes run here from Fethiye, and some long-distance buses will stop if you ask.

Walk up the hill to the site. Xanthos, for all its importance and grandeur, had a chequered history of wars and destruction. Several times, when besieged by clearly superior enemy forces, the city was destroyed by its own inhabitants. You'll see the theatre at once, and opposite it is the agora. Though Xanthos was a large and important city, the acropolis is now badly ruined. Many of the finest sculptures and inscriptions were carried off to the British Museum in 1842; many of the inscriptions and decorations you see here today are copies of the originals. Excavations by a French team in the 1950s have made Xanthos worth visiting, however. One does enjoy the spicy smells of sage and mint which come up while trudging through the ruins. Try to get here before the heat of the day.

Patara

Heading east again, seven km brings you to the turning for Patara. The ruins here are of some interest and they come with a bonus in the form of a wonderful white sand beach some 50 metres wide and 20 km long.

Look for the Patara turning in the village of Ovaköy; from here it's 3½ km to the village of Patara, with its pensions, hotels and restaurants, or five km to the ruins; the beach is one km past the ruins. At the end of the road, by the beach, is a little restaurant where you can buy snacks and drinks.

Dolmuşes run several times a day to Patara from Fethiye and Kaş. They tend to fill up so you should make careful arrangements about getting there and back. Buy your tickets in advance to assure a seat.

The Ruins The ruins at Patara include a **triumphal arch** at the entrance to the site and just past it a **necropolis** with a **Lycian tomb**. Next are the **baths** and a much later **basilica**. You'll approach a car park attended by a guardian, but there is no fee for visiting the ruins.

The **theatre** is of good size and striking because it is half-covered by wind-driven sand, which seems intent on making a dune out of it. Climb to the top of the theatre for a good view of the whole site.

Several other baths, two temples and a Corinthian temple by the lake are also here, though the swampy ground may make them difficult to approach. Across the lake is a **granary**.

The Beach What was once a completely pristine swath of sand has now suffered the damage of discovery. Patara has incipient problems with litter and itinerant vendors, but it is still a beautiful and very large beach. Bring something for shelter if you can as there are few places to get out of the sun and bad burns are a real problem. The restaurant by the parking area at the beach is run by the people who own the Patara Pension.

You can get to the beach by following the road in through the ruins, or by turning right at the Golden Pension and following the track which heads for the sand dunes on the other (western) side of the archaeological zone. It's about a 30-minute walk. Sometimes you can hitch with vehicles passing along the main road.

Excursion boats come for the day from Kaş, so you needn't stay overnight in Patara to enjoy the beach.

Places to Stay The lodging situation at Patara is complicated because this is an archaeological zone, which means it is public property and camping is not allowed due to the danger of theft of antiquities.

The best known of the pensions is the *Golden Pension & Restaurant* (tel (3215) 1166), with 15 rooms – six with private shower, nine without – and a restaurant on the roof. The charge for a double room with shower is US$15 in season, slightly less off season. The owner, Muzaffer Otlu, speaks some English and French and is very friendly. There are many similarly priced pensions around, including the *St Nicholas*, the *Akgül* and the *Sisyphos*. The *Patara Pension* also calls itself the Patara Motel and is a newer building with double rooms with shower for US$18 to US$20 in season, almost half price off season. There are much cheaper pensions in town and your best plan is to allow some time after you arrive to shop around. I assure you that if I put the names of the cheaper pensions in this guide, they wouldn't remain cheap for very long.

Up on the hillside to the left as you enter the village, above the road, are several hotels and lots of holiday villas. The *Hotel Delfin* has nice little standard Turkish hotel rooms with shower and balcony, and a terrace restaurant. The *Hotel Xanthos*, higher on the hill above the Delfin, even has a swimming pool and tennis court. Another place on this hillside is the *Ekizoğlu Motel* (tel (3215) 4007) where double rooms with bath and breakfast cost US$18. Building is so furious here that by the time you arrive there will be many other lodging choices, both cheap and not so cheap.

Places to Eat Most of the hotels and some of the pensions (including the Golden and the Patara) have restaurants. The *Eucalyptus Restaurant*, on the western road to the beach (the 'back' road), has very good food and reasonable prices – about US$3 for a full meal.

Kalkan

About 11 km east of the Patara turning, or 81 km east of Fethiye, the highway skirts

Kalkan (kahl-KAHN), an old village with a burgeoning interest in tourism. New installations include a yacht marina in the serene, unspoilt bay and several hotels as well as inexpensive pensions. Kalkan is one of those idyllic villages which offer nothing to do, and everything to enjoy.

Orientation Kalkan is built on a hillside sloping down to the bay, and you will find yourself trekking up and down it all day. Coming in from the highway the road descends past the Belediye then takes a switchback turn by the Ziraat Bankası to pass the Orman Genel Müdürlüğü (Directorate of Forests) office and the PTT before entering the main shopping area. The Kalkan Han hotel is here, though most other little hotels and pensions are on terraces below the shopping area, all the way down to the harbour's edge.

Places to Stay As the selection of accommodation is limited, and because Kalkan is visited exclusively by tourists, prices for lodgings tend to be higher than normal, but are still very affordable.

Places to Stay - bottom end Cheapest are the pensions rated 2nd class by the town – the *Akın Pansiyon* (ah-KUHN) (tel (3215) 1025) and the *Akgül* around the corner, charging US$12 for a double without running water. The Akın has lots of clean bathrooms off the hall, though. First-class pensions such as the *Ay Pansiyon* (AHY) (tel 1058) provide double rooms with showers for US$16 per night; the Ay is family-run and popular with British tour groups. Similar accommodation is provided at the *Pension La Boheme* (tel 1219), Yalıboyu Mahallesi 40, where the rooms are tiny, the shower is always hot (so they tell me), breakfast is included and a double with twin beds goes for US$22. The *Pension Dalkıran* is similar. The *Şahin Pension* (tel 1104), Yalıboyu Mahallesi, charges US$18 for a double, breakfast included, for one of its

nine rooms with private shower. Some English and German is spoken here.

The pensions in the market area, on the same street as the expensive Kalkan Han, remain fairly low in price because they're simple and don't have views of the sea. The *Holiday, Deniz* and *Balkan*, for instance, charge US$12 for double rooms with or without shower. They may be upgraded in future, however, with a consequent rise in prices.

Places to Stay - middle Among the hotels, perhaps the most atmospheric is the *Kalkan Han* (kahl-KAHN) (tel 1151), Köyiçi Mevkii, an old village house wonderfully restored and now equipped with 16 rooms, each with private bath, for US$58 a double, breakfast included. The decor is of stone, wood, local crafts and Turkish carpets. The hotel's terrace provides a good view of the stars at night. According to Herodotus, Kalkan is the place 'closest to the stars' (thereby edging out Hollywood, no doubt). The small number of rooms means that the hotel is often full; to reserve in advance, call Evren Seyahat, Cumhuriyet Caddesi 245, İstanbul (tel (1) 146-6172).

Another old village house beautifully restored is the *Balıkçı Han* (tel 1075), Yalıboyu Mahallesi, with several old fireplaces, red tile floors throughout, and panels of coloured faïence in the walls, with Turkish carpets and craft items added as accents. Some rooms have brass beds. Rooms with private shower cost US$45 a double, breakfast included.

Among the nicer additions to Kalkan's range of accommodation is the *Famous Pansiyon* (tel 1286), a short walk from the centre of the village on the hillside to the west of the harbour. Most rooms have views of the bay, the town and the surrounding olive groves. The bright guest rooms have nice touches such as monogrammed pillowcases, wooden latticework on the wardrobes and glass-enclosed shower stalls (toilets are shared, down the hall). Coloured kilims are used in the decor; there's a lobby bar and TV lounge. Rates are US$35 for a double with shower and breakfast. Here you're only a five-minute walk from town.

The new *Hotel Pirat* (tel 1178) has added an unwelcome six storeys to the village skyline, but does provide 65 comfortable, modern rooms with balconies for US$36/48 a single/double, breakfast included. It was built to cater for tour groups, which it often does. The morning-glory-covered terrace restaurant is a good place from which to gaze at the harbour just to the east.

Places to Eat Dining has yet to approach the level of an art in Kalkan, but you can have a very pleasant and not overly expensive dinner down on the waterfront at the *Yakamoz, Pala'nin Yeri, Kalamaki, Han, İlyana* or *Pandora*. Pala'nin Yeri has nice vine-covered terraces, and the İlyana, beneath the little mosque (obviously a former church), was offering a full meal for US$3.50 last time I visited. On the terrace above are the *Kalkan* and the *Doy Doy* with more panoramic views. Least expensive fare is at the top of the town not far from the PTT in the market street. Look for the *Köşk Restaurant* (tel 1046) (that's KURSHK), the *Smile* and the *Çetin*.

Kalkan to Kaş

At 87 km from Fethiye is Kaputaş (or Kapıtaş), a striking mountain gorge crossed by a small highway bridge. The marble plaque on the east side of the bridge, embedded in the rock wall, commemorates four road workers who were killed during the dangerous construction of this part of the highway. Below the bridge is a perfect little sandy cove and beach, accessible by a long flight of stairs.

A short distance past Kaputaş, 20 km before Kaş, is the Blue Cave (Mavi Mağara). It is beneath the highway and marked by a sign. You may see boats approaching, bringing tourists for a glimpse of this Turkish Capri. You can climb down from the road for a look and a swim.

KAŞ

Fishing boats and a few yachts in the harbour, a town square with teahouses and restaurants in which one can hear half a dozen languages spoken, inexpensive pensions and hotels, classical ruins scattered about: this is Kaş (KAHSH, population 5000), the quintessential Turkish seaside village. But Kaş has been discovered by the vanguard of foreign travellers and by some Turkish vacationers, so you won't have it all to yourself. The town has awoken to its tourism potential and the main street is now hung with little signs reminding the local people to do their best: 'The Tourist is our guest!', and 'Let's all treat the Tourist well!'

Kaş is not popular because of its beaches – they are small, not sandy but pebbly and a good distance out of town. But Kaş is pleasant for itself, and it can be used as a base for boat excursions to several fascinating spots along the coast.

Orientation

Life centres on the town square by the harbour, with its teahouses, restaurants, mosque, police station and shops. Come down the hill into the town from the bus station and turn left to the town square; if you turn right you will go to the ancient theatre along Hastane Caddesi. The theatre is about all that's left of ancient Antiphellus, which was the Lycian town. On the sheer rock mountain wall above the town are a number of Lycian rock tombs, which are illuminated at night.

Information

The Tourism Information Office (tel (3226) 1238) is on the main square. They speak English and have numerous handouts on local lodgings and sights.

Boat Excursions

Local boatmen will take you along the

coast for cruising and swimming on several standard excursions. No matter which excursion you take, check to see what the provisions are for lunch. If you take an all-day trip you'll have to eat, and I've had some reports of rip-offs on the price of lunch.

One popular excursion is to Kekova and Üçağız, about two hours away by boat, where there are several interesting ruins, also accessible by road. The cost is US$5 to US$8 per person. You can go over to Kastellorizon (Meis Adası, meh-YEESS ah-dah-suh, in Turkish), the Greek island just off the coast, visible from Kaş, for the day, returning to Kaş in the evening, or perhaps enter Greece and go on to other islands. Check on the current diplomatic status of Kastellorizon as a port of entry. The cost to charter a fishing boat for the excursion is about US$50; a single fare is about US$6 round-trip.

Other standard excursions go to the Blue Cave, Patara and Kalkan for US$7 per person, lunch included; or to Liman Ağzı, Longos and several small islands for the same price, lunch included.

For a three-day (two-night) yacht cruise along the coast, expect to pay about US$100 per day for the entire boat. If you have a car, drive out of town on Hastane Caddesi past the theatre, and make the 11-km scenic loop around the western peninsula, which has nice views though not really any good swimming spots. At the tip of the peninsula you're surprisingly close to Kastellorizon.

Other Sights

Walk up the hill on the street to the left of the Tourist Information Office to reach the **Monument Tomb**, a Lycian sarcophagus mounted on a high base. It is said that Kaş was once littered with such sarcophagi but that over the years most were broken apart to provide building materials. This one, on its lofty perch, survived very well.

Walk to the **theatre**, half a km west of the main square, for a look. It's in very good condition and was restored some

time ago. Over the hill behind the theatre is the **Doric Tomb**, cut into the hillside rock in the 3rd century BC. You can also walk to the rock tombs in the cliffs above the town, but as the walk is strenuous go at a cool time of day.

Places to Stay

You can ignore the hawkers who will greet you at the bus station and want to take you to a hotel, or you can ask some questions about price and facilities, and then follow them home. Most of the town's lodgings are within a five-minute walk.

Places to Stay – bottom end

Pensions are everywhere; sometimes it seems that every house in town is a pension. The cheapest charge US$5 or US$6 per bed in high season, but prices range up to US$10 or US$11 per bed in places with more comforts. There are many pensions behind the Hotel Mimosa, just down the hill from the bus station, and pension owners will probably meet you at the bus and make their offers.

Among the pensions within a few minutes' walk of the bus station is the excellent *Limyra Pansiyon* (tel 1080), Meltem Sokak, a good clean place with hot showers and rooms for US$13 a double in season. The *Pension Orion* (tel 1938), Yeni Cami Caddesi, is on the same street despite the different address. The top floor is a quiet terrace with a fine view of the town and the sea, and tidy rooms go for US$17 a double, breakfast included. Some rooms have balconies; and a few are triples. Mr Birol Bayraktar, the owner, is very friendly.

Nearby are many other pensions, including the *Doğan* (doh-AHN) (tel 1223), *Meltem* (mehl-TEHM) (tel 1055), *Bahar* (baa-HAHR) (tel 1323), *Hilal* (hee-LAHL) (tel 1207), *Melisa* (tel 1162), *Oba* and *Keskin* (kess-KEEN). At the end of the street, by the mosque, is the *Ay Pansiyon* (tel 1020), a new and clean place. Front rooms have sea views. The

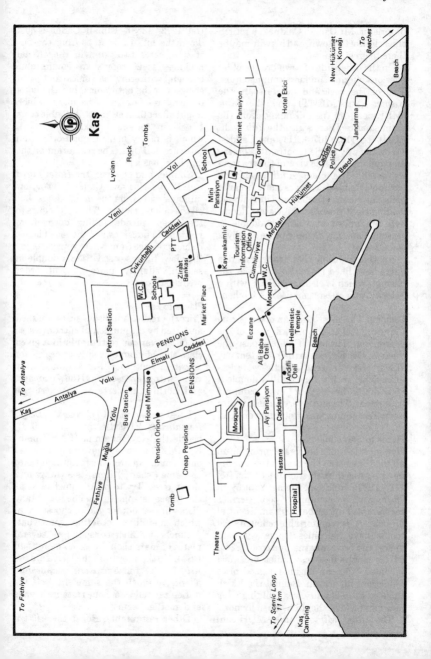

proprietor, Mr Osman Çakmak, a retired chief clerk of the town, and his wife may be there to greet you.

On the other side of town are the older pensions offering similar accommodation. Two of the best and quietest are the *Kısmet* (kuss-MEHT) and the *Mini* (MEE-nee), up the hill inland from the main square. There's also the *Yalı* (yah-LUH) (tel 1132, 1070), Hastane Caddesi 11, on the way to the theatre. It is breezy and quiet with a fine view of the sea from its porch. The older *Andifli*, also on Hastane Caddesi, charges more because of its fine views of the bay and its stairway leading right down to the water. Rooms here are priced at US$26 a double in season. A similar, cheaper place nearby is the *Özdemir*.

Another pension that readers of this guide have liked is the *Koştur*, near the Kısmet, which is clean, spacious, with a balcony, and guests can use the kitchen.

Camping The most popular place is *Kaş Camping* (tel 1050), one km west of the centre, out Hastane Caddesi past the theatre. Two persons in their own tent pay US$3; you can rent a little waterless 'bungalow' shelter for US$10 a double if you don't have your own camping equipment. The site is very pleasant, with a small swimming area, restaurant and bar.

Places to Stay - middle
New middle-range hotels are springing up all the time here. The best in town at my last visit was the two-star *Hotel Ekici* (tel 1417, 1823), Hükümet Konağı Yanı. With 75 rooms, a swimming pool, terrace restaurant, Turkish bath, lifts and central air-con, it is comfortable enough. All rooms have balconies (some with sea views) and private baths, and cost US$44/54 for singles/doubles, buffet breakfast included. You can haggle for good price reductions off season. Behind the Ekici, the Kaş Municipality was building a big new hotel which should be open by now.

The *Hotel Mimosa* (mee-MOH-sah)

(tel 1272, 1368), Elmalı Caddesi, just down the hill a few steps from the bus station, rates two stars in the official ranking. Its 20 rooms are comfortable enough, with tiny balconies and tiled showers in the bathrooms, but the hotel disco blares late into the night, which might affect light sleepers. A double costs US$65 in season, breakfast included, which is pretty high, though off-season rates are half that. The restaurant on the 2nd level has a good view.

Simpler and cheaper, the *Hotel Likya* (tel 1270), Hastane Caddesi, is a few minutes' walk from the main square, but all the quieter for that. The hotel clings to the steep hillside falling down from Hastane Caddesi toward the sea. There's a shady terrace from where you can enjoy the view. Rooms cost US$28 a double in season, slightly more if you order breakfast.

Places to Eat
Prices for restaurant dishes are established and fixed by the municipal authorities, so all of the various restaurants in a given class should charge exactly the same for any item you order. Restaurant quality varies with the seasons and the patronage, and nothing is certain, but here are some tips.

Local people tend to choose the *Derya Restaurant* (DEHR-yah) (tel 1093), beside the Kaymakamlık (KAHY-mah-KAHM-luhk, county government house) on the main square. The restaurant takes its name ('shady') from its awnings and shady trees. Try to pick a quiet table as this place is sometimes chaotic. Many dishes are set out for you to choose from, which simplifies ordering somewhat. A lunch or dinner consisting of several plates of meze should cost no more than US$4. Up the alley from the Derya are the *Aslı*, *Reis'in* and *Eva Kent* restaurants, all pretty much the same. In fact, it's difficult to tell where one restaurant ends and another begins.

Other restaurants are at the eastern

edge of the square near the Belediye; look for the *Mercan* (mehr-JAHN) (tel 1209), which has a waterfront location with tables under awnings. The waiters are inexperienced but willing. Choose a fish, have it weighed, get the price, then say 'evet' if you want it, or 'hayır' if you don't. A fish dinner with mezes and wine can cost US$10 to US$15 per person.

Across the street, the *Morning Star Café* (tel 1517), Hükümet Caddesi 15, has a small street-level dining room, but upstairs there's a covered terrace with a view of the harbour and the traffic along Hükümet Caddesi. Choose your dinner before you climb the stairs; they have a good selection of salads and mezes, fish and kebaps.

The *Çınar*, on the main square next to the Tourism Information Office, is among the simplest restaurants in town. For snacks, pastries and puddings, the *Noel Baba Pastanesi* (Father Christmas) on the main square is the favourite, and the best for people-watching when its outdoor tables are in shade. I paid less than US$1 for an éclair and a cup of Turkish coffee.

Among the prominent restaurants on the main square is the *Eriş*, with shady pseudo-rustic tables in front. Prices are not bad and better food can be found elsewhere, but the candle-light dining atmosphere makes it a very popular place in the evenings.

Up Hükümet Caddesi to the southeast, past the jandarma post, is the *Bacchus Restaurant* which readers have found to have excellent food and service. Also in this part of town is the *Melis Bar*, with familiar English food and cakes, and an English-speaking owner.

For lighter, cheaper fare try the sandwich shop near the PTT, where a huge sandwich costs less than US$1; they have good home-made cake as well. On Hastane Caddesi toward the theatre look for the *Pizza Funghi Restaurant*, where a full meal can be had for US$3 or less.

Getting There & Away

Bus Most of the buses in and out of Kaş are handled by the Aydın Turizm company, but there is some competition, so shop around for good ticket prices. Some destinations include:

Antalya – 185 km, five hours, US$3.50; at least four buses daily

Bodrum – 375 km, seven hours, US$7.50; three buses daily

Fethiye – 110 km, 2½ hours, US$3; eight buses daily, dolmuşes as well, some going directly to Ölüdeniz

Göreme (Cappadocia) via Antalya – 775 km, 15 hours, US$12; several times daily

İzmir (via Selçuk) – 510 km, nine hours, US$9; two night buses

Marmaris – 280 km, 5½ hours, US$6; four buses daily

Pamukkale (via Denizli) – 500 km, 10 hours, US$9; two buses daily; or go via Aydın

Patara – 36 km, one hour, US$2; several dolmuşes daily

KEKOVA

Fourteen km east of Kaş you will see signs for a turning (south, right) to Kekova. A 30-minute drive of 19½ km along this dirt road (rough at times) brings you to the village of Üçağız, the ancient Teimiussa, in an area of ancient ruined cities, some of them partly submerged in the Mediterranean's waters. This area is regularly visited by day-trippers on boats and yachts from Kaş, but is just now being discovered by travellers wanting to stay overnight. For a short time it remains an unspoilt Turkish fishing and farming village hidden away behind the mountains, hardly known to the rest of the world.

The setting of the village is absolutely idyllic, on a bay amidst islands and peninsulas. The old village houses are of the local stone and are often whitewashed. The largest building in town is the modern İlk Okul (primary school). Cows and chickens wander the streets, villagers heft sacks of carob beans down to the town

wharf, fishers repair their nets on the quay
as yachts glide through the harbour.
Village girls sell hand-printed scarves
(*yazma*) with hand-made lace borders;
you can see village women sitting outside
making lace and doing embroidery. Here
and there, perhaps by a football pitch or in
a house's back garden, are remnants of
ancient Lycian tombs. Üçağız, at this
writing, is for real, not yet commercialised
by the force of investment and
advertisement. However, a few carpet
shops have already opened and the
dreaded discos cannot be far behind.

Orientation

The village you enter is Üçağız ('Three
Mouths'; that is, entrances to the
harbour), the ancient Teimiussa. Across
the water to the east is Kale, a village on
the site of the ancient city of Simena,
accessible by boat. South of the villages is
a larger harbour called Ölüdeniz (not to be
confused with the famous beach spot near
Fethiye), and south of that is the channel
entrance, shielded from the
Mediterranean's sometime fury by a long
island named Kekova.

Kale

Though Üçağız is where you arrive, Kale
is where you will go by motorboat to see
the ruins of ancient Simena and the
mediaeval Byzantine **fortress** perched
above the picture-perfect hamlet. Within
the fortress is a little **theatre** cut into the
rock. Near the fortress are ruins of several
temples and public baths, several
sarcophagi and Lycian tombs; the city
walls are visible on the outskirts. It's a
delightfully pretty spot. Boats from
Üçağız will take you on a tour of the area
lasting one to 1½ hours; the price to
charter an entire boat is about US$7 to
US$10, but haggle as prices are subject to
what the traffic will bear.

Your boat excursion may follow this
route around the bay clockwise. First you
go to Kale, where there are a dozen little
seaside restaurants (*Palmiye, Balıkçı'nın

Restaurant and *Mehtap* up on the
hillside, *Simena* and *Yacht* down by the
harbour) and a few tiny pensions; the
restaurants tend to be a bit expensive as
everything comes by boat, and yachting
types are the most frequent customers.
From Kale, the boat goes to the **sunken
Lycian tombs** just offshore, and then to
Kekova Adası (Kekova Island). Along the
shore of the island are more foundations
and ruins, partly submerged in the sea,
and called the Batık Şehir, the Sunken
City. Signs say 'No Skin-Diving Allowed',
indicating that this is an archaeological
zone and the authorities are afraid of
antiquity theft. The boat stops at the
island dock in a little cove to let you have a
swim and wander around and explore the
ruins on land. The town here dates from
Byzantine times. After a swim it's back to
Üçağız. Don't neglect to walk around the
town itself as it has a few old Lycian tombs
also. Next to the football field are two
Lycian sarcophagi (one of them in the
shape of a house) and a rock-cut tomb.

Places to Stay

There are only small pensions in Üçağız,
charging US$4 to US$6 per person. The
Onur Pansiyon has rooms with two or
three beds, and all rooms have solar-
heated water. The toilets are a bit smelly
(bring your own paper) but there's an
agreeable waterfront terrace dining area
and you are allowed to use the fridge. Ali
and Susan Haykır's *Antique Pension* has
very tiny, basic rooms with bed and
wardrobe only, but trim is natural wood
and the shared bathroom is tiled, with a
fired hot-water tank guaranteeing lots of
hot water if you notify the owners in
advance.

Places to Eat

Most of the food and all of the drinks
served in the village's simple restaurants
must be brought in by boat from Kaş, or
even farther away, so prices are higher
than you would expect, but still quite
cheap. On the waterfront are half a dozen

little eateries, including the *Kordon, Liman, Yazır* and *Kekova*, all charging about US$4 for a meal. The Liman is currently favoured. The menu at my last visit included a salad of beans in tomato sauce, cubes of white cheese with sliced green olives, *sigara böreği* (tubes of flaky pastry filled with white cheese), marrow (squash) fritters, potato and egg salad, and fish or lamb kebap, followed by fruit. Wine and beer are served.

There are a few simple shops in the village at which you can buy basic food supplies and, of course, souvenirs and Turkish carpets.

Getting There & Away

There is no regular or daily road transport to Üçağız, though there will no doubt be a minibus service from Kaş in the near future when tourism develops and as the road is improved. For the moment, though, travellers without their own car, or the money to hire a taxi, must come by motorboat or yacht from Kaş or Demre. Motorboats can be chartered at Demre's western beach, called Çayağzı, for US$20; often it is possible to buy one place in the boat for a one-way journey for about US$2. You may be able to do this from Kaş as well.

DEMRE (Myra)

The road descends from the mountains to a very fertile river delta, much of it covered in greenhouses. At Demre (DEHM-reh), also called Kale, sometimes even Kale-Demre, 43 km east of Kaş, is the Church of St Nicholas. It is said that the legend of Father Christmas (Santa Claus) began here when a 4th-century Christian bishop gave anonymous gifts to village girls who had no dowry. He would drop bags of coins down the chimneys of their houses, and the 'gift from heaven' would allow them to marry. This is perhaps why he is the patron saint of virgins; he went on to add sailors, children, pawnbrokers and Holy Russia to his conquests. His fame grew, and in 1087

a raiding party from the Italian city of Bari stole his mortal remains from the church. In mediaeval Europe relics were hot items. (They missed a few bones, which are now in the Antalya Museum.)

The Roman city of Myra (the name comes from myrrh) was important enough to have a bishop by the 4th century. Several centuries before, St Paul stopped here on his voyage to Rome. Though Myra had a long and significant history as a religious, commercial and administrative town, Arab raids in the 7th century and the silting of the harbour led to its decline. Today that same silting is the foundation of the town's wealth. The rich alluvial soil supports the intensive greenhouse production of flowers and vegetables.

Church of St Nicholas

The Church of St Nicholas ('Noel Baba' in Turkish) has been restored and offers a rare chance to see what a 5th-century Byzantine church looked like. A symposium on St Nicholas is held here each year in December. Admission costs US$3.

Orientation

Demre sprawls over the alluvial plain. At the centre near the main square is the famous church, several small pensions and restaurants, shops and bus ticket offices. The better hotels are one km south of the centre, near the shore. Four km west of the centre is Çayağzı beach, with several places to camp for free and several which charge a small amount. The impressive rock tombs and ruins of ancient Myra are about two km north of the main square.

Myra

A few km inland from the church are the ruins of Myra, with a striking honeycomb of **rock-hewn tombs** and a very well-preserved **Roman theatre**. They're well worth a look. Taxi drivers in town will offer to take you on a tour but it's not really necessary. The walk from the main

Lycian rock tombs

square takes only about 20 minutes and the site is pretty much self-explanatory.

Places to Stay

The town's two best hotels are quite simple and are one km south of the main square at the junction with the highway to Antalya. The *Kıyak Otel* (kuh-YAHK) (tel (3224) 2092/3), Merkez İlk Okul Arkası, Şehir Girişinde, is set in its own gardens and charges only US$14 for a double room with private shower and one large bed, US$16 for a double with two beds; prices drop out of season. Its only disadvantage is that it is a 10-minute walk (one km) south of the main square. Across the street is the newer *Otel Topçu* (TOHP-choo) (tel 2200/1/2) which charges about the same.

The *Myra Pension* near the main square is slightly cheaper. Next to it is the *Akdeniz Restaurant*.

On the road to the rock tombs are the *Noel Pansiyon* and the *Palmiye Pansiyon*, charging US$4 per person, breakfast included. The *Star Pension*, on Myra Caddesi, is clean, friendly and has hot showers included in the price.

Places to Eat

The food from the little restaurants near the main square and the church can fill you up, but for a pleasant (if somewhat more expensive) lunch or dinner, head for the restaurants at Demre's harbour, the ancient port settlement of Andriake. To find it, head south from the main square, past the Kayık and Topçu hotels, and turn right. When the highway turns sharp right, continue straight along the river bank to the port. Apart from the pleasant restaurants (meals for US$5 to US$10) there is also a good beach.

FİNİKE

Thirty km along the twisting mountain road brings you to Finike (FEE-nee-keh, population 7000), the ancient Phoenicus, now a sleepy fishing port and way-station on the burgeoning tourist route. Most of the tourists are Turks who have built ramshackle dwellings on the long pebble beach to the east of the town. The beach looks very inviting but parts of it have pollution problems and insects can be a problem at certain times of the year.

A short distance inland from Finike are the ruins of ancient Limyra, not really worth the effort unless you're out to see every antique town along the coast. Arycanda, 35 km north along the Elmalı road, is well worth seeing with its dramatic setting and many well-preserved buildings, but this requires a special excursion. Finike itself is uninteresting and you should not make a special plan to stop here.

Places to Stay

Finike has only a few very modest hotels downtown. The *Hotel Sedir* (seh-DEER) (tel (3225) 1183, 1256), Cumhuriyet Caddesi 37, is in the market district behind the Belediye building. A double room with shower costs a high US$18, with breakfast included. There are also some cheap pensions and lots of camp grounds out near the beach. There are several better motels back from the beach

Top: Slicing döner to make *Bursa Kebabı*
Bottom: Turkey's first republican parliament building in Ankara

Top: The Library of Celsus, Ephesus
Bottom: Angelic figure in high relief, Ephesus

on the eastern outskirts of town, including the *Urallı Motel* and the *Hotel Finike*. The *Hotel Eker* (tel (3229) 1427), eight km east of Finike, charges US$32 for a double with shower, breakfast included.

HEADING EAST

As you leave Finike the highway skirts a sand-and-pebble beach which runs for about 15 km. Signs at intervals read 'Plaj Sahası Halka Açıktır', which means 'The Beach Area is Open to the Public'.

Upon leaving the long beach the road passes through the town of **Kumluca** (population 13,000), a farmers' market town surrounded by citrus orchards and plastic-roofed greenhouses. A few small pensions can put you up in an emergency. After Kumluca the highway winds back up into the mountains. You may see crews of wood-cutters, a reclusive people called Tahtacılar who hold to their own unique culture and traditions.

About 28 km from Finike there is an especially good panorama. Three km later you enter Beydağları Sahil Milli Parkı, the Bey Mountains Coastal National Park. Another six km and you get splendid views of the mountains.

Olympos

After a half-hour drive from Kumluca a road on the right (east) is marked for Olympos, another Lycian city now badly ruined. The road into the site (nine km) is not good, there is little transport (no dolmuşes, few cars to hitch with) but if you're up to it, take a picnic, walk in, and enjoy the beach, which you will enjoy more than the ruins. A few very basic pensions, camp grounds and restaurants will take care of your needs if you decide to stay the night.

By walking 1½ hours from Olympos you can see the Chimera, a perpetual flame issuing from a hole in the rock. Ruins of a temple to Hephaistos (Vulcan) are at the site. Though the Chimera was once quite spectacular, there is not much to see today, though the natural phenomenon of

an eternal flame, still unexplained, is intriguing.

Phaselis

At 55 km from Finike, about 16 km past the Olympos turning and 13 before the turning to Kemer, is a road marked for Phaselis, a Lycian city on the shore. The sign on the highway indicates that the archaeological site is one km from the turning, but that is the distance only to the entrance of the area; the distance to the ruins themselves is two km.

The site is open from 8 am to 6 pm daily, for US$3. Near the entrance to the site is a small modern building where you can buy soft drinks, snacks and souvenirs, use the WC, and visit a small one-room museum.

About one km past the building, shaded by soughing pines, are the ruins of Phaselis, arranged around three small perfect bays, each with its own small beach. Among the ruins there is not a lot to see, and it is all from Roman and Byzantine times, but the setting is incomparably romantic. You will want to have a look at the aqueduct, but that's about all.

Prominent signs read 'No Picnicking in the Ruins!', and point the way to a designated picnic area. Turkish visitors largely ignore the signs and picnic where they like.

Two or three km south-west of Phaselis is the village of Tekirova, with small restaurants, a few pensions (the simple *Ölmez* and *Melissa*), and the enormous five-star *Phaselis Princess Hotel*. Perhaps the best accommodation is at the *Martı Pension-Motel*, about half a km off the highway. This friendly, family-run place has good rooms with bath and breakfast for US$12 a double. You'll enjoy the large garden and pool, too, and meals are available.

Kemer

Kemer (keh-MEHR), 42 km south-west of Antalya, is a burgeoning beach holiday resort being built under government

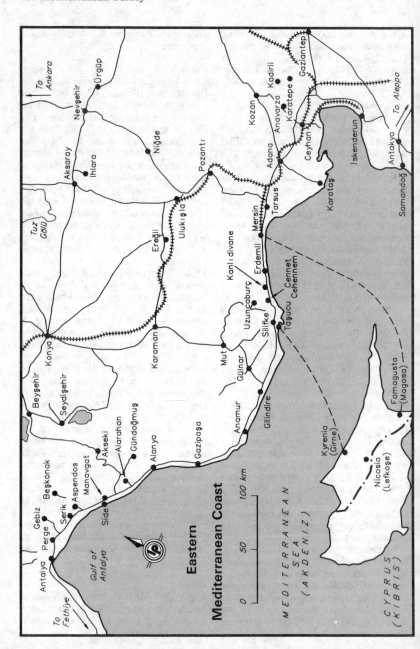

Eastern

Mediterranean Coast

supervision. Accommodation is available in all price ranges so you should be able to find whatever you like. Laid out by a city planner, it is meant to attract groups on package tours, and to provide sun, fun, and a controlled 'Turkish experience'. Dolmuşes run between Kemer and Antalya frequently.

Orientation The main street in town, Liman Caddesi (Harbour Ave), is lined with white waffle-front hotels, palm trees, banks, shops and pensions, with a citrus orchard thrown in for colour. At the end of the main street to the north is the large yacht marina and dry-dock; to the south is a peaceful cove with a beautiful crescent of sand-and-pebble beach backed by emerald grass and fragrant pine trees. Stands here rent equipment for parasailing, water-skiing and windsurfing. Motorboat excursions run from the beach as well. The town has outdoor cafés and restaurants and of course lots of carpet and leather clothing shops. Inland from the town a wall of evergreen-clad, jagged mountains forms a dramatic backdrop.

Information The Tourism Information Office is in the Belediye Binası (Town Hall) (tel (3268) 1536/7).

Yörük Parkı On a promontory north of the cove beach is Kemer's Yörük Parkı, an ethnographic exhibit meant to usher you into some of the mysteries of the region. Local nomads (yörüks) lived in these black camel-hair tents now furnished authentically with carpets and grass mats. Typical nomad paraphernalia includes distaffs for spinning woollen yarn, looms on which Turkish carpets are being woven, musical instruments and churns for butter and ayran. Among the tents, in the shade of the pines, are little rustic tables with three-legged stools at which a 'nomad girl' will serve you refreshments and snacks. The view is very pretty from here. At night, Antalya, to the

north, is a long string of shore lights in the distance.

Places to Stay Kemer's lodgings are of all classes, from family pensions to five-star luxury hotels. The *Barbaros Pansiyon*, a German-style villa in the villa ghetto just off Liman Caddesi, is very clean and charges US$20 a double; other pensions are similar. Hotels are expensive (if you're not on a package tour), from the two-star *Adonis Hotel* (tel 2481), Karayel Mevkii, with doubles for US$65, to the four-star *Otem Oteli* (tel 3181), Yat Limanı Karşısı, facing the yacht marina, charging only slightly more.

Beldibi
North of Kemer a side road (actually the old highway) follows the shoreline more closely between the main highway and the sea. After a few km you pass the **Kımdıl Çeşme Kamp Yeri**, a forest camp ground. About 12 km north of Kemer brings you to the centre of Beldibi, another planned resort area. The beach here is stones, not even pebbles, but the water is clear, the pines cool and the mountain backdrop dramatic. Lodgings along this shore run the gamut from the new *Ramada Hotel* and the *Club Alba* resort to little motels and pensions, and lots of camping areas. Transport between Beldibi and Antalya is by dolmuş (frequent in high summer).

ANTALYA
Antalya (ahn-TAHL-yah, population 400,000, altitude 38 metres) is the chief city of Turkey's eastern Mediterranean coast. Agriculture, light industry and tourism have made Antalya boom during the past few decades, and this mostly modern Mediterranean city is still growing at a fast pace.

Though Antalya is well worth a visit, one doesn't normally come here for a beach vacation, as the city's beaches are out of town. Rather, people come to see the large museum packed with the archaeological and ethnographic wealth

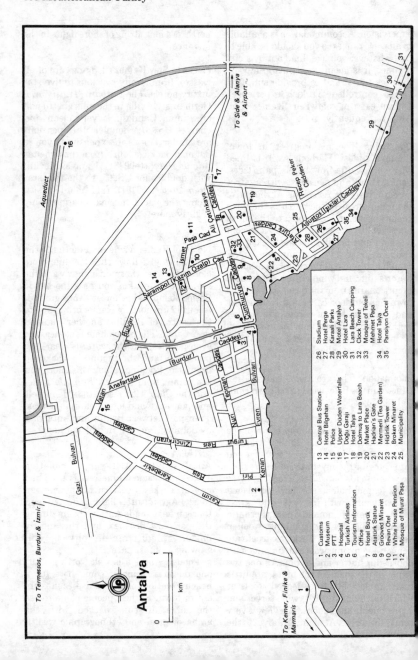

Antalya

To Termessos, Burdur & İzmir

To Kemer, Finike & Marmaris

To Side & Alanya & Airport

Aqueduct

To Termessos, Burdur & İzmir

Recep Peker Caddesi

Paşa Cad Ali Çetinkaya Caddesi

Atatürk Caddesi

4 Ağustos (Işıklar) Caddesi

İsmet

Sarampol (Kazım Özalp) Cad

Tuzcular Caddesi

Cumhuriyet Caddesi

Bulvarı

Burdur

Teoman Caddesi

Vatan

Anafartalar

Nuri

Evren

Caddesi

Bulvarı

Kenan

İnhanı

Gazi Bulvarı

Karabekir

Hela Caddesi

Zincirkıran

Reis

Kazım

Pırı

1 Customs
2 Museum
3 PTT
4 Hospital
5 Turkish Airlines
6 Tourism Information Office
7 Hotel Büyük
8 Atatürk Statue
9 Grooved Minaret
10 Revan Otel
11 White House Pension
12 Mosque of Murat Paşa

13 Central Bus Station
14 Hotel Bilgehan
15 Police
16 Upper Düden Waterfalls
17 Doğu Garajı
18 Hotel Talya
19 Dolmuş to Lara Beach
20 Market Place
21 Hadrian's Gate
22 Mermerli (Tea Garden)
23 Hıdırlık Tower
24 Broken Minaret
25 Municipality

26 Stadium
27 Hotel Perge
28 Karaali Parkı
29 Motel Antalya
30 Hotel Lara
31 Lara Beach Camping
32 Clock Tower
33 Mosque of Tekeli
34 Mehmet Paşa
35 Hotel Talya
    Pansiyon Öncel

0   1
km

of this deeply historical coast. Other attractions include the Old Town and its cosy harbour, which date back several centuries before Christ. This pleasant city can also be used as a base for excursions to the dramatic ruins at nearby Termessos, Perge and Aspendos.

History

Antalya is not as old as many other cities which once lined this coast, but it is still prospering while the older cities are dead. Founded by Attalus II of Pergamum in the 1st century BC, the city was named Attaleia after its founder. When the Pergamene kingdom was willed to Rome, Attaleia became a Roman city. Emperor Hadrian visited here in 130 AD and a triumphal arch (Hadrian Kapısı) was built in his honour.

The Byzantines took over from the Romans. In 1207 the Seljuk Turks based in Konya took the city from the Byzantines and gave Antalya a new version of its name, and also its symbol, the Yivli Minare (Grooved Minaret). After the Mongols broke Seljuk power, Antalya was held for a while by the Turkish Hamidoğulları emirs. It was later taken by the Ottomans in 1391.

During WW I the Allies made plans to divide up the Ottoman Empire, and at the end of the war they parcelled it out. Italy got Antalya in 1918, but by 1921 Atatürk's armies had put an end to all such foreign holdings in Anatolia.

Though always a busy port (trading to Crete, Cyprus and Egypt), Antalya has grown rapidly since the 1960s and is now Turkey's 15th largest city. The 1990 census will no doubt have moved it up a few more notches on the population list.

Orientation

The city sprawls well beyond its ancient limits. A *çevre yolu* (ring road or bypass) named Gazi Bulvarı carries long-distance traffic around the city. To the west is Konyaaltı Plajı, a pebble beach 10 km long, now partly sullied by industrial development. To the east are the sandy bathing beaches, especially Lara Plajı (12 km) which has its own hotels, motels and pensions.

In the centre the main streets have been renamed in recent years, which leads to some confusion since maps and street signs may bear the new names but citizens may use the old names. The street which has the bus terminal is officially called Kâzım Özalp Caddesi, but you may also hear Şarampol, the old name. As it heads north and west from the bus station the name changes to Abdi İpekçi Caddesi, then Vatan Bulvarı before it meets the bypass highway.

Cumhuriyet Caddesi, the main thoroughfare, used to be called Hastane Caddesi. In the western part of town, out toward the Antalya Museum, it becomes Kenan Evren Bulvarı. Ali Çetinkaya Caddesi is the eastern continuation of Cumhuriyet Caddesi. Atatürk Caddesi goes from Cumhuriyet/Ali Çetinkaya Caddesi down to the large Karaali Parkı.

Antalya's landmark and symbol is the Yivli Minare (yeev-LEE mee-nah-reh), built in the early 13th century during Seljuk rule. It is on Cumhuriyet Caddesi, next to the plaza and at the top of the Old Town.

Across Cumhuriyet Caddesi is a currency exchange place that stays open later, until 8 pm during the summer months, and charged no commission when I was here. Another local landmark is the dramatic statue of Atatürk in Cumhuriyet Meydanı (Republic Square), very near the Yivli Minare on Cumhuriyet Caddesi.

The Old Town is called Kaleiçi (kah-LEH-ee-chee, 'within the fortress') or Eski Antalya (ehss-KEE, 'old'). It is down the hill beneath the Yivli Minare and the Atatürk statue.

There are two bus stations, the Oto Garajı, which is the central station for the long-distance inter-city buses, and the Doğu Garajı or Eastern Garage, a parking area in the eastern part of town from which minibuses depart for villages and points as far east as Manavgat and Side.

Information

The Tourism Information Office (tel (31) 11 17 47, 11 52 71) is at Cumhuriyet Caddesi 91 in the Özel İdare İş Hanı building, several blocks west of the Yivli Minare, but there is also an office in a restored house in the Old Town. The local tourism and information association, the Antalya Turizm ve Tanıtma Derneği, has a small information booth at the back of the plaza with the Atatürk statue, on the terrace overlooking the harbour.

Yivli Minare

Start your sightseeing at the Yivli Minare. The handsome and unique minaret was erected by the Seljuk Sultan Alaeddin Keykubat I in the early 13th century, next to a church which the sultan had converted to a mosque. There is an old **stone clock tower** (Saat Kulesi, saa-AHT koo-leh-see), a landmark in the plaza just above it. The view from the plaza, taking in the Old Town, the bay and the distant ragged summits of the Beydağları (Bey Mountains), is spectacular. Teahouses behind the Büyük Otel and the Atatürk statue offer the opportunity to enjoy the view at leisure.

Old Town (Kaleiçi)

Go down the street at the eastern end of the plaza which descends into the Old Town. Note another old clock tower at the beginning of the street. Just below this is the **Mehmet Paşa Camii**, the Mosque of Mehmet Pasha, another Seljuk structure with beautiful Arabic inscriptions above the doors and windows.

Wander down to the harbour, now used for yachts. It was Antalya's lifeline from the 2nd century BC up until very recently when a new port was constructed about 12 km west of the city, at the far end of Konyaaltı beach.

The Old Town has been declared a historic zone and is slowly undergoing restoration. This will take some time though the port area is already well restored. The quaint, twisted streets and picturesque Ottoman houses are certainly charming. East of the harbour you might come across the **Kesik Minare**, or Broken Minaret. Its mosque was once a church, built in the 5th century. The Old Town has lots of little hotels and pensions at low to moderate rates, and a few expensive small hotels.

Bazaar

Antalya's tidy bazaar is north of Cumhuriyet Caddesi between Kazım Özalp and Atatürk Caddesis. Don't go in the heat of a summer afternoon as many of the shops are closed.

Hadrian's Gate & Karaali Park

Down Atatürk Caddesi is Hadrian Kapısı, Hadrian's Gate, erected during the reign of that Roman emperor (117-138). The monumental marble arch, which now leads to the Old Town, makes a shady little park in the midst of the city.

Farther along Atatürk Caddesi toward the sea is Karaali Parkı, a large, attractive, flower-filled park good for a stroll and for views of the sea. Sunset, the prettiest time, is when most Turks come here to stroll. An old stone tower in the park, the Hıdırlık Kulesi, was once a lighthouse and a bastion in the city walls.

Antalya Museum

Antalya's large and rich museum (Antalya Müzesi) is at the western edge of town, two km from the Yivli Minare, reached by bus along Cumhuriyet Caddesi. Ask the driver: *Müzeye gider mi?*, (mew-ZEH-yeh gee-DEHR mee?), 'Does this go to the museum?'. The collections include fascinating glimpses into the popular life of the region, with crafts and costume displays as well as a wealth of ancient artefacts. Opening hours are 9 am to 6 pm, closed Monday; admission costs US$1.

The exhibits, most of them labelled in

English as well as Turkish, start with fossils, proceed chronologically through the Stone and Bronze ages (in which Turkey is especially rich in artefacts) and continue through the Mycenaean, Classic and Hellenistic periods. The Gods Gallery has statues of 15 classical gods from Aphrodite to Zeus, some of them very fine. Among the exceptionally good smaller objects are jewellery, vases, glass items and statuettes. The Tomb Room is also quite good.

The museum has a small collection of Christian art, including a room for icons which also contains a few of the bones of St Nicholas. There are also several sections of mosaic pavement.

The collection continues through Seljuk and Ottoman times, with costumes, armour, calligraphy, implements, faïence, musical instruments, carpets and saddlebags. The ethnographic exhibits are fascinating and include a fully furnished nomad's tent, a room with a carpet loom from a village home and several rooms from a typical Ottoman household.

A shady patio has tables where you can sit and have a cool drink or hot tea.

Places to Stay – bottom end

Kaleiçi Undoubtedly the nicest places to stay are the little pensions in Kaleiçi. Some are in modern buildings, others in historical houses; some are very comfortable, even fancy, while others are quite spartan.

Perhaps the best way to guide you is to describe a route through the twisting streets of the Old Town which you can follow, looking at the various pensions, seeing which have the right prices and also beds available. Start your explorations at Hadrian's Gate (also called Üçkapılar, the Three Gates), on Atatürk Caddesi. Walk through the gate, bear left around the Urartu Rug Store and you're on Hesapçı Sokak. If you follow this street straight to its end you'll reach the Kesik Minare.

First up is the *Yunus Pansiyon* (tel 11 89 73), Hesapçı Sokak 14, a friendly place with rooms in an old house. The small interior court is half sheltered and half open to the sun so you can choose your exposure. Crafts decorate the walls and backpacks are stacked here and there. Rates are US$14 for a double with shower.

Turn left just before the Yunus to find the *Patara Pansiyon* (tel 11 22 68), Barbaros Mahallesi, Kandiller Sokak 21, a newer building with spartan but clean rooms without running water for US$16 a double. All the tea and hot showers you want are included in the price. Haggle like mad, though, and you'll get a better rate, especially if you're staying more than a day or two.

Just past the Yunus is the *Kemer İki Pansiyon* (tel 12 43 99), Hesapçı Sokak, a simple building without charm, but with bare rooms without plumbing at the lowest price: US$10 for a double. I wouldn't recommend this one for females. Farther along is the *Bahar Aile Pansiyon* (tel 18 20 89), Akarçeşme Sokak 5, with similarly low prices (US$10 a double) for simple, basic clean waterless rooms good for men or women. The showers are clean, tiled and fired by şofbens. On the same very narrow street as the Bahar is the *Pansiyon Olea* (tel 12 34 60), Akarçeşme Sokak 11, with surprisingly nice gardens with trees, a fountain and a little outdoor bar where drinks and light meals are served. Rooms are equipped with insect screens and washbasins and are priced at US$14 to US$18 a double.

The *Sabah Pansiyon* (tel 17 53 45), Hesapçı Sokak 60/A, is run by the friendly Sabah family (Ali, the manager, speaks English and German) and has its own garden and dining room serving three meals a day. Rates for the 16 rooms are US$14 a double, breakfast included. You can stay for less if you roll out your sleeping bag on the sleeping terrace.

Before Hesapçı Sokak reaches the Kesik Minare a street goes off to the left to the *Kale Pension* (tel 12 57 97), a house covered in grape and bougainvillaea vines, with a 2nd-storey vine-covered terrace and clean rooms. There's a bit of traffic noise here, though.

Turn right on Kurtuluş Sokak before coming to the Kesik Minare and walk one block to Hıdırlık Sokak. Then turn left to reach the *Erken Pansiyon* (tel 17 60 92), Kilınçaslan Mahallesi, Hıdırlık Sokak 5, a well-preserved (not restored) old Antalya house with lots of dark wood and white plaster. Ottoman times come alive here. One room on the ground floor has its own private bath; the upstairs rooms have no running water but are large and airy with high ceilings. You pay a bit for the antiquity here – the charge per person is US$10. The *Dedekonak Pansiyon* nearby is similar.

At Hıdırlık Sokak 17 is the *Turistik Frankfurt Pansiyon* (tel 17 62 24), a restored house with white plaster walls and bright honey-coloured wood trim on door frames and lattice-covered windows. A little marble fountain burbles in the courtyard. It's pleasant, and you pay a bit more for that: US$26 a double in high summer for a room with shower, breakfast included.

Next along the street is the *Hadriyanus Pansiyon* (tel 11 23 13), Kılınçarslan Mahallesi, Zeytin Çıkmazı 4/A-B, an old house fronting on a refreshingly green walled garden. The owners are very friendly and charge US$14 for a double room without running water, breakfast included.

The *Villa Mine* (VEE-lah MEE-neh) (tel 17 62 29), Hıdırlık Sokak, is more a hotel than a pension as all rooms have private showers and piped music, and it also has a restaurant, gift shop, garden café and TV lounge. The price (US$28 a double in high summer, breakfast included) is good value for money.

Walk in the opposite direction along Hıdırlık Sokak to reach the pleasant *Mini Orient Pansiyon* (tel 12 44 17), Barbaros Mahallesi, Civelek Sokak 30, an old house

nicely restored but still simple. The six rooms grouped around the small but pleasant courtyard all have tiny private facilities, and there's a cosy little dining room for meals. Prices in summer are US$22/28 for a single/double, with reductions off season.

Bus Station Area A place near the bus station is the quaint and funky old *Otel Sargın* (sahr-GUHN) (tel 11 14 08), Tahıl Pazarı, 459 Sokak 3, behind the prominent Revan Otel on Kâzım Özalp (Şarampol) Caddesi. A real traditional old Turkish market-place hotel in a stone building freshly painted, the Sargın charges US$10 for a double room (some have washbasins), US$0.65 for a hot shower.

Across the street from the Sargın is the modern white *Kaya Oteli* (tel 11 13 91), Kâzım Özalp Caddesi, 459 Sokak 12, a quiet, clean place renting double rooms with washbasin for US$11 a double.

If you're tired enough to want to spend a bit more for more comfort, consider the *Revan Otel* (tel 11 20 44, 11 49 79), Kâzım Özalp Caddesi 122, where a room with private shower costs US$30, breakfast included.

As soon as you alight from your bus you're likely to see signs pointing the way to the *Sima Pension* (tel 18 19 54), Balbey Mahallesi, 426 Sokak 13, and following the signs is about the only way to find this place, 400 metres away in a maze of tiny streets. Plain double rooms without running water go for US$10. If the Sima is a bit stark, try the more expensive but much more comfortable *White House Pansiyon*, with its pleasant front garden; it's just down the street.

Near the Yivli Minare, a five-minute walk from the bus station, is the *Ülker Pansiyon* (eurl-KEHR) (tel 12 96 36), Posta Sokak 6, behind the Turkish Airlines cargo building, which is directly across Cumhuriyet Caddesi from the dramatic statue of Atatürk. The pension, which charges US$22 in waterless rooms, might best be described as new, neat, tidy, spartan and central.

If you'd rather have a Turkish bath than a shower ask directions to the Cumhuriyet Hamamı in the bazaar just north of Cumhuriyet Caddesi.

Places to Stay - middle

Old faithful of the mid-range hotels is the two-star, 48-room *Hotel Yayla* (YAHY-lah) (tel 11 19 13/4), Ali Çetinkaya Caddesi 14, not far from the corner of Atatürk Caddesi. Though an older hotel, it is well kept, with an accommodating staff and a lift. Singles cost US$36 in high summer, doubles cost US$45.

Near the Oto Garajı (visible from its centre in fact) is the *Hotel Bilgehan* (BEEL-geh-hahn) (tel 11 51 84, 12 53 24) on Şarampol Caddesi (walk out the front gate of the Oto Garajı and turn right), a comfortable, undistinguished place charging US$36 for a double with bath, breakfast included.

For three-star comfort try the *Hotel Start* (tel 11 12 80), Ali Çetinkaya Caddesi 19, just a short stroll east of the Otel Yayla. The 56 rooms at the Start (where did they get that name?) have TV, bath and air-con, and go for US$60/76 a single/double. If it's full try the nearby *Hotel Bergen*.

Places to Stay - top end

The best of the big places is the *Talya Oteli* (TAHL-yah) (tel 11 56 00), Fevzi Çakmak Caddesi 30, a bright and modern 150-room palace overlooking the sea. For the price of US$135 a single, US$165 to US$200 a double, you get a modern air-con room of an international standard, swimming pool, tennis court, restaurant, bar and nightclub, hairdressers and exercise room.

Prices are considerably lower at the *Turban Adalya Oteli* (TOOR-bahn ah-DAHL-yah) (tel 11 80 66), Yat Limanı, an old building with a sense of history. Once a bank, then a warehouse, it has been restored and is now a very pleasant little

hotel of 26 rooms, all with private showers, direct-dial telephones and TV. It is down by the old harbour in the Old Town and a quiet air-con room costs US$60/85 for a single/double in the high summer season, breakfast included.

Another restored hotel in the Old Town is the beautiful *Marina Hotel* (tel 17 54 90; fax 11 17 65), Mermerli Sokak 15, managed by Kuoni of Switzerland. If the restored pensions of Kaleiçi are village houses, this is an Ottoman mansion, with opulent decoration and all the comforts, including air-con, TV, mini-bars and direct-dial phones in the rooms, as well as a swimming pool and courtyard garden café. Turkish carpets, kilims, mirrors and gilt are used throughout. Depending on the size of your room and its view, prices range from US$35 to US$100 for a single, US$60 to US$160 a double.

Places to Eat - bottom end

Those in search of low-cost meals should go to the intersection of Cumhuriyet and Atatürk Caddesis and find the little street (parallel to Atatürk Caddesi) called Eski Sebzeciler İçi Sokak. The name means 'The Old Inner Street of the Greengrocers' Market' and it is now lined with little restaurants and pastry-shops, many of which have outdoor tables. Most of the food is kebaps, including Antalya's speciality, tandır kebap (tahn-DUHR) - mutton baked in an earthenware pot buried in a fire pit; it's rich and flavourful, but pretty greasy, served on a bed of fresh pide with vegetable garnish. It's sold by weight so you can have as many grams as you like. A normal portion is 150 grams (*yüz elli gram*), a small portion 100 grams (*yüz gram*). A full meal costs anywhere from US$3 to US$5; ask prices before you sit down. Wine and beer are not stocked by the restaurants but your waiter may be willing to scoot over to a nearby shop and fetch your beverage of choice.

To enjoy the view of the harbour and the sea find the *Park Café* across from the

Vilayet (Provincial Government Building) on Cumhuriyet Caddesi. The views are splendid. Tea or coffee and pastry should cost between US$2 and US$4. A few steps down the hillside from the Park Café is *Pizza Margerita*, sharing that excellent view and serving pizzas and burgers of various sorts for US$3 to US$6.

There are other inexpensive restaurants along Kazım Özalp (Şarampol) Caddesi. Look for the two places, side by side, advertising *Canlı balık* (live fish), fried to order. For a pastry and tea pick-me-up try the *Tektat Pastanesi* just a few steps farther north toward the bus station.

Places to Eat - middle

One goes to the *Hisar Restaurant* (tel 11 52 81) as much for the view as for the food. Diners peer out from holes in the sheer cliff behind Cumhuriyet Meydanı to the harbour and the sea beyond. As you might have guessed, the restaurant is set up in some old vaulted stone chambers within the retaining wall; the stone is exposed, with Turkish kilims and copper utensils added for decoration. Cuisine is Turkish and a three-course meal with wine or beer should cost only US$8 to US$10. Come early for lunch (12 noon) or dinner (6 to 7 pm) if you want to get one of the few tables with the view; most of the seats are within the vaulted rooms. To get to the restaurant walk from the Atatürk statue to the edge of the cliff and find the flight of stairs descending to the harbour. The restaurant has erected some signs.

Down by the Old Harbour near the Turban Adalya Oteli are numerous patio restaurants such as the *Ahtapot*, featuring standard Turkish cuisine with prices marked on a signboard and meals of meat or fowl for US$5 to US$7, of fish for about US$8 to US$10, appetisers, main course, sweet and beverage included. The *Yat Restoran* (tel 12 48 55) is in a stone building close by, with a nice terrace dining area out front graced by two marble fountains. The Yat is ambitious in its menu, listing onion soup, beef stroganoff and other such non-Turkish dishes. Prices are similar to those at the Ahtapot.

A funky old place in the heart of town is the *Şehir Restaurant* (tel 11 51 27), close to Cumhuriyet Meydanı. It's a taste of the old Antalya before the gloss of tourism was laid on. The plaster walls are painted to look like brick and the lighting is by little ersatz chandeliers, but the waiters are in black and white, the tablecloths snowy and the prices very satisfying. The cooking is Turkish and a meal with drinks might cost US$6 to US$8 per person. The Şehir is a local place of long standing, not yet discovered by tourists. To find it cross Cumhuriyet Caddesi to its northern side. More or less parallel, and just a few more steps up a rise to the north, is Birinci Sokak (written '1 Sokak' on street signs). Turn left on Birinci Sokak and look down the second street on the right to see the restaurant.

Finally, Atatürk Caddesi between Cumhuriyet Caddesi and Hadrian's Gate has several sidewalk café-restaurants serving meals for about US$5 to US$7 per person.

Places to Eat - top end

The top restaurants are in the *Talya Oteli* and the *Marina Hotel*, of course, and they're very good. In fine weather tables are set out on the Talya's terrace overlooking the sea. At the Marina, food and service are first-rate due to the Swiss management. A good dinner for two costs between US$25 and US$50.

Getting There & Away

Air The Antalya airport is about seven km east of the city on the Alanya highway. Turkish Airlines (tel 11 28 30, 12 34 32, 11 52 38; at the airport 11 27 86, 12 32 93), Cumhuriyet Caddesi, Özel İş Hanı Altı, has non-stop flights in summer between Antalya and Ankara (Thursday), Frankfurt (Thursday), İstanbul (twice daily), Lefkoşa (Cyprus; Sunday), London (Monday), Munich (Saturday and Sunday), and Zurich (Saturday). Direct flights to many other destinations in Turkey, Europe and the Middle East stop in İstanbul en route. Walk west on Cumhuriyet Caddesi from the Yivli Minare and you'll see the Turkish Airlines office on the north side of the street.

Istanbul Airlines (tel 12 48 88; at the airport 12 24 44), Anafartalar Caddesi 2, Selekler Çarşısı 82, has Sunday flights to and from Dalaman, and Friday flights to and from İzmir in summer. The İzmir to Antalya one-way fare is US$30.

Bus Because Antalya is such a popular tourist and commercial city, bus transport is frequent and convenient from all points in Turkey. Antalya's Oto Garajı is on Kâzım Özalp (Şarampol) Caddesi, several blocks north of Cumhuriyet Caddesi and the Yivli Minare.

For minibuses to places east of Antalya (such as Perge, Aspendos, Manavgat and Side) go the the Doğu Garaji, which is not a building but a parking lot and staging area for the minibus traffic. You can take a dolmuş between the Oto Garaji and the Doğu Garaji. The minibus to Lara Plaj leaves from here.

Some destinations served from Antalya's Oto Garaji include:

Adana – 555 km, 12 hours, US$10; a few buses daily
Alanya – 115 km, two hours, US$2; hourly buses in summer
Ankara – 550 km, 10 hours, US$9; frequent buses daily
Denizli (Pamukkale) – 300 km, 5½ hours, US$6; several buses daily
Fethiye – 295 km, eight hours, US$6.50; several buses daily
İstanbul – 725 km, 15 hours, US$12; frequent buses daily
Kaş – 185 km, five hours, US$3.50; at least four buses daily
Konya – 365 km, seven hours, US$6; several buses daily
Marmaris – 590 km, nine hours, US$8; a few buses daily
Side/Manavgat – 65 km, 1½ hours, US$1.50; very frequent buses and dolmuşes in summer
Ürgüp – 485 km, 11 hours, US$10; several buses daily in summer

AROUND ANTALYA

You can use Antalya as a base for excursions to Olympos and Phaselis, Termessos, Perge, Aspendos and Side, but you might find it easier to visit Olympos and Phaselis on your way to or from Kaş, and Perge and Aspendos on your way to Side. With your own car you can stop at Termessos on your way north or west to Ankara, İstanbul or İzmir. Otherwise, Termessos is the one city you must visit using Antalya as your base.

Travel agencies in Antalya operate tours to all of these sites. For instance, a half-day tour to the Düden Waterfalls (Düden Şelalesi) and Termessos costs US$14 per person and is perhaps a bit rushed – there's a lot to see at Termessos. A full-day tour to Perge, Aspendos and Side costs almost US$30. Or you can organise your own transport. If you can scrape together a party of four or five people you can negotiate with a taxi or minibus driver for a private excursion. The private taxi method is especially pleasant and useful for getting to Termessos, and is a lot cheaper than taking an organised tour.

Düden Waterfalls

The Upper Düden Falls, north of the city, can be reached by dolmuş from the Doğu Garajı. Within view of the falls is a nice park and teahouse. This is a relaxing spot on a hot summer afternoon.

The Lower Düden Falls are down where the Düden Çayı, the stream, meets the Mediterranean at Lara Plaj. You'll need a boat to see them properly. Dolmuşes run to Lara Plaj from the Doğu Garajı.

Termessos

High in a rugged mountain valley 34 km inland from Antalya lies the ruined city of

Termessos (tehr-MEH-sohs), once a
Pisidian city of warlike people. They lived
in their impregnable fortress city and
guarded their independence fiercely.
Alexander the Great did not attack them,
and the Romans accepted them as allies,
not as a subject people.

Start early in the day as you have to
walk and climb a good deal to see the
ruins. Though it's cooler up in the
mountains than at the shore, the sun is
still quite hot. Do this visit in the morning
and spend the afternoon at the beach.

Leave Antalya by the highway toward
Burdur and Isparta, turning after about
12 km onto the road for Korkuteli. Signs
mark the entrance to Termessos Milli
Parkı (National Park). Entry to the park
costs US$0.75 for a car, US$0.25 per
person. About 800 metres into the park is a
small museum with photographs and
artefacts from the ruins, plus displays
touching on the botany and zoology of the
park. Near the museum are camping and
picnic sites. Continue another 8½ km up
the road to the ruins, which are open daily
from 8 am to 5 pm; entry is US$3.

The road winds up through several
gates in the city walls to the agora, the
largest flat space in this steep valley.
From here you must explore the ruins
on foot.

At the agora are the remains of a small
Temple of Hadrian, now little more than a
doorway. Head up the path to the city
gate, the theatre (the best preserved
building here), gymnasium, a Corinthian
temple and the upper city walls.

Your goal is the **necropolis** at the very
top of the valley, three km up from the
agora. It's a hike but the necropolis is a
fantastic sight and the mountain vistas
are breathtaking. As you toil upward
you'll notice a wire running alongside the
path. It goes to a fire tower at the top of the
valley, where a man sits, drinks tea,
smokes cigarettes, reads newspapers and
keeps a lookout for fires. He has to carry
up from the agora all the water he uses.

The necropolis (*mezarlık*) is really

something – a vast field of huge stone
sarcophagi tumbled about by earthquakes
and grave-robbers. The scene is reminiscent
of mediaeval paintings portraying the
Judgement Day, when all tombs are to be
cast open.

Isparta

Famous for its carpets, Isparta (altitude
1035 metres, population 125,000) is also at
an important highway junction. It is
surprising, therefore, that there are few
good places to stay.

Places to Stay The best in town for years
was the one-star *Otel Bolat* (tel (327)
18998, 15506), Demirel Bulvarı 71, 1½ km
from the bus station at the main traffic
roundabout in the city. The rooms have
private baths but few other comforts and
rent for US$14 to US$20 for a single,
US$16 to US$26 for a double; the lower
prices are for rooms with washbasin, the
higher for rooms with private shower.
There is a lift, though. By the time you
arrive the new two-star *Büyük Bolat Oteli*
should be open, with more modern and
comfortable rooms.

Right across the street in a shopping
complex is the very simple *Otel Ün* (tel
19852), Mimar Sinan Caddesi, Üslü Ün
Pasajı, where double rooms cost US$8,
shower charge included; this is for
emergencies only. Other cheap hotels are
farther along the same street past the
Belediye.

For three-star comfort you must head
east 36 km to the lakeside town of Eğridir
where the 42-room *Eğridir Hotel* (tel
(3281) 1798), Kuzey Sahil Yolu 2, will put
you up in comfort for US$34/44 a single/
double.

Places to Eat Right next door to the Otel
Ün is the *Başkent Kebapçı ve Pideci*
where I had soup, pide and a soft drink for
US$1. It fills the bill.

Getting There & Away Living up to its
reputation as a transfer point, Isparta's

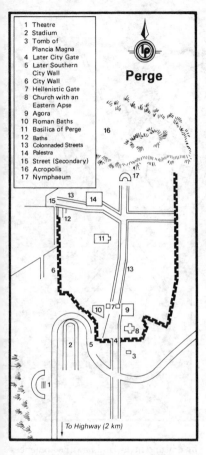

1 Theatre
2 Stadium
3 Tomb of Plancia Magna
4 Later City Gate
5 Later Southern City Wall
6 City Wall
7 Hellenistic Gate
8 Church with an Eastern Apse
9 Agora
10 Roman Baths
11 Basilica of Perge
12 Baths
13 Colonnaded Streets
14 Palestra
15 Street (Secondary)
16 Acropolis
17 Nymphaeum

Perge

To Highway (2 km)

ancient towns. Greek colonists came here after the Trojan War and probably displaced even earlier inhabitants. The city prospered under Alexander the Great and the Romans but dwindled under the Byzantines. The substantial remains of a great theatre, stadium, huge Hellenistic and Roman gates and an impressive colonnaded street are worth seeing. At the acropolis, on a rise behind the other ruins, there is nothing much to see. For a fine view of the site climb to the top of the theatre.

A visit to Perge can be included in the trip eastward to Aspendos and Side. Leave early in the morning. Ride the 13 km east from Antalya to Aksu and the turning for Perge, then two km north to the ruins; you may have to hitch or hike these last two km. Opening hours are 8 am to 6 pm in summer; admission is US$3.

Aspendos (Belkis)

The land east of Antalya was called Pamphylia in ancient times. The Taurus Mountains (Toros Dağları) form a beautiful backdrop to the fertile coast, rich with fields of cotton and vegetables. Irrigation troughs of concrete radiate like spider webs through the lush agricultural land.

Aspendos (ahs-PEHN-dohs) lies 47 km east of Antalya in the Pamphylian plain. Go as far as the Köprüçayı stream, and notice the old Seljuk humpback bridge. Turn left (north) along the western bank of the stream, following the signs to Aspendos.

The great theatre is less than four km from the highway. Opening hours for the site are 8 am to 7 pm daily in summer; admission is US$3.

What you see here remains from Roman times, though the history of the settlement goes back to the Hittite Empire (800 BC). In 468 BC the Greeks and Persians fought a great battle here (the Greeks won, but not for long). Under the Romans, during the reign of Marcus Aurelius (161-180 AD), Aspendos got its theatre.

bus station, 1½ km from the main traffic roundabout in the centre, has buses to many destinations including:

Afyon – 175 km, 2½ hours, US$2.50
Antalya – 175 km, two hours, US$2.50
Denizli – 175 km, 2½ hours, US$2.50
Konya – 270 km, four hours, US$4.50

Perge

Perge (PEHR-geh), 15 km east of Antalya near the town of Aksu (take a minibus from the Doğu Garajı), is one of those very

Side

0   50   100 m

To Manavgat

Parking Lot

1 City Wall
2 Main Gate
3 City Fountain
4 Aqueduct
5 Colonnaded Street
6 Colonnaded Street
7 Building with
   a Sacred Fountain
8 House of Peristyle Type
9 House of Peristyle Type
10 Agora
11 Theatre
12 Roman Baths & Museum
13 Monumental Gate
14 Dionysos Temple
15 Colonnaded Street
16 Christian Basilica
17 Harbour Baths
18 Temple of Apollo
19 Temple of Athena
20 Christian Basilica
21 Main Temple
22 A Byzantine Fountain
23 The Most Imposing Baths
   of Side
24 Byzantine House
25 Building the State Agora
   of the City
26 Byzantine House
27 Small Byzantine Church
28 Byzantine Basilica
29 Inner City Wall

There are many fine Hellenistic and Roman theatres in Anatolia but the one at Aspendos is the finest of all. Built by the Romans, maintained by the Byzantines and Seljuks, it was restored after a visit by Atatürk. A plaque by the entrance states that when Atatürk saw the theatre he declared that it should be restored and used again for performances and sports.

Purists may question the authenticity of the restorations, but more than any other, the theatre at Aspendos allows the modern visitor to see and feel a true classical theatre: its acoustics, its lighting by day and night, and how the audiences moved in and out. Don't miss it.

Other ruins of a stadium, agora and basilica offer little to look at. Note, however, the arches and several towers of a long aqueduct out in the fields.

Selge & Köprülü Kanyon

About six km east of the Aspendos road along the main highway, a road on the left (north) is marked for Beşkonak, Selge and Köprülü Kanyon Milli Park (Bridge Canyon National Park). The road is good for the first 40 km to the town of Beşkonak but deteriorates thereafter. There is a famous **Roman Bridge** over the canyon of the Köprü Irmağı (Bridge River, anciently called the Eurymedon) some six km beyond Beşkonak. Across the bridge and another km along over a very rough track are the ruins of ancient Selge, now partly occupied by a small Turkish village. Though the theatre is well preserved, the rest of the city is badly ruined, but the setting, high in this mountainous country, is spectacular.

SİDE

Cleopatra and Marc Antony chose Side (SEE-deh, population 1500) as the spot for a romantic tryst, and today lots of Turkish couples follow their example. Side has everything: a km of fine sand beach on either side, good Hellenistic ruins, an excellent little museum and a Turkish village.

It is perhaps too good. In recent years Side has been overrun by tourists in the summer months, mostly from Ankara but also from Germany and Britain. During the season even moving down the streets can be difficult. The quaint main street is now lined with carpet and clothing shops, some with air-cons roaring and venting their hot blasts into the street. In summer this is no longer a tranquil seaside village. In spring and autumn the town is quieter and less crowded however, and the swimming is still excellent.

History

Ancient Side's great wealth was built on piracy and slavery. Many of its great buildings were raised with the profits of such dastardly activities. Slavery flourished only under the Greeks and was stopped when the city came under Roman control.

No-one knows where Side got its name, though it probably means 'pomegranate' in some ancient Anatolian language. The site was colonised by Aeolians about 600 BC but by the time Alexander the Great swept through, the inhabitants had abandoned much of their Greek culture and language.

After the period of piracy and slave-trading, Side turned to legitimate commerce and still prospered. Under the Byzantines it was still large enough to rate a bishop. The Arab raids of the 7th century AD diminished the town, which was dead within two centuries, but it revived in the late 19th century under the Ottomans.

Orientation

Side is several km south of the east-west highway. The road to the village is littered with trashy signs and billboards and is dotted with little hotels and pensions, often bearing signs which read *Boş Oda Var* ('Rooms Available'). The road passes through the archaeological zone and past the museum, beneath an arch and around the theatre before ending at a barrier by a car park. In high season you will not be allowed to drive a car into the village proper. You must pay a fee and park in the car park, which is also Side's bus terminal.

Information

The Tourism Information Office (tel (3213) 1265) is somewhat inconveniently located on the outskirts of the village on the road out to the highway, a walk of about one km.

The Ruins

Side's impressive ruins are an easy walk from the village. Look first at the **theatre**, one of the largest in Anatolia, with 15,000 seats. Originally constructed during Hellenistic times, it was enlarged under the Romans.

Next to the theatre and across the road from the museum is the **agora**. The **museum** is built on the site of the Roman baths. It has a very fine small collection of statuary and reliefs. Opening hours are 8 am to 5.15 pm daily; admission is US$1.50.

To the east, between these buildings and the Hellenistic city walls, lie a

Byzantine basilica and some foundations of Byzantine houses. Down at the edge of the eastern beach is another agora.

At the very southern tip of the point of land upon which Side lies are two temples, the **Temple of Athena** and **Temple of Apollo**, which date from the 2nd century AD. Who knows that Cleopatra and Marc Antony didn't meet at exactly this spot? Though they met (42 BC) before these great columns (some of limestone, newly erected) were standing, might they not have sat in earlier marble temples to enjoy one of Side's spectacular sunsets? Wandering among these marble remains at dusk is one of the finest things to do here.

Horseback Riding
The Özcan Atlı Spor Kulübü (Equestrian Sport Club) (tel 1230), on the road to the motels on the western beach, has horses you can ride.

Manavgat
The larger town five km to the north and east is a farmers' market and commercial town. Its **Manavgat Şelalesi** (waterfall) is famous and has a cool, shady teahouse by it. About six km past the falls are the ruins of the ancient city of Seleucia, with many buildings still recognisable.

Places to Stay
You may have difficulty finding a room in high summer so try to arrive early in the day. Before May and after early October you should have no problem finding the lodgings you want, but the 'tourist season' lasts from April to October these days. Prices are highest from June to September, slightly lower in April, May and October, and much lower in winter at the few places which remain open.

Places to Stay – bottom end
In the village proper, little pensions abound. There are dozens to choose from and your choice is dictated by availability as much as price. I can't help you much

with these because ownership and facilities change every season to a surprising degree. Prices depend upon season, demand, facilities, and even your nationality, and range from US$10 to US$15 for double rooms with running water; some have private showers.

The *Şen Pansiyon* (Shen) is a simple place on a quiet street not far from the water. A good one near the eastern beach is the *Martı* (mahr-TUH). Some readers of this book have enjoyed the *Çiğdem* and the small wooden bungalows at the İkimiz. *Heaven's Gate Pension* has cheap triple rooms with toilet and shower. As you comb the town for good lodgings look for little signs which say Boş Oda Var.

Camping
There are camp grounds on the road into town from the main highway, and along the roads going to motels on the western beach.

Places to Stay – middle
The *Huzur Yasemin Motel* (tel 1023) is very pleasant, with lots of rooms (US$36 for a double with breakfast) in a modern building topped by a wonderful, airy rooftop restaurant and café. Similar in some ways is the *Köseoğlu Otel* (kurr-SEH-oh-loo) (tel 1110, 1166), on the other side of the village. It's a glorified pension with simple modern rooms priced at US$42 a double with private shower, breakfast included. This rate drops by about 30% if demand is not great.

Near the Köseoğlu is the *Sidemara Motel* (tel 1083), not far from the eastern beach. Double rooms with private shower go for US$34 to US$38, breakfast included.

Side has a few comfortable motels on its western beach, among which the best is the *Motel Side* (tel 1022). Close to the village, attractive and with a pretty patio restaurant, the motel charges US$30 for a double room, breakfast and dinner included.

Other motels along the western beach

are reached by a road going west, outside the antique city walls. Lodgings here include the *Subaşı Motel* (SOO-bah-shuh) (tel 1215, 1047), one of the first places you come to along this road. The location is good as it's only a 15-minute walk to the village, and the motel's rooms (with balconies) face east and west to take full advantage of beach views, sunrises and sunsets. Two people pay US$42 for a double room with bath and breakfast. If the Subaşı is full, the nearby *Temple Motel* (tel 1119, 1414) is the place to check next. It's considerably cheaper at US$22 a double but is not right on the beach.

Places to Stay - top end

Among the several luxury hotels which have sprung up around Side in recent years, my favourite is the five-star, 154-room *Hotel Asteria* (tel 1830; fax 1830; in İstanbul, make reservations at Halitağa Caddesi, Ekşioğlu İş Hanı, Kat 1 No 52, Kadıköy) (tel (1) 338-4870, 337-4885, 338-9454), about three km north-west of the village proper, on the western beach. Set on a rise overlooking the beach and the sea, the hotel's extensive grounds are fenced and kept private. Between the hotel and the beach are swimming pools, sunning areas, bars and cafés, and lots of equipment for water sports. Rooms have good quality furnishings, mini-bar, TV, private baths with marble vanities and both tubs and showers. Each room has a 'lanai', or patio, with chairs and table, and plants. Ask for a room with an eastern sea view. The hotel's restaurant is excellent, and a casino with one-armed bandits will take your money if you like. Rates are US$135/175 for a single/double, breakfast included.

Places to Eat

When looking for a pension, ask about cooking facilities. Most have them and this allows you to make substantial savings. At the motels you may be required to buy at least two meals a day, so the food problem is solved that way

whether you like it or not. As for cheap restaurants, there aren't any. The names, prices, staff and quality of food change every season.

The better restaurants in town tend to be expensive for what you get. An exception is the *Kalamar*, which has reasonably good food at decent prices considering the pleasant garden-terrace atmosphere with lamps glowing inside basket shades. You can usually get a good full meal here (perhaps including octopus, squid or fish) for US$6 to US$9, drinks included.

For a gratifying lunch or romantic dinner try the very pleasant *Afrodit Restaurant* (tel 1171) at the beach end of the main street. A large place with lots of garden terrace dining tables, the Afrodit usually has a very good selection of mezes and salads, as well as fish. To eat lightly and cheaply, order three or four meze plates with bread and a drink. If you go for fish, remember to ask prices; they speak English and German here. The average meal costs around US$10 per person.

The *Nergiz Tea Garden & Cocktail Place*, at the beach end of the main street, is excellent for a cool rakı in the evening while watching the sunset and the fishing and excursion boats come in.

Ask your pension *hanım* (lady) for tips on other current restaurant favourites.

Getting There & Away

Bus Side, 75 km east of Antalya, is so popular as a resort that it has its own direct bus service to Ankara, İzmir and İstanbul. The numerous buses which run along the coast between Antalya and Alanya will drop you in Side or in Manavgat, the town on the highway. From Manavgat dolmuşes frequently travel the few km down to the shore.

To catch the bus eastward to Alanya you may find it best to take a dolmuş from Side to the highway junction or to Manavgat.

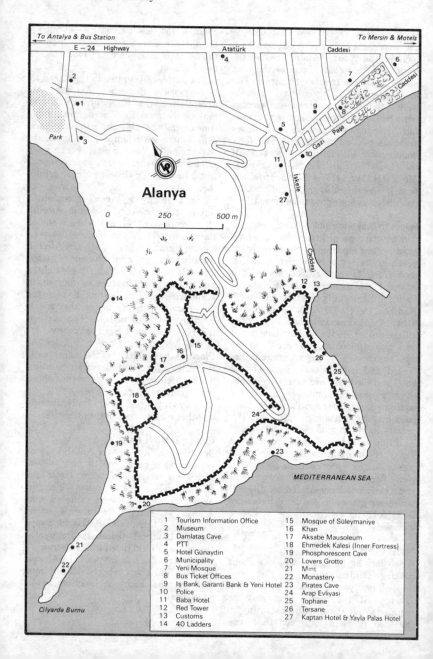

Alanya

To Antalya & Bus Station
E – 24 Highway
Atatürk
Caddesi
To Mersin & Motels
Park
Gazi Paşa Caddesi
İskele Caddesi
0   250   500 m
MEDITERRANEAN SEA
Cılyarda Burnu

1	Tourism Information Office	15	Mosque of Süleymaniye
2	Museum	16	Khan
3	Damlataş Cave	17	Aksabe Mausoleum
4	PTT	18	Ehmedek Kalesi (Inner Fortress)
5	Hotel Günaydın	19	Phosphorescent Cave
6	Municipality	20	Lovers Grotto
7	Yeni Mosque	21	Mint
8	Bus Ticket Offices	22	Monastery
9	İş Bank, Garanti Bank & Yeni Hotel	23	Pirates Cave
10	Police	24	Arap Evliyasi
11	Baba Hotel	25	Tophane
12	Red Tower	26	Tersane
13	Customs	27	Kaptan Hotel & Yayla Palas Hotel
14	40 Ladders		

EAST TO ALANYA

The journey from Manavgat to Alanya is 60 km and takes about an hour. About 12 km east of Manavgat a highway heads north up to the Anatolian plateau and Konya (280 km) via Akseki, twisting its way through an endless expanse of mountains. Though the road appears on the map to be far shorter than that via Antalya or Silifke, it has some narrow, winding stretches where you can drive only very slowly; buses do not take this route because of the curves. However, the scenery is spectacular and it is an area rarely seen by tourists. Soon you should be able to choose this route to Konya, as great efforts are being made to widen and straighten the highway through the mountains. At present it can take six hours to reach Konya by this route; soon it may be down to four.

Back on the road heading east the coastal highway skirts good sandy beaches virtually the whole way to Alanya. Here and there a modern motel, posh holiday village or government rest camp has been built to exploit the holiday potential. On the landward side you see the occasional bit of aqueduct or the foundations of some old caravanserai or baths. Thirteen km before Alanya notice the Şarapsa Hanı, a Seljuk caravanserai reportedly about to be turned into yet another raucous disco. Another one, the Alarahan, is accessible (30 km) by a side road heading north.

ALANYA

The Seljuk Turks built a powerful empire, the Sultanate of Rum (ROOM, Rome), which thrived from 1071 to 1243. Its capital was in Konya, but its prime port was Alanya.

Like Side, Alanya (ah-LAHN-yah, population 50,000) occupies a point of land flanked by two great sweeping beaches. Once a pleasant, sleepy small agricultural and tourist town, Alanya has been heavily affected by the recent tourism boom. With its wide swath of sandy beach stretching more than six km eastward from the town, it has the potential for becoming Turkey's Miami, and it is rushing to achieve that status. The pleasant, sleepy character of the town has been driven out by an army of construction workers, cement trucks and lofty cranes as Alanyans struggle to keep up with the soaring demand for hotel rooms, holiday villas and condominiums.

Orientation

The bus station is on the coastal highway (Atatürk Caddesi) three km west of the centre. It is served by city buses which take you into town every half-hour for US$0.20. You can buy bus tickets in town at the open lot from which dolmuşes leave.

Information

The Tourism Information Office (tel (323) 11240), Çarşı Mahallesi, Kalearkası Caddesi, is at the north-western foot of the promontory, near the Alanya Müzesi and Damlataş cave. City buses to the top of the promontory depart from the office every hour.

Seljuk Sites

Head for the Seljuk sites early in the day as Alanya gets very hot in summer. Walk down to the harbour for a look at the **Red Tower** (Kızıl Kule, KUH-zuhl koo-leh), constructed in 1226 in the reign of the Seljuk Sultan Alaeddin Keykubad I by a Syrian Arab architect. The five-storey octagonal tower, now restored to its former glory, was the key to Alanya's harbour defences. Past it, out toward the sea, a path leads to the old Seljuk **Tersane**, or shipyard (1228).

Fortress

Alanya's most exciting historical site is of course the fortress (kale, KAH-leh) atop the promontory, reached by hourly city bus from the Tourism Information Office. Otherwise it's a very hot one-hour walk (three km), or take a taxi (US$5); with your own car you can drive right up to the fort.

The ancient city was enclosed by the rambling wall (1226) which makes its way all around the peninsula. At the top is the **Ehmedek Kalesi**, the inner fortress. From the İç Kale (EECH-kah-leh, inner fort or keep) you get a dazzling view of the peninsula, walls, town and great expanses of beautiful coast backed by the blue Taurus Mountains.

Boat Excursions

You can hire a boat for an hour's coastal tour around the promontory, during which you'll approach several caves, including those called the **Lovers' Grotto** (Aşıklar Mağarası, ah-shuk-LAHR mah-ah-rah-suh), **Pirates' Cave** (Korsanlar Mağarası, kohr-sahn-LAHR), **Phosphorescent Cave** (Fosforlu, fohs-fohr-LOO) and **Cave of Dripping Stones** (Damlataş, DAHM-lah-tahsh), as well as **Cleopatra's Beach** on the west side of the promontory. To hire the entire boat for such a tour costs US$12 to US$15; a boat can take seven or eight passengers. By the way, Damlataş and Cleopatra's Beach are accessible on foot from the western side of the promontory, not far from the museum and the Tourism Information Office.

Museum

Alanya has a tidy little museum on the west side of the peninsula, near the Tourism Information Office on the way to Damlataş cave; it's open daily from 9 am to 6.30 pm and admission is US$1. Exhibits span the ages from Old Bronze through Greek and Roman to Ottoman. Don't miss the Ethnology Room at the back, with a fine assortment of kilims (woven mats), *cicims* (embroidered mats), Turkish carpets, wood and copper inlay work, gold and silver, and beautifully written and illuminated religious books.

Pages from an 18th-century Turkish prayer book

The Prophet's Rose Tree. The stamen is identified with God; the petals with the Prophet; the leaves with the Caliphs.

The Tree of Bliss. Planted by the Prophet in Paradise, it grows from the heavens towards earth.

Places to Stay

The most comfortable and luxurious lodgings are well out on the eastern beach, but they're inconvenient if you want to stroll in town. Downtown hotels are moderately priced or quite cheap.

Places to Stay – bottom end

Small hotels and pensions in the town rent rooms for as little as US$10 a double. My favourite is the Hotel Günaydın (gurnahy-DEEN) (tel 11943), Kültür Caddesi 30, in a quiet location a long block inland from the hotels along İskele Caddesi. Prices for a tidy room with shower are US$12/16 a single/double; breakfast is included. The warmth of the solar-heated water depends upon the sun and upon the level of demand.

Other choices are along İskele Caddesi on the way to the Red Tower. The Yayla Palas (YAHY-lah pah-LAHS) (tel 11017, 13544), a converted house at İskele Caddesi 48, has waterless rooms, some with sea views. It's been serving budget travellers for several decades. At the nearby Baba Hotel (tel 11032), İskele Caddesi 8, doubles without bath cost about the same; they also have some rooms with private shower. The tidy hotel at İskele Caddesi 12, (tel 12754), is a cut above its neighbours and charges a bit more for a double with bath (US$20).

If you can't find the room you want here, start from the Tourism Information Office and walk along the western beach, where there are several pensions charging US$5/10 for a single/double. Pensions on the eastern beach tend to charge twice as much.

Camping

The Perle Campground, back from the beach east of town (reached by dolmuş) is one of the better ones.

Places to Stay – middle

I prefer hotels in the centre of the town as they allow you to easily walk to restaurants and attractions. If you prefer

them too, head for the three-star Kaptan Otel (kahp-TAHN) (tel 12000, 11094), İskele Caddesi 62, very near the Red Tower. The modern 45-room hotel faces the harbour, town and beach; air-con singles cost US$32 to US$40, doubles are US$44 to US$55, breakfast included. The nearby, newer Bayırlı Hotel (tel 14320), İskele Caddesi 66, has 40 three-star rooms for similar prices. In the bazaar the Çınar Oteli and the Eren Oteli are very cheap.

The eastern beach holds several more three-star hotels, including the Banana Motel (tel 11548) at Cikcikli Köyü.

Places to Stay – top end

Alanya's most comfortable rooms are at the 300-room Club Alantur (ah-LAHN-toor) (tel 11224, 11924), Çamyolu Köyü, also sometimes called the Alantur Motel. It is six km east of the centre, has a good layout with lawns and gardens, sea views, tennis courts, sailboats, water-skiing equipment and a swimming pool. Comfortable air-con singles go for US$65 to US$75, doubles cost US$90 to US$110.

Places to Eat

Though Alanya has several inexpensive hazır yemek restaurants, you should have at least a few meals at one of the little waterfront restaurants along Gazi Paşa Caddesi in the centre. Walk along the street and you'll see the Şirin, Yönet and Havuzbaşı. A full lunch or dinner here costs about US$6 to US$9 per person. In the market streets off Gazi Paşa Caddesi are several even cheaper restaurants, including a very inexpensive pide and kebap place, the Konya Etli Pide ve Kebap Salonu. Here the price for a tuck-in drops to US$3. Another good one is the Saray Lokantası.

Readers have also liked the Blue Knight Restaurant, west of the Alaadin Hotel on the main road, overlooking the beach.

While you're here try a few of the local fish: levrek (sea bass), barbunya (red mullet) or kuzu balığı ('muttonfish').

An unusual treat is the local ice cream, made with flavours such as şeftali (peach), *kavun* (melon), *dut* (mulberry) and *sakız* (pine resin).

Getting There & Away

Bus Much of Alanya's bus traffic travels via Antalya and you may find yourself switching buses there. When the Manavgat to Beyşehir road is finally widened and straightened you can expect to find direct buses between Alanya and Konya, making the 340-km trip in about seven hours. Presently the trip takes 10 hours. Travel times and distances to other northern cities (Ankara, Nevşehir/Ürgüp) will be shortened by about three hours also.

Compared to the rest of Turkey, traffic is sparse eastward around the 'bulge' of Anamur. Few buses originate in Alanya so you have to rely on passing buses having empty seats, which they don't always have, so make your departure arrangements as far in advance as possible. Also keep in mind that the road eastward is mountainous and curvy and takes a good deal longer to traverse than you might think from looking at the map.

Some destinations include:

Adana – 440 km, 10 hours, US$9; eight buses daily in summer
Anamur – 135 km, three hours, US$3; several buses daily in summer
Antalya – 115 km, two hours, US$2; hourly buses in summer
İstanbul – 840 km, 17 hours, US$14; several buses daily, more from Antalya
İzmir – 660 km, 12 hours, US$12; via Antalya
Kaş – 300 km, seven hours, US$7; via Antalya
Konya – 480 km, 10 hours, US$9; via Antalya
Marmaris – 700 km, 11½ hours, US$10; via Antalya
Mersin – 375 km, 8½ hours, US$8; eight buses daily in summer
Silifke – 275 km, seven hours, US$6.50; eight buses daily in summer

Ürgüp – 600 km, 13 hours, US$12; via Antalya

Boats to Turkish Cyprus You can make arrangements in Alanya to catch a ferry to northern Cyprus. Boats leave from Taşucu, just west of Silifke, 265 km east of Alanya. At Alanya's Otogar you can make a boat reservation and also buy a ticket for the very early morning bus from Alanya to the ferry docks. For more information on these boats, see the Taşucu section.

ALANYA TO SİLİFKE

From Alanya you may want to head north to Konya, Cappadocia and Ankara. The eastern Mediterranean coast has a few sights of interest, but the cities of Mersin, Tarsus, Adana and İskenderun have very little to hold your interest. Agriculture, commerce and shipping, not the tourist trade, are what keep them going.

From Alanya to Silifke is 275 km along a twisting road cut into the cliffs which rise steeply from the sea. Every now and then the road passes through the fertile delta of a stream, planted with bananas or figs. Views of the sea and stretches of cool evergreen forest are nice but there's little else to look at until Anamur.

This region was called Cilicia by the ancients, a somewhat forbidding part of the world because of the mountains. Anyone wanting to conquer Cilicia had to have a navy, as the only practicable transport was by sea. If you just had a ship, you were in for it as this coast was a favourite lair of pirates. In the late 1960s the Turks put the finishing touches on a good paved road stretching from Alanya to Silifke. Though this has opened the country to progress considerably, transport is still slow, though the going is scenic.

Anamur

Anamur (AH-nah-moor, population 32,000), at the southernmost point along the Turkish coast, is near the ruined Byzantine city of Anamurium, which you should see, south-west of the town on the beach. To the east of the town are two Crusader castles also worth a look: the Mamure Kalesi and the Softa Kalesi. Each of these points of interest has a handy beach close by.

Orientation The town itself is to the north of the highway (one km to the main square) but it has a beachside 'suburb' two km south of the highway. The Otogar is at the junction of the highway and the main street north of the main square. To reach the beach head east a short distance and turn right (south) at the signs; the beach is two km down the road.

Anamurium The ruins of Anamurium are 8½ km west of the centre of the modern town of Anamur. Coming down from the Cilician mountains the highway finally reaches some level ground and a straight section. At this point, six km from the main square in Anamur, a road on the right (south) is marked for the ruins. Another 2½ km brings you past fields and through the ruins to a dead end at the beach. There is no regular dolmuş service to the ruins; you will probably have to take a taxi.

Founded by the Phoenicians, Anamurium flourished through the Roman period. Its Golden Age may have been around 250 AD, after which it lost some importance, but nothing like what it was about to lose. When the Arab armies stormed out of Arabia in the 7th century they raided and pillaged this coast, including Anamurium. Despite its mighty walls and remote location, the city fell. It never recovered from the devastation and no-one was interested in settling here afterwards.

Had new settlers come, they doubtless would have torn down these old buildings and used the cut stones to build their own houses, stores, wharves and bridges, as they did everywhere until this century. Anamurium escaped this pillage and today it is an authentic Byzantine ghost town, with dozens of buildings perched eerily on this rocky hillside above an unsullied pebble beach. Churches, aqueducts, houses and defensive walls stand silent and empty, their roofs caved in but their walls largely intact. It's quite surprising that Anatolia's earthquakes did so little damage.

Anamurium's **baths** are well-preserved, even to some of the wall decoration; many of the tombs in the **necropolis** have traces of decoration as well.

Mamure Kalesi Seven km east of Anamur, just off the highway, stands Mamure Kalesi – you can't miss it. There has been a fortress at this point since the 3rd century AD, but the present structure dates from the time of the Crusades when it was used by the Crusader rulers of Cyprus, and later the emirs of Karaman. The Ottomans took over in the middle of the 15th century and kept the castle in good repair until the empire ended in this century. The fortifications, with crenellated walls and towers, are very impressive. You can visit every day from 8 am to 5 or 6 pm; entry is US$1.

Softa Kalesi Heading east from Anamur, 2¾ km past the Mamure Kalesi, is a new harbour (a yacht marina?), and four km east of the harbour the town of **Bozyazı**, a town spread, like Anamur, on a fertile alluvial plain backed by rugged mountains. Eastward across the plain, clearly visible as you travel, is the Softa Kalesi, surrounded by the little hamlet of **Çubukkoyağı**. As you leave Bozyazı, a road on the left (north, inland) is marked for the Softa Kalesi, perched atop its rocky crag and looming over the highway. This castle, built by the Armenian kings who ruled Cilicia for a short while during the Crusades, is now fairly ruined inside but the walls and situation are still quite impressive. From the Softa Kalesi it's 20 km west back to Anamur, or 140 km east to Silifke.

Places to Stay There are cheap pensions and camp grounds near each of the three points of interest. On the road to ancient Anamurium you pass the *Alper Pension* and the *Anamuryum Pension & Restaurant*, open in summer only. Down on the beach (bear left at the Alper Pension and go 650 metres) is the fancy *Anamuryum Mocamp* for campers. Prices are the standard US$4 or US$5 per person, depending upon season and demand.

Just across the road from the Mamure Kalesi is the *Mamure Pension*, a tidy place which is handy but suffers from road noise. To the east of the castle in the next 1½ km are lots more little pensions. Staying at one of these allows you to visit the castle and take a swim from the same base. Exactly 1½ km east of the castle is the *Pullu Orman İçi Dinlenme Yeri*, a forest camp ground operated by the General Directorate of Forests. The cost is US$1 for a tent, US$2 for a caravan, plus US$0.40 per person. There is a fine sandy beach just below.

On the little cove beneath the Softa Kalesi are several little pensions, some condominiums and the *Alinko Motel*.

Down at Anamur beach, due south of the town, are numerous little pensions and camp grounds. The configuration changes every few months as new construction gets under way. The one-star *Dragon Motel* (tel (7571) 1572), İskele Caddesi, has 35 rooms with shower in little bungalows set amid evergreens on the beach, for which the charge is US$24/36 for a single/double, breakfast included. The *Hotel Dolfin* is a bit newer, and by the time you arrive there will be several places newer still.

In the town of Anamur itself the *Hotel Saray* (tel 1191), Tahsin Soylu Caddesi, near the Otel Alahan, is simple and cheap, with cleanish rooms for US$14 a double.

The fanciest place in town is the fairly simple two-star *Otel Anahan* (tel 3511/2), Tahsin Soylu Caddesi 109, Anamur, İçel.

It has 22 fairly comfy rooms (with balcony and private shower) reached by a marble staircase (no lift), a restaurant and a café-bar. It's one km east of the main square, 1½ km from the Otogar, and almost three km from the beach.

Places to Eat Many pensions provide meals, as do the hotels and motels. A few metres south of the main square is the *Bulvar Restaurant*. It's nothing fancy, but it provides food.

Getting Around Anamur is spread out and somewhat difficult to get around if you haven't got your own wheels. To get to Anamurium, ask at the bus station; sometimes drivers going a longer distance will drop you at the crossroads, from where it's 1½ km to the archaeological zone entrance. A taxi will no doubt run you out to the ruins, wait for an hour, and run you back into town for US$4 or US$5.

During the summer there are sometimes dolmuşes to the beach south of Anamur, and you may also be able to hitch here. East of Anamur the transport situation brightens as there are frequent dolmuşes to Bozyazı from the Anamur Otogar. You can use these to visit the Mamure Kalesi, the Softa Kalesi and the beach.

East to Silifke

From Anamur it's 160 km to Silifke. The highway winds up into the mountains again, and then winds on and on, occasionally dipping down to another alluvial valley with its requisite farming hamlet and semi-tropical crops. If you'd like to climb into the mountains and see yet another mediaeval castle, turn left (north) a few km east of Gilindire and head up toward **Gülnar** (25 km) for a look at the **Meydancık Kalesi**, which has stood here in one form or another since Hittite times.

After interminable curves and switchbacks the highway finally comes down from the cliffside to the Cilician Plain, the fertile littoral at the foot of the Taurus

Mountains which stretches from Silifke to Adana. Before coming to Silifke proper, you pass its port of Taşucu, from where ferries and hydrofoils depart for Turkish Cyprus.

Taşucu

Taşucu (TAHSH-oo-joo) lives for the ferries. This pleasant little village has always been the port for Silifke. Hotels put up voyagers, and car ferries and hydrofoils take them to and fro across the sea.

Orientation The main square by the ferry dock has a PTT, a customs house, a Tourism Information Office (tel (7593) 1234), various shipping offices and a few restaurants. It's only a few dozen metres south of the highway. The village bazaar is east of the main square.

Places to Stay About the cheapest is the *Işık Otel* (tel 1026), Atatürk Caddesi, an old waterfront building facing the main square with rooms for US$10 a double without running water. It's right next door to a *pavyon* (Turkish nightclub) and thus may be noisy.

The *Hotel Fatih* (tel 1125, 1248) is better. It's on the highway behind the Gümrük only metres from the square. Rooms have private showers, little balconies and prices of US$18/26/34 a single/double/triple, though you can haggle them down out of season. There's a restaurant as well.

You may have noticed two fancy motels on the highway as you approached Taşucu. The *Lades Motel* (tel 1008, 1190) is the older of the two. It is also comfortable and commodious with a swimming pool, a wading pool for children, a playground, a restaurant and rooms with private bath. Many rooms also have balconies looking right out to the ferry dock directly below.

The *Taştur Motel* (tel 1045, 1090, 1290), a hundred metres west of the Lades, has 54 quite comfortable rooms with private

showers and sea-view balconies furnished with table and chairs. Public spaces include a dramatic restaurant and terrace, a lobby, and a bar all done in sea blues with bits of nautical decoration. A small garden reaches down to the seashore beyond the large swimming pool and the smaller children's pool. Rates in summer are US$50/66 for a single/double, breakfast included.

Places to Eat The *Denizkızı Restaurant* (mermaid), opposite the bust of Atatürk in the main square, is the favourite of the locals at lunch and dinner, and is fairly cheap. The fancy *Baba Restaurant* (tel 1210) adjoining the Taştur Motel has good views of the harbour, good fish and moderate prices (about US$6 for a meat meal, US$8 or more for fish).

Boats to Cyprus Passenger boats to Kyrenia (Girne, Turkish Federated Republic of Northern Cyprus) depart from Taşucu, 11 km west of Silifke's Otogar.

The air-con, 250-passenger MV *Barbaros*, a deniz otobüsü, is operated by Kıbrıs Express (tel 1434, 1334), Atatürk Caddesi 82. It departs Taşucu on the two-hour voyage to Kyrenia daily at 11.30 am, returning from Kyrenia at 2.30 pm. Tickets cost US$18 one way, US$32 round trip; children less than four years of age travel free, those from five to 12 pay US$13 one way. There is a Cypriot port tax which is added to your fare. The *Barbaros* has a snack bar but no restaurant so bring your own supplies. Tickets are on sale at the Kıbrıs Express office on Taşucu's main square.

Tickets are also sold at Mersin Seyahat (tel (741) 18789, 13644) at ticket counter 5 in Mersin's new bus station. Direct Mersin to Taşucu buses depart daily at 8.30 am, arriving in Taşucu in time for the *Barbaros'* departure. Other Kıbrıs Express offices are in Kyrenia at İskenderun Caddesi 4 (tel (581) 53-544, 52-900); in Mersin at İnönü Bulvarı, Güvenç İş

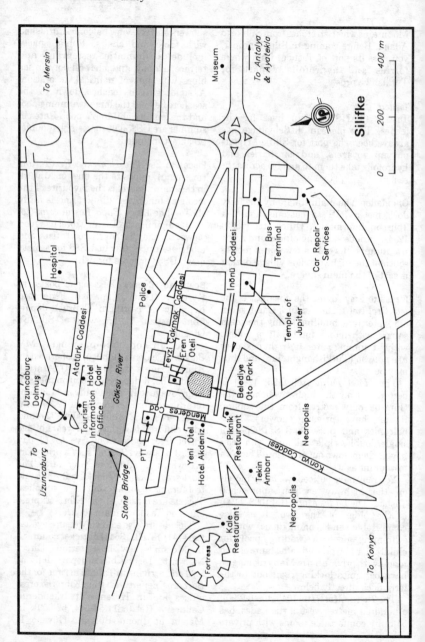

Silifke

Merkezi 10 (tel (741) 16731, 11550); and in Lefkoşa (Nicosia, Turkish Cyprus) across from the İş Bankası.

For the car ferry, tickets cost less but the trip is longer. The Ertürk company operates boats at midnight on Sunday, Monday, Tuesday, Wednesday and Thursday, arriving Kyrenia the next day at 7.30 am. From Kyrenia the ferries depart at 12 noon on Monday, Tuesday, Wednesday, Thursday and Friday, arriving in Taşucu at 4 pm. Tickets cost US\$22 one way, US\$33 round trip. Buy your tickets at Fatih Ferryboat (tel 1249, 1386) in Taşucu's main square, or at these offices: in Kyrenia (tel (081) 54880, 54977, 52840); in Lefkoşa call the Jen-Tur agency (tel (020) 78824).

Getting Around Dolmuşes run between Taşucu and Silifke's Otogar frequently throughout the day. The Silifke terminus is not the Otogar proper, but a petrol station across the road from it.

SİLİFKE

Silifke (see-LEEF-keh, population 25,000) is the ancient Seleucia, founded by Seleucus I Nicator in the 3rd century BC. Seleucus was one of Alexander the Great's most able generals and founder of the Seleucid dynasty which ruled ancient Syria after Alexander's death.

Silifke's other claim to fame is as the place where Emperor Frederick I Barbarossa (1125-1190), while leading his troops on the Third Crusade, drowned in the river. What an end for a soldier!

A striking castle dominates the town from a Taurus hillside and promises good sightseeing. To many people, however, Silifke is just a place to catch the boat to Cyprus or a bus to Mersin, Adana or Konya.

Orientation

The bus terminal is near the junction of highways to Alanya, Mersin and Konya. From the bus terminal into the centre of the town is exactly one km; at the half-

way mark you pass the Temple of Jupiter.

The town is divided by the Göksu River, called the Calycadnus in ancient times. Most of the services are on the southern bank of the river, along with the bus station. Exceptions are the Tourism Information Office, several hotels and the dolmuş to Uzuncaburç, which are on the river's northern bank.

Information

Silifke's Tourism Information Office (tel (7591) 1151) is at Atatürk Caddesi 1/2, on the traffic roundabout just at the northern end of the bridge across the river. The staff speak some English and French and have interesting material on Silifke and its history.

Sights in Town

The fortress on the hill dates from mediaeval times. From the hilltop you can gaze down at the **Tekir Ambarı**, an ancient cistern some 46 metres long, 23 metres wide and 12 metres deep, carved from the rock. A circular stone staircase provides access to what was an important feature of the ancient city's water supply. To get to the Tekir Ambarı from the junction of İnönü and Menderes Caddesis, walk up the hill on the street to the left of the Emlak Kredi Bankası. Perhaps the most striking ruin is that of the **Temple of Jupiter**, which dates from the 2nd or 3rd century AD.

Cave of St Thecla

Another site of interest for those up on their biblical lore is the cave of St Thecla. The saint (Ayatekla in Turkish) is known as St Paul's first Christian convert. She was also the first woman to be threatened with death for the young faith. An outcast from family and society, legend has it that she retreated to a cave outside present-day Silifke, where she pursued good works, particularly healing the sick. The Byzantines built a church over the cave in her honour in 480 AD. The site is four km from the Otogar in Silifke, south past the museum, then to the right up a narrow road. Rubble from the Byzantine settlement is scattered over a large area. Ruins of the basilica and a nearby cistern are evident, but the entrance to the cave is not. As soon as you arrive (probably by taxi or on foot), a guardian will appear, sell you a ticket (US$1) and unlock the iron gate to the cave. In it are several vaulted chambers, some arches and columns. It's exciting if you are a fan of the saint.

Uzuncaburç

The ancient temple-city of Olbia, 28 km north of Silifke, was renamed Diocaesarea in Roman times and is now called Uzuncaburç. The place began its history (as far as we know) as a centre of worship to Zeus Olbius. It was ruled by a dynasty of priest-kings, who also managed the ceremonies in the large temple and arranged for the burial of many devout visitors, some of them quite wealthy.

You can take a dolmuş to the site, but then you have the problem of getting back to Silifke; dolmuşes are not frequent. You might decide to find a few other explorers and hire a taxi (US$6 to US$8 for the car, for the round trip, waiting time included).

Because it was a holy place, many people wanted to be buried near it, and you will see lots of curious tombs on your detour into the mountains. Only eight km up the road from Silifke you encounter the first group of tombs, and at 8.7 km the Twin Monument Tombs (Çifte Anıt Mezarları) in the village of Demircili, plainly visible from the road. Turn right at 22.7 km and proceed through a lovely pine forest to the archaeological site, just over 28 km from Silifke. Entry costs US$2. A village girl will find you out and sell you a ticket.

From the car park you enter the site along a colonnaded way, passing the famous Temple of Zeus Olbius on your left. The temple, among the earliest (circa 300 BC) examples of Corinthian architecture, was converted to a church by the Byzantines, who removed its central portion (cella) for this purpose. Just past the temple, on the right, is a city gate, after which you come to the Temple of Tyche (circa 100 BC).

Along a road leaving the right side of the car park is the city tower. Other ruins hidden among the undergrowth include a Roman theatre and a temple-tomb.

There is a small restaurant at the site, the Burç, but no lodgings, though I expect that simple pensions will open at some time in the future.

If you are driving you may be curious about what lies farther along the road. You can indeed continue via Kırobası to Mut and thus to Konya. Winding up into the forests you may pass huge stacks of logs cut by the Tahtacılar, the mountain wood-cutters who are a breed apart. About 40 km before coming to Mut the road skirts a fantastic limestone canyon which extends for quite a number of km. High above in the limestone cliffs are caves which seem to have been inhabited at one time or another. The land in the valleys here is rich and well-watered, exploited by diligent farmers. The air is cool, clean and sweet.

Other Sights

The Archaeological Museum is not far from the bus terminal, and includes a large number of Hellenistic coins and several mosaics, among many other exhibits from the area's deep and eventful past.

The town's mosques include the Ulu Camii, originally constructed by the Seljuks but much modified, and the Reşadiye Camii, an Ottoman work. The bridge across the river, which you cross to reach the Tourism Information Office, was originally built in Roman times.

Places to Stay

There are very comfortable motels along the highway at Taşucu, 11 km west of Silifke. In Silifke proper the hotels are much more modest. As this is a transportation junction, hotels can fill up.

Arrive early in the day or, better yet, make your connection and head out of town the same day.

The *Hotel Akdeniz* (AHK-deh-neez) (tel 1285), Menderes Caddesi 96, is at the western end of İnönü Caddesi. Simple but presentable, it charges US$7 for a double without private bath, or US$9 for a double with private shower. The *Hotel Taylan* next door is similar. Menderes Caddesi was formerly named Mut Caddesi and may still be called that by locals.

The nearby *Eren Oteli* (eh-REHN) (tel 1289) is in a quiet location north of İnönü Caddesi. It charges US$7/11 for a single/double room with private shower.

Across the river on the north side is the *Hotel Çadır* (tel 1244, 2449), Gazi Mahallesi, Atatürk Caddesi 8, which currently can boast of being this town's finest hotel. In the past comfort and style were not its hallmarks but renovations are underway and the future promises better. Its situation, overlooking the river, is pleasant and convenient. Rates are US$20 to US$22 for a double room with shower.

Places to Eat

The best place in town at my last visit (not counting the seaside restaurants in Taşucu and other shoreline enclaves) was the *Piknik Restaurant* (tel 2810), İnönü Caddesi 17, at the corner with Menderes Caddesi in the centre of town. They provide ready food or grills for about US$3 or US$4 per person.

Up near the fort on the hilltop above the town is the aptly named *Kale Restaurant* (tel 1521), right at the upper end of the road. It's a wonderful place for lunch or dinner in summer, with meals costing US$6 to US$8 per person.

Getting There & Away

Bus Being at the junction of the coastal highway and the road into the mountains and up to the plateau, Silifke is an important transportation point with pretty good bus service.

Frequent dolmuşes to Taşucu for the Cyprus ferries depart frequently from a Mobil fuel station across the highway from the bus station.

Dolmuşes north to Uzuncaburç depart from near the Tourism Information Office at 11 am and 12 noon daily (but check these schedules at the Tourism Information Office).

The highway east from Silifke to Adana is well travelled by buses. The Silifke Koop company buses depart for Adana about every 20 minutes throughout the morning and afternoon and will stop to pick you up on the road should you be visiting one of the many archaeological sites east of town.

Some other likely destinations include:

Adana – 155 km, two hours, US$1.25; three buses per hour until early evening

Alanya – 275 km, seven hours, US$6.50; eight buses daily in summer

Ankara – 520 km (via Konya), eight hours, US$6.50; frequent buses daily

Antalya – 390 km, nine hours, US$8; eight buses daily in summer

Kızkalesi – 20 km, 30 minutes, US$0.65; three buses per hour

Konya – 260 km, 4½ hours, US$4; frequent buses daily

Mersin – 85 km, two hours, US$1.75; three buses per hour

Narlıkuyu – 23 km, 30 minutes, US$0.65; three buses per hour

Ürgüp (via Mersin) – 400 km, 6½ hours, US$6; several buses daily (change at Mersin)

SİLİFKE TO ADANA

East of Silifke the Cilician Plain opens to an ever-widening swath of arable land which allowed civilisation to flourish. The ruins come thick and fast until Mersin, where modern commerce and industrialisation takes over.

Susanoğlu is a holiday village 16 km east of Silifke with a very nice little beach, but also an enormous amount of construction underway. With all the condos for well-to-do Mersinli and Adanalı vacationers, there's little room for the passing traveller.

The wildly romantic castle offshore, about 20 km east of Silifke, is the **Maiden's Castle** (Kız Kalesi, KUHZ kah-leh-see); another, much more ruined castle, is near it on the shore. These two edifices account for many legends, but historically the castles were built by the Byzantines and later used by the Armenian kings with the support of the Crusaders. The castles and good beach are served by a few small restaurants, some pensions, camping areas and a motel or two.

Inland from the Kız Kalesi a road winds two km north-west up the mountainside to the **Caves of Heaven & Hell** (Cennet ve Cehennem). This limestone coast is riddled with caverns but the Cennet (jeh-NEHT) is among the most impressive. Little soft-drink and snack stands cluster at the top. Walk down a long path of many steps to reach the cavern mouth. Along the way notice the strips of cloth and paper tied to twigs and tree branches by those who have come to this 'mystical' place in search of cures. The bits of cloth and paper are reminders to a saint or spirit that a supplicant has asked for intercession. At the mouth of the cave are the ruins of a small Byzantine church. The cave is not lit so the immense mouth is about as far as you can go without a guide. Near Cennet is Cehennem (jeh-HEHN-nehm), or Hell, a deep gorge entered by a ladder.

The village of Narlıkuyu, on the seashore at the turning for Cennet ve Cehennem, has a few seaside restaurants, a little shop for snacks and necessities, a water pump, a little pension and the remains of a Roman bath (4th century AD) with a nice mosaic of the Three Graces – Aglaia, Thalia and Euphrosyne. Entry to the museum which protects the mosaic costs US$1. The fish restaurants here are very nice but surprisingly expensive; a little tea garden and kebapçı serves meals for much less.

Some 8½ km east of Kız Kalesi, at a place called Kumkuyu (KOOM-koo-yoo), is a turning to **Kanlıdivane**, the ruins of ancient Elaiussa-Sebaste-Kanytelis, which lie three km off the highway. The ancient city occupies a vast site around limestone caverns. As you ride the four km up into the hills the ruins become more prolific. The main part of the old city has many buildings, mostly in great ruin. The necropolis, with its tombs built as little temples, is interesting. If you have camping equipment you can make camp at Kumkuyu.

Back on the highway you see unmarked ruins at various points along the roadside, testifying to the long and confused history of the area. It served as a pathway between the Anatolian plateau and Syria.

Just before Mersin, at a place called Mezikli, is a turning on the right (south) to **Viranşehir**, the ancient Soles or Pompeiopolis. Two km down the road is a row of Corinthian columns in a field, while in the distance is part of an aqueduct; all date from the 3rd century AD.

MERSİN (İÇEL)

Mersin (mehr-SEEN, population 350,000), also called İçel (ee-CHEHL), is a modern city built less than half a century ago to give Anatolia a large port conveniently close to Adana and its agriculturally rich hinterland. It has several good hotels in each price range and can serve as an emergency stop on your way through.

Information

The Tourism Information Office (tel (741) 16358) is down near the docks, east of the park, at Yenimahalle, İnönü Bulvarı, Liman Giriş Sahası. Near the office is the stop for city buses going out to Viranşehir.

Places to Stay – bottom end

Downtown, several small hotels are at the centre of the action. The *Hotel Kent* (tel 11655), İstiklal Caddesi 51 near Kuvayi Milliye Caddesi, charges US$12 for a double with shower. The *Erden Palas*

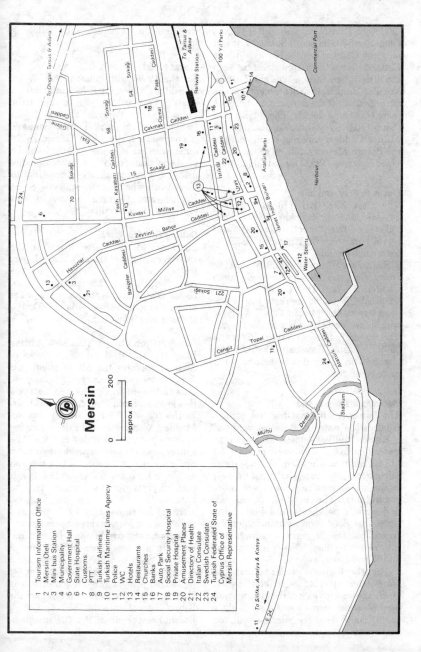

Mersin

0 — 200

approx m

1 Tourism Information Office
2 Mersin Oteli
3 Mini bus Station
4 Municipality
5 Government Hall
6 State Hospital
7 Customs
8 PTT
9 Turkish Airlines
10 Turkish Maritime Lines Agency
11 Police
12 WC
13 Hotels
14 Restaurants
15 Churches
16 Banks
17 Auto Park
18 Social Security Hospital
19 Private Hospital
20 Amusement Places
21 Directory of Health
22 Italian Consulate
23 Swedish Consulate
24 Turkish Federated State of
     Cyprus Office of
     Mersin Representative

To Silifke, Antalya & Konya

E 24

Oteli (ehr-DEHN pah-lahss) (tel 11329), Cami Şerifi Mahallesi, 3 Sokak 19, is just off Uray Caddesi east of Kuvayi Milliye Caddesi (follow the narrow street between the little square mosque and the Türkiye Vakıflar Bankası). Quiet except for the amplified call of the muezzin, it charges a mere US$9 for a double. The *Büyük Otel* (beur-YEURK) (tel 12606), on Kuvayi Milliye Caddesi only one block north of the deluxe Mersin Oteli, is a last resort place charging US$10 for a double.

Places to Stay – middle

The *Otel Ege* (EH-geh) (tel 21419), İstiklal Caddesi, 33 Sokak 24, is bright, folksy and fairly quiet. Decorated with lots of Turkish crafts, it charges US$28/36 for a single/double.

Rooms are cheaper but still good at the *Hosta Otel* (tel 14760), Fasih Kayabalı Caddesi 4, Yeni Hal Civarı, near the wholesale vegetable markets just a few blocks from the Mersin Oteli. A single with shower costs US$18, a double US$22. The two-star, 45-room *Sargın Hotel* (tel 35815), Fasih Kayabalı Caddesi 10, charges a bit more but provides somewhat more comfort.

Places to Stay – top end

The four-star *Mersin Oteli* (tel 21640), Gümrük Meydanı 112 at the seaward end of Kuvayi Milliye Caddesi, is down on the waterfront in the very centre of town. Its 116 air-con rooms have comfortable beds, refrigerator, private bath, mini-bar, telephone and balcony, and are quite comfortable. The location is central; underground parking is available nearby. Rates are US$50/66/86 for a single/double/triple, but they'll grant a reduction if they're not too busy. There's a restaurant on the hotel roof.

The other four-star place in town is the *Hotel Atlıhan* (tel 24153), İstiklal Caddesi 16, on the western side of the city, with 80 very pleasant rooms which cost slightly more than those at the Mersin Oteli. You can find the hotel easily by following its signs.

Places to Eat

Try the *Ali Baba Restaurant* (tel 33737), off Silifke Caddesi (one block inland from Atatürk Caddesi), on a little side street between the Türkiye Emlak Kredi Bankası and the Türk Ticaret Bankası; it's across from the Silifke Garajı. Fairly quiet, with bright lights, café chairs and a good selection of food, it is very reasonably priced with average meals costing US$3 to US$5 (somewhat more for seafood). Some English and German is spoken and seafood is the speciality.

Getting There & Away

Bus From Mersin's new Otogar on the eastern outskirts of the city buses depart for all points, including up to the Anatolian Plateau through the Cilician Gates. Distances, travel times and prices are similar to those from Adana, 70 km to the east over a fast four-lane highway.

Ferries to Cyprus & Syria Turkish Maritime Lines (tel 31513), down at the docks in Mersin, operates the MF *Yeşilada* car ferry service to Famagusta (Magosa, mah-GOS-sah) in Cyprus and Lattakia (Laskiye) in Syria from Mersin all year. Ferries depart Mersin at 10 pm on Monday, Wednesday and Friday arriving in Famagusta the next day at 8 am. The Friday departure arrives in Famagusta on Saturday at 8 am, departs at 11 pm and arrives in Lattakia at 7 am on Sunday. It then departs for the return trip to Famagusta at 12 noon on Sunday, arriving in Famagusta at 7 pm and departing for Mersin three hours later.

Fares for the trip between Mersin and Famagusta range from US$18 for a Pullman chair to US$36 per person for a luxury cabin; mid-range cabins rent for US$26 per person. The fare for an auto is US$18. Agents for the ferry service are the Kıbrıs Türk Denizcilik Şirketi Ltd, 3 Bülent Ecevit Bulvarı, PK 37, Famagusta (tel 65995); and the Lattakia Shipping Agencies Company, Port Said St, PO Box 28, Lattakia (tel 33163, 34263).

MERSİN TO ADANA

Transport between Mersin and Adana is fast and frequent, with buses leaving every few minutes. There are even some trains.

Going east, 27 km brings you to Tarsus, where St Paul was born almost 2000 years ago. There is very little left of old Tarsus – certainly not enough to stop for.

Three km east of Tarsus the E5 highway heads north through the Cilician Gates, a wide gap in the Taurus Mountains, to Ankara, Nevşehir and Kayseri.

ADANA

Turkey's fourth largest city, Adana (AH-dah-nah, population 950,000), is commercial. Its wealth comes from the intensely fertile Çukurova (CHOO-koor-oh-vah), the ancient Cilician Plain formed by the rivers Seyhan and Ceyhan, and by the traffic passing through the Cilician Gates. The city has grown rapidly and chaotically during the last few decades. Though the local people take pride in their city, many look upon it as an over-grown village – an adolescent metropolis.

Adana has one or two sights of touristic interest, but if you are not here on business you will find yourself in and out of town in no time. This is good, as Adana suffers from high humidity in summer and the clammy air doesn't cool off very much, even at night.

Orientation

The Seyhan River skirts the eastern edge of the city; the highway rushes right through the centre from west to east. Adana's airport (Şakirpaşa Havaalanı) is several km west of the centre on the highway. The bus station is in the eastern part of town, a 20-minute walk from the centre just north of the highway, on the west bank of the river. The railway station is at the northern end of Ziya Paşa Bulvarı,

several km north of the centre. The main commercial and hotel street is İnönü Caddesi; it will serve as your reference point for everything else in town.

Information

The Tourism Information Office (tel (71) 11 13 23) is at Atatürk Caddesi 13, a block north of İnönü Caddesi, in the centre of town.

Museums

Adana has a little gem of a museum, the **Adana Ethnography Museum** (Adana Etnoğrafya Müzesi; tel 22417), housed in a former church built by the Crusaders. Nicely restored, the building now houses displays of carpets and kilims, weapons, manuscripts, inscriptions and funeral monuments. Opening hours are 9 am to 12 noon and 1.30 to 5.30 pm, closed Monday; admission costs US$1. The museum is on a little side street off İnönü Caddesi, just to the left of the Adana Sürmeli Oteli.

Adana's other museum is the **Adana Regional Museum** (Adana Bölge Müzesi; tel 43856), beside the Otogar on the bank of the Seyhan just north of the east-west highway. Admission costs US$2, and hours are 8.30 am to 12.30 pm and 1.30 to 5.30 pm. It has lots of Roman statuary as the Cilician Gates were an important transit point even in Roman times.

Other Sights

Have a look at the long Taş Köprü, or **Roman bridge**, built by Hadrian and repaired by Justinian, which spans the Seyhan. Sullied by lots of modern traffic, it is impressive, though not romantic. The bridge is one long block south of the Regional Museum.

Places to Stay

Adana has lots of hotels in all classes. There are a few cheap emergency hotels near the Otogar but most of the mid-range and top-end hotels are downtown on İnönü Caddesi. There are no hotels near the airport or the railway station.

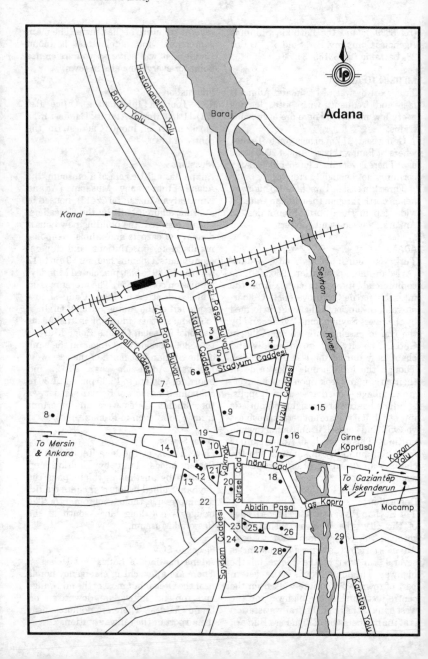

1	Railway Station
2	National Parks Office
3	American Consulate
4	Sports Arena
5	Turkish Airlines Office
6	Atatürk Park
7	Swimming Pool
8	Airport
9	Municipality (Belediye)
10	Tourism Information Office
11	Adana Sürmeli Oteli
12	Ethnographic Museum
13	Büyük Sürmeli Oteli
14	Otel İnci
15	Bus Station
16	Regional Museum
17	Cultural Centre
18	Atatürk Museum
19	Hotel Çavuşoğlu
20	Church
21	New Mosque (Yeni Cami)
22	Kemeraltı Camii
23	PTT
24	Yağ Camii
25	Clock Tower
26	Ulu Cami
27	Bazaar
28	Government House (Vilayet)
29	Hospital

Places to Stay - bottom end

The *Otel Köşk Palas* (KERSHK pah-lahss) (tel 13 72 15), at the corner of Türkkuşu Caddesi and Ordu Caddesi one block west of the Otogar, is a big old building on a back street well away from the intense traffic noise, yet conveniently close to the Otogar. The plain rooms contain nothing but beds and rent for US$5/8/11 a single/double/triple. To find it, leave the Otogar, cross the boulevard (Fuzuli Caddesi), turn left and look for a little sign pointing the way west (right) to the hotel.

The downtown hotels are more congenial and comfortable. They include the little *Mehtap Oteli* (mehh-TAHP) (tel 12 19 54), İnönü Caddesi, 123 Sokak 6, on a tiny street opposite the Adana Sürmeli Oteli. The entrance to the Mehtap is populated

with public scribes banging out citizens' petitions to the government. It's quiet here, yet central, and waterless rooms cost only US$3/5 a single/double.

The *Öz Otel* (EURZ) (tel 11 78 44), İnönü Caddesi 34, is right on the main street and so is noisy. Doubles without shower go for US$8, with shower for US$12.

Two hotels on İnönü Caddesi offer a good deal more comfort for a modest increase in price. The *Otel Duygu* (dooy-GOO) (tel 11 67 41), İnönü Caddesi 14/1, has a lift, a bar and rooms with private baths and fans for ·US$12/18 a single/ double. Nearby, the two-star, 84-room *Otel İpek Palas* (ee-PEHK) (tel 11 87 43), İnönü Caddesi 103, charges just US$12/16 for single/double rooms with private bath and ceiling fan.

Across the street from the prominent Büyük Sürmeli Oteli, the modest old *Pehlivan Palas* charges only US$10 for a huge old room with private bath, although there may be no hot water.

Places to Stay - middle

The 94-room *Otel İnci* (tel 15 83 68, 15 82 34), Kuruköprü Meydanı, Kurtuluş Caddesi, is rated at four stars, has two lifts, air-con and baths in the rooms, and offers a sauna and Turkish bath as well as the standard restaurant and bar. All rooms have natural wood trim and some come with TV and fridge. Prices in summer are a very reasonable US$30/38 for a single/ double.

The *Otel Çavuşoğlu* (tel 11 13 06), Ziyapaşa Bulvarı, Atilla Altıkat Köprüsü Yanı, is at the southern end of the overpass which spans the highway on Ziyapaşa Bulvarı, on the right-hand (east) side. Rated at two stars, the Çavuşoğlu has a restaurant, bar, nightclub, car park and decent rooms with bath for US$22/36 a single/double. Discounts are readily granted if they're not full.

If you're willing to spend a bit more you can get luxury at moderate prices; this is not a tourist town. The next-to-top place, with 116 air-con doubles officially priced at US$100, but discounted to as low as US$45, is the four-star *Adana Sürmeli Oteli* (tel 12 27 01), İnönü Caddesi 142. Its sister establishment behind it, the five-star, 210-room *Büyük Sürmeli Oteli* (bew-YEWK sewr-meh-LEE) (tel 12 19 44), is an even fancier place, with listed prices of US$120/160 a single/double, but discounts of up to 50% if they're not crowded.

My favourite in this class is the very pleasant (and therefore very popular, and often full) *Zaimoğlu Oteli* (zah-EEM-oh-loo) (tel 11 34 01), Özler Caddesi 72, between the two Sürmeli hotels. Opened in the summer of 1986, the Zaimoğlu charges US$45/57 for singles/doubles, US$68 for a suite and US$80 for an apartment, all with air-con, TV, mini-bar fridge and bath. These prices might be discounted somewhat if there are rooms to spare, however.

Places to Eat

If you like spicy food try Adana kebap, the local speciality. Ground lamb is mixed with hot pepper and wrapped around a flat skewer then grilled over charcoal. You'll find other Arab-inspired dishes as the Syrian influence is strong.

Once among the best places for Adana kebap, the *Yeni Onbaşılar Restorant* (yeh-NEE ohn-bah-shuh-LAHR) (tel 11 41 78), on Atatürk Caddesi more or less opposite the Tourism Information Office, has changed character recently. By mentioning it here I'm hoping it can regain its old standards of cuisine and service. It's up a flight of stairs in the building called the Özel Sancak İşhanı, with an open-air terrace in good weather (which is most of the time). A full meal of soup, kebap, salad, dessert and beverage (wine and beer are served) should not cost more than US$4 or US$5, probably less.

For even cheaper fare try the *Üç Kardeşler Lokanta ve Kebap Salonu* (EWCH kahr-desh-lehr) (tel 11 73 14), İnönü Caddesi, to the right of the Adana Sürmeli Oteli. The kebaps are good, the hummus spectacular, the service friendly and the prices low. There are lots of similar simple eateries in this area.

Getting There & Away

As an important transfer point for centuries, Adana is well served by all means of transport.

Air Turkish Airlines (tel 13 72 47, 14 31 43), Stadyum Caddesi 1, operates daily non-stop flights between Adana and İstanbul (1¼ hours), and Ankara (one hour). There are also four flights weekly in each direction between Adana and Nicosia (Lefkoşe), Cyprus.

An airport bus runs between the airport (tel 11 26 37) and the Turkish Airlines office (US$0.60), meeting all flights. A taxi into town costs about US$2.

Bus Adana's large Otogar is active, as you might imagine, with direct buses to everywhere. Some destinations include:

Adıyaman (for Nemrut Dağı) – 370 km, six hours, US$5; seven buses per day, two of these go on to Kâhta for an extra US$1

Antalya – 555 km, 12 hours, US$10; a few buses daily

Alanya – 440 km, 10 hours, US$9; eight buses daily in summer

Ankara – 490 km, 10 hours, US$8; frequent buses daily

Diyarbakır – 550 km, 10 hours, US$8; several buses daily

Gaziantep – 220 km, four hours, US$3.25; several buses daily

Haleb (Aleppo, Syria) – 300 km, 12 hours, US$16; at least once daily

Kayseri – 335 km, 6½ hours, US$6; several buses daily

Konya – 350 km, 6½ hours, US$6; frequent buses daily

Malatya – 425 km, eight hours, US$6.75; a few buses daily

Nevşehir (Cappadocia) – 285 km, 5½ hours, US$5; several buses daily

Şanlıurfa – 365 km, six hours, US$4.75; several buses daily
Van – 950 km, 18 hours, US$13; at least one bus daily

Train The façade of the Adana Gar (tel 13 31 72), at the northern end of Ziyapaşa Bulvarı, is decorated with pretty faïence panels. Trains depart six times daily for Mersin via Tarsus, a 75-minute trip.

Car Rental As a town for Turkish business travellers, not foreign tourists, Adana has particularly good prices for services such as car rentals. If you want a car to explore the eastern parts of the country it may make sense to fly to Adana and hire the car here. A local agency with a good reputation, well-maintained cars and very good prices is Seytur Ltd (tel 14 41 57, 14 42 16), Ziyapaşa Bulvarı, Libya Dostluk Derneği Yanı, 290 Sokak 40, 01060 Adana. Rates for cars rented on a weekly basis, with unlimited km and collision damage waiver (insurance) included, range from US$30 to US$60 per day. Right next door is a convenient travel agency, Nextour (tel 14 00 88, 14 53 63), 290 Sokak 40/B.

ADANA TO ANTAKYA
The very eastern end of the Turkish Mediterranean coast surrounds the Bay of İskenderun and includes the cities of İskenderun and Antakya, in the province of Hatay. Inland from the bay are ruins of a very old Hittite city at Karatepe, and a later Roman one (Anazarbus). On the road are several mediaeval fortresses. Dolmuşes from Adana run to the town of Kadirli, beyond Anazarbus and before Karatepe. You should be able to reach Anazarbus by dolmuş and a short hitchhike without too much trouble; you may want to stay the night in Kadirli. The hitch from there to Karatepe is not an easy one. If you have your own transport this detour is a breeze.

About 45 minutes (35 km) east of Adana is the **Snake Castle** (Yılankale), a fortress

perched on a hilltop 2½ km south of the highway. Built by Armenians and Crusaders in the 12th or 13th century, it is said to have taken its name from a serpent which was once entwined in the coat-of-arms above the main entrance (today you'll see a king and a lion, but no snake); other versions have it that this area was once full of snakes. If you have the time, feel free to drive or walk up and have a look around. It's about a 20-minute climb over the rocks and up to the highest point in the fort. There are no services here, no guardian and no admission charge.

To see Anazarbus and Karatepe, make a detour north and east just after the Snake Castle. About 37 km east of Adana is an intersection marked on the left (north) for Kozan and Kadirli, on the right (south) for Ceyhan. Take the Kozan/Kadirli road.

Anazarbus
When the Romans moved into this area around 19 BC they built this fortress city atop a hill dominating the fertile plain. They called it Caesarea ad Anazarbus. Later, when the Roman province of Cilicia was divided in two, Tarsus remained the capital of the west, and Anazarbus became capital of the east. In the 3rd century AD Persian invaders destroyed the city along with a lot of others in Anatolia. The Byzantine emperors rebuilt it and in later centuries, when earthquakes destroyed it several times, they rebuilt it again.

The Arab raids of the 8th century gave Anazarbus new rulers and a new Arabicised name, Ain Zarba. The Byzantines reconquered and held it for a brief period, but Anazarbus was an important city at a strategic nexus, and other armies came through and took it, including the Hamdanid princes of Aleppo, the Crusaders, a local Armenian king, the Byzantines again, the Turks and the Mamluks. The last owners didn't care about it much and it fell into decline in the 15th century. Today it's called Anavarza.

The Road to Anazarbus From the main highway follow the Kozan/Kadirli road north to the village of Ayşehoca, where a road on the right is marked for Anavarza/Anazarbus, 4½ km to the east. If you're in a dolmuş or bus you can get out here and usually hitch pretty easily with a tractor or truck.

At a T-junction you come upon a large **triumphal arch** in the city walls. Through the gate was the ancient city, now given over to crops and pasture, with not much to see. If you turn left, a walk of 650 metres will bring you to the remains of an **aqueduct** of which several arches are still standing. Sometimes there's a gypsy camp set up around them.

Turn right at the T-junction and a 200-metre walk brings you to a little private 'open-air museum' on the right-hand side of the road. Bits of column and sarcophagi are set in the garden, and an ancient pool has a nice **mosaic** of the goddess Thetis (Nereid), a sea nymph. A young lady named Ayfer, who lives here, may welcome you, and splash some water on the mosaic to brighten its colours. Ayfer, despite her youth, has already seen the world (or part of it), having visited Delaware in the USA.

To reach the impressive **fortress** on the hilltop dominating the old city and the plain, you can traipse across the fields to a rock-cut stairway, or continue past the open-air museum for several km to a defile cut in the hill. An unpaved road leads through the cut to the far side of a hill, where a farmer's track along the base provides access to the **necropolis**. Ascent of the hill is much easier on this side. Inside are the ruins of a church.

The village of Anavarza has no services though you can get a glass of hospitality tea or a cool drink of water. As the flow of visitors increases, there will probably be some simple eateries and perhaps a pension. If you have camping equipment you can probably find a place to set up here.

Heading onward to Karatepe, return the 4½ km to Ayşehoca and the road north to Çukurköprü and Kozan.

Karatepe

From Ayşehoca head north to Çukurköprü, where the road divides. The left is marked for Kozan and Feke, the right for Kadirli. Take the right fork.

Kadirli (population 50,000), 20 km east of Çukurköprü, is a farming town with a useful little bazaar, a few small restaurants and hotels. The *Aktürk Lokantası* (tel 4691), facing the shady park with the teahouses in the centre, is simple, cleanish, cheap and good.

From Kadirli to Karatepe the gravel road is easily passable in dry weather, but perhaps a bit uncertain after heavy rains. Hitchhiking is very chancy, though. You might have an easier time hitching if you approach from the south, taking a bus from Adana to Osmaniye, then a dolmuş toward Tecirli and Kadirli and hitchhiking the last 8.6 km to Karatepe; or you can hire a taxi or minibus in Osmaniye to take you round.

It's 21 km from Kadirli to Karatepe through pretty hill country given over to farms and evergreen forests. The **Ceyhan Gölü** (Lake Ceyhan, JEY-hahn) is an artificial lake for hydroelectric power and recreation. Karatepe (follow the signs) is in the Karatepe-Aslantaş Milli Park (National Park) and Orman Dinleme Yeri (Forest Retreat).

From the Kadirli to Osmaniye road it's two km to the Forest Retreat, which has picnic tables and charcoal grills. A bit farther along is the car park (US$0.50 fee), from which it is a five-minute, 400-metre walk uphill through the forest to the hilltop archaeological zone of Karatepe. A building above the car park has toilets, and soft drinks for sale. Campervans seem to get away with camping in the car park, though this is probably not officially permitted and there is no dependable source of water (bring your own).

The Hittite City This hilltop site, now officially called the Aslantaş Müzesi (Lion-Stone Museum), has been inhabited for almost 4000 years, but the ruins you see date from the 13th century BC when this was a summer retreat for the neo-Hittite kings of Kizzuwatna (Cilicia), the greatest of whom was a fellow named Azitawadda.

Halfway up the hill a guard will collect the US$2 admission fee, take your camera (no photography is allowed as excavations are still under way) and offer to lead you around (tip expected). Opening hours for the site are 8 am to 6 or 7 pm daily in summer.

The remains here are significant. The city was defended by walls one km long, traces of which are still evident. Before arriving at the south gate there is a **lookout point** giving a fine view of the lake, which was not here in Hittite times, of course. The southern entrance to the city is protected by four lions and two sphinxes and lined with fine reliefs showing a coronation or feast complete with sacrificial bull, musicians and chariots. Across the hill at the north gate the lions are even scarier (from an evil spirit's point of view, that is) and the reliefs are even sharper as the stones were buried for centuries and thus protected from weathering. The eyes in the volcanic lion statue are of white stone held in by lead. There are inscriptions in Hittite script; a very long one, with a Phoenician translation, was discovered here and deciphered, which is how we know the history of the city.

Continue past the north gate and bear left to make a circle of the hilltop, ending back at the guard's shed. The road south from Karatepe to the main east-west highway is easier and passes by the ruins of a Roman town.

Hierapolis Castalba

From Karatepe a gravel road goes south down through the hills 8.6 km (the sign reads nine) before joining a paved road. The gravel is fine in dry weather but be careful in rain when there may be mudslides. Once on the paved road head for Osmaniye.

Nineteen km south of Karatepe and six km north of the east-west highway are the ruins of Hierapolis Castalba, with a little castle on a rocky outcrop above the plain about 500 metres east of the road, and columns from a colonnaded street standing in a field. If you clamber up to the fortress, do so for the wonderful view, and not for the building itself, which is badly ruined inside. From the fort you can see the city's **theatre** to the east. Hierapolis Castalba was the capital of a little semi-independent principality paying tribute to Rome. Unfortunately its king, Tarcondimotus I, sided with Pompey in his struggle with Julius Caesar and died at the great battle of Actium. Tarcondimotus II never quite got it together and the little principality faded away not long afterward.

The road south goes across a bridge and through the village of Cevdetiye before reaching the highway. Head west to reach Toprakkale, about 12 km along.

Toprakkale

At a point 72 km east of Adana the highway divides, skirting the **Earth Castle** (Toprakkale), built of dark volcanic stone about the same time as the Snake Castle. The access road up to the fortress turns off from the westward branch of the highway (Adana to İskenderun); it's 600 metres to the fortress walls, then a few minutes' easy walk into the ruins.

When you're finished seeing the fortress, head south for İskenderun and Antakya along a fairly perilous road heavy with truck traffic. At Erzin, just over eight km south of Toprakkale, there's a long **aqueduct** in the fields to the right.

Payas (Yakacık)

At Payas, also called Yakacık, 35 km south of Toprakkale, look for the inconspicuous signs in the centre of town (north of Payas's big steel factory) pointing the way (right, west) to the

Kervansaray and Cin Kule, one km toward the sea.

The huge Ottoman **Sokullu Mehmet Paşa Kervansaray** was built for the Grand Vizier of Süleyman the Magnificent and Selim II in the 1570s. Opening hours are from 8 am to 4 or 5 pm daily. It's an elaborate complex of courtyards, Turkish baths, mosque, medrese and covered bazaar – a fortified city in what was then a recently conquered (1516) and still hostile territory. Parts of it look positively Burgundian, which makes me think that Sokullu Mehmet Paşa's architects, who worked under the guidance of Sinan's school, may have restored and expanded the ruins of a Crusader church.

Next to the caravanserai is the **Cin Kalesi**, or Fortress of the Genies, a restored little bastion protected by a moat now filled with fig trees. The main gate is a double-bend defensive one which leads to a grassy interior now used as pasture for cattle. The ruins of a small mosque are the only other item of interest. If you walk around the outside of the castle walls you can descend to the moat by means of a stone subterranean stairway at the moat's westernmost point and pick figs.

Farther along down the tarmac road from these two buildings is another little **fortress** with a bent-gate entrance, a keep and gun ports, and there's the ruins of yet another fortress down by the water's edge. You can wander into all three forts at any time of day.

After Payas the road is lined with factories for making steel, cement, fertiliser and the like, all taking advantage of the historic port of İskenderun, 22 km to the south.

İskenderun

İskenderun (ees-KEHN-deh-roon, population 150,000), 130 km east of Adana, was founded by Alexander the Great in 333 BC and once bore the name Alexandretta, of which İskenderun is a translation. It was the most important port city on this part of the coast until Mersin was developed in the 1960s, but it has retained its importance as a port. It was even added to recently with the opening of an oil pipeline from Iraq.

İskenderun was occupied by the English in 1918, turned over to the French in 1919, and included under the French Protectorate of Syria as the Sanjak of Alexandretta. Atatürk reclaimed it for the Turkish Republic (with French acquiescence) in 1938, as he knew it would be of great strategic importance in the coming war (WW II).

There is nothing to hold you in İskenderun as it is just a sailors', brokers' and shippers' town. If you must stop, there are several good places to stay in this clean and pleasant city.

Orientation Turn right (west) from the highway to reach the waterfront street, Atatürk Bulvarı, with its hotels, banks and restaurants. The centre of town is marked by a pretentious patriotic statue on the waterfront and several old buildings dating from the French Protectorate. Most of the town's cheap hotels are here, on the street running inland beside the city hall.

Information The Tourist Information Office (tel (881) 11620), is at Atatürk Bulvarı 49/B, across the street from the odd Belediye Büfesi and next to the Başak Pasta Salonu.

Places to Stay Two blocks inland from Atatürk Bulvarı in the French centre of town is the modest *Kavaklı Pansiyon* (tel 14608, 17890), Şehit Pamir Caddesi, 52 Sokak 14, a basic but adequate place with a friendly staff, lift and rooms with running water for US$8/12 a single/ double.

The *Kıyı Otel* (tel 13680/1), on Atatürk Bulvarı, charges US$11/17 for its 30 rooms with balcony (many with sea views), private bath and fan. Tidy marble-topped café tables are set out front on the sidewalk for breakfast, lunch or a snack, or you can dine in the cheerful, sunny restaurant. They have some large multi-bedded rooms for families.

Best in town is the three-star *Hataylı Oteli* (tel 11551, 18751, 19790), Osman Gazi Caddesi 2, which you may pass as you come in from the highway on your way westward to the waterfront. The Hataylı has a terrace restaurant on the 5th floor, a breakfast room on the mezzanine and 60 rooms with private baths for US$23/32 a single/double, and US$40 for a double suite.

South of İskenderun

Past İskenderun the road winds uphill toward Antakya, 60 km away, through the town of Sarımazı (10 km from İskenderun) to Belen, the town at the head of a gorge 15 km south of İskenderun. Belen looks to be an old settlement, and indeed it is, as archaeological excavations nearby have unearthed evidence of settlements dating back to the time of Hammurabi, king of Babylon.

At 147 km from Adana the road passes over the Belen Pass (Belen Geçidi; altitude 740 metres) and then descends to the fertile Amik Plain, the source of Antakya's prosperity.

ANTAKYA

Antakya (ahn-TAHK-yah, population 150,000), also called Hatay (HAH-tahy), is rather Arabic in its culture and language. Many people speak Arabic as a first language, Turkish as the second. You will soon see that there are two Antakyas: the tidy, modern one on the western bank of the Asi River (the ancient Orontes) which divides the town; and the older, ramshackle, sympathetic, Arabic one, with many buildings left from the times of the Ottoman Empire and the French Protectorate, on the eastern bank.

In the city there's a Roman bridge built under the reign of Diocletian (3rd century AD), an aqueduct, the old city walls, several Arab-style mosques (very different from the Turkish) and, most importantly, the Antakya Museum, on the western

bank at the southern side of Cumhuriyet Alanı by the bridge. The museum is justly famed for its marvellous Roman mosaics.

History

This is the ancient Antioch, founded by Seleucus I Nicator in 300 BC. Before long it had a population of half a million. Under the Romans it developed an important Christian community (out of its already large Jewish one), which was at one time headed by St Paul.

Persians, Byzantines, Arabs, Armenians and Seljuks all fought for Antioch, and the Crusaders and Saracens battled for it as well. In 1268 the Mameluks of Egypt took the city and wiped it out. It was never to regain its former glory.

The Ottomans held the city until Muhammed Ali of Egypt captured it in his drive for control of the empire (1831), but with European help the Ottomans drove their rebellious vassal back. The French held it as part of their Syrian protectorate until 1939. Atatürk saw WW II approaching and wanted the city rejoined to the republic as a defensive measure. He began a campaign to reclaim it, which came to fruition by means of a plebiscite shortly after his death.

Orientation

The modern town is on the western bank, with its Tourism Information Office, PTT, government buildings and museum all ranged around the traffic roundabout named Cumhuriyet Alanı; the Büyük Antakya Oteli, the best hotel in town, is just up the street. The older Ottoman town on the eastern bank is the place to find the bus station (Santral Garajı), a few blocks north of the centre. The city's cheaper hotels are in the eastern part along the river bank promenade.

Information

The provincial Tourism Information Office (tel (891) 12636) is two km north of the PTT, on the western bank at a traffic

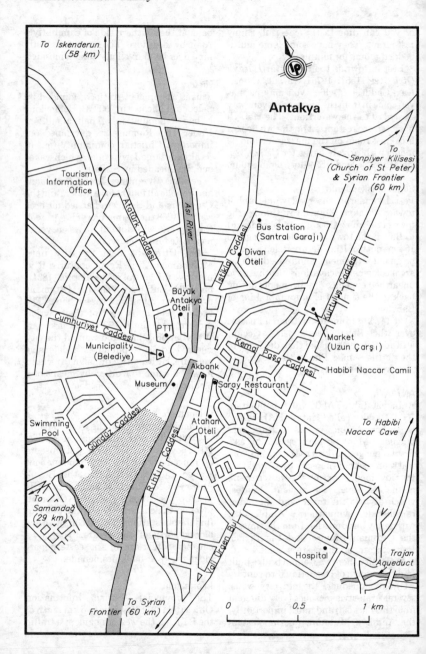

roundabout. It's open from 8 am to 12 noon and 1.30 to 6.30 pm daily.

Antakya Archaeological Museum

The Antakya Arkeoloji Müzesi is the prime reason for journeying all the way to Antakya. Admission costs US$2; opening hours are Tuesday to Sunday from 8 am to 12 noon and 1.30 to 5 pm, Monday from 1 to 5 pm. Most labels are in English as well as Turkish. Photographs of the mosaics are permitted for a fee.

The first four 'salons' in the museum (Salons I to IV) are filled with Roman mosaics – and what mosaics! Photographs show how they looked in situ, and the tall, naturally lit exhibit rooms show them off well. Seasonal themes, fishing, hunting, war and mythological subjects are all astonishingly well portrayed using the little coloured stone chips. Many of these came from Roman villas at the seaside and in the suburban resort of Daphne (Harbiye).

Salon V holds exhibits of artefacts recovered from the *tells* (mounds) at Açana and Cüdeyde. The pair of lions serving as column pediments, dating from the 8th century BC, are especially good.

Salon VI has Roman and Byzantine coins, statues, pots, glassware and tools, some dating from the Eski Tunç Devri II (Second Old Bronze Age, 2600-2500 BC). The cuneiform inscriptions are from the Açana excavations.

Cave-Church of St Peter

On the outskirts of town (two km from the centre) is the **Senpiyer Kilisesi** or Church of St Peter. In this grotto, enclosed by a wall in Crusader times, it is said that St Peter preached. There is no bus service to Senpiyer; you must take a taxi (US$4 return trip), or plan to walk the three or four km from town.

Daphne (Harbiye)

Dolmuşes run frequently from Antakya's bus station to the hill suburb of Harbiye,

the ancient Daphne, nine km to the south; there are less-frequent city buses as well. Through a modern residential area and up the hill you come to the **waterfall** on the right (west), just past the Hotel du Liban. Walk down into the wooded valley, which is usually full of Antakyalı vacationers enjoying the cool shade, the little tea gardens (each with scratchy cassette player), and the rivulets, pools and falls of cooling water.

Past Harbiye, 42 km farther on, is the Yayladağı Yazılıtaş Orman Piknik Yeri, a forest picnic spot near some ancient inscriptions. Along the way the road passes near the village of Sofular, next to which is a Crusader castle.

Samandağ

Dolmuşes and Samandağ city buses (Samandağ Belediyesi) run frequently to this seaside suburb 28 km away, following the road south-east past the Antakya Archaeological Museum and over the mountains to the sea.

Samandağ itself is very uninspiring, but go six km north along the beach to Çevlik to see the ruins of **Seleucia ad Piera**, in ancient times Antioch's port town. Dolmuş service is not regular to Çevlik so talk your dolmuş driver into continuing to Çevlik for a small additional fare. Several restaurants here by the sea offer meals in pleasant surroundings; there are a few simple pensions as well.

Seleucia's ruins are not much to look at but a nearby feat of Roman engineering is quite interesting. During its heyday Seleucia lived daily with the threat of inundation from the stream which descended the mountains and came through the town. To remove the threat, Roman emperors Titus and Vespasian ordered their engineers to dig a diversion channel around the town. This they did. From the car park in Çevlik, ascend the steps to the Titus ve Vespasiyanus Tüneli, pay the US$1 admission fee and a guide will accompany you up the hillside, along the channel and through a great gorge. At the upper end of the channel is an inscription dating the work.

Places to Stay – bottom end

Closest to the bus station is the dumpy Şeker Palas Oteli (sheh-KEHR pah-lahss) (tel 11603), İstiklal Caddesi 79, west across the street. It's nothing special but it's the closest, and it charges US$4/6 for singles/doubles without water. Walk south on İstiklal Caddesi a few blocks to find the much better Hotel İstanbul (tel 11122), İstiklal Caddesi 14, above the Garanti Bankası halfway between the bus station and the bridge, charging the same prices as the Şeker Palas for much better rooms. The hotel's façade is more appealing than its rooms, however.

The Hotel Kent (tel 11670), Köprübaşı, opposite the bridge but back from the river bank a few metres, is no beauty either, but it has double rooms without bath for US$7.50 and a few with bath for US$8.

Continuing southward into the bazaar, south of the bridge and inland a bit, is the one-star, 28-room Atahan Oteli (AH-tah-hahn) (tel 11036, 11407), Hürriyet Caddesi 28, at one time the best in town. The lobby is up one flight. Rooms are somewhat overpriced at US$17/21 for singles/doubles, but comfortable all the same.

The one-star Divan Oteli (dee-VAHN) (tel 11518, 11735), İstiklal Caddesi 62, just a few steps south of the bus station, offers the best accommodation within the immediate vicinity of the bus station, with 23 rooms going for US$10/14/17 a single/double/triple. There are no fans but the cross-ventilation is fairly good. Look for the Pamukbank on the corner; the hotel is close by.

Places to Stay – middle

The best in town is the new Büyük Antakya Oteli (tel 13426, 14659), Atatürk Caddesi 8, a three-star, asymmetrical seven-storey white building a few steps away from Cumhuriyet Alanı. The hotel has lots of services including a restaurant, a

pastry-shop, nightclub and bar, and 72 air-con rooms looking onto the river or the town, and some have TV. Prices for this cool comfort are US$32/40 a single/double. If tourism to Antakya picks up you can expect these prices to rise dramatically.

Places to Eat

Except for the hotel restaurants, Antakya's eateries tend to be simple and cheap, and are on the eastern bank near the bridge. With most meals you will be offered a plate of pimientos (peppers) and mint, an Arabic touch. Also, you will find hummus readily available here, something one does not find easily in other parts of Turkey. The spring water served with the meal is the sweetest I have ever tasted.

I had a good lunch at the Saray Restaurant (tel 17714), Hürriyet Caddesi, Akbank Karşısı, just off the little plaza by the eastern end of the bridge. Go inland from the square and the Akbank a few steps and look for the restaurant. A plain, bright place done in white plastic laminate, it is clean and popular with the locals. Mahmut Akar is the chef and brother Sami tends the cash register. Tas kebap (the ever-present lamb and vegetable stew), pilav, bread and beverage cost me US$2. The eastern section of town has lots of similar places; the bus station area has even cheaper ones.

Getting There & Away

Bus Dolmuşes run frequently from the southern end of Antakya's bus station to Harbiye (nine km, 15 minutes), Samandağ (28 km, 35 minutes) and the Turco-Syrian border stations at Reyhanlı (for Aleppo) and Yayladağ (for Lattakia and Beirut) throughout the day. Antakya city buses run to and from Harbiye and Samandağ.

Antakya bus station also has direct buses to most western and northern points (Ankara, Antalya, İstanbul, İzmir, Kayseri, Konya), most going via Adana and up through the Cilician Gates. There are also direct buses to major cities in neighbouring countries; travel times to these cities do not include border crossing formalities, which may add several hours to the trip. Have your visas in advance to hasten formalities.

Adana – 190 km, 2½ hours, US$2.75; very frequent buses daily

Amman (Jordan) – 675 km, 10 hours, US$13; daily buses

Damascus (Syria) – 465 km, eight hours, US$9; daily buses

Gaziantep – 200 km, four hours, US$4; frequent buses daily

Haleb (Aleppo, Syria) – 105 km, four hours, US$5.50; several buses daily

Şanlıurfa – 345 km, seven hours, US$7; several direct buses daily, or change at Gaziantep, from which buses head east to Urfa every half-hour

Into Syria Syrian visas are not normally issued at the border, but this depends partly upon your nationality and partly upon current regulations. If you plan to travel to Syria and other Middle Eastern countries, plan ahead and obtain the necessary visas in your home country, in İstanbul or in Ankara. At the border you must change the equivalent of US$100 into Syrian currency at the official exchange rate, which is currently only 25% of the black market rate.

Central Anatolia

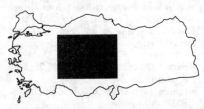

When nomadic Turkish shepherds moved into Anatolia around the year 1100, they found a land which reminded them of Central Asia: semiarid, rolling steppe covered with grass, perfect for their flocks. Mountains and great lakes (some of them salt) broke up the vast expanse of steppe. By the numerous streams, marked with rows of tall, spindly poplars, the nomads finally established villages.

In spring, Central Anatolia is a sea of wild flowers. Great swaths of vivid colour are splashed across the spare landscape in an annual extravagance born of the spring rains. Days are pleasantly warm, nights chilly. In summer the rain disappears and the Anatolian plateau is hotter and drier, but never humid as on the coasts. As you ride across Anatolia in summer, you will see the dark red of newly ploughed furrows, the straw yellow of grass, the grey and green bands of sandstone in a rockface. Winter is cold and rainy, with numerous snow falls. You shouldn't be surprised at the snow, for the plateau has an average altitude of 1000 metres.

Though Central Anatolia yields a first impression of emptiness, this is deceptive. The armies of a dozen empires have moved back and forth across this 'land bridge' between Europe and Asia; a dozen civilisations have risen and fallen here, including the very earliest established human communities, which date from 7500 BC. Crumbling caravanserais scattered along the modern highways testify to rich trade routes which flourished for several millennia.

Today, Central Anatolia is still flourishing. Wheat and other grains, fruits and vegetables (including delicious melons) are grown in the dry soil, and livestock is still a big concern. Ankara, Turkey's capital city, is a sprawling urban mass in the midst of the semidesert; Konya and Kayseri, fuelled by the wealth of agriculture and light industry, are growing at a remarkable pace. These cities are quite modern with wide boulevards, apartment blocks and busy traffic. At the heart of each is an old town, a fortress dating to Roman times and a few foundations going back to the dawn of civilisation.

Ankara

Capital of the Turkish Republic, Ankara (AHN-kah-rah), with a population of three million and an altitude of 848 metres, was once called Angora. The fine, soft hair (*tiftik*) on Angora goats became an industry which still thrives. Today, Ankara's prime concern is government. It is a city of ministries, embassies, universities, medical centres, gardens, vineyards and some light industry. Vast suburbs are scattered on the hillsides which surround the centre; and most are filled by country people who have moved here in search of work and a better life. Many have found it.

Until recently, the principal heating fuel was a soft brown coal called lignite which produces thick, gritty smoke. During the heating season (15 October to 15 April), Ankara's air was always badly polluted, but now a pipeline brings clean-burning natural gas to Ankara from the Soviet Union. Air quality is expected to improve dramatically as the city converts to this superior fuel. But natural gas will not prevent car exhaust pollution, which is as bad in Ankara as in any other large, car-dependent city.

Your stay in Ankara need not be as long as in İstanbul. The city has several significant attractions, but you should be able to tour them all in 1½ to two days, or even one day if you're in a hurry.

History
It was the Hittites who named this place Ankuwash before 1200 BC. The town prospered because it was at the intersection of the north-south and east-west trade routes. After the Hittites, it was a Phrygian town, then taken by Alexander, claimed by the Seleucids and finally occupied by the Galatian tribes of Gaul who invaded Anatolia around 250 BC. Augustus Caesar annexed it to Rome in 25 BC as Ankyra.

The Byzantines held the town for centuries, with intermittent raids by the Persians and Arabs. When the Seljuk Turks came to Anatolia after 1071, they made the town they called Engüriye into a Seljuk city but held it with difficulty. Ottoman possession of Angora did not begin well, for it was near the town that Sultan Yıldırım Beyazıt was captured by Tamerlane, and the sultan later died in captivity. After the Timurid state collapsed and the Ottoman civil war ended, Angora became merely a quiet town where long-haired goats were raised.

Modern Ankara is a planned city. When Atatürk set up his provisional government here in 1920, it was a small, rather dusty Anatolian town of some 30,000 people, with a strategic position at the heart of the country. After his victory in the War of Independence, Atatürk declared this the new capital of the country (October 1923), and set about developing it. European urban planners were consulted, which resulted in a city of long, wide boulevards, a large forested park with an artificial lake, a cluster of transportation termini and numerous residential and diplomatic neighbourhoods.

From 1919 to 1927, Atatürk did not set foot in the old imperial capital of İstanbul, preferring to work at making Ankara the country's capital city in fact as well as in name.

For republican Turks, İstanbul is their glorious historical city, still the centre of business and finance, but Ankara is their true capital, built on the ashes of the empire with their own blood and sweat. It is modern and forward-looking and they're proud of it.

Orientation
The main boulevard through the city is, of course, Atatürk Bulvarı, which runs from Ulus in the north all the way to the Presidential Mansion in Çankaya, six km to the south.

The old city of Ankara, dating from Roman times and including the Hisar (fortress), is near Ulus Meydanı, called simply Ulus (oo-LOOS), the centre of 'old Ankara'. This is an area with many of Ankara's cheapest hotels, restaurants and markets. The most important museums and sights are near Ulus. You can recognise the square by the large equestrian statue of Atatürk at the south-east corner.

Kızılay (KUH-zuh-lah-yee) is the intersection of Atatürk Bulvarı and Gazi Mustafa Kemal Bulvarı/Ziya Gökalp Caddesi. Officially called Hürriyet Meydanı, everyone knows it by the name Kızılay, the 'Red Crescent' (Turkish 'Red Cross') headquarters which used to be here but were demolished long ago. This is the centre of 'new Ankara', called Yenişehir (yeh-NEE-sheh-heer). It holds several moderate hotel and restaurant choices. There are also bus and airline ticket offices, travel agencies and department stores. On Kocatepe hill in Yenişehir is the Kocatepe Camii, a modern mosque in Ottoman style which is among the largest in the world.

At the southern end of Atatürk Caddesi, in the hills overlooking the city, is Çankaya, the residential neighbourhood which

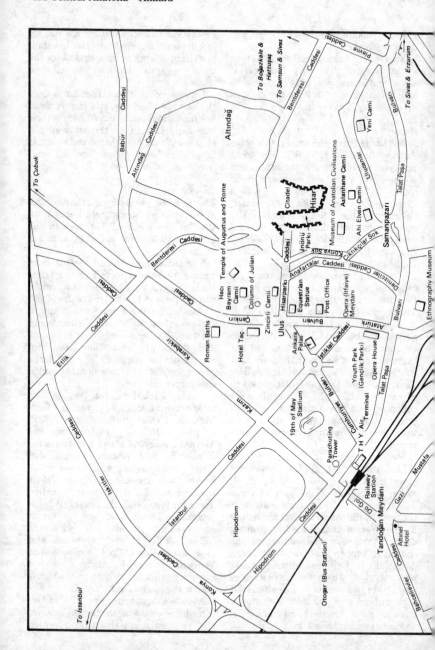

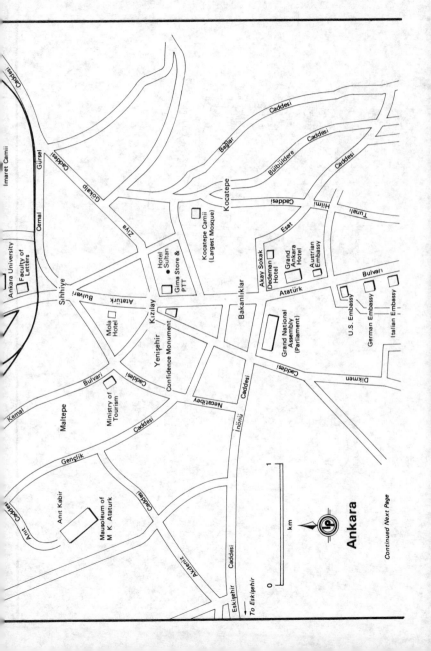

Ankara

km

Continued Next Page

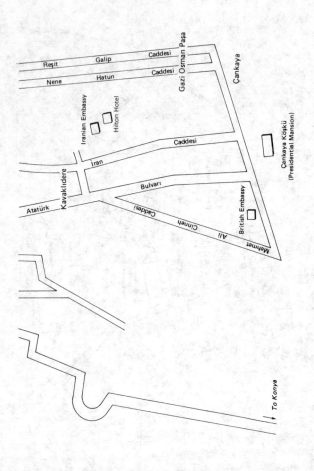

holds the Cumhurbaşkanlığı Köşkü, the Presidential Mansion, plus many of the most important ambassadorial residences. Between Kızılay and Çankaya along Atatürk Bulvarı are most of the city's important embassies and many government ministries, plus the Büyük Millet Meclisi, the Grand National Assembly, parliament of the Turkish Republic.

First goal of most sightseers is the Hisar (hee-SAHR) or Kale, the citadel atop the hill. Near the Hisar, on the south-western slope of the hill, is the important Anadolu Medeniyetleri Müzesi or Museum of Anatolian Civilisations, also called the Anadolu Uygarlıkları Müzesi, Hitit Müzesi or Arkeoloji Müzesi.

Information

There are Tourism Information Offices at Ankara's otogar and at Esenboğa Airport. For information in central Ankara, direct your feet and your questions to the office at İstanbul Caddesi 4, Ulus (tel (4) 311-2247, 310-6818, 312-3525), or to the Ministry of Tourism (Turizm Bakanlığı) (tel 230-1911, 231-7380/95), Gazi Mustafa Kemal Bulvarı 33, a 10-minute walk west of Kızılay. The entrance to the information office is actually on the right side of the Ministry building, around on Özveren Sokak.

Anadolu Medeniyetleri Müzesi

If you're a walker and the day is not too hot, you can climb the hillside to the museum; otherwise take a taxi. Walk east from Ulus on Hisarparkı Caddesi and turn right into Anafartalar Caddesi, then bear left along Çıkrıkçılar Sokak to reach the museum, which is open from 8.30 am to 5.30 pm, seven days a week; admission costs US$4. Photographs are permitted (for free) only in the central room of the museum; photography in other rooms must be approved by the director and a fee paid.

The museum building is made up of a restored covered market built by order of Grand Vizier Mahmut Paşa in 1471, and the adjoining Kurşunlu Han, an Ottoman warehouse. Exhibits heavily favour the earlier Anatolian civilisations such as the Urartu, Hatti, Hittite, Phrygian and Assyrian. Among the more fascinating items are those brought from Çatal Höyük, the earliest known human community. You'll also enjoy the graceful, lively Hittite figures of bulls and stags and the early water vessels.

As you stroll through the museum's exhibits, you should know that MÖ is the Turkish abbreviation for BC.

By the way, there are several decent, inexpensive restaurants down the hill on Konya Sokak, including the Yavuz. See Places to Eat for details.

Hisar

The imposing fortress just up the hill from the museum took its present form in the 800s with the construction of the outer walls by the Byzantine Emperor Michael II. The earlier inner walls date from the 600s.

Enter the citadel by the gate called **Parmak Kapısı** (pahr-MAHK kah-puh-

Hittite deer statue - a symbol of divine power

suh), and you're in a Turkish village right at the centre of Ankara! The small mosque here, the **Alaettin Camii**, dates originally from the 1100s, but much has been rebuilt. Wander into the village, following any path that leads higher and soon you'll arrive at the **Şark Kulesi** (SHARK koo-leh-see, Eastern Tower), where there's a magnificent view over the entire city, all the way to Yenişehir and Çankaya. The tower at the north, **Ak Kale** (AHK kah-leh, White Fort), also offers fine views. The area inside the citadel is being restored. The village ambience will be preserved along with the fortress itself.

Bazaar

Come down from the Hisar, exit by the Parmak Kapısı, and you'll be in the bazaar. Warehouses here are filled with Angora goat hair and merchants busy themselves with its trade. Turn left and walk down through the bazaar area, lined with vegetable stalls, copper and iron-mongers and every variety of household item. Soon you will come to the **Aslanhane Camii** (ahs-LAHN-hah-neh, Lion House), which dates from the 1200s and is very Seljuk in aspect. Go inside for a look.

Continue down the hill on Can Sokak and turn right into Anafartalar Caddesi for Ulus.

Railway Museum

Rail enthusiasts passing by Ankara's railway station will want to have a look at Atatürk's private white railway coach, on display at the station. Enter from the street, walk through the main hall and out to the platforms, turn right, and walk along until you come to the coach, on the right. It was constructed in Breslau in 1935 and looks very comfy. You can't go inside the coach but you can tour the Demiryolları Müzesi (deh-MEER-yoh-lah-ruh mew-zeh-see), the Railway Museum, just past the coach. It's supposedly open from 8.30 am to 12 noon and from 1 to 5.30 pm, closed Monday. As there are few visitors, it may be locked. Find an official and

request, *Müzeyi açarmısınız?* (mew-zeh-YEE ah-CHAR-muh-suh-nuhz, 'Would you open the museum?'). If the time is within the hours given, he should oblige.

Roman Ankara

At the north-east corner of the square in Ulus are some buildings and behind them is the first stop on your tour of Roman Ankara. Set in a small park (Hükümet Meydanı), surrounded by the Ankara provincial government house and the Ministry of Finance & Customs, is the **Jülyanüs Sütunu** (zhewl-YAH-news sew-too-noo), the Column of Julian. The Roman Emperor Julian (the Apostate, 361-363), last of the scions of Constantine the Great, visited Ankara in the middle of his short reign and the column was erected in his honour. Turkish inhabitants later gave it the name Belkız Minaresi, the Queen of Sheba's Minaret.

Walk east from the park, up the hill; turn right, then left to reach Bayram Caddesi and the **Hacı Bayram Camii** (hah-JUH bahy-RAHM), Ankara's most revered mosque, built on the ruins of the **Temple of Augustus & Rome**. Hacı Bayram Veli was a Muslim saint who founded the Bayramiye order of Dervishes around the year 1400. Ankara was the centre of the order and Hacı Bayram Veli is still revered by the city's pious Muslims.

The temple walls that you see were once surrounded by a colonnade. Originally built by the kings of Pergamum for the worship of Cybele, the Anatolian fertility goddess, and Men, the Phrygian phallic god, it was later rededicated to Emperor Augustus. The Byzantines converted it to a church and the Muslims built a mosque and saint's tomb in its precincts. The gods change, the site stays the same.

From Hacı Bayram, walk north on Çiçek Sokak until it meets Çankırı Caddesi. Across this main road, up the hill on the opposite side, is the fenced enclosure of the **Roma Hamamları** or Roman Baths. The layout of the 3rd-century baths is clearly visible, as is much of the water system.

Hours are from 8.30 am to 5.30 pm; admission costs US$0.75. If you're short on money or pressed for time, you can ignore the baths.

Republican Ankara

In the 1920s, at the time of the War of Independence, Ankara consisted of the citadel and a few buildings in Ulus. Atatürk's new city grew with Ulus as its centre and many of the buildings here saw the birth and growing pains of the Turkish Republic. A short tour through a few of the buildings tells a great deal about how a democratic nation-state grew from the ruins of a vast monarchy.

Kürtülüş Savaşı Müzesi

The War of Salvation Museum is on Cumhuriyet Bulvarı at the north-west corner of Ulus. Photographs and displays recount great moments and people in the War of Independence; captions are in Turkish only. The republican Grand National Assembly held its early sessions here (earlier called the TBMM Müzesi for Türkiye Büyük Millet Meclisi, Grand National Assembly). Before it was Turkey's first parliament, this building was the Ankara headquarters of the Committee of Union & Progress, the political party which overthrew Sultan Abdül Hamid in 1909 and attempted to bring democracy to the Ottoman Empire. Hours are from 8.30 am to 5 pm, closed Monday; admission is only a few pennies.

Cumhuriyet Müzesi

The Republic Museum is on Cumhuriyet Bulvarı, just down the hill from Ulus. This was the second headquarters of the Grand National Assembly, the parliament founded by Atatürk in his drive for a national consensus to resist foreign invasion and occupation of the Anatolian homeland. The early history of the assembly appears in photographs and documents; all captions are in Turkish only but you can visit the assembly's meeting room and get a sense of its modest beginnings. The Grand National Assembly is now housed in a vast and imposing building in Yenişehir. Hours are from 8.30 am to 5 pm, closed Monday; admission is only a few pennies.

Across Cumhuriyet Caddesi from the museum is the former **Ankara Palas** hotel, built as the city's first luxury lodging. It has been beautifully restored and now serves as guest quarters for important official visitors.

Gençlik Parkı & Opera House

Walk south from Ulus along Atatürk Bulvarı and you'll soon reach the entrance to Gençlik Parkı, the Youth Park. A swamp on this site was converted to an artificial lake on Atatürk's orders and the park was included in the city's master plan. It has a permanent fun fair with amusements for children and, in the evening, outdoor cafés with musical performances. Single women should find a café with the word 'aile' in its name.

Notice the small Opera House just past the entrance to the park. Atatürk became enamoured of opera during a tour of duty as military attaché in Sofia (1905), and saw to it that his new capital had a suitable hall for performances as well. The opera has a full season, beginning in autumn. The new Atatürk Cultural Centre will no doubt supplant the quaint old opera house as the preferred venue for operatic productions.

Ethnography Museum

The Etnografya Müzesi is perched above Atatürk Bulvarı, to the east of the boulevard and south of Ulus past Gençlik Parkı. It's an eye-catching white marble oriental structure (1925) with an equestrian statue of Atatürk in front, reached by walking up Talat Paşa Bulvarı from Atatürk Bulvarı. Recently restored, it has fine collections of Seljuk and Ottoman art, craftwork, musical instruments, weapons, folk costumes, jewellery and household items. Also on view is a large and elaborately decorated room used by

Kemal Atatürk as his office. Hours are from 8.30 am to 5.30 pm, closed Monday; admission costs US$0.50.

Next door to the Ethnography Museum is the **Resim ve Heykel Müzesi** or Painting & Sculpture Museum in the former headquarters of the Turkish Hearths (Türk Ocağı) movement, open at the same times for the same price.

Ulus Markets

Walk up the hill on Hisarparkı Caddesi out of Ulus and turn right at the first traffic signal onto Susam Sokak; a Ziraat Bankası will be on your right. Bear left, then turn left and on your right will be Ankara's **Yeni Haller** or Vegetable Market, a good place for buying supplies or photographing colourful local life.

Behind the Vegetable Market, on Konya Caddesi, is the **Vakıf Suluhan Çarşısı**, a restored han with lots of clothing shops, a café, toilets and a free-standing small mosque at the centre of its courtyard.

Anıt Kabir

Atatürk's mausoleum, called the Anıt Kabir (ah-NUHT-kah-beer, Monumental Tomb), stands atop a small hill in a green park about two km west of Kızılay along Gazi Mustafa Kemal Bulvarı. If you saw Ankara from the Hisar or the terrace of the Ethnography Museum, you've already admired from a distance the rectangular mausoleum with squared columns around its sides on the hill. A visit to the tomb is essential when you visit Ankara.

Walking along Gazi Mustafa Kemal Bulvarı from Kızılay, you can make a short cut by turning left onto Maltepe Sokak. This becomes Erdönmez Sokak and then meets Gençlik Caddesi. Turn right onto Gençlik, then left onto Akdeniz Caddesi and you'll see the back entrance to the park. You may not be allowed to enter by the pedestrian gate, but past it is the auto exit road and you can enter there.

Should you take a taxi to the Anıt Kabir's main entrance, from Tandoğan

Meydanı up Anıt Caddesi, you'll see the mausoleum as it is meant to be approached. Up the steps from the car park you pass between allegorical statues and two square kiosks; the right-hand one holds a model of the tomb and photos of its construction. Then you pass down a long monumental avenue flanked by Hittite stone lions to the courtyard.

To the right as you enter the courtyard, beneath the western colonnade, is the sarcophagus of İsmet İnönü (1884-1973), Atatürk's close friend and chief of staff, a Republican general (hero of the Battle of İnönü, from which he took his surname), diplomat, prime minister and second president of the republic.

Across the courtyard, on the east side, is a museum which holds memorabilia and personal effects of Atatürk. You can also see his official automobiles, several of which are American-made Lincolns.

As you approach the tomb proper, the high-stepping guards will probably jump to action. Past the colonnade, look to left and right at the gilded inscriptions, which are quotations from Atatürk's speech celebrating the 10th anniversary of the republic (1932). As you enter the tomb through its huge bronze doors, you must remove your hat (if you don't, a guard will remind you that this is correct protocol). The lofty hall is lined in red marble and sparingly decorated with mosaics in timeless Turkish folk designs. At the northern end stands an immense marble cenotaph, cut from a single piece of stone. (The tomb is beneath the cenotaph.)

The Anıt Kabir was begun in 1944 and finished in 1953. Its design seeks to capture the spirit of Anatolia: monumental, spare but beautiful. Echoes of several great Anatolian empires, from the Hittites to the Romans and Seljuks, are included in its design. The final effect is modern but somehow timeless.

Çankaya Köşkü

One last museum in Ankara is well worth a visit. At the far southern end of Atatürk

Bulvarı in Çankaya is the Presidential Mansion. Within the mansion's beautiful gardens is the Çankaya Köşkü, or Çankaya Atatürk Müzesi. This quaint chalet was Atatürk's country residence, set amid vineyards and evergreens. In the early days of the republic it was a retreat from the town, but now the town spreads beyond it. Visits to the mansion gardens and grounds and to the museum are permitted on Sunday afternoons from 1.30 to 5.30 pm, and on holidays from 12.30 to 5.30 pm, free of charge. Bring your passport.

Take a bus (Nos 8 or 13) or taxi to the far southern end of Atatürk Bulvarı, where you will find an entrance to the grounds of the Presidental Mansion. Tell the bus or taxi driver that you want to go to the Çankaya Köşkü, (CHAHN-kah-yah Kursh-kur). At the guardhouse, exchange your passport for an identity badge, leave your camera, and a guide will accompany you to and through the museum.

The house is preserved as Atatürk used it, with decor and furnishings very much of the 1930s. You enter a vestibule, then turn right into a games room, complete with tables for billiards and cards (the British ambassador was a favourite card partner). The next room is a green parlour, Atatürk's favourite colour. The large dining room at the back of the house has its own little nook for after-dinner coffee, cigars and brandy.

Upstairs is a formal office, the bedroom and bath, another work room and the library (note the many books in foreign languages).

Downstairs again, to the left of the vestibule is a reception room for dignitaries.

Places to Stay - bottom end

Ulus holds numerous very inexpensive hotels in its back streets. Most are quiet. The first area to explore is İtfaiye Meydanı, also called Opera Meydanı, across Atatürk Bulvarı from the Opera House. At the far eastern end of the square are several small streets, including Sanayi

Caddesi and Kosova Caddesi, with almost a dozen cheap little places.

The Otel Devran (dehv-RAHN) (tel 311-0485/6), has, as its official address, Opera Meydanı Tavus Sokak 8, but you'll find it most easily by looking for Gazi Lisesi (a high school) on Sanayi Caddesi, across Atatürk Bulvarı from the Opera House and Gençlik Parkı. It's an older building, well used, but with nice touches such as marble staircases, brass trim and little chandeliers. Doubles cost US$14 with shower, US$16 with bath. This is a family hotel.

The two-star, 49-room Otel Akman (ahk-MAHN) (tel 324-4140/1/2/3), İtfaiye Meydanı, Tavus Sokak 6, is next to the Otel Devran. It's much more modern, has a lift, car park and bar with colour TV and charges US$16 for a single, US$24 for a double with bath. The hotel's grilled-meat restaurant is right next door. Though it costs more, single women may prefer to stay here rather than at the simpler places in this neighbourhood.

The Otel Erden (ehr-DEHN) (tel 324-3191/2), İtfaiye Meydanı, Gazi Lisesi Yanı 23, is beside the Gazi Lisesi, a semi-modern building where double rooms rent for US$14 with washbasin, US$16 with private shower. There's a lift, a car park and a TV room with videos. Here too they cater to couples and single women and discourage single men.

The Otel Sipahi (SEE-pah-hee) (tel 324-0235/6), İtfaiye Meydanı, Kosova Sokak 1 at Azat Sokak, across the little side street from the Uğur Lokantası and the Otel Mithat, is another small family hotel. Tidy, friendly and not too noisy, it costs US$15 for a double with shower.

The 50-room Mithat Otel (tel 311-5410), İtfaiye Meydanı, Tavus Sokak 2, has a lift and quite suitable budget rooms for US$14 a single.

Cheaper is the Otel Uğur Palas (oo-OOR) (tel 324-1296/7), İtfaiye Meydanı, Sanayi Caddesi 54, also called simply the Otel Uğur. It is older, but this is an advantage. Once an important Ankara hotel many

Opera Meydanı

0   50   100 m

To Ulus Meydanı

İstiklal Caddesi

To Trains & Otogar

Gençlik Parkı

Atatürk Bulvarı

Parking Area

Opera House

Kosova Sokak

To Trains & Otogar

• Hotel Ugrak
• Hotel Uğur Palas
  — Gaziantep 3 Lokanta
• Hotel Devran
• Hotel Erden
• Hotel Akman
• Uğur Lokantası
• Hotel Sipahi
  • Öz Urfa Salonu
• Hotel Üçler
  Hacıbey Salonu   Hotel Kösk

years ago, it has an assortment of rooms with washbasin (US$14 a double), with shower (US$15 a double) and with bath (US$18 a double). There's no lift and the rooms are quite simple but clean and proper. This, too, is a family hotel.

Just off Atatürk Bulvarı near the big Ulus PTT, on the north side, is the fairly quiet *Otel Oba* (OH-bah) (tel 312-4128/9), Şehit Teğmen Kalmaz Caddesi 9, with an assortment of rooms. Bathless doubles with washbasin are US$14; with shower, US$15; with bath, US$17.

Cheapest rooms are in the *Sahil Palas*

Oteli (sah-HEEL pah-lahss) (tel 310-6935), Anafartalar Caddesi, Hal Sokak 5, next to the Yeni Haller. Where it got its name, the 'Shoreline Palace', I can't say, but on its business card the hotel touts its wares with a little verse which might be translated, 'Clean, quiet, nice; for any purse, good price!' Waterless rooms go for only US$8 a double. On the opposite side of the building is the similar *Otel Avrupa* (tel 311-4300), Susam Sokak 9. (Susam Sokak, by the way, translates as 'Sesame St'.)

On the northern side of Ulus, going east off Çankırı Caddesi, is a little street named Beşik Sokak. The *Otel Turan Palas* (too-RAHN pah-lahss) (tel 312-5225/6/7), Çankırı Caddesi, Beşik Sokak 3, Ulus, is quiet though dark and in an area that's developing commercial importance; it may not survive the wrecker's ball for long. At present, however, rooms with washbasin go for US$6/12 a single/double. There's hot water for five hours each morning.

A few steps up Beşik Sokak, at its eastern end, is the *Lâle Palas* (lyaa-LEH pah-lahss) (tel 312-5220/1/2), Hükümet Meydanı, Telgraf Sokak 5 (look for the jauntily named Frizbi Birahanesi directly across the street). The Lâle is a bit of old Ankara with its marble and brass trim, faded grace and welcome quiet. Doubles with washbasin cost US$12, with private shower US$14.

Near Kızılay, the *Otel Ertan* (ehr-TAHN) (tel (4) 118-4083, 4), Selanik Caddesi 70, Kızılay, a half-block south off Meşrutiyet Caddesi, is the best bet. On a quiet street, with a grape arbour and flowers in the front, it has rooms with shower for only US$11/21 a single/double; a few bathless singles on the top floor are tiny and unappealing but priced at only US$7.

Places to Stay – middle
Near Kızılay Perhaps the best value for money in this price range is at the two-star *Hotel Sultan* (sool-TAHN) (tel 131-5980/1), Bayındır Sokak 35 off Ziya Gökalp Caddesi. It's a quiet and fairly pleasant if simple establishment of some 40 rooms, with a lift and its own covered car park, only two blocks from Kızılay. Doubles with bath cost US$44, including breakfast.

More expensive, but also newer and nicer, is the *Hotel Melodi* (tel 117-6414), Karanfil Sokak 10, Kızılay, with two stars and 35 rooms, all with private baths (shower). Rooms are comfortable and the hotel has services such as a bar in the lobby and a little patio out front set with umbrella-shaded café tables in fine weather. Rates are US$42/54 a single/double, but you may be able to haggle for a

lower price if business is slack. To find the hotel, walk up the hill on Atatürk Bulvarı from Kızılay and take the first street on the left (a tree-shaded, pedestrian-only walk) named Yüksel Caddesi. The Hotel Melodi is a block along this street, on the left-hand side.

Also convenient to Kızılay is the *Erşan Oteli* (ehr-SHAHN) (tel 118-9875/6/7), Meşrutiyet Caddesi 13, a block east of Atatürk Bulvarı. The 64 rooms are nothing special, and the whole place seems darkish and male-oriented but the location is very convenient, the price is not bad and the rooms will do if all else is full. Rooms with shower go for US$30/40 a single/double, breakfast included.

On the opposite (north) side of Kızılay stands the two-star, 50-room *Hotel Apaydın* (tel 135-4950), Bayındır Sokak 8, Yenişehir, right next to the building which was once the Turkish Airlines air terminal (it's now a restaurant). Despite the fading of the business next door, the fairly modern and comfortable Apaydın does a brisk trade lodging the business types and families who visit Ankara. Rates are US$45/55 a single/double with bath, but hesitate and the price should drop substantially – unless they're full up. To find it, walk north along Bayındır Sokak (the same street on which you'll find the Hotel Sultan), cross Ziya Gökalp Caddesi and keep walking 1½ blocks; or walk north along Atatürk Bulvarı one long block until you see an open space on the right with the Beyaz Saray Restaurant at the back. Walk up to the restaurant and the Hotel Apaydın is to the right.

Near Ulus Newest and nicest in this area is the three-star *Otel Karyağdı* (tel 310-2440), Sanayi Caddesi, Kuruçeşme Sokak 4, Ulus, Ankara, with more comforts than any of the hotels already mentioned. It has good wooden furniture, wall-to-wall carpeting, bathrooms with little tubs (showers also), marble trim and even bedside lights bright enough for reading! Some rooms have TVs. Prices are US$35/50

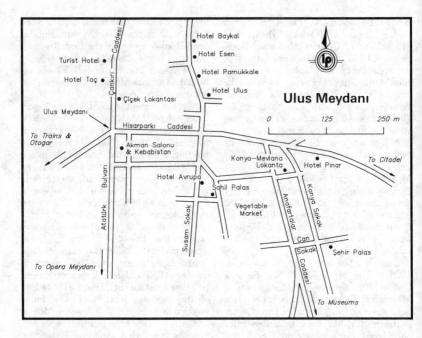

a single/double, though you may be able to haggle here as well. Kuruçeşme Sokak, by the way, is just east of İtfaiye Meydanı, and the Otel Karyağdı is just a few steps off the square.

Also in the midst of the cheap hotel area of İtfaiye Meydanı is the two-star *Otel Güleryüz* (geur-LEHR-yeurz, Smiling Face) (tel 310-4910), İtfaiye Meydanı, Sanayi Caddesi 37, Ulus, a clean, modernish place overlooking the square, with 50 bath-equipped rooms, an enclosed car park, a lift and prices of US$25 a double.

Two blocks north of Ulus along Çankırı Caddesi (the northern continuation of Atatürk Bulvarı) is the three-star, 154-room *Turist Hotel* (tel 310-3980), Çankırı Caddesi 37, Ulus, a big old square building that was one of this city's prime hostelries in its early days. It now offers nominal three-star comforts at decent prices, though in a noisy location. Rooms

with bath cost US$30/42 a single/double. A block back toward Ulus is a cheaper alternative (also on this noisy street), the one-star *Hotel Taç* (TAHCH) (tel 324-3195, 311-1663), Çankırı Caddesi 35, Ulus, with 35 rooms, over half of them with private bath. Rooms cost US$18/22 a single/double, with shower. You can walk to many of Ankara's sights from here but watch out for street noise when selecting a room.

There is a hotel next to Ankara's otogar, the one-star, 110-room *Terminal Oteli* (TEHR-mee-NAHL) (tel 310-4949), Hipodrom Caddesi 3; it's fairly dingy but serviceable and convenient if you're exhausted. Double rooms cost US$16 without bath, US$27 with bath, but haggle over the price.

Places to Stay - top end

With the opening of a Hilton International Hotel in Ankara, the city has a full range of top-end hotels, with even more being built.

The *Hilton International Hotel* (tel 168-2888; fax 168-0909), Tahran Caddesi 12, Kavaklıdere, 06700 Ankara, is the city's prime place to stay, with 327 plush, modern rooms and suites on 16 floors, near Çankaya and the embassy district, four km south of Kızılay. The hotel's architecture is bold and modern, using traditional Anatolian materials such as coloured stone, brass, glass and lots of greenery too. The covered swimming pool has an open air terrace in summer, a health club, disco, business centre, covered car park, casino and numerous restaurants and bars. The very comfortable guest rooms are air-conditioned and have radio and colour TV (with local and satellite programming), mini-bar, direct-dial telephones and electronic locks opened with a plastic card. Some rooms have good views of the city from this hillside perch. Rates are US$100 to US$125 a single, US$115 to US$150 a double.

Before the opening of the Hilton, the five-star, 194-room *Büyük Ankara Oteli* (bew-YEWK AHN-kah-rah, the Grand Ankara Hotel) (tel 125-6655; fax 125-5070) was the city's best place to stay. Located near the parliament at Atatürk Bulvarı 183, this air-conditioned high-rise has all amenities including a swimming pool (summer only), health club, sauna, tennis court and several shops, bars and restaurants. Service is smooth, polished, experienced. Many rooms have fine views. The price for staying here, on Atatürk Bulvarı near parliament, is US$85 a single, US$95 to US$140 a double.

Less dramatic but equally comfortable is the four-star *Ankara Dedeman Oteli* (DEH-deh-mahn) (tel 117-6200; fax 117-6214), Büklüm Sokak 1, Akay, a block east of Atatürk Bulvarı at Akay Sokak, also near parliament. The Dedeman has 308 air-con rooms and suites in two sections – the older Section B has slightly smaller but somewhat cheaper rooms. All

rooms have colour TVs, private baths and direct-dial telephones. The hotel has a good restaurant, a snack bar, several bars, a night club and a swimming pool (summer only). One person pays US$60 to US$75, doubles are US$75 to US$90.

The five-star *Hotel Pullman Etap Altınel* (tel 231-7760; fax 230-2330), Tandoğan Meydanı, 06570 Tandoğan, Ankara, is the larger of the two Ankara hotels operated by the French Pullman Etap chain. Comfortable in every regard, it has several unique features including a formal Japanese restaurant and a tiny rooftop swimming pool usable in winter and summer. Another restaurant serves good Turkish and continental cuisine. The 171 air-con guest rooms have colour TVs with satellite channels, mini-bars, direct-dial phones and hair dryers in the bathrooms. Staff are experienced and helpful. The only problem here is that the architecture and decoration are positively outlandish – a Turkish interpretation of space age hipness. Rooms are priced at US$95 to US$110 a single, US$120 to US$155 a double. The hotel is often busy with foreign tour groups.

Only a few steps north of Kızılay, on Atatürk Bulvarı, is Pullman Etap's other Ankara hostelry, the three-star *Hotel Pullman Etap Mola* (eh-TAHP MOH-lah) (tel 117-8585; fax 117-8592), İzmir Caddesi, 06440 Kızılay. Comfortable and convenient though not overly fancy, the Mola has 60 air-con rooms with bath, mini-bar, colour TV with satellite channels and direct-dial phones. There's a restaurant too and many more in the neighbourhood. You pay US$66/85 a single/double.

Finally, a very different sort of accommodation is the *First Apart-Hotel* (tel 125-7575/6/7), İnkilap Sokak 29, Kızılay, a small modern building on a quiet back street three blocks east of Kızılay. There are 15 comfortable apartments, each with two bedrooms, living/dining room, bathroom and fully equipped kitchen. All apartments have direct-dial phones, colour TVs and furnishings equal to those in a three or four-star hotel. The official rate per apartment for one to four persons is US$110, but I was quoted a reduced rate of US$75 because they weren't too busy. To find the hotel, walk east on Ziya Gökalp Caddesi from Kızılay to the third street (İnkilap Sokak) and turn right; or walk or drive east on Yüksel Caddesi from Atatürk Bulvarı to the third left, which is İnkilap Sokak.

Places to Eat – bottom end
Near Ulus The Ulus area has lots of good, cheap restaurants. North of the square on Çankırı Caddesi are two full-service restaurants with good food, a pleasant atmosphere and low prices. The better is perhaps the *Çiçek Lokantası* (chee-CHEK) (tel 311-5997), Çankırı Caddesi 12/A, a half-block north of the square on the right-hand side. Dine on soup, kebap, salad and spring water for US$3 or so. There's a pleasant little *havuz* (pool, fountain) in the dining room.

Similar is the *Yıldız Restaurant*, Çankırı Caddesi 17, across the street from the Çiçek.

Perhaps the closest restaurant to the Museum of Anatolian Civilisations is the *Yavuz Lokantası* (yah-VOOZ) (tel 311-8508), Konya Sokak 13/F, a clean, airy, bright place with some English speaking staff, open long hours every day of the week. Good food at low prices (kebaps for only US$1 to US$1.50 or so) is the rule. The restaurant is 1½ blocks east off Hisarparkı Caddesi, about a 10-minute walk downhill (20 minutes uphill!) from the museum.

Just a few steps up the hill from Ulus, on the left-hand (north) side of Hisarparkı Caddesi, is a building named the Şehir Çarşısı and, at the back of its courtyard, two small kebap places, the *Başkent* and the *Misket*. Both have upstairs family dining rooms and both serve that delicious İskender kebap from Bursa at about US$2. The *Arı Pasta Salonu* (tel 311-1081), Şehir Çarşısı 30, is right next door to the

Başkent and Misket and serves pastry and cakes, plus light meals, in quietish surroundings (there's an upstairs family dining room at great prices). Other shops in the general area of the Şehir Çarşısı serve similarly cheap, good eats. For flaky pastry, try the *İstanbul Börekçisi*, just up Hisarparkı Caddesi from the equestrian statue of Atatürk, on the opposite side of the street from the statue.

Just south of the centre of Ulus is the *Akman Boza ve Pasta Salonu*, Atatürk Bulvarı 3, in the courtyard of the large building at the south-east corner of the square (there are several courtyards – keep looking until you find the right one). Breakfasts, light lunches (sandwiches, omelettes, etc) and pastries are the specialities, consumed at tables in the little artificial garden on the open-air terrace. Boza is a winter favourite. Food is not cheap here, as this is a gathering place for the young and leisured, but the surroundings are very agreeable.

Located right above the Akman Boza is *Kebabistan* (tel 310-8080), a budget traveller's dream come true. This busy family-oriented kebap and pide parlour serves good, fresh, cheap pide and kebap all day, every day, to large and appreciative crowds. You can have a filling meal of pide for as little as US$1.50 or US$2.

Slightly more expensive is the *Uğur Lokantası* (tel 310-8396), Tavus Sokak 2, near Opera Meydanı and the bottom-end hotels. The Uğur specialises in Turkey's regional lamb kebaps. Expect to spend US$3.50 to US$5 for a full meal here.

Near Kızılay There are several concentrations of restaurants in this area. On Selanik Caddesi, north of the square off Ziya Gökalp Caddesi, are numerous little eateries including *Cihan Kebap* (jee-HAHN) (tel 133-1665), Selanik Caddesi 3/B. It has dinky chandeliers in the dining room, shaded tables out the front by the pedestrian street and good kebaps. A full meal with soup, bread and kebap costs from US$3 to US$3.50. The next street east of Selanik Caddesi is all cafés, beer gardens, pizza joints, grilled chicken emporia and lokantas.

Places to Eat – middle

Near Ulus Near Opera Meydanı and the budget hotels already described is an interesting, even entertaining restaurant. The *Akman Et Lokantası* (tel 311-1086), Tavus Sokak 4, is right next to the Otel Akman. It is a meat restaurant, specialising in kebaps and grilled meats, but this one does it with a difference: the decor is half timber with a mock rustic stone wall complete with bucolic fountain at the back of the dining room. The upstairs eating area has numerous exotic caged birds. Waiters are in uniform and quite attentive. The list of dishes is long, from soups and assorted meze plates to such meats as tandır kebap, döner kebap and even beef stroganoff. Pide is available for the thrifty. Prices are moderate for Turkey, low for anywhere else, and you can get a full meal for US$5 to US$8 per person; hours are from 11.30 am to 11 pm daily.

Near Kızılay The place to look for good, moderately priced food near Kızılay is on Bayındır Sokak, to the east of Atatürk Bulvarı and south of Ziya Gökalp Caddesi. You can't go wrong at the *Körfez Lokantası* (keur-FEHZ) (tel 131-1459), Bayındır Sokak 24, a half-block south of Ziya Gökalp Caddesi. Though there are indoor dining rooms, the terrace is better in fine weather. It's simple, pleasant and unpretentious, with many kebaps priced under US$2.50 and fish dishes for about US$3 to US$6. The bread served here is freshly made, flat, unleavened village bread, which is wonderful. The restaurant's name means 'gulf' and the specialty is fish, so feel free to order that; it will be good, even in this land-locked city.

Next door to the Körfez is the *Washington Restaurant* (tel 131-2219), Bayındır Sokak 22/A, which has much fancier surroundings, diligent service,

Turkish and continental cuisine, and slightly higher prices.

Getting There & Away

In Turkey, all roads lead to Ankara. Its role as governmental capital and second-largest city guarantees that transportation will be convenient.

The Ankara Otogar is one block north-west of the Ankara Railway Station. In a wing of the railway station is the Turkish Airlines Air Terminal. The railway station and the otogar are separated, appropriately, by the Ministry of Transportation (Ulaştırma Bakanlığı). This whole transportation complex is about 1¼ km from Ulus and three km from Kızılay. Many buses heading down the hill on Cumhuriyet Bulvarı from Ulus will take you there; from Kızılay and Bakanlıklar, take bus No 44 (Terminal).

Air Ankara has good international and domestic connections by air to Esenboğa Airport, 33 km north of the city. Pan Am (tel 168-2808), Tunus Caddesi 85/8, Kavaklıdere, takes its daily New York/Europe/İstanbul flights onward to Ankara several times a week, as does Air France.

Turkish Airlines (tel 312-4910 for information, or 312-6200 for reservations) operates non-stop flights from Ankara's Esenboğa Airport to and from the following foreign and domestic cities (there are many other direct and connecting flights as well):

Adana – daily
Antalya – Thursday and Saturday
Berlin East (GDR) – Friday
Cologne – Saturday
Dhahran – Wednesday and Sunday
Diyarbakır – daily
Erzurum – daily
Frankfurt – Friday
Gaziantep – Monday, Wednesday, Thursday, Friday, Sunday
Hamburg – Friday
İstanbul – six or more flights daily

İzmir - daily, with extra flights on Thursday and Friday

Jeddah - Wednesday and Sunday

Nicosia - Monday, Tuesday, Wednesday, Friday, Saturday

Malatya - Tuesday, Thursday, Saturday, Sunday

Munich - Saturday

Sivas - Tuesday, Sunday

Trabzon - daily

Van - Monday, Wednesday, Friday, Sunday

The Turkish Airlines Air Terminal at the railway station has a bank branch for currency exchange, a restaurant and bar and is open daily from 7 am to 8 pm; ticket sales and reservations counters are open between 8.30 am and 7.45 pm, on Sunday from 8.30 am to 5.15 pm.

Bus Every city or town of any size has direct buses to Ankara's huge otogar. From İstanbul there is a bus to Ankara at least every 15 minutes throughout the day and late into the night.

To the Turks, the Ankara Otogar is a busy terminus. To foreigners not knowing the place or the language, it is a frightful chaos of crowds, touts, noise, roaring behemoths and indecipherable signs. Take courage. After a little bit of reconnoitring and searching and with the help of the touts and the ticket agents, you can be on your way before too long. It may be confusing but it is not sinister.

As Ankara has many buses to all parts of the country, it is often sufficient to arrive at the otogar, baggage in hand, and let a barker lead you to a ticket window for your chosen destination (no charge for the lead). However, it might be well to wander through the rows of ticket kiosks to see if there is a more convenient departure time. If you arrive in Ankara by bus, take a few moments to check on schedules to your next destination. Buy your ticket and at the same time reserve your seat, if you can.

Numerous bus companies have offices

near Kızılay on Ziya Gökalp Caddesi, Gazi Mustafa Kemal Bulvarı, İzmir Caddesi and Menekşe Sokak. Buying your ticket here will save you a trip to the otogar.

Here are some destinations from Ankara:

Adana - 490 km, 10 hours, US$8; frequent buses daily

Amasya - 335 km, six hours, US$4.50; frequent buses daily

Antalya - 550 km, 10 hours, US$9; frequent buses daily

Bodrum - 785 km, 13 hours, US$12; a dozen buses daily

Bursa - 400 km, 6½ hours, US$5; hourly buses

Diyarbakır - 945 km, 13 hours, US$10; several buses daily

Erzurum - 925 km, 15 hours, US$11.50; several buses daily

Gaziantep - 705 km, 12 hours, US$10; frequent buses daily

İstanbul - 450 km, eight hours, US$6.50 to US$8.50; virtual shuttle service

İzmir - 600 km, nine hours, US$8.50; buses at least every hour

Kayseri - 330 km, five hours, US$4; very frequent buses daily

Konya - 260 km, 3½ hours, US$4; very frequent buses daily

Nevşehir - 285 km, 4½ hours, US$4; very frequent buses daily

Samsun - 420 km, eight hours, US$7; frequent buses daily

Sivas - 450 km, eight hours, US$6.50; frequent buses daily

Sungurlu (for Boğazkale) - 175 km, three hours, US$2; hourly buses

Trabzon - 780 km, 12 hours, US$12; several buses daily

You can also buy through tickets to Damascus (Şam) for US$25, Tehran for US$32, and to other eastern destinations.

Train Train service is fairly convenient and comfortable on the top trains. Any train not named mavi tren, ekspres or mototren will be very cheap but fantastically slow.

Even if you're out to save money, don't take a slow yolcu or posta train. You may literally be on it for days.

Numerous daily express trains run between Ankara and İstanbul. There are three top trains. The Mavi Tren is an all-reserved, 1st-class (supplement payable) train with club cars and a dining car – Turkey's version of a Trans-Europe Express. It departs both Ankara and İstanbul at 1 pm and 11 pm on the eight-hour trip, arriving at 9 pm and 7.30 am. A one-way ticket costs US$10.

For the comfort of a bed, there's the Ankara Ekspresi, an all-sleeping car train with 1st and 2nd-class berths and a dining car for breakfast only. It departs at 9.40 pm and arrives at 8.30 am; fares, bed fees and service charges in a two-person sleeping compartment come to about US$32 per person (US$64 total). The Anadolu Ekspresi (ah-nah-doh-LOO, Anatolia) is another night train with 1st and 2nd-class sleeping cars but it also hauls regular 1st and 2nd-class coaches. It leaves at 9.05 pm and arrives the next morning at 8.10 am. Sleeping car charges are the same as on the Ankara Ekspresi.

Two other express trains take a bit longer but offer similar comfort and convenience at lower prices. The 1st-class Boğaziçi Ekspresi (boh-AHZ-ee-chee, Bosphorus) is a day train with club cars and a dining car. It leaves at 8 am and arrives at dinner time, making the run in about nine hours. A one-way ticket costs US$6.

The 'third tier' of express trains are through-trains which stop at Ankara. They are not as dependable or as comfortable as the other trains, though you may pay as much for a seat. Don't assume these trains will be on time, particularly if you are going west from Ankara to İstanbul.

The Doğu Ekspresi (doh-OO, east) goes from İstanbul via Ankara, Sivas and Erzurum to Kars daily.

The Vangölü Ekspresi and Güney Ekspresi share a common route from İstanbul (daily at 7.10 pm) via Ankara (arrive 5.40 am, depart 6.40 am), to Sivas, Malatya and Elazığ Junction. East of the junction, the train continues on some days to Tatvan and other days to Diyarbakır and Kurtalan (east of Diyarbakır). These trains haul sleepers, 1st and 2nd-class coaches and diners.

The İzmir Mavi Tren hauls Pullman coaches only, no sleeping cars, and departs both İzmir and Ankara daily at 8.05 pm to arrive the next morning at 10.35 am. The İzmir Ekspresi departs each city at 6.05 pm daily and arrives at 9.18 am, hauling 1st and 2nd-class sleepers and coaches and a dining car.

There are also two daily trains to and from Zonguldak on the Black Sea coast, the morning Karaelmas Ekspresi departing at 7.55 am, arriving at 7.12 pm, and the evening Zonguldak Mavi Tren departing at 1.15 pm, arriving at 10.25 pm.

The Erzurum Mavi Tren runs daily, departing each city at 9 pm, arriving the next day at 5.16 pm and running via Kayseri, Sivas and Erzincan.

The Gaziantep Mavi Tren departs at 7 pm, arriving at 11.50 am. Trains run from Ankara on Monday, Wednesday, Friday and Saturday; from Gaziantep on Monday, Wednesday, Friday and Sunday. They connect the cities of Ankara, Kayseri, Niğde, Adana and Gaziantep.

Getting Around

Airport Transport The airport is 33 km north of the city. Havaş airport buses, US$1, are supposed to depart the air terminal in Ankara 1½ hours before domestic flight times, 2¼ hours before international flight times, but they may leave sooner if they fill up, so claim your seat on the bus at least two hours before flight time. Minimum check-in time at the airport for any flight is 45 minutes.

When your flight arrives in Ankara, don't dawdle in the terminal because the Havaş bus will depart for the city within a half-hour after the flight has landed and there may not be another bus for several hours depending upon flights. Taxis between the airport and the city cost about US$15.

Bus Ankara is served well and frequently by an extensive bus and minibus network. Some of the important bus routes are: Route No 8 (Çankaya) between Ulus and Çankaya runs the entire length of Atatürk Bulvarı; Route No 16 (Bahçelievler) and Route No 64 (Emek) run between Ulus and the railway station; Route No 44 (Terminal) runs past the otogar, air terminal and railway station, then on to Kızılay and Bakanlıklar; Route No 63 (Anıttepe) will take you from Ulus to Atatürk's mausoleum.

City bus tickets cost US$0.20 and can be bought from the little ticket kiosks at major bus stops.

Taxi The drop rate is US$0.55 and an average trip costs US$2 to US$2.50. The lower fare would be for a trip from the otogar or railway station to Ulus; the higher fare, to Kızılay or Kavaklıdere.

Konya & Aksaray

Standing alone in the midst of the vast Anatolian steppe, Konya (KOHN-yah), at an altitude of 1016 metres and with a population of 550,000, is like some traditional caravan stopping-place. The windswept landscape gives way to little patches of greenery in the city, and when you're in the town you don't feel the loneliness of the plateau.

In recent years Konya has been booming. The bare-looking steppe is in fact good for growing grain and Konya is the heart of Turkey's very rich 'breadbasket'. Light industry provides jobs for those who are not farmers. Much of the city was built within the last 10 years but the centre is very old. No-one knows when the hill in

the centre of town, the Alaettin Tepesi, was first settled but it contains the bones of Bronze Age men and women.

Plan to spend at least one full day in Konya, preferably two, but not a Monday as the museums will be closed. If your interest in Seljuk history and art takes flame you could easily spend another half or full day. As it takes a good half-day to reach Konya from anywhere, and another half-day to get from Konya to your next destination, you should figure on spending at least two nights in a hotel here.

It's important to remember that Konya is a favourite with devout Muslims and a fairly conservative place. Take special care not to upset the pious and look tidy when you enter mosques and the Mevlana Museum. If you visit during the holy month of Ramazan, do not eat or drink in public during the day. This is a courtesy to those who are fasting. (For Ramazan and other religious dates see the Calendar in the Facts for the Country chapter.) Also, the Dervishes do not whirl all the time. They usually only dance during the Mevlana Festival in December.

History

The city has been here a very long time. Neighbouring Çatal Höyük, 50 km to the south, is thought to be the oldest known human community, dating from 7500 BC.

The Hittites called Konya 'Kuwanna' almost 4000 years ago but the name has changed over the years. It was Kowania to the Phrygians, Iconium to the Romans and now Konya to the Turks.

Under Rome, Iconium was an important provincial town visited several times by the saints Paul and Barnabas, but its early Christian community does not seem to have been very influential.

Konya's heyday was during the 1200s, when it was capital of the Seljuk Sultanate of Rum, the last remnant of an earlier Seljuk empire.

The Seljuk Turks ruled a powerful state in Iran and Iraq, the Empire of the Great Seljuks, during the 1000s. Omar Khayyam was their most noted poet and mathematician. But Great Seljuk power was fragmented in the early 1100s, and various parts of the empire became independent states. One of these states was the Sultanate of Rum, which encompassed most of Anatolia. Konya was its capital from about 1150 to 1300. In that period, the Seljuk sultans built dozens of fine buildings in an architectural style decidedly Turkish, but with its roots in Persia and Byzantium.

Mevlana The Sultanate of Rum also produced one of the world's great mystic philosophers – Celaleddin Rumi (jeh-LAH-leh-DEEN roo-MEE). The founder of the order of Whirling Dervishes, Rumi was called Mevlana (Our Guide) by his followers. His poetic and religious work, mostly in Persian (the literary language of the day), is some of the most beloved and respected in the Islamic world.

Mevlana (1207-1273) was born in Balkh (near Mazar-i Sharif in modern Afghanistan). His family fled the impending Mongol invasion by moving to Mecca and then to the Sultanate of Rum by 1221, reaching Konya by 1228. His father was a noted preacher and Rumi grew to be a brilliant student of Islamic theology. After his father's death in 1231, Rumi studied in Aleppo and Damascus but returned to live in Konya by 1240.

In 1244 he met Mehmet Şemseddin Tebrizi, called Şemsi Tebrizi, one of his father's Sufi (Muslim mystic) disciples. Tebrizi had a profound effect on Rumi, who became devoted to him. An angry crowd of Rumi's own disciples put Tebrizi to death in 1247, perhaps because of his overwhelming influence on the brilliant Rumi. Stunned by the loss of his spiritual master, Rumi withdrew from the world for meditation and, in this period, founded a Dervish order. Its members called Rumi 'Mevlana' and the order came to be called Mevlevi (Those who Follow the Guide).

Rumi's great poetic work, the *Mesnevi*, has 25,000 verses. He also wrote many *ruba'i* and *ghazal* poems, collected into his 'Great Opus', the *Divan-i Kebir*.

The Mevlevi Dervishes The way of the Mevlevis spread throughout Turkey, Syria and Egypt. Wherever there was a branch of the order there would be a Dervish monastery.

The worship ceremony is a ritual dance representing union with God. The Dervishes' long white robes, with full skirts, represent their shrouds, and the tall conical red hats represent their tombstones, as they relinquish the earthly life to be reborn in mystical union with God. They pass before the şeyh, spiritual descendant of Mevlana, with their arms folded and he whispers in their ears. Each Dervish then moves on, unfurling his arms and starting the dance.

By holding their right arm up, palm upwards, they receive the blessings of Heaven and communicate them to Earth by holding their left arm down, palm downwards. Pivoting on their left heel, the Dervishes whirl ever faster, reaching ecstasy with a blissful expression. The Dervishes, still whirling, form a 'constellation' which slowly rotates. They stop suddenly and kneel down. The dance is repeated three times, with the şeyh joining the last repetition. An orchestra with small drums, *rebap* (a gourd viol), *kemançe* and *ney* (an open-tube reed flute) and a male choir, provides the music. After the whirling, a *hafız* (man who has memorised the entire Koran) chants poetical passages from the holy book.

The breathy, haunting music of the ney is perhaps the most striking sound during the ceremony. Each musician 'opens' (makes) his own instrument from a carefully chosen length of bamboo-like reed, burning the finger-holes to a mathematical formula. The ney is thought to have its own soul, like a human, and 'opening' it liberates the soul, which comes out in its music.

Rumi's teachings were ecumenical. He

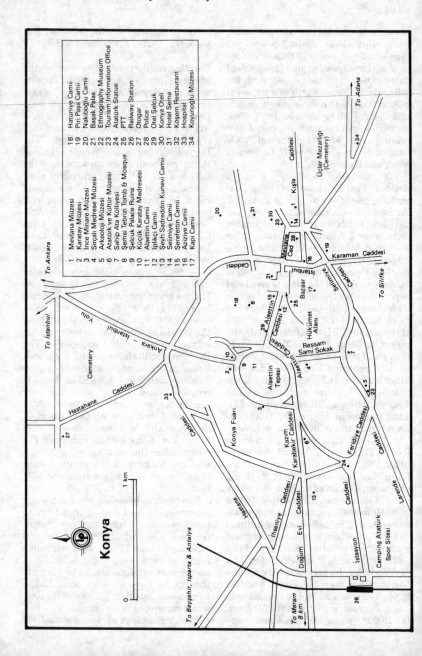

Konya

0   1 km

1	Mevlana Müzesi
2	Karatay Müzesi
3	Ince Minare Müzesi
4	Sırçalı Medrese Müzesi
5	Arkeoloji Müzesi
6	Atatürk ve Kültur Müzesi
7	Sahip Ata Külliyesi
8	Şemsi Tebrizi Tomb & Mosque
9	Selçuk Palace Ruins
10	Küçük Karatay Medresesi
11	Alaettin Camii
12	İplikçi Camii
13	Şeyh Sadreddin Kunevi Camii
14	Seiimiye Camii
15	Serefettin Camii
16	Aziziye Camii
17	Kapı Camii
18	Hatuniye Camii
19	Piri Paşa Camii
20	Nakiboğlu Camii
21	Başak Palas
22	Ethnography Museum
23	Tourism Information Office
24	Atatürk Statue
25	PTT
26	Railway Station
27	Otogar
28	Police
29	Otel Selçuk
30	Konya Oteli
31	Hotel Sema
32	Kösem Restaurant
33	Hospital
34	Koyunoğlu Müzesi

To Ankara

To İstanbul

To Adana

To Silifke

To Beyşehir, Isparta & Antalya

To Meram 8 km

Üçler Mezarlığı (Cemetery)

Cemetery

Ankara – İstanbul Yolu

Karaman Caddesi

stressed the universality of God and welcomed any worshipper, of any sect or following, to join in worshipping Him. Non-Muslims were regularly invited to witness the ceremony.

Republican Reforms Under the Ottoman Empire, Dervish orders exerted a great deal of influence in the country's political, social and economic life. Their world-view was monarchist, arch-conservative and xenophobic in most cases. Committed to progress, democracy and separation of religion and state, Atatürk viewed the Dervishes as a block to advancement for the Turkish people, so he saw to it that the Dervish orders were proscribed in 1925. Many of the monasteries were converted to museums. The Mevlana opened as a museum in 1927.

Though outlawed, several of the Dervish orders survived as fraternal religious brotherhoods, stripped of their influence. The Whirling Dervishes of Konya are now officially a 'cultural association' which preserves a historical tradition. The annual Festival of Mevlana, held in mid-December, is officially encouraged as a popular – not a religious – event. Groups of Dervishes are also sent on cultural exchange tours to other countries, performing the ceremony from Leningrad to Los Angeles.

The Dervishes are no longer interested in politics but neither are they truly a 'cultural association'. Young novices are recruited as early as grammar school, and devotion to the principles of the order can still be lifelong. Konya's Dervishes whirl today to celebrate a great tradition and, as they have been doing for over 700 years, to worship and to seek mystical union with God as Mevlana taught.

Orientation
Though you will want to ride in from the bus and rail terminals, (both one km from the centre), you can easily walk to most of Konya's attractions once you get downtown. The city's historic axis is Alaettin Caddesi/Mevlana Caddesi, the main street which runs between the hill called Alaettin Tepesi and the Mevlana Museum. Half-way along this street it broadens into Hükümet Alanı, Government Square, also called Konak. By the way, the Mevlana Museum shelters Rumi's tomb and was the first Whirling Dervish monastery. It's the most important building to visit in Konya.

The distance from the hill to the museum is about one km, a 10 to 15-minute walk.

Information
Konya's official Tourism Information Office (tel (33) 11 10 74) is at Mevlana Caddesi 21, across the square from the Mevlana Museum. Hours are from 8.30 am to 5 pm, Monday to Saturday. They speak English, French and German here and will offer to sell you a swell carpet along with the free information.

Across the street is the Konya Kültür ve Turizm Derneği (Konya Culture & Tourism Association, (tel 11 62 55, 11 82 88), where you can buy books on Konya and cassette tapes of Mevlevi music.

Buildings
The centre of Konya is Turkey's best 'outdoor museum' of Seljuk architecture. While the buildings themselves are often starkly simple on the outside, the main portal is always grand and imposing, sometimes huge and wildly baroque. The Seljuks built wondrous doorways to which small buildings were attached. The interiors are always very harmonious and often decorated with blue and white tiles. Tiles of other colours are sometimes found but they rarely have red in them as the fusing of vivid reds on faïence was a later Ottoman accomplishment.

You can walk to all of the buildings described here but it would be tiring to do so in one day.

Mevlana Müzesi
First place to visit is the Mevlana Müzesi

or Mevlana Museum, the former monastery of the Whirling Dervishes, open every day from 9 am to 12 noon and from 1 to 5 pm (3 to 5 pm on Monday); admission costs US$3. Admission tickets are sold until 5.10 pm. On religious holidays the museum (really a shrine) may be open for longer hours. Women may want to cover their heads and shoulders when they enter. You will see many people praying and pleading for Mevlana's intercession. For Turkish Muslims, it is a very holy place.

Enter through a pretty courtyard with an ablutions fountain and several tombs, then remove your shoes and pass into the Mevlana Türbesi, or Tomb of Rumi. The sarcophagi of Rumi and his illustrious followers are covered in great velvet shrouds heavy with gold embroidery. It gives the powerful impression that this is a sacred place. Those of Mevlana and his son have great symbolic turbans on them.

The tomb dates from Seljuk times. The mosque and room for ceremonies were added later by Ottoman sultans (Mehmet the Conqueror was a Mevlevi adherent and Süleyman the Magnificent made large charitable donations to the order). Selim I, conqueror of Egypt, donated the Mameluke crystal lamps.

In the rooms adjoining the sepulchral chamber are exhibits of Dervish parapher-nalia: musical instruments, vestments, illuminated manuscripts and ethnographic artefacts. The rooms off the courtyard by the entrance, once offices and quarters for the Dervishes, are now furnished as they would have been at the time of Mevlana (1200s), with mannequins dressed in Dervish costumes.

Outside the entrance to the Mevlana Museum is the **Selimiye Camii**, endowed by Sultan Selim II (1566-1574). Construction on the Ottoman-style mosque started during Selim's term as Governor of Konya, before his accession to the throne.

Leave the museum, turn left, walk between the Selimiye Camii and the museum and cross the wide street. You'll see a verdant cemetery, the **Üçler Mezarlığı** (urch-LEHR meh-zahr-luh) where you can take a stroll. If you cut through the cemetery at the proper angle, you will emerge near the Koyunoğlu Müzesi.

Koyunoğlu Müzesi

This fine museum, 750 metres from the Mevlana Museum, was donated to the city by a private collector who seemed to collect everything. Hours are from 9.30 am to 12 noon and from 2 to 5 pm; admission costs US$0.50. The few labels are in Turkish only.

The modern museum building has three levels. Downstairs are collections of minerals, weapons, fossils, stuffed birds and an atrium filled with plants and live birds. The main floor has exhibits of ancient coins: Roman, Seljuk and Ottoman; sculptures, glass, jewellery, Bronze Age implements and a photo display of old Konya. Upstairs is the ethnographic section including kilims and carpets (one bears a map of Turkey); illuminated manuscripts and Korans; miniature paintings and clocks; and 19th-century clothing, bath clogs, weapons, household items, coffee sets, musical instruments, embroidery and needlework.

Next door to the museum is the **Koyunoğlu Konya Evi**, a quaint and delightful little old-fashioned house which shows vividly how a Konyalı family lived a century ago. Leave your shoes at the carved wooden door, put on sandals as all Turks used to do and inspect the small ground-floor room with its silk carpet. There is another, smaller salon on the ground floor as well. Upstairs the rooms are traditionally furnished with lots of carpets, kilims, low benches, pillows, a fine tray-table and lots of turned wood. The picture is of the museum's founder.

Alaettin Camii

Except for the Mevlana Museum, many of Konya's principal sights are near the

Alaettin Tepesi or Aladdin's Hill, at the western end of Alaettin Caddesi. The eastern slopes of the hill are set with tea gardens. The ancient Alaettin Camii is right atop the hill.

The Mosque of Aladdin Keykubat I (or Alaettin), Seljuk Sultan of Rum, is a great rambling building designed by a Damascene architect in the Arab style and finished in 1221. Over the centuries it was embellished, refurbished, ruined and restored. Restoration began over a decade ago and is still under way, so you will have to view the mosque from the outside. Though hardly as harmonious as an Ottoman work of Sinan, it is very sympathetic and impressive. The interior is a forest of old columns surmounted with Roman and Byzantine capitals, with a fine, carved wooden pulpit (1156) and a marble prayer niche.

On the north side of the Alaettin Tepesi, the scant ruins of a **Seljuk palace** are protected by a modern concrete shelter.

Büyük Karatay Medresesi

Now called the **Karatay Müzesi** (KAH-rah-tah-yee) or Karatay Museum, this Seljuk theological seminary just north of the Alaettin Tepesi houses Konya's outstanding collection of ceramics and tiles. It is open from 8.30 am to 12 noon and from 1.30 to 5.30 pm for US$2.

The school was constructed in 1251 by the Emir Celaleddin Karatay, a Seljuk diplomat and statesman. It has a magnificent sculpted marble doorway.

Inside, the central dome is a masterpiece of Seljuk blue tilework with gold accents. The effect suggests the heavens with stars of gold. The Arabic inscription in Kufic style around the bottom of the dome is the first chapter of the Koran. The triangles below the dome are decorated with the names of the first four caliphs who succeeded Muhammed; the Arabic letters are highly stylised.

Note especially the curlicue drain for the central pool: its curved shape made the sound of running water a pleasant background 'noise' in the quiet room where students studied.

The museum's collection of tiles includes interesting coloured ones from Seljuk palaces in Konya and Beyşehir. Compare these to the later Ottoman tiles from İznik.

İnce Minare Müzesi

Around the Alaettin Tepesi on its western side is the İnce Minare Medresesi (een-JEH mee-NAH-reh) or Seminary of the Slender Minaret, now the Museum of Wood & Stone Carving. Don't enter the building immediately, for half of what you came to see is the elaborate doorway with bands of Arabic inscription running up the sides and looping overhead. As this religious school was built in 1258, it may be that the architect was trying to outdo a rival who had designed the Karatay Medresesi only seven years earlier.

The doorway is far more impressive than the small building behind it. The minaret beside the door is what gave the seminary its popular name of 'slender minaret'. Over 600 years old, most of the very tall minaret was knocked off by lightning less than 100 years ago.

As of this writing, the museum is closed for renovation but go anyway as the exterior is the most impressive part of the building. When it was last open, the exhibits showed Seljuk motifs used in wood and stone carving, many of them similar to those used in the tile and ceramic work. In Islam, images of creatures with souls (humans and animals) are forbidden as idolatry, but most great Islamic civilisations had artists who ignored the law from time to time. Most Islamic art is geometrical or nonrepresentative, but you will still see birds (the Seljuk double-headed eagle, for example), men and women, lions and leopards, etc. Though the Ottomans seem to have observed the law more strictly than the Seljuks, there were some lapses. Mehmet the Conqueror, for instance, had his portrait painted by the great Bellini. But, as the finished masterpiece was hung in the palace, the masses were none the wiser to this 'sacrilege'.

South of the Hill

Several other significant Seljuk monuments lie south of the city, in a warren of little streets. If you can find Ressam Sami Sokak, it will lead you to the following sights.

Not far from the Alaettin Tepesi on Ressam Sami Sokak is another Seljuk seminary. Now a museum of funerary monuments, it is the Sırçalı Medrese Müzesi (sirr-chah-LUH). As always, the portal is grand and highly decorated. The tiles on the exterior give the seminary its name (sırçalı means crystalline). Construction was completed in 1242, sponsored by a Seljuk vizier. The inscriptions on the gravestones inside are often very fine, done in a variety of Arabic scripts. Symbols of rank – headgear, usually – served to tell the passer-by of the deceased's important role in life. The museum is closed for renovation as of this

writing, but you can still enjoy a view of the marvellous facade.

Konya's small **Archaeological Museum** is a few blocks south along Ressam Sami Sokak, in the grounds of the **Sahip Ata Külliyesi**. Museum hours are from 8.30 am to 12 noon and from 1.30 to 5.30 pm; admission costs US$1. A külliye is a complex of buildings surrounding a mosque. These might include soup kitchens, religious schools, an orphanage or hospital, a library and other charitable works. Sahip Ata was the man who funded the İnce Minare Medresesi. There is also a Dervish monastery and a Turkish bath. The entire complex was finished in 1283. Note especially the portal to the mosque with its tiled minaret and prayer niche. Sahip Ata, by the way, was a Seljuk prime minister and obviously very rich.

Not far from the Sahip Ata Külliyesi is the city's small **Ethnography Museum**, open during the same hours as the Archaeological Museum for US$1.

Other Mosques & Tombs

As you wander around town, you will pass other buildings of interest. The **Şemsi Tebrizi Camii**, containing the tomb (1300s) of Rumi's spiritual mentor, is just north of Hükümet Alanı, off Alaettin Caddesi. The **Aziziye Camii** (1874) is a work of Ottoman late Baroque in the bazaar; it's the one with twin minarets bearing little sheltered balconies. The **İplikçi Camii** (1202) on the main street is perhaps Konya's oldest mosque. The **Şerefettin Camii** was constructed in 1636. Near the PTT on Hükümet Caddesi is the **Hacı Hasan Camii**.

The Bazaar

Konya's market area is behind the modern PTT building. Walk through the city bus parking area, along the east side of the Koli PTT (the parcel branch) and to the left of the shoeshine stand, then straight along Çıkrıkçılar Caddesi. Besides shops selling all manner of things, there are lots of inexpensive eateries here.

Meram

If you have a spare morning or afternoon, take an excursion (less than 10 km) to Meram, a pleasant, shady suburb west of the city. It's been a getaway destination for Konya city dwellers for at least 1000 years. Minibuses depart the market area not far from the Mevlana Museum for the 15-minute trip to Meram. The fare is US$0.25.

Çatal Höyük

You can drive or arrange a taxi excursion to Çatal Höyük, the world's oldest human community, 50 km south-east of Konya, but there is little to see except the setting. The prehistoric artefacts have been removed to museums.

Places to Stay – bottom end

Being a God-fearing sort of town, Konya has lots of inexpensive, clean, proper little hotels. The cheap lodging situation here is better than in most other Turkish cities.

On a quiet street near the Mevlana Museum is the *Otel Köşk* (KEURSHK) (tel 12 06 71), Mevlana Caddesi, Bostan Çelebi Sokak 13, also called the Yeni Köşk Oteli. Look for the street opposite the Töbank building on Mevlana Caddesi. It's a tidy and convenient place which charges US$7/10 for a single/double room with washbasin, US$14 for a double with shower. Many rooms have three and four beds, good for families or small groups. The same people run the tidy *Petek Oteli* (tel 11 25 99), Çıkrıkçılar Caddesi 42, Vali Konağı Arkası, behind the PTT in the bazaar, which charges the same prices for even nicer rooms; but the Köşk is only steps from the Mevlana Museum.

The nearby *Otel Tur* (TOOR) (tel 11 98 25), Eşârizade Sokak 13, is also very close to the museum. It has very basic barebulb double and triple rooms which go for a high US$19 a double with shower, but it's modern and clean and you can often haggle them down. The hotel is only a half-block from the traffic roundabout by the museum.

The *Otel Selimiye* (seh-LEEM-ee-yeh) (tel 111-2306), Mevlana Caddesi 17, a half-block from the Tourism Information Office, is very clean and tidy and charges US$7/10 for a single/double room with cold-water washbasin; a hot shower costs another US$1. Be sure to get a room away from the noisy street.

An excellent choice is the *Hotel Ulusan* (OO-loo-sahn) (tel 11 50 04), PTT Arkası, Kurşuncular Sokak 2, behind the PTT (follow the little signs). Clean, tidy and quiet, it seems to be run by a little old lady who keeps everything in good shape and who charges US$7/10 a single/double with hot and cold-water washbasin. This may be a good choice for women travelling without men.

Near the Alaettin Tepesi is the *Otel Kanarya* (kah-NAHR-yah, Canary Hotel) (tel 11 15 75), Alaettin Caddesi, Emirpervane Sokak 4 (turn off the main street by the Anadolu Bankası). This is a homey place where rooms with three beds and no water go for US$7/10/13 a single/double/triple. Be sure to note the safe in the lobby which bears the legend 'Milner's Patent Fire-Resisting Strong Holdfast Safe'.

Kara Hüyüklü Sokak is a little street running south from Alaettin Caddesi between the Ağazade Eczanesi (a pharmacy) and the Tekel building – ask for the Tekel Binası, (teh-KEHL bee-nah-suh). On it are no less than five small, cheap, clean hotels charging about US$6 or US$7 a double, US$7 or US$8 a triple for waterless rooms. Look for the *Otel Roma, Pak Otel, Otel Nur, Bulvar Oteli* and *Yeni Doğan Oteli* (tel 11 25 92), all within one block of one another.

Finally, for a bit more colour and homey feeling, seek out the *Çatal Aile Pansiyonu* (tel 11 49 81), Mevlana Caddesi, Nacifikret Sokak 4/2, above the Çatal Restaurant behind the Tourism Information Office. Simple but folksy it has lots of character and is fairly quiet. Rooms with private shower cost US$14/18 a double/triple.

Camping You can camp at the *Şehir Stadı*, the sports complex just east of the railway station on İstasyon Caddesi.

Places to Stay – middle

Conveniently located next to the otogar are two middle-range hotels.

The two-star *Özkaymak Park Oteli* (EURZ-kahy-mahk) (tel 13 37 70/2), has 90 clean and comfortable (if simple) rooms with shower going for US$36/49 a single/double; it's generally regarded as one of the town's best places to stay and is popular with tour groups. The staff are not particularly friendly; breakfast is priced at a high US$4, and they will insist you take it with your room. Demand that they not include it, then go over to the Uludağ Pasta Salonu, a pastry shop right next to the Hotel Sema 2, and have a big breakfast for US$1. A set-price meal at the Özkaymak Park Oteli is also fairly expensive at US$10, plus drinks and tip.

Hotel Sema 2 (tel 13 25 57, 13 01 38), Yeni Terminal, is also next to the otogar. With 33 rooms priced at US$15 for a double without running water, or US$28 for a double with bath, this is the second choice. A bathless single here goes for US$11.

The other moderately priced hotels are central. The two-star *Konya Oteli* (tel 11 92 12, 11 66 77), Mevlana Meydanı, Turizm Yanı 8, 42040 Konya, just behind the Tourism Information Office and very near the Mevlana Museum, is a fine choice. At this quiet, recently renovated hotel the desk clerk will quote you prices of US$36/49 a single/double for one of the 27 rooms with shower, but he's amenable to haggling which should bring the price down considerably. Some rooms have mini-bars.

Also here is the three-star, 100-room *Hotel Dergah* (tel 11 11 97, 11 76 61), Mevlana Meydanı 19, 42040 Konya, which has been renovated and modernised with new furniture and wall-to-wall carpeting in recent years. It is now a pleasant and convenient hostelry charging US$30/48 a single/double for rooms with private bath (some with tubs as well as showers). The rooms at the front have views of the Mevlana Museum but are also subject to street noise; there are many quieter rooms as well.

Konya's other three-star hotel is the *Hotel Selçuk* (SEHL-chook) (tel 11 12 59, 11 41 61; fax 11 33 78), Alaettin Caddesi, Babalık Sokak, 42050 Konya, not far from the Alaettin Tepesi hill, on a side street running north from Alaettin Caddesi. The 75 fairly spacious guest rooms with bath and balcony here have recently undergone complete renovation and are now bright with new paint and natural wood accents. Prices are moderate at US$34/48 a single/double.

The one-star *Başak Palas* (bah-SHAHK pah-LAHS) (tel 11 13 38/9), Hükümet Alanı 3, 42050 Konya, facing the provincial government house midway along Alaettin Caddesi, is an older place with 40 rooms kept brightly painted. Rooms are US$16/28 a single/double with washbasin; with private bath (tub and shower), US$24/34. You can often haggle over these prices.

The *Şahin Oteli* (tel 11 33 50, 11 23 76), Hükümet Alanı 6, 42050 Konya, is an older hotel offering good value and location. The rooms have been used a good deal and the ones facing the busy street are quite noisy. The staff are polite and helpful and prices are US$24 a single, US$35 for a double with shower.

Places to Eat

Konya's speciality is fırın kebap, a rich joint of mutton roasted in an oven. It is not normally prepared to order, so you must trust to luck for a taste of it. If you see it offered, give it a try.

The *Çatal Lokantası* (chah-TAHL) (tel 14439) is just behind the Tourism Information Office, near the Mevlana Museum. This is a simple, tidy kebap place (no booze) next to the Konya Otel, with good food at low prices. Expect to pay US$3.50 for a full lunch or dinner.

Mesut Bolu Lokantası, Mevlana Caddesi 3, across from the Hotel Dergah, has white tables and chairs, lots of air and light, and serves an assortment of Turkish dishes including Konya's fırın kebap. No alcoholic beverages are available. Fırın kebap with salad, bread and soft drink might cost US$2 or so. The 'Bolu' in the restaurant's name refers to the town of Bolu, in the mountains on the Ankara to İstanbul highway, where most of Turkey's best chefs come from.

Nearby is the popular *Şifa Lokantası* (shee-FAH, health) (tel 12 05 19), Mevlana Caddesi 30, only a short stroll from the Mevlana Museum. It's a modern if simple dining room with tablecloths and full meals for US$3 or US$4. No booze served here either.

Even cheaper fare is available on Çıkrıkçılar Caddesi in the bazaar, behind the PTT. At No 19 is the *Şambaba Börekçi*, serving pide called etli ekmek (bread with meat) for only US$0.75. See it made fresh right before your eyes. Nearby is the *Çağlar Lokantası* (tel 12 40 42), Çıkrıkçılar Caddesi, with lots of ready-food dishes as well as etli ekmek; the upstairs aile salonu may be more pleasant than the downstairs room.

Just off Çıkrıkçılar on Başaraldı Sokak is the *Örnek Lokantası* with ready food, etli ekmek, and *tereyağlı börek* (flaky pastry made with butter), all at low prices. The upstairs aile salonu is for couples and women alone. There are many other, similarly cheap and good restaurants in this area.

Near the Yeni Köşk Oteli, Bostançelebi Sokak has several cheap eateries, including the good *Yeni Şamdan Lokantası*.

Readers of this book have written to recommend the *Hanedan Restaurant* (HAH-neh-DAHN, dynasty), on Kışla Caddesi, for its good pide and baklava; downstairs you share tables, upstairs is more formal, with individual tables and tablecloths.

Getting There & Away

Konya has some air and rail access, but most transport is by road (bus).

Air Turkish Airlines, Alaettin Caddesi 22 Kat 1/106, Konya (tel 112000, 112032), on the north side of the street not far from the Alaettin Tepesi, flies between Konya and İstanbul on Monday and Friday.

Bus Konya's otogar is one km or so from Hükümet Alanı, which is called Konak by the minibus drivers. To travel from the otogar into town there are municipal buses and more convenient minibuses (Konak-Otogar, US$0.25) waiting at a rank near the Özkaymak Park Oteli, just outside the otogar. Climb in, and you'll be quickly transported to Hükümet Alanı at the very centre of things on Alaettin Caddesi. Some of the minibuses continue to Mevlana Meydanı, next to the Tourism Information Office and the Mevlana Museum.

When the road south via Beyşehir and Akseki is fully improved and opened to bus traffic, travel times and distances to Alanya, Antalya and Side will decrease dramatically, perhaps to only four or five hours.

Adana – 350 km, 6½ hours, US$5; frequent buses daily
Adıyaman (Nemrut Dağı) – 720 km, 16 hours, US$15; change at Adana
Aksaray – 140 km, 2½ hours, US$2.25; frequent buses daily
Alanya – 500 km, 10 hours, US$11; change buses at Silifke
Ankara – 265 km, four hours, US$4.50; very frequent buses
Antalya – 365 km, eight hours, US$6; several buses daily
Bursa – 500 km, 8½ hours, US$7; several buses daily
İstanbul – 660 km, 12 hours, US$10; very frequent buses daily
İzmir – 575 km, eight hours, US$8; buses at least every two hours

Nevşehir (Cappadocia) – 226 km, 3½ hours, US$3; several buses daily

Silifke – 218 km, four hours, US$3; very frequent buses daily

Side – 440 km, nine hours, US$10; a few buses daily, or change at Antalya

If you can't find a direct bus or minibus from Konya to Nevşehir, take something to Aksaray then ask for directions to the ticket office for the onward journey. The phrase is *Nevşehir'e giden otobüs nereden kalkar?* (NEHV-sheh-heer-eh gee-dehn oto-beurss NEH-reh-dehn kahl-KAHR, 'From where does the Nevşehir bus depart?') Going to Konya, you must ask *Konya'ya giden otobüs nereden kalkar?* (KOHN-yah-YAH. . ., 'From where does the bus to Konya depart?') People in Aksaray are used to foreigners passing through and will gladly and quickly point the way.

Train There is no direct rail link across the steppe between Konya and Ankara. Bus is the best way to make this journey.

Between İstanbul (Haydarpaşa) and Konya you can ride the Meram Ekspresi which departs each city at 8.25 pm and arrives the next morning at 10.15 am, almost 14 hours later, with 1st-class coaches and a dining car. The alternative is the Anadolu Mavi Tren, departing each city at 11.30 pm, arriving the next day at 12.16 pm, making the journey in under 13 hours. It hauls 1st-class Pullman coaches and a dining car (morning only).

City buses connect the railway station with the centre of town, running at least every half-hour. If you take a taxi from the railway station to Hükümet Alanı, it will cost about US$2.

SULTAN HANI

The highway between Konya and Aksaray crosses quintessential Anatolian steppe: undulating grassland, sometimes with mountains in the distance. Along the way, 95 km from Konya and 45 km from Aksaray, is the village of Sultan Hanı,

which has one of several Seljuk hans bearing that name. The Sultan Hanı is 500 metres from the highway. You can visit it any day from 8 am to 5 or 6 pm for US$0.50, and you should, if possible, as it is a fine and impressive example. It was constructed between 1232 and 1236, in the reign of the Seljuk Sultan Aladdin Keykubat I. Nearby is the *Kervan Pansyion & Camping* (tel (4817) 1411, 1325); follow the signs from the han to the pension.

AKSARAY

Aksaray, with a population of 85,000, is another of those farming towns (lots of potatoes) where a bed and a meal are its most important features, though you can amuse yourself well enough if you have a spare hour. More to the point, Aksaray is a good base for visits to Ihlara.

It's one km from Aksaray's otogar to the main square. For tourism information, apply to the local Tourism Information Office in the Jandarma headquarters on the main square with the other government buildings; signs point the way.

Things to See

The Zinciriye Medresesi dates from Seljuk Turkish times, when it was built by the local dynasty of Karamanoğulları. It has been restored several times over the past seven centuries. It is now the local museum, with displays of pots and inscriptions arranged around the courtyard and in the rooms. But it's the building itself which is interesting. It served as a theological college and a han as well. To find it, walk downhill past the Toprak and Çardak hotels, turn right, and walk one short block to the museum.

If you have an evening free, wander into the older part of town to Çerdiğin Caddesi (also called Nevşehir Caddesi), where there are some old stone houses and a curious **brick minaret** leaning at a pronounced angle. Built in 1236 by the Seljuks, it is touted by a nearby sign as the 'Turkish Tower of Pisa'.

The **government buildings** on the town's main square have been nicely restored. A short way up the hill is the **Ulu Cami**, with a good facade and an interesting pulpit.

Places to Stay – bottom end
Aksaray has several bottom-end hotels behind the Vilayet (Government House) on the main square. The *Toprak Oteli* (tel (481) 11308), *Çardak Oteli* (tel 11246) and *Mutlu Oteli* (tel 11073) all charge US$3 a single, US$5 for a waterless double.

Across the street and up a few steps from the Otel Ihlara is the *Hitit Pansiyon* (tel 11996), Kılıçaslan Mahallesi, Otel Ihlara Karşısı, Aksaray, Niğde, a little apartment house turned into a pension 'alla turka'. You remove your shoes and put on clean slippers when entering. The lobby is decorated with carpets, kilims, low couches (called *sedir*) and pillows. The guest rooms upstairs are bare and waterless but the front ones are large and have balconies. Bathrooms down the hall are small but tiled and clean. The price for a double room is US$18.

If you're camping, head for the *Ağaçlı Turistik Tesisleri*, a luxury camping ground at the main highway intersection, where you can pitch your tent or park your campervan for US$3, plus the same amount again for each person in your party.

Places to Stay – middle
The two-star *Otel Vadi* (VAH-dee) (tel 14326/7), one block from the main square, is the best value. With 35 rooms with shower and a restaurant, it's comfortable for one night, and charges US$18/24 a single/double. Breakfast is an additional US$2 per person.

The alternative is the three-star, 64-room *Otel Ihlara* (tel 11842, 13252), Kılıçaslan Mahallesi, Eski Sanayi Caddesi, Aksaray, Niğde, two blocks from the main square on a quiet back street (follow the signs, or ask). A bit plusher with a lift, restaurant and fairly quiet rooms with private baths, its official rates are US$35/55 a single/double, breakfast included,

but on my last visit I was quoted rates only a third as high as these.

The top place in town is the *Ağaçlı Turistik Tesisleri* (Ağaçlı Touristic Establishments) (tel 14910; fax 14914), Ankara-Adana Asfaltı, Nevşehir Kavşağı, Aksaray, Niğde, out on the highway at the main intersection with the roads to Nevşehir and Niğde. If you have a car, this place will be convenient. Two motels are within its green and shady gardens. The *Melendiz Motel* charges US$35/45 a single/double, breakfast included. The *Ihlara Motel* charges a bit less, US$30/40 a single/double. Other services abound, including an inexpensive cafeteria, a more formal restaurant, gift shops, swimming and wading pools and a petrol station.

Places to Eat
Except in the better hotels, there are only simple restaurants. The place to look is behind the Vilayet building, near the cheap hotels. Here you'll find the *Zümrüt Restaurant* (zurm-RURT) (tel 12233), *Çardak* (chahr-DAHK) (tel 11926) and *Aksaraylı Restaurant* (AHK-sah-rahy-luh) (tel 13386), all serving tasty if simple meals for under US$3.

Getting There & Away
There are direct buses from Aksaray to Ankara (230 km, 4½ hours), Nevşehir (65 km, 1½ hours), Niğde (115 km, two hours) and Konya (140 km, 2½ hours). There are also regular dolmuşes in summer to Ihlara Köyü (45 km, one hour), the starting place for visits to the Ihlara valley.

IHLARA (Peristrema)
Forty-five km south-east of Aksaray, partly along a rough unpaved road, is Ihlara, at the head of the Peristrema gorge. This remote and somewhat forbidding valley was once a favourite retreat of Byzantine monks, and dozens of painted churches, carved from the rock or built from the local stone, have survived. The area, wildly beautiful, is visited by

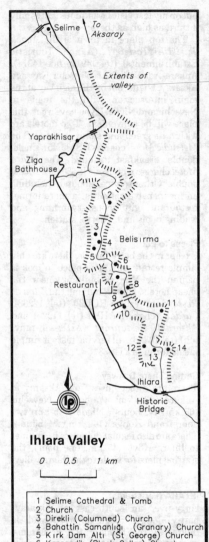

Ihlara Valley

```
0        0.5        1 km
```

1 Selime Cathedral & Tomb
2 Church
3 Direkli (Columned) Church
4 Bahattin Samanlığı (Granary) Church
5 Kırk Dam Altı (St George) Church
6 Karagedik (Black Collar) Church
7 Eski Baca (Old Chimney) Church
8 Yılanlı (Serpent) Church
9 Sümbüllü (Hyacinth) Church
10 Ağaç Altı (Beneath–a–Tree) Church
11 Karanlık Kale (Dark Castle) Church
12 Kokar (Fragrant) Church
13 Pürenli Seki (Platform) Church
14 Eğritaş (Crooked Stone) Church

the occasional tour bus but it is far less touristy than Göreme.

The trip up the gorge, along the course of the Melendiz Suyu stream, is something of a mini-expedition, wilder and more exciting than touring the rock-hewn churches at Göreme. If you've got an adventurous spirit or a car of your own and haven't had enough of rock churches, you will enjoy a visit here. Start early in the day and you'll enjoy the trip more, particularly in the middle of summer.

If you decide to make this trip, you will probably have to pass through Aksaray and make it your base, though lodging does exist at the site.

Things to See

The scenery on this trip, especially on the descent into the gorge, is as wonderful as the ancient churches themselves. Plan for a full day to see Ihlara. If you're coming out from Aksaray, the drive will take some time. If you're taking the minibus, you will have to spend two nights here.

At the south-eastern (upper) end of the gorge, on the rim near Ihlara Köyü, is a modern installation with a restaurant, souvenir shop and ticket booth, where you buy a US$2 ticket and enter anytime from 8.30 am to 5.30 pm.

You must descend a very long flight of stairs to the floor of the gorge and wander for several hours to see the various churches. Pack a picnic or at least take snacks so you won't have to climb back up to the restaurant at the rim of the gorge and then go down all those steps again.

Signs mark the **churches**. The most interesting, with the best paintings, are the Yılanlı Kilise, Sümbüllü Kilise, Kokar Kilise and Eğritaş Kilisesi. Farther down the valley are the Kırk Dam Altı Kilise, Bahattin Samanlığı Kilisesi, Direkli Kilise and Ala Kilise.

Places to Stay

There are a few small pensions between the village and the entry to the gorge. The *Vadibaşı Pansiyon* (VAH-dee-bah-shuh) is a neat village house charging US$8 per person for bed & breakfast. It's 750 metres from the entry at the rim of the gorge, and the same distance into the village. A similar place is the *Pension Anatolia*, new and clean, charging US$16 a double for a waterless room, breakfast included.

Places to Eat

There is only the restaurant at the rim entry to the gorge, which is nice enough but has a limited menu. Though it has a lock on the trade, a full meal still costs only about US$4.

Getting There & Away

Road If you have a car, your visit is made much easier. From the main Aksaray to Nevşehir highway, turn south (right, if you're coming from Aksaray) at a point 11 km east of the intersection of the Ankara to Adana and Aksaray to Nevşehir highways. On my last visit there was no sign marking the turning; it seems to have been removed. After making this turn, go about 23 km to another right turn marked for Ihlara Vadisi. The road passes through Selime village, with numerous rock-hewn buildings, and then three km farther on it runs through Yaprakhisar; both villages are dramatically surrounded by rock and marked by Göreme-style fairy chimneys. After 13 km you come to Ihlara Köyü, where you turn left to reach, after another km or so, the entry point at the rim of the gorge.

It is also possible to come to Ihlara from the underground cities of Kyamaklı and Derinkuyu, or vice versa. From Derinkuyu, proceed south toward Niğde, but turn west (right) at the village of Gölcük (signs mark the turning). Drive up into the mountains through Sivrihisar and Güzelyurt. Güzelyurt has its own underground dwellings and a mosque built in Byzantine times as a church dedicated to the theologian Gregory of Nazianza (born 330 AD). The scenery on this drive is dramatic and beautiful. Sixty km after

Gölcük, turn left for Selime and the road to Ihlara.

Bus The rim entry to the gorge is 1½ km from the village of Ihlara Köyü, 45 km from Aksaray and 95 km from Nevşehir. Dolmuşes run several times daily from Aksaray's otogar, charging US$0.80 for the trip (one-way).

UZUN YOLU

The drive from Aksaray or Ihlara to Nevşehir takes you along one of the oldest trade routes in the world, the Uzun Yolu or Long Road. It linked Konya, the capital of the Seljuk Sultanate of Rum, with other great cities of the sultanate (Kayseri, Sivas and Erzurum) and ultimately with the birthplace of Seljuk power in Persia. Following the Long Road today takes you past the remains of several hans, including the impressive and well-preserved **Ağızkarahan** (1243) on the south side of the road about 13 km east of Aksaray, open daily from 7 am to 6 pm for a small fee; the **Tepesidelik Hanı** (also called the Öresin Hanı, 13th century) on the south side about 20 km east of Aksaray; and the **Alay Hanı** (12th century), badly ruined, on the north side of the highway about 33 km east of Aksaray. All are marked by signs.

KIRŞEHİR

Midway along the road from Ankara (190 km) to Cappadocia (100 km) lies Kırşehir with a population of 70,000 and an altitude of 978 metres. It's an ancient city famous in Ottoman times as the centre of the mystical Akhi (ahi) brotherhoods. The brotherhoods – the Muslim equivalent of the Masons – began in the 14th century as secret religious societies among members of the crafts guilds, particularly the tanners' guild. Their political power grew to the point where the sultans had to reckon with them.

The founding father and inspiration of the Akhi brotherhoods was Ahi Evran

(1236-1329), a tanner whose family came from Khorasan. He lived and died in Kırşehir. His mosque and tomb are Muslim places of pilgrimage.

Kırşehir is a provincial capital with a few old buildings and a few cheap, basic hotels. If you decide to stop for the night, here's what to see and where to stay.

Things to See

Everything is a short walk from the main traffic roundabout with the ugly modern clock tower, off which you'll see the local tourism office, the Kırşehir Valiliği İl Turizm Müdürlüğü. If it's open (hours are supposedly from 8 am to 12 noon and from 1 to 5 pm daily), the chances of finding a knowledgeable person who speaks English are virtually nil. All the sights are well marked by signs, though, usually with wonderful, hilarious translations.

The **Ahi Evran Camii ve Türbesi** or Ahi Evran Mosque & Tomb, also called the Ahi Evran Zaviyesi (Dervish Lodge), are simple stone structures, obviously very old. The amusing translated sign notes that Ahi Evran 'was founder of saints philosophy and he had striven hard with skin art', meaning he was a tanner. Pilgrims in their 'Friday best' are usually crowded into the small rooms in prayer.

Just off the traffic roundabout is the **Cacabey Camii** (JAH-jah-bey), built by the Seljuk Turks in 1272 as a meteorological observatory and theological college. It's now used as a mosque. The black and white stonework draws the eye here. The **Alaettin Camii** dates from Seljuk times as well. You may also see a number of tombs dating from the 1300s.

Places to Stay

All the hotels in town charge about the same prices for the same well-used, spartan, somewhat unhappy rooms, about US$3/5 a single/double for a room with washbasin, or US$3.50/6 for a room with shower. The *Ahi Oteli* (tel (487) 11700), Ahi Evran Zaviyesi Karşısı, faces the Ahi Evran Camii. The *Otel Anadolu* (tel 11826), Ankara Caddesi 20, across the main street from Ahi Evran, has a lift and at least 100 different cigarette packets tacked to the wall behind the reception desk. The *Otel Banana* (tel 11879), Ankara Caddesi 26, is next door; it also has a variety of cigarette packets on the wall, but not nearly as many as the Otel Anadolu, though this may change by the time you arrive.

Cappadocia

The region between Ankara and Malatya, between the Black Sea and the Taurus Mountains, with its centre at Kayseri, was once the heart of the Hittite Empire, later an independent kingdom, then a vast Roman province. Cappadocia is mentioned several times in the Bible.

Today the word survives as a name for one of Turkey's most visited tourist areas, the moonlike landscape around the town of Ürgüp and the Göreme Valley. You won't find the name on an official road map, so you must know that the area is between Kayseri to the east of Ürgüp, Aksaray to the west, and Niğde to the south.

For all its apparent barrenness, the mineral-laden volcanic soil is very fertile and Cappadocia today is a prime agricultural region with many fruit orchards and vineyards. Little wineries experiment with the excellent grapes, sometimes with pleasant results. Irrigation schemes should greatly increase the productivity of the region.

Another source of wealth is carpet making and while the women in Cappadocian villages toil at their looms, Kayseri is a hotbed of persistent rug dealers. But Cappadocia's new economic dimension is tourism. People come from all over the world to visit the open-air museum of the Göreme Valley, to explore the rock-hewn churches and dwellings in surrounding valleys, to gaze on the fairy chimneys and

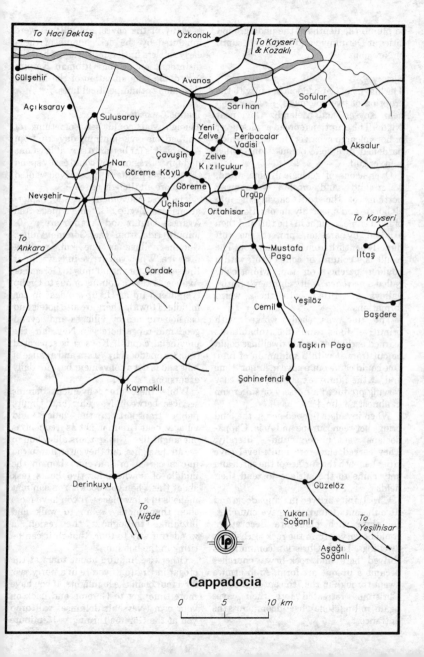

Cappadocia

0   5   10 km

to plumb the depths of the underground cities at Derinkuyu and Kaymaklı, south of Nevşehir.

History

The history of Cappadocia began with the eruption of two volcanoes, Erciyes Dağı near Kayseri and Melendiz Dağı near Niğde. The eruptions spread a thick layer of hot volcanic ash over the region which hardened to a soft, porous stone called tufa, or tuff.

Over aeons of geological time, wind, water and sand erosion wore away portions of the tuff, carving it into elaborate and unearthly shapes. Boulders of hard stone, caught in the tuff and then exposed by erosion, protect the tuff directly beneath from further erosion. The result is a column or cone of tuff with a boulder perched on top, whimsically called a *peribaca*, 'fairy chimney'. Entire valleys are filled with these weird formations.

The tuff was easily worked with primitive tools and the inhabitants learned early that sturdy dwellings could be cut from it with a minimum of fuss. One could carve out a cave in a short time and, if the family expanded, more easy carving produced a nursery or storeroom in almost no time!

When invaders flooded across the land bridge between Europe and Asia, Cappadocians went underground – literally. They carved elaborate multi-level cave cities beneath the surface of the earth and only came to the surface to tend their fields.

Christianity arrived in Cappadocia and its adherents found that cave churches, complete with elaborate decoration, could be carved from the rock as easily as dwellings. Large Christian communities thrived here and rock-hewn churches became a unique art form. Arab armies swept through in the 7th century but the Christians retreated into their caves again, rolling stone wheel-doors across the entrances.

Many of the caves and villages were inhabited by the descendants of these early settlers until our century, when the disintegration of the Ottoman Empire forced the reorganisation of the Middle East along ethno-political lines.

Touring Cappadocia

Though you could see something of Cappadocia on a lightning day-trip from Ankara, it is far better to stay at least one night in the region. You could easily spend three or four nights or a week if you wanted to explore all there is to see.

The most convenient bases for explorations are Ürgüp, Göreme village and Avanos. Ürgüp and Avanos are a 10-minute ride from the Göreme Valley; Göreme village is one km, walking distance. When you arrive in Nevşehir or Kayseri, ask for the dolmuş to Göreme or Avanos, or take a dolmuş or bus to Ürgüp (you'll end up at Ürgüp's otogar in the middle of town). There are also hotels and pensions in nearby villages and several good mid-range hotels in Nevşehir, the provincial capital. Kayseri is separated from Cappadocia by 70 km and a range of hills and is not a convenient base for daily excursions.

While there are convenient dolmuş services between Nevşehir and Ürgüp, public transport to the valleys and villages near Ürgüp is not as frequent as one might like. Cheap tours allow you to see all the sights, but they often dump you into a carpet or souvenir shop in the middle of nowhere for two hours (ask about this when you book). You can rent mopeds in a few places. If you have more time than money, plan to walk and hitchhike throughout the region, a wonderful way to tour, though it can be tiring in the hot sun.

Otherwise, inquire about tours at the otogar in Ürgüp. If you're in a hurry, ask for a tour of all the highlights. If you have more time, get to Göreme and back on your own (Nevşehir dolmuşes will drop you at the Göreme turning, a 15-minute walk to the site). Also, plan to take a dolmuş from Nevşehir to the underground cities at Derinkuyu and Kaymaklı. For the remaining places (Uçhisar, Zelve, Avanos, Sarı Han, Peribacalar Vadisi, etc), arrange a one-day tour.

NEVŞEHİR

Nevşehir (NEHV-sheh-heer), with an altitude of 1260 metres and a population of 60,000, is the provincial capital and the largest town in the region. The moonlike landscape of Cappadocia is not much in evidence here but it's very close by. There is nothing to see in Nevşehir proper except, perhaps, Monday's market or a climb up to the citadel to enjoy the view. Nevşehir is a transfer point and a base for visiting the underground cities at Kaymaklı and Derinkuyu.

Orientation

Buses will drop you at the otogar which is a large square west of the centre. Walk downhill along the highway, which is also the city's main street, called Atatürk Bulvarı, to reach the business district of banks, shops, restaurants and hotels. Near the major intersection in the centre of town, minibus dolmuşes depart for nearby towns and villages.

Information

The Tourism Information Office (tel (4851) 2717), Atatürk Bulvarı, is one km east of the otogar along the main road; look for a small white building on the right-hand side. It's open every day. There is a convenient little information booth at the otogar too, just below the Hotel Hisar, open from 8.30 am to 12 noon and from 1 to 5.30 pm.

Nevşehir Müzesi

The Nevşehir Müzesi, or Nevşehir Museum is one km out along Kayseri Caddesi on the road to Göreme and Ürgüp. Hours are from 8 am to 12 noon and from 1.30 to 5.30 pm; admission is US$1. The arrangement is the familiar one: an archaeological section with Phrygian, Hittite and Bronze Age pots and implements, up through Roman, Byzantine and Ottoman articles; and an ethnographic section with costumes, tools, manuscripts and jewellery.

Underground Cities

For sheer fascination and mystery, the places to see are the underground cities at Kaymaklı, 20 km south of Nevşehir along the road to Niğde, and at Derinkuyu, 10 km farther south. Board a bus or minibus at the central intersection in Nevşehir; they depart every 30 minutes or so and charge US$0.75 for the ride. Kaymaklı Belediyesi operates regular buses, and there are others to Niğde.

Kaymaklı The countryside here is without enchanting fairy chimneys or sensuously carved valleys. Yet the stone is the same soft volcanic tuff and it allowed early residents to develop the real estate cheaply.

At Kaymaklı, an unprepossessing farming village of white houses and unpaved streets, an unimpressive little cave in a low mound leads down into a vast maze of tunnels and rooms. Follow the signs which indicate a left (east) turn, or ask for the Yeraltı Şehri (YEHR-ahl-tuh shehh-ree, Underground City). The entrance is one block from the highway and it's open from 8.30 am to 6.30 pm every day; admission costs US$3.50.

Little arrows guide you into the cool depths. (Space yourself to travel in a gap between larger groups.) As you go down, it's like entering a huge and very complex Swiss cheese. Holes here, holes there, 'windows' from room to room, paths going this way and that, more levels of rooms above and below. Without the arrows and the electric wires, it would be fearfully difficult to find the way out again. If you wander off along another passage, separated from the group by only a few metres, you can hear what they say, you can converse with them, but you can't

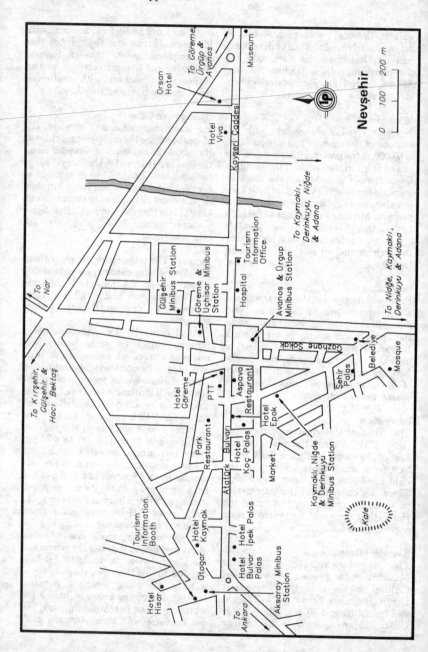

find your way back to them! Suddenly a foot comes into view and you realise that they're on the next level, almost above your head!

If you look carefully, signs of the troglodyte life style are everywhere: storage jars for oil, wine and water, communal kitchens blackened by smoke, stables with mangers, incredibly deep wells. Soon you no longer find it impossible to believe that tens of thousands of people could have lived here happily year-round, deep within the earth. It's even suspected that there were underground passages which connected Kaymaklı with its sister city of Derinkuyu, seven km away, though the tunnels have yet to be fully excavated.

Derinkuyu Having seen Kaymaklı, catch a bus or minibus south along the highway 10 km to Derinkuyu (deh-REEN-koo-yoo, Deep Well) for a look at another such city, this one with larger rooms on eight levels.

Prices and opening times are the same as at Kaymaklı. Derinkuyu is perhaps a bit less touristy than is Kaymaklı, but they've both been discovered.

Derinkuyu has several restaurants near the main square. There's also the Hotel Ali Baba.

If you continue to Niğde, have a look at the troglodytic monastery of Eski Gümüşler.

Places to Stay – bottom end
You probably won't want to use Nevşehir as your sightseeing base but if you need to stay here hotels are easy to find and cheap.

The *Hotel Kaymak* (kahy-MAHK) (tel 5427), Eski Sanayi Meydanı 11, is opposite the vast bus station to the east; you'll see its sign. Older but presentable and convenient, it has elephant-foot toilets (but regular baths in the common bathrooms) and charges US$5/7.50/8.50 a single/double/triple for a waterless room. The lobby bears a primitive mural showing a steel factory.

Just above the otogar is the new and bright *Hotel Hisar* (hee-SAHR) (tel 3857, 5672), Aksaray Caddesi 17. It looks fancy with its posh lobby and lift, but prices at my last visit were a reasonable US$14/18/22 a single/double/triple with shower or bath. Singles and doubles have showers, but triples have larger bathrooms with showers and tubs.

About 500 metres back up the hill toward Ankara, look on the left for a sign identifying *La Maison du Turc,* Beddik Mahallesi, Haşimi Sokak 3, a pension catering to French travellers and others as well. Clean rooms here go for US$3 per person, plus another US$0.50 for a hot shower.

Walking down the hill on the main street from the bus station, you pass several small hotels which suffer badly from street noise. There's the *Bulvar Palas* (bool-VAHR pah-lahss) (tel 1695), Atatürk Bulvarı 101, which rents clean waterless rooms at US$3/5.50/8 a single/double/triple. The triples have washbasins in them. The *İpek Palas Oteli* (ee-PEHK pah-lahss) (tel 1478), Atatürk Bulvarı 99, a few doors down to the left, is somewhat nicer and charges US$5/7.50 a single/double with washbasin. You have a better chance of actually getting hot water here.

A bit farther down the hill is a quieter place, the *Koç Palas Otel* (KOHCH pah-lahss) (tel 1216), Hükümet Caddesi 1, facing a little square not too far from the bus station. The charge for a waterless double is US$8.

Walking downhill on the main street, you pass the Hotel Epok. Around the corner from it is the little *Otel Sunar Palas* (tel 1444), Belediye Caddesi 2, which is quieter than those right on the boulevard, and just as cheap, with rooms costing US$3.75/7 a single/double.

Camping There are several camping places along the road to Ürgüp. Rates are generally US$2 per person, and another US$2 or so for a tent or caravan.

Follow the signs to Ürgüp and shortly after leaving Nevşehir you will come to a *Dinler Turizm Mocamp*, behind a BP petrol station. Farther along on the right is the *Koru Mocamp* (tel 2157), with room for 240 campers and water and electricity hook-ups for camping vehicles. The *Kervansaray Göreme Mokamp* (tel 1428) has room for some 600 campers and is more elaborate than most. Rates are a bit higher, about US$3.50 per adult, almost as much for tent or vehicle.

For other camping areas near Göreme, see the Ürgüp section.

Places to Stay – middle

The two-star, 60-room *Hotel Epok* (tel 1168), Atatürk Bulvarı 39, is on the main street in the middle of town. Though it's nice enough, it suffers from street noise and I'd suggest that you look first at its even more attractive and comfortable sister hotel, the *Şehir Palas Hotel* (tel 5329), Camii Kebir Caddesi 41, not far away. Walk downhill past the Epok, turn right at the next street, and walk two blocks to the large tawny stone building which is the hotel. Designed with echoes of the local architecture and traditional building materials, the Şehir Palas offers comfy, quiet rooms with bath and balcony; the only noise here is from the minaret. The price for a room here (and at the Epok) is US$25/38 a single/double, breakfast included.

The *Hotel Viva* (tel 1326, 1760), Kayseri Caddesi 45, is farther down the hill past the Tourism Information Office, on the left-hand (north) side of the road. This is a small, cosy, homey hotel of 24 rooms, all with private showers and balconies, at rates of US$38 a double, breakfast included. Rooms on the front of the hotel may be noisy.

Among the old stand-bys is the *Hotel Orsan* (tel 1035, 2115), Kayseri Caddesi 15, the road east to Ürgüp. The lobby and public rooms are covered in the wonderful Turkish carpets of the area, many of which feature crimson; they make a strong impression. The 80 rooms (with bath) rent for US$40 to US$45 a double, breakfast included. It's slightly dearer than other hotels because the Orsan has a small swimming pool.

Places to Stay – top end

About a km east of Nevşehir on the Ürgüp road stands the huge *Nevşehir Dedeman Hotel* (tel 5619), Nevşehir-Kayseri Yolu, Nevşehir, the town's first five-star accommodation with all the luxury accoutrements. Construction was nearly finished when I visited and prices weren't set but they should be about US$80/100 a single/double for a brand-new luxury room with all the amenities. This hotel will be popular with tour groups.

Places to Eat

Nevşehir does not have many restaurants and none of them is fancy.

For general purposes, the *Aspava Lokantası* (AHSS-pah-vah) (tel 1051), Atatürk Bulvarı 29 in the centre of town, is a good bet for ready food, kebaps and pide at low prices. There's a nicer family dining room upstairs. Other cheap restaurants are near the otogar.

Try the *Park Restaurant* (tel 4487) across Atatürk Bulvarı from the Hotel Epok and up the hill through the park. Nevşehir's movers and shakers come here in the evening to have a drink and talk politics, sports and business as waiters quietly bring plate after plate of meze, grilled meat or chicken, various soups and stews and a few desserts. It's not a fancy place at all, but there's a view and one of the waiters speaks English. A full lunch or dinner costs US$6 to US$7.

Getting There & Away

Bus Nevşehir has good bus transport to points north, south, east and west.

For Ürgüp, catch a bus at the otogar or a minibus from the centre of town. Minibus is also the way to reach Göreme village and Avanos. To get to the underground cities at Kaymaklı or Derinkuyu, catch a bus or minibus from the centre; they leave about every half-hour. Minibuses to Niğde leave from the same spot every hour.

Here are details for other destinations:

Adana – 285 km, 5½ hours, US$5; several buses daily

Aksaray – 65 km, 1½ hours, US$1.25; frequent minibuses and buses

Ankara – 285 km, 4½ hours, US$4; very frequent buses daily

Denizli (Pamukkale) – 665 km, 10 hours, US$9; one bus daily

İstanbul – 725 km, 12 hours, US$10; a few buses nightly

İzmir – 785 km, 12 hours, US$10; one bus daily

Kayseri – 105 km, 2½ hours by bus, 1½ hours by minibus, US$2; very frequent buses and minibuses

Konya – 226 km, 3½ hours, US$3; several buses daily

Yozgat (via Kayseri) – 300 km, five hours, US$4

From Nevşehir you might be going south to the underground cities of Kaymaklı and Derinkuyu, already described. If so, you may want to visit Niğde as well. If not, skip the following section and head for Ürgüp and Göreme.

NIĞDE

Niğde (NEE-deh), at an altitude of 1200 metres and with a population of 65,000, was built by the Seljuks 85 km south of Nevşehir, and if you are passing through you might want to have a look at the buildings they left behind. Not far out of town is an ancient monastery hewn from the volcanic stone.

Orientation

The marketplace is conveniently marked by a clock tower (*saat kulesi*). The centre of town life is between the clock tower and the Vilayet (government building), which is a few short blocks to the north-west on Atatürk Meydanı (sometimes called Hükümet Meydanı), the main square. The Tourist Information Office (tel (483) 11168, 11856), İstiklal Caddesi, Vakıf İş Hanı 1/D, is open daily (except Sunday) from 9 am to 12 noon and from 1.30 to 6.30 pm. It's one km from the otogar to the Vilayet; you pass near the hill with the Alaeddin Camii on the way.

Süngür Bey Camii

The Alaeddin Camii (1223), on the hill with the fortress which dominates the town, is the grandest mosque. But the Süngür Bey Camii at the foot of the hill by the marketplace (Thursday is market day) is, for me, the city's most interesting building. Restored by the Mongols in 1335, it is a curious and affecting blend of architectures. Windows around the ground floor are of differing styles and highly carved; on the upper storey are blind lancet arches instead of windows. The rose window above the north window bears a six-pointed 'Star of David', a motif you'll see used elsewhere. The big, stolid, square doors with fine carving are unusual. The new restorations have done wonders for the exterior stonework but have filled the interior with reinforced concrete which is quite ugly and jarring. The north galleries are a conglomeration of architectural styles. The mihrab is wonderfully carved and almost Chinese in appearance.

The Ak Medrese (1409) is now the town's museum. Also take a look at the Hüdavend Hatun Türbesi (1312), a fine example of a Seljuk tomb; and the Dış Cami, an Ottoman mosque with a carved mimber inlaid with mother-of-pearl.

Eski Gümüşler Monastery

It's 10 km from the clock tower in Niğde to the rock-hewn monastery of Eski Gümüşler, east of town. Coming from Nevşehir, an intersection near a Mobil petrol station on the main highway is marked for Niğde (right, west) and Eski Gümüşler (left, east), four km. It's actually 4¾ km. Minibuses operated by the Gümüşler

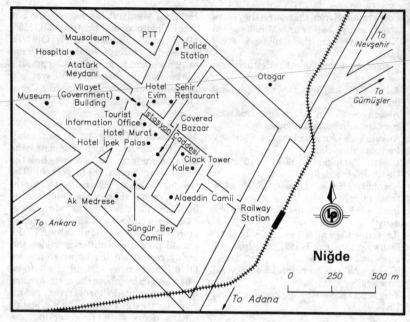

Niğde

0   250   500 m

Belediyesi run out here from Niğde; ask for Eski Gümüşler (ess-KEE gur-murshlehr) and take the bus to the end of the line. You can also hitch to the site. In the village of Gümüşler you can find refreshing tea, soft drinks and snacks. Follow the sign pointing to the left at the far end of the village to reach the site.

The monastery, discovered in 1963, is open daily from 8 am to 12 noon and from 1.30 to 5.30 pm. The guardian may not be around and the gates locked, but don't worry. He was probably sitting in the teahouse as you passed by and will follow you to open the gates. The admission fee is US$1.

The monastery doesn't look like much from the front but as you enter along a rock-cut passage you will come to a large courtyard surrounded by rock-hewn dwellings, a refectory, churches and crypts. Eski Gümüşler is noteworthy because its coloured paintings, dating from the 7th to the 11th centuries, are so

well preserved (much better than at Göreme), with many faces intact. The main church is lofty, with big, completely unnecessary columns. The cross-hatch line motif here shows the influence of the Iconoclasts, when images were prohibited and artists had to stick to geometric representations. The guard shows you the kitchen (*mutfak*) and refectory, the wine and oil reservoirs, bathroom and the crypt. If you're nice, he may also point out a small hole in the ground which seems to be nine metres deep from which a gentle wind always issues (he puts a little pinwheel in it to show you). No-one yet knows where the hole leads or what other rooms and tunnels there may be in this labyrinth.

Places to Stay

Should you want to stay, Niğde can offer several small hostelries. There are restaurants near the otogar and also the *Hotel Stad* (tel 17866), Yeni Terminal

Yanı, charging US$15 for a double with bath.

Otel Evim (tel 11860), Hükümet Meydanı, has simple rooms with private baths (showers and short tubs) and balconies. The hotel is in the midst of everything, has a lift, and charges a reasonable US$15/20 a single/double. When you search for it, look for the Türkiye Halk Bankası, which is easier to see than the neighbouring hotel.

Otel Murat (tel 13978), İstasyon Caddesi, Belediye Yanı, has a facade on the main street but its entrance is at the back near the clock tower. Well kept, clean and quite presentable like the Hotel Evim, this hotel has no lift, no large lobby and no tubs (only showers) in the rooms and so charges less: US$10/14 a single/double.

Hotel Taciroğlu (tel 13047), a half-block from the Hotel Murat on İstasyon Caddesi, is comparable.

Niğde Oteli (tel 11826, 11208), İstasyon Caddesi 83, at the clock tower end of İstasyon Caddesi, is clean, with over-enthusiastic help, but passable, and certainly cheap: rooms with washbasin cost US$4/6 a single/double.

İpek Palas Oteli (tel 18255), to the right of the old Belediye building near the clock tower, has presentable, simple rooms with clean sheets (but no running water) for US$3/5 a single/double.

Places to Eat

Besides the restaurants near the otogar, you might try the *Niğde Şehir Lokantası*, to the right of the Pamukbank on İstasyon Caddesi; it's closed Sunday, though. The *Aile Pastanesi*, near the statue of Atatürk on the main square, has an outdoor shaded terrace.

Getting There & Away

Niğde's otogar has buses to most nearby destinations, but perhaps only one or two per day. There is frequent service to Adana (205 km, 3½ hours, US$3), Aksaray (115 km, two hours, US$1.75), Kayseri (130 km, 1½ hours, US$1.75) and Konya (250 km, 3½ hours, US$4).

Service to Nevşehir (85 km, 1½ hours) is fast and frequent, with minibuses departing the otogar every hour on the hour from 5 am to 6 pm.

CAPPADOCIAN VALLEYS

East out of Nevşehir, the rolling terrain is sandy. After a few km the panorama of Cappadocia begins to unfold: distant rock formations become visible as fairy chimneys, and valleys with undulating walls of soft volcanic ash fall away from the road. In the distance, the gigantic snow-capped peak of the volcano, Erciyes Dağı (Mt Aergius), floats above a layer of cloud.

No matter where you make your base, several moonscape valleys with painted churches and troglodyte dwellings will draw your attention. Göreme Valley is the most famous of these, but nearby Zelve is less touristy, and the valleys at Soğanlı even less so. Here are descriptions of these Cappadocian wonders, followed by details of places which make convenient base camps: Göreme village, Ürgüp, Avanos, Gülşehir and Hacıbektaş.

Dolmuşes run from some of the villages to the Göreme Valley in summer. From Ürgüp, look for the Göreme Müze dolmuş at the otogar. It leaves when it fills up and costs US$0.45.

Tours of the sights in the region are offered by several agencies for about US$8 to US$12 per person, and considering the heat of the sun and the difficulties of transport, it's not a bad idea. The catch, of course, is that you spend some of your valuable time sitting in shops to which the minibus has brought you. The tour company gets as much as 30% commission on everything you buy in the shops. But the tea is free and the 'shopping' can be just a rest from walking in the sun. If you don't want to waste time in a shop, find a company which does not have the enforced shopping.

To hire an entire taxi or minibus, with

driver, for a full-day tour of all Cappadocia, starting at Ürgüp or Nevşehir, costs US$35 to US$60.

Whichever way you go, wear flat shoes for going up the metal-rung ladders and stairways, and take a torch (flashlight) if you have one. Refreshments, snacks and light meals are available at all of the valleys.

Göreme Valley

Of all the Cappadocian valleys, Göreme is without doubt the most famous, and rightly so. Approaching it from the Ortahisar intersection by the Lapis Inn, the road descends steeply into a maze of little valleys, ridges and cones. The rich bottomland of each valley blazes with bright patches of green crops or is dotted with tidy rows of grapevines. Halfway down the hill is the entrance to the **Göreme Açık Hava Müzesi** or Göreme Open-Air Museum, open from 8.30 am to 5.30 pm; admission costs US$5.

It's easy to spend most of a day walking the paths here, climbing stairways or passing through tunnels to reach the various churches. The primitive 11th-century paintings and frescoes in several are outstanding. In between churches, the utter improbability of the landscape floods over you: the lovely, soft textures in the rock, the fairytale cave dwellings, the spare vegetation growing vigorously from the stark but mineral-rich soil. If you're smart, you'll get to the valley early in the morning in summer and space yourself between tour groups. When lots of people crowd into one of these little churches they block the doorway, which is often the only source of light. They then 'look at the paintings' in the dark!

Walking into the valley from the entrance, you come first to the **Rahibeler Manastırı**, or Nun's Convent, a large plain room with some steps up to a smaller domed chapel with frescoes. Across the way is the similar Monk's Monastery. From this point you can follow a loop path around the valley in either direction. Here

are the sights you come to if you walk clockwise.

The path winds past various vistas and unmarked churches; the large grooves in the church floor are burial crypts. The **Çarıklı Kilise** or Sandal Church is named for the 'sandals' in the floor opposite the doorway. This one has lots of good frescoes, especially one showing Judas's betrayal (in the arch over the door to the left). Near the Sandal Church is a small unmarked chapel with a fresco of a man on horseback – St George, no doubt.

The **Karanlık Kilise** or Dark Church, among the most famous and fresco-filled, is currently undergoing two years of restoration work by Turkish and Italian artisans. It will probably be open by the time you visit. The church took its name from its former condition when it had very few windows. The lack of light preserved the vivid colour of the frescoes which, among others, include scenes of Christ as Pantocrator, Christ on the cross and his betrayal by Judas. Past the Dark Church is a **refectory** with tables and benches cut right from the rock.

The **Yılanlı Kilise**, Snake Church or Church of the Dragon, has frescoes on part of the vault and iconoclast designs on the other. On the left wall, St George and St Theodore attack the dragon yet again.

The **Barbara Kilise**, or Church of St Barbara, is a good example of the severely plain decoration used during the Iconoclastic period (726-842) when images were outlawed. There are a few fairly worn post-Iconoclast frescoes of the Virgin Mary and St Barbara. On the right are three more chapels, with carved crosses in the apse and primitive line drawings.

The **Elmalı Kilise** or Apple Church has a stunning display of frescoes. There are eight small domes and one large one, and lots of well-preserved paintings. Where's the apple? Some say the Angel Gabriel, above the central nave, is holding it.

Last church on the loop is that of **St Basil**, with somewhat disappointing frescoes.

Outside the enclosure and down the hill

a few steps along the road is the **Tokalı Kilise** or Buckle Church, among the biggest and finest of the Göreme churches, with frescoes telling the stories of Christ's miracles. There's a little chapel downstairs. If a guardian is not on duty and the gate to the church is locked, get someone to come. Then get them to turn on the lights (*ışıklar*, uh-shuk-LAHR).

Farther down the hill and along the road to Göreme village are many more churches, most minor and unimpressive. The region once had hundreds of little chapels. Signs point the way to the **Nazar Kilise** and the **Saklı Kilise**, which are worth a visit.

Göreme village (formerly called Avcılar), 1½ km past the Open-Air Museum, is small but busy with backpackers, farm wagons and tractors. If you take the time to explore the village's winding streets, you will see many buildings carved in the rock. There's even a flour mill.

Çavuşin & Zelve

From Göreme village, the Avanos road leads north to Çavuşin, with its Church of John the Baptist near the top of the cliff which rises behind the village. A half-km north of the village, along the road, is the Çavuşin Church (look for the iron stairway).

A side road from Çavuşin heads up another valley five km to Zelve, almost as rich in churches and strange panoramas as Göreme, but much less well organised. Half-way along the road are groupings of curious 'three-headed' fairy chimneys near a row of souvenir stalls. If you're walking from Göreme village, a footpath starts from Çavişin and saves you a few km to the road junction, but it is more difficult walking on the path than on the road; take your pick. Zelve is seven km from Avanos, by the way.

Zelve was a monastic retreat. The several valleys here do not have nearly as many impressive painted churches, though there are a few you should see. They are marked by signs. The **Balıklı Kilise** or Fish Church has fish figuring in one of the primitive paintings, and the more impressive **Uzümlü Kilise** or Grape Church has obvious bunches of grapes, but mostly iconoclastic decoration. Look also for the **Değirmen** (Mill). Hours are from 8.30 am to 5.30 pm and entry costs US$3. There are restaurants and tea gardens for refreshments.

Peribacalar Vadisi

From Zelve, an unpaved road on the right is marked for Aktepe. It leads up to the Avanos to Ürgüp road (several km away) by way of the Valley of the Fairy Chimneys (Peribacalari Vadisi). Though many valleys hold collections of strange cones, these are the best formed and most thickly clustered. Most of the rosy rock cones are topped by flattish, darker stones which have caused the cones to form. Being harder rock, the dark cap-stones sheltered the cones from the rains which eroded all the surrounding rock.

Uçhisar

In Uçhisar you can climb up to the top of

the tall rock outcrop riddled with tunnels and windows, which is the most prominent landmark in the region. The view is magnificent.

Soğanlı

This valley, about 35 km south of Ürgüp by way of Mustafa Paşa and Güzelöz, is much less touristy than Göreme or even Zelve. But the pressure of tour buses is getting so bad at these places that the tour operators are searching for new parking places and Soğanlı may be one of them. Even so, it's an interesting and beautiful place to explore. It is not easy to get to, however. Try to find a dolmuş from the otogar in Nevşehir or Ürgüp, but this is chancy. If not, it's taxi or hitch.

The valleys of Aşağı Soğanlı (Lower Onion Valley) and Yukarı Soğanlı (Upper Onion Valley) were, like Göreme and Zelve, largely monastic. Turn off the main road and proceed five km to the village, where signs point out the **Tokalı Kilise** or Buckle Church on the right, reached by a steep flight of worn steps, and the **Gök Kilise** or Sky Church to the left across the stream bed. Follow the signs, walk up the stream bed 50 metres, then go up on the left to the church. The Gök is a twin-nave church, the two naves separated by columns, ending in apses. The double frieze of saints is badly worn.

At the point where the valleys divide, the villagers have posted a billboard map indicating the churches by number. The village square is to the left. In the village square are the Soğanlı and Cappadocia restaurants, toilets, shops and a telephone.

The churches are open from 8.30 am to 5 or 6 pm with a break for lunch; an admission fee of US$0.50 to US$1 is payable at each church. Here are the churches according to the villagers' numbering scheme:

1 **Ballık** (Honey-Hive) – this church is of little interest.
2 **Tokalı** – described in Soğanlı section.
3 **Gök** – described in Soğanlı section.

4 **Karabaş** (Black Head) – in the right-hand valley, this church is covered in paintings showing the life of Christ and also Gabriel and various saints. Look for the pigeon in the fresco, showing the local influence. Pigeons were very important to the monks, who wooed them with dovecotes cut in the rock. The dovecote across from the Karabaş Kilise has white paint around its small window entrances to attract the birds; the sides of the entrance are smoothed so the birds cannot alight, but must enter. Inside, a grid of poles provides roosting space for hundreds of birds that dump manure by the kg onto the floor below. The monks gather the manure, put it on their grapevines and get the sweetest grapes and the best wine for miles around. In the yard between the church and the dovecote is a refectory, with tandoor ovens in the ground (note the air-holes for the fires). The monks lived apart but dined communally.

5 **Kübbeli** and **Saklı** (Cupola and Hidden Churches) – these two are also in the right-hand valley, across the stream bed and high on the far hillside. The Kübbeli is interesting for its unusual eastern-style cupola. The Hidden Church is just that – hidden from view until you get close.

6 **Yılanlı** (Snake Church) – farthest up the right-hand valley, this church has frescoes darkened by smoke and age, but you can still make out the serpent to the left as you enter.

7 **Geyikli** (Deer Church) – this is up the left-hand valley, above the village square, but it's not very impressive.

8 **Tahtalı** (Wooden Church) – the farthest of the churches up the left-hand valley, it is also dull.

Sarı Han

This Seljuk-era Yellow Caravanserai (Sarı Han, sah-RUH hahn) is six km east of Avanos along the eastern road back to Ürgüp. It has recently undergone complete renovation and may be in commercial use by the time you arrive. The elaborate Seljuk portal is, as usual, quite impressive.

Inside, it is the standard plan with a large court where animals were loaded and unloaded, and a great hall where people and animals could escape the weather. Above the portal is a small mosque.

GÖREME VILLAGE

This little village one km from the Göreme Open-Air Museum has grown explosively over the last decade as Turkey's tourism boom expands. What was once a sleepy farming village is now chock-a-block with little pensions, camping grounds, restaurants, as well as a little tourist office and town hall – go there with any complaints about local businesses. It is the prime place to stay for those travelling on a budget because the beds and meals are cheap and you can walk to the sights.

Though there are lots of pensions, they change character frequently as the friendliness, cleanliness and cheapness of a place depend almost completely on the owner or manager. Owners and managers come and go, and so do pensions. I'll recommend some of my current favourites but I don't guarantee that Göreme's lodging picture will remain unchanged. In any case, you'll find a good place if you spend an hour looking.

Places to Stay

Pensions are found everywhere in the village and along the road to the Göreme Open-Air Museum. Prices for beds range from US$3 to US$5 or even US$6 per person, but most are of the cheaper variety.

Melek Hotel-Pansiyon (tel (4857) 1463) is run by an energetic Dutch woman (J V Boekhout) who keeps everything in excellent shape. You enter a small patio, then a village-type lounge with low seats and a fireplace. It's quiet here as well. Rooms cost US$11 waterless, US$18 with private shower.

Paradise Pension (tel 1248), right at the turning for the Göreme Valley, has generic waterless pension rooms for US$10 a double, and a good view of the procession along the road.

Köse Pansiyon (tel 1294), well up the valley behind the village centre, is run by Mehmet and Dawn Köse and has hosted backpackers for years. It's very plain, with beds on the floor village-style; there's a dining room and camping ground as well. Rates are low, US$9 a double for waterless rooms.

SOS Motel-Pansiyon-Restaurant (tel 1134) has two types of lodgings: the pension with beds in dorms at US$5 each, or 'motel' rooms with private showers for US$14 a double. Modest but attractive in the Greek Islands way, it has some rooms carved from the rock. Look for it near the popular but posh Ataman Restaurant.

Just down the road from the SOS is the *Halil Carved Pansiyon*, which is similar, with some rooms carved right from the rock.

Other pensions which readers have liked in the past include *Nazar, Paradise, Esen, Ufuk, Divan* and *Peri's Pansiyon*.

Places to Eat

Most pensions in Göreme provide cheap meals and most are similar. The best place in town is the *Ataman Restaurant* (tel 1310/1/2), up the valley behind the village in rock-hewn chambers. Clearly aimed at the bus-tour clientele which arrives frequently and abundantly, it provides good food and service in pleasant and certainly unusual surroundings. The rock-hewn dining rooms are decorated with Turkish crafts. The menu is limited but passable; wine and beer are served. Expect to spend US$6 to US$10 per person for a full meal with drinks here.

ORTAHİSAR

The village of Ortahisar is near the intersection of the Nevşehir to Ürgüp and Göreme roads. A Cappadocian farming village at heart, Ortahisar's new-found importance comes from its strategic location so close to the access roads and the famous painted churches.

Places to Stay

The village centre, 1½ km from the intersection, has several small pensions. Try the *Dönmez* and the *Gümüş* on the street by the PTT, the *Yalçın* (on the way to Ürgüp) and the more comfortable *Hotel Göreme* (tel (4869) 1005) on the main square, a simple but clean, airy and cheerful place renting rooms with new tiled baths for US$10/12/15 a single/double/triple. If it's full, try the *Hotel Selçuk* across the street.

For campers, the *Kaya Camping* on the road to the Göreme Valley can't be beaten. This small camping ground has showers, a restaurant and a fabulous view of the landscape. It's within walking distance (600 metres) of the Open-Air Museum. Rates are US$2 for a tent and US$3 per person. At the turning to Göreme, only one km from the entrance to the site, is the *Paris Motel & Camping,* with 24 good double rooms and a swimming pool at US$28 a double, breakfast included. In the camping area you'll find room for 600 campers, most services and the standard low prices.

Ortahisar's prime place to stay is the *Lapis Inn Hotel* (tel 1470; fax 1480), Göreme Kavşağı, Ortahisar, 50560 Ürgüp, Nevşehir, right at the Göreme, Ürgüp, Nevşehir intersection across from the Motel Paris. A large, blocky, modern place, it features a rich use of black-and-white marble and polished limestone in the spacious lobby. Wide hallways lead to the 250 comfortable guest rooms equipped with dark wood furniture, twin beds and bathrooms with marble vanities and tub and shower baths. Hotel services include a TV lounge, games room, piano bar, restaurant and a large shopping area. Rates are US$50/65 a single/double, US$85 for a 'suite' (a larger double room with TV and mini-bar).

ÜRGÜP

Twenty-three km east of Nevşehir is the village of Ürgüp (EWR-gewp), with a population of 10,000, at the very heart of the Cappadocian wonderland. Life in Ürgüp is divided between farming and tourism, and a hotel might share a stretch of land with a vineyard or alfalfa field. Because of the volcanic soil, sufficient water and abundant sunshine, the town is surrounded by a rich landscape of grain fields, vineyards and clusters of beehives.

Many of the buildings in the town are made of the local tawny limestone with a pronounced grain. Some of the older houses have fine bits of carved stone decoration. Quite a number of Ürgüp's citizens still live or work, at least part of the time, in spaces carved out of the rock. Surrounding villages such as Ortahisar and Uçhisar are also inhabited by cave-dwellers.

Ürgüp's main street has a sprinkling of antique and carpet shops, a Tourism Information Office and several restaurants.

Information & Orientation

Ürgüp is a small town and, with the help of the map in this book, you'll find your way around in no time. The Tourism Information Office (tel (4868) 1059) is at Kayseri Caddesi 37, on the main street down the hill from the main square behind a garden. The town's museum is right next door, open every day from 8.30 am to 5.30 pm.

Places to Stay – bottom end

Ürgüp has numerous pensions in which you can get a bed in a clean but spartan room for about US$3 to US$5 per person. The prime area for cheap pensions and hotels is the quarter called Sivritaş Mahallesi, especially Elgin Sokak, which has four small pensions and hotels.

Cheapest is the *Hotel Villa* (VEE-lah) (tel 1906), Elgin Sokak, which is OK inside, though not much to look at from the outside. Doubles rent for US$10, with bath for US$14. A new hotel is going up across the street.

Hotel Divan (dee-VAHN) (tel 1705), Elgin Sokak 4, has its own tiny camping area in the garden, as well as rooms that

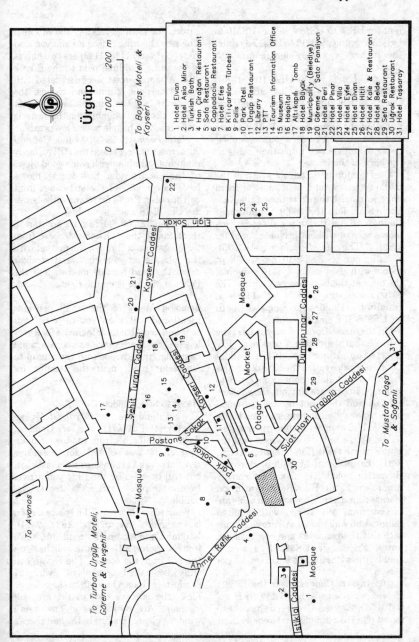

Ürgüp

0   100   200 m

1   Hotel Elvan
2   Hotel Asia Minor
3   Turkish Bath
4   Han Çirağan Restaurant
5   Sofa Restaurant
6   Cappadocia Restaurant
7   Hotel Efes
8   Kılıçarslan Türbesi
9   Polis
10 Park Oteli
11 Ürgüp Restaurant
12 Library
13 PTT
14 Tourism Information Office
15 Museum
16 Hospital
17 Altı kapılı Tomb
18 Hotel Büyük
19 Municipality (Belediye)
20 Göreme / Sato Pansiyon
21 Hotel Peri
22 Hotel Pınar
23 Hotel Villa
24 Hotel Eyfel
25 Hotel Divan
26 Hotel Hitit
27 Hotel Kale & Restaurant
28 Hotel Belde
29 Sefa Restaurant
30 Uğrak Restaurant
31 Hotel Taşsaray

To Boydaş Moteli & Kayseri

To Avanos

To Turban Ürgüp Moteli; Göreme & Nevşehir

To Mustafa Paşa & Soğanlı

Elgin Sokak

Kayseri Caddesi

Mosque

Dumlupınar Caddesi

Mosque

Şehit Turan Caddesi

Market

Kayseri Caddesi

Otogar

Sokak

Postane

Park Sokak

Suat Hayri Ürgüplü Caddesi

Mosque

Ahmet Refik Caddesi

İstiklal Caddesi

Mosque

rent for US$5 to US$8 a single, US$10 to US$15 a double, US$12 to US$17 a triple; the higher prices are for rooms with shower.

Hotel Eyfel (ey-FEHL) (tel 1325), Elgin Sokak 8, is the class act on the street, with a tiny swimming pool. The watering hole raises the prices somewhat but all of the rooms have private showers and cost US$12/17/20 a single/double/ triple. Campers can pitch their tents at the back of the house.

On Dumlupınar Caddesi south of the market are several hotels, most of them not cheap, with the exception of the *Kale Otel* (KAH-leh) (tel 1069), Dumlupınar Caddesi 26, on the upper floor, renting rooms with or without private shower for US$10. The *Hotel Belde* (tel 1970), Dumlupınar Caddesi 8-10, has well-kept rooms with showers for US$16 a double; the ones at the back are very quiet. The *Hitit Hotel* (hee-TEET) (tel 1481) on Dumlupınar Caddesi has rooms with bath for US$16/21 a single/double.

Up the street from the otogar past the Turkish bath are more pensions. The *Hotel Asia Minor* (tel 1645), İstiklal Caddesi 38, also called the Küçük Asya, is a nice stone village house converted to lodgings. Rooms are tiny but the showers are OK and the front terrace is a good place to take it easy. Prices are moderate at US$11/16 a single/double, with shower.

Also up the hill on a side street past the Turkish bath is the *Hotel Elvan* (tel 1191, 1291), Dutlu Cami Mahallesi, Barbaros Hayrettin Sokak 11, a pension run by Ahmet and Fatma Bilir. Rooms are in odd places around a small courtyard; some are carved from the stone, with vaulted ceilings and wall niches. All are well kept, with tidy tiled showers and plenty of hot water. Prices are US$12/18 a single/ double; breakfast costs an extra $2 per person.

Off Kayseri Caddesi near the Büyük Hotel are more pensions. The *Peri Hotel* (tel 1055), Kayseri Caddesi 5, has cheap rooms (US$10 a double) and a shady front

garden for sitting, talking and sipping. The neighbouring *Göreme Pansiyon* and *Hotel Şato* (tel 1146, 1149) are two halves of the same building, next to the Büyük Otel. A homey, quiet place decorated with lots of carpets, kilims and cicims, the rooms are fairly cool in summer and cost US$12/18 a single/double, but the owner is often ready to haggle over a lower rate.

Hotel Park (tel 1883), Avanos Caddesi 20, across the street from the PTT, is fairly plain but suitable, with some good views of the countryside. East-facing rooms have balconies, but the street out front can be noisy. Prices for rooms with shower are US$12/18 a single/double.

Readers of this guide have written to recommend the *Pension Merkez*; from the otogar, walk through the market with the mosque on your right and straight down the road for 300 metres, and the Pension Merkez is on the right.

Camping Many of the small pensions mentioned will allow you to pitch your tent and use all of their facilities for a very low fee. For more spacious and congenial camping grounds, look on the Ürgüp to Nevşehir road, near the turning for Göreme.

Places to Stay – middle

The old stand-by is the *Büyük Otel* (bew-YEWK) (tel 1060/1), Kayseri Caddesi, down the hill a bit from the town's main square. It was closed for extensive renovation and expansion on my last visit, but will be open by the time you arrive. I estimate prices at US$38/48 a single/ double.

Want to live in a cave? The place for you is the *Hotel Eyvan* (tel 1822, 2424), İstiklal Caddesi, on the road into town from Nevşehir, a 10-minute walk back up the hill from the otogar. The Eyvan can truly be called troglodytic, with 27 comfortable rooms hewn from the volcanic rock (the cutter's tool marks are still visible). All rooms have one small window, clean, modern baths and there's a pleasant terrace restaurant so you can escape your cave-person existence now and then. The price, at US$40 a double, is hardly prehistoric, but how many times do you get the chance to live in a cave? This place is not for claustrophobes, though.

The *Taşsaray Hotel* (tel 2344, 2444), Mustafa Paşa Caddesi 10, made of tawny sandstone, is 400 metres from the otogar along the Mustafa Paşa road. It's a comfortable, modern hotel with restaurant, lobby and lift; the rooms have a bath and a balcony. Some have nice views. Prices are moderate at $42 a double with shower, breakfast included.

Besides these downtown hotels, Ürgüp has several motels on its outskirts. The *Boydaş Moteli* (BOY-dahsh) (tel 1259, 1659), PK 11, is on the eastern edge of town along the Kayseri road next to several other hotels. Opened in 1986, the Boydaş was designed for group tours. There are 127 guest rooms, three bars and a discotheque. Rates are US$45/65 a single/double, breakfast included. The Boydaş also owns the *Tepe Oteli*, on the hilltop across the highway. Many rooms here have fabulous views of the valley.

Just as nice as the Boydaş is the modern 240-room *Turban Ürgüp Moteli* (TOOR-bahn) (tel 1490), at the top of the hill as you leave Ürgüp on the road to Nevşehir and Göreme. Operated by the government's Tourism Bank, it's a nice place with comfortable rooms in small bungalows designed in harmony with the landscape and the traditional architecture of Cappadocian villages. Doubles with breakfast cost US$55. The motel is walking distance from Ürgüp, a short ride from Göreme.

Places to Eat – bottom end

On the main square is the popular *Cappadocia Restaurant* (tel 1029), with a few outdoor tables and many more indoor, fairly attentive service and decent three-course meals for about US$4 or US$5. The nearby *Sofa Restaurant* (tel 2300), across

the square in the courtyard of an old han provides the competition, and many readers prefer it to the Cappadocia. Meals cost about the same.

Cheaper restaurants are found on Dumlupınar Caddesi, south of the market. The *Erciyes Restaurant* is one, with a few tiny sidewalk tables and main courses such as şiş kebap for only US$1 or US$1.50. The *Köşk* is similar. Even cheaper fare is the pide served at the *Kent Restaurant & Pide Salonu*. They have ready food as well. The *Buhara Restaurant* (tel 1182) is at the western end of the street, with prices like those at the Cappadocia. It has an outdoor terrace dining area and is right next door to a fragrant bakery.

On Suat Hayri Ürgüplü Caddesi, near the entrance to the otogar, is the *Uğrak Restaurant*, with a few outdoor tables on the busy street corner and full meals for US$3.

For pastries and sweets, there's the *Zümrüt Pasta Salonu* on Dumlupınar Caddesi next to the Kent Restaurant & Pide Salonu, and the *Merkez Pastanesi* (tel 1281), the best in town, on the main square. A large glass of tea and a portion of cake costs less than US$1.

Places to Eat – middle

The *Han Çırağan Restaurant* (tel 1169, 1621) is at the far end of the main square in an old village stone house behind a vine-covered garden. The plain, vaulted interior dining room is simple but not unpleasant. The menu offers a welcome change from the standard kebaps and ready foods, listing some regional dishes. I had a good dinner of soup, salad, meat course, melon for dessert and a half-bottle of local wine for less than US$10. If you skip the wine you'll spend much less.

Getting Around

The transport situation for Ürgüp is similar to that at Nevşehir. Indeed, many of the buses departing Nevşehir actually begin their journeys in Ürgüp, so you can pile onto a bus going directly to Adana, Ankara, Mersin, Konya, Antalya, Alanya, İstanbul, İzmir and other destinations. Direct buses to Kayseri depart every hour from 7 am to 6 pm.

Minibuses connect Ürgüp with neighbouring towns. There is at least one minibus per hour to Nevşehir from 7.30 am to 7.30 pm, operated by the Ürgüp Belediyesi at a fare of US$0.50. There are occasional minibuses to Avanos, but few to any of the smaller villages such as Göreme.

AVANOS

North of Göreme, on the banks of the Kızılırmak River, lies Avanos (AH-vah-nohs), with a population of 12,000. It's a town famous for pottery making and workshops turn out ashtrays, lamps, chess sets and other utensils and souvenirs moulded from the red clay of the Red River (Kızılırmak). On the outskirts along the Gülşehir road are several tile factories making clay construction blocks (tuğla) and roof-tiles (kiremit).

If you're not staying here overnight, Avanos is a good place to have lunch or at least a çay break. Wander around the town a bit, looking in the workshops.

Avanos has banks, a PTT, pensions, hotels, restaurants, pharmacies and other such necessities.

Information & Orientation

Most of the town is on the north bank of the river, but several pensions are on the south. The town is small enough, in any case, that you won't have trouble getting around on foot. There is a small Tourism Information Office (tel (4861) 1360) next door to the prominent Hotel Venessa, on the traffic roundabout at the northern end of the bridge across the river.

Özkonak

North of Avanos is the village of Özkonak, beneath which is a small version of the underground cities to be seen at Kaymaklı

and Derinkuyu. It's not nearly so dramatic or impressive as the larger ones, but it is less crowded. The town's muezzin found it in the garden of his house, and now opens it to visitors for a fee.

Dolmuşes run infrequently from Avanos to Özkonak. Leave Avanos on the Gülşehir road; after 4½ km, look for a road on the right (badly marked) for Özkonak, 9½ km farther along. Once you arrive in the village, turn right at a crude sign pointing the way to the Özkonak Yeraltı Şehri (underground city). There is another right turn and, at a petrol station, yet another right. Less than two km brings you to the car park. (You can also reach Özkonak via the main road to Kayseri; a sign points the way.)

The muezzin, Mr Latif Acer, will greet you in bits of German, English or French, and show you to the entrance, right beneath the car park. Take a jumper or jacket and a torch (flashlight) if you have them. The muezzin fixed the place up himself, adding the electric lights. He says that he's shown so many visitors through the chilly rooms that he's contracted rheumatism. The admission fee is a tip given after the tour. He or a boy will take you through, pointing out a room with a wine reservoir (the wine press is on the other side of the wall in the next room – you'll see it), air shafts, rolling stone doors, grindstones, etc. Some of the passages and tunnels from room to room are quite low, requiring you to duck.

Latif Acer may invite you in for some tea, show you his collection of photos and articles dealing with his underground city and attempt to sell you textiles at inflated prices. If you like, he'll also show you the village mosque (where he works) and an old monastery called the Belha Kilisesi.

Other Sights

This is a handicrafts town and its citizens sponsor the annual Avanos Elsanatları Festivalı (Avanos Handicrafts Festival) for three days in late August. Have a look in one of the pottery workshops. Several in

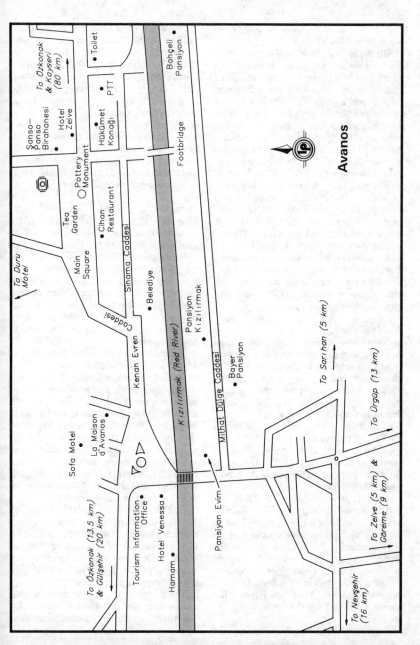

the town welcome visitors and even sponsor pottery classes.

On the main square, by the shady little park-cum-tea garden, is a marvellous **monument** in a pool. Made entirely of red clay pottery, it shows an amazingly lifelike potter at work. Below it is a scene of a woman and a girl weaving a Turkish carpet, another Avanos craft. On the left side is a bearded, short-clad, camera-carrying tourist holding a bunch of grapes and laughing while standing on a huge pair of hands: is this God's gift to Avanos? At the back of the monument is a woman on a donkey with a child peering out of a saddlebag. On the right side is a self-portrait of the monument's creator, H Ömer Taşkın, who finished the work in 1974.

The town's **hamam** is in Orta Mahalle, behind the Hotel Venessa, newly built in a traditional style with local sandstone and a red-tile roof. Something was wrong with the heating system at my last visit, but perhaps it's fixed by now.

Places to Stay

Avanos has several good hotels and pensions and can serve well as a base for your Cappadocian explorations. Noise in this town comes from dogs, roosters, donkeys and a nuclear-powered muezzin.

Places to Stay – bottom end

Try *La Maison d'Avanos* (tel 1587), run by Erol of Poterie d'Erol, an artist in the local bohemian community. Beds in waterless rooms cost US$3. Living at Erol's is like bringing the best of the hippie years back to life.

Another pension in an old Avanos house is the *Çardak Pansiyon* (chahr-DAHK) (tel 1403), with eight rooms, two WCs, two showers and prices of US$3 per person. The pension is 100 metres up from the main square; follow the signs. You might also try the 17-room *Kirkit Pension* charging US$5 per person, breakfast and shower included. Find the Kirkit Halı carpet shop and ask the owner about the pension.

Also explore the cluster of pensions on Mithat Dülge Caddesi on the southern bank of the river, near the bridge. The *Evim Pansiyon* (eh-VEEM) (tel 1614), Mithat Dülge Caddesi 1, is by the bridge; the *Kızılırmak Pansiyon* (KUH-zuh-luhr-mahk) (tel 1634) is several blocks from the bridge along the river, as is the *Bayer* (tel 1287). The Bayer was built as an apartment building with shop (now the lobby) below and rooms above. It's well-kept and homier than some of the others, and charges US$6/12 a single/double for a clean, cheerful, waterless room.

Places to Stay – middle

The *Sofa Motel* (tel 1489), Köprübaşı, Venessa Oteli Yanı, 50500 Avanos, is four nice old village houses joined into one (ignore the word 'Motel'), up the hill from the traffic roundabout near the Hotel Venessa. Several of the 23 rooms are partially built into the rock, and all are quite nicely kept. You can live the troglodytic life here for US$24 a double, breakfast included. The rooftop terrace has a fine view.

High above the town stands the *Duru Motel* (tel 1005), Kenan Evren Caddesi 38, 50500 Avanos, a modern white two-storey block with a grassy terrace and wonderful views over the town, the river and the valley. Rooms have wall-to-wall carpeting, little tiled bathrooms with showers (solar-heated water) and friendly management. You can have breakfast on the terrace, enjoying the view. Prices are US$13/23 a single/double, breakfast included. To find it, follow the signs up the winding, narrow street to the top.

By the bridge is the *Hotel Venessa* (tel 1201), Köprübaşı, 50500 Avanos, a big, modern place which has recently undergone a complete facelift and now has 83 comfortable rooms, each with shower and balcony, priced at US$30/40 a single/double, breakfast included.

The *Hotel Zelve*, on the main square across from the Hükümet Konağı (Sub-province Government House) is modern and quite suitable, with kilims in the lobby and functional guest rooms with bath going for US$23/32 a single/double, buffet breakfast included.

Across the bridge on the road to Göreme, a number of three and four-star hotels have recently been built, mostly for the group trade but available to individual travellers as well. These include the *Hotel Altınyazı*, *Hotel Büyük Avanos* and *Hotel Ergün*.

Places to Eat

Outside the hotels, there's nothing fancy. The *Cihan Restaurant* (jee-HAHN) (tel 1045) on the main square is a popular ready food and broiled chicken place open for all three meals. Lunch or dinner might cost US$3 or US$4. The *Sofra Restaurant* (tel 1324), Hükümet Konağı Karşısı, next to the Hotel Zelve and facing the government building, is similar. Nothing fancy, but serviceable. The *Kuş*, likewise; the *Tuvanna* is slightly fancier and more expensive, but not by much. *Şanso-Panso Birahanesi*, up the slope of the main square behind the pottery monument, on the right, serves beer and food and is the closest you'll come in Avanos to a taverna.

GÜLŞEHİR

Some 23 km west of Avanos is Gülşehir with a population of 7000. It has several unimpressive rock formations on the outskirts: Karşı Kilise, or St John Church; an unexcavated underground city; and Açık Saray, rock formations with a few insignificant churches. In the centre of the village stands the **Karavezir Mehmet Paşa Camii & Medrese** (1778), an Ottoman mosque and its college (now a library).

Gülşehir has several good hotels, including the fancy Swiss-run *Kepez Hotel* (tel 1163), on the flat-top hill in the midst of the town. The Kepez is attractively built of local sandstone, with finish work by Swiss craftsmen brought in expressly for the job. Rooms have marble floors and showers, with the heating in the floor; reading lights of a special design invented by the hotel's owner and builder, Mr H W Peter; and three cosy restaurants. 'All is to a Swiss standard,' says owner Peter. The cost to stay here, breakfast and dinner included, is US$40 per person.

Hotel Gülşehir (tel 1028), on the northern outskirts by the river, is a new three-storey hostelry surrounded by greenery, with older rooms in a motel-style block, newer ones in the hotel. Airy, decently furnished rooms with bath go for US$45 a double, breakfast included. They have a camping area and a swimming pool, as well as a restaurant.

HACIBEKTAŞ

A clean and pleasant town on the north-western outskirts of the Cappadocian region, Hacıbektaş, 27½ km west of Gülşehir, is famous not for its churches or troglodyte dwellings, but as the birthplace of Hacı Bektaş Veli, founder and spiritual leader of the Bektaşi order of Dervishes. Hacı Bektaş, who lived in the 1200s, inspired a religious and political following that blended aspects of Islam (both Sunni and Shiite) and Orthodox Christianity. Bektaşi Dervishes, who were often scorned by mainstream Islamic clerics, developed a wide following in Ottoman times, attaining considerable political and religious influence. They were outlawed along with all other Dervish sects when the Turkish Republic was founded.

The Bektaşi spiritual philosophy developed in the borderlands between the Turkish and Byzantine empires, where guerrilla fighters from both sides had more in common with one another than they did with their sovereigns in Konya or Constantinople. Their liberal beliefs caught on with the common people, and the ideas of the Bektaşis are still an important force in Turkish religious life today. The believers gather in Hacıbektaş each August on pilgrimage to the saint's tomb.

Things to See

There's only one really, the **Hacı Bektaş Monastery**, officially called the Hacıbektaş Müzesi, open from 8 am to 12 noon and from 1.30 to 5.30 pm, closed Monday. Admission costs US$0.50. Plaques are in Turkish, with some in English. Though it's called a museum, you should remember that it is a sacred place.

Several rooms in the museum are arranged as they might have looked when the Dervishes lived here, including the **Aş Evi**, or kitchen, with its implements; and the **Meydan Evi**, where novice Dervishes were inducted into the order. Other rooms have musical instruments, costumes, embroidery, turbans and other artefacts of the order, as well as relevant old photographs.

You can enter the saint's tomb in the garden at the far end of the building; remove your shoes before stepping inside, as this is a place of prayer.

Places to Stay

Across the street from the monastery is a market and shopping complex, and in it the simple *Hotel Hünkar* (tel (4867) 1344), with clean rooms and telephone-style showers going for US$6 a double. The management is friendly, too.

Out on the main road, one km from the monastery, is the *Hotel Village House* (tel 1628, 1046), with 26 modern rooms priced at US$17/22 a single/double, breakfast included. It's a nice little three-storey hotel with restaurant and bar. Guest rooms have balconies and tiny private 'telephone' showers.

KAYSERİ

Once the capital of Cappadocia, Kayseri (KAHY-seh-ree), with an altitude of 1054 metres and a population of 450,000, is now a booming farm and textile centre. In the shadow of Erciyes Dağı (Mt Aergius, 3916 metres), the sleepy old conservative town surrounding the ancient black citadel has become a city of modern, apartment-lined boulevards in only a few years. These two aspects of Kayseri aren't completely comfortable together, and something remains of old Kayseri's conservative soul.

In Turkish folklore, the people of Kayseri are the crafty dealers. Though every merchant you meet in the bazaar will not fit this image, you are sure to be persecuted by at least one carpet dealer. Kayseri is at the centre of a region which produces many of Turkey's loveliest carpets, and you may do well shopping here. But if you don't buy, the rug merchant who has been following you for days will be there at the bus station, waving and weeping, as you pull out of town. (The carpet pushers are getting more polite as time goes on, though.)

If you're passing through on your way to Cappadocia, take a few hours to tour Kayseri, as it has many Seljuk buildings and a nice bazaar. Those heading east might want to see the sights, spend the night, and get an early start the next morning. Besides the sights in town, there are two superb Seljuk hans north-east of the city, off the Sivas road. Taxi drivers in Kayseri will quote you a price for a three or four-hour tour including both of them.

History

This was Hittite country, so its history goes way back. The first Hittite capital, Kanesh, was earlier the chief city of the Hatti. It's located at Kültepe, north-east of Kayseri on the Sivas road. There was probably an early settlement on the site of Kayseri as well, though the earliest traces which have come to light are from Hellenistic times.

Under the Roman emperor Tiberius (14-37 AD), the town received its name, Caesarea, and later became famous as the birthplace of St Basil the Great, one of the early Church Fathers. Its early Christian history was interrupted by the Arab invasions of the 600s and later.

The Seljuks took over in 1084 and held the city until the Mongols' arrival in 1243, except for a brief period when the

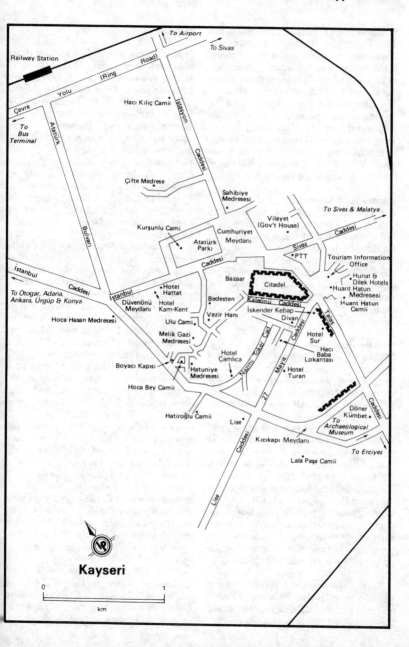

Kayseri

To Airport
To Sivas

Railway Station

Yolu (Ring Road)

İstasyon Caddesi

Çevre

To Bus Terminal

Atatürk Bulvarı

Hacı Kılıç Camii

Çifte Medrese

Sahibiye Medresesi

Vilayet (Gov't House)

To Sivas & Malatya

Kurşunlu Cami

Cumhuriyet Meydanı

Atatürk Parkı

Caddesi

Sivas Caddesi

PTT

Tourism Information Office

İstanbul Caddesi

To Otogar, Adana, Ankara, Ürgüp & Konya

İstanbul

Düvenönü Meydanı

Hotel Hattat

Hotel Kam-Kent

Bazaar

Bedesten

Vezir Hanı

Citadel

Kaleönü Caddesi

İskender Kebap

Divan

Hunat & Dilek Hotels

Huant Hatun Medresesi

Huant Hatun Camii

Hoca Hasan Medresesi

Ulu Cami

Melik Gazi Medresesi

Hotel Çamlıca

Talas

Hotel Sur

Hacı Baba Lokantası

Boyacı Kapısı

Hatuniye Medresesi

Nazmi Toker Cad.

Maris

Hotel Turan

Hoca Bey Camii

27

Döner Kümbet

To Archaeological Museum

Caddesi

Hatiroğlu Camii

Lise

Kıcıkapı Meydanı

To Erciyes

Caddesi

Lise

Lala Paşa Camii

0   1
km

Crusaders captured it on their way to the Holy Land. After Kayseri had been part of the Mongol Empire for almost 100 years, its Mongol governor set up his own emirate (1335) which lasted a mere 45 years. It was succeeded by another emirate (that of Kadı Burhaneddin), then captured by the Ottomans (seized during the Ottoman interregnum by the Karamanid emirs), later taken by the Mamelukes of Egypt, and finally conquered by the Ottomans again in 1515, all in just over 100 years. Those were exciting times in Kayseri.

Information & Orientation

For orientation, use the black-walled citadel at the centre of the old town. The railway station is at the end of İstasyon Caddesi, one km from the citadel. Kayseri's otogar is in the western part of town. The Tourism Information Office (tel (351) 11190, 19295) is beside the citadel at Kağnı Pazarı Honat Camii Yanı No 61.

Near the Hisar

Many of Kayseri's interesting buildings are either found near the citadel, on Cumhuriyet Meydanı or on nearby Düvenönü Meydanı. In this district you will have to spend half your time fighting off the carpet dealers.

The hisar, which has been restored and turned into a tourist shopping bazaar, was built by Emperor Justinian in the 500s, and extensively repaired by the Seljuk Sultan Keykavus I around 1224. In 1486, the Ottoman sultan, Mehmet the Conqueror, made major repairs. With Erciyes looming over the town, it's not surprising that the hisar should be made of black volcanic stone. At several points within the citadel you can climb flights of stairs up to the top of the walls (no guardrails, though).

East of the hisar is a complex which includes the **Huant Hatun Camii** or Mosque of Huant Hatun (1228), built by the wife of the Seljuk sultan Alaettin Keykubat,

plus the tomb of the lady herself, and bits of a Turkish bath.

Next to the mosque is the **Huant Hatun Medresesi** or Seminary of Huant Hatun (1237), now Kayseri's Ethnographic Museum open from 8 am to 5 pm; admission costs US$1. Displays in the historic building include ceramics and faïence, weapons, glassware, kitchen utensils, coins, costumes for both men and women and the interior of a Kayseri household as it was a century ago. You can also visit Lady Huant's tomb, an octagonal room with a high domed ceiling. Besides the lady, the tomb contains the remains of her grandchild and of an unknown person. Remove your shoes before entering the tomb.

The **Sahibiye Medresesi** or Sahibiye Seminary is at the north side of Cumhuriyet Meydanı, the large square by the citadel. It dates from 1267 and has an especially beautiful Seljuk portal.

You can spot the Ottoman-style **Kurşunlu Cami** or Lead-Roofed Mosque by its lead-covered dome, unusual in old Kayseri, north of İstanbul Caddesi and west of Cumhuriyet Meydanı and Atatürk Parkı. Also called the Ahmet Paşa Camii after its founder, it was completed in 1585 to plans that may have been drawn, and were certainly influenced, by the great Sinan.

Two adjoining religious schools, the Gıyasiye ve Şifaiye Medreseleri, are sometimes called the **Çifte Medrese** or the Twin Seminaries. They're in a maze of narrow back streets north of the Kurşunlu Cami. Sultan Gıyaseddin Keyhüsrev I ordered the schools built, and they were finished by 1206. For much of their history they functioned as a combined theological school, medical college and clinic. They now serve as a museum of medical history.

North of the Çifte Medrese, near İstasyon Caddesi, is the mosque (1249) of the Seljuk vizier Abdül Gazi, called the **Hacı Kılıç Camii**, with some very fine Seljuk architectural detail, especially in the doorways.

Near Düvenönü Meydanı

West of the hisar is Kayseri's tidy, shady bazaar, which you should definitely explore, fending off carpet dealers as you go.

Kayseri's **Ulu Cami** (oo-LOO jah-mee) or Great Mosque is near Düvenönü Meydanı. It was begun in 1135 by the Danışmend Turkish emirs and finished by the Seljuks in 1205. There's been a lot of repair and 'restoration' over the centuries, but it's still a good example of early Seljuk style.

South of the Hisar

Among Kayseri's other Seljuk archaeological treasures are several tombs. The **Döner Kümbet** (deur-NEHR kewm-beht) or Revolving Tomb is about one km southeast of the hisar along Talas Caddesi. Though it doesn't (and never did) revolve, its cylindrical shape suggests turning, and as you view its marvellous and elaborate Seljuk decoration (1276), you will at least revolve around it. This was a lady's tomb. Nearby is another, the Sırçalı Kümbet (1300s), which used to be covered in coloured tiles and topped by a pyramidal roof. You may spot other kümbets in and near Kayseri.

The city's **Archaeological Museum** is out near the Döner Kümbet, to the east by the railway. The museum houses the finds from Kültepe, site of ancient Kanesh, including the cuneiform tablets which told historians much about the Hittite Empire. Hittite, Hellenistic and Roman statuary, plus exhibits of local ethnography, help to make it worth a visit. Hours are from 8 am to 12 noon and from 1 to 5.30 pm daily except Monday; admission costs US$2.

In the bazaar, the historic **Kapalı Çarşı** or Covered Market was nicely restored in 1988. The shops here serve the residents, not the tourist trade.

Hans

Haggle with a taxi-driver for an excursion to the Sultan Han and Karatay Han, and you will probably end up with a figure of US$12 to US$18 for the entire car. If time and money are short, bargain for just the Sultan Han. If only money is short, try to find a bus which will drop you at the Sultan Han (start early in the day!), and then trust luck to catch something back to Kayseri.

Head out on the Sivas road. Twenty km from Kayseri there is a left turning to **Kültepe**, site of ancient Kanesh. You may want to take a quick look at the site of this incredibly old Hittite city (2000 BC), but there's not a lot to see.

The **Sultan Han** is on the highway, 45 km north-east of Kayseri. Besides being a fine example of the Seljuk royal caravan lodging, it has been beautifully restored so it is easy to appreciate the architectural fine points. The han was finished in 1236; restoration was carried out only a few decades ago. Don't let the locked gate worry you. Shortly after your car draws up, a boy will come running with the key and a booklet of tickets; admission costs US$0.14. Hours are supposedly from 9 am to 1 pm and from 2 to 5 pm, but in fact it is open whenever the guardian can be found.

Tour the inside, noticing particularly the elegant snake motif on the little mosque's arches. Climb up to the roof if you like, but don't neglect a walk around the exterior as well. Note the lion-faced water spouts on the walls, and the plain towers of varying design.

If you have time, take your taxi to the **Karatay Han**, in a Turkish village now well off the beaten track. From the Sultan Han, head back toward Kayseri and take the turning south or east to Bünyan. Pass through Bünyan toward Malatya, and about 30 km along there is a road on the right for Elbaşı. Follow this track five km to Elbaşı, and four km beyond to Karatay, also called Karadayı.

The Karatay Han, built in 1240 for the Seljuk vizier Emir Celaleddin Karatay, was once on the main east-west trade route. It was restored in the 1960s, and is yet another fine example of high Seljuk art.

A visit to the Karatay Han gives you a glimpse into the life of a Turkish village as well.

Climbing Erciyes

Mountaineers may like to know that at Kayak Evi there is a mountain hut of 100 beds, 26 km south of Kayseri on the mountain road. Leave the city by the road to the airport (*havaalanı*) and the village of Hisarcık (14 km), and continue to Kayak Evi. Even if you don't plan to climb, the outing will give you a look at some spectacular scenery.

Places to Stay – bottom end

Behind the Huant Mosque and Ethno-graphic Museum near the Tourism Information Office is the *Hotel Hunat* (tel 24319), Hunat Sokak 5, a simple, cheap, convenient, quiet place with waterless rooms priced at US$3/5 a single/double. The *Hotel Dilek*, right next door, takes the overflow.

Hotel Sur (SOOR) (tel 19545, 13992), Cumhuriyet Mahallesi, Talas Caddesi 12, offers good value in a convenient location. Doubles cost US$14 for one large bed or twin beds, or US$16 for two beds (one double, one single), both with private shower. The hotel is not far from the citadel, behind the city walls and the Sivas Kapısı (Sivas Gate) off Talas Caddesi. Walk south-east on Talas Caddesi from the citadel, with a remnant of the city walls on your right. Turn right after passing the wall, then right again, and you'll see the hotel. Don't mind the crowd of men gathered in the street; they're waiting to do business at the local employment office.

The *Hotel Kam-Kent* (tel 12454), Camikebir Mahallesi, Camikebir Caddesi 2, near Düvenönü Meydanı and the Hotel Hattat, is more modest and much-used. Double rooms with shower here go for US$15.

In the bazaar is the tidy and fairly quiet *Hotel Çamlıca* (CHAHM-luh-jah)(tel 19426), Bankalar Caddesi, Gürcü Sokak 14, with serviceable rooms priced at US$15 double with washbasin, US$18 with shower. It's a bit difficult to find. From the Divan Pastanesi (see Places to Eat), turn right off 27 Mayıs Caddesi, and take the third street on the left, Nazmi Toker Caddesi, known to the locals as Bankalar Caddesi (Banks Street), for obvious reasons. After you come to an intersection, walk one block more along the curving street to the hotel.

Places to Stay – middle

Kayseri is ripe for some new hotel construction, and I expect that in the next few years some comfortable, modern hotels will open. But at the time of this writing, you face a bad situation.

The two-star *Hotel Turan* (too-RAHN) (tel 11968, 12506), 27 Mayıs Caddesi, Turan Caddesi 8, is Kayseri's old faithful, having served travellers for several decades now. This is obvious from the rooms, but they're still serviceable, especially as long as nothing better is available, and priced at US$25 to US$30 a single, US$30 to US$50 a double; the higher prices are for larger rooms with larger closets and baths as well as showers. They're ready to haggle here, and if business is slack you'll pay much less. The hotel has a roof terrace and a Turkish bath.

Hotel Hattat (hah-TAHT) (tel 19331, 19829), İstanbul Caddesi 1, is similar but less so, with 67 rooms quite clearly overpriced at US$37/50 a single/double, private bath and breakfast included. They probably won't ask these official prices of you.

Next to the otogar is an emergency-only lodging, the nominally one-star *Terminal Oteli* (TEHR-mee-NAHL) (tel 64674), Osman Kavuncu (İstanbul) Caddesi 176, with 21 rooms for US$22 a double with private shower, US$18 a double with just a washbasin.

Places to Eat

Kayseri is noted for a few special dishes,

among them *pastırma* (from the same root-word as *pastrami*?) – sun-dried beef coated with garlic and savoury spices. It has a very strong flavour, tends to stick in your teeth and despotically rule your breath for hours, but once you acquire the taste you look forward to a return to Kayseri. Shops in the centre will sell it to you for picnics (try 100 grams); before you buy, ask for a sample (*Bir tat, lütfen*, beer TAHT lewt-fehn, 'A taste, please').

Other Kayseri specialities include *sucuk* (soo-JOOK), a spicy sausage; *salam* (sah-LAHM), Turkish salami; *tulum peynir* (too-LOOM pehy-neer), hard cheese cured in a goatskin; and *bal* (BAHL), honey. Few of these things, with the exception of pastırma, will appear on restaurant menus, so you must buy them in food shops for picnics.

The town's best restaurants are in the top hotels, the *Hattat* and the *Turan*. For cheaper, less elegant, but dependably good food (for 20 years now), the *İskender Kebap Salonu* (tel 12769), 27 Mayıs Caddesi 5, is by the citadel, one floor above street level; good döner kebap served Bursa-style, good view of the busy street, low prices of about US$2 or US$3 for a meal of kebap, ayran and salad. The general dining room is one flight up; the much nicer aile salonu with flowers on every table is another flight up via a stairway from the general dining room.

Across the street is the *Merkez Kebap ve Pide Salonu* (tel 12962), with similar fare, including fresh pide. The nearby *Cumhuriyet Lokantası* (tel 14911), two doors down 27 Mayıs Caddesi from the Divan Pastanesi, is a good choice for ready food or roast chicken.

The *Hacı Usta Lokanta ve Kebap Salonu*, Serdar Caddesi 3 & 7, has two locations in the bazaar. To find them, walk from the citadel on 27 Mayıs Caddesi, pass Vatan Caddesi on the right, and then turn right onto Serdar Caddesi. Or, turn right off 27 Mayıs Caddesi at the Divan Pastanesi, turn left at the second street, and look for the restaurant on the

left. Both these places are very simple, cheap and tasty, with ready food meals going for US$1.50 to US$2.50.

The *Divan Pastanesi* is a good, fancy pastry shop on 27 Mayıs Caddesi a block south of the citadel, at the corner of Mevlevi Caddesi. As there are few places to sit, it's mostly good for take-away.

Getting There & Away
Air Kayseri's Erkilet Airport is connected with İstanbul by two flights per week, on Tuesday and Thursday, by Turkish Airlines (tel (351) 13947), Sahibiye Mahallesi, Yıldırım Caddesi 1. As of this writing, there is no air service to Ankara. An airport bus US$0.49 connects the city with Erkilet airport. Catch the bus 1¼ hours before flight departure time, or be at the airport at least 20 – preferably 30 – minutes before scheduled departure time.

Bus Buses run very frequently – at least every hour – between Kayseri's otogar and Ankara, a five-hour, 330 km, US$4 trip. You can also get convenient buses to Adana (335 km, 6½ hours, US$6), Malatya (360 km, six hours, US$5), Sivas (195 km, four hours, US$4) and points east.

Dolmuşes run frequently to Ürgüp and Nevşehir, operating at least hourly in the morning and afternoon during the summer. The fare is US$1.75.

To get to the hisar from the otogar, walk out the front door, cross the avenue and board any bus. Or take a dolmuş marked 'Terminal-Şehir'. A taxi to the citadel costs less than US$2.

Train Several daily trains connect Kayseri with Ankara and points east; see the Ankara section for details. There are trains eastward to Sivas (3½ hours) and Erzurum (22 hours); the trains are not luxurious. The train between Kayseri and Malatya takes 10 hours, if it's on time; the bus is much quicker. There are no good train connections north to the Black Sea;

better to take the train to Sivas, then a bus to Samsun.

To get into town from the railway station, walk out of the station, cross the big avenue and board any bus heading down Atatürk Bulvarı.

YOZGAT

About 35 km south of Boğazkale is Yozgat. At an altitude of 1301 metres and with a population of 45,000, Yozgat is on the Ankara to Sivas highway. It's an unprepossessing provincial capital founded by the Ottomans in the 1700s. Now the main highway through town is lined with modern Turkish waffle-front apartment buildings. In contrast is the Nizamoğlu Konağı, a 19th century Ottoman house now used to hold ethnographic exhibits. But Yozgat has those two things travellers need, hotels and an otogar.

Orientation

The old main road, a block north of the highway, is more sympathetic than the highway, Ankara Caddesi. Walk two blocks north to reach the main square, Cumhuriyet Meydanı, with its old clock tower, Vilayet building, PTT and an old Ottoman building now serving as local army offices; the sultan's monogram is still emblazoned in the tympanum. The Büyük Cami (or Çapanoğlu Camii, 1778), one long block west of the clock tower, is a late Ottoman work. Yozgat's otogar is less than one km east of the main square, an easy walk. To find your way to the main square from the otogar, go out the front door and turn right.

Five km south of Yozgat is Çamlık Milli Parkı (Pine-Grove National Park).

Places to Stay - bottom end

Right next door to the otogar is the Pınar Otel & Lokanta (tel (473) 11997), Ankara Caddesi. The inauspicious entry is past redolent toilets; rooms are OK, nothing special, but noise is a big factor here: the highway is out front, the otogar is at the side, and a mosque is behind! There is a

wonderfully luxuriant vine in the second storey hall. Double rooms with washbasin cost US$7.

On the main square are two more places. The Otel Saraylar (tel 11269), Cumhuriyet Meydanı, has almost been worn out by long and frequent usage. Doubles with washbasin go for US$7, with shower for US$9. Next door is the Hotel Saray (tel 12032, 14333), Cumhuriyet Meydanı 1, an old place with high ceilings and dated decor. Here you have a choice of rooms with shower (US$10 a double) or with washbasin (US$8); the ones with shower sell out fastest.

Places to Stay - middle

The nicest place in town is the one-star, 44-room Turistik Yılmaz Oteli (tel 11361, 11107), Ankara Caddesi 3, 66200 Yozgat, on the highway in the middle of town. The serviceable rooms here, all with private shower, are supplemented by a lift, restaurant, bar and a Turkish bath. Rates are US$17 to US$19 a single, US$26 to US$32 a double, but you should haggle for a reduction; higher prices are for rooms with bathtub as well as shower.

Places to Eat

The dining room in the Yılmaz Oteli is the most genteel, but the locals like the Ömür Lokantası down the hill a few steps from the clock tower. It's basic, but I had a good biftek, salad, ayran, fıstıklı baklava and a large glass of tea for US$3. The Merkez Restaurant, facing the main square near the clock tower, is more light and airy, with similar prices.

Getting There & Away

As with Sungurlu, getting to Yozgat is easy: catch a bus from the otogar in Ankara (220 km), Kayseri (250 km), or Sivas (230 km). For most other destinations, you must change buses at one of those cities. All three are a three-hour, US$3 ride from Yozgat.

Occasional minibuses run from Yozgat to Alaca, from which you can hitch to

Alacahöyük, or catch an onward minibus to Sungurlu. But to get to Boğazkale, the best course is to hire a taxi (US$20, up to four persons) or minibus (US$35, up to a dozen persons) to give you a full tour around: the ride to the site, two hours to look around, and return to Yozgat.

SUNGURLU

Going to Boğazkale from Ankara takes you through Sungurlu, where you must change buses. You may want to stay the night here as well. A commerce and farming town 175 km (three hours) east of Ankara, Sungurlu has nothing to detain you except its transport and lodging services.

Orientation

The otogar is one km west of the centre (Şehir Merkezi) just off the main highway. In the centre, an old clock tower marks the main ceremonial and government square; the commercial centre (Çarşı) is 200 metres up the hill. Minibuses to Boğazkale depart from this commercial square (villagers come into 'the big city' to do their shopping). There may also be direct Boğazkale minibuses from the bus terminal also.

Places to Stay

The cheap hotel situation in Sungurlu is not particularly good. The Çarşı has the *Hattuşaş Oteli*, but it was closed for renovation when I visited; no doubt it will open to receive a more upscale clientele. The little old *Masatlı Oteli* (tel (4557) 1968) is also on the main commercial square, a cheap han-style place advertising that it is *elektrikli battaniyeli* (equipped with electric blankets).

In the middle range, the situation is much better. One km east of the commercial square, on the highway, stands the *Hitit Motel* (tel 1042, 1409), Ankara-Samsun Yolu, Sungurlu, Çorum, with 23 rooms on two floors set amidst pretty gardens surrounding a swimming pool. The restaurant has good food and

service, the guest rooms have private showers and balconies looking onto the grounds, and prices are quite reasonable: single rooms cost US$15/20/30 a single/double/triple. In the restaurant, expect to spend US$5 to US$7 per person for lunch or dinner, drinks included.

Getting There & Away

Getting to Sungurlu is easy: take one of the hourly buses from Ankara's otogar. Getting away from Sungurlu demands a choice. You can catch a Boğazkale Belediyesi minibus operated by the village (US$1) for the 30-km, one-hour ride to Boğazkale; this is the cheapest way to go. Minibuses run throughout the day, with the last run departing Boğazkale at 5 pm, the return trip from Sungurlu departing at 6 pm. Or you can hire a taxi or minibus to give you a tour of Boğazkale and Alacahöyük, including a ride to the top of that exhausting hill, for US$20 for the entire car, about twice as much for a 15 to 20-person minibus.

BOĞAZKALE & THE HITTITE CITIES

Before our own century very little was known about the Hittites, a people who commanded a vast empire in the Middle East, conquered Babylon, and challenged the Egypt of the pharaohs over 3000 years ago. Though their accomplishments were monumental, time has buried Hittite history as effectively as it has buried the Hittites themselves. Only a few references to them, in the Bible and in Egyptian chronicles, remain.

In 1905 excavations began at the site of Hattuşaş, the Hittite capital near the Turkish village of Boğazkale (also called Boğazköy), 200 km east of Ankara off the highway to Samsun. The digging produced notable works of art, most of which are now preserved in Ankara's Museum of Anatolian Civilisations; also brought to light were the Hittite state archives, written in cuneiform (wedge-shaped characters) on thousands of clay tablets. From these tablets, historians and

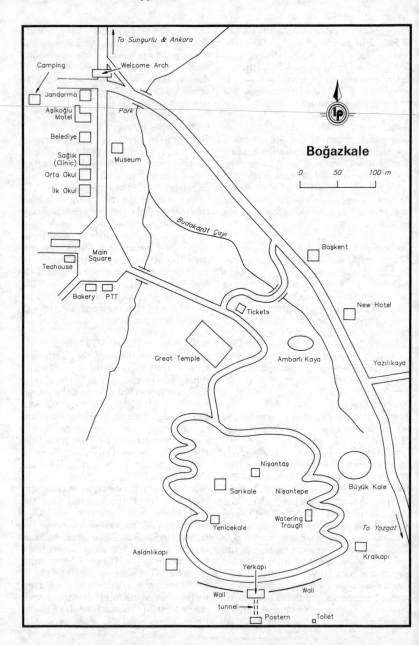

To Sungurlu & Ankara

Welcome Arch

Camping

Jandarma

Aşikoğlu Motel

Park

Belediye

Sağlık (Clinic)

Orta Okul

İlk Okul

Museum

Boğazkale

0   50   100 m

Budaközüt Çayı

Başkent

Main Square

Teahouse

Bakery   PTT

Tickets

New Hotel

Great Temple

Ambarlı Kaya

Yazılıkaya

Nişantaş

Sarıkale   Nişantepe

Büyük Kale

Yenicekale   Watering Trough

To Yozgat

Aslanlıkapı

Kralkapı

Yerkapı

Wall   Wall

tunnel →

Postern   Toilet

archaeologists were able to construct a history of the Hittite Empire.

The Hittites spoke an Indo-European language. They swept into Anatolia around 2000 BC and conquered the Hatti, from whom they borrowed both their culture and their name. They established themselves here at Hattuşaş, the Hatti capital, and in the course of a millennium enlarged and beautified the city. From about 1375 BC to 1200 BC, this was the great and glorious capital of the Hittite Empire.

Most of the Hittite artefacts are now in Ankara's museum, though there is also a small museum in Boğazkale, open from 8 am to 12 noon and from 1.30 to 5.30 pm. One US$3 admission ticket allows you entry to both the ruins and the museum.

Orientation

Coming from Sungurlu, you arrive in the village of Boğazkale, which has several hotels, camping grounds and restaurants, a teahouse and a few shops. It's a small farming village with a sideline in tourism. From the welcoming arch over the road at the entrance to the village, it's 100 metres up the street to the museum. Across the street from the museum is the İlçe Sağlık Ocağı (county clinic), the primary school and the grammar school.

If you are coming from Yozgat, you follow a road which comes over the mountains from the south-east and skirts the eastern part of the archaeological zone. The view of the ruined city from this road is very fine.

South of the village, up on the hillside, sprawl the extensive ruins of Hattuşaş. It's exactly one km from the welcome arch to the ticket kiosk, and another 2½ km up the hillside to the farthest point, the Sphinx Gate (or Yerkapı) along the road which loops through the ruins. The separate site of Yazılıkaya is about three km uphill from the ticket kiosk along another road.

Hattuşaş

This was once a great and very impressive city, well defended by stone walls over six km in length. Today the ruins consist mostly of reconstructed foundations, walls and a few rock carvings, but there are several more interesting features, including a tunnel. The site itself is strange, almost eerie, exciting for its ruggedness and high antiquity rather than for its extant buildings or reliefs.

The road looping around the entire site of Hattuşaş (not including Yazılıkaya) is five km long, from the ticket kiosk all the way around and back. The walk itself takes at least an hour, plus time spent exploring the ruins, so figure about three hours or so to see the site. You might want to take some water with you, and start early in the day before the sun is too hot. I'll describe the loop going anti-clockwise.

The first site you come to, 300 metres up from the ticket kiosk, is the **Büyük Mabed** or the Great Temple of the Storm God, a vast complex that's almost a town in itself, with its own water and drainage systems, storerooms and ritual altars. It dates from the 14th century BC; it seems to have been destroyed around 1200 BC.

About 350 metres past the Great Temple, the road forks; take the right fork and follow the winding road up the hillside. On your left in the midst of the old city are several temples and inscriptions, including the **Nişantaş**, a rock with a long but severely weathered Hittite inscription in it; the **Sarıkale**, which may be a Phrygian fort on Hittite foundations; and the **Yenicekale**, where Hittite engineers transformed the very uneven site into a flat plain on which to build their structures.

From the fork in the road it's about one km uphill to the **Aslanlıkapı** or Lion Gate which has two stone lions (copies of the originals, which are now in Ankara) defending the city against all comers. The city's defensive walls have been restored along the ridge, and this allows you to appreciate the scope of the construction effort that took place almost 4000 years ago.

Continue another 700 metres up to the top of the hill and the **Yerkapı** or Earth Gate, once defended by two great sphinxes, now domesticated in the museums of İstanbul and Berlin. The most interesting feature here is the long, 70-metre **tunnel** running beneath the walls to a postern on the southern side of the hill. As the true arch was not discovered until much later, the Hittites used a corbelled arch, two flat faces of stones leaning toward one another. Primitive or not, the arch has done its job for millennia, and you can still pass down the tunnel as Hittite soldiers did, emerging from the postern. Your reward is a WC, off to the left at the base of the slope. Climb back up to the Sphinx Gate by either of the monumental **stairways** placed on either side of the wide stone glacis beneath the walls. Once back up top, enjoy the wonderful view from this highest point, sweeping down over Hattuşaş, Boğazkale and beyond.

Another 600 metres eastward down the slope brings you to the **Kralkapı** or King's Gate, named after the regal-looking figure in the relief carving; the one you see is a copy, as the original was removed to safekeeping in the Ankara museum. Actually, the figure is not a king at all, but the Hittite war god.

The ruins of the **Büyük Kale** or Great Fortress are 800 metres downhill from the Kralkapı. This elaborate fortress also held the royal palace and the Hittite state archives. The archives, discovered in 1906, contained a treaty between the Hittite monarch, Hattusili III, and Ramses II, Pharaoh of Egypt, written on a clay tablet in cuneiform. From the fortress it's just over one km back to the ticket kiosk.

Yazılıkaya

The Turkish name (yah-zuh-LUH kah-yah) means 'inscribed rock', and that's what you find at this site just under three km from Boğazkale. Follow the signs from the ticket kiosk. The road circles a hillock called Ambarlı Kaya, atop which there

were more Hittite buildings, before crossing a stream and climbing the hill past the Başkent restaurant, pension and camping ground (you might want to stop here for refreshments or lunch).

Yazılıkaya was always a naturalistic religious sanctuary open to the sky, but in the later Hittite times (13th century BC) monumental gateways and temple structures were built in front of the natural rock galleries. It is the foundations of these late structures that you see as you approach Yazılıkaya from the car park.

There are two natural rock galleries, the larger one to the left, which was the empire's sacred place, and a narrower one to the right, which was the burial place of the royal family. In the large gallery, the low reliefs of numerous conehead gods and goddesses marching in procession indicate that this was the Hittite's holiest religious sanctuary. The Hittites had 1000 gods, but fewer than 100 are represented here. The most important Hittite deities were Teshub, the Storm God, and Hepatu, the Sun Goddess, which pretty much covered the bases back in 1200 BC.

Alacahöyük

There is less to see at Alacahöyük, but Hittiteophiles will want to make the trip to the site, 25 km north of Boğazkale. As at the other Hittite sites, movable monuments have been taken to the museum in Ankara, though there is a small museum on the site and a few worn sphinxes, and good bas-reliefs have been left in place. This is a very old site, settled from about 4000 BC.

To get there, leave Boğazkale heading north-west on the Sungurlu road, and after 13½ km turn right at the road marked for Alaca and Alacahöyük. (Coming from Sungurlu, turn left about 11 km after turning onto the Boğazkale road.) Go another 11½ km and turn left for Alacahöyük, nine more km along. As of this writing there is no dolmuş service. The villagers told me they preferred to get rides with trucks, as the truck drivers charge less than the minibus drivers. Thus you will have to do the same, or hire a taxi or minibus to take you to the ruins and back. (You should be able to get dolmuşes as far as the town of Alaca, 18 km from Alacahöyük; from there you must hitch rides.)

Alacahöyük is now a farming hamlet with a humble main square on which stands a fountain, a PTT, a souvenir shop, a bakery and a modest grocery. The Kaplan Restaurant & Hotel, basically a spartan pension, was not open when I was last in town, though it may re-open if demand warrants.

The little museum is right by the ruins, and both are open from 8.30 am to 12 noon, and from 1.30 to 5.30 pm, closed Monday; as this is a small village operation, you may even be able to beg your way in on Monday. Admission fee for everything is US$0.50.

In the tidy little museum you can inspect tools used in the excavations, and finds from the Chalcolithic and Old Bronze ages. A handy ant farm-style glass case shows the stratigraphy of Alacahöyük's 15 layers of history:

1	Phrygian Age (1200-600 BC)
2 to 4	Old Hittite and Great Hittite Empire Age (2000-1200 BC)
5 to 9	Old Bronze Age (3000-2000 BC)
10 to 15	Chalcolithic Age (5500-3000 BC)

The exhibits are not labelled except by period; I have included a table to help you translate. Note also the Hitit Çağı Banyo Teknesi, a Hittite-Age bathtub! Downstairs in the museum is its ethnographic section, which many people find more absorbing than the ancient potshards.

At the ruins, signs are in Turkish and English. The site is self-explanatory. The monumental gate is what you've come to see, with its lions guarding the door and its very fine reliefs down in front. The reliefs show Storm God worship ceremonies and festivals, with musicians, acrobats, priests and the Hittite king and queen.

Off to the left across the fields is a **secret escape tunnel** leading to a postern as at Hattuşaş.

Leaving Alacahöyük, signs for Sungurlu lead you seven km out to the Sungurlu to Çorum highway by a road not shown on many maps; turn left (south-west) for Sungurlu (27 km), right for Çorum (42 km) and Samsun (210 km).

Still interested in Hittites? You can visit the very earliest Hittite capital at **Kültepe**, near Kayseri in Cappadocia, but there is much less to see there. **Karatepe**, east of Adana, is worth a visit, though.

Places to Stay

There are several small hotels in Boğazkale. First one you'll see as you enter from Sungurlu is the 25-room *Aşıkoğlu Turistik Moteli* (ah-SHUK-oh-loo) (tel (4554) 1004), Boğazkale, Çorum, right by the welcome arch, open from mid-March to November. A very simple but clean double room with washbasin and shower (no toilet) costs US$12 – but the price goes up and down depending on who's asking, and when. The hotel also has a restaurant with edible food at premium prices, about US$5 or US$6 per person for a meal. Both places are heavily used by tour groups.

Behind the Jandarma post by the welcome arch is the Aşıkoğlu's camping ground, which is pretty basic but will do for a night.

If, before passing under the welcome arch, you take the road to the left across a stream and up the hill, after one km you will come to the *Başkent Restoran, Pansiyon & Campink* (tel 1037), Yazılıkaya Yolu Üzeri, Boğazkale, Çorum, with six tidy little rooms with twin beds but no running water. Hot water (flash) heater) showers at the end of the block are also clean. They ask US$12 a double, but you can haggle if they're not full and it's late in the day. You can camp here as well. The restaurant, with its white laminate tables, dark wood trim and red tile roof is pleasant, and has a nice view of the ruins.

Just 400 metres farther up the hill from

the Başkent is a newer, fancier three-storey hotel which was not finished when I visited, but is no doubt open now.

Getting There & Away

You can make a day's excursion from Ankara to Boğazkale. Ankara travel agents sell bus tours of the ruins, which are a good way to make your visit. With your own car you can stop at Boğazkale on the way to the Black Sea coast at Samsun. Otherwise, come by bus as described in the Sungurlu section.

If you don't want to make the hike around the ruins when you arrive in Boğazkale, you may be able to find a taxi to give you a tour for around US$10.

Black Sea Coast

Turkey's Black Sea coast is a unique part of the country; it's lush and green throughout the year with plentiful rainfall. Dairy farming, fishing and tea production are big industries, and there are bumper crops of tobacco (*tütün*), cherries (*kiraz*) and hazelnuts or filberts (*fındık*). The hazelnut crop picked for export every year is close to 140,000 tons.

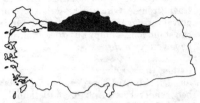

History

The coast was colonised in the 700s BC by Milesians and Arcadians, who founded towns at Sinop, Samsun and Trabzon. Later it became the Kingdom of Pontus. Most of Pontus's kings were named Mithridates, but it was Mithridates IV Eupator who gave the Romans a run for their money in 88-84 BC. He conquered Cappadocia and other Anatolian kingdoms, finally reaching Nicomedia (İzmit), which was allied with Rome. When the latter came to its defence, Mithridates pushed onward to the Aegean. The Roman response was hampered by civil war at home, but Rome's legions finally drove into Cappadocia and Pontus (83-81 BC), and Mithridates was forced to agree to peace based on pre-war borders.

In 74-64 BC Mithridates was at it again, encouraging his son-in-law Tigranes I of Armenia to seize Cappadocia from the Romans. He tried, but the Romans conquered Pontus in response, forcing Mithridates to flee and later to commit suicide. The Romans left a small client-kingdom of Pontus at the far eastern end of the coast, based on Trebizond (Trabzon).

The coast was ruled by Byzantium, and Alexius Comnenus, son of Emperor Manuel I, proclaimed himself emperor of Pontus when the Crusaders sacked Constantinople and drove him out in 1204. His descendants ruled this small empire until 1461, when it was taken by Mehmet the Conqueror.

While Alexius was in Trabzon, Samsun was under Seljuk rule and the Genoese had trading privileges. But when the Ottomans came, the Genoese burned Samsun to the ground before sailing away.

After WW I, the Ottoman Greek citizens of this region attempted to form a new Pontic state with Allied support. Turkish inhabitants, disarmed by the Allied occupation authorities, were persecuted by ethnic Greek guerilla bands which had been allowed to keep their arms. It was fertile ground for a revolt. Mustafa Kemal (Atatürk) used a bureaucratic ruse to escape from the sultan's control in İstanbul, and landed at Samsun on 19 May 1919. He soon moved inland to Amasya, and began to organise what would become the battle for independence.

Touring the Coast

Travelling along the coast from İstanbul east to Sinop is not all that easy by road. From Sinop east to Hopa, near the Soviet frontier, the road is excellent and very scenic, though with little of historic or artistic interest. The 360-km ride from Samsun to Trabzon can even be done in a day if you wish. You must take a few hours to see the sights in Trabzon, before heading up onto the plateau to Erzurum, or eastward along the coast through the tea plantations to Rize and Hopa. Past Hopa is Sarp, a border crossing point on the Soviet frontier, opened in 1988.

At Hopa you can climb into the mountains to Artvin, a ride with exceptionally beautiful views. Roads south and east from Artvin may be impassable in winter. Public transport is scarce, as are hotel facilities. Plan to travel from Artvin to Kars or Erzurum only if you have an adventurous spirit and can stand long, bumpy bus rides, or if you have your own car.

Getting There & Away

Air Turkish Airlines has daily flights between Trabzon, Ankara and İstanbul; there are no flights to any other Black Sea city at this writing. İstanbul Airlines flies between İstanbul and Trabzon on Monday, Wednesday and Friday.

Bus Buses to and along the coast are, as usual, fast, frequent and cheap. Plan to take the bus to Samsun from Ankara (420 km), Kayseri (450 km) or Sivas (340 km). On the eastern reaches of the coast, the route to take is between Trabzon and Erzurum via Gümüşhane.

Train The passenger rail service to Samsun via Sivas is slow and inconvenient. There are daily trains to and from Sivas to connect with the Güney Ekspresi and Vangölü Ekspresi, but the trip takes 12 mostly daylight hours. You can save time by taking the bus. There is no rail service east of Samsun.

Boat Turkish Maritime Lines operate car ferries on what amounts to a mini-cruise service between İstanbul and Trabzon, departing İstanbul each Monday evening, arriving in Samsun on Tuesday evening, and departing a few hours later to arrive in Trabzon Wednesday morning. Departure from Trabzon for the return trip is late Wednesday evening, reaching Samsun on Thursday morning, stopping for only about 90 minutes, then embarking again for İstanbul, arriving Friday at 12 noon. The only problem with this service is that tickets sell out fast – and well in advance in summer.

A reclining seat between İstanbul and Samsun costs US$14; between İstanbul and Trabzon, US$19. For the comfort of a bed in a cabin you pay from US$22 to US$55 per person between İstanbul and Samsun, US$25 to US$60 per person between İstanbul and Trabzon. Meals are not included in these prices; buy whatever you like on board. The fee for a car between İstanbul and Samsun is US$25, between İstanbul and Trabzon it's US$42.

The cruise is fun, but much of the time you will be steaming at night, with no chance of seeing the passing scenery. Also, food and drink on board tend to be expensive, so pack your own supplies. You can stock up at Samsun, as well. If you find the Pullman seat uncomfortable for sleeping, or noisy, or the room smoky, stake out some deck space, roll out your sleeping bag, and spend the night in the fresh air.

AMASYA

On the way to Samsun, you may pass through Amasya (ah-MAHSS-yah). This city, with a population of 65,000, was capital of the province of the same name and one-time capital of the Pontic kings. At an altitude of 392 metres, on the banks of the Yeşil Irmak (Green River), surrounded by high cliffs, Amasya is an old-time town with a number of things to see including the rock-hewn tombs of the kings of Pontus, some fine old mosques, picturesque Ottoman half-timbered houses and a good little museum. Set away from the rest of Anatolia in its tight mountain valley, Amasya has a feeling of independence, self-sufficiency and civic pride. Preservation of history is respected.

History

Despite appearing a small, sleepy provincial capital, Amasya has seen very exciting times. It was a Hittite town, and was conquered by Alexander the Great. When his empire broke up, Amasya became the capital of a successor-kingdom ruled by a family of Persian satraps. By the time of King Mithridates

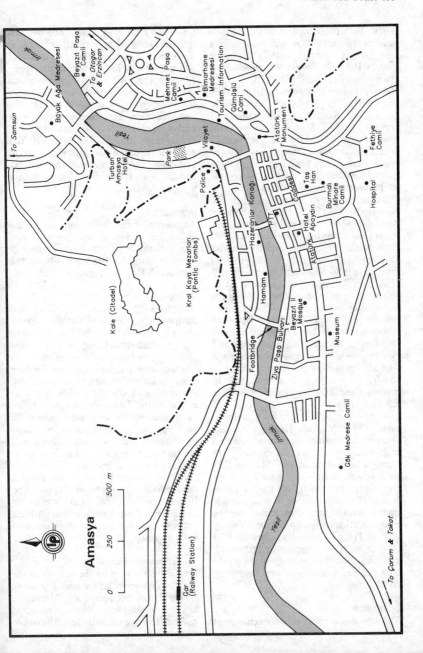

Amasya

0   250   500 m

To Samsun

Irmak

Yeşil

Büyük Ağa Medresesi

Beyazıt Paşa Camii

To Otogar & Erzincan

Mehmet Paşa Camii

Bimarhane Medresesi

Tourism Information

Gümüşlü Camii

Atatürk Monument

Fethiye Camii

Turban Amasya Hotel

Park

Vilayet

Police

Kral Kaya Mezarları (Pontic Tombs)

Kale (Citadel)

Hazeranlar Konağı

PTT

Taş Han

Çarşı

Burmalı Minare Camii

Hotel Apaydın

Atatürk

Hospital

Hamam

Footbridge

Beyazıt II Mosque

Ziya Paşa Bulvarı

Museum

Yeşil

Irmak

Gök Medrese Camii

Gar (Railway Station)

To Çorum & Tokat

II (281 BC), the Kingdom of Pontus was entering its golden age and ruled over a large part of Anatolia. During the latter part of Pontus's flowering, Amasya was the birthplace of Strabo (c 63 BC-25 AD), the world's first historian. Perhaps he felt constrained by Amasya's surrounding mountains, for Strabo left home and travelled through Europe, West Asia and North Africa, and wrote 47 history and 17 geography books. Though his history books have mostly been lost, Strabo was quoted by many other classical writers, so we know something of their content.

Amasya's golden age ended when the Romans decided it was time to take all of Anatolia (47 BC) and call it Asia Minor. After them came the Byzantines, who left little mark on the town, and the Seljuks (1075) and Mongols (early 1300s), who built numerous fine buildings which still stand. In Ottoman times, it was an important power-base when the sultans led military campaigns into Persia, and a tradition developed that the Ottoman crown-prince should be taught statecraft in Amasya, and test his knowledge and skill as governor of the province. The town was also noted as a centre of Islamic theological study, with as many as 18 medreses and 2000 theological students in the 19th century.

At the end of the Ottoman Empire, after WW I, Mustafa Kemal (Atatürk) escaped the confines of occupied İstanbul and came to Amasya via Samsun. At Amasya he met secretly on 12 June 1919 with several friends and hammered out the basic principles of the Turkish struggle for independence. The monument in the main square commemorates the meeting; other scenes depict the unhappy state of Turks in Anatolia before the War of Independence. Each year, Amasyalı commemorate the meeting with a week-long Art and Culture Festival beginning on 12 June.

Orientation

The otogar is at the north-eastern edge of

town, the railway station at the western edge. It's several km from either terminal to the main square, marked by a statue of Atatürk and a bridge across the river. Most of the town (including the main square, the bazaar and the museum) is on the southern bank of the river. On the northern bank are various government and military offices, the tombs of the Pontic kings, and the Kale (citadel). You may want to take a bus, minibus, or taxi to and from the otogar and the railway station, but everything else is within walking distance.

Information

Amasya has no proper Tourism Information Office, but a kiosk on the riverbank just north of the main square is staffed in summer. Some leaflets are available; the staff speak English, French or German.

Buildings

Start your sightseeing with a walk around the town, admiring the old Ottoman houses along the river. One of them on the north bank, the **Hazeranlar Konağı**, dates from the 1800s. It was finely restored in the early 1980s, and has been set up as an ethnology museum and gallery for travelling exhibits. Restoration of the old houses is highly prized by the Amasyalı. However, many local residents would like to replace old buildings they own (which are expensive to renovate) with more efficient modern structures, so the battle between conservation and progress goes on.

Also on the north bank of the river are the Vilayet (Government House) and Belediye Sarayı (Town Hall); beside the latter is the shady **Belediye Parkı** with tea and soft drink service, and entertainment some evenings.

Pontic Tombs & Citadel

Looming above the northern bank of the river is a sheer rock face with the easily observed rock-cut Kral Kaya Mezarları, or Tombs of the Pontic Kings, carved into it. Cross the river, climb the well-marked path toward them and you'll come to the **Kızlar Sarayı** (kuhz-LAHR sah-rah-yuh), or Palace of the Maidens. Though there were indeed harems full of maidens here, the palace which stood on this rock terrace was not theirs, but that of the kings of Pontus and later of the Ottoman governors.

Follow the path upward; you may find yourself accompanied by a youthful unappointed guide repeating a few words of German and hoping for a tip. If you don't want a guide, say *Istemez* (eess-teh-MEHZ). In a few minutes you will reach the royal tombs of Pontus, cut deep in the rock as early as the 300s BC, and used for cult worship of the deified rulers. There are 14 tombs in all, but only a few are worth a look.

Above the tombs, perched precariously on the cliffs, is the **kale** or citadel which can be reached by a path, or by road (two km) if you have a car. The remnants of the walls date from Pontic times, perhaps from those of King Mithridates; the fortress was last repaired by the Ottomans. It's from here that an old Russian cannon is fired during the holy month of Ramazan to mark the ending of the fast. The view is magnificent.

Museum

There's a tidy little museum on Atatürk Caddesi, open from 8am to 12 noon and from 1.30 to 5.30 pm; admission costs US$1. The collection includes artefacts from Pontic, Roman, Byzantine, Seljuk and Ottoman times, and there is an ethnographic exhibit. In the museum garden is a Seljuk tomb, the Sultan Mesut Türbesi, now containing some fairly gruesome mummies which date from the Seljuk period and were discovered beneath the Burmalı Cami.

Amasya's Mosques

Across Atatürk Caddesi from the museum is the **Sultan Beyazıt Camii** (1486), Amasya's principal mosque, with its

medrese, *kütüphane* (library) and a nice garden.

West of the museum about a half km is the **Gök Medrese Camii** (GEURK mehdreh-seh) or Mosque of the Blue Seminary, built in 1276 by the Seljuks; it has a wonderfully ornate Seljuk doorway once covered in blue tiles. Near it are several Seljuk türbes, including the **Toruntay Türbesi** (1266). The neighbouring **Yörgüç Paşa Camii** is an Ottoman work dating from 1428.

East of the museum, across Atatürk Caddesi from the Kapalı Çarşı (Covered Market), is the **Taş Han** (1758), an Ottoman caravanserai still used by local traders and artisans. It was originally much larger, but much of it has fallen to ruins. Behind it to the south is Amasya's famous **Burmalı Minare Camii** (BOORmah-LUH) or Spiral Minaret Mosque. It's of Seljuk construction (1242), with elegant spiral carving on the minaret, true to its name.

Just to the east of the main square and Atatürk's statue, perched on a rise, is the **Gümüşlü Cami** (Silver Mosque) which was built in 1326, and rebuilt in 1491 after an earthquake; in 1612 after a fire; and again in 1688. It was added to in 1903, and the latest restoration was carried out in 1988.

Other Sights

North of the main square along the river are Amasya's other historic buildings. The **Bimarhane Medresesi** (Insane Asylum Seminary) was built by the Ilkhanid Mongol governors of Amasya in 1308. The Ilkhans were the successors to the great Mongol Empire of Ghengis Khan; their architecture reflects styles and motifs borrowed from many conquered peoples. Today only the outer walls of the building stand, stabilised to prevent further deterioration. With the pretty garden in front, this place gains a sort of brooding presence.

By the way, that large, obtrusive building on the opposite bank of the river is an army recreation facility, contributing little to the beauty of the town.

Next along the river is the pretty **Mehmet Paşa Camii** or Mehmet Paşa Mosque, a fairly early Ottoman mosque (1486), which now serves as the girls' Koran study centre of Amasya. The **Beyazıt Paşa Camii** or Beyazıt Paşa Mosque, a few hundred yards north and just past the bridge, was finished in 1419, and bears many similarities to the famous early-Ottoman Yeşil Cami in Bursa. Note especially the porch with marble arches in two colours of stone, the entranceway with gold and blue and the carved doors.

Across the river from the Beyazıt Paşa Camii is the **Büyük Ağa Medresesi** (Seminary of the Chief White Eunuch), built to an octagonal plan in 1488 by Sultan Beyazıt II's Chief white eunuch, Hüseyin Ağa. Nicely restored, it still serves as a seminary for boys who are training to be *hafız*, theologians who have memorised the entire Koran. The medrese is not open to the public, but if the door is open you may peep in to see local boys at their Koranic studies, or playing a quick and refreshing game of football in the spacious yard.

On the southern bank of the river, Ziya Paşa Bulvarı is shady and cool with huge old plane trees. The market section south of here includes an ancient (1483) covered bazaar or bedesten in its narrow streets. As you walk along the river you may see two traditional waterwheels, called *dolap* in Turkish; one is by the footbridge across the river, the other is opposite the Tourism Information kiosk. These are recreations of the devices once used extensively to lift water from the deep river channel up to fields and houses.

Yedi Kuğular Gölü

About 15 km west of town is the recently man-made Yedi Kuğu Gölü (Seven Swans Lake), a favourite stopping-place for birds on their spring and autumn migrations. Trees have been planted and when they mature this *Kuş Cenneti* (Bird Paradise) may be as welcoming to humans as to birds.

Places to Stay – bottom end

There are few hotels in Amasya, and even fewer good ones, but at least they're cheap. The 31-room *Apaydın Oteli* (AHP-ay-duhn) (tel 1184), Atatürk Caddesi 58, is perhaps the most presentable, charging US$3/$4.50 a single/double for a room with washbasin (cold water only). The common bathrooms have showers with electric-heater shower-heads; there is a Turkish-style splash bath as well. The paint here is perhaps a bit brighter and the lobby has a TV, but the spartan rooms are similar to those in the town's other cheap places.

The *Konfor Palas* (kohn-FOHR, Comfort Palace) (tel 1260), Ziya Paşa Bulvarı 4, by the river, has 36 rooms and charges even less: US$2/4 a single/double; your room may have a balcony looking onto the river. The similarly priced *Örnek Oteli* (tel 1108), Ziya Paşa Bulvarı 2, is across the courtyard, with 13 basic rooms without baths. The *Aydın Oteli* (tel 2463), Atatürk Caddesi 86, charges least of all for its seven bathless rooms.

Places to Stay – middle

The two-star *Turban Amasya Hotel* (tel 4054/5/6), Helkis Mahallesi, Emniyet Caddesi 20, north of the centre near the Büyük Ağa Medresesi, is a small 34-room hotel on the riverbank which has a restaurant and bar, a games room and TV lounge, and rooms with shower for from US$16 to US$20 a single, US$22 to US$28 a double, with breakfast. In the past this has been Amasya's only comfortable place to stay and was often filled to capacity by tour groups. However, a new hotel right on the main square should be finished by the time you arrive.

About 28 km north of Amasya on the Samsun road, at Suluova, is the *Saraçoğlu Muzaffer Turistik Tesisleri* (Muzaffer Saraçoğlu's Touristic Installations) (tel 1010, 1783), a small highway motel and restaurant next to a fuel station. Rooms are simple but acceptable, though there is some highway noise. The price for a room with bath is from US$12 to US$18 a single, US$20 to US$26 a double.

Places to Eat
Look for small restaurants in the narrow market streets off the main square (the one with the statue of Atatürk), such as the *Çiçek Lokantası*, which is very basic but cheap and serviceable, and the *Zafer Lokantası*, three short blocks farther along. Both are very basic, but cheap, with meals for US$2 or so. The *Elmas Kebap ve Pide Salonu* (tel 1606), on the same street more or less behind the Hotel Apaydın, is similar, and stays open late in the evening. For tea in a pleasant garden setting, go to the *Belediye Parkı*, across the river from the main square, by the Town Hall.

For nicer dining at a higher price (from US$5 to US$8 for a full meal with drinks), go to the dining rooms in the Turban Amasya Hotel or the new hotel on the main square.

Getting There & Away
Amasya is not far off the busy route between Ankara and Samsun, so buses are frequent. It is also on the Samsun to Sivas railway line, but the daily trains are quite slow. Some bus companies maintain ticket offices at the main square. Here are some bus times and distances:

Adıyaman & Kahta (for Nemrut Dağı) – 650 km, 10 hours, US$10; one bus daily
Ankara – 335 km, five hours, US$4; several dozen buses daily
Çorum – 95 km, two hours, US$1.75; at least eight buses daily
İstanbul – 685 km, 11 hours, US$9.50; a dozen buses daily
Kayseri – 405 km, eight hours, US$8; three buses daily
Malatya – 460 km, nine hours, US$9.50; five buses daily
Samsun – 130 km, 2½ hours, US$2; 10 buses daily
Sivas – 225 km, four hours, US$4; five buses daily
Tokat – 115 km, two hours, US$2; nine buses daily

In addition, there are direct buses to many other destinations, including Adana, Alanya, Antakya, Antalya, Bursa, Diyarbakır, Erzurum, Gaziantep, Izmir, Marmaris and Şanlıurfa.

SAMSUN
Burned to the ground by the Genoese in the 1400s, Samsun (sahm-SOON) with a population of 300,000 has little to show for its long history. It is a major port and commercial centre and the largest city on

Nomads outside their goat-hair tent

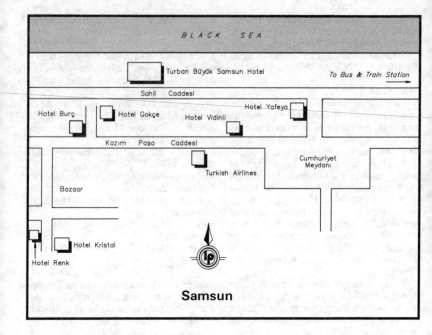

the coast. Your reason to stop here would be to change buses, have a meal or find a bed.

Orientation

The railway station is one km east of the centre; the Otogar is slightly more than two km east of the centre. Come out of the terminal (either one) and cross the coastal road so you can catch a bus heading into town. The centre of town is Cumhuriyet Meydanı (Republic Square); the Otel Yafeya is a handy landmark here. Many bus companies have ticket offices facing the square. The Turban Büyük Samsun Hotel is a few blocks west of the centre, on the shore.

The main business street, with banks, PTT and restaurants, is Kazım Paşa Caddesi (sometimes called Bankalar Caddesi) one block inland from the shore road, running westward from Cumhuriyet Meydanı. A few blocks west of the square along Kazım Paşa Caddesi, Hacı Hasur

Sokak turns left (inland, south) past the Hacı Hasur Camii in the bazaar. Look on this street for cheap hotels, and in the bazaar for cheap restaurants.

Information

Samsun's Tourism Information Office is at 19 Mayıs Bulvarı 2, Kat 1 (tel (361) 10014, 21158).

Places to Stay – bottom end

On Hacı Hasur Sokak in the bazaar you'll find the *Renk Otel* (tel 17350), Gaziler Meydanı, Hacı Hasur Sokak, 55000 Samsun; the reception desk is one flight up. Clean and basic rooms here go for US$7 a double with washbasin, US$9 with private shower. The nearby *Kristal Otel* (tel 11713), Gaziler Meydanı, Hastane Sokak 5, 55000 Samsun, offers even nicer, brighter rooms with stylish blankets. Official prices are from US$6 to US$8 a single, US$12 a double with shower, but

I was quoted rates several dollars lower when I haggled: US$8 for a double (one bed) with private shower.

The chances of both these hotels being full is small, but there are several other, similar hostelries nearby in the bazaar.

Right at the otogar is the 44-room *Otel Terminal* (tel 15519), Samsun Otogar, 55000 Samsun, fairly beat-up but serviceable if you've been on a bus all day. Rates for room with bath are US$10/15 a single/ double.

Places to Stay – middle

The city's best is the four-star *Turban Büyük Samsun Oteli* (tel 10750; fax 10740), Sahil Caddesi, 55002 Samsun, on the shore just west of Cumhuriyet Meydanı, set in its own spacious gardens. Services abound: swimming pool, tennis court, nightclub, pastry shop-café, games room and, of course, a comfortable bar and dining room. The 117 air-con rooms cost from US$25 to US$30 a single, US$32 to US$42 a double, depending upon whether you have a sea view (more expensive) or a land view; breakfast is included.

The three-star, 96-room *Hotel Yafeya* (tel 51131; fax 51135), Cumhuriyet Meydanı, 55000 Samsun, is newer than the Büyük Samsun and, though it ranks a star lower in the official ratings and has fewer facilities, it is more modern and equally as comfortable. Furnishings are modern and attractive, with lots of natural wood. The roof restaurant and bar offer good food and good views of the city. Prices for the comfortable rooms with bath are from US$18 to US$22 a single, US$20 to US$26 a double; larger suites with TV and mini-bar cost slightly more.

Walk west along Kazım Paşa Caddesi to find three more good hotels. A few blocks along and one block inland from the Büyük Samsun is the small, modern *Hotel Burç*, (BOORCH) (tel 15480), Kazım Paşa Caddesi 36, 55000 Samsun. The 38 rooms with bath go for US$18/

22 a single/double. Get a quiet one off the main street.

Just near the Burç, around the corner, is the one-star, 35-room *Gökçe Otel* (tel 17952), Kazım Paşa Caddesi, Ferah Sokak 1, 55000 Samsun, just across the coastal highway from the Turban Büyük Samsun Hotel. All rooms here seem to have small balconies opening onto a quiet side street; some have partial views of the sea. Services include a lift, rooftop bar, TV lounge and restaurant. Rates are a reasonable US$20/24 a single/double.

Not far away is the older, two-star *Vidinli Oteli* (vee-deen-LEE) (tel 16050), Kazım Paşa Caddesi 4, 55000 Samsun, having 65 rooms with shower, priced at US$15/20 a single/double. Services are similar to those of the neighbouring hotels.

Places to Eat

All of the middle-range hotels have dining rooms, the one at the *Büyük Samsun* being especially noted, and not overly expensive. In the evening they feature live entertainment and full meals for US$10 if you order Turkish dishes, about twice as much if you go for the *kordon blö* (cordon bleu steak), *fileminyon mantarlı* (filet mignon with mushrooms), fish or fondue.

The bazaar, as usual, is the place to look for cheap eats. There's also a clean and pleasant place just a few steps from Cumhuriyet Meydanı, the *Saray Restoran* (tel 12313), Kazım Paşa Caddesi 14, with plastic laminate tables, a ceiling fan and a huge mural of an alpine scene. It's not fancy, but they serve good döner kebap and lots of hazır yemek. I had a nice yayla çorbası (yoghurt and barley soup), İzmir köfte, pilav, ayran, kadayıf, bread and tea for US$2.25.

Getting There & Away

Samsun seems to offer at least one bus per day to every important destination in Turkey, and very frequent buses to logical next destinations. Though there are daily trains between Samsun and Sivas, the trip takes over 12 daylight hours, and is hardly worth it when the bus makes the same trip in about half the time. Here are some bus-travel examples:

Amasya – 130 km, 2½ hours, US$2; 10 buses daily
Ankara – 420 km, seven hours, US$6; frequent daily buses
Artvin – 615 km, 10 hours, US$9; several buses daily
Giresun – 220 km, four hours, US$4; frequent buses daily
İstanbul – 750 km, 12 hours, US$10; several buses daily
Kayseri – 530 km, nine hours, US$8; a few buses daily
Sinop – 155 km, three hours, US$2.75; several buses daily
Sivas – 345 km, 6½ hours, US$6; a few buses daily
Trabzon – 365 km, six hours, US$6; frequent buses daily
Yozgat – 275 km, 7½ hours, US$6.50; a few buses daily

SİNOP

On the road west of Samsun you pass through Bafra (BAHF-rah), a tobacco-growing centre. Sinop (SEE-nohp), with a population of 28,000, is 155 km west of Samsun. It enjoyed a long history as a port beginning from Hittite times, almost 4000 years ago. Successive empires made it a busy trading centre, but the Ottomans preferred to develop Samsun, subordinating Sinop to this eastern neighbour. Sinop has reminders of its prominence as a Seljuk port in the Alaettin Camii (1214), Alaiye Medrese (now the museum) and Seyyit Bilal Camii. The *Hotel 117* (tel (3761) 1579, 5117), Rıhtım Caddesi 1, has fairly cheap rooms.

EAST TO TRABZON

Two of Anatolia's great rivers, the Kızıl Irmak and the Yeşil Irmak, empty into the sea here on either side of Samsun. The rivers have built up fertile deltas which are now filled with corn and tobacco amidst Balkan scenes of bucolic contentment.

Each house has a lush lawn from its dooryard to the roadway, and each lawn has its own fat cow.

Ünye

Ünye (EURN-yeh), a small port town amidst hazelnut groves, has a population of 40,000 and is 95 km east of Samsun. In the centre there's a pleasant, tree-lined seaside promenade. Five km west of the town are numerous camping places along the beach, including the *Gölevi, Europa* and *Camping Derya* (tel 3473); more development is on the way. The *Turistik Çamlık Motel* (too-rees-TEEK CHAHM-luhk) (tel 1333), in a pine forest on the shore 1½ km west of Ünye, is well-used but inexpensive. A double room with bath and sea view costs from US$10 to US$15; you must haggle here.

There are other small hotels in the town such as the *Otel Ürer* (eur-REHR) (tel 1729), Atatürk Bulvarı, on the shore road, charging US$10/15 a single/double for a room with bath, breakfast included. Some rooms have sea views (and road noise); there is a restaurant. This is the choice of business travellers coming to town to buy nuts.

Ordu

Seventy km east of Ünye is Ordu (OHR-doo), with a population of 90,000, another fishing port with some nice old houses. When approaching the town from the west, you pass a small Orman Piknik Yeri (Forest Picnic Spot). In the town there's a provincial Tourism Information Office (look for the sign at the Town Hall), a port for Turkish Maritime Lines ships, a little museum, and the 39-room *Turist Oteli* (too-REEST) (tel 14273, 19115), Atatürk Bulvarı 134, a bit noisy perhaps but moderately priced at US$15/20 a single/double. This is where the hazelnut traders stay. The *Divan Palas* is even cheaper, at US$6 a double.

Travelling another 46 km brings you to Giresun.

Giresun

The town of Giresun (GEE-reh-SOON), with a population of 75,000, was founded 3000 years ago. Legend has it that Jason and the Argonauts stopped here on their voyage to the fabled kingdom of Colchis, on the eastern shores of the Black Sea, in search of the Golden Fleece. The Argonauts supposedly stopped at a nearby island (Büyük Ada) where Amazon queens had erected a shrine to Ares, god of war.

After the Romans conquered the Kingdom of Pontus, they discovered that the locals had orchards full of trees bearing delicious little red fruits. One theory holds that the ancient name for the town, Cerasus, is the root for many of the names for the fruit – *cherry*, *cerise* (French), *kiraz* (Turkish) – as well as for the town's modern name. Cherries are still important here 20 centuries later. You can see the ruins of a mediaeval castle (Giresun Kalesi) above the town. In the eastern part of the city, a disused Greek Orthodox church has been turned into the town's Şehir Müzesi (City Museum).

Bus companies have offices near the Town Hall. The PTT is on the main street from the Town Hall up the hill.

Places to Stay – bottom end The *Hotel Bozbağ* (tel 11249, 12468), Arifbey Caddesi 8, is in a quiet location up the street from the As Turizm bus office, one block from the Town Hall. The spacious lobby/lounge has a TV and a canary (the canary's programme is better than the TV's), and shower-equipped rooms that are decently maintained and clean. Rates are US$7/10 a single/double; hot water is on in the evenings only.

Places to Stay – middle Stay overnight in the *Giresun Oteli* (tel 12469, 13017), Atatürk Bulvarı, the town's most comfortable hotel, on the Black Sea side of the highway one block from the Town Hall. It's often filled by tour groups; if it's not,

you can get a decent room with shower for US$20/27/32 a single/double/triple.

Places to Eat The *Deniz Lokantası*, next to the Belediye, is simple, cheap and open from early morning to late at night. Directly behind the Hotel Bozbağ (on the other side of the block) is the more modern but still cheap *Halil Usta Lokantası*. Up the hill by the Town Hall are several pastry shops.

Giresun to Trabzon

From Giresun, it's another 150 km to Trabzon. Along the way, the road passes through several small towns, including Espiye with its castle Andoz Kalesi, and the attractive town of Tirebolu, with a tree-lined shore drive (the highway), and two castles, the St Jean Kalesi and Bedrama Kalesi. At Akçakale are the ruins of a 13th-century Byzantine castle on a little peninsula, marked by a prominent sign.

TRABZON

Once called Trapezus, and later Trebizond, the modern town of Trabzon (TRAHB-sohn) with a population of 200,000 has a purpose in life. Iran's oil wealth has led to massive purchases of western goods, and many of these goods come to Trabzon by sea, continuing overland by road.

Though it is the 20th-century oil boom which has given Trabzon new life, the town actually performed a similar role in the 1800s, when the trade was mostly British. The English-speaking world still thinks of Trabzon as some remote and romantic outpost, though its cosmopolitan days of traders, consulates and international agents are long past.

Its recorded history begins around 746 BC, when colonists originally from Miletus, south of Kuşadası, came to Sinop and founded a settlement with its acropolis on the *trápeza*, or 'table' of land above the harbour. The town did reasonably well for 2000 years, occupying itself with port activities, until in 1204 the

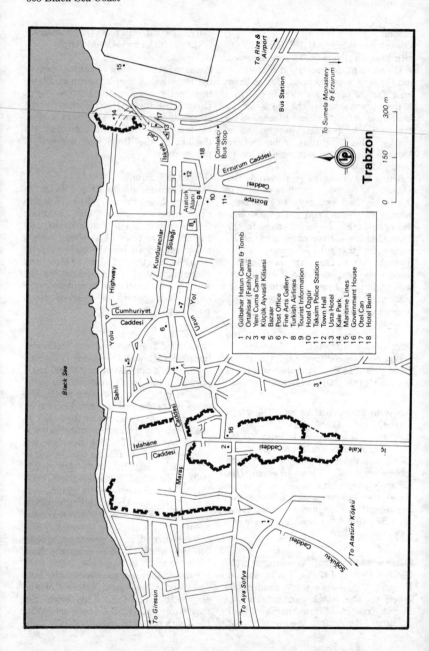

Black Sea

Trabzon

To Rize &
Airport

Bus Station

To Sumela Monastery
& Erzurum

To Giresun

To Aya Sofya

To Atatürk Köşkü

0   150   300 m

Çömlekçi
Bus Stop

Erzurum Caddesi

Boztepe Caddesi

İskele Caddesi

Atatürk Alanı

Kunduracılar Sokağı

Cumhuriyet Caddesi

Highway

Sahil Yolu

Uzun Yol

İslahane Caddesi

Maraş Caddesi

Kale Caddesi

İç Kale

Soğuksu Caddesi

1   Gülbahar Hatun Camii & Tomb
2   Ortahisar (Fatih) Camii
3   Yeni Cuma Camii
4   Küçük Ayvasıl Kilisesi
5   Bazaar
6   Post Office
7   Fine Arts Gallery
8   Turkish Airlines
9   Tourist Information
10 Hotel Özgür
11 Taksim Police Station
12 Town Hall
13 Usta Hotel
14 Kale Park
15 Maritime Lines
16 Government House
17 Otel Can
18 Hotel Benli

soldiers of the Fourth Crusade seized and sacked Constantinople, driving its noble families to seek refuge in Anatolia. The imperial family of the Comneni established an empire along the Black Sea coast in 1204, with Alexius Comnenus I reigning as the Emperor of Trebizond. The Trapezuntine rulers became skilful at balancing their alliances with the Seljuks, the Mongols, the Genoese and others – it didn't hurt to be cut off from the rest by a wall of mountains, either. Prospering through trade with eastern Anatolia and Persia, the empire reached the height of its wealth and culture during the reign of Alexius II (1297-1330), after which the place fell to pieces in 'Byzantine' factional disputes marked, as one historian put it, 'by unbelievable degeneracy and cruelty'. Even so, the Empire of Trebizond survived until the coming of the Ottomans in 1461.

When the Ottoman Empire was defeated after WW I, the many Greek residents of Trabzon sought to establish a Republic of Trebizond echoing the old Comneni Empire, but Atatürk's armies were ultimately victorious.

The main reasons for visiting Trabzon are to see the church of Aya Sofya (1200s), to poke around in the old town, to visit Atatürk's lovely villa on the outskirts and to make an excursion through the gorgeous alpine scenery to Sumela, a dramatic Byzantine monastery carved out of a sheer rock cliff.

Orientation

Trabzon is built on a mountainside. The port is at the centre of town, with the ancient acropolis on the 'table', now occupied by the main square called Atatürk Alanı, rising to the west of it. Most government offices, airline offices, hotels and restaurants are in and around Atatürk Alanı. The PTT is just west of the square on Uzun Yol (oo-ZOON yoh-loo) or Uzun Sokak (Long Road). Buses bearing the legend 'Park' are going to Atatürk Alanı. Many of Trabzon's principal sights

are to the west of the main square along Uzun Yol. Trabzon's otogar is three km east of the port on the landward side of the shore road. The airport is several km east of the town.

Information

The Tourism Information Office (tel (031) 14659, 35818), Atatürk Alanı at Boztepe Caddesi, is on the main square, very convenient to most of the town's hotels. Staff speak English, French or German and are very helpful and well-informed. The office of Turkish Maritime Lines is here as well.

Atatürk Alanı

The centre of Trabzon's social life is undoubtedly Atatürk Alanı, with a shady park in its midst. It has a fountain, a statue of Atatürk, tea gardens and lots of trees. A few moments' rest in the park reveals a secret about Trabzon: it is a city crowded by its hillside location and there always seem to be lots of people around. The humid air and overcast skies add to the feeling of claustrophobia. In daylight the park is pleasant enough, with men and women, boys and girls going about their business or taking their leisure. At night it's somewhat depressing, with only men hanging around.

Churches

Trabzon has lots of old churches, many of which were converted to mosques after the Ottoman conquest of the city. If you stroll along the Uzun Yolu west from Atatürk Alanı, you'll pass the remains of the Küçük Ayvasıl Kilisesi Church of St Anne Basilica built in the 7th century, with later renovations. The Yeni Cuma Camii (New Friday Mosque), up the hill, was once the Church of St Eugenios.

Cross the gorge of the Tabakhane Deresi (stream), turn left into Kale Sokak, and enter the Kale, the heart of the old part of town. Within the ancient walls is the Fatih Camii (sometimes called the Ortahisar Camii), which began life in the 900s as the

Church of Panaghia Chrysokephalos,

Trebizond's chief place of worship (the more famous Aya Sofya was built later as a monastery church).

Gülbahar Hatun Camii

Past the Fatih Camii and inland a bit farther is the Gülbahar Hatun Camii or Lady Gülbahar Mosque, constructed by Selim the Grim, the great Ottoman conqueror of Syria and Egypt, in honour of his mother Gülbahar in 1514.

Boztepe Picnic Area

Up the hillside above the main part of town is a lookout and the Boztepe Piknik Alanı with a fine view of the city and the sea. To get there from Atatürk Alanı, take a bus labelled 'Park – Boztepe Bld Dinlenme Tesisleri' (Park-to-Boztepe Municipal Recreation Facilities). It goes uphill 1½ km to the local orthopaedic hospital, then another 700 metres to a beautiful forest with the picnic facilities.

Up the hill past the picnic area about three or four km are the ruins of the former **Kaymaklı Monastery**, now part of a farm. At this writing it is unmarked, so finding it in the maze of hillside paths can be difficult. Perhaps in future there will be signs.

Aya Sofya

The Aya Sofya, Haghia Sophia or Church of the Divine Wisdom is three km west of the centre on a terrace which once held a pagan temple. The site is above the coastal highway, reachable by city bus or dolmuş (look for dolmuşes on the north (lower) side of the square with an 'Aya Sofya' sign in the windscreen). The church is now a museum, open daily except Monday from 8.30 am to 5 pm; admission costs US$1.

Built between 1238 and 1263, its design was influenced by eastern Anatolian and Seljuk motifs, though the excellent wall paintings and mosaic floors follow the style of Constantinople. Tombs were built into the north and south walls. Next to the church is its bell tower, finished much later, in 1427. This was a monastery church, but nothing remains of the monastery.

Atatürk Villa

The Atatürk Köşkü or Atatürk Villa, accessible by city bus or dolmuş, is five km south-west of Atatürk Alanı, above the town with a fine view and lovely gardens. The white villa was designed in a Black Sea style seen much in the Crimea, and built between 1890 and 1903. The citizens gave it to their leader when the republic was founded. He visited Trabzon and stayed here only three times briefly, the last time in 1937. Upon his death in 1938 the villa, and all the rest of his estate, became national property. The villa is now a museum with various bits of Atatürk memorabilia. To get there, take a city bus from the bus stop on the lower side of the square, more or less behind the Tourism Information Office; buses depart at 20 minutes past the hour, arriving at the villa 25 minutes later. Get off at the Atatürk Köşk stop. The return trip takes only 15 minutes. The round trip costs US$0.40.

Being a patriotic site, the villa is open every day, from 9 am to 5 pm; admission is US$0.25. Local students who are studying foreign languages act as volunteer guides, though you can stroll through on your own if you like.

Sumela Monastery

The Greek Orthodox Monastery of the Virgin Mary at Sumela, 54 km south of Trabzon, was founded in Byzantine times (500s), and was abandoned (1923) upon the founding of the Turkish Republic, after hopes of creating a new Greek state in this region were dashed. It clings to a sheer rock wall high above evergreen forests and a rushing mountain stream; it is a mysterious, eerie place, especially when mists swirl among the tops of the trees in the valley below. Don't miss it, as it is among the most impressive and fascinating sights in Turkey. Note that on

Wednesdays, when the ferry from İstanbul arrives in Trabzon, Sumela is crowded with its cruise passengers.

Transport to Sumela is fairly easy during the summer tourist season. Look for the Çömlekçi bus stop near the Hotel Dünya and Hotel Hitit, across from the port on the shore road; minibuses depart from here daily at 10 am (with another at 11 am on Sunday), returning about 3 pm, for US$3. Or you can take a taxi-dolmuş (tel 11328) round-trip for US$5 per person; stop by and reserve your seat the day before at the taxi stand facing the Hotel Özgür. For a taxi proper, look in the main square; wait under banners proclaiming prices of US$30 or so for a car holding five persons. The price includes the ride there, a two-hour wait and the ride back to Trabzon.

With your own car, head out of Trabzon on the Erzurum road. At Maçka (31 km), turn left for Sumela, also signposted as Meryem Ana, as the monastery was dedicated to the Virgin Mary. For the next 23 km until you reach the monastery, you won't believe you're in Turkey or, indeed, anywhere in the Middle East.

The road winds into dense evergreen forests, following the sinuous course of a rushing mountain stream. Mists may hang about the tops of the trees and the air becomes much cooler. Peasant houses look like something out of central Europe.

At the end of the road is a small park, picnic and camping area (free) and the head of the trail up to the monastery. This trail is steep but easy to follow, and is the one most people use. There is another trail which begins farther up the valley. To find it, follow the unpaved road past the picnic and camping area, cross the stream and head up into the forest.

Climb through forests and alpine meadows, ascending 250 metres in about 30 to 45 minutes. There are glimpses of the monastery as you climb. In the autumn a beautiful sort of crocus, called *kar çiçeği* (snowflower) blooms in the meadows; the

flowers bloom just before the snows arrive.

The monastery is open from 9 am to 6 pm. At the entrance, a guardian will sell you a ticket for US$2.

The various chapels and rooms here are mere shells or facades but have a good deal of fine fresco painting, some of it with gilt. Many of the paintings are the worse for wear, as bored shepherd boys used them as targets for pebble attacks. In recent years, antiquity thieves and black marketeers have been a problem as well.

Places to Stay - bottom end

Several streets in town are lined with little cheap hotels, including İskele Caddesi, the street between the port and Atatürk Alanı. But for quieter, more convenient accommodation, find Güzelhisar Caddesi, off İskele Caddesi not far from the Hotel Usta. My favourite here is the funky old 19th-century *Erzurum Oteli* (tel 11362), Güzelhisar Caddesi 6. In the little fenced front garden-cum-café, old men play tavla (backgammon) and dominos amidst the honeysuckle. The old-fashioned high-ceilinged guest rooms are clean, and some even have views of the sea. Rates are US$5 a double with washbasin, or US$7.50 a double with shower.

Nearby is the *Hotel Anıl* (tel 19566, 22617), Güzelhisar Caddesi 10, a modern place with friendly staff, bright and clean rooms (some with good tiled showers), and only a little bit of street and nightclub noise. A double with washbasin costs US$8, with shower US$10.

Otel Can (JAHN) (tel 14762), Güzelhisar Caddesi 2, is modern and tidy, with tiny but good rooms, a TV lounge on the upper floor, and friendly management. But its thoroughfare location means it is not for light sleepers. Rooms cost US$7 a double with washbasin, US$8.50 with shower.

Hotel Benli (behn-LEE) (tel 11022, 11750), İskender Paşa Mahallesi, Cami Çıkmazı Sokak 5, is just off the eastern end of Atatürk Alanı, up the hill behind the İskender Paşa Camii. It's an odd place with some strange staff, but the rooms are OK (check the sheets, though). The 42 rooms here rent for US$6 a double with washbasin, US$7.50 a double with shower.

Places to Stay – middle

Otel Horon (hoh-ROHN) (tel 11199, 12289), Sıra Mağazalar Caddesi 125, 61100 Trabzon, is a fairly modern and quite presentable one-star, 42-room place on Atatürk Alanı which has a variety of rooms with a variety of beds and plumbing options. Rooms are priced at US$16 to US$20 a single, US$20 to US$26 a double; lower prices are for rooms with washbasins only, higher priced rooms have private shower. They have some triple rooms as well. By the way, the hotel's street may also be marked Şehit Teğmen Kalmaz Caddesi.

The *Hotel Usta* (OOSS-tah) (tel 12843, 12195), Telgrafhane Sokak 1, 61100 Trabzon, on Atatürk Alanı, has 72 rooms, all of them due for renovation (they're very spartan and old-fashioned), though the lobby and restaurant have been modernised. Services include a lift and car park; it's a fairly quiet location just off the square. Rates are a somewhat high US$20/26 a single/double.

Also on the square is the nominally two-star *Hotel Özgür* (eurz-GEUR) (tel 11319, 12778), Atatürk Alanı 29, 61100 Trabzon, with 45 modernish rooms, all with bath or shower, most suffering from the noise of the square, and renting for US$24/33/40 a single/double/triple. Though most rooms have twin beds, others have double beds, five have three beds, and five are junior suites.

Places to Stay – top end

By the time you arrive, Trabzon will finally have a four-star hotel just off Atatürk Alanı. The *Pullman Etap Trabzon Hotel* will have 170 guest rooms with TV, mini-bar, hair dryer and air-con. No doubt many of the rooms will be booked by tour groups, so if you are looking for a top-class room, reserve one in advance. Contact Pullman International hotels in your home country, a Pullman Etap hotel in İstanbul, İzmir or Ankara, or the Pullman International office in İstanbul (tel (1) 1344-4415; fax 141-7628).

Places to Eat

Look around Atatürk Alanı and you will see many small restaurants. The *Meydan Kebap ve Yemek Lokantası*, opposite the statue of Atatürk, is a good choice for a cheap lunch or dinner, as is the *Durak 2 Kebap Salonu*. The *Gaziantep Kebabcısı & Baklavacısı* has good, cheap kebaps and sweets.

The *Cici Lokantası* (the name means Cute Restaurant) offers decent, cheap food, fluorescent lights, a ceiling fan and a tactile stalactite ceiling that is a finish-plasterer's nightmare. The *Café Kuğu*, on the north side of the park, is good for breakfast.

Off the square, across from the alleyway entrance to the Hotel Usta, are more, even cheaper places: the *Bolkepçe, İmren* and *Çiçek Lokantası*.

The *Kıbrıs Restaurant* (tel 17679, 18179), Atatürk Alanı 17, has a small and rather plain dining room at street level, but a bigger, more pleasant one upstairs. Dishes include the Turkish classics, and a meal might cost US$5 or US$6, though it can be more if you have fish.

The rooftop restaurant at the *Otel Trabzon* (tel 12788) on Atatürk Alanı across the square from the Hotel Özgür attracts customers by posting signboards on the sidewalk. Prices are good, with full meals for from US$3 to US$5.

At the *Güven Pastahanesi* (tel 12372), Güzelhisar Caddesi 5/A, across from the Erzurum Oteli, you can get a good breakfast and, later in the day, excellent pastries and puddings. The place has nice touches, such as embroidered Turkish cloth on the glass-topped tables. The proprietor, Mr Gündüz Akay, can also lead you on a trek to Çamlıhemşin in the Kaçkar Mountains where there are hot

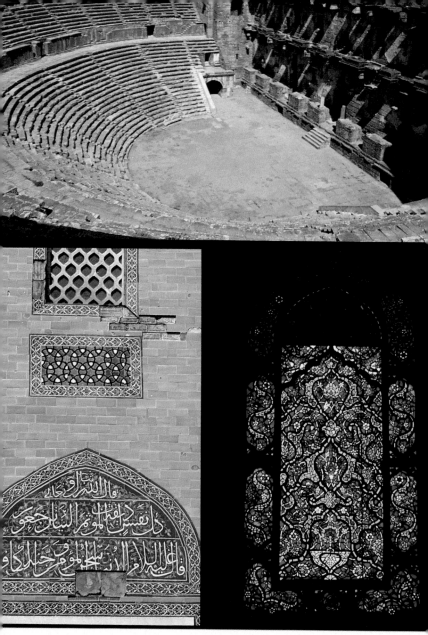

Top: The restored Theatre at Aspendos, near Antalya
Left: Detail from the Green Tomb, Bursa
Right: Stained-glass window in Süleymaniye Mosque

Top: The troglodyte dwellings, Göreme
Bottom: Roman busts and modern syntax in the Ephesus museum

springs, lots of wildlife and beautiful mountain scenery. Gündüz Bey speaks German as well as Turkish.

Getting There & Away

As the commercial hub of the eastern Black Sea coast, transport to and from Trabzon is easy by bus, air and sea. For information on the İstanbul, Samsun and Trabzon ferries, see the beginning of this chapter.

Air Turkish Airlines has nonstop flights between İstanbul and Trabzon on Monday, Wednesday and Saturday. On other days, flights to İstanbul travel via Ankara; there are daily flights between Trabzon and Ankara. The Turkish Airlines office (tel (031) 13446, 11680) is on Atatürk Alanı. The airport bus leaves for the airport 90 minutes before departure time.

İstanbul Airlines also flies nonstop between İstanbul and Trabzon on Monday, Wednesday and Friday, at fares lower than the competition. Their office (tel (031) 23806, 23346; at the airport, 23327) is on Atatürk Alanı at Kazazoğlu Sokak 9, Sanat İş Hanı.

Bus Trabzon's modern otogar, three km east of the port, is served by buses and dolmuşes running along the coastal road and up to Atatürk Alanı. From the otogar, cross the shore road in front of the terminal, turn left, walk to the bus stop and catch any bus with 'Park' in its name; the dolmuş to catch for Atatürk Alanı is 'Garajlar-Meydan'. A taxi between the otogar and Atatürk Alanı costs less than US$2.

The new otogar has a left-luggage area with prices posted, a maternity room for nursing and changing, a restaurant, cafeteria, barber shop and shops in which to buy food and sundries for the journey.

As for buses, they go daily to many parts of the country, including Adıyaman, Ağrı, Amasya, Bursa, Diyarbakır, Gaziantep, Kayseri, Malatya, Mardin, Marmaris and Tokat.

Buses operated by the town of Rize (Rize Belediyesi) shuttle along the coast between Trabzon and Rize frequently, charging US$1 for a ticket.

The Aydın-Sezar-Rizeliler company (ticket window No 4) runs a bus to Hopa every half-hour throughout the day, with onward minibuses to Artvin. The Ulusoy company has the most comfortable buses; they run trips every hour to Hopa. Some Ulusoy buses are the two-level, air-con Neoplan models. These run on the major routes (to Ankara, İstanbul) and offer luxury travel at a slightly higher price. Here are details on some logical destinations from Trabzon:

Ankara – 780 km, 12 hours, US$12; frequent buses daily
Artvin – 255 km, five hours, US$6; frequent buses daily
Erzurum – 325 km, eight hours, US$7.50; several buses daily
Hopa – 165 km, three hours, US$3; buses at least every half-hour
İstanbul – 1110 km, 18 hours, US$14; several buses daily
Kars – 525 km, 12 hours, US$10; change at Erzurum or Artvin
Rize – 65 km, one hour, US$1; very frequent buses daily
Samsun – 365 km, six hours, US$6; frequent buses daily
Van – 745 km, 17 hours, US$15; a few daily, direct or via Erzurum

South to Erzurum

Heading south into the mountains by road, you're in for a long, but wonderfully scenic ride. Before you get in the bus, take charge of any liquid-filled containers in your luggage. The atmospheric pressure here at sea level is much greater than it will be in the mountains. If you have a full water bottle in your pack at Trabzon, it will have burst or at least leaked by the time you reach Gümüşhane. If you're descending to Trabzon from Erzurum, your water bottle will *collapse* and leak due to the increase in pressure as you descend. It's best to carry liquids with you and adjust the pressure as you travel.

Along the highway south, you zoom straight to Maçka, 35 km inland from Trabzon, and then begin the long, slow climb along a serpentine mountain road through active landslide zones to the breathtaking **Zigana Geçidi** (Zigana Pass) at an altitude of 2030 metres. The landscape is one of sinuous valleys, cool pine forests with dramatic light. At the pass there is a small restaurant, grocery and teahouse. The dense, humid air of the coast disappears as you rise and becomes light and dry as you reach the south side of the Doğu Karadeniz Dağları (Eastern Black Sea Mountains). Along with the landscape, the towns and villages change. Black Sea towns have a vaguely Balkan appearance, while those higher up look distinctly central Asian. Snow can be seen in all months except perhaps July, August and September.

An extensive programme of road improvement is under way; the widening of this ancient caravan route will cause traffic delays for years to come.

Gümüşhane, about 125 km south of Trabzon, is a small town in a mountain valley with a few simple travellers' services, but not much to stop for except the scenery. By the time you reach Bayburt, 195 km from Trabzon, you are well into the rolling steppe and low mountains of the high Anatolian plateau. Bayburt has a big mediaeval fortress and simple travellers' services. The road from Bayburt passes through green, rolling farm country; in early summer wildflowers are everywhere.

Exactly 80 km west of Erzurum is the Kop Geçidi (Kop Pass) at an altitude of 2400 metres. A monument here commemorates Turks who fought for this pass for six months under the most dire conditions during the War of Independence. Countless soldiers lost their lives. A memorial ceremony is held annually on 15 May.

From Kop Pass, the open road to Erzurum offers fast, easy travelling.

EAST FROM TRABZON
Rize
Seventy-five km east of Trabzon, Rize (REE-zeh), with a population of 55,000, is at the heart of Turkey's tea plantation area. The steep hillsides which sweep upward from the shore are thickly planted with tea bushes. Local men and women bear large baskets on their backs, taking the leaves to the processing plants. The tea is cured, dried and blended here, then shipped throughout the country. A few years ago there was a shortage of processed tea due, some say, to bad industry planning, and at that time all Turkish eyes were on Rize. In this country, a shortage of tea could spell imminent social collapse.

Çamlıhemşin
East of Rize about 40 km, just before Ardeşen, a road on the right (south) points the way to Çamlıhemşin (22 km), a village deep in the Kaçkar Mountain range that serves as the jumping-off place for treks into the mountains or overland trips to the hot springs (with water reaching temperatures of 56°C) at Ayder. Peaks in the range rise to almost 4000 metres. You can explore the area on your own or organise a tour by talking to Mr Gündüz Akay at the Güven Pastahanesi in Trabzon. In Çamlıhemşin, treks are organised by Savaş and Doris Güney.

Hopa
The easternmost Turkish port on the Black Sea coast, 165 km east of Trabzon, is Hopa (HOH-pah) with a population of 18,000. The locals are friendly people who are curious about the few tourists who pass through and about why they come to Hopa at all. Many of the tourists seem to want to get a look at the Soviet frontier, 30 km to the east. In 1988, thanks to glasnost, a new border-crossing point was opened on the Turco-Soviet frontier at Sarp, so if you have a Soviet visa you can cross here. If you do, you can continue on

to Batum, the pretty Soviet seaside resort which was once an Ottoman town.

Places to Stay Should you find yourself in Hopa, you can stay at the *Cihan Hotel* (jee-HAHN) (tel 1897), Orta Hopa Caddesi 7, right on the shore. It's a comfortable lodging charging US$16/26 a single/double for rooms with bath. If they're not busy, they're amenable to haggling.

Getting There & Away Direct buses from Hopa to Erzurum depart early in the morning. If you miss the direct bus, you can catch a later bus to Artvin (1½ hours, US$1.50), then an onward bus from Artvin. For information on Artvin, see the following chapter, after Erzurum and Kars.

Eastern Anatolia

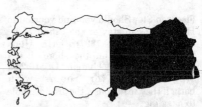

Eastern Turkey is a land of adventure, almost a magical place where each event of the day seems to take on the character of some fabled happening. You might go to bed at night disappointed because Mt Ararat was covered in cloud. But early next morning the mountain will take you by surprise, intruding into your consciousness, shining in the sun outside your hotel window. Or you might be riding along a rough road and suddenly come upon the ruins of a mediaeval castle, not marked on any map, not described in any guidebook. Every day reveals some new notion of epic events.

The east is not as well developed as western Turkey. You will see fewer tractors in the fields and more draught animals. Instead of grain-harvesting machinery, you might come across farmers threshing and winnowing in the ancient manner.

The people are no less friendly than in other parts of Turkey but they are not, generally speaking, used to seeing and dealing with foreigners (except in the hotels and tourist offices). It may take a little more time for the friendliness of the adults to emerge, but not so with the children. Every single one will simply *have* to find out where you come from and what language you speak.

Be prepared for the distances. You may ride for hours to get from one town to the next. When you get to that town, there may not be many hotels to choose from. And the one you want – particularly if it's the best in town – may be booked solid. Travelling in eastern Turkey is certainly not as comfortable as in the west. But if you are adaptable and out for adventure, this is the place to find it.

Touring the Region

The eastern mountains and high plateaux are subject to long and severe winters.

I don't recommend travelling out east except from May to September and preferably in July and August. If you go in May or September, be prepared for some quite chilly nights. A trip to the summit of Nemrut Dağı (2150 metres) should not be planned for early morning except in July and August. In other months the mountaintop will be very cold at any time and bitterly cold in early morning. There may also be snow.

Most visitors touring this part of the country make a loop through it, starting from Ankara, Kayseri, Trabzon, Adana or Antakya. Such a trip might follow one of these itineraries:

From Kayseri, head via Sivas and Malatya to Adıyaman then Kâhta to see Nemrut Dağı, then to Şanlıurfa and via Mardin to Diyarbakır for its ancient walls and mosques.

Starting from Adana or Antakya, go to Adıyaman and Kâhta via Gaziantep. After seeing Nemrut Dağı, head south to Şanlıurfa, east to Mardin and north to Diyarbakır.

From Diyarbakır, head east through Bitlis and around the southern shore of Van Gölü (Lake Van), stopping to see the Church of the Holy Cross on the island of Akdamar, before reaching the city of Van. Then head north to Ağrı and east to Doğubeyazıt to see Mt Ararat and also the İşak Paşa Sarayı, the dramatic Palace of Ishak Pasha.

From Doğubeyazıt head north to Kars to see the ruins of Ani, then to Erzurum. At Erzurum you can catch a plane westward, or toil through the mountains to Artvin, or head for the Black Sea coast at Trabzon, or start the return journey westward to Sivas and Ankara. This itinerary, from Kayseri or Adana to Van to Kars to Erzurum to Sivas, is about 2500 km and would take an absolute minimum of 10 days to complete by bus and/or train. It's better to take two weeks or more.

Getting There & Away

If you're touring by public transport, you may want to consider flying to or from the eastern region. Buses, as always, go everywhere; there are even direct buses to İstanbul from most large eastern cities such as Erzurum, Van and Diyarbakır. Though there are some trains, they're usually not as comfortable nor as fast as the bus.

Air Turkish Airlines flies between İstanbul/ Ankara and Diyarbakır (daily), Erzurum (daily), Gaziantep (daily), Malatya (Tuesday, Thursday, Saturday, Sunday), Sivas (Wednesday, Sunday), Trabzon (daily) and Van (Monday, Wednesday, Friday, Sunday).

İstanbul Airlines has a service from İstanbul to Trabzon on Monday, Wednesday and Friday. Check with the airline for schedules.

Bus Services to and from Ankara are frequent. Routes running east-west are generally not a problem, but north-south services can be infrequent, so allow plenty of time and check departure schedules as soon as you can.

Train From Ankara via Kayseri, there are three major eastern rail destinations: Erzurum, Kurtalan/Diyarbakır and Tatvan/Van. The Erzurum line goes on to Kars and the Soviet frontier, with a connecting train to Moscow. The Van line used to go on to Iran, with a connection to Tabriz and Tehran; this connection has been severed for years, but because of recent developments in Iran it may be

revived. South of Elazığ, this line branches for Diyarbakır and Kurtalan.

Except perhaps for the Blue (Mavi) Trains, don't expect any of the following trains to be on time; they may be hours late.

The Erzurum Mavi Tren runs daily, departing Ankara and Erzurum at 9 pm, arriving the next day at 5.16 pm, and running via Kayseri, Sivas, and Erzincan. All seats are reclining Pullman style.

The Gaziantep Mavi Tren departs Ankara and Gaziantep at 7 pm, arriving at 11.50 am; trains run from Ankara on Monday, Wednesday, Friday, and Saturday, and from Gaziantep on Monday, Wednesday, Friday, and Sunday, connecting the cities of Ankara, Kayseri, Niğde, Adana, and Gaziantep. There are Pullman seats only.

Then there are the trains with 1st and 2nd class seats, couchettes, sleeping cars, and (sometimes) dining cars. The Doğu Ekspresi (doh-OO, east) goes from İstanbul via Ankara, Sivas and Erzurum to Kars daily. The Vangölü Ekspresi and Güney Ekspresi share a common route from İstanbul (daily at 7.10 pm) via Ankara (arrive 5.40 am, depart 6.40 am), to Sivas, Malatya and Elazığ Junction. East of the junction, the train continues on some days to Tatvan, and on others to Diyarbakır and Kurtalan (east of Diyarbakır). The train trip between Malatya and Diyarbakır takes about six hours.

GAZİANTEP

Known throughout most of its long history as Aintab, this city (population 500,000, altitude 855 metres) was called Antep by the Ottomans. In April 1920, when the Great Powers were carving up the Ottoman lands, Antep was attacked and besieged by French forces. The city's nationalist defenders held out for 10 months before finally surrendering, a feat later recognised by the Grand National Assembly when it granted the city the title of Gazi, meaning Defender of the Faith (or War Hero). Since that time, the city has been called Gaziantep.

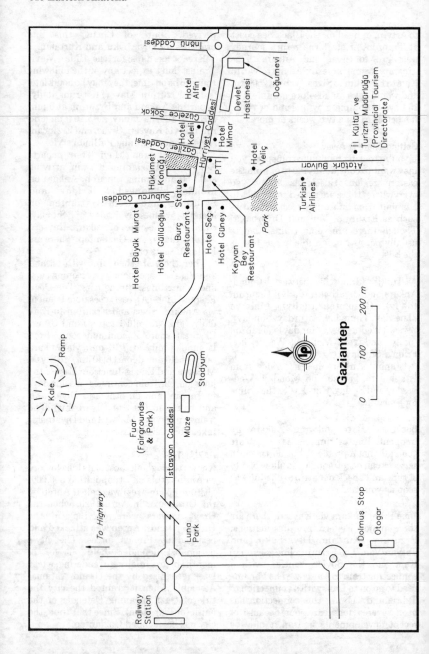

Gaziantep

Despite its remarkably long history, Gaziantep today is a large, modern city with only two sights to interest visitors: the kale and the museum.

Otherwise, Gaziantep offers a number of comfortable hotels at mid-range prices. As a bonus, you can enjoy a good number of culinary treats: the city and the region are known for excellent grapes and olives, for the soft Arabic 'pizza' called lahmacun and for pistachios. This is the pistachio nut (şam fıstığı, SHAHM fuhss-tuh) capital of Turkey. By the way, the phrase fıstık gibi, 'like a (pistachio) nut', is the way Turks describe a particularly attractive young woman.

You can bypass this city without great feelings of guilt. If you do stay the night, have some lahmacun, buy a supply of delicious pistachios (about US$6 per kg in the shells; more without shells), spend an hour looking at the kale and museum the next morning, then get back on the road.

History
Archaeologists have sifted through some of the dirt which forms the artificial hill beneath the kale, and have found prehistoric artefacts dating from Neolithic times (7000-5000 BC). But the history begins when small proto-Hittite, or Hatti, city-states grew up between 2500 and 1900 BC.

Hittites and Assyrians battled for this region until it was taken by Sargon II, king of Assyria, in 717 BC. The Assyrians ruled for almost a century before being overcome by the Cimmerians, a Crimean people driven from their traditional lands by the Scythians. The Cimmerians swept through Anatolia destroying most everything that lay in their path, setting an example that would be followed by numerous uncreative hordes which showed up in later history.

The Cimmerians cleared out and the Persians took over from 612 to 333 BC. They were followed by Alexander the Great, the Romans and the Byzantines. The Arabs conquered the town in 638 AD and held it until the Seljuk Turks swept in from the east in the 1070s.

With the Crusades, Antep's history perks up a bit, but most of the action and romance took place in Urfa. The Crusaders didn't stay long before the Seljuks took over again, and Antep remained a city of Seljuk culture, ruled by petty Turkish lords until the coming of the Ottomans under Selim the Grim in 1516.

Orientation
Gaziantep is fairly large, and you will have to take public transport to get from the bus or train station to the centre. For reference purposes, the centre of the city is the intersection of the main roads named Atatürk Bulvarı and Hürriyet Caddesi next to the Hükümet Konağı (hew-kew-MEHT koh-nah-uh), or Provincial Government House.

The Devlet Hastanesi or State Hospital, another useful landmark, is a few blocks past the Hükümet Konağı on Hürriyet Caddesi. Most of the services you might need, including banks, post office, pharmacy, cheap and moderate restaurants, pastry shops, florists, pistachio-nut shops, a newsagent and even a hamburger joint are within one block of the intersection of Atatürk Bulvarı and İstasyon Caddesi.

The most recommendable hotels are also within a block or two of the Hükümet Konağı. The museum is about half a km from here and the kale is about half a km from the museum – an easy and pleasant walk.

The otogar is two km from the Hükümet Konağı; walk out the front door of the otogar to the main road, turn right, walk half a block to the 'D' sign, and take a 'Devlet Hastanesi' minibus, or one of the less frequent city buses from the nearby bus stop. Don't listen to the taxi drivers when they say, 'There are no minibuses that take you into town'. The railway station is almost as far out. The 'Devlet Hastanesi' minibus passes near it; walk from the station to the first large intersection to find the minibus. A taxi to the centre costs about US$1.

You can see the hill which bears the kale from many places in the city, and thus it serves as a handy landmark. Look for the highest hill, which bears a two-minaret mosque as well as the kale.

Information

Gaziantep does not have a Ministry of Tourism office. There is a provincial tourism directorate (İl Turizm Müdürlüğü) on Atatürk Bulvarı. Very few of the staff speak anything but Turkish and only a few hand-out materials are available.

Kale

Head for the citadel first. The road to it begins just opposite the museum, which is next to the stadium.

The citadel was first constructed, as far as is known, by the Emperor Justinian in the 6th century AD, but was rebuilt extensively by the Seljuks in the 12th and 13th centuries. The massive doors to the fortified enclosure may well be locked, but at least have a look at them. As you approach the kale bear right around the massive walls. Don't go through what appears to be an enormous stone gateway; this is actually the fosse (dry moat), straddled in ancient times by a drawbridge high above. Around to the right of the fosse you will come to a small mosque, opposite which is a ramp leading up to the citadel doors. If they're open, proceed across the wooden bridge which spans the fosse and into the kale.

The surrounding quarter is one of artisans workshops, old stone houses and little neighbourhood mosques. Lorries for hire are gathered at one side of the kale, heirs to the ancient carters and teamsters.

Gaziantep Müze

The museum (tel (851) 11171), next to the stadium on İstasyon Caddesi, is open from 9 am to 5.30 pm, closed Monday; admission costs US$1. Surrounded by the requisite sculpture garden, the museum holds something from every period of the province's history, from mastodon bones

through Hittite figurines and pottery to Roman mosaics (three fairly good ones) and funeral stones complete with portraits of husband and wife, to an Ottoman ethnography room of kilims, carpets and furniture heavily worked in mother-of-pearl.

Places to Stay

Gaziantep accommodation is resolutely middle-range, with nothing much at the bottom and top ends of the price scale. There are no hotels near the otogar or the railway station. Most of the hotels are within a block or two of the Hükümet Konağı, either on Atatürk Bulvarı or on Hürriyet Caddesi between the Hükümet Konağı and the Devlet Hastanesi. I'll start with the cheaper places and end with the best place in town.

The 35-room *Hotel Veliç* (tel 22341, 11726), Atatürk Bulvarı 23, is fairly bright and modern, with a lift and its own car park. All rooms have private showers and cost US$10 a single, US$16 a double.

Nearby is the 50-room *Hotel Güney* (tel 16886), Atatürk Bulvarı 10, also bright and modern, with lift and sauna; singles with shower go for US$15, doubles for US$22, but the hotel has two bathless rooms which rent for less. The hotel has its own car park.

Just a few steps from the crossroads at Hükümet Konağı is the *Hotel Seç* (tel 15272) at Atatürk Bulvarı 4/B. Equipped with a lift and central heating, it charges US$7 a single with private shower, US$8 for a double room without private bath, or US$11 a double with private shower; watch out for street noise.

On the opposite side of the intersection Atatürk Bulvarı becomes Suburcu Caddesi. The *Hotel Güllüoğlu* (tel 24363/4), Suburcu Caddesi 1/B, 27010 Gaziantep, has all the standard medium-class comforts, is clean, and charges only US$12/16 a single/double for a room with shower. Enter the hotel around the corner from the baklavacı on the side street.

Three more hotels are on Hürriyet Caddesi between the Hükümet Konağı and the Devlet Hastanesi. *Hotel Alfin* (tel 19480/1), Hürriyet Caddesi 25, 27010 Gaziantep, just across from the Devlet Hastanesi, has rooms with bath, lift, breakfast room and bar, and charges US$14/19/27 a single/double/triple.

The one-star, 45-room *Hotel Mimar* (tel 17992), Hürriyet Caddesi 24/C, 27010 Gaziantep, has eight storeys of comfortable bath-equipped rooms, a lift and a garage. It's the newest hotel in town and offers good value at US$15/22, a single/double.

The best place in town, which has accommodated tourists for years, is the two-star *Hotel Kaleli* (tel 13417/12728), Hürriyet Caddesi, Güzelce Sokak 50, 27010 Gaziantep, between the Hotel Alfin and the Hükümet Konağı. Rooms go for US$22/28 a single/double, or US$48 a triple in a suite. The hotel has two lifts, 70 large guest rooms with good cross-ventilation and small tiled showers, a rooftop restaurant and several small private parking spots.

Places to Eat

Gaziantep's recommendable restaurants are likewise clustered at the intersection of Atatürk Bulvarı and Hürriyet Caddesi.

Just across Hürriyet Caddesi from the Hükümet Konağı and its plaza is the *Keyvan Bey Restaurant* (tel 12651), on the upper floor, with an outdoor terrace section festooned with green vegetation. A full meal here based on kebap need cost only US$3 or US$4.

Slightly fancier is the *Burç Restaurant* (tel 13012) at the corner of Suburcu and İstasyon caddesis, on the upper floor of the Ticaret Sarayı building. Glassed-in dining rooms with lots of crimson drapes provide a fine view of the plaza and busy crossroads. They are favoured by pistachio magnates, government chiefs and other local notables, but meals here are priced similarly to those at neighbouring places, and the average meal price is between US$4 and US$6. The restaurant features live entertainment on some evenings.

Right across the street from the entrance to the Ticaret Sarayı is *Best Burger*, a modern fast-food hamburger shop with edible, if not wildly authentic, burgers for US$1.50.

Finally, there's the roof restaurant at the Hotel Kaleli. Green and blue fluorescent lights make everyone look somewhat ghostly, but it's pleasant and airy and well above the street noise. A full dinner can cost as little as US$5 or US$6.

Getting There & Away

Air Turkish Airlines (tel 20505, 20446, 20406), Atatürk Bulvarı 38/C, operates non-stop flights between Gaziantep's Sazgın Airport and İstanbul on Tuesday, and between Gaziantep and Ankara on the other days of the week; connecting at Ankara for İstanbul. The flight from Ankara takes just over an hour; from İstanbul, one hour and 40 minutes. An airport bus departs the downtown office on Atatürk Bulvarı 90 minutes before flight time and costs less than US$0.75.

Bus The modern otogar is two km from the town centre and the bus service is frequent and far-reaching. Here are destinations:

Adana - 220 km, 3½ to four hours, US$2.75; several buses daily

Adıyaman & Kâhta (Nemrut Dağı) - 210 km, four hours, US$4; several buses daily

Ankara - 705 km, 12 hours, US$10; frequent buses daily

Antakya - 200 km, four hours, US$4; frequent buses daily

Diyarbakır - 330 km, five hours, US$5.50; frequent buses daily

Mardin - 330 km, 5½ hours, US$6; several buses daily

Şanlıurfa - 145 km, 2½ hours, US$2.75; frequent buses daily

Train Only one train is a serious contender for your attention, and that is the Gaziantep Mavi Tren which departs Ankara at 7 pm Monday, Wednesday, Friday and Saturday, and departs

Gaziantep on Monday, Wednesday, Friday and Sunday, at 7 pm also, arriving the next morning at 11.50 am. It has 1st-class Pullman seats only. The train runs via Kayseri, Niğde and Adana.

There is a 6 am train to Akçakale, near Harran, which is not too far from Şanlıurfa, but then you must make your way to Şanlıurfa by taxi (probably). Take the bus instead of the train. Likewise, a 9 pm posta train to Diyarbakır takes an astounding 15 hours, while the bus makes the trip in one-third of the time.

NORTHWARD & EASTWARD
You are probably heading north to visit Nemrut Dağı, but just in case your itinerary takes you due east, here's what to expect.

The road from Gaziantep to Şanlıurfa is very hot in summer, yet the land is fertile, with fig orchards, olive trees, cotton and wheat. At Nizip, there is a turning south for Karkamış (Carchemish), a neo-Hittite city which flourished around 850 BC, about the time Akhenaton occupied the throne of Egypt. Though Karkamış assumed the role of Hittite capital after the fall of Hattuşaş, there is little left to see, and you must see it with a military escort so you don't get shot at as a smuggler – it's hardly worth the trip. The only regular tourist group to arrive in Karkamış these days is the small

Girl from Gaziantep holding her prize kid

remaining flock of bald ibises, gawky but near-extinct birds which favour Karkamış from mid-February to July, after which they fly off for autumn in Egypt's Nile Valley. (Bald ibises figured prominently in ancient Egyptian mythology.)

At Birecik you cross the Euphrates. The town has a ruined fortress, rebuilt and used by the Crusaders. In spring (March or April), the town holds a traditional festival to welcome back the 37 wild bald ibises (14 more are in captivity for breeding). Authorities establish an ibis feeding and protection station to give them meat and eggs. Construction of wooden apartments for ibis is underway, following plans provided by the Turkish Wildlife Protection Society and World Wildlife Fund.

As you head east, the land becomes rockier and less fertile. The highway is crowded with oil tankers shuttling between the Turkish oilfields and the refineries in Batman and Siirt. By the time you approach Şanlıurfa, the land is parched, rolling steppe roasting in the merciless desert sun. This landscape will change when the gigantic South-east Anatolia Project (Güney Anadolu Projesi) is complete, bringing irrigation waters to vast tracts of otherwise unarable land.

NEMRUT DAĞI
The Commagene Nemrut Dağı (NEHM-root dah-uh), not to be confused with a mountain of the same name on the shores of Lake Van, rises to a height of 2150 metres between the provincial capital of Malatya to the north and the village of Kâhta in the Adıyaman province to the south. It's part of the Anti-Taurus range.

The temples on this bare mountaintop in south-eastern Anatolia are certainly unique. The mountain peak was formed when a petty, megalomaniac pre-Roman king cut two ledges in the rock, filled them with colossal statues of himself and the gods (his 'relatives'), then ordered an artificial mountain peak of crushed rock

50 metres high to be piled between them. The king's tomb may well lie beneath those tons of rock. Nobody knows for sure.

Earthquakes have toppled the heads from most of the statues, but many of the colossal bodies sit silently in rows, and the two-metre-high heads watch from the ground. It's something to see.

Plan your visit to Nemrut between late May and mid-October, and preferably in July or August. The road to the summit is still partially unpaved and it becomes impassable in spring when the snow melts, turning it to mud. Remember that at any time of year, even in the heat of summer when the sun bakes the valleys below, it will be chilly and windy atop the mountain. This is especially true at sunrise, the coldest hour of the day. Take warm clothing and a windbreaker on your trek to the top, no matter when you go.

History

Nobody knew anything about Nemrut Dağı until 1881, when an Ottoman geologist making a survey was astounded to come across a remote mountaintop full of statues. Archaeological work didn't begin until 1953, when the American School of Oriental Research undertook the project.

From 250 BC onwards, this region was the borderland between the Seleucid empire (which followed the empire of Alexander the Great in Anatolia) and the Parthian empire to the east, also occupying a part of Alexander's lands. A small but strategic land which was rich, fertile and covered in forests, it had a history of independent thinking ever since the time of King Samos at about 150 BC.

Under the Seleucid Empire, the governor of Commagene declared his kingdom's independence. In 80 BC, with the Seleucids in disarray and Roman power spreading into Anatolia, a Roman ally named Mithridates I Callinicus proclaimed himself king and set up his capital at Arsameia, near the modern village of Eski Kâhta. Mithridates prided himself on his royal ancestry, tracing his forebears back to Seleucus I Nicator, founder of the Seleucid Empire to the west, and to Darius the Great, king of ancient Persia to the east. Thus he saw himself as heir to both glorious traditions. He married a Parthian princess.

Mithridates died in 64 BC and was succeeded by his son Antiochus I Epiphanes (64-38 BC) who, born of a Parthian mother, consolidated the security of his kingdom by immediately signing a non-aggression treaty with Rome, turning his kingdom into a Roman buffer against attack from the Parthians. His good relations with both sides allowed him to grow rich and to revel in delusions of grandeur. As heir to both traditions, he saw himself as equal to the great god-kings of the past. It was Antiochus who ordered that the fabulous temples and funerary mound be built atop Nemrut.

Antiochus must have come to believe in his own divinity, for in the third decade of his reign he sided with the Parthians in a squabble with Rome, and the Romans deposed him in 38 BC. Commagene was alternately ruled directly from Rome or by puppet kings until 72 AD, when Emperor Vespasian incorporated it for good into Roman Asia. So the great days of Commagene were limited to the 26-year reign of Antiochus.

Orientation

Visitors to Nemrut Dağı have traditionally used the provincial capital of Adıyaman (ah-DUH-yah-mahn, population 75,000, altitude 725 metres) or the nearby village of Kâhta (ky-YAHH-tah, population 32,000) as a base for their ascent, though the route via Malatya is popular too. In recent years the Malatya route has gained in popularity as the people are nicer. Adıyaman's citizens are not particularly welcoming to foreign tourists, and the minibus drivers and tour touts in Kâhta are very crooked and positively pestilential the way they follow and badger you to take

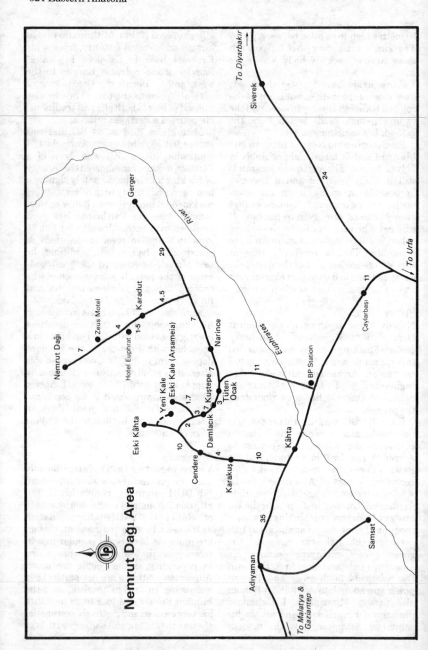

To Diyarbakır

Siverek

24

To Urfa

Gerger

River

29

Karadut

4.5

Zeus Motel

4

Hotel Euphrat

1.5

7

Nemrut Dağı

7

Narince

Euphrates

11

Çaylarbaşı

11

BP Station

Eski Kâhta

Yeni Kale

1.7

Eski Kale (Arsameia)

7

Kuştepe

3

3

Tüten Ocak

7

2

Damlacık

Kâhta

10

Cendere

4

Karakuş

10

35

Samsat

Adıyaman

To Malatya &
Gaziantep

Nemrut Dağı Area

their overpriced tours. But there's more to see along the Kâhta route.

The road to the top from Malatya via Tepehan can also be done in a day, or with an overnight stay in the village of Büyüköz near the summit, where there are simple pensions and a basic but adequate new hotel. By taking the Malatya route, visitors miss seeing the several sights along the Kâhta-Nemrut road, such as Arsameia. Cost is about the same by either route (if you don't get ripped off in Kâhta, a big 'if'). If you decide to go via Malatya, refer to the section on that city.

Distances among these points are as follows: Kâhta to the summit of Nemrut 70 km; Kâhta to Adıyaman 35 km; Adıyaman to Gölbaşı 65 km; Gölbaşı to Malatya 121 km; Malatya to the summit of Nemrut 110 km.

Whichever way you go, pack a bottle of water and some snacks such as dried fruit, biscuits and nuts, as the journey can take between six and eight hours and services along the way are limited. Plan between two and 2½ hours of driving (or riding) for the outward trip from Kâhta to the summit. The return trip takes almost as long. Add to these two or three hours of sightseeing at the various sites.

Information

The Tourism Information Office in Adıyaman (tel (8781) 2478, 1008), Atatürk Bulvarı 41, is next to the PTT on the main street, which is also the highway. If no one is around, check at the Hükümet Konağı, the Government House. You may not get much help.

Touring from Kâhta

Over the years, as the flow of travellers to Kâhta increased, so has the number of unpleasant characters who interject themselves between you and your Nemrut Dağı experience. It is difficult to find a decent hotel at a decent price, difficult to find an honest minibus driver and a tour worth the money. The local people don't welcome tourists because they believe, incredibly, that tourists venture to the top of Nemrut to *worship* the idols, not just to see an archaeological wonder. (It makes no sense to them that someone would come halfway around the world at great expense just to look and take photographs.) As for the people involved in tourism, some valiantly struggle against the odds to provide good services at a fair price, but they are in the minority.

At one point, the minibus drivers removed all the road signs on the road to Nemrut in order to make it difficult for tourists to get up the mountain in their own cars. Other tricks involve bait-and-switch: you agree with a minibus driver on a tour price and a departure time to get to the summit by sunrise, but the driver never shows up. However, another driver *just happens* to be waiting across the street from your hotel and will take you up for twice the price!

If you run into difficulties in Kâhta, write to the Ministry of Tourism, Gazi Mustafa Kemal Bulvarı 33, Demirtepe, Ankara, to let them know about it; with evidence in hand, they can do something to straighten out the situation.

Minibus In theory, there are two standard minibus tours. The short tour takes you from Kâhta to the summit, allows you about an hour there, then comes right down to Kâhta again. The long or complete tour takes you to the summit, and on the trip down stops at Eski Kale (Arsameia), Yeni Kale (next to Eski Kâhta) and Karakuş. The normal price to rent a 10-person minibus for the short tour is US$35, US$50 for the long tour. Though sunrise and sunset are popular times to be at the summit, either one condemns you to a long ride in the dark. I recommend going in the middle of the day when it's warmer and you can enjoy the scenery in both directions.

If you are one of those romantics who plan to stay the night at a pension in Eski Kâhta and ascend at midnight on muleback or on foot, you can get to your base at Eski Kâhta very inexpensively by taking a dolmuş from Kâhta toward Gerger, which passes by Eski Kâhta.

It is possible to take a minibus tour up Nemrut from Şanlıurfa, departing that city at 9 am, seeing everything, with lunch in Kâhta, returning to Urfa by evening, all for less than US$20 per person.

Private Car You can easily make the trip on your own using the map in this guidebook. Make sure you have plenty of fuel for at least 200 or 250 km of normal driving. Though the trip to the summit and back down is only about 150 km, much of that will be driven in low gear, which uses more fuel. Should you run out of fuel, villagers may be able to sell you a few litres from a barrel or another vehicle's fuel tank.

You can approach Nemrut via Karakuş, Eski Kâhta and Eski Kale, or via the road north from the BP petrol station on the highway east of Kâhta. To see all the sights on the way up, go via Karakuş and Eski Kâhta.

To Eski Kâhta
The road is paved and fairly well signposted as far as the village of Damlacık. It's 24 km from Kâhta to Eski Kâhta. After 15 km you come to a fork in the road; take the right fork. The road from Kâhta passes through the villages of Karakuş and Cendere, and the sights begin 10 km after leaving Kâhta. A mound by the roadside at Karakuş, marked with columns, holds the graves of royal ladies from the Kingdom of Commagene. A black eagle (*karakuş*), its head missing, tops one of the columns.

Nineteen km from Kâhta and five km before Eski Kâhta, you'll cross a Roman bridge built in honour of Emperor Septimius Severus (194-211 AD), his wife and sons, long after Commagene had become part of Roman Asia. Of the four original columns (two at either end), three are still standing. Some historians think that the missing column was removed by one of the sons, Caracalla, when he murdered the other son, Geta, in 212.

As you leave the bridge, there should be a sign pointing to the right for Nemrut Dağı and Gerger; the road to the left is for Eski Kâhta.

You approach Eski Kâhta along the valley of a stream called the Kâhta Çayı. Opposite the town are the ruins of a Mameluke castle (1300s), now called Yeni Kale (yeh-NEE kah-leh, New Fortress), which you can explore. It bears some Arabic inscriptions; the Mamelukes were originally a Turkic people, but they were assimilated into Egyptian society. It's difficult to imagine that this region was once very fertile, cloaked in forests and noisy with the sound of great herds of cattle. Deforestation and consequent erosion have turned it to semi-desert.

Eski Kale (Arsameia)
Just after leaving Eski Kâhta, the old road passes through a dramatic, beautiful gorge spanned by an ancient bridge which appears to be Seljuk in design. The new road, however, bypasses the gorge.

About a km up the road from Eski Kâhta, a turn-off to the left takes you the two km to Eski Kale, the ancient Commagene capital of Arsameia. Walk up the path from the car park and you'll come to a large stela with a figure (maybe female) on it. Further along are two more stelae, a monumental staircase and, behind them, an opening in the rock leading down to a cistern.

Another path leads from the first path to the striking stone relief which portrays the founder of Commagene, Mithridates I Callinicus, shaking hands with the god Heracles. Next to it is a long inscription in Greek and to the right is a tunnel descending through the rock. The locals will tell you the tunnel goes all the way to the valley floor below, though it has not yet been cleared of the centuries of rubble.

Above the relief on the level top of the hill are the foundations of Mithridates' capital city. The view is magnificent from here. If you stop at Arsameia on your way down from Nemrut, this is the perfect site for a picnic.

To the Summit
Driving three km upward from Eski Kale, you pass through **Damlacık** where there are humble restaurants and camping places, a Jandarma post and a Red Crescent first-aid station. After Damlacık the paved road gives way to one of stabilised gravel.

The next settlements are **Kuştepe** (seven km), then **Tüten Ocak** (three km). Shortly after Tüten Ocak you come to a bridge and a road leading south marked for Kâhta, which goes back to BP station on the main highway. This road fords the river at one point and is impassable if the river is in flood, usually during spring or after heavy rains.

Seven km east of this junction is the hamlet of **Narince**, after which the road becomes rougher and steeper. Another seven km east of Narince is a turning to the left marked for Nemrut, which you want to take; to continue straight on would take to the village of Gerger. At this road intersection is the *Boğaz Café*, on the right.

Continue up the mountain five km to the hamlet of **Karadut**, which has a few small pensions and restaurants. The backpackers' choice here is the *Apollo Pansiyon, Restaurant & Camping* (tel 1246). The price of a bed is US$3.50, shower fee included. If you stay you'll have to take a minibus from Karadut to reach the summit. A passing minibus may charge US$1 to US$2; to rent an entire minibus for a trip to the summit and back to Karadut costs about US$14. At the upper end of Karadut village is the *Karadut Kamping & Restaurant.*

North of Karadut, the last half-hour's travel to the top is on a steep road paved in black basalt blocks and still fairly rough. There are two lodging places along the road. The 30-room *Hotel Euphrat* (tel (1)

144-6583 in İstanbul), 9½ km from the summit, charges US$14 per person for bed & breakfast and dinner.

The *Zeus Motel* (tel (8781) 2180, 3054 in Adıyaman) has offices at Atatürk Bulvarı 43, Vilayet Karşısı, Adıyaman, or Mustafa Kemal Caddesi 50 (PO Box 50), Kâhta. Contact the offices for reservations. The 'motel' is a modern, simple but comfortable mountain inn of 20 rooms, some with tiled baths and electrically heated water. Most rooms have fireplaces, and some have three or four beds. There is a restaurant and a terrace café. Rooms are priced at US$16/25 a single/double, with breakfast an additional US$2.50 per person. Note that the motel is open from May to October only. From the Zeus Motel, it's seven km to the summit.

At the Summit
You're well above treeline when you climb the final ridge and pull into the car park at the summit. Just up from the car park is a building with toilets, a café for snacks and hot tea, soft drinks and souvenirs. There are also dormitory-type beds going for US$4 each or sleeping-spots on the roof for less than US$2, but it's *very* cold. No doubt better dormitory space will be arranged in future. Note also that the attendants don't seem to mind if you park a camper van in the car park overnight.

Beyond the building is the pyramid of stones; it's a hike of less than one km (15 or 20 minutes) over the broken rock to the western temple. Sometimes donkeys are on hand to carry you, but this is not much help since staying on the donkey is almost as difficult as negotiating the rocks on your own. Admission to the archaeological site costs US$5.

Antiochus I Epiphanes ordered the construction here of a *hierothesium*, or combination tomb and temple.

I, great King Antiochus, have ordered the construction of these temples, the ceremonial road, and the thrones of the gods, on a foundation which will never be demolished...

I have done this to prove my faith in the gods. At the end of my life I will enter my eternal rest here, and my spirit will join that of Zeus-Ahura Mazda in heaven.

Approaching from the car park, you see first the western temple and behind it the conical tumulus, or funerary mound, of fist-sized stones. At the western temple, Antiochus and his fellow gods sit in state, though the bodies have mostly been tumbled down along with the heads. But at the eastern temple the bodies are largely intact, except for the fallen heads, which seem more badly weathered than the heads at the west. On the backs of the eastern statues are inscriptions in Greek.

Both terraces have similar plans, with the syncretistic gods, the 'ancestors' of Antiochus, seated in this order, from left to right: first is Apollo, the sun god, Mithra to the Persians, Helios or Hermes to the Greeks; next is Fortuna, or Tyche; in the centre is Zeus-Ahura Mazda; to the right is King Antiochus; and at the right end is Heracles, also known as Ares or Artagnes. The seated figures are several metres high, their heads alone about two metres tall.

Low walls at the sides of each temple once held carved reliefs showing royal processions of ancient Persia and Greece, Antiochus' 'predecessors'. Statues of eagles represent Zeus.

The flat space next to the eastern temple, with an 'H' at its centre, is a helipad which accepts the arrival of the wealthy, the important and the fortunate. It stands on the site of an ancient altar. In the valley below, about three km from the summit, is the *Güneş Hotel*, of use mostly to those coming up Nemrut from Malatya. The Güneş charges US$18 per person for bed & breakfast and supper, hot shower included.

Places to Stay

You can lodge in Adıyaman, Kâhta, Eski Kâhta, Malatya or on the mountain slope;

for lodgings on the mountain, refer to the description of the trip up Nemrut Dağı.

Adıyaman Though Adıyaman has some budget hotels such as the *Hotel Uyanık* (tel (8781) 1179), the *Hotel Yolaç* (tel 1301) and the *Konak Oteli* (tel 2392), there are few advantages to staying here rather than in Kâhta. In fact, the hotels here often suffer from underuse as most visitors prefer Kâhta, and underuse means musty rooms, inexperienced staff and low maintenance budgets.

As for middle-range places, the three-star *Bozdoğan Hotel* is under construction and may be open by the time you arrive, with rooms priced from US$25 to US$30 a single and from US$35 to US$40 a double.

The *Motel Beyaz Saray* (tel 4907), Atatürk Bulvarı 136, 02100 Adıyaman, on the highway in the eastern part of town, has a small swimming pool and acceptable but unexciting rooms with shower at US$8/12 a single/double with washbasin, or US$12/16 with private shower. The hotel's nightclub-restaurant does a booming business (and I do mean 'booming'; watch out for the noise).

Not far away is the *Motel Sultan* (tel 3493, 3377), Atatürk Bulvarı YSE Yanı, 02100 Adıyaman, charging US$10/12 a single/double for a room with private shower. Like the Beyaz Saray, the Sultan has a swimming pool which may or may not have water in it.

Next door to the Sultan stands the *Motel Arsameia* (tel 2112, 3131), Atatürk Bulvarı 148, 02100 Adıyaman, a standard Turkish hotel with double rooms and shower renting for US$16. The Arsameia has a restaurant and camping area and is not far from Adıyaman's bus and dolmuş station.

Off the highway is the *Ünal Pansiyon* (tel 1508), Harıkçı Caddesi 14/A-B, 02100 Adıyaman, which is open all year. Its 24 rooms are priced at US$15 to US$18 a single, US$18 to US$24 a double, depending on whether you want a room with washbasin or with private bath.

Kâhta There are several hotels in town which I emphatically do not recommend. If you don't see a hotel mentioned, either it was built after my last visit or it should be avoided. All of the hotels in Kâhta are quite overpriced.

The one-star, 28-room *Hotel Merhaba* (MEHR-hah-bah) (tel (8795) 1098, 1139), two short blocks south of the highway, was the first real hotel in town. It is now very worn but there's not much choice hereabouts. It has a restaurant. Prices are US$15/26 a single/double for small, old rooms with private showers and inter-mittent water. This is Kâhta quality at İstanbul prices.

The more presentable *Hotel Selçuk* (tel 1838), Adıyaman Yolu, 02400 Kâhta, is on the highway west of town. With a shady terrace restaurant, swimming pool and presentable guest rooms with private showers, it is Kâhta's most comfortable lodging-spot, charging US$35/42 a single/double – İstanbul prices again. The pool may not have water and the restaurant certainly does not have alcoholic drinks, as the hotel is owned by fundamentalists. It also has a camping area but charges US$3 per person for the privilege.

At the junction with the Nemrut road is the *Hotel Kommagene* (tel 1092), PK 4, 02400 Kâhta, a converted house with fly-screens on the windows, lots of Turkish carpets and kilims to lend atmosphere and prices of US$11/17 a single/double with bath for its much-used and very basic rooms. The hotel has a bar and a camping area.

Eski Kâhta This tiny village, 25 km north of Kâhta, can be reached by two direct dolmuşes daily; or take a Gerger dolmuş and mention the village (ESS-kee ky-YAHH-tah) to the driver. The village has two very basic pensions, one of which is run by the Demiral (DEH-meer-ahl) family (no phone). For US$3 per person you can bed down (it helps to have your own sleeping bag). There's running water from a can. With a camper van, you can camp in their front yard.

The Demirals will serve you simple but tasty meals for about US$2 each, whether you sleep here or not; order well before meal time. They have beer and soft drinks but no wine or spirits. Their house was once occupied by Professor Dörfer, a German archaeologist who worked at Nemrut. The Demirals will find a guide you can employ to lead you up the mountain, a three or four-hour trek whether you go on foot or on donkey-back.

A newer pension is just across from the newly built mosque at the foot of the fortress; it's run by friendly young people who charge about the same as the Demirals and who may beat you at cards.

Places to Eat

Besides the dining places in the various hotels mentioned in the Places to Stay, Kâhta has several little restaurants. Typical is the *Kent Restaurant* on the north side of the main highway in the centre of town. A hazır yemek restaurant, it fills you up at rock-bottom prices. Two plates of food and a drink will cost about US$2.50. There are plenty of restaurants on the south side of the highway as well. Also, the *Güney Restaurant*, next to a tea house and facing the Hotel Merhaba, was conveniently open for me early one morning when I needed a good bowl of breakfast soup.

Getting There & Away

Adıyaman and Kâhta are served by frequent buses, but nothing else. There are air and rail services to Malatya.

Bus From Kâhta you can reach Diyarbakır (192 km, three hours, US$4) and Malatya (221 km, three hours, US$3.50). Dolmuşes run between Kâhta and Adıyaman (US$1) throughout the day.

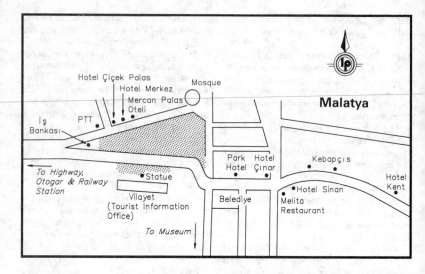

AROUND KÂHTA

From Kâhta you have a choice of roads in all directions. To the north lies Malatya, an agricultural centre without tourist significance except for the alternate route up Nemrut Dağı; and Divriği, Sivas and Tokat, three towns important to the history of Seljuk Turkish architecture.

To the east is Elâzığ, a rarity in that it has no deep history, having been founded by the Ottomans in 1862. The museum at Euphrates University (Fırat Üniversitesi) holds many Urartian and other artefacts scavenged from the valleys flooded when the great Keban Dam was finished in 1974. Five km outside Elâzığ are the ruins of old Harput. This city was ruined by an earthquake, and Elâzığ rose to take its people and its place in history.

Also eastward lies Diyarbakır, the most important city in south-eastern Turkey.

To the south lies Şanlıurfa, perhaps the most fascinating and pleasant town in the region. If you're heading east rather than north, I'd suggest that you make the detour south to Şanlıurfa, then continue to Mardin and/or Diyarbakır.

On this ride you will enter that fabled cradle of civilisation, the watershed of the Tigris (Dicle, DEEJ-leh) and Euphrates (Fırat, fuh-RAHT) rivers. The shortest route is east from Kâhta via Çaylarbaşı to the east-west highway (53 km). Turn right (west) at the highway for Şanlıurfa, 70 km from the junction; or left (east) 23 km to Siverek, and another 116 km to Diyarbakır, a total distance of 192 km.

MALATYA

A modern town grown large and rich on agriculture, Malatya (mah-LAHT-yah, population 252,000, altitude 964 metres) has virtually nothing to offer the tourist except the alternative route up Nemrut Dağı, and apricots. This happens to be the apricot capital of Turkey. An apricot festival is held in late July. Look in the shop windows at all the packages of dried apricots. There is also a small museum near the Vilayet (vee-lah-YEHT, Provincial Headquarters) building; follow the Müze signs.

Orientation

Malatya is ranged along its main street for many km. Everything you'll want is in the centre, near the main square with its statue of Atatürk and Vilayet building, and the neighbouring Belediye (beh-leh-DEE-yeh, City Hall).

The otogar and train station (İstasyon) are on the outskirts of town, several km from the centre. City buses marked 'Vilayet' operate between the stations and the centre.

Information

The Vilayet holds the local Tourism Information Office (tel (821) 17733). There is also a small tourist information office in the otogar, where a tourism official will be on hand to greet you and urge you to sign up for one of the tours to the top of Nemrut Dağı. A third office, more for administration than information, is at İzzetiye Mahallesi, Atmalı Sokak, Esnaf Sarayı, Kat 4-5, No 10, Malatya.

Going to Nemrut

Though this route is in some ways less convenient than the route via Kâhta, it is more pleasant because of the people. Minibus tours can be made in a day, but it's more comfortable to stay overnight. The transport costs about US$10 per person, a mattress in a hut US$10 and a hotel bed with supper, breakfast and hot shower US$18. The ride to the summit takes about five hours, but the scenery is marvellous.

You can in fact arrange a trip on your own, but it might turn out to cost more. Start by taking the first of the two daily minibuses to the village of Büyüköz (berr-YERRK-erz) via Tepehan. At the end of the run, you must strike a bargain with the driver to take you to the summit, 110 km from Malatya. He must wait and bring you down to the village again. As the day will be mostly gone by the time you arrive in the village, you will have to spend the night in one of the village homes. The next morning you can catch a minibus back to Malatya.

It is possible to ascend from Malatya and descend via Kâhta. Hike across the

summit with your baggage to the car park and café building and ask around for a minibus with an empty seat; or hitch a ride with a tourist going down to Kâhta.

Places to Stay

You must be particularly wary of noise in this town. The last night I stayed here (a week night), heavy traffic along the main street did not abate until 2 am, and started up again in earnest at 5 am. I got less than four hours' sleep.

Places to Stay – bottom end

Several small, simple and very inexpensive places are just east of the PTT in the centre. The *Mercan Palas Oteli* (tel 11570), PTT Caddesi 14, is typical of these, charging US$3 per person for bathless rooms. Next door to the Mercan Palas are the *Merkez* and the *Çiçek Palas*. Though these places lack the comforts of the more expensive hotels, they are quiet, which is difficult to find in this active town.

Places to Stay – middle

The two best hotels in town are just to the east of the Vilayet. The one-star, 35-room *Hotel Sinan* (tel 12907, 13007), Atatürk Caddesi 16, has eight floors, a lift, restaurant and bar and car park, and charges US$20 to US$28 a single, US$25 to US$32 a double. The more expensive rooms have private baths and more amenities. Being right on the main street, the front rooms suffer from noise.

A bit farther east, up the hill on the opposite side of the main street, is the one-star, 50-room *Kent Otel* (tel 12175, 12813), Atatürk Caddesi 151. Prices and services are similar to those at the Hotel Sinan.

If these two hotels are full, the clerks may suggest the *Hotel Çınar*, across the road from the Hotel Sinan. While OK in some regards – friendly staff and well-used rooms renting for US$8 a double with washbasin, or US$10 a double with private shower – it suffers badly from the street noise.

Places to Eat

Besides the top two hotels, try the *Restaurant Melita* next door to the Hotel Sinan on the upper floor. Clean, bright and cheerful, with attentive and experienced waiting service, it is still surprisingly moderate in price, charging about US$4 to US$6 for a full dinner.

The main street holds much cheaper kebapçıs, such as the *Çınar* on the main street between the Sinan and Kent hotels, where a meal need cost only US$2 or even less.

Getting There & Away

There are many people interested in buying, selling, trading, growing and eating apricots, so Malatya is served by air, rail and bus.

Air Turkish Airlines (tel 11922, 14053), Kanalboyu Caddesi 10, Ordu Evi Karşısı, has flights serving Malatya's Erhaç Airport to and from İstanbul and Ankara on Tuesday, Thursday, Saturday and Sunday. The airport bus costs US$0.75 and leaves the Turkish Airlines office 90 minutes before flight departure time.

Bus Service includes frequent daily trips to these destinations:

Adana – 425 km, eight hours, US$6.75; a few buses daily
Adıyaman – 221 km, three hours, US$3.50; frequent buses daily
Ankara – 685 km, 11 hours, US$10; frequent buses daily
Diyarbakır – 260 km, 4 hours, US$4; frequent buses daily
Kayseri – 360 km, six hours, US$6; several buses daily
Sivas – 235 km, five hours, US$6; several buses daily

Train Malatya's İstasyon can be reached by a dolmuş or a city bus of that name.

The city is served daily by express train from İstanbul (Haydarpaşa) and Ankara via Kayseri and Sivas. On some days it's the Vangölü Ekspresi; on other days it's the Güney Ekspresi, heading eastward for Diyarbakır and Kurtalan.

Malatya and Adana are connected by daily express trains in each direction. From Malatya, departure is at 9.20 am, arriving in Adana at 6.12 pm.

SİVAS

The highway comes through Sivas, the railway comes through Sivas, and over the centuries the dozens of invading armies have come through Sivas (SEE-vahss, population 200,000, altitude 1285 metres), often leaving the town in ruins when they left. It started life, so far as we know, in Roman times under the name Megalopolis and later changed to Sebastea which the Turks shortened to Sivas. Today it is a fairly modern and unexciting place which is full of farmers, yet at its centre are a few of the finest Seljuk Turkish buildings ever erected. And outside Sivas, deep in the countryside, is a Seljuk masterpiece hidden among the hills.

History

In recent times Sivas gained fame as the location for the Sivas Congress, which opened on 4 September 1919. Atatürk came here from Samsun and Amasya, seeking to consolidate the Turkish resistance to Allied occupation and partition of the country. He gathered as many delegates from as many parts of the country as possible, and confirmed decisions which had been made at a congress held earlier in Erzurum. These two congresses were the first breath of the revolution and heralded the War of Independence.

Orientation

The centre of town is Konak Meydanı; near it are most of Sivas' important sights, hotels and the Tourism Information

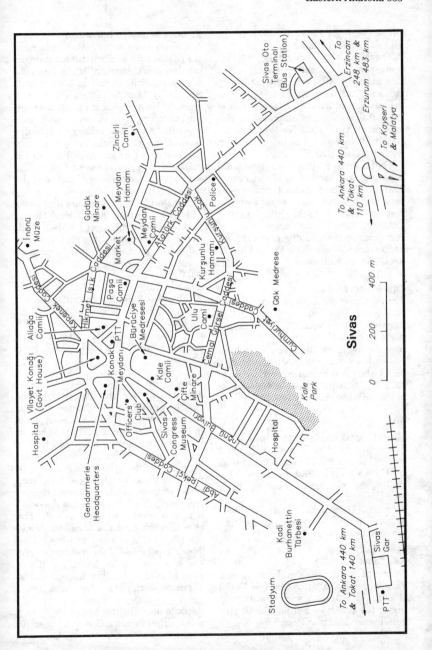

Sivas

Office (tel (477) 13535 or 13506) in the Vilayet Konağı building.

The railway station (Sivas Gar) is 1½ km south-west of Konak Meydanı along İnönü Bulvarı. After you arrive in Sivas by rail, walk out the station's front door to the bus stop on the station (south) side of İnönü Bulvarı. Any bus running along this major road will trundle you to or from the station. If in doubt, just ask the driver, 'Konak?' (koh-NAHK).

The bus terminal (Sivas Oto Terminalı) is several km south-east of the centre. Transport to and from the terminal is by taxi, with a ride to Konak Meydanı costing US$2, less to the cheap hotels.

All of the sights except one are conveniently grouped in a pleasant park at Konak Meydanı; the other building to see is a short walk away.

Çifte Minare Medrese

The Seminary of the Twin Minarets has, as its name explains, a pair (çift) of minarets. Along with its grand Seljuk portal, that's about all it has, as the medrese building itself has long been ruined. It was commissioned by the Mongol vizier who ruled here and was finished in 1271. It is among the greatest monuments of the Seljuk architectural style.

Şifaiye Medresesi

Directly opposite the Çifte Minare is the Şifaiye Medresesi, or Darüşşifa, a hospital medical school built in the same year as the Çifte Minare by Sultan Keykavus I of the Seljuks, who chose to be buried here. His tomb is just to the right of the entrance. Inside, the court has four *eyvans*, or niche-like rooms; note the remnants of tilework.

Kale Camii

Near the Çifte Minare, back toward Konak Meydanı a bit, is the Kale Camii (1580), an Ottoman work constructed under the orders of Sultan Murad III's grand vizier Mahmut Paşa.

Bürüciye Medresesi & Museum

A few steps east of the Kale Camii, near the gazebo with an ablutions fountain up top and a WC beneath, is the Bürüciye Medresesi, built in 1271 (a busy year in Sivas!) by Muzaffer Bürücirdi, who is entombed in it (inside, to the left, with the fine tilework). It now serves as Sivas' museum. As of this writing, it is under renovation, with sacks of cement and stacks of tools here and there. If the door is unlocked, you should have a look inside, as this is the best preserved building of the three Seljuk works in the park.

The town's other sights are south-east of Konak Meydanı along Cemal Gürsel Caddesi and Cumhuriyet Caddesi. Walk to the southern end of the park and turn left (east) onto Cemal Gürsel Caddesi.

Ulu Cami

The Ulu Cami, or Great Mosque (1197) is Sivas' oldest building of significance. It's a large, low room with a forest of 50 columns. The brick minaret was added later. Though it's not as grand as the more imposing Seljuk buildings, it does have charm.

Gök Medrese

Just east of the Ulu Cami, turn right (south) on Cumhuriyet Caddesi to reach the Gök Medrese, or Blue Seminary, built in that bumper year of 1271 at the behest of Sahip Ata, the same fellow who funded the Sahip Ata mosque complex in Konya. Although built to the traditional Seljuk medrese plan, in this one the fancy embellishments of tiles, brickwork designs and carving are not just on the doorway, but on windows and walls as well. The blue tilework gave the school its name, *gök* (sky) being an old Turkish word for 'blue'. The facade of the building is wild and exuberant in its decoration. If you want to take a photograph, come in the afternoon when the shadows have gone.

Places to Stay – bottom end

Sivas suffers from a lack of tourists, so its

hotels are not kept up to visitor standards. There are no hotels near the bus or railway stations.

The cheaper hotels are a bit farther from Konak Meydanı, at the junction of Atatürk Caddesi and Kurşunlu Sokak.

At the junction, facing Atatürk Caddesi, is the tidy *Otel Evin* (tel 12301), Atatürk Caddesi 160, offering rooms with and without a washbasin for US$5/7 a single/double. Around the corner on Kurşunlu Sokak is the very similar *Otel Yuvam* (tel 13340), which may be slightly quieter.

If both of these places are full, try the much larger *Otel Çiçek* (tel 14081, 15667), farther east on Atatürk Caddesi. Its facilities are well worn and very plain, but many of its rooms are quiet and cost only US$6/8 a single/double, with a washbasin.

The *Otel Sultan* (tel 12986), Eski Belediye Sokak 18, has 30 double rooms which are sombre and basic, a lift and solar-heated water. When I stayed, the sun must not have shone on the heater (though it certainly shined on me), as the water was always cold. Prices are US$16 for a double with a shower or US$12 without, while singles cost US$10 with a bath or US$8 without.

Places to Stay - middle

The two-star *Otel Köşk* (KURSHK) (tel 11150), Atatürk Caddesi 11, one short block east of Konak Meydanı, has a restaurant, a lift and 44 double rooms with bath priced from US$35 to US$40. Singles cost from US$25 to US$28. A buffet breakfast is included.

Competing with the Köşk for the carriage trade (such as it is) is the 33-room *Otel Madımak* (tel 12489), around the corner at Eski Belediye Sokak 4. The lobby and restaurant are bright and fancy and may actually rate the two stars the hotel has been awarded, but the rooms tend to be much plainer and only functional. Rooms cost from US$20 to US$25 a single and US$30 a double.

Places to Eat

The top two hotels, as is usual in these little-touristed towns, have the two best restaurants, but for general eating purposes, including breakfast and sweets, try the *Hacı Kasımoğulları Baklava ve Kebap Salonu* at Atatürk Caddesi 17, very near the Otel Köşk, where a simple breakfast of yoghurt and tea costs US$1 or less. Lunches and dinners of kebap, with some of their own baklava afterwards, cost US$3 or US$4.

Getting There & Away

As it's on Turkey's main east-west highway and is also a transit point from north to south, Sivas is well served by air, rail and bus.

Air Turkish Airlines (tel 11147, 13687), Belediye Sitesi, H Blok No 7, has flights on Tuesday and Sunday to and from Ankara and İstanbul. The route is İstanbul to Ankara (change planes), then to Sivas, continuing to Malatya and vice versa. An airport bus (US$0.75) to Sivas Airport leaves the Turkish Airlines office 105 minutes before flight departure.

Bus The modern Sivas Oto Terminalı has its own PTT branch, a restaurant and pastry shop, a shoeshine stand and an *emanetçi* (eh-mah-NEHT-chee, baggage check room).

Bus traffic is intense in all directions, though many of the buses are passing through, so it's impossible to know what seats are available until a bus arrives. Here's an idea of the schedules:

Amasya – 225 km, four hours, US$4; several buses daily
Ankara – 450 km, eight hours, US$6.50; frequent buses daily
Divriği – 175 km, 3½-hours, US$4; several buses daily
Diyarbakır – 500 km, nine or 10 hours, US$8; several buses daily
Erzurum – 485 km, nine hours, US$9; several buses daily

Kayseri – 195 km, 3½ hours, US$3; hourly buses

Malatya – 235 km, five hours, US$6; several buses daily

Tokat – 105 km, two hours, US$2; frequent buses daily

Train Sivas is a main rail junction for both east-west and north-south lines. The fastest and most comfortable train is the Erzurum Mavi Tren, departing Ankara each evening at 9 pm, stopping at Kayseri, Sivas and Erzincan before rolling into Erzurum.

Otherwise, the two main east-west expresses, the Doğu Ekspresi and the Güney/Vangölü Ekspresi, pull through Sivas daily.

DİVRİĞİ

South-east of Sivas, 175 km over recently improved roads and on the rail line, lies Divriği (DEEV-ree, population 20,000), a town hidden beyond a mountain pass 1970 metres high in a fertile valley. It is visited by few tourists, foreign or Turkish. Above the town, a ruined castle stands guard over two magnificent Seljuk buildings, the Ulu Cami or Great Mosque and the Darüşşifa or hospital. Both were built in 1228 by the local emir Ahmet Şah and his wife, the lady Fatma Turan Melik. Beautifully restored and preserved, they sit, far from anywhere, and are a wonderful work of art hidden in the boondocks.

Divriği has a few very basic lodging places, some simple restaurants and banks for changing money.

Ulu Cami

Both of Divriği's architectural treasures are actually part of the same grand structure. Say 'Ulu Cami' (OO-loo jah-mee) to anyone in town, and they'll point the way up the hill to the complex.

The portal of the Ulu Cami is simply incredible, with geometric patterns, medallions, luxuriant stone foliage and intricate Arabic-letter inscriptions in a richness that is simply astonishing. It is the sort of doorway which only a provincial emir, with more money than restraint, would ever conceive of building. In a large Seljuk city, this sort of extravagance would have been ridiculed as lacking in taste. In Divriği, it's the wonderful, fanciful whim of a petty potentate shaped in stone.

The portal is most of what there is to see. Seljuk buildings were traditionally plain outside, other than the portals. Past a side door on the south wall, to the south-east, is the door to the Darüşşifa.

Darüşşifa

Adjoining the Ulu Cami is the hospital, plainer and simpler except for its requisite elaborate portal. The octagonal pool in the court has a spiral run-off, similar to the one in Konya's Karatay Medresesi, which allowed the soothing tinkle of running water to break the silence of the room.

Seljuk Tombs

As this was once an important provincial capital, you will notice several hexagonal or octagonal drum-like structures throughout the town. These are the traditional *kümbet* or Seljuk tombs. Ahmet Şah's tomb is near the Ulu Cami, as are several earlier ones from 1196 and another dating from 1240.

A Walk About Town

Divriği is a nice, old-fashioned Turkish mountain town based on agriculture. Its narrow streets are laced with grapevines and paved in stone blocks and its houses are still uncrowded by modern construction. It's a pleasant enough place to spend a few hours, which you may have to do if you come by bus or rail.

Places to Stay

Even those travellers on the lowest budget will have to make hard decisions once they look at the hotels in Divriği. But at least there are hotels and, as more tourists come, these will no doubt improve.

The *Otel Ninni* (tel 1239) charges US$5 for a double room without water; the common shower and toilet are down one floor from some of the rooms. The *Hotel Değer* next door is even more basic. Both hotels are on the main commercial street in the centre of town.

Getting There & Away

Road With your own car, you can drive in and out; there is no road onward toward Erzincan. In spring, late autumn and winter, the road may be slippery, washed out, difficult or snowed over.

Bus Three or four buses run between Divriği and Sivas daily, continuing to Ankara and İstanbul. The trip between Sivas and Divriği takes about 3½ hours and costs US$4. Divriği's bus station is on the highway south-west of the village.

Coming from Malatya, you can take a bus as far as Kangal, near the turning for Divriği, and wait for the Divriği bus to stop on its way through.

Train The rail line from Sivas to Erzurum passes through Divriği. Check the schedules, allow for late arrival of trains in Sivas, and you may be able to catch a train to get you to Divriği conveniently. However, buses are faster and more frequent.

You can continue eastward by train from Divriği to Erzurum, about 6½ hours away, though you may have to stay overnight in Divriği and catch a train the next day.

The Divriği railway station is about two km south of the Ulu Cami.

TOKAT

From Sivas, go west to Yıldızeli, then north into the Çamlıbel Dağları mountain range, up over Çamlıbel Geçidi (Çamlıbel Pass, 2038 metres), down again, then up to

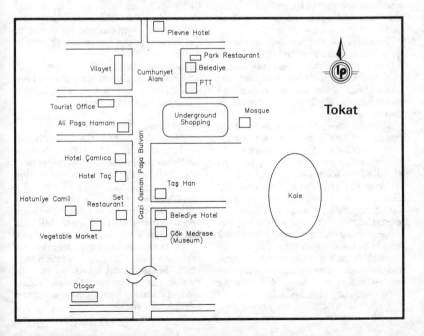

Kızıliniş Pass (1150 metres) before going down into Tokat. Along the way, you leave the dry red soil of the Anatolian Plateau and enter the lushness of the Black Sea littoral.

Tokat (TOH-kaht, population 105,000, altitude 623 metres) is on the southern edges of the Black Sea region and shares in its fertility. It's one of those towns that is half Ottoman and half modern.

History

Its history is very deep and long, starting in 3000 BC and proceeding through the sovereignty of 14 various states, including the Hittites and Phrygians, the Medes and the Persians, the empire of Alexander the Great, the kingdom of Pontus, the Romans, the Byzantines, the Turkish principality of Danismend, the Seljuks and the Mongol Ilkhanids.

Tokatlıs are proud that it was near their town that Julius Caesar said *Veni, vidi, vici* (I came, I saw, I conquered) in 47 BC after having defeated Pharnaces II, King of Pontus, in a quick and easy four-hour battle.

By the time of the Seljuk Sultanate of Rum, Tokat was the sixth largest city in Anatolia and on important trade routes. The roads approaching the city are littered with great Seljuk bridges and caravanserais testifying to its earlier importance.

After the Mongols rushed in and blew away everyone's composure in the mid-1200s, their Ilkhanid successors took over, followed by a succession of petty warlords who did little for Tokat.

Under the Ottomans, who took the town in 1402, it resumed its role as an important trading entrepôt, agricultural town (the grapes are especially good) and copper mining centre (the copper artisans have been famous for centuries).

Tokat doesn't get too many tourists, and those who come usually have a quick look at the famous Gök Medrese, the town's museum, then leave.

Orientation

The town centre is the big open square named Cumhuriyet Alanı, where you will find the Vilayet, the Belediye, the PTT and the coyly named Turist Otel. A new sunken shopping centre has added lots of retail space without ruining the spaciousness of the square. Across the main street from the shopping centre is the Tarihi Ali Paşa Hamamı, an old Turkish bath that's a fantasy of domes studded with bulbous glass to let sunlight in.

Looming above the town is a rocky promontory crowned by the obligatory ancient fortress. At its foot is clustered the bazaar and the town's old Ottoman-style houses.

The main street, Gazi Osman Paşa Bulvarı, runs downhill past the Gök Medrese to a traffic roundabout near which is the otogar, two km from the main square.

From Tokat, roads lead westward to Amasya and Samsun (see the Black Sea Coast chapter) and to Yozgat and Boğazkale in Central Anatolia. Resuming the eastern tour, though, takes you to Şanlıurfa near the Syrian border.

Information

The Provincial Government maintains a small Tourist Office (tel (475) 15499); follow the signs in the main square.

Gök Medrese

The Blue Seminary is the first thing to see. It was constructed in 1275 by Pervane Muhineddin Süleyman, a local potentate, after the fall of the Seljuks and the coming of the Mongols. Although once used as a hospital, it's now the town museum, next to the Taş Han and the Belediye hotels several hundred metres down the hill from Cumhuriyet Alanı.

The museum is open from 8.30 am to 5 pm each day except Monday; admission is US$1. Some exhibit labels are in both English and Turkish, though young students learning English may be on hand to guide you around.

Gök (sky) is also a name for blue, and it is the building's blue tiles which occasioned the name. Very few are left on the facade, which is now well below street level, but there are enough tiles on the interior walls to give an idea of what it must have looked like in its glory.

Museum exhibits include Stone Age and Bronze Age artefacts from excavations at Maşat Höyük, relics from Tokat's churches (before WW I there were good-sized Armenian and Greek communities here), tools and weapons, Korans and Islamic calligraphy and an excellent display of costume. Also, an ethnographic section has examples of local kilims and Tokat's famous *yazma* art of wood-block printing on gauze scarves.

One corner of the museum is dedicated to Gazi Osman Paşa, a boy from Tokat who made good as an Ottoman general. After commanding with distinction in the Crimean War, Gazi Osman Paşa led the heroic but doomed 1877 defence of Plevne (in Bulgaria) against a Russian force twice the size of the Ottoman's.

Other Sights

A few steps from the Gök Medrese, on the other side of the Belediye Hotel, is the **Taş Han**, an Ottoman caravanserai and workshop building which is still in use.

Several hundred metres down the hill from the Gök Medrese, on the same side of the street, is the **Sümbül Baba Türbesi**, A Seljuk-style tomb dating from 1292. Beside it is a road up to the kale, of which little remains but the fine view.

Behind the Taş Han are bazaar streets lined with old half-timbered Ottoman houses, including several of the best examples of Tokat's Ottoman mansions which have been beautifully restored and opened as museums. Note especially the **Madımağın Celal'ın Evi** or House of Madımak Cemal, and the **Latifoğlu Konağı** or Latifoğlu Mansion.

Across Gazi Osman Paşa Bulvarı from the Taş Han, in the fruit and vegetable market, stands the **Hatuniye Camii** and its

medrese, dating from the reign of Sultan Beyazıt II (1485). You may run across several other old hans and a covered market.

The bazaar's shops have lots of copperware, yazma printed scarves and local kilims and carpets, some of which have Afghan designs because of the many Afghan refugees who settled here during the Russian invasion of that country.

Places to Stay

Tokat does not have many hotels and most are simple, though a new two or three-star hotel should soon be finished.

Among the cheapest places is the old *Belediye Hotel* (tel 16327), Gazi Osman Paşa Bulvarı, which charges US$6 for a double room with a bathroom, but only the washbasin has water! Rooms have two or three beds. Check the sheets for freshness!

Up the hill 100 metres is the 26-room *Hotel Çamlıca* (tel 11269), Gazi Osman Paşa Bulvarı 85, which although simple, is bright, clean and modern, with tidy private baths in the rooms and non-tourist prices of US$5 a single with a washbasin or US$7 with a shower and US$8 a double with a washbasin or US$12 with a shower. Get a back room if you need peace and quiet. The nearby *Hotel Taç* occupies the top two floors of an office building and charges slightly lower rates.

Facing the Vilayet building, just off Cumhuriyet Alanı, is the *Turist Otel* (tel 11610, 12049), Cumhuriyet Alanı, Tokat's first very simple entry into the tourist lodging sweepstakes. Actually, it's not as bad as it looks from the outside, as the rooms with private showers are neat, clean and serviceable, and the cosy lobby is decorated with bits of old sculpted stone and local woven and embroidered crafts. Rooms cost US$8/12 a single/double, with a shower.

The 16-room *Hotel Plevne* (tel 12207), Gazi Osman Paşa Bulvarı 83, rates one star in the official government list but offers about the same accommodation as the Turist Otel, at the same prices.

Camping Tokat has no organised camping grounds, but you can camp at several recreation areas nearby, including Gümenek (the ancient town of Comana, nine km east); Almus, on the shores of the lake, 35 km east; Niksar Ayvaz hot springs and Çamiçi forest, 53 km north-east.

Places to Eat
The *Set Restaurant* across the street from the Taş Han and the Belediye Hotel is a simple split-level place with ready food, döner kebap and a selection of grilled meats. Meals for US$2 are easy to get, though you can spend a bit more. Behind the Set, in the fruit and vegetable market near the Hatuniye Camii, are little köfte and kebap shops with even lower prices.

Across the street, the *Belediye Lokantası*, on the ground floor of the Belediye Hotel, is fancier than the hotel and is the chosen place for local potentates coming to chat, sip and munch in the evening. Expect to spend about US$3 or US$4.

The Turist Otel has a dining room with decent food and service and is the place to meet other travellers.

The most pleasant place in town is the *Park Restaurant*, to the left of the Belediye on the main square. True to its name, dining tables here are set on terraces amidst evergreens and cooled (in spirit at least) by a tinkling fountain and pool. Come here for a meal or just a relaxing glass of çay. It costs from US$4 to US$6 for a good feed.

Getting There & Away
Bus Tokat's modern little otogar is not as

busy as some, but it still manages to get you where you want to go pretty easily. Buses run between the otogar and Cumhuriyet Alanı, but these are infrequent and you may find yourself hiring a taxi for less than US$2 for the ride into town. Destinations from Tokat include:

Amasya – 120 km, under two hours, US$1.50; frequent buses daily

Ankara – 440 km, eight hours, US$7; frequent buses daily

İstanbul – 800 km, 14 hours, US$10; several buses daily

Samsun – 245 km, 4½ hours, US$3; frequent buses daily

Sivas – 105 km, two hours, US$2; frequent buses daily

Yozgat – 240 km, 4½ hours, US$3; hourly buses south to Yıldızeli, then hourly buses west to Yozgat

ŞANLIURFA

Dry, dusty and hot – this is the way Şanlıurfa (population 207,000, altitude 540 metres) appears at first glance. You may think, 'What importance could such a town in the middle of nowhere possibly have?' When you get to know Urfa (as it's commonly called), you'll find that it's known for a shady park with several pools and great religious significance, a richness of agricultural produce, a cool and inviting labyrinthine bazaar, and its great historical importance.

Urfa is the Ottoman Empire come alive. In the shadow of a mighty mediaeval fortress, saintly old men toss chickpeas into a pool full of sacred carp or gather at a cave said to be the birthplace of Abraham. In the cool darkness of the covered bazaar, shopkeepers sit on low platforms in front of their stores, as was the custom in Ottoman times. The chatter of Turkish is joined by a babble of Kurdish and Arabic, with the occasional bit of English, French or German.

Urfa's character is in for a change in the 1990s when the South-east Anatolia Project (GAP) comes on line, bringing irrigation waters to large arid regions and generating enormous amounts of hydro-electricity for industry. Parched valleys will become fish-filled lakes and dusty villages will become booming market towns, factory cities or lakeside resorts. One element in the project is the Urfa Irrigation Tunnel which, at 26 km, will be the longest in the world.

You must spend at least one night in Urfa and a full day, or at least a morning, to see the sights and get lost in the bazaar. You may also want to make an excursion south to Harran, the Biblical town of beehive houses near the Syrian frontier.

History

The mysterious laws of geography ruled that this dusty spot would be where great empires clashed again and again over the centuries. Far from Cairo, Tehran and Constantinople, Urfa was nevertheless where the armies, directed from those distant capitals, would often meet. Urfa's history, then, is one of wreckage.

Urfa has been sizzling in the sun for a long time. It is thought that more than 3500 years ago there was a fortress on the hill where the kale now stands. Called Hurri (cave) by the Babylonians, the people built a powerful state by military conquest simply because they knew what a chariot was and how to use it in battle (few of their neighbours had heard of the chariot). But the Hittites finally got the better of the Hurrites, despite the latter's alliance with the pharaohs of Egypt. Around 1370 BC, the Hittites took over. After the fall of Hattuşaş, Urfa came under the domination of Carchemish.

The alliance with Egypt produced an interesting cultural exchange. After Amenhotep IV (Akhenaton) popularised worship of the sun as the unique and only god, a similar worship of Shemesh (the sun) was taken up here. Sun-worship (one would think it might be shade worship instead!) was not just a religious belief, but a political posture. It defied the cultural, political and religious influence of the nearby Hittites, by adopting the customs of the Egyptians, who were a safe distance away.

After a period of Assyrian rule, Alexander the Great came through. He and his Macedonian mates named the town Edessa, after a former capital of Macedonia, and it remained the capital of a Seleucid Province until 132 BC when the local Aramaean population set up an independent kingdom and renamed the town Orhai. Though Orhai maintained a precarious independence for four centuries, bowing only slightly to the Armenians and Parthians, it finally succumbed to the Romans, as did everyone hereabouts. The Romans did not get it easily, however. Emperor Valerian was badly defeated here in 260 AD and subsequent Roman rulers had a hard time over the centuries keeping the Persians out.

Edessa pursued its contrary history (witness the sun-worship) by adopting Christianity at a very early time (about 200 AD), before it became the official religion of the conquerors. The religion was so new that for Edessan Christians the liturgical language was Aramaic, the language of Jesus and not the Greek on which the church's greatness was built. Edessa, having pursued Christianity on its own from earliest times, had its own patriarch. It revelled in the Nestorian monophysite heresies as yet another way to thumb its nose at its faraway rulers, whose armies so often trooped through and flattened everything.

Edessa was at the outer edge of the Roman Empire near the frontier with Persia, and as the two great empires clashed, Edessa was shuttled back and forth from one to the other, as in a tug-of-war. In 533 AD the two empires signed a Treaty of Endless Peace which lasted seven years. The Romans and Persians kept at it until the Arabs swept in and cleared them all out in 637 AD. Edessa enjoyed three centuries of blissful peace under the Arabs, after which everything went to blazes again.

Turks, Arabs, Armenians and Byzantines battled for Edessa from 944 until 1098, when the First Crusade under Count Baldwin of Boulogne arrived to set up the Latin County of Edessa. This odd European feudal state lasted until 1144 when it was conquered by a Seljuk Turkish emir. The 'loss' of Edessa infuriated the Pope, who called for the Second Crusade, which never set foot near Edessa and accomplished little except to discredit itself. But the Latin county made its mark in history by giving Europeans a look at Eastern architecture and some of what they saw turned up later in the Gothic style.

The Seljuk Turkish emir, from the Zengi family, was succeeded by Saladin, then by the Mamelukes. The Ottomans under Selim the Grim conquered most of this region in the early 1500s, but Edessa did not become Urfa until 1637 when the Ottomans finally took over.

As for its modern sobriquet, Urfa became Şanlıurfa (Glorious Urfa) a little more than a decade ago. Even since the War of Independence, when Heroic Antep was given its special name, the good citizens of Urfa have been chafing under a relative loss of dignity. Now that their city is 'Glorious', the inhabitants can look the citizens of 'Heroic' Antep straight in the eye.

Orientation

Except in the bazaar, it is fairly easy to find your way around Urfa. You will see the kale to the right (south) as you enter the town along the highway from Gaziantep. The otogar is next to the highway by a stream bed which is usually dry. Most of the time you must take a taxi to the centre, which will cost less than US$1. Ask to go to the Belediye in order to reach most hotels and the Tourism Information Office , or to Dergâh (dehr-GYAH), also called Gölbaşı (GURL-bah-shuh), for the mosques, pools and bazaar. The latter is 1½ km from the otogar.

Once in town from the otogar, you

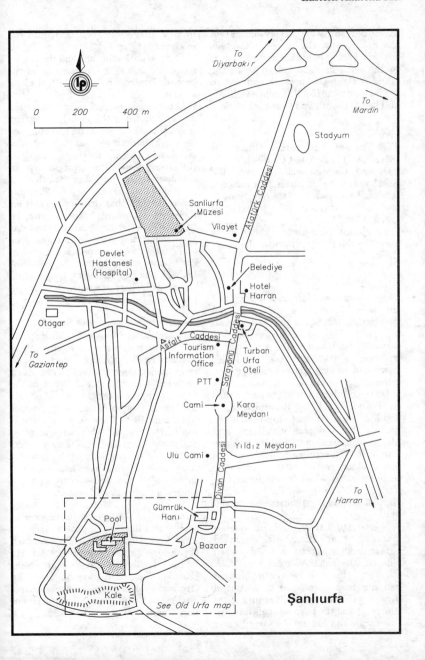

Şanlıurfa

should be able to walk to everything. From the Belediye, at the centre of the new town, it is about half a km north and west to the museum, one km south to the Gümrük Hanı, 1½ km south and west to the pool with the fish (Dergâh or Gölbaşı) and two km south and west to the kale.

Information

The Tourism Information Office (tel (8711) 2467) is at Asfalt Caddesi 3/B, off Sarayönü Caddesi, not far from the Belediye and the top hotels. In summer, it tends to be open most of the day, Sunday too, though there may be a break for lunch.

Except for the museum, Urfa's sights are in the oldest part of town, at the foot of the kale.

Gölbaşı

This is the area which includes the pools of the sacred carp, the Rızvaniye and Abdurrahman mosques and the surrounding park. The name means 'at the lakeside', and while the pools hardly constitute a lake, it is easy for Urfa's citizens to amplify the size of these cool, refreshing places in their minds.

On the northern side of the pool, called the Balıklı Göl, is the Rızvaniye Camii and Medresesi. At the western end of the pool is the Abdurrahman Camii and Medresesi, also called the Halil ur-Rahman Camii, a 17th-century building with a much older (early 1200s) Arab-style square minaret which looks suspiciously like a church's bell tower. You may walk in and look around the Abdurrahman as you like.

Legend had it that Abraham, who is a great prophet in Islamic belief, was in old Urfa destroying pagan gods one day when Nimrod, the local Assyrian king, took offence at this rash behaviour. Nimrod had Abraham immolated on a funeral pyre, but God turned the fire into water (the pool) and the burning coals into fish (the carp). You can sip the sacred water

from a subterranean spring within the mosque.

The two pools, this one and the nearby Ayn-i Zeliha, are fed by a spring at the base of Damlacık hill, on which the kale is built.

Local legend-makers have had a field day with the fish in the pool, deciding that they are sacred to Abraham and must not be caught lest the catcher go blind. You can buy food for the fish from vendors at the poolside, even though signs say: 'In the interests of the fishes' health, it is requested that they not be fed.' The signs ignore the fact that people will do it for their own enjoyment, not to nourish the fish. Instead of feeding the fish, take a seat and a shady table in one of the tea gardens and have a cool drink or bracing glass of çay to ward off the heat of the day. (Hot tea will make you perspire, thus cooling you down.) There are restaurants in the park (see Places to Eat).

Dergâh

This area, to the south-east of the pools and the park, has several mosques. The Mevlid-i Halil Camii holds the tomb of a saint named Dede Osman, a cave which harbours a hair from the Beard of the Prophet and another cave called Hz İbrahim'in Doğum Mağarası or Prophet Abraham's Birth Cave, in which, legend has it, the Prophet Abraham was born. You can visit any and all of these wonders for free, but do so quietly and decorously. Abraham's birth cave has separate entrances for men and women, as it is a place of pilgrimage and prayer.

A new, large, Ottoman-style mosque stands to the west of the birth cave to supplement the smaller prayer places.

Next door to the birth cave is a complex of mosques and medreses called Hz İbrahim Halilullah (Prophet Abraham, Friend of God), built and rebuilt over the centuries as an active place of pilgrimage. To the east, on Göl Caddesi, is the Hasan Paşa Camii, an Ottoman work.

Top: İshan Paşa Palace, Doğubeyazıt
Bottom: Nomad's tent, Doğubeyazıt

Top: Jumbled headstones atop Nemrut Dağı (Mt Nimrod)
Bottom: Mosque inscription, Antalya

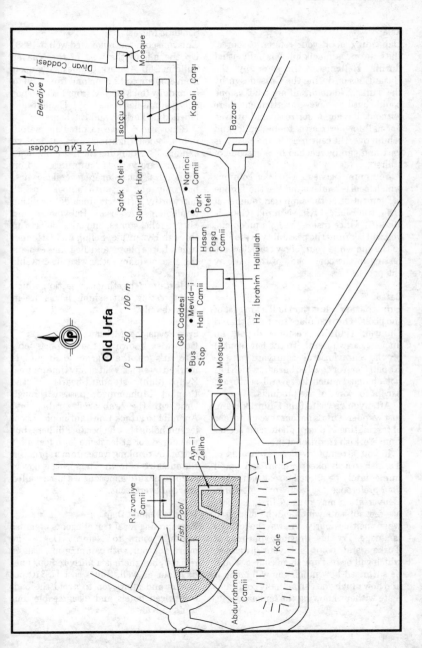

Old Urfa

0   50   100 m

Divan Caddesi

To
Belediye

12 Eylül Caddesi

İsotçu Cad

Mosque

Kapalı Çarşı

Bazaar

Şafak Oteli

Gümrük Hanı

Narinci Camii

Park Oteli

Hasan Paşa Camii

Hz İbrahim Halilullah

Göl Caddesi

Bus Stop

Mevlid-i Halil Camii

New Mosque

Ayn-i Zeliha

Rızvaniye Camii

Fish Pool

Abdurrahman Camii

Kale

Kale

Depending upon your reference source, the kale on Damlacık hill was built either during Hellenistic times or by the Byzantines or during the Crusades or by the Turks. No doubt all are true, as one could hardly have a settlement here without having a fortress, and it was normal for fortresses to be built and rebuilt over the centuries. In any case, it is vast and can be reached by a cascade of stairs.

You enter between a pair of columns which local legend has dubbed the Throne of Nemrut after the supposed founder of Urfa, the Biblical King Nimrod (Genesis 10:8-10). Once inside the kale precincts, you will confront the possibility of broiling in the sun while your fellow travellers are resting in the cool shade of the park by the pools.

Bazaar

Urfa's bazaar is less than half a km east of the pools. The first place to visit is the old Gümrük Hanı or customs depot, an ancient caravanserai. To the left (south) of the caravanserai courtyard is the Kapalı Çarşı or covered bazaar, which has not changed much in several centuries, except for some of the products.

After you've visited the Gümrük Hanı, just wander. Urfa's bazaar reveals dozens of fascinating and very photogenic scenes from Turkish traditional life.

If you attempt even a few words of Turkish to a shopkeeper or artisan, you'll immediately be offered a seat and asked your preference: tea, coffee or a soft drink. Conversation may drag at first, as there are few subjects which can be discussed when neither party knows the other's language. Try this: drag out your map of Turkey and point out your itinerary, which will be in Turkish, of course. You'll be surprised how much you will enjoy it and how much you can actually communicate without knowing the language.

Şanlıurfa Müzesi

This museum was renovated well in 1988. Up the hill to the west of the Vilayet building, off Atatürk Caddesi, it's open from 8.30 am to 12 noon and from 1.30 to 5 pm daily (on Monday, from 1.30 to 5 pm only); admission costs US$1. Exhibits are labelled in Turkish and English.

Renovations have resulted in marble floors, good lighting and attractive exhibits. Surrounding the museum, in its gardens, are various sculptures, and on the porch as you enter are several mosaics, but only one is worth a look. Inside, noteworthy artefacts include neolithic implements, Assyrian, Babylonian and Hittite relief stones, and other objects up through Byzantine, Seljuk and Ottoman times. Large photos and diagrams explain the use of many otherwise inscrutable objects.

Upstairs is the ethnology section, which is interesting, but exhibit labels are in Turkish only.

Eyüp Peygamber Makamı

Otherwise known as the Prophet Job's Site, it's off the Harran road and is marked by signs. Visit at any time for free. Eyüp (Job), standard-bearer of the Prophet Muhammed, passed through Urfa with the Arab armies riding into Anatolia to attack Constantinople. Local legend holds that he became ill here, but was cured (or at least made to feel a bit better) by drinking water from a spring on the outskirts of town. The spring is now in a grotto next to a mosque within a walled grove of evergreens.

Tours to Nemrut Dağı

Enterprising local travel agents organise minibus tours to Nemrut Dağı. The overnight tour, with camping out, is more relaxed, but there is a fairly tedious one-day tour as well. Tours cost US$10 per person and allow you to avoid the bad, overpriced hotels and disagreeable tour touts in Kâhta.

Places to Stay - bottom end

Urfa has numerous inexpensive hotels and two relatively fancy places, grouped conveniently in two areas: the centre of the town and near Abraham's Cave. There are no lodgings in the vicinity of the bus station.

Two cheap hotels are next to the bazaar and Gölbaşı. The Şafak Oteli (tel 1157), Göl Caddesi 4, is the better, with rooms (no private baths) renting for US$3.50/6 a single/double. Haggle! The hotel faces the Gümrük Hanı across Göl Caddesi. Unfortunately, it also catches the full sun and can be oppressively hot. When it is, the manager (İbrahim) allows you to sleep in the cooler courtyard where there's a breeze.

Rooms at the Park Otel (tel 1095), Göl Caddesi 101, 100 metres to the west, are even plainer and without washbasins, but doubles are priced even cheaper.

Between Dergâh and the centre of town is the modern shopping district. Just off the main street here is the quietly located Otel İstiklal, Sarayönü Caddesi, Zincirli Kapı 4/E. It has a vine-shaded courtyard and a small terrace restaurant. Its cool, fairly quiet rooms and usually hot showers cost US$6 a double, without a private bath.

In the town centre near the Belediye, several cheap hotels face the expensive Turban Urfa Oteli. The Otel 11 Nisan (tel 1089), Sarayönü Caddesi 141, is a small, simple family place with bathless rooms renting for US$5.50 a double. Nearby on Sarayönü, the Hotel Güven (tel 1700) charges just a bit more for its bathless rooms.

Behind the Turban Urfa Oteli are several other cheap hotels at similar prices. The Hotel İpek Palas (tel 1546), Köprübaşı 4, has doubles for US$7 with a washbasin or for US$4.50/8.50 a single/double with a private shower. The proprietors are adding showers to more rooms and the prices will rise along with the comforts. Just around the corner is the Cumhuriyet Palas (tel 4828), Köprübaşı 6, which is similarly small and quiet, but lower in price.

Hotel Kapaklı (tel 5230, 2016), Sarayönü Caddesi near the corner with Asfalt Caddesi, is very near the Tourism Information Office and offers a choice of rooms with or without a bath and with or without air-con. The cheaper rooms have washbasins but not bathrooms and cost US$11 a double. The more expensive rooms have both private baths and evaporative air-cons and cost US$8/14 a single/double. Some rooms are quiet and some aren't. Keep this in mind when you inspect them.

Places to Stay - middle

Middle and top-end hotels may have evaporative air-cons in the guest rooms. These machines do cool the air, but are very noisy and the cooled air blows at gale force. They're a mixed blessing.

Urfa's best hotel is the three-star Hotel Harran (tel 4743, 2860), Atatürk Bulvarı, directly across from the Belediye. All 54 rooms have evaporative air-cons and private bathrooms, and some have TVs and refrigerators. The hotel also has a good terrace restaurant and a Turkish bath. This is a favourite place for Arab tourists and business travellers. Rooms cost US$35/50 a single/double, but discounts are available when they're not busy.

A few steps to the south (right) is the one-star Turban Urfa Oteli (tel 3520, 3521), with 53 basic but serviceable rooms, all with telephone, twin beds and a tiny private shower bath. Some of the guest rooms, as well as the lobby, restaurant and bar, are air-conditioned. Rooms cost US$28/38 a single/double. Prices include breakfast, dinner and air-con. The rooftop restaurant is pleasant, but some of the prices aren't. A 14% reduction is in order for rooms without air-con and for all rooms from October to May. The staff have a reputation for brusqueness.

Places to Eat

Urfa's culinary specialties include çiğ köfte (minced uncooked mutton), içli köfte (a deep-fried croquette with a mutton filling) and Urfa kebap (skewered chunks of lamb or ground lamb rissoles, broiled on charcoal and served with tomatoes, sliced onions and hot peppers). For a snack, try *künefe*, a sweet pastry with a cheese filling.

Places to Eat - bottom end

Inexpensive eateries are plentiful, and the richest concentration of them is near the Hotel İpek Palas and Cumhuriyet Palas on Köprübaşı Çarşısı. The *Güney Lokantası* (tel 2237) at 3/D is an example. Ceiling fans keep the hot air moving, refrigerated cases keep the drinks cold, its location keeps the noise at bay and the chef fills his steam table with various stews, vegetable dishes, pilavs and soups each day. A simple meal of tas kebap (mutton and vegetable stew), beans, bread and soft drink costs US$2. Similar restaurants are only a few steps away.

Perhaps the most pleasant place for an inexpensive meal is in the park at Göbaşı. The *Turistik Göl Gazinosu, Lokanta & Aile Çay Bahçesi* or Touristic Lake Club, Restaurant & Family Tea Garden, next to the Balıklı Göl, has a family dining area, a video cassette player and a prohibition against alcoholic beverages. I had domatesli kebap, köfte grilled with chunks of tomato and served with chopped scallions, grilled hot peppers and huge flaps of flat village bread. With a tankard of cool ayran, the cost was US$3. Tea costs US$0.20, Turkish coffee twice as much and soft drinks three times as much. The food is good, but what you're paying for is the pleasant location.

If you're in the market for picnic supplies, stop at the *Uğur Pide Fırını* on Göl Caddesi, where delicious flat pide bread comes fresh from the wood-fired oven throughout the day. A loaf costs US$0.35. The bakery's official address is Akarbaşı Çarşısı.

Places to Eat - middle

Urfa is one of those towns in which the best hotels also hold the best restaurants. There is general agreement that the terrace restaurant of the Hotel Harran is the best place to dine. Service is attentive and polite, the food is good, alcoholic beverages are served and the open-air terrace at the back of the hotel several floors up is very pleasant. All this comes at a price, however. A dinner of tavuk şiş (chicken brochettes), mixed salad, bread and beer costs about US$7 or US$8.

Getting There & Away

Although Urfa is supposedly served by rail, the station is at Akçakale on the Syrian frontier, 50 km south of the town. The nearest airport is at Diyarbakır. Therefore, Urfa is best reached by bus.

Bus The otogar has a restaurant and pastry shop and a left-luggage depot. As it is on the main highway serving the southeast, Urfa has plenty of bus traffic, but few buses start from here. Instead, most are passing through, so you must take whatever seats there are:

Adana – 365 km, six hours, US$4.75; several buses daily

Ankara – 850 km, 13 hours, US$10; several buses daily

Diyarbakır – 190 km, three hours, US$4; frequent buses daily

Erzurum – 665 km, 12 hours, US$14; a few buses daily

Gaziantep – 145 km, 2½ hours, US$3; frequent buses daily

İstanbul – 1290 km, 24 hours, US$20; a few buses daily

Kâhta (for Nemrut Dağı) – 375 km, four hours, US$6; a few buses daily to Adıyaman, change for Kâhta

Malatya – 395 km, seven hours, US$7.50; a few buses daily

Mardin – 175 km, three hours, US$4; several buses daily

Van – 585 km, 10 hours, US$10; a few buses daily

HARRAN

And Terah took Abram his son, and Lot the son of Haran his son's son, and Sarai his daughter in law, his son Abram's wife; and they went forth with them from Ur of the Chaldees, to go into the land of Canaan; and they came unto Harran, and dwelt there.

Genesis 11:31

So says the Bible about Harran's most famous resident, who stayed here for a few years back in 1900 BC. It seems certain that Harran, now officially called Altınbaşak, is one of the oldest continuously inhabited spots on earth. Now its ruined walls and Ulu Cami, its crumbling fortress and beehive houses give it a feeling of deep antiquity.

Harran's ancient monuments are interesting, though not really impressive. It is more the lifestyle of the residents that you may find fascinating. They live by farming and smuggling and now await expectantly the completion of the Atatürk Barajı (dam) which will bring water to the irrigation system under construction. Once the longed-for waters arrive, farming might actually become safer and more profitable than smuggling.

History

Besides Abraham's sojourn, Harran is famous as a centre of worship of Sin, god of the moon. Worship of the sun, moon and planets was popular hereabouts, in Harran and at neighbouring Sumatar, from about 800 BC until 830 AD, although Harran's temple to the moon god was destroyed by the Byzantine Emperor Theodosius in 382 AD. Battles between Arabs and Byzantines amused the townfolk until the coming of the Crusaders. The fortress, which some say was built on the ruins of the moon god's temple, was restored when the Frankish crusaders approached. The Crusaders won, and maintained the fortress for a while before they too moved on.

Things to See

Before even reaching the town you'll see the hill surrounded by crumbling walls and topped with ruined buildings. Besides the gates and city walls, the most impressive of the ruins, in which some good mosaics were found, is the **Ulu Cami**, built in the 8th century by Marwan II, last of the Umayyad caliphs. You'll recognise the square minaret (very un-Turkish) of the mosque.

On the far (east) side of the hill is the fortress, in the midst of the beehive houses. As soon as you arrive, children will run to you and crowd around, demanding coins, sweets, cigarettes, empty water bottles and ballpoint pens. Whether you pass out some of these treats or not, they'll continue their demands. Expect to have an escort as you tour the ruins.

Several of the residents are happy to welcome foreign visitors, have their photographs taken and show you their homes. A tip is not really expected, but a small gift would be in order, preferably something from your home country. If you take a photograph, send a copy to your hosts.

Getting There & Away

If you have your own car, you must go to Harran. Without a car, you must decide whether the three to four-hour 100-km return trip from Urfa should be done by taxi (US$25 or US$30 for the car and driver) or by minibus tour (US$3 to US$5 per person). If by minibus, be advised that there are several in town and that not all give good service. Ask other travellers who have just taken the tour, and see what they say. The minibus normally departs Urfa at 9.30 am, returning at 1.30 pm from Harran.

While Harran is now officially called Altınbaşak, you will see signs in both names. Leave Urfa by the Akçakale road at the south-east end of town and go 37 km to a turning left (east). From there, it's another 10 km to Harran. As you approach the site you come to a Jandarma post, across from which is a small restaurant, a camping ground and a souvenir shop.

There is no accommodation in Harran, though this will no doubt soon change.

MARDİN

About 175km east of Urfa and 100 km south of Diyarbakır is Mardin (mahr-DEEN, population 40,000, altitude 1325), an odd and very old town crowned with a castle and a set of immense radar domes, all overlooking the vast, roasted Syrian plains. There is a certain amount of smuggling trade with Syria (sheep for example, which are much more expensive in Syria than in Turkey) and Kurdish separatist activity, but other than that, Mardin sizzles and sleeps.

This town had a large Christian community and there are still a few Syriac Christian families and churches. On the outskirts is the monastery of Deyrul Zafaran in which Aramaic, the language of Jesus, is still used as the liturgical tongue.

Mardin is not particularly well equipped with hotels and restaurants and is perhaps best visited on a day-trip from Diyarbakır if you prize your comforts. Travelling on the cheap, it makes sense to take a bus from Urfa to Mardin, stay the night if you're in no hurry, then take a minibus north to Diyarbakır.

History

The history of Mardin, like that of Diyarbakır, involves disputes by rival armies over dozens and dozens of centuries, though now nobody cares. A castle has stood on this hill from time immemorial.

Assyrian Christians settled in this area during the 5th century. In the 6th century, Jacobus Baradeus, bishop of Edessa (Urfa), had a difference of opinion with the patriarch in Constantinople over the divine nature of Christ. The patriarch and official doctrine held that Christ had both a divine and a human nature. The bishop held that he had only one (mono) nature (physis), that being divine. The bishop was branded a Monophysite heretic and excommunicated. He promptly founded a church of his own, which came to be called the Jacobite (or Syrian Orthodox) after its founder.

At the same time and for the same reason, the Armenian Orthodox Church and the Coptic Church in Egypt were established as independent churches. In the case of the Jacobites, control from Constantinople was no longer a problem, as the Arabs swept in and took control soon afterwards. The Monophysites were also able to practice their religion as they chose under the tolerant and unconcerned rule of the Arabs.

The Arabs occupied Mardin between 640 and 1104. After that, it had a succession of Seljuk Turkish, Kurdish, Mongol and Persian overlords until the Ottomans under Sultan Selim the Grim took it in 1517.

Information & Orientation

There is no Tourism Information Office in Mardin because it has few tourists.

Perched on the hillslope, Mardin has one long main street, Birinci Caddesi, running for about two km from the Belediye Garajı at the western end of town through Cumhuriyet Meydanı, the main square, to Konak, a small square with the Hükümet Konağı and military buildings at the eastern end. Everything you'll need is along this street or just off it. City buses and intra-city dolmuşes run back and forth along the street. If you are driving your own car, leave it in the car park at Cumhuriyet Meydanı and walk to the hotels and things to see.

Sultan İsa Medresesi

Dating from 1385, this seminary is the town's prime attraction. Walk east from the main square to the Hotel Başak Palas, then left (north) up the stairs to a large and imposing doorway. The doorway is what you have come to see, as there is little to see inside; the ancient building is used in part as a private residence.

Mardin Müzesi

Set up in one courtyard of the Sultan İsa Medresesi, you can enter this museum (tel 1664) at the door with the flagpole and sign. You may have to shout for the watchman. The museum hours are from 8.30 am to 5.30 pm every day; admission is free. It holds bits of statuary, but you've really come to admire the building and the view across the vast plains towards Syria.

Kasım Paşa Medresesi

Built in the 1400s near the western end of town, below the main street, you'll have to ask for guidance to find this seminary.

Ulu Cami

This ancient mosque, built in the 11th century, is an Iraqi Seljuk structure. It's below (south of) the main street at Cumhuriyet Meydanı. As Mardin's history has been mostly one of warfare, the mosque has suffered considerably over the centuries, particularly in the Kurdish rebellion of 1832.

Deyrul Zafaran

In the rocky hills east of the town, six km along a good but narrow road, is the monastery of Mar Hanania, called Deyrul Zafaran. This means the Saffron Monastery in Arabic, a name which perhaps originated from the tawny colour of its stone walls. It was once the seat of the Syrian Orthodox patriarch. Though the patriarchate is now in Damascus, the monastery still has the modest trappings due to the patriarch and continues its charitable work of caring for orphans.

You can visit the monastery any day without prior arrangement. As there is no public transport, you must take a taxi from the town centre, which will cost about US$5. Haggle for a set price to include the return journey and about 45 minutes waiting time.

As you drive to the monastery, you will doubtless notice a hillside on which a motto has been written with white stones: 'Ne Mutlu Türküm Diyene' (What Joy to

Him Who Says, 'I am a Turk'). Atatürk originally uttered the phrase as part of his campaign to overcome the Turkish inferiority complex imposed by Europe and the United States. Here, though, it has a different significance, reiterating the government's commitment to the unity of the country against the efforts of Kurdish separatist groups.

Enter the walled enclosure through a portal bearing a Syriac inscription. An Orthodox priest will greet you and hand you over to one of the orphans for a guided tour.

First comes the underground chamber, an eerie place with a flat ceiling of huge, closely fitted stones held up by magic, without the aid of mortar. It is thought that this room may have been used ages ago by sun worshippers, who viewed their god rising through a window at the eastern end. A niche on the southern wall is said to have been for sacrifices.

The guide then leads you to the tombs of the patriarchs and metropolitans who have served here. The doors to the room are 300 years old.

In the chapel, to the left of the altar as you face it, is the patriarch's throne. It bears the names of all the patriarchs who have served since the monastery was founded in 792. To the right of the altar is the throne of the metropolitan. The present stone altar was carved to replace a wooden one which burnt about half a century ago. A candle started the fire. The chapel is fairly plain and simple, but the primitive art is wonderful, especially the carved furniture and paintings. Services use the original Aramaic.

The next rooms on the tour hold several litters used to transport the church dignitaries, and also one of several wells in the monastery. In a small side room is a 300-year-old wooden throne. The mosaic work in the floor is about 1500 years old.

A flight of stairs takes you up to the suite of guest rooms, which is very simple accommodation for travellers and those coming for meditation. The patriarch's suite, a small, simple bedroom and parlour, are here. On the walls of the parlour are pictures of the patriarch (who lives in Damascus) with Pope John Paul II. Another picture shows an earlier patriarch with Atatürk. As you leave the parlour, take a moment to enjoy the fine view of the mountains. Other monasteries, now in ruins, once stood farther up the slope. Some of the water for Deyrul Zafaran comes from near these ruins, through underground channels excavated many centuries ago.

At the end of the tour you may want to tip the guide. He'll refuse at first, but will probably accept when you offer a second or third time.

Places to Stay

All of Mardin's hotels are very basic and very cheap. Few are really pleasant.

East of Cumhuriyet Meydanı are several small, modest hotels, such as the *Yıldız Oteli* (tel 1096), Birinci Caddesi 391, where plain rooms without plumbing go for US$3/5 a single/double. The public showers have cold water only.

The *Hotel Bayraktar* (tel 1338, 1645) is on the main street facing Cumhuriyet Meydanı, with its other side overlooking the plains. It is Mardin's best hotel, with 50 rooms on eight floors reached by a lift, and a terrace restaurant where the notables gather. All rooms have showers and cost US$10 a double.

In the unlikely event that both these places are full, continue east to the *Hotel Başak Palas* and the even simpler *Hotel Şirin Palas*, on the main street beneath the Sultan İsa Medresesi.

Places to Eat

The only real restaurant, although nothing special, is at the Hotel Bayraktar (tel 1647), which overlooks the square. Ask about prices before you order, as my simple meal turned out to be surprisingly expensive at US$4.50.

There are several small, very inexpensive eateries east of the Bayraktar along the main street. I would ask about prices at these too.

Getting There & Away

Several buses run daily from Urfa to Mardin. As for transport to and from Diyarbakır, it is by minibus. They run about every hour between Mardin's Belediye Garajı and Diyarbakır's Mardin Kapısı (Mardin Gate in the city walls), for US$1.50. The 100-km journey takes about 1¾ hours.

DİYARBAKIR

The Tigris (Dicle, DEEJ-leh) flows by the mighty black walls of Diyarbakır (dee-YAHR-bah-kuhr, population 250,000, altitude 660 metres). As with many Turkish cities, this one has grown beyond its ancient walls only in the last few decades. Farming, stock raising, some oil prospecting and light industry fuel the Diyarbakır economy.

The city prides itself especially on its watermelons. A brochure published for the annual Watermelon Festival in late September states: 'In olden times, our watermelons had to be transported by camel as they weighed 90 or 100 kg. They were carved with a sword and sold in the market.' The brochure also says that nowadays the prize-winning melons at the festival weigh a mere 40 to 60 kg!

Today this city, lying in the midst of a vast, lonely plain, is like a desert oasis full of traders. Many of the men wear the traditional baggy trousers called *şalvar* (SHAHL-vahr), and older women have black head coverings which often serve unofficially as veils. Visiting men from Syria and Iraq have the long jellabah robes and keffiyeh (headscarves) of Arab lands, and the women may even be in purdah, wearing the black chador.

The tawdry chaos of signs at the city's centre, the narrow alleys, the mosques in the Arab style with black-and-white banding in the stone – all these give Diyarbakır a foreign, frontier feeling. The people tend to be taciturn and not

particularly outgoing in their dealings
with foreigners, and the street urchins are
annoying. In summer it is very hot here, so
avoid hotel rooms just beneath the
building's roof or rooms that get full late-
afternoon sun.

History

Considering that Mesopotamia, the land
between the Tigris and Euphrates valleys,
saw the dawn of the world's first great
empires, it's no surprise that Diyarbakır's
history begins with the Hurrian Kingdom
of Mitanni around 1500 BC, and proceeds
through domination by the civilisations of
Urartu (900 BC), Assyria (1356 to 612 BC),
Persia (600 to 330 BC), Alexander the
Great and his successors the Seleucids.

The Romans took over in 115 AD, but
because of its strategic position the city
continued to change hands numerous
times until it was conquered by the Arabs
in 639 AD. Until then it had been known
as Amida, but the Arabs settled it with the
tribe of Beni Bakr, who named their new
home Dıyar Bakr, The Realm of Bakr.

I'd like to make this city's history
simple for you, and say that when it was
conquered by the Seljuks in 1085 or the
Ottomans in 1515 it became a peaceful
place, but this isn't so. Because it stands
right in the way of invading armies from
Anatolia, Persia and Syria, it was
clobbered a lot more.

It is still a bit unsettled, for south-
eastern Turkey has a large Kurdish
population. The authorities in Ankara
want the Kurds, who are Muslims, to
assimilate, and will not permit any talk of
secession. Among the Kurds there are
nationalists who dream of a Kurdish state
encompassing the areas in Turkey, Syria,
to more than a century of Turkoman rule
in this area.

Orientation

Although the city has grown, your concern
will be with the old part within the walls,
except for the bus and rail stations west of
the old city.

Old Diyarbakır has a standard Roman
town plan, with the rough circle of walls
pierced by four gates at the north, south,
east and west. From the gates, avenues
travel to the centre where they meet.
Since Roman times, several sections of
wall have been razed and a few new gates
opened.

The railway station is at the western
end of İstasyon Caddesi. From the
station, this street travels east to the Urfa
Kapısı (OOR-fah kah-puh-suh, Edessa
Gate), the city's eastern gate. Inside the
walls, the continuation of İstasyon
Caddesi is named Melek Ahmet Caddesi
or sometimes Urfa Caddesi. To go
downtown from the station, walk out the
front door, go to the first big street and
wait on the left (north-east) corner of the
far side for a dolmuş going to Dağ
Kapısı.

The otogar is north-east of the city
where Elazığ Caddesi (also called Ziya
Gökalp Bulvarı) intersects the highway.
Travel along Elazığ Caddesi to the centre
and you will pass the Turistik Oteli just
before penetrating the walls at the Dağ
Kapısı (DAAH kah-puh-suh, Mountain
Gate), the northern gate, sometimes also
called the Harput Kapısı. From this gate,
Gazi Caddesi leads to the centre. To get
downtown from the otogar, take a dolmuş
to Dağ Kapısı, 3½ km away. Don't let
them tell you that there are no dolmuşes
and that you must take a taxi.

Information

The Tourism Information Office (tel (831)
12173, 17840) is in the new city north of the
walls at Lise Caddesi 24, Onur Apartımanı.
Ask for LEE-seh jah-deh-see, which runs
west from Elazığ Caddesi about three
blocks north of the Dağ Kapısı. The office
is about 3½ blocks along. The central
tourism office is in the Kültür Sarayı on
the 6th and 7th floors (tel 10099, 17840).

The Walls

The city's old walls are extensive – almost

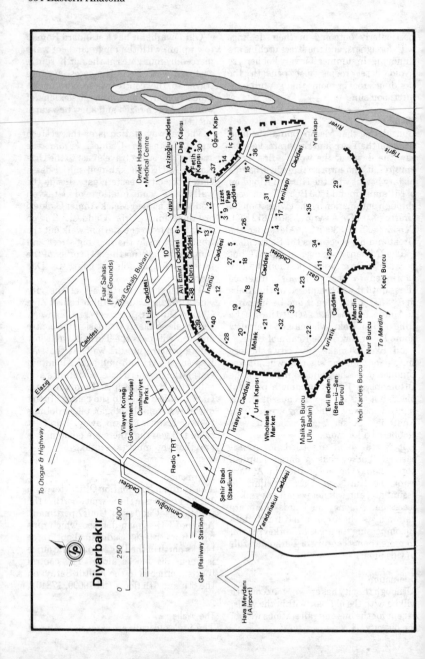

Diyarbakır

0 — 250 — 500 m

Map labels:
- To Otogar & Highway
- Elazığ
- Caddesi
- Camiloğlu Caddesi
- Gar (Railway Station)
- Hava Meydanı (Airport)
- Yenidanakul Caddesi
- Şehir Stadı (Stadium)
- Radio TRT
- Vilayet Konağı (Government House)
- Cumhuriyet Parkı
- Fuar Sahası (Fair Grounds)
- Ziya Gökalp Bulvarı
- Lise Caddesi
- İstasyon Caddesi
- Urfa Kapısı
- Wholesale Market
- Melikşah Burcu (Ulu Badan)
- Evli Beden (Ben-u-Sen Burcu)
- Yedi Kardeş Burcu
- Nur Burcu
- Mardin Kapısı
- To Mardin
- Turistik Caddesi
- Keçi Burcu
- Gazi Caddesi
- Ahmet Caddesi
- Melek Caddesi
- İnönü Caddesi
- Kıbrıs Caddesi
- Ali Emiri Caddesi
- Yusuf
- Azizoğlu Caddesi
- Devlet Hastanesi (Medical Centre)
- Dağ Kapısı
- Fetih Kapısı
- Oğun Kapı
- İç Kale
- Yenikapı
- Yenikapı Caddesi
- İzzet Paşa Caddesi
- River
- Tigris

six km long – and are the first item on most people's list of things to see.

Although there were Roman and probably earlier walls here, the present walls date from early Byzantine times (330 to 500 AD).

The historic names for the gates in the walls are the Harput Kapısı (north), Mardin Kapısı (south), Yenikapı (east) and Urfa Kapısı (west). The massive black basalt walls are defended by 72 bastions and towers, many of them gathered around the İç Kale (EECH-kaleh, citadel or keep) at the north-eastern corner, overlooking the Tigris. Of the gates, the Harput Kapısı or Dağ Kapısı is in the best condition.

Perhaps the most rewarding area of the walls to explore for inscriptions and decoration is the portion between the İç Kale and the Mardin Kapısı, going westward (away from the river). Start at the Mardin Kapısı near the Deliller Han, a stone caravanserai now restored and turned into a hotel. Climb up to the path atop the walls, walk along and you'll pass by the **Yedi Kardeş Burcu** (Tower of Seven Brothers) and **Malikşah Burcu** (Tower of Malikşah, also called Ulu Badan). The view of the city from atop the walls is good and enables you to get your bearings and to see how the Diyarbakırlıs live. You must descend at Urfa Kapısı, but you can climb up again on the opposite side of İstasyon Caddesi.

Mosques

Diyarbakır has many mosques, but the most interesting is the **Ulu Cami**, built in 1091 and extensively restored in 1155 after being damaged by fire. The mosque is rectangular in plan – Arab-style, not Ottoman. Its founder was Malik Şah, an early sultan of the Seljuks. Across the courtyard from the Ulu Cami is the Mesudiye Medresesi, now used as offices. Across the street from these buildings is the Hasan Paşa Hanı, a caravanserai dating from the 16th century, now used by carpet sellers and souvenir vendors.

Black-and-white stone banding is a characteristic of Diyarbakır's mosques, many of which date from the reign of the Akkoyunlu (White Sheep Turkomans) Dynasty. One of these is the **Nebi Camii** (1530) at the main intersection of Gazi Caddesi and İzzet Paşa/İnönü Caddesi.

The **Behram Paşa Camii** (1572), in a

residential area deep in the maze of narrow streets, is Diyarbakır's largest mosque and is in a similar style. The **Safa Camii** (1532) is in a more Persian style, with a grand and highly decorated minaret.

The **Kasım Padişah Camii** (1512) is also famous for its minaret, but it's the engineering that draws the interest, for the huge tower stands on four slender pillars about two metres high, lending it the name Dört Ayaklı Minare or Four-Legged Minaret.

Atatürk Villa

The Atatürk Köşkü or Villa is interesting not because the Turkish leader spent much time here (he didn't), but as an example of upper-class Diyarbakır architecture, with horizontal zebra stripes and an airy eyvan court facing pretty gardens.

Museum

Diyarbakır's new museum is in the Fuar Sahası (fair grounds) off Ziya Gökalp Caddesi, next to the Devlet Hastanesi. To get there, leave the old city through the Dağ Kapısı. Besides the usual archaeological and classical finds and the obligatory ethnological rooms, it has collections showing the accomplishments of the Karakoyunlu (Black Sheep Turkomans) and Akkoyunlu, powerful tribal dynasties which ruled a lot of Eastern Anatolia and Iran between 1378 and 1502. The Akkoyunlu formed a pact with the Venetian Empire against the Ottomans, but were defeated by Mehmet the Conqueror in 1473. After 1497, the Safavid Dynasty founded by Shah Ismail took over Iran, putting an end to more than a century of Turkoman rule in this area.

Places to Stay – bottom end

Diyarbakır's hotels are fairly simple, with no truly luxurious places.

The area around Dağ Kapısı has numerous little inexpensive hotels. Some are on İnönü Caddesi, as are the more expensive places. A favourite is the *Van Palas Oteli*, in a narrow side street off the south side of İnönü Caddesi, next to the Hotel Derya. The manager is into his work and sits around the courtyard fountain trading stories with visitors, playing backgammon or helping them to apply henna. Simple rooms are inexpensive, from US$2 to US$4 per person, but it's the spirit of the place that makes it popular.

The *Hotel Köprücü* (KEURP-reu-jeu, tel 12963/4), İnönü Caddesi, Birinci Çıkmaz, is on a tiny dead-end street off İnönü Caddesi near the Büyük Otel. It's quiet, except for the call of the muezzin from the Nebi Camii next door, and offers a choice of rooms without running water or with a private shower, costing from US$3.50 to US$4.50 a single and from US$6 to US$7 a double.

Near the Derya and Büyük hotels are two more cheap places. The *Hotel Malkoç* (tel 12975), İnönü Caddesi, Sütçü Sokak 6, is an aile hotel charging US$6/7 a single/double with shower. Next door is the *Hotel Kaplan* (tel 13358, 16617), İnönü Caddesi, Sütçü Sokak 14, in a very quiet location with clean rooms, lots of hot water, big towels and similar prices.

If you can't find a room at the places named, take a look at the *Otel Kenan* (tel 16614), İzzet Paşa Caddesi 20/B, next to the Otel Saraç. It's well worn, but the rooms are kept up fairly well. Some rooms have private baths and all smell a bit musty, but cost only US$7 a double with a private shower. The hotel has a lift.

Moving up in quality a little, the first choice is the one-star *Hotel Derya* (tel 14966, 19735), İnönü Caddesi 13, among the recently renovated places in town. It's less pretentious than some others and offers very good value at US$11/16 a single/double for its 28 rooms with shower. It's often full.

Next in line is the one-star, old and fairly beaten-up *Otel Saraç* (sah-RAHCH, tel 12365), İzzet Paşa Caddesi 16, almost next door to the more expensive Demir Otel. The 35 rooms are drab and simple, but cost only US$9.50/13 a single/double, with shower or bath.

The older, one-star, 29-room *Hotel Aslan* (ahss-LAHN, tel 13971), Kıbrıs Caddesi 53, is a few steps from the Dağ Kapısı. It costs US$10/15 a single/double for older rooms overlooking the gate in the city walls, but it has a lift. Don't confuse it with the *Aslan Palas* next door.

Places to Stay – middle

Of the moderately priced places along İzzet Paşa Caddesi, several, such as the *Akdağ* and *Sürmeli*, are under long-term lease to oil prospecting companies and do not rent rooms to others.

Most of the middle-range hotels are on İnönü Caddesi or its continuation, İzzet Paşa Caddesi. The two-star *Demir Otel* (tel 12315/6/7), İzzet Paşa Caddesi 8, at the intersection with Gazi Caddesi, a short distance south of the Dağ Kapısı, is the old standard. The 39-room Demir, popular with tour groups, has fairly good housekeeping standards, phones in the bathrooms (!) and what passes for luxury in Diyarbakır. It rents its rooms for US$25/35 a single/double, subject to haggling.

The nearby two-star, 75-room *Büyük Otel* (beur-YEURK, tel 15832/3), İnönü Caddesi 4, charges a bit more for similar rooms, but has a fancier lobby. It has the trappings, but not the comforts, of a luxury hotel. Rooms cost US$25/38 a single/double with bath.

Just outside the Dağ Kapısı is the veteran 39-room, two-star *Turistik Oteli* (tel 12662/3, 25003), Ziya Gökalp Bulvarı 7, built in 1953 but well kept, with spacious public rooms and guest rooms. It's a comfortable period piece and prices reflect this extra comfort. Rooms cost US$30/42/50 a single/double/triple with a private bath. Due to street noise, it's best to get a room at the back.

Places to Eat

Kebap places are everywhere and solve the dining problem easily and cheaply (US$2 to US$3) most of the time. Many are near the junction of İnönü/İzzet Paşa and Gazi caddesis, near the hotels.

A stroll along Kıbrıs Caddesi from Dağ Kapısı westward will reveal several small, cheap places to eat, including the *Büryan Salonu* (tel 24372), Kıbrıs Caddesi 17, for kebaps (a sign notes that you can pay in US$ or DM); the *7 Kardeşler,* and the *Kent Restaurant* (tel 10899), Kıbrıs Caddesi 31/A, which has outdoor tables in the alleyway.

The *Babaman Lokantasi* (tel 15887), Kıbrıs Caddesi, serves a sebzeli kebap (vegetable and lamb stew), pilav and soft drink for less than US$2.50. It even has a summer dining area on the upper level, overlooking the walls and tea gardens.

For slightly fancier meals, head for the hotel restaurants in the *Demir* (a rooftop terrace) and the *Turistik*, or the air-conditioned *Güneydoğu 21 Sofra Salonu* (tel 42597), İnönü Caddesi 32/A, near the Derya and Büyük hotels. The Turkish classics are served behind huge front windows in a Diyarbakır-style white decor; this is where the city's gilded youth (and gilded elders, for that matter) meet to eat, paying from US$5 to US$7 for a full meal.

There are also some pastanes in the centre, good for breakfast or a snack. I always seem to end up having a breakfast of su böreği (steamed noodle-like pastry with white cheese) at the *Şeyhmus Pastanesi* at the north-eastern corner of the intersection of İnönü/İzzet Paşa and Gazi caddesis. Despite being one of the town's fanciest pastry shops, the breakfast costs less than US$1, even with a large glass of tea.

Late in the afternoon, get baklava at the *Ünal Pastanesi,* a few steps south of the intersection on Gazi Caddesi in a building called the Merkez İş Hanı. Plush easy chairs and fake marble tables provide the decor while the cook provides a fine selection of various styles of baklava selling for between US$0.50 and US$0.75 per portion.

Getting There & Away

Bus Many bus companies have ticket offices downtown on Kıbrıs Caddesi or in other spots near the Dağ Kapısı. Minibuses to Mardin depart not from the otogar but from the centre of town, leaving by the Urfa Gate hourly. Main routes are:

Adana – 550 km, 10 hours, US$8; several buses daily

Ankara – 945 km, 13 hours, US$10; several buses daily

Erzurum – 485 km, 10 hours, US$8; several buses daily

Kâhta (Nemrut Dağı) – 192 km, three hours, US$4; several buses daily

Malatya – 260 km, 4 hours, US$4; frequent buses daily

Şanlıurfa – 190 km, three hours, US$4; frequent buses daily

Sivas – 500 km, nine or 10 hours, US$8; several buses daily

Van – 410 km, seven hours, US$7; several buses daily

Train Diyarbakır is connected to Ankara and İstanbul by the Güney Ekspresi which runs eastward on Monday, Wednesday, Friday and Saturday, departing Ankara at 6.40 am and stopping at Kayseri, Sivas and Diyarbakır before heading east to Batman (!) and Kurtalan. The return service from Diyarbakır is on Monday, Wednesday, Friday and Sunday at 5 pm. Train services are neither frequent nor dependably on time, so you may prefer to take the bus.

BİTLİS

Travel eastward from Diyarbakır 88 km and you'll reach the town of Silvan from where it's another 22 km to Malabadi. Just east of here is the Batman Suyu, a stream spanned by a beautiful hump-backed stone bridge built by the Artukid Turks in 1146. It is thought to have the longest span (37 metres) of any such bridge in existence. With its engaging bend in the middle, it's truly a work of art.

Restoration in 1988 has returned it to much of its former stateliness.

Another 235 km brings you to Bitlis (BEET-lees, population 40,000, altitude 1545 metres), an interesting but dusty and somewhat chaotic old town squeezed into the narrow valley of a stream. A castle dominates the town and a hump-backed bridge and another old bridge span the stream.

The Ulu Cami here was built in 1126, while the Şerefiye Camii and Saraf Han (a caravanserai) were built in the 16th century. The town was the capital of a semi-autonomous Kurdish principality in late Ottoman times.

Walnut trees surround the town and in autumn children stand by the highway with bags of nuts for sale.

Up the hill at the eastern side of the town, on the left (north) side of the road, is an old caravanserai, the Pabsin Hanı, built by the Seljuks in the 13th century. Often there are nomads camped near it, their sprawling black tents pitched beneath its crumbling walls.

It's only 26 km to Tatvan, a railhead and western port for lake steamers.

TATVAN

Tatvan is a crossroads town, built for and surviving on the commerce which moves through by road and rail. This includes the Turkish army which is here to protect the country's eastern borders at the traditional invasion points from north, east and south.

The town, several km long and only a few blocks wide, is not much to look at and has only a few, poor tourist services. However, its setting on the shores of an inland sea, backed by bare mountains streaked with snow, is magnificent.

You will have to pass through Tatvan, and you may even make it your base for explorations along the north-western shore of the lake, so here's what you need to know.

Nemrut Dağı

The mountain rising to the north of Tatvan is Nemrut Dağı, not to be confused with the one near Adıyaman and Malatya with the statues on top. This Nemrut Dağı (3050 metres) is an inactive volcano with a crater lake on top which is beautiful, clear and cold and which should be visited for the view or for a swim if you normally swim among icebergs. If not, there are hot springs as well. Nemrut is the volcano which dammed up the outflow of Lake Van, causing it to take its present vast size of 3750 square km, and to become highly alkaline.

In summer, dolmuşes make the run up the mountain if there are enough people interested, charging about US$4 per person. If you have your own transport, leave Tatvan by the road around the lake to the north marked for Ahlat and Adilcevaz. On the outskirts of Tatvan, look for a left turn near a Türk Petrol station, as this road will take you up the mountain.

Ahlat

Continue northward by car or dolmuş along the lake shore for 42 km and come to the town of Ahlat, famous for its Seljuk Turkish tombs and graveyard.

To the right (south) of the highway as you approach the town is Ulu Kümbet, the Great Tomb, now in the midst of a field near some houses. Across the highway from it is a little museum, and beyond the museum is a unique Muslim cemetery with stela-like headstones. Over the centuries, earthquake, wind and water have set the stones at all angles, giving the graveyard an unsettling and eerie look.

On the north-western side of the graveyard is the Çifte Kümbet (Twin Tomb) and Bayındır Türbesi (Bayındır Tomb), with a colonnaded porch and its own small prayer room.

Ahlat, and indeed this whole region, was conquered by the Ottomans during the reign of Süleyman the Magnificent in

the 16th century. The fortress on the shore in Ahlat dates from that period.

Malazgirt

About 60 km north of Ahlat is Malazgirt (Manzikert), which is greatly important in Turkish history. On 26 August 1071, the Seljuk Turkish Sultan Alp Arslan and his armies decisively defeated the Byzantine Emperor Romanus Diogenes and took him prisoner. The Byzantine defeat effectively opened Anatolia to Turkish migration and conquest. The Seljuks established the Sultanate of Rum with its capital at Konya, and other nomadic Turkish tribes came from Central Asia and Iran to settle here. A band of border warriors, following a leader named Osman, later spread its influence and founded a state which would become the vast Ottoman Turkish Empire. It all started here, in 1071, when the heir of the Caesars lost to a Turkish emir.

Adilcevaz

Twenty-five km east of Ahlat is the town of Adilcevaz, once an Urartian town but now dominated by a great Seljuk Turkish fortress, the Kef Kalesi, and the even greater bulk of Süphan Dağı (4434 metres).

Meltwater from the year-round snow-fields on Süphan Dağı flows down to Adilcevaz, making its surroundings lush and fertile. As you enter town along the shore, the highway passes the nice little Tuğrul Bey Camii, built in the 13th century and still used daily for prayer. You can climb Süphan Dağı in summer. For details, see Lonely Planet's *Trekking in Turkey*.

Dolmuşes run between Adilcevaz and Van (Beş Yol) several times daily. If you continue around the lake, you will pass through Erciş, a modern town which covers settlements that date from Urartian times.

Places to Stay

Ahlat and Adilcevaz have a few small, cheap pensions. In Tatvan, the few cheap hotels (such as the *Otel Trabzon*, where rooms cost US$3/5 a single/double with washbasin) are very basic and well used, but so is the best hotel in town, the *Vangölü Denizcilik Kurumu Oteli* (tel (8497) 1777). Hidden on the shore a short walk from the centre, the old stone building looks as though it is left from Ottoman times, though it may have been built to accommodate passengers on the railway. It has a serviceable restaurant and the 23 drab, basic and old-fashioned rooms cost from US$10 to US$15 a double, some with private showers. Despite its lack of comforts, this, the best hotel in Tatvan, is often fully booked with tour groups.

Getting There & Away

Tatvan's railway station is about two km north-east of the centre along the road to Ahlat and Adilcevaz; there are infrequent city buses. The Vangölü Ekspresi departs Tatvan at 7 am on Tuesday, Thursday and Saturday. The more desirable couchettes and sleeping car berths should be reserved well in advance.

Ferries operated by Turkish Maritime Lines cross the lake from Tatvan to Van on an irregular schedule, for while there are supposed to be four boats per day, there often is only one. Don't believe the departure times you're told. You can make the 156-km journey to Van more quickly (two hours) by bus around the southern shore.

AKDAMAR

From Tatvan to Van, the scenery is beautiful, but there is no reason to stop except at a point eight km west of Gevaş, where you *must* see the 10th-century Akdamar Kilisesi or Church of the Holy Cross. One of the marvels of Armenian architecture, it is perched on an island in the lake. Motorboats ferry sightseers back and forth. You can also make this trip as an excursion from Van.

In 921, Gagik Artzruni, King of Vaspurakan, built a palace, church and monastery on the island, three km out in the lake. Little remains of the palace and monastery, but the church walls are in superb condition and the wonderful relief carvings on the walls are among the masterworks of Armenian art.

If you are familiar with biblical stories, you'll immediately recognise Adam and Eve, Jonah and the Whale, David and Goliath, Abraham about to sacrifice Isaac (but he sees the heaven-sent ram, with its horns caught in a bush, just in time!), Daniel in the Lions' Den, Sampson, etc.

The paintings inside the church are not in the best of condition, but their vagueness and frailty seem in keeping with the shaded, partly ruined interior.

The church and its setting are incomparable, so don't miss this place. It's one of the main reasons you've come to eastern Turkey.

Bring a picnic and swimming gear for your outing to Akdamar.

Getting There & Away

Dolmuşes run from Beş Yol in Van to Gevaş for US$1. Some of the dolmuş drivers have a racket whereby they take you to Gevaş, then set a high price for the remaining eight km to the boat dock for Akdamar. To beat this, agree on a price all the way to the dock (Akdamar İskelesi) before you board the dolmuş in Van.

Boats to the island (US$2 round trip) run about every 30 minutes if traffic warrants this, which it usually does in the warm months, especially on Sundays. (If it doesn't, you may have to charter a boat for a special trip, at a cost of US$20 or US$25.) The voyage takes about 20 minutes and an admission ticket to the church costs US$1.

A fairly expensive teahouse and camping area are near the dock.

HAKKÂRI

The absolute, positive dead end of Turkey is Hakkâri (hah-KYAH-ree, population 25,000, altitude 1700 metres), 210 km south of Van over a zig-zagging mountain road. The scenery is spectacular. However, there is often trouble in these regions and the newspapers are full of items about Turkish border guards being killed by smugglers and Kurdish separatists.

Buses depart daily from Van for Hakkâri. At 112 km is Başkale, notable for its altitude (2450 metres). Yeni Köprü, at 160 km, is the point at which a road left goes to Yüksekova, on the road to Iran, an alternative base for climbs into the mountains.

Finally, 210 km from Van you arrive in Hakkâri, which has two small, cheap hotels, the better of which is the *Hotel Çelli*, which charges US$10 for a double room. The Çelli also has the best restaurant in town.

VAN

At the south-eastern edge of the vast Van Gölü (VAHN gew-lew), almost 100 km across the water from Tatvan, lies Van (population 130,000, altitude 1727 metres), the eastern railhead on the line to Iran and the largest Turkish city east of Diyarbakır and south of Erzurum.

Van has several claims to fame. It was the Urartian capital city and at the Rock of Van near the lakeshore are long cuneiform inscriptions. Van is also the market centre for the Kurdish tribes who live in the mountain fastnesses of extreme south-eastern Turkey. An excursion to the south-east takes you past the ancient Urartian city at Çavuştepe and the picture-perfect mountain fortress of Hoşap to Hakkâri and Yükselova, deep in the breathtaking scenery of the Cilo Dağı mountains.

History

The kingdom of Urartu, called Ararat in the Bible, flourished in these parts from the 13th to the 7th centuries BC. The Urartian capital, Tooshpa, was near present-day Van. The Urartians were traders and farmers, highly advanced in the art of metalwork and stone masonry. They borrowed much of their culture from the neighbouring Assyrians, including their cuneiform writing. Yet although they emulated the Assyrians, they were at war with them more or less permanently. Even though Urartu was less powerful than Assyria, the Assyrians never completely subdued the Urartians. But when the battle was joined by several waves of Cimmerians, Scythians and Medes who swept into Urartu, the kingdom met its downfall.

With the downfall of Urartu, the region was resettled by a people whom the Persians called Armenians. By the 6th century BC the region was governed by Persian and Mede satraps.

The history of the Armenians is one of repeated subjugation to the rule of other peoples as they occupied a strategic crossroads at the nexus of three great empires in Syria, Persia, and Anatolia. Tigranes the Great succeeded in gaining control of the kingdom from its Parthian overlords in 95 BC, but his short-lived kingdom was soon crushed in the clash of armies from Rome in the west and Parthia in the east.

In the 8th century AD, the Arab armies flooded through from the south, forcing the Armenian prince to take refuge on Akdamar Island. Unable to fend off the vast number of Arabs, he later agreed to pay tribute to the Caliph. When the Arabs retreated, the Byzantines and Persians took their place, and overlordship of Armenia see-sawed between them as one or the other gained military advantage.

The next wave of people to flood through were the Turks. Upon defeating the Byzantines at Manzikert, north of Lake Van, in 1071, the Seljuk Turks marched in to found the Sultanate of Rum and were followed by a flood of Turkoman nomads. Domination of the powerful Karakoyunlu and Akkoyunlu Turkish tribes followed until the coming of the Ottoman armies in 1468.

During WW I, Armenian guerrilla bands intent on founding an independent Armenian state worked with the Russians to defeat the Ottoman armies in the east.

The Armenians, former loyal subjects of the sultan, were looked upon as traitors by the Turks. Bitter fighting between Turkish and Kurdish forces on the one side and Armenian and Russian on the other brought wholesale devastation to the entire region and to Van.

The Ottomans destroyed the old city of Van (near the Rock of Van) before the Russians occupied it in 1915. Ottoman forces counterattacked but were unable to drive the invaders out, so Van remained under Russian occupation until the armistice of 1917. Under the Turkish Republic, a new planned city of Van was built several km from the old site.

Information & Orientation

The Tourism Information Office (tel (061) 12018) is at the southern end of Cumhuriyet Caddesi, at No 127.

The highway passing between the town and the lake is the ancient Silk Road (İpek Yolu). In the city, the main commercial street is Cumhuriyet Caddesi, with banks, hotels, restaurants, the Turkish Airlines office and the Tourism Information Office. At the northern end of Cumhuriyet Caddesi, where it meets five other streets, is the square called Beş Yol (Five Roads), with a huge concentration of dolmuş and bus stops.

The city's bus terminal is on the north-western outskirts, just off the Silk Road.

The two railway stations are the İskele İstasyon or lakeside Dock Station and the Şehir İstasyon or City Station. The City Station is north-west of the centre near the bus terminal, while the Dock Station is several km north-east on the shore.

Van Kalesi (Rock of Van), the only significant sight, is about five km west of the centre.

Müze

Off Cumhuriyet Caddesi, not far from the Bayram Oteli, is the museum, which holds exhibits dating back to before Urartian times. Other exhibits include beautiful Urartian gold jewellery, some with amber and coloured glass, Urartian cylindrical seals, and pots from the Old Bronze Age (5000 BC). The Urartu Süsleme Plakaları (jewellery breastplates) from the 9th to 7th centuries BC are particularly fine, as are the bronze belts. Another exhibit has At Gemleri (horse bits) from the 9th and 8th centuries BC.

The ethnographic exhibits upstairs include countless kilims, the flat-woven rugs superbly made by the Kurdish and Turkoman tribes who live in the mountains. At the far end of the room is a *sedir* or low couch such as is found in village houses, covered with traditional crafts.

The museum is open from 9 am to 5.30 pm; admission costs US$1. Cameras are not permitted inside, so you must check yours in at the door.

Van Kalesi

Dolmuşes to the Rock of Van depart from Beş Yol and cost almost US$1. Many people hitchhike, which is fairly easy, or walk it if it's not too hot a day.

On the north side of the rock is the tomb of a Muslim saint which is visited frequently by pilgrims. A stairway from the car park at the north-western corner leads to the top, where you can see the fortifications and several cuneiform inscriptions dating from about 800 BC. On the south side is a narrow walkway with an iron railing leading to several funeral chambers cut from the rock. Before reaching these you pass a long cuneiform inscription.

The view south of the rock reveals a flat space broken by the grass-covered foundations of numerous buildings. This was the site of Tushpa, an Urartian city which flourished almost 3000 years ago. The foundations you see, however, are those of the old city of Van, destroyed during the upheavals of WW I and the futile struggle for an Armenian republic. The sight is stunning – a dead city, buried as though in a grave, with only two 16th-century mosques, the Hüsrev Paşa and Kaya Çelebi.

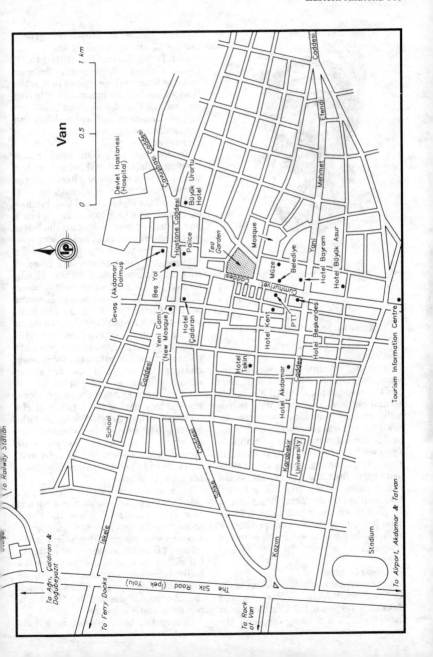

Kurdish man from Lake Van area

Lake Van

This highly alkaline lake was formed when the volcano named Nemrut Dağı (not the one with the statues!) blocked its natural outflow. The water level is now maintained by evaporation which results in a high mineral concentration. It's not good to drink, but it's fine to swim in, and if you wash your clothes in it, you need no soap! For swimming, pick a spot on the shore away from the city of Van, as the waters right by the city are polluted. A better place for swimming is Edremit on the road to Akdamar and Tatvan. Don't swim if you have sunburn or open cuts or sores, as the alkaline water will burn you intensely.

Çavuştepe & Hoşap

A day excursion south-east of Van along the road to Başkale, Yüksekova and Hakkâri takes you to the Urartian site at Çavuştepe, 25 km from Van, and the

Kurdish castle at Hoşap (Güzelsu), another 33 km further along.

Old Tuşba Turizm (tel (061) 14561), Posta Caddesi 9, operates full-day minibus tours to these sites as well as the Rock of Van and Akdamar, also allowing for a swim in the lake, for about US$15 per person. Departure is after breakfast and the minibus returns in the evening in time for supper.

To do it on your own, catch a bus heading to Başkale (US$1.50) and say you want to get out at Hoşap. After seeing the castle, hitch back to Çavuştepe, 500 metres off the highway, and then hitch or catch a minibus back to Van. Pack a lunch and water and plan to be gone the better part of the day, as rides can be scarce.

The narrow hill on the right side of the highway at Çavuştepe was once crowned with the fortress-palace Sarduri-Hinili, home of the kings of Urartu, built between 764 and 735 BC by King Sardur II, son of Argisti. Climb the hill to the car park, where there is a guardian to keep you from taking photos (excavations are still underway) and perhaps to show you what there is to see. No admission fee is being charged as yet and no drinks or refreshments are available at the site.

Climb the rocky hill to the temple ruins, marked by a gate of black basalt blocks polished to a high gloss. A few of the blocks on the left side of the doorway are inscribed in cuneiform. As you walk around, notice the cisterns for water and, at the far end where the palace once stood, the royal Urartian loo.

Back on the road, another half-hour's ride (33 km) brings you up over a hill and down the other side, where the Hoşap Kalesi stands perched and photogenic atop a rocky outcrop. Beneath it is the village of Güzelsu, along a stream. On the left side of the road before the village is a badly ruined caravanserai or medrese. Cross the bridge into the village and follow the signs around the far side of the hill to reach the castle entrance.

The castle, built in 1643 by a local

Kurdish chieftain, has a very impressive entrance portal in a round tower. A guardian is supposed to be on duty from 8.30 am to 12 noon and from 1.30 to 5 pm. The guardian will sell you a ticket for less than US$1 and let you walk up into the fortress via a passage cut through the rock. Many of the castle's hundreds of rooms are still clearly visible and the view is good. Across the valley are the remains of mud-brick defensive walls, now badly eroded to look like a dinosaur's spine. Soft drinks are on sale at the castle entrance.

Places to Stay – bottom end

Van has one decent, modern, comfortable hotel and a good selection of cheaper places.

The *Bayram Oteli* (BAH-yee-RAHM, tel 11136/7), Cumhuriyet Caddesi 1/A, is very near the intersection of Cumhuriyet and Yani Mehmet Efendi caddesis. It could use a sandblasting from top to bottom and all new paint, but for now its 72 rooms with beaten-up showers and balconies cost US$7/10 a single/double. Other services available are a lift, car park, hamam and TV lounge.

A similar but slightly cheaper place is the one-star *Hotel Beşkardeş* (BEHSH-kahr-desh, tel 11116/7), Cumhuriyet Caddesi 34, which has 40 rooms with balconies going from US$7 to US$9 a single, from US$10 to US$12 a double and from US$13 to US$15 a triple. Prices are lower for rooms with washbasins and higher for rooms with a private shower. The hotel has five floors but no lift.

The cheapest of the more modern hotels is the 63-room *Hotel Kent* (tel 12519, 12404), behind the Türkiye İş Bankası. Its 63 rooms cost from US$5 to US$7 a single and from US$8 to US$10 a double, with a washbasin or private shower. The paint is fairly new, though the place still looks well used.

The *Hotel Çaldıran* (CHAHL-duh-RAHN, tel 12718), on Sıhke Caddesi, two short blocks down toward the lake from Beş Yol and near the Yeni Cami, has 48

clean, cheap rooms priced at US$7/10 a single/double with private shower.

Very popular among backpackers is the old *Hotel Van*, behind the Tekel building not far from the Çaldıran and near the fruit and vegetable market. It's a big old place with minimal maintenance carried out but lots of beds priced at only US$2 a night.

In the bazaar area not far from the Yeni Cami and Beş Yol is the *Lüks Aslan Oteli* (tel 12469), Eski Hal Civarı, a small and simple family concern with pale yellow doors, yellow-striped wallpaper, hot water morning and evening and many light and airy rooms, some with views of the town (the three-bed corner rooms numbered 103, 203, 303, etc are the best). Prices are good at US$4/7/9 a single/double/triple.

The *Hotel Tekin* (tel 11366, 13010), Küçük Cami Civarı, near the Little Mosque west of Cumhuriyet Caddesi, has an easily visible sign on its roof. There are 52 rooms in this quiet place and each has its small problems, such as leaky washers, but it's cleaner than most and offers a bit more comfort for a bit more money. A room costs US$11/16/20 a single/double/triple with private shower.

Camping There is camping at Edremit, 18 km from Van on the way to Gevaş and Akdamar.

Places to Stay – middle

The best hotel in town is the 75-room, three-star *Büyük Urartu Oteli* (tel 20660), Cumhuriyet Caddesi 60, 65100 Van, a fairly new, modern and attractive place with a spacious lobby, restaurant and bar, mezzanine breakfast room and comfortable guest rooms with private baths. Rooms cost US$32 a single and from US$45 to US$52 a double. The decor draws from Urartian themes as the hotel's designer is a professor of archaeology. (The hotel is on Hastane Caddesi, near the hospital, despite its Cumhuriyet Caddesi address).

Also quite comfortable is the three-star, 75-room *Hotel Akdamar* (AHK-dah-mahr, tel 18100), Kazım Karabekir Caddesi 56, 65200 Van, running west from Cumhuriyet Caddesi near the Tourism Information Office. Rooms cost US$23/32 a single/double with bath. The hotel has lifts, a car park, a terrace restaurant which is among the best in town, and a bar.

The older, more modest two-star *Büyük Asur Oteli* (beur-YEURK ah-SOOR, tel 18792/3), Cumhuriyet Caddesi 126, has 48 rooms in muted colours lit by fluorescence. It also has all the basic services such as lifts, a restaurant and parking. Like the other middle-range hotels, it is heavily used by European tour groups. Rooms cost US$14/28 a single/double with bath.

Places to Eat – bottom end
Van's simple lokantas are bright, big and unfancy. Try the *Şölen Lokantası* (tel 12855), Kazım Karabekir Caddesi, across from the Hotel Akdamar, or the *Şafak Lokantası* (tel 11922) next door to the Hotel Akdamar. A plate of İzmirli kebap (meatballs and vegetables in broth), rice pilav and a soft drink costs less than US$2.

Cumhuriyet Caddesi has more small restaurants. The *Altın Şiş Fırınlı Kebap Salonu* or Golden Skewer Oven-Equipped Kebap Salon (tel 12265), is a modern, smokey place down past the PTT, with a good selection of cheap kebaps.

The *Saray Lokantası* (tel 11756) is down a side street off Cumhuriyet Caddesi by the Türkiye İş Bankası, toward the Hotel Kent. It's just as cheap as the place on the main street, but quieter.

Up the hill a few steps from the intersection of Cumhuriyet and Kazım Karabekir caddesis is the *Turistik Köşk Restoran* (tel 12160), with similar food and prices, but a garden dining area behind the main dining room.

For pastries or breakfast, try the *Tuşba Pasta Salonu* (tel 11069), the fanciest in

town, to the right of the Belediye on Cumhuriyet Caddesi between the Sümer-bank and Garanti Bankası. The *Güven Pastanesi* (tel (16578), across the street from the Hotel Nuh and south of the tea garden next to the Töbank, is a bit less fancy.

Places to Eat – middle
The fanciest and probably the best food is at the *Büyük Urartu Oteli* and *Hotel Akdamar*, where a great dinner can cost US$7 but represents good value for money.

Things to Buy
In the shops of Van you will see handwoven craft items, such as kilims and saddlebags, finer than you've ever seen before. The dealers, however, realise that these finely made things will fetch high prices in Paris, London and New York, so you won't find many bargains. Instead, settle for the finest selection of the finest such items anywhere. Prices for the normal, common kilims, etc will be reasonable. If you don't buy, and there is no obligation to, don't feel pressured! Looking at these crafts is a wonderful experience. Some of the dealers speak English.

Getting There & Away
As the 'capital' of the extreme south-east, Van has ready transport. For dolmuşes to the Rock of Van (Kale), the ferry dock (İskele), the Akdamar boat dock (Gevaş) and Adilcevaz on the lake's northern shore, go to Beş Yol at the northern end of Cumhuriyet Caddesi.

Air Turkish Airlines (tel 11241), Cumhuriyet Caddesi 196, Enver Perihanoğlu İş Merkezi, has flights between Ankara and Van on Monday, Wednesday, Friday and Sunday. The airport bus departs the downtown office 90 minutes before departure time.

Bus Many bus companies maintain ticket offices along Cumhuriyet Caddesi, including the Van Gölü and Van Turizm companies. The larger companies have servis arabası minibuses to shuttle passengers between the downtown office and the bus terminal. As usual, bus traffic to and from Van is fast and frequent:

Ağrı – 230 km, four hours, US$4; frequent buses daily

Diyarbakır – 410 km, seven hours, US$7; several buses daily

Doğubeyazıt via Erçiş, Patnos & Ağrı – 315 km, 5½ hours, US$6; several daily to Ağrı, then change for Doğubeyazıt

Doğubeyazıt via Çaldıran – 185 km, five hours, US$6; direct dolmuş every few days; more frequent service planned

Erzurum – 420 km, 7½ hours, US$9; several buses daily

Hakkâri – 210 km, four hours, US$4.50; several buses daily

Malatya – 585 km, 10 hours, US$12; several buses daily

Tatvan – 156 km, three hours, US$3; frequent buses daily

Train Van used to be served by the Vangölü Ekspresi which rode right on to the lake steamer at Tatvan and huffed across the lake, resuming its eastward journey to Tehran at Van's İskele (dock). Service to Iran has been suspended for several years, but perhaps it will be resumed as Turkish-Iranian relations improve. The ferries still run at irregular intervals, taking four hours to cross the lake to Tatvan. Bring your own food, as only drinks are served on the boats.

NORTH FROM VAN

Having come this far, your next goal must be Doğubeyazıt, the town in the shadow of Mt Ararat, at the Iranian frontier on the E23 highway. There is an alternative to the normal Erçiş to Patnos to Ağrı route. Where the lake ring-road turns westward at the town of Bendimahi, continue north towards Muradiye, Çaldıran and Ortadirek. (Dolmuşes leave Van every few days in summer along this route). The road is

unpaved after Çaldıran and is extremely rough in spots between Çaldıran and Ortadirek, but it's usually passable. The road is being improved and is wonderfully scenic. Dolmuşes often stop at a scenic waterfall, at volcanic rock formations and at a nomad camp.

This route to Doğubeyazıt is only 185 km, so it saves a few km, but you shouldn't drive it after 5 pm. It's officially closed after that hour and Turkish army patrols are on duty to stop smugglers. The patrollers are very friendly if you obey the regulations, but will be strict after 5 pm. Even during daylight hours, keep your passport handy for identity checks.

AĞRI

The Turkish name for Mt Ararat is Ağrı Dağı, and the town of Ağrı (ah-RUH, population 60,000, altitude 1640 metres) is 100 km west of the snow-capped peak. It is a strong contender for the title of the drabbest town in Turkey. There is nothing to hold you here except the few small, very modest hotels – the *Otel Can* and *Otel Salman* – within a block of the main crossroads in the town centre. The otogar is a mud lot 500 metres from the main crossroads. I'd advise you to head for Doğubeyazıt in the east or Erzurum in the west.

DOĞUBEYAZIT

It's only 35 km between the Iranian frontier and Doğubeyazıt (doh-OO-bey-yah-zuht, population 30,000), a town that is dusty in summer and muddy in winter. Behind the town is a range of bare, jagged mountains, while before it there is a table-flat expanse of wheat fields and grazing land. On the far northern side of this flatness rises Ağrı Dağı (altitude 5165 metres), an enormous volcano capped with ice and often shrouded in dark clouds.

The name Ararat is derived from Urartu. The mountain has figured in legends since time began, most notably as

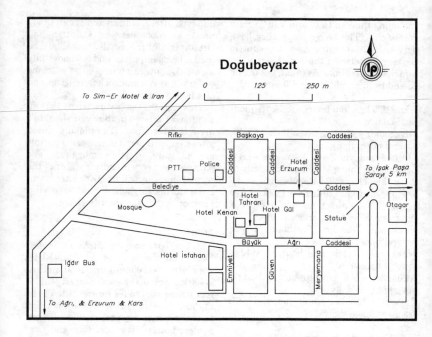

the supposed resting place of Noah's Ark. But more on that later.

Doğubeyazıt's other attraction is the İşak Paşa Sarayı, a fortress-palace-mosque complex perched on a terrace five km east of town.

İşak Paşa Sarayı

Head east, five km from town, to get to İşak Paşa Sarayı (ee-SHAHK pah-shah sah-rah-yuh). It's a pleasant walk and you'll have lots of company. Dolmuşes often pass nearby, especially on weekends, otherwise a taxi driver will demand about US$6 for a return-trip tour, waiting time included. Admission to the site costs US$2 and it's supposedly open from 8 am to 5 pm, but it may close earlier in winter. Drinks are available at the site.

Although ruined, the 366-room fortress-like palace has many elements which are in good condition. The mosque was used for prayers until about a decade ago and

the central heating system, which needs some work, is a surprise in that it's there at all.

The building was begun in 1685 by Çolak Abdi Paşa and completed in 1784 by his son, a Kurdish chieftain named İşak (Isaac). The architecture is an amalgam of Seljuk, Ottoman, Georgian, Persian and Armenian styles. A grand main portal leads to a large courtyard. The magnificent gold-plated doors which once hung on the portal were removed by the Russians, who invaded in 1917 and took the doors to the Hermitage Museum in Leningrad.

The palace was once equipped with a central heating system, running water and a sewerage system. You can visit the mosque and the various palace rooms. Note especially the little türbe in a corner of the court, with very fine relief work on it.

Fortress & Mosque

Across the valley are a mosque and the

ruins of a fortress. The fortress foundations may date from Urartian times (13th to 7th centuries BC), though the walls will have been rebuilt by whoever needed to control this mountain pass.

The mosque is thought to date from the reign of the Ottoman Sultan Selim I (1512 to 1520), who defeated the Persians decisively near the town of Çaldıran, 70 km south of Doğubeyazıt, in 1514. Selim thus added all of Eastern Anatolia to his burgeoning empire and went on to conquer Syria and Palestine.

The ruined foundations you see rising in low relief from the dusty plain are of Eski Bayazıt, the old city, which was probably founded in Urartian times at about 800 BC.

Mt Ararat

Mt Ararat (Ağrı Dağı) has two peaks when seen from Doğubeyazıt. The left-hand peak, called Büyük Ağrı (Great Ararat) is 5165 metres high, while Küçük Ağrı (Little Ararat) rises to about 3925 metres.

The best time to view the mountain is at sunrise or within an hour or two thereafter before the clouds obscure it. Any viewing requires good, clear weather.

You can climb Mt Ararat but you need written permission from the authorities in Ankara, and then you must have an approved guide. The mountain is dangerous: severe weather, ferocious sheep dogs, rock and ice slides, smugglers and outlaws can turn an adventure into a disaster. Getting the necessary permission can take several months unless you do it through a Turkish agency, when it may get done in six weeks.

The only legal way to go up the mountain is with an organised group, which will have made the necessary official arrangements. A Turkish agency that operates such trips is Trek Travel (tel (1) 155-1642/4772, fax 143-3625), Aydede Caddesi 10, 80090 Taksim, İstanbul. In Doğubeyazıt, the Trek Travel office will arrange a group for about US$100 per person, as will the AMTA agency.

Your guide will take you to Eli, a hamlet at 2100 metres, the starting point for the trek. You will stay at two other camps before the final ascent, for which you should have ice-climbing gear. For full details see Lonely Planet's *Trekking in Turkey*.

The Ark Over the years, several people have reported sighting a boat shape high on the mountain, and in 1951 an expedition brought back what was presumed to be a piece of wood from the ark, found in a frozen lake. But so far no-one, not even American astronaut James Irwin who climbed the mountain in 1982, has brought back a full report. If it's there, it will be found, for the activity nowadays is intense, with scientists, archaeologists, fundamentalist Christian sects, the Turkish Mountaineering Federation and various universities all sending expeditions.

Meteor Crater

A bit of celestial refuse arrived on the earth about 35 km from Doğubeyazıt, and its mark has now been added to the regular circuit of things to see near Doğubeyazıt. Ask at your hotel for more information.

Places to Stay – bottom end

My favourite among the cheap places is the tidy *Hotel Tahran* (tel (0278) 2223), Büyük Ağrı Caddesi 86, up the street from the big Hotel İsfahan. Modern and clean, it charges US$8 for a double room with a private shower. Another good choice is on the main street several blocks from the Hotel İşak Paşa. It's the *Hotel Erzurum* (tel 1708, 1080), Belediye Caddesi, a bit more expensive for what you get, with waterless rooms going for US$8, but it's fairly new as Doğubeyazıt hotels go.

There are three small hotels on Emniyet Caddesi, the street between the prominent İşak Paşa and İsfahan hotels. The *Hotel Kenan* (tel 1303, 2009), Emniyet Caddesi, has a restaurant, a nice lobby and good rooms, though the hallways are shabby. The price is a bit high at US$7/10 a single/double with bath. The *Hotel İlhan* (tel 2055), Emniyet Caddesi, has very plain, basic accommodation in waterless rooms, but free hot showers and it charges US$7 a double. The *Hotel Nur*, nearby, is similar.

The *Hotel Gül* (tel 1176, 1479), Güven Caddesi 34, behind the Hotel Kenan in the next block, is very cheap, but is often fully booked with religious Iranian tourists. Double waterless rooms cost US$5 a double, plus another US$1 for a bath. The *Hotel Kıbrıs* (tel 1407), Güven Caddesi, is a better choice at US$4 per person. Some rooms have views of Mt Ararat.

Places to Stay - middle

Rising above the mud-brick roofs and TV aerials of Doğubeyazıt is the two-star *Hotel İsfahan* (tel 1139, 1159, 2045), Emniyet Caddesi 26, 04410 Doğubeyazıt, Ağrı. Its 73 double rooms with showers on five floors cost US$20/34/42 a single/double/triple. It's modern and comfortable, with lots of kilims and carpets in the lobby and lounge, as well as its own lift and car park. The restaurant is the best in town. The hotel often caters to high-energy trekking groups.

Perhaps the most comfortable accommodation in Doğubeyazıt is at the *Sim-Er Moteli* (SEEM-ehr, tel 1601, 2254), PK 13, İran Transit Yolu, 04410 Doğubeyazıt, Ağrı, a modern 130-room establishment five km east of town on the highway to Iran. It's a comfortable, quiet, light and pleasant place surrounded by its own grounds. The rooms are decorated in restful colours and have shiny-clean tiled bathrooms, locally made woollen blankets and craftwork decorations. With a shower, rooms cost US$18/25 a single/double, and the set-price meal costs US$8; children receive a 30% reduction on room rates.

The two-star *İşak Paşa Hotel* (tel 1245, 2406), Emniyet Caddesi 10, 04410 Doğubeyazıt, Ağrı, at the intersection of

Emniyet and Belediye caddesis a block from the Hotel İsfahan, is simpler than the aforementioned hotels, but lower in price. It has 18 rooms on four floors, each with a tiled shower and balcony. There is a restaurant and bar and rooms cost US$12/22 a single/double.

Places to Eat

The main street holds three or four kebapçıs, one of which advertises (in English) 'All Kinds of Meals Found Here'. The *Gaziantepli Kebap Salonu* is not bad. The restaurants in the two top hotels are good. The *Kristal Pastahanesi* on Emniyet Caddesi, to the left of the Hotel Kenan, offers a Turkish breakfast for US$1 and afternoon tea and pastry for about the same price. It's a fancy place for this town, with photo-wood-grain tables, ice-cream parlour chairs and a separate aile salonu at the back.

Getting There & Away

From Doğubeyazıt, bus travel is limited and mostly goes via Erzurum. Here are a few destinations:

Ankara – 1210 km, 22 hours, US$18; one direct bus daily

Erzurum – 285 km, 4½ hours, US$5; five buses daily

Iğdır – 51 km, 45 minutes, US$0.75; several dolmuşes daily

İstanbul – 1550 km, 28 hours, US$24; two direct buses daily

Kars – 236 km, five or six hours, US$4; change at Iğdır

Van via Ağrı, Patnos & Erçiş – 315 km, 5½ hours, US$6; several buses daily to Ağrı, change for Van

Van via Çaldıran – 185 km, five hours, US$6; direct dolmuş every few days; more frequent service planned

NORTH TO IĞDIR & KARS

If you want to see Kars and the ruins of Ani, go north via Iğdır (UH-duhr), Tuzluca and Kağızman, a distance of 236 km.

A minibus service runs from Doğubeyazıt

to Iğdır and there are several suitable cheap hotels on the way. These include the one-star Yıldız Oteli, the 51-room Parlar Oteli (tel 2509), charging US$6/12 a single/double with a shower, and the cheaper Hotel Polat, charging US$4 per person.

At Tuzluca, there are salt caves to visit. North of Kağızman, above the village of Çamuşlu Köyü (chah-moosh-LOO kur-yur), there are 12,000-year-old rock carvings (*kaya resimleri*, kah-YAH reh-seem-leh-ree) which the villagers can show you.

As this route passes very close to the Soviet frontier between Iğdır and Tuzluca, it's important to know that the border zone is a no-man's land, 700 metres deep on each side of the frontier line, and that the Soviet border guards have been known to shoot at anyone who enters that strip, on either the Turkish or the Soviet side.

INTO IRAN

Unless you're an international driver who does it frequently and has all the right visas and papers, entry to Iran is difficult. You must have a visa, which can theoretically be obtained from an Iranian embassy or consulate. But visas depend upon the political winds. See the sections Visas and Embassies & Consulates in the Facts for the Visitor chapter or contact your embassy in Ankara for the latest situation. Once in Iran, it's good to have US dollars in cash, which trade easily. US dollars travellers' cheques cannot be changed.

ERZURUM

Erzurum (EHR-zoo-room, population 260,000, altitude 1853) is the largest city on the high plateau of Eastern Anatolia. It has always been a transportation centre and military headquarters – the command post for the defence of Anatolia from Soviet invasion (and in the days of the empires, from Persian invasion as well). Under the republic, it is assuming a new role as an eastern cultural and commercial city. The city has a university.

Erzurum lacks the colour and complexity of İstanbul or İzmir, but makes up for it with a rough frontier refinement. The severe climate and the sparse landscape make you think that this is the beginning of the vast, high steppe of Central Asia.

The people, too, reflect the severity of the climate and remoteness of location by their steadfast conservatism. Although unused to seeing a lot of foreigners, the people here still give travellers a warm welcome. Many more women wear the veil here and a few are in purdah. The old men go to prayer early and often.

In contrast, the town is busy with armed forces officers striding purposefully through its streets and squadrons of troops being trucked here and there. They may well be on their way to a new tree-planting site. When there's no fighting to do, Turkish commanders tend to order that the troops plant trees. The trees are everywhere in Erzurum. The orderly, modern tree-lined boulevards provide a welcome contrast to the arid, almost lifeless appearance of the surrounding oceans of steppe.

For tourists, Erzurum is a transfer point with air, rail and bus connections. But if you stay the night (or even two nights) here, you'll be able to occupy your free time with visits to some very fine Turkish buildings and a lively market area. You can also take a scenic excursion to the Tortum Vadisi Valley and the village of Yusufeli in the mountains on the road to Artvin.

History

The Byzantines called the city Theodosiopolis after the emperor who founded it on the ruins of an earlier settlement in the late 5th century. The powers in Constantinople had their hands full defending this town from Arab attack on several occasions. The Seljuks took it after the Battle of Manzikert (1071) effectively opened Anatolia to Turkish settlement. Being in a strategic position at the confluence of roads to Constantinople, Russia and Persia, Erzurum was conquered and lost by armies (in alphabetical order)

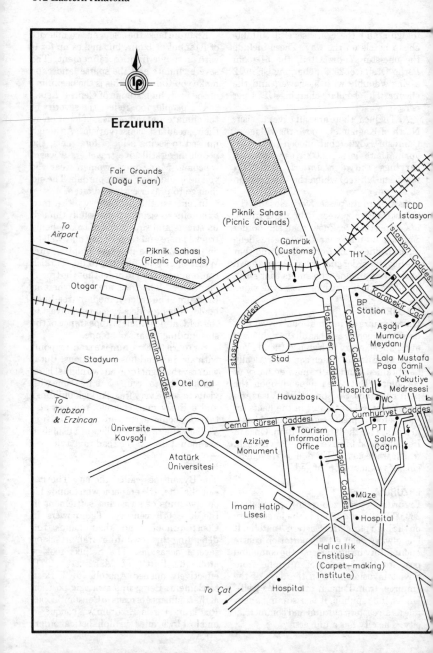

Erzurum

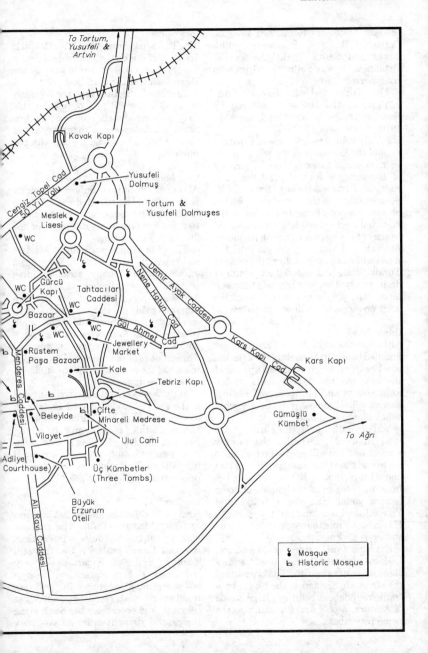

To Tortum, Yusufeli & Artvin

Kavak Kapı

Cengiz Topel Cad
50 Yıl Yolu

Yusufeli Dolmuş

Tortum & Yusufeli Dolmuşes

Meslek Lisesi

WC

Demir Ayak Caddesi

Gürcü Kapı

WC

Tahtacılar Caddesi

Nene Hatun Cad

WC

Bazaar

WC

WC

Gül Ahmet Cad

Jewellery Market

Kars Kapı Cad

Kars Kapı

Rüstem Paşa Bazaar

Kale

Tebriz Kapı

Menderes Caddesi

Beleyide

Çifte Minareli Medrese

Gümüşlü Kümbet

Vilayet

Ulu Cami

To Ağrı

Adliye (Courthouse)

Üç Kümbetler (Three Tombs)

Ali Ravi Caddesi

Büyük Erzurum Oteli

Mosque
Historic Mosque

of Arabs, Armenians, Byzantines, Mongols, Persians, Romans, Russians, Saltuk Turks and Seljuk Turks. As for the Ottomans, it was Selim the Grim who conquered the city in 1515.

The Turks feel the Soviet threat acutely, as the city was captured by Russian troops in 1882 and again in 1916.

In July 1919, Atatürk came to Erzurum to hold the famous congress which, along with the one at Sivas, was the rallying cry of the struggle for independence. The Erzurum Congress is most famous for its determination of the boundaries of what became known as the territories of the National Pact – those lands which would be part of the foreseen Turkish Republic. Atatürk and the congress claimed the lands which, in essence, form the present Turkish state and rejected any claim or desire to any other formerly held Ottoman lands. The phrase at the time was: 'We want no more, we shall accept no less.'

Orientation

Although the old city of Erzurum was huddled beneath the walls of the kale, the new Erzurum, which has grown up around the old, has broad boulevards, traffic roundabouts and an open, airy feeling, part of which comes from the dry wind which blows constantly.

You can walk to everything in the centre (Old Erzurum), including the railway station, but you will need a taxi or bus to get to and from the otogar, the airport and one of the top hotels. It is almost three km from the otogar to the centre of town (where you'll find the Belediye and Vilayet), and two km from the otogar to Havuzbaşı. From the otogar to the railway station is 2½ km.

Erzurum's main street is Cumhuriyet Caddesi, renamed Cemal Gürsel Caddesi along its western reaches. The two parts of the street are divided at the centre by a traffic roundabout bearing a large statue of Atatürk, a pool and fountain and the name Havuzbaşı.

Information

The Tourism Information Office (tel (011) 15697, 19127) is on the south side of Cemal Gürsel Caddesi, one block west of the Havuzbaşı traffic roundabout.

Erzurum's sights are conveniently grouped in the old part of town, within easy walking distance of one another. Start your sightseeing with the city's most famous Seljuk building, the one with two minarets.

Çifte Minareli Medrese

At the eastern end of Cumhuriyet Caddesi is the Çifte Minareli Medrese (1253) or Twin Minaret Seminary. Admission is free and it is open every day, more or less during daylight hours.

The Çifte Minare was built by Alaettin Keykubat II, son of the Seljuk sultan known for his many great building projects. Enter through the towering limestone portal topped by its twin minarets made of brick and decorated with small strips of blue tile. The main courtyard has four large niches and a double colonnade on the eastern and western sides of the courtyard. Stairways in each of the corners lead to the students' cells on the upper level.

At the far (southern) end of the courtyard is the grand 12-sided domed hall which served as the Hatuniye Türbesi or Tomb of Huant Hatun, the sultan's daughter. Beneath the domed hall is a small room with ingenious vents to allow the entry of light and air. This may have been a mescit prayer room or the tomb proper.

Ulu Cami

Next to the Çifte Minareli is the Ulu Cami or Great Mosque (1179). The contrast between the two buildings is interesting: the Ulu Cami, built by the Saltuklu Turkish Emir of Erzurum, is very restrained, though elegant, with seven aisles running north-south and six running east-west, resulting in a forest of columns. You enter from the north along the central (fourth) aisle. As you walk straight in, at the fourth east-west aisle is a stalactite dome with an opening to the heavens. At the far southern end of the central aisle is a very interesting wooden dome and a pair of bull's-eye windows.

Üç Kümbetler

To reach the complex of three Seljuk tombs, walk south between the Çifte Minareli and the Ulu Cami; you come to a T-intersection. Turn left then immediately right and walk a short block up the hill to the tombs, which are in a fenced enclosure on the right-hand side. The gate to the enclosure may be locked, but you can see most of what there is to see from the street. They have some good decoration, the best being on the octagonal Emir Sultan Türbesi, dating from the 12th century.

Erzurum Kalesi

Erzurum castle, erected by Theodosius around the 5th century, is on the hilltop to the north of the Çifte Minareli and the Ulu Cami. Walk up the hill toward the curious old clock tower topped by a Turkish flag. The tower was built as a minaret in the time of the Saltuks but was converted later to its time-keeping function. It stands by the entrance to the kale.

The kale is open from 8 am to 12 noon and from 1.30 to 7.30 pm in summer; admission costs US$0.50.

Within the kale walls you will probably encounter a group of boys playing football. Once they notice you, the game will end and they will run up to ask where you come from and to try their one phrase in English, which is usually 'Do you speak English?' or 'What is the time?'.

Besides the boys, the kale harbours a few old cannons with Russian or Ottoman inscriptions and a disused prayer room. It's difficult to get to the top of the walls for a view. The boys will recommend that you climb an electricity tower, but this is probably not a good idea.

Ottoman Mosques

Return to Cumhuriyet Caddesi then head west and you will pass on the north (right) side the small Ottoman **Caferiye Camii**, constructed in 1645 upon the order of Ebubekiroğlu Hacı Cafer.

Cross over the busy intersection, at the south-eastern corner of which stands the Vilayet, and you come to the Lala Mustafa Paşa Camii (1563), at the north-western corner. Lala Mustafa Paşa was a grand vizier during the golden age of the Ottoman Empire, and his mosque is a classical Ottoman work of the high period. It may have been designed by Sinan or someone in his following.

Yakutiye Medresesi

Just to the west of the Lala Mustafa Paşa Camii is the Yakutiye Medresesi, a Mongol theological seminary dating from 1310 and built by the local Mongol emir. Its portal copies the Seljuk style and is well worth a look at, especially the lions. The minaret borrows from Seljuk architecture as well. There is a türbe adjoining the school at the back, which was meant to be used as the emir's tomb but never was. The school is not open to visitors, though many Erzurumlus enjoy the surrounding park.

Erzurum Müzesi

The museum (tel 11406) is several long blocks south-west of the Yakutiye Medresesi. Walk west along Cumhuriyet Caddesi to the Havuzbaşı roundabout, then turn left (south) and walk up the hill. The museum is just before the next intersection, on the left (east) side of the street. It's a 15-minute walk, or you can take any bus climbing the hill from Havuzbaşı.

The museum is open from 8 am to 12 noon and from 1.30 to 5.30 pm, closed on Monday; admission costs US$1. Some exhibit labels are in English.

The museum's collection is interesting primarily for its ethnological displays. There are beautiful carpets and kilims galore, a hanging cradle (beşik) from the Caucasus (Kafkas), a shepherd's traditional heavy woollen cape, Ottoman costumes and home furnishings, a purloined Russian church bell, a traditional local carpet loom and an exhibit on the making of prayer beads (*tespih*) from the lightweight jet-black mineral called *oltutaş*. These can be bought in the market.

Besides the ethnological collection, the museum has some fragments of Seljuk tiles and Urartian pottery, and some pottery and jewellery found in Hellenistic and Roman tombs.

Upstairs (don't bash your head on the low overhang!) are more exhibits, including weaponry, some fine Ottoman suits of chain mail and a complete coin collection beginning with examples from the Egypt of the Ptolemys through the many Turkish princedoms to Ottoman times.

Bazaar

Erzurum's market areas are scattered through the old part of the city. As the streets are narrow and winding (as usual), it is not easy to direct you on your walk. Start your wanderings at the Lala Mustafa Paşa Camii, then walk north along the street next to the mosque. You will pass the Rüstem Paşa Çarşısı or Market of Rüstem Pasha, which is the centre for the manufacture and sale of black prayer-beads. For a look at the shops, go to the upper floor.

Just down the street from the Rüstem Paşa Çarşısı is the small **Pervizoğlu Camii** (1715), with a small, bright blue wooden screen in front. On Kavaflar Çarşısı Sokak are many tinsmiths who sell handmade cookers, heaters and samovars.

Continuing downhill in the market district will bring you, finally, to İstasyon Caddesi, the street to the railway station and the numerous hotels in this district.

The **Erzurum Hamamı** at the bazaar end of İstasyon Caddesi has received praise from many readers of this guide as one of the better hamams in Turkey.

Tortum Vadisi

Many visitors to Erzurum make an excursion northward into the Tortum Valley to enjoy the dramatic mountain scenery and to visit some of the old Georgian churches in little farming villages. For details, refer to the following section on travelling from Erzurum to Artvin.

Places to Stay - bottom end

Erzurum is a low-budget traveller's dream come true, with many very cheap places not far from the town centre. As for the upper end, there are no hotels in the luxury class, but several sufficient, comfortable places.

Erzurum's inexpensive lodging places are scattered throughout the old part of town and are especially thick along Kâzım Karabekir Caddesi (KYAA-zumm kah-rah-beh-KEER), north of the centre, not far from the railway station and the bazaar.

Among the cheapest hotels in the old city is the *Otel Evin* (tel 12349), Ayaz Paşa Caddesi, Bedendibi Sokak 12, down the street from the better known Hotel Çınar. The Evin has clean beds for US$2.50 and double rooms for US$5. Some rooms have views of the town. Hot water for Turkish splash-baths comes from the simple water heaters in which the hotel owner builds a fire half an hour before your appointed shower time. The patron is a congenial and helpful man.

The *Otel Çınar* (tel 13580), Ayaz Paşa Caddesi, a favourite with dolmuş and bus drivers, is a little more comfortable, but also costs more. To find these two hotels, look for the Gürpınar Sineması (a cinema) in the bazaar. Across the street from it is a little street leading to the Çınar.

Beyond the Çınar, the *Otel Arı* (tel 13141) is on Ayaz Paşa Caddesi, one of the main streets in the bazaar, and charges US$4 a double for a tidy room without running water. There are several similar hotels on Ayaz Paşa Caddesi.

Beginning in Aşağı Mumcu Meydanı, the little square at the eastern (bazaar) end of Kâzım Karabekir Caddesi, you'll see the *Nur Palas Oteli* (tel 11706), behind the more expensive Hotel Sefer. Rooms with no baths cost US$2/3.50 a single/double.

Walking along Kâzım Karabekir Caddesi, you will see these hotels:

The 32-room *Hitit Otel* (tel 11204), at No 26, is just off the little square. A room with washbasin costs US$7/9 a single/double, US$9/11 with private shower. It's one of the better places on the street, being more modern, comfortable and pleasant. Next door is the *Örnek Otel* (tel 11203), Kâzım Karabekir Caddesi 8, a similar place with 35 rooms, all with private showers. It's a bit like a barrack though, and has a weird colour scheme, but Turkish families love it. Rooms cost US$6/11 a single/ double with shower.

Next along the street is the 55-room *Otel San* (tel 15789/90), Kâzım Karabekir Caddesi 10, which has friendly management, a lift, cracked linoleum but tidy beds and towels. Rooms cost US$10/15 a single/double with shower, US$7 for a double with washbasin and US$17 for a triple with bath.

The one-star *Otel Polat* (tel 11623/4), Kâzım Karabekir Caddesi 3, next along the street, has a lift, a family atmosphere, pretensions to modernity and style and 60 rooms, each with a bath, for US$13/19/22 a single/double/triple. The lift does not inspire confidence. It is the one on the left; the 'lift' on the right is actually a telephone booth.

At the western end of Kâzım Karabekir Caddesi are two more places, which are very simple but willing to give reductions in price. The *Otel Serhat* (tel 12139), Gez Mahallesi 49, has only one single room with bath for US$5, but numerous doubles without bath for US$9, before haggling. Rooms with a washbasin only cost US$4/7 a single/double.

The nearby *Otel Çam* (tel 13025), Gez Mahallesi BP Karşısı, is close to the Turkish Airlines office and has very basic rooms with beds only and no running water, for US$3/5.50 a single/double, before haggling.

Places to Stay – middle

Otel Oral (tel 19740), Terminal Caddesi 3, 25100 Erzurum, is perhaps the best hotel in the city. Its 90, two-star rooms and suites all have showers or baths and telephones, and cost US$28/36 a single/double and US$48 for a suite. Although it's comfortable and has a willing staff and a good restaurant, it is out of the centre which means that you will have to travel everywhere by taxi. Also, being on the main thoroughfare, it suffers from the noise of heavy vehicles. In the warm months, when you will need to have the windows open for ventilation, request a room at the back (*arka tarafta*) without fail.

The 50-room, nominally three-star *Büyük Erzurum Oteli* (tel 16528/9, 16201), Ali Ravi Caddesi 5, 25100 Erzurum, is older than the Oral but has a better location just up the hill from the Belediye and Vilayet. The staff speak some English. The hotel is a bit old-fashioned, with small rooms and slightly faded furnishings, but it's comfortable enough. Rates are US$26/34 a single/double and from US$42 to US$50 for suites. Dinner in the hotel's dining room costs from US$7 to US$10 per person. As always, front rooms may be noisy.

Other hotels are distinctly more modest than the Oral and Büyük Erzurum and are basically at the bottom end. They are mentioned here because their more desirable locations may cause their prices and quality to rise in future.

One middle-range hotel is very near the railway station and the bazaar. It's the 36-room, two-star *Hotel Sefer* (tel 13615, 16714), İstasyon Caddesi, near Aşağı Mumcu Meydanı. Modern and convenient, but certainly not fancy, it officially charges US$20/28 for a single/double room with bath, but almost always offers substantial reductions.

On Cumhuriyet Caddesi in the heart of town are two more choices. The *Kral Hotel* (tel 16973, 11930), Erzincankapı 18, 25100 Erzurum, is across Cumhuriyet

Caddesi from the Yakutiye Medresesi in a very convenient location. Its 51 rooms with showers are fairly shabby but still serviceable, and cost US$11/15/18 a single/double/triple, but they are open to bargaining. The Kral is a favourite with Turkish families. The staff speak some English.

The *Akçay Otel* (tel 17330), Cumhuriyet Caddesi 2, 25100 Erzurum, has a lift and 32 fairly nice, well-kept rooms with showers for US$10/15 a single/double. The entry to the hotel is via Kâmil Ağa Sokak, a small side street opposite the Yakutiye Medresesi and Lala Mustafa Paşa Camii.

Places to Eat

As with hotel prices, meal prices in Erzurum are delightfully low. In fact, all are cheap enough to qualify as bottom-end places, though they are suitable for all tastes and budgets. The only exception might be the dining room of the Otel Oral, but even this is budget-priced compared to a similar place in İstanbul. Restaurants have not sprouted like mushrooms in this town but there are plenty to use, mostly along Cumhuriyet Caddesi.

Kebap places are, as usual, among the cheapest and best. Just opposite the Akçay Otel on Kâmil Ağa Sokak is the *Mulenruj Kebap Salonu* (that's Moulin Rouge!) (tel 19783) which has a large main dining room and a smaller mezzanine at the rear. On the west wall is an ersatz rock grotto with toy electrical power lines on top, connected to a rustic stone waterwheel which, at one time, appears to have generated the electricity to fire the power lines and to light several small bulbs. The whole assemblage does not appear to have worked properly for some time and its presence in a restaurant is a total mystery. I guess it's just one of those wonderful Turkish *jeux d'esprit*. The döner kebap tends to be a bit salty for my taste, but a meal of it, along with some kuru fasulye (beans in tomato sauce), pilav and a soft drink came to US$2.50. Several other

kebapçıs are within a few steps of the Mulenruj.

A stroll along Cumhuriyet Caddesi reveals several slightly fancier places, without waterwheels or fake rocks but with similarly low prices. The *Salon Çağın* (tel 19320) is near the traffic roundabout nearest the Yakutiye Medresesi, on the south side of the street. Clean, bright and cheery, it has very tasty food and on Sunday they make the house specialty, *mantı* (Turkish ravioli). A light lunch of sebzeli kebap (lamb stew with vegetables), bread and soft drink cost a mere US$1.75.

Across the street is the fancier *Salon Asya* (tel 21243). How much fancier? White tablecloth and napkin fancier! The menu includes a large variety of kebaps, including *tereyağlı* (with butter) and Bursa kebap. Meals cost US$3 to US$4.

The *Güzelyurt Restoran* (tel 11514), directly facing the Yakutiye Medresesi across Cumhuriyet Caddesi, is also fancier than the Çağın, with a menu listing prices of US$2 for a small fillet beefsteak, even less for şiş kebap or lamb chops. A sign on the door says: 'Please do not drive after having used alcohol.'

For cheap pide, try the *Park Pide Salonu* (tel 22554), facing the front door of the Yakutiye Medresesi from across the park and across the side street. A tiny place, it's clean, the pide is good and the price is only US$0.50 to US$0.75.

Getting There & Away

Being the main city in eastern Turkey, Erzurum is well served by all modes of transport.

Air Turkish Airlines (tel 18530, 11904) at 100 Yıl Caddesi, SSK Rant Tesisleri 24, at the north-western end of Kâzım Karabekir Caddesi, has a daily flight from İstanbul via Ankara to Erzurum, and return. The fare for the one-hour flight from Ankara to Erzurum is US$75, between İstanbul and Erzurum US$92. The airport bus (US$0.75) meets every flight and stops at the otogar on the way into town. For the trip back to the airport, it leaves the Turkish Airlines office 1¾ hours before flight time and stops at the otogar along the way. A taxi to or from the airport, 10 km from town, costs about US$3.50.

Bus The otogar is several km from the centre along the airport road, a 12-minute walk from the Otel Oral. City bus No 2 passes by the otogar and will take you into town for US$0.07. The otogar has snack shops and a restaurant. Just up the hill from the railway station along İstasyon Caddesi, at Gürcü Kapı Meydanı where the bazaar begins, are the offices of numerous bus companies. You can buy your onward tickets here and save yourself a trip out to the otogar.

Services to and from Erzurum include these destinations:

Ankara – 925 km, 15 hours, US$11.50; several buses daily
Artvin – 215 km, four hours, US$6; several buses daily
Diyarbakır – 485 km, 10 hours, US$8; several buses daily
Doğubeyazıt – 285 km, 4½ hours, US$5; five buses daily
Erzincan – 192 km, four hours, US$3.75; frequent buses daily
İstanbul – 1275 km, 21 hours, US$19; several buses daily
Kars – 205 km, 3½ hours, US$3; several buses daily
Sivas – 485 km, nine hours, US$9; several buses daily
Tortum – 53 km, one hour, US$1; several dolmuşes daily
Trabzon – 325 km, eight hours, US$7.50; several buses daily
Van – 420 km, 7½ hours, US$9; several buses daily
Yusufeli – 129 km, three hours, US$3; several dolmuşes daily

For Iran, take a bus to Doğubeyazıt, where you can catch a minibus to the Iranian frontier.

For dolmuşes to the Tortum Vadisi and Yusufeli, see the Around Erzurum section.

Train The Erzurum Garı is at the northern end of İstasyon Caddesi, about half a km north of the centre. You can easily walk to or from the station to most hotels, except the Oral. City buses depart the station forecourt every half-hour and circulate through the city. A taxi should cost less than US$2, no matter where you go in town.

Erzurum has good rail connections with Ankara via Kayseri, Sivas, Divriği and Erzincan. The daily Erzurum Mavi Tren departs Ankara at 9 pm, arriving in Erzurum the next day at 5.16 pm; from Erzurum, departure is at 10 am, arriving in Ankara the next morning at 6.15 am. The trip takes about 20 hours if it's on time. Besides the normal Pullman seat cars, this Mavi Tren hauls a car with blanketed couchettes. Tickets between Erzurum and Ankara cost US$12 on the Mavi Tren; couchettes cost 10% more.

Express trains cover the distance between Erzurum and Ankara in about 28 hours – if they're on time. The Doğu Ekspresi (Eastern Express) departs Ankara at 10.40 am daily, arriving in Erzurum at 1.22 pm the next day if all goes well (which it usually doesn't). The train continues to Sarıkamış, arriving at 6.11 pm, then Kars, arriving at 7.30 pm more or less (usually much more). The Doğu hauls 1st and 2nd-class coaches, couchettes and sleeping cars. A ticket costs from US$8 to US$10 and a sleeping berth costs between US$30 and US$50, depending upon the class, which depends upon the number of people in the sleeping compartment (one to three).

AROUND ERZURUM
Tortum Vadisi
For a look at the countryside around Erzurum, take an excursion into the Kaçkar Mountains through the Valley of Tortum. The town (population 6000) and the valley, about 53 km north of Erzurum,

are most beautiful in mid-June, when the orchards of cherries and apricots are in bloom.

Georgian Churches

Beyond Tortum, in villages near the highway, are some old Georgian churches worth visiting if you have the time and energy. The *Gürcü* or Georgians are a people who occupied the Caucasus, the mountainous country to the north of Artvin and Kars in the Soviet Union. The people are of lighter complexion than the Turks or Iranians. During the times when slavery was practised, Georgian Caucasian girls were in great demand as wives, concubines and harem girls, and many were sold by Christian families with too many mouths to feed in this rugged country.

The Georgians, like the Armenians, have usually been subjected to rule by another people, but in mediaeval times the Georgians had a splendid monarch, Queen Tamara, who by military might and diplomatic prowess brought the Georgian kingdom to rule over Armenians, Turks, Persians and Kurds in this area. At her death in 1212 the Kingdom of Georgia was at its height, but the Mongol conquest, which ruined everybody's day (except Ghengis Khan's), was only a few decades in the future.

Learning to play friend against foe, the Georgians maintained cordial relations with Byzantium in order to keep the local Armenian princes at bay. This policy may also have led them to convert to Islam in the 17th century, after the coming of the Ottomans. Yet early Georgian architecture, as you will see, borrowed heavily from the Armenian, Seljuk and Persian styles.

Bağbaşı About 25 km north of Tortum is a turning on the left (west), near a hump-back bridge, to this village called Haho by the Georgians. Go 7½ km up the unpaved road through orchards and fields to the village. Stop at the Belediye and teahouse and ask for the *kilise anahtarı* or church

key; no doubt a guide will accompany you for the last 600 metres up the road to the church, which is now the village mosque. The church, which dates from the 10th century, is still in fairly good repair, thanks to its continued use for worship. The guide will show you several reliefs reminiscent of those at Akdamar.

Vank Another 15½ km north of the Bağbaşı turning, in a wide valley with the river to the left (west) of the highway, is the road to Vank, seven km off the highway and up into the mountains. You must ford the river and wind up the road to the village, where you can't miss the big, impressive church. Most of the roof is gone, but there are still traces of reliefs and paintings. This was a monastery church, built in the 10th century. The Coşkun Çay Evi, to the right of the church, is used by foreigners dropping in for a glass of tea.

Tortum Gölü

North of Vank, the highway skirts the western shore of Tortum Lake, which was formed by a landslide about three centuries ago. You can visit the 48-metre Tortum Şelalesi (waterfall), which is only worth seeing in the winter when there's plenty of water. In summer, the meagre flow of water is diverted to the nearby hydroelectricity plant. The lake is a beautiful spot for a picnic and will surely have inns on its shores in future years.

İşhan

Heading north from the lake, take the road on the right marked for Olur and go six km (exactly 50 km from the Vank road) to a turning on the left for İşhan. This village is another six km up a rough, steep, muddy road carved out of the mountainside and probably impassable during wet or icy weather. If there have been heavy rains, the road may be washed out.

The scenic mountain village is worth seeing. Its **Georgian church** is 100 metres past the village and down the hill. On one side of the church is a fountain and a toilet, while on the other side is pasture land. The front of the church faces an open space, while the back is nestled into the hillside. This was the Church of the Mother of God, built in the 8th century and enlarged in the 11th century. There are several reliefs on the exterior, including one of a lion, some traces of a fresco inside and a horseshoe arcade in the apse.

Return to the Olur road, go back the six km to the highway and go north toward Artvin. In the 8½ km between the Olur road and the Yusufeli road, the highway goes through a dramatic gorge, wild and scenic, with striking bands of colour in the tortured rock of the sheer canyon walls. At the Yusufeli turning a sign reads, 'Meyve Cenneti Yusufeline Hoş Geldiniz' (Welcome to Yusufeli, Paradise of Fruit). From the turning, it's 10 km to the town.

Yusufeli

The swift Çoruh River rushes noisily through Yusufeli (population 4500), a place which is kept neat and tidy in the best tradition of alpine towns. The local people are friendly, though they think it a bit much that foreigners spend vast sums of money and come long distances to risk their lives rushing down the Çoruh River in little boats. (The Çoruh is a favourite white-water rafting and kayaking river.)

A one-minute stroll shows you all of metropolitan Yusufeli: the Belediye facing the main market street next to the river and the few little hotels and restaurants.

Places to Stay The hotels are of the most basic type, with beds (that's all) in waterless rooms. These include the *Çiçek Palas Oteli* (tel (0589) 1393, 1033), charging US$2 per bed and offering free showers, and the *Çilek Palas* (tel 1507), around the corner next to the mosque. It charges US$2 per bed in triples and US$3 per bed in doubles. It has a restaurant on the ground floor.

Places to Eat As for restaurants, the *Saray Lokantası* on the main street beneath the Lale Oteli is perhaps the nicest, though the *Mahzen Fıçı Bira* (Draught Beer Cellar) on the far side of the river below the Öğretmenler Lokalı (Teachers' Club) has a more dramatic setting, with a porch hanging over the turbulent river.

Getting There & Away It's 53 km from Erzurum to Tortum and another 77 km from Tortum to Yusufeli.

Minibuses to Tortum Vadisi and Yusufeli do not leave from the otogar in Erzurum, but from several locations, not easy to find, in the old part of town. The fastest way to find the minibus offices is to have a taxi take you to the Otel Çoruh (choh-ROO), near the Atatürk Endüstri Meslek Lisesi, a technical training high school. Look then for signs with the name Tortum, Yusufeli or Artvin on them. The Artvin-Yusufeli Otobüs İşletmesi, for example, operates minibuses about every hour as far as Tortum (US$1.50), with some continuing to Yusufeli (US$4). Another company is the Öz Tortum Birlik. There may be dolmuşes to Artvin which will drop you at the Yusufeli turning, whence you must hitch the last 10 km to the town.

From Yusufeli, there are dolmuşes several times daily to Artvin, 75 km to the north.

Without your own transport, it's difficult to get to the Georgian churches. Perhaps the best plan is to catch an early morning dolmuş north, hop out at the turning for one of the churches, hike in and see it, hike back out and see what can be caught to take you to the next one. If time runs out, return to Erzurum or head onward to Yusufeli for the night.

ARTVİN

Artvin (ahrt-VEEN, population 28,000, altitude 600 metres) is the capital of the province bearing the same name. You can approach Artvin from Yusufeli (75 km, 1¾ hours) or from Hopa on the Black Sea coast (70 km, 1½ hours). Sit on the right-hand side of the bus coming up from Hopa so as to get the best views.

If you come from Hopa, or go there from Artvin, remember that any liquid-filled containers in your luggage will expand as you ascend into the mountains or contract as you descend to the Black Sea coast. They will leak in either case. Keep liquid-filled containers with you and open them periodically to adjust the atmospheric pressure.

The ride to Artvin via either route is wonderfully scenic. As you approach Artvin you will notice mediaeval castles guarding the steep mountain passes. During three days in mid-June, a pasture seven km from Artvin called the Kafkasör Yaylası becomes the scene of an annual festival, the Kafkasör Kültür ve Sanat Festivalı (Caucasus Culture and Arts Festival). The main events are the bull wrestling matches (boğa güreşleri). Enquire in town.

Orientation

Artvin's new otogar is at Çarşı, the market district at the foot of the high hill which bears the town. The two main companies, Artvin Express and As Turizm, have servis arabası to take you the five km up the hill to the centre called Hükümet Konağı. This is a modern building with a statue of Atatürk in front. The PTT and hamam are nearby. Both companies also have ticket offices in the town centre.

Places to Stay

The centre of town has several good, cheap hotels and restaurants. The *Hotel 7 Mart* (YEH-dee MART), on the main street, is a good, friendly place with low prices and good value for money. The *Otel Genye* (GEHN-yeh) is another modest place to stay where the obliging staff will rent you a small, simple but tidy double room with a washbasin for US$7; a shower and flat toilet are down the hall.

For better rooms at a moderate price, check into the fairly new and modern two-

star *Hotel Karahan* (tel (0581) 1800), İnönü Caddesi 16, a 48-room hostelry with a lift, restaurant and comfortable rooms priced from US$18 to US$22 a single and from US$24 to US$30 a double.

Getting There & Away

The roads between Artvin and Hopa and Artvin and Erzurum are fairly good, smooth and fast. Take some water and snacks along on the trip between Artvin and Kars, whether you go by bus or car. If you have your own car, it's a good idea to fill your fuel tank in Artvin before setting out for Kars. Some distances and times from Artvin are:

Erzurum – 215 km, four hours, US$6; several buses and dolmuşes daily
Hopa – 70 km, 1½ hours, US$2; frequent dolmuşes daily
Kars – 270 km, six hours, US$7; two buses daily (6 and 10 am)
Trabzon – 255 km, five hours, US$6; frequent buses daily
Yusufeli – 75 km, 1¾ hours, US$2.25; several dolmuşes daily

EAST TO SARIKAMIŞ

The highway leaves Erzurum and climbs into a landscape of wide vistas, rich irrigated fields and the inevitable flocks of cattle and sheep.

At **Pasinler**, a farming town, the Hasankale fortress dominates the town from its rock promontory. There are hot springs here.

Between Pasinler and Horasan are more wide-open views of broad, fertile mountain valleys. In **Horasan** you may see the Çoban Köprü, a 16th-century stone bridge designed, it is said, by the great Sinan. The highway follows the river valley of the Aras Nehri, as does the rail line.

After Horasan and Karakurt, the road leaves the river valley to climb into the mountains through pine forests, passing one fertile mountain pasture after another.

Sarıkamış

This lumbering town 152 km east of Erzurum has a small ski resort, a huge army base, a forestry headquarters and, on its eastern outskirts, a big shoe factory. The army base is a reminder that in December 1914, in the early days of WW I, Ottoman troops defended the pass at Sarıkamış against the traditional invader along this route, the armies of Imperial Russia, losing tens of thousands of soldiers in the savage fighting.

East of Sarıkamış, the highway climbs out of the lush mountain valleys and away from the evergreen forests to vast rolling steppe with mountains in the distance. It is in this sea-of-grass setting that you find Kars.

Places to Stay Sarıkamış has two hotels, better than any found in Kars. If you normally stay in middle-range hotels, consider staying in Sarıkamış and taking day trips to Kars.

The *Turistik Hotel Sarıkamış* (tel 1176, 2152), Halk Caddesi 64, Sarıkamış, Kars, is in the centre of town, marked prominently by signs. Although the hotel is not fancy, the lobby is colourfully decorated with local carpets and kilims, and the rooms are well kept and fairly cheerful. The dining room is quite serviceable. Rooms cost US$16/32 a single/double with bath and breakfast.

A small resort motel, the *Sartur Moteli*, stands above the town and is the centre of skiing activity in winter. In summer, it offers an alternative to the Hotel Sarıkamış and, more importantly, another alternative to the hotels in Kars. Prices are similar to those at the Hotel Sarıkamış.

KARS

Kars (KAHRSS, population 80,000, altitude 1768 metres) is an odd place which is chilly and drab most of the time. There are lots of police and soldiers, and every one of them can tell you without hesitation the precise number of days he has yet to serve in Kars before he can go

west to 'civilisation'. And they will want to talk to you! As a foreigner, you bring them a breath of culture. As for the locals, a harsh climate and a rough history has made them, for the most part, dour and sombre, though not impolite.

Kars doesn't look like any other Turkish town. It is dominated by a stark, no-nonsense mediaeval fortress (rebuilt in 1855) which is still used as part of the city's defences. Many of the public buildings, and even some of the residences, look Russian, not Turkish. The school gymnasium was obviously built as a Russian Orthodox church.

Kars was indeed held by the Russians for a time (1878 to 1920), which accounts for the 19th-century Russian aspect of the town. The mood of the inhabitants comes from the fact that Kars, although set in the midst of fertile agricultural land, is a garrison town. What people do is grow wheat, make carpets and watch out for the Soviets.

Orientation

Kars is laid out on a somewhat grandiose grid. The Russians must have had great plans for the town when they laid it out but, unable to keep it, they never realised their goals. Nonetheless, almost everything in Kars is within easy walking distance, except perhaps the railway station and the museum.

Information

The Tourism Information Office (tel (021) 12300), Lise Caddesi, is in the Turizm Müdürlüğü (Tourism Directorate) building across from the Vilayet and the Jandarma. Go up several flights of steps to the top floor to find the office. This is where you go with questions and to fill in forms to obtain permission to visit Ani.

You have no doubt come to Kars with the intention of visiting Ani, for without that intention it doesn't make much sense to come here. But while in Kars, there are a few things well worth seeing.

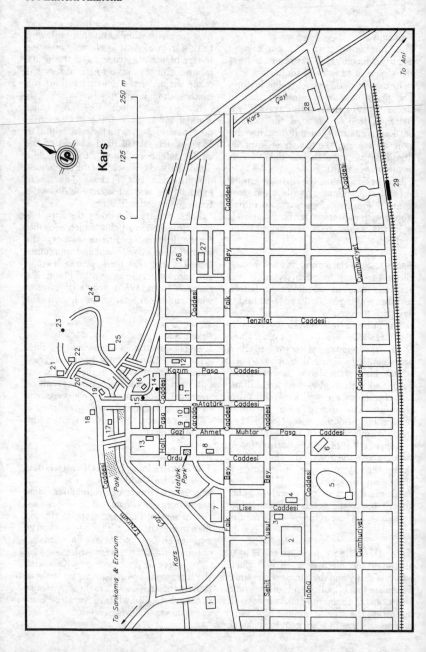

Kars

1	Unknown Soldier Monument
2	Vilayet
3	Jandarma
4	Tourist Information Office
5	Stadyum
6	Hospital
7	Emniyet (Police)
8	PTT
9	Merkez Camii
10	Belediye
11	Asya Oteli
12	Hotel Temel
13	Yusuf Paşa Camii
14	Güngören Hotel
15	Aliağa Camii
16	Evliya Camii
17	Cuma Hamamı
18	Lacin Bey Camii
19	Namık Kemal House
20	Taş Köprü
21	Mazlum Ağa Hamamı
22	İlbeyioğlu Hamamı
23	Kars Kalesi
24	Kümbet Camii
25	Beylerbeyi Sarayı
26	Otogar
27	Hotel Yılmaz
28	Müze
29	Railway Station

Kars Müzesi

This fine, new little museum is open from 8 am to 5.30 pm; admission costs US$0.75. Its oldest exhibits date from the Old Bronze Age. Roman and Greek periods are represented, as are the Seljuks and Ottomans. Several photo exhibits show excavations at Ani and there are shots of Armenian churches in Kars. The chief exhibit is a pair of carved doors from an orthodox church and a Russian church bell from the time of Tsar Nicholas II (1894 to 1917).

You should not miss the ethnographic exhibits upstairs, as this area produces some very fine kilims, carpets and *cicims* (embroidered kilims). Costumes, saddle-bags, jewellery, samovars and a home carpet loom complete the exhibit.

Behind the museum is the railway coach in which representatives of the new Russian Bolshevik Government and the new Turkish Republic signed the 1920s protocol which ended the Russian occupation and annexation of Kars.

Kümbet Camii

Although called the Drum-Dome Mosque in Turkish, this building by the river was built as the Church of the Apostles by the Bagratid King Abas, between 932 and 937. It was repaired extensively at about 1579 when the Ottomans rebuilt much of the city. The relief carvings on the drum are of the apostles and the porches were added to the ancient structure in the 19th century. The church awaits restoration again and it's not possible to see the interior.

Not far from the church is an old bridge, the Taş Köprü, which dates from the 15th century. It was repaired in 1579 along with everything else in town, but was later ruined by an earthquake after which it was rebuilt to its present form by the local Karaoğulları emirs in 1719. Ruins of the Ulu Cami and a palace called the Beylerbey Sarayı are beneath the kale.

Kars Kalesi

No doubt there has been a fortress at this strategic spot since the earliest times, but records show that one was built by the Saltuklu Turks in 1152 and torn down by Tamerlane in 1386. It was rebuilt upon the order of the Ottoman sultan Murat III by his grand vizier Lala Mustafa Paşa in 1579. Further repairs were made in 1616 and 1636.

Although the fortress is still an active military base, it is open to visitors a few days a week (Thursday, Saturday and Sunday from 9 or 9.30 am to 5 pm), for free.

The kale was the scene of bitter fighting during and after WW I. When the Russian armies withdrew in 1920, the control of Kars was left in the hands of the Armenian forces which had allied themselves with Russia during the war. Civilians, whether Christian or Muslim, suffered oppression and worse when under the control of irregular troops of the opposing religion. As the slaughter of Christian Armenians occurred in some parts of eastern Turkey, there was also slaughter of Muslim Turks and Kurds around Kars until the republican armies took the kale.

Places to Stay – bottom end

Hotel Nur Saray on Faik Bey Caddesi charges US$2.66 for a double room with washbasin; cold showers are free. While this is about the best, there are similar, cheap places.

Places to Stay – middle

The hotel situation in Kars is not particularly bright, but it's passable if you're travelling on a very low budget. Most of the small, cheap hotels are on Faik Bey Caddesi, the main street. These include the 38-room *Otel Kervansaray* (tel 11990), Faik Bey Caddesi 129; the *Topçu Palas* (tel 11946), Faik Bey Caddesi 169; and the *Nur Saray Oteli* (tel 11364), Faik Bey Caddesi 26. All charge US$3/5/6 a single/double/triple in waterless rooms.

The other hotel street is Küçük Kâzımbey Caddesi, where you'll find the 33-room *Asya Oteli* (tel 12299), Küçük Kâzımbey Caddesi 48, where rooms cost slightly more; and the 30-room *Yılmaz Oteli* (yuhl-MAHZ, tel 11074, 12387), Küçük Kâzımbey Caddesi 14, next to the bus terminal. It has 30 rooms and charges US$10/16 a single/double with shower. It is the best place in town, which is not saying much.

You might also look at the 22-room *Temel Oteli* (tel 11287), Kâzım Paşa Caddesi 39, which is second to the Yılmaz with similar prices.

Places to Eat – bottom end

Kars is noted for its excellent honey. If you're lucky (or if you ask), you might get it for breakfast.

The town has several cheap, suitable restaurants, including the popular *Manolya* on Atatürk Caddesi, the main street, the *Yeni Nil Kebap Salonu* on Atatürk Caddesi and the *Başkent Lokantası* near the otogar, which has good döner kebap. The *Esmeray* on Pazar Caddesi offers a good breakfast with excellent Kars honey and the traditional Turkish breakfast beverage, hot sweetened milk.

Places to Eat – middle

The best restaurant in town is in the *Yılmaz Hotel*. It serves alcoholic beverages, which is not the case in most places.

Things to Buy

I bought several of the local carpets in Kars. The weave of the modern rugs is coarse. The local wool is not dyed, so its earthy colours are retained. Any dealer in town can show you some *Kars halıları* (KAHRSS hah-luh-lah-ruh, Kars carpets) and will quote you a price of so many liras per square metre. There are several grades of carpets, and thus several price ranges. Once you've found a carpet you like and have agreed on a price per square metre (haggle!), the carpet is measured, yielding the final, exact price.

These are not fine Turkish carpets, but they are earthy, attractive, sturdy and inexpensive, although heavy and bulky to carry home. I'm not sure that I'd trust having them shipped.

Getting There & Away

Bus There is direct bus service between Kars and Adana, Ankara, Ardahan, Bursa, Denizli, Diyarbakır, Erzurum, Iğdır, İskenderun, İstanbul, İzmir, Kahramanmaraş, Kayseri, Konya, Malatya, Mersin, Samsun, Sivas and Trabzon. Most of these buses (except those to Ardahan, Iğdır and Doğubeyazıt) go via Erzurum.

For Doğubeyazıt, change buses at Iğdır; there is one bus per day to Iğdır, departing at 9 am.

Buses take 3½ to four hours to cover the 205 km between Erzurum and Kars.

Train The Doğu Ekspresi is scheduled to depart Erzurum for Kars each afternoon at 2 pm, arriving in Sarıkamış at 6.11 pm and Kars at 7.30 pm, but it is invariably late. The trip is supposed to take 5½ hours. The return trip to Erzurum and points west departs Kars at 8 am daily, arriving in Erzurum at 1.03 pm. A single ticket costs US$1.50 1st class and US$1 2nd class. In the Kars switching yard you might see some marvellous old steam locomotives.

There are supposedly express trains on Tuesday (and Friday in summer) from Kars to Ahuryan in the Armenian SSR. Obtain your Soviet visa in advance from the Soviet Embassy at home or at Ankara.

ANİ

The ruined city at Ani (AH-nee), 48 km east of Kars, is striking. It's a mediaeval ghost town set in grassy fields overlooking the ravine cut by the Arpaçay stream, which forms the boundary between the Turkish Republic and the Soviet Armenian Republic. On the far side are somewhat ominous Soviet watchtowers. The frontier no-man's land extends to a distance of 700 metres on either side of the Arpaçay.

The walls of Ani, over a km in length, will impress you as you drive across the wheat-covered plains toward the border.

History

This was the capital of an Urartian state and later of an Armenian Bagratid kingdom (953 to 1045), when it was taken by the Byzantines. After that, the city was taken by the Great Seljuks of Iran, then by the King of Georgia, then by Kurdish emirs. The struggle for the city went on among these groups until the Mongols arrived in 1239 and cleared everybody else out. The Mongols, who were nomads, had no use for city life, so Ani became a ghost town after their victory.

Information

To visit Ani, you must have permission from the authorities. The Turks and the Soviets have signed a protocol agreement laying down the rules to be obeyed while visiting Ani, so everyone going into the no-man's land must be accounted for. Ani lies so close to the border that under normal conditions anyone spotted there would be considered to be violating the Soviet frontier.

Go to the Tourism Information Office in Kars and ask for the simple application form to visit Ani. After filling it out you'll be referred to the Emniyet Müdürlüğü (ehm-nee-YEHT mew-dewr-lew, Security Headquarters), two blocks away, where police officials in green uniforms will consider your application. Approval is routine usually.

At present the Turco-Soviet protocol on visitors to Ani requires that you follow these rules: no staring or pointing toward the Soviet side; no use of binoculars or cameras whatsoever; no taking notes; and no picnicking or remaining in one spot for too long.

A soldier guide was once necessary to tour the ruins, but that requirement has been relaxed so you can now tromp around the site on your own, with several guards watching to see that the rules are obeyed. With *glasnost* and *perestroika*, even these simple rules may be relaxed.

Touring the Ruins

About eight km before you come to Ani, your vehicle stops at a Jandarma post where there will be a check to make sure you have official permission to visit. You will be required to leave your camera in a check room. Hand it over. You can get yourself (and the soldiers) in big trouble if you're discovered taking photos in Ani, contrary to international protocol.

When you reach Ani, enter through the **Alp Arslan Kapısı**, a double gate. Your first view of Ani, the wrecks of buildings in a ghost city where once hundreds of thousands of people lived, is stunning. The site is open from 8.30 am to 5 pm daily; admission costs US$2.

Within the walls are the ruins of eight churches, a convent and the İç Kale.

The **cathedral** is the most impressive of

the churches. Ani became the seat of the Armenian Catholicos in 993 and this church was built between 989 and 1010. As the grandest religious edifice in the city, it was transformed into a mosque whenever Muslims held Ani, but reverted to a church when the Christians took over.

Other than the cathedral, the most interesting churches are the **Church of the Holy Saviour** (1036) and the **Church of St Gregory of Tigran Honentz** (1215). The latter is to the left as you enter and is the only one with frescoes.

The İç Kale may be off limits. Obey the guards if they signal you not to approach it. Also, don't get too near the river.

Getting There & Away

In summer, many Kars hotels arrange minibuses out to Ani at a cost of about US$4 per person both ways. The Tourism Information Office may set one up as well and your driver may even take care of the police permission for you once you've filled in the form. An even cheaper way to go is via the city bus, which departs at 6.30 am and 2 pm for the village of Ocaklı, next to Ani. It will even wait for you while the jandarmas check your permit and ask for your camera. Have your permission form completed the day before if you intend to catch the early bus.

Turkish Language Guide

From the time when Turks first encountered Islam about the year 670, Turkish had been written in the Arabic alphabet, the letters of the Koran. However, the Arabic letters did not suit the sounds of Turkish well and made the task of literacy very difficult.

Even under the empire, alphabet reform had been proposed in order to promote literacy and progress. But it was Atatürk, of course, who did it in 1928. The story is typical of him: when told that it would take several years of expert consultation to devise a suitable Latin alphabet for Turkish, and then about five years at the least to implement it, he replied, 'The change will be carried out in three months, or not at all'. Needless to say, the new alphabet was ready in six weeks, and three months later the old alphabet was forbidden in public use. And it worked! The president of the republic himself got a slate and chalk, went into the public parks, and held informal classes to teach the people the new letters.

Lonely Planet's new *Turkish Phrasebook* (available mid-1990) has words and phrases that are geared to travellers' needs. Ask for it at your bookshop.

For more complete and systematic help, I've made up a cassette keyed to both this guidebook and the Lonely Planet *Turkish Phrasebook*. For a copy of the cassette, please send your name and address, and a cheque payable to Tom Brosnahan for US$10, A$12.50, UK£6, CN$12, or SFr 16, to Turkish Cassette, c/o Tom Brosnahan, PO Box 563, Concord, MA 01742, USA.

PRONUNCIATION

Despite daunting oddities such as the soft 'g' (ğ) and undotted 'i' (ı), Turkish is phonetic and simple to pronounce. In a few minutes you can learn to pronounce the sounds reasonably well.

Here are some tips on correct pronunciation in Turkish. Most letters in Turkish are pronounced as they appear. Here are the tricky ones, the vowels and the exceptions.

A, a	short 'a' as in 'art' or 'bar'
â	very faint 'y' sound in preceding consonant, eg Lâleli is lyaah-leh-LEE
E, e	'eh' as the first vowel in 'ever' or 'fell'
İ, i	as 'ee' in 'see'
I, ı	'uh' or the vowel sound in 'were' or 'sir'
O, o	same as in English
Ö, ö	same sound as in German, or like English 'ur', as in 'fur'
U, u	'oo', like the vowel in 'moo' or 'blue'
Ü, ü	same as in German, or 'ew' in 'few'
C, c	pronounced like English 'j' as in 'jet'
Ç, ç	'ch' as in 'church'
G, g	always hard like 'get', not soft like 'gentle'
ğ	not pronounced; lengthens preceding vowel; ignore it!
H, h	never silent, always unvoiced, as in 'half'
J, j	like French 'j', English 'zh', or the 'z' in 'azure'
S, s	always 'sss' as in 'stress', not 'zzz' as in 'ease'
Ş, ş	'sh' as in 'show'
V, v	soft, almost like a 'w'

W, w exists only in foreign words; not really Turkish
X, x only in foreign words; Turks use 'ks' instead

An important point for English speakers to remember is that each Turkish letter is pronounced; there are no diphthongs as in English. Thus the name *Mithat* is pronounced 'meet-HOT', not like the English word 'methought', and Turkish *meshut* is 'mess-HOOT', not 'meh-SHOOT'. Watch out for this! Your eye, used to English double-letter sounds, will keep trying to find them in Turkish, where they don't exist.

These examples also demonstrate that the 'h' is pronounced as an unvoiced aspiration (like the first sound in 'have' or 'heart', the sound a Cockney drops), and it is pronounced every time it occurs; it is never combined to make a diphthong. So your Turkish friend is named not 'aa-meht' but 'ahh-MEHT'; the word *rehber*, 'guide', is not 're-ber' but 'rehh-BEHR'. In the old days, English writers used to spell the name *Achmet* just to get people to breathe that 'h', but it didn't work: people said 'otch-met'. Say, 'a HALF'. Now say 'Ah MEHT' the same way.

GRAMMAR

Grammar is another matter entirely. Though supremely logical and unencumbered by genders and mountains of exceptions, Turkish structure is so different from that of the Indo-European languages that it is completely unfamiliar at first. A few hints will help you comprehend road and shop signs, schedules and menus.

Suffixes

A Turkish word consists of a root and one or more suffixes added to it. Though in English we have only a few suffixes (-'s for possessive, -s or -es for plural), Turkish has lots and lots of suffixes. Not only that, these suffixes are subject to an unusual system of 'vowel harmony' whereby most of the vowel sounds in a word are made in a similar manner. What this means is that the suffix might be *-lar* when attached to one word, but *-ler* when attached to another; it's the same suffix, though.

Sometimes these suffixes are preceded by a 'buffer letter', a 'y' or an 'n'.

Here are some of the noun suffixes you'll encounter most frequently:

-a, -e	to
-dan, -den	from
-dır, -dir, -dur, -dür	emphatic (ignore it!)
-(s)ı, -(s)i, -(s)u, -(s)ü	for object-nouns (ignore it!)
-(n)ın, -(n)in	possessive
-lar, -ler	plural
-lı, -li, -lu, -lü	with
-sız, -siz, -suz, -süz	without

Here are some of the common verb suffixes:

-ar, -er, -ır, -ir, -ur, -ür	simple present tense
-acak, -ecek, -acağ-, -eceğ-	future tense
-dı, -di, -du, -dü	simple past tense
-ıyor-, -iyor-	continuous (like our '-ing')
-mak, -mek	infinitive ending

Nouns

Suffixes can be added to nouns to modify them. The two you will come across most frequently are -*ler* and -*lar*, which form the plural: *otel*, hotel; *oteller*, hotels; *araba*, car; *arabalar*, cars.

Other suffixes modify in other ways: *ev*, house; *Ahmet*, Ahmet; but *Ahmet'in evi*, Ahmet's house. Similarly with *İstanbul* and *banka*: it's *İstanbul Bankası* when the two are used together. You may see -*i*, -ı, -u or -*ü*, -sı, -sı, -su or -*sü* added to any noun. A *cami* is a mosque; but the *cami* built by Mehmet Pasha is the *Mehmet Paşa Camii*, with a double 'i'. Ask for a *bira* and the waiter will bring you a bottle of whatever type he has; ask for an *Efes Birası* and that's the brand you'll get.

Yet other suffixes on nouns tell you about direction: -*a* or -*e* means to; *otobüs* is bus, *otobüse* (oh-toh-bews-EH), to the bus; *Bodrum'a* (boh-droom-AH), to Bodrum. The suffix -*dan* or -*den* means 'from': *Ankara'dan*, from Ankara; *köprüden*, from the bridge. Stress is on these final syllables (-*a* or -*dan*) whenever they are used.

Verbs

The infinitive form is with -*mak* or -*mek*, as in *gitmek*, to go; *almak*, to take. The stress in the infinitive is always on the last syllable, 'geet-MEHK', 'ahl-MAHK'.

The simple present form is with -*r*, as in *gider*, he/she/it goes; *giderim*, I go. The suffix -*iyor* means about the same, *gidiyorum*, I'm going. For the future, there's -*ecek* or -*acak*, as in *alacak* (ah-lah-JAHK), he will take (it).

Word Order

The nouns and adjectives usually come first, then the verb; the final suffix on the verb is the subject of the sentence:

I'll go to İstanbul.
   İstanbul'a gideceğim.
I want to buy (take) a carpet.
   Halı almak istiyorum (literally 'Carpet to buy want I').

Some Useful Words & Phrases

Greetings & Civilities
Hello	*Merhaba*	MEHR-hah-bah
Good morning	*Günaydın*	gew-nahy-DUHN
Good day	*Günaydın*	gew-nahy-DUHN
Good evening	*İyi akşamlar*	EE ahk-shahm-LAHR
Good night	*İyi geceler*	EE geh-jeh-LEHR
Good-bye	*Allaha ısmarladık*	ah-LAHS-mahr-lah-duhk (said only by the person who is departing to go somewhere)
Bon voyage	*Güle güle*	gew-LEH gew-LEH (said only by the person who is staying behind; literally, 'Go smiling')

How are you?	*Nasılsınız?*	NAHS-suhl-suh-nuhz
I'm fine, thank you.	*İyiyim, teşekkür ederim.*	ee-YEE-yihm, tesh-ek-KEWR eh-dehr-eem
Very well	*Çok iyiyim*	CHOHK ee-YEE-yeem
Pardon me	*Affedersiniz*	af-feh-DEHR-see-neez
May it contribute to your health!	*Afiyet olsun!*	ah-fee-EHT ohl-soon (said to someone sitting down to a meal)
May your life be spared!	*Başınız sağ olsun!*	bah-shuh-nuhz SAAH ohl-soon (said to someone who has just experienced a death in the family)
May your soul be safe from harm!	*Canınız sağ olsun!*	jah-nuh-nuhz SAAH ohl-soon (said to someone who has just accidentally broken something)
May it be in your past!	*Geçmiş olsun!*	gech-MEESH ohl-soon (said to someone who is ill, injured, or otherwise distressed)
May it last for hours!	*Saatler olsun!*	saaht-LEHR ohl-soon (said to someone who just emerged from a bath or shower, a shave or a hair cut. It's a corruption of *sıhhatler olsun*)
'In your honour!' or 'To your health!'	*Şerefinize!*	sheh-rehf-ee-neez-EH

Small Talk

yes	*evet*	eh-VEHT
no	*hayır*	HAH-yuhr
please	*lütfen*	LEWT-fehn
thanks	*teşekkürler*	teh-sheh-kewr-LEHR
thanks	*mersi*	mehr-SEE
thank you very much	*çok teşekkür ederim*	CHOHK teh-sheh-KEWR eh-deh-reem
you're welcome	*bir şey değil*	beer SHEHY deh-YEEL
pardon me	*affedersiniz*	AHF-feh-DEHR-see-neez
pardon	*pardon*	pahr-DOHN
help yourself	*buyurun(uz)*	BOOY-roon-(ooz)
friend	*arkadaş*	AHR-kah-DAHSH
what?	*ne?*	NEH
how?	*nasıl?*	NAH-suhl
who?	*kim?*	KEEM
why?	*niçin, neden?*	NEE-cheen, NEH-dehn
when?	*ne zaman?*	NEH zah-mahn

Which one?	*Hangisi?*	HAHN-gee-see
What's this?	*Bu ne?*	BOO neh
Where is .... ?	*........ nerede?*	NEH-reh-deh
At what time?	*Saat kaçta?*	saht-KAHCH-tah
How much/many?	*Kaç/kaç tane?*	KAHCH/tah-neh
How many liras?	*Kaç lira?*	KAHCH lee-rah
How many hours?	*Kaç saat?*	KAHCH sah-aht
How many minutes?	*Kaç dakika?*	KAHCH dahk-kah
What does it mean?	*Ne demek?*	NEH deh-mehk
Give me	*........ bana verin*	bah-NAH veh-reen
I want	*........ istiyorum*	ees-tee-YOH-room
this	*bu(nu)*	boo(NOO)
that	*şu(nu)*	shoo(NOO)
the other	*o(nu)*	oh(NOO)
hot/cold	*sıcak/soğuk*	suh-JAHK/soh-OOK
big/small	*büyük/küçük*	bew-YEWK/kew-CHEWK
new/old	*yeni/eski*	yeh-NEE/ehss-KEE
open/closed	*açık/kapalı*	ah-CHUHK/kah-pah-LUH
not	*........ değil*	deh-YEEL
none	*yok*	YOHK
and	*ve*	VEH
or	*veya*	veh-YAH
good	*iyi*	EE
bad	*fenah*	feh-NAH
beautiful	*güzel*	gew-ZEHL

Accommodation

Where is .... ?	*........ nerede?*	NEH-reh-deh
Where is a hotel?	*Bir otel nerede?*	BEER oh-TEHL NEH-reh-deh?
Where is the toilet?	*Tuvalet nerede?*	too-vah-LEHT NEH-reh-deh?
Where is the manager?	*Patron nerede?*	pah-TROHN NEH-reh-deh?
Where is someone who knows English?	*İngilizce bilen bir kimse nerede?*	EEN-geh-LEEZ-jeh bee-lehn beer KEEM-seh NEH-reh-deh?

To request a room, say:

I want	*........ istiyorum.*	ees-tee-YOH-room
a double room	*iki kişilik oda*	ee-KEE kee-shee-leek OH-dah
a twin-bedded room	*çift yataklı oda*	CHEEFT yah-tahk-LUH OH-dah

If you want to be fully correct, say *istiyoruz* for the plural ('We want ....'). For the courageous, string them together:

We want a quiet bathless double room with a wide (double) bed.
   Sakin iki kişilik geniş yataklı banyosuz oda istiyoruz.

room	*oda*	OH-dah
single room	*bir kişilik oda*	BEER kee-shee-leek OH-dah
double room	*iki kişilik oda*	ee-KEE kee-shee-leek OH-dah
triple room	*üç kişilik oda*	EWCH kee-shee-leek OH-dah
room with one bed	*tek yataklı oda*	TEHK yah-tahk-LUH OH-dah
room with two beds	*İki yataklı oda*	ee-KEEyah-tahk-LUH OH-dah
room with twin beds	*çift yataklı oda*	CHEEFT yah-tahk-LUH OH-dah
double bed	*geniş yatak*	geh-NEESH yah-tahk
room with bath	*banyolu oda*	BAHN-yoh-LOO OH-dah
room without bath	*banyosuz oda*	BAHN-yoh-SOOZ OH-dah
room with shower	*duşlu oda*	doosh-LOO OH-dah
room with washbasin	*lavabolu oda*	LAH-vah-boh-LOO oh-dah
a quiet room	*sakin bir oda*	sah-KEEN beer oh-dah
It's very noisy.	*Çok gürültülü.*	CHOHK gew-rewl-tew-lew
What does it cost?	*Kaç lira?*	KAHCH lee-rah
cheaper	*daha ucuz*	dah-HAH oo-jooz
better	*daha iyi*	dah-HAH ee
very expensive	*çok pahalı*	CHOHK pah-hah-luh
bath	*banyo*	BAHN-yoh
Turkish bath	*hamam*	hah-MAHM
shower	*duş*	DOOSH
soap	*sabun*	sah-BOON
shampoo	*şampuan*	SHAHM-poo-AHN
towel	*havlu*	hahv-LOO
toilet paper	*tuvalet kağıdı*	too-vah-LEHT kyah-uh-duh
hot water	*sıcak su*	suh-JAHK soo
cold water	*soğuk su*	soh-OOH soo
clean	*temiz*	teh-MEEZ
not clean	*temiz değil*	teh-MEEZ deh-YEEL
laundry	*çamaşır*	chah-mah-SHUHR
dry cleaning	*kuru temizleme*	koo-ROO teh-meez-leh-meh
central heating	*kalorifer*	kah-LOH-ree-FEHR
air-conditioning	*klima*	KLEE-mah
light(s)	*ışık(lar)*	uh-SHUHK(-LAHR)
light bulb	*ampül*	ahm-PEWL

Getting Around

Where is a/the .... ?	*........ nerede?*	NEH-reh-deh
railway station	*gar/istasyon*	GAHR, ees-tah-SYOHN
bus station	*otogar*	OH-toh-gahr
cheap hotel	*ucuz bir otel*	oo-JOOZ beer oh-TEHL

toilet	*tuvalet*	too-vah-LEHT
restaurant	*lokanta*	loh-KAHN-tah
post office	*postane*	POHSS-tah-neh
policeman	*polis memuru*	poh-LEES meh-moo-roo
checkroom	*emanetçi*	EH-mah-NEHT-chee
luggage	*bagaj*	bah-GAHZH
suitcase	*bavul*	bah-VOOL
left	*sol*	SOHL
right	*sağ*	SAH
straight on	*doğru*	doh-ROO
here	*burada*	BOO-rah-dah
there	*şurada*	SHOO-rah-dah
over there	*orada*	OH-rah-dah
near	*yakın*	yah-KUHN
far	*uzak*	oo-ZAHK
A ticket to	*........ bir bilet*	BEER bee-LEHT
A ticket to İstanbul	*İstanbul'a bir bilet*	ih-STAHN-bool-AH
map	*harita*	HAH-ree-TAH
timetable	*tarife*	tah-ree-FEH
ticket	*bilet*	bee-LEHT
reserved seat	*numaralı yer*	noo-MAH-rah-LUH yehr
1st class	*birinci mevki*	beer-EEN-jee mehv-kee
2nd class	*ikinci mevki*	ee-KEEN-jee mehv-kee
for today	*bugün için*	BOO-gewn ee-cheen
for tomorrow	*yarın için*	yah-ruhn ee-cheen
for Friday	*Cuma günü için*	joo-MAH gew-new ee-cheen
one-way trip	*gidiş*	gee-DEESH
round-trip	*gidiş-dönüş*	gee-DEESH-dew-NURSH
student (ticket)	*talebe (bileti)*	tah-leh-BEH
full-fare (ticket)	*tam (bileti)*	TAHM
daily	*hergün*	HEHR-gurn
today	*bugün*	BOO-gurn
tomorrow	*yarın*	YAHR-uhn

Getting Around – arrivals & departures

When does it ....?	*Ne zaman ....?*	NEH zah-mahn
depart?	*kalkar?*	kahl-KAHR
arrive?	*gelir?*	geh-LEER
eight o'clock	*saat sekiz*	sah-AHT seh-KEEZ
at nine-thirty	*saat dokuz buçukta*	sah-AHT doh-KOOZ boo-chook-TAH
in 20 minutes	*yirmi dakikada*	yeer-MEE dahk-kah-dah
How many hours does it take?	*Kaç saat sürer?*	KAHCH sah-aht sew-REHR
.... hours	*........ saat*	sah-AHT
.... minutes	*........ dakika*	dahk-KAH
early/late	*erken/geç*	ehr-KEHN/GECH
fast/slow	*çabuk/yavaş*	chah-BOOK/yah-VAHSH

upper/lower	*yukarı/aşağı*	yoo-kah-RUH/ah-shah-UH
next/last	*gelecek/son*	geh-leh-JEHK/SOHN

Getting Around – air

airplane	*uçak*	oo-CHAHK
airport	*havaalanı*	hah-VAH-ah-lah-nuh
flight	*uçuş*	oo-CHOOSH
gate	*kapı*	kah-PUH

Getting Around – bus

bus	*otobüs, araba*	oh-toh-BEWSS
bus terminal	*otogar*	OH-toh-gahr
direct (bus)	*direk(t)*	dee-REK
indirect (route)	*aktarmalı*	ahk-tahr-mah-LUH

Getting Around – train

railway	*demiryolu*	deh-MEER-yoh-loo
train	*tren*	tee-REHN
railway station	*gar, İstasyon*	GAHR, ees-tahs-YOHN
sleeping car	*yataklı vagon*	yah-tahk-LUH vah-gohn
dining car	*yemekli vagon*	yeh-mehk-LEE vah-gohn
couchette	*kuşet*	koo-SHEHT
no-smoking car	*sigara içilmeyen vagon*	see-GAH-rah eech-EEL-mee-yehn

Getting Around – boat

ship	*gemi*	geh-MEE
ferry	*feribot*	FEH-ree-boht
dock	*iskele*	ees-KEH-leh
cabin	*kamara*	KAH-mah-rah
berth	*yatak*	yah-TAHK
class	*mevki, sınıf*	MEHV-kee, suh-nuhf

Getting Around – highway terms

hitchhike	*otostop*	OH-toh-stohp
diesel fuel	*mazot, motorin*	mah-SOHT, MOH-toh-reen
petrol	*benzin*	behn-ZEEN
regular	*normal*	nohr-MAHL
super	*süper*	seur-PEHR
motor oil	*motor yağı*	moh-TOHR yah-uh
air (tyres)	*hava (lâstik)*	hah-VAH (lyaass-TEEK)
exhaust (system)	*egzos(t)*	ehk-ZOHSS
headlamp	*far*	FAHR
brake(s)	*fren*	FREHN
steering (-wheel)	*direksiyon*	dee-REHK-see-YOHN
electric repairman	*oto elektrikçi*	oh-TOH ee-lehk-TREEK-chee
tyre repairman	*oto lâstikçi*	oh-TOH lyass-TEEK-chee
car washing	*yıkama*	yuh-kah-MAH

lubrication	*yağlama*	YAH-lah-MAH
highways	*karayolları*	KAH-rah-yoh-lah-ruh
road repairs	*yol onarımı*	YOHL oh-nah-ruh-muh
road construction	*yol yapımı*	YOHL yah-puh-muh
overtaking lane	*tırmanma şeridi*	tuhr-MAHN-mah sheh-ree-dee
low verge (shoulder)	*düşük banket*	deur-SHEURK bahn-KEHT
mountain pass	*geçit, -di*	geh-CHEET, GEH-chee-dee
careful! slow!	*dikkat! yavas!*	dee-KAHT, yah-VAHSH
landslide (zone)	*heyelan (bölgesi)*	heh-yeh-LAHN burl-geh-see
vehicles entering	*araç çıkabılır*	ah-RAHCH chuk-kah-buh-luhr
dangerous cargo	*tehlikeli maddè*	teh-LEE-keh-LEE mahd-deh
'liquid fuel'	*akaryakıt*	ah-KAHR-yah-kuht
military vehicle	*askerî araç*	ahss-keh-REE ah-rahch
forbidden zone	*yasak bölge*	yah-SAHK beurl-geh
rest area	*dinlenme parkı*	deen-lehn-MEH pahr-kuh
spring (potable)	*çeşme*	CHESH-meh
motorway	*otoyol*	OH-toh-yohl
long vehicle	*uzun araç*	oo-ZOON ah-rahch
wide vehicle	*ğeniş araç*	geh-NEESH ah-rahch
population	*nufüs*	noo-FEURSS
altitude	*rakım*	rah-KUHM
car park	*park yeri*	PAHRK yeh-ree
multi-level parking garage	*kat oto parkı*	KAHT oh-toh pahr-kuh
God protect me!	*Allah korusun*	ah-LAH koh-roo-soon
Wonder of God!	*Maaşallah*	MAASH-ah-lah

Note Towns are marked by blue signs with white lettering; villages are marked by white signs with black lettering. Yellow signs with black lettering mark sights of touristic interest. Yellow signs with blue lettering have to do with village development projects.

Post Office

post office	*postane, postahane*	POHSS-tah-NEH
post office	*PTT*	peh-teh-TEH
open	*açık*	ah-CHUHK
closed	*kapalı*	kah-pah-LUH
postcard	*kartpostal*	kahrt-pohs-TAHL
letter	*mektup*	meht-TOOP
parcel	*koli*	KOH-lee
parcel	*paket*	pah-KEHT
small packet (mail category)	*küçük paket*	kew-CHEWK pah-keht
printed matter (mail category)	*matbua*	MAHT-boo-ah

postage stamp	*pul*	POOL
registered mail	*taahhütlü*	TAA-hewt-LEW
express mail, special delivery	*ekspres*	ehks-PRESS
by air mail	*uçakla, uçak ile*	oo-CHAHK-lah, oo-CHAHK-ee-leh
money order	*havale*	hah-vah-LEH
poste restante	*postrestant*	pohst-rehs-TAHNT
customs	*gümrük*	gewm-REWK
inspection (prior to mailing)	*kontrol*	kohn-TROHL
telephone token (large, small)	*jeton (büyük, küçük)*	zheh-TOHN (bew-YEWK, kew-CHEWK)

Bank

money	*para*	PAH-rah
small change	*bozuk para*	boh-ZOOK pah-rah
Turkish liras	*lira*	LEE-rah
dollars	*dolar*	doh-LAHR
foreign currency	*döviz*	durr-VEEZ
cash	*efektif*	eh-fehk-TEEF
cheque	*çek*	CHEK
equivalent	*karşılık*	kahr-shuh-LUHK
exchange	*kambiyo*	KAHM-bee-yoh
exchange rate	*kur*	KOOR
commission	*komisyon*	koh-mees-YOHN
charge, fee	*ücret*	eurj-REHT
purchase	*alış*	ah-LUSH
sale	*veriş*	veh-REESH
stamp	*pul*	POOL
tax	*vergi*	VEHR-gee
identification	*kimlik*	KEEM-leek
cashier	*kasa, vezne*	KAH-sah, VEHZ-neh
working hours	*çalışma saatleri*	chal-ush-MAH sah-aht-leh-ree

Days of the Week

day	*gün*	GEWN
week	*hafta*	hahf-TAH
Sunday	*Pazar*	pah-ZAHR
Monday	*Pazartesi*	pah-ZAHR-teh-see
Tuesday	*Salı*	sah-LUH
Wednesday	*Çarşamba*	char-shahm-BAH
Thursday	*Perşembe*	pehr-shehm-BEH
Friday	*Cuma*	joo-MAH
Saturday	*Cumartesi*	joo-MAHR-teh-see

Months of the Year

month	*ay*	AHY
year	*sene, yıl*	SEH-neh, YUHL

January	*Ocak*	oh-JAHK
February	*Şubat*	shoo-BAHT
March	*Mart*	MAHRT
April	*Nisan*	nee-SAHN
May	*Mayıs*	mah-YUSS
June	*Haziran*	HAH-zee-RAHN
July	*Temmuz*	teh-MOOZ
August	*Agustos*	AH-oo-STOHSS
September	*Eylül*	ehy-LEWL
October	*Ekim*	eh-KEEM
November	*Kasım*	kah-SUHM
December	*Aralık*	AH-rah-LUHK

Health

hospital	*hastane*	hahss-tah-NEH
dispensary	*sağlık ocağı*	saah-LUHK oh-jah-uh
I'm ill	*Hastayım*	hahss-TAH-yuhm
My stomach hurts	*Karnım ağrıyor*	kahr-NUHM aah-ruh-yohr
Help me	*Yardım edin*	yahr-DUHM eh-den

Shopping

shop	*dükkan*	dyook-KAHN
market	*çarşı*	chahr-SHUH
price	*fiyat*	fee-YAHT
service charge	*servis ücreti*	sehr-VEES ewj-reh-tee
tax	*vergi*	VEHR-gee
cheap/expensive	*ucuz/pahalı*	oo-JOOZ/pah-hah-LUH
very expensive	*çok pahalı*	CHOHK pah-hah-luh
which?	*hangi?*	HAHN-gee
this one	*bunu*	boo-NOO
Do you have .... ?	*........ var mı?*	VAHR muh
We don't have	*........ yok*	YOHK
I'll give you	*........ vereceğim*	VEH-reh-JEH-yeem
this much	*bu kadar*	BOO kah-dahr

Cardinal Numbers

¼	*çeyrek*	chehy-REHK
½	*yarım*	YAH-ruhm (used alone, as 'I want half')
½	*buçuk*	boo-CHOOK (always used with a whole number, as '1½', *bir buçuk*)
1	*bir*	BEER
2	*iki*	ee-KEE
3	*íç*	EWCH
4	*dört*	DURRT
5	*beş*	BEHSH
6	*altı*	ahl-TUH
7	*yedi*	yeh-DEE
8	*sekiz*	seh-KEEZ

9	*dokuz*	doh-KOOZ
10	*on*	OHN
11	*on bir*	ohn BEER
12	*on iki*	ohn ee-KEE
13	*on üç*	ohn EWCH
20	*yirmi*	yeer-MEE
30	*otuz*	oh-TOOZ
40	*kırk*	KUHRK
50	*elli*	ehl-LEE
60	*altmış*	ahlt-MUSH
70	*yetmiş*	yeht-MEESH
80	*seksen*	sehk-SEHN
90	*doksan*	dohk-SAHN
100	*yüz*	YEWZ
200	*iki yüz*	ee-KEE yewz
1000	*bin*	BEEN
2000	*iki bin*	ee-KEE been
10,000	*on bin*	OHN been
1,000,000	*milyon*	meel-YOHN

Ordinal Numbers

Ordinal numbers consist of the number plus the suffix *-inci, -ıncı, -uncu* or *-üncü*, depending upon 'vowel harmony'.

1st	*birinci*	beer-EEN-jee
2nd	*ikinci*	ee-KEEN-jee
6th	*altıncı*	ahl-TUHN-juh
13th	*onüçüncü*	ohn-ew-CHEWN-jew
100th	*yüzüncü*	yewz-EWN-jew

Turkish Food

Except in the fanciest restaurants, Turks don't have much use for menus. This is a society in which the waiter (*garson*, gahr-SOHN) is supposed to know his business and to help you order. Nonetheless, the waiter will bring a menu (*menü*, meh-NEW or *yemek listesi*, yeh-MEHK lees-teh-see) if you ask for one. The menu will at least give you some prices so you'll know what you will be asked to pay.

Otherwise, you may choose from the menu several times only to get the response *Yok!* (YOHK, None!). The menu, as I said, is not much use. Instead, the waiter will probably say *Gel! Gel!* (Come! Come!) and lead you into the kitchen for a look. In the glass-fronted refrigerator cabinets you'll see the *şiş kebap, köfte, bonfile* steaks, lamb chops, liver, kidneys and fish which are in supply. Also in the cabinet may be the cheeses, salads and vegetable dishes, if meant to be served cold. Then he'll lead you right to the fire for a look at the stews, soups, pastas and *pilavs*. With sign language, you'll have everything you want in no time. It's a good idea to ask prices. Some general words to know are:

| restaurant | *lokanta* | loh-KAHN-tah |

pastry-shop	*pastane*	PAHSS-tah-neh
'oven' (bakery)	*fırın*	FUH-ruhn
'pizza' place	*pideci*	PEE-deh-jee
köfte restaurant	*köfteci*	KURF-teh-jee
kebap restaurant	*kebapçı*	keh-BAHP-chuh
snack shop	*büfe*	bew-FEH
alcoholic drinks served	*içkili*	eech-kee-LEE
no alcohol served	*içkisiz*	eech-kee-SEEZ
family (ladies) dining room	*aile salonu*	ah-yee-LEH sah-loh-noo
no single men allowed	*aileye mahsustur*	ah-yee-LEH mah-SOOS-tuhr
breakfast	*kahvahltı*	KAHH-vahl-TUH
lunch	*öğle yemeği*	ury-LEH yeh-meh-yee
supper	*akşam yemeği*	ahk-SHAHM yeh-meh-yee
to eat; meal, dish	*yemek*	yeh-MEHK
portion, serving	*porsyon*	pohr-SYOHN
fork	*çatal*	chah-TAHL
knife	*bıçak*	buh-CHAHK
spoon	*kaşık*	kah-SHUHK
plate	*tabak*	tah-BAHK
glass	*bardak*	bahr-DAHK
bill, cheque	*hesap*	heh-SAHP
service charge	*servis ücreti*	sehr-VEES ewj-reh-tee
tax	*vergi*	VEHR-gee
tip	*bahşiş*	bah-SHEESH
error	*yanlış*	yahn-LUSH
small change	*bozuk para*	boh-ZOOK pah-rah

Here is a guide to restaurant words, arranged (more or less) in the order of a Turkish menu and a Turkish meal. I've given the names of the courses (*çorba*, *et*, etc) in the singular form; you may see them in the plural (*çorbalar*, *etler*, etc).

Soup

soup	*çorba*	CHOHR-bah
broth with mutton	*haşlama*	hahsh-lah-MAH
chicken soup	*tavuk çorbası*	tah-VOOK chor-bah-suh
egg & lemon soup	*düğün çorbası*	dew-EWN chor-bah-suh
fish soup	*balık çorbası*	bah-LUHK chor-bah-suh
lentil soup	*mercimek çorbası*	mehr-jee-MEHK chor-bah-suh
lentil & rice soup	*ezo gelin çorbası*	EH-zoh GEH-leen chor-bah-suh
mutton broth with egg	*et suyu (yumurtalı)*	EHT soo-yoo, yoo-moor-tah-LUH
tripe soup	*işkembe çorbası*	eesh-KEHM-beh chor-bah-suh
trotter soup	*paça*	PAH-chah
tomato soup	*domates çorbası*	doh-MAH-tess chor-bah-suh
vegetable soup	*sebze çorbası*	SEHB-zeh chor-bah-suh

| vermicelli soup | *şehriye çorbası* | shehh-ree-YEH chor-bah-suh |
| yoghurt & barley soup | *yayla çorbası* | YAHY-lah chor-bah-suh |

Hors d'Oeuvres

Meze (MEH-zeh), or hors d'oeuvres, can include almost anything, and you can easily – and delightfully – make an entire meal of *meze*. Often you will be brought a tray from which you can choose those you want.

aubergine/eggplant puree	*patlıcan salatası*	paht-luh-JAHN sah-lah-tah-suh
cold white beans vinaigrette	*pilaki, piyaz*	pee-LAH-kee
flaky pastry	*börek*	bur-REHK
red caviar in mayonnaise	*tarama salatası*	tah-rah-MAH sah-lah-tah-suh
stuffed squash/marrow	*kabak dolması*	kah-BAHK dohl-mah-suh
stuffed vine leaves	*yaprak dolması*	yah-PRAHK dohl-mah-suh
	yalancı dolması	yah-LAHN-juh dohl-mah-suh
stuffed with lamb (hot)	*etli*	eht-LEE
stuffed with rice (cold)	*zeytinyağlı*	zehy-teen-yah-LUH
white cheese	*beyaz peynir*	bey-AHZ pehy-neer

Fish

A menu is of no use when ordering fish (*balık*, bah-LUHK). You must ask the waiter what's fresh, and then ask the approximate price. The fish will be weighed, and the price computed at the day's per-kg rate. Sometimes you can haggle. Buy fish in season (*mevsimli*, mehv-seem-LEE), as fish out of season are very expensive.

Aegean tuna	*trança*	TRAHN-chah
anchovy (fresh)	*hamsi*	HAHM-see
black bream	*karagöz*	kah-rah-GURZ
bluefish	*lüfer*	lew-FEHR
caviar	*havyar*	hahv-YAHR
crab	*yengeç*	yehn-GECH
grey mullet	*kefal*	keh-FAHL
lobster	*istakoz*	uhss-tah-KOHZ
mackerel	*uskumru*	oos-KOOM-roo
mussels	*midye*	MEED-yeh
plaice	*pisi*	PEE-see
red coralfish	*mercan*	mehr-JAHN
red mullet	*barbunya*	bahr-BOON-yah
roe, red caviar	*tarama*	tah-rah-MAH
sardine (fresh)	*sardalya*	sahr-DAHL-yah
sea bass	*levrek*	lehv-REHK
shrimp	*karides*	kah-REE-dess
sole	*dil balığı*	DEEL bah-luh
swordfish	*kılıç*	kuh-LUHCH

trout	*alabalık*	ah-LAH-bah-luhk
turbot	*kalkan*	kahl-KAHN
tunny, bonito	*palamut*	PAH-lah-moot

Meat & Kebap

In *kebap* (keh-BAHP), the meat (*et*, EHT) is always lamb, ground or in chunks; preparation, spices and extras (onions, peppers, bread) make the difference among the kebaps. Some may be ordered *yoğurtlu* (yoh-oort-LOO), with a side-serving of yoghurt.

aubergine/ eggplant & meat	*patlıcan kebap*	paht-luh-JAHN keh-bahp
beef	*sığır*	suh-UHR
boiling chicken	*tavuk*	tah-VOOK
chateaubriand	*şatobriyan*	sha-TOH-bree-YAHN
chicken in walnut sauce	*çerkez tavuğu*	cher-KEHZ tah-voo
cutlet (usually lamb)	*pirzola*	peer-ZOH-lah
döner with tomato sauce	*bursa kebap*	BOOR-sah keh-bahp flat
flat bread with ground lamb	*etli pide, ekmek*	eht-LEE PEE-deh, ehk-MEHK
grilled ground lamb patties	*köfte*	KURF-teh
kidney	*böbrek*	bur-BREHK
lamb stew	*tas kebap*	TAHSS keh-bahp
lamb & vegetables in paper	*kağıt kebap*	kyah-UHT keh-bahp
liver	*ciğer*	jee-EHR
meat & vegetable stew	*güveç*	gew-VECH
milk-fed lamb	*kuzu (süt)*	koo-ZOO (SEWT)
mixed grill (lamb)	*karışık ızgara*	kah-ruh-shuk uhz-gah-rah
pit-roasted lamb	*tandır kebap*	tahn-DUHR keh-bahp
pork (forbidden to Muslims)	*domuz*	doh-MOOZ
ram's 'eggs' (testicles)	*koç yumurtası*	KOHCH yoo-moor-tah-suh
roast lamb with onions	*orman kebap*	ohr-MAHN keh-bahp
roast skewered chicken	*tavuk/piliç şiş*	tah-VOOK/ pee-LEECH SHEESH
roast skewered lamb	*şiş kebap*	SHEESH keh-bahp
roasting chicken	*piliç*	pee-LEECH
small fillet beefsteak	*bonfile*	bohn-fee-LEH
spicy-hot roast köfte	*Adana kebap*	ah-DAH-nah keh-bahp
spit-roasted chicken slices	*tavuk/piliç döner*	tah-VOOK/pee-LEECH dur-NEHR
spit-roasted lamb slices	*döner kebap*	dur-NEHR keh-bahp
sun-dried, spiced beef	*pastırma*	pahss-TUHR-mah
tiny bits of skewered lamb	*çöp kebap*	CHURP keh-bahp
veal	*dana*	DAH-nah
wok-fried lamb	*saç kavurma*	SAHTCH kah-voor-mah
wienerschnitzel	*şinitzel*	shee-NEET-zehl

Salads

Each one of the names would be followed by the word *salata* (sah-LAH-tah) or *salatası*. You may be asked if you prefer it *sirkeli* (SEER-keh-LEE), with vinegar or *limonlu* (LEE-mohn-LOO), with lemon juice; most salads (except *söğüş*) come with olive oil. If you don't like hot peppers, say *bibersiz* (BEE-behr-SEEZ), though this often doesn't work.

chopped mixed salad	*karışık*	kah-ruh-SHUHK
	çoban	choh-BAHN
green salad	*yeşil*	yeh-SHEEL
mayonnaise, peas, carrots	*Amerikan*	ah-meh-ree-KAHN
	Rus	ROOSS
pickled vegetables	*turşu*	toor-SHOO
roast aubergine/eggplant puree	*patlıcan*	paht-luh-JAHN
romaine lettuce	*marul*	mah-ROOL
sheep's brain	*beyin*	behy-EEN
sliced vegetables, no sauce	*söğüş*	sur-EWSH
tomato & cucumber salad	*domates salatalık*	doh-MAH-tess sah-LAH-tah-luhk

Vegetables

vegetable	*sebze*	sehb-ZEH
cabbage	*lahana*	lah-HAH-nah
carrot	*havuç*	hah-VOOCH
cauliflower	*karnabahar*	kahr-NAH-bah-hahr
cucumber	*hıyar*	huh-YAHR
	salatalık	sah-LAH-tah-luhk
green beans	*taze fasulye*	tah-ZEH fah-sool-yah
marrow/squash	*kabak*	kah-BAHK
okra	*bamya*	BAHM-yah
onion	*soğan*	soh-AHN
peas	*bezelye*	beh-ZEHL-yeh
peppers	*biber*	bee-BEHR
potato	*patates*	pah-TAH-tess
radish	*turp*	TOORP
red beans	*barbunye*	bahr-BOON-yeh
spinach	*ıspınak*	uhs-spuh-NAHK
tomato	*domates*	doh-MAH-tess
white beans	*kuru fasulye*	koo-ROO fah-sool-yah

Fruits

fruit	*meyva*	mehy-VAH
apple	*elma*	ehl-MAH
apricot	*kayısı*	kahy-SUH
banana	*muz*	MOOZ
cherry	*kiraz*	kee-RAHZ
fig	*incir*	een-JEER
grapefruit	*greyfurut*	GREY-foo-root
grapes	*üzüm*	ew-ZEWM

morello (sour cherry)	*vişne*	VEESH-neh
orange	*portakal*	pohr-tah-KAHL
peach	*şeftali*	shef-tah-LEE
pear	*armut*	ahr-MOOT
pomegranate	*nar*	NAHR
quince	*ayva*	ahy-VAH
strawberries	*çilek*	chee-LEHK
tangerine, mandarin	*mandalin*	mahn-dah-LEEN
watermelon	*karpuz*	kahr-POOZ
yellow melon	*kavun*	kah-VOON

Sweets

sweet, dessert	*tatlı*	taht-LUH
baked caramel custard	*krem karamel*	KREHM kah-rah-MEHL
baked rice pudding (cold)	*fırın sütlaç*	foo-roon SEWT-lach
'bottom of the pot' (cold baked pudding)	*kazandibi*	kah-ZAHN-dee-bee
cake	*kek*	KEHK
candied marrow/squash	*kabak tatlısı*	kah-BAHK TAHT-luh-suh
cheese cake	*peynir tatlısı*	pehy-NEER TAHT-luh-suh
chocolate pudding	*krem şokolada*	KREHM shoh-koh-LAH-dah
crumpet in syrup	*ekmek kadayıf*	ehk-MEHK kah-dah-yuhf
flaky pastry, nuts & milk	*güllaç*	gewl-LACH
fruit	*meyve*	mehy-VEH
ice cream	*dondurma*	dohn-DOOR-mah
'Lady's navel', doughnut in syrup	*kadın göbeği*	kah-DEEN gur-beh-yee
many-layer pie, honey, nuts	*baklava*	bahk-lah-VAH
milk & nut pudding	*keşkül*	kehsh-KEWL
pastry	*pasta*	PAHSS-tah
rice flour & rosewater pudding	*muhallebi*	moo-HAH-leh-bee
rice pudding	*sütlaç*	sewt-LAHCH
saffron & rice sweet	*zerde*	zehr-DEH
semolina sweet	*helva*	hehl-VAH
semolina cake in syrup	*hurma tatlısı*	hoor-MAH
shredded wheat in syrup	*tel kadayıf*	TEHL kah-dah-yuhf
shredded wheat with pistachios & honey	*burma kadayıf*	boor-MAH kah-dah-yuhf
stewed fruit	*komposto*	kohm-POHSS-toh
sweet of milk, rice & chicken	*tavuk göğsü*	tah-VOOK gur-sew
Turkish delight	*lokum*	loh-KOOM
walnut, raisin, pea pudding	*aşure*	ah-shoo-REH
yoghurt & egg pudding	*yoğurt tatlısı*	yoh-OORT taht-luh-suh

Other Dishes & Condiments

English	Turkish	Pronunciation
aubergine baked with onions & tomatoes	*imam bayıldı*	ee-MAHM bah-yuhl-duh
aubergine & lamb (hot)	*karnıyarık*	KAHR-nuh-yah-RUHK
aubergine & lamb pie	*musakka*	moo-sah-KAH
biscuits	*bisküvi*	BEES-koo-VEE
black pepper	*siyah biber*	see-YAH bee-behr
	kara biber	kah-RAH bee-behr
bread	*ekmek*	ehk-MEHK
butter	*tereyağı*	TEH-reh-yah
cheese	*peynir*	pehy-NEER
'cigarette' fritters	*sigara*	see-GAH-rah
flaky or fried pastry	*börek*	bur-REHK
fruit jam	*reçel*	reh-CHEHL
garlic	*sarmısak*	SAHR-muh-SAHK
honey	*bal*	BAHL
ice	*buz*	BOOZ
lemon	*limon*	lee-MOHN
macaroni, noodles	*makarna*	mah-KAHR-nah
mild yellow cheese	*kaşar peynir*	kah-SHAHR pey-neer
mustard	*hardal*	hahr-DAHL
oil, fat	*yağ*	YAH
olive oil	*zeytinyağı*	zehy-TEEN-yah-uh
olives	*zeytin*	zehy-TEEN
pastry (not noodles)	*pasta*	PAHSS-tah
pizza, flat bread	*pide*	PEE-deh
salt	*tuz*	TOOZ
spaghetti	*spaket*	spah-KEHT
stuffed (vegetable)	*........dolma(sı)*	DOHL-mah(-suh)
cabbage leaves	*lahana*	lah-HAH-nah
green pepper	*biber*	bee-BEHR
marrow/squash	*kabak*	kah-BAHK
vine leaves	*yalancı*	yah-LAHN-juh
vine leaves	*yaprak*	yah-PRAHK
sugar, candy, sweets	*şeker*	sheh-KEHR
vinegar	*sirke*	SEER-keh
white (sheep's cheese)	*beyaz peynir*	bey-AHZ pey-neer
with ground lamb	*kıymalı*	kuhy-mah-LUH
with white cheese	*peynirli*	pehy-neer-LEE
water	*su*	SOO
yoghurt	*yoğurt*	yoh-OORT
yoghurt & grated cucumber	*cacık*	jah-JUHK

Drinks

İçki (eech-KEE) usually refers to alcoholic beverages, *meşrubat* (mehsh-roo-BAHT) to soft drinks. If your waiter says *İçecek?* or *Ne içeceksiniz?*, he's asking what you'd like to drink.

As for Turkish coffee (*kahve*, kahh-VEH) you must order it by sweetness; the sugar is mixed in during the brewing, not afterwards. You can drink it *sade* (sah-DEH), without sugar; *az* (AHZ) if you want just a bit of sugar; *orta* (ohr-TAH), with a middling amount; çok or şekerli or even çok şekerli (CHOHK sheh-kehr-LEE), with lots of sugar. When the coffee arrives, the waiter may well have confused the cups, and you may find yourself exchanging with your dinnermates.

Nescafé is readily found throughout Turkey but tends to be expensive, often around US$0.70 per cup.

American coffee	*Amerikan*	ah-meh-ree-KAHN
aniseed-flavoured brandy	*rakı*	rah-KUH
beer	*bira*	BEE-rah
dark	*siyah*	see-YAH
light	*beyaz*	bey-AHZ
coffee	*kahve(si)*	kah-VEH(-see)
coffee & milk	*Fransız*	frahn-SUHZ
fizzy mineral water	*maden sodası*	mah-DEHN soh-dah-suh
fruit juice	*meyva suyu*	mey-VAH soo-yoo
gin	*cin*	JEEN
hot milk & tapioca root	*sahlep*	sah-LEHP
instant coffee	*neskafe*	NEHSS-kah-feh
lemonade	*limonata*	lee-moh-NAH-tah
milk	*süt*	SEWT
mineral water	*maden suyu*	mah-DEHN soo-yoo
tea	*çay*	CHAH-yee
thick millet drink	*boza*	BOH-zah
Turkish (coffee)	*Türk*	TEWRK
vermouth	*vermut*	vehr-MOOT
vodka	*votka*	VOHT-kah
water	*su*	SOO
whisky	*viski*	VEE-skee
wine	*şarap*	shah-RAHP
red	*kırmızı*	kuhr-muh-ZUH
rose	*roze*	roh-ZEH
sparkling	*köpüklü*	kur-pewk-LEW
white	*beyaz*	bey-AHZ
yoghurt drink	*ayran*	AH-yee-RAHN

Cooking Terms

baked, oven-roasted	*fırın*	fuh-RUHN
boiled, stewed	*haşlama*	hahsh-lah-MAH
broiled	*kızartma*	kuh-ZAHRT-mah
charcoal grilled	*ızgara*	uhz-GAH-rah
cold	*soğuk*	soh-OOK
hot, warm	*sıcak*	suh-JAHK
puree	*ezme(si)*	ehz-MEH(-see)
roasted	*rosto*	ROHSS-toh
steamed	*buğlama*	BOO-lah-MAH
well-done, –cooked	*iyi pişmiş*	ee-YEE peesh-meesh
	pişkin	peesh-KEEN
with egg	*yumurtalı*	yoo-moor-tah-LUH
with ground lamb	*kıymalı*	kuhy-mah-LUH
with cheese	*peynirli*	pehy-neer-LEE

with meat	*etli*	eht-LEE
with sauce	*soslu*	sohss-LOO
	terbiyeli	TEHR-bee-yeh-LEE
with savoury tomato sauce	*salçalı*	sahl-chah-LUH
with yoghurt	*yogurtlu*	YOH-oort-LOO

Index

MAPS

612

THANKS

Writers (apologies if we've misspelt your names) to whom thanks must go include:

A Moe & D Brown (US), Simon Allen (UK), Graham Aller (A), Ralf Andersen (Dk), Duncan Angus (UK), Jackie Aplin (UK), Graeme Archer (A), M J Armitage (UK), Georgina Arnold (UK), Mark Ashby (NZ), P & J Aughey (UK), Lisa Austin (D), A Barzilai (Isr), Bonnie Baskin (US), A L Bayliss (UK), Sahin Baynut (Tur), Mark S Beiley (UK), Bec & Andy Bell (UK), Kirsten Bender (Tur), Garrett Bennett (A), E M Bentley (UK), Michael Berendt (Dk), Pollak Bernhard (Aust), Murray Berrie (US), R Blackie (UK), Rhonda Boddie (UK), Helen Borsky & Dan Thompson (UK), Robin Braithwaite (A), Nicolas Brault (F), Joyce Bregman (US), Craig Breskin (UK), Graeme Broughton (A), Jan & Geoff Brown (A), Martin Brown (UK), M Bruce (A), Mr S Burge (?), Dr Paul Burns (UK), Refik Carikci (Tur), N Chadwick (UK), Robyn Chaplin (A), Mr S J Cheetham (UK), Judy Chrastina (C), Margie Christopherson (?), Mr M W Clark (UK), M & M Clark (A), John Clarke (UK), Soren Henrik Clausen (DK), Dr Philip Clendenning (US), Mrs J Collinson (A), Kerry Collinson (A), Dennis Costello (Ire), Nick Crawley (UK), Kiran Curtis (UK), Tyler Cutfork (C), David & Shahar Dahan (Isr), Magnus Dahlbring (Sw), Sven Dano (Dk), Sven Dano (UK), Sue Darlow, Reverend Andrew Davey (UK), William M David (US), G J Davis (UK), J de Koning (NL), Jochem de Koning (NL), Jean-Louis Demers (C), Suayip Demircan (Tur), Jack D Derry (UK), K L Dickhaut (C), K L Dickhaut (C), S Dolman (UK), John & Frances Drummond (UK), Susan Duckworth (UK), Rita & Brian Eatock (UK), Rita Eatock (UK), R H Edge (UK), Cardine J Ellis (UK), Ingiliz Enstitusu (Tur), Gugor Evrensel (Tur), Michael Finnelston (A), Jeanette Floyd (UK), Lennart H Forsell (Sw), Mark Fox (UK), Mario Franchi (I), Ms K R George (UK), Gina Georgiou (D), Kate Gillispie-Jones (A), Alan Ginsberg (US), Hugh Goddard (UK), Andrew Green (A), Phil Greenwood (UK), Chris Gregg, Sjoerd Groenewold (NL), E J Groeskamp (NL), Anders Hagen Hansen (Dk), Doris Haggett (UK), Alan & Nora Hague (UK), Carol Hahn (US), Susan Hall (?), Ishai Hammer (Isr), Sven Hansen (Dk), Soren V Hansen (Dk), Anette Hansen (Dk), Glenn Harbott (UK), David Harrington (UK), Lance Hartland (UK), Suzie Harvey (UK), Michael Hatch (UK), Jill Hauser (A), Michael Hawley (US), Andy Hazell (UK), Lucy Casson (UK), Rick Heeks (UK), Mark Henderson (NZ), George Henke (D), Victoria C H Hope (UK), Derek Hill (UK), Yael Hirshfeld (Isr), Alice Hitchings (UK), M J Horner (UK), Chris Humphrey (US), Barbara Inan (UK), Guy Jenkin (UK), Tina Jensen (Dk), Michael Johansson (Dk), Kryss Kats (UK), Julie Kendall & Mark Vernon (UK), Dr H J Kisch (Isr), Noel Kitching (UK), Inger Klaboe (NL), Bart Kleijer (NL), Joanne Knight (US), Irene Knirck (C), Dovotny R Knowes (UK), Willem Jan de Kogel (NL), A Cenk Konusur (Tur), Dawn Kose (Tur), Niels W Kundsen (Dk), Salman Kurt (Tur), O & H Kurtoglu (Tur), Harry Langeveld (NL), Lauren (US), Joanne Learry (UK), Rob Lee (UK), L M Lefeaux (UK), Joseph Jr Lemak (US), Carol Leong (US), Bernice Lewis (UK), J van der Lierop (NL), Constance Lim (C), Chris Line (UK), Neil Longthorne (B), Eric & Marg Louwersheimer (NL), Amanda Jane Lowry (UK), Ms Ginny Lunn (UK), Connie Madsen (Dk), George main (UK), A A C Matthaei (UK), Steve McDowell (C), Chris McGarvey (UK), M & C McGrath (A), Capt Barry Mclauchlan (NZ), Paul McLean (UK), Patrick McNamara (A), Graeme McQueen, Geoffrey Medcalf (UK), Mehmet Irdem (Tur), Fons Meijer (NL), Arnout Menkveld (NL), W A Menzies (NZ), Frank Mercer (Tur), Maria Meylan (CH), Jacqueline Miller (UK), Claudia Mills & Tom Schroeder (US), F Mitehell & S Davies (UK), John & Rosemary Morris (UK), Stella Mulder (NL), Donald Newton (Swit), Henrik de Nielson (NL), David Nishimura (US), Eamon O'Flynn (Ire), Robert Oakley (UK), Sam Oddie (UK), Avny Ohad (Isr), W Orennan (C), David Palmer (A), H & S Parr, Bruce Pierini (US), Mrs F Mary Poole (UK), Bram Posthumus (NL), Dorothy Potter (NZ), Stephanie Lee Raby (Tur), L Ravestein (NL), Prue Richard (A), C M Ridley (UK), Choni Rimat (Isr), Rupert Robin (UK), James Romaine (US), H E Rose, Paul Sargent (US), Anya Schiffrin (UK), Peter Scola (UK), I W Searle (UK), Mark Seltzer (US), Andrew Senior (UK), Mrs & Capt Serrano (US), Deborah Shadovitz (A), Laura Shiller (US), Sare Sikstrom (C), Jean Sinclair (UK), Helen Singer (UK), Lilian Six (US), E M Skeens (UK), Karl Smith (UK), Alexander Duval Smith (UK), Jane Southern (UK), Ryan & Speirs (A), Sally Spencer (A),

David St Vincent (UK), Alex Stewart (A), Doug Strachan (NZ), Raewyn Sulzberger (NZ), Margaret Sutherland (A), Suzanne Swan (C), Lorne Talbot (C), Osman Tan (Tur), Celal Taskiran (Tur), Jacqueline Ter Veer (NL), Joan Thomas (US), Helle N J Thomsen (Dk), Ewan & Fiona Thomson, Peter Thorne (UK), S E Tongijc (Tur), Riky van Og (NL), Magda Verdonck (B), Ben Versteegen (NL), Nancy Waerts (NL), Kate Wakeman (A), Simon Wallis (UK), Mrs D E Walter (US), Dimitri Waring (UK), Jane Webb (NZ), Ron & Georgie Webb (UK), N Welman (NL), Albert Welsh (US), S Wheeler & M Bavatie (UK), Tim & Mark Wildy (A), Ann Williams (UK), Claire Williams (UK), A Vasey & J Williams (UK), Brian Wilson (UK), Walter & Eileen Wiseman (UK), Jennifer Woodhouse (A), Suzanne Woolcott (D), Jason Wright (UK), Kerry Wright (A), Marijke Wurtheim (C), Rifat Yildez (Tur), Claudia Zeiler (US), G Zwiers (NL).

A - Australia, Aust - Austria, B - Belgium, C - Canada, D - West Germany, Dk - Denmark, F - France, I - Italy, Ire - Republic of Ireland, Isr - Israel, NL - Netherlands, NZ - New Zealand, Sw - Sweden, Swit Switzerland, Tur - Turkey, UK - UK, US - USA.

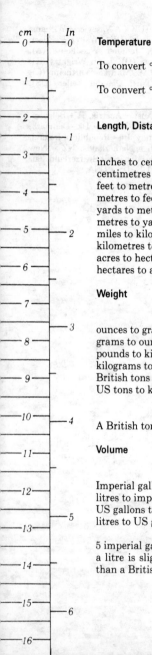

Temperature

To convert °C to °F multiply by 1.8 and add 32

To convert °F to °C subtract 32 and multiply by ·55

Length, Distance & Area

	multiply by
inches to centimetres	2.54
centimetres to inches	0.39
feet to metres	0.30
metres to feet	3.28
yards to metres	0.91
metres to yards	1.09
miles to kilometres	1.61
kilometres to miles	0.62
acres to hectares	0.40
hectares to acres	2.47

°C	°F
50	122
45	113
40	104
35	95
30	86
25	75
20	68
15	59
10	50
5	41
0	32

Weight

	multiply by
ounces to grams	28.35
grams to ounces	0.035
pounds to kilograms	0.45
kilograms to pounds	2.21
British tons to kilograms	1016
US tons to kilograms	907

A British ton is 2240 lbs, a US ton is 2000 lbs

Volume

	multiply by
Imperial gallons to litres	4.55
litres to imperial gallons	0.22
US gallons to litres	3.79
litres to US gallons	0.26

5 imperial gallons equals 6 US gallons
a litre is slightly more than a US quart, slightly less
than a British one

More guides to the region

Trekking in Turkey
Western travellers have discovered Turkey's coastline, but few people are aware that just inland there are mountains with walks that rival those found in Nepal. This book, the first trekking guide to Turkey, gives details on treks that are destined to become classics.

Eastern Europe on a shoestring
With all the facts on beating red tape, and detailed information on the GDR, Poland, Czechoslavakia, Hungary, Romania, Bulgaria, Yugoslavia, Albania and the USSR, this book opens up a whole new world for travellers.

West Asia on a shoestring
A complete guide to the overland trip from Bangladesh to Turkey. Updated information on Bangladesh, Bhutan, India, Iran, Maldives, Nepal, Pakistan, Sri Lanka, Turkey and the Middle East, even Afghanistan as it used to be!

Egypt & the Sudan – a travel survival kit
The sights of Egypt and the Sudan have impressed visitors for more than 50 centuries. This guide takes you beyond the spectacular pyramids to discover the villages of the Nile, diving in the Red Sea and many other attractions.

Israel – a travel survival kit
This is a comprehensive guidebook to a small, fascinating country that is packed with things to see and do. This guide will help you unravel its political and religious significance – and enjoy your stay.

Some other Lonely Planet guides

Africa on a shoestring
From Marrakesh to Kampala, Mozambique to Mauritania, Johannesburg to Cairo – this guidebook gives you all the facts on travelling in Africa. It provides comprehensive information on more than 50 African countries – how to get to them, how to get around, where to stay, where to eat, what to see and what to avoid.

South-East Asia on a shoestring
For over 10 years this has been known as the 'yellow bible' to travellers in South-East Asia. It offers detailed travel information on Brunei, Burma, Hong Kong, Indonesia, Macau, Malaysia, Papua New Guinea, the Philippines, Singapore, and Thailand.

Australia – a travel survival kit
Australia is Lonely Planet's home territory so this guide gives you the complete low-down on Down Under, from the red centre to the coast, from cosmopolitan cities to country towns.

Canada – a travel survival kit
Canada offers a unique combination of English, French and American culture, with forests mountains and lakes that cover a vast area.

Brazil – a travel survival kit
A complete guide to all the travel possibilities of this huge, exciting country. Whether you're trekking up the Amazon, lazing on Ipanema beach or partying at the Rio carnival you'll find all the information you need in this travel survival kit.

Lonely Planet Guidebooks

Lonely Planet guidebooks cover virtually every accessible part of Asia as well as Australia, the Pacific, Central and South America, Africa, the Middle East and parts of North America. There are four main series: 'travel survival kits', covering a single country for a range of budgets; 'shoestring' guides with compact information for low-budget travel in a major region; trekking guides; and 'phrasebooks'.

Australia & the Pacific
Australia
Bushwalking in Australia
Papua New Guinea
Papua New Guinea phrasebook
New Zealand
Tramping in New Zealand
Rarotonga & the Cook Islands
Solomon Islands
Tahiti & French Polynesia
Fiji
Micronesia

South-East Asia
South-East Asia on a shoestring
Malaysia, Singapore & Brunei
Indonesia
Bali & Lombok
Indonesia phrasebook
Burma
Burmese phrasebook
Thailand
Thai phrasebook
Philippines
Pilipino phrasebook

North-East Asia
North-East Asia on a shoestring
China
China phrasebook
Tibet
Tibet phrasebook
Japan
Japanese phrasebook
Korea
Korean phrasebook
Hong Kong, Macau & Canton
Taiwan

West Asia
West Asia on a shoestring
Trekking in Turkey
Turkey

Indian Ocean
Madagascar & Comoros
Mauritius, Réunion & Seychelles
Maldives & Islands of the East Indian Ocean

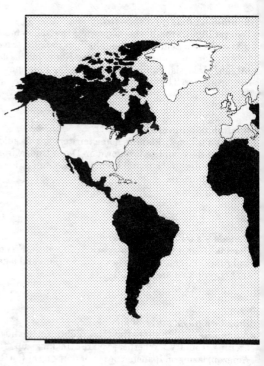

Mail Order

Lonely Planet guidebooks are distributed worldwide and are sold by good bookshops everywhere. They are also available by mail order from Lonely Planet, so if you have difficulty finding a title please write to us. US and Canadian residents should write to Embarcadero West, 112 Linden St, Oakland CA 94607, USA and residents of other countries to PO Box 617, Hawthorn, Victoria 3122, Australia.

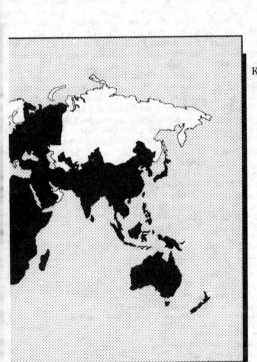

Lonely Planet

Lonely Planet published its first book in 1973. Tony and Maureen Wheeler had made a lengthy overland trip from England to Australia and, in response to numerous 'how do you do it?' questions, Tony wrote and they published *Across Asia on the Cheap*. It became an instant local best-seller and inspired thoughts of a second travel guide. A year and a half in South-East Asia resulted in their second book, *South-East Asia on a Shoestring*, which they put together in a backstreet Chinese hotel in Singapore in 1975. The 'yellow book', as it quickly became known, soon became *the* guide to the region and has gone through five editions, always with its familiar yellow cover.

Soon other writers came to them with ideas for similar books – books that went off the beaten track with an adventurous approach to travel, books that 'assumed you knew how to get your luggage off the carousel,' as one reviewer put it. Lonely Planet grew from a kitchen table operation to a spare room and then to its own office. Its international reputation began to grow as the Lonely Planet logo began to appear in more and more countries. In 1982 *India – a travel survival kit* won the Thomas Cook award for the best guidebook of the year.

These days there are over 70 Lonely Planet titles. Over 40 people work at our office in Melbourne, Australia and another half dozen at our US office in Oakland, California.

At first Lonely Planet specialised in the Asia region but these days we are also developing major ranges of guidebooks to the Pacific region, to South America and to Africa. The list of walking guides is growing and Lonely Planet now has a unique series of phrasebooks to 'unusual' languages. The emphasis continues to be on travel for travellers and Tony and Maureen still manage to fit in a number of trips each year and play a very active part in the writing and updating of Lonely Planet's guides.

Keeping guidebooks up to date is a constant battle which requires an ear to the ground and lots of walking, but technology also plays its part. All Lonely Planet guidebooks are now stored and updated on computer, and some authors even take lap-top computers into the field. Lonely Planet is also using computers to draw maps and eventually many of the maps will be stored on disk.

The people at Lonely Planet strongly feel that travellers can make a positive contribution to the countries they visit both by better appreciation of cultures and by the money they spend. In addition the company tries to make a direct contribution to the countries and regions it covers. Since 1986 a percentage of the income from each book has gone to aid groups and associations. This has included donations to famine relief in Africa, to aid projects in India, to agricultural projects in Central America, to Greenpeace's efforts to halt French nuclear testing in the Pacific and to Amnesty International. In 1989 $41,000 was donated by Lonely Planet to these projects.

Lonely Planet Distributors

Australia & Papua New Guinea Lonely Planet Publications, PO Box 617, Hawthorn, Victoria 3122.
Canada Raincoast Books, 112 East 3rd Avenue, Vancouver, British Columbia V5T 1C8.
Denmark, Finland & Norway Scanvik Books aps, Store Kongensgade 59 A, DK-1264 Copenhagen K.
India & Nepal UBS Distributors, 5 Ansari Rd, New Delhi - 110002
Israel Geographical Tours Ltd, 8 Tverya St, Tel Aviv 63144.
Japan Intercontinental Marketing Corp, IPO Box 5056, Tokyo 100-31.
Kenya Westland Sundries Ltd, PO Box 14107, Nairobi, Kenya.
Netherlands Nilsson & Lamm bv, Postbus 195, Pampuslaan 212, 1380 AD Weesp.
New Zealand Transworld Publishers, PO Box 83-094, Edmonton PO, Auckland.
Singapore & Malaysia MPH Distributors, 601 Sims Drive, #03-21, Singapore 1438.
Spain Altair, Balmes 69, 08007 Barcelona.
Sweden Esselte Kartcentrum AB, Vasagatan 16, S-111 20 Stockholm.
Thailand Chalermnit, 108 Sukhumvit 53, Bangkok 10110.
Turkey Yab-Yay Dagitim, Alay Koshu Caddesi 12/A, Kat 4 no. 11-12, Cagaloglu, Istanbul.
UK Roger Lascelles, 47 York Rd, Brentford, Middlesex, TW8 0QP
USA Lonely Planet Publications, PO Box 2001A, Berkeley, CA 94702.
West Germany Buchvertrieb Gerda Schettler, Postfach 64, D3415 Hattorf a H.
All Other Countries refer to Australia address.